ENCYCLOPEDIA OF EARLY CINEMA

The *Encyclopedia of Early Cinema* is a unique one-volume reference work on the first twenty-five years of the cinema's international emergence, approximately from the early 1890s to the mid-1910s. These early years of the history of cinema have lately been the subject of resurgent interest and a growing body of scholarship, and have come to be recognized as an extraordinarily diverse period, when moving pictures were quite unlike the kind of cinema that later emerged as the dominant norm.

This encyclopedia covers all aspects of scholarship on early cinema, both traditional and revisionist. It contains articles on the technological and industrial developments, the techniques of film production, the actors and filmmakers of the time, and on the changing modes of representation and narration, as well as the social and cultural contexts within which early films circulated, including topics such as distribution, exhibition, and audience. Beyond the USA and Europe, attention is also given to the wider international picture, including those regions in Asia, Africa, the Middle East, and South and Central America where filmmaking may have been relatively undeveloped but movie-going was significant.

More than 950 entries have been commissioned from internationally recognized specialists. Alphabetically organized, the entries range in length from short factual articles to full essays that offer clear and stimulating discussions of the key issues, people, practices, and phenomena of early cinema. A thematic list of entries is a useful guide through the book, and all entries contain detailed cross-references. The longer articles have considered suggestions for further reading, which are complemented by a general bibliography of specialized works on early cinema.

The *Encyclopedia of Early Cinema* is an invaluable and fascinating resource for students and researchers interested in the history of cinema.

Richard Abel is Robert Altman Collegiate Professor of Film Studies at the University of Michigan, USA.

ENCYCLOPEDIA OF EARLY CINEMA

Edited by Richard Abel

Routledge
Taylor & Francis Group

LONDON AND NEW YORK

First published 2005
by Routledge
2 Park Square, Milton Park, Abingdon, Oxon, OX14 4RN

Simultaneously published in the USA and Canada
by Routledge
270 Madison Avenue, New York, NY 10016, USA

Routledge is an imprint of the Taylor & Francis Group

© 2005 edited by Richard Abel

Typeset in Goudy and Optima by Newgen Imaging Systems (P) Ltd, India

Printed and bound in Great Britain by TJ International Ltd, Padstow, Cornwall

British Library Cataloguing in Publication Data
A catalogue record for this book is available from the British Library

Library of Congress Cataloging in Publication Data
Encyclopedia of early cinema/edited by
Richard Abel.
p. cm.
Includes bibliographical references and Index.
1. Motion pictures–History–Encyclopedias.
I. Abel, Richard, 1941–

PN1993.45.E53 2005
791.43′09′03–dc22   2004051460

ISBN 0–415–23440–9

Contents

Illustrations   vii

Contributors   xi

Thematic entry list   xvii

Introduction   xxix

Entries A–Z   1

Bibliography   711

Index   719

Illustrations

1   Frame still from *Sortie d'usine* (Lumière, 1895).   5
2   Flip book showing a clown juggling boxes of Church and Co.'s Arm and Hammer baking soda, *c*. late 1880s or early 1890s.   8
3   Production photo of G. M. Anderson as Broncho Billy.   23
4   Poster for Cherry Kearton, *Bioscope*, 1912.   26
5   Frame still from Emile Cohl's *Fantasmagorie* (1908).   27
6   Eadweard Muybridge, *Animal Location*, 1887: plate 202.   33
7   Emile Reynaud's Théâtre Optique, from *La Nature*, 1892.   34
8   Louis Aubert, from a palace cinema program, 1913.   41
9   Drawing from *Cleveland Leader*, 11 May 1911.   43
10   Wladyslaw T. Benda, "The Line at the Ticket Office"—illustration for Mary Heaton Vorse, "Some Moving Picture Audiences," *Outlook*, 24 June 1911.   44
11   Luisen-Kino, Berlin, *c*. 1910.   48
12   Edmond Benoît-Lévy.   66
13   Frame still from *The Life of Christ* (Gaumont, 1906).   69
14   Biograph studio exterior, 14th Street, Manhattan.   72
15   Frame still from *Corbett-Fitzsimmons Fight* (Veriscope, 1897).   81
16   Café-concert "Kursaal", Paris. Behind the rows of benches can be seen small tables where drinks could be ordered.   90
17   Cinématographe Lumière in use as a camera, from *La Nature*, 1896.   95
18   Pathé-Frères camera (engraving).   96
19   Frame stills from Lumière's *Inauguration par Guillaume II du monument de Guillaume 1er* (4 September 1896). 35mm nitrate print with one round perforation on each side of frame.   107
20   Frame still from *Meet Me at the Fountain* (Lubin, 1904).   111
21   Home model Schnellseher by Ottomar Anschütz; barely visible is one image from the 1892 Anschütz chronophotograph *Card Players*. From Oskar Messter, *Mein Weg mit dem Film* (Berlin, 1936).   119
22   Frame still from *Joueurs de cartes arrosés* (Lumière, 1896).   144
23   Poster for Max Linder, 1911.   146
24   Poster for Prince, 1910.   146
25   The last two rows of a Buster Brown comic strip, *New York Herald*, 1903.   149
26   Poster for Éclair's *Zigomar*, 1911.   158
27   Poster for Éclair's *Nick Carter* series, 1908.   181
28   Miles Bros advertisement, 1908.   184
29   Jean Desmet's Cinema Royal, Rotterdam, with a poster of Cines' *La tutela* [Guardianship] (1913) in four languages.   190
30   Edison cameramen, *c*. 1910.   202

31   35mm nitrate print of *Le chevalier mystère* [The Mysterious Knight] (George Méliès, 1899): (a) A cement splice on the positive copy is visible as a dark line between the frames; (b) A cement splice made on the negative source shows on the positive copy as a pale area near the top of the frame. 205

32   Sequential frame stills of a doctor and his threatened wife in spaces distant from one another but linked by telephone, in Pathé-Frères' *A Narrow Escape* (1908). 208

33   Theatre des fleurs program, Beirut, Syria, *c.* 1911. From *Moving Picture World*, 1912. 217

34   Dranem in Pathé's *Ma Tante* [My Aunt] (1904). 226

35   From *Mitchell and Kenyon 772*: Sedgwick's bioscope showfront at Pendlebury Wakes, August 1901. James Kenyon of Mitchell and Kenyon is standing to the left of the poster. 228

36   Production photo from *Le Voyage dans la lune* [Trip to the Moon] (Méliès, 1902). 232

37   Poster for *La Poule aux Oeufs d'Or* [The Hen with Golden Eggs] (Pathé 1905). 234

38   Poster for *L'Assassinat du duc de Guise* [Assassination of the Duke of Guise] (Film d'Art 1908). 236

39   Pathé-Frères' film splicing lab, Vincennes, *c.* 1910. 239

40   American Film Company editing room, Santa Barbara. 240

41   Pathé-Frères' Vincennes studio. 251

42   Modern Palast fairground cinema. 252

43   Poster for the Cinéma Pathé, *c.* 1907. 253

44   Poster for the Kinema Gab-Ka, Paris, December 1910. 255

45   Poster for the Gaumont-Palace, 1913. 256

46   Georges Specht, Léonce Perret, and René Poyen in the Gaumont studio, *c.* 1913. 266

47   Léon Gaumont. 268

48   "Inside a picture palace," *The Sphere*, April 1913. 285

49   D. W. Griffith directs *Death's Marathon* (1913), with Henry Walthall. 289

50   Interior of Hale's Tours train car. 294

51   Production photo for *Napoleon* (Pathé, 1903). 300

52   Production photo for *Notre Dame de Paris* (SCAGL, 1911). 300

53   Lyman Howe program, 1906. 308

54   Cover of *Le Petit Journal*, illustrated supplement, 16 May 1897. 310

55   Sheet music cover for "Beautiful Eyes," 1909. 311

56   Thomas Ince seated with his Bison-101 Indian actors, *c.* 1912. 317

57   D. S. Phalke. 319

58   Frame still from *A Visit to Peak Fraen and Co.'s Biscuit Works* (Cricks and Martin, 1906). 323

59   Four intermittent movements. 326

60   Thanhouser title card set up. 329

61   Marking for editing or title insertion, Pathé, 1912. 330

62   Frame still of Nero singing to Rome burning, in *Quo Vadis?* (Cines, 1913). 338

63   Frame still of Lyda Borelli in *Ma l'amore mio non muore* [Love Everlasting] (Gloria, 1913). 339

64   American Entertainment Co. poster, *c.* 1900 342

65   Frame still from *Momijigari* [Viewing Scarlet Maple Leaves] (1899). 346

66   Kalem Company exterior set, with Alice Joyce, *c.* 1912. 354

67   Engraving of a Kinetoscope, 1894. 359

68   Ticket for the Red Cinema, Amsterdam, *c.* 1912. 367

69   Carl Laemmle. 371

70   *Cooper-Hewitt* mercury vapor lamps, Biograph studio. 389

71   Production photo of *Max Linder contre Nick Winter* (Pathé, 1911). 391

72   Lubin studio interior, Philadelphia, Pennsylvania. 395

73   Louis and Auguste Lumière, 1895. 399

74 "Bob the Fireman" set of four magic lantern slides.   407
75 Docwra triple lantern.   409
76 Georges Méliès (left) in his Montreuil studio.   420
77 Frame still from Edison's *Uncle Tom's Cabin* (1903).   422
78 Poster for Pathé-Frères' *Nuit de noël* [Christmas Eve Tragedy] (1908).   426
79 Frame still from *The Black Hand* (American Mutoscope and Biograph, 1906).   427
80 The Pests of our Pacific and Atlantic Coasts: Uncle Sam: "There shall be no
    discrimination. I will shut you both out." *Judge*, 23 (17 December 1892).   434
81 *Moving Picture Boys* book cover.   450
82 Frame enlargement of Asta Nielsen and Poul Reumert in the "Gaucho Dance"
    scene from *Afgrunden* [The Abyss] (Nordisk, 1910).   455
83 Poster for *Traffic in Souls* (Universal, 1913).   457
84 Clyde Martin Plays the Pictures, *Film Index*, 27 June 1911.   462
85 "A rare moment of silence from an effects set-up and the pianist too," from
    "Jackass Music," *Moving Picture World*, 1911.   462
86 Studio of Anton Nöggerath Jr., at Sloterdijk (now Amsterdam), 1911, from *De Kunst*,
    193, p. 8.   471
87 From *Le Petit Journal*, 1911.   475
88 Poster for *Pathé Journal*, 1908.   478
89 Exterior of the Normal Theater, Chicago, 1909.   480
90 Interior of the Keith Bijou theater, Boston, c. 1910.   480
91 Interior of the Wonderland Theater, Troy, New York, c. 1908.   480
92 *Pollice verso*, by Jean-Léon Gérôme (1859).   495
93 Frame still from *Quo Vadis?* (Cines, 1913).   496
94 Saxe Theatre, Minneapolis, 1912.   498
95 Ferdinand Zecca and Charles Pathé in the latter's office.   503
96 Pathé advertisement, *Views and Films Index*, 1906.   504
97 Poster for Pathé-Frères, c. 1906.   509
98 Omnia-Pathé program, 1913.   509
99 Poster for Herbert Ponting, *Bioscope*, 1912.   524
100 Preservation pattern of a 35 mm silent positive print. (Paolo Cherchi Usai.)   532
101 Palace Theatre of Varieties program, London, December 1897.   535
102 Keith Bijou projection room, Boston, 1910.   537
103 Pre-fabricated Gaumont projection booth, c. 1906.   537
104 Powers Cameragraph, 1906.   539
105 Cinématographe Lumière in use as a projector, from *La Nature*, 1896.   539
106 Cartoon from *Motion Picture Story Magazine* (September 1912).   543
107 Poster for Urban's *Unseen World*, 1903.   569
108 Interior of the American Theater, Salt Lake City, 1913.   574
109 Stage of the Strand Theater, Newark, 1914.   576
110 Selig Polyscope West Coast Studio, Los Angeles.   581
111 Group of technicians performing sound effects behind the screen, 1908.   597
112 Wladyslaw T. Benda "They were permitted to drink deep of oblivion of all the trouble in
    the world"— illustration for Mary Heaton Vorse, "Some Moving Picture Audiences,"
    Outlook, 24 June 1911.   603
113 Frame enlargement from *Ingeborg Holm*, (Victor Sjöström, 1913).   607
114 Frame enlargement of Mary Pickford in *The New York Hat* (Biograph, 1912).   609
115 Exterior of the Svenska Biografteatern studio, Kyrkviken, Lidingö, 1912.   615
116 Interior of the Lilla Elite Teatern, Härnösand, 1910.   617

117 Gaumont Chronophone advertisement, *Motion Picture World*, 1909. 621
118 George Kleine advertisment, *Film Index*, 4 February 1911. 643
119 Production photos of *Magic Bricks* (Pathé, 1908). 645
120 Frame still from *Le Cakewalk chez les nains* [The Dwarfs' Cakewalk] (Pathé 1903). 645
121 Entrance to Universal City, *c.* 1915. 650
122 Central Square, Lynn, Massachusetts, *c.* 1910. 653
123 Edison studio interior, Bronx. 658
124 Laemmle Film Service ad, 1908. 662
125 Theatre Row, Broad Street, Richmond, Virginia, 1910. 664
126 Mutual Movies advertisement, *St. Paul News*, Minnesota (November 1913). 666
127 Exterior of Keith's Theatre, Boston, 1894. 674
128 Keith's Theatre program, Providence, Rhode Island, 1905. 675
129 Vitagraph studio exterior, Brooklyn, *c.* 1907. 680
130 Frame still from *Indian Massacre* (Bison-101, 1912). 691
131 Minnesota moving picture theater exterior be-decked with posters for white slave films, *c.* 1913. 694
132 Ohio Woman Suffrage Party advertisement, *Cleveland Leader* (1 September 1912), Metropolitan Section, 4. 701

Contributors

Richard Abel
University of Michigan, USA

Antti Alanen
Finnish Film Archive, Finland

Rick Altman
University of Iowa, USA

Barry Anthony
UK

S. M. Ardan
Sinematek, Indonesia

Kaveh Askari
University of Chicago, USA

Jonathan Auerbach
University of Maryland, USA

Constance Balides
Tulane University, USA

Timothy Barnard
Canada

Jennifer M. Bean
University of Washington, USA

Janet Bergstrom
University of California, Los Angeles, USA

Dave Berry
Sgrîn, Media Agency for Wales, UK

Giorgio Bertellini
University of Michigan, USA

Ina Bertrand
University of Melbourne, Australia

Robert S. Birchard
USA

Gretchen Bisplinghoff
Northern Illinois University, USA

Ivo Blom
Vrije University, the Netherlands

Stephen Bottomore
UK

Eileen Bowser
USA

Marta Braun
Ryerson University, Toronto, Canada

Ben Brewster
University of Wisconsin-Madison, USA

Richard Brown
UK

Judith Buchanan
University of York, UK

Alan Burton
De Montfort University, UK

Carlos Bustamante
Berlin University of the Arts, Germany

Paolo Caneppele
Filmarchiv Austria

Alain Carou
Bibliothèque nationale, France

Suresh Chabria
India

Paolo Cherchi Usai
National Film and Sound Archive, Australia

Ian Christie
University College London, UK

Guido Convents
Belgium

Mark Garrett Cooper
Florida State University, USA

Roland Cosandey
École centrale d'art Lausanne, Switzerland

Donald Crafton
University of Notre Dame, USA

Richard Crangle
University of Exeter, UK

Scott Curtis
Northwestern University, USA

Marina Dahlquist
Stockholm University, Sweden

Angela Dalle Vacche
Georgia Institute of Technology, USA

Nico de Klerk
Filmmuseum, Amsterdam, the Netherlands

François de la Brèteque
University of Montpelier, France

Aurelio de los Reyes
Mexico

Leslie Midkiff DeBauche
University of Wisconsin-Stevens Point, USA

Jonathan Dennis
New Zealand

Nick Deocampo
Mowelfund Film Institute, the Philippines

Victoria Duckett
University of Manchester, UK

Claire Dupré la Tour
University Paris IX Dauphine, France

Joseph Eckhardt
Montgomery County Community College, USA

Thomas Elsaesser
University of Amsterdam, the Netherlands

Bo Florin
Stockholm University, Sweden

Annette Förster
The Netherlands

Paul Fryer
Rose Bruford College, UK

John Fullerton
Stockholm University, Sweden

Jane Gaines
Duke University, USA

Dorin Gardner Schumacher
USA

Joseph Garncarz
University of Cologne, Germany

André Gaudreault
Université de Montréal, Québec, Canada

Aaron Gerow
Yale University, USA

Alan Gevinson
Johns Hopkins University, USA

Maurice Gianati
France

Douglas Gomery
University of Maryland, USA

Frank Gray
University of Brighton, UK

Lee Grieveson
University College London, UK

Alison Griffiths
City University of New York, USA

Tom Gunning
University of Chicago, USA

Stephen Herbert
UK

Joanne Hershfield
University of North Carolina-Chapel Hill, USA

Steven Higgins
Museum of Modern Art, New York, USA

Nicholas Hiley
University of Kent, UK

Bert Hogenkamp
Netherlands Audiovisual Archives, the Netherlands

Gunnar Iversen
University of Trondheim, Norway

Lea Jacobs
University of Wisconsin-Madison, USA

Uli Jung
Trier University, Germany

Charlie Keil
University of Toronto, Canada

Frank Kessler
University of Utrecht, the Netherlands

Robert King
University of Michigan, USA

Jeffrey Klenotic
University of New Hampshire, USA

Hiroshi Komatsu
Waseda University, Japan

Richard Koszarski
USA

Germain Lacasse
Canada

Jean-Marc Lamotte
Institut Lumiére, France

James Latham
University of California, Irvine, USA

Laurent Le Forestier
France

Eric Le Roy
Centre nationale de la cinématographie

Thierry Lefebvre
Centre de Calcul Recherche et Réseau Jussieu, France

Martin Loiperdinger
Trier University, Germany

Ana M. López
Tulane University, USA

Patrick Loughney
Library of Congress, USA

Laurent Mannoni
La Cinémathéque française, France

Madeline F. Matz
Library of Congress, USA

David Mayer
University of Manchester, UK

Janet McBain
Scottish Screen, UK

Luke McKernan
British Universities Film and Video Council, UK

Alison McMahan
USA

Jean-Jacques Meusy
CNRS, France

Joan M. Minguet
Universitat Antónoma de Barcelona, Spain

Ingrid Muan
Cambodia

Corinna Müller
Germany

Charles Musser
Yale University, USA

Glenn Myrent
France

Hamid Naficy
Rice University, USA

Kathleen Newman
University of Iowa, USA

Panivong Norindr
University of Southern California, USA

Jan Olsson
Stockholm University, Sweden

William Paul
Washington University, USA

Roberta E. Pearson
University of Nottingham, UK

Jennifer Lynn Peterson
University of California, Riverside, USA

Michael Quinn
College of New Rochelle, USA

Lauren Rabinovitz
University of Iowa, USA

Isabelle Raynauld
Université de Montéal, Québec, Canada

David Robinson
UK

Kevin Rockett
Trinity College, Ireland

Deac Rossell
UK

Mark B. Sandberg
University of California, Berkeley, USA

Viola Shafik
American University in Cairo, Egypt

Charles Silver
Museum of Modern Art, New York, USA

Ben Singer
University of Wisconsin-Madison, USA

Jean Pierre Sirois-Trahan
Université Laval, Quebec, Canada

Sheila Skaff
University of Texas-EL Paso, USA

Astrid Söderbergh Widding
Stockholm University, Sweden

Paul Spehr
USA

Shelley Stamp
University of California, Santa Cruz, USA

Jacqueline Stewart
University of Chicago, USA

Dan Streible
University of South Carolina, USA

Kristin Thompson
University of Wisconsin-Madison, USA

Vanessa Toulmin
University of Sheffield, UK

Hillel Tryster
Hebrew University of Jerusalem,
Israel

Yuri Tsivian
University of Chicago, USA

Maureen Turim
University of Florida, USA

Casper Tybjerg
University of Copenhagen, Denmark

William Uricchio
MIT, USA/Utrecht University, the Netherlands

Ansje van Beusekom
The Netherlands

Nanna Verhoeff
Utrecht University, the Netherlands

Gregory A. Waller
Indiana University, USA

Eva Warth
Ruhr-Universität Bochum, Germany

Michael Wedel
Hochschule für Film und Fernsehen
Potsdam–Babelsberg, Germany

Kristen Whissel
University of California, Berkeley, USA

Denise J. Youngblood
University of Vermont, USA

Zhen Zhang
New York University, USA

Thematic entry list

Categories listed in small upper case do not correspond to entries; all other categories and topics are entry headwords.

ARCHIVE SOURCES, SITES, AND POLICIES
    access
    archives
    authentication
    collections: public and private
    film festivals and occasional events
    preservation

AUDIENCES/SPECTATORSHIP
    audiences: research issues and projects
    audiences: surveys and debates
    spectatorship: issues and debates

CULTURAL CONTEXTS
    advertising
    amusement parks
    cafés-concerts
    Chatauqua
    comic strips
    department stores
    dime museums: USA
    dioramas and panoramas
    fairs/fairgrounds: Europe
    Hale's Tours
    illustrated lectures
    illustrated magazines
    illustrated songs
    intermediality and modes of reception
    magic lantern shows
    magicians
    moving picture fiction
    moving picture fiction: juvenile series
    museum life exhibits
    music hall

    newspapers
    opera
    painting and the visual arts
    penny arcades
    phonography
    photography
    postcards
    saloons
    shadow theater
    stereography
    theater, legitimate
    theater, melodrama
    vaudeville
    wax museums: Europe
    world's fairs

DEVELOPMENTS IN FILM STYLE
    acting styles
    camera movement
    cinema of attractions
    classical Hollywood cinema
    color
    costume
    editing: early practices and techniques
    editing: spatial relations
    editing: tableau style
    editing: temporal relations
    framing: camera distance and angle
    intertitles and titles
    lighting
    set design
    SOUND ACCOMPANIMENT
        benshi
        cue sheets

dialogue accompaniment
lecturer
musical accompaniment
musical scores
sound effects
sound machines
staging in depth

FILM COMPANIES
   AUSTRALIA
      Australasian Films
      Johnson and Gibson
      Pathé (Australia)
      Salvation Army
   AUSTRIA-HUNGARY
      Saturn
      Wiener Kunstfilm
   BELGIUM
      Belge Cinema SA, La
   CANADA
      Bioscope Company of Canada
   CHINA
      Asia Film Co.
      Commercial Press Motion Picture
        Department
      Fengtai Photography Studio
   CUBA
      Santos y Artigas
   DENMARK
      Biorama
      Dania Biofilm
      Dansk Biograf Kompagni
      Filmfabrikken Danmark
      Fotorama
      Kinografen
      Nordisk Films Kompagni
   FINLAND
      Atelier Apollo
      Finlandia Film
      Lyyra Filmi
   FRANCE
      AGC
      American Biograph (France)
      Aubert, Etablissements L.
      Cinéma du people, Le
      Cinéma-Halls, Compagnie des
      Comica
      Éclair

      Eclipse
      Film d'Art
      Gaumont
      Lumière et fils
      Lux
      Maison de la Bonne Presse
      Pathé-Frères
      Raleigh & Robert
      SCAGL
      STAR FILM (see Méliès, Georges)
      Théophile Pathé
      Valetta
   GERMANY
      AGFA
      Continental-Kunstfilm
      Deutsche Mutoskop & Biograph
      Messter consortium
      PAGU/AKGUT
      Vitascope
      Weltkinematograph/Express-Film
   GREAT BRITAIN
      Alpha Trading Company
      Bamforth
      Barker Motion Photography
      Blair Camera Company, European
      British & Colonial Kinematograph
        Company
      British Gaumont
      British Mutoscope & Biograph
      Butcher's Film Service
      Charles Urban Trading Company
      Clarendon Film Company
      Hepworth
      Mitchell and Kenyon
      Miles Brothers
      National Color Kinematograph
      Pathé-Frères (Great Britain)
      Sheffield Photo
      Topical Film Company
      Walturdaw
      Warwick Trading Company
      Wrench Film Company
   INDIA
      Aurora Cinema
      Hindustan Cinema Films Company
      Kohinoor Film Company
      Madan Theatres Limited
      Maharashtra Film Company
      Patankar Friends & Company

Phalke Films
Royal Bioscope
ITALY
  Ambrosio
  Aquila Films
  Cines
  Comerio Films
  Dora Film
  Film d'Arte Italiana (Pathé-Frères)
  Gloria Films
  Itala
  Milano Films
  Pasquali & C.
JAPAN
  Fukuhodo
  Komatsu Shokai
  Konishi Photographic Store
  M. Pathe
  Nikkatsu
  Tenkatsu
  Yokota Shokai
  Yoshizawa Shoten
NETHERLANDS, THE
  Dutch Mutoscope & Biograph
  Hollandia
  Hollandsche Film (Pathé-Frères)
POLAND
  Kosmofilm
  Sfinks
RUSSIA
  Drankov
  Khanzhonkov & Co.
  Pathé russe
  Thiemann & Reinhardt Company
SPAIN
  Barcinógrafo
  Cuesta Valencia
  Hispano Films
SWEDEN
  Numa Peterson's Trading Company
  Orientaliska teatern
  Pathé Film (Sweden)
  Svensk-Amerikanska Filmkompaniet
  Svenska Biografteatern
USA
  American Film Manufacturing
    Company
  American Mutoscope and Biograph
    (AM&B)

Biograph
Blair Camera Company
Centaur/Nestor
Chicago Film Exchange
Eastman Kodak Company
Éclair American
Edison Manufacturing
Essanay Film Manufacturing Company
Famous Players Motion Picture Company
General Film Company
Greater New York Film Rental Company
IMP
Kalem
Keystone Film Company
Klaw & Erlanger
Kleine Optical Company
Lubin Manufacturing Company
Maguire & Baucus
Majestic
Miles Brothers
Motion Picture Distributing and Sales
  Company (Sales)
Motion Picture Patents Company
Mutual Film Corporation
New York Motion Picture Company
North American Phonograph
Pathé Cinematograph
Raff & Gammon
Reliance
Rex
Selig Polyscope Company
Solax
Thanhouser Film Company
Universal Film Manufacturing Company
Vitagraph Company of America
Warner's Features, Inc.
World Film Corporation

INDUSTRY DEVELOPMENTS
  distribution: Europe
EXHIBITION
  airdomes
  churches and exhibition
  cinema circuits or chains
  itinerant exhibitors
  nickelodeons
  palace cinemas
  program formats
  projectionists

modes of production: issues and debates
publicity: issues and debates
    fashion
    star system
screenwriting

KEY FIGURES
  ARGENTINA
    Gallo, Mario
    Glücksmann, Max
    Py, Eugenio
  AUSTRALIA
    Gavin, John
    Higgins, Ernest
    Lincoln, W. J.
    Longford, Raymond
    Perry, Joseph
    Rolfe, Alfred
    Spencer, Cozens
    West, T. J.
  AUSTRIA-HUNGARY
    Arche, Alto
    Hintner, Cornelius
    Kolm, Louise Veltée
    Kolowrat-Krakowsky, Alexander
      "Sascha" Joseph
    Lowenstein, Hans Otto
  BELGIUM
    Belot, Charles
    Krüger, Fréderic
    Machin, Alfred
    Thévenon, Etienne
    Van Goitsenhaven, Louis
  BRAZIL
    Auler, William
    Botelho, Alberto Màncio
    Campos, Antônio
    de Barros, Luis
    Ferrez, Julio
    Hirtz, Eduardo
    Leal, Antônio
    Medina, José
    Reis, Luis Tomás
    Requião, Anibal Rocha
    Rossi, Gilberto
    Santos, Francisco
    Santos, Silvino
    Segreto, Afonso

    Segreto, Paschoal
    Serrador, Francisco
  CANADA
    Bianchi, Joseph
    Freer, James Simmons
    Green, John C.
    Griffin, John J.
    Schuberg, John
  CANADA: QUEBEC
    De Grandsaignes d'Hauterives, Henry
    Gauvreau, Georges
    Mason, Bert
    Minier, Louis
    Ouimet, Léo-Ernest
    Silvio, Alexandre
  CHILE
    Giambastiani, Salvador
    Sienna, Pedro
  CHINA
    Ramos, Antonio
    Zhang Shichuan
    Zhang Zhengqiu
  COLOMBIA
    Di Doménico family
  CUBA
    Casasús, José
    Diaz Quesada, Enrique
    Peón, Ramón
  DENMARK
    Ankerstjerne, Johan
    Blom, August
    Christensen, Benjamin
    Elfelt, Peter
    Gad, Urban
    Glückstadt, Vilhelm
    Holger-Madsen
    Larsen, Viggo
    Lind, Alfred
    Nielsen, Asta
    Olsen, Ole
    Psilander, Valdemar
    Skaarup, Frede
  FRANCE
    Andréani, Henri
    Andreyor, Yvette
    Andriot, Josette
    Arnaud, Etienne
    Arquillière, Alexandre
    Aubert, Louis

Baron, Auguste
Benoît-Lévy, Edmond
Bernhardt, Sarah
Bosetti, Romeo
Bourbon, Ernest
Bourgeois, Gérard
Boutillon, Edmond
Breteau
Brézillon, Léon
Bull, Lucien
Bünzli, Henri René
Burguet, Charles
Calmettes, André
Canudo, Ricciotto
Capellani, Albert
Capellani, Paul
Carl, Renée
Carpentier, Jules
Carré, Michel
Chautard, Emile
Clément-Maurice
Cohl, Emile
Coissac, Guillaume-Michel
Comandon, Jean
Continsouza, Pierre-Victor
de Bedts, Georges William
de Morlhon, Camille
Debrie, Joseph and André
Decourcelle, Pierre
Decroix, Charles
Deed, André
Delac, Charles
Demaria, Jules
Demenÿ, Georges
Denola, Georges
Desfontaines, Henri
Doublier, Francis
Doyen, Eugène-Louis
Dranem
Duhamel, Sarah
Durand, Jean
Dureau, Georges
Fescourt, Henri
Feuillade, Louis
Floury, Edmond Louis
Froissart, Georges
Gabet, Françisque
Gasnier, Louis
Gaumont, Léon Ernest

Grandais, Suzanne
Grimoin-Sanson, Raoul
Gugenheim, Eugène
Guy Blaché, Alice
Hamman, Joë
Hatot, Georges
Heuzé, André
Isola, Emile and Vincent
Janssen, Pierre-Jules-César
Jasset, Victorin-Hippolyte
Joly, Henri
Jourjon, Charles
Kirchner, Albert (a.k.a. Léar)
Krauss, Henry
Laffitte, Paul
Le Bargy, Charles
Le Prince, Louis Aimé Augustin
Lépine, Charles-Lucien
Leprince, René
Levesque, Marcel
Linder, Max
Londe, Albert
Lordier, Georges
Lumière, Auguste and Louis
Marey, Etienne-Jules
Mary, Clément
Méliès, Georges
Mendel, Georges
Mercanton, Louis
Merzbach, Saul and Georges
Mesguich, Felix
Migé, Clément
Mistinguett
Modot, Gaston
Monca, Georges
Musidora
Nalpas, Louis
Napierkowska, Stacia
Natan, Bernard
Navarre, René
Noguès, Pierre
Nonguet, Lucien
Parnaland, Ambroise-François
Pathé, Charles
Perret, Léonce
Pirou, Eugène Louis
Popert, Siegmund
Pouctal, Henri
Poyen, René-Georges

Prince, Charles
Promio, Alexandre
Reulos, Lucien
Reynaud, Emile
Riche, Daniel
Robinne, Gabrielle
Rogers, George
Sandberg, Serge
Tourneur, Maurice
Vandal, Marcel
Velle, Gaston
Veyre, Gabriel
Werner, Michel and Eugène
Zecca, Ferdinand

GERMANY
Altenloh, Emilie
Anschütz, Ottomar
Bartling, Georg
Bassermann, Albert
Becce, Giuseppe
Bolten-Baeckers, Heinrich
Davidson, Paul
Decroix, Charles
Delmont, Joseph
Dentler, Martin
Duskes, Alfred
Ewers, Hanns Heinz
Foersterling, Hermann
Froelich, Carl
Gärtner, Adolf
Giampietro, Josef
Gliewe, Max
Gottschalk, Ludwig
Häfker, Hermann
Hofer, Franz
Lange, Konrad
Lautensack, Heinrich
Lubitsch, Ernst
Mack, Max
May, Joe
Messter, Oskar
Misu, Mime
Müller-Lincke, Anna
Oliver, David
Piel, Harry
Pinschewer, Julius
Pinthus, Kurt
Porten, Henny
Reicher, Ernst

Reinhardt, Max
Rye, Stellan
Seeber, Guido
Skladanowsky, Max and Emil
Stollwerck, Ludwig
Tannenbaum, Herbert
Trautschold, Gustav
Valentin, Karl
von Woringen, Paul
Wegener, Paul
Weisse, Hanni
Wolff, Philipp

GREAT BRITAIN
Acres, Birt
Barker, William George
Brown, Theodore
Cheetham, Arthur
Collins, Alfred
Darling, Alfred
Donisthorpe, Wordsworth
Duncan, Francis Martin
Evans, Fred ("Pimple")
Fitzhamon, Lewin
Friese-Greene, William
Furniss, Harry
Green, George
Haggar, William
Hepworth, Cecil
Holland, Annie
Hopwood, Henry Vaux
Jeffs, Waller
Jury, Sir William Frederick
Kamm, Leonard Ulrich
Kearton, Cherry
Mason, Bert
McDowell, John Benjamin
Newman, Arthur Samuel
Norton, Charles Goodwin
Paul, Robert William
Pike, Oliver
Ponting, Herbert
Pringle, Ralph
Pyke, Montague Alexander
Raymond, Matt
Redfern, Jasper
Relph, Harry ("Little Tich")
Rosenthal, Joseph
Smith, F. Percy
Smith, George Albert

Smith, John William
Stow, Percy
Taylor, Alma and White, Chrissie
Thomas, Arthur Duncan
Urban, Charles
von Herkomer, Sir Hubert
Walker, William
West, Alfred
Williams, Randall
Williamson, James

INDIA
Bhatavdekar, Harishchandra Sakharam
Esoofally, Abdulally
Ganguly, Dhirendranath
Madan, Jamshedji Framji
Mudaliar, Nataraja
Phalke, Dhundiraj Govind
Sen, Hiralal
Singh, Suchet
Venkaiah, Raghupati

ITALY
Alberini, Filoteo
Almirante Manzini, Italia
Ambrosio, Arturo
Bertini, Francesca
Bonnard, Mario
Borelli, Lyda
Calcina, Vittorio
Capozzi, Alberto
Caserini, Mario
Collo, Alberto
D'Annunzio, Gabriele
De Liguoro, Giuseppe
De Riso, Camillo
Del Colle, Ubaldo Maria
Duse, Eleonora
Fabre, Marcel
Falena, Ugo
Frau, Raymond
Fregoli, Leopoldo
Frusta, Arrigo
Ghione, Emilio
Guazzoni, Enrico
Guillaume, Ferdinando
Gys, Leda
Jacobini, Maria
Lo Savio, Gerolamo
Maggi, Luigi
Martoglio, Nino

Menichelli, Pina
Morano, Gigetta
Negroni, Baldassarre
Nepoti, Alberto
Novelli, Amleto
Notari, Elvira Coda
Omegna, Roberto
Oxilia, Nino
Pagano, Bartolomeo
Pasquali, Ernesto Maria
Pastrone, Giovanni
Roberti, Roberto
Rodolfi, Eleuterio
Rossi, Carlo
Serena, Gustavo
Vidali, Enrico
Vitrotti, Giovanni
Zacconi, Ermete

JAPAN
Edamasa Yoshiro
Kaeriyama Norimasa
Kobayashi Kisaburo
Komada Koyo
Makino Shozo
Maseo Inoue
Onoe Matsunosuke
Sawamura Shirogoro
Tachibana Teijiro
Tanaka Eizo
Tokugawa Musei
Umeya Shokichi
Yokota Einosuke

MEXICO
Alva, Carlos, Guillermo
and Salvador
Becerril, Guillermo
Bernard, Fedinand "Bon"
Derba, Mimi
Rosas, Enrique
Toscano, Salvador

NETHERLANDS, THE
Binger, Maurits Herman
Bos, Annie
Desmet, Jean
Frenkel, Theo
Gildemijer, Johan Hendrik
Hartlooper, Louis
Ivens, Cees A. P.
Lamster, Johann Christian

Mullens, Bernard and Willy
Nöggerath, Franz Anton Jr.
Nöggerath, Franz Anton Sr.
Slieker, George Christiaan
Stokvis, Simon B.
Wolf, Nathan Hyman
NORWAY
Gladtvet, Ottar
Gundersen, Jens Christian
Lykke-Seest, Peter
POLAND
Matuszewski, Bóleslaw
Prószynski, Kazimierz
RUSSIA
Bauer, Evgenii
Chardynin, Petr
Drankov, Aleksandr
Gardin, Vladimir
Goncharov, Vasilii
Hansen, Kai
Khanzhonkov, Aleksandr
Kholodnaia, Vera
Maître, Maurice Andrá
Mosjoukine, Ivan
Protazanov, Jakov
Starewicz, Wladyslaw
Thiemann, Pavel
Yermoliev, Iosif
SPAIN
Chomón, Segundo de
Gelabert, Fructuoso
Gual, Adrià
Marro, Albert
Ors, Eugeni d'
Togores, José de
SWEDEN
Bergqvist, John
Friberg, C. A.
Klercker, Georg af
Lundberg, Frans
Magnusson, Charles
Nilsson, N. P.
Sjöström, Victor
Stiller, Mauritz
SWITZERLAND
Burlingham, Frederick
Dussaud, François
Joye, Joseph-Alexis
Lavanchy-Clarke,

François-Henri
Le Blond, Elizabeth Alice Frances
Sivan, Casimir
USA
Addams, Jane
Aitken, Harry
Anderson, Gilbert M.
Arbuckle, Roscoe ("Fatty")
Armat, Thomas
Baggot, King
Bakshy, Alexander
Balaban, Barney and A. J.
Balshofer, Fred J.
Baumann, Charles O.
Bedding, Thomas G.
Berst, Jacques A.
Bitzer, Wilhelm ("Billy")
Blackton, J. Stuart
Boggs, Francis
Bonine, Robert Kates
Bosworth, Hobart
Brady, William Aloysius
Brulator, Jules E.
Buckwalter, Harry H.
Bunny, John
Bush, W. Stephen
Bushman, Francis X.
Cabanne, W. Christy
Chaplin, Charles
Clement, Josephine
Clune, William H.
Cody, William F. ("Buffalo Bill")
Collier, John
Corbett, James J.
Costello, Maurice
Cunard, Grace
Davis, Harry
Dawley, J. Searle
DeMille, Cecil B.
Dickson, William Kennedy Laurie
Dintenfass, Mark M.
Dwan, Allan
Dyer, Frank L.
Eastman, George
Edison, Thomas Alvin
Farnum, Dustin
Finch, Flora
Ford, Francis
Foster, William

Fox, William

Freuler, John L.

Fuller, Loïe

Fuller, Mary

Fynes, J. Austin

Gardner, Helen

Gauntier, Gene

Gilmore, William E.

Gish, Lillian

Grau, Robert

Grauman, Sid

Gregory, Carl Louis

Griffith, David Wark

Harrison, Louis Reeves

Hart, William S.

Heise, William

Hodkinson, W. W.

Holmes, Elias Burton

Holmes, Helen

Horsley, David

Howe, Lyman H.

Hulfish, David S.

Hutchinson, Samuel S.

Ince, Ralph

Ince, Thomas H.

Jenkins, C. Francis

Johnson, Arthur

Johnson, Jack

Johnson, Noble M.

Jones, Aaron J.

Joyce, Alice

Katz, Sam

Keith, B. F.

Kennedy, Jeremiah J.

Kessel, Adam

Kleine, George

Laemmle, Carl

Lasky, Jesse

Latham, Gray and Otway

Lauste, Eugene

Lawrence, Florence

Leonard, Marion

Lindsay, Vachel

Loew, Marcus

Long, Samuel

Lubin, Siegmund

Mace, Fred

Marion, Frank J.

Mark, Mitchell H.

Marvin, Arthur

Marvin, Harry

Mastbaum, Jules and Stanley

McCay, Winsor

McCutcheon, Wallace

McRae, V. H.

Méliès, Gaston

Miller, Arthur C.

Mix, Tom

Moore, Annabelle

Moore, Owen

Munsterberg, Hugo

Murdock, J. J.

Muybridge, Eadweard

Normand, Mabel

Olcott, Sidney

Paley, William ("Daddy")

Pickford, Mary

Poli, Sylvester

Porter, Edwin S.

Power, Nicholas

Powers, Patrick A.

Richardson, Frank Herbert

Robertson, D. W.

Rock, William T. ("Pop")

Roland, Ruth

Rothapfel, S. L. ("Roxy")

Sandow, Eugen

Sargent, Epes Winthrop

Saunders, Alfred Henry

Saxe, John and Thomas

Schenck, Nicholas and Joseph

Schneider, Eberhard

Selig, William Nicholas

Sennett, Mack

Shepard, Archibald

Shipman, Nell

Skouras, Spyros

Smalley, Phillips

Smith, Albert E.

Spoor, George K.

Steiner, William

Sterling, Ford

Storey, Edith

Swanson, William H.

Sweet, Blanche

Tally, Thomas Lincoln

Talmadge, Norma

Turner, Florence

Turpin, Ben
Walthall, Henry B.
Warner brothers
Waters, Percival Lee
Weber, Lois
White, James Henry
White, Pearl
Williams, Kathlyn
Woods, Frank
Young Deer, James
Zukor, Adolph

news event films
newsreels
phantom train rides
polar expedition films
propaganda films
re-enactments
religious filmmaking
scientific films: Europe
scientific films: USA
sports films
travelogues

KINDS OF FILMS
    amateur film
    FICTION
        animal pictures
        animation
        Autorenfilme
        biblical films
        chase films
        comedy
        comic series
        crime films
        detective films
        facial expression films
        féeries or fairy plays
        filme cantante (sung films)
        film d'art
        historical films
        melodramas, domestic
        melodramas, sensational
        mythologicals
        phonoscènes
        pornography
        serials
        Shakespeare films
        Tonbilder
        trick films
        westerns: cowboy and Indian films
        white slave films
        women's suffrage films
    NON-FICTION
        actualités
        advertising films
        boxing films
        dance films
        ethnographic films
        expedition/exploration films
        industrial films

LAW AND THE CINEMA
    copyright
    law and the cinema: regulating exhibition
    National Board of Censorship
    trade marks
    US patent wars

MULTIPLE-REEL FILMS
    multiple-reel films: Europe
    multiple-reel films: USA

NATIONAL CINEMAS
    AFRICA
        Africa: Belgian Colonies
        Africa: British Colonies
        Africa: French Colonies
        Africa: German Colonies
        South Africa
    ASIA
        Australia
        Cambodia
        China
        India
        Indonesia
        Japan
        Malaya
        New Zealand
        Oceania/South Pacific
        Philippines, the
        Thailand (Siam)
        Vietnam
    EUROPE
        Austria-Hungary
        Balkans, the
        Belgium
        Denmark
        Finland
        France

Germany
Great Britain
Greece
Ireland
Italy
Luxemburg
Netherlands, the
Norway
Poland
Portugal
Russia
Scotland
Spain
Sweden
Switzerland
Wales
MIDDLE EAST
    Egypt and other Arab countries
    Iran
    Palestine
    Turkey/Ottoman Empire
NORTH AMERICA
    Canada
    Canada, Quebec
    Cuba
    Mexico
    USA
        black cinema, USA
SOUTH AMERICA
    Argentina
    Bolivia
    Brazil
    Chile
    Colombia
    Peru
    Uruguay
    Venezuela

SOCIAL CONTEXTS
    colonialism: Europe
    consumer cooperatives: Europe
    education
    imperialism: USA
    labor movement: Europe
    labor movement: USA
    leisure time and space: USA
    migration/immigration: USA
    modernity and early cinema

    monopoly capitalism: USA
    racial segregation: USA
    TECHNOLOGIES
        communication
        electricity
        transportation
    urbanization
    women's movement: Europe
    women's movement: USA
    World War I

TECHNOLOGY AND MATERIAL
    archaeology of cinema/pre-cinema
    celluloid
        film developing, printing, and assembly
    chronophotography
    COLORING PROCESSES
        Chronochrome Gaumont
        Pathécolor
    intermittent movements
    magic lanterns and stereopticons
    PROJECTING MOVING IMAGES
        projectors
            Biograph 70mm projector
            Cinématographe Lumière
            double-film-band projectors
            Edison Home Kinetoscope
            Ernemann Imperator projector
            Gaumont projectors
            glass-plate projectors
            Kinetoscope
            Kinora
            Nuremberg toy projectors
            optical intermittent projectors
            Pathé-Frères projectors
            Pathé KOK projector
            Phantoscope
            Powers Cameragraph No. 5 projector
            Simplex projector
            Warwick Bioscope projector
        screens
    RECORDING MOVING IMAGES
        cameras
            Aeroscope camera
            Bell & Howell studio camera
            Biograph 70mm camera
            Cinématographe Lumière
            Debrie "Parvo" camera

Edison Kinetograph camera
English pattern cameras
Newman & Sinclair Reflex camera
Pathé-Frères cameras
lighting apparatus
synchronized sound systems
films sonores: Pathé-Frères
Chronophone Gaumont
Kinetophone
Messter Biophon

TRADE PRESS
DENMARK
Filmen
FRANCE
Ciné-Journal
Cinéma et l'Echo du cinéma réunis, Le
Courrier cinématographique, Le
Phono-Ciné-Gazette

GERMANY
Kinematograph, Der
Lichtbild-Bühne, Die
GREAT BRITAIN
Bioscope
Optical Lantern Weekly/Kinematograph
and Lantern Weekly
ITALY
Cine-Fono e la Rivista Fono-
Cinematografica, La
Vita Cinematografica, La
USA
Moving Picture News
Moving Picture World
New York Dramatic Mirror
New York Morning Telegraph
Phonogram, The
Phonoscope, The
Views and Films Index

Introduction

For the purposes of this encyclopedia *early cinema* refers to the first twenty or twenty-five years of the cinema's emergence at the end of the 19th and beginning of the 20th centuries. That is, if one thinks of Europe and North America, early cinema "begins" approximately in the early to middle 1890s and "ends" in the middle 1910s. However, certain entries discuss the "pre-cinema" period not only to describe the apparatuses (and their inventors) on which early cinema would be predicated but also to explore the cultural, philosophical, and socio-economic contexts within which it emerged. Likewise, certain entries extend beyond the middle 1910s, especially for countries or regions outside Europe and North America.

Those initial decades, again thinking of Europe and North America, encompass at least two overlapping periods. The first period is perhaps best described as a "cinema of attractions," whose defining characteristic was not so much storytelling or narrative but rather attractions—that is, forms of spectacle or display. In other words, it assumed venues of exhibition that primarily featured novelties foregrounding acts of shock, surprise, and/or amazement. The second is characterized by the transition to a cinema in which attractions generally were subordinated to narrative yet in different ways, with a variety of alternatives developing (in Europe and elsewhere) in parallel, and sometimes in competition, with the American model of what would become the "classical Hollywood" cinema. At the same time, however, an aesthetic of attractions continued to strongly mark certain kinds of fiction films, predominated in nonfiction, and also emerged in animation.

Until the early 1980s, the basic story of early cinema history focused on film production or filmmaking—whether that involved apparatuses, companies, filmmakers, or groups of film texts—and on developing modes of representation and narration. Since then, however, interest has been focused almost equally on film exhibition, and not only changes in the sites or venues of exhibition but also the cultural contexts and social spaces within which early films were distributed and shown. This shift has drawn new attention to those regions in Asia, the Middle East, South and Central America, and Africa where filmmaking initially may have been minimal but movie-going was significant. Moreover, it has led to greater consideration of who actually made up the audiences for early cinema, what was the use value of going to the movies—for pleasure, distraction, education, communality or sociality—and what was its impact on spectators for the social construction of identity or subjectivity, particularly given a historical context of heightened nationalism and growing mass consumption in Europe and North America.

This encyclopedia presents as much information as possible from the basic story of early cinema history, with its traditional focus on film production, filmmakers, kinds of films, and even individual films. Yet it also is committed to presenting information from the "revisionist" history of early cinema, with its focus on the changing nature of film distribution and exhibition and changing patterns of reception. Of particular importance is the notion that early cinema was inextricably bound up with other forms and practices of mass culture, that it emerged as a *combinatoire* of existing and innovative elements (audio as well as visual), and that it was a hybrid medium which only gradually coalesced into something more or less distinct as *cinema*.

The recent renewal of interest in early cinema has been spurred by special events as well as a variety of sustained activities. What perhaps most caught public attention were the 1990s centennial celebrations of the cinema's "origins," from well-publicized exhibitions to scholarly conferences, from catalogues focused on film manufacturers to essay collections and special journal issues. Long before those celebrations, however, the 1978 Congress of the International Federation of Film Archives (FIAF), held in Brighton, England, probably did more to revive this interest by bringing together archivists and academics from across the world for a full week to view and discuss nearly 600 fiction films made between 1900 and 1906, many of them newly rediscovered and available in new viewing prints. The so-called Brighton Conference soon led to long-term archive efforts to collect, preserve, and restore as much as possible of what early film material has survived and related efforts to present those "restorations" in annual festival venues such as Le Giornate del Cinema Muto (Pordenone/Sacile, Italy) or in special museum film series and workshops such as those held at the Nederlands Filmmuseum. As academics and archivists began to realize how unique and distinct early cinema had been from the "classical Hollywood" cinema and other later cinemas, they created, in 1987, an international organization, Domitor, specifically devoted to its study. This, in turn, led certain universities, especially in North America and Europe, to encourage and support theses and dissertations on the subject of early cinema, increasing numbers of which have researched little-known collections of material related to the circulation, exhibition, and reception of moving pictures.

In any enterprise of this scope and magnitude, certain caveats are in order. In choosing consultants, selecting contributors, and determining what entries would be included, I have sought, as general editor, to be as broadly representative as possible. However successful those efforts may have been, it has proved impossible, inevitably perhaps, not to seem to privilege North America and Europe, where cinema initially was so predominant and where cinema studies as an academic discipline has been most institutionalized. Similarly, it has been impossible to include or adequately cover every country or region, every company or "pioneer," every relevant concept or category that readers might wish or even expect to find in seeking to become more knowledgeable about early cinema and its emergence (perhaps certain gaps or lacks will be addressed in a subsequent edition). Moreover, having contributors write entries in English or having those entries translated from another language has revealed certain differences between cultures that may produce discrepancies in terminology and even conceptualization. This is especially the case when considering legal or business terms as well as patterns of social behavior: for instance, in the case of companies, the distinction between *société anonyme* and *société en nom collectif par actions* in French has no precise equivalent in English. Indeed, the sheer dominance of English as the *lingua franca* of academic culture in the early 21st century inevitably has had its "imperial" effects on this volume, not all of them perhaps recognized.

That said, I am deeply indebted to the ten consultants and nearly 150 contributors from around the world for the stellar work they have achieved (including their generosity in negotiating revisions), in order that this encyclopedia be completed. For his initial translations of entries written in French by François de la Bretèque, Roland Cosandey, André Gaudreault, Germain Lacasse, Laurent de Forestier, Eric Le Roy, Thierry Lefebvre, Laurent Mannoni, Jean-Jacques Meusy, and Jean-Pierre Sirois-Trahan, I humbly thank Franck Le Gac, at the time a Ph.D. candidate in Cinema and Comparative Literature at the University of Iowa. Finally, I am immensely grateful for the consistent support and dedicated work of the editorial team at Routledge, especially Fiona Cairns, Stephanie Rogers, Aileen Harvey, and Faye Kaliszczak. Such a global cooperative effort is all the more to be applauded, given that this text is being written during and after the depressing days of my own country's divisive, arrogantly misguided, even deceptive war on Iraq.

Richard Abel

access

Research on early cinema is primarily conducted in moving-image **archives** (through public screenings and in structures designed for individual study) and specialized **film festivals and occasional events** (Pordenone, Bologna). Because of their fragility, original nitrate prints can be consulted only in exceptional cases. This is unfortunate because much of the visual quality of the film is lost in the **preservation** process through the creation of a duplicate, normally a 35 mm or 16 mm viewing print. Although useful as a reference tool, a reproduction through electronic media is not considered a proper substitute for film, as it lacks the basic component of the cinematic work: a series of complete, consecutive photographic images projected through an intermittent mechanism.

A moving-image archive does not function like a library: a film is not a text, and access to a film print cannot be granted as quickly as in a repository of books and journals. Before being given to the researcher, a print is retrieved from a climatized vault, slowly brought to ambient temperature (this procedure takes at least 24 hours), and inspected. The most complete listing of extant films of the early period is published by the International Federation of Film Archives (FIAF); however, a surviving film is not necessarily available for viewing, because it may not yet have undergone preservation.

Research in the archive is greatly facilitated by the adoption of a few practical rules. Requests are to be submitted in writing with reasonable advance, specifying the original title and, if possible, the production year. Viewing sessions are scheduled by appointment in a study center where prints are seen on editing tables (the preferable method for in-depth analysis, as the film can be run slowly through the machine), or projected on a large screen. No more than three features or a dozen shorts can be viewed during an average working day. Film prints must be treated with the utmost care for their physical integrity: replacing a damaged copy is very costly in terms of laboratory work and staff labor. Information on the provenance of the print is sometimes subject to restrictions imposed by the donors. Finally, the results of the viewing session should be shared with the archive's staff for their cataloguing and documentation records in order to foster better public knowledge of the collection. With the exception of the Library of Congress in Washington D. C. and a few other institutions where research can be done at no cost, archives normally charge for access to their holdings.

Archives may loan their prints for showings outside the institution's premises to non-profit organizations and festivals with an established reputation for quality of presentation (variable speed **projectors**, three-blade shutters) and care for the archival elements. In doing so, they request that prints are shown with changeover (non-platter) projectors in order to minimize physical damage to the artifact. Many films of the early period are in public domain; however, borrowers are asked to obtain **copyright** clearance from the legal owners when this is required by law.

Further reading

Footage: The Worldwide Moving Image Sourcebook (1997) New York: Second Line Search.

International Federation of Film Archives (2001ff.) *Database of Archival Holdings*, Brussels: FIAF (CD-ROM).

Klaue, Wolfgang (1993) *World Directory of Moving Image and Sound Archives*, Munich: K. G. Saur.

Magliozzi, Ronald S. (1988) *Treasures from the Film Archives*, Metuchen, N.J. and London: Scarecrow Press.

PAOLO CHERCHI USAI

Acres, Birt

b. 1852; d. 1918

inventor/filmmaker, Great Britain/Germany

A photographic technician, Acres designed a cinematographic **camera** by early 1895. He took the first British films during a short-lived partnership with Robert **Paul**, notably *Arrest of a Pickpocket* and *The Derby*; then, in June 1895, he took the first films in Germany, for Ludwig **Stollwerck**, at the opening of the Kiel Canal. Acres exhibited these films with his own **projector** in London in January 1896, then elsewhere, chiefly to scientific and photographic societies. Temperamentally unsuited to life as a showman, he marketed a 17.5 mm amateur camera, the Birtac, in 1898, and then retreated to work in his small film laboratory and apparatus manufacturing firm.

DEAC ROSSELL

acting styles

The earliest instances of acting on film consist of photographic reproductions of pre-existing acts: several **Edison Kinetoscopes** show the strong man Eugene **Sandow** flexing his muscles; others include Annabelle Whitford performing one of her fan dances. Slightly later, in the popular **chase** and **trick films**, people go through the requisite actions with only minimal attention to performance. Film acting as a profession, and as a set of specifiable techniques, does not really begin until after 1908, as story film production increased and the major producers formed their own stock companies, drawing from the pool of available theatrical talent. It is only after this point that one can begin to think about the development of cinematic acting styles as such.

Discussions of acting in the American, British, and French **trade press** in 1908–1909 frequently compared it to pantomime as another form of acting without words. However, the overt substitution of gesture for dialogue soon came under criticism for being artificial, too obviously directed toward the audience. Filmmakers rapidly found other ways of conveying the kind of information normally conveyed in dialogue on the legitimate stage: using **intertitles and titles**, stage business, props, or **editing**. The evolution of film acting lay, rather, in the elaboration of devices for expressing emotion, underscoring dramatic situations, and blocking scenes in ways that were pictorially coherent and pleasing.

Film actors drew upon a panoply of 18th- and 19th-century acting styles—styles elaborated in the legitimate **theater** (and in **opera** and ballet, as well as pantomime—which relied upon poses, sometimes called attitudes, to control how the actor looked and moved on stage. Actors were enjoined to study statues and **paintings**, and to practice poses, and there was a consistent use of illustrative drawings in manuals on acting and oratory. Actors struck poses upon entering or exiting a scene, to indicate their interior states, to call attention to significant bits of stage business, and to signal major turning points in the action. Poses by the entire acting ensemble, called tableaux, were used at scene and act ends, and carefully planned by directors and playwrights. If, by the 1910s, stage actors eschewed posing in certain genres—naturalist drama, and light, sophisticated comedy set in a contemporary, urban milieu—these techniques still widely were employed and appreciated in opera, in many stagings of Shakespeare and classical tragedy, and for melodrama, romantic drama and history plays. In addition, some avant-garde stage directors associated with anti-naturalist movements such as symbolism and expressionism also sought to re-institute a highly posed acting style. Thus, these techniques remained available, and proved highly adaptable to the medium of silent film.

The cinematic use of poses varied by actor and genre as on the stage but was also affected by other stylistic developments: as filmmakers moved to closer camera **framing**, actors frequently adopted more restrained attitudes, and as cutting rates increased, actors necessarily shortened the sequences of poses that they employed, and the way they handled the problems of the acting ensemble. In particular, the rapid development of editing techniques in the USA, and the predilection for **staging in depth** as an alternative to editing in Europe, meant that the two film acting traditions developed differently.

One of the first companies celebrated for its acting was **Film d'Art** in **France**, which used highly trained actors from major theatrical companies, including the Comédie Française in Paris. These films demonstrate the way that the acting ensemble could accommodate, and even benefit from, the stylistic parameters of the earliest films: scenes presented in a single take with long-shot framing. Actors pose in turn to direct the spectator's attention within the frame, while larger groupings form harmonious compositions. In *La Tosca* (1909), in the famous scene in which Tosca (Cécile Sorel) kills Scarpia (Charles **Le Bargy**), Sorel rests very still on a couch in the foreground so that the action of Le Bargy, gesturing to his lieutenant in the rear, becomes prominent. Later, Le Bargy is at the rear of the set with his head down writing when Sorel in the foreground sees a knife on a table and strikes a pose indicating that she has conceived the idea of Scarpia's murder. *L'Assassinat du duc de Guise* [The Assassination of the Duc de Guise] (1908) is structured through the contrast between the poses assumed by a single actor (in some scenes Le Bargy as Henri III, in others Albert Lambert as the Duc de Guise) and the group poses assumed by the courtiers. In the scene in which Henri III plans the murder, for example, the courtiers cluster around Le Bargy as he moves from the bed, front left, to the window, rear right, and back again; often they strike attitudes in unison, as when they raise their swords together or kneel together at the king's command.

The **multiple-reel film**, which began to develop in Europe in 1910, had significant consequences for European acting styles. Some of the earliest, made in Denmark, featured one of the first

international **stars**, Asta **Nielsen**. In Italy, as manufacturers moved into long film production, they too began to make films based around star performances and performers, most notably Lyda **Borelli** and Francesca **Bertini**. Although this phenomenon is most often thought of in connection with "diva" acting, there were films based upon the work of male performers as well, for example the Danes Valdemar **Psilander** and Viggø **Larsen**, or the Italian Bartolomeo **Pagano** (Maciste).

The length of the feature film made possible more elaborate successions of poses. In *Ma l'amor mio non muore!* [Love Everlasting] (1913), the heroine (Borelli) writes a letter calling off her love affair with a prince, for his own good and the good of their country. The scene, presented in a medium-shot framing interrupted by a title, lasts over three minutes, and provides no new narrative information: the acting functions to embellish a situation which has already been clearly established. Borelli alternates the business of writing the letter with expressive poses: trying to suppress tears, giving way to them, burying her face in her hands, assuming an attitude of prayer. In addition to a deliberately slow pace, the highly ornamented acting characteristic of the diva film was produced by tailoring other stylistic elements to the demands of the performance. Closer framings or cut-ins displayed nuances of facial expression and gesture, staging in depth provided for highly choreographed entrances and exits, and the figure and movement of the actor were set off both by **camera movement** and by any number of visual devices within the frame: mirrors, windows, hats, and veils.

While the diva film prototypically focusses attention on a single performer, one often left alone on camera to express her reaction to her plight, this style also encompasses highly intricate ensemble acting, with gestural duets or trios in which the actors sometimes trade off expressive gestures, sometimes come together to form group poses or tableaux. In Albert **Capellani**'s *Les Misérables* (1912), Fantine (Marie Venture), ill and dying, is terrified by the appearance of Javert (Henri Étiévant), who has previously tried to arrest her, and who has followed the disguised Jean Valjean (Henry **Krauss**) to her bedside in order to arrest him. Krauss leans over talking to Venture, who lies in bed midground left. Suddenly, the door midground right opens and Étiévant enters, standing on the threshold. Venture sees him and assumes an attitude expressing terror. Étiévant folds his arms over his cane forming a barrier as if to prevent his prisoner from the leaving the room. Venture points to Étiévant and maintains this pose. Krauss turns, keeping his back to Étiévant and moves to front center, then turns again, glances at Étiévant, and turns to face front once more. All of the actors then hold their positions in a tableau. In this simple entrance, the postures of the actors are varied to form striking visual compositions, to shift attention from one to another, and to represent each character's reaction to the situation: the terror expressed by Venture, the aggressive threat indicated by Étiévant's pose, and the cool indifference and protective stance assumed by Krauss, accentuated by his front center position.

The films produced by the members of the **Motion Picture Patents Company** (MPPC) provide a clear contrast with the European tradition. In 1908–1909, no American company could have achieved the sophisticated ensemble work of the Film d'Art actors, although a film like D. W. **Griffith**'s *Confidence* (1909) suggests that he was trying to replicate that style at **Biograph**. Further, by the time the first important generation of American film actors had developed a following, and their own individual acting styles—people like Florence **Turner** and Maurice **Costello** at **Vitagraph** or Henry **Walthall** and Blanche **Sweet** at Biograph—conventions of filmmaking had altered, and with them, the way that actors handled blocking and the assumptions of attitudes. Closer framings meant that actors in the foreground were now "bigger," positioned at the nine-foot line, framed from knees to head, simplifying the problem of directing the spectator's attention in the frame. Thus, in Vitagraph's *Red and White Roses* (1913), the vamp Lida (Julia Swayne Gordon) slouches on a divan in the right foreground, dominating our attention and the space, while the politician she seeks to seduce moves forward through the depth of the hotel-room set. In addition, as the MPPC manufacturers adopted faster cutting rates, there was less time and less necessity for posing. Blanche Sweet's

performance in *The Painted Lady* (1912) is an often-discussed example. Sweet plays a girl deceived by a thief who courts her in order to gain access to her father's house. On the night of the attempted robbery, she shoots and kills the man, and then, after lifting the kerchief which had obscured his face, discovers his identity and goes mad with grief. The scene of the murder and discovery takes place in 18 shots with two titles, the action largely split between two adjacent rooms. A single gesture or a small number of them are contained within each shot, obviating the need to repeat and vary poses, and helping the actress engineer the transitions from one pose and emotional mood to another. There is only one pose when she realizes she has killed the masked intruder at the end of shot 12, while shot 13 similarly makes room for only two, a call for help which also functions as an expression of horror, with hands raised above head, and a turn and start at the sight of the body. The interpolation of a title, "Shattered," and the move to another room articulates the onset of madness, and it is accompanied by a cut to a closer framing that permits Sweet to act out her madness with smaller gestures. But such editing also means that the transition between one phase of the action and the next is no longer a matter of how and when she poses. Thus, while actors do strike attitudes in the more highly edited American cinema, one is much less likely to find the sequences of poses, or the methods for directing the spectator's attention in ensemble scenes that characterize European acting.

See also: *Autorenfilme*; biblical films; historical films

Further reading

Brewster, Ben (1999) "*Confidence*," in Paolo Cherchi Usai (ed.) *The Griffith Project: Volume 2, Films Produced in January–June 1909*, 87–89, London: British Film Institute.

Brewster, Ben and Lea Jacobs (1997) *Theatre to Cinema: Stage Pictorialism and the Early Feature Film*, Oxford: Oxford University Press.

Merritt, Russell (1976) "Mr. Griffith, *The Painted Lady* and the Distractive Frame," *Image*, 19.4.

Pearson, Roberta (1992) *Eloquent Gestures: The Transformation of Performance Style in the Griffith Biograph Films*, Berkeley: University of California Press.

LEA JACOBS

actualités

A word of French origin, *actualités* can refer to different types of films. In its most general meaning it can be seen as synonymous with "factual film." The French term quite often takes this sense in Anglo-American writings, probably because of its consonance with the English word "actuality," commonly used as a synonym for "reality." Consequently, all sorts of non-fiction pictures such as **travelogues**, **industrial films**, **scientific films**, **sports films, boxing films**, etc. can be considered *actualités*. In the light of this broad conception of *actualités* as early non-fiction films, John Grierson's famous definition of the documentary as the "creative treatment of actuality" has been understood by several historians as an attempt to distinguish films like those made by Robert Flaherty from the earlier practice of factual filmmaking.

The original French term, however, clearly implies a temporal reference: an *actualité* is a current event or something which happened relatively recently. In this narrower sense, commonly used on the European continent, *actualités* are topical films and can be seen as an early form of **news event films** and **newsreels**. *Actualités* defined as pictures presenting topical events can in fact be found among the earliest films: a considerable part of the **Lumière** production consists of views depicting state visits, inaugurations of monuments, parades, processions or other affairs that were of interest to the public and treated by other media as well. These were sold not only as single views but as series of views that exhibitors could arrange in their programs in different ways.

Yet another important sense of the term came from the French company **Pathé-Frères**, who wrote in their 1904 catalogue: "By this we mean scenes of general and international interest, which are so important that they will be able to thrill the

Figure 1 Frame still from *Sortie d'usine* (Lumière, 1895).

masses." In short, the subject matter of *actualités* had to be sensational enough to attract audiences.

These two characteristics—the reference to current events and the search for the sensational—were indeed the main ingredients of *actualités*, at least when defined according to the European use of the term. In late 19th-century France, the word also appeared in advertisements for other forms of visual entertainment, such as **dioramas and panoramas** or the displays of **wax museums** presenting recent events or the celebrities of the day. Thus *actualités* contributed to the emerging modern media landscape, adding moving pictures as a means to record or represent current political and social affairs.

In contemporary catalogues both "actuality" films (for instance, pictures taken while the event occurred) and **re-enactments** appear as *actualités*. Sometimes these are clearly separated as in a 1903 R. W. **Paul** catalogue distinguishing between "Pictures of the Transval War" and "Reproductions of Incidents of the Boer War." In other cases staged and unstaged *actualités* appear under the same heading. Battle scenes in war films, for instance, almost always were re-enactments since it was hardly possible for cameramen to capture any of the fighting except from a very great distance. Georges **Méliès** filmed a number of well-known re-creations of topical events such as his series of films on the "Maine" incident (1898) during the Spanish–American War, on the Dreyfus affair (1899), and on the coronation of King Edward VII (1902).

It would be anachronistic to consider these films as "fakes." There is hardly any evidence that contemporary audiences distinguished factual views from staged ones, at least in the way they might acknowledge the difference between a drawing and a **photograph** illustrating an article in a newspaper. In a short story published in *L'Illustration*, in 1900, and translated into German the same year, Maurice Normand has a young Irish maid watch pictures of the Boer War in a Paris theater. Believing she has witnessed her fiancé being shot in one of the films, she faints away. Later a Parisian gentleman assures her that these battle scenes were staged. This very interesting source suggests that an educated, urban (male) spectator could recognize a staged view, whereas a naïve and credulous (female) spectator could not. However, after 1907–1908, re-enactments sharply decline and *actualités* generally use "documentary" footage recorded at the scene.

During the early years of cinema, especially once the novelty effect of the moving picture machine had worn off, *actualités* contributed to building an **audience** for moving picture shows, sustaining their interest and attracting new groups of spectators. In the Netherlands, the **British Mutoscope and Biograph**'s pictures of the 1898 coronation of Queen Wilhelmina were immensely popular: they were screened throughout the country for many weeks. About the same time, in the United States, images of the Spanish–American War, which were shown mainly in **vaudeville** theaters, had a similar effect. In Germany, before the coming of permanent cinemas, variety theaters catering to the middle and upper classes differentiated films from the rest of the program by focusing on *actualités* which appeared on the bill as *Optische Berichterstattung* or "optical reports." In this context, even a film like Edwin S. **Porter**'s *The Great Train Robbery* (1903) could be presented as an "optical report," giving a true-to-life account of a train hold-up in the United States. As early as 1901 the Musée Grevin in Paris organized special programs with *actualités* presented first as *Journal lumineux* and then, from 1904 on, as *L'actualité par le cinématographe*. From 1906 on, the Kinema-Théâtre Gab-Ka in Paris also specialized in *actualités*, showing new programs every Friday. Others followed this model all over the world.

In the following years, *actualités* continued to draw audiences and were often highlighted on the programs. Public events such as coronations, jubilees, visits of state, and other ceremonies, natural disasters such as volcanic eruptions or floods, but also the exploits of daring criminals—such as the rise and fall of the French automobile gang of Jules Bonnot in 1911–1912—were extensively covered, both through actuality footage and re-enactments. In Germany, images of the Kaiser were so popular that the monarch and his family could even be considered to have been the first German film **stars**.

In 1909 Pathé launched its first newsreel series, *Pathé faits divers*, which then became *Pathé Journal* (*Pathé Weekly* in the USA). Other companies soon followed suit. These newsreels consisted of about eight to twelve different items presenting a broad range of subjects from political events to crime, sports, fashion, and beauty contests. However, individual *actualités* continued to exist alongside newsreels, now more often than not as news event films.

Further reading

Kessler, Frank, Sabine, Lenk, and Martin, Loiperdinger, (eds.) (1997) *KINtop. Jahrbuch zur Erforschung des frühen Films—6: Aktualitäten*, Basel/Frankfurt: Stroemfeld/Roter Stern.

Malthête, Jacques (1989) *Les actualités reconstituées de Georges Méliès* (Archives #21), Perpignan: Institut Jean Vigo/Cinémathèque de Toulouse.

Musser, Charles (1990) *The Emergence of Cinema: The American Screen to 1907*, New York: Scribner's.

FRANK KESSLER

Addams, Jane

b. 1860; d. 1935

reformer, USA

Jane Addams, a major figure during the Progressive era, worked for legal reforms to ameliorate social conditions associated with industrialization, **migration/immigration**, and **urbanization**, held key positions in trade-union (see **labor movement**), social-work, and **women's suffrage** organizations, and viewed recreation as an important municipal responsibility. In 1889, she co-founded Hull House, a model social settlement in Chicago. Addams critiqued commercial moving pictures for their lessons in crime, the trite morality of **illustrated songs**, and lurid **advertising** in posters. She also observed the communal atmosphere in **nickelodeons**; in an attempt to redirect their popularity, Hull House, in 1907, briefly ran its own nickelodeon.

CONSTANCE BALIDES

advertising

Neither those who made films nor those who viewed them came to their places in early cinema history in a vacuum. Producers and consumers of film enacted an exchange that was monetary but predicated on the expectation of meaningful or otherwise useful **communication**. As such, they brought with them the tendencies and resources of their cultures, and there was no more visible and influential signpost strewn across those cultures than advertising. For capitalist nations in particular, advertising formed a pervasive cultural context that influenced how films were made, how they were packaged and promoted, and how they were understood by audiences.

The practice of advertising has long roots that stretch back into the histories of many countries including Great Britain, France, Germany, and the USA. In the USA, which offers a prime example, an industry devoted exclusively to crafting and circulating commercial messages first developed in the 1840s. At that time, agencies emerged in response to the needs of penny **newspapers**, which increasingly relied on advertising to defray expenses, and the needs of manufacturers, who sought broader markets for mass-produced goods. Agencies built a profitable bridge between mass media and modern business.

As agencies multiplied—by 1861 there were twenty in New York City alone—so did the number of advertising messages. Advertising became the privileged discourse for educating people about the qualities and uses of branded

commodities, and it communicated a vision of life in which consumption was heralded as a means for shaping personal identity, communicating status, and establishing successful social relationships.

Before moving pictures, advertising appeared in many forms. Handbills were distributed to people in public spaces, and outdoor advertising (broadsides, posters, billboards, signs painted on rocks and buildings) was widespread. Newspapers sold increasingly large amounts of advertising, much of it to **department stores**, and in the 1860s advertising appeared regularly in **illustrated magazines** such as *Harper's Bazaar* and *Vanity Fair*. During the 1870s and 1880s, trade cards were a popular form of advertising. These small but vibrant images were distributed inside packaged goods and collected by consumers. **Postcards** were used to communicate with consumers as well.

When moving pictures were introduced in the 1890s businesses and agencies quickly became involved in producing **advertising films**. Like newspaper editors who deftly inserted messages into a loosely connected layout of diverse stories and images, theater showmen used advertising films as part of the assembled mix that formed the **cinema of attractions**. Because these films were thought of as "animated posters" or "animated billboards," showmen occasionally projected them on open-air **screens** at crowded intersections, in keeping with existing practices for outdoor advertising.

If businesses used the film medium as a resource for advertising, so too did film manufacturers use advertising as a resource for films. During the pre-**nickelodeon** era, films were short and did not possess a high degree of internal coherence. Manufacturers depended on exhibitors (perhaps using **lecturers** or **dialogue accompaniment**) and movie-goers to supply missing information. Filmmakers chose images, topics, and stories familiar to **audiences**. Advertising campaigns provided a ready-made stock of knowledge.

In the 1890s, American Tobacco Company controlled nine-tenths of the domestic cigarette market and inserted trade cards depicting famous or exotic women into the packs of some of its brands. A person familiar with this practice thus had little trouble understanding the visual pun in *Admiral Cigarette* (1897), where a woman in striking costume bursts from a large pack of Admiral cigarettes.

Edison's *The Great Train Robbery* (1903) based its famous image of a robber firing his pistol directly at the audience on Sam Hoke's "Highwayman" poster for Gold Dust brand powdered cleanser (a poster that gave new meaning to the phrase "cleaning up crime"). This shot intensified the audience's reaction by associating the film with an advertising image that was controversial for its alleged power to mesmerize those who stared too long at it.

Edison's *Romance of the Rail* (1904) spoofed a popular advertising series done for Lackawanna Railroad by famed copywriter Earnest Elmo Calkins. The company sought to differentiate its passenger service, which used "clean-burning" anthracite coal, from competing services using bituminous coal (which produced heavy clouds of soot that clung to clothes). To personify the distinction, Calkins created Phoebe Snow, whose white hat and dress remained spotless throughout her many travels on Lackawanna Railroad— dubbed the "Road of Anthracite." In *Romance of the Rail*, Snow and a new acquaintance fall in love and are married in the course of a single trip. Lackawanna's trademark appears prominently on the suitor's luggage and train's box cars. At film's end, two tramps crawl from beneath a train car and rebuff a porter who tries to brush their clothes, an unnecessary gesture on the "Road of Anthracite."

Film companies also used advertising for ideas about how to market the film product itself. Early exhibitors showed continuous programs of shorts, often changed daily, and had little advance knowledge about the content and release dates of new films. This made it difficult for nickelodeons to advertise individual films. However, with the development of a reliable distribution system, exhibitors received more information about upcoming releases and film producers began to differentiate their brands by supplying lithographed posters and other materials to promote company **trade marks** and advertise specific film titles.

Manufacturers hired advertising agencies to develop organized marketing campaigns. Film posters became highly artistic, like much advertising generally, because agencies believed beauty and style stimulated visual interest and consumer desire. A film's genre, spectacle, and the **star system** became increasingly important as marketing elements that were tied-in with other products (such as designer **fashions**) and repeated across a variety of advertising mediums and formats. By 1910, advertising slides—long a source of revenue for exhibitors who used **magic lanterns** to project commercial messages for a variety of goods and services onto movie screens—were being used to build studio brand names, generate anticipation for upcoming releases, and promote stars. By 1915, a new type of advertising—the movie trailer— developed to help stimulate and control demand for individual films that increasingly could be conceived and produced with their advertising potential in mind.

Figure 2 Flip book showing a clown juggling boxes of Church and Co.'s Arm and Hammer baking soda, *c*. late 1880s or early 1890s. (Courtesy of Jeffrey Klenotic.)

See also: consumer cooperatives: Europe; industrial films; monopoly capitalism: USA; program formats; publicity; travelogues

Further reading

Goodrum, Charles and Helen Dalrymple (1990) *Advertising in America*, New York: Harry N. Abrams.

Luckett, Moya (1999) "Advertising and Femininity: The Case of *Our Mutual Girl*," *Screen*, 40.4: 363–383.

Staiger, Janet (1990) "Announcing Wares, Winning Patrons, Voicing Ideals: Thinking about the History and Theory of Film Advertising," *Cinema Journal*, 29.3: 3–31.

Strasser, Susan (1989) *Satisfaction Guaranteed: The Making of the American Mass Market*, New York: Pantheon.

JEFFREY KLENOTIC

advertising films

With their emergence as a new form of screen practice and mass **communication**, moving pictures were perceived as a dynamic medium for **advertising** and promotion. Film manufacturers cultivated the market for advertising by creating **travelogues**, **industrial films**, and other types of short films to stimulate demand for consumer goods and services and promote product brand names and company **trade marks**.

The idea of using moving pictures for advertising was not radically new. Rather, it extended and synthesized existing forms of advertising and screen practice. For well over a decade before the development of cinema, advertisers personalized and animated the expanding world of anonymous mass-produced objects, giving life and movement to commodities by inserting their trade-marked packages into the ephemeral images and fleeting narratives of thumb books and mechanical trade cards. When motion-picture projection was achieved and films captured a place in the landscape of commercial imagery and amusement, advertisers were there. Like billboards vying for the attention of distracted urbanites, advertising films

(and slides) were projected as part of the showman's **cinema of attractions.** Better than billboards, though, advertising films reached an invested (paying) and relatively immobilized public that was not likely to turn away. This "captive" aspect of the cinema audience has intrigued advertisers ever since.

As with the emergence of cinema generally, advertising films were an international phenomenon. In Great Britain, Arthur Melbourne Cooper was hired in 1897 by Bird's Custard Powder to make a film based on one of the company's advertising posters. Some manufacturers purchased equipment and made films themselves, as when Nestlé and Lever Bros. jointly produced *The Sunlight Soap Competition* (1897) and other advertisements.

French filmmaker Felix **Mesguich** created "animated posters" in 1898 that were projected onto an open-air billboard affixed to the third floor of a Montmartre building in Paris. Georges **Méliès**, celebrated for his **trick films**, was also a prolific producer of innovative advertising films. These were sometimes shown on a screen above the entrance to the Robert-Houdin Théâtre. Among his clients: Bornibus mustard, Chocolat Ménier, Delion hats, Dewar's whiskey, Mystère corsets, Orbec beer, Widow Brunot's wax, and the hair-restoring Xour lotion.

In the USA, the International Film Company employed Edwin S. **Porter** in 1897 to project a mix of advertising films (Haig whisky, Pabst beer, Maillard's chocolate) and topical subjects for an open-air show in New York. When Porter projected the films onto a large **screen** atop the Pepper building on 34th Street and Broadway, he was reportedly charged with creating a public nuisance for inciting pedestrians to crowd the sidewalks below. **Edison**, Porter's next employer, also produced advertising films, such as *Admiral Cigarette* (1897), *Crawford Shoe Store* (1897), *Lickmann's Cigar and Photo Store* (1898), and *North Side Dental Rooms* (1898).

While some films made direct pitches to spectators, many more took an indirect approach. Serving as sponsors, businesses and other organizations—primarily **transportation** companies, but also heavy industry, the military, and chambers of commerce—subsidized production costs for films that subtly promoted their interests and brand names. Between 1896 and 1900, nearly half of all Edison films were financed this way.

These films were presented by exhibitors as entertainment that was exciting and educational. Travel films offered vivid glimpses of life in distant and sometimes exotic settings that were increasingly open to tourists by rail or steamship. Military films depicted the daily life of soldiers and sailors, and granted privileged battlefield views, thereby visually punctuating recruiting efforts. An industrial film demonstrating wine production in California educated the consumer, promoted the wine industry, and fostered West Coast tourism. Other industrials presented an attractive vision of factory production as a safe, clean, and well-organized process.

In addition to their covert appeals, sponsored films were used by sales people to make a more direct and targeted pitch, as when prospective clients were treated to a pre-meeting screening of the sponsor's film at a local theater. With the development of positive safety film stock around 1908, sales agents could even use portable **projectors** to show films in their offices or take films for meetings on the road.

Although the number of advertising films as a percentage of total film output probably peaked between 1896 and 1900, such films were produced throughout the period of early cinema and beyond. The efforts of Germany's Julius **Pinschewer** in the 1910s were especially significant. He commissioned and distributed internationally advertising films made by avant garde **animation** artists like Lotte Reininger, Walter Ruttmann, and Guido **Seeber**. Another trend in the 1910s was the production of fiction films that concealed their advertising intent within an entertaining narrative. Thus the dramatic resolution of Edison's *The Stenographer's Friend* (1910) hinged on the effectiveness of the company's business **phonograph**, while the harried housewife in *The Family Jar* (1913) solved her husband's chronic indigestion by providing "pure food" Beech-Nut bacon. One exhibitor who recognized the advertising intent behind *Chew Chew Land* (1910) complained to *Moving Picture World* that it was unfair "to deal out for amusement and edification a picture embellished with the trade marks of the certain manufacturer of the goods it is desired to advertise."

Although no one knew if advertising films actually stimulated demand, no one knew for sure they didn't. So advertisers continued to use the film medium. By the 1910s, when advertising films averaged 1,000 feet in length, sponsors were willing to pay one dollar per foot for the original negative and initial positive print, and fifteen cents per foot for additional prints. There were also costs for travel when outdoor scenarios were used and costs for portable lights when indoor sets applied. On average, the subsidy to produce and distribute an advertising picture was roughly $5,000. Yet agents estimated that such a film, distributed in theaters across the USA for seven months, reached fifteen to twenty-five million people.

See also: consumer cooperatives: Europe; department stores; fashion; monopoly capitalism: USA; publicity

Further reading

Musser, Charles (1997) *Edison Motion Pictures, 1890–1900: An Annotated Filmography*, Pordenone/Washington D. C.: Le Giornate del Cinema Muto/Smithsonian Institution Press.

Perkins, Daniel J. (1985) "Sponsored Business Films: An Overview 1895–1955," *Film Reader*, 6: 125–132.

Perkins, Daniel J. (1990) "The American Archives of the Factual Film," *Historical Journal of Film, Radio, and Television*, 10.1: 71–80.

Thompson, Kristin (1985) *Exporting Entertainment: America in the World Film Market, 1907–1934*, London: British Film Institute.

JEFFREY KLENOTIC

Aeroscope camera

Patented in 1909 by Poland's Kasimir de **Prószynski**, but manufactured from 1912 on by **Newman and Sinclair** in London and then commercialized by Cherry **Kearton**, the Aeroscope was one of the first cameras whose claw mechanism was driven by compressed air, which required tanks that had to be filled with a pump. The advantage of such a system was that it gave the camera greater autonomy, because a cameraman no longer needed to turn a crank to advance the film. Abel Gance used the Aeroscope camera for the horse chase scene in *Napoleon* (1927), shot in Corsica.

LAURENT MANNONI

Africa: Belgian colonies

The first films successfully shot in the Congo Independent state occurred in the summer of 1908, probably taken by a Belgian officer in the northern part of the country: the Uélé river, Redjaf, and the enclave of Lado. The films were presented at the Club Africain-Cercle d'Etudes Coloniales in Antwerp the following November.

In 1909, when the Congo became a Belgian colony, scenes of life in the harbor towns of Boma and Matadi and along the railroad between Matadi and Leopoldville (Kinshasa) already were circulating in Brussels as a means of propagating the Belgian presence in Africa. Le Cinématographe des Colonies was founded to exhibit films of the new territories in Africa in the company's own cinema in Brussels. Its cameraman Léon Reinelt shot urban centers, harbors, new railways and the Belgian military presence in such films as *L'Estuaire du fleuve Congo, Banana, Boma, Le marché de Boma, Le défilé de la Force Publique, Le chemin de fer des Cataractes, Au Kasai, Voyage dans le Mayumbé*. He also gave special attention to the natural resources in such nonfiction films as *Travaux forestiers au Congo* and *Le Poste et la ferme de Duma*.

Between 1909 and 1913, a number of personalities were filmed on their travels to the Belgian Congo: i.e., *Le voyage du prince Albert au Congo, Le comte de Turin au Congo, l'Arrivée du Ministre des Colonies à Banana, Boma et Matadi, Les manoeuvres de la Force Publique Noire devant le prince Albert*.

For the British weekly, *The African World and Cape Cairo Express*, published in the Belgian Congo, the South African cameraman R. C. E. Nissen filmed daily life in the newly built mine town of Elizabethville (Lubumbashi), the copper mines of Katanga, the commercial city of Stanleyville (Kisangani), and the Kambove mines.

In 1913, this footage was edited into a two-hour program entitled *From Rhodesia via Katanga to Angola, Bulawayo to Elisabethville and Kambove to Lobito Bay*, which met with success throughout the British and Belgian colonial world.

The first films seem to have been projected in the Belgian Congo about 1910 in Leopoldville. A year later a travelling showmen from Italy showed films from **Méliès** and **Pathé-Frères** in both Stanleyville and Elisabethville. By 1913 **itinerant exhibitors** had reached the most remote parts of the Congo: i.e., in Yungu and Lemfu near Ngidinga at the Angolan border (Upper Congo). Of the first cinema halls opened in Leopoldville in 1916, one was owned by a Belgian, Henri Legaert, who showed French and British films about the battlefields of **World War I**. Soon after, a cinema also opened in Elizabethville, as did the Cinéma Hennion (with French **projectors**), on the site of a former café-restaurant in Boma.

During the war, the Ministry for the Belgian colonies created a special service to produce films in the Congo. Between 1917 and 1919, cameraman Ernest Gourdinne worked almost everywhere in the colony. He shot films about the copper mines in Katanga, the industrial center of Lusambo, Catholic mission work, the palm oil industry, the cacao plantations in Mayumbe, colonial farms in the Kasaï, and the newly constructed railways. These films were shown in Belgium and elsewhere after the war.

See also: Africa: British colonies; colonialism: Europe; ethnographic films; industrial films; travelogues

Further reading

Convents, Guido (1986) *Préhistoire du cinéma en Afrique 1897–1918. A la recherche des images oubliées*, Brussels: OCIC.

Convents, Guido (1988) "Documentaries and Propaganda before 1914. A View on Early Cinema and Colonial History," *Framework*, 35: 104–113.

GUIDO CONVENTS

Africa: British colonies

In British-controlled Africa, the first moving pictures were made in the Sudan, in 1897, by John Bennet Stanford (1870–1947), who shot a film of the battle of Omdurman, entitled *Alarming Queen's Company of Grenadier Guards at Omdurman*. Fifteen years later, Charles **Urban** had a Kinemacolor film shot in Khartoum of Lord Kitchener, the "hero" of Omdurman, reviewing Egyptian troops. During these years, numerous filmmakers travelled up the Nile to the Sudan and even Kenya because there was no tropical forest to hinder their filming. One of the more famous, Félix **Mesguich**, filmed for **Charles Urban Trading Company** in Khartoum in 1906. Later that year, the Colonial Office in London, also now interested in showing the British presence on the continent, granted **Warwick Trading** (cameraman E. L. **Lauste**) special privileges to film around Mombassa in East Africa. Other well-known filmmakers active in the area of Sudan, Uganda, and Kenya were Alfred **Machin**, Cherry **Kearton**, Paul Rainey, and Theodore Roosevelt. Between 1909 and 1913, moving pictures also were projected in theaters as well as in the open air by **itinerant exhibitors** in cities such as Nairobi.

By 1903, the British government set about making films to demonstrate economical development and modernization in its African colonies. Between late 1906 and late 1908, British cameramen filmed in Rhodesia, Mashona, and Barotseland. An impressive surviving image was that of the Victoria Bridge, the highest in the world at the time, near Victoria Falls on the Zambezi River. Specifically, as a result of the Urban-Africa Expedition, films such as *Life on the Zambezi River*, *Amongst the Central African Natives*, and *A Trip on the Rhodesian Railway* were shown around the world. Because investment in the colonies was a long-term financial adventure, moving pictures could assure "anxious shareholders" that their money was being well spent so far from home. British investors such as the British South Africa Company (BSAC) used films about the construction of railways and bridges—for instance, connecting the diamond, copper, and tin mines in Rhodesia—not only to attract shareholders but also to present themselves as essential in conquering the world for the Empire.

In 1912, BSAC produced *Rhodesia To-Day*, shot by Alfred Kaye and R. C. E. Nissen in the region between Bulawayo and the Zambesi. That film especially nourished the British Imperial dream of constructing a Cape to Cairo railway. Itinerant showmen also were active in the mining areas of Rhodesia and densely populated cities such as Bulawayo or Salisbury early in the century. Around 1910, films were being programmed (for whites) at theaters such as the New London Bioscope and Empire in Salisbury (Rhodesia). In 1912, as film screenings in theaters became accessible to the black population, Rhodesia's Native Affairs Department, along with the industry, was pressured by (white) women's groups to censor those films presented to blacks.

Moving pictures also arrived relatively early to Nigeria on the west coast. The first screenings took place at Glover Memorial Hall in the capital of Lagos, on ten consecutive nights, beginning 12 August 1903. Ten years later, a BSAC film expedition shot more than 10,000 feet of high quality film showing the tin mines of Nigeria and the countryside as far inland as Kano. By 1913, itinerant showmen had brought moving pictures to most of the coastal cities of British West Africa (Nigeria and Ghana).

See also: Africa: Belgian colonies; Africa: French colonies; Africa: German colonies; colonialism: Europe; racial segregation: USA; travelogues

Further reading

Convents, Guido (1986) *Préhistoire du cinéma en Afrique 1897–1918. A la recherche des images oubliées*, Brussels: OCIC.

Convents, Guido (2001) "Cinéma coloniale," in G. P. Brunetta (ed.) *Storia del Cinema Mondiale*, IV: 335–386, Torino: Catedra.

MacKenzie, John M. (1984) *Propaganda and Empire: The Manipulation of British Public Opinion, 1880–1960*, Manchester: Manchester University Press.

MacKenzie, John M. (1986) *Imperialism and Popular Culture*, Manchester: Manchester University Press.

GUIDO CONVENTS

Africa: French colonies

French cameramen probably shot the most films in Africa. The first moving pictures from North Africa (Algeria and Tunisia) were produced for the **Lumière** Company by Alexandre **Promio** in 1896–1897. In 1903, he filmed again in this area. In 1902, **Pathé-Frères** also sent cameramen to Algeria and Tunisia, where they produced such films as *Marché à Biskra* and *Laveuses, Baigneurs dans l'Oued Senia* (Algeria), and *Place principale à Tunis* and *Panorama de Constantine* (Tunisia).

Films from tropical French Africa seem to have been made regularly from 1905 on. One of the pioneers was the Pathé cameraman Léo Lefébvre, who filmed daily life and natural resources in French West Africa (Senegal and Guinée). His films, such as *Panorama en Guinée*, were shown at the colonial exhibition in Marseilles in 1906. For Pathé, Alfred **Machin** entered French Africa via Egypt and the Nile in 1909. He brought back moving pictures from Fachoda in the French Sudan, a mythical space for French colonial history: i.e., *En Afrique Centrale: Fachoda*. During this expedition, he also shot hunting scenes such as *Voyages et grandes chasses en Afrique*. Later, Pathé cameramen were active in Madagascar (*Fabrication Malgache des Sobikons*) as well as West Central Africa (*Au Congo*).

Around 1910 other French companies began to produce films in Africa, and eventually almost every city of French colonial Africa found its way onto film. **Gaumont** even had a policy of collecting a full range of moving pictures from this part of the world: i.e., dozens of scenes from Senegal (Kayes, Saint-Louis, Dakar), Brazzaville-Congo, Niger (Bamako, Timbuktu, Koudoussou, Kankan), etc. These were shot entirely from the colonialist point of view, as can be seen in *Vues de Soudan Français-Tombouctou*, which contained scenes of the chief of the Ouled Mechdouff (a Touareg tribe) offering his submission to the French military governor.

From the moment cameramen became active in the French colonies in the Magreb and the tropics, films also were shown in the open air or in existing theaters or halls. In the Magreb, for instance, **itinerant exhibitors** already were operating before 1905. Europeans had an important presence in cities such as Algers, Casablanca, and Tunis, where they owned and frequented **music halls**. In 1911, the Excelsior Cinéma opened in Casablanca and was a success among not only Europeans but also the Arab population. About the same time, theaters like the Splendide Cinéma opened in the small Algerian city of Mostagane. Most French distributors bought rental rights for Italian, German, American, Spanish or British films not only for France but also for the "colonies." By 1910, for instance, A. Bonaz in Paris had agencies in Algers, Tunis, Alexandria, and Cairo. In the early 1910s, exhibitors became active in Dakar, Saint-Louis and other important centers in West and Central Africa.

In the **World War I**, the French army initiated film production in Africa; among its films were *L'aide des colonies à la France* (1917).

See also: colonialism: Europe; Egypt and other Arab countries; ethnographic films; travelogues

Further reading

Aubert, Michelle and Jean-Claude Seguin (1996) *La Production cinématographique des Frères Lumière*, Paris: Editions Mémoires de cinéma.

Bousquet, Henri (1990–1996) *Catalogue Pathé des années 1896 à 1914*, Bassac: Editions Henri Bousquet.

Convents, Guido (1986) *Préhistoire du cinéma en Afrique 1897–1918. A la recherche des images oubliées*. Brussels: OCIC.

GUIDO CONVENTS

Africa: German colonies

In South West Africa (Namibia) and German East Africa, Karl Müller probably shot the first films in 1904, recording the natural environment of the colonies and the work of the colonists. Due to their successful exhibition among colonial pressure groups in Germany, he returned to Africa in early 1906 and shot 2,000 meters of film in the German Sudan (Togo), Cameroon, and Namibia.

Through an arrangement with Deutsche Kolonial Gesellschaft, he then showed these films all over Germany to thousands of school children and anyone interested in the German colonies.

The collection of scientific data in the colonies was important to Europe, and cinematography became an essential means of collecting. Karl Weule (1864–1926), from the Museum of Ethnology in Leipzig, used an **Ernemann** camera to record the rituals of the Wakonda in the German East African colonies in 1906. Adolf Friedrich (1874–1969) of Mecklenburg brought similar films back from Urundi, Ruanda and the regions of the Uele and the Aruwimiriver in 1908. Appointed governor of Togo in 1911, he encouraged filming there as well.

German companies also produced a small number of films in the African colonies before 1914. For Bioscop-, Kolonial- und Eisenbahngesellschaft, Georg Furkel filmed in Namibia, where he captured images of the victorious Germans as well as the Hereros and Namas who had survived the gruesome colonial war. Deutsche-Bioscop Gmbh sent several cameramen into German Africa to make such films as *Leben und Treiben in Tangka*, *Linienlaufe unter dem Aequator*, *Die Sigifälle in Cameroun und Togo*. Other specialized film companies included Deutschkoloniale Kino-GmbH and Deutsche Jagdfilm Gmbh, the latter of which hired the big game hunter Robert Schumann to shoot *Nashorn Jagd in Deutsch Ostafrika* in East Africa (Ruanda/Urundi). The most famous producer, however, was Hans Schomburgk (1880–1967) who, with cameraman Georg Bürli, crossed the territories from Liberia to Northern Togo just before **World War I**. He made both documentaries (i.e., *Aus dem Kriegsleben in Süd-Westafrika*, *Unsere Polizeitruppe in Togo* and *Im Deutschen Sudan*) and fiction films (i.e., *The White Goddess of The Wangora* and *The Outlaw of the Sudu Mountains*).

The first screenings in German East Africa were organized by a German travelling showman by the name of Wexelsen in April 1908, specifically in the city of Tanga (north-eastern Tanzania) on the Indian Ocean. In September, he had a cameraman film daily life there. In May 1909, the same showman came to Dare salaam, where he exhibited films to both black and white audiences. It was Wexelsen who also organized film shows in June 1911 in Usumbura (the capital of western Burundi,

on the northeastern shore of Lake Tanganyika). By then he had been joined by other **itinerant exhibitors** such as Ohlmanns Kinematograph and Prinsenschaums Kino, all of whom regularly received new films from Germany. Ohlmanns and Prinsenschaums also organized film screenings on a regular basis in Swakopmund and Windhoek in German West Africa. According to the local press in Swakopmund, in June 1911, Ohlmanns opened a cinema hall and nearby garden restaurant, where he offered not only music with an electric organ and presented **synchronized sound** films but served excellent beer. Prinsenschaum also is known to have travelled with his films to South Africa (i.e., the city of Bloemfontein).

See also: colonialism: Europe; ethnographic films; travelogues

Further reading

Convents, Guido (1990) "Film and German Colonial Propaganda for the Black African Territories to 1918," in Paolo Cherchi Usai and Lorenzo Codelli (eds.) *Prima di Caligari. Cinema tedesco, 1895–1920*, 58–77, Pordenone: Biblioteca dell'Immagine.

Fuhrmann, Wolfgang (1999) "Lichtbilder und kinematographische Aufnahmen aus den deutschen Kolonien," *Kintop*, 8: 101–116.

Gehrts, Megh (1915) *A camera actress in the wilds of Togoland; the adventures, observations & experiences of a cinematograph actress in West African forests whilst collecting films depicting native life and when posing as the white woman in Anglo-African cinematograph dramas*, London: Seeley, Service & Co.

Waz, Gerlinden (1997) "Auf der Suche nach dem letzten paradies. Der Afrikaforscher und Regisseur Hans Schomburgk," in Jörg Schöning (ed.) *Triviale Tropen*, 95–109, München: CineGraph.

GUIDO CONVENTS

AGC

The Agence Générale Cinématographique (AGC) emerged eventually from American Kinetograph, a small company specializing in exhibition founded in 1904 by Théophile Michault, Maurice Astaix and François Lallement, three former Georges

Méliès employees. On 10 May 1907, their company was taken over by the Compagnie des **Cinéma-Halls**, which operated, among other theaters, the Hippodrome (the future Gaumont-Palace). In August 1909, Cinéma-Halls went bankrupt, and American Kinetograph set up a new business renting films and apparatuses. Early in 1910, Michault sold his shares to his two associates, and in April–May, Astaix, Lallement and Paul Kastor (co-owner of the moving picture theaters, Le Panthéon and Les Mille-Colonnes, in Paris) created a general partnership under the designation of Agence Générale Cinématographique and the corporate name "Astaix, Kastor et Lallement." The company acquired the exclusive rental rights to the films of **Film d'Art**, after the latter was taken over by Charles **Delac** (in 1911), and shared rights to **Éclair** films with the Union des Grands Editeurs. In late 1912, AGC could boast weekly rental purchases of 18,000 to 20,000 meters of films. Besides Éclair and Film d'Art, it also rented and distributed American films from **Biograph**, **Kalem**, **New York Motion Picture (Bison)**, **Edison**, and **Vitagraph**; French films from **Eclipse**, Le Lion and **Lux**; Italian films from **Ambrosio**, **Itala**, **Milano-Films**, **Cines** and **Aquila**; and English films from Kineto and **Clarendon**. From 1915 on, AGC distributed Charlie **Chaplin** films which quickly had tremendous success. It was taken over by Franco-Films in 1927.

See also: distribution: Europe

JEAN-JACQUES MEUSY

AGFA

In 1892, Dr. Momme Andresen, inventor of Rodinal, Metol, Amidol, and Glycin, set up a photographic department to research and eventually manufacture photographic material at the Actien-Gesellschaft für Anilin-Fabrikation (AGFA) in Berlin. Early in 1908, AGFA began to supply French production companies with **celluloid** film stock (positive nitrate). By summer's end in 1913, AGFA was supplying 40% of the European market and was **Eastman Kodak**'s main competitor. AGFA's customers included **Gaumont**, **Eclipse**, **Éclair**, **Lux** and **Raleigh & Robert** in Paris as well as **Ambrosio**, **Itala**, Comerio, and Ottalinghi in Italy. In 1908, AGFA also began producing an acetylcelluloid nonflammable photographic base.

CARLOS BUSTAMANTE

airdomes

A very common, generic term used in the USA to describe one type of outdoor venue for screening moving pictures from the **nickelodeon** era through the 1910s. Unlike storefront moving picture shows, airdomes were open-air, usually roofless theaters designed exclusively for warm-weather climates or for summertime use. Though they were in most cases operated as seasonal amusement venues, airdomes differed from traveling carnivals (which sometimes included moving pictures) and tent shows because they were permanent theaters typically run by local entrepreneurs. Open-air moving picture theaters operating in small commercial **amusement parks** or in municipally owned parks sometimes also were referred to as airdomes. If airdomes in certain ways looked forward to the drive-in theaters of the post-World War II era, they also were very much a product of the early 20th century, when communal, outdoor, warm-weather venues were an essential part of the leisure-time experience across the USA.

As David **Hulfish** notes in *Motion-Picture Theater Management* (1911), an airdome could be set up in a country town as well as a large city, since it required only a fenced-in vacant lot, a **screen**, chairs, and a projection booth or platform. A more elaborate airdome might include an ornate entryway, a separate area with tables and chairs, concession stands for food and drink, and a small stage. Airdomes offered programming that was comparable to indoor moving picture venues, at first combining films with live performances, including **illustrated songs** and **vaudeville** acts, then introducing more "balanced" film programs by the early 1910s. In a time before air conditioned theaters, airdomes filled a lucrative niche in the marketplace, most notably in places where indoor theaters traditionally had been closed once summertime heat and humidity set in. As a result, airdomes helped establish film exhibition as an everyday, year-round business in the USA.

Moving Picture World duly noted the spread of airdomes in 1907, which were most likely to be found in midwestern states like Missouri, Kansas, Indiana, and Oklahoma. Well into the 1910s, airdomes remained a significant site for film exhibition in this region and elsewhere. In the summer of 1915, for example, there were permanent open-air movie theaters from Bar Harbor, Maine to Fresno, California, and in a number of large cities as well, including Washington, D. C., Nashville, and Kansas City. Urban airdomes could contain fancy gardens and 2,000 or more seats. Sometimes they were joined with an indoor theater, allowing patrons to see the show regardless of thunderstorms or unseasonable cold spells. In cities like St. Louis, Missouri, and Louisville, Kentucky, the many airdomes operating in residential areas helped to spread film exhibition out of the central business district and to foster investment in "neighborhood" theaters.

See also: leisure time and space: USA

GREGORY A. WALLER

Aitken, Harry

b. 1878; d. 1956

distributor, producer, entrepreneur, USA

Aitken was a Milwaukee exchange man who, in order to supply clients after his **Motion Picture Patents Company** (MPPC) licenses were revoked in 1910, founded and acquired production companies, eventually owning outright **Majestic** and **Reliance** and having some stake in **American Film Manufacturing**, **New York Motion Picture**, and **Keystone**. In early 1912, together with John **Freuler**, C. J. Hite, and Samuel **Hutchinson**, he founded **Mutual**, soon a national distributor of short film programs. In 1913, he hired D. W. **Griffith** away from **Biograph** to supervise Reliance and Majestic production in a new studio in Los Angeles. Aitken supported Griffith's project

for *The Birth of a Nation* and, when his partners refused backing, set up the Epoch Producing Corporation to produce and distribute the film. In 1915, he left Mutual and established the Triangle Distributing Corporation to provide a national program of feature films made by Fine Arts (the renamed Reliance-Majestic Studio), Keystone, and Thomas **Ince**. In 1917, he had to cede control of Triangle, which rapidly lost its product suppliers to Paramount and First National. Although Aitken remained a film distributor for the rest of his life, never again was he a major player in the industry.

BEN BREWSTER

Alberini, Filoteo

b. 1865; d. 1937

inventor, producer, Italy

Nine months after the patenting of the **Cinématographe Lumière** and four years after the **Edison** had submitted a claim for the **Kinetograph**, on 11 November 1895 Alberini patented a *Kinetografo*, a device for recording and projecting moving pictures. Without industrial support, however, Alberini moved into moving picture exhibition in 1901 and then film production in 1904. He established the first Italian production company, Alberini & Santoni (sold to **Cines** in 1906), and produced *La presa di Roma* [The capture of Rome] (1905), Italy's first fiction film. In later years, he invented **cameras** that recorded stereoscopic and panoramic images.

GIORGIO BERTELLINI

Almirante Manzini, Italia

b. 1890; d. 1941

actor, Italy

Born to a Southern Italian family of travelling actors, Almirante Manzini began her acting at **Itala**, as the most matronly of all Italian divas, in such films as *Sul Sentiero della Vipera* [In the Viper's Path] (1912) and *Bacio della Zingara* [Gypsy's Kiss] (1913). Her career peaked with the role of Sofonisba, a North-African queen lying on leopard skins all day long, in Giovanni **Pastrone**'s *Cabiria* (1914). After *Patria* [Homeland] (1915), she lost her place in the company to Pina **Menichelli**. Throughout the late 1910s and 1920s, she continued to act in films, in Rome and Turin. In 1935, after appearing in one sound film, she moved to Brazil and did stage work in the theaters of Rio de Janeiro and San Paolo.

ANGELA DALLE VACCHE

Alpha Trading Company

In 1901, the Alpha Trading Co. was established at St. Albans, Hertfordshire, England, by Arthur Melbourne Cooper (1874–1961), who had worked for Birt **Acres** in the 1890s. Alpha produced **trick films**, **animation** films, and a variety of nonfiction films, often for distribution by other companies. Its engaging stop-motion *Dream Of Toyland* (1908) featured animated toys careening around a miniature replica of High Street in St. Albans. Cooper himself opened two local cinemas, later established the Kinema Industries production company, and in the 1920s made some **advertising films**.

STEPHEN HERBERT

Altenloh, Emilie

b. 1888; d. 1985

economist, politician, Germany

Altenloh's dissertation, "Zur Soziologie des Kino" (1914), is the sole study of early cinema **audiences** in any country. Based on inadequate, quickly gathered empirical evidence, it reflects the attitude of the German educated class toward moving pictures as an amusement for the "uneducated masses." However overrated (it fares better as an

economic study), the dissertation makes some valuable observations: for instance, the young and unmarried had the greatest interest in moving pictures, and boys attended more often because girls had far more duties at home. Later Altenloh would become seriously engaged in local politics and environmental research.

CORINNA MÜLLER

Alva, Carlos, Guillermo and Salvador

producers, cameramen, exhibitors, Mexico

Natives of Morelia, the family of Guillermo, Carlos, and Salvador Alva owned a bicycle factory, which the brothers abandoned in order to dedicate themselves to moving picture exhibition in Morelia and later to film production in Mexico City. They created a characteristic structure for Mexican films by appropriating the apotheosis finale from Georges **Méliès** and the strategy of parallel **editing** from **Pathé-Frères** and other companies in the USA. This format first appeared in October 1908, in a 45-minute film presenting President Porfirio Díaz's interview with William Taft, his counterpart in the USA. In May 1911, they filmed the taking of Ciudad Juarez by the Revolutionaries in parallel with President Maderos' journey from that city to Mexico City. Their most ambitious film, *The Orozquista Rebellion* (May 1912), portrayed both the federal and revolutionary sides of the battle, with a finale representing the victors. The National Autonomous University of Mexico has preserved a large part of the Alva film archive.

AURELIO DE LOS REYES

amateur film

Before about 1910, it can be misleading to separate professional and amateur film apparatuses and/or activity. The renowned **Cinématographe**

Lumière began life in its inventors' eyes as a lightweight multi-purpose domestic moving picture machine that would provide French photographic plate manufacturers with years of steady sales of film and developing services, modeled on the business success that the Kodak system had provided for the American plate-making company of George **Eastman**. Yet it turned out to be a consummate professional apparatus that could— and did—go anywhere and take and exhibit films under almost any circumstances. We remember John Montagu Benett-Stanford for his Boer War films and a striking film portrait of Lord Kitchener, the British commander, released by **Warwick Trading**, but his own curiosity about moving pictures paled in comparison to his Eton education, long Army career, and management of the family estate in Wiltshire: he failed to mention his film work in either his account of the Boer War or his unpublished autobiography. Conversely, the "amateur" productions of Robert A. Mitchell, a lawyer from County Down, Ireland, or William Henry Youdale, a draper from Cockermouth, England, show little difference from "professional" work of the late 1890s, and include a shipboard comedy, street scenes, a fire company answering an alarm, a parade, sea waves, and a train entering a station.

In the early years, there were many varied ideas about how to use moving pictures and what marketplace would secure their future; consequently, most apparatuses retrospectively called "amateur" were designed for film narrower than the 35 mm bands that later became the standard size. These included the 17.5 mm Birtac camera and projector of Birt **Acres**, introduced in October 1898; T. C. **Hepworth**'s Biokam of 1899, another 17.5 mm design sold with accessories allowing it to be used as a **camera, projector**, or printer, with the additional facility of taking single-frame still **photographs**; and J. A. Prestwich's Junior Prestwich of the same year, using 13 mm wide film. **Ernemann** in Germany, **Reulos** and Goudeau in France, and many others also sold small-format apparatuses designed for home use, while some companies made attempts to convert the longstanding experience of photographers in working with glass plates with apparatuses that made rows or spirals of tiny images on glass, like those of Leonard Ulrich **Kamm**, Robert Krayn, and Theodore Brown. By 1912, when **Edison** introduced the **Edison Home Kinetoscope** using 22 mm film, and **Pathé-Frères** marketed its **Pathé Kok projector** Home Cinematograph for 28 mm film, both intended for non-flammable safety film stock, an amateur home market was clearly distinguished from professional users dependent on the public sale and distribution of their work. Both systems were attempts to reach new markets for existing theatrical films supplied in reduced-size prints.

Not until the early 1920s were substantial amateur filmmaking apparatuses introduced, with the Pathé-Baby system for 9.5 mm film in France (1922) and the Eastman Kodak 16 mm system in the USA (1923).

See also: glass plate projectors

Further reading

Coe, Brian (1981) *The History of Movie Photography*, Westfield, NJ: Eastview Editions, especially "Movies in the Home," 162–173.

Kuball, Michael (1980) *Familienkino, Bd. 1: 1900–1930*, Reinbek bei Hamburg: Rowohlt.

Zimmerman, Patricia (1995) *Reel Families: A Social History of Amateur Film*, Bloomington, IN: Indiana University Press.

DEAC ROSSELL

Ambrosio

The Ambrosio film company was founded in 1906 in Turin by Arturo **Ambrosio** and Alfredo Gandolfi, first as "Società Ambrosio & C." and then, in 1907, as a public corporation "Società Anonima Ambrosio, Torino." From 1908, when it opened its new studio complex, until 1912, it flooded the world with its short films and, from 1911 on, with its **multiple-reel/feature films**, beginning with *L'ultimo dei Frontignac* [The Last of the Frontignacs] (1911). In 1912 and 1913, Ambrosio managed to release around 200 films per year and shared with **Cines** the role of leading Italian manufacturer on the international market. Ambrosio first established its worldwide reputation, and that of Italian cinema, with the historical dramas, *Gli ultimi giorni di Pompei* [The Last Days of Pompei] (1908) and *Nerone* [Nero] (1909), both directed by Luigi **Maggi**. Ambrosio's **historical films**, released from 1909 on as "serie d'oro" [Golden Series], were the firm's business card. Among them were the first in the "serie d'oro", *Spergiura!* [Swear!] (1909), *Il granatiere Roland* [Grenadier Roland] (1911), and the second version of *Gli ultimi giorni di Pompei* in 1913, released in competition with that of **Pasquali**. In 1911 the company received the prize for the best artistic film and best documentary at the International Exposition in Turin with the Risorgimento drama *Nozze d'oro* [The Golden Wedding] (1911), featuring the leading Ambrosio actors Alberto **Capozzi** and Mary Cléo Tarlarini, and the documentary *La vita delle farfalle* [Life of the Butterflies] (1911), based on a text by Guido Gozzano.

Considering other genres, Ambrosio promoted itself mainly through **comic series** with the tall and anarchic Marcel **Fabre**, alias Robinet, and the corpulent but swift Ernesto Vaser, alias Fricot. It also became well known for its boulevard-style **comedies** with Gigetta **Morano**, Eleuterio **Rodolfi** and Camillo **de Riso**. The company also was famous for its *actualités* and **travelogues** from all over Europe, sometimes including remarkable split-screen effects such as in *Tripoli* (1912), and its **scientific films** such as *La nevropatologia* [The Neuropathology] (1908) on hysteria. Ambrosio's distribution reached as far as Russia. In 1909–1910, Ambrosio cameraman Giovanni **Vitrotti** shot films there and contributed to the beginnings of Russian film production. In 1912 Ambrosio hired lion tamer Alfred Schneider and his lions for a series of sensational **melodramas** such as *La nave dei leoni* [The Ship with the Lions] (1912). Ambrosio never really was a production company for diva films, notwithstanding the sole production with stage star Eleonora **Duse**: *Cenere* [Ashes] (1916).

After 1911, Ambrosio's international market share began to decline in favor of that of Cines. The most serious problems, however, arose with the outbreak of the **World War I** and Italy's decision to join the Allied forces. The government requisitioned the studio complex for the construction of airplane propellers, and production dropped to just nine films in 1917. After the war Ambrosio tried to revive itself through expensive productions such as *La Nave* [The Ship] (1921) and *Teodora* [Theodora] (1922), but they were economic failures. When Arturo Ambrosio left the company, production halted in 1923; one year later the company was dissolved.

In the two decades of its productivity, Ambrosio released 1400 films, of which a little more than ten per cent survives, mainly in the film archives of Turin, Amsterdam, London, Gemona, Bologna, and Rome.

Further reading

Bertetto, Paolo and Gianni Rondolino (eds.) (1998) *Cabiria e il suo tempo*, Turin: Museo Nazionale del Cinema/Il Castoro.

Gianetto, Claudia (2000) "The Giant Ambrosio, or Italy's Most Prolific Silent Film Company," *Film History*, 12.3: 240–249.

IVO BLOM

Ambrosio, Arturo

b. 1870; d. 1960

cameraman, producer, Italy

After a trip to Paris, London, and Berlin in 1904, Ambrosio (an amateur photographer and professional accountant) began shooting local *actualités* in Turin with Roberto **Omegna**. One year later, also in Turin, he created the Arturo Ambrosio & Co. supported by financier Alfredo Gandolfi. Soon this "Italian Zukor" built larger studios, recruited the best technical, acting, and literary talents in Italy and abroad, and established worldwide commercial links by directly visiting foreign competitors and markets. From 1908 until **World War I**, Società Anonima Ambrosio (or **Ambrosio** Film) represented a most modern and cosmopolitan film company.

GIORGIO BERTELLINI

American Biograph (France)

The Biograph and Mutoscope Company for France, a branch of the **British** and **American Mutascope and Biograph** companies, was established in 1898 to produce films and distribute its own product and that of other branches. Julian Orde managed the Paris office and a studio was opened in the Paris suburb of Courbevoir with Eugene **Lauste** as manager. Although the studio only operated for a short time, it produced more than 300 films. Lauste and Orde left the company in the fall of 1900, after which it was converted into a distribution branch that supplied large-format Biograph films for projection at the Casino de Paris and Folies Bergère.

PAUL SPEHR

American Film Manufacturing Company

The American Film Manufacturing Company was founded in Chicago by John L. **Freuler** and Samuel S. **Hutchinson**, when the **Motion Picture Patents Company** (MPPC) licenses of their film exchanges were revoked in 1910, in order to help supply product for their theatrical clients. Harry **Aitken** also had a stake in the company until he abandoned **Mutual** in 1915, but Freuler remained the executive director of American until its demise in 1921, and Hutchinson continued to operate its Chicago laboratories.

At its foundation, American hired most of its initial personnel, including actor J. Warren Kerrigan and scenarist Allan **Dwan**, from one of the MPPC-licensed Chicago production companies, **Essanay**. It also imitated Essanay, starting in November 1910, by producing three titles a week: a drama, a comedy, and a **western**. In 1911, it sent its unit for westerns to California under director Frank Beal, with Kerrigan as the lead player. The western company was initially based in San Diego county, at San Juan Capistrano, Lakeside, and then La Mesa, but in the summer of 1912, well after Dwan had replaced Beal, it moved permanently to a studio in Santa Barbara. There, Wallace Reid directed social dramas, while Dwan made westerns. By late 1912, American was releasing three reels a week under the "Flying A" logo, with their distribution by Mutual. In 1913, Dwan left the company with his wife, western lead Pauline Bush, after a dispute with Kerrigan, and was replaced by Lorrimer Johnston and Sydney Ayres. From 1914, American concentrated on producing **comedies** under the Beauty label. A dispute over Mutual's handling of the first Flying A feature, *The Quest* (1915), contributed to Aitken's leaving Mutual the same year, taking with him a large share of Mutual's product suppliers, after which Freuler quickly expanded American's output. For instance, American jumped on the **serial** bandwagon with *The Diamond from the Sky* (1915), and made the sensational **melodrama** feature, *Damaged Goods* (1915). By 1916, the company was producing twelve reels a week, mostly as feature films. The expansion could not be sustained, however, and when Mutual went bankrupt in 1918, American released a declining number of titles, many of them re-releases, through Pathé-Exchange, until it ceased operations in 1921.

See also: multiple-reel/feature films

Further reading

Lyons, Timothy J. (1974) *The Silent Partner: The History of the American Film Manufacturing Company 1910–1921*, New York: Arno Press.

BEN BREWSTER

American Mutoscope and Biograph (AM&B)

The American Mutoscope Company was a production and distribution company established at the end of 1895 by KMCD, a syndicate of four friends, Elias B. Koopman, Harry **Marvin**, Herman Casler, and W. K. L. **Dickson**. With substantial financial backing from a consortium of bankers, railroad men and industrialists, it offered Thomas **Edison** stiff competition in the US market, and it became one of the first multi-national film companies. The initial intent was to market a peep-show device, the Mutoscope, but the popularity of the **Lumière Cinématographe** and Vitascope led KMCD to introduce a projector, the **Biograph**, which they leased to large **vaudeville** theaters under a contract which included an operator and a changing program of films. Biograph's film stock was 2 3/4 inches wide by 2 inches high, larger than conventional 35 mm film and about the size of today's Imax film. This produced a striking image, and Biograph's programs earned a reputation as the most spectacular of early projections. The Biograph was featured at Keith-Albee's vaudeville theaters for a decade, beginning in 1896. The peep-show machines were leased in a similar, but less dramatic package.

In 1897, the company expanded to Europe, establishing the **British Mutoscope and Biograph**, then set up production and distribution in England, France and Germany; branches in Holland, Belgium and Austria, as well as offices in London to distribute to other parts of Europe, South Africa, and India.

Dickson organized film production in the USA, then in Europe. Dickson designed a roof-top studio in New York City, and outdoor studios in London and Paris. Films were made by a team consisting of a director and camera operator. From 1896 until 1901, AM&B specialized in producing short *actualité* films for middle-class family audiences and saucier fare for the peep show's fans. After 1901, **comedies** and melodramas dominated its programs. AM&B films generally stressed action and quality camera work, and they pioneered two "genres" that were very popular in the early years, the **phantom train ride** and the **chase film**.

In 1903, after one court decision, AM&B started making films in the more commonly used 35 mm format. This made it possible for the company to make longer, more complicated productions which could be sold to anyone with a standard **projector**. Although they still made some large-format films, the more popular smaller format soon dominated production and distribution.

From 1897 until 1908 the company was involved in a lawsuit with Edison's company that was pivotal in the so-called, **US patent wars**. After several inconclusive decisions, in 1908 the two companies negotiated an agreement to combine their patents, along with some others, to form the **Motion Picture Patents Company**. Although other American companies joined this trust, Edison and Biograph were the dominant members.

In 1899, the company changed its name to the American Mutoscope and **Biograph** Co., and in 1909 it became the Biograph Co. By this time, D. W. **Griffith** had become principal director, inaugurating a period when the company created a standard for production quality and creativity.

Further reading

Hendricks, Gordon (1964) *Beginnings of the Biograph (New York, The Beginnings of the American Film)*, reprinted in Gordon Hendricks (1972) *Origins of the American Film*, New York: Arno Press/New York Times.

Niver, Kemp R. and Bebe Bergsen (eds.) (1971) *Biograph Bulletins, 1896–1908*, Los Angeles: Locare Research Group.

PAUL SPEHR

amusement parks

In the years before **World War I**, there were more than 1,500 amusement parks in North America and scores more scattered across Europe. Most operated during the summer months and went by the names of Luna, Wonderland, Dreamland, White City, and Electric. They evolved out of certain turn-of-the-century amusement venues: international expositions or **world's fairs**, seaside bathing resorts, country fairs, and European pleasure garden. Most of these parks featured moving pictures, especially since urban theaters tended to "go dark" in the summer due to the heat. They were shown either in nickel theaters or at free outdoor **airdomes**. In 1906, as many as thirty moving picture venues were operating in the three parks that made up Coney Island. In addition, **Hale's Tours** and Scenes of the World was a popular amusement park attraction, one that incorporated moving pictures into its simulation of a train ride. In short, amusement parks were an important site for early moving picture exhibition.

Amusement parks were so widespread because new electric streetcar and interurban railroad companies across the United States built them at the end of their rail lines. These traction companies, as they were called, did not need to make a profit at their parks so long as the parks encouraged excursions on their trolleys and railways, especially in evenings and on weekends. Metropolitan centers such as New York and Chicago each had as many as eight parks operating at one time. Medium-sized cities such as Cleveland, Pittsburgh, Toronto, or Washington, D. C. had at least three at any given time during this period. Even small cities in rural states almost always had at least one amusement park on the outskirts of town. Some European cities also built parks that capitalized on the success of their American counterparts.

Amusement parks, sometimes also called electric parks or trolley parks, featured mechanical thrill rides, games of chance, dancing, roller skating, band concerts, disaster shows, live acts and ethnographic displays, fireworks shows, food and drink, and swimming as well as moving pictures. The architecture of the parks often provided fanciful, exotic backdrops with ornate electrified towers, boldly painted facades, brilliant flags waving, and vividly colored gardens. Barkers attempting to lure customers to attractions, gramophone music, band performances, and mechanical pianos and orchestras filled the air. The moving pictures shown in the parks, therefore, always were experienced in the context of an atmosphere of visual and auditory excitement or kinesthesia, a showcase of new mechanical technologies, and crowds of diverse peoples.

Amusement parks were also among the first important subjects of moving pictures. As early as

1896, **Edison** began filming the shoot-the-chutes ride at Coney Island. This attraction was filmed several more times by both Edison and **American Mutoscope and Biograph** over the next ten years. Because of its proximity to the chief New York manufacturers, Coney Island was filmed more than any other amusement park in the USA. For Edison, especially in *Coney Island at Night* (1905), the brilliant electric illuminations also provided an opportunity to showcase both the dramatic spectacle that his company could offer and the product that his New York electric company supplied to Coney Island. Numerous other rides and outdoor acts of acrobats, dancers, and diving elephants and horses at Coney Island continued to be filmed during cinema's first decade.

Probably the most memorable film shot during this time at Coney Island is Edison's *Electrocuting an Elephant* (1903), which also demonstrates the power of Edison-supplied **electricity**. In this real-time electrocution, the film simply shows the elephant being led to an electrified plate and strapped in place. After several seconds, smoke rises from her feet, and she topples over. The film was made both to solve the problem of what to do with Lucy, the Coney Island elephant who had stomped to death a caretaker who had fed her a lighted cigarette, and to advertise electrocution by direct current as an improved method of capital punishment.

As narrative films increased in number, amusement parks also became an ideal setting for early **chase films** and slapstick **comedy**. Representative titles include: *Rube and Mandy Go to Coney Island* (Edison, 1903), *Boarding School Girls* (Edison, 1905), *Fat Jack and Slim Jim at Coney Island* (**Vitagraph**, 1911), and *Gavroche à Luna-Park* (**Éclair**, 1912). Amusement parks were particularly apt places for showcasing the comedy of the human body in motion as it was whirled, bounced, and turned upside down on mechanical rides. The excitement of the amusement park as a place of perpetual motion could best be captured only through the medium of cinema.

Most amusement parks went out of business either sometime before the end of World War I or by the Great Depression of the 1930s. Various factors led to their demise: devastating fires (in 1911 alone, five major parks burned to the ground)

and mismanagement were often singled out as major causes. Park land also became increasingly valuable real estate as cities grew beyond their boundaries. But the chief factor was that the railroad companies who had built the parks generally went out of business or became public utilities. Competition from the automobile proved too much for the streetcar and interurban railroad companies that had been running the parks as a means of attracting people to ride their trains. By the Great Depression, approximately only 400 amusement parks were left across North America and fewer than a dozen in Europe.

See also: advertising; advertising films; leisure time and space; nickelodeons; melodrama, sensational; transportation

LAUREN RABINOVITZ

Anderson, Gilbert M. [Max Aaronson]

b. 1880, Pine Bluff, Arkansas; d. 1971, Woodland Hills, California

actor, director, scriptwriter, executive, USA

Anderson, who came to be known by his screen persona "Broncho Billy," was a minor stage actor and male model when he made his first screen appearances for the **Edison** Manufacturing Company. Among his earliest screen credits were *The Messenger Boy's Mistake* (October 1903) and *What Happened in the Tunnel* (November 1903). He also played several different roles in Edwin S. **Porter**'s *The Great Train Robbery* (December 1903). After leaving Edison, Anderson joined **Vitagraph** and found his first opportunities as a director. *Raffles, the Amateur Cracksman* (August 1905) was well received, but he had strong ideas about the pictures

Figure 3 Production photo of G. M. Anderson as Broncho Billy. (Courtesy of the Robert S. Birchard Collection.)

he wanted to make and decided to become his own producer.

Moving to Chicago, Anderson became associated with the **Selig** Polyscope Company, and in Anderson's words, "With this start I took two women who could act and went to Montana to make 'hold-up' stuff." He then approached George K. **Spoor** with a similar proposition, and they incorporated the **Essanay Film Manufacturing Company** on February 5, 1907, with Anderson supervising production and Spoor managing business affairs. Anderson spent little time in the Chicago studio, preferring to shoot his films on location—first in Golden, Colorado, and later in Los Angeles, San Rafael, Los Gatos, and finally Niles, California. He developed several **comic series** with this traveling unit, including the *Hank and Lank*, *Alkali Ike*, and *Snakeville* films, but his most popular creations were the **westerns** in which Anderson himself took the leading role. His early films bore standard western titles like *Under Western Skies* (1910) or *The Two-Gun Man* (1911), but by late 1911 Essanay began to regularly identify his screen character as "Broncho Billy" and incorporated the name in such titles as *Broncho Billy's Christmas Dinner* (1911) and *Broncho Billy's Narrow Escape* (1912). Audiences seemed to love his rather beefy screen hero, and Anderson churned out a bi-weekly series of *Broncho Billy* films (mostly one-reelers) through 1915.

As a filmmaker Anderson was more than competent; as a person, given to extravagences. Residents of Niles recalled that he would often explode at his employees and fire them on the spot, only to re-hire them a few minutes later. He exploited his wealth and position in the community by sponsoring a semi-pro baseball team called the Essanay Indians and managed several prizefighters who doubled as actors between bouts.

The adverse Supreme Court decision against the **Motion Picture Patents Company**, declining revenues, and the high costs of maintaining Anderson's West coast operation led Spoor to buy out Anderson's interest in Essanay in 1916. Anderson himself remained active in the industry for several years, but with limited success. After producing a handful of features and a series of Stan Laurel shorts in the early 1920s, Anderson left the film business. When asked in later years what he

had been doing since his retirement, he replied: "Just drifting along with the breeze".

Further reading

Kiehn, David (2003) *Broncho Billy and the Essanay Film Company*, Berkeley: Farwell.

ROBERT S. BIRCHARD

Andréani, Henri [Gustave Sarrus]

b. 1877, La Garde-Freinet; d. 1936, Paris

filmmaker, producer, France

Sarrus chose "Andréani" as a pseudonym, probably to take advantage of the vogue for Italian cinema. He started working for **Pathé-Frères** around 1910 and was an assistant to Gaston **Velle** and Ferdinand **Zecca** before becoming a filmmaker himself. He soon specialized in directing period pieces such as *Le Siège de Calais* [The Siege of Calais] (1911), as well as producing the *Le Film Biblique* series (1911), for which he shot about fifteen **biblical films** based on scenarios by Eugène Creissel. In 1913, he created his own company, Les Films Andréani, which then became part of Les Grands Films Populaires in 1914. To this day, many questions about his career remain unresolved.

FRANÇOIS DE LA BRETÈQUE

Andreyor, Yvette [Yvette Roye]

b. 1892; d. 1962

actor, France

After a theatrical debut in Belgium and at the Théâtre Antoine in Paris, Andreyor was hired by **Gaumont** and, from 1910 to 1918, appeared in numerous **historical films**, contemporary dramas, and **crime films** directed by Louis **Feuillade**. She was an accomplice of Fantômas in *Juve contre Fantômas* [Juve Against Fantomas] (1913) and Judex's "fiancée" in *Judex* (1917), where her gentle appearance, in sharp contrast to **Musidora**'s, embodied the new moral tone of Feuillade's later serials. During the 1920s, Andreyor scored memorable roles in Henri **Fescourt**'s *Mathias Sandorf* (1920), Germaine Dulac's *Âme d'artiste* [The Artist's Soul] (1925), and René Clair's *Les Deux timides* [Two Timid Souls] (1928). She performed in minor parts well into the 1940s.

MARINA DAHLQUIST

Andriot, [Camille-] Josette

b. 1886; d. 1942

actor, France

Andriot was *the* action actress of French silent films—as elegant as she was remarkably athletic. At the time, the only female characters with such physical edge and prowess were found in American sensational **melodramas**. Until Andriot retired in 1919, she appeared in about sixty **Éclair** films, among them Victorin **Jasset**'s **crime films** and adventure stories—*Zigomar* (1911–1913), *Tom Butler* (1912), *Balaoo* (1913)—and as the title figure in *Protéa* (1913). Despite Jasset's death in 1913, Andriot starred in four more *Protéa* features (1914–1919). Her character displayed a penchant for disguises and wore a tight black body-stocking years before **Musidora** appropriated the outfit in Louis **Feuillade**'s *Les Vampires* (1915–1916).

MARINA DAHLQUIST

animal pictures

Three basic types of animal pictures emerged and co-existed during the early cinema period: (1) **scientific** or educational films, (2) hunting or safari films, and (3) narrative adventures in which animals play a central or important role. All three reveal the common impulse to capture and to tame what is "wild" in wildlife, often via an analogy between the camera and the rifle, a metaphor that very often became deadly in hunting or safari films.

Etienne-Jules **Marey** literalized this analogy with his "photographic gun," a camera in the shape of a rifle designed to capture the movements of birds, suggesting the importance of animals as subjects for early moving picture experiments. The first serial photographs of Eadweard **Muybridge** featured Leland Stanford's racehorse, Occident; and Muybridge went on to "capture" photographically hundreds of wild animals at the Philadelphia Zoo. At one point, he set a tiger loose on a water buffalo in the interest of these photographs, inaugurating a tradition of "disposable subjects" and staged confrontation in animal pictures.

Animals were even featured in the earliest projected moving pictures: in Germany, Max **Skladanowsky**'s program included *Mr. Delaware and the Boxing Kangaroo* (1895). Titles from **Edison**'s *The Sea Lions' Home* (1897) or *Wild Bear at Yellowstone* (1897) to **Lubin**'s *Feeding the Hippopotamus* (Lubin, 1903) or **Charles Urban Trading Company**'s *Feeding the Otters* (1905) indicate that wild animals in their natural habitat or in zoos were useful as educational subjects. On the other hand, these relatively tame **actualités** did not compare to more dramatic confrontations of animals, in Edison's *Cock Fight* (1896), or to the gruesome and violent stagings of animal deaths, in the same company's *Electrocuting an Elephant* (1903).

By 1909, hunting or safari films (which often borrowed conventions from **chase films**) had outrun educational wildlife films in popularity. Although **Selig** Polyscope's *Hunting Big Game in Africa* (aka *Roosevelt in Africa*) (1909) featured a fake Roosevelt shooting a real lion in a staged scene in Chicago, it circulated widely and often in theaters and prompted adventurers and filmmakers to journey to Africa. Safari films such as *Paul J. Rainey's African Hunt* (1912) left an enduring legacy of onscreen killings, seen in the 1920s films of Martin and Osa Johnson.

A few narratives, such as **Hepworth**'s *Rescued by Rover* (1905), featured animal protagonists, but they were relatively rare in early cinema. However, filmmakers were not opposed to spicing up a story with lions, tigers, and bears; indeed, "jungle films" set in faraway (that is, colonial) locales were extremely popular in the early 1910s. In the USA, Selig Polyscope often included exotic animals housed in the Selig Zoo to lend a bit of dramatic excitement—from *Lost in the Jungle* (1911) to the

Figure 4 Poster for Cherry Kearton, *Bioscope*, 1912.

serial, *The Adventures of Kathlyn* (1914). In France, **Gaumont** and **Pathé-Frères** exploited their own menageries, respectively, in such **multiple-reel films** as *Au pays des lions* [In the Land of Lions] (1912) and *La Grotte des supplices* [The Grotto of Torture] (1912). Adventures featuring anthropomorphized animal protagonists—for instance, **Vitagraph**'s *Baree, Son of Kazan* (1917)—would become common only after the establishment of the studio system.

See also: ethnographic films; melodramas, sensational; museum life exhibits; scientific films; travelogues

Further reading

Bousé, Derek (2000) *Wildlife Films*, Philadelphia: University of Pennsylvania Press.

SCOTT CURTIS

animation

Animation appeared near the beginning of cinema history, and may be defined as a technique, as a mode of production, and as a cinematic genre. Its historical development was international, but it did not become a regular feature of the movie program until the subject matter and technology became somewhat standardized. Animation technique is any method of designing images that will appear to move when displayed in a sequence. When the positions of nearly identical figures are changed sequentially when displayed, we see them as one figure moving.

Non-cinematic methods of producing animation include flipbooks, **magic lantern** "slip slides," and the many optical toys and motion-study experiments that often are cited as forerunners of cinematography. Emile **Reynaud**'s "Luminous Pantomimes" (1889–1892) were well-known animated films made before cinematography. He painted frames on long celluloid strips which, when projected sequentially onto a screen by a system of mirrors, created the illusion of moving drawings.

The cinematic animation method consists of exposing the camera negative discontinuously, that is, one frame (or a few) frames at a time, rather the standard continuous exposure, and moving the object/drawing each time. In the pre-1915 era, this was accomplished by a quick turn of the camera crank to open and close the shutter rapidly. Some **cameras** were specifically adapted for the "one turn one frame" option. Between exposures the filmmaker would make small changes in the position of the subjects, which could be drawings, Plasticine (clay), household objects, toys or models, and, in at least one film by Segundo de **Chomón**, human beings. When projected normally, the filmed subjects would appear to move as convincingly as any other moving picture subject.

Film animation's mode of production during the pre-1915 period occurred in three phases: **trick film**, cartoonist, and industrialized. In the pre-1912 trick film period, a few artisan filmmakers experimented with the technique as a novelty effect. The resulting "attraction" often was a short section in a longer nonanimated film. Around 1912–1913, the cartoonist phase began with the release of entire films (one reel in length) consisting entirely or mostly of animation. The films borrowed content from the newspaper **comic strips** of famous or would-be famous cartoonists. Around 1914, important technological changes and efficiency work methods were introduced that would change the cartoon to an industrial mode of production, anticipating the Hollywood studio system. Because of the outbreak of the **World War I**, the cartoonist and industrialized phases were delayed in Europe.

As early as 1898, filmmakers in Great Britain, the USA, and other countries started experimenting with animation. Because of the spottiness of the early cinematic record, the search for a "first" is futile. The rudimentary animated sequences that have come to light from cinema's first decade highlight the technique by calling attention to itself as a novelty. Around 1907, filmmakers began integrating their animated sequences into longer works with more narrative complexity.

Among the early pioneers of animation is Edwin S. **Porter**. Some of his trick film shots, for instance in *Bluebeard* (1901), verged into crudely executed frame-by-frame animation. Later, Porter introduced "jumble announcements," or animated title cards in three **Edison** films of 1905. In *The "Teddy" Bears* (1907), he integrated a scene of animated toy bears into the narrative as a POV shot.

J. Stuart **Blackton** was among the most prominent innovators. His **Vitagraph** studio released at least eight films with prominent animation sequences before1910, beginning with *Humorous Phases of Funny Faces* (1906). This film made drawings move. The others animated various objects and Plasticine, a clay, oil, and wax compound invented in 1897. The success of Vitagaph's films inspired the **Biograph** company, in early 1907, to use object animation in three films photographed by Billy **Bitzer**. Bitzer also shot a dream sequence with Plasticine for *The Sculptor's Nightmare* (1908), in which Mack **Sennett** and D. W. **Griffith** appear as actors.

The two most important practitioners of trick film animation in Europe worked for rival French companies: Chomón (**Pathé-Frères**) and Emile **Cohl** (**Gaumont**). Chomón moved to Paris in 1905 (going by the name Chomont) and worked as Pathé's special effects wizard. He shot scenes for Gaston **Velle**, Ferdinand **Zecca**, and others who later were credited with the trick shots. Chomón experimented with single-frame cinematography, visible in the extant *Le théâtre du Petit Bob* [Bob's Electric Theater] (1906, remade in 1910). In July 1907, Pathé released *La silhouette animé* [Animated Silhouettes], which consisted of shots of paper animals with moving limbs, and *Le sculpteur express* [Express Sculptor], using clay. In *Pas possible s'asseoir* [Impossible Seating] (1908), Chomón animated a man sitting on a chair to make him travel across a room. He accomplished more large-object animation with real furniture in *Le déménagement* [Moving Day] (1908) and in *Jim le glisseur* [Slippery Jim] (1908–1909). Animation remained a Pathé specialty until Chomón returned to Barcelona to co-found the Ibérico company in 1910.

Cohl was Gaumont's chief trick photography specialist, hired in the summer of 1908. He made animated sequences for Louis **Feuillade**, Roméo **Bosetti**, and others before becoming a director in his own right in 1909. Cohl's *Fantasmagorie* [Metamorphosis] (1908), although short (about two minutes), is a full-fledged animated drawing film, executed with at least 700 drawings on sheets of paper, photographed individually. The subject was a clown character going through fantastic transformations. Cohl directed or

Figure 5 Frame still from Emile Cohl's *Fantasmagorie* (1908).

collaborated on over 70 films at Gaumont between 1908 and 1910, many of them containing animation sequences. He explored many formats, including animated paper cutouts, two-dimensional figures with articulated joints, clay, dolls and puppets, and drawings. In the latter, he developed a distinctive style in which one image metamorphoses into another to create an unexpected or strange juxtaposition, a sort of visual non sequitur.

Cohl's career became peripatetic after 1910. In 1912, his employer **Éclair** transferred him to the Fort Lee, New Jersey, branch, where he stayed for a little less than two years. During this time Cohl began animating a regular series of short films featuring the characters of the popular comic strip, "The Newlyweds." This was the beginning of the cartoonist mode of production. The influence was direct and immediate; dozens of American comic strip artists decided to try their hand at the new technique and find broader audiences for their work. In 1913, the **trade press** began using the term "animated cartoons" for the new film genre.

Because film distribution was international before the 1914 war, the technique of animation spread globally. A few of the many pioneers who might be cited include: Wladyslaw **Starewicz** (aka Ladislas Starevich) in Russia (beginning in 1911); Julius **Pinschewer** in Switzerland (beginning in 1911); and Erik Wasström, in Finland (beginning in 1914).

One of the most renowned American comic strip artists was Winsor **McCay**, an employee of the Hearst newspapers and a friend of Blackton. In 1911, McCay finished a short animated film officially called *Winsor McCay*, but generally known as *Little Nemo* (1911). It was adapted from his weekly comic, "Little Nemo in Slumberland." The film was shown on movie programs, and McCay built a live vaudeville act around it. The medium was drawings on paper, retraced laboriously hundreds of times to create moving images. Unlike Cohl's line-drawing figures, McCay retained the three-dimensional form of the comic strip characters. They exhibited consistent and characteristic quirks of expression and movement that later would be labeled character animation. McCay followed up with two further ink-on-paper works, *The Story of a Mosquito* (1912), and what would become the most widely seen pre-1915 animated film, *Gertie* (aka Gertie the Dinosaur) (1914).

Newspaper magnate William Randolph Hearst was a fan of comic strips and was responsible for publishing some of the American masters of the form, including, besides McCay and McManus, Frederick Burr Opper ("Maud"), George Herriman ("Krazy Kat"), and Rudolph Dirks ("The Katzenjammer Kids"). In 1915, his **newsreel**, the *International Film Service*, began including a weekly cartoon produced under the supervision of future comedy director, Gregory LaCava.

Also in 1915, Edison began releasing the "Animated Grouch Chasers" series drawn by Canadian comic strip pioneer Raoul Barré. In addition to his talents as a graphic artist, Barré was technically proficient. The sheets of drawings were uniformly punched with alignment holes designed to fit precisely over pegs on the drawing board and on the animation stand. This made retracing easier, more accurate and made the photographed drawings much more stable. Barré also organized his studio efficiently to enable his staff to release animated films on a regular basis.

The basic animation procedure, placing a drawing or object before the camera and exposing single frames, was inescapably laborious. Filmmakers like Chomón and Cohl chose media like paper cut-outs and object animation in part because they adhered to pre-cinema traditions (such as the puppet theater and **shadow theater**), but also because they offered production shortcuts. The work remained tedious and demanding, but easier than creating thousands of individual drawings, as McCay, for instance, had done for Gertie.

In 1913, John Randolph Bray, another newspaper comic strip artist, released *An Artist's Dream*. This film used the retraced paper technique but with added labor-saving techniques. Bray elaborated on McCay's "cycling," that is, reusing a set of drawings to create repetitive motion and thus extend screen-time with less retracing. He also prepared the sheets by mechanically reproducing the nonmoving parts of each picture on many pages through the process of etching. Thus only the moving figures in the shot had to be drawn individually on each prepared sheet. Reflecting the vogue of scientific management that was prevalent in pre-World War I America, he also instituted an assembly-line approach to production with specialized divisions of labor. Under contract with **Pathé**

Cinematograph, Bray's studio released Colonel Heeza Liar's African Hunt in January 1914. Following the "Newlyweds" precedent, it was a comic-strip-based series of episodes.

Bray's signal contribution was his patent on a means of making animated drawing films with relative efficiency using transparent sheets of **celluloid** (cellulose nitrate, the same as film stock). Backgrounds and other nonmoving elements were made on opaque cardboard, while anything that was to move was drawn and/or painted on the "cel," as it came to be called. During photography, the cel sequences were laid over the same background one by one. Incorporating prior patents by another animator, Earl Hurd (and possibly Paul Terry as well), resulted in the "Bray-Hurd Process Company." This initiated the industrialized mode of production for animation. Eventually cel **photography** nearly monopolized studio animation and remained the dominant technique until the widespread use of computers.

During the period of 1895 to 1915, animation came to be defined as a style or genre. While the subjects of most of the films on movie programs became increasingly less associated with popular theater (**vaudeville**, the *féeries* **or fairy plays**, children's theater), these traditional subjects remained robust in animated films. The phantasmagorical content of films by Blackton, Chomón, Cohl, and McCay created an aura of the magical and the irrational in animation. The comic strip, which had been a minor influence in standard movie production, came to the fore in animation as a provider of content and character. Thus for many years thereafter, animation was often considered a curious relative of "live" cinema, nonrealistic, flippant, and perhaps more suitable for children, until critics and historians began to appreciate their importance in the panoply of popular cultural sources of early cinema.

Further reading

Bendazzi, Giannalberto (1994) *Cartoons: One Hundred Years of Cinema Animation*, trans. Anna Taraboletti-Segre, Bloomington, IN: Indiana University Press.

Crafton, Donald (1993) *Before Mickey: The Animated Film, 1898–1928*, Chicago: University of Chicago Press.

Frierson, Michael (1994) *Clay Animation: American Highlights 1908 to the Present*, New York: Twayne.

Gifford, Denis (1987) *British Animated Films, 1895–1985*, Jefferson, NC: McFarland & Company.

Gifford, Denis (1990) *American Animated Films: The Silent Era, 1897–1929*, Jefferson, NC: McFarland & Company.

Tharrats, Juan Gabriel (1988) *Los 500 films de Segundo de Chomón*, Zaragosa: Unversidad de Zaragoza, Prensas Universitarias.

DONALD CRAFTON

Ankerstjerne, Johan

b. 1896; d. 1959

cinematographer, Denmark

Until the spring of 1911, when Ankerstjerne was hired, all films at **Nordisk** had been shot by just one cameraman, Axel Graatkjaer. Thereafter, Ankerstjerne became the close collaborator of the company's leading filmmaker, August **Blom**, and was responsible for the atmospheric images of his masterpiece, *Atlantis* (1913). He left Nordisk in 1915 to shoot the visually stunning *Haevnens Nat* (1916) for Benjamin **Christensen**, for whom he also shot *Häxan* [Witchcraft Through the Ages] (1922) with its elaborate optical effects work.

CASPER TYBJERG

Anschütz, Ottomar

b. 1846; d. 1907

photographer, chronophotographer, inventor, exhibitor, Germany

A respected photographer specialising in capturing movement, rather than a scientist and physiologist like Etienne-Jules **Marey** or Georges **Demenÿ**, Anschütz not only took exceptional series photographs but also created a disk-based exhibition apparatus that reproduced his images in crisp, life-like motion that were widely used in both Europe and North America in the late 1880s and early 1890s. The key to his ability to achieve richly detailed and natural photographs of movement was his development of the first practical focal-plane shutter, which was incorporated for over a quarter-century in influential hand-held **cameras** manufactured by C. P. Goerz in Berlin.

Born in Lissa (now Leschnow, Poland), Anschütz was the son of a decorative painter who took up **photography** late in life and had him apprenticed to the leading photographers. Taking over the family business in 1868, Anschütz gained a national reputation for his "instantaneous" photographs, especially of military manoeuvres, captured with very short exposures. He caught the attention of Crown Prince Friedrich (later Kaiser Friedrich III); as his reputation grew, he moved to Berlin and began exhibiting across Europe, winning medals for portraits, enlargements, animals in natural settings, and large-scale official ceremonies.

Inspired by Eadweard **Muybridge**, he began taking **chronophotographs** (series photographs) in 1885 with a set of twelve cameras using his own shutters. The next year, he built a second camera specifically designed to make chronophotographs that could be reproduced in a zoetrope or other circular viewing device as brief moving pictures. This camera, which used 24 lenses, shutters, release mechanisms, and glass plates built into three cases, often is mistakenly considered to be 24 separate cameras, but it was a unique construction made as a single unit with sophisticated adjustments to produce "closed" movements: i.e., series photographs where the first and last images were matched so that they could be exhibited in a continuously repeating cycle without apparent interruption.

Having designed the first of several improved zoetropes in 1887, Anschütz built an exhibition apparatus for his chronophotographs later that year, calling it the Schnellseher (sometimes Electrical Tachyscope). Through 1893 Anschütz devised at least eight models of the Schnellseher, all of which operated on this principle: intermittent light from a Geissler tube briefly illuminated each image on a continuously revolving disk as it passed a viewing screen. Early models (1888–1891) were viewed by six to eight people simultaneously; later models were coin-operated automatons for individual peep-show exhibition. At least 160 Schnellsehers were made, most in automaton form, and one brief stage of the **Kinetoscope**'s development at the **Edison** laboratory replicated Anschütz's technology.

The Schnellseher was widely exhibited publicly throughout Europe and North America, and some individual **itinerant exhibitors** kept the apparatus in use until *c.* 1902 in Central and South America. From 1891 on, multiple-apparatus installations in "Schnellseher parlors" were established in Berlin, London, New York, Hamburg, and elsewhere by the Electrical Wonder Company of London, which also exhibited at the Chicago **World's Fair** in 1893, just as the undercapitalised company was in financial decline. 17,000 people saw the Schnellseher at the Frankfurt Electrical Exhibition in 1891; 34,000 people saw it in Berlin in the summer of 1892; a further 10,152 saw ten machines at a fair in Lübeck in 1895; and 56,645 visited an installation at the Italian Exhibition in Hamburg in 1895, a show that ran concurrently with the exhibition of the Edison Kinetoscope in the city.

Few of Anschütz's chronophotographs survive: existing or published images mostly record the galloping horses or walking animals that Anschütz considered would receive favorable comment in comparison with the work of Marey and Muybridge from photographic societies, which they did. Over a hundred series of dancers (1888–1889) intended for teaching dance have disappeared, as has commercial work documenting the German Post Office (1891). Also missing are amusement chronophotographs, which included short comic scenes and **facial expression** sequences; one published image remains from *Skatspieler* [Card Players], showing three men in hats outdoors playing cards around a table; this series and *Einseifen beim Barbier* [Barber Shop Scene], which used elaborate props and timed action to comically illustrate a barber lathering an impatient customer, have close affinities with the earliest films of **Lumière**, Edison, and **Méliès**. The plea of one exhibitor for more exciting series and his comment that changing old pictures for new ones created repeat attendance, is further evidence that Anschütz's moving picture system, technologically overtaken by the development of films on **celluloid** bands, was an important precursor of cinematic practice and institutional apparatuses. From mid-1893, after the failure of the Electrical Wonder Company nearly bankrupted him, Anschütz abandoned moving picture work and returned to high society still photography and the design of cameras and photographic accessories, establishing a studio and an association to support amateur photography. He died suddenly, of appendicitis, in 1907.

See also: archaeology of cinema

Further reading

Rossell, Deac (2001) *Faszination der Bewegung. Ottomar Anschütz zwischen Photographie und Kino,* Frankfurt a. M./Basel: Stroemfeld/Roter Stern.

DEAC ROSSELL

Aquila Films

One of the most commercially oriented Italian film companies, with a unique penchant for stories of sensationalism, crime, and mystery. Aquila was founded as a private company in Turin, on 24 July 1907, by eight partners headed by a small businessman from Turin, Camillo Ottolenghi. His name regularly appeared in the company's early advertisements (Aquila Films Camillo Ottolenghi). Despite its modest size, the company gained international prominence in 1909 when Ottolenghi took part in the Congress of European film producers, in Paris, and publicly committed Aquila to the conference's technical and commercial resolutions.

Initially engaged in the production of all kinds of films, Aquila soon distinguished itself for its sensational **melodramas**, based on violent murders, international espionage, and egregious villains, often set in exotic locales such as India, Russia, and an unspecified "Orient." Its early works, which Italian film critics punctually deemed too commercial and photographically flawed, included *Il bandito nero* [The Black Bandit] (1908) and *L'imperatore* [The Emperor] (1908).

After releasing five titles in 1907 and twenty in 1908, Aquila's production of fiction films increased greatly after 1909, with 55 films released in 1910 and 73 in 1911. In this period Aquila made a name for itself with **comedy**, especially the **comic series** of *Jolicoeur* (1910) and *Pik-Nik* (1911). In 1912 several events occurred. Aquila shifted to producing **multiple/reel feature films**, releasing 27 titles in 1912 and 32 in 1913, and became a public company. One of its original co-founders, lawyer Lino Pugliese, became main shareholder and artistic director. Ottolenghi briefly remained as chief administrator.

Aiming to become the new **Nordisk**, that year the Turinese company launched two new sensational **crime film** series, "Terrore" and "Grand Spectacles Aquila," as well as a Golden series in 1913. After 1914, the company began alternating crime narratives with passionate melodramas of love and death. In these years, Aquila's most notable successes included *Lo Spettro di Jago* [The Vengeance of Jago] (1912), *Fedora* (1913), *La Bibbia* [The Bible] (1913), *Teodora* (1914), and two 1916 films directed by Roberto **Roberti**, *La peccatrice* [The Sinful Woman] and *Tenebre* [Darkness].

Apart from its sensationalist and highly commercial preferences, what helped Aquila compete against other Italian companies was its dense network of international distributors. As early as 1908, Ottolenghi had established commercial alliances with a number of distributors for the British and the French markets, from **Williamson** and **Gaumont** to Charles Heffer and **Raleigh & Robert**. Aquila reached also Spain, Russia and several nations in South America. In the USA, the Turinese company found a partner in the independent circuit of Film Import & Trading Co. The outbreak of **World War I** radically affected Aquila's capacity to sustain production and commercialize its films abroad. As a result, in 1917, AF closed its doors.

Further reading

Bernardini, Aldo (1999) "Aquila Films: profilo di una casa 'editrice'," *Bianco & Nero*, 60.2: 107–125.

GIORGIO BERTELLINI

Arbuckle, Roscoe ("Fatty")

b. 1887; d. 1933

actor, director, USA

Following a brief career as a **vaudeville illustrated song** performer and several unexceptional appearances in **Selig comedies** during 1909, Arbuckle eventually found success in joining **Keystone** in 1913. Popularly known as "Fatty" to the movie-going public, Arbuckle appeared most notably alongside Mabel **Normand** in a self-directed **comic series** called *Fatty and Mabel*, often distinguished by Arbuckle's playful and remarkably sophisticated handling of comic narrative. After completing the three-reel *Fatty and Mabel Adrift* (1916), Arbuckle and Normand left California and established a new Keystone unit for their productions in New Jersey. In 1917, Arbuckle was signed by Paramount, where he made two-reel comedies (sometimes partnered with Buster Keaton) and starred in comic features until a notorious scandal in 1921 cost him his career.

Further reading

Edmonds, Andy (1991) *Frame-up!: The Untold Story of Roscoe "Fatty" Arbuckle*, New York: W. Morrow.

ROB KING

archaeology of cinema/pre-cinema

According to G.-Michel **Coissac**, in *Histoire du cinématographe* (1925), or Will Day, in "25,000 Years to Trap a Shadow" (an unpublished manuscript from the 1930s), the archaeology of cinema might date back to the Pharaohs, or indeed even to the Magdalenian period. "Writing in movement" may indeed be found, for instance, on Greek vases. Yet the first concrete evidence of animated images or luminous images projected through a natural, optical, or catoptric artifice came with the invention of the *camera obscura*, whose principle had been known since Antiquity. The camera obscura came into existence in the 16th century, notably through the work of Italian inventor Giambattista

della Porta, who, in 1589, first presented projected animated color images in a dark room with sound accompaniment. The idea was both simple and subtle: some comedians performed outside a room plunged into darkness and in whose wall a hole had been drilled and a set of lenses had been placed. The images of the comedians were thus projected, by bright sunlight, onto the opposite inner wall, and the representation was accompanied by music and various noises. It was the desire to retain and capture the fugitive images seen inside such a dark room that triggered Nicéphore Niepce's and Louis J. M. Daguerre's **photography** research in the 19th century: the daguerreotype was introduced in 1839.

In 1645, *Ars magna lucis et umbrae*, a treatise written by the German Jesuit, Athanase Kircher, provided early scientists with a summary of optical, catoptric, and dioptric techniques necessary for the projection of luminous images. A Dutch Protestant, Christiaan Huygens, then simplified older processes and, in 1659, invented the "lantern of fright," or **magic lantern**, a box equipped with lenses which made possible the magnified projection of images painted on glass. These images could be animated as well as fixed or still, thanks to the juxtaposition of mobile plates. The magic lantern, one of the most spectacular instruments of entertainment and **education** in the prehistory of cinema, quickly spread throughout the world.

Over the following century the lantern was transformed through the invention of achromatic lenses, the solar microscope, and the megascope. It was now able to project the temporal passage of objects, living animals, human faces, opaque objects, and microscopic preparations. Other "curiosities" swamped collectors' "wonder cabinets": anamorphoses, perspectival views, optical boxes for the viewing of colored engravings with dissolving day-and-night effects. In the latter spectacle, a fundamental notion came into play: the representation of elapsed time within space, which later would become characteristic of **chronophotography** as well as cinematography.

During the 1790s, several slightly unscrupulous physicists revived the notorious past of Huygens's lantern (which in 1659 projected a frightening "Dance of Death" inspired by Hans Holbein) and created a spectacle called the "fantasmagoria." As such spectacles gained in sophistication, they included projections from behind a **screen** or over a smoke screen, animated and three-dimensional images that grew or shrank in size as the lantern was moved on rails (as in a tracking shot). Noises and magic tricks often accompanied these nerve-racking visions. The fantasmagoria was popular throughout the 19th century, notably thanks to Robert Houdin, and was later transposed into Georges **Méliès**'s work.

Since Antiquity, the phenomenon of the persistence of impressions produced by light on the eye also had been a consistent object of study. Research intensified during the 19th century, led by Michael Faraday and Peter Mark Roget (England), Joseph Plateau (Belgium), Simon Stampfer (Austria), and others. In 1833, as strobe lights (with their obdurating discs) were marketed, they inspired myriads of new scientists. Indeed, stroboscopy and photography were soon combined. In the 1860s, a fresh wave of research sketched out a major principle of cinematography: a light-sensitive plate or strip that could be moved intermittently would halt momentarily in front of a lens as it was uncovered by an obdurating disc (Henry Du Mont, 1861; Louis Ducos du Hauron, 1864).

In 1874, the French astronomer, Pierre J. C. Janssen, exploited this principle and managed to photograph the various phases of the passage of Venus between the Sun and the Earth on a sensitive disc. His "photographic gun" inspired physiologist Etienne-Jules **Marey**, who perfected his own "gun" (1882) after British photographer Eadweard **Muybridge** had obtained the first successive negatives of galloping horses in the United States, in 1878.

Marey was the propagator of a "graphic method" of recording (thanks to electric or pneumatic captors and rotating cylinders) all kinds of human and animal movement as well as that of mobile objects. This graphic method or "chronostylography" was but the first phase of Marey's research, which led, without epistemological rupture, to the photography of movement or "chronophotography."

Marey greatly advanced the analytical and synthetic study of movement. He studied subjects as diverse as the blood stream, breathing processes, muscular effort, acoustics, hydrodynamic and aerodynamic phenomena, insect and bird flight. Compiling thousands of glass plates and some 800

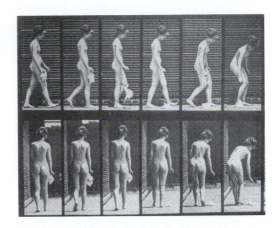

Figure 6 Eadweard Muybridge, *Animal Location*, 1887: plate 202.

chronophotographic films, Marey's legacy is a sort of encyclopedia of movement and forms nobody had seen before. He was the first to slow down and accelerate time, to measure and master space, to "recreate life" through images or machines. An "engineer of life," an atypical scientist, he was able to rally disciples around himself—for instance, Nicolas C. E. François-Franck, Georges **Demeñy**, Lucien **Bull**, Pierre **Noguès**—and create two important research laboratories: the Station physiologique and the Institut Marey. Marey's glass plate cameras (1882) and **celluloid** strip **cameras** (1889) influenced all those researching cinematography in the 1890s.

Among them were William **Friese-Greene** and Louis **Le Prince** in Great Britain, Albert **Londe**, Hippolyte Sébert, Léon Bouly, and Demeñy in France, and Ottomar **Anschütz** in Germany, all of whom explored other means of recording movement and produced an uneven quantity of films throughout the 1890s. In 1892, Emile **Reynaud**'s "Théâtre Optique" indicated a new direction of research: the projection, on a large screen, of animated drawings. Some speculated on the next logical step, chronophotographic projection, which Demeñy and Anschütz both attempted with, respectively, the "Phonoscope" (1892) and the "Electrotachyscope" (1894).

Indeed, in 1894, an industry of moving photographs began to emerge in both the United States and Europe with the marketing of the **Edison**

Figure 7 Emile Reynaud's Théâtre Optique, from *La Nature*, 1892.

Kinetoscope, patented in 1891. In Edison's hands, Marey's chronophotography was no longer a purely scientific endeavor: it also became a popular spectacle and generated important revenues. In 1895 Otway and Gray **Latham**, Thomas **Armat** and Francis **Jenkins** (United States), Max **Skladanowsky** (Germany), George William **de Bedts**, Henri **Joly**, and particularly Louis **Lumière** (France) managed to combine satisfactorily the projection (magic lantern) and recording of successive images of movement. Chronophotographic or cinematographic projection then spread quickly around the world, much as did the magic lantern during the 17th century.

During a 1955 filmology conference, Professor Francastel first formulated the idea of a "pre-cinema"; soon after, Paul Léglise published a literary study entitled *Une oeuvre de pré-cinéma: L'Enéide* [A Work of Pre-Cinema: The Aeneid] (1958); more recently, there has been Hermann Hecht's monumental *Pre-Cinema History* (1993). The term now has become common, even if equivalents such as "proto-cinema" and "archeocinema" have been proposed. Theoretically,

"pre-cinema" refers to the period running from the earliest instances of "writing in movement" down to 1895, when moving picture screenings began in Europe and the United States. This would imply, however, that Marey's chronophotographs (1882–1904) as well as Edison's kinetoscope films (1891–1895) belong to pre-cinema, not cinema, which in turn makes the notion of pre-cinema very problematic, if only from an etymological perspective. "Cinematograph," a word coined by Léon Bouly in 1892 for the reversible camera he had patented, means "writing in movement" in Greek. Yet Marey and Edison had been "writing in movement" with quite some virtuosity since the 1880s. But what if "cinematograph" means "projecting images," as sycophants of the Lumière brothers claim? The mere projection of film images alone hardly encompasses the complexity of cinematographic techniques.

There is a temptation, especially among Lumière defenders, to equate the "birth" of cinema with the invention of the Lumière's machine. All the research and discoveries done before would thus pertain to "pre-cinema." Conversely, the opposite camp nurtures the teleological desire of a cinema going back to the dawn of time, thereby invalidating the term "pre-cinema" altogether.

This entry has opted for the "archaeology of cinema" (a more technical term first used by Ceram and others in 1966) to designate the early history of cinema as an object of study and research. Whether conceived as a technology, an industry, an amusement, or an art, cinema history is punctuated by complex discoveries and transformations in any number of domains. Among them are numerous experiments in physics and physiology, seemingly unrelated problems derived from such specific sciences as hippology, aerodynamics, and neurology, and thousands of patents registered by an extremely diverse group of individuals. Also included are diverse social practices in the areas of economics, politics, culture, religion, and private life. Even so, this loose conglomeration presents some coherence. This Hecht brilliantly demonstrates in a bibliography of 3,700 articles and books, and that the bibliography is still incomplete strongly suggests the incredible richness of the subject.

Thus, an "archeology of cinema" involves different currents of thought. One, which appeared at least as early as the Renaissance, combines physical science, the study of optics and light, physiology, the practice of magic, **painting** and perspective, the persistence of light impressions, chemistry, acoustics, and mechanics. This was what Charles Patin, a French traveler of the 17th century, called the "trickster art," as its object was to transfigure images through light, to sublimate them through optics, to animate them, even to distort them sometimes. Articulated shadows, **shadow theater**, sets of mirrors, the *camera obscura*, anamorphoses, optical boxes, dioptric paradoxes, magic lanterns, fantasmagoria, stroboscopic discs, zootropic films, magic shows, **dioramas and panoramas** all belong in this current and comprise an immense set of materials in the history of the sciences and arts.

Much later, the history of photography also has its "pre-history" (della Porta) and "inventors" (Niépce, William Henry Fox Talbot). Photography was quickly combined with the most serious applications of stroboscopy and stereoscopy. The first "animators" of the 19th century had as their utopian dream the animation of photography, in three dimensions and in **color**. Marey and other "photographers of movement" of the late 19th century were the leaders of this essential current.

The study of experimental physics and of the physiology of animal and human movement generated another type of research. Physics rooms of the 18th century were rich in extremely sophisticated machines that attempted to re-create human animation artificially. Experimental instruments of the 19th century also re-created phenomena related to visual, auditory, and mental perceptions—for instance, Faraday's wheels, Koenig's revolving mirrors.

Whether in the domain of the "trickster art" or in that of photography and pure scientific study, there existed a dream, one of a demiurge-like nature, whose ambition was not only to observe phenomena invisible to the naked eye, but also (and mainly) to re-create life.

Further reading

Campagnoni, Donata Pesenti (1995) *Verso il cinema, Macchine spettacoli e mirabili visioni*, Turino: Utet Libreria.

Hecht, Hermann (1993) *Pre-Cinema History: An Encyclopaedia and Annotated Bibliography of the Moving Image before 1896*, London: British Film Institute/Bowker Saur.

Mannoni, Laurent (2000) *The Great Art of Light and Shadow, Archaeology of the Cinema*, trans. and ed. Richard Crangle, Exeter: University of Exeter Press.

Musser, Charles (1990) *History of the American Cinema 1: The Emergence of Cinema: The American Screen to 1907*, New York: Scribner's.

Rossell, Deac (1998) *Living Pictures, The Origins of the Movies*, Albany: State University of New York Press.

LAURENT MANNONI

Arche, Alto

b. 1854; d. 1940

scientist, filmmaker, Austria

A professor of chemistry and natural history at the Staatsreal Schule of Vienna, Arche obtained, in 1907, a government subsidy to produce educational films. He became one of the first to make and use such films as pedagogical tools. The subjects of surviving titles include artisans at work—*Zeugfärberei* [Dyeworks], *Glasbläser* [Glassblowers], and *Hafner an der Drehscheibe* [On the Potter's Wheel]—and gymnastic exercises for students—*Kürturnen der Schüler der k.k. Franz Joseph-Realschule* [Voluntary Exercises of the Pupils from the k.k. Franz Joseph School]. In 1912, he founded the Vienna Club of Cinematography.

See also: scientific films: Europe

PAOLO CANEPPELE

archives

Moving image archives are broadly defined as repositories for the long-term **preservation** of, and permanent **access** to, motion picture artifacts. These two functions are described by other languages with different terms: in French and German, *cinémathèque* and *kinemathek* refer to institutions whose main focus is film exhibition (hence the English term *cinematheque* as synonymous of a screening venue specialized in repertoire programs), while *archive du film* and *filmarchiv* are adopted by entities where preservation is the main priority; on the other hand, the Spanish terms *filmoteca* and *cinemateca* are more or less equivalent (although the latter is used mainly in South America), the Russian *filmoteka* is far more common than *kinoarchiv*, and there is no specific word for it in Japanese. There is some agreement, however, on the difference between "film archives" and "film museums" in relation to the scope of their collections; the aim of an "archive" is to preserve as many films as possible, while "museums" have the mandate to select the most representative examples of cinema as art, technology, or historical document.

Research conducted in 1993 identified 577 public moving image archives operating worldwide. Their number has increased exponentially in the last decade of the 20th century and is likely to grow even further, but not all of them include early films among their holdings. The majority of titles from the beginnings of cinema are held

by members of the International Federation of Film Archives (FIAF), an association of non-profit archives and museums established in 1938 and now counting well over one hundred affiliates worldwide. According to a provisional survey made in August 2001, among 83 FIAF institutions, 12,016 fiction films produced between 1893 and 1915 are known to survive in some form; not surprisingly, most of them are from the USA (6,700), France (2,875), Italy (759), the United Kingdom (738), Germany (347) and Denmark (207), leaders in the film industry during its formative years. However imposing, this number represents a modest percentage of the films actually produced (33,664 titles were released in the USA between July 1907 and December 1920, for instance, according to Einar Lauritzen and Gunnar Lundquist), and a tiny fraction of the prints actually struck during the era (from a few for some of the first **Edison** or **American Mutoscope and Biograph** films to several hundreds for a Charlie **Chaplin** comedy of 1915).

The reasons why the survival of an early film is a relatively rare phenomenon can be summarized in two categories. First, almost all films of the period were printed onto nitrate stock, a chemically unstable and extremely fragile carrier whose short life span is affected by temperature and humidity, and by mechanical damage derived from repeated handling and projection. The second reason is of an economic nature: from the beginnings to 1905, film producers and distributors were selling prints to exhibitors, who could project them as many times as they wanted and then dispose of them when they were no longer useful. The destruction of prints after repeated viewings was considered not only inevitable as much as desirable, insofar as their demise would encourage the demand for new subjects. This tendency was further enhanced by the gradual transition to the rental practice, formally agreed upon during a meeting between film producers and manufacturers held in Paris on February 2–4, 1909: at the end of the exploitation period, prints were to be returned to the producer and destroyed.

Other waves of destruction of the early film heritage occurred after 1915. With the increasing success of multiple-reel/feature films, distributors eliminated their remaining copies of early shorts;

silent cinema was deemed unprofitable as a whole after the transition to sound in the late 1920s, and thousands of copies were burned at that time; the final blow came with the introduction of acetate film in February 1951, when nitrate was abandoned altogether because of its flammability and potential danger. As film was not regarded as an art form, only a handful of visionaries fought for its survival as a cultural artifact, from filmmaker Robert William **Paul**, who deposited one of his films to the reluctant curators of the British Museum in 1896, to the Polish writer Boleslaw **Matuszewski** in his pioneering essays "Une Nouvelle source pour l'histoire" and "La Photographie animée" (both 1898). The deposit of copies on paper from nitrate negatives at the Library of Congress began in 1893, but its goal was the legal protection of images from plagiarism and copyright infringement, not conservation as such.

Film archives began to exist as separate entities in the 1910s, with the purpose of keeping a document of notable events and people: the first institutions of this kind are documented in Stavanger (Norway) and Prague (1910), Vienna (1912), Copenhagen (1913), Brussels, Hamburg, Berlin, Madrid, and the Vatican. The word *cinémathèque* was coined in 1913 by a member of the French cabinet, but became a reality in the modern sense of the term only twenty years later at the Svenska Filmfundet of Stockholm (1933). In the 1930s, the corpus of early films known to archivists and historians was reduced to a few dozen titles; after half a century, the list included several thousand titles, and a ground-breaking retrospective of 548 shorts from the period 1900–1906 held in Brighton in 1978, under the auspices of David Francis for the National Film Archive (London), marked the beginning of an international effort toward the rediscovery and scholarly appraisal of early cinema.

Early films are still found all over the world, and acquired by archives, mainly through deposits and donations (purchase of nitrate prints is generally discouraged on the basis of the expenses necessary to restore the films and to maintain them in adequate storage conditions; donors are often encouraged to leave them to the care of the archives in exchange for a copy of the restored film). George Eastman House (Rochester), Library of Congress (Washington D. C.), Museum of Modern Art (New York) have the largest collections of early films in the United States; the Archives du Film (Bois d'Arcy, France), British Film Institute (London), Det Danske Filmmuseum (Copenhagen) and the Nederlands Filmmuseum (Amsterdam) are the main sources in Europe. Historical research for **authentication**, cataloguing, and research purposes is conducted by their teams in collaboration with academics and independent scholars. Most films made before 1916 are in public domain (legislation varies between Europe and North America), and of modest commercial appeal (with the notable exception of some non-fiction films, often used for broadcast documentaries). They are restored and made available in formats as close as possible to the original, often with severe financial constraints (particularly in developing countries) and with the additional challenges of ongoing decomposition of the surviving artifacts, **color** degradation, and increasing pressure from the entertainment industry.

Further reading

Borde, Raymond (1983) *Les Cinémathèques*, Paris: L'Âge d'Homme.

Bowser, Eileen and John Kuiper (eds.) (1980/1991) *A Manual for Film Archives*, Brussels: FIAF/New York–London: Garland.

Holman, Roger and André Gaudreault (eds.) (1982) *Cinema 1900–1906: An Analytical Study*, 2 Vols., Brussels: FIAF.

Houston, Penelope (1994) *Keepers of the Frame: The Film Archives*, London: British Film Institute.

PAOLO CHERCHI USAI

Argentina

Argentina's economic and cultural connections with Paris and New York swiftly brought news of moving pictures to Buenos Aires, and film equipment was imported shortly thereafter. Recent scholarship indicates that the **Edison Kinetoscope** was exhibited in the city on September 18, 1894, five months after its appearance in New York, and films by the **Lumière** company and R. W. **Paul** were exhibited for several months beginning in July 1896. Research by the Fundación Cinemateca Argentina reveals that, in 1896, Federico Figner established an exhibition venue with one or more Vitascopes, Kinetoscopes, and X-rays machines in downtown Buenos Aires. It also credits Figner with first exhibiting Argentine views filmed by José Steimberg in early November 1896, predating by one year the activity of Eugenio **Py**, usually credited as the first to present local views.

Several photographic supply stores imported film equipment and material and became involved in the moving picture business. One owner, Gregorio Ortuño, opened the Salon Nacional, the first moving picture theater in Buenos Aires, in 1900. As owner of Casa Lepage, Enrique Lepage (an immigrant from Belgium) employed two very important figures in early Argentine cinema, Py and Max **Glücksmann**. Py became a major cameraman, especially known for filming *actualités*. Although active as early as 1897, he is best remembered for filming the Brazilian president-elect in *El viaje del Doctor Campos Salles a Buenos Aires* [The Visit of Doctor Campos Salles to Buenos Aires] (1900). Py also worked for Casa Lepage on synchronizing **phonographs** and moving pictures and created thirty-two **phonoscènes** between 1907 and 1911. By contrast, Glücksmann, became a leading producer and distributor and, after purchasing Casa Lepage in 1908, a well-known theater owner.

Others became involved in different kinds of filmmaking. Dr. Alejandro Posadas is credited with filming two surgical operations, possibly in 1899 and 1900. Eugenio Cardini, an amateur photographer, used a **Cinématographe Lumière** to film *Escenas callejeras* [Street Scenes] (1900), considered a precursor of fiction films. Mario **Gallo** made the country's first long fiction film, *La revolución de Mayo* [The May Revolution] (1909) as well as *El fusilamiento de Dorrego* [The Execution of Dorrego] (1910), for the centenary celebrations of Argentine independence.

During the 1910s, foreign distributors made available packages of French, Italian and American films (and **serials**), with the latter finally dominating exhibition by the end of **World War I**. The first Argentine **multiple-reel/feature film** to be considered a major box office success was *La nobleza gaucha* [Gaucho Nobility] (1915), although *Amalia* (1914) and *Juan sin ropa* [Juan without Clothes] (1919) also were notable. Glücksmann, Gallo, and Federico Valle all established weekly **newsreels** by the end of the decade (the exact dates are still disputed), which continued into the 1920s. Valle also was responsible for producing Quirino Cristiani's *El apóstol* [The Apostol] (1917), considered the country's first feature **animation** film.

Throughout the early period, film exhibition received significant coverage in the national press and in cultural magazines. Only later did a **trade press** appear, with *La película* (1917) and *Imparcial Film* (1919).

Further reading

Caneto, Guillermo, Marcela Cassinelli, Héctor González Bergerot, César Maranghello, Elda Navarro, Alejandra Portela, and Susana Strugo (eds.) (1996) *Historia de la primeros años de cine en la Argentina, 1895–1910*, Buenos Aires: Editorial Fundación Cinemateca Argentina.

Couselo, Jorge Miguel (1984) "El período mudo," in Couselo *et al.* (eds.) *Historia del cine argentino*, 11–45, Buenos Aires: Centro Editor de América latina.

Kriger, Clara and Alejandra Portela (eds.) (1997) *Diccionario de realizadores: Cine latinoamericano 1*, Buenos Aires: Ediciones del Jilguero.

KATHLEEN NEWMAN

Armat, Thomas

b. 1866; d. 1948

inventor, USA

A railway mechanic and bookkeeper, Armat went into partnership with C. Francis **Jenkins** in late 1894 to develop a moving picture projection apparatus used for public demonstrations beginning in September 1895. Buying out Jenkins, Armat sold an improved beater-mechanism **projector** to **Raff & Gammon**, who persuaded

Thomas **Edison** to lend his name to their machine, which was exhibited on 23 April 1896 as the Edison Vitascope. Armat defended his intellectual rights in this machine for the next twelve years, eventually joining the **Motion Picture Patents Company**. He was given a special Academy Award in 1947.

DEAC ROSSELL

Arnaud, Etienne

b. 1879; d. 1955

filmmaker, scriptwriter, France, USA

Arnaud began his career as a director and scriptwriter for **Gaumont** in late 1905. Active with the company until 1911, he made more than 230 films, from *phonoscènes* and comic **chase films** such as *La course aux potirons* [The Pumpkin Chase] (1908) to melodramas and **trick films** such as *Le Korrigan* [The Breton Goblin] (1908). From 1912 to 1914, he served as artistic director at **Éclair**'s American studios in Fort Lee (New Jersey). After his return to France at the outbreak of **World War I**, Arnaud was unable to regain his former stature in the French film industry.

LAURENT LE FORESTIER

Arquillière, Alexandre

b. 1870; d. 1953

actor, France

Arquillière was an important actor at André Antoine's Théâtre Libre, where he collaborated with Firmin Gémier and also authored several plays. Although his first film appearances included **SCAGL**'s *L'Assommoir* (1909), it was at **Éclair** that he became an early film **star** as the master criminal in Victorin **Jasset**'s *Zigomar* series (1911–1913). There, realism blended with fantastic trick effects—i.e., "fantastic realism"—to highlight Zigomar's deceptive machinations. Arquillière also played another mysterious bandit in Jasset's *Tom*

Butler (1912). His later career included several powerful psychological roles, among them the crude husband in Germaine Dulac's *La Souriante Madame Beudet* [The Smiling Madame Beudet] (1923) and the gardener in Julien Duvivier's *La Fin du jour* [Day's End] (1939).

MARINA DAHLQUIST

Asia Film Co.

The first production company in China founded by the Russian-American showman Benjamin Polaski in 1909. Before leaving Shanghai in 1912, Polaski sold his assets to two American expatriates, who, in collaboration with the Xinmin theater group led by **Zheng Zhengqiu** and **Zhang Shichuang**, formed a joint venture. Its productions included a number of *actualités*, short **comedies**, and a feature-length fiction film, *Nanfu nanqi* [A Couple in Trouble] (1913), a parody of arranged marriage written by Zheng and directed by Zhang. In 1914, the company ceased operation due to a shortage of film stock in the wake of the **World War I**.

ZHEN ZHANG

Atelier Apollo

Atelier Apollo was established in 1889 by K. E. Ståhlberg (1861–1919), a visionary pioneer of **photography** and cinematography in Finland. Having bought **Pathé-Frères** equipment on his Paris honeymoon in 1896, he started a touring moving picture show. In 1904, he established a cinema in Helsinki called *Maailman Ympäri* [Round the World] and proceeded to build a **cinema chain**. In 1906, he became the country's first film producer, with a total of 110 shorts by 1913—half the entire national production. He also produced the first Finnish fiction film, *Salaviinanpolttajat* [The Moonshiners] (1907), and built Finland's first film laboratory in the same year. Atelier Apollo was always known for its high standards of photography and for employing talent like Frans Engström, Hjalmar Hårdh, and Oscar Lindelöf.

ANTTI ALANEN

Aubert, Etablissements L.

In 1909, Louis **Aubert** bought Couture et Carré, a small company in Paris which purchased and then sold and rented films on a very limited scale. By the end of the year, he had become the exclusive agent for an Italian company, Vesuvio Films. For some time, he provided rental services for a number of foreign producers such as Crick & Martin, **Hepworth**, Roma, Unitas, Victoria, and **Hispano Films**. In 1910, Aubert gained a significant advantage over his competition when he became the exclusive representative of **Nordisk Films**, the Danish company which had released several successful **multiple reel films**, including *The White Slave Trade*.

In August 1911, Aubert turned his enterprise into a public limited company (société anonyme), the Compagnie Générale du Cinématographe. With a capital of 500,000 francs and activities in distribution and exhibition, the company remained under Aubert's tight control—he received 4,000 of the original 5,000 100-franc shares, in exchange for a number of assets, and purchased 415 of the 1,000 shares open to subscription. Within a year the company's capital doubled, and its name was changed, in February 1914, to Etablissements L. Aubert.

One of Aubert's masterstrokes, in 1911, was to obtain an exclusive concession from the prestigious Italian company **Cines** for the sale of its films in France, Belgium and the Netherlands. Cines was to bring the genre of the peplum or toga film to its highest level of success, notably in Enrico **Guazzoni**'s *Quo Vadis?* (1913). Over the four months prior to its release, Aubert repeatedly promoted the film in professional journals, so that its presentation at the Gaumont-Palace proved a major event.

The Compagnie Générale du Cinématographe also distributed, sometimes in conjunction with other companies, important films from a variety of foreign and domestic producers and negotiated exclusive rights for those that seemed most promising at the box office. Such was the case with Mario **Caserini**'s *The Last Days of Pompei* (1913), a 2,000-meter film produced by **Ambrosio**, an Italian company represented in Paris by Charles Helfer. From 1912 on, the Compagnie also owned exclusive rental rights for Georges **Lordier**'s Grands Films Populaires, several of which met with public success: for instance, *Tire au flanc* [The Layabout], *Le Bossu* [The Hunchback], and *Les Cinq sous de Lavarède* [Lavarède's Five Sous].

As early as October 1910, Aubert sought to complement his activities in the rental business by purchasing the Cinéma-Théâtre Voltaire (a neighborhood theater in Paris), one of the assets exchanged for shares in the Compagnie Générale du Cinématographe. He developed a network of such theaters, owning five at the time **World War I** war broke out. In May 1915, in partnership with Serge **Sandberg**, he opened the Cinéma des Nouveautés-Aubert Palace, a **palace cinema** located in the Grands Boulevards.

Late in 1913, Aubert also decided to venture into production. He had a studio built in Joinville-le-Pont near Paris, and the first production, *Fille-Mère* [An Unmarried Mother], sought to emulate *The White Slave Trade*. The scenario was written by Arthur Bernède who, during the war, would write the scenario and serialized story for Louis **Feuillade**'s *Judex*. *Fille-Mère* was released early in 1914 and also was exhibited in some theaters under the more explicit title, *L'Abandonnée* [The Abandoned Woman].

In the 1920s, Etablissements L. Aubert developed an extended network of "Aubert-Palace" theaters, remained very active in the rental and distribution business, and engaged in many European co-productions. By 1929, when Louis Aubert sold his business to Franco-Films, it was ranked third among French film companies.

See also: distribution: Europe

Further reading

Meusy, Jean-Jacques (1995) *Paris-Palaces ou le temps des cinémas, 1894–1918*, Paris, CNRS Editions.

JEAN-JACQUES MEUSY

Aubert, Louis

b. 1878; d. 1944

exhibitor, distributor and renter,
producer, France

The son of a big civil engineering contractor in western France, Félix Hippolyte Louis Aubert received his high school education in Paris before taking up an internship abroad to prepare himself for a career in agriculture. He was attracted to the burgeoning film industry, however, and, in 1909, acquired a small business in Paris specializing in selling and renting films. The following year, he ventured into exhibition and, by the time of **World War I**, owned several neighborhood theaters. Yet he owed his swift rise to prominence to his rental business. He managed to sign contracts with large (mostly foreign) companies and distributed several very successful films, including *Quo Vadis?*. In 1912, he became the president of the renters' branch of the newly created Chambre Syndicale Française de la Cinématographie et des Industries qui s'y rattachent (French Trade Association of Cinematography and Related Industries). Late in 1913, he built a studio in Joinville-le-Pont near Paris, and moved into film production. In May 1915, he opened the first of what would become a circuit of luxury Aubert-Palaces in Paris.

An authoritarian figure, Aubert described his business in these oft-quoted lines: "Two drawers, one for receipts, the other for expenses ... It's all very simple ... I am a tradesman, that's all!" In 1929, at the height of his success, he sold his company to Franco-Film, in order to pursue a career in politics as an "independent radical" and was a representative for the Vendée region from 1932 to 1942.

JEAN-JACQUES MEUSY

Figure 8 Louis Aubert, from a palace cinema program, 1913. (Courtesy of Jean-Jacques Meusy.)

audiences: research issues and projects

Speculations about the composition, function, and responses of early motion-picture audiences have produced some of the liveliest, most extended, and productive debates in cinema studies. In a nutshell, the tendency in early cinema studies (hereinafter ECS) has been away from concentrating on the producers, exhibitors and the films themselves as agents of influence and management of consumers, and toward emphasizing viewers, communities of viewers, and the historical junctures of film practice. The crucial issues concerning audiences in ECS have been: identifying spectators and audiences and the exhibition context; assessing what reliable evidence is available, how generalizable is it, and how should it be interpreted; determining the composition of audiences; conjecturing about the relationship between the form and content of films and their social effects; examining societal constraints on audiences; and trying to learn about audience behaviors before, during and after shows.

Inquiries into the patterns of cinema exhibition and the identity and behavior of attendees were among the first research programs of early film scholarship when academic interest in the subject escalated in the 1970s. At the same time, film studies in general was beginning to include the end-use as part of the "cinema system." Evaluating semiotics, structuralism, neo-Marxism, psychological, feminism, Russian formalism and other "isms," ECS absorbed some of these theoretical discourses, but also qualified and reacted against them. Fundamentally, ECS began to doubt that one way of explaining the films of 1893–1915 could ever be adequate.

The development of ECS played out against a heady and rapidly evolving theoretical background. Many theories centered around the idea that film texts stipulated an ideal spectator, not only optically with respect to mise en scène, point of view and so on, but also ideologically. Films, following Roland Barthes, were palimpsests that analysts like Christian Metz and Noël Burch could read to recover residues of meaning and the mechanisms by which films implied or constructed subjectivity. Textual approaches ranged from looking at films as linguistic communication systems, as equivalent to psychological processes, and as vivid demonstrations of the mechanisms of patriarchal determination, especially in the case of the movies' seemingly omnipresent "male" gaze. The ideas of Louis Althusser, Walter Benjamin, Antonio Gramsci, Raymond Williams, and Pierre Bourdieu, to name a few social theorists, motivated authors who focused on how social hierarchies affected or determined **spectatorship**. The spectator—a word used in the special sense of connoting this idealized hypothetical viewer—was a function of the film text, not a person. One beneficial aspect of reconstituting an implied audience from film texts was that researchers developed critical techniques and a vocabulary for closely analyzing films.

Exhibition site research in the 1970s sparked interest in early cinema outside of a pre-existing circle of specialists. Did the patterns of **nickelodeon** exhibition in Boston and Manhattan indicate that film thrived with lower-class audiences, the prevailing view for the previous decades, or did exhibitors target middle-class audiences from the start? (For a concise summary of the controversy, which went on for nearly a decade, see Stokes, 2–8.) As theories evolved in the 1980s, ECS scholars tended to conceptualize audiences as less unitary and passive, and admitted more discretionary behavior. Formal properties were not innate in films, but existed in viewer recognition and use. Increasingly, ECS borrowed concepts from contemporary movements in history, sociology and communication theory, which valorized the political power of non-mainstream groups. The application of cultural studies has taken audience analysis outside the walls of theaters to include fan response, the development and circulation of movie discourses (e.g., **star** vs. picture personality), and the behavior of viewers after the show as they pursued other social practices.

The actual experiences of "real people" watching a film can never be known, but researchers have been locating data about sites of exhibition, demographics of specific neighborhoods, and patterns of film distribution that enable us to infer the circumstances of movie-going. Among the sources that have been used are theater handbills, **newspaper** accounts and advertisements, social services files, insurance company documents, business directories, fire district maps, census figures, municipal tax records, city ordinances, immigration statistics, police reports, travel narratives, **postcards** and photographs, memoirs and the occasional oral history. Historical materialist approaches augment such documentation with interpretations about how individuals would have derived meanings from the films being documented, with the larger goal of situating movie-going in the context of other social practices and institutions.

Unfortunately, the documents that would provide clues about early cinema audiences are mostly lost or never existed. Extant reviews, memoirs, censorship files and so on may be tainted by their authors' elite status as members of the dominant social groups. Much evidence is contradictory. Estimates of the number of nickelodeons in New York City in 1908, for instance, have been given variously as from a little more than 300 to nearly 1000.

In ECS of the 1970s the "bourgeoisification" thesis emerged as a way to explain the apparent radical change in the movies' clientele from plebeian to middle class. After the novelty among the predominantly working class consumers of films wore off around 1902–1903, producers and exhibitors struggled to attract more respectable audiences to their showings. Presumably the

ameliorated **program format** would entice affluent patrons, women and children into the nickelodeons and movie houses and help immigrants
assimilate American culture through the movies.
As a corollary, the new audience of sophisticated
literate viewers who were accustomed to **legitimate theater** conventions were better equipped
to understand the complicated narrative structures that filmmakers like Louis **Feuillade**
and D. W. **Griffith** were developing around
1908–1909.

The bourgeoisification thesis has been challenged on numerous fronts. Subsequent research on
exhibition may not support the postulated
"upward" direction from low- to highbrow venues.
Rather, it could be that the trend was toward
greater diversity during the nickelodeon era as
new groups of consumers joined the mixture of
movie-goers without necessarily displacing established groups. Even if viewership was upwardly
mobile in dynamic urban melting pots of American
cities, the case might be different in rural America
where the composition of audiences was more or
less homogeneous. Recent research further pro-
blematizes bourgeoisification; Richard Abel argues,
for instance, that the "vacuum" during 1903–1906
was only in American production. Meanwhile, the
audience for films continued to expand, but viewers
around the world—including those in the USA—
saw mostly French exports. It was only around 1909
that US trade journals began calling for more
"Americanness" in subject matter. Finally, the
apparent meaning of a film for us today or the
meaning intended by producers back then may not
have matched the meaning produced by individual
groups of viewers, who were free to filter content
through idiosyncrasies and local customs. Producers
and exhibitors may have anticipated that immigrant audiences would profit from the "assimilative," "democratic" and "bourgeois" messages
delivered in their films, but this might not have
been the case. Actual audiences had opportunities
to recall and reassert their national identities in
travelogues, imported films, **musical accompaniment** and in vocal interaction with the screen.
In the post-nickelodeon period, however, as the
control of the program tilted toward the producers
and distributors intent on consolidating regional
markets and building **palace theaters**, there was

undoubtedly less reflection of local tastes and
interests in programs.

Issues related to audiences also include controlling the content of films, delineating the location of screenings, and disciplining attendees. Most
countries implemented state censorship of cinema
early on. In the USA, despite many efforts, there
was no national censorship of the movies. Instead,
censoring was local, sporadic, and enforced by
assorted agents, including city and state boards of
review and a 1909 **National Board of Censorship**, established with the complicity of the
Motion Picture Patents Company (MPPC).

Another issue pits exhibitors against their
audiences. Because of the inherent risks to health,
property, and fear of incurring the displeasure of
civic authorities, managers employed strategies for
managing customers. But was this an ethnically
tinged conflict or an ordinary business practice?
One interpretation is that, while the atmosphere in
a nickelodeon may have been raucous, it was not
necessarily disorderly. The deportment of audiences in a nickelodeon probably differed little
from the audience in the neighboring **vaudeville**
theater. The "continuous performance" policy of
American theaters, without definite show times,
entr'actes or intermissions, may have made the
audiences seem more tumultuous and distracted
than they really were. Another point of contention
is that cultural antagonism between exhibitor and
audience may have varied widely depending on
whether the owners of the show were of the same
background as their customers.

Early cinema studies of the 1970s and 1980s had
theorized audiences based on exhibition studies of
big American cities. Later researchers expanded to
locales such as Chicago, Atlanta and Milwaukee.

Figure 9 Drawing from *Cleveland Leader*, 11
    May 1911.

Figure 10 Wladyslaw T. Benda, "The Line at the Ticket Office"—illustration for Mary Heaton Vorse, "Some Moving Picture Audiences," *Outlook*, 24 June 1911.

Special cases, such as theaters in blue-collar towns and the segregated South have also been studied, as well as small town audiences in New England, Kentucky and the Midwest. It has been found that American filmgoers developed indigenous patterns of attendance and preferences in film subjects inflected by local religious, labor, and cultural practices.

The motives for attending cinema, the nature of the pleasures attained there, the ambiance of the theater, the discussions that followed the screening and the lasting effects are among the most elusive aspects of studying the first film viewers. One component of the phenomenology of cinema, sound, has been neglected until recently in studies of early audiences. The spoken commentaries by on-stage **lecturers** was a widespread pre-nickelodeon practice in the USA, and remained common into the sound era in Canada and European regions with a mixed linguistic culture. Musical accompaniment of silent films had important implications for audience expectations, for the appreciation of film as an aesthetic experience, for its relationship to narrative form, and for audience participation. Efforts to record sound synchronously while recording the pictures, and accompanying films with recorded **synchronized sound**, date from the earliest days of cinematography.

Prior to the intensification of research into early cinema that began in the 1970s, film audiences were portrayed in broad strokes according to assumptions of class, ethnicity, and perceived sophistication.

Current studies parse the original audiences much more finely. Although "The Audience" is chimerical as a critical concept as well as an historical entity, investigations of spectators as subjects in the film system, research into viewing patterns, demographics, and the historical and cultural milieu of specific groups, and the social practices that led to the development of a relatively unified mass audiences are crucially important features of early cinema scholarship. This eclectic and inter-disciplinary approach ultimately reveals much about the significance of the films themselves.

While ECS has highlighted audience formation and response in scholarship, the geographical focus has been predominantly American. There have been significant studies of viewers of Quebeçois, British, French, German, Russian and Chinese cinemas, but a truly international assessment of early film audiences has yet to be initiated.

See also: law and the cinema: regulating exhibition; migration/immigration: USA

Further reading

Abel, Richard (1999) *The Red Rooster Scare: Making Cinema American, 1900–1910*, Berkeley: University of California Press.

Austin, Bruce (1995) "The Motion Picture Audience: A Neglected Aspect of Film

Research," *The Film Audience: An Annotated Bibliography*, Metuchen, N.J.: Scarecrow Press.

Fuller, Kathryn H. (1996) *At the Picture Show: Small-Town Audiences and the Creation of Movie Fan Culture*, Washington: Smithsonian Institution Press.

Hansen, Miriam (1991) *Babel and Babylon: Spectatorship in American Silent Film*, Cambridge: Harvard University Press.

Rabinovitz, Lauren (1998) *For the Love of Pleasure: Women, Movies, and Culture in Turn-of-the-Century Chicago*, New Brunswick: Rutgers University Press.

Staiger, Janet (1992) "Toward a Historical Materialist Approach to Reception Studies" and "Rethinking 'Primitive' Cinema: Intertextuality, the Middle-Class Audience, and Reception Studies," in *Interpreting Films*, 79–123, Princeton: Princeton University Films.

Stokes, Melvyn and Richard Maltby (eds.) (1999) *American Movie Audiences: From the Turn of the Century to the Early Sound Era*, London: British Film Institute.

Uricchio, William and Roberta Pearson (1993) *Reframing Culture: The Case of the Vitagraph Quality Films*, Princeton: Princeton University Press.

DONALD CRATTON

audiences: surveys and debates

Late in 1905, in the USA and Germany, and shortly thereafter in other Western countries, the spread of moving picture theaters enabled audiences who had not previously frequented commercial entertainments to attend the new "cheap amusement" on a regular basis. City recreation surveys conducted in the 1910s emphasized the sheer size of this audience: an estimated 900,000 people a week visited moving picture shows in New York City in 1910; weekly attendance in Kansas City, Missouri, surpassed the city's total population in 1912; a total of 100,229 spectators in a single day attended the movies in Cincinnati in 1913, more than one-fourth of the city's population; a total of 21 million cinema tickets were sold in Great Britain in 1917. Working-class groups often were identified as central to the audience,

closely aligned in the USA with immigrant groups. Hence a 1910 New York City survey estimated that 72% of the audience was working class, 25% "clerical," and 3% "leisured"; a 1912 survey of 2400 movie-goers in Mannheim, a mid-size industrial city in Germany, found that the audience comprised mainly blue-collar and lower-status, white-collar workers. Women also frequently were singled out as core components of the new urban audience, and surveys suggested they formed the largest group in, for example, Mannheim, Cincinnati, Waltham (an industrial city on the outskirts of Boston), San Francisco (in neighborhood theaters but not downtown, where men dominated), and a significant percentage elsewhere. Children, too, were seen to be important to the audience, comprising, for example, 25% in New York City in 1910; indeed, the general consensus was that children and young adults ranging in age from 15 to 25 constituted the bulk of the movie audience (estimates ranged from two-thirds to three-quarters). Still, the surveys and anecdotal evidence indicated that there was audience diversity between regions as well as among locations within cities, and subsequent scholarship has emphasized important differences between rural, small town, and urban audiences.

Simple enumeration, however, was only one aspect of the surveys. Equally important, often providing the motivation for elite groups to undertake research on audiences, were questions about what drew people to cinemas, what experiences they had there, and what the possible effects of movie-going might be. Investigators initially expressed concerns about the deleterious effects of movies and movie-going both on the morality of audiences, particularly on children and women (besides adult immigrant and working-class groups), and on public order. Here survey information often was connected to anecdotal evidence about the psychological effects of movies. One of the first sustained considerations of the seemingly intense pleasures of movie-going, informed in part by anxieties about such effects, was Harvard psychologist Hugo **Munsterberg**'s *The Photoplay: A Psychological Study* (1916). Using perceptual psychology to describe the hold moving pictures had on audiences, Munsterberg inaugurated a concern to describe the pleasure and desire underpinning movie-going that was central to later work on **spectatorship**; but he also warned that the effects of this for both individuals and society as a whole could be grave. Other commentators alternatively suggested that cinema could provide the space for emotional sustenance and communal gathering. Sociologist Emilie **Altenloh**, for example, investigated early audiences in Mannheim. Whereas reform and psychology-influenced writing generally treated the audience as a troublesome phenomenon of mass society, Altenloh categorized audience members, their consumption patterns, and their film preferences according to a range of social and demographic characteristics and tried to understand their experiences in the spirit of ethnographic research. Working-class groups, women, adolescents, and children were drawn to moving pictures, Altenloh suggested, as a space for experiences and forms of communality that were largely excluded from other public arenas in the modern world. Cinema, for Altenloh, appealed to those seeking to escape the monotony of new forms of industrial labor and to relax from the demands of everyday modern life. Leftist commentators and historians in the 1920s and 1930s replicated this sense of cinema's social function for the supposedly working-class audiences who attended **nickelodeons** in the USA, implicitly following Altenloh's suggestion that cinema could be seen as a democratic and progressive alternative public space. In negotiating the contradictory experiences associated with modernity, so this argument contended, working-class and immigrant audiences shaped the American cinema as an institution.

Later debates were central to the sustained scholarship on early cinema that flourished in the 1970s. Here, the working-class basis of nickelodeon and other cheap moving picture show audiences became a starting point for, on the one hand, theoretical reflections on audiences and spectatorship from a psychological perspective or, on the other, historical accounts of the role cinema played in the everyday life of audiences from the perspective of social history. Noël Burch's influential work on the relation between films and audiences in early cinema, later gathered together in *Life to Those Shadows* (1990), was informed by prevalent theoretical accounts of spectatorship. **Classical Hollywood cinema** worked to bind and

realign audiences with dominant ideological norms, he argued, but other textual formations of cinema—notably the avant-garde—could challenge that. Linked by Burch (and later others) to the avant-garde, early cinema was read now as a cinema inextricably enmeshed with working-class audiences and their desires, until the emergence of narrative norms around 1907–1909 began to realign cinema with bourgeois norms and (implicitly in Burch) middle-class audiences.

Later scholars have argued, however, that it was regulatory concerns about audiences, coinciding with the rise of palace cinemas in many countries in the 1910s, driven by entrepreneurs seeking an affluent and stable middle-class audience (whose national or regional circuits tended to eliminate local differences), that curtailed cinema's role as an alternative public space. Here, Miriam Hansen's work was crucial. Linking the traditions of work on spectatorship and social history via traditions of German theorizing on the public sphere, Hansen argued that early cinema in Germany and the USA functioned in part as an alternative public sphere in terms both of physical and psychic space, but that regulatory and commercial imperatives to attract a middle-class audience delimited the communal experiences of audiences, in effect de-realizing and privatizing theater/public space and aligning spectators with dominant positions of ideology. Very different traditions of scholarship effectively combined then to propose that only during the nickelodeon period could working-class, immigrant, and women audiences seek a physical and psychic space apart from hegemonic norms because a variety of factors—narrative, national cinema markets, movie palaces, regulation—brought middle-class audiences into cinemas and effectively "tamed" the former's radical potential.

Various revisions to this account have been proposed, linked both to specific arguments about the nickelodeon audience and to the broader imperative to extend research beyond the urban nickelodeon in order to better account for the diversity of audiences in the early period and the growth of cinema as a mass medium. Here, Robert C. Allen's claim that middle-class audiences were more prevalent in the nickelodeon audience in New York City than scholars had hitherto allowed was crucial. Locating the city's nickelodeons by using a number of empirical sources—business directories, insurance maps, trade journals—Allen concluded that most were located either in busy commercial or theatrical areas or in what he characterized as middle-class neighborhoods. His claims did not go uncontested. Robert Sklar questioned some of Allen's sources and contended that his arguments downplayed the important role of working-class and immigrant groups in shaping American cinema. Later, Ben Singer revisited the question of nickelodeons in Manhattan and argued that there were more working-class nickelodeons than Allen's resource materials allowed and that the neighborhoods characterized as middle-class were more likely working-class. Singer's work in turn prompted a flurry of responses, including one from Allen himself calling for, among other things, further analysis of the types of shows on offer to better delineate audiences within the city. Equally important, as Allen and Singer effectively agreed, was further attention to theorizing the historical formation of class distinctions in the USA. Lower middle-class groups made up of low-paid white-collar workers arguably were extremely important components of the audience; moreover, their class affiliation was uncertain, for, depending on circumstances, they may have understood their interests to lie with either working-class or middle-class groups.

Leaving aside the focus on urban nickelodeon audiences and on class, scholars increasingly have sought to account for the audience in various countries before the establishment of cheap cinemas and beyond urban areas, asking: where were moving pictures seen prior to the nickelodeon? How regular were such shows, and who was the audience for them? When, where, and how did non-urban audiences have access to the movies? Were the movies the same in similar exhibition sites? Were they the same kinds of audiences? In short, were there regional and/or national differences in moviegoing, and how can we account for those?

Vaudeville and other types of variety entertainment were frequently the first place movies were shown relatively regularly, attracting middle-class audiences in the USA and Germany. Lower-middle-class audiences were important for slightly cheaper variety theater entertainment, notably the so-called family vaudeville that emerged in the

USA around 1903, mixing moving pictures together with a few live acts and costing less than high-class vaudeville but more than later nickelodeons. Yet such venues were principally an urban phenomenon. Outside of major urban areas, audiences often saw moving pictures initially by way of **itinerant exhibitors** as part of a traveling show, sometimes in combination with **fairs**, festivals, and markets that attracted a broad spectrum of people. Likewise, showmen traveling independently or managing small companies attracted broad audiences, partly because their shows were pitched to appeal to middle-class and/or religious audiences—often in multi-media presentations that included moving pictures, slides, and a lecture—and partly simply because rural and small town dwellers were likely to attend shows in the absence of much other commercial entertainment. Other traveling showmen relied more exclusively on moving pictures, prefiguring the establishment of nickelodeons everywhere. Of the estimated ten thousand nickelodeons in the USA in 1910, seven thousand were located outside big cities.

Even so, some groups had less access to moving picture shows than others and significant regional variations can be discerned in audience attendance. Dispersed and often poor rural populations, like those in the southern and western USA, did not have regular access to moving pictures. Conservative religious groups often chose not to attend. Women and children often had their attendance curtailed as a result of both social customs and economic strictures. Often black audiences were denied access to moving pictures in the rural areas of the south or in small towns in the USA; otherwise, they were restricted to segregated areas in most theaters. Even so, black-only theaters emerged—numbering perhaps 200 in 1913— often featuring prominent black performers live and so enabling black audiences to contest the norms embodied in the dominant white films. Here scholars have emphasized both how audiences can contest dominant norms and how reception and experience are framed in important ways by the conditions of presentation.

Linked to the concern to map the diversity of exhibition contexts, then, is the effort to rethink reception in relation both to individual films and in the broad terms that Allen has described as the confrontation of the semiotic and the social. Here, scholarship draws on traditions of social history and British cultural studies to investigate further how audiences engaged actively with the cinema and how the historical and social positioning of audiences, their cultural repertoires, and the broad intertextual framework surrounding particular texts influenced reception in various ways. Work on black audiences, women audiences, and fan culture has been especially important, again linking the study of audiences with broad questions about resistance and hegemony.

Perhaps no sweeping characterization of the early cinema audience is possible; social composition varied within towns and cities, between different regions and rural and urban spaces, and no doubt also between different countries. Still, local studies of audiences will continue to increase our knowledge of this diversity. Like previous studies, this future work will need to make use of, as well as interrogate, varied data in order to reconstitute a historical audience that left only scattered and incomplete traces of itself. No doubt the task of identifying that audience and the experiences it had at the cinema will continue to be important to scholars, drawn to the task by the belief that a crucial part of cinema's significance depends on the

meaning and pleasure that audiences took from their movie-going.

See also: law and the cinema: regulating exhibition; migrations/immigration; racial segregation: USA

Further reading

Allen, Robert C. (1979) "Motion Picture Exhibition in Manhattan, 1906–1912: Beyond the Nickelodeon," *Cinema Journal*, 18.2: 2–15.

Allen, Robert C. (1990) "From Exhibition to Reception: Reflections on the Audience in Film History," *Screen*, 31.4: 347–356.

Altenloh, Emilie (1914) *Zur Soziologie des Kino: Die Kino-Unternehmung und die sozialen Schichten iher Besucher*, Jena: Diederichs. A translation of the Introduction and Part II appears in *Screen*, 42.3 (Autumn 2001): 249–293.

Fuller, Kathryn H. (1996) *At the Picture Show: Small Town Audiences and the Creation of Movie Fan Culture*, Washington: Smithsonian Institution Press.

Hansen, Miriam (1991) *Babel and Babylon: Spectatorship in American Silent Film*, Cambridge: Harvard University Press.

Singer, Ben (1995) "Manhattan Nickelodeons: New Data on Audiences and Exhibitors," *Cinema Journal*, 34.3: 5–35.

Sklar, Robert (1988) "Oh! Althusser!: Historiography and the Rise of Cinema Studies," *Radical History Review*, 41: 10–35.

Stokes, Melvyn and Richard Maltby (eds.) (1999) *American Movie Audiences: From the Turn of the Century to the Early Sound Era*, London: British Film Institute.

LEE GRIEVESON

Auler, William

b. 1865, Rio de Janeiro; d. 1927, Rio de Janeiro

exhibitor, producer, Brazil

A major figure of the Brazilian *bela época*, Auler provided furnishings for the earliest exhibition venues in Rio de Janeiro. In 1907, he created

Figure 11 Luisen-Kino, Berlin, *c.* 1910.

Williams & Cia. and opened his own theater, Grande Cinematógrafo Rio Branco. Imitating the practice of synchronizing films and phonograph recordings, Auler substituted singers behind the screen and created the *filme cantante* genre. He also made **crime films** popular and, later, developed other national genres like the musical review film. Alberto Moreira's *Paz e amor* [Peace and Love] (1910), a wily satire of Rio's social and political elites, was wildly successful, filling his 700-seat theater to capacity for more than 1000 screenings. However, shortly thereafter, Auler abandoned production to return to his furniture businesses.

ANA M. LÓPEZ

Aurora Cinema

Much like J. F. **Madan**'s Elphinstone Bioscope Company, Aurora Bioscope was founded by a theater owner, Anadi Nath Bose. Buying used **projectors**, Bose first added moving pictures to the variety programs in his tent shows and Manmohan Theatre in Calcutta. In 1911, the company was renamed Aurora Cinema when it became a partnership firm, but it remained primarily an exhibition concern until winning a contract in 1917 to make short films for the army during **World War I**. In 1921, Aurora released its first feature, *Ratnakar*, directed by Surendra Narayan Roy; but the company's forte was **newsreels**, especially a popular news review compilation called *Aurora Tidbits*.

SURESH CHABRIA

Australasian Films

In March 1911, Amalgamated Pictures was formed by the merger of **Johnson and Gibson** with J. & N. Tait. In November 1912, the interests of T. J. **West**, Cozens **Spencer** and Amalgamated Pictures were merged, joined in January 1913 by J. D. Williams and **Pathé** (Australia). The new company had an exhibition branch (Union Theatres) and a distribution branch (Australasian Films), but no interest in feature film production, although it retained Spencer's Rushcutter's Bay studio, and distributed a weekly **newsreel**. Known familiarly (but not affectionately) as "The Combine," this remained the most powerful Australian-based film company of the silent period.

INA BERTRAND

Australia

Australia may have been geographically distant from the main centers of film production, but it was integrated into the international market early, through entrepreneurial exhibitors and distributors. Indigenous production also began early, with non-fiction films at first, followed by fiction films, and features developing earlier than in many other countries.

Peepshow **kinetoscopes** appeared in Sydney on 20 November 1894, and projected moving pictures arrived with **magician** Carl Hertz, who, after a private preview, presented a season at Melbourne Opera House beginning on 22 August 1895. Early attempts to present programs devoted exclusively to moving pictures in Brisbane, Sydney and Melbourne in September and October 1895, however, were short-lived. Until 1906, moving pictures were more commonly presented as supplements to a theatrical presentation or as one of several acts in **vaudeville**, or in an outdoor entertainment venue such as Ye Olde Englishe Fayre in Perth. Showmen were soon traveling through the suburbs and country areas by horse-drawn vehicle (in the 1920s, by automobile) or train, presenting moving pictures in Town Halls and Mechanics Institutes or in open air "picture gardens." In the cities, they were screened in legitimate **theaters** and in premises converted from skating rinks and dancehalls, before the first permanent cinemas appeared around 1909, followed in 1916 by the first sustained building boom. Australia had no exact equivalent of the American **nickelodeon**: but the local cinema or picture garden was soon a favorite family entertainment venue.

The films to supply these venues came mainly from Great Britain, or from Europe (particularly France) via Britain. Nonfiction films were popular, particularly **news event films** on major events such as the death of Queen Victoria or the Boer War, presented by touring companies as a full evening's entertainment.

Local film production was early and innovative, but never challenged the imported product in quantity. The first Australian production was *Passengers Alighting from the Paddle Steamer "Brighton" at Manly* (October 25, 1896), made by **Lumiere** representative Marius Sestier. The earliest film to survive in an archive is footage of the 1896 Melbourne Cup carnival. There were short-lived film production ventures in both Sydney and Melbourne before the turn of the century, and the earliest Government film production had the Queensland government contracting Frederick Charles Wills, in October 1898, to make thirty one-minute **advertising films** for distribution in Great Britain. Most government film was produced on contract by companies such as **Pathe (Australia)** or the **Salvation Army** Limelight Department, which made some of Australia's first long films: *Inauguration of the Commonwealth*, *Visit to Australia of the American Fleet*, and a series of royal visits (all 1900–1901).

Beginning in 1897, the Salvation Army's evangelical program added moving pictures to their lantern lectures, culminating in Commandant Booth's ambitious multi-media presentations, consisting of lecture, lantern slides, motion pictures, live music and audience participation. The most famous of these was *Soldiers of the Cross* (1901), telling the story of the early Christian church and including thirteen one-minute films (most produced in Melbourne using Salvation Army premises and personnel).

Multiple-reel films were common in Australia before other parts of the world, largely as a result of the huge success of *The Story of the Kelly Gang* (1906), an action adventure about bushranger and anti-establishment hero Ned Kelly, who had been hanged in 1880. This three-reel, 40-minute feature was screened with actors providing dialogue behind the screen and **sound effects** simulating galloping horses, gun shots, and crowd noises. Other feature-length films followed in 1907 and

1908, then in growing numbers until, in 1911, Australia produced at least twenty films of more than 3000 feet in length, most of them fiction.

The producers of *The Story of the Kelly Gang* (**Johnson and Gibson** and J. & N. Tait) joined to form Amalgamated Pictures and employed W. J. **Lincoln** as director. Their St. Kilda studio was the best in Melbourne (after the closure of the Salvation Army studio in 1910), and when Amalgamated joined **Australasian Films**, the Lincoln-Cass company took over the studio lease.

In Sydney, several theatrical companies (including George Marlow, and E. I. Cole's Bohemian Company) produced films of their stage repertoire, and specialist film companies were also formed (such as Australian Life Biograph and Southern Cross Motion Pictures). Cozens **Spencer** embarked on an ambitious production program in 1910. His *The Fatal Wedding* (1911) was the first feature film of the talented team of Raymond **Longford** (director), Lottie Lyell (Australia's first movie star), and Arthur Higgins (cinematographer brother of Ernest **Higgins**). Spencer opened Sydney's best studio in Rushcutter's Bay in 1912, which was retained by Australasian Films for lease to other producers.

In this flowering of fiction film, two genres predominated: the theatrical melodrama, such as *Called Back* (1911) and the outdoor action or bushranger film, including much of the output of John **Gavin** and Alfred **Rolfe**. Non-fiction films, however, continued to be popular. Professor Walter Baldwin Spencer filmed anthropological expeditions in 1901, and again in 1910–11. The first commonwealth government cinematographer, in 1911, was James Pinkerton Campbell, replaced in 1913 by Bert Ive, who held the position until his death in 1939. Francis Birtles pioneered the outback expeditionary film, a **Gaumont** production recording his 1911 bicycle journey from Sydney to Darwin; on later expeditions he did his own filming.

Australia's first **newsreel** was *Pathe's Animated Gazette* (the Australian edition), in November 1910, followed by several others, some of which eventually were amalgamated into *Australasian Gazette* produced by Australasian Films from 1916 until the introduction of sound in 1929. Pioneer animator Harry Julius contributed cartoons to *Australasian Gazette* during **World War I**.

Up to the formation of Australasian Films in 1912, this was a vibrant and innovative industry, integrated into the international film community through entrepreneurs such as T. J. **West**, Cozens Spencer and J. D. Williams, but retaining its local flavor through the production of non-fiction films and fiction films on national themes. After Australasian's decision not to produce feature films, and then the arrival of distribution agencies for major Hollywood studios, local producers became embattled, leading eventually to bitter exchanges before the 1927–1928 Royal Commission into the Moving Picture Industry. Australian feature film production did not again reach the assurance of that early period until the 1970s.

See also: *actualités*; animation; biblical films; ethnographic films; expedition/exploration films; melodrama, sensational

Further reading

Bertrand, Ina and William D. Routt (1989) "The Big Bad Combine: Some Aspects of National Aspirations and International Constraints in the Australian Cinema, 1896–1929," in Albert Moran and Tom O'Regan (eds.) *The Australian Screen*, 3–27, Ringwood: Penguin.

McFarlane, Brian and Geoff, Mayer and Ina, Bertrand (eds.) (1999) *The Oxford Companion to Australian Film*, South Melbourne: Oxford University Press.

Pike, Andrew and Ross, Cooper (1998) *Australian Film 1900–1977*, Melbourne: Oxford University Press.

INA BERTRAND

Austro-Hungary

The development of Austro-Hungarian cinema initially was slow. Some years passed from the first official projection of the **Cinématographe Lumière** in the capital of Vienna, on March 27, 1896, until the establishment of sustained film production. The vast expanse of the Empire's territory, which included modern-day parts of Poland, the Czech Republic, Slovakia, Hungary, Bosnia, and Northern Italy and a diverse ethnic mix of peoples means that it is particularly difficult to create a unified picture. Accordingly, this entry focuses principally on the areas of the Empire in which German was spoken.

The first attempts at filming in the Habsburg territories were made by **Lumière** cameramen. An example is the brief film sequence shot by Charles Moisson, entitled *Entrée du cinématographe* (June 1896), in which the building which first housed Viennese projections is featured. However, an act of legislation, perhaps the first relating to the cinema promulgated by the Empire and one of the first in Europe, soon outlawed the work of the French company in Austrian territories. The prohibition was ordered because Lumière cameramen, having projected films many times in 1896–1897, left the imperial territory without having paid the taxes which they owed.

From 1897, cinematographic activity passed to entrepreneurs who shot film and travelled from cities to small towns and into the countryside, showing the marvels of moving pictures. Aside from metropolitan areas, the first cinemas were opened in the far-flung corners of the Empire in 1907–1910. In its first stages of development, however, cinema mainly was diffused through **itinerant exhibitors** who travelled with their projectors from city to city, from fair to fair.

The first of these entrepreneurs came from the tradition of busking showmen, circus people, traveling salesmen, and funambulists who for centuries had wandered through Europe. A character who neatly summarizes this tradition and its multiple forms of pre-cinematic showmanship is Louis Geni (born in 1856). After a long career as an illusionist and owner of a panopticon and a museum collection of nature's curiosities, he became an important itinerant exhibitor in the Austro-Hungarian Empire and ended up as owner of a moving picture theater.

Until 1898, moving picture projections often were advertised as "technical experiments" produced by the cameraman. This term indicates how they were initially conceived of as demonstrations of the new technology which reproduced movement. It was sufficient for the image to move and the content of the film was secondary. Only subsequently, once the novelty had worn off, did it become necessary to depict something which had intrinsic artistic value.

In this initial period, moving pictures had no fixed venue and, in urban areas, were projected in the halls of hotels, beer halls, or **music halls**. From 1901 on, an important change occurred with the development of mobile projection booths. Initially booths measured 12×8 meters, but within a few years they had reached much larger proportions of up to 20×8 or even 30×12 meters. The booths could be erected and dismantled at every stop on an exhibition circuit. The pavilion, equipment, and owner's family and workers moved from location to location, often associated with **fairs**, in carriages or by train. Their growing success meant that the booths were replaced by circular pavilions, similar to the big-tops of the circus, which could seat from 1,000 to 2,000 people. Indeed, the first Austrian films were made by pavilion owners so that they themselves could increase their repertoire of films.

The first company to make films continuously was founded in Budapest in 1898 by Moritz Ungerleider and Josef Neumann. Named Projectograph-Filmgesellschaft, the company produced nonfiction films beginning in 1905. The company then earned its reputation by renting its films and soon achieved a dominant position in Hungary.

In Vienna, the first company to produce films continuously was **Saturn**, founded between 1905 and 1906. Its exclusive product was erotic films, advertised in the pages of the German **trade press**. The first Austrian magazines devoted to moving pictures were *Die Kinematographische Rundschau* and *Anzeiger für die gesamte Kinematographen-Industrie*, beginning in 1907, and *Österreichischer Komet*, beginning the following year.

In 1906, also in Vienna, Josef Halbritter began making nonfiction films. One year later, thanks to the efforts of Professor Alto **Arche**, moving pictures began to serve educational purposes. This interest became so strong in Austria that, in 1912, a magazine called *Kastalia* appeared, with the aim of promoting the educational value of moving pictures in the schools and wider society.

The major pioneers of Austrian cinema were Gustav Anton Kolm, his wife Louise Veltée **Kolm**, and photographer Jakob Julius Fleck. After four years of making short films, in 1910, thanks to the financial assistance of Louise's father, owner of the Viennese Panopticum, the three partners founded the Erste österreichische Kinofilms-Industrie AG. At the beginning of 1911, the company was renamed Österreichische-ungarische Kinoindustrie. On 15 October 1911, economic difficulties and management disputes doomed the venture. However, within a few months, the three founded another company, **Wiener Kunstfilm**. The output of this company was prodigious, especially given the constraints under which it operated; by December 1912, the company had released more then ten films, including dramas, **comedies**, and documentaries.

At the same time, Count "Sascha" **Kolowrat-Krakowsky** was making his first cinematographic experiments in the castle of Gross-Meierhöfen in Bohemia. Having relocated to a studio in 1912, he began releasing films through his company, Sascha-Filmfabrik.

In the period between 1912 and 1913, other film companies were set up in Vienna, including Vindobona-Film (founded by the writer Felix Dörmann), Kallos-Film-Industrie Gesellschaft, Jupiter-Film Gesellschaft, Hida-Film, Emel-Film-Gesellschaft Lutze & Co., Dramagraph-Film, Halbritter Film, and Wiener Spezialfilmfabrik.

In all, approximately 350 films were made in Austria from the time of cinema's inception up until 1918, with more than 200 nonfiction films produced by 1914.

A separate sector of filmmaking was involved in **advertising**. The idea of using moving pictures for commercial ends was well established in the first decade of the 20th century, but the first company to specialize in making such films did not appear in Austria until 1913, when Adam Julius founded Erstes österreichische konzessionierte Reklamefilm-Institut. The company's aim was to produce **advertising films** for distribution in Austria and abroad. This innovative enterprise did not manage to gain a firm footing, however, and folded within less than a year. Another, more successful advertising film company, Handels- und Industrie-Film-Gesellschaft, also emerged slightly later that year, founded by the Viennese businessmen, Josef Fuchs, Paul Schönwalder, and Friedrich Landau.

If filmmaking tended to be a rather fragmented, dispersed affair, film distribution had a more linear development. Up until 1906, picture theater owners and itinerant exhibitors bought their films and, after projecting them for a while, sold them on to others. In Austria the practice of renting films only began to appear in 1908–1909. Before that, the sales agents of important French producers such as **Pathé-Frères** and **Gaumont** dominated the trade in Vienna. The honor of being the first company to rent films in Austria had many companies among its contenders, all of them founded between 1906–1907: they included Sigge H. Lundén and Max Rády Maller, Erste Film-Verleihanstalt (specializing in erotic films), Filmhaus Christensen, Universal Film et Kinematograph Company, and Josef Quester.

In 1909, in the city of Vienna alone, these rental companies had 76 cinemas as clients, with a capacity of over 20,000 seats. By 1913, moving pictures were so widely diffused throughout the empire that a total of 869 licences were issued: 720 for picture houses, and 149 for itinerant exhibitors. The specific numbers were as follows in the diverse parts of the Imperial territory: Upper Austria: 20 permanent cinemas, 10 itinerant exhibitors; Salzburg: 3 permanent cinemas, 3 itinerant exhibitors; Styria: 17 permanent cinemas, 8 itinerant exhibitors; Carinthia: 7 permanent cinemas, 2 itinerant exhibitors; Krain: 2 permanent cinemas, 2 itinerant exhibitors; Küstenland: 56 permanent cinemas, 1 itinerant exhibitor; Tyrol: 44 permanent cinemas, 4 itinerant exhibitors; Bohemia: 151 permanent cinemas, 46 itinerant exhibitors; Mähren: 55 permanent cinemas, 23 itinerant exhibitors; Silesia: 15 permanent cinemas, 10 itinerant exhibitors; Galicia: 105 permanent cinemas, 9 itinerant exhibitors; Dalmatia: 8 permanent cinemas, 2 itinerant exhibitors; Vienna, 154 permanent cinemas, 25 itinerant exhibitors; Lower Austria: 71 permanent cinemas; Bukowina: 12 permanent cinemas and 4 itinerant exhibitors.

The rapid spread of moving pictures gave rise to censorship and also to **publicity** materials (photographs, advertisements, posters, and leaflets) which accompanied the films. In Austro-Hungary the regulations which governed the cinema came into existence in 1912. Before then, moving pictures were governed by pre-existing laws which regulated theatrical performances or by specific regulations introduced at a local level by the police. These laws established the police's role in enforcing public morality. As a result, the local authorities and police exercised their powers in differing ways from locality to locality. Theater owners and itinerant exhibitors first had to screen their films for local officials who then could ban those they deemed offensive.

As expected, Vienna, the city which boasted a number of international film companies and the first Austrian production companies, became the center of the Empire's regulation of film. In the capital, regulation and systematic censorship was instituted in 1907, with power entrusted explicitly to the chief of police. The system put in place was relatively complex. Police officials in each district visited the theaters located in their area every time the moving picture program changed (generally once a week), in order to view the forthcoming films. A film which had been viewed by police officials in one district had to be rescreened for other officials if it was to be shown in another district. In a city which, in 1909, was divided into 21 quarters and had 76 moving picture theaters, this practice was laborious. The system finally was revised in 1909, when the press published the news that henceforth all new films to be distributed would be screened at Stiller's Prater cinema. Police officials who attended these screenings then would authorize distribution.

The enormity of the task before the Vienna censors is apparent when one considers the number of films in circulation. In the first half of 1914 (January–June), the censors had to view 1,314,176 meters of film or approximately 3000 titles. Of these, 500 were totally censored and never distributed.

The growth in the number of moving picture theaters and the regulatory chaos which ensued forced legislators to consider introducing a more modern and up-to-date law. In order to prepare drafts of the legislation, an official inquiry was undertaken with the participation of the police, teachers, prominent figures from the theater world, tourist bodies, women's groups, and the film industry itself. The industry was in favor of a single regulating body whose decisions would apply to the whole of the Imperial territory. On September 18,

1912, the Home Office finally issued the "Verordnung" ordinance (# 191) which took effect on January 1, 1913, stipulating that films licensed in Vienna also would be licensed in the other thirteen administrative regions of the territory. Not all of these administrative regions, however, decided to accept the films which already had been licensed in Vienna. In 1916, for instance, there was further censorship in Prague, Innsbruck in Tyrol, and Troppau in Silesia. The fragmentation of censorship accentuated the subjectivity of the law and generated resentment in the film industry.

Perhaps the most significant contribution which Austro-Hungary made to world cinema was the filmmakers who later forged careers abroad: they included Erich von Stroheim (born 1885, in Vienna), G. W. Pabst (born 1885, in Raudnitz, Bohemia), Michael Curtiz (Kertesz) (born 1888, in Budapest), Fritz Lang (born 1890, in Vienna), Josef von Sternberg (born 1894, in Vienna), and Samuel Wilder (born 1906, in Vienna) who found success under the pseudonym of Billy.

See also: cinema and the law; distribution: Europe; scientific films: Europe

Further reading

Achenbach, Michael, Paolo Caneppele, and Ernst Kieninger (1999) *Projektionen der Sehnsucht. Saturn.Die erotischen Anfänge der österreichischen Kinematografie*, Wien: Filmarchiv Austria.

Armin, Loacker (1993) "Die österreichische Filmwirtschaft von den Anfängen bis zur Einführung des Tonfilms," in *Maske und Kothurn*, 4: 75–123.

Bono, Francesco, Paolo Caneppele, and Günter Krenn (1999) *Elektrische Schatten. Beiträge zur österreichischen Stummfilmgeschichte*, Wien Filmarchiv Austria.

Fritz, Walter (1997) *Im Kino erlebe ich die Welt… 100 Jahre Kino und Film in Österreich*, Wien: Brandstätter.

Knezevic, Srdan (1997) *Lebende Photographien kommen . . . Die Anfänge der Kinematographie auf dem Gebiet des Kaisertums Österreich (1896–1897)*, Wien: ÖGFKM.

Schwarz, Werner M. (1992) *Kino und Kinos in Wien*, Wien: Turia & Kant.

PAOLO CANEPPELE

authentication

Very much as in **painting** and sculpture, identification of early films is a matter of a long acquaintance with the field, and requires a thorough knowledge of film history, aesthetics, economic practices, and technology. This expertise can be acquired with the aid of analytical tools, which may be broadly divided in two categories. The first is drawn from the actual viewing of as many films as possible, in suitable reproductions of the original prints. Evidence directly drawn from the image is often a useful starting point: an actress' face, a building, a car licence plate, the design of clothing, or a sign on a door may help determining where the film was made, when, and who played in it, thus narrowing down the range of possibilities. A hypothesis can also be established through the observation of stylistic recurrences: for example, a fiction film with parallel editing or eyeline match should be dated after 1906, as no example of these devices is known in films released before that date; stencil **color** was not used until 1905; and so forth. In order to discourage plagiarism, several firms incorporated their trademark into the scenes (for instance, an eagle for the **Vitagraph Company**, the silhouette of a rooster for **Pathé-Frères**, a bear surmounting a globe for **Nordisk**) or in the **intertitles**, whose style and typeset also changed from time to time. The serial numbers often seen at the bottom corner of the intertitles may correspond to the catalogue numbers, thus also providing clues to be interpreted with the help of corporate bulletins.

The second category of indicators is found exclusively in nitrate prints made at the time of a film's commercial release. Perforation size and shape varied considerably until 1905. Inscriptions on the edge of the prints were applied by manufacturers and production companies: Pathé employed a dozen different wordings and styles between April 1905 and 1914; **Eastman Kodak** introduced a similar system in 1913, further developed in 1916 into an edge code (a sequence of geometric figures) used throughout the 20th century. A company's name or **trademark** could be embossed or punched on the fronts of its films. The dimensions and shape of the frame aperture, and the frame line between images, are also typical of various producers. All these features are lost in the transfer of the vintage print into a reference copy, and are bound to disappear forever as the nitrate base of the original element decomposes. A further potential source of information—the shape of the splice joining two film segments—is often visible upon close examination of a 35 mm duplicate.

It must be stressed that all the above criteria are used comparatively, as none of them taken individually provides definitive proof of the film's precise identity. Identification work is integrated by the scrutiny of primary and secondary sources, from historical and scholarly literature to moving picture **cameras** and **projectors**.

See also: archives; preservation

Further reading

Brown, Harold (1990) *Physical Characteristics of Early Films as Aids to Identification*, Brussels: FIAF.
Richard, Suzanne (1991) "Pathé, marque de fabrique," *1895*, 10 (October): 13–28.

PAOLO CHERCHI USAI

Autorenfilme

In 1913, just before **World War I**, the generic term *Autorenfilme* (authors' films) began to be applied in Germany to films either based on well known literary motifs or involving stage writers or theater actors who participated, directly or indirectly, via literary adaptations.

In 1908, Heinrich **Bolten-Baeckers** set up a "Society for the Utilization of Literary Ideas for Cinematic Purposes," inspired by French *films d'art* which had entered the German market the same year. However, it was not until 1913 that the first German *Autorenfilme* were released. In November 1912, the Danish company **Nordisk**

announced future collaboration with such prominent German writers as Gerhart Hauptmann, Arthur Schnitzler, Hugo von Hofmannsthal, Felix Salten, and Jakob Wassermann. In a parallel move, **PAGU** signed an exclusive contract with the Verband Deutscher Bühnenschriftsteller (Association of German Stage Writers) and established a joint distribution company. Yet the first German *Autorenfilm* was released in January 1913 by **Vitascope**: *Der Andere* [The Other One] was directed by Max **Mack**, based on a screenplay by Paul Lindau, and had Albert **Bassermann** playing the lead role. Other companies followed suit. Bioscop contracted writer Hanns Heinz **Ewers** and stage actors Paul **Wegener**, Grete Berger and Alexander Moissi for films such as *Der Student von Prag* [The Student of Prague] (1913), *Das schwarze Los* [The Black Lot] (1913), and *Die Augen des Ole Brandis* [The Eyes of Ole Brandis] (1914). PAGU assured itself of the collaboration of Germany's leading theater director Max **Reinhardt**, who made two films in 1913, *Die Insel der Seligen* [The Island of the Happy Ones] and *Eine venezianische Nacht* (A Venetian Night). **Messter** made three films based on works by Richard Voss, and **Continental-Kunstfilm** produced a series of screenplays by Heinrich **Lautensack**. Nordisk achieved major successes on the German market with screen versions of Hauptmann's *Atlantis* (1913), Schnitzler's *Liebelei* (1914) and, in collaboration with the Swedish **Svensk-Amerikanska Filmkompaniet**, adapted von Hofmannsthal's *Das fremde Mädchen* [The Strange Girl] (1913).

Set up in opposition to the popular *Sensationsfilm* or sensational **melodrama**, the *Autorenfilm* met some of demands of the *Kinoreformbewegung* (cinema reform movement), calling for "higher artistic standards" in the **multiple-reel feature film**. Apart from their literary input, the *Autorenfilme* were promoted through exceptionally large budgets, expensive **advertising** campaigns, and exclusive premieres. *Autorenfilme* also helped to legitimate the building of architecturally more ambitious palace cinemas, signalling the industry's intention to make upper middle-class audiences its preferred audience. The emergence of professional film criticism in Germany also was due to the

Autorenfilm, as was the introduction of new production facilities: for instance, the opening of glass-house studios in Neubabelsberg by Bioscop, in Tempelhof by PAGU, and in Weissensee by Vitascope.

Stylistically, *Autorenfilme* not only pioneered the combination of literary themes and experiments in cinematic form, for which the German cinema would become known in the early 1920s, but they also naturalized fantastic motifs and trick photography, location footage and studio compositions into integrated film narratives.

Further reading

Quaresima, Leonardo (1990) "Dichter heraus!: The Autorenfilm and the German Cinema of the 1910s," *Griffithiana*, 13: 38–39.

MICHAEL WEDEL

B

Baggot, King

b. 1879, St. Louis, Missouri; d. 1948, Los Angeles, California

actor, director, USA

A popular leading man, **trade press ads** proclaimed that Baggot had "A Face as Well Known as the Man in the Moon." On stage from 1900, his first film appearance was for **IMP** in October 1909, opposite Florence **Lawrence**. At IMP, and later **Universal**, he scored successes in *The Scarlet Letter* (1911), *Dr. Jekyll and Mr. Hyde* (1912), *Ivanhoe* (1913), and *The Cricket on the Hearth* (1915). Baggot was later a director until alcoholism made him unemployable. He ended his career as a Hollywood extra.

ROBERT S. BIRCHARD

Bakshy, Alexander

b. ? d. ?

critic, USA

An innovative early theorist of film and theater, Bakshy was one of the first critics to apply to cinema early discourses of reflexive modernism (prizing anti-illusionist medium-awareness and perceptual self-consciousness) that had emerged in theater criticism in the early 1900s. Bakshy also theorized about the implications of different spatial positions of **spectatorship** in theater and film, drawing on Nietzchian aesthetic categories and anticipating subject-position theory of the 1970s. A Russian emigré, Bakshy began writing on film in English in 1913, published books of collected essays in 1916 and 1923, and was film critic for *The Nation* between 1928 and 1933.

Further reading

Bakshy, Alexander (1916) *The Path of the Russian Stage and Other Essays*, London: Palmer and Heywood.

BEN SINGER

Balaban, Barney & A. J.

b. June 8, 1887; d. March 7, 1971

b. 1889; d. November 1, 1962

exhibitors, USA

In Chicago, in 1908 the Balaban brothers opened the Kedzie **nickelodeon**; a year later came the Circle, a small-time **vaudeville** theater. Before 1915, they were still minor players in exhibition. Thereafter, they teamed with Sam **Katz** and built a chain of influential **palace cinemas** in Chicago, with Barney handling finances, and A. J. live entertainment. By 1936, Barney had become the head of **Paramount**, whereas A. J. faded into obscurity.

DOUGLAS GOMERY

Balkans, the

Cinema arrived at varying times in the different countries of the Balkans, depending on the degree of West European influence in a particular nation. Romania was the first, on 27 May 1896, when **Lumière** films were shown in the offices of a Francophone **newspaper**. Serbia followed, on 6 June, when a Lumière operator, André Carré, gave a show at a Belgrade café. In the autumn it was the turn of the Lumières' competitors: on 8 October in Zagreb (possibly followed in Fiume and Sarajevo), Croatia's first film show was given with a German **projector**, and in Slovenia in October and November shows were given by Charles Crassé. Further away from Western Europe's sphere of influence, Bulgaria had to await the arrival of moving pictures until late February 1897, when a film show was given in the town of Rouse. Macedonia may have had screenings in Bitola in 1897, although some believe the country's first film show was not until 1906; and Albania apparently had to wait until as late as 1908.

By that time the first permanent cinemas were being established in more advanced parts of the Balkans: from 1906, in Zagreb; from 1907, in Sarajevo and Ljubljana; and from 1908, in Cetinje (Montenegro). Belgrade had ten cinemas by 1911, and several years later the US consul reported that moving pictures' influence was such that the inhabitants of Serbia were becoming noticeably Americanized in their taste for clothes and other US goods. Romania was, as ever, in the Balkan advance guard, with 450 cinemas by 1913. Trieste became an important film center in this period, and James Joyce briefly set up in the exhibition business there.

In terms of film production, again Romania led the way. Local photographer Paul Menu filmed the King and Queen of Romania for the Lumières in May 1897. Another Romanian, Dr. Gheorghe Marinescu, made medical films in Bucharest from 1898 to 1901. But in the early years it was foreign cameramen who primarily filmed in the Balkans. In 1898, Lumière operator Alexandre **Promio** shot some scenic views on the coast of Dalmatia (Croatia). In 1903, Charles Rider Noble filmed in Macedonia and Bulgaria to highlight the anti-Turkish rebellion taking place there. This was a turbulent time in the region, and the Serbian King and Queen were horribly murdered the same year (**Pathé-Frères** made a film version of the murder). The following year the new King Peter was crowned, and British cameraman Frank Mottershaw was invited by the Serbian authorities to come and record the event. In the spring of 1905, explorer Harry DeWindt and cameraman John McKenzie toured through Bosnia, Montenegro, Serbia, Bulgaria, and Romania, working for Charles **Urban**: the films later were released as *Across the Balkans*. Urban was behind another early Balkan enterprise, for the Manaki brothers began documenting their region of Macedonia and its surroundings in 1907, using an Urban Bioscope acquired in London. The Balkan wars of 1912–1913 were a magnet for cameramen, including foreigners such as Thomas Sarll and Jessica Borthwick, and Balkan nationals such as Josip Halla.

Nationalism and the continuing struggle against the Ottoman empire were important themes in the first Balkan **multiple-reel/feature films**. Serbia's first was *Karadjordje*, made in 1910, and Romania followed in 1911. The superproduction, *The Independence of Romania* (1926), documented Romania's national liberation war of the 19th century. Bulgaria's first feature was made in 1915.

See also: Greece; Turkey

Further reading

Kosanovic, D. (1992) "Cinema muto italiano all'est dell'Adriatico," in V. Martinelli (ed.) *Cinema Italiano in Europa 1907–1929*, 111–130, Rome: Associazione italiana per le ricerche di storia del cinema.

Stoyanov-Bigor, Georgi (1993) "The Balkans and 'The Wonder of the Century'," *Balkanmedia*, 4: 12–18.

STEPHEN BOTTOMORE

Balshofer, Fred J.

b. 1877; d. 1969

cameraman, producer, writer, director, USA

A lab technician and cameraman for the **Lubin** company beginning around 1905 and then founder in 1908 of the Brooklyn-based Crescent Film Company, Balshofer formed the **New York Motion Picture Company** (NYMPC) with Adam **Kessel** and Charles O. **Baumann** in 1909, releasing films under the Bison brand. Acting as writer, director, and cameraman, Balshofer specialized in **westerns** and soon moved his company from the northeast to southern California, setting up a studio in Edendale. He returned east when the company was reorganized in late 1911. After leaving NYMP, he formed Sterling Camera and Film Company (1913) and Quality Pictures Corporation (1915).

STEVEN HIGGINS

Bamforth

Based in Holmfirth, Yorkshire, Bamforth originated as a portrait **photography** shop; by the 1890s, it had become a lantern slide manufacturing business, claiming to be the world's largest supplier of "life model" posed photographic slides. The company produced a few short **comedies** around 1898, in collaboration with Riley, another Yorkshire slide firm. Bamforth resumed filmmaking around 1913, producing a series of longer comic films whose actors also appeared on comic **postcards**, which had meanwhile become its principal product. **World War I** curtailed its filmmaking, and Bamforth remained an important postcard publisher, trading until the 1990s.

RICHARD CRANGLE

Barcinógrafo

Production company founded in 1913 in Barcelona (Spain) that produced several films between 1914 and 1917, first under the direction of Adrià **Gual** and later Magí Murià. It was the first company to involve the Catalan bourgeoisie, traditionally opposed to cinema. Gual made eight cultural films in 1914. Between 1915 and 1916, Murià opted for more commercial films, making five Italian-influenced melodramas starring Margarida Xirgu, including *El nocturno de Chopin* [Chopin's

Nocturne] and *El beso de la muerte* [The Kiss of Death]. The company closed in 1918.

JOAN M. MINGUET

Barker Motion Photography

Barker Motion Photography was founded by William **Barker** after he left **Warwick Trading** in 1909. With Barker himself as managing director, the company took over the old Warwick studio in Ealing, constructing three daylight studios (supplemented by arc **lighting**) and making extensive use of the property's large gardens.

Aiming to create a prestigious "all British" rival to American imports, in 1911 Barker paid Sir Herbert Tree £1,000 for a day's work on *Henry VIII*, the first British two-reel feature—then caused a sensation by making only twenty prints, and burning them after six weeks' exclusive distribution. In May 1913, he released a two-hour adaptation of the novel *East Lynne*. Although he later claimed to have run the company "entirely on his own money," in July 1913, he had to raise a mortgage to finance *Sixty Years a Queen* (1913), which allegedly cost £8,000 in salaries alone.

On the outbreak of war in 1914, Barker began producing short war films such as *The Looters of Liege* and *Your Country Needs You*. Once British audiences wearied of the war, he returned to large-scale **historical films**, releasing *Jane Shore* in March 1915, and *Brigadier Gerard* in September 1915. Thereafter, the company's feature production declined, and Barker retired in December 1918.

NICHOLAS HILEY

Barker, William George
b. 1861; d. 1951

businessman, producer, filmmaker, Great Britain

"Bill" Barker, owner of a photographic equipment company in London, bought a **Lumière** camera in 1896 and began filming local subjects. In 1901, he formed the Autoscope Company, specializing in news event films and, in 1906, merged it with the **Warwick Trading Company**, of which he became managing director. In 1907, at the top of his profession, Barker became the first chairman of the Kinematograph Manufacturers' Association; two years later he left Warwick to form his own company, **Barker Motion Photography**, filming spectacular dramas as well as news events. In 1912, Barker was instrumental in creating the British Board of Film Censors, but in 1918 he retired from production and devoted the rest of his life to commercial film developing and printing.

NICHOLAS HILEY

Baron, Auguste

b. 1855; d. 1938

inventor, engineer. France

On April 3, 1896, after seeing an **Edison** kineto-phone, Baron registered a patent for a machine that would record images and **synchronized sound**. That same year, he also registered patents for a film stock perforator and for panoramic projection. A 1898 patent describes a reversible **camera**, called a "graphophonoscope," equipped with an electrical synchronism motor connected to a cylinder phonograph. In 1899, Baron built a glass studio in Asnières, where he recorded sound films, thanks to a revolutionary process: four graphite microphones were set above the stage to capture the actors' voices, a camera was placed on tracks, and both were connected to a phonograph equipped with an electrical engine, a receptor similar to the telephone, an ear trumpet, and an electro-magnetic recorder. Unfortunately, Baron was not able to commercialize his devices, nor could he present them at the 1900 Paris Exposition.

Further reading

Basile, Giusy and Laurent Mannoni (1998) "Le centenaire d'une rencontre: Auguste Baron et la synchronisation du son et de l'image animée," *1895*, 26 (December): 3–88.

LAURENT MANNONI

Bartling, Georg

b. ? d. ?

showman, filmmaker, manufacturer, Germany

An experienced **fairs/fairgrounds** showman from Hamburg, Bartling constructed his own film projection apparatus by late spring 1896, when it was in use at the Berlin **World's Fair**. After two years of both exhibiting and manufacturing this machine, he joined up with Johann Nitzsche in 1898 and moved to Leipzig in 1903, where the two established a factory for projection apparatuses, introducing first the "Vitagraph" and then the Saxonia I in 1907. The firm was incorporated into Zeiss Ikon AG, Dresden, in the late 1920s.

DEAC ROSSELL

Bassermann, Albert

b. 1867; d. 1952

actor, Germany

Bassermann began his acting career in his hometown of Mannheim, but eventually settled in Berlin in 1895, where he worked with such theater directors as Otto Brahm and Max **Reinhardt**. By 1913 he was perhaps the most important stage actor in Germany. His appearance in *Der Andere* [The Other One] (1913), the first *Autorenfilm*, gave that film and the medium of moving pictures itself a legitimacy that cannot be underestimated. Despite occasional negative reviews of the film's Jekyll-and-Hyde story—and of moving pictures in general—Bassermann remained loyal to cinema: he continued to act in film until 1948.

SCOTT CURTIS

Bauer, Evgenii

b. 1867; d. 1917

filmmaker, Russia

Born in Moscow into an Austrian-Russian family, Bauer belonged to the Russian Orthodox Church and remained an Austrian citizen all of his life. After attending (but not graduating from) the Moscow College of Painting, Sculpture and Architecture, he won recognition as a resourceful stage designer of *féeries*/**fairy plays** and musical comedies. In 1912, he was hired as production designer for the **Pathé-Frères** company in Moscow; a year later he became a director for **Drankov** & Taldykin. Only one of the seven films he made for the latter company survives, the sensational **melodrama**, *Twilight of a Woman's Soul* (1913). In 1914, Bauer began directing films for **Khanzhonkov** and soon became its leading director, working with Vera **Kholodnaya** in such films as *Children of the Age* (1915) and *A Life for a Life* (1916); eventually he became one of the company's shareholders.

His fine arts studies and prior work as a stage designer help to explain the unusual significance Bauer gave to **set design**, often fashioned according to current trends within Russian *art nouveau* architecture. Along with other European directors such as Léonce **Perret**, Giovanni **Pastrone**, Benjamin **Christensen**, and Franz **Hofer**, he experimented with **lighting** effects, **camera movement**, **staging in depth**, and other visual uses of spacious interior architecture, often taking those techniques to new extremes. With Yakov **Protazanov**, Bauer also became known for developing an "aesthetics of immobility," prompting actors, for instance, to hold a posture or pause so as to rivet an audience's attention on a single image of psychological or spiritual intensity. Among the salient features of Bauer's visual style (at least based on the twenty-six surviving films of a total number of eighty-two) are darkened foregrounds, gauzed middle grounds, and velvet-draped backgrounds. He also was interested in deploying curtains and doors to flank scenes, as in *Child of the Big City* (1914), in positioning mirrors to complicate the blocking of actors, as in *King of Paris* (1917), and in long, slow dolly shots that could last more than three minutes, as in *After Death* (1915).

Bauer died of stagnant pneumonia five months before the October Revolution of 1917.

Further reading

Tsivian, Yuri (1999) *Immaterial Bodies: Cultural Anatomy of Early Russian Film* (CD-ROM), Philadelphia/Los Angeles: Annenberg Center of Communication/University of Southern California.

YURI TSIVIAN

Baumann, Charles O.

b. ? d. ?

executive, USA

Charles O. Baumann first entered the film business when Adam **Kessel** enlisted him to run an unlicensed sub-exchange affiliated with Kessel's Empire Film Exchange. In 1909, he and Kessel then established the **New York Motion Picture Company** which was the parent company for the Bison, **Reliance**, **Keystone**, and Kay-Bee film brands. The partners became familiar names to moving picture audiences because aside from the titles and company logos the only credits on their films and posters read: "Kessel & Baumann, Executives." Baumann sold his film interests to Harry **Aitken** in 1917.

ROBERT S. BIRCHARD

Becce, Giuseppe

b. 1877 d. 1973

composer, Germany

Italien-born Guiseppe Becce moved to Berlin in his early 20s and came in contact with Oskar **Messter**, for whom he began to write musical arrangements and occasionally compose original **musical scores**: for instance, for the *Autorenfilm* drama, *Schuldig* [Guilty] (1913). That year he was contracted to play Richard Wagner in the bio-pic of the same title, and, when the Wagner estate refused permission to use original compositions, Becce "arranged and partially composed" a neo-romantic score himself. In 1915, he was made conductor of Messter's orchestra at the Mozartsaal cinema, becoming the Wilhelmine cinema's outstanding theoretician and practician of film music.

MICHAEL WEDEL

Becerril, Guillermo

b. ? d. ?

producer, cameraman, Mexico

A native of the city of Puebla, Guillermo Becerril was a professional photographer. He acquired a moving picture **camera** with which he filmed President Francisco Madero's trip to Puebla and to the spa at Tehuacán. In 1912, he recorded the massacre of the Zapatistas in the Plaza of Bulls in Puebla, an early example of clandestine political filmmaking.

AURELIO DE LOS REYES

Bedding, Thomas G.

b. ? d. ?

editor, Great Britain/USA

Editor in the 1890s of the *British Journal of Photography*, Bedding's first practical contact with early cinema was when he helped Birt **Acres** film the Diamond Jubilee in 1897. He wrote extensively on cinematography in 1897 and 1898, and in 1903 became chairman of the **Charles Urban Trading Company** (with financially disastrous results for himself). He moved to the USA in 1907, hired by the technical department of the Cameraphone Company. From 1909 to May 1911, Bedding was an associate editor of *Moving Picture World* and wrote technical and critical articles, including acclamations of *The Assasination of the Duc de Guise*, in March 1909, and of **Biograph** films the following year. A scenario editor and perhaps the first **publicity** director, he was associated with the **IMP** company by 1911, and edited their house journal. He worked with the **World Film Corporation** until the end of 1915.

STEPHEN BOTTOMORE

Belge Cinéma SA, La

La Belge Cinéma SA was founded by **Pathé-Frères** on 14 February 1908, with a capital of one million French francs, mainly from French investors. Its objective was to organize for Belgium, the Netherlands, and Luxemburg the sales of French Pathé films and film material, the production and distribution of its own films, and the construction of a large exhibition circuit. Between 1908 and 1913, the company controlled the most prestigious moving picture theaters in the main cities of all three countries. Eventually it also produced **multiple-reel/feature films**, most notably those of Alfred **Machin**, in Belgium and the Netherlands.

GUIDO CONVENTS

Belgium

In late 1894, the French poet Henri de Fleurigny or Henri Micard (1846–1916) obtained the **Edison Kinetoscope** concession for France and its colonies. With Belgian and French investors, in January 1895, he founded the Edison Kinétoscope Français in Brussels. The first kinetoscopes arrived in Belgium from France in March 1895 and soon were a great success. In May, investors such as Emile Sepulchre (1849–1933), who had links with the French kinetoscope company, founded the Edison Kinétoscope Belge in Brussels. This had the support of Ladislas–Victor Lewitzki, who now had the exclusive rights for Belgium. The company disbanded by the summer of 1896, but kinetoscopes remained a Belgian amusement for some years.

The **Cinématographe Lumière** was first presented to Belgian industrialists, scientists, photographers and businessmen in November 1895. From March through August 1896, a Belgian company obtained the concession to exhibit the Cinématographe in Belgium and the Netherlands. This company organized screenings in Brussels and sent Camille Cerf (1862–1936) and Francis **Doublier** to Amsterdam to do the same. That summer, competitors with other kinds of film **projectors** appeared on the market. Charles Schram (1851–1909) was one of these, with his own device called the Cinématographe Géant, a projector that easily could be adapted to all available film standards. From the autumn of 1896 on, he showed moving pictures in a canvas theater that he toured through the **fairgrounds** of Belgium, the Netherlands, and France.

From 1897 on, film exhibitions quickly became part of fairs, circuses, **music halls**, cafés, and all kinds of theaters. Although the opening of the **World's Fair** in Brussels in May 1897 had to be postponed a few days—because relatives of the Belgian royal family died in the Bazar de la Charité catastrophe in Paris—moving pictures would become a main attraction at the World's Fair. Daily screenings were organized by colonial businessmen who had links with the royal family, using the Zoograph, a kind of Cinématographe.

Almost every city and village had its annual fair; and some had even more than one. From the moment that moving picture apparatuses and films came on the market, showmen who worked the fairs picked them up as an attraction. Between 1896 and 1913 there were approximately fifty, either Belgians or foreigners, who already had lived for generations in the country. In general, the first moving picture showmen—for instance, Etienne **Thévenon**, Philippe Claeys, or Fréderic **Krüger**—didn't belong to the fairground families. They were technicians who recognized the fair as a market possibility even before the traditional fairground showmen did. From 1899 on, traditional fairground showmen with a canvas museum or circus often integrated moving pictures into their shows, or changed completely to a canvas film theater. The best known amongst them were the families of Grünkorn, Opitz, Lemeur, Grandsart, and Gérardy-Xhaflaire, all of whom entered the business between 1900 and 1906, at the moment of the heyday of these shows. Most didn't risk abandoning their existing successful show—for instance, a merry-go-round or a **wax museum**—for the latest attraction. But the German Henri Grünkorn was an exception. In 1897, he replaced his mechanical museum with a show using the American Bioscope. He presented his screenings in a canvas theater luxuriously decorated in the Louis XV style. After five years, Grünkorn sold his theater to Krüger but continued to work the fairgrounds. One of the most ostentatious of the itinerant shows also came from abroad, namely the Albert Frères (**Mullens** Brothers) from the Netherlands. They were very professional. Between 1905 and 1908, they visited Belgian cities during, but also after, the time of the fairs. For them, as for most non-traditional fairground showmen, unlike Grünkorn, moving pictures were their business and not the fairground itself.

Simultaneous with their appearance in fairground shows, moving pictures also became part of the program in about twenty existing Belgian music halls. Some of these halls, like that of Antonio Wallenda in Liège, could seat more than 5,000 spectators. Initially foreign **vaudeville** artists presented a few moving pictures as one act on programs, often using the name of the apparatus for the act—for instance, American Bioscope, American Biograph, Vitoscope, Wargraph, Edison's Ideal, or Vitographe Américaine Froissart. There also was another kind of traveling film entrepreneur who appeared at the end of the music-hall season and rented the building during the summer months, showing variety programs of moving pictures. The most famous were The Royal Bio of the Frenchman Edmond Oger, the Pioneer Cinématographe American, the Barnum Excelsior of the Frenchmen Deroubaix and Delgrange as well as the Imperial Bio of Krüger. They worked solely with a projector and films. Soon they also began to rent other kinds of theaters or even empty rooms on a temporary basis. Their success led music hall directors like Wallenda to begin installing their own moving picture apparatuses, ordered from **Messter**, **Lubin**, **Gaumont**, **Mendel** or **Pathé-Frères**.

In 1907–1908, moving picture exhibitors were confronted with a crisis. There were too many of them, and they all were purchasing the same, latest (expensive) films. At that time, exhibitors ran three-hour programs that changed every day, which meant a huge investment. The competition was enormous because most cities accepted only a limited number of fairground theaters. Due to the success of moving pictures, travelling variety theaters, museums and circuses also began to include them in their shows. One example was the French circus of François Bidel (1839–1909), who used films to show his animals in their natural environment. Local authorities also began to invite open-air picture shows at any time of the year because it meant extra income. Combined with the music of a local band, these shows attracted thousands. The showmen themselves—Louis Van Neck, Maurice De France, and Charles **Belot**—were mainly Belgians who worked with optics, **phonographs**, photographical products, or even owned a **publicity** agency. Outside city centers, moving pictures also became popular in cafes. These café-cinés showed their customers films either for free or else very cheaply. There were thousands of cafés and event-halls that used the projection of films to attract customers.

In June 1908, special legislation restricting film projections in public made it almost impossible for traveling shows to work with moving pictures. The traditional showmen dropped them and put their money into the latest fairground successes, like toboggans. Consequently, traditional fairground exhibitors did not make the transition to permanent film theaters; instead, entrepreneurs like Krüger or Thévenon, who had no traditional links with the fairgrounds or music halls, were the ones to become cinema owners.

The first permanent moving picture theater opened its doors in the center of Brussels in late 1904. Dozens soon followed, with the important ones financed by the Belgian investors. Many outside the city centers were integrated into cafés. The legislation of June 1908 set up strict rules for building theaters and for obtaining governmental authorization. These rules, and the decision of film producers not to sell but to rent films, favored the permanent film theaters. From that moment on, they rapidly conquered cities and even villages. By 1913, there were more than 650 theaters for 7.5 million Belgians, although many still were linked to a brewery or a café. One exception in Brussels was Le Congo Cinéma, which mainly showed its own films produced in the Belgian Congo. In 1913, the first modern cinema, the Pathé-Palace, opened in the center of Brussels with seats for 2,500 spectators.

Generally the moving picture programs in Belgium consisted mostly of foreign film because the country's own production was insignificant in quantity. Before 1907, exhibitors bought their films mainly in France or from Pathé-Frères, which opened a sales office in Brussels around 1900, although films produced in Germany, Italy, Great Britain, and even the USA were not totally absent on the market. Some owners of the first moving picture theaters, such as Louis **Van Goitsenhoven**, also entered the business by distributing foreign films. This changed quickly after 1907. More and more distribution companies—**Ambrosio**, **Cines**, **Vitagraph**, **Edison**, and **Warwick**—entered the expanding Belgian market. Pathé sought to maintain its dominance by establishing its own production company, La **Belge Cinéma SA**, and by distributing its films on an exclusive basis, but its position was challenged by the rapid development of dozen of specialized international film distribution houses in Brussels and Liège.

Although the majority of films shown in Belgium came from abroad, a small number were produced locally from the autumn of 1896 on. It was then that the inventor Raoul **Grimoin-Sanson** seems to have shot some scenes of city life in Liège. Lumière produced a few titles in early 1897, the same year the Zoograph filmed dozens of *actualités* of city life and events—in Brussels, Ostend, Charleroi, La Louvière and Bruges—for its program. It became standard policy for fairground showmen to film local events, in order to let the public recognize themselves on the screen. Among the many films produced by Opitz was *La Procession du Saint Sang à Bruges* in 1901 with a duration of 35 minutes (850 meters). In 1904, Belot shot probably the first Belgian fiction film, *Aventure sur la plage d'Ostende*. Krüger produced **synchronized sound** films with local vaudeville singers for music-hall programs, and he also put on filmed vaudeville plays like *Bruxelles-Scies-Némas* (1907). Around 1907, both Krüger and Van Goitsenhoven initiated a kind of **newsreel**. La Belge Cinéma consistently offered its customers newsreel items shot in Belgium and especially fiction films directed by Alfred **Machin**. Other French companies like Gaumont, **Eclipse**, **Éclair**, **Lux**, and Le Lion also had cameramen in the country in order to regularly have a Belgian item in their newsreels. Belgians like Isidore Moray and Hippolyte de Kempeneer, who experimented with their own weekly newsreels, also financed a handful of fiction films. The Belgian Kinemacolor company used special **cameras** and projectors and **color** films to make nonfiction films, which were shown in special Kinemacolor theaters in Brussels, Antwerp, Ostend and Leuven.

See also: distribution: Europe; itinerant exhibitors; law and the cinema; program formats

Further reading

Convents, Guido (1994) "Motion Picture Exhibitors on Belgian Fairgrounds," *Film History*, 6.2: 238–249.

Convents, Guido (1999) "Edison's kinetoscope in Belgium, or, Scientists, Admirers, Businessmen, Industrialists and Crooks," in Claire Dupré la Tour, André Gaudreault, and Roberta Pearson (eds.) *Le cinema au tournant du sicèle* [Cinema at the Turn of the Century], 249–258, Laval/ Laussanne: Les Presses de l'Université Laval/ Editions Payot Laussanne.

Convents, Guido (2000) *Van Kinetoscoop tot Café-Ciné. De eerste jaren van de film in België 1894–1908*, Leuven: Universitaire Pers Leuven.

De Kuyper, Eric (1995) *Alfred Machin, cinéaste, filmmaker*, Brussels: Koninklijk Belgisch Filmarchief.

Thys, Marianne (1999) *Belgian Cinema/Le Cinéma Belge/De Belgische Film*, Gent: Koninklijk Belgisch Filmarchief/Ludion.

GUIDO CONVENTS

Bell & Howell studio camera

h 15", w 7", d 15"; c. 27 lb

This expensive cast aluminium camera, with a four-lens turret and variable opening shutter, first appeared in 1912 and became the standard American studio camera from around 1915 through the late 1920s. The camera was moved sideways ("racked over") on its base plate for accurate focussing and framing, and registration pins held each frame steady during exposure. The camera's unusual **intermittent movement**, where a reciprocating gate lifted the film onto twin claws for each change of frame, proved noisy and impossible to insulate for sound filming.

DEAC ROSSELL

Belot, Charles

b. 1860; d. 1935

exhibitor, producer, distributor, Belgium

Belot is an important film pioneer in Belgium. He attended the first presentation of moving pictures in Brussels on 10 November 1895, probably because he had a shop selling photographic material, optics, **phonographs**, and bicycles. Around 1900, he began to organize open-air moving picture shows and developed a touring show named The Modern Cinema. In 1904, he directed probably the first Belgian fiction film, *Aventure sur la plage d'ostende*. From 1909 until his death, he worked chiefly in film distribution.

GUIDO CONVENTS

Benoît-Lévy, Edmond [Lévy, Benoît]

b. 1858; d. 1929

lawyer, businessman, exhibitor, promoter, scriptwriter, France

Born in Paris of an Alsatian school teacher, Edmond Benoît-Lévy originally was a business lawyer (1879–1898). He became a Free Mason in 1881 in the Alsace-Lorraine lodge, to which Jules Ferry also belonged. After lecturing at the Société nationale des conférences populaires, he founded the Société populaire des Beaux-arts (1894) and then became a member of the Ligue des droits de l'homme (League for the Rights of Man) when, provoked by the Dreyfus court case, it was established in February 1898.

In 1905, Benoît-Lévy launched *Phono-Gazette*, which soon became *Phono-Ciné-Gazette*, the first professional trade journal in France dedicated to moving pictures as well as the **phonograph**. In December 1906, in partnership with **Pathé-Frères**, he opened the Omnia-Pathé, the first luxury moving picture theater on the Grands Boulevards of Paris.

He argued for royalties and **copyrights** on the occasion of the production and release of one of his commissioned projects, *L'Enfant prodigue* [The Prodigal Son] (1907), an exceptionally long film for its time (1,600 meters). The film initiated the movement that led to the creation of **Film d'Art** and **SCAGL** the following year.

Benoît-Lévy founded or administered many film organizations and film companies, particularly in the exhibition sector (again in partnership with Pathé). During **World War I**, he wrote scripts for a number of patriotic productions and defended French cinema against the "invasion" of imported

Figure 12 Edmond Benoît-Lévy. (Courtesy of the Jean-Jacques Meusy Collection.)

American films. He was the uncle of filmmaker Jean-Benoît Lévy.

See also: education; law and the cinema; trade press

Further reading

Meusy, Jean-Jacques (1995) "Qui était Edmond Benoit-Lévy?," *Les vingt premières années du cinéma français*, Paris, Presses de la Sorbonne Nouvelle–AFRHC.

JEAN-JACQUES MEUSY

benshi

Benshi refers to the professional performers who narrated the story of a moving picture screened during the silent era in Japan. So-called **lecturers** performed elsewhere in the world during this period, but the *benshi* were so popular that they dominated moving picture exhibition in Japan until the end of the silents. Arguably, they even retarded the full development of sound in Japan's film industry.

In the Meiji era (1868–1912), the word *benshi* originally designated a person who gave political speeches, but it shifted to signify a film lecturer in the early 1900s. The shift began with the arrival of the first imported cinematic apparatus. In 1896, when the **Edison Kinetoscope** was shown for the first time in Kobe, a man named Ueda Tsunejiro explained the apparatus and the contents of the images for viewers. In 1897, when the Vitascope was first shown in Tokyo, there was a similar person, named Jumonji Daigen, who explained the moving pictures. But these people were never professional *benshi*. The first professional *benshi* was **Komada Koyo**, who succeeded Jumonji Daigen at the Kinkikan theater in Tokyo.

In the early years, the *benshi* explained the contents of the very brief films on a program before they were projected. When the films grew in length and their details became more complicated, the *benshi* began to narrate during the film's projection, even adding dialogue to the images on occasion. After 1907, when the production of fiction films in Japan accelerated, a unique convention for narrating evolved. Seven or eight *benshi* sat in front of the screen and spoke the dialogue of different characters on the screen while traditional Japanese music instruments accompanied their voices. This method of *benshi* narration for Japanese films continued until the early 1920s. By contrast, the exhibition of foreign films did not involve such a multi-vocal practice. A single *benshi* narrated a foreign film, although sometimes the most senior *benshi* on a theater's staff would take over and narrate the final reel.

Each theater employed several *benshi*, with each assuming a different position within a well established hierarchy. The most famous *benshi* were so powerful that their popularity could determine the success of a film, and sometimes even influence production. The *benshi* preferred scenes done in long takes so that they could display their monologuist skills to advantage. Shorter takes and a brisk alternation of shots were not suited to the special convention of multi-vocal narration. Throughout the 1910s and up to the early 1920s, the normative form of Japanese film was regulated by the practice of *benshi*.

See also: dialogue accompaniment; editing: temporal relations; staging in depth

HIROSHI KOMATSU

Bergqvist, John

b. 1874; d. 1963

distributor, producer, Sweden

In the city of Linköping, John Bergqvist expanded his Electro Biograf company to become Viking Film, in order to encompass both exchange activities and film production, principally *actualités* and **industrial films**. A major drawback for Bergqvist was his involvement with the Kinemacolor venture—he acquired the rights for Sweden—which eventually ended up in the courts after an array of mishaps. In 1912, he shot two features in the far north of Sweden, but this initiative met with only limited success, and his company was later restructured as Discus Film, a business that folded after producing only a couple of shorts.

JAN OLSSON

Bernard, Ferdinand "Bon" (*sic*)

b. ? d. ?

exhibitor, Mexico

Possibly the son of German immigrants, Ferdinand "Bon" Bernard was born in Santa Fe, Argentina. He signed a contract with the **Lumière** company to exploit the **Cinématographe** in Mexico, Cuba, and the Caribbean. For a time, Gabriel **Veyre** served as the cameraman or technician for his company. In Mexico, Bernard acquired a second apparatus so that he could give performances simultaneously in Mexico City and Guadalajara. An unscrupulous character, at a crucial point he dissolved his company, sold the

second apparatus, and returned to his beloved Santa Fe with the money.

AURELIO DE LOS REYES

Bernhardt, Sarah

b. 1844; d. 1923

actor, France

A famous French stage actress who made nine theatrical tours of the USA between 1880 and 1918, Bernhardt was a crucial figure in early attempts to associate moving pictures with the prestige of legitimate **theater**. Her first released film, *La Dame aux Camélias* [The Lady of the Camelias] (1911), was very successful, breaking box office records in the USA. Her second film, *La Reine Elisabeth* [Queen Elizabeth] (1912), was imported into the USA by Adolph **Zukor**, who used the venture's profits to found the **Famous Players Motion Picture Company**. Although Bernhardt continued to be involved with the industry until her death, she is remembered as an anachronistic performer who had little understanding of the nascent medium.

VICTORIA DUCKETT

Berst, Jacques A.

b. ? d. ?

sales agent, executive, USA

Sent from France by Charles **Pathé** to run the **Pathé-Frères** sales office in New York City in 1904, Berst soon made **Pathé Cinematograph** into the largest film supplier on the US market and a key factor in the **nickelodeon** boom. In 1907, he oversaw the company's construction of a laboratory for printing positive film stock in Fort Lee, New Jersey; three years later, he directed the construction of a studio for producing American films. For several years in the early 1910s, Berst served as an officer of the **General Film Company**. When Pathé Cinematograph was transformed into Pathé-Exchange in 1914, he headed the company until his retirement in 1918.

RICHARD ABEL

Bertini, Francesca

b. 1888; d. 1985

actor, Italy

Born to a middle-class Florence family, Francesca Bertini (Elena Seracini Vitiello) was the most versatile of Italian silent film divas. She first worked in film adaptations of operas for **Film d'Arte Italiana**, but then, inspired by Asta **Nielsen**'s performance in *The Abyss* (1910), she moved on to more contemporary roles with Celio. There, she starred in two important films: the pantomime, *L'Histoire d'un Pierrot* (1913), and the social melodrama, *Sangue Bleu* [Blue Blood] (1914). Bertini's greatest triumph came in *Assunta Spina* (1915), a Neapolitan melodrama of female sacrifice and male revenge. Playing a Neapolitan laundress who attracts several men, Bertini found the perfect role for her spontaneous, somewhat intuitive, yet codified acting style which resonated with class and regional connotations.

In 1921 she married the wealthy Swiss, Paul Cartier, and retired from the screen. The marriage eventually failed, and towards the end of her life, she shared a basement apartment with her former seamstress. Forgotten, she died alone and in poverty. In *The Last Diva* (1982), through interviews and archival footage, Gianfranco Mingozzi has eloquently documented Bertini's career as well as her last days.

ANGELA DALLE VACCHE

Bhatavdekar, Harishchandra Sakharam

b. 1868; d. ?

photographer, exhibitor, filmmaker, India

Aka Save Dada, Bhatavdekar may be India's first filmmaker. A professional still photographer, equipment dealer, and film exhibitor, he shot several typical early cinema subjects in Bombay before filming the **news event** footage for which he is best remembered, *The Return of Wrangler Paranjpye* (1902). This widely exhibited, now lost film was perhaps the first filmed document of 20th-century Indian history because it featured a watershed event in India's rising national movement. Bhatavdekar retired into obscurity in 1907, and the date of his death is not known.

SURESH CHABRIA

Bianchi, Joseph

b: ? d: ?

inventor, Canada

Based in Toronto, Bianchi was an inventor who devised a shutterless moving picture **camera** in 1908. His training at the Columbia Phonograph Company, an **Edison** rival, doubtless led him to concoct a camera whose operating mechanism would circumvent Edison patents. For that reason, the Bianchi camera proved useful for the Independent companies wishing to produce films without infringing on those patents. Although *American Photography* reported in 1909 that the Bianchi camera's resulting images were stable and produced little flicker, perhaps the invention simply provided Independent companies with a legally viable, but technologically inferior alternative whose chief virtue was strategic.

CHARLIE KEIL

biblical films

In a world markedly less secular than that of the 21st-century West, early cinema drew heavily for both non-fiction and fiction films upon the Judeo-Christian religious tradition. *Actualités* of the Holy Land came from nearly every American and European manufacturer: in 1903 alone, **Edison** released *Tourists Taking Water From the River Jordan*, *A Jewish Dance at Jerusalem*, *Herd of Sheep on the Road to Jerusalem*, and *Jerusalem's Busiest Street Showing Mount Zion*. **Historical films** sometimes illustrated the trials undergone by true believers, as in **Cines'** *Quo Vadis?* (1913) about the Christians of Emperor Nero's Rome. Domestic **melodramas** often had religious themes, as in **Biograph**'s *The Spirit Awakened* (1912), which the company described as "a story of the Christian and the renegade." Rather than attempting to discuss the entire range of religious films, this entry will focus on biblical dramas and even more specifically upon those featuring the most important figures, respectively of the Old and New Testaments of the Christian Bible, Moses and Christ. The New Testament mentions Moses more often than any other Old Testament figure, and contemporary rhetoric often drew parallels between Moses and Christ.

The French and American industries produced several films illustrating key moments in Christ's life, with some following him "From the Manger to the Cross," as **Kalem** titled its 1912 feature-length film, and others following the age-old tradition of depicting Christ's "passion": that is, his suffering and death at the hands of the Roman Empire. In the cinema's first decade, the Passion Play constituted a distinct "genre," with several of them even made before the turn of the century. American producers tended to reference the live Passion Play performed every decade by the inhabitants of Oberammergau, a small Bavarian town. Rather than waiting for the 1900 staging of the Oberammergau Play, the **Klaw and Erlanger** theatrical syndicate filmed a Passion Play put on by the inhabitants of the Austrian village of Horitz in the spring of 1897. The resulting film premiered that November in Philadelphia, accompanied by a lecture that would previously have been illustrated with lantern slides. Opening *actualité* footage of Horitz was followed by shots of the principal actors and then by the Play. The Eden Musee, the only entertainment center in New York City that showed moving pictures on a full-time basis, quickly countered with its own *Passion Play*. The **dime museum**'s hastily put together version used the costumes and script from a never-staged 1880s theatrical Passion Play and was shot on a city rooftop: it had twenty-three scenes and lasted for roughly nineteen minutes. The Eden Musee's **publicity** implied that it had filmed the 1890 Oberammergau Play, but critics, knowing that the cinema had not then existed, quickly derided the pretence. Despite its lack of authenticity relative to the Klaw and Erlanger version, the Eden Musee's *Passion Play* had greater

box office success and inspired Siegmund **Lubin** and William **Selig** to produce yet more rival versions.

During the last years of the 1890s, the French contributed two more Jesus biographies to the world's screens, *La Vie et la Passion de Jesus-Christ*, directed by Georges **Hatot** for the **Lumière** Company, and *La Vie de Christ* (1899), shot by the world's first woman director, Alice **Guy**, for Gaumont. Between them, the French firms of **Gaumont** and **Pathé-Frères** went on to win the Passion stakes, with Gaumont producing another (also directed by Guy) in 1906 and Pathé producing a total of four, in 1900, 1902–1903, 1907, and 1913. Indeed, the 1907 *Passion Play* probably was seen by more people in North America and Europe (and more than once) than any other film of the period. Pathé also made two films about Moses, *La Vie de Moise* [The Life of Moses] (1905) and *Moise sauvé des eaux* [The Infancy of Moses] (1911), but **Vitagraph**'s five-reel spectacular, *The Life of Moses* (1910), far surpassed them in ambition, taking its hero from the bulrushes to Mount Pisgah.

The Vitagraph film's clever blending of cinematic special effects with Biblical authority helps to explain the prevalence and success of biblical films during the early cinema period. Biblical films, whether relating the lives of Moses, Christ, or other Old and New Testament heroes, had a clear advantage relative to films derived from other

Figure 13 Frame still from *The Life of Christ* (Gaumont, 1906).

source material. They conformed perfectly to the **cinema of attractions** which depended for its appeal upon spectacle and narrative familiarity, that is, upon combining visually pleasing shots with well-known stories rather than constructing "new" narratives and spatio/temporal continuity. No stories were more familiar to the majority of Europeans and Americans than those of the Bible, and few offered more opportunities for the insertion of "miracles" derived from filmic manipulation. The early cinema had quickly developed a battery of special effects techniques, often showcased in **trick films**, which biblical films appropriated. *The Life of Moses* includes the six most "cinematic" of the ten plagues, including stop-motion transformation of a rod into a snake, water changed into blood through tinted film stock, and the Angel of Death walking through walls with the aid of double exposure. The five reels also present other miracles: the burning bush that is never consumed, the striking of the rock to bring forth water, and the raining down of manna upon the starving Israelites. Reel three even features the most crowd-pleasing miracle in the Pentateuch: double exposure permits the Israelites to walk through the Red Sea, walls of water looming up on either side of them. Although perhaps not especially convincing to modern eyes accustomed to computer-generated images, the effect was fairly spectacular for 1910.

Biblical films also maintained the tradition of the cinema of attractions by drawing heavily upon prevalent period intertexts such as a long tradition of biblical illustration, including illustrated Bibles, stereoscope cards, **magic lantern** slide series, and **illustrated lectures** (among them, John L. Stoddard's lecture/magic lantern show of the Oberammergua Passion Play in 1880). *The Life of Moses*, for instance, corresponded closely to Biblical images familiar to the respectable middle classes that the industry wished to attract to moving picture shows. Vitagraph's publicity claimed that the producers had consulted the works of several painters well-known for their religious art: among them, James Tissot, Jean-Léon Gérôme, Gustav-Doré, and Sir Lawrence Alma-Tadema. Some films actually reproduced these painters' work upon the screen, matching composition, **set design**, and **costumes** to the original. *From the Manger to the Cross* used as its sourcebook the so-called Tissot Bible, *La Vie de Notre Seigneur Jésus Christ* (1896–1897), in which commentary and selected passages from the Gospels supplemented the French painter's illustrations, the book's chief appeal. Tissot's "five-act" presentation of Christ's life—Holy Childhood, The Ministry, Holy Week, the Passion, and the Resurrection—structured the film's five reels while the composition of many shots "realized" his illustrations.

By drawing on an unimpeachable source as well as other culturally respectable and widely circulating intertexts, biblical films made a bid for legitimacy at a time when the new film medium was not yet fully accepted by social and educated elites. Religious authorities across Western Europe and the USA at first had embraced moving pictures, even advocating them as a teaching tool, but as the new medium's popularity increased, many clerics began to fear its possible deleterious effects. In the USA, progressive elements within organized religion had used illustrations, in the form of both magic lanterns slides and films for years, but the growing dominance of fiction films, coupled with the rapid emergence of **nickelodeons** as the primary exhibition venue, suddenly made moving pictures objectionable. By 1909, many influential religious figures were waging all-out war upon the cinema. *The Life of Moses* thus constituted a major attempt to make religious subjects that would placate clergymen and aid the unfettered operation of the nickelodeons. The American clergy objected to their operating on the Christian Sabbath in a country which had a strong tradition of "Blue Sundays," that is the banning of all public entertainments on that day. Yet some venues had evaded the ban by showing moving pictures of an educational or religious nature. In the cinema's transitional period, biblical films still provided acceptable subjects for Sunday shows, while also legitimating attendance by women and children, encouraging attendance during the slack Lenten season, and perhaps attracting new viewers from classes other than those which usually patronized nickelodeons. The **trade press** engaged in a concerted effort to form an alliance between the film industry and organized religion, happily reporting any film use by churches and constantly urging film producers to turn out appropriate subjects for religious venues. Perhaps for this reason, Vitagraph advertised *The Life of Moses* as corresponding closely to the versions of the story learned in Sunday Schools.

Biblical films played an important part in the film industry's maturation not only by placating the critics but also by pushing the transition to the **multiple-reel/feature film**. At a time when most films ran for no more than a few minutes, the *Passion Plays* of necessity consisted of several reels, making them, together with the popular **boxing films**, among the earliest multiple-reel films. This is not to say, however, that the *Passion Plays* were always shown in their entirety. Rather, in a practice typical of the early film industry, their producers marketed different combinations of shots, enabling exhibitors to make the final decisions about what audiences would view. In the transitional period, when the single-reel film still dominated distribution and exhibition practices, significant biblical films ran for two or more reels. *From the Manger to the Cross*, one of the first American feature films, ran for eighty minutes, while D. W. **Griffith**'s first feature was the four-reel biblical story, *Judith of Bethulia* (1926). *The Life of Moses*, Vitagraph's longest production until March 1914, is an early example of practices of multiple-reel release and exhibition that briefly became the norm. While the five reels could be shown in successive weeks in nickelodeons, the film also could be exhibited in its entirety and in venues, such as opera houses or churches, outside the usual distribution networks. In a departure from period norms, *The Life of Moses* received relatively intensive advance publicity, with Vitagraph suggesting a range of promotional strategies to exhibitors such as draping the house with **color** posters and planting stories in local **newspapers**.

See also: churches and exhibition; law and the cinema; religious filmmaking

Further reading

Cosandey, Roland, Andre Gaudreault, and Tom Gunning (eds.) (1992) *Une Invention du Diable? Cinema Des Premiers Temps et Religion/An Invention of the Devil? Religion and Early Cinema*, Sainte-Foy/Lausanne: Les Presses de l'Universite Laval/ Editions Payot Lausanne.
Lindvall, Terry (2001) *The Silents of God: Selected Issues and Documents in Silent American Film and Religion, 1908–1925*, Lanham: Scarecrow Press.
Uricchio, William and Roberta E. Pearson (1993) *Reframing Culture: The Case of the Vitagraph Quality Films*, Princeton: Princeton University Press.

ROBERTA E. PEARSON

Binger, Maurits Herman

b. 1868; d. 1923

producer, director, the Netherlands

The owner of a printing business in Haarlem, Binger opened the **Hollandia** "film factory" in an adjacent building in 1912. He regarded moving pictures as an extension of his hobbies, **photography** and theater, both of which he practiced as a dedicated amateur. In 1915, he became the company's principal director, changing the studio style from typically Dutch "wooden-shoe-and-windmill" films to international society dramas that provided a rich setting for his **star**, Annie **Bos**. He wrongly assumed this strategy would attract foreign audiences after **World War I**. Ironically, his last films were mostly adaptations of popular Dutch plays.

ANSJE VAN BEUSEKOM

Biograph

In 1907, **American Mutoscope and Biograph** was facing liquidation because of the economic downtown as well as the defections by key production personnel: Wallace **McCutcheon** had been hired by rival **Edison**, and Francis **Marion** had left to found a new company, **Kalem**. Jeremiah J. **Kennedy** emerged to reorganize the company simply as Biograph and become its new president. At the same time a legal victory over Edison made it clear that the **Biograph camera** did not infringe on Edison's patents. The field of US film production, even more potentially lucrative with the enormous expansion of **nickelodeons**, was now in the hands of Edison and Biograph. Edison licensed all other existing US production companies, along with **Pathé-Frères**, and challenged Biograph to match its ability to supply the market with films. Biograph solidified alliances with other foreign producers and particularly importers like George **Kleine** and took the challenge head on. By the end of 1908 it was clear that Edison and Biograph would merge on terms favorable to Biograph, resulting in the **Motion Picture Patents Company** (MPPC).

Essential to Biograph's ability to face down Edison was a steady supply of story films on a regular schedule. The company had problems finding a director for such films, but finally settled in 1908 on a sometime actor and scriptwriter, D. W. **Griffith**. Griffith not only made films at a steady and reliable rate, but also transformed the narrative style of American cinema through systematic use of parallel editing, new styles in performance, and a new attention to character psychology. Through most of 1909, Griffith was Biograph's only director and, as other Biograph directors appeared (such as Mack **Sennett** who specialized in **comedies**), they were all trained by Griffith and reflected his reliance on editing as a narrative device. Through the summer of 1913, at which time he had personally directed over 400 one-reel films, Griffith gave the Biograph company a unique style and reputation as a leader of the industry, creating some of the masterpieces of American film history, such as: *A Corner in Wheat* (1909), *The Country Doctor* (1926), *The Lonedale Operator* (1926), and *The Informer* (1926), and introducing such performers as Mary **Pickford**, Lillian **Gish** and her sister Dorothy, Mae **Marsh**, Clare McDowell, Henry **Walthall**, Lionel Barrymore, and Bobby Harron.

Until 1913, Biograph stuck to a policy of producing, with few exceptions, one-reel and split-reel films for the variety programs distributed by **General Film**. That year, however, the company decided to begin producing **multiple-reel films**, based on stage plays. Special arrangements were made with **Klaw & Erlanger**, a theatrical production house, to adapt works they controlled. A new studio in the Bronx was built. Griffith

Figure 14 Biograph studio exterior, 14th Street, Manhattan. (Courtesy of the Robert S. Birchard Collection.)

supervised a few of these productions, but soon left the company to join **Mutual**. Like most of the companies associated with the MPPC, Biograph quickly declined in the feature era and ceased important production after 1914. The success of the government suit against the MPPC under anti-trust laws finalized its demise in 1915.

See also: acting styles; editing: spatial relations; editing: temporal relations

TOM GUNNING

Biograph 70mm camera

h: 18"; w: 16³/4"; d: 18"

Using normal unperforated still camera roll film 68mm wide, thinner and cheaper than 35mm roll film, the Biograph camera was designed to produce mutoscope reels. It had a unique "gripper" friction **intermittent** with two counter-rotating protrusions pulling across the entire film, and ran at

30 fps (frames per second). To register mutoscope cards, it punched two holes at either side of the image during exposure. When **American Mutoscope and Biograph** (AM&B) decided to build a film **projector**, the uneven spacing of the frames was corrected in a complex printing apparatus.

Further reading

Rossell, Deac (2001) "The Biograph Large Format Technology," *Griffithiana*, 66/70: 78–115.

DEAC ROSSELL

Biograph 70mm projector

The Biograph system with its unperforated film for producing Mutoscope reels seemed especially unsuited to film projection, but the projector that Herman Casler developed used the same gripper **intermittent** as did his camera and was widely contracted to large **vaudeville** theaters and **music halls** up to about 1903. The apparatus completely enclosed its mechanics and lamp house, along with the film path, to preserve expensive 68mm prints and required constant attention to a sophisticated clutch that kept the image properly framed, yet the Biograph projector was regularly praised for the quality of its image.

See also: American Mutoscope and Biograph

Further reading

Rossell, Deac (2001) "The Biograph Large Format Technology," *Griffithiana*, 66/70: 78–115.

DEAC ROSSELL

Biorama

This Danish film company took its name from a Copenhagen moving picture theater founded by former **fairground** showman Søren Nielsen in 1905. Its success allowed Nielsen to establish a chain of picture theaters in Denmark, Norway, and the Netherlands. Biorama became an important

distributor and, in 1909, began producing its own films, including the bawdy farce, *København ved Nat* [Copenhagen by Night] (1910). Of the substantial output of the company (renamed Filmfabrikken Skandinavien in 1912), very few films survive, but the uncanny thriller, *Dødsvarslet* [Mememto Mori] (1912) demonstrates the talent of its leading director, Aage Brandt.

CASPER TYBJERG

Bioscope Company of Canada

The Canadian Pacific Railway, built across the country's western provinces, engaged the **Charles Urban Trading Company** to extol the virtues of the west to potential immigrants via moving pictures. Urban's English partner, F. Guy Bradford, and Bradford's brother-in-law, Clifford Denham, joined forces with cameraman Joseph **Rosenthal** to film a series of scenic views—in the process becoming the Bioscope Company of Canada, the nation's first production company. Using Urban's Bioscope **camera**, the group spent nearly a year, in 1902–1903, filming scenes of Canadian life that became known as the "Living Canada" series. Shown to acclaim in Great Britain, the series also was taken across Canada by Bradford and Denham, as a lengthy **illustrated lecture**.

CHARLIE KEIL

Bioscope, The

Launched in September 1908, *The Bioscope* was one of three important trade journals in the early years of British cinema, the others being *The Cinema* and **Kinematograph and Lantern Weekly**, its chief rival. Although it began a year after the latter, *The Bioscope* could be called the first British film trade journal for it did not grow out of an existing, and part **magic lantern**, predecessor. Founded and edited by a genteel ex-lawyer and actor, John Cabourn, *The Bioscope* was a 'lighter' read than its rivals, for, while maintaining all the usual apparatus of the **trade press**—film listings and reviews, critical articles, and analyses of trade conditions—there was always room for the quirky and comic piece. Many cartoons appeared on its pages, by its regular artists 'Glossop' and 'Peter' and by others such as Harry Furniss (in 1912–1913). *The Bioscope* always had excellent foreign coverage, through correspondents such as John Cher in Paris. It continued publication until 1932 when it was acquired by *Kinematogaph Weekly*.

STEPHEN BOTTOMORE

Bitzer, Wilhelm ("Billy")

b. 1872; d. 1944

cameraman, USA

Primarily known as D. W. **Griffith**'s cameraman, Bitzer worked with him throughout his **Biograph** career beginning in 1908, and nearly exclusively after 1911 (before 1912, Griffith also worked with cameraman Arthur **Marvin**).

From **American Mutoscope and Biograph's** inception in the 1890's, Bitzer worked as "operator" of the **Biograph 70mm camera** (and, for its premiere performance, the **Biograph projector**). He shot *actualités*, including subjects from William McKinley's presidential campaign to the Spanish–American War, **boxing film re-enactments**, and **phantom train rides**. He also shot brief **comedies**, and, as AM&B films began to lengthen, several important early narrative films: the **chase film**, *Personal* (1926); the elaborately staged *Tom the Piper's Son* (1926); and the **trick film**, *The Sculptor's Nightmare* (1905). The claim (even implied by Bitzer himself) that he directed any fiction films after 1903 remains unlikely, given Wallace **McCutcheon**'s role as AM&B principal director. Although Bitzer indicates that Griffith exerted control over the company's visual style after 1908, the innovations of later Biograph films in editing and composition undoubtedly were the result of collaboration between the two men. Bitzer's pre-Griffith films show many technical innovations, such as the extended pan in *Love in the Suburbs* (1926) or the directional **lighting** in *The Music Master* (1926). Yet under Griffith, images were tailored for narrative expressivity—through a psychological use of

lighting, as in *The Drunkard's Reformation* (1926), a new lyrical sense of landscape, as in *The Country Doctor* (1926); and broad panoramas, as in *The Massacre* (1926).

TOM GUNNING

black cinema, USA

While black subjects appeared in moving pictures from the mid-1890s on, it was not until the early 1910s that African Americans entered the field of film production.

Many scholars have assumed that black filmmaking began as a response to D. W. **Griffith**'s landmark film, *The Birth of a Nation* (1926), which contained numerous inflammatory black stereotypes. Although two of the silent era's most successful black film companies—the Lincoln Motion Picture Company (co-founded by Noble **Johnson** in 1916) and the Micheaux Book and Film Company (founded by Oscar Micheaux in 1918)—emerged as part of the black community's efforts to challenge that film's racist ideologies, black cinema has a longer and more complex history.

African Americans had patronized moving pictures throughout the **nickelodeon** era. While early cinema has been credited with helping to assimilate diverse European immigrants into the American mainstream, for African Americans early moving pictures rarely offered satisfying representations of black life. In addition, the venues of film exhibition were frequently regulated by race. Black moviegoers experienced various types of **racial segregation**: they were forced to sit in balconies, to attend separate screenings from whites, or restricted to second-run theaters in their own neighborhoods. These conditions suggested that blacks were a ripe market for films catering to their particular desires and viewing conditions. Thus black-cast films for black audiences—commonly known as "race films"—were born.

Race films also emerged out of the vibrant black business, theatrical, and musical cultures that were developing at the turn of the 20th century, particularly in urban areas. Black entrepreneurs owned and operated theaters and **newspapers**, and black performers appeared on the **vaudeville** stage and in jazz clubs. These sources provided venues, on-screen talent, **musical accompaniment**, and **publicity** for early black filmmakers.

The first black film producer, William **Foster**, used his Chicago connections to cast, promote, and exhibit his first film, *The Railroad Porter* (1926). The following year, the Peter P. Jones Photoplay Company was founded in Chicago by a prominent black portrait photographer, and debuted with the **comedy**, *Sambo and Dinah* (1926). Foster, Jones, and other early black filmmakers attempted to present new black images in familiar genres. Foster produced several short comedies, *The Butler* and *The Fall Guy* (1926), trying to avoid long-standing stereotypes by representing members of the black middle-class. After joining the Afro-American Film Company in 1913, Hunter C. Haynes, a New York City-based entrepreneur, then founded the Haynes Photoplay Company in 1914. Haynes' *Uncle Remus' First Visit to New York* (1926) juxtaposes a Southern rube with an urban New Negro to illustrate "race progress" into **modernity**. In **news event films** such as Foster's *The Colored Championship Base Ball Game* and Jones' *For the Honor of the 8th Ill. U.S.A.* (1926) as well as Haynes' footage of prominent blacks in New York and Boston, black filmmakers sought to entertain with images of black community, patriotism, and achievement.

Further reading

Sampson, Henry T. (1995) *Blacks in Black and White: A Source Book on Black Films*, 2nd ed., Metuchen, N.J.: Scarecrow.

Stewart, Jacqueline (2003) *Migrating to the Movies: Black Urban Film Culture, 1893–1920*, Berkeley: University of California Press.

JACQUELINE STEWART

Blackton, J. (James) Stuart

b. 1875, England; d. 1941, USA

actor, director, producer, USA

Born in Sheffield, Blackton's family emigrated to the USA when he was a child. Allegedly, he entered the film industry after an encounter with Thomas **Edison**, while working as a journalist and cartoonist for the *New York Evening World*. During an interview, Edison was impressed with Blackton's drawings and asked him to perform a sketch for a moving picture **camera**; this became *Blackton, the Evening World Cartoonist* (1926). Another result of this meeting was Blackton's purchase of an Edison projecting machine. Later the same year, he founded the American **Vitagraph Company** together with Albert E. **Smith** (Ronald Reader joined as a third partner in 1897), and became responsible for the company's production, directing most of the films during the company's formative period.

Blackton was an innovative force in the development of moving pictures and also one of the more seminal figures in the American film industry's development. Although he worked within a wide range of films—*actualités*, **propaganda films**, **comic series**, **westerns** and stage adaptations, including many **Shakespeare films**—perhaps his most important achievement was to put American **trick films** on a par with the French. He became one of the pioneers of **animation**—at this time considered a trick device—and he even claimed to have been the first to use the frame-by-frame technique of shooting. In 1906, Blackton directed the influential *Humorous Phases of Funny Faces*, a series of animated drawings of caricatured faces, usually considered the first animated cartoon. He experimented with object-animation techniques in *A Mid-Winter Night's Dream; or, Little Joe's Luck* (1926) and *The Haunted Hotel* (1926) at a time when animation still was in its infancy as a mode of production. The success of the latter helped Vitagraph to establish a European office in Paris. In 1909, his last year of making trick films proper, Blackton produced the much praised *Princess Nicotine, or The Smoke Fairy*. In 1911, together with other members of the **Motion Picture Patents Company**, he founded and edited *Motion Picture Story Magazine*, initially a **publicity** organ for the industry that would become the first fan magazine. Blackton also organized and was president of the Motion Picture Board of Trade, forerunner to the Association of Motion Picture Producers and Distributors of America.

Blackton left Vitagraph in 1917 to become an independent producer of adaptations of literary masterpieces, eventually going to England to produce and direct three films, among them *The Glorious Adventure* (1926), the first British feature in **color**. Unsuccessful as an independent, he returned to Vitagraph in 1923, again partnered with Smith. After Vitagraph was sold to **Warner Brothers**, he retired in 1926, only to lose his fortune in the 1929 stock market crash. His final film project was *The Film Parade* (or *The March of the Movies*)—a history of the motion-picture industry—in the early 1930s.

Blackton was killed by a bus while crossing a street close to his home in Los Angeles in 1941.

Further reading

Crafton, Donald (1993) *Before Mickey: The Animated Film 1898–1928*, Cambridge: MIT Press.
Slide, Anthony (1976) *The Big V: A History of the Vitagraph Company*, Metuchen, N.J.: Scarecrow.

MARINA DAHLQUIST

Blair Camera Company

Founded by the Canadian Thomas Henry Blair (1855–1919) to produce a portable wet collodion **photography** system in 1877, this Boston-based company was a major competitor of George **Eastman**, offering a range of mass-market cameras, photographic plates, and, particularly, roll-film systems. Blair's **celluloid** film was used for most **Edison Kinetoscope** prints, and the company supplied both negative and positive film stock for many American producers until it was bought out by Eastman in 1899, who then converted his film stock production to the patented Blair continuous casting method.

See also: Blair Camera Company, European

DEAC ROSSELL

Blair Camera Company, European

Removed from the management of his American company, Thomas Henry Blair replicated its offerings of cameras, film stock, and accessories by founding the European Blair Camera Company on 28 April 1893, with a factory at Foots Cray, Kent, and offices in London. Initially, the most significant manufacturer of **celluloid** film stock in Europe, Blair provided film for the experiments of **Lumière**, **Acres**, **Paul**, **Joly** and others, and later was a regular supplier to **Messter**, **de Bedts**, G. A. **Smith**, Charles **Urban** and others until it went out of business in 1903.

See also: Blair Camera Company

DEAC ROSSELL

Blom, August

b. 1869; d. 1947

filmmaker, Denmark

A key figure in the Danish silent cinema, Blom was a stage actor whom **Nordisk** hired as a filmmaker in 1910 and who then served as the company's artistic supervisor from 1911 to 1921. Among the most important of his nearly 100 films are the **white slave film** *Den hvide Slavehandel* [In the Hands of Impostors] (1910), the erotic melodrama *Ved Faengslets Port* [Temptations of the Big City] (1911), and the big-budget *Autorenfilm Atlantis* (1926), which combines a complex psychological drama with a spectacular Titanic-like shipwreck. Blom's films were distinguished by their carefully composed images and subtle, compelling performances.

CASPER TYBJERG

Boggs, Francis

b. 1870; d. 1911

director, producer, USA

Francis Boggs was hired as a director for the Chicago-based **Selig Polyscope Company** in September of 1907; his earliest documented film is *The Two Orphans* (23 December 1907). After scouting and filming locations throughout the southwest and west, Boggs established a studio in the Edendale section of Los Angeles in the spring of 1909, hiring Hobart **Bosworth** as his company's lead actor. Tragically, Boggs was shot and killed by a studio employee on 27 October 1911. A highly regarded craftsman, Boggs' contemporaries considered him among the best filmmakers of his generation.

STEVEN HIGGINS

Bolivia

Although for years it was believed that moving pictures arrived late in Bolivia, recent research indicates that Bolivia was not really out of synch with the rest of the continent. On 21 June 1897, the newspaper *El Comercio* announced a film screening at the Municipal Theater and subsequent notices have led researchers to believe that it was a screening of **Lumière** films. Nevertheless, there are few other reports until 21 September 1905, when **newspapers** announced a screening of "views," including one about the Sino-Soviet war, at the Coliseo de La Paz. Echoing this late development, sound production did not begin until late: the silent period in Bolivia extends until 1938.

There is disagreement about when the first Bolivian moving pictures appeared. Carlos Mesa has located a newspaper advertisement announcing *Retratos de personajes históricos y de actualidad* [Portraits of Historical and Contemporary Figures] on 15 August 1904, while others have argued that the first Bolivian views were shot by Kenning, impresario of a "Biógrafo" theater, who, on 19 July 1906, exhibited *La exhibición de todos los personajes ilustres de Bolivia* [The Exhibition of All the Important Figures of Bolivia], featuring portraits of the power elite. This latter film was extraordinarily well-received, and Kenning continued to produce views such as *Un paseo en el Prado el día de todos los santos* [A Promenade on the Prado on All Saints Day] (1906). Other "biógrafos" appeared and their owners entered production as well, filming the typical array of military parades, views of the city, and civic events throughout the period of 1906–1912.

Perhaps the first consistent filmmaker of the Bolivian cinema was Luis G. Castillo: in December 1912, he shot images of the city and exhibited them a few days later, on 4 January, 1913. He continued shooting "views" of various civic events throughout 1913–1917 and exhibiting them in his theater, the Cine Teatro, which aggressively advertised its programs. In 1918, Castillo founded Andes Films and began to produce commissioned documentaries. Later he joined forces with archeologist Arturo Posnasky and, in 1925, founded Condor Mayku Films to produce *La Gloria de la Raza* [The Glory of the Race] (1926). In this film, an archeologist (Posnasky himself) meets an Uru Indian (a community extinct since the 1950s) on Lake Titicaca and asks him to tell the story of his people. The Indian's tale ends with the destruction of Tiwanaku, a city that was the center of millenarian Aymara culture. Although the film has been lost, the script, published by Castillo and Posnansky at the time of its release, still exists. Throughout the 1920s, Castillo shot many documentaries, among them some of great historical value, for example, a 1926 record of the demonstrations in favor of the USA incited by President Coolidge's announcement that the provinces of Tacna and Arica (given to Chile and Peru after the Great War) would be returned to Bolivia.

Much like other Andean nations, Bolivia did not have a flourishing film culture until the 1920s, and its first fiction film—José María Velasco Maidana's *La Profecía del lago* [The Prophecy of the Lake]—did not appear until 1925.

Further reading

Mesa, Carlos D. (1976) *El cine en Bolivia*, La Paz: Cinemateca de la Paz.

Susz, Pedro (1992) "Orígines de la expresión cinematográfica en Bolivia," in *Cine Latinoamericano, 1896–1930*, Caracas, Consejo Nacional de la Cultura/Foncine/Fundacine UC.

ANA M. LÓPEZ

Bolten-Baeckers, Heinrich

b. 1871; d. 1938

director, Germany

A successful stage manager, playwright, and publisher, Bolten-Baeckers set up a film studio in Berlin-Steglitz in 1906, where he experimented with sound pictures and directed a version of *Der Hauptmann von Köpenick* [The Captain of Köpenick]. In 1908, five years before the *Autorenfilme* movement emerged, he initiated an attempt to win over literary writers to moving pictures in collaboration with **SCAGL** and **Pathé-Frères**. Between 1909 and 1915, for his own BB-Film company, co-financed by Pathé, but also then for **Duskes**, Literaria-Film, and (in 1914/15) for **Gaumont**'s German subsidiary, he directed over fifty films, mostly **comedies**, but also fast-paced **crime films** and war films.

MICHAEL WEDEL

Bonine, Robert Kates

b. 1862; d. 1923

photographer, cameraman, lecturer, USA

A well-known photographer from Altoona, Pennsylvania, Bonine began working for **Edison Manufacturing** in 1898, mostly taking **travelogues** (and slides)—for instance, of the 1899 Klondike gold rush. Joining **American Mutoscope and Biograph** (AM&B) in 1901, Bonine filmed in China, Japan, Hawaii, and Yosemite Park. In 1902–1903, he was cameraman at AM&B's New York studio. In January 1905, he rejoined Edison to take charge of the company's **film developing** facilities yet continued to take *actualités*, filming San Francisco devastated by the earthquake. Feeling that Edison was committed to making fiction films, Bonine resigned in May 1907 and traveled around the world taking films for the U.S. government before settling in Hawaii.

CHARLES MUSSER

Bonnard, Mario

b. 1889; d. 1965

actor, director, Italy

One of the most familiar figures of silent Italian cinema, Bonnard starred in such **Ambrosio** classics as Luigi **Maggi**'s *Satana* [Satan] (1912) and Eleuterio **Rodolfi**'s *Gli Ultimi giorni di Pompei* [The Last Days of Pompeii] (1913). His 1913 role in Mario **Caserini**'s decadent melodrama *Ma l'amore mio non muore!* [Love Everlasting], also starring Lyda **Borelli**, launched his career as an indolent young lover modeled after Gabriele **D'Annunzio**'s novels. Unsuccessful with his own short-lived Bonnard Films (1915), after 1917 he directed popular, but unremarkable films, most of them love melodramas, **comedies**, and uncomplicated adaptations of famous novels.

GIORGIO BERTELLINI

Borelli, Lyda

b. 1887; d. 1959

actor, Italy

When Lyda Borelli performed in her first film, *Ma l'amor mio non muore* [Love Everlasting] (**Gloria**, 1913), she already was an acclaimed theatre actress and had played opposite such "monstres sacrés" as Eleonora **Duse**. That film, one of the first **star** vehicles in Italy, launched Borelli as the country's first film diva. Borelli's melodramatic characters, her sophisticated body language, her aristocratic appearance, and her long blonde hair caused women on and off the screen to imitate her in a **fashion** called "borellismo." In 1914, Borelli switched to the **Cines** company, where she performed in such films as *Rapsodia satanica* [Satanic Rhapsody] (1917), for which Pietro Mascagni wrote an original score. In 1918 Borelli married the Venetian count Giorgio Cini and withdrew from the film world.

IVO BLOM

Bos, Annie

b.1886; d. 1975

actor, Netherlands

The dark-eyed and dark-haired Bos was the first and only Dutch diva of the silent film era. She appeared in most of the melodramas produced and directed by Maurits **Binger** at **Hollandia** between 1912 and 1920. After starring in a series of three **comedies** about Mijntje en Trijntje (The Adventures of Mijntje and Trijntje) (1913) directed by Louis Crispijn Sr., she specialized in leading dramatic roles. Her Carmen in *Carmen van het noorden* [A Carmen of the North] (1919) and Jo in *Op hoop van zegen* [The Good Hope] (1918) are among her best performances.

ANSJE VAN BEUSEKOM

Bosetti, Roméo [a.k.a. Bosetti, Romulus Joseph]

b. 1879; d. 1946

actor, filmmaker, France

Bosetti started his film career performing a handful of comic parts for **Pathé-Frères** before being hired by **Gaumont** in March 1906. From 1909 to 1910, he directed Clément **Migé** in the *Calino* series, short burlesques that were so successful that Pathé-Frères hired him away. Given the direction of two production units located in Nice, **Comica** and Nizza, Bosetti specialized in **comic series** such as *Little Moritz* and *Rosalie* (1911–1912), *Roméo* (1912–1913), and *Bigorno* (1912–1914). Wounded in **World War I**, he returned to act in minor roles in the 1920s.

LAURENT LE FORESTIER

Bosworth, Hobart

b. 1867; d. 1943

actor, producer, USA

Born in Ohio, Bosworth had a successful stage acting career before signing with **Selig** in 1907 to act in moving pictures. From 1911 on, he also directed films for Selig, until forming the Bosworth Film Company in 1913 to produce **multiple-reel/feature films** based on the novels of Jack London, most notably *The Sea Wolf* (1926). In 1914, Bosworth handed over production duties to the noted writing/directing team of Lois **Weber** and Philip **Smalley**. That same year Bosworth Film was one of the earliest producers to distribute through Paramount Pictures Corporation.

MICHAEL QUINN

Botelho, Alberto Mâncio

b. 1885, Rio de Janeiro; d. 1973, Rio de Janeiro

photographer, filmmaker, Brazil

One of the first professional filmmakers in Brazil, Botelho had a long and productive career and was wholly responsible for more than 2,000 *actualités*, documentaries, and **newsreels**. After working as a reporter, he associated with Francisco **Serrador** in São Paulo, who provided him with a **Lumière** camera. *Desfile de un tiro de Guerra* [Parade of a War Cry] (1907) made him the best known local cinematographer. Botello shot *actualités*, stage shows and *filmes cantantes* (sung films), represented *Pathé-Journal*, and achieved a journalistic scoop when he filmed a contentious navy uprising, *A revolta da esquadra* [The Rebellion of the Squadron] (1910), the first Brazilian film to be censored. Although he experimented with fiction, Botelho's love was nonfiction, and he was active in the field until his retirement in the 1960s.

ANA M. LÓPEZ

Bourbon, Ernest

b. 1886; d. 1954

actor, France

In 1910, Bourbon became part of *les Pouit(t)es*, a group Jean **Durand** had formed to shoot comic films for **Gaumont**. Given the title role in the *Onésime* **comic series** (1912–1914), Bourbon embodied this romantic, elegant young man in more than sixty films, lending him acrobatic grace. A character who combined naiveté and stubborness, Onésime often ended up shaping the world according to his desires: in *Onésime horloger* [Onésime Clock-maker] (1912), he accelerated the unfolding of time so that he could receive his inheritance sooner. After the war, Bourbon produced a sequel to the series, but without much success.

LAURENT LE FORESTIER

Bourgeois, Gérard

b. 1874; d. 1944

filmmaker, scriptwriter, France

After a career as a stage actor, Gérard Bourgeois became the artistic director at **Lux** in 1908, before joining **Pathé-Frères** in 1911 and then **Éclair** in 1914. During his tenure at Pathé, he directed several films in the *Nick Winter* detective series (1911), starring Georges Vinter, as well as the **multiple-reel** *Les Victimes de l'alcool* [In the Grip of Alchohol] (1911), adapted from Emile Zola's novel, *L'Assommoir*. His work for Éclair included the script for *Protéa II* (1926) and direction of *Protéa IV* (1917), starring Josette **Andriot**. In 1916–1917, Bourgeois went to Spain to shoot *Christophe Colomb*, financed by the Paris Association of Theater Directors and released in two parts in 1919. After the war, he specialized in **serials**.

THIERRY LEFEBVRE

Boutillon, Edmond

b. 1872, Paris; d. 1952, Paris

exhibitor, France

A wine merchant in Vincennes, where **Pathé-Frères** located its first factory and studios, Boutillon occasionally acted in such films as Lucien **Nonguet**'s *Le Chat botté* [Puss in Boots] (1903). Between 1904 and 1907, he became an important **itinerant exhibitor** of Pathé films in several towns around Paris. In 1907, after selling the rights to his exhibition circuit to Cinéma-Exploitation, one of Pathé's concessionary companies, he was hired as the firm's general manager for three districts in the Paris area. On his own, he also constructed four moving picture theaters, including one in Saint-Denis and another on rue de Belleville in Paris. In 1908, he left Cinéma-Exploitation to set up the Casino d'Ivry and Casino de Clichy, the latter of which he sold in 1910 to the Société des Cinémas Modernes, just founded by Edmond **Benoît-Lévy**, who hired him as manager of its suburban Paris theaters. Boutillon retired from the exhibition business in 1929, but he was president of the Société de Secours Mutuel (mutual insurance company of cinema exhibitors) from its founding in 1921 until World War II.

JEAN-JACQUES MEUSY

boxing films

Scenes of boxers were common in early moving pictures, particularly in the USA. Although prize-fights were illegal in many locales, in the 1890s the sport was in ascendancy. Moving pictures brought boxing a wide new audience, while publicized bouts gave producers topical subject matter that was easy to shoot. Promoters also sought motion picture contracts for significant matches, as film profits outstripped gate receipts. Despite the commercial success of prizefight pictures (more than one hundred had been released by 1915), violent content, interracial provocations, and gender politics stigmatized the genre.

Boxing films included three categories: sparring scenes, prizefight recordings, and **re-enactments**. Before the first genuine contest was filmed in 1897, dozens of boxing subjects had already been shot. The majority of these one-shot films recorded sparring performances. A spate of films followed **Edison**'s *Corbett and Courtney before the Kinetograph* (1926), in which champion James J. **Corbett** posed for a well-publicized set of moving pictures taken in the Black Maria studio.

Corbett's popularity led to the first recording of a genuine prizefight. Using specially engineered

cameras, Enoch Rector shot all fourteen rounds of the *Corbett-Fitzsimmons Fight* (1926) in Nevada. Marketed by promoter Dan A. Stuart's Veriscope Company, this **multiple-reel film** toured for five years, earning an estimated $750,000. The film was promoted to female spectators, bringing pugilism to a previously excluded **audience** and stirring debate about the power of the new medium.

Attempts to replicate Veriscope's success met with mixed results. Technical and legal problems interfered with many productions, including attempts by Edison, **Vitagraph** and **American Mutoscope and Biograph** to record the title bouts of heavyweight champion James J. Jeffries (1899–1901). To capitalize on publicized fights, re-enactments proliferated. During 1899–1906, faked film bouts outnumbered actual recordings. The **Lubin** company produced dozens of films such as *Reproduction of the Fitzsimmons-Jeffries Fight* (1926). When location shooting became reliable, the practice ceased. After several years of commercial decline for boxing, prizefight recordings returned to profitability with several multiple-reel films shot by the **Miles Brothers** (1905–1909).

However, the genre reached its zenith during the reign of Jack **Johnson** (1908–1915). The first black heavyweight champion, the controversial Johnson received major film coverage. Interest peaked with the *Jeffries–Johnson Fight* (1926). The **Motion Picture Patents Company** invested $100,000 in the bout, billed as a contest for racial supremacy. When the "white hope" Jeffries lost, white backlash led to frequent censorship of the films. In 1912, Congress banned interstate transportation of prizefight pictures. When Johnson lost to a white challenger in Havana, many expected the USA would ignore the ban for the *Willard–Johnson Fight* (1926). But federal authorities confiscated the pictures when producer Lawrence Weber attempted to import them.

The prohibition of fight film distribution remained on the books until 1940, but was increasingly ignored after 1915.

See also: the law and the cinema; spectatorship: issues and debates; sports films

Figure 15 Frame still from *Corbett-Fitzsimmons Fight* (Veriscope, 1897). (Courtesy of George Eastman House.)

Further reading

Streible, Dan (2002) *Fight Pictures: A History of Boxing and Early Cinema*, Washington: Smithsonian Institution Press.

DAN STREIBLE

Brady, William Aloysius

b. 1863; d. 1950

actor, entrepreneur, producer, author, USA

A flamboyant and influential impresario, Brady was born in San Francisco and spent his early years on the Lower East Side of New York City. In the 1880s, he began acting and touring in his own company; by the 1890s, he was managing several touring companies and, as a fight promoter, two world heavyweight champions, James J. **Corbett** and James J. Jeffries. In 1899, he arranged for **American Mutoscope and Biograph** to film, indoors under artificial lights, the Jeffries-Sharkey bout at the Coney Island Athletic Club. After some years, he returned to producing, writing, and adapting works for the stage and built two Broadway theaters. Around 1906, while still producing plays, Brady partnered with Adolph **Zukor** in operating several **nickelodeons**. In 1915, he became president of the **World Film Corporation**, producing some of his own stage plays with original casts. From 1915 to 1922, he headed the National Association of the Motion Picture Industry. Brady wrote two books about his early career, *The Fighting Man* (1926) and *Showman* (1926). He was the father of Alice Brady, stage and screen actress.

MADELINE F. MATZ

Brazil

The first cinematographic apparatus to arrive in Brazil was the **Edison Kinetoscope**, imported by Argentine Federico Figner and exhibited in Rio de Janeiro in December 1894. The first cinematographic projection proper took place on 8 July 1898, also in Rio de Janeiro, by a French entrepreneur using a modified **Lumière** apparatus dubbed the "Omniógrapho." Contemporary research indicates that the first indigenous films were shot and exhibited in Petrópolis, a summer resort near Rio, on 1 May 1897, by Vittorio de Maio. The program for the show at the Teatro Casino-Fluminense featured European films and four Brazilian scenes: a trapeze artist, a children's dance, the end of the trolley line in Botafogo (Rio), and the arrival of a train at the Petrópolis train station.

Rio de Janeiro was a bustling city, teeming with European immigrants and internal migrants who eagerly sought alternative forms of entertainment (and would contribute greatly to the development of the medium). As elsewhere, exhibition was at first nomadic and sporadic; because entrance fees were significantly lower than in legitimate theaters, the medium quickly gained popular acceptance. As various urban renewal projects took shape (1903–1907), the city nourished a popular sector in which the cinema would thrive among other entertainments.

The first entrepreneurs were the **Segreto** brothers, who invested heavily in the medium and opened the first exhibition locale in Rio de Janeiro. For years, it was believed that Afonso Segreto had shot the first Brazilian images in 1898, although no evidence of a film has been found in the press. He was, however, responsible for the first filming in São Paulo in September 1899. By the turn of the century, the Segretos had their own studio and laboratory. de Maio also inaugurated several exhibition venues, especially in São Paulo (Cinematógrado Paris, 1900), but could not compete with the Segretos' better infrastructure.

Pathé-Frères established a sales agency in Rio early on (with the **Ferrez** company), and later in São Paulo with Alberto **Botelho**. Edison also began to sell apparatuses in Rio and São Paulo, and moving pictures rather quickly took root throughout the entire national territory as pioneer exhibitor-producers emerged in other regions: **Hirtz** in Porto Alegre, de Baños in Belém, **Requião** in Paraná.

From 1906 through 1908, there was continued experimentation and development, spurred by the availability of consistent electrical power in Rio de Janeiro after 1907. Exhibition locales multiplied, with more than 20 in Rio by the end of the year.

Many of these exhibitors turned to production, among them José Labanca, who employed William **Auler** to direct the most spectacular film of the era, *Os estranguladores* [The Stranglers] (1906). The **re-enactment** of a crime shot on locations with a documentary spirit, the film is an early example of narrative construction driven by the chronology of a real event. The popularity of this film (800 screenings in two months) defined the **crime film** as a significant genre of national production and also established a commercial base for further innovation. The genre would prove to be profitable and led to other popular films by Ferrez, Francisco **Serrador**, and others. This was the *bela época* or "golden age" of the Brazilian silent cinema, defined as such by national producers who—aligned with or themselves exhibitors—came to dominate the film market for the first (and last) time in Brazilian film history. In addition to crime films, *filmes cantados* (*filmes cantantes*), domestic **melodramas**, and literary and theatrical adaptations also played an important role as popular national films. The epoch is marked by a series of "firsts." The first Brazilian fiction film, *Nhô Anastacio chegou de viagem* [Mr. Anastacio Arrived from a Trip] was directed by Julio Ferrez in 1908. A picaresque tale about the exploits of a newly arrived immigrant to Rio, this short film exhibited a distinct *carioca* sensibility, featuring its most recognizable locations and gently sarcastic humor. The first literary adaptation was *A cabana do Pai Tomás* [Uncle Tom's Cabin] (1909) directed by Antonio Serra, which included images of Brazilian abolitionist leaders in its last tableaux. The first **multiple-reel/feature film** was João Stamato's *Imigração e comércio* [Immigration and Commerce] (1910).

At the same time, a battle was being waged among those in the business to become the representatives of prestigious European producers; it was a big coup for Giacomo Staffa, for example, to become the sole representative in Brazil in 1910, of **Italia**, **Filme d'Arte Italiana**, and **Nordisk**. In 1911, by contrast, Serrador created the exhibition trust Companhia Cinematográfica Brasileira and achieved vertical integration in association with American capital and distributors which privileged imported films. National audiences, perhaps exhausted by the dominance of crimes and music, but also seduced by the novelty of the different narrative strategies and the **star system** developing in US cinema, soon came to choose the new imported films which were shown in bigger and better theaters. National producers gradually closed their doors (many switched to commissioned documentary and **newsreel** production); distribution became the key to the business. After a production average of 80 films per year between 1908 and 1910, eight fiction films were produced in 1912, and only three in 1913. The "golden age" was essentially over. In Rio, production continued throughout 1913–1914 and thereafter, but with inconsistent financing and success. Perhaps the most significant figure of the period was Luiz **de Barros**, who would produce more than 60 features throughout his long career, working in every genre, but especially literary adaptations such as *Ubirajara* (1926), from José de Alencar's novel.

São Paulo was then the most prosperous region in the country (coffee and industrialization) with a vast immigrant working class that developed a rich theatrical tradition and nourished the cinema after 1915. Although few fiction films were produced, documentary and newsreel productions flourished. Filmmakers such as Antônio **Campos**, Gilberto **Rossi** and José **Medina** managed to sustain sufficient commissioned documentary and newsreel production to finance a significant number of fiction films (about 50 in the 1920s), many of them adaptations of national literary and patriotic themes. Among these, Medina and Rossi's *O exemplo regenerador* [The Regenerative Example] (1919) was significant for demonstrating the filmmakers' mastery of continuity editing à la D. W. **Griffith** circa 1910.

Of greater significance in the late 1910s were the various cycles that began to emerge throughout the provinces—Minas Gerais, Recife, Amazônia, Cataguases, Pelotas—that eventually produced some of the most interesting work of the silent period in the late 1920s: Humberto Mauro, for example, whose career would flourish with sound.

See also: electricity; migration/immigration

Further reading

Araújo, Vincente de Paula (1976) *A Bela época do cinema brasileiro*, São Paulo: Perspectiva.

Galvão, Maria Rita (1987) "Le Muet," in Paulo
Antônio Paranaguá (ed.) *Le cinema Brasilien,*
51–64, Paris: Editions du Centre Pompidou.
Gonzaga, Alice. (1996) *Palácios e poeiras,* Rio de
Janaeiro: FUNARTE.
Ramos, Fernão (ed.) (1987) *História do cinema
brasileiro,* São Paulo: Art Editora.
Ramos, Fernão and Luiz Felipe Miranda (eds.)
(2000) *Enciplopédia do cinema brasiliero,* São
Paulo: Editora Senac.

ANA M. LÓPEZ

Breteau

b. 1865; d. ?

actor, scriptwriter, director, France

Breteau and Georges **Hatot** met at the Théâtre des
Menus-Plaisirs (headed by André Antoine), and
both became walk-on coordinators for Firmin
Gémier at the Odéon (1894–1896). Breteau then
worked as an actor, scriptwriter, and director in
more than fifty films for the three main French
manufacturers: **Lumière**, between 1897 and 1898
(*Assassinat du duc de Guise, Vie et Passion de Jésus-
Christ*—in which he played the part of Christ);
Gaumont in 1898 (*Chez le magnétiseur* [At the
Magnetic Healer's], *Scène d'escamotage* [A Filch-
ing]; and **Pathé-Frères** between 1899 and 1904
(*Vie et Passion de Notre Seigneur Jésus-Christ, Histoire d'un crime* with Ferdinand **Zecca**). No trace of
his later activities survives.

MAURICE GIANATI

Brézillon, Léon

b. 1870; d. 1936

exhibitor, trade association leader, France

A charismatic and colorful figure in the Syndicat
français des Directeurs de Théâtres cinématographiques (French Trade Association of Film
Theater Owners), over which he presided from
1912 to 1931, Brézillon led several vigorous
corporate actions defending exhibitors' interests.

In March 1912, he organized the first Congrès
International des Exploitants du Cinématographe
(International Conference of Film Exhibitors) in
the reception halls of the Palais des Fêtes, the large
moving picture theater he had opened in 1910 near
Les Halles in Paris (its two halls had a total of
2,000 seats). That same year, he also founded a
music publishing company, La Liberté musicale,
and a trade weekly, *L'Ecran.*

JEAN-JACQUES MEUSY

British and Colonial Kinematograph Company

British and Colonial Kinematograph (B&C) was
established in 1908 by Albert Bloomfield, former
head of **Walturdaw**'s darkroom, and John
Benjamin McDowell, the company's former chief
cameraman. They began producing **news event
films** and short dramas, using one camera and a
rented basement in central London, and developing their films in McDowell's house. Soon they
could afford to move to larger premises, and, in
March 1910, B&C received a major commission to
film the Canadian Pacific Railway. McDowell
returned in time to film the funeral of Edward VII
in May 1910.

Although best known for news filming, the
company expanded its fiction production by renting a large house in East Finchley and building a
50-foot daylight studio. B&C now became known
for such series as the *Lieutenant Daring* films (from
1911) and the *Dick Turpin* and *Don Q* films (from
1912). B&C also was noted for its location
shooting when, in 1912, Bloomfield took a film
unit to Jamaica.

In May 1913, Bloomfield left for the Broadwest
Film Company, but McDowell pressed ahead with
an ambitious **multiple-reel/feature film** project.
He used hundreds of extras and re-mortgaged the
company to produce *The Battle of Waterloo* (1926),
which proved very successful worldwide. In October, B&C opened a second, larger studio in Wal-
thamstow.

After the outbreak of war in 1914, B&C made
several patriotic films, but greater efforts were put
into news film production. In October 1915, B&C

was one of several companies to take over British filming on the Western Front; in June 1916, McDowell left to become an official cameraman. Meanwhile, B&C's fictional production declined.

NICHOLAS HILEY

British Gaumont

Gaumont established a British agency in 1897, under John Le Couteur, that flourished once Alfred Bromhead took over in 1898. Although its business was dominated by French films and equipment, the British company distributed native production, handling the work of **Clarendon**, **Mitchell & Kenyon**, William **Haggar** and others, and made its own fiction films (mostly comic **chase films**), directed by Alf **Collins**. British Gaumont became most identified with **news event films**, notably the *Gaumont Graphic* **newsreel** which began in 1910. Bromhead bought out the French interests in 1922, and in 1927 the company reformed as the Gaumont British Picture Corporation, eventually becoming part of the Rank empire.

See also: distribution: Europe

LUKE McKERNAN

British Mutoscope and Biograph

The Mutoscope and Biograph Syndicate Ltd., a British-financed branch of the **American Mutoscope Co.,** was incorporated 21 July 1897 to produce and distribute the latter company's films outside North America. Elias B. Koopman was business manager with W. K. L. **Dickson** in charge of production. Throughout Europe, Biograph films were exhibited at prominent **vaudeville** theaters and **music halls** and shown on the company's peep-show Mutoscopes. To provide local fare, films also were made by other branch companies in several European countries. Production was active from 1897 until 1903, but then slowed and came to an end in 1905. The company disbanded in 1908.

PAUL SPEHR

Brown, Theodore

b. 1870, Salisbury; d. 1938, London

inventor, journalist, England

An indefatigable inventor, Brown was obsessed with his patented idea of 3-D moving pictures made with an oscillating camera, previewed in 1903 but never perfected. In 1904, he re-launched the defunct *Optical Magic Lantern Journal* as the *Optical Lantern and Cinematograph Journal*, serving as editor until he went bankrupt in 1907. Four years later he patented an English version of the Kinoplastikon (originating in Germany); combining a real stage set with filmed actors, this modern "Pepper's Ghost" enjoyed some success at London's Scala Theatre. Brown also devised the ill-fated Spirograph, a home projector using acetate discs, many optical toys, and successful pop-up books.

STEPHEN HERBERT

Brulatour, Jules E.

b. 1870, New Orleans; d. 1946, New York City

sales agent, financier, USA

Beginning in 1909, Brulatour acted as **Lumière**'s representative in the USA, supplying negative film stock to the independent manufacturers. Two years later he convinced George **Eastman** to make him the principal sales agent for **Eastman Kodak**'s negative, and quickly made a fortune. Brulatour served as a more or less "silent partner" in a number of major companies, among them the **Motion Picture Distributing and Sales Company**, **Universal Film Manufacturing**, and **World Film Corporation**, where he arranged financing for Maurice **Tourneur**'s initial American films.

RICHARD ABEL

Buckwalter, Harry H.

b. 1867; d. 1930

photographer, exhibitor, filmmaker, USA

A resident of Denver from the age of 16, Buckwalter went into the **newspaper** business and became the city's first press photographer. He developed an interest in moving pictures around 1900, and soon became Colorado's first established filmmaker. He was filming ranching and Native American scenes by 1902, and even experimenting with fictional subjects. Buckwalter's films of Colorado were distributed by **Selig** from 1903, and he continued to film *actualités* to promote the state and its railways. He made a number of trips to Latin America, beginning in 1904, and filmed the Panama Canal under construction in 1913. He also became an important exhibitor in Colorado in the early years, was ever interested in new technologies (introducing X-rays to Denver), and was involved in aviation, automobiles, and radio (he operated Denver's first radio station).

Further reading

Jones, W. (1990). "Harry Buckwalter: pioneer Colorado filmmaker," *Film History*, 4.2: 89–100.

STEPHEN BOTTOMORE

Bull, Lucien

b. 1876; d. 1972

scientific filmmaker, France

An assistant of Etienne-Jules **Marey** beginning in 1896, the Irish-born Bull accepted a permanent position at the Marey Institute in 1902. He first worked on stop-motion, then dedicated his efforts to the opposite technique, fast-motion, and came up with extremely innovative systems. By combining electrical sparks, a lens with a rotating prism, and fast 35mm film, Bull recorded at a rate of 800 images/second, as in *Vol d'une mouche ordinaire* [Flight of a Common Fly] (1903), then at 2,000 images/second (1905). By increasing the frequency of sparks, Bull achieved rates of 15,000 images/second in *Décharge d'un revolver* [Firing a Gun] (1914) and finally reached a rate of one million images/second in the late 1940s, with *L'onde de choc* [Shockwave]. The technique he had developed in the first years of the century still is in use in some nuclear research laboratories today.

See also: scientific films: Europe

LAURENT MANNONI

Bunny, John

b. 1863 [possibly 1856], New York; d. 1915, New York

actor, USA

John Bunny was the most beloved early American screen comedian. He made his professional acting debut in 1883, and later worked in every phase of show business. He joined **Vitagraph** on 24 October 1910, and during his years with the company, his salary went from $40 to $1,000 per week. In 1914–1915, he attempted to become a legitimate stage star, but without success; if he made little impression as a stage attraction, film fans regarded Bunny as the best the movies had to offer.

See also: comic series; Finch, Flora

ROBERT S. BIRCHARD

Bünzli, Henri René

b. 1876; d. ?

inventor, craftsman, manufacturer, France

The graduate of a clockmaking school, Bünzli attended one of the first shows of the **Cinématographe Lumière** and, on November 14, 1896, registered a patent with his associate Victor **Continsouza** for a reversible **camera** equipped with a "Maltese cross." In 1897, manufacturer Claude Grivolas took over Bünzli and Continsouza's workshops and founded the Manufacture française d'appareils de précisions, which then was absorbed by **Pathé-Frères** in August 1900. Thanks to Bünzli and Continsouza, Pathé could sell excellent Maltese-cross **projectors** as early as 1897. The 'Maltese cross' system soon was copied by manufacturers around the world and is still in use today. Bünzli himself created an independent company manufacturing precision appliances in 1914.

LAURENT MANNONI

Burguet, Charles

b. 1872; d. 1957

filmmaker, France

After acting on stage for ten years, Burguet briefly managed the Théâtre Réjane in Paris and then directed shows at several casinos in the south of France. In 1912, he founded his own company, Films d'Azur, in Nice, where he produced and directed more than a dozen films, starring Regina Badet, over the next two years. After the war, he and René Le Somptier were hired by Louis **Nalpas**, to direct *La Sultane de l'amour* [The Sultan of Love] (1919) at what would become the Victorine studio near Nice. Burguet went on to direct **serials**, establish a second production company (1925–1929), and preside over the Société des Auteurs des Films (Society of Film Directors) (1925–1940).

RICHARD ABEL

Burlingham, Frederick

b. 1877; d. 1924?

cameraman, France, Switzerland

A red-bearded eccentric born in Baltimore, from the early years of the 20th century Burlingham was based in Paris, where he wrote for US **newspapers**. He was a keen Alpinist and became an equally keen filmmaker: he ascended the Matterhorn in 1913, and his film of the climb attracted great public interest. Early the following year he filmed his descent into the crater of Vesuvius, which drew even wider attention. In 1915, he founded his own company in Switzerland, and produced several mountaineering and other films. Leaving Europe in 1918, he continued filming as a "globe-trotting" cameraman, from the southern USA to the Far East, especially Borneo. In total he may have made as many as sixty films, some of which were deposited at the American Museum of Natural History (New York) and the Field Museum (Chicago).

See also: travelogues

STEPHEN BOTTOMORE

Bush, W. Stephen

b.? d.?

journalist, critic, lecturer, editor, USA

From 1908 to 1916, Bush wrote articles, film reviews, and critical observations for **Moving Picture World**. While he respected the value of original screenplays, he especially championed adaptations of the classics for the screen in order to promote lofty aesthetic values and high educational standards. He himself served as a **lecturer** around Philadelphia and New York for prestigious films based on the works of **Shakespeare**, Dickens, and others and for notable foreign imports such as **Pathé-Frères**' *Passion Play* and **Milano**'s *Dante's Inferno*. An active opponent of state censorship boards and local censorship groups, Bush advocated a self-regulating board, different from the **National Board of Censorship**, made up solely of manufacturers, exchange men, and exhibitors. From January 1917 to March 1918, he served as editor of *Exhibitors Trade Review*.

MADELINE F. MATZ

Bushman, Francis X.

b. 1883; d. 1966

actor, USA

One of the American screen's first sex symbols, Francis X. Bushman was hired by the **Essanay Film Manufacturing Company** in 1911, after many years as an itinerant actor and artist's model. In 1912, he teamed professionally with actress Beverly Bayne and the pair enjoyed great success in a series of formulaic love stories. In 1915, they moved to Fred J. **Balshofer**'s Quality Pictures, releasing feature-length films through Metro. The team's popularity declined quickly after the public discovered they were married, and Bushman soon was relegated to bit parts, most notably as Messala in Fred Niblo's *Ben-Hur* (1926).

STEVEN HIGGINS

Butcher's Film Service

William Butcher established Butcher's as a photographic business in 1896; by the following year, W. Butcher & Son was dealing in cinematographic supplies, with a factory in Blackheath, London. Some film production was undertaken, but the firm chiefly sold equipment. Butcher committed suicide in 1903, and the business was headed thereafter by F. W. Baker, who turned it into Butcher's Film Service. Primarily a renting concern, Butcher's also produced some *actualités* and, during the war, moved into producing **multiple-reel/feature films**. Butcher's stayed on the fringes of film production to the 1940s, and in one form or other remained in business until very recently.

LUKE McKERNAN

C

Cabanne, W. Christy

b. 1888, St Louis; d. 1950, Philadelphia

actor, director, USA

W. Christy Cabanne (pronounced Ca-ban-ay) learned his craft working with D. W. **Griffith**. After a hitch in the Navy prior to going on stage, he joined the **Biograph Company** in 1910, and remained with Griffith through his moves to the **Reliance**, **Majestic**, and Fine Arts companies. In the late 1910s, he connected with Metro, and later worked at nearly every studio in a long, slowly declining career that ended on poverty row. However, he was a better director than many of his later credits would seem to indicate.

ROBERT S. BIRCHARD

cafés-concerts

In France, up to 1906, theaters devoted exclusively to moving pictures were few. In Paris and other large cities, moving pictures were screened mostly in cafés-concerts and **music halls**.

During the last two decades of the 19th century, cafés-concerts (caf'conc') multiplied both in the center of major cities and in their outlying neighborhoods. A show at a café-concert would unfold according to specific conventions. The orchestra opened with stirring tunes. Most of the program was comprised of singers who would generally perform two songs each; these were often risqué, and their subject matter was frequently related to military life. Following the songs (although this was not always the case), comic artists, acrobats, dialogists, or dancers performed attractions. After an intermission, the show usually would end with a one-act play, often a comic vaudeville. French music halls followed the tradition of cafés-concerts, yet their programs involved more attractions and fewer songs. As variety revues became the fashion, their place in the program grew in importance.

In 1900, *Le Nouvelliste des Concerts, Cirques et Music-Halls* defined the café-concert as follows: "Lights, music, and women, in a usually packed theater, on whose seats you could digest your dinner, entertained by the scene, a cigar in your mouth and a glass in front of you; a place where the spectators' daily worries, like the smoke from their cigars, vanish for an evening: that's what the Café-concert is . . . ."

Moving pictures did not have a set place in these programs, but they frequently occurred in the middle or at the end. Several films were shown so as to provide an interlude of about ten minutes. Like other numbers in the program, the screenings were put together by an outside service contracted for a specific period. In large cities, some businesses specializing in screenings would set up in the same theater for extended periods of time. In Paris, for instance, beginning in 1901, Georges **Froissart** (American Vitograph) worked with the Eldorado for twelve years or so. Beginning in October 1905, Georges Petit (Booston-Vio) was responsible for screenings at the Etoile-Palace for nearly three years. American Vitograph had enough equipment and personnel to be in charge of screenings simultaneously in several locations in Paris, in provincial cities, and even abroad. Other businesses were much more limited and shared certain similarities with **itinerant exhibitors**: they owned all the projection equipment needed, including the films, but lacked the premises. However, they did not systematically tour places they had booked in advance (as did itinerant exhibitors) and charged a one-time contract fee rather than collect any of the receipts. The difference between these two types of exhibition, however, was not always so clear-cut, especially in the provinces.

Screenings in cafés-concerts peaked around 1905–1908, before declining with the emergence of permanent moving picture theaters. As a certain loss of interest in cafés-concerts occurred, some of them even turned into moving picture theaters. Such screenings disappeared almost completely by **World War I**.

Further reading

Meusy, Jean-Jacques (1995) *Paris-Palaces, ou le temps des cinémas (1894–1918)*, Paris: CNRS Editions.

JEAN-JACQUES MEUSY

Calcina, Vittorio

b. 1847; d. 1916

photographer, cameraman, exhibitor, inventor, Italy

In 1896, Turinese photographer Vittorio Calcina was **Lumière**'s agent for Northern Italy and the owner of the first Italian movie theater. After making several *actualités* about Italy's reigning nobility, he became the royal family's authorized

Figure 16 Café-concert "Kursaal", Paris. Behind the rows of benches can be seen small tables where drinks could be ordered. Photo Bernard Chevojon.

operator as he filmed formal events, ceremonies, and official visits. Between 1908 and 1911, he devised an apparatus consisting of camera, printing machine, and projector that used a special film stock format, smaller than the established 35 mm gauge. Called *Cine Parvus*, it failed to gain widespread commercial exploitation, unlike Pathé Baby, a similar product profitably launched in 1922.

GIORGIO BERTELLINI

Calmettes, André

b. 1861; d. 1942

filmmaker, France

Between the spring and fall of 1908, Calmettes organized shooting on the first three dramas released by **Film d'Art**, under the artistic direction of Charles **Le Bargy**: *L'Assassinat du duc de Guise* [The Assassination of the Duke de Guise] (1908), *Le Retour d'Ulysse* [The Return of Ulysses] (1909), and *Le Baiser de Judas* [The Kiss of Judas] (1909). Between the time of the **Laffitte** management's departure and the takeover of the company by Agence générale de cinématographie (**AGC**), he was the main director for Film d'Art, most notably on *Madame Sans-Gêne* (1911). In 1913, he still directed *Les Trois Mousquetaires* [The Three Musketeers], his longest **multiple-reel/feature film** for the company.

ALAIN CAROU

Cambodia

During the period of early cinema, the region today known as Cambodia was under a French Protectorate, forming part of the larger colonial administrative unit of Indochina. During the early 1900s, local audiences began to attend screenings of foreign films while Protectorate Cambodia became a subject for foreign cinematographers. No films were made by Cambodians themselves, however, until the late 1940s and early 1950s.

As a European technological innovation of the late 19th and early 20th centuries, cinema seems to have first come to Cambodia in 1909. But if we think of cinema as a lighted screen on which stories are told, then it could be said that Cambodia already had a long-standing tradition of such narratives since troupes of shadow puppeteers had for centuries brought stories to life through the movement of pricked leather images projected on screens set in front of blazing fires. These shadow puppet theaters retrospectively were dubbed *kon Khmer* or "Khmer cinema," thus underscoring the similarities between modern cinema and older local forms of performance.

Early 20th-century Cambodia was filled with encounters between existing local practices and unfamiliar technologies brought from abroad. Under colonial rule, goods, images, and ideas infiltrated and affected the region. The introduction of moving pictures was part of this colonial influx. Records in the National Archives of Cambodia indicate that the French entrepreneur Brignon established a riverside cinema in the capital city of Phnom Penh in October 1909. The Brignon Cinema probably was simply an open air projection stand or a roofed but open enclosure. Although this venue seems to have been frequented primarily by the small European population of the city, moving pictures soon were being shown to local **audiences** since the cinema was thought to be an exemplary tool by which colonial authorities could publicize French culture and France itself to their colonial subjects. By 1914, evenings of short French **comedies**, **travelogues**, and **scientific films** were being presented to Cambodian students from a range of schools in Phnom Penh. Film viewing quickly spread throughout Cambodia. Letters from the provinces in the early 1920s indicate that several **itinerant exhibitors** were traveling through the countryside, showing a variety of French, American, and Chinese films.

The rapid spread of cinema not only in Cambodia but throughout Indochina was considered a mixed blessing by colonial authorities. Although top French officials considered the cinema as "a marvelous tool for intellectual and moral education," they soon realized that it could also have negative effects on what they called the "rather impressionable heads of the youth." By 1921, censoring commissions had been established in Saigon and Hanoi to control the films that could be shown in Indochina. The concerns of colonial authorities seem to have focused on the import of "Bolshevik" and other kinds of "revolutionary propaganda."

By the 1920s, films also began to be shot in Cambodia, although exclusively by foreign cinematographers. The majority seem to have been documentaries which presented the region as both an exotic tourist destination and a successful example of French colonial policy to audiences at the frequent Colonial Exhibitions held in France and Indochina throughout the 1920s and 1930s. More extravagant projects included the **re-enactment** filming of a historical procession at Angkor intended for screening at the 1922 Colonial Exposition in Marseilles. By the late 1920s, a small number of fictional films by French film-makers were at least being proposed for filming in Cambodia: e.g., Jacques Feyder's "Le Roi lépreux."

See also: colonialism: Europe; shadow plays; Vietnam

Further reading

Muan, Ingrid and Ly Daravuth (2000) "A survey of film in Cambodia," in David Hanan (ed.) *Film in Southeast Asia: Views from the Region*, Hanoi: SEAPAVAA/Vietnam Film Institute.

INGRID MUAN

camera movement

Camera movement has generally been subordinated in filmmaking and film theory to **editing** as a way of changing camera viewpoint. This is as true in the era of early cinema as it has been throughout most of film history. However, close examination of films from different periods within early cinema reveals that in a number of contexts camera movement played an unusually important role. Although special apparatuses for moving the camera, such as dollies and tracks, generally did not appear until the very end of the period of early cinema—for instance, the camera transports designed for Giovanni **Pastrone**'s *Cabiria* (1914)—a variety of means for moving the camera were found prior to the mid-1910s, including mounting films on various modes of

transportation (boats, trains, automobiles, even wheel chairs). Yet the must frequently encountered camera movement during the era of early film remains the simple pan, pivoting the camera from left to right. Camera movement appeared most often in non-fiction films, defining one of the key genres of early cinema, the **phantom train ride** film, in which the camera reproduces the movement through space that a rider would experience in a trolley car, railway carriage, or automobile. These elaborate tracking shots were sometimes integrated into fictional films, and occasional films after 1908 make use of extended pans, or tracks, especially films in the early 1910s by such directors as Pastrone, or Evgenii **Bauer**.

As *actualité* filmmaking dominated the output of many film companies before 1906, most examples of early camera movement appear in nonfiction. Traditionally, the origin of camera movement is assigned to **Lumière** cameraman Alexandre **Promio** with an 1897 film of the Venice Grand Canal shot from a moving boat. Whether or not this was the *first* example of a mobile camera (always a dubious claim in early cinema, given how many films no longer exist), there is no question that the idea of placing a camera on a moving vehicle occurred to a number of cameramen. Practically any vehicle that moved was used in such films. Railway trains were especially popular, and films of trains going through tunnels were shot by Lumière, **Edison**, **American Mutoscope and Biograph**, and many other companies. But extraordinary films were also shot from unusual forms of transportation such as the titanic industrial transports moving through a modern factory in AM&B's Westinghouse films from 1904, or intimate views of children in an Indochinese village racing after the camera in a rolling chair held by Lumière cameraman Gabriel **Veyre** in 1897.

If the defining feature of cinema during the novelty period lay in portraying movement, films that could maximize this movement were especially prized. Films of locomotives—Edison's *Black Diamond Express* (1895), Lumière's *Arrival of a Train at the Station* (1895), AM&B's *Empire Express*—moving towards the camera had especially excited audiences. It made sense to intensify the experience by placing the camera on the moving vehicle itself. Promio explained his decision to place a camera on a moving boat in this manner. Whatever audience reactions to these films may have been, their fascination is unquestionable. One reviewer spoke of the effect as almost hypnotic, describing his attention as being held as if in a vice of fate, as "an unseen energy swallows up space." Undoubtedly, camera movement endowed objects and locations with a greater solidity and an appearance of three dimensions. Noël Burch argues that the identification of the spectator with the point of view of the camera in these phantom rides set up a central spectator relation used in all of cinema to follow. Charles Musser has described this experience as the "spectator as passenger" convention and indicated its importance in the early **travelogue**.

Many such films were designed to reproduce the viewpoint of a tourist, whether from a train, a boat, or the elevator ascending the Eiffel Tower. Transporting the viewer through space simulated the literal experience of travel (it is no coincidence that the tracking shot is often referred to as a "traveling shot"). Simulated travel formed a basic attraction of **world's fairs** and **amusement parks** at the turn of the last century, usually accomplished by other means than films, primarily moving panoramas—enormous lengths of canvas painted to represent landscapes which were unrolled to simulate voyages. Thus the fascination with portrayed movement (what Anne Friedberg has termed "the virtual mobile gaze") definitely preceded film, as moving panoramas had appeared in the middle of the 19th century. The 1900 Paris Exposition included several elaborate moving panoramas, to simulate voyages along the Mediterranean or through Russia and Siberia. The application of these forms to cinema was more or less natural, although they often encountered technical problems. The most ambitious example, the Cinéorama designed by Raoul **Grimoin-Sanson** for the 1900 Exposition, attempted to project overlapping films taken from aerial balloons within a 360 degree screening space in which audience members were seated in a mock-up of a balloon's gondola. However, the Cinéorama never actually opened due to technical problems and perceived fire dangers.

Although first appearing in 1897, phantom rides eventually led to a scheme of film exhibition that premiered in 1904, known as **Hale's Tours**. The innovation of Hale's Tours consisted of presenting films shot from trains within a screening room that was constructed to resemble a train car. This attraction had various degrees of elaboration, some even involving a short actual train ride. Most relied on the movement portrayed in the film for their illusion of motion, aided by the realism of the surroundings, a ticket taker and **lecturer** dressed as a train conductor, a mechanically induced swaying of the train compartment, and **sound effects** which added to the illusion of being on an actual train. Although their popularity was brief, it was substantial, and in many cities Hale's Towers were the first theaters that showed moving pictures outside of **vaudeville** programs, thus opening the way for the **nickelodeon** theaters that followed them.

If phantom ride films derived from the moving panoramas of the 19th century, the more common if less spectacular form of camera movement, the pan (short for "panorama"), takes its name from the older form, although in this case the stationary panorama, the painted canvases of landscapes and battles which encircled a spectator. Very early on (Barry Salt attributes the first "real" panning head camera to Robert W. **Paul** in 1897, designed to allow more flexible filming of Queen Victoria's Diamond Jubilee) **cameras** were fitted with moveable heads that allowed them to pivot in either direction (although the smoothness of this operation depended on both the camera mount and the skill of the operator). While a few 360-degree panorama shots do exist, most panorama shots consist of an arc of 180 degrees or less. The initial use of these was for picturesque landscapes, increasing the range of the camera frame by panning across an expansive location.

Camera movement also was integrated into narrative films. The most frequent camera movement was the pan, generally used to follow the movement of characters as they reached the limits of the frame, as in AM&B's *Love in the Suburbs* (1900), a single shot film in which the camera somewhat jerkily follows a woman and her would-be suitors as they walk to the left of the frame. Pans reframe action most frequently in films shot in exteriors, such as Edison's *The Great Train Robbery* (1903) or **Pathé-Frères**' *Indiens et cow-boys* [Indians and Cowboys] (1904). Less frequently, pans appear in scenes shot within studio sets, but a number of Pathé films using elaborate sets do use pans, such as *Les Martyrs de l'Inquisition* [Christian Martyrs] and *La Poule aux oeufs d'or* [The Hen with the Golden Eggs] (both 1905). Upon occasion, these pans do not follow character movement, but rather lead the spectator's attention to a narratively important action, as in Edwin S. **Porter**'s *Stolen by Gypsies* (1904).

The tracking shots so remarkable in phantom rides, while not disappearing entirely, became rather rare in fiction films. A few titles from 1906, during the height of the popularity of Hale's Tours, integrated tracking shots from locomotives into fictional films, such as AM&B's *Hold-up on the Rocking Mountain Express*, although the sense of a discontinuous pastiche between the two forms is very strong. Tracking shots in front of a moving vehicle also appear in such films as Edison's *Boarding School Girls* (1905). In these cases the camera was mounted on either an automobile or a train. A pair of **facial expression films** from AM&B, *Hooligan in Jail* (1903) and *Subject for Rogues Gallery* (1904), used camera movements which move progressively (and smoothly) closer to the characters, emphasizing their expressions. We know from photographs of AM&B's earlier rooftop studio that tracks were used for changing camera position, but we have no other example of the camera actually filming this movement.

In the period of increased dominance of fiction films, after 1906 or so, camera movement rarely dominates a film; the development of this aspect of style never matches the elaboration of editing during this period. However, even in the work of a master editor like D. W. **Griffith** there are strong uses of camera movement, especially in 1909. A pair of remarkable pans sweeping over the valley of Stillwater that open and close *The Country Doctor*, bracket the film in a lyrical circularity, while an elaborate panning shot moves back and forth across a mountainside location and picks up a number of actions in a Civil War film, *In Old Kentucky*. Charlie Keil finds that, in the period from 1908 to 1913, pans occur in about 25% of American films, becoming increasingly frequent from 1911, and especially frequent in films from the **Lubin** studio. Shots from moving trains and automobiles appear in films of this period: for instance, while Pathé's *Nick Winter: le pickpocket mystifié* [The Mysterious Pickpocket] (1911) slowly marches the handcuffed detective through several city streets in one long take, Griffith repeatedly tracks rapidly alongside a charging locomotive in *A Girl and her Trust* (1912). Cameras in a fast-moving automobile also form an exciting and visually innovative sequence in Lois **Weber**'s extraordinary *Suspense* (1913) as well as in Léonce **Perret**'s *Main de fer: L'Evasion de forçat de Croze* [The Iron Hand: Convict de Croze's Escape] (1913).

However, the principle innovation in camera movement comes in the first **multiple-reel/feature films**, as tracking shots moving through dramatic space take on new roles. George Loan Tucker's early feature *Traffic in Souls* (1913) presents a climactic shot which tracks past the villains of the film in jail. Maurice **Tourneur**'s *The Wishing Ring* (1914) also climaxes with a circular pan around a happy wedding party. These films recognize the tour de force nature of camera movement and use it as a culminating image, rather than simply following action.

The most through use of camera movement in the early feature era comes from Europe with the systematic use of oblique tracking shots in Pastrone's epic of the Roman empire, *Cabiria* (1914). Here the camera movement frequently has an independence from the action and moves across the playing area, largely, it was claimed at the time, to increase a sense of the third dimension and to underscore the spectacular nature of the sets. Rather than being reserved for a climactic shot, the tracking shots here (operating on a mechanical system devised by Segundo de **Chomón**, former master of **trick films** at Pathé) are sprinkled throughout. The other great exploiter of the tracking shot, the Russian director Evgenii Bauer, liberates camera movement from character movement to explore interior spaces, as in *Twilight of a Woman's Soul* (1913), or track down deserted city streets in *Day Dreams* (1915).

See also: dioramas and panoramas

Further reading

Friedberg, Anne (1993) *Window Shopping: Cinema and the Post Modern*, Berkeley: University of California Press.

Gartenberg, Jon (1982) "Camera Movement in Edison and Biograph Films 1900–1906," in Roger Holman (ed.) *Cinema 1900/1906: An Analytic Study*, 169–180, Brussels: FIAF.

Keil, Charlie (2001) *Early American Cinema in Transition: Story, Style and Filmmaking 1907–1913*, Madison: University of Wisconsin Press.

Musser, Charles (1984) "The Travel Genre in 1903–1904: Moving towards Fictional Narrative," *Iris*, 2: 47–60.

Salt, Barry (1983) *Film Style and Technology: History and Analysis*, London: Starword.

TOM GUNNING

cameras

Work in **chronophotography** after the mid-1870s advanced camera technology able to record sequential images of movement so that, when rolls of photosensitive film became available in 1888, many experimenters were encouraged to work on what would become moving picture cameras. In the first years, however, cameras were scarce and the supply of positive films was both expensive and limited, particularly compared to the plethora of cinematographic **projectors** that flooded the market from mid-1896 on.

With two exceptions, chronophotographic cameras were built to analyze or arrest movement for scientific or didactic purposes. Etienne-Jules **Marey**'s film band camera of 1888 and its improved versions of 1889 and 1891, plus Georges **Demenÿ**'s beater movement addition (1894) to his camera of 1893 are examples, along with Ernst Kohlrausch's cameras of 1892 and *c.* 1894, and Victor von Reitzner's intriguing intermittent camera of 1891. The first exception was Ottomar **Anschütz**'s second chronophotographic camera of 1887: still using multiple plates and lenses and not paper or **celluloid** bands, this complex apparatus was equipped with sophisticated shutters and elaborate adjustments to record "closed" movements, or repetitive motion where the first and last images would match so they could be reproduced in a zoetrope or in Anschütz's own disk exhibition machine, the Schnellseher. The second exception was Thomas **Edison** and William K. L. **Dickson**'s camera (1888–1892) that produced films for the peep-show **Kinetoscope**, intended from the first, like the Anschütz camera, as part of an integrated moving picture display system.

The imprecise boundary between chronophotographic developments and the first avowed moving picture experiments is well illustrated by the successful cameras of Louis Aimé Augustin **Le Prince** and Wordsworth **Donisthorpe**, from which only six and ten frames, respectively, survive; their attempts to build projectors, however, floundered. George William **de Bedts** was more successful, incorporating von Reitzner's intermittent in a camera/projector that was ready in late 1895 and sold publicly from February 1896 on. The most famous of these early devices was the elegantly compact **Cinématographe Lumière**, developed throughout 1895 and publicly exhibited on 28 December. A combination camera, projector and printer, the business model of the Cinématographe, much like the **Eastman Kodak** system, was intended as moving picture hardware for popular use, so as to expand Lumière's principal activity as a manufacturer of photographic

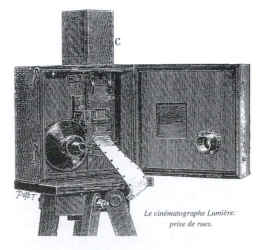

Le cinématographe Lumière: prise de rues.

Figure 17 Cinématographe Lumière in use as a camera, from *La Nature*, 1896.

supplies. But by the time the Cinématographe was finished, Lumière was challenged by a host of new inventors with moving picture apparatuses for public entertainment—the **Latham** brothers, Thomas **Armat** and C. Francis **Jenkins**, Herman Casler, Birt **Acres**, Robert **Paul**, de Bedts, Henri **Joly**, Demenÿ, and others.

Some early filmmakers improvised cameras from early projection apparatuses, or copied briefly glimpsed cameras to begin production: examples include Georges **Méliès**, who adapted a Paul theatrograph projector, and Georg Furkel, who converted his Joly projector in mid-1896. Others employed mechanics to make a one-off apparatus, as did Peter **Elfelt**, who had a copy of the Cinématographe made in late 1896. At first, cameras were almost exclusively in the hands of companies principally engaged in manufacturing projectors for a rapidly expanding number of exhibitors, to whom they wanted to sell films, sometimes in a proprietary width, and for whom most also provided a filmmaking service. Hermann **Foersterling**, Oskar **Messter**, Philipp **Wolff**, **Pathé-Frères**, de Bedts, Paul, Acres, Méliès, Lumière (after early 1897), the Edison Manufacturing Company, Joly, and **Lubin** produced 35mm films, sometimes with proprietary variations in perforations. **Gaumont**, James Albert Prestwich, European **Blair Camera**, and **American Mutoscope and Biograph** (AM&B) used proprietary apparatuses to produce films with widths of from 48 mm to 68 mm; and some entrepreneurs already making 35mm cameras, such as Acres and Charles **Urban** also attempted to expand their markets by offering more economical production in a narrow width, usually 17.5 mm. When not made in a company's own workshop, this first generation of cameras was made to order by a few precision machinists, such as Alfred **Darling** in Brighton or Karl Grahner in Berlin. Specialist manufacturers, such as Pierre-Victor **Continsouza**, aligned with Pathé-Frères, continued in some countries for the next two decades.

By 1899, the moving picture camera had settled into a relatively stable normative form: a claw (with two or four prongs) movement intermittently pulled down the film, internal or external magazines held a maximum of 400 feet of film, a crank handle (sometimes a clockwork drive)

geared for eight frames per turn or two turns per second drove the mechanism, all fitted inside a wooden case. Notable cameras supplied to a small but steady market included those made by: Prestwich, with detachable 400-foot external magazines (1898); Oskar Messter, with 200-foot magazines and a four-sided Maltese Cross (Geneva) movement (1900); James **Williamson**, with a subtle oscillating claw moving in a curved slot (1904); and Heinrich **Ernemann**, with single-frame exposure and an early two-lens turret (1910). Many of these cameras (and others) were widely used in the USA as patent disputes distorted the domestic market and severely limited the availability of native apparatuses.

After 1905, rugged cameras with a full range of accessories and adjustments began to appear, mainly for use in professional studios. The **Debrie "Parvo"** (1908) with an all-metal chassis inside a wooden case and an adjustable shutter was one of the first of the new breed, and influenced camera design throughout the silent period. The Pathé professional camera manufactured by Continsouza,

Figure 18 Pathé-Frères camera (engraving).

introduced in 1905, with its distinctive top-mounted magazines and back-mounted crank was in use for over twenty years both in the USA and across Europe. **Newman & Sinclair** provided a reflex viewfinder using a prism behind its adjustable shutter (1911) in a camera that was both robust and lightweight. When **Bell & Howell** introduced its 2709 studio camera in 1912, with its unique pin-registration intermittent plate that kept the film perfectly steady during exposure, a new era of precision camera design based on the requirements of experienced cameramen began. This camera became the standard studio camera for the next two decades and found use in almost every corner of the world.

See also: intermittent movements; US patent wars

Further reading

Coe, Brian (1981) *The History of Movie Photography*, Westfield, N.J.: Eastivew Editions.

Rossell, Deac (1998) *Living Pictures: The Origins of Movies*, Albany: State University Press of New York.

Salt, Barry (1992) *Film Style & Technology: History & Analysis* (2nd ed.), London: Starword.

DEAC ROSSELL

Campos, Antônio

b. 1877, Baependi, Minas Gerais; d. 195?, Rio de Janeiro

filmmaker, Brazil

Although not prolific, Campos was a persistent and innovative pioneer filmmaker. His first film, *O diabo* [The Devil] (1908), was inspired by Georges **Méliès' trick films** and *féeries or fairy plays*, and he thrived commercially by making commissioned films. In partnership with actor Vittorio Capellaro, he came to specialize in literary adaptations: their adaptation of the national classic, *Os guaranis* [The Guaranties] (1916), was a tremendous critical and popular success. Campos ended his career as Brazil's first official movie censor, a job he held from 1921 until his forced retirement in 1946.

ANA M. LÓPEZ

Canada

Early cinema in Canada was shaped by three distinctive factors: the colonial status of the country, the geographical singularity of a small population spread over the largest national land mass in the world, and interventionist government policies that affected cinema's production, distribution, exhibition, and reception. Operating in the shadow of dominant producers, Canada produced few films and found its distribution networks soon integrated with those of established US concerns. Only in exhibition strategies adapted to specific national and regional demands did Canada exercise some autonomy.

Originally a French colony, Canada came under British rule in 1763. Its inhabitants were concentrated along the continuous border shared with the USA, the Atlantic shoreline, and the valley of the St. Lawrence River, while nomadic native peoples populated its northern reaches. In 1850, 98 percent of its population, predominantly from the British Isles, could be found in Ontario and the Atlantic provinces on either side of the French-speaking community in the province of **Quebec** (which for this encyclopedia is treated separately in the next entry). By the end of the century, the population had doubled to close to five million, much of the increase occurring in the recently settled farmlands of the west precipitated by newly-built railway lines. Although urban areas saw rapid growth during this period, the country remained predominantly rural.

Befitting the country's colonial status, Canadian cinema began with the importation of foreign-based technologies into major urban centers: Toronto, Montreal, the capital Ottawa, the maritime city of Halifax on the east coast, and Vancouver on the west. Familiar names (**Edison**, **Lumière**, **Paul**, and so forth), dominated these first years. The **Kinetoscope** was the motion picture device initially introduced, brought to Toronto's Industrial Fair in August of 1894, several months after Edison's eastern agents, the Ottawa-based Holland brothers, had opened the first kinetoscope parlor in New York City. Subsequent appearances included Montreal and St. Thomas in November of the same year, Halifax in December, and Ottawa in February 1895.

The Holland brothers also held the license for the **Vitascope**, which they exhibited in Ottawa on 27 July 1896, in Toronto on 31 August, and in Halifax on 10 September. But the Vitascope exhibition was not the first motion picture screening in Canada. That distinction belongs to the **Cinématographe** demonstration to a private audience in Montreal in June 1896. The Cinématographe appeared next in Toronto on 1 September, a day after the Vitascope's debut. H. J. Hill, manager of the Industrial Fair, had secured rights for the Lumière apparatus, and after the fair's closing screened British films in a storefront opposite Robinson's **wax museum** until December. The Edison Projecting Kinetoscope appeared in Toronto in October 1896, and was placed on the open market with no territorial restrictions by November. Other **projectors** including the Animatograph, Motograph, Veriscope, and **Biograph** followed in rapid succession throughout the balance of the decade. Their debuts spread across the country in a westerly fashion as the nation's population moved westward. In 1898, for example, John **Schuberg**, introduced Vancouver to the cinema with Vitascope films of the Spanish–American War. He then traveled eastward to Winnipeg and worked as an **itinerant exhibitor** for communities along the main railway line.

As was typical of this period, moving pictures were not the sole selling point of most early screenings. In urban centers, projectors such as the Biograph were not sold on the open market but tied to **vaudeville** theaters, where screenings were part of the show. They also were inserted into magic and hypnotist acts and wax museum galleries, freak shows, and X-ray demonstrations. In both urban and rural areas, films were shown at summer resorts and **amusement parks**, in **churches** and storefronts. These different presentational models allowed exhibitors leeway in supplementing moving pictures as a form of entertainment, adapting their screenings to local conditions and **audiences**; and it was here, despite broad similarities to the US pattern of exhibition, that the infusion of a particularly Canadian cultural inflection could be instigated. The presence of music and commentary in programs often provided the opportunity for the inclusion of Canadian content, whether in the form of a distinctly "Canadian" accent, cultivated by some **lecturers**, or of locally resonant songs performed by musicians accompanying the projection. The appearance of the Canadian Prime Minister, Sir Wilfred Laurier, in Lumière films of the Queen's Diamond Jubilee (30 August 1897), for instance, was picked out by the lecturer, as would be similar subjects of national import. Programs also worked to fuel patriotism. During the Boer War, patriotic concerts held in Toronto's Massey Hall accompanied Edison's films of Canadian battalions embarking from Halifax to fight for Great Britain. By the turn of the century, it was not uncommon for locally-made *actualités* to be inserted into some programs. Although the production of these *actualités* was definitely minimal, it cropped up from time to time: examples include **American Mutoscope and Biograph**'s *Panorama of the Bay of Fundy* (1900), *Crowd on St. Catherine Street* (Montreal, March 1901), and *Sleighing in High Park*, (Toronto, December 1902). Whatever Canadian content was constructed within the exhibition context was all the more important because the majority of films shown were imported. As did Quebec, English Canada depended initially on Edison and AM&B films from the USA, but Lumière, **Pathé-Frères**, and Georges **Méliès** subjects could also be found.

The first attempts at indigenous production were the product of private and government expansionist policies. British Columbia, had entered the confederation on the promise of a railway connecting the west coast province to the rest of the country. Completed in 1885, the Canadian Pacific Railway (CPR) fused business and political interests. The federal government soon initiated policies to encourage immigration to the west from the British Isles, seen within the framework of the British Empire providing the most desirable immigrants. Thus in 1898 and again in 1901, the CPR sponsored a British film tour for James S. **Freer**, a Manitoba farmer (from Bristol) who had filmed the scenic wonders of his adoptive country and projected them locally. The Freer films were only the beginning of the railway's exploitation of film to entice immigrants; the company subsequently contracted with the **Charles Urban Trading Company** to film across the country in 1902. Under the name **Bioscope Company of**

Canada, the CPR released 35 *Living Canada* films that toured both Canada and the British Isles. They included views of the British Columbia salmon industry, *Bees at Work*, and *The CPR Transcontinental Train*.

As these few early attempts at Canadian production aimed at promoting the country abroad, they constructed an image of a land of snow and scenic wonders like Niagara Falls that soon became a cliché. Similarly, between 1900 and 1914 almost one hundred films produced in Canada by US companies, including Edison, AM&B and **Kalem**, defined the landscape and national identity of the country. Among the earliest, AM&B cameraman Billy **Bitzer** filmed the Canadian Rockies in May–June 1900, and Edison copied films of the Klondike gold rush in 1900–1901. This tendency of US producers to exploit Canadian landscapes and subjects persisted into the studio era. The rugged, spectacular scenery of Canada made it an ideal substitute for, and useful variation on, the images of isolation and wilderness that defined the American psyche.

As in the USA, the growth of the story film precipitated a more regularized distribution system that in turn ushered in the **nickelodeon** era. Although far less dramatically than in the USA, permanent movie theaters in Canada began to proliferate noticeably after 1906. Credit for the first nickelodeon usually is given to Léo Ernest **Ouimet**, whose Ouimetoscope opened in Montreal that year. Ouimet also was responsible for Canada's first film exchange, which included branches in Toronto and St. John, New Brunswick. The American-born brothers, Jules and Jay Allen, who opened their Theatorium in Brantford, Ontario, in 1906, established a film exchange in 1908. Other Canadian exhibitors set up fledgling exchanges prior to the formation of the **Motion Picture Patents Company**, but once the trust was in place the Canadian marketplace became a virtual extension of the American. From then on, the most expedient and profitable direction for Canadian entrepreneurs was that of affiliation with US producers and exchanges, guaranteeing a ready supply of non-Canadian products. Thus the story film inaugurated the incorporation of Canadian towns and cities into a pattern of US distribution networks.

Larger moving picture houses supplanted nickelodeons in the early 1910s. In Toronto, for example, a boom in construction of such theaters occurred between 1913 and 1914, leading the *Toronto World* to state that one moving picture house existed for every 5,000 inhabitants. The boom culminated in the opening of the 3,000-seat Loew's Yonge Street Theatre, which had the largest floor area of any in the city and a staff of 134 people. Featuring more luxurious interiors and enticing facades, improved ventilation and projection and larger screens, these theaters also engaged in competitive promotional schemes to lure customers. Patrons were invited to feel part of the movie-going experience by submitting essays describing their favorite photoplay of the week or even devising names for newly built theaters.

The economic democracy that movie-going promised, as a new mass entertainment, also had social implications that conservative, English, middle-class Canadians often found disconcerting, for they initially viewed the activity in nickelodeons with some alarm. The 1908 moral reform movement in the USA translated into the "social gospel" movement in anglophone Canada. Social pressure to reform led to different forms of government intervention, ranging from legislative control to state-sponsored production. Municipal and provincial governments first attempted to regulate the exhibition context with fire concerns as the stated motivation. By 1911, they were acting to ensure that all reels or spools were enclosed in fire-proof boxes; fire-proof projection booths became standard in towns and cities by 1912; and **projectionists** were subject to examinations by 1913. The 1911 introduction of the Theatres and Cinematographs Act in Ontario dictated the licensing of apparatuses by the provincial treasurer. It also forbade unaccompanied children under 15 from attending cinemas. The Ontario Act's provisions for a board of censors was followed by similar legislation in Quebec and Manitoba (1911), British Columbia and Alberta (1913), and Nova Scotia (1915). Censors objected not only to predictable suggestions of infidelity but also to such contentious matters as excessive display of the US flag.

Canadian antagonism toward the USA emerged during the free-trade debate of 1911 (and continued throughout **World War I**), setting the stage for the 1914 enactment of tariffs on all foreign film production. This protective gesture never translated into a federally imposed quota system, however, because the provinces regulated motion picture projection. Whether afraid of reprisals from a powerful trading partner that essentially controlled distribution networks within Canada, or reticent to engage in the risky business of funding **multiple-reel/feature films**, the Canadian government declined to support domestic production in any way. For that reason, the dearth of Canadian films made before the war testifies to the strength of factors militating against indigenous film production. The results of this non-intervention dictated the shape of Canadian cinema to come: theaters prey to purchase by US production companies, and distribution deals with US producers which excluded independents.

During the war, cinema's potential as a unique tool of mass communication and propaganda led to the establishment of government-sponsored film bureaus to foster the production of films which, it was hoped, would encourage social harmony, educate the country's new inhabitants, promote its beauties at home and abroad, and stimulate foreign capital to invest in and develop its resources. These films marked the entry of the provincial and federal governments into Canadian filmmaking and the emergence of the nonfiction film and documentary as Canada's most important film forms.

See also: advertising films; law and the cinema; colonialism: Europe; migration/immigration: USA; musical accompaniment; transportation; travelogues

Further reading

Gittings, Christopher E. (2002) *Canadian National Cinema: Ideology, Difference and Representation*, London/New York: Routledge.

Gutteridge, Robert W. (2000) *Magic Moments: First 20 Years of Moving Pictures in Toronto (1894–1914)*, Whitby, Ontario: Gutteridge-Pratley Publications.

Morris, Peter (1992 [1978]) *Embattled Shadows: A History of Canadian Cinema, 1895–1939*, Montreal: McGill-Queen's University Press.

MARTA BRAUN AND CHARLIE KEIL

Canada: Quebec

The advent of cinema in Quebec occurred in a context marked by certain colonial aspects: by contrast with the usual chronology, exhibition appeared before production, which was to begin only a decade later and remain mostly nonfiction. This scarce production, a consequence of the massive importation of films, was nevertheless offset by strategies of local appropriation: the important role played by exhibitors, the long-lived and crucial presence of **lecturers**, and the integration of moving pictures with theatrical spectacles. These practices would prove decisive in the subsequent evolution of cinema in Quebec, notably in the predominance of the documentary genre and in a consistent concern with "national" identity.

Cinema appeared in a Quebec society strongly divided, historically and culturally. The territory, initially occupied by native peoples before its conquest by the French in the 17th century, fell under British rule in 1763. The French-speaking community then rallied around a culture where tradition and religion impeded the advances of **modernity**. Mostly rural, that community began to assert a separate identity from the middle of the 19th century on, while the English-speaking community was taking advantage of colonial domination to lay the foundations of a dynamic industrial capitalism. At the end of the 19th century, Quebec society thus was comprised of two communities relatively isolated from each other. Quebec had as its main political and economic partners, Ontario and the rest of Canada as well as the British Empire, but commercial relations with the USA, already very important, were fast-expanding. The French-speaking community still maintained influential and continued, if diffuse, relationships with France.

It comes as no surprise, then, that while no research tied to the invention of moving pictures occurred in Quebec, the province was nevertheless the site of the first screening in Canada. It took place in Montreal on 27 June 1896, and was organized by Louis **Minier**, sent from France by the **Lumière** brothers, inventors of the **Cinématographe**. While it was reserved for an invited audience, public screenings took place over several weeks at the same location, the Théâtre Palace. It was not until the beginning of the following fall that other prototypes manufactured in Europe or in the USA (Animatographe, Phantascope, Kinetograph, etc.) came to Montreal and that theaters began to use them in competition.

These screenings did not immediately stimulate local inventors or producers, but moving pictures quickly became an extremely popular form of mass entertainment. They were presented as attractions in **vaudeville** theaters and **amusement parks**, where they shortly took up almost permanent residence. Once again, thanks to a strong French presence, exhibition soon followed a remarkable path. A skillful French exhibitor, countess Marie de Kerstrat, established a traveling cinema called the Historiographe with her son Henry **De Grandsaignes d'Hauterives** acting as lecturer. Their show was so successful that they were booked in most towns and created an infatuation for the lectured film that was to last until the advent of sound. Spoken commentary in French thus made it possible to adapt films, which for the most part were imported, to local tastes.

The French may also have produced the first moving pictures made in Quebec. In September 1898, another representative of the **Lumière** company, Gabriel **Veyre**, shot *Danse indienne* [Indian Dance] in the Kahnawake Mohawk reservation, carefully staged to fit into the European stereotype of a wild Canada. Veyre expressed his intention to shoot others, but no other film survives. This colonialist vision of Quebec characterized all the early moving pictures that were shot there by foreigners.

The available information on the first films made by Americans is questionable. In the spring of 1897 a **projectionist**, Allan May, announced that he was presenting a moving picture of local firemen as well as an advertisement for the **newspaper** *La Presse*. There is no evidence that these films were made in Montreal; nor is it certain that the Quebec *actualités* featured in the 1903

American Mutoscope and Biograph (AM&B) catalog (*Snow Shoe Club*, *Hockey Match*, etc.) were actually shot in Quebec in the winter of 1898. A few American cameramen, however, visited Quebec on important occasions which warranted shooting: **Edison**'s *2nd Special Service Battalion Canadian Infantry Embarking for South Africa* (1898), *Duke of York at Montreal and Quebec* (1901), and *Arrival of Governor General Lord Minto at Quebec* (1902). These early films recorded mainly the visits of officials, the remnants of a **colonialism** which may have entertained the American public as much as the winter scenes shot by the same cameramen during their stay in Quebec: AM&B's *Dog Sleighing* and *Toboggan Slide* (1902), Edison's *Quebec Winter Carnival Series* (1902).

The most ambitious production project came from the British **Charles Urban Trading Company**, which the railway company Canadian Pacific commissioned in 1902–1903 to make a series of films with the purpose of attracting English immigrants to Canada. The shooting was overseen by Joseph **Rosenthal**, who spent several months in Canada and directed a series of more than 100 films titled *Living Canada*, among which about 30 were shot in Montreal: *Electric Tram Ride Through St. Catherine Street Montreal*, *C. P. R. Imperial Ltd Leaving Montreal Station*, *Montreal Fire Department*, *Montreal on Skates*, etc. Within a colonial series designed mostly to enhance natural resources and the plains of the West, the films made in Montreal were almost the only ones showing a modern, urban Canada—although they ignored the cultural duality of the city.

The immense popularity of moving pictures in Montreal probably explains why the first permanent theater in Canada, the Ouimetoscope, was opened there by Léo-Ernest **Ouimet** in January 1906. Phenomenally successful, it rapidly spawned competition, including the Nationoscope built in the spring of 1907 by theater producer Georges **Gauvreau**, who wanted to make his one of the first theaters in the world devoted exclusively to moving pictures. Looking to increase his theater's visibility, in the fall of 1906, by contrast, Ouimet began to shoot his own *actualités*, featuring local characters or events. Shooting on location enabled him to capture action in the making, which gave his films a feel of authenticity and made them very popular. The titles of his films (almost all of which have been lost) thus coincided with local or regional contemporary events.

Ouimet never attempted to produce fiction films in Quebec, contenting himself with shooting three medium-length films mixing nonfiction and fiction in 1918: *Le Feu qui brûle* [The Fire that Burns], *Sauvons nos bébés* [Let's Save Our Babies], and *L'Appel de la liberté* [The Call of Freedom]. As one of the strategies of appropriation that marked filmmaking practices in Quebec, nonfiction even influenced the reception of foreign films, especially American titles, which by then dominated its market. The other strategy was lecturing, which made it possible to comment on foreign films orally in French and to better integrate them into vaudeville shows, where they were long an attraction. Quebecois vaudeville had mixed programs of dance numbers, burlesque comedy acts, and lectured films, and some lecturers were local stars, with careers that lasted until the advent of sound. The most famous lecturer, Alexandre **Silvio**, even became the director of five theaters, and he and his employees themselves performed the commentary on the films.

The first significant effort to produce fiction films in Quebec was by Americans attracted by the exotic aspect of the city of Quebec. It was used as a setting for about ten American fiction films in 1912, some of which—*A Sailor's Heart* and *Pirate's Gold*—were supervised by D. W. **Griffith**. Others included **Vitagraph**'s *The Old Guard* and *Put Yourself in Their Place* and **Lubin**'s *A Gay Time in Old Quebec*. American expertise was later called upon for the first Canadian **multiple-reel/feature film**, *Dollard des Ormeaux* [Battle of the Long Sault], shot near Montreal by Frank Crane for the British-American Film Co., in 1913. The next feature-length local fiction films did not appear until the early 1920s, and they were produced and directed by professionals: Joseph-Arthur Homier's *Madeleine de Verchères* (1922) and Jean Arsin's *Aimez-vous* [Love Each Other] (1925). At the time, these did not benefit from a wide distribution, as the sector was almost completely under American domination.

Exhibition, however, was very much a local affair. Many exhibitors were immigrants who

swiftly developed a wide theatrical network: there were 15 theaters in Montreal in 1907, 25 in 1908, 50 in 1912. Many of these catered to a popular audience (factory and clerical workers), but several luxurious theaters depended mainly on bourgeois or middle-class patrons who associated moving pictures, whether domestic or foreign, with modernity and the affirmation of national culture. Several theaters actually alternated moving pictures and stage plays in their program, depending on the season or even the day. The variety of **audiences**, practices, and genres probably was most visible in Quebec vaudeville. According to the artists who worked there, the audience was primarily working-class yet split between the two linguistic communities.

A large majority of the moving pictures shown in Quebec were American and the main U. S. distributors promptly opened offices in Montreal as soon as picture theaters mushroomed there between 1906 and 1908. The **Motion Picture Patents Company** (MPPC), for instance, was represented in Montreal through its subsidiary, **General Film**. Others, such as **Gaumont**, **Laemmle** and Toronto's Canadian Films Ltd, also had branches there. Ouimet ventured into distribution in 1906, but had to give up this activity barely two years later as the MPPC threatened to cut off his supply of films. In 1915, he became a pan-Canadian distributor again, but only after the Trust had disbanded.

The immense popularity of moving pictures quickly made them the obsession of the Catholic Church, which tried every means to limit their diffusion. A French-speaking and Catholic province, Quebec was home to many religious figures affiliated with some of the more puritan and traditional currents of the Church. They waged a twenty-year legal battle against exhibitors, focusing mainly on seeking to prohibit screenings on Sundays. In 1912, in the Canadian Supreme Court Ouimet won the right to show moving pictures on Sundays, but the clergy continued to use its influence to restrict cinema's spread as much as possible. When censorship appeared in 1913, it was implemented with such severity that American distributors threatened several times to stop exporting films there. The Quebec government backed the censors, who continued to follow stringent rules. The clergy also often exerted pressure on municipal authorities, asking that drastic safety rules apply to theaters and requiring those that failed to be closed down.

The particular conditions within which moving pictures appeared in Quebec deeply influenced later developments. Only around 1950 did fiction film production begin in earnest, but it was (and remains to this day) indebted to the long-standing nonfiction tradition initiated by Ouimet. Quebec cinema truly took off during the 1960s and 1970s, again through the work of documentary filmmakers who had first worked with the National Film Board and who emerged in the course of a struggle to produce works better reflecting Francophone presence in Quebec. The same factors that had once produced the lecturer and a substantial number of nonfiction films were determinant yet again in the emergence of a production marked by the assertion of a separatist identity.

Further reading

Gaudreault, André, et al. (1996) *Au pays des ennemis du cinéma . . . Pour une nouvelle histoire des débuts du cinéma au Québec*, Québec: Nuit Blanche Éditeur.
Lacasse, Germain (1989) *Histoires de scopes. Le cinéma muet au Québec*, Montréal: Cinémathèque québécoise.
Lacasse, Germain (2000) *Le bonimenteur de vues animées*, Québec: Éditions Nota Bene.

GERMAIN LACASSE

Canudo, Ricciotto

b. 1877; d. 1923

film theoretician, Italy/France

Born in Italy but living in Paris after 1901, Canudo was fanatical in winning over French intellectuals and artists for the new film medium and in stimulating the production of more artistic films. Already in 1911, he wrote in his *Manifesto of the Seventh Art* that film was the twentieth-century *Gesamtkunstwerk* in which the other arts merged: literature, sculpture, **painting**, music, dance, and

architecture. After **World War I**, he founded the first ciné-club, the Club des amis du septième art (CASA), and the film magazine *La Gazette des sept arts*. His influential writings were posthumously edited as *L'Usine aux images* (1926).

IVO BLOM

Capellani, Albert

b. 1874; d. 1931

filmmaker, France

Born in Paris in 1874, Albert Capellani studied at the Paris Conservatory (drama academy) with Charles **Le Bargy**. He began his career as a theater actor for André Antoine at the Théâtre Libre and then as stage manager and administrator for Firmin Gémier. In 1905, Ferdinand **Zecca** hired him as a director at **Pathé-Frères**, where he directed everything from *féeries*/**fairy plays**, **historical films**, and **biblical films** to domestic and sensational **melodramas** and **comedies**. In 1908, Charles **Pathé** appointed him artistic director of a new subsidiary company, Société Cinématographique des Auteurs et Gens de Lettres (**SCAGL**). An energetic and enterprising man, Capellani supervised and advised SCAGL directors such as Georges **Monca**, Michel **Carré**, Henri **Desfontaines**, Georges **Denola**, René **Leprince**, and Henri Etiévant. Besides supervising the writing of scripts, he also introduced many theater actors to the cinema, from Jacques Grétillat and Berthe Bovy to his brother Paul **Capellani** and, most notably, Henry **Krauss**. Until the war broke out, he supervised on average the production of one film a week at SCAGL.

In his own films, Capellani brought the "Pathé" style to its highest level, directing adaptations from the classics of popular literature. Among the earliest were *L'Arlésienne* [The Girl from Arles] (1908), adapted from Alphonse Daudet's novel, and *L'Assommoir* (1909), adapted from Emile Zola, which, at 740 meters, could be considered the first feature film in French cinema. His later **multiple-reel films** were characterized by a strong sense of verisimilitude, an unusual skill in deploying a variety of **editing** techniques, and a particular adeptness at **staging in depth**, which often involved deftly choreographing characters and crowds of extras in deep outdoor spaces. Many of these films received very favorable reviews from both the public and the press: among them, *Le Courrier de Lyon* [The Attack of the Lyon Post] (1911), *Notre-dame de Paris* (1911), *Les Mystères de Paris* [The Mysteries of Paris] (1913), and *Germinal* (1913). The most famous of these, of course, was *Les Misérables* (1912), whose four parts (totaling nearly 3,500 meters) brought worldwide recognition.

As France entered the war in 1914, production at Pathé and SCAGL came to a halt. Capellani was sent to the USA, where he first continued his work as artistic director among a small community of French filmmakers, especially at **World Film**. He eventually directed quite succesful films for companies such as Metro Pictures, Empire, Cosmopolitan, and Nazimova Productions, before briefly working as an independent with Capellani Production Inc. After several setbacks, he finally returned to France in 1923 to rest and work on new projects despite his failing health. He died in Paris in 1931 at the age of 57.

Further reading

Ford, Charles (1984) *Albert Capellani, précursor méconnu*, Bois d'Arcy: Archives du Film.

ERIC LE ROY

Capellani, Paul

b. 1873; d. 1960

actor, France

After working in the theater in Paris, Paul Capellani moved into the cinema under the aegis of his older brother, Albert **Capellani**. With his brooding good looks and stage experience, Paul had a successful career in both France and the USA. For **SCAGL**, he was especially noted for his roles in his brother's **historical films**: Armand Duval in *La Dame aux camélias* [Camille] (1911), Captain Phébus in *Notre-Dame de Paris* (1911), and Prince Rodolphe in *Les Mystères de Paris*

[The Mysteries of Paris] (1913). In 1914, Paul followed Albert to the USA and acted in several of the latter's films. When Clara Kimball **Young** formed her own company, she hired him to co-star in several films of European inspiration directed by Emile **Chautard**. Returning to France after **World War I**, he performed off and on as a character actor throughout the 1920s.

ERIC LE ROY

Capozzi, Alberto

b. 1886; d. 1945

actor, Italy

Originally a stage actor, Capozzi joined **Ambrosio** in 1909, where he soon became the company's leading man, often coupled with Mary Cleo **Tarlarini**. In the early 1910s, he was the principal actor for both Ambrosio and **Pasquali**, visible in a wide range of heroic and romantic roles, particularly in Ambrosio's **historical films** such as *Nerone* [Nero] (1909), *Nozze d'oro* [The Golden Wedding] (1911), and *Il granatiere Roland* [Grenadier Roland] (1911). In the mid-1910s he often co-starred with the diva Diana Karenne. From 1918 on, his career declined, although he continued to act for numerous film companies including foreign ones in Austria, France and Britain in the early 1920s.

IVO BLOM

Carl, Renée

b. ?; d. 1954

actor, France

A fiery-eyed brunette, Renée Carl entered the troupe of players directed by Louis **Feuillade** at **Gaumont** in 1907. Often cast as a noble mother or a persecuted woman, she also played the harassed mother in the *Bébé* series (1910–1912) and later became a lead actor in Feuillade's dramatic series, *La Vie telle qu'elle est* [Life As It Is] (1911–1913). René **Navarre** was her regular male co-star and their pairing was immortalized in *Fantômas* (1913–1914), where she played Lady Beltham.

Carl left Gaumont just before **World War I** and later briefly formed her own production company.

LAURENT LE FORESTIER

Max **Reinhardt** in Vienna. His last film was a new version of *L'Enfant prodigue* in 1916.

LAURENT LE FORESTIER

Carpentier, Jules

b. 1851, Paris; d. 1921, Joigny

engineer, scientific equipment manufacturer, France

In 1878, Carpentier opened his own workshop in Paris to manufacture electric and telegraphic equipment, scientific measuring devices, and photographic cameras (including the famous "twin-photo" commercialized by Léon **Gaumont**). In March 1895, he attended the **Cinématographe Lumière** screening at the Société d'encouragement, after which Louis **Lumière** asked him to mass-produce his machine. In late October 1895, Carpentier launched the production of the first twenty-five Cinématographes Lumière, followed by a new series of 200 machines in 1896. Later, he also manufactured the "Carpentier-Lumière winder," the 75 mm camera and projector for the 1900 World Fair, and the Cinématolabe (1909). Carpentier may be considered the inventor of the Maltese-cross projector (patent dated March 28, 1896), a month before **Continsouza**'s patent (April 28, 1896). He died in a car accident.

LAURENT MANNONI

Carré, Michel

b. 1865; d. 1945

scriptwriter, filmmaker, France

Carré had a background in the theater and wrote the play, *L'Enfant prodigue* [The Prodigal Son], which **Gaumont** adapted to film in 1907. The film's success gave Carré the opportunity to become a scriptwriter for **SCAGL** in 1908. The following year, he became a full-fledged filmmaker, directing dramas he had written or adapted such as *Athalie* (1910). After leaving SCAGL in 1912, he made a film version of *Le Miracle* (1913), a play staged by

Casasús, José

b. 1871, Caibarién, Las Villas; d. 1948, Havana

actor, producer, exhibitor, Cuba

Casasús began his professional career as an actor, working with the theatrical company directed by the well-known Cuban diva, Luisa Martínez Casado, with whom he traveled throughout Latin America.

Enchanted by the early moving pictures and by Gabriel **Veyre**, the **Lumiére** representative who brought the **Cinématographe** to Cuba, Casasús convinced a national brewery, "La Tropical," to produce the first Cuban film, *El brujo desapareciendo* [The Disappearing Magician] (1898). Enrique **Díaz Quesada** (then 15 years old) collaborated in the filming. A year later, Casasús purchased a **Pathé-Frères projector** and, equipped with a generator, traveled throughout the countryside, bringing moving pictures—and in many instances—**electricity** into the interior for the first time. Later, he also participated in early experiments to bring sound to the cinema via synched projection apparatuses.

He remained involved in the growing industry as a distributor and exhibitor, organizing film screenings in cultural societies, theaters, and even his own home until he moved to Mexico City to run the Apolo Theater.

ANA M. LÓPEZ

Caserini, Mario

b. 1874; d. 1920

director, Italy

A prolific filmmaker, Caserini began at **Cines** (1907–1911), making **historical films** such as *Beatrice Cenci* [Beatrice Cenci] (1909). He then moved to **Ambrosio**, where he directed

Santarellina [Mam'selle Nitouche] (1912), one of the earliest Italian **multiple-reel** film **comedies**. In 1913, for **Gloria Films**, he directed *Ma l'amore mio non muore!* [Love Everlasting] (1913), Italy's most successful pre-war love melodrama, starring Lyda **Borelli** and Mario **Bonnard**. The film's success established Caserini's talent for the genre, catalyzed the phenomenon of Italian divas, and revealed to Italian producers that blockbusters did not need to be historical epics.

GIORGIO BERTELLINI

celluloid

The development of transparent celluloid as the flexible support for a photographic emulsion in 1889, intended for roll-film cameras like the **Eastman Company**'s Kodak and the **Blair Camera Company**'s Hawk-Eye, was the last key element necessary for modern photographic moving pictures. Although no longer used in films, and rarely in other fields, "celluloid" today remains a potent symbol synonymous with the world of the movies. Used at the outset as a synthetic substitute for ivory, tortoise shell, horn, and rubber in billiard balls, combs, buttons and electrical insulators, celluloid was the first man-made plastic and opened a new area of organic chemistry which would develop rapidly throughout the 20th century.

The discovery of celluloid came from experiments saturating the cellulose fibers of wood chips, plants, paper, or other natural materials with sulphuric and nitric acids in combination with a solvent. Early researchers included the Frenchmen Henri Bracconot (1833) and Théophile-Jules Pelouzé (1838), and the Swiss chemist Christian Friedrich Schönbein (1846); their substances were at first called Pyroxyline or Xyloidine, names that lingered in celluloid terminology. The British metallurgist and inventor Alexander Parkes exhibited his cellulose nitrate, called Parkesine, in 1862, and began commercial production in 1866, but his company went bankrupt. The precise amounts of acids to use in relation to the cellulose, plus the choice of any number of different solvents including camphor, acetanilic

acid, alcohol, ether, and various exotic oils, each of which changed the hardness, color, and characteristics of the final material, remained difficult questions: as late as 1907 a standard textbook on celluloid manufacture stated frankly that the chemical reaction causing the mix of ingredients to form into a useful substance remained unknown.

Celluloid was successfully marketed by the brothers Isaiah Smith Hyatt and John Wesley Hyatt in Albany, New York, in 1870, where they founded a company to make dental plates and false teeth to replace the hard rubber then used by dentists. Moving to Newark, New Jersey, in 1872, as the Celluloid Manufacturing Company, they began using a new process that manufactured their product under heat and pressure, a risky undertaking for a flammable substance closely related chemically to gunpowder. A rapidly expanding urban middle class that saw value in inexpensive celluloid shirt collars and cuffs, costume jewelry, hairbrushes, cutlery, and picture frames helped fuel their success. One use for the new material in the 1880s was as a substitute for the heavy glass plates used by photographers to carry photosensitive emulsions. When George **Eastman** introduced his Kodak camera system with its paper-backed roll film in 1888, its success in rapidly broadening the market for **photography** caused great problems for his company, which could not keep up with customer demand due to the complicated processes needed to replace the opaque paper backing of the film before making prints. After trying several substitutes (Irish moss, Japanese Isinglass, seaweed), Eastman settled on celluloid produced with an amyl acetate solvent as the transparent backing to replace paper; his solution was copied by other companies, and several experiments with chronophotographic cameras also switched from paper films to celluloid.

The leading work with moving pictures on celluloid was undertaken by W. K. L. **Dickson** at Thomas **Edison**'s laboratory in West Orange, New Jersey. After beginning with celluloid photographic plates supplied by the Carbutt Dry Plate Company, Edison's team, together with Eastman, slowly developed a special-order roll film that was 1 and 1/4 inches (35 mm) wide and decidedly thicker than still camera film so that it could take the stress of **intermittent movement** in the **Kinetograph** camera. Ultimately, Edison ordered his clear negative film stock from Eastman, but turned to the **Blair Camera Company**, which produced celluloid films with a different formula so that they were slightly translucent, for positive viewing prints for the **Kinetoscope**—the frosted celluloid from Blair was better suited to viewing by transmitted light. These two companies, plus Carbutt and the small Goodwin Film and Camera Company owned by the photographic supply house of Anthony & Scoville (later Ansco) provided most of the film stock for early moving pictures in the USA. In Europe, the significant suppliers to early moving picture producers were: Dr. J. H. Smith & Co. in Zurich; the **Blair Camera Company (European)** in Great Britain: Victor Planchon, Georges Balagny, and **Lumière** in France: and, briefly, the Schering Chemical Company in Germany. Some firms, like E. H. Fitch & Co, the Northern Photographic Works of Birt **Acres** and the Reliance Roller Film & Dry Plate Company in Great Britain purchased celluloid and coated it with their own proprietary emulsions for use in moving picture work. Until about 1900, raw film was usually cut specially to order for customers, who then perforated the film to their own specifications.

Because the chemistry of celluloid was so little understood, early manufacturers including Eastman were periodically "out of business" when personnel changed or the composition of the photographic emulsion was improved. There were constant problems of adhesion between the emulsion and the celluloid, and manufacturing problems like static **electricity** added to the difficulty of making a consistent product. These complexities and the dangers of working with the volatile material, along with patent fights in the USA, limited the production of nitro-cellulose films to a relatively few companies. By 1910, the leading suppliers worldwide were Eastman, who had bought out Blair in 1899; Aktien-Gesellschaft für Anilin-Fabrikation (**AGFA**), which began producing in 1907; **Pathé-Frères**, which began in 1911; Lumière; and Gaevert in Belgium. A secret agreement in 1913 between AGFA and Eastman sought to divide the European market between these two dominant firms.

Figure 19 Frame stills from Lumière's *Inauguration par Guillaume II du monument de Guillaume 1er* (4 September 1896). 35mm nitrate print with one round perforation on each side of frame. (Courtesy of Paolo Cherchi Usai.)

Further reading

Harding, Colin (1995) "Celluloid and Photography," Parts I–III, *Photographica World*, 75: 23–6; 76: 34–6; 77: 7–11.

Rossell, Deac (2003) "Exploding Teeth, Unbreakable Sheets, and Continuous Casting: Nitrocellulose, from Guncotton to Early Cinema," in Carol Sobiezek and Roger Smither (eds.) *This Film is Dangerous: A Celebration of Nitrate*, Brussels: FIAF.

Spehr, Paul (2000) "Unaltered to Date: Developing 35mm Film," in John Fullerton and Astrid Soderbergh Widding (eds.) *Moving Images: From Edison to the Webcam*, 3–27, Sydney: John Libby.

DEAC ROSSELL

Centaur/Nestor

Founded in 1908 by David **Horsley**, the Centaur Film Manufacturing Company operated initially out of Bayonne, New Jersey. The first independent film company to release without a license from the **Motion Picture Patents Company** (MPPC), Centaur folded in 1910, when Horsley reorganized his business as the Nestor Film Company. Nestor established a studio in Hollywood in October of 1911, becoming the first company to do so, and released through the **Motion Picture Distributing and Sales Company**. Its directorial staff included Al E. Christie, Milton Fahrney, and Thomas Ricketts. Horsley moved the studio back to Bayonne in 1913.

STEVEN HIGGINS

Chaplin, Charles

b. 1889, London; d. 1977, Switzerland

actor, filmmaker, USA

Arguably, Chaplin is the cinema's greatest actor and one of its leading creators. Indeed, Richard Koszarski has written: "Charlie Chaplin remains the most significant figure in the history of the silent film." Although the evidence of his first year (1914–1915) provides little compelling support for these judgments, as often has been said, "Genius has to start somewhere."

Chaplin's familiar story of childhood poverty, abandonment by his father, and his mother's intermittent madness seems to have been written by Charles Dickens. Rescued by becoming a performer in **music halls**, he soon achieved a moderately successful career (including as part of a small company touring the USA) that eventually brought him to the attention of Mack **Sennett**, purveyor of cheap, broad comedies at **Keystone**.

Chaplin debuted in a slap-dash **chase film**, *Making a Living*, in February 1914, where his character's appearance seems fashioned after Max **Linder**. There is some dispute over whether *Mabel's Strange Predicament* or *Kid's Auto Race* (both released during the following week) marked the first time Chaplin donned his "tramp" outfit (derby, tattered jacket, baggy pants, oversized shoes, and cane). Legend has it that the costume arose spontaneously from a visit to the Keystone prop room.

So much of what was to come in his later career exists in the improvised split-reel of *Kid's Auto Race*—Charlie hogging the frame, running afoul of the police, directly appealing to the audience—that this surviving fragment of a film now seems especially prescient. Over the course of the Keystone year, the Tramp gradually accreted a defined personality, and Charlie was to keep him as his world-renowned alter ego for a quarter-century.

Although he worked with Fatty **Arbuckle**, Mack Swain, Chester Conklin, Hank Mann, and others who would (except for Fatty) become part of his stock company in later years, Chaplin established a special rapport with the talented Mabel **Normand**. It was Normand who championed his cause to Sennett, finally permitting him to direct his thirteenth film, *Caught in a Cabaret* (1914).

Over a ten-month period, Chaplin appeared before the public thirty-five times, nearly once a week. Although **World War I** broke out during this period, he quickly became an established figure for European audiences. For Americans, the Tramp became, in René Clair's phrase, "Our Friend." Although the Keystone films never fully transcended the burlesque comedy of the Sennett model, Charlie's character gradually became more nuanced, and audiences became more familiar with him and took pleasure in anticipating his gags. Often, a bit of business in Chaplin's Keystone films would be developed more subtly in his later work.

Chafing under the restraints imposed by Sennett's limited vision and pocketbook, at the end of his contract, Chaplin signed on with **Essanay**. There he had bigger budgets, more freedom, and a less-frenetic production schedule, and he molded Edna Purviance into a suitable replacement for Mabel Normand. Although a less gifted comedienne, Purviance's malleability provided the opportunity to explore the more romantic nature of the Tramp, thus opening up the possibility for the more rounded and deeply felt films that were soon to follow.

See also: comedy; comic series

Further reading

Chaplin, Charles (1964) *My Autobiography*, London: The Bodley Head.
Robinson, David (1985) *Chaplin: His Life and Art*, New York: McGraw-Hill.

CHARLES SILVER

Chardynin, Petr

b. 1873/1877?; d. 1934

filmmaker, Russia

After studying drama in Moscow in the 1890s, Chardynin became a successful actor in provincial theaters. In 1908, he was hired to act in a **Khanzhonkov** drama; the following year, he directed his first film. Early on, he worked on quality productions, mostly adaptations of literary classics; his style, initially dependent on **Pathé-Frères**, as in *The Queen of Spades* (1910), grew less so in the critically acclaimed *Precipice* (1913) and *House in Kolomna* (1913).

Unlike Evgenii **Bauer**, Chardynin was not a visual stylist; instead, he was an "actors' director," generous with rehearsals and mindful of actors' techniques. He even published an essay (1916), noting how and why screen acting differed from stage acting.

In 1916, Chardynin joined a new company, Kharitonov, where he directed all-star salon melodramas, some of which—*Don't Speak, Sorrow, Don't, The Tale . . . at the Fireplace*—became record hits in pre-Revolutionary cinema. In 1920, he emigrated to Latvia, where he made four films; in 1923, he returned to the USSR, where he continued to direct until 1930. He died of liver cancer in 1934.

YURI TSIVIAN

Charles Urban Trading Company

The Charles Urban Trading Company (CUTC) was formed in 1903, when Charles **Urban** broke away from the **Warwick Trading Company**. The company realized Urban's ambitions for the production of **travelogues**, educational and **scientific films**, and swiftly became one of the leading British film concerns, despite the industry as a whole becoming increasingly committed to the fiction film. The CUTC first made its name with coverage of the Russo-Japanese war of 1904–1905 from Joseph **Rosenthal** (with the Japanese) and George **Rogers** (with the Russians). Other notable cameramen working for Urban were Charles Rider Noble (the Balkans), H. M. Lomas (Malaya, Borneo, hunting films), John Mackenzie (the Balkans, the early Kinemacolor experiments), and mountaineer F. Ormiston-Smith (Switzerland, Sweden). Rosenthal became the most traveled Urban employee, his most notable peacetime exploit being a visit to Canada in 1903, with sponsorship from the Canadian Pacific Railways. The CUTC catalogues became increasingly encyclopedic, exemplified by the slogan, "We Put the World Before You." As a showcase for his particular view of film as a medium of popular **education**, Urban initiated a series of "Urbanora" film shows at London's Alhambra, beginning in 1904, with "The Unseen World," which highlighted the micro-cinematography of F. Martin **Duncan**. Urban in particular attracted naturalists: the wildlife photographer Cherry **Kearton**, and most notably F. Percy **Smith**, whose eye-catching *The Strength and Agility of Insects* (1911) perfectly encapsulated the Urban approach.

The CUTC became the parent company for Urban's business interests, which diversified to include the French company **Eclipse**, the travel and scientific branch Kineto (founded in 1907), and in 1909 the **Natural Color Kinematograph** company, producers of Kinemacolor. The CUTC also produced fiction films, never Urban's forte, so most of the fiction material distributed by Urban came from Eclipse. Most interesting among the CUTC's own fiction productions were the science fiction **trick films**, such as *The Airship Destroyer* (1909), made by Walter Booth. In 1908, the CUTC moved its London address to Wardour Street, at "Urbanora House," thus becoming the first film business to be located at what was to become (and remains) the heart of the British film industry. The CUTC was also an important agency for film equipment, much of it designed by Alfred **Darling**, and a distributor of foreign films in Great Britain, in particular **Vitagraph**. The company's trademark name was "Urbanora."

The growing importance of Kinemacolor led Urban to devote all of his energies to its production and promotion, and he resigned from the CUTC in January 1910. The company continued without Urban's direct leadership, but gradually lost its authoritative position within the industry, and declined swiftly during **World War I**. It ceased as a viable concern once Urban decided to relocate in the USA in 1917.

See also: expedition/exploration films; propaganda films

Further reading

Low, Rachael (1949) *The History of the British Film: 1906–1914*, London: George Allen & Unwin.

McKernan, Luke (ed.) (1999) *A Yank in Britain: The Lost Memoirs of Charles Urban, Film Pioneer*, Hastings: The Projection Box.

LUKE McKERNAN

chase films

The term chase films refers to a large group of early multi-shot movies devoted almost exclusively to representing the activity of pursuit, most often a group of women or men running outdoors after a solitary man. From late 1903 to 1906, these films were among the most popular in the USA and abroad. Although elements of "the chase" certainly can be found in prior films, as well as precursory cultural forms such as **vaudeville** routines and dime novels, this particular group of moving pictures provides an especially significant insight into how early cinema began shifting from showing (as in a **cinema of attractions**) to telling stories. In its relentless focus on repeated movement mainly for movement's sake, the chase film helped audiences as well as filmmakers understand how images that move could be employed to sustain a coherent narrative from one shot to the next.

A pair of British **crime films** made in 1903, *A Daring Daylight Burglary* by Frank **Mottershaw** and *Desperate Poaching Affray* by **William Haggar** set the tone for chase films to come: a man (or two) is spied in the act of committing a crime and then hunted down by police in a frenzy of action. Across the Atlantic, American filmmakers soon converted high drama into low comedy by exploiting the farcical potential of figures running frantically after one another. One of the earliest, longest, and most interesting of these, *The Escaped Lunatic*, a fifteen-shot extravaganza made in November 1903 by **American Mutoscope and Biograph** (AM&B), featured a madman dressed as Napoleon who breaks free from his confining asylum cell, only to return ultimately to the same cell, for no apparent reason, after being chased over hill and dale, shot after shot, by three exasperated attendants. AM&B followed up this tremendous hit with an even bigger success, *Personal* (June 1904), in which an aristocratic French bachelor advertising for a wife in a **newspaper** "personal" column is chased by a group of American women desperately seeking matrimony. This chase comedy proved so popular that it spawned a number of imitations, including **Edison**'s *How a French Nobleman Got a Wife through the New York Herald Personal Columns* (August 1904), **Lubin**'s *Meet Me at the Fountain* (November 1904), and, in France, **Pathe-Frères**'s *Dix Femmes pour un mari* [Ten Wives for One Husband] (April 1905). While filmmakers commonly imitated one another in early cinema, this quick succession of nearly identical remakes (which remarkably all survive) suggests a deeper connection between modes of repetition within each pursuit film and the repetition between them.

Whether cops chasing a robber, insane asylum attendants trying to catch an escaped lunatic, or women pursuing an eligible bachelor, these early cinematic chases are all marked by a fascination with the biomechanics of running itself. Thematically, such frenetic pursuit dramatizes how forces of social order—law, reason, marriage—manage to contain and subdue irrational, anarchistic, disruptive energies and fears that are located in the individual being chased. The final apprehension of the pursued thus represents the restoration of social rule. Formally, the start of the chase (what initially motivates the running) as well as its eventual denouement is less important than the middle sections, which emphasize sheer repetitious movement. As several early cinema historians have pointed out, the chase created an imagined synthetic space greater than its individual parts that enabled viewers to follow the figures running through the frame from one scene to the next. Whereas many films of this era still required some outside information (such as an accompanying lecture) to supplement and clarify the story being told within the film, in its redundancy the chase enabled the audience to construe meaning without recourse to external sources. Hence the importance of the chase film for tracing the development of cinematic storytelling during a key period of transition.

Yet given the chase's emphasis on representing shot after shot of the same activity without much difference, this narration remains largely based on a curious kind of compulsive reiteration rather than a plot built and sustained by cause and effect. For each shot the lone runner usually enters the frame from the back, moves diagonally towards the front, and then exits the frame, chased by his pursuers who follow each other in a single file line. This same linear pattern is repeated for the next several shots, but a new shot is not introduced until all the running figures have exited the frame, and have been accounted for, one by one. There is little or no cutting on action, with the implication that running bodies might be missed or lost by viewers if shots were switched too quickly. Although these films are obsessed by linear trajectory, there is very little local continuity between shots, so that an individual who is second in line in one scene may be seventh in line in the following one. Similarly, these movies lack spatial consistency: the pursuit's specific geographical terrain varies from scene to scene, with a steep hill in one long shot suddenly shifting to a medium range shot of a fence in the next.

So if the chase anticipates cinematic narration as we now know it by allowing viewers to imagine a single dynamic thread of action running throughout its entirety, it also harkens back to earlier single-shot films in its concern for the integrity of the human body and in its ceaseless repetition of the same motion in varying locales. This tension

Figure 20 Frame still from *Meet Me at the Fountain* (Lubin, 1904).

between the single shot as a film's basic unit of meaning versus a broader concept of a continuous story line underscores the important 1904 copyright infringement lawsuit brought by AM&B against Edison for its imitation of *Personal*, as filmmakers, lawyers, and judges all struggled to figure out whether movies were simply a discrete succession of individual shots (all of which had to be separately copyrighted, as Edison's lawyers reasoned), or whether the emerging medium, like the novel, told distinct stories which could be grasped in their totality. Played out in the courtroom, these crucial theoretical questions about how films convey meaning are dramatized in the early chase itself.

See also: comedy; cinema and the law; editing: spatial relations; editing: temporal relations

Further reading

Auerbach, Jonathan (2000) "Chasing Film Narrative: Repetition, Recursion, and the Body in Early Cinema," *Critical Inquiry*, 26: 4.

Burch, Noël (1990) *Life to those Shadows*, Berkeley: University of California Press.

Gunning, Tom (1984) "Non-Continuity, Continuity, Discontinuity: A Theory of Genres in Early Film," *Iris*, 2.1: 100–112.

Musser, Charles (1990) *The Emergence of Cinema: The American Screen to 1907*, New York: Scribner's.

JONATHAN AUERBACH

Chautard, Emile

b. 1881; d. 1934

actor, producer, filmmaker, France

A famous actor on the Grands Boulevards theater scene, in 1909 Chautard became an administrator and artistic director of the **Éclair** affiliate, ACAD (Association cinématographique des auteurs dramatiques), a company that worked within the *film d'art* movement. Chautard directed several literary adaptations as well as Grand Guignol plays such as *Le Mystère du pont Notre-Dame* [The Mystery of Notre Dame Bridge] (1912). He also apparently directed Henry Hertz's production of *L'Aiglon* [The Eagle] (1914), the last major French film made before **World War I**. After the outbreak of hostilities, Chautard emigrated to the USA.

ALAIN CAROU

Chautauqua

Chautauqua refers to three sites: the original Chautauqua Assembly, independent chautauqua assemblies, and circuit chautauqua. In its different manifestations, chautauqua offered uplifting or at least "wholesome" entertainment to an overwhelming white, Protestant, native-born, middle-class audience from the later 19th century well into the 1920s. Moving pictures served as a novelty attraction at the original Chautauqua and a regular entertainment feature at independent assemblies. Circuit chautauqua, introduced after the nickelodeon boom, made little or no use of moving pictures.

The original Chautauqua Assembly, located at Lake Chautauqua in northwestern New York state, was founded in 1874 as a summer institute for Sunday school teachers. It successfully blended non-denominational Christianity, practical instruction, and self-described "entertainments," such as readings, musical performances, and stereopticon lectures. This model was soon imitated at what were called independent chautauqua assemblies. By 1904 there were 157 annual independent assemblies across North America—primarily in the midwestern USA—providing 2–4 week summer programs that were held in rural settings easily accessible from nearby towns and small cities. Finally, after 1908, "chautauqua" came primarily to refer to the many traveling tent shows comprising "circuit" chautauqua, a summer mainstay in midwestern and southern small towns from 1910 through the 1920s. Circuit chautauqua reduced the independent assembly's offerings to a seven or ten-day program of inspirational lectures, musical performances, and stage plays.

Vitascope films were introduced at the New York Chautauqua Assembly in 1896 and returned for the next two seasons. Moving pictures fit comfortably into a Chautauqua schedule that had long featured lectures illustrated with stereopticon slides, firework displays, spectacular scientific experiments, dramatic monologues, and Alexander Black's "picture plays." Lyman H. **Howe** brought his **illustrated lectures** to Chautauqua in 1907 for the first of several appearances.

Beginning with touring "war films" in 1897 and continuing for at least the next decade, moving pictures were a mainstay of many independent chautauqua assemblies, such as the Northern Chautauqua on Lake Michigan and the Midland Chautauqua in Des Moines, Iowa. Traveling film exhibitors like D. W. **Robertson** were frequently the top-billed entertainment attraction at independent assemblies. Along with moving pictures, independent assemblies also offered **magicians**, costumed readers, illustrated travel lectures, vocal quartets, and dialect recitations. Regardless of the deep-seated anxiety among Protestant churchgoers concerning "cheap amusements," moving pictures gained a measure of legitimacy when presented under the auspices of a chautauqua assembly, where they were deemed suitable for children as well as adults.

The role of moving pictures at independent chautauqua assemblies underscores the cultural, social, and geographical diffusion of moving pictures in the USA and Canada, well beyond the urban **vaudeville** stage and even the ubiquitous **nickelodeon**.

See also: audiences: surveys and debates; churches and exhibition; itinerant exhibitors

Further reading

Morrison, Theodore (1974) *Chautauqua: A Center for Education, Religion, and the Arts in America*, Chicago: University of Chicago Press.

Waller, Gregory A. (1990) "Motion Pictures and Other Entertainment at Chautauqua," in R. Pearson, C. Dupré la Tour, and A. Gaudreault (eds.) *Cinema at the Turn of the Century*, 81–89, Quebec: Editions Nota Bene.

GREGORY A. WALLER

Cheetham, Arthur

b. 1864; d. 1936

filmmaker, exhibitor, Great Britain

An ebullient British entrepreneur, Derby-born Arthur Cheetham settled in Wales in the 1880s, began showing moving pictures in hired halls in January 1897, and made his own first film, of children playing on a Rhyl beach, North Wales, the following January. As the first Welsh-based filmmaker, he shot more than 20 *actualités* between 1898 and 1903. His *Blackburn Rovers vs. West Bromwich Albion* (1898) is the oldest known surviving soccer film. Other extant titles include *Mailboat Munster's Arrival at Holyhead* (1898), *Royal Visit to Conway* (1899), and *Buffalo Bill Cody's Visit to Rhyl* (1903). In 1906, he opened the first permanent cinema in Rhyl, the first of a circuit of cinemas he would run in Wales and the Manchester area into the 1920s.

DAVE BERRY

Chicago Film Exchange

Owned by Max Lewis, the Chicago Film Exchange (one of the earliest and largest rental exchanges in the city) became embroiled in controversy when

Gaston **Méliès**, brother of French filmmaker Georges **Méliès** and custodian of his American interests, attempted to go into production for himself. Trading on a promised license for Méliès Star Films, Gaston raised capital from investors, who in turn sold their interest to Lewis. This chicanery led to the cancellation of licenses for both Star Film and Chicago Film Exchange in 1909. Gaston survived as a small independent producer; Chicago Film Exchange did not.

ROBERT S. BIRCHARD

Chile

As in other coastal Latin American countries from **Peru** to **Uruguay**, moving pictures arrived early to Chile: on 25 August 1896, the capital of Santiago welcomed the "Cinematógrafo **Lumière**" at the Salón de Patinar of the Galeria Union Central, through the agency of a prosperous French merchant. Although audiences were enchanted by these first films, interest waned when programs were not regularly renewed. Another entertainment venue imported the **Edison** Vitascope in June 1897 with great fanfare, but its popularity also declined quickly.

The Odeón theater in Valparaíso exhibited the first national production on 26 May 1902: shot by an unknown cameraman, *Ejército General de Bombas* [Firefighters' Corps] was a three-minute view of the city's firefighters on parade (as in Cuba, firefighting was a recent profession and of great local interest). In June 1902, unknown cameramen minutely recorded the activities of an official Argentine delegation visiting Chile to sign the May Peace Pacts. These and other imported films were shown in centrally-located Santiago theaters such as the Variedades, Apolo, Biographe Lumière, and Imperial which catered primarily to the city's elite.

With only 300,000 inhabitants at the turn of the last century, Santiago had a small elite sector and a far larger sector of crowded *conventillos* (ghettos). Construction on the city's sewage system had only begun in 1898; electrical street lighting would not be widespread until 1925. At first, the popular classes viewed moving pictures with suspicion and continued to seek entertainment at circuses and variety theaters. They would not take to movies until 1910, when screening venues began operating in populous neighborhoods.

The celebration of Chile's Centenary in 1910 generated a number of social and cultural activities which were filmed and successfully exhibited. For the first time, cameramen were identified by name. Julio Chevenay and Arturo Larraín Lecaros were the most prominent, but little is know about them: Chevenay worked in a **photography** store and Larraín (from a well-off family) later became a diplomat. Larraín filmed the funeral of President Pedro Montt in 1910 and included an extended "traveling" shot from the last wagon of the train carrying his body to the capital from the port in Valparaíso (Montt died in Germany). A good portion of this material survives and is included in Edmundo Urrutia's *Recordando* [Remembering] (1960).

Another important figure was Adolfo Urzúa, a theater teacher in a Santiago conservatory, who was hired by a new company, the Compañía Cinematográfica del Pacífico (or Pacífico Filmes) to train actors and direct fiction films. In the spirit of the centenary celebrations, in 1910 he directed the first fiction film, *Manuel Rodríguez*, about the life and exploits of the hero of Chile's war of independence from Spain.

As in many other Latin American countries, European immigrants played a significant role in developing an infrastructure for national filmmaking. A French photographer, Fédier Vallade, created the Franco Chilena Films company in 1914 and announced the production of two fiction films. Although neither were completed, the venture was important because Vallade became associated with a 19-year-old amateur actor, Jorge Délano (also known as "Coke"), who later became Chile's best-known illustrator and a film director/producer in the late 1920s.

Of greater immediate impact was the 1915 arrival of Salvador **Giambastiani**, an Italian photographer who soon set up a studio in Santiago. His first production, a fiction film based on a notorious criminal case, was *La Baraja de la Muerte* [The Card of Death] (1916). Slated to premiere in Santiago before the real-life trial had ended, it was banned and premiered in Valparaíso. The following year,

Giambastiani's common-law wife, 17-year-old Gabriela von Bussenius, wrote and directed *La Agonía de Arauco* [Arauco's Agony] for Chile Films, a company formed by Giambastiani and two local businessmen. Although her only solo directorial effort—she was subsequently Giambastiani's silent collaborator—von Bussenius was one of the first women to venture into filmmaking in Latin America. Giambastiani produced many documentaries: best known because of its restoration in the 1950s is *Recuerdos del Mineral El Teniente* [Remembrances of the El Teniente Mine] (1918), Chile's first socially conscious documentary.

Giambiastini also introduced the theatrical actor Pedro **Sienna** in *El hombre de acero* [The Man of Steel] (1917), who became a director in the 1920s. Although he made only five films, he is considered the most significant director of Chilean silent cinema.

The late 1910s and 1920s were productive years: filming became widespread throughout the nation, from Iquique to Punta Arenas, and production companies proliferated: Estudios Hans Frey, Condor Film, Compañía Cinematográfica del Pacífico, Patagonia Films. Regular **newsreels** also were produced in Santiago, affiliated with **newspapers** such as *La Nación* and *El Mercurio*. These and other papers featured regular cinema columns, in conjunction with the appearance of a specialized **trade press**, including *Cine Gaceta* and *Farándula*.

Seventy-eight fiction films were produced in Chile during the silent period, with a record 25 in 1925 alone. This was, without a doubt, the "golden age" of Chilean cinema, encompassing **historical films**, contemporary melodramas, and **comedies**. Unfortunately, less than a handful of these films have survived. Notable among these is Sienna's *El húsar de la muerte* [The Hussar of Death] (1925), particularly for its skillful narrative construction and extraordinary photography: it was declared a national "monument" in 1978.

Further reading

Jara Donoso, Eliana (1994) *Cine Mudo Chileno*, Santiago: CENECA.

Godoy Quezada, Mario (1966) *Historia del Cine Chileno*, Santiago: Arencibia.

ANA M. LÓPEZ

China

Cinema was first introduced in Hong Kong and Mainland China by European and American traveling showmen. From the first reported exhibition in the Xu Garden in Shanghai on 11 August 1896 to the establishment of the Mingxing Company in 1922, early film practices in China, although erratic and uneven, laid a crucial foundation for a metropolitan film culture centered in Shanghai.

Early film exhibition in China took place largely in urban teahouses, theaters, and amusement halls. Film programs were often mixed with native **operas**, drum storytelling, magic shows, fireworks displays, and acrobatics. Foreign showmen and travelers first shot *actualités* and **news event films** for inclusion in local programs as well as for export. Variously called the "Occidental Shadowplay" or "Electric Shadowplay," early moving pictures enthralled Chinese audiences, who regarded the new medium as at once a variation of the puppet **shadow play** and a form of modern magic. In 1902, moving pictures appeared in teahouses in Beijing and even inside the Forbidden Palace. The interest of the imperial family waned, however, after an explosion during a projection in the court in 1904. Yet before long, film exhibition spread beyond urban centers and into the countryside.

In the 1900s, several permanent moving picture theaters opened in Hong Kong, Taipei, and Shanghai, including Antonio **Ramos**'s 250-seat Hongkew in Shanghai. Along with other foreigners, notably S. G. Hertzberg and G. Goldenberg, Ramos monopolized the movie theaters in Shanghai in the ensuing decade, showing predominantly European imports. Film exhibition as part of variety shows continued, however, in venues such as the Great World and the New World, two prominent amusement centers, as well as theaters in Shanghai and elsewhere.

From 1905 on, a number of Chinese began to take up filmmaking. In response to the popularity of the Peking opera, the **Fengtai Photography Studio** in Beijing started making short films featuring famous opera stars. The first of these was an episode in *Dingjunshan* [Conquer the Jun Mountain], starring Tan Xinpei. These films emphasized spectacular martial arts over singing and were well received by Beijing residents. Fentai was forced to abandon film production, however, after a fire in 1909.

While Beijing was the birthplace of Chinese cinema, the crucible of a vibrant domestic film industry unquestionably was Shanghai, which by then had become the largest metropolis and the commercial, industrial and cultural center of China. In 1913, **Zhang Shichuan**, **Zheng Zhengqiu**, and other associates formed the Xinmin Theater Research Society, in partnership with the **Asia Film Co.**, originally founded by Benjamin Polaski. The Society contracted all aspects of film production, including **screenwriting**, directing, and **acting**. Within a year, Asia made scores of *actualités* and **comedies**. Actors engaged in filming during the day and performing in the theater at night. Many of these films were shown at intermissions during theater performances. Due to the particular historical context, all the female parts, both on stage and on screen, were played by male actors. Among Asia's productions, the four-reel *A Couple in Trouble* (1913) is considered the first Chinese narrative **multiple-reel/feature film**. A satire on arranged marriage, it anticipated the **domestic melodrama** that was to become a trademark of Zheng and Zhang's Mingxing Company.

During the same period, Li Minwei, also in collaboration with Polaski, made *Zhuangzi shiqi* [Zhuangzi Tests His Wife] (1913) in Hong Kong. Li played Zhuang's wife while his own wife, Yan Shanshan, played the maid, becoming the first Chinese woman to appear on the silver screen.

The outbreak of **World War I** in Europe seriously affected film production in China as it cut off the supply of film stock for a period of time. Yet it was during the war that the Civilized Play, a modern spoken drama appealing to urban dwellers, began to heavily influence the content and style of early Chinese cinema. For instance, together with Guan Haifeng, Zhang made the four-reel *Heiji yuanhun* [Victims of Opium] based on an eponymous popular Civilized Play in 1916.

The **Commercial Press Motion Picture Department** was the most important enterprise engaged in producing and promoting Chinese cinema in the late 1910s. Its productions were wide-ranging, from scenics or **travelogues**, educational films, and opera films to features, all for the purpose of mass enlightenment. In 1920, the company upgraded its facilities and built the first glass studio. Several independent companies that emerged in this period relied heavily on the Commercial Press for technical support in the making of a number of early feature-length films.

Chinese narrative films carried strong imprints of the **cinema of attractions** characteristic of earlier filmmaking. *Yan Ruisheng* (1921), for example, was adapted from a Civilized Play, itself derived from sensational news reporting on a murder case in Shanghai. This "docu-drama" premiered at Ramos' Olympic Theater and made a large profit unprecedented for a Chinese film, which spurred the development of other similar ventures. Dan Duyu's family business, the Shanghai Motion Picture Company, produced *Haishi* [Sea Oath] (1921), a six-reel tale of romance between a modern girl and a painter. Dan's wife, the legendary Yin Mingzhu, known as Miss F F (Foreign Fashion), played the female lead. Meanwhile, Guan Haifeng, co-director of *Victims of Opium*, applied his expertise in theater mechanics to *Hongfeng kulou* [Ten Sisters] (1921), a ten-reel feature liberally adapted from a French detective novel and mixed with elements of romance, action, comedy and horror. While serving to consolidate narrative cinema in China, these early experiments in feature filmmaking also exploited and synthesized elements of early cinema that would resurface in several mixed genres of the 1920s, in particular, the melodrama and martial arts film.

See also: melodrama, sensational

Further reading

Leyda, Jay (1972) *Electric Shadows: An Account of Films and the Film Audience in China*, Cambridge, MA: MIT Press.

Li Suyuan and Hu Jubin (1997) *Chinese Silent Film History*, Beijing: China Film Press.

Zhen Zhang (1999) "Teahouse, Shadowplay, Bricolage: *Laborer's Love* and the Question of Early Chinese Cinema," in Yingjin Zhang (ed.) *Cinema and Urban Culture in Shanghai, 1922–1943*, 27–50, Stanford: Stanford University Press.

ZHEN ZHANG

Chomón, Segundo de

b. 1871; d. 1929

filmmaker, Spain, France, Italy

Segundo de Chomón was the most international Spanish filmmaker of the early cinema. In 1895, he travelled to Paris, where he met and married Julienne Mathieu, a stage performer who introduced her husband to the studios and laboratory facilities of Georges **Méliès** and **Pathé-Frères**, for whom she worked as an actress. In 1901, Chomón and his family returned to Barcelona, where he first worked with Albert **Marro**. Between 1902 and 1905, Chomón operated as a concessionary for Pathé-Frères in Barcelona: he distributed the company's films to Spanish-speaking countries; he shot *actualités* of the city and its surroundings; and he opened a workshop to **color** the French company's films. He also made several fiction films, experimenting with special effects, and participated in the Modernist movement at the Sala Mercè (1904), along with Adrià **Gual**.

During the spring of 1905 he and his wife returned to Paris to work for Pathé. Chomón was soon put in charge of the company's **trick films** and special effects, making some of the best then being produced: *Le roi des dollars* [The King of Dollars] (1905), *Les cent trucs* [The Hundred Tricks] (1906), *Les fleurs animées* [The Animated Flowers] (1906), *Kiriki, acrobates japonais* [Kiriki, Japanese Acrobats] (1907). From his experience with trick films, Chomón went on to master film narrative and **animation** (objects, puppets, drawings), and it was this speciality that made him one of the great filmmakers of the early silent period: *La légende du fantôme* [The Legend of the Phantom]

(1908), *Electric hotel* (1908), *Voyage au planète Jupiter* [Journey to the Planet Jupiter] (1909), *Le voleur invisible* [The Invisible Thief] (1909), *Le théâtre électrique de Bob* [Bob's Electric Theater] (1909), *Une excursion incohérente* [An Incoherent Excursion] (1910).

Chomón returned to Barcelona in 1910 and founded the Chomón & Fuster company, where he made 37 films within a ten-month period, some of which were distributed by Pathé. From 1911 to 1912, he worked for Ibérico, a Pathé subsidiary in Barcelona, among other films making the intriguing *Superstition andalouse* [Andalusian Superstition] (1912). At that time he also patented a technically advanced film coloring system, "cinemacoloris."

In 1912, Chomón was hired by **Itala** Film, in Turin, to serve as director of photography, specializing in special effects, and he participated in such large-scale productions as *Cabiria* (1914) by **Pastrone**. There he also created the animated scenes with puppets for *La guerra e il sogno di Momi* [Momi's War and Dream] (1916). Chomón continued to work as cameraman and as a specialist in special effects until his death. One of his last collaborations was on *Napoléon* (1927) by Abel Gance.

See also: *féeries* or fairy plays

Further reading

Abel, Richard (1994) *The Ciné Goes to Town: French Cinema, 1896–1914*, Berkeley: University of California Press.

Minguet Batllori, Joan M. (1999) *Segundo de Chomón, beyond the cinema of attractions (1904–1912)*, Barcelona: Filmoteca de la Generalitat de Catalunya.

Tharrats, Juan Gabriel (1988) *Los 500 films de Segundo de Chomón*, Zaragoza: University of Zaragoza.

Vidal, Agustín Sánchez (1992) *El cine de Segundo de Chomón*, Zaragoza: Caja de Ahorros de la Inmaculada de Aragón.

JOAN M. MINGUET

Christensen, Benjamin

b. 1879; d. 1959

actor, filmmaker, Denmark

Forced by vocal problems to abandon a promising stage career, in 1912 Christensen began acting in moving pictures produced by **Dania Biofilm** and **Dansk Biograf Kompagni**. His directorial debut, *Det hemmelighedsfulde X* [The Mysterious X, aka Sealed Orders] (1914), was a masterfully produced and elaborately shot spy thriller with brilliant **lighting** effects. Even more visually impressive was *Haevnens Nat* [The Night of Vengeance, or Blind Justice] (1916), inspired by Victor Hugo's novel *Les Misérables*. Christensen played leading roles in both films. Only in 1922 did the slow-working Christensen complete his third film, the weird and extravagant *Häxan* [Witchcraft through the Ages].

CASPER TYBJERG

Chronochrome Gaumont

The chronochrome, whose patent Léon **Gaumont** registered on February 11, 1911, relied on a three-**color** process invented during the 19th century, whose principle already was being applied to film screenings by Lee and Turner in 1902. A camera equipped with three lenses and three filters (blue, red, green) would record a given scene (usually an outdoor, well-lit scene). The resulting positive was projected by a machine also equipped with three lens and filters. Three images in different colors would thus overlap on the screen. A servoengine installed on the projector would correct parallax problems. The chronochrome image measured only 14 mm in height (the standard was 19 mm), which resulted in a panoramic format on the screen. In France, Gaumont managed to use the chronochrome in a number of theaters, including the Gaumont-Palace, in the early 1910s. Chronochrome images still produce an amazing spectacle, as the films restored by the George Eastman House reveal.

LAURENT MANNONI

Chronophone Gaumont

On 7 November 1902, **Gaumont** demonstrated the chronophone (a patent had been registered on July 11, 1901) using three films synchronized with a phonograph. After several lean years of unsuccessful exploitation, in 1906, a more reliable chronophone was devised by Georges Laudet, a Gaumont engineer, and marketed as the Elgéphone. During the recording process (which used an electromagnetic microphone invented by Frely), a performer mimicked (and lip-synced) a song played by a **phonograph** connected to a Gaumont **camera**. In projection, an electric impulse would start a phonograph connected to a **Gaumont projector** and synchronize the sound with the image; a synchronizing engine controlled by a master deck allowed the speed to be corrected. Gaumont built one Chronophone recording studio in Paris, in 1905, and another in New York, in 1908. Although several models of the Chronophone were marketed for exhibition (only three survive, in Paris and in Rochester), the most sophisticated was the Chronomegaphone, which relied on compressed air and was used at the Gaumont-Palace, beginning in 1911. Chronophone films or *phonoscènes* were seen by thousands of spectators in France, Germany, and the USA. Most were musical numbers by cabaret artists (Mayol, Polin, **Dranem**, Fragson), **opera** arias, and dances, usually four minutes in length.

LAURENT MANNONI AND ALISON McMAHAN

chronophotography

The rapid taking of multiple sequential photographs of a subject in motion was called chronophotography, or series **photography**, and in the last quarter of the 19th century it was at the cutting edge of photographic technology, principally used by scientists analysing physical phenomena, including animal locomotion and the physiology of flight. There were two methods: single-plate chronophotography, where moving images were either slightly overlapped or placed consecutively on a single photosensitive surface, and multiple-plate chronophotography, where an apparatus equipped with several lenses or a series of separate cameras exposed individual photographic plates for each phase of movement recorded. The introduction of nitrocellulose-backed flexible roll film after 1888 allowed special single-lens cameras to record multiple phases of movement on a single photographic band. Because this last evolution of chronophotography has only minimal differences with a moving picture film, which in its essence is a continuous row of individual photographs recording the separate phases of movement, some chronophotographers have been closely studied as important precursors of the cinema, while others have been largely ignored. But any multiple-plate chronophotograph can be exhibited and reconstitute the original motion of its subject when arranged for a stroboscopic viewer such as a phenakistiscope, zoetrope, or even a simple flip-book, and chronophotographic apparatus and techniques were of great interest to many of the pioneering inventors of moving pictures, including Thomas **Edison**, the **Lumière** brothers, Henri **Joly**, C. Francis **Jenkins**, Birt **Acres**, and others.

Single-plate chronophotography began in 1860 when Professor Wilhelm Feddersen exposed sparks from a leyden jar on a photographic plate and calculated both the spark's duration and the amount of energy produced by his electrical source. Elaborate single-plate work also was carried out by Robert von Lendenfeld to measure and analyze the wing movements of dragonflies, and, before 1888, by the outstanding physiologist Étienne-Jules **Marey** to study human locomotion and motor functions, as well as the flight of birds. Multiple-plate work was first undertaken by Eadweard **Muybridge** in Palo Alto, California, in 1877, using 12 Scoville plate cameras with the support of the industrialist Leland Stanford, who wanted to improve the training methods for his racehorses. Muybridge quickly applied his method to both people and animals, and his images astonished the photographic world and the public alike. By the early 1890s, the method had been used for a variety of purposes by John Annan, Dr. William Gilman Thompson, Albert **Londe**, Colonel Hippolite Sébért, Thomas Eakins, Ernst Kohlrausch, Victor von Reizner, and others. But the leading figures in chronophotography, for each of whom the claim of "inventor of the cinema" has been made, were Muybridge, Marey, Georges **Demenÿ**, and Ottomar **Anschütz**. Muybridge inspired them all, but never achieved the projection of reconstituted movement using photographic images. Marey and his long-standing assistant Demenÿ fought and eventually split up over the issue of using Marey's ingenious cameras for non-scientific purposes such as producing moving pictures: working on his own, Demenÿ made delightful pioneering films and useful cinematographic apparatuses. Anschütz spent the decade from 1885 to 1895 developing a moving picture system that was widely seen in Europe and North America but ultimately collapsed in bankruptcy. As cinematographic apparatuses using **celluloid** film stock matured after 1900, scientists adopted the new medium, particularly Marey's successor in Paris, Lucien **Bull**, and the time-and-motion analyst of workplace efficiency, Frank Taylor in the USA.

Figure 21 Home model Schnellseher by Ottomar Anschütz; barely visible is one image from the 1892 Anschütz chronophotograph *Card Players*. From Oskar Messter, *Mein Weg mit dem Film* (Berlin, 1936).

See also: archaeology of cinema/pre-cinema; cameras; projectors

Further reading

Braun, Marta (1992) *Picturing Time. The Work of Etienne-Jules Marey (1830–1904)*, Chicago/London: University of Chicago Press.

Haas, Robert Bartlett (1976) *Muybridge. Man in Motion*, Berkeley: University of California Press.

Mannoni, Laurent (1999) *Étienne-Jules Marey. La memoire de l'Oeil*, Milan/Paris: Mazzola/Cinémathèque française.

Mannoni, Laurent, with Mard de Ferrière and Paul Demeny (1997) *Georges Demenÿ, Pionnier du Cinéma*, Paris/Lille: Pagine Editions: Cinémathèque française/Université Lille 3.

Rossell, Deac (2001) *Faszination der Bewegung. Ottomar Anschütz zwischen Photographie und Kino*, Frankfurt a. M.: Stroemfeld/Roter Stern.

DEAC ROSSELL

churches and exhibition

Churches were frequent venues for moving picture exhibitions throughout the entire period of early cinema. In these noncommercial settings, the purpose and meaning of moving pictures were tailored to the cultural, educational, and institutional interests of distinctive religious groups around the world.

In most countries, showing moving pictures in churches initially was an outgrowth of the activities of **itinerant exhibitors**: see Cecil **Hepworth**, Lyman H. **Howe**, and D. W. **Robertson**. Since the middle of the 19th century, itinerant showmen had sought reputable sponsors and paying audiences for programs of high-class entertainments that included science demonstrations, lectures, **magic lantern shows**, **stereographs**, phonographic concerts, and other educational exhibits. By the 1890s, churches (and nondenominational religious associations such as **chautauquas**, the YMCA, and the **Salvation Army**) were among the showmen's most reliable and longstanding partners. Even Methodists, with strict rules forbidding attendance at commercial amusements, sanctioned traveling exhibits sponsored by the Epworth League, the denomination's affiliated social organization.

Soon after the innovation of film **projectors** in 1895, itinerant exhibitors introduced moving pictures, first as a novelty and later as a main attraction, to church audiences. Religious leaders saw first-hand the medium's appeal and sought to harness this power as a source of edification for their communities. Churches were especially eager for **travelogues** of distant lands (whether holy or heathen), **industrial films** or other educational subjects, and **biblical films** such as the *Passion Play*. Fictionalized entertainment films were also acceptable so long as these had redemptive moral themes and were otherwise unobjectionable.

As sponsors for traveling exhibitions, churches publicized shows to the broader community, mobilized constituent audiences, and provided screening space. In exchange they received a share of the receipts, typically 30% but as high as 50% if turnout greatly exceeded expectations. This money helped finance church activities and facilities. Just as important as the financial benefits, sponsorship allowed religious leaders to ally with traveling emissaries of **education** and cultural uplift in the growing struggle against **saloons** and cheap commercial amusements for moral authority over community life and popular leisure. In 1905, the French Catholic publisher, **Maison de la Bonne Presse**, opened a Paris office for renting projectors as well as selected programs of films to serve as "teaching aids" in diocese schools and "illuminated sermons" in churches.

During the **nickelodeon** era in the USA, itinerant showmen endured tough times and survived only to the extent that they could reach the larger audiences available in secular halls and commercial theaters. Although churches were not wholly abandoned as venues for traveling shows, both urban and rural religious leaders found themselves increasingly at odds with highly popular nickelodeons for the time, loyalty, and financial support of their congregations. Churches did not shrink from the challenge. When Sunday nickelodeon shows cut into church attendance and collection coffers, attempts to mobilize political support for "Blue Laws" banning Sunday movies at theatrical venues were widespread, especially in the USA.

Church leaders also began presenting moving pictures directly to their constituents. A voluntary donation of 1–3 cents was common, thereby undercutting the price of nickelodeons. Saturday matinees were offered in church vestibules for devout parents and their children. To reach the wayward, however, required bolder programming strategies. In 1907, Rev. Charles McClellen of Philadelphia told *Moving Picture World* of plans to draw "unsaved men and women from the playhouse, the card table and the saloon" by building a "rooftop garden" above his Baptist church. Here open-air programs of moving pictures, **vaudeville** acts, and **illustrated songs**, along with the promise of free food and concluding gospel services conducted by laymen, would be irresistable Saturday night attractions on hot summer nights.

As nickelodeons found ways to sidestep Blue Laws, Sunday movie-going proliferated, especially by workers for whom Sunday was the only day off. Many church leaders eventually responded to declining attendance among young working-class adults by offering entertaining motion pictures as added attractions after Sunday evening religious services. Here, moving pictures replaced stereopticon views, which were uplifting in a genteel way but not exciting enough to draw audiences away from commercial theaters. Some ministers went further, projecting moving pictures directly from the pulpit as part of the Sunday service itself. For instance, in 1907 at St. Mary Axe church in London, Rev. Wilson Carlisle's sermons were illustrated with special subjects based on religious scripture or with general entertainment films dramatizing relevant moral dilemmas.

The main problem facing churches as exhibition venues in the early 1910s was a limited supply of what were deemed suitable films. The educational catalogues of George **Kleine** and Charles **Urban** were widely used, as were industrial and **advertising films** (often distributed at no cost to churches). Still many believed the availability of scripturally accurate religious films and morally acceptable entertainment films was insufficient, and most ministers did not have sufficient time to locate and order the few suitable pictures that did exist. In response, new distributors catering to the church market emerged, such as Edwin Dunham Foster's Community Motion Picture Bureau (1913) and

Rev. William Carter's Church and Social Service Bureau (1914). For a small fee, these organizations provided weekly programs of short films and mainstream features handpicked for the education, uplift, and entertainment of religious audiences. The films were prescreened for quality and pre-censored to eliminate any incidental objectionable material. Church leaders were thus assured no unwanted surprises would occur during projection.

By 1915, the presentation of motion pictures in churches was common enough to precipitate changes in distribution but not lucrative enough to precipitate increased film production targeting the religious market. Still, the vitality of church movie shows attests to the diversity of exhibition practices throughout early cinema and to the enduring struggle of religious groups to bend the context of film reception, and the meaning of film, to suit their own agendas.

Further reading

Fuller, Kathryn H. (1996) *At the Picture Show: Small-Town Audiences and the Creation of Movie Fan Culture*, Washington. D.C.: Smithsonian Institution Press.

McConoughey, Edward M. (1916) *Motion Pictures in Religious and Educational Work, with Practical Suggestions for Their Use*, Boston: Methodist Federation for Social Service.

JEFFREY KLENOTIC

Cine-fono e la Rivista Fono-Cinematografica, La (1909–1927)

This important Italian trade weekly emerged out of various mergers occurring in 1908 and 1909, first between the Neapolitan *Il Cafè-Chantant* (1900) and the Milanese *La Rivista Fono-Cinematografica* (1907) and then, after their fusion, with the Milanese *La Cine-Fono* (1908). Directed by Francesco Razzi, over the years *La Cine-fono* became a favorite within the Italian film industry for the comprehensiveness of its coverage. Its pages comprised columns devoted to film reviews, technical information, financial updates on current productions,

distribution deals, national box-office figures, and much appreciated regular reporting on local film exhibitions.

GIORGIO BERTELLINI

Ciné-Journal (1908–1937)

On 15 August 1908, Georges **Dureau**, previously editor of *l'Argus-Phono-Cinéma* and *Phono-Cinéma-Revue*, launched *Ciné-Journal*, which quickly became the "mouthpiece of the film industry." Like **Phono-Ciné-Gazette**, which disappeared in December 1909, *Ciné-Journal* dealt with economic and legal issues concerning the cinema and devoted numerous articles to its evolving techniques. It also listed the latest "cinematographic novelties" and patents as well as printed ads for traveling **fair/fairground** exhibitors. **Advertising** came to occupy a prominent position during the 1910s, particularly in the form of inserts praising the qualities of French and foreign films. After taking over *Le Journal du Film* in June 1923, *Ciné-Journal* lasted until September 1937. For historians of cinema, it remains an invaluable resource.

Further reading

Toulet, Emmanuelle (1989) "Au sources de l'histoire du cinéma ... Naissance d'une presse sous influences," *Restaurations et tirages de la Cinémathèque française*, 4 (14–25), Paris: Cinémathèque française.

LAURENT MANNONI

cinema circuits or chains

A business practice whereby one company or corporation owns and operates more than a single motion picture theater. Before 1915, this was common in the largest cities of the USA. National or regional chains did not commence until after that. Yet most of the noted major studios—save RKO and United Artists—began as local chain exhibition operations during the early cinema era, and this chain ownership helped them dominate the movie business.

The **nickelodeon** era lasted less than a decade and spawned only small chains except in the largest cities: a circuit of twenty or more, for instance, could be found in New York. During this era, the **Motion Picture Patents Company** failed in its attempt to corner the market, but it set into play the forces which led to the development of cinema circuits or chains across the USA. By owning more than one theater, a booker could demand better terms from the MPPC. And owning a score of cinemas meant the costs of operation for each cinema were lower than simply controlling one. Two or more theaters could be serviced by one accountant, one booker, and hence costs could be spread out over the circuit. Nickelodeon-era entrepreneurs saw this in action in **vaudeville** circuits such as Keith's and Orpheum, legitimate **theaters** in the Shubert chain, and burlesque chains such as Columbia.

All these theatrical circuits or chains followed the lead of far larger organizations, particularly department store and grocery store chains that precipitated significant changes in mass selling in the USA during the years before and coinciding with early cinema. Moving picture theater chains did not operate in a vacuum. Indeed, entertainment followed a national trend. In the latter part of the 19th century and during the first two decades of the 20th century, the U.S. economy was altered radically by the innovation of chain store retailing which increased sales volume, speeded delivery of services, standardized products and services, cut costs, and increased profits.

In short, chain stores became a significant force in the United States economy. They emerged in the form of grocery stores (A&P, Grand Union, Krogers), variety stores (Woolworths, McCrory, Kresge), and then others for drugs and sundries, auto parts, gas stations, and clothing. Moving picture exhibitors simply sought to follow suit, usually first at some regional or citywide level. For example, a former "small time vaudeville" company, Loew's Theatrical Enterprises, based in New York City, was able to use the advantages of chain ownership—called by economists economies of scale—to dominate film exhibition in all five boroughs of the USA's largest market. One hundred miles to the south, Jules and Stanley **Mastbaum**'s Stanley Company seized power in the same manner in the country' third largest city, Philadelphia.

By the middle 1910s, chains based in the biggest cities in the USA were learning to take full advantage of the savings that could be gained from "scientific management." Owners began to hire university-trained experts to study conditions and propose methods by which to minimize costs and maximize sales. Each department of the modern chain store enterprise was simply asked to perform its specialty at maximum speed and minimum cost. Only those tasks necessary to that goal needed to be learned. Owners and operators of single store outlets had to be jacks-of-all-trades. Masters of specialties could do their jobs faster and cheaper—and encompass hundreds of operations. Scientific management came to the moving picture business, not through production—which struggled to standardize—but through exhibition.

The greatest lesson these pioneer chains learned from the MPPC was that power came with numbers. The monopsony buying power of a chain organization kept other operating costs low (monopsony buying power refers to the economic advantage that results when a firm is one of a limited number of buyers of a necessary input). For example, as A&P grew to become the dominant grocery chain, it could seek and secure discounts from its suppliers, be they farmers or mass producers of household items. A&P would buy in bulk, at lower than normal unit prices. Sellers were happy to secure the sizable sale guaranteed by signing up with A&P. Cinema chains would do the same in booking theaters with the same films, labor, and buildings.

Cinema chains or circuits came to this form of business organization late in the game. By 1912, A&P's 400 red-fronted outlets came to represent the modern age of self-service grocery shopping, revolutionizing a major institution in the nation's economic life. Marcus **Loew**, William **Fox**, Thomas and John **Saxe**, Barney & A. J. **Balaban**, and others aspired to earn the millions A&P stores took in each year.

If the "chain store revolution" began to emerge in the movie business toward the end of the early cinema period, its effect was strongest during the years between 1916 and 1924, when exhibitors diligently copied the efficiencies of their retail cousins down the street, in order to gain greater power within a city, to increase profits every year, and eventually to become giants in the new industry. In time five national chains would dominate the USA, amassing 90% of the dollars collected at the movie show.

See also: monopoly capitalism; palace cinemas

Further reading

Conant, Michael (1960) *Antitrust in the Motion Picture Industry: Economic and Legal Analysis*, Berkeley: University of California Press.

Gomery, Douglas (1992) *Shared Pleasures: A History of Movie Presentation in the United States*, Madison: University of Wisconsin Press.

Kennedy, Joseph P. (ed.) (1927) *The Story of Films*, Chicago: A. W. Shaw.

Lebhar, Gedfrey M. (1963) *Chain Stores in America, 1859–1962*, third edition, New York: Chain Store Publishing Corporation.

DOUGLAS GOMERY

Cinéma du peuple, Le

In 1913, the French anarchist movement decided to respond to what it saw as film propaganda originating from the Catholics (**Maison de la Bonne Presse**), the bourgeois class (represented by **Pathé-Frères, Gaumont, Éclair**), and military and patriotic circles. On the model of a "Theater of the People" created in 1912, Yves Bidamant and Robert Guérard, founded the "Cinema of the People," a cooperative public limited company, on October 28, 1913. Through May 1914, the Cinéma du peuple released 4,895 meters of film: among them, *Les misères de l'aiguille* [Miseries of the Needle]; *Les obsèques du citoyen Francis de Pressensé* [The Funeral of Citizen Francis de Pressensé]; *L'hiver, plaisirs de riches! Souffrances des pauvres!* [Winter, Pleasures for the Rich, Sufferings for the Poor!]; *Le Vieux docker* [The Old Docker]; *Biribi*; *Francesco Ferrer*; *Les Actualités ouvrières* [The Workers' News]. Armand Guerra directed certain titles such as *La Commune*, recently found at the Cinémathèque française. **World War I** put an end to the efforts of the Cinéma du peuple.

Further reading

Mannoni, Laurent (October 1993) "28 octobre 1913: création de la société Le Cinéma du Peuple," in Thierry Lefebvre et Laurent Mannoni, "L'année 1913 en France," *1895*, 100–107.

LAURENT MANNONI

Cinéma et L'Écho du cinéma réunis, Le

Le Cinéma was founded in March 1912 by Armand Dennery. Some of its writers soon seceded and established a rival trade paper, *L'Écho du cinéma*, in April 1912. After competing for four months, the two weeklies merged, and the first issue of *Le Cinéma et L'Écho du cinéma réunis* came out on 19 July 1912, with film producer Georges **Lordier** (from Grands Films Populaires) at the helm. The magazine adopted a folio format and made the principles guiding the Paris arts **newspaper**, *Comœdia*, its own: it addressed a large **audience** of movie-goers while "serving as an advocate of the film industry." Its publication was interrupted during the war but resumed between 1917 and 1923.

THIERRY LEFEBVRE

Cinéma-Halls, Compagnie des

Founded by merchant Henri Daniel in June 1907, the Compagnie des Cinéma-Halls was, at the time, the most capitalized French public limited company (*société anonyme*) in the business of exhibition, with 1.5 million francs. Among its main subscribers were two bankers (Maurice Gallet and Adrien Caro), Louis Morénas (co-founder, several months before, of **Théophile Pathé** et Cie), as well as most of the main investors in the future

Film d'Art. The company quickly established a network of moving picture theaters, taking over American Kinetograph and acquiring its flagship, the Hippodrome (the future Gaumont-Palace) in Paris. Very poorly managed and plagued by considerable debts, Cinéma-Halls disbanded in April 1909, after the bankers went broke, and was itself declared bankrupt in August.

JEAN-JACQUES MEUSY

cinema of attractions

The phrase "the cinema of attractions," introduced by Tom Gunning and André Gaudreault in 1985, characterized the earliest phase of cinema as dedicated to presenting discontinuous visual attractions, moments of spectacle rather than narrative. This era of attractions was followed by a period, beginning around 1906, in which films increasingly *did* organize themselves around the tasks of narrative. These later films employed extensive actions over time, a strong sense of cause and effect, the development of characters with motivations and purposes, and the creation of suspense. By contrast, the cinema of attractions presented visual delights (**color**, spectacular **costumes** or **set design**), surprises (unusual physical feats, or magical trick effects), displays of the exotic, beautiful, or grotesque (views of foreign sites or indigenous peoples, scantily clad women, or physical freaks), or other sorts of sensational thrills (speeding trains, explosions, tricks of fast motion). Using the term "monstration" (from *monstre*, to show) rather than narration to characterize this style, Gaudreault emphasized that this is a cinema of "showing" rather than "telling."

The term "attractions" had two sources. First, in the late 19th and early 20th centuries show business, such as the **fair/fairground**, **vaudeville**, or circus, "attractions" referred to anything which would attract an audience: an act within a variety program (singing, dancing, acrobatics, trained animals); a technological thrill ride in the new **amusement parks** (the roller coaster, loop-the-loop, merry-go-round); or even a display of oddities within a dime museum. In the 1920's, Soviet director Sergei Eisenstein appropriated the term to describe his avant-garde practices in theater and film, which he referred to as a "montage of attractions." Eisenstein defined "attractions" as any aggressive moment designed for maximum emotional or psychological effect on the spectator, such as eyes being gouged out in a Grand Guignol horror play, or the acrobatic tightrope balancing in his own stage production of *The Sage*. Rather than attempting to create a fictional world (as narrative tends to do), attractions address the spectator directly, even aggressively, subjecting him or her to emotional shocks.

The practice of direct audience address distinguished the "cinema of attractions" from the later cinema of narrative integration. In much of early cinema, typified by the **trick films** of Georges **Méliès**, a **magician** or impresario acknowledges the audience, looking towards the camera during filming, frequently bowing and gesturing towards it as well, even soliciting the viewer's attention by pointing out aspects of the spectacle as it unfolds. With the rise of narrative cinema, performances that acknowledge the camera became taboo, as early film critics claimed that such looks at the camera ruined the illusion essential to fiction. This stricture on looking at the camera created what Christian Metz described as the "voyeur" nature of **classical Hollywood cinema**, in which one watches a film, but the film does not acknowledge (at least directly) the viewer's presence. By contrast, the cinema of attractions operates outside this stricture, and could be described as an "exhibitionist" cinema well aware of the act of being seen, flaunting the act of display.

This display of visual novelties or spectacular arrangements motivated the very first exhibition of motion pictures. In this fairly brief "novelty period" the motion picture itself—photographs which appeared to move—constituted the main attraction, beyond any interest in the subject matter of individual films. After the initial exploitation of the new apparatus, early filmmakers widely adopted **newspapers** and **illustrated magazines** as models, and the most popular films frequently became those that reflected current events. Consequently, the display of such images in *actualités* and **news event films** (e.g., the Derby Race, Queen Victoria's Diamond Jubilee, U.S. Presidential candidate McKinley appearing at his home) also came to exemplify the cinema of attractions. In place of the dichotomy proposed by French film historian Georges Sadoul between the style of **Lumière** and Méliès (which contrasted a style rooted in documentary realism to a style rooted in fictional fantasy), therefore, both the fiction and non-fiction film of early cinema could be considered attractions, emphasizing the display of novel events, whether real or constructed.

The temporality of the cinema of attractions tends towards suddenness, rather than duration. Narrative stretches out an action, delaying its resolution. Attractions, in contrast, feature sudden appearances. The substitution tricks found in a Méliès trick films typify this burst of attraction, as an object or character suddenly transforms into something else. However, longer films of attractions could be formed through a concatenation of several attractions (a Méliès film with a number of substitutions or transformations), by a succession of various visual effects, or occasionally by presenting actions which simply unfold (the many films of surf crashing on the shore, or the famous **phantom train rides** which showed a landscape passing by a camera mounted on some means of **transportation**—train, tram, or motor boat). Furthermore, some films could use a story as an excuse to present attractions.

Whether attractions really dominated the first decade of early cinema has generated discussion. Gunning admits that a number of early films, such as Méliès' more elaborate **féeries/fairy-tale films**—*Le Voyage dans la lune* [Trip to the Moon] (1902), *Le Royaume de fées* [The Kingdom of Fairies] (1903)—involve narrative development. However, following Méliès' own claim that the film's story only served as the pretext for the display of a series of tricks or elaborate sets, Gunning claims such hybrid films are dominated by the succession of attractions rather than the story. Instead of developing characters or dramatic suspense, these films foreground spectacular moments of non- narrative display. Yet audience reception in vaudeville houses in the USA indicates that Méliès' longer narrative films enjoyed considerable popularity and that their narrative aspect may have played a role in this.

Charles Musser has challenged the claim that narrative played a subordinate role in cinema's first decade. Since many early cinema programs were accompanied by oral commentaries given by **lecturers**, Musser points out, the role of narrative might have been greater than is evident today from watching a film without such accompaniment. For Gunning, however, such verbal accompaniments convey narrative as an extraneous element, outside the film rather than organizing it. Indeed, it is not clear that all such commentary was primarily narrative in form; lecturers could emphasize the spectacular or non-narrative aspects of the film. Moreover, the use of direct audience address by such lecturers relates strongly to the realm of attractions, much like the Méliès magicians.

Musser also argues that narrative plays a stronger role in the multi-shot films of Edwin S. **Porter** between 1903 and 1906, an era he says represents "the rise of story film" (thus claiming an earlier date for the dominance of narrative films, at least in popularity). Acknowledging that aspects of narrative exist from nearly the beginning of cinema, Gunning argues that the first decade is best characterized by interrelation between narrative and attractions, rather than the exclusion of one or the other—albeit he claims that attractions dominate this era. Musser's and Gunning's contrasting reading of such elements as the close-up of the bandit leader shooting at the camera in *The Great Train Robbery* (for Gunning, an example of aggressive address to the spectator; for Musser, a narrative strategy to make the audience identify with the outlaw's victims and thus condemn him) or the close-up of the lady's ankle in *The Gay Shoe Clerk* (for Gunning, an erotic attraction enlarged for the spectator's delight; for Musser, a dramatic emphasis of a key narrative moment) demonstrate that critical analysis can plausibly find both elements in Porter's early films, accenting what Noël Burch terms the filmmaker's Janus-like nature between two eras. Clearly Gunning finds Porter more interesting in his differences from later practices, those moments that relate him to the cinema of attractions. Musser would rather emphasize Porter's pioneering of later narrative devices. Neither could absolutely deny the possibility of the other point of view.

Musser rightly emphasizes the importance of the context of presentation and reception for early cinema. But even he agrees that the attractions aspect of early films was probably increased by their presentation in vaudeville theaters as an act within the variety format, a discontinuous and generally non-narrative form of entertainment. Early films were presented in other circumstances as well, and no doubt certain presentations of the *Passion Play* (such as **Pathé-Frères** 1903 version), if accompanied by lectures and quotations from the Bible, could be received as a coherent narrative experience. The same would be true of Porter's *Uncle Tom's Cabin* (1903), if accompanied by a lecture which identified characters and provided motivations and causes and effects not evident in the film itself. As Janet Staiger and Musser have pointed out, in the case of such well-known stories, audiences could provide much of this information themselves. However, the fact that such narrative elements had to be supplied as a supplement from outside the film shows how different this form of narrative would be from later forms in which the films would be self-contained. For Gunning, this porous and often incoherent style of early narrative indicates that the style of attractions still dominates. The Cake Walk and Steamboat Race in *Uncle Tom* are coherently presented attractions, and Eliza's escape across the ice floes forms an attraction in itself, whether or not one knows the narrative context (only alluded to in the film). Likewise, *The Passion Play*, far from giving a coherent account of the life of Jesus, illustrated key moments with eye-popping visual spectacle. It would be hard to maintain that either a narrative or an attractional form of reception dominated the era enough to exclude the other.

There is, of course, a danger in making an absolute opposition between attractions (or spectacle) and narrative. As theorists of narrative have pointed out, narrative tends to absorb things rather than exclude them. Thus, rather than excluding one term or the other from early film analysis, the most useful approach is to observe their interaction. While Porter or Méliès can be taken as narrative filmmakers, it diminishes our understanding of their films if their reliance on attractions is not acknowledged. The reverse also is true for certain of their films. However, the sort of film produced through the interaction of narrative and attractions in early cinema differs greatly from the narrative films increasingly produced after 1906, in which character's motives and narrative suspense not only is hinted at but determines the style of the film.

While narrative aspects certainly exist in early cinema before 1906, it must also be emphasized that attractions persist as a key element of cinema thereafter. While most kinds of fiction film seem dominated by narrative, some continue the display of attractions (**animation**, **pornographic** films, later experimental films), while others seem to seesaw back and forth between narrative and attractions (slapstick **comedies**, sensational **melodramas**, **biblical films**, later musicals, the current special effects blockbuster). However, a number of film industry practices (not the least being the role of the script as blueprint for production planning) seem to demand that even films such as *Jurassic Park*, while clearly dependent on special effect attractions for their box office appeal, nonetheless maintain characterization and cause and effect to a degree unheard of in *A Trip to the Moon* or *The Gay Shoe Clerk*. Still, one has to ask, what is it that audiences remember from these films and what ultimately attracts them to them?

See also: editing: early techniques and practices; editing: tableau style

Further reading

Abel, Richard (1994) *The Ciné Goes to Town: French Cinema, 1896–1914*, Berkeley: University of California Press.

Eisenstein, Sergei (1988) "The Montage of Attractions," 33–38, in Richard Taylor (ed.) *1922–1934*, London: British Film Institute.

Gaudreault, André and Tom Gunning (1989) "Le cinéma des premiers temps, un défi à l'histoire du cinéma?," in J. Aumont, A. Gaudreault, and M. Marie (eds.) *Histoire du Cinema: Nouvelles Approches*, Paris: La Sorbonne nouvelle.

Gunning, Tom (1990) "The Cinema of Attractions: Early Film, Its Spectator and the Avant-Garde," 56–62, in Thomas Elsaesser and Adam Barker (eds.) *Early Film Space Frame Narrative*, London: British Film Institute.

Gunning, Tom (1995) " 'Now You See it, Now You Don't': The Temporality of the Cinema of

Attractions," 71–84, in Richard Abel (ed.) *Silent Cinema*, New Brunswick: Rutgers University Press.

Musser, Charles (1994) "Rethinking Early Cinema: Cinema of Attractions and Narrativity," *Yale Journal of Criticism*, 7.1: 203–232.

TOM GUNNING

Cinématographe Lumière

The Cinématographe **Lumière**, patented on February 13, 1895, was a camera, projector, and contact printer, all in one. Shifting from one function to another simply required changes in various accessories and lenses. After being demonstrated by Lumière operators around the world, the machine was marketed in 1897, but by then customers already preferred separate **cameras** or **projectors** because they were easier to handle and could accommodate more than 60 meters of film. **Pathé-Frères**, for instance, was beginning to sell excellent Maltese-cross projectors made by René **Bünzli** and Victor **Continsouza**. The Lumière brothers thus decided to make a sprocketed machine designed secifically for projection. Because they had difficulty establishing their two round perforations (one on each one side of the frame) as the standard for 35 mm film, two models were produced: one for their own films, another for films with "American perforations" (two square perforations on each side of the frame), promoted by **Edison**. Around 1901, a device developed by Jules **Carpentier** allowed the Lumière projector to use longer reels, and it was still featured in a 1905 company catalogue.

LAURENT MANNONI

Cines

In 1905, the first major Italian film studio was founded by Filoteo Alberini and Dante Santoni as "Alberoni & Santoni," then changed in 1906 to the public corporation "Società italiana Cines." In *La presa di Roma* [The Taking of Rome] (1905), Alberini & Santoni produced a prototype for the

Italian **historical film** shot in a studio and using trained actors. In 1906, the management lured the French filmmaker Gaston **Velle** away from **Pathé-Frères** to produce a series of *féeries* or **fairy plays**. In 1907, the former actor Mario **Caserini** joined the company as director. From then on, Cines began to excel at the genre of historical films. By 1910, the former painter, art director, and pupil of Caserini, Enrico **Guazzoni**, began to distinguish himself as the director of historical productions such as *Brutus* (1910), *Agrippina* (1910), and *La sposa del Nilo* [The Bride of the Nile] (1910).

In the same period (1909–1910), Cines was confronted with the first worldwide crisis in the film industry caused by overproduction. Count Alberto Fassini, ordered to liquidate the company, reorganized it instead, attracting several aristocrats onto the board and providing an enormous increase of capital. From then on the company could guarantee a steady production schedule. The studio was equipped with modern utilities and populated by a cast (i.e., Amleto **Novelli**, Maria Caserini-Gasperini, Gianna Terribili Gonzales) and crew with long-term contracts, all of whom worked simultaneously on different productions. A **screenwriting** office was installed for the regular output of scenarios. The production of historical films came to a climax with the epic *Quo vadis?*, produced in 1912 but not released until 1913. The large three-dimensional sets, the revival of the "grandeur" of Roman antiquity, the countless extras, and the spectacular scenes such as the burning of Rome and the Roman arena, thrilled audiences all over the world. *Quo vadis?* not only put Cines among the best of the world's film companies but also contributed greatly to the acceptance of cinema as a "respectable" entertainment and even an art form. The success of *Quo Vadis?* led to the production of two other big-budget epics set in classical times, *Marcantonio e Cleopatra* [Antony and Cleopatra] (1913) and *Cajus Julius Caesar* [Julius Caesar] (1914).

Besides historical films, Cines was well known for its steady output of **comedies**, from farces with Tontolini (Ferdinando **Guillaume**) and Kri Kri (Raymond **Frau**) to boulevard-style comedies such as *Una tragedia al cinematografo* [A Tragedy at the Cinematograph] (1913), in which Pina **Menichelli** had one of her first roles. Cines also produced modern dramas, in which future diva, Francesca **Bertini**, excelled, after her roles in historical films at **Film d'Arte Italiana** and before moving to Celio, an affiliate of Cines. Cines produced many non-fiction films as well, with many of them **travelogues** that glorified the beauties of natural scenery, mainly in Italy itself. Cines even produced the first Italian **westerns**, foreshadowing the later spaghetti-westerns of the sixties and seventies.

After the outbreak of **World War I**, Cines survived the war crisis by releasing films with such stars as Lyda **Borelli** and by employing a new generation of outstanding directors such as Nino **Oxilia**, Giulio Antamoro, Carmine Gallone, Augusto Genina, and Amleto Palermi. By the war's end, however, decline was inevitable. In 1919 Cines merged with the Unione Cinematografica Italiana, and in 1923 activity halted altogether. Most early Cines films are to be found today in the film archives of London, Amsterdam, and Bologna.

See also: comic series

Further reading

Redi, Riccardo (1990) *La Cines. Storia di una casa di produzione italiana*, Roma: CNC Edizioni.
Tomadjoglou, Kimberly (2000) "Rome's premiere film studio: Società Italiana Cines," *Film History*, 12.3: 262–275.

IVO BLOM

Clarendon Film Company

Founded in 1904, Clarendon established itself with **comedies** (directed by Percy **Stow**) that mixed gentle social comment with absurdity, notably *A Glass of Goat's Milk* (1909) and the suffragette satire *Milling the Militants* (1913). Such inventive productions have yet to receive their critical due. Clarendon enjoyed success with the *Lieutenant Rose* series of adventure stories (1909–1914), and gained prestige among a class-conscious industry for its scenarios by the Marchioness of Townshend. Clarendon grew ambitious with the feature-length

historical films, *King Charles* (1913) and *Old St Paul's* (1914). Never at the forefront of British film production, but modestly prosperous, the company and its Croydon studios were taken over by Harma in 1918.

LUKE McKERNAN

classical Hollywood cinema

Historians often apply the term, "classical Hollywood cinema," to a general approach to storytelling that arose roughly between 1903 and 1917 in the USA and has continued in its basic principles to the present day. This approach differs from that in use in the earliest years of moving pictures, sometimes termed the **cinema of attractions**, because films' appeal then lay mainly in brief gags and minimally developed situations. Classical films instead tell sustained, unified stories, using cinematic techniques in such a way as to make them easily comprehensible to the spectator.

Although there had been narrative films from the beginning of cinema, nonfiction films dominated until around 1904. As the rapid spread of **nickelodeons** increased the demand for moving pictures, producers responded by making longer films. By 1908, the standard length for individual releases was set at one reel, lasting about fifteen minutes in projection. A film of that length could not be a simple gag, and although the **chase films** so popular in the early years could be stretched out, other types of stories were needed.

Longer stories required scenarios for the dozens of narrative films released each week. Since there were no professional scriptwriters, film manufacturers solicited submissions from the huge pool of freelance writers working in other narrative arts. Thus influences from **melodrama theater**, **vaudeville**, novels, and short stories of the day helped shape the classical Hollywood narrative. During the late 19th century, the spread of the railroad system and improvements in publishing methods had created a boom in popular fiction magazines, dime novels, and touring theatrical companies. Writers experienced in these areas began writing film scenarios as well.

These freelancers drew on models of narrative structure that were current during the 19th century. During that era, the notion of the well-made play took shape, and the short story arose as a form that strives for unity of effect. Writers revived the principle of narrative described by Aristotle, who had advocated a unified plot with a clear beginning, middle, and end. During the early 1910s, as the number of freelancers writing film scenarios grew, advice manuals were published, laying out these Aristotelian principles in detail and helping to standardize what became the classical Hollywood narrative system. In the late 1910s and 1920s, when studios began employing staff writers, they continued to use these principles.

In classical film narratives, events occur in a linear chain of cause and effect. Unexplained actions are avoided. Typically the causes for events arise from the characters' clearly established traits and desires. The main character desires something and pursues that desire. This goal-oriented protagonist encounters obstacles, often in the form of countering goals of the antagonist or other characters.

As films grew to feature length during the first half of the 1910s, filmmakers faced challenges in sustaining longer, more complex stories without confusing the spectator. Great emphasis was laid on unity of action. Films would have a clear-cut progression, with a complete resolution to all lines of action. Rather than following a single goal, the protagonist often had two, one of which would involve a romance. Goals might change in the course of the film as the protagonist faced new situations. Classical narratives establish information about action clearly and typically repeat that information; redundancy helps further orient the spectator.

Lacking spoken dialogue, silent films began using **intertitles** to convey story information. From Edwin S. **Porter**'s *Uncle Tom's Cabin* (1903) on, brief, third-person expository titles were inserted before each shot to summarize its action, as well as to cover time gaps between scenes. By 1910, intertitles giving key lines of the characters' dialogue came into common use.

In the early era of moving pictures, actors stayed at long-shot distance from the camera and conveyed information about their characters' thoughts and dialogue largely through pantomime. Such acting included many standardized gestures. For example, an actor telegraphed that the character was getting an idea by pointing to his/her temple and smiling broadly. By the early 1910s, however, with the camera framing the actor from the knees or even the waist up, facial expressions were easier to see. With intertitles to help convey information, actors could use more sophisticated facial expressions and smaller gestures. This new style was termed "American" acting because it contrasted with the more flamboyant, virtuoso displays of emotion appreciated in countries such as Italy and Russia.

In the classical system, film techniques usually do not call attention to themselves, as they often had done in the era of the cinema of attractions. Rather, style is subordinated to the demands of telling the story.

In the early years, the camera also tended to be aimed straight into a flat backdrop and to view the action from a distance. The result was often a shallow playing space far from the spectator's viewpoint. As the principles of classical storytelling developed, however, filmmakers brought the spectator into the space of the action. In part this resulted from changes in **set design** and in part from new editing techniques that brought the viewer closer to the action.

In exterior scenes shot in the studio, early backdrops often suggested a deep space behind the actors by using perspective paintings. For interiors, however, the camera faced perpendicularly toward the back wall. At most, backdrops might include a corner of a room, suggesting a bit of depth. By 1910, theater-style flats were used to construct actual corners, and real furniture was placed relatively close to the camera to create a deeper playing space. From about 1913 on, rising budgets for two-reelers and feature films made bigger sets possible. A large doorway at the center rear could show part of a second room in depth. If a single room were shown, it was typically deeper than it was wide, with side walls and more furniture. As a result, actors could move more freely in any direction, and editing could guide the spectator's eye instantly to the most important narrative actions.

Those instantaneous changes of time and space at the cuts, however, also risked confusing the spectator about the space and time of the action.

Filmmakers devised techniques for aiding understanding by keeping space, time, and action clear, consistent, and continuous. By 1912, this ideal was referred to as "continuity," and the guidelines of classical film editing form the continuity system. As its name implies, continuity editing aims to make actions continue uninterrupted across a series of shots within a scene.

In early multi-shot films, each scene tended to be played out in one shot, followed by another one-shot scene in another space, and so on. In the period from about 1910 on, however, filmmakers increasingly used "cut-ins" to closer views of important details that were important to the spectator's understanding of the action: most often a photograph or a letter. But by the mid-1910s, a filmmaker might cut in to reveal an actor's expression or a detail of gesture. During the trial scene of *Intolerance* (1916), D. W. **Griffith** famously cut to close views of the Dear One's anguished face and her hands clutching a handkerchief. By the mid-1910s, filmmakers would often begin with an establishing long shot but then cut fairly often within the scene to guide the viewer's attention. Matching the actors positions and gestures across the cut avoided making the editing confusing or distracting; it also conveyed a sense of time continuing smoothly over the cut. Cutting around within a single space came to be known as "analytical" editing.

Other editing devices allowed filmmakers to cut freely around in a single space. A shot of a character looking off-screen could be followed by a second of what he/she sees; the cut creates an "eye-line match." Two characters facing each other could be shown in separate shots, one looking off left, the other looking off right. This "shot/reverse shot" pattern came into frequent use by the mid-1910s and has remained one of the most common ways of staging and editing dialogue scenes ever since.

All this cutting around could become confusing if the camera placements were merely random. The spatial relations among the characters and objects in the separate shots then would be unclear. To avoid such problems, filmmakers began to adhere to a "180-degree system." In cutting to different views of a scene, the camera would be placed on one side of the space, within a generally semi-circular area defined by the "axis of action," an imaginary line through the main figures in the scene. With the camera always placed on one side of that axis, the shots keep the spatial relations of the actors consistent. Two actors appearing on the left and right, respectively, in one shot will still be on the left and right in the next, whereas a shot from the opposite side would make them switch positions. By maintaining consistent screen direction in eye-line matches, cut-ins, and shot/reverse shot, filmmakers can build a scene of many shots and not confuse the spectator.

If two actions were taking place simultaneously in widely separated places, the filmmakers convey this fact to the viewer by using editing to move back and forth between them, a technique variously known as "intercutting," "crosscutting," or "parallel editing."

Techniques of **lighting** changed considerably during the development of the classical system. Initially sets and actions had been lit by a flat wash of light coming in from the upper front of the set, either from the sun or from studio lamps. Such lighting illuminated actors and sets alike but had this disadvantage: actors could cast obvious shadows that distracted viewers from the story. During the 1910s, cameramen gradually learned to light the space of the action from more than one direction. Bright "key" lights concentrated attention on the actors, while dimmer "fill" light eliminated the distracting shadows they cast and made the backgrounds subdued and unobtrusive. "Back" light from lamps at the top rear of the set, illuminating the actors from behind, created a rim of brightness around their bodies that further helped to make them stand out against the backgrounds and created a sense of depth (as well as a glamorous look from glowing hair and costumes). This "three-point" lighting system (key, fill, back) became the standard for Hollywood for decades to come.

All of these principles and techniques of classical Hollywood cinema were fully formulated and consistently used by 1917. Many refinements and small changes would take place over succeeding decades. By 1919, for instance, filmmakers shooting a conversation scene would occasionally place the shoulder of the second actor in the foreground while filming the face of the other; the purpose was simply to give a bit more spatial information to help orient the viewer in relation to the action. Such placement became extremely common during the 1920s and is referred to as "over-the-shoulder shot/reverse shot."

Such refinements, however, left the basic classical system intact. Even such major later technical changes as sound (in the late 1920s), **color** (in the 1930s), and wide-screen images (in the 1950s) have not altered the narrative and stylistic principles underlying classical Hollywood cinema.

See also: acting styles; camera movement; editing: spatial relations; editing: tableau style; editing: temporal relations; facial expression films; framing; multiple-reel/feature films: USA; screenwriting; spectatorship: issues and debates; staging in depth

Further reading

Bordwell, David, Janet Staiger, and Kristin Thompson (1985) *The Classical Hollywood Cinema: Film Style and Mode of Production to 1960*, New York: Columbia University Press.

Bowser, Eileen (1990) *The Transformation of Cinema, 1907–1915*, New York: Scribner's.

Cherchi Usai, Paolo and Lorenzo Codelli (eds.) (1988) *Sulla via di Hollywood, 1911–1920* (The Path to Hollywood, 1911–1920), Pordenone: Biblioteca dell'Immagine.

Gunning, Tom (1991). *D. W. Griffith and the Origins of American Narrative Film: The Early Years at Biograph*, Urbana: University of Illinois Press.

Keil, Charlie (2002) *Early American Cinema in Transition: Story, Style, and Filmmaking, 1907–1913*, Madison: University of Wisconsin Press.

Thompson, Kristin (1997) "Narration Early in the Transition to Classical Filmmaking: Three Vitagraph Shorts," *Film History*, 9.4: 410–434.

KRISTIN THOMPSON

Clement, Josephine [Mrs. Edward]

b. ?; d. ?

exhibitor, USA

A Boston social leader and wife of the former editor of the *Boston Transcript*, Clement managed the prestigious Bijou Theatre in Boston for the **Keith** circuit between 1908 and early 1914. Along with S. L. **Rothapfel**, she established a model of the "artistic and wholesome" moving picture theater thought to appeal to a "refined" clientele. By late 1910, according to "a handsomely printed booklet describing its aims" and amenities, the Bijou ran five daily shows of two hours each, with programs comprised of several **Motion Picture Patents Company** films, a one-act play, vocal and instrumental music (not **illustrated songs**), and "camera chats" using **magic lantern slides** and "stereoptican views." This "high-class" variety program enjoyed strong support in the US **trade press**.

RICHARD ABEL

Clément-Maurice [Clément Maurice Gratioulet]

b. 1853, Aiguillon; d. 1933, Sanary-sur-Mer

photographer, industrialist, France

Clément-Maurice was a Paris photographer, whose shop was next to Georges **Méliès**'s Robert Houdin theater. A close friend of Antoine **Lumière**, he organized the first **Cinématographe** screenings at the Grand Café, starting 28 December 1895. In March 1896, he also organized Cinématographe screenings at the Olympia **music hall**. In 1900, he served as technical supervisor for the **Phono-Cinéma-Théâtre**. With A.-P. **Parnaland**, he also made films of Dr. **Doyen**'s surgical operations. In March 1907, he created a general-partnership film company with his son Léopold and Félix **Mesguich**, a well-known Lumière cameraman. Shortly thereafter (July 1907), the company was turned into a public limited company, the "Société générale des Cinématographes Radios," with studios in Boulogne-sur-Seine. Clément-Maurice was the father of Léopold Maurice, who in 1919 founded the CTM ("Cinéma-Tirage-Maurice") laboratories, as well as Georges Maurice, a cameraman and film technician.

LAURENT MANNONI

Clune, William H.

b. 1862; d. 1927

exhibitor, distributor, producer, USA

William H. Clune's business interests moved from trains to musical instruments before he set up a **penny arcade** in turn-of-the-century Los Angeles. He later built several lavish moving picture theaters in the city's downtown and then all over southern California before taking over the Los Angeles Auditorium in 1914. Besides his exhibition activities, Clune owned a licensed exchange as well as a **vaudeville** circuit, Clune's Vodville, managed by Robert Brackett. His substantial real-estate interests included acquiring Mary **Pickford**'s studio, later leased to the Tec-Art Company, when Clune dismantled his film activities in the early 20s. Around 1910, Clune backed several **boxing films**; later he produced *Ramona* (1914) and invested in D. W. **Griffith**'s *The Birth of a Nation* (1915) and *Intolerance* (1916).

See also: cinema chains; nickelodeons

JAN OLSSON

Cody, William F. ("Buffalo Bill")

b. 1846; d. 1917

promoter, producer, actor, USA

Cody was the purveyor of "Buffalo Bill's Wild West" (1883–1914), which had a great influence on the development of **westerns**. In 1894, the **Edison Manufacturing Co.** filmed *Buffalo Bill, Indian War Council, Sioux Ghost Dance, Buffalo Dance*, and *Bucking Broncho*, all of which feature performers from Cody's "Wild West." Other films such as **American Mutoscope and Biograph's** *Buffalo Bill's Wild West Parade* (1902) document the "Wild West's" standard pre-show parade. Cody himself became involved in producing **multiple-reel films** towards the end of his career. *The Life of Buffalo Bill* (1912) depicts events previously represented in the "Wild West." **Essanay**'s *Indian War Pictures* (1914), shot on location, reenacts

the battles of Summit Springs, War Bonnet Creek, and Wounded Knee.

KRISTEN WHISSEL

Cohl [Courtet], Emile

b. 1857; d. 1938

animator, France

Cohl had been a well known caricaturist when **Gaumont** hired him as a writer in 1908. He quickly ascertained the technique of **animation** and developed a character, Fantoche, that continued over several films, using different animated media, from paper drawings to puppets. His intellectual roots in the 19th-century Incoherent Art movement contributed to his idiosyncratic aesthetic and influenced the subsequent films and cartoons that he directed for **Pathé-Frères**, **Éclair**, and others. He directed or animated over 250 short films before retiring in 1924.

Further reading

Crafton, Donald (1990) *Emile Cohl, Caricature, and Film*, Princeton: Princeton University Press.

DONALD CRAFTON

Coissac, Guillaume-Michel

b. 1868; d. 1946

journalist, editor, historian, France

In 1890, Coissac began working for the **Maison de la Bonne Presse**, the major French publisher for Catholic education, and, in 1896, became director of its visual **education** division. In 1903, he became editor of the Catholic bi-weekly, *Le Fascinateur*. He wrote several early technical manuals, including *La Théorie et la pratique des projections* [The Theory and Practice of Projections] (1905), *Le coloris des diapositives de projection et de bandes cinématographiques* [Coloring Slides and Films] (1906), and *Le Manuel pratique du conférencier projectionniste* [The New Manual of the Lecturer-Projectionist] (1907). Coissac is considered one of the first French historians of cinema, and his *Histoire du Cinématographe de ses origines à nos jours* [History of Cinema from its Origins to the Present] (1925), triggered much controversy.

LAURENT MANNONI

collections: public and private

The undisputed father of cinema collectors was the London-born Will Day or William Ernest Lytton Day (1873–1936). In 1897, Day bought a Theatrograph **projector** from Robert W. **Paul**, and thereafter dedicated his life to the film business, eventually broadening his interests to include radio and television. With a precocious regard for the detritus of cinema history, he preserved his original Paul projector and begged or bought discarded apparatuses from other pioneers. He also recognized the significance for motion pictures history of the optical shows and toys of earlier centuries, and enthusiastically collected then unconsidered books, prints, manuscripts, **magic lanterns**, peepshows, and a host of devices whose names generally ended in -scope or -trope or -rama.

In 1922, Day loaned the collection to the Science Museum, South Kensington, London, where, housed in two large galleries, it constituted the world's first museum of cinema. It remained there until 1961, when (with no British institution prepared to buy it) Day's heirs sold it to the Cinémathèque française, to establish a combined collection that today remains unequalled.

The collections of the Cinémathèque, constituting documents and artefacts as well as films, had been built up since its foundation in 1936 by an inspired collector, Henri Langlois. From 1945, Langlois showed off his collections in a series of memorable exhibitions, but not until 1972 did he establish a permanent museum in the Palais de Chaillot, Paris. A fire in 1997 forced its eventual closure and, as of this writing, plans for its reopening had still not been realized. A major part of the Cinémathèque's paper-based collections—6,000 boxes, including thousands of posters—was destroyed in a fire in a storage facility in February 2002.

The Museo Nazionale del Cinema of Turin preceded the Cinémathèque's museum. In 1941, in the midst of the World War II, Maria Adriana Prolo (1908–1991) conceived the idea of a museum to commemorate Turin's pioneer cinema industry of the early 20th century. Her interests broadened as she succumbed to the fascination of pre-cinematic objects, particularly the 18th-century peepshows in which Turin's collection, now housed in the Mole Antonelliana, is today unrivalled.

The Will Day collection inspired several generations of British collectors, most notably twins John and William Barnes (b.1920). From the 1930s through the early 1950s, they were able to mine virgin ground in amassing artefacts, books, and ephemera of cinema archaeology. In 1995, the Turin museum acquired the pre-cinematic objects from the Barnes collection, while a considerable portion representing the beginnings of cinema in Britain went to form the nucleus of a new museum in Hove, the birthplace of British film. From a slightly later generation, broad-ranging collections illustrating the **archaeology of the cinema** were established from the 1960s by David Francis, David Robinson, and filmmaker Bill Douglas (1934–1991), whose collection was donated to establish the Bill Douglas Centre at the University of Exeter. In Switzerland, an important, long-standing collection was formed by Thomas Ganz, successor to several generations of a 19th-century optical manufacturer famous for **magic lanterns**.

The innovation by British auction houses of sales devoted to photographic and pre-cinematic artefacts in the 1960s served to bring much undiscovered material out of hiding, and to transform cinema pre-history from an esoteric field of research to a mainstream field of collecting. Important new private collectors and collections proliferated in the USA, Great Britain, and continental Europe, particularly in France, still the richest hunting grounds for collectors of cinema archaeology. In Padua, Italy, Laura Minici Zotti, a practising lanternist, established a museum to house her impressive private collection in 1998. One of several successive collections established by the German filmmaker Werner Nekes (b. 1944) forms the nucleus of the collection at the J. Paul Getty Museum in Los Angeles. Laurent

Mannoni, curator of the Cinémathèque française museum, also created a private collection exceptional for books, ephemera, and documentation.

In terms of the survival of actual films, two early collectors contributed much to the evidence of early cinema that has come down to us. The film element of Will Day's collection, although comparatively small, included the first experiments of William **Friese-Greene** from the early 1890s and examples of the work of French and British pioneers. The Swiss Jesuit Abbé Joseph **Joye** was a pioneer of audio-visual **education** who made extensive use of the magic lantern before using films to enliven his spiritual teachings from the late 1890s. Joye was, apart from all else, a dedicated film enthusiast, who left behind 2,500 films as well as 16,000 lantern slides, now mostly conserved by the National Film and Television Archive (London).

The private collecting of films has been widespread since the introduction, early in cinema history, of sub-standard gauges (principally 8 mm, 9.5 mm, and 16 mm) for home use. Discerning and scholarly collectors such as Kevin Brownlow, David Shepherd, and William K. Everson (whose collection is now housed in the archive of the George Eastman House) have saved many works which would otherwise have vanished. Our first-hand knowledge of Japanese silent cinema also is to a major extent due to Shunsui Matsuda, a latter-day practitioner of the art of the *benshi*, who began to collect 16mm prints in the 1920s for use in his shows. In 1952, his collection formed the basis of the Matsuda Film Company (Matsuda Eigasha), which now boasts some 1,000 films in 6,000 reels—the largest body of work from an important but largely vanished area of production.

Matsuda is an instance of a private collection self-funded by commercial exploitation of its materials. Similar organizations that have done exemplary work in collection and conservation include the Kobal Collection (stills) and the Cinema Museum (Ronald Grant Collection; stills and films) in London as well as the Lobster Film Archive (films) in Paris.

See also: archives; festivals; preservation

Further reading

Aubert, Michelle, Laurent Mannoni, and David Robinson (eds.) (1997) *The Will Day Historical Collection of Cinematograph and Moving Picture Equipment*, Paris, AFRHC.

Barnes, John (1967–1970) *Catalogue of the Collection*, 2 vols., St Ives: Barnes Museum of Cinematography.

Matsuda Film Company website: www.infoasia.co.jp/sub.dir/matsudae.html

Prolo, Adriana and Luigi Carluccio (1978) *Il Museo nazionale del cinema*, Turin: Museo nazionale del cinema.

DAVID ROBINSON

Collier, John

b. 1884; d. 1968

social worker, USA

John Collier holds a prominent place in early cinema history by virtue of his post as Secretary of The People's Institute, a New York civic reform organization much concerned with the film industry. Collier authored several influential reports on film content and exhibition and played an important role in setting up and running the **National Board of Censorship**, founded in 1909 together with the **Motion Picture Patents Company**. Renamed the National Board of Review in 1913, the Board helped to stave off state censorship through self-regulation. Yet Collier probably is best remembered for his later work with Native Americans as Commissioner of Indian Affairs during the Roosevelt administration.

ROBERTA PEARSON

Collins, Alfred

b. 1865/1866; d. 1952

filmmaker, Great Britain

Collins began his career as a stage actor, and by the 1880s was playing various minor roles, including in pantomime. While he continued to appear on stage in **music-hall** comedy, he began to work in the film industry in 1902, and swiftly became a director at **British Gaumont.** Through 1912, he may have made over 200 films, many of them slapstick **comedies**, featuring fights and chases, often filmed on the streets of London. With their working-class heroes, accident-prone policemen and chaotic pursuits, many of Collins' films, like those of William **Haggar**, had an implicit anti-establishment message. In 1903–1904, several were widely distributed in North America and continental Europe and popularized the **chase film**. Collins' films were innovative in other ways too: *The Runaway Match* (1903), for example, includes point of view tracking shots and a close-up.

Further reading

Anthony, Barry (2000) "Alfred Collins: Britain's Forgotten Filmmaker," in Alan Burton and Laraine Porter (eds.) *Pimple, Pranks and Pratfalls: British Film Comedy before 1930*, 14–16, Trowbridge: Flicks Books.

STEPHEN BOTTOMORE

Collo, Alberto

b. 1883; d. 1955

actor, Italy

Born in Turin, Collo is mostly known for his roles opposite Francesca **Bertini**, in at least fifteen films between 1913 and 1915. Originally trained in the theater, he began doing comic roles for **Ambrosio** in 1907. Two years later, he was working for **Itala**, where he often impersonated funny female characters. Finally he landed at Celio, where Baldassarre **Negroni** turned him into a romantic male lead. Besides his collaborations with Bertini, Collo's most successful films were *Oberdan* (1915) and *La Cuccagna* (1917), both for Tiber Film. In a famous routine, the cabaret artist and comedian Ettore Petrolini lampooned Collo's languid expressions and delicate manners.

The transition to sound caused Collo's retirement from the cinema, with the exception of a few minor roles from 1939 onward.

ANGELA DALLE VACCHE

Colombia

After traveling through Mexico and Cuba, **Lumière** cameraman Gabriel **Veyre** went to Colombia in 1897, but, apparently bankrupt, did not hold any screenings before moving on to Venezuela. The first screenings thus featured **Edison**'s Vitascope, which premiered in Colón in 1897 and, following coastal routes, arrived in Bogotá's Teatro Municipal in August 1897. Within two years most major cities had held their premieres.

The Thousand Days civil war (1899–1902) and the secession of the province of Panama (1903) slowed the cinema's progress. There is evidence of the screening of a local *actualité* in Cali in 1899, but no notice of other productions until the Compañía Cronofónica, about which little is known, exhibited eleven local views and civic events in Bogotá on May 1907.

An exhibition infrastructure and more consistent production efforts did not emerge until the efforts of the **Di Doménico** family in the 1910s. After emigrating to Panama from Italy, the Di Doménicos acquired European equipment and films and traveled through the Antilles, Venezuela, and the Colombian provinces before settling in Bogotá on March 1911.

With fewer than 100,000 inhabitants, in 1911, Bogotá had **electricity**, but few paved roads or sewage lines; it was still essentially a colonial city in which Europeanized elites contrasted sharply with the indigenous classes. The Di Doménicos' film programs were exotic and immediately successful. In 1912, they opened the Salón Olympia, the first theater specifically designed for moving pictures, which soon became the center of Bogotá nightlife. In 1914, the family established a distribution house for the region (which eventually including Venezuela); shortly thereafter, they moved into production. They produced **news event films**, culminating with *El drama del 15 de Octubre* [The Drama of October 15th] (1915), the first Colombian feature, which reconstructed the notorious and violent assassination of a general in 1914 and starred the assassins themselves (filmed in their jail cells). The film was ambivalently received and even censored in some municipalities, which set back the family's commitment to **newsreel** and documentary production.

Three successful melodramas marked the 1920s: two literary adaptations—*María* (1921–1922), by Alfredo del Diestro and Máximo Calvo, and *Aura o las violetas* [Dawn or the Violets] (1923), by the Di Doménico family—and *Bajo el cielo antioqueño* [Under the Antioquian Sky] (1925) by the newly-formed company Acevedo e Hijos or Acevedo and sons. The Acevedos subsequently founded *Noticiero Nacional* [The National Newsreel], which was released until 1948. Production averaged two or three fiction features per year throughout the 1920s.

Established in 1927 as an exhibition chain in the provinces, Cine Colombia purchased the Di Doménico company the following year and immediately closed its studios and labs in order to focus on exhibition. Cine Colombia's hegemony over exhibition, together with the coming of sound, fractured the fragile infrastructure that had developed during the 1920s; with the exception of the Acevedos, producers simply disappeared.

Further reading

Duque, Edda Pilar (1992) *La aventura del cine en Medellín*, Bogotá: Ancora Editores.

Martínez Pardo, Hernando (1978) *Historia del cine colombiano*, Bogotá: Librería y Editorial América Latina.

Nieto, Jorge y Diego Rojas (1992) *Tiempos del Olimpia*, Bogotá: Fundación Património Fílmico Colombiano.

Salcedo Silva, Hernando (1981) *Crónicas del cine colombiano 1897–1950*, Bogotá: Carlos Valencia Editores.

ANA M. LÓPEZ

colonialism: Europe

Before **World War I**, European countries involved in territorial expansion sought to affirm and explain their actions through film. This was especially the case with specific pressure groups in those countries such as the army, geographical societies, missionary congregations, colonial museums, and other kinds of colonial associations. They often were the first to produce, distribute, and screen colonial films. Colonialism was not accepted unanimously as contributing to the common good, however, for there were serious doubts expressed by other groups about the occupation and (violent) acquisition of overseas territories or "colonies."

From 1896 on, colonialism became an essential part of national and international expositions. Belgian colonialists, for instance, were represented at the 1897 Brussels **World's Fair** in two pavilions where they intended to screen films shot in the Congo with a special film camera, the zoographe, in order to show investors that their money was being used well in the Independent Congo State. Although the plan for film production in the Congo failed, they did use other films to assure the public that their enterprise was trustworthy.

At the 1900 Paris Exposition, several pavilions were dedicated to colonial expansion, and images from the colonies were omnipresent. The **Lumière** Company, an active player in French economic expansion, produced most of the films in the Asian and North African colonies. One film shot in Indochina, for instance, showed the colonial army in Saigon, the coal mines of Hong Gay, factories in Hanoi, and so on. Six years later the Colonial Exposition in Marseille showed that cinema had become a very important propaganda tool for the French. For that exposition, the world's largest film manufacturer, **Pathé-Frères**, which also contributed to French economic and cultural expansion, produced a special series of films of the West African French colonies as well as Indochina. Likewise, at the first important colonial fair in Germany, in 1907, organized by both private and public institutions, the Deutsche Armee, Marine und Kolonialausstellung represented their country's colonies on the screen.

Many of these early films were made by cameramen linked to colonial pressure groups. Those shot by a German brewer in the German colonies between 1904 and 1906, for instance, were programmed during meetings of the numerous local associations of the Deutsche Kolonialgesellschaft, which could be found in almost every German city. In late 1908, a Belgian officer of the colonial army presented films from the Belgian Congo all over Belgium for colonial groups. At the same time, Portuguese colonialists used films from their cacao plantations in Sao Tomé é Príncipe to demonstrate that they were not the cruel exploiters that the

British press had depicted. In Great Britain the big mining and railway companies active in Southern Africa financed the **illustrated magazine** *The African World*, to propagate the British presence in Africa. It sent cameramen all over that continent to film the riches of nature (e.g., timber, diamonds, and copper) for potential investors and to show what was accomplished in the name of western civilization. One of these productions, *Across Africa on Film via Rhodesia to Katanga and Lobito Bay: The Tanganyika Concessions at Work*, shot in 1912 by Albert Kaye, R. C. Nissen and Arthur Pereira, was presented to thousands of spectators (investors and potential investors as well as school children) in Belgium and Great Britain before 1914. The images also highlighted the presence of military, civil and religious authorities in the overseas territories.

An essential element of colonial exploitation was scientific information. It brought order out of "disorder," informed the mother country about natural resources, and represented Asians and Africans as pagans and non-civilized beings, exemplified by rituals, dances, or clothing. In short, it provided the incentive to "civilize" overseas peoples. European scientists—above all, Germans like Karl Weule from the Ethnological Museum of Leipzig and active in Africa (1904–1906), the ethnologist Rudolf Pöch who went to New Guinea (1907), and others from the Museum für Völkerkunde in Berlin (1908–1910), who travelled through German New Guinea—produced films which were shown either in their institutions or for colonial associations. The most famous scientific expedition was that of Adolf Friedrich zu Mecklenburg in 1908. He took thousands of meters of film in Eastern Africa, which were much appreciated in the German colonial world as well as German schools. Likewise, Belgian, Dutch, and French scientists used not only pen and pencil but also the camera to report back home with moving images of their work.

Around 1903, special commercial film companies were founded to produce and also (often) distribute colonial films in Europe. The most famous undoubtedly was the **Charles Urban Trading Company** which, in 1903, launched the Urban Bioscope Expedition Through Borneo. Films of the expedition were needed to attract money for a commercial company active in British Borneo. With the help of French bankers, in Paris in 1905, Urban also founded the production company **Eclipse**, which offered special colonial films: e.g., *Du Caire au Centre d'Afrique* by Felix **Mesguich** (1906). Pathé, of course, was active world-wide, producing colonial films en masse. In other countries like Germany and Belgium, companies such as Die Bioscop-Kolonial-und Eisenbahngesellschaft also were very explicit in interweaving film and colonialism for commercial ends. In Brussels, at least from late 1908 on, Le Cinématographe des Colonies had as its main objective to convince people of the civilizing presence of Belgians in the Congo. Most of its films were *actualités* programmed first in the company's own cinema hall, Cinéma Colonial, and then in other halls in Belgium and even in France.

As colonialism became more widely accepted in European societies, major events in the colonies appeared on the screen—and were very popular. These films—often expressing a strong sense of nationalism and heroism—were first shown in **fairs/fairgrounds** and in **music halls**. Producers began to make colonial (fiction) films such as James **Williamson**'s *Attack on a China Mission— Blue Jackets to the Rescue* (1900) or others about the Anglo-Boer war in South Africa. Soon commercial companies were producing films about colonial wars—e.g., **Cines**'s *Corrispondeza Cinematografica dal teatro della guerra italo turca* (1911–1912) about the Italians in Libya and **Raleigh & Robert**'s *La France contre les beni-Snassem* (1907) or Pathé's *La prise de Taza par les troupes françaises* (1914) about the French in Asia or Africa. Perhaps the most interesting colonial films at the time were produced in India. At the end of 1902, **Gaumont**, **Warwick Trading** , and the Englishman, Robert W. **Paul** all filmed the Delhi Durbar, an exaltation of British colonial rule in India. Nine years later, the crowning of George V as Emperor of India (the Delhi Durbar) was filmed by dozens of film companies, among them Pathé, Gaumont, and **Natural Color Kinematograph**. Here film producers were guided by Cecil Rhodes's dream of a dominant British colonial empire. In 1907, Raleigh & Robert distributed *From the Cape to Cairo*, with its images of Cape Horn and Johannesburg as well as of the construction of railways by black workers considered as savages. White supremacy and its challenges in the colonies were the theme of hundreds of films about hunting in Africa and Asia, among them those Alfred **Machin** made in Africa for Pathé in 1908–1909. Another Pathé film shot in Vietnam, *Chasse au tigre dans la province de Nam Dihn, Tonkin* (1913) proved that films about hunting were not restricted to Africa. The famous hunter-cameramen Cherry **Kearton** also was active in Asia and Africa. Much like his contemporary filmmakers, he saw the world through Social Darwinian eyes, and his film, *A Primitive Man's Career to Civilisation* (1911), was one of the more palatable examples. These films were distributed by companies such as Pathé, Gaumont, Éclair, Raleigh & Roberts, Le Lion, and **Ambrosio**, not only for their own national public but also for the world market.

Colonialism also quickly became an important ingredient in fiction films. Africans or Asians had mostly stereotypical roles, which corresponded to colonial "values": servants, slaves, comedians, savages or villains. When they were confronted with white Europeans, the latter inevitably turned out to be the masters, as serious, civilized people with manners and honor. Even prior to 1914, the French Foreign Legion had become a symbol of the defence of western civilisation against barbarian Arab tribes—as in French films such as *Little Moritz Soldat d'Afrique* (1911) or *Le Legionnaire* (1914), an adaptation of a popular book by Yves Mirande. In such early colonial films, a crucial melodramatic element was the act by which a servant or other colonized character sacrificed himself/herself for the white colonialists—as in *A Zulu's Devotion* (1916) by the South African Joseph Albrecht or *L'Otage* (1912) by Camille **de Morlhon**. In the colonial ideology white Europeans were presented as the masters of Africans and Asians, almost god-like; white women were close to divine. A good example of the latter was *The White Goddess*, shot in Cameroon by the German traveller and hunter Hans Schomburgk, who made dozens of documentaries, with the British actress Meg Gehrts playing the Goddess.

During and after World War I, colonial cinema became an important medium for European governments to explain and propagandize the idea that colonies were necessary for a country's well being. Production became better organized, and the colonial film developed into a popular genre and not only in those countries that possessed colonies.

See also: Africa, Belgian; Africa, French; Africa, German; animal pictures; distribution: Europe; ethnographic films; industrial films; travelogues

Further reading

August, Thomas G. (1985) *The Selling of the Empire: British and French Imperialist Propaganda, 1890–1962*, Westport, CT: Greenwood Press.

Bottomore, Stephen (1995) "An Amazing Quarter Mile of Moving Gold, Gems and Geneology. Die Filmaufnahmen des Delhi Durbar von 1902–03," *KINtop*, 4: 74–97.

Boulanger, Pierre (1975) *Le cinéma colonial. De L'Atlantide à Lawrence d'Arabie,*. Paris: Seghers.

Chowdry, Prem (2000) *Colonial India and the Making of Empire Cinema: Image, Ideology and Identity*, Manchester: Manchester University Press.

Convents, Guido (1986) *La préhistoire du cinéma en Afrique, 1897–1918: A la recherche des images oubliées*, Brussels: OCIC.

De Kuyper, Eric (1995) *Alfred Machin, cinéaste, film-maker*, Brussels: Koninklijk Belgisch Filmarchief.

Gray, Frank (1998) "James Williamson's Composed Picture Attack on a China Mission—Blue Jackets on the Rescue (1900)," in John Fullerton (ed.) *Celebrating 1895. The Centenary of Cinema*, 203–311, London: John Libbey.

Vints, Luc (1981) *Het miskende Eldorado op het Zilveren Scherm. Exotische films en Kongopropaganda, 1895–1940*, Leuven: Kritak.

GUIDO CONVENTS

color

The great majority of the films produced between the beginnings of cinema and the outbreak of **World War I** were endowed with color. The fact that non-specialized audiences are accustomed to think of early or silent films as moving images in black and white is largely the result of the preservation strategies implemented by film **archives** in the course of their activity. Three factors may contribute to explain this cultural bias. First, a large number of films made after 1920 were indeed released in black and white, thus endorsing the belief that all the cinema of the past was deprived of color, according to an evolutionist view of the history of technology. Second, archives have been accustomed to restoring their most ancient holdings through duplicates in black and white, partly because of the prohibitive costs involved in color preservation until the 1990s, partly out of a legitimate concern for the instability of modern color film (Eastmancolor, the most common color stock between 1960 and 1980, was doomed by the quick fading of its emulsion); from the point of view of long-term conservation, a black and white print was (and still is) believed to have a much longer life span. A third rationale for this course of action—shared by the archives and their public—was the assumption that early color techniques were not sophisticated enough to justify the effort to reproduce them for modern audiences (so that tinted nitrate copies were not catalogued as "color" prints). Because color was regarded as "primitive" as the films themselves, disregarding it in the restoration process was considered an acceptable compromise for the sake of saving thousands of endangered prints from complete oblivion.

While this approach to film history has finally changed at the twilight of the 20th century (the color of most nitrate elements is now recreated in the restoration work), our knowledge of the first twenty years of cinema is dramatically affected by this prejudice, thus concealing the inherent continuity between the aesthetics of color in the arts and that of moving pictures. Color photography was actively researched in the late 19th century, with outstanding results such as those achieved by the **Lumière** autochrome process; **magic lantern** slides had been hand-painted since the 1700s; some mechanical color processes adopted by production companies were even borrowed from techniques which were widely implemented by manufacturers of **postcards** and popular engravings. The early appearance of color in moving pictures is the logical outcome of this tradition: one of the earliest known films in color, *Les Dernières cartouches* (Lumière, 1896), has strokes of bright red manually applied (with the aid of a magnifying lens) onto each positive print with a tiny brush; several colors are present in a version of **Edison**'s *Serpentine Dance* shown in the same year. Up to a half-dozen different hues of aniline dyes could be used on each frame, thus creating effects of remarkable beauty and complexity. Georges **Méliès** brought the art of hand-coloring to its zenith in *féeries*/**fairy tale films** such as *Le Royaume des fées* [Kingdom of the Fairies] (1903) and *Le Palais des Mille et une nuits* [Palace of the Arabian Nights] (1905), whose chromatic palette has often been compared to medieval miniatures.

The transparency and luminosity of hand-applied color was especially suitable for **trick films** and views of imaginary worlds. In order to maximize its impact, filmmakers were keen to shoot their films in sets painted in various shades of grey in order to minimize the shortcomings of orthochromatic film (its emulsion was sensitive to ultra-violet, violet, and blue light, and partially sensitive to yellow and green radiations, whereas red would appear on the screen as a dark area). As much as it enhanced the abstract, bi-dimensional qualities of cinema, hand-coloring was less successful in giving depth to scenes of real life. It also was extremely expensive, as it would take several days and a whole team of workers (mostly female, each one responsible for applying a single color to the entire print) to put color on a short reel of film. The obvious solution to the problem was to attribute one color to the whole image, a procedure already visible in films made between 1900 and 1902. This was first obtained by applying the color with a large brush on the film emulson, then by immersing the film stock in an aqueous solution containing the coloring agent.

The latter system, widely employed throughout the early years of cinema, would have important consequences in the development of editing. In a film tinted green for outdoor scenes, yellow for interiors, and blue for night settings, all the shots corresponding to each color were put together in tiny black and white negative rolls, printed as they were, then tinted and finally assembled in the appropriate sequence according to a continuity sheet provided to the editing crew (again, mostly female). Therefore, each positive print was composed of several segments joined by hand-made splices (few attempts at creating prints with multiple tinting without splices are documented before 1916). With tinting, the entire surface of the film—both on the image itself (including its lighter areas) and on its edges—is uniformly colored. Soon after the discovery of this method, a variation on the dye immersion process was devised by coloring only the sensitized portions of the frame—the dark areas of the image—through a chemical process called toning: a colored compound binds to the silver of the emulsion, without coloring the gelatin of the film (the lighter areas of the image remain white). This was more expensive than tinting, but would also produce a crisper image (heavy tinting could conceal details, thus forcing filmmakers to process their negatives with lighter contrast) and enhance photographic values such as composition and depth of field.

Tinting and toning were used separately or together (by toning the image and then immersing it in a dye bath), in often exquisite and complex combinations which can hardly be reproduced with modern techniques; their subtlety (such as a red-tinted, orange-toned image) often defy the attention of today's viewer. This major gap between the color aesthetics of the early period and our own perception of it points to a crucial question about the role played by tinting and toning in the development of film style. It has been often said that primary colors for tinted scenes were basic indicators of physical features of the scene being depicted: red tinting in James **Williamson**'s *Fire!* (1901) evoked the conflagration in an apartment building; blue would often represent an action occurring in the moonlight or at dark, as in D. W. **Griffith's** *The Lonedale Operator* (1911); green could be chosen for a scene taking place in a meadow, and amber was the most common choice for candlelit interiors. However, an explanation of tinting and toning in purely naturalistic terms does not account for the frequent "inconsistencies" in its use (often due to economic factors such as the costs of multiple tinting, and the distribution of a film in a foreign country where local taste would dictate a different color scheme for prints created from a duplicate negative for export) and the great number of color combinations with no evident dramatic purpose. Plausible interpretations of this phenomenon are the greater importance attributed to the

pictorial over the dramatic approach to filmmaking (especially through toning); the use of tinting and toning as editing tools (separating a given shot or scene from the rest of the film, or determining the tempo of a sequence); tinting as a soothing device against the harshness of black and white (evident in prints uniformly tinted in amber), or as a symbol of color itself (black and white being identified with "poverty row" companies or prints for lower-class audiences).

Moreover, tinting and toning were no less "abstract" than hand-coloring in their attempt at presenting a single color as a symbol of chromatic perception of the physical world. The effort to achieve a synthesis of reality by means other than symbolism and simplification resulted in the work of those who sought to endow film with the presumed qualities of the human eye. Such endeavors were initiated with a clever development of hand-coloring: the areas of the frame to be colored were cut (by hand or by needles connected to pantographs) onto matrix copies which were then placed on the positive prints; each color was applied to the film through the outlines thus obtained, with brushes or pads soaked in the appropriate aniline dye. First adopted by **Pathé-Frères** for trick films and *féeries* such as *La Poule aux œufs d'or* [The Hen With the Golden Eggs] (1905) and *Aladin ou la lampe merveilleuse* [Aladdin] (1906) and quickly followed by **Gaumont** and few others, stencil color—also known as "au pochoir" in France—established cinematography "in natural colors" as a criterion of taste in the evolution of moving images, as important as the "talking picture" (the coupling of color and sound came to be considered at a certain point as the ultimate goal of film experiments). The Pathé *Films d'Art* series and the adaptations from drama and literature produced by **SCAGL** and **Film d'Arte Italiana** between 1909 and 1912 displayed a refinement of color and precision of outline (impossible with manual hand-coloring) unequalled in the period; their palette and their audience mirrored an appreciation for academic painting then common among middle-class viewers (many films were made available in two versions—black and white and hand-tinted or stenciled—at varying prices for different audiences).

A further breakthrough in the quest for "natural color" came with a dramatic shift from the principle of producing color by applying it onto the film to its re-creation with the help of multiple colored lenses converging onto a single image (**Chronochrome Gaumont**, 1912), frames tinted alternatively with primary colors (William **Friese-Greene**, 1909), or colored filters rotating in front of them at a higher projection speed (Kinemacolor, 1906). Initiated in Great Britain by George Albert **Smith**, the Kinemacolor process developed from an idea introduced in 1897 by a German technician, Hermann Isensee, who theorized the possibility of producing color moving images by projecting them in rapid sequences of red, blue and green. For a brief period of time, Kinemacolor and Chronochrome fought for supremacy in the field, but they both ultimately failed, because they either required non-standard projection apparatuses or had to be run at higher speeds, with considerable waste of film stock for a shorter screening time. A very large number of similar experiments between 1911 and 1916 had a similar fate.

However unsuccessful, one of these systems—the first Technicolor process (1916)—marked the beginning of a revolution in the ideology of "natural color." The process involved two reels of film running in parallel before two lenses and two filters (red and green), using a single light source split by a prism; a projector with two lenses equipped with filters superimposed the two complementary images using a complex and uneven registration mechanism. No example of this system—the first of four designed by Technicolor during the silent era—is known to survive, a demonstration of the difficulty inherent in the study of color in early cinema. As much as tinting, toning, and stencil were by far the most widespread ways of giving color to the moving image, they were not the only ones; the years between 1906 and 1916 witnessed a vast array of patents, experiments, prototypes, and processes—mostly documented only through secondary sources—with no print available to demonstrate how they worked. The fact that about 85 per cent of the nitrate copies of early films displays some kind of color does not mean that we have an adequate knowledge of its meaning in the visual culture of the period. With very few exceptions, the color of all modern viewing prints of early films is the outcome of processes (and

cultural values) which are radically different from those in use at the time; they approximate the look of early cinema, but they somehow betray the technological and aesthetic rationale of its original identity. Inevitably, any discourse on color aesthetics as applied to the cinema of the early years is to a large extent still a work of fiction.

See also: access; archaeology of cinema

Further reading

Cherchi Usai, Paolo (2000) *Silent Cinema: An Introduction*, 21–43, London: British Film Institute.
Coe, Brian (1972) "The Development of Colour Cinematography," in Roger Manvell (ed.) *The International Encyclopedia of Film*, 29–32, New York: Crown.
Hertogs, Daan and Nico De Klerk (eds.) (1996) *"Disorderly Order": Colours in Silent Film. The 1995 Amsterdam Workshop*, Amsterdam: Stichting Nederlands Filmmuseum.
Hulfish, David S. (1918) *Cyclopedia of Motion-Picture Work*, vol. 1, 262–277, vol. 2, 149–154, Chicago: American Technical Society.
Nowotny, Robert A. (1983) *The Way of All Flesh Tones: A History of Color Motion Picture Processes, 1895–1929*, New York and London: Garland.
Talbot, Frederick A. (1912) *Moving Pictures. How They are Made and Worked*, 287–300, London: Heinemann.

PAOLO CHERCHI USAI

Comandon, Jean

b. 1877; d. 1970

physician, filmmaker, France

A pioneer of microcinematography, Dr. Jean Comandon was hired by **Pathé-Frères** in October 1909 to develop a department of scientific popularization. He thus directed an impressive series of films on microorganisms, on which he continued to work under the sponsorship of banker Albert Kahn (1929–1932) and the Institut Pasteur (1932–1966). As early as 1910, Comandon also had perfected an effective technique in radiocinematography with radiologist André Lomon. During **World War I**, he oversaw the production of many hygienist films which were distributed in France by the Commission for the Prevention of Tuberculosis (Rockefeller Foundation).

See also: scientific films: Europe

THIERRY LEFEBVRE

comedy

Comedies were the first form of fiction film, for brief gags appeared among the single-shot films that made up the premiere programs shown internationally in the years 1895–1896. Drawing on a variety of sources, including cartoons and **comic strips**, **vaudeville** skits and traditional practical jokes, these films were among the first to introduce characters and narrative actions, although the actions were generally very brief and the characters merely sketched types. For the first decade or so, such comedies continued to make up the bulk of fiction filmmaking. Longer comedy films appeared around 1904 in two dominant forms: "linked vignettes," in which a series of gags were strung together around a common character, and chases. In 1908, responding perhaps to widespread criticism of films as vulgar, a number of film companies began introducing domestic comedies usually focused on a married couple and the crises caused by infractions of social proprieties. However, the vein of "vulgar" or slapstick comedy, deriving from the **chase film** and burlesque never disappeared. In the USA, Mack **Sennett**'s **Keystone** studio (founded in 1912) paved the way for fast-paced, wildly exaggerated styles of action and acting. But Sennett also hired Charles **Chaplin** whose first films in 1914 introduced a different style of comedy based more centrally on a single comedian with more elaborate and individualized gags and a more unique sense of character type. Yet Chaplin undoubtedly was influenced by European models. In France, comedian comedy began appearing around 1907, with such actors as André **Deed**, Max **Linder**, and Charles **Prince** and their characters, respectively, Boireau (later, Cretinetti in Italy), Max, and Rigadin. The comedies of

Pathé-Frères and **Gaumont** especially devised elaborate sight gags and a frequently exaggerated (almost surrealist) sense of humor, producing the first golden age of silent comedy, unfortunately overshadowed by the later American silent comedians and therefore neglected.

Genre poses a fascinating problem in early cinema. Since genre indicates an already established expectation on the part of audiences, it might be asked if genres were possible when cinema itself was a novelty. Yet the first film programs certainly included different types of film, including vaudeville acts (jugglers, dancers, and other performers); *actualités* (street scenes, family scenes, factory gate films); **news events** (dignitaries and celebrities, parades, public ceremonies), as well as single-shot gag films. The earliest comedies appear mainly as versions of vaudeville gags, although the sources could just as easily be a comic strip (**Lumière**'s *Arroseur Arrosée* [The Waterer Watered] (1895), a joke **post card** (**Edison**'s *The Whole Dam Family and the Dam Dog*, 1905), a vaudeville or burlesque skit (**American Muttoscope and Biograph**'s *The Sausage Machine*, 1897), a political cartoon (Eidson's *Terrible Teddy, The Grizzly King*, 1901), or even a minstrel song (AM&B's *Everybody Works but Father*, 1905).

Until about 1905, comedies made up the vast majority of fiction films. Designed to provoke an immediate laugh or chuckle rather than to develop characters or stories, single-shot comedies seemed perfectly suited to a silent, visual and, in this period, usually quite brief format. Limited in length (and sometime offered in the peepshow format of the Mutoscope), they usually relied on a gag to provide interest and entertainment. Almost impossible to define, the gag could be described as the visual, acted-out equivalent of a joke: an action that, as a rule, involves a comic reversal of expectations, generally leading to a violation of social proprieties. An obvious form of such films would be what I have called the "besmirching films" in which some unwitting figure either is doused with liquid, stained with filth, or otherwise dirtied. For instance, in AM&B's *Toodles and Her Strawberry Tart* (1903) a well-dressed man sits down in the tart Toodles has placed on the seat beside her in the streetcar. The *Biograph Bulletin* summarized the film's gag: "The dude jumps up and bringing around the tails of his coat, shows the havoc wrought by the accident. A thoroughly funny and cleverly enacted scene."

Frequently these moments of embarrassment are the result of willfully laid traps, and therefore one of the major characters in early film comedy is the prankster, usually a mischievous boy (sometimes a girl, but the gender roles are fairly fixed). Examples include such titles as: Edison's *The Bad Boy's Joke on the Nurse* (1901), **Hepworth**'s *When Daddy Comes Home* (1902), AM&B's *The Katzenjammer Kids and the School Marm* (1903), Pathé's *Horrible fin d'un concierge* [The Terrible Fate of a Concierge] (1903), and **Paul**'s *Drat that Boy!* (1904). Highly visual, very brief and based in physical humor, such material gave early cinema its first simple scenarios. Thus comedy could be seen as one of the principal examples of narrative in early cinema. Gags can also be related to the **cinema of attractions**—the aspect of early cinema based in non-narrative spectacle. However, most gags seem to exist between non-narrativized attractions (such as ocean waves, a juggling act, or magic transformations) and what we usually think of as a story. Because cause and effect plays a key role in gags, and they require some minimal—yet essential—character roles (such as, the joker and his victim), gags possess some key elements of stories. Yet in their brevity, their sudden catastrophic nature that seems to curtail any further development, gags also operate in a different way than most stories. Don Crafton contrasts these two elements of comedy, attractions and story, in terms of "the pie" (as in "pie in the face", a besmirching gag and an attraction) and "the chase" (a comic action which stretches out over time and space, allowing the delay essential to most stories).

If simple gags were beautifully suited to early cinema, other sorts of attractions also seemed to have a comic effect. Grotesque sights or performances, such as the facial acrobatics of the many **facial expression films** in which a performer made a succession of grimaces at the camera—for instance, **Williamson**'s *Comic Faces* (1897), Pathé's *Masques et grimaces* (1902), Edison's *Goo Goo Eyes* (1903)—or even actions such as Edison's *The May Irwin John Rice Kiss* (1896) seem to have caused hilarity for early audiences. Likewise most early **trick films**, with their sudden unexpected and frequently grotesque

transformations or substitutions, probably should be considered comedies, if by the term we mean something as simple as: films greeted with laughter (or films produced with that intent).

Multi-shot comedy films appear frequently after 1900, but rather than establishing more complex narrative structures, most are additive in structure. The form I have termed "linked vignettes" involves stringing a number of gags together through a recurrent character and/or action. For instance, Williamson's *The Dear Boys Home for the Holiday* (1903), Pathe's *Ah le salle gosse* [That Dirty Kid] (1906), or Edison's *The Terrible Kids* (1906) all pile on a number of pranks engineered by bad boys, usually concluded by a punishment meted out by an adult. The other additive form of comedy was the chase film, one of the most popular of the early film genres. Instead of simply adding together pranks, the chase followed a single action through a series of locations, as someone (often a mischievous boy) or something (such as a hat blown by the wind, as in Gaumont's *Une Coup de vent* [A Gust of Wind] (1907) is pursued by a group of people. Frequently gags and pranks are combined with the chase, and the chasers then are a group that grows from scene to scene (for instance, when new victims of a mischievous boy join the chase). Chases were by no means restricted to comedies and could be melodramatic as well. But comic chases, which appeared with AM&B's *Escaped Lunatic* and *Personal*, both from 1904, remained popular through 1909, and, with some further development, remained part of slapstick comedies throughout the silent era. As a synthetic form interrelating actions and extensive spaces and supplying the delay usually associated with narrative development (will they catch him? not yet . . .), chases provide a clear form of narrative integration in comedies, albeit still including gags.

Comedies based on characters and more elaborately plotted situations appear around 1907 and might also be divided into two forms. One features grotesque or eccentric comedians whose costumes and make-up as well as bizarre behavior seem derived from the clowns of the circus or **music hall**. Deed in his various manifestations (Boireau in France, later Cretinetti in Italy), Clément **Migé** as Calino and Ernest **Bourbon** as Onésime at Gaumont, Pimple at the British company Phoenix, and the Keystone actors (Fred Mace, Mabel

Normand, Ford **Sterling**) usually fall into this category. The other form relies more on a sort of comedy of manners, dealing with domestic situations and features actors who are more realistically costumed and tend to behave more realistically. Although this division can be blurred, Linder at Pathé, Léonce **Perret** (Léonce) and René **Poyen** (Bout-de-zan) at Gaumont, and John **Bunny** and Flora **Finch** at **Vitagraph** would serve as examples. Although gags still abound, especially in the films of the more clown-like characters, plots involving deceptions, misunderstandings and conflicts between character types frequently hold these films together.

If comedies dominate fiction filmmaking until about 1905, dramas and action melodramas make up a greater proportion of the fiction film output after that date. In 1910, in fact, a trade journal estimated comedies to make up about one fifth of the films released in the USA. During the **nickelodeon** period (1906–1912 or so) the single-reel film format shared by most films (although comedies occasionally came as "split reels", taking less than a full reel) interacted with a desire for variety in programming, so that most theaters offered a varied assortment of films, balancing comedies with dramas. By 1912 certain studios, at least in the USA (Keystone, the Joker Comedy Company), specialized in comedy films and the market for them was steady.

Trading generally on reversals of expectations, comedies often deal with the socially forbidden or the grotesque. Early comedies abound with moments that still cause laughter and often amazement, as much as amusement. Let me list a few unforgettable moments from early comedies: the scatological humor of Pathe's *Erreur du Port* [The Wrong Door] (1904) in which a peasant in a train station mistakes a telephone booth for a WC; Max Linder calling his dog on the phone in Pathé's *Max et son chien Dick* [Max and His Dog Dick] (1912); Rosalie being followed down the street by her furniture after she has sold it (one of many examples of tricks employed in comic films) in Pathé's *Rosalie et ses meubles fideles* [Rosalie and Her Faithful Furniture] (1911); Dorothy Gish playing a banjo to Eddie Dillon, covered with pasted-on hair, in Biograph's *Almost a Wild Man* (1912); a baby growing to manhood in a few

Figure 22 Frame still from *Joueurs de cartes arrosés* (Lumière, 1896).

seconds in Gaumont's *Onésime horloger* [Onesime, the Clockmaker] (1912); the infectious, irresistible dance in Gaumont's *Le Bous-Bous Mie* (1910); Mack Sennett firing a revolver wildly at the screen, trying to save his former girlfriend from the villain in Keystone's *Mabel's Dramatic Career* (1913); Boireau fused at the back with an Apache by a building accident, the two wandering through Paris like Siamese twins in Pathé's *Une Extraordinaire aventure de Boireau* [Boireau's Extraordinary Adventure] (1914).

The history of American slapstick comedy of the teens mainly has focused on male comedians, in spite of the popularity of such figures as Marie Dressler (the featured star of Chaplin's first feature, *Tillie's Punctured Romance*, 1914), or Mabel Normand. But the earlier comedies starred women of enormous comedic talent as well, to name a handful: Flora Finch, Florence **Lawrence** (Mrs. Jones), Mary **Pickford** (initially called the "Biograph comedy girl"), and, perhaps most extraordinarily, Sarah **Duhamel** (Rosalie) at Pathé.

See also: comic series

Further reading

Abel, Richard (1994) *The Cine Goes to Town: French Cinema 1896–1914*, Berkeley: University of California Press.

Gordon, Rae Beth (2001) *Why the French Love Jerry Lewis: From Cabaret to Early Cinema*, Stanford: Stanford University Press.

Karnick, K and Jenkins, H. (eds.) (1994) *Classical Hollywood Comedy*, London: Routledge.

TOM GUNNING

Comerio Films

Comerio Films, also known as Luca Comerio & C., was founded in 1907 by a Milanese photographer, Luca Comerio (1878–1940). In the 1890s, Comerio had become famous as a photojournalist and by 1907 he was one of the King of Italy's favorite cameramen. His expertise in *actualités* of military parades and public ceremonies determined the company's most lucrative domain. Comerio Films, which became SAFFI-Comerio in 1908, before turning into **Milano Films** in 1909, also produced adaptations of renowned literary works and biopics, including *I promessi sposi* [The Bethrothed], *Amleto* [Hamlet], and *Lorenzino De' Medici* [Lorenzino De Medici], all released in 1908.

GIORGIO BERTELLINI

comic series

Although probably unintended and unplanned, the earliest distinct comic series, arguably, was the extensive run of "Tramp" films, of which at least 40 appeared between 1897 and 1902. Tramps and hobos figured large in the popular imagination at the turn of the 20th century; familiar real-life figures, they combined the potent appeal of romance, menace, and pathos. **American Mutoscope and Biograph** initiated these films with *The Tramp and the Bather* (June 1897), and went on to make at least seventeen *Tramp* films by 1900. **Edison** competed with a mere six comparable films in the same period, while other contemporary firms made their contribution throughout the cinema's first decade. The elements were fairly constant: the tramp forever plotting to steal a slice of pie or an item of clothing, but regularly frustrated by ferocious dogs and virago cooks, and generally finishing with a beating or a soaking. Tramp films did however inspire at least one early experiment in **editing**: both **Lubin**'s and Edison's *The Tramp's Dream* (respectively, 1899 and 1901) cut from the tramp's present misery to his dream of good fortune, and then back to reality— early examples of a cutaway to subjective fantasy.

A similar accidental comic series was the proliferation of **chase films**, notably in France, in the years 1906–1908. Filmmakers discovered moving pictures' potential to capture the dynamic progression of a chase, and the excitement and laughter that it could generate. Everything that could be chased—pumpkins, barrels, policemen, umbrellas, wigs, bicycles, dogs, mothers-in-laws, automobiles, and nurses—was pursued with frenetic energy. The most prolific producer of chase films was André **Heuzé** at **Pathé-Frères**, who also claimed to be their inventor, although one of the best remembered today, **Gaumont**'s *La Course aux potirons* [The Pumpkin Race] (1907) was directed by Emile **Cohl**.

Out of the chase films emerged the first major comedy **star**, André **Deed**, who first appeared in Heuzé's *La course à la perruque* [The Wig Chase] (1906). From 1907, Deed was firmly established in the character of Boireau, a small, grotesque figure, grinning demoniacally—except when exploding, in moments of disaster, into wild howling. The characteristic form of his films cast him in some metier—boxer, gendarme, concierge, or sailor-suited infant—which would permit him to precipitate an orgy of chaos or destruction.

In 1909, having already won an international following in some 30 films, Deed was lured away from Pathé by **Itala**, where he changed his *nom d'art* to Cretinetti. Pathé found an instant replacement, who was rapidly to eclipse Deed's fame: Max **Linder**. A former stage actor, Linder already had been working in Pathé films for four years, sometimes already under the screen name of Max, when, in 1910 he definitively launched the character which was to achieve world fame in a series which, by 1916, would extend to more than a hundred films. While Deed was grotesque and absurd, Max was handsome, neat, elegant, the perfect man-about-town. The essence of his comedy was the contrast between this impeccable persona and the grotesque incidents which befell him. Linder was the cinema's first comic genius: his invention was inexhaustible; his performance (done without re-takes) phenomenal in its precision.

Figure 23 Poster for Max Linder, 1911.

Figure 24 Poster for Prince, 1910.

Linder's international triumph encouraged comedy production in France, with every company competing to build up its own troupe of star comics. Another Pathé star, the moon-faced Charles **Prince**—a comic actor rather than a clown—created the durable Rigadin, who was to feature in two hundred comic shorts between 1910 and 1920. Pathé also engaged the former circus and **music hall** clown, Roméo **Bosetti**, to organize two studios, Nizza and **Comica**, dedicated to comedy, on the Côte d'Azur. Their most successful series featured the diminutive Little Moritz (the German-born Moritz Schwartz), the stout Rosalie (Sarah **Duhamel**), generally playing obstreperous maid-servants, and the more elegant Léontine (the actor remains unknown). Bosetti was succeeded as chief of Comica by Alfred **Machin** who inaugurated the *Babylas* series, in which the principal performers were animals, including Machin's pet panther Mimir. Pathé quickly followed up its Babylas success with a short-lived series starring the dog comedians, Médor and Moustache.

Previously, Bosetti had worked briefly for **Gaumont**, where, besides featuring in his own

Roméo series, he took charge of the company's comedy production. Under Bosetti's guidance, Gaumont developed a successful series with Clément **Migé** as the acrobatic and destructive Calino (1909–1913). When Bosetti returned to Pathé, he was succeeded by Jean **Durand**, who then prefigured Mack **Sennett**'s **Keystone** in creating a whole troupe, Les Pouics, specialists in mindless, surreal destruction. The most remarkable figure to emerge from the Pouics was Ernest **Bourbon** as Onésime (1912–1914), a lean, stooping figure with the face of a grinning Pierrot, topped by a flattish grey bowler. The memory of Onésime's strange fantasies and sense of incongruity continued to excite the Surrealists of the 1920s when most of his contemporaries were forgotten.

Gaumont's production chief, Louis **Feuillade** created two outstandingly successful comedy series starring children. As Bébé, Clément **Mary** appeared in 74 films between December 1910 and January 1913 (and ages five through seven). Just like the adult stars, Bébé was thrown into a variety of roles and situations—as Flirt, Moralist, Millionaire, Tramp, Strong Man, Prestidigitatuer, Sleepwalker, and Socialist. He was in time usurped by the clever, charming, and even younger Bout-de-Zan (René **Poyen**), whose style, in 52 films (1912–1916), had a more plebeian quality than the essentially bourgeois Bébé. The **Éclair** company endeavored to compete with upwards of 70 episodes of its *Little Willy* series (1912–1914), starring a precocious English child, Willy Saunders, of considerably less appeal than the French children.

Gaumont's *Léonce* films (1912–1916) stand apart from the rest of the French series of the era, for their visual elegance and the sophistication of their comic variations on marital manners. As director and star, Léonce **Perret** worked with a succession of beautiful young women, including Suzanne **Grandais**, who played his on-screen wives or temptresses.

The arrival of Deed at Itala was to precipitate the Italian cinema's own rush to emulate French comic series production. Following the instant success of Deed's Italian debut in January 1909, in his new character of Cretinetti, Itala launched Pacifico Aquilanti in a *Coco* series, while rival **Ambrosio** transformed its contract actor Ernesto Vaser into Fricot. Ambrosio's most significant capture, however, was to be the brilliant and inventive young Spaniard Marcel **Fabre** (often partnered with Nilde Barrachhi as Robinette), whose 150 *Robinet* films, made between 1910 and 1915, represented some of the most original comedy invention of the era.

After Deed's Cretinetti, the most successful of the Italian series comedians was Ferdinando **Guillaume**, as Tontolini at **Cines** from 1909, then Polidor at **Pasquali** from 1911. Guillaume represented the fifth generation of a distinguished line of circus performers, and more than any of the other comedians his anecdotes can truly be said to have elements of the *commedia dell'arte* tradition. While Cretinetti was demonic, producing chaos with his crazed, single-minded enterprises, Polidor was quaint and innocent, the victim of a universe of ever-imminent disaster. The Cines company's Kri Kri (the French-born Raymond **Frau**) was closer to Linder in his dandified knowingness, and even anticipates some Linder gags, including the anachronistic d'Artagnan of *Un sogno di Kri Kri* (1913). Italy also had its child comics to rival Bébé and Bout-de-Zan: Ambrosio had Firuli (Maria Bay) while Cines had Frugolino (Ermanno Roveri) and Cinessino (Eraldo Giunchi).

No other European countries could compete with the comedy stars of France and Italy. In Germany, for instance, from 1913, Ernst **Lubitsch** starred brightly in a few films of the *Meyer* series, while the **Messter** company made several comedies with the precocious, 10-year-old Curt Bois, although without giving him a series name. Russia also boasted its own rather later series comedians, the suave Arkadi Boitler as Arkasha and Antonin Ferner as Antosha.

The international market conquered by the comic stars of France and Italy was immense: it was characteristic that their characters were renamed in every country, so that Cretinetti was Foolshead in England and the USA, Gribouille in France, Muller in Germany, Lehman in Hungary, Toribio in Spanish-speaking countries, and Glupishkin in Russia. **World War I** closed down that rich market, however, and at a moment when the overall film economy was already shaky. Many of the bright young performers went off to war. More significantly, a new generation of comedy, technically more sophisticated and with a New World repertory and vocabulary, rapidly was consolidating in the USA. Europe's comedy empires collapsed overnight.

American filmmakers had studied the European imports attentively. Sennett recalled that D. W. **Griffith**'s *The Curtain Pole* (1908) was a comedy "in the French style"; and Griffith seemed to be consciously following the European format in the group of films featuring the adventures and misadventures of Mr. and Mrs. Jones (1908–1909), played by John Compson and Florence **Lawrence**. Compson thereafter moved to **Edison** for the short-lived *Bumptious* series of 1910–1911.

The first American company systematically to exploit the commercial advantage of a series built around a personality, however, seems to have been **Essanay**. In 1910, Essanay embarked on the production of a comedy series, with several episodes of *Hank and Lank*, featuring Augustus Careny and Victor Potel as two working-class hopefuls, somewhere between the old tramp characters and the working class duo of Bud Fisher's *Mutt and Jeff* **comic strip**, who were themselves to figure in Nestor's live-action series (1911) and in short **animation films** from 1913. Carney discovered a more effective comic character in Alkali Ike (1911–1913), usually partnered with his wife Margaret Joslin. In 1914, Carney defected to **Universal**, to become Universal Ike in a new series, but the fictional locale which had been created around him provided material for Essanay to make some 30 Snakeville comedies, generally starring Potel, although any Essanay artists might be involved. One of Essanay's most successful comic series followed with the 24 *Sweedie* films (1914–1915), featuring Wallace Beery; although these shortly were to be eclipsed by the fourteen films the company made with Charles **Chaplin** in 1915.

Other studios rushed to establish comic series. In 1912, **Selig** made a few episodes of *The Katzenjammer Kids,* from Rudolph Dirks' comic strip, featuring Guy Mohler and Emil Nuchberg as Hans and Fritz in their constant battle against authority. Hobo characters retained their attraction, with Lloyd Hamilton and Bud Duncan featured in **Kalem**'s *Ham* series (1914–1915) and Bobby Burns and Walter Stull as Poke and Jabbs in the Wizard/World series of 1915. **Vitagraph** specialized in a more refined style of comedy, of bourgeois pretensions, with the *Bunny* series. John **Bunny** and Flora **Finch** already were prominent Vitagraph actors before Bunny was featured as Bunny, the well-intentioned if easily tempted bourgeois, with Finch generally playing his watchful wife. The *Bunny* films were the first American comic series to find wide acceptance in Europe—to such an extent that on Bunny's death in 1915 the Libken company of Moscow created its own imitator, Pokson played by V. Zimovoi.

The Keystone Studios, established in 1912, for a while would dominate American comedy production. Yet it was the name "Keystone" on a film that constituted the attraction of its series comedy; for the company generally refrained from promoting character-based series. Although the films of Mabel **Normand** and Roscoe **Arbuckle** frequently (although not invariably) were titled with Mabel or Fatty respectively, no film by Keystone's greatest discovery, Chaplin, ever featured his name in the title. Hence, the best years of the American comic series based on personalities would only commence with World War I.

Further reading

Abel, Richard (1994) *The Ciné Goes to Town: French Cinema, 1896–1914,* Berkeley: University of California Press.

Lacassin, Francis (1972) "Les fous rires de la belle époque," *Pour une contre historie du cinema,* 73–87, Paris: Union générale d'editions.

Robinson, David (1986) "The Italian Comedy," *Sight and Sound.*

Robinson, David (1987) "Rise and Fall of the Clowns," *Sight and Sound,* 56: 198–203.

DAVID ROBINSON

comic strips

Comic strips, which date as far back as the Renaissance, developed a complicated relationship with moving pictures in the first decades of the new medium. The salient issues are formal influence, content influence, individual interactions, and a shared social milieu. Comics and moving pictures flourished together in the age of technological innovation and the rise of mass consumers. Nevertheless, their symbiotic relation, if any, has to be evaluated with caution.

The formal properties of the European comic strip were standardized in the 19th century. The German *Bilderbogen* (picture stories) were internationally known, especially those of Wilhelm Busch who drew the exploits of two brats, "Max und Moritz," in 1865. Improvements in mechanical reproduction in the 1880s, as well as distribution by railway, led to a boom in popular graphic humor in Europe in the last quarter of the century. During the early cinema period there were 120 different **satirical illustrated magazines** in Great Britain, 105 in France, 29 in Germany, 24 in Spain, 20 in Austria, and 16 in Italy. By comparison, only 20 humor journals appeared (and disappeared) in the USA during the same period.

In the USA, the European humor magazines were well known to illustrators, since they were distributed in original and translated versions, and their form and content influenced early American comic strips. The transformative event was the rise of the daily newspaper during the "circulation wars" of the 1890s. Joseph Pulitzer's *New York World* began running **color** comics in its Sunday edition in 1894. His arch rival William Randolph Hearst not only enjoyed comics and cartoonists; he recognized the value of comic strips in building brand loyalty to the paper. He aggressively recruited—frequently from Pulitzer—the best comic strip artists in the country. Rudolph Dirks' "The Katzenjammer Kids," inspired by "Max und Moritz," began in 1897, in Hearst's **New York Journal**. The distinctive features of the American comics were a continuing cast of characters, daily or weekly installments in mass-circulated papers, and dialogue conveyed by speech balloons. In 1903, there were 48 **newspapers** in 33 American cities carrying comic strips; in 1908, there were 83 newspapers in 50 cities. Three-quarters of the strips were supplied by Hearst.

Despite several efforts to show an evolutionary link between comic strip form and early cinema narration, it is a difficult case to make. The way comic strips are "read" as a discursive medium is fundamentally different from the way movies are "watched." Their panels are like "snap shots" of key parts of a narrative, while moving pictures, especially at the turn of the century, when they told stories, tended to show actions in their entirety (sometimes more than once). Analytic editing in film did not emerge until later, but even then, the technique probably derived little from comic art. It is likely, however, that comics influenced film as a source for characters and plots.

Before the **star system** circa 1910, films with continuing casts of characters were rare. The exceptions were films that actually borrowed characters from strips, a common practice by the earliest filmmakers, evidenced by Cecil **Hepworth**, Alice **Guy Blaché**, and Victorin **Jasset**. The **Lumière** *vues comiques*, made in 1896–1897, found the "stories without words" a rich source of material. The most famous, *Arroseur et arrosé* [Tables Turned on the Gardener] (1896), was derived from an 1889 print version of the story. To illustrate the persistence of the naughty boy motif, the inaugural "Katzenjammer Kids" comic strip in 1897 used the same story of causing the gardener to squirt himself. In the USA, there were filmed adaptations of the most popular strips, including Alphonse and Gaston, Buster Brown, Happy Hooligan, Foxy Grandpa, and the Katzenjammer Kids. In Great Britain, there was Ally Sloper.

Later examples of comics adaptation include **Edison**'s *The Rivals* (1907), from a T. E. Powers strip, and *Dream of a Rarebit Fiend* (1907), from Winsor **McCay**'s. Neither film seems to utilize any "comic strip" formal effects. Editorial cartoons also provided occasional inspiration, as when Edwin S. **Porter** based The "Teddy" Bears (1907) on a satire of Theodore Roosevelt. There were even isolated

Figure 25 The last two rows of a Buster Brown comic strip, *New York Herald*, 1903. (Courtesy of Charles Musser.)

efforts to adapt comic strip speech balloons to live action films, as in Edison's *Looking for John Smith* (1906). Nestor began a *Mutt and Jeff* series in 1911 that utilized superimposed speech. The first series of animated cartoons, *The Newlyweds* (1913–1914), was adapted from a comic strip by George McManus. Many short films used conventional chases, sight gags, and anarchic actions that might have antecedents in comics—but they also developed as autonomous film forms.

Turning the tables, early films frequently provided grist for the cartoonists' mill. Film subjects, the risks of movie-going and the rapidity of scene changes were remarkably popular topics during the introduction of moving pictures, especially among British satirists. Many popular graphic humor artists eventually entered the film profession, a list that includes: Storm Peterson (Denmark), Georges **Méliès**, Emile **Cohl**, Jean **Durand**, Lortac, O'Galop (France), Heinrich Zille (Germany), Anson Dyer, Harry Furniss, George Studdy (Great Britain), J. Stuart **Blackton**, John Randolph Bray, Bud Fisher, Rube Goldberg, Hy Mayer, and Winsor McCay (USA).

The significance of comics and cinema's relation lies not so much in the realm of formal influence as in their sharing of personnel, their common narrative sources, and their coexistence in the sphere of emerging popular entertainment and **leisure-time** consumption. Significantly, reformers often lumped film and comics together and condemned their erotic and violent content.

Further reading

Bottomore, Stephen (1995) *I Want to See This Annie Mattygraph: A Cartoon History of the Coming of the Movies*, Pordenone: Le Giornate del Cinema Muto.

Crafton, Donald (1990) "Graphic Humor and Early Cinema," in *Emile Cohl, Caricature, and Film*, 221–256, Princeton: Princeton University Press.

Gordon, Ian (1998) *Comic Strips and Consumer Culture 1890–1945*, Washington, D.C.: Smithsonian Institution Press.

Musser, Charles (1990) *The Emergence of Cinema: The American Screen to 1907*, New York: Charles Scribner's Sons.

DONALD CRAFTON

Comica

Comica was registered as a commercial brand on 17 December 1910 by **Pathé-Frères**. Apparently it was created at the instigation of actor-director Roméo **Bosetti**, who had just left **Gaumont**. Its productions, most of which were shot in Nice, carried on the tradition of eccentric burlesque comedy that had become Bosetti's specialty over the previous years. Several **comic series** met with much success: *Little Moritz* (played by Maurice Schwartz), *Rosalie* (Sarah **Duhamel**), *Bigorno* (René Lantini), etc. Directors such as Henri Gambart and Alfred **Machin** also lent their support to Bosetti. **World War I** brought Comica's activities in production to an end.

THIERRY LEFEBVRE

Commercial Press Motion Picture Department

The Commercial Press, established in 1897, was the largest Chinese multimedia enterprise that promoted national culture and modern **education**. In 1917, it opened its Motion Picture Department to make *actualités* (for example, *Workers Leaving the Commercial Press*), scenics or **travelogues**, educational films, and **opera** films (particularly those featuring Mei Lanfang). It also rented its equipment, facilities (including a glass studio) and technical expertise to other Chinese film companies that lacked such resources. In the early 1920s, it began producing feature-length narrative films. Although dissolved in 1926, the Department continued to operate as the independent Guoguang Film Co. for another year.

ZHEN ZHANG

communication

Communication technologies are inextricably bound up or imbricated with early moving pictures in a multitude of ways: as embedded models for filmic narration, as a horizon of expectations for the medium's engagement with absent yet visible realities and displaced realms, and as allegorical versions of spectatorship.

In 1898, **Edison** already was producing two slightly different versions of the telephone, toying with—in a science-fiction-like fashion—liquid transfers via versatile telephone lines. If **transportation** technologies were grafted onto the new medium of moving pictures from the very outset for purposes of introducing dynamism in the non-edited, but progressively shifting frame or view, telephones later offered motivational links for **editing** by inscribing an entire communication scenario—or allegory of communication—within the frame by way of split-screen or superimposition. Filmic special effects, then, revealed both the telephone's and the film technology's shared opportunities for spatial connections in real time and diegetical time, respectively.

Trick films brimmed with askew versions of communicating and split-second time and space shifting, transfers and transferences, for instance in Georges **Méliès'** *Photographie electrique à distance* (1908). Here Méliès underscores the film medium's unique combination of indexical accuracy and deft trick work by mounting less dexterous attempts at communicating and transferring photographic or pixel-like information. **Pathé-Frères** seems to have pioneered split-screen shots for telephone situations, a device quickly emulated by many other studios, not least by **Gaumont**. Nonetheless, Pathé resorted to editing proper in some of the studio's key telephone titles—from *Terrible angoisse* (1906) to *Le Médecin du château* (A Narrow Escape) (1908). D. W. **Griffith** enhanced his early line of suspense by clever telephone situations—all parallel edited, however— *The Medicine Bottle* (1908), *The Lonely Villa* (1909), *Love in an Apartment Hotel* (1912) among others.

In many cases, both telephone and telegraph messages were graphically displayed by various trick devices: for instance, the scrambled letters traveling across the screen in both directions for the telephone conversation in Edison's *College Chums* (1907) or the telegraph letters standing and later traveling on wires in Gaumont's *L'Homme qui à mangé du tareau* (The Man Who Ate a Calf's Head) (1908).

The space compression in real time, which provided the principal rationale for invoking communication technologies in moving picture contexts, took on interplanetary dimensions in an array of films. Links to the planet Mars were very much on the agenda around 1910 and not least in vogue in the Sunday newspaper magazines and on screen. Communication fantasies of all kinds were triggered in the wake of Nikola Tesla's attempt at broadcasting wireless messages, images, and more from his tower on Long Island. His efforts coincided with upgraded telescopic access to other planets. In Latium's *Un Matrimonio interplanetario* (1910), an astronomer on earth, via telescope, spots a girl on Mars with whom he falls in love. After a telegraphic exchange, space ships are built on the respective planets, and eventually the couple is united on the moon.

Likewise, telegraphy and recording devices played a prominent part in **crime films**. Already in 1903, **Sheffield Photo** affected a resolution to a crime film, *Daring Daylight Burglary*, by way of telegraphy, yet only as catalogue information to be delivered by a **lecturer** or exhibitor explaining why the burglar eventually was caught when he disembarked a train after having successfully outrun the police. Soon enough, such information was interiorized and unequivocally delivered within the story diegesis to spectators; a case in point is offered by Pathé's *Un Drame en express* (1906). Here the *apache* is apprehended when his train stops at a station, but this time a detailed telegraph scene is crucial for connecting the story's two plotlines. Telegraphy later proved crucial in Gaumont's 1912–1913 *Main de fer* series (directed by Léonce **Perret**), Pathé's 1911–1912 *Nick Winter* series, as well as more melodramatic suspense thrillers such as Griffih's *The Lonedale Operator* (1911) and *The Girl and Her Trust* (1912). Universal's *Traffic in Souls* (1913) even anthologized communication devices by sporting both a writing-pad link between building floors for tracking the influx of vice cash, and an audio storing device to incriminate the nefarious "white slave" traffickers by recording the voice of "the man higher up."

Éclair's *Amour et science* (1912), by contrast, stages a love affair temporarily put on hold by the fiancé's efforts to invent a television-like telephone. Impatient with his dedication to work only, his girlfriend plays a prank (creating a fictional rival) over the visual phone, which has a traumatic effect on him. The young man's mental bearing, however, is eventually restored via a complex routine involving a replay of the call. This is secured by way of filming it, but with a revelation that effects a happy resolution, dispersing his love doubts and temporary mental affliction.

Overall, communication devices—contemporary as well as futuristic ones—introduced and represented a sense of televisual liveness that compressed the time frame of a "slow" medium, with its several phases between recording and exhibition. This desire for liveness embellished cinema with the modus operandi of electrical, real-time media. In addition, the communication situations displayed in specific films updated audiences on the progress of these affiliated technologies, both extant everyday ones and those in the pipeline. Moreover, blueprints for the future of communication technologies and cinema were negotiated in titles, toying with versions of communication having a pedigree that went back to media utopias of Albert Robida and others. In addition to such concerns, telephone calls offered a handy alternative to letters and telegrams, which in the early phase of narrative cinema provided filmmakers with yet another convenient means to push stories ahead.

See also: editing: spatial relations; editing: temporal relations; electricity

Further reading

Marvin, Carolyn (1988) *Old Technologies Look New Again*, Oxford: Oxford University Press.

JAN OLSSON

consumer cooperatives: Europe

Consumer cooperatives made tremendous progress in many European countries in the last quarter of the nineteenth century. The British Movement with its influential model of "Rochdale Cooperation" was particularly impressive, successfully developing a range of economic activities including retail, wholesale, manufacture, and financial services. By the turn of the century, the British Movement controlled £50 million of business and claimed 1,707,000 members. Much of this success was replicated around Europe, where ordinary working-class

families organised their consumption according to collective ideals. Faced with the new film medium the movement in Great Britain and on the Continent resorted to various strategies to incorporate it.

In Belgium, the so-called Maisons du Peuple (People's Houses) built by the socialist consumer cooperatives were the most visible expression of the power of the labor movement. They housed offices, shops, a library or reading room, a bar and restaurant and one or more large halls to be used for political as well as entertainment purposes. The most famous was undoubtedly the Brussels Maison de Peuple, designed in art deco style by the celebrated architect Victor Horta. For a medium so popular among their working-class customers, it is no surprise that the cooperatives soon started using their main halls for moving picture shows. By 1910, leading cooperatives such as the Vooruit (Forward) in Ghent, the Proletaar (Proletarian) in Louvain, the Populaire (Popular) in Liège and the Maison du Peuple in Brussels were all giving moving picture shows on a regular basis. Although the **lecturer**'s words accompanying the films may have had a left-wing perspective and tickets were somewhat cheaper, the kinds of films they screened hardly differed from other cinemas. This was a complaint taken up by Belgian Labor Party rebel Henri De Man in 1911. In a scathing attack on the Party's reformism, published in the German socialist monthly, *Die neue Zeit*, De Man pointed out that "meeting halls which used to be available exclusively to the Party are now used for film shows during which the most vulgar stupidities are screened, but which bring in more money; as regards the meetings, they have to be held elsewhere." Yet De Man held no bias against moving pictures as such, for in 1913 he helped to set up a Cinema Bureau within the Labor Party's Federation for Workers' Education, to further "the use of still and moving pictures in the interest of socialist propaganda and **education**."

In France, similar cooperative societies developed in parallel with those in Belgium. The most prominent were part of the Bourse des coopératives socialistes in Paris (influenced by Jules Guesde, a leading French Marxist), which, after a lengthy rivalry, joined with the more moderate "School of Nimes" cooperatives (led by Charles Gide), in 1912, to form the Fédération nationale des sociétés françaises de consommation. An anarchist wing of the Paris cooperatives one year later founded the **Cinéma du peuple** movement.

In Great Britain, the coops became engaged with moving pictures from an early date as a natural development of the visual propaganda achieved through the **magic lantern**. Local societies began sponsoring moving picture shows in 1897, and by 1899–1900 the central Co-operative Wholesale Society was filming its own productive activities for screening at local educational events. By this latter date a typical coop show comprised of general interest subjects (**travelogues**, royal visits, *actualités* or topicals) leavened with a few subjects informing members of the extent and achievements of cooperation. This conformed to the traditional labor movement ideal of rational recreation that eschewed frivolous entertainments. By 1914, it was claimed that all of the British movement's productive facilities, including some of the overseas depots, had been filmed. There was a collection of forty films, fitted with titles, averaging 1,000 feet in length. From 1905, the Scottish Co-operative Wholesale Society was operating an equivalent service for members in that country.

In 1908, there emerged a debate in the British movement's press as to the most effective use of moving pictures. A film series at the Leeds Society that ran from 1908 to 1909 was prepared "with an eye to making every member a Cooperator," while the Eccles Society, providing "cinematographic entertainments" for its children, noted that, "though bored by dry discourse, [the children] are briefly imbued with the idea that the evening's delight is associated with the coop store, and thus taught by a striking object-lesson to expect good things from cooperation." Some of this activity was motivated by the desire to counter the "harmful" influence of commercial pictures, and in the time-honored tradition of cooperative distribution sought to displace the vulgar dramas of the capitalist purveyor by the wholesome product of working men's association. It was thought expedient to put before member audiences moving pictures of educational and cooperative subjects— those that "educate the eye."

By the eve of **World War I**, cooperators, virtually alone within the British labor movement, were particularly sensitive to the potential of the cinema. As a contributor to the *Co-operative News* put

it: "The great advantage to us would be its spread of a knowledge of Cooperative activities in a way that the rank and file of the Movement would come to see and learn. We are always talking about the necessity of reaching the masses and bringing the masses together. The cinema would do this for us."

See also: labor movement: Europe

Further reading

Burton, Alan (1996) "The Emergence of an Alternative Film Culture: Film and the British Consumer Co-operative Movement before 1920," *Film History*, 8.4: 446–457.

Burton, Alan (1997) *The British Co-operative Movement Film Catalogue*, Trowbridge: Flicks Books.

Burton, Alan (2001) " 'To gain the world but to lose our soul': Visual Spectacle and Working Class Consumption before 1914," in Simon Popple and Vanessa Toulmin (eds.) *Visual Delights. Essays on the Popular and Projected Image in the 19th Century*, 25–37, Trowbridge: Flicks Books.

Hogenkamp, Bert and Rik Stallaerts (1986) *Pain noir et film nitrate*, Bruxelles: Revue Belge du Cinéma.

Man, Henri de and Louis de Brouckère (1985) *Un épisode de la lutte des tendances socialistes: Le mouvement ouvrier en Belgique (1911)*, Bruxelles: Editions de la Fondation Joseph Jacquemotte.

Williams, Rosalind H. (1982) *Dream Worlds: Mass Consumption in Late Nineteenth-Century France*, Berkeley: University of Calfornia Press.

ALAN BURTON

Continental-Kunstfilm

A successor to businessman (and figure-skater) Max Rittberger and director Walter Schmidthässler's Schmidthässler-Film, Continental-Kunstfilm was founded in February 1912 and initially specialized in psychological melodramas, mostly written by Heinrich **Lautensack** and directed by Max **Mack** or Joe **May**. Whereas its biggest international success was Mime **Misu**'s *Titanic In Nacht und Eis* [Titanic—In Night and Ice] (1912), domestic audiences were smitten in 1913 by one-reelers starring Gerhard Dammann as the comic figure "Bumke." Early in 1914, May and Theodor

Mülleneisen took over the company from Rittberger (Schmidthässler had left in April 1912), inaugurating Continental's last successful phase with the first four parts of May and Ernst **Reicher**'s popular *Stuart Webbs* **detective film** series, for which a separate production company was established in 1915.

MICHAEL WEDEL

Continsouza, Pierre-Victor

b. 1872; d. 1944

engineer, film equipment manufacturer, France

On August 6, 1896, Continsouza registered a patent for his invention of a reversible camera and joined with René **Bünzli** to manufacture the first 35 mm Maltese-cross projectors, commercialized by Charles **Pathé** and others from 1897 on. In January 1898, manufacturer Claude Grivolas founded the Manufacture française d'appareils de précision, a public limited company, which acquired Bünzli and Continsouza's workshops. In August 1900, the company became affiliated with **Pathé-Frères**. Between 1901 and 1909, Continsouza provided Pathé-Frères with all of its **projectors**, **cameras**, contact printers and other laboratory equipment. In October 1909, Continsouza created his own public limited company, with Pathé as one of its shareholders. In 1914, the company employed a thousand workers, exported 7 million francs' worth of film equipment, and represented 60% of European production overall.

LAURENT MANNONI

copyright

Copyright deposits of films and scenarios from the early years of cinema have provided historians with invaluable research material. Yet, whereas manufacturers had no difficulty in using available patent and **trade mark** legislation to engage in litigation, existing photographic copyright proved to be an inadequate and problematic area ultimately requiring the establishment of new case law.

As early as 1899, a British parliamentary select committee concerned with copyright law amendment had recognized the problem in registering films for copyright protection, but when a successful infringement action was undertaken, as in **British Mutoscope and Biograph** vs. *Burns and Oates* (UK 1899), it was on the basis that a single photograph taken from a filmed sequence had been subsequently reproduced without authority in a magazine.

In the USA, **Edison** vs. **Lubin** (US 1902) was a key case. The lower court supported the defendants' contention that Edison ought, in accordance with the 1870 Copyright Act, to have registered each frame individually to obtain protection for the entire film. The Appeals Court (1903) reversed judgment and held that a film could be protected in the USA by the registration of a single frame. However, in **American Mutoscope and Biograph** vs. *Edison Manufacturing Company* (US 1904), both the lower court and appeals court decided that copyright in a film only related to unauthorized duplication of the images and did not extend to its thematic elements. A film could, however, be registered separately as a dramatic production. Not until several years later, in *Harper Brothers* vs. **Kalem** *Company and* **Kleine** *Optical* (US 1908)—a case concerned with a filmed version of *Ben Hur* (1907)—did the court definitively hold that the content of a film (providing that it had previously been expressed in words and was not simply a narrative idea) could be protected as a mime, and that an author had the sole right to permit use of his work in a film.

In an English test case, *Karno vs.* **Pathé-Frères** (UK 1908), the plaintiff lost on a technicality, but the court nonetheless clearly indicated that a dramatic work would be infringed by its use in a film without permission. It should be noted that neither in this ruling, nor in the American Harper Brothers case, was a film recognized as a creative work in itself. In a rather similar French case, the Paris Court of Cassation in 1910 rejected Georges Courteline's claim that his farce, *Boubouroche*, had been illegally reproduced on film but decided that an author's copyright did extend to a filmed copy of his work, even though dialogue was omitted.

These later cases took place against a background of growing dissatisfaction with copyright law. The Berlin Convention of 1908 represented a coordinated international attempt to simplify procedure and to extend full protection to newer forms of communication such as film and sound recording. Article 74 of the Convention dealt specifically with film and recommended that a film production should be recognized as a literary and artistic work. The International Copyright Act of 1911 ratified these recommendations.

See also: law and the cinema; screenwriting; US patent wars

Further reading

Allen, Jeanne Thomas (1985) "Copyright and Early Theater Vaudeville, and Film Competition," in John L. Fell (ed.) *Film Before Griffith*, 176–187, Berkeley: University of California Press.
Brown, Richard (1996) "The British Film Copyright Archive," in Colin Harding and Simon Popple (eds.) *In the Kingdom of Shadows: A Companion to Early Cinema*, 240–245, London/ Madison: Cygnus Arts/Farleigh Dickinson University Press.

RICHARD BROWN

Corbett, James J.

b. 1866; d. 1933

boxer, actor, USA

As heavyweight champion (1892–1897), Corbett gained a celebrity that was abetted by early cinema. William **Brady** managed the fighter, using film appearances to supplement his growing career in **vaudeville** and melodrama theater. In 1894, Corbett signed with the **Edison**-licensed Kinetoscope Exhibiting Company, created by the **Latham** brothers to record prizefights. *Corbett and Courtney before the Kinetograph* captured six rounds of sparring and became one of the most widely-seen **Kinetoscope** attractions. The Veriscope Company then filmed the extravagantly-publicized *Corbett-Fitzsimmons Fight* (1897), a **multiple-reel**, wide-screen **boxing film** that toured the world with great success. Although "Gentleman Jim" was dethroned, the film was promoted to female fans of the matinee idol, eliciting commentary about cinema's role in exposing women to taboo subject matter. In 1900, Corbett and Kid McCoy re-enacted their New York

bout for **Lubin** cameramen in Philadelphia. From 1913 through 1930, the retired champion starred in fiction films for **Warner's Features** and other companies.

DAN STREIBLE

Costello, Maurice

b. 1877; d. 1950

actor, USA

One of the most popular actors of the early cinema period, Costello was among the first to receive on-screen credit as well as to gain the status of movie **star**. After learning his craft on the stage, Costello first appeared in films for **Edison** in 1905 and then moved to **Vitagraph** in 1907, where he appeared in such romantic roles as Lysander in *A Midsummer Night's Dream* (1910) and Sidney Carton in *A Tale of Two Cities* (1911). But bad **publicity** related to domestic difficulties tarnished his image, and he ended his film career as an extra.

ROBERTA E. PEARSON

costume

The heritage of film costuming may be seen as theatrical in numerous ways. Consider the migration of costumes from Georges **Méliès**' stage magic acts to his early films, exemplified by his direct representation of himself as a devilish **magician** and his assistants in alluring, abbreviated costumes. In *Cendrillon* [Cinderella] (1899), the costumes mimic those of the ballet renditions of this **féerie or fairy play**, whereas *Le Voyage dans la lune* [Trip to the Moon] (1902) **music hall** costumes seem to inspire the sailor blouses and shorts that adorn the "chorus girls" who load the space capsule so fetchingly. Numerous Méliès' films highlight costume changes by combining them with substitution editing to create marvelous transformations, including those which turn fairy princesses into monsters, men into women, and commonplace dress into sinister guises. Méliès' costumes, like his sets, were designed in black and white to facilitate filming. **Color** was added by painting on the film.

The iconographic tradition of costuming **western** characters in bandana, cowboy hat, and six-shooter was inaugurated by the famous close shot in **Edison**'s *The Great Train Robbery* (1903), directed by Edwin S. **Porter**. The garb of the hold-up men and the sheriff in this film contrasted with the more urbane costumes of their robbery victims. In 1912, Lou Burns, a former trader who collected Indian tribal weapons and clothing, established the Western Costume Company in Los Angeles, initially to supply companies producing Indian and Wild West pictures, in which the dress of various tribes, including the elaborate feathered headdresses of the Plains Indians, was such an attraction. Western Costume soon branched out into other costumes and was responsible, for example, for those in D. W. **Griffith**'s *The Birth of a Nation* (1915), including all of the Civil War uniforms.

Sources for costumes in early cinema included theater cast-offs scavenged and stored in trunks, the actors' own wardrobes, and cobbled together imitations of the dress of the poor and various ethnic groups. Much of our specific knowledge of early costume practices comes from memoirs. Lilian **Gish** speaks of selecting costumes with her sister Dorothy for **Biograph**'s *An Unseen Enemy* (1912), from a "rack of second hand clothes reeking with fumigant"; in the film they wear matching striped shirtwaists with an asymmetrical row of buttons and ruffles on the bodice. She also writes that "an elderly man in the company combed second-hand stores and pawnshops for cheap clothes to be used as costumes," that leading players always had first choice, and that Griffith then personally approved the choices, sometimes seizing the opportunity to create rivalry among his players.

Gish also claims that her mother's skills as a seamstress provided the sisters with elegant clothes in their own wardrobes that they would use in films. In speaking of Arthur **Johnson**, Gish remarks that he wore his sole dark blue serge suit in at least twenty films. In fact, this tradition of actors supplying their own wardrobes may have contributed to the inclusion of designer **fashion** in early films, as the **stars** began to frequent designers for their own wardrobes, which they then wore in their roles, such as Gish's taffeta gown trimmed in velvet and ermine made by Madame Francis and worn in *Captain Macklin* (1915). **Serial** stars Pearl

White and Eleanor Woodruff also wore designer gowns for their roles; indeed, **Vitagraph** advertised the elegance of Woodruff's Maison Maurice dresses as part of the film's appeal to distributors.

Pathé-Frères' Films d'Art not only borrowed actors from the legitimate **theater** and adapted literary classics; it prided itself on the status of its set and costume design, advertising its adaptation of Balzac's short story, *La grand bretèche* (1909) as authentic in scenery, costumes, and furnishings. Italian companies such as **Ambrosia** and **Cines** began a cycle of historical spectacles with *Gli Ultimi giorni de Pompei* [The Last Days of Pompeii] (1908) that led to the extravagant *Quo Vadis?* (1913), which drew on costume designers of **opera**. When Pathé established **Film d'Arte Italiana**, it too concentrated in part on historical spectacle, with ancient, medieval, and renaissance costuming as one of its draws, including in some credits and ads a named "artistic director."

Avant-garde costume design for the stage, such as Bakst's designs for the Ballets russes, had little direct influence on film costuming during the early period, but one can see in the costumes designed for divas, vamps, and seductresses some costumes bearing similar geometrically imaginative embellishments and flowing lines. More generally, orientalism and decadence shaped the costumes of such Italian divas as Francesca **Bertini** as well as the American vamp, Theda Bara. Griffith's *Judith of Bethulia* (1914) displayed similar fanciful exoticism in its costumes, including striking headdresses and large bracelets, on both males and females.

Comedies often based their humor on costumes that poked fun at fashion, as is the case with Porter's *Aunt Sallie's Wonderful Bustle* (1901). In attempting to regain her balance after her hat is swept off by the wind, Sallie falls over a stone wall, landing on her bustle. She immediately rebounds upward and disappears off screen, only to drop down safely beside her startled companion. Italian comic Ferdinando **Guillaume** borrowed alternatively from the tramp and the gentleman about town in designing costumes for his characters, Polidor and Tontolini. Max **Linder** dressed in impeccable elegance. Charlie **Chaplin** costumed his tramp in the scavenger elegance of worn formal suits too large for his frame, accompanied with a cane and top hat that not only became wonderful props, but spoke of his character's aspirations.

Marked as a period initially influenced by theatrical costumes, early cinema quickly integrated everyday life into filmic costuming through the practice of having players use their own clothes or help design their own costumes. It also laid the foundation for companies like Western Costume to service Hollywood studios and the emergence of the costume designer, once the duties of the artistic director were divided into more specialized positions.

Further reading

Abel, Richard (1994) *The Ciné Goes to Town: French Cinema, 1896–1914*, Berkeley: University of California Press.

Gish, Lillian and Ann Pinchot (1969) *Lillian Gish: the Movies, Mr. Griffith, and Me*, Englewood Cliffs, N.J.: Prentice-Hall.

LaVine, W. Robert and Allen Florio (1980) *In a Glamorous Fashion: The Fabulous Years of Hollywood Costume Design*, New York: Scribner, 1980.

Leese, Elizabeth (1991) *Costume Design in the Movies*, New York: Dover.

Maeder, Edward (ed.) (1987) *Hollywood and History: Costume Design in Film*, Los Angeles: Los Angeles County Museum of Art.

Owen, Bobbi (1987) *Costume Design on Broadway: Designers and their Credits, 1915-1985*, New York: Greenwood Press.

Traphagen, Ethel (1918) *Costume Design and Illustration*, New York: Wiley.

Turim, Maureen (1994) "Seduction and Elegance: The New Woman of Fashion in Silent Cinema," in Shari Benstock and Suzanne Ferris (eds.) *On Fashion*, 140–158, New Brunswick: Rutgers University Press.

MAUREEN TURIM

Courrier cinématographique, Le

Le Courrier cinématographique was a weekly Paris trade paper whose first issue appeared on 8 July 1911. Charles Le Fraper, formerly an exhibitor and a collaborator with Serge **Sandberg** in the Loire region, was the demanding editor of the journal as well as an indefatigable advocate for the profession for more than twenty-five years. Resolutely "modern, independent, and rebellious," *Le Courrier cinématographique* rivalled **Ciné-Journal**, as the leading French trade journal during the 1910s. After a hiatus during **World War I**, the journal reappeared on 12 January 1917 and continued publishing until 1937.

THIERRY LEFEBVRE

crime films

Among the sensational **melodramas** that comprised much of early fiction film production in the USA, Great Britain, France, Germany, Brazil, and other countries, crime films were unusually significant. They indicate that early cinema often shared with sensational **newspapers** (and other media) an interest in exploiting shocking criminal behavior in order to attract and hold audiences; and that, in turn, led some government authorities and moral reform groups eventually to seek to regulate or censor their circulation as a threat to the social order. Nevertheless, crime films were an important factor in establishing the dominance of single-reel fiction films and later in supporting the transition to **multiple-reel/feature films**, especially in France.

Crime films initially emerged as **re-enactments** of notorious historical subjects, as in **Lumière**'s *La mort du Marat* [The Death of Marat] (1897). Soon, however, they began to re-enact either representative or especially shocking contemporary crimes and their consequences, as in **Edison**'s *Execution of Czolgosz* (1901) or **Pathé-Frères'** *Histoire d'un crime* [Story of a Crime] (1901), the latter of which reproduced a popular exhibit in the Paris **wax museum**, the Musée Grévin. The most famous early crime film, often still mistaken as the first **western**, was Edison's *The Great Train Robbery* (1903), inspired by a popular 1890s stage melodrama. Although this last film includes a short chase near the end, British crime films such as **Sheffield Photo**'s *A Daring Daylight Burglary* (1903) and Walter **Haggar**'s *Desperate Poaching Affray* (1903) were more crucial in the development of **chase films**, which culminated in such titles as Cecil **Hepworth**'s *Rescued by Rover* (1905), Haggar's *The*

Life of Charles Peace (1905), and Pathé's *Brigandage moderne* [Highway Robbery Modern Style] (1905) and *Les chiens contrebandiers* [Dog Smugglers] (1906), the latter being one of the first films to deploy sequences of extended parallel editing—before the format largely turned into a means of stringing together a series of comic gags.

Between 1905 and 1908, Pathé seemed to specialize in crime films, which had widespread distribution through its global network of sales agencies. Like the *grand guignol* plays of Alfred de Lorde from which some derived, they tended to be set in modern urban milieux, to involve attacks on bourgeois or upper-class characters (often women) and/or property, and to end with the crimes sometimes going unpunished. Although some criminals came from the lower classes, as in *A Narrow Escape* (1908), just as often they were desperate or deceptive bourgeois gentleman, struck by remorse, as in *Pour un collier!* [All for a Necklace] (1907), or trapped ironically for a crime they did not commit, as in **SCAGL**'s *L'Homme aux gants blancs* [The Man in White Gloves] (1908). Beyond France, a Brazilian sensational film, William **Auler**'s, *Os estranguladores* [The Stranglers] (1906), which reconstructed an actual crime shot on location, was so popular that it made the crime film a significant subject of national production. In the USA, by contrast, **Lubin**'s *Unwritten Law* (1907), which re-enacted the lurid Thaw–White case, was condemned, as was Pathé's *Nuit de noël* [Christmas Eve Tragedy] (1908), in which, on the coast of Brittany, a man and horse are pushed off a cliff into the sea (which provoked a court case and fine). Much more acceptable were D. W. **Griffith**'s crime melodramas, from *The Lonely Villa* (1909) to *The Girl and Her Trust* (1912), in which the villains (all marginal types) consistently were thwarted in the nick of time.

Sensational melodramas played an important role in the transition to multiple-reel films in Denmark, Germany, and the USA, but only in France did that involve the crime film in a major way. Although historical subjects such as Albert **Capellani**'s *Le Courrier de Lyon* [The Orleans Coach] (1911), based on a popular stage melodrama, again could be said to initiate this transition, the crucial films were driven by modern criminal figures, now drawn from pulp fiction. Leading the pack was Victorin **Jasset**'s three-reel *Zigomar*

(1911), focused on the master criminal of Eugène Sazie's popular serial novel (1909–1910), which enjoyed a stunning success worldwide. That success led **Éclair** to have Jasset direct not only two more *Zigomar* films, in 1912 and 1913, but also other crime films in multiple reels, such as *Tom Butler* (1912) and *Balaoo* (1913). The exploits, capture, and execution of the infamous Bonnot gang in early 1912 provoked Pathé and **Gaumont** to join Éclair in producing up-to-the-minute crime films, but some of these now began to face censorship by local authorities. Their appeal was strong enough, however, for Gaumont to encourage Louis **Feuillade** to begin producing a series constructed around another master criminal (and master of disguise), drawn from the immensely popular *Fantômas* novels written by Marcel Allain and Pierre Souvestre (1911–1913). In each of what became five separate, feature-length *Fantômas* films (1913–1914), the "hero" (played by René **Navarre**) eludes capture at the end and makes audiences anticipate a further sequel. Not only does Fantômas prey on the rich, arranging murders whenever expedient (as in the case of a painter who has the skin removed from one hand in order to create a human glove), and

Figure 26 Poster for Èclair's *Zigomar*, 1911.

repeatedly slip deftly away from the police, but, in the final film, he also perverts the French legal system and Catholic Church, disguised first as a magistrate and then as a priest.

Although they share certain features, **detective films** became somewhat distinct from crime films by the early 1910s, and also especially characteristic of the USA and Germany. The US **trade press** in particular came to see this as an important mark of the US cinema's distinction and superiority *vis-à-vis* the French, which continued, in its view, to "indulge" in disreputable crime films.

See also: editing: spatial relations

Further reading

Abel, Richard (1994) *The Ciné Goes to Town: French Cinema, 1896–1914*, Berkeley: University of California Press.
Gunning, Tom (1991) *D. W. Griffith and the Origins of American Narrative Film: The Early Years at Biograph*, Urbana: University of Illinois Press.
Musser, Charles (1990) *The Emergence of Cinema to 1907*, New York: Scribner's.

RICHARD ABEL

Cuba

Barely two years after its Parisian premiere—on 24 January 1897—the **Cinématographe Lumière** arrived in Havana, via Mexico, with cameraman Gabriel **Veyre**. Two weeks later, Veyre inaugurated the Cuban cinema with *Simulacro de un incendio* [Simulation of a Fire], a one-minute film about a staged fire-fighting incident that promoted the colonial government as well as the incipient **modernity** of the city's new firefighting system.

Shortly thereafter, with the onset of the Spanish–American war, Cuba became a privileged location for US cameramen intent on producing *actualités* and **news event films**. **Edison** cameramen shot *Burial of the Maine Victims* "on location" as early as February 1898. Camera limitations prevented the filming of actual battles, so Edison also produced **re-enactments** of the fighting shot for the most part in New Jersey using National Guard troops. The war was of such interest that **Vitagraph** also produced

several famous battle re-enactments in New York, and even George **Méliès** reconstructed the sinking of the Battleship Maine in late 1898 in France.

Notwithstanding the war, a Cuban actor, José **Casasús**, used the new medium in the service of commercial interests with *El brujo desapareciendo* [The Disappearing Magician] (1898). Sponsored by a brewery, this first Cuban film was inspired by Méliès' **trick films** and featured a **magician** who "disappeared" to drink a beer. Throughout 1901–1905, the business of exhibition prospered in Havana, with a growing number of entertainment venues advertising film programs and the creation, in 1905, of several distribution companies, most notably, **Santos y Artigas** (representatives of **Gaumont**) and the Moving Picture Company, owned by Enrique **Díaz Quesada** and entrepreneur Francisco Rodríguez (the two companies later joined forces).

Between 1906 and 1920, Díaz Quesada and Santos y Artigas led efforts to develop a national cinema. Díaz Quesada filmed *El parque de Palatino* [Palatino Amusement Park] (1906) to promote a recently inaugurated **amusement park** on the outskirts of Havana. Commissioned by the park's US-owners to promote its rides abroad, this is the oldest extant Cuban film. In addition to recording many of the social and political events of the time, he also shot the first fiction film, *Un duelo a orillas del Almendares* [A Duel on the Banks of the Almendares River] (1907).

Slowly, the cinema business expanded beyond Havana, with the opening of exhibition venues in other provincial capitals and with various local productions, most notably, in 1909, Díaz Quesada's *Los festejos de la Caridad en la ciudad de Camagüey* [The St. Charity Festivities in the City of Camagüey]—for which he produced a traveling shot aboard a streetcar—and Chas Pérez's ten-minute fiction film, *La leyenda del charco de Güije* [The Legend of the Güije Lake], significant for reenacting a popular legend about river sprites.

In 1906, businessman Eusebio Azcue founded the Actualidades in Havana, the first theater designed to show moving pictures exclusively (and until recently still functioning). By 1914, Havana had forty theaters, with an additional 300 (the seating capacity averaged 650) in the rest of the country, for a population of only 2.5 million.

Besides several more or less successful experiments to sonorize films via behind-the-screen actors and synched recordings, most theaters featured live accompaniment with performers such as Ernesto Lecuona, who later would achieve great notoriety.

Throughout the 1910s, Santos y Artigas consolidated its control of distribution and exhibition—importing the most popular European films, including special "festivals" devoted to figures such as Max **Linder** (1909) and Francesca **Bertini** (1916); showing Díaz Quesada's films in exclusive first runs; and operating a number of theaters in Havana and the provinces. The company also sponsored the first trade journal, *Cuba Cinematográfica* (1912), and several national scriptwriting contests. Other exhibitors and distributors included Enrique **Rosas**, a Mexican entrepreneur (1906–1908); Blanco y Martínez (1916–1928), and, after the creation of Paramount's subsidiary, Caribbean Films, in 1916, direct representatives of US studios. However, until 1920 (when the association with Díaz Quesada ended), Santos y Artigas remained the dominant force.

The 1920s were difficult for Cuba and its film business. The economy was in a shambles due to the crash of world markets for sugar and there was tremendous political instability; moreover, subsidiaries of US companies had established a firm stronghold in distribution and exhibition and vanquished the European competition. National production continued, but it was sporadic and barely registered against the continued popularity of US films. The one exception was the work of Ramón **Péon**, whom Georges Sadoul would later hail as a neorealist precursor.

Further reading

Agramonte, Arturo (1966) *Cronología del cine cubano*, Havana: Ediciones ICAIC.

Douglas, María Eulalia (1996) *La Tienda Negra: El cine en Cuba (1897–1990)*, Havana: Cinemateca de Cuba.

Rodríguez, Raúl (1992) *El cine silente en Cuba*, Havana: Letras Cubanas.

ANA M. LÓPEZ

cue sheets

Originally, the term "cue music" was reserved for music required to match a visible sound source, such as a bugle call or dance. By the mid-1910s, the term "cue" had taken on a new meaning, referring instead to any designated point during a film when music is to be played.

The first published musical suggestions for film accompaniment, in the 1909–1910 **Edison** *Kinetogram*, were split between two different accompaniment practices. Suggestions for several films followed contemporary theatrical practice, calling for the conductor or pianist to select an available "andante," "allegro," "hurry," or "march," while other recommendations emulated contemporary **nickelodeon** practice, suggesting instead specific popular songs: e.g., "Take Me Out to the Ball Game" for *A Great Game* (1909), "Everybody Works But Father" for *The Man With a Weak Heart* (1910), or "A Hot Time in the Old Town To-night" for the end of *A Warrior Bold* (1910). When, in 1910–1912, the **trade press** began to devote columns to **musical accompaniment**, writers typically offered suggestions of a similar nature, stressing general types of music from the theatrical collections then available, or specific popular songs matched to the film action by title or lyrics. Soon, music publishers began to issue compilations specifically aimed at film accompaniment, using labels such as "Hurry Music," "Plaintive Music," or "Mysterioso-Burglar Music." The increasing availability of such collections fostered continued use of generic designations, along with persistent recourse to popular favorites, in music suggestion lists like those found in mid-1910s issues of the **Vitagraph** *Bulletin of Life Portrayals*.

During the 1910s, music publishers progressively replaced trade press columnists and manufacturers as primary purveyors of musical suggestions for film accompaniment. The "cue sheets" they produced were often compiled by current or former music publishing personnel, and served in part to publicize the products of specific music publishers (especially Carl Fischer, Schirmer, and Belwin). By the time cue sheets became generalized, accompaniment styles had changed substantially. Postwar cue sheets thus rarely recommend popular songs, and, when they call for a piece of generic music (e.g., a hurry or plaintive number), they typically designate a specific composition from a published collection. Most selections suggested by cue sheets are light classical pieces identified by composer name and title. For each number, the cue sheet provides a beginning cue, tempo, duration, and sometimes an ending cue, although the continuous accompaniment style of the period usually makes ending cues superfluous. Because of the musicians' need for a stable running time, many cue sheets indicate projection speed, often our best indication of silent film projection rates. After 1917, when composers succeeded in establishing their right to royalties on music played in film theaters, many cue sheets were issued with two separate sets of musical suggestions, one recommending copyrighted or "taxable" music and the other sticking to "non-taxable" music.

Cue sheets were usually prepared by a classically trained music professional, either a **palace cinema** musical director or a publishing house employee. They thus often featured music that was difficult for local pianists or orchestras to obtain or play. For this reason, cue sheets were not always used.

RICK ALTMAN

Cuesta Valencia

Founded in Valencia (Spain) in 1905, Cuesta Valencia primarily produced films but also sold and rented them along with apparatuses. Its first films were *actualités*, especially about bullfighting, but it also made fiction films, such as *El ciego de la aldea* [The Blind Man of the Village] (1906). Until 1911, the company's artistic director was photographer Angel García Cardona, author of the comedy, *Benitez quiere ser torero* [Benitez Wants to be a Bullfighter] (1910). From then on, J. M. Codina served as artistic director; he is best known for making the first Spanish **crime film** series, *Los bandidos de Sierra Morena* [The Bandits of Sierra Morena] (1911–1912).

JOAN M. MINGUET

Cunard, Grace [Harriet Mildred Jeffries]

b. 1891; d. 1967

actor, scriptwriter, director, USA

Remembered as a daring jewel thief, a madcap reporter with a nose for news, and a circus tamer of ferocious cats, Grace Cunard starred in over 100 silent films. She also wrote the screenplays and treatments for 44 of these, while directing at least eight. Teamed with actor/director Francis **Ford**, Cunard's most prolific period began at **Universal** in 1913, where she created her popular criminal character Lady Raffles, as well as the *Twin Sisters Double* cycle. In 1914, Cunard and Ford co-starred in *Lucille Love, Girl of Mystery*, inaugurating a string of action-crime **serials** popular throughout the 1910s.

JENNIFER M. BEAN

D

dance films

Thomas **Edison** once referred to his invention of the **Kinetoscope** as "a machine to make little pictures that danced." The statement reveals an affinity between the new invention and our most ancient art. The vast majority of the **Edison** company's early films recorded trained bodies in motion, principally acrobatic and athletic performers as well as dancers. In 1894, the first year of Kinetoscope production, the dances filmed included: Carmencita in Spanish dances; Scotch Highlanders performing a reel; Ruth [St.] Dennis performing high kicks; Annabelle **Moore** performing both a butterfly and a serpentine dance; Sioux warriors enacting several native dances; "The Gaiety Girls" in a number of their well-known dances; Japanese women performing a ribbon dance; Rosa doing a Turkish belly-dance; and Wilson and Waring in an eccentric "tramp" dance.

Dance films became one of the most stable genres of early cinema before 1904. Basically, subjects oscillated between foreign, even **ethnographic** dances, and more familiar theatrical dances. The **Lumière** company catalogue emphasized the foreign (Tyrolese, Javanese, Russian, Italian, Egyptian, Mexican, Ashanti, Spanish, Scotch), but included some more theatrical performances, such as serpentine dances and a series of films of the Ballet Excelsior. Beginning in 1899, **Pathé-Frères** offered a series of international dance films (Russian, Abyssinian, Greek, Spanish, belly dances from Tunisia, Egypt, and Greece), but also filmed highly theatrical performances: stars of the Moulin Rouge, a film supposedly of Loïe

Fuller, and the ballet companies of the Paris Opera and Châtelet. Richard Abel estimates that fully half of the films **Gaumont** released between 1900 and 1902 were dance films, including both international dances and ballet numbers. The **American Mutoscope and Biograph Company** (AM&B) initially gave less emphasis to dance but, after 1902, featured comic **vaudeville** performances such as: *The Betsy Ross Dance*, *The Comedy Cake Walk*, *The Franchonetti Sisters*, *The Dance in Pajamas*, *Foxy Grandpa and Polly in a Little Hilarity*, and *The Princess Rajah Dance*.

After 1904, films consisting entirely of dances became less frequent, but dances were integrated into longer narrative films. Pathé included dance numbers in genres as different as **trick films**—the dancing chicken women in *Le Poule aux oeufs d'or* [The Hen with the Golden Eggs] (1905)—and **detective films**—the Japanese dance number in *Tour de monde policier* [Police's Tour of the World] (1906). Following theatrical models, spectacle films included dance numbers often with little narrative motivation, such as the Cake-Walk number in Edison's *Uncle Tom's Cabin* (1903). Trick films frequently featured dances, as in Georges **Méliès'** *Cake-Walk Infernal* (1903), or the extraordinary serpentine dance in **Cines'** *Farfalle* (1907). Pathé's **historical films** such as *Cleopatra* and *Le festin Balthazar* [Balthazar's Feast] (both 1910) featured Stacia **Napierkowska**'s exotic dances. Dances could play a key role in comedies as well, as in Gaumont's delightful *La Bou-Bou-Mie* (1909), in which a concierge cannot stop reenacting the oriental dance she saw at a cabaret, or in AM&B's

The Hypnotist's Revenge (1907), in which a hypnotist makes a disrespectful audience member dance in a variety of embarrassing situations. Early **Keystone** films include dances by Charlie **Chaplin**, Roscoe **Arbuckle**, or Mabel **Normand** that anticipate their later nearly balletic performances.

A number of early multiple-reel films highlight dances. The melodramatic *The Whirl of Life* (1915) featured the dancing duo of Vernon and Irene Castle. Numerous Italian diva films also included dance numbers. Whereas Asta **Nielsen**'s erotic gaucho dance in *Afgrunden* [Abyss] (1910) helped launch her stardom, the tango sequence in Evgenii **Bauer**'s *Child of the Big City* (1914) both reflected and fostered a dance craze in Russia.

TOM GUNNING

Dania Biofilm

A Danish production company founded with large ambitions, following the model of **Film d'Art** and **SCAGL**, in 1913. Gyldendal, the most important Danish publishing house (especially its literary director, writer Peter Nansen), was closely involved with Dania Biofilm. The company acquired rights to famous novels at considerable expense and hired well-known actors (including Benjamin **Christensen**); but filmmaking skills seem to have been in short supply. Although the company did not close down until 1918, it consistently was unprofitable and never produced any major successes.

CASPER TYBJERG

D'Annunzio, Gabriele

b. 1863; d. 1938

novelist/poet/dramatist, Italy

Italy's Belle Epoque was suffused with Gabriele D'Annunzio's influence; as was early Italian cinema, even if D'Annunzio was cynical about its possibilities. His late-romantic influence is clear in diva films. In a literary sense, D'Annunzio's influence also is visible in the many adaptations of his works, with **Ambrosio** making no less than six films in the 1911–1912 season. His most well-known association with early Italian cinema came

in the marketing strategy for the epic *Cabiria* (1914). For 50,000 francs, **Itala** producer-director Giovanni **Pastrone** convinced the forever-in-debt D'Annunzio to promote himself as the author of the film, to write the turgid **intertitles**, and to create some of the exotic names of the characters. These literary pretensions and D'Annunzio's aura, however, long delayed recognition of the innovating aspects of the film and of the actual filmmaker.

IVO BLOM

Dansk Biograf Kompagni

The origin of this Danish film company lay in the international success of Alfred **Lind**'s *De fire Djaevle* [The Four Devils] (1911). German investors enabled one of the men behind this film, actor Carl Rosenberg, to establish a production company in 1912. It was a commercial failure, however, until its backers put Benjamin **Christensen** in charge. His *Det hemmelighedsfulde* X [The Mysterious X] (1914) was a huge hit, and Christensen took over the company and renamed it Benjamin Christensen Film. His subsequent film, *Haevnens Nat* [The Night of Vengeance] (1916), also was very successful, but uncertain wartime conditions made him decide to close the company down.

CASPER TYBJERG

Darling, Alfred

b. 1862; d. 1931

engineer, Britain

The active 1890s filmmaking scene on England's south coast, which Georges Sadoul later dubbed "The Brighton School," owed much to the presence and inventive genius of Darling, a local engineer who manufactured cinematographic equipment for Esme Collings, G. A. **Smith**, James **Williamson**, and most notably Charles **Urban**, for whom Darling began producing equipment in 1898, including the celebrated **Watwick Bioscope projector** and the Biokam 17.5mm camera-projector for amateur use. Darling's business prospered, and he was one of the original investors and directors of the **Charles Urban Trading Company**. His projectors, cameras, tripods, winders and printers had widespread use the world over.

See also: amateur films

LUKE McKERNAN

Davidson, Paul

b. 1867; d. 1927

producer, distributor, exhibitor, Germany

After having worked in the textile and security service industries, Davidson built up AKGT, Germany's largest cinema chain (showing mainly Pathé-Frères films) between 1906 and 1910, from which emerged the country's first vertically-integrated film company, Projektions-AG "Union" (PAGU). In 1913, Davidson re-modelled the U.T. Alexanderplatz in Berlin into the country's biggest movie palace with a capacity of 1,200 seats, converted his distribution contract with Asta Nielsen and Urban Gad into a long-term production agreement, and contracted Max Reinhardt to produce prestigious *Autorenfilme*. In 1914 Davidson began his collaboration with Ernst Lubitsch, which lasted well beyond 1918, when he sold the majority of PAGU's shares to the newly founded UFA (Universum Film AG). He committed suicide in a sanatorium in 1927.

MICHAEL WEDEL

Davis, Harry

b. 1861, London; d. 1940, Pittsburgh

exhibitor, entrepreneur, USA

By 1900, Davis was an important figure in the entertainment industry of Pittsburgh. When a fire destroyed one of his downtown theaters in June 1905, he quickly opened the legendary Nickelodeon; so successful was this venture that, with associate John Harris, he soon financed more storefront theaters in Pittsburgh and other major cities. By 1907, he and Harris owned or managed a chain of twenty-five Bijou Dream moving picture theaters throughout the East and Midwest. Although his fortunes rose and fell several times over the next few years, Davis remained one of the biggest exhibitors in Pittsburgh at least through the 1910s.

RICHARD ABEL

Dawley, J. Searle

b. 1878, Del Norte, Colorado; d. 1949, Woodland Hills, California

director, USA

J. Searle Dawley gave D. W. Griffith his first screen acting work in Edison's *Rescued From an Eagle's Nest* (1907). He left home as a teenager and was stage manager for a Brooklyn stock company in 1906, when he was hired by the Edwin S. Porter at Edison. In 1913, Dawley joined Porter at Famous Players Motion Picture Company and directed Mary Pickford, Marguerite Clark, and John Barrymore in their earliest feature roles. He later directed for Metro, Fox and others. Illness forced his early retirement.

ROBERT S. BIRCHARD

de Barros, Luis

b. 1893, Rio de Janeiro; d. 1981

filmmaker, Brazil

With the longest career in the history of Brazilian cinema, de Barros directed over 100 fiction and nonfiction films. The scion of a bourgeois family, he dabbled in theater initially; during a sojourn in Paris, he met Max Linder and eventually obtained work as an actor with Gaumont. Returning to Brazil in 1914, he dedicated himself to cinema; his first film was the melodrama, *Perdida* [Lost] (1915). Later he would explore literary and theatrical adaptations such as *Ubirajara* (1919) and adventure films and become one of the most respected directors of the early 1920s. In order to sustain production, he filmed sensational nude scenes in *Alma sertaneja* [Soul of the Sertão] (1919), commissioned documentaries, and staged revues for Francisco Serrador's exhibition chain. Later he directed the first Brazilian talkie and had a successful career in sound films.

ANA M. LÓPEZ

de Bedts, George William

b. ? d. ?

inventor, manufacturer, France

De Bedts, who first worked in the photographic equipment trade, took an interest in **chrono-photography** in 1895. In his Paris shop, where Georges **Demenÿ** and other pioneering figures occasionally stopped, de Bedts (also the franchise holder in Paris for **Blair**) sold **Edison kinetoscope** films and negative film stock (to **Gaumont**, among others, in September 1895). In November 1895, according to Jules **Carpentier**, de Bedts devised a reversible camera called the Kinétographe which he patented on January 14, 1896. On October 29, 1896, he registered another patent for a non-professional 35mm camera, which was commercialized in December. He created the first French company exclusively dedicated to the exploitation of "animated images" (January 15, 1896). His film catalog, published in three languages around 1897, featured 310 titles. "All our films were made in our company and with the de Bedts Kinétographe," de Bedts wrote. Historically a highly interesting figure, he nevertheless remains little known.

Further reading

Mannoni, Laurent (1995) "George William de Bedts et la commercialisation de la Chrono-photographie," in Michèle Lagny and Michel Marie (eds.) *Les vingt premières années du cinéma français*, 39–51, Paris: PSN/AFRHC.

LAURENT MANNONI

De Grandsaignes d'Hauterives, Henry

b.1869; d. 1929

lecturer, exhibitor, Quebec/USA

A Breton aristocrat ruined by gambling debts, De Grandsaignes d'Hauterives emigrated to Quebec in 1897 and went into the film business. A talented speaker, he would accompany film screenings with didactic or entertaining comments. His reputation as an exhibitor grew to such a point that he was engaged by major theaters as well as museums and schools, and almost every early moving picture theater in Quebec took up the popular tradition he initiated by featuring its own **lecturer**. After working as an exhibitor in New York and Saint Louis from 1908 to 1913, he returned to France where he abandoned his cinema activities, and became a civil servant.

GERMAIN LACASSE

De Liguoro, Giuseppe

b. 1869; d. 1944

actor, director, scriptwriter, Italy

Following a career as a stage actor between 1894 and 1908, De Liguoro began working at **Milano Films** in 1909. As a director, he specialized in highly choreographed adaptations of literary, historical, and adventure dramas, such as *Edipo Re* [Oedipus the King] (1910) and *Il coraggio della paura* [Courage of Fear] (1911). Although not an original artistic talent, De Liguoro nonetheless had a prolific career at **Gloria Film**, Etna Film, Caesar Film, and Lux-Artis. In 1916, for Caesar, he directed Francesca **Bertini** in such notable films as *Odette* [Odette] and *Fedora* [Fedora].

GIORGIO BERTELLINI

de Morlhon, Camille

b. 1869; d. 1952

filmmaker, scriptwriter, France

As a writer-director, de Morlhon made nearly 160 films between 1908 and 1930, but he was especially important to French cinema in the 1910s.

Born in Paris of an aristocractic background (his actual name was Louis Camille de la Valette de Morlhon), de Morlhon served as Secretary General of the Automobile-Club de France (1895–1901), where he met Léon **Gaumont**. While serving as Henry Deutsch de la Meurthe's personal secretary, he began to direct revues and comedies in Paris theaters. In 1908, encouraged by Gaumont, he turned one of his own scripts into a film, which Gaumont then refused to distribute (the plot too reminiscent of the Dreyfus affair). After this debacle, he met Charles **Pathé**, who immediately hired him as a scriptwriter and director at **Pathé-Frères**.

de Morlhon's first films included original scripts such as *Le Spectre du passé* [The Ghost of the Past] (1910) and *Soldat et Marquise* [Soldier and Marquess] (1910) and adaptations from France's literary and dramatic heritage, such as *Madame Tallien* (1911) from Victorien Sardou and *L'Affaire du collier de la Reine* [The Affair of the Queen's Necklace] (1911) from Frantz Funck-Brentano. In late 1911, he went to Algeria to shoot seven films, casting actors from the principal national theaters (Henri Étiévant, Léontine Massart, and Valentine Tessier) in films such as *Le Fils prodigue* [The Prodigal Son] and *Pour voir les mouquères* [To See the Women], which met with great success in 1912.

An enterprising man, de Morlhon created his own company, **Valetta**, in 1912, to produce films for distribution by Pathé. His films increased in length, with more elaborate sets, and the screenplays became more complex. Although he engaged many celebrated actors—Jean Hervé and Romuald Joubé for *Britannicus* (1912), Claude Garry and Jane Grumbach for *Don Quichotte* [Don Quixote] (1913)—his fetish performer was Massart, who starred in films that now epitomize the early 1910s: *La Calomnie* [Slander], *L'Escarpolette tragique* [Tragedy in the Stirrup], and *Une Brute humaine* [A Human Beast] (all 1913). The following year, he directed two films in Hungary, including *La Dette de l'aventurière* [The Adventuress's Debt], before the war temporarily halted his production. It resumed in 1915, at a slower pace, but with equally acclaimed films such as *Les Effluves funestes* [Deathly Effluvia] (1915), *Coeur de Gavroche* [Street Urchin's Heart] (1916), *L'Orage* [The Storm] (1917), and *Expiation* (1918).

In 1917, de Morlhon founded the Société des Auteurs de Films, through which he defended the rights of French filmmakers and wrote legislation as well as numerous polemical articles on authors' rights. Although he finished his career collaborating with René Jeanne on radio plays in the 1930s, he died in complete oblivion in Paris on November 24, 1952.

Further reading

Le Roy, Eric (1997) *Camille de Morlhon, homme de cinéma (1869–1952)*, Paris: L'harmattan.

ERIC LE ROY

De Riso, Camillo

b. 1854; d. 1924

actor, Italy

De Riso had a long theater career before entering the film industry. Beginning at **Ambrosio** in 1912, he formed a successful comic trio with Gigetta **Morano** and Eleuterio **Rodolfi**, contributing a rotund face and the generous look of a bourgeois *bonhomme*. The trio's films often were based on Italian and French fin-de-siècle *pochades* or sketches and grew in length over the years. In late 1913, De Riso switched to the **Gloria** company, where he created the gay epicure and shameless libertine character of "Camillo" and also performed opposite Lyda **Borelli** in the feature film, *Love Everlasting* (1913). In the second half of the 1910s, De Riso directed films with such actresses as Leda **Gys** and Francesca **Bertini**. He continued working in the light comedy genre into the early 1920s.

IVO BLOM

Debrie, Joseph and André

Joseph: b. ?; d. 1919

André: b. 1891; d. 1967

film equipment manufacturers, France

A foreman in the Boucot company, Joseph Debrie made the first film perforation machine for Lucien **Reulos**'s Mirographe around 1898. In 1900, he created his own precision tools workshop in Paris. He commercialized a new film perforation machine called the "Optima" (he provided Georges **Méliès** with one), then an industrial film contact printer, the "Nova," in 1905. In 1908, his son André, now his collaborator, devised the "Parvo" **camera**, a landmark in the history of film technology. The latter also expanded the company through the development of extremely reliable and innovative equipment between 1919 (when he took over the helm) and the 1950s.

LAURENT MANNONI

Debrie "Parvo" camera

On September 19, 1908, Joseph **Debrie** registered the patent for the "Parvo" camera, which was marketed the following year. It had been developed by André **Debrie**, his son, who eventually assumed leadership of the company in 1919. Precision-tooled, very steady, and unusually compact (weighing only slightly more than ten pounds), the Parvo supplanted the famous **Pathé** Professional, which had become outdated during **World War I**. The magazines, which could accommodate 120 meters of film, were opened in the center and placed inside the boxes on either side of the camera. Direct vision of the image on the film was thus made possible. An automatic dissolve mechanism was added to the Parvo in 1920 and often was used by French avant-garde filmmakers.

LAURENT MANNONI

Decourcelle, Pierre

b. 1856; d. 1926

writer, producer, executive, France

Decourcelle grew up in a family of playwrights to become a master of popular fiction, as in *Les Deux Gosses*. In 1908, he founded **SCAGL**, which he co-administered with Eugène **Gugenheim**. He played a key role in securing exclusive rights to other popular writers' work for the company. He was among the first to foresee the synergy between popular literature and moving pictures as well as the replacement of theater by cinema. In 1914, he

hired André Antoine as a director before distancing himself from SCAGL to dedicate himself to the *cinéroman*, beginning with his newspaper serialization of Pathé-Frères' *Les Mystères de New York* (1915–1916).

ALAIN CAROU

Decroix, Charles

b. ?; d. ?

director, France/Italy/Germany

The son of an Alsatian shoemaker, Decroix started as a writer for Louis **Feuillade** at **Gaumont** in 1908, before he directed his first *films d'art* for **Pathé-Frères** and its affiliates, **Film d'Art** and **SCAGL**, in 1909/10. Mostly based on literary sources, these included Goethe's *Werther* (1910), adapted for the screen by Decroix himself. In 1911, he went to Germany, where he remade a number of his French films for **Deutsche Mutoskop & Biograph**. After a brief stint at **Milano Films** in Italy in 1912, Decroix returned to Germany in 1913, as writer, director and independent producer of his own series for the Monopol-Film Co. His dramas, such as *Die Czernowska* [The Czernowska] (1913), but especially his comedies, starring the former Gaumont comedian "Pyp," became hugely popular, influencing other German filmmakers. In 1914, Decroix joined **Continental-Kunstfilm**, but soon was forced to leave Germany with the outbreak of **World War I**. In Switzerland he made films until 1919, then retired from filmmaking and returned to his native Alsace.

MICHAEL WEDEL

Deed, André [Chapuis, André, a.k.a. de Chapais, André]

b. 1879, Le Havre, France; d. 1935, Paris, France

actor, filmmaker, France, Italy

Deed started his career as a circus artist and then appeared in a number of **music hall** revues in Paris, including the Folies-Bergère. It is probably in shows at the Châtelet that he came to the attention of Georges **Méliès**, who hired him to act in a few **trick films** such as *Dislocation mystérieuse* [Mysterious Dislocation] (1901). They collaborated until 1904.

At that point Deed was contracted by **Pathé-Frères**, for whom he acted in short **comic films** such as *La course à la perruque* [The Wig Chase] (1906), which showcased his agility through multiple acrobatic feats. That same year, Georges **Hatot** shot the first installment in the *Boireau* **comic series**: *Boireau déménage* [Boireau Moves Out]. Pathé programs explicitly mention Deed's presence in only four films in the series, but there were many others in which his character was assumed to bear that name. Boireau was not a clearly defined, unique character: he could be a teenager, as in *Les Apprentissages de Boireau* [Boireau as an Apprentice] (1907) or a bourgeois adult living alone with a housekeeper, as in *Boireau a mangé de l'ail* [Boireau Ate Garlic] (1908). The unity of the series resided in the singularity of Deed's acting, which pervaded other films such as *Un duel à la dynamite* [A Dynamite Duel] (1908). Deed excelled in the roles of somewhat dim-witted, dreamy characters who triggered (often absurd) disasters. His comic ability lay in his rich repertoire of somersaults and grimaces, which emblematic close shots sometimes helped to enhance. In a way, Deed prefigured Clément **Migé** as Calino and Ernest **Bourbon** as Onésime.

By 1908, he enjoyed such popularity throughout Europe that **Itala** Films, through its artistic director Giovanni **Pastrone**, hired him away to launch a comic series in Italy. Known there previously as Beoncelli (Little Drunkard), this time Deed would triumph under the name of Cretinetti (translated as "Gribouille" in France) in more than 90 films, some of which he directed himself. His character was recognizable by his outfit, among other distinctive signs: he donned a white suit, an opera hat, and a stick.

In late 1911, Deed returned to France with his then regular partner, Valentina Frascaroli, to resume his role as Boireau for Pathé in about fifty films directed by Henri Gambard. The first in the new series was aptly titled *Gribouille redevient Boireau* [Gribouille Is Back as Boireau] (1912). During this period, Deed also appeared on stage in shows combining moving pictures and theater.

In 1915, Pastrone asked him back to Turin in order to restart the *Cretinetti* series, which was interrupted by the war shortly thereafter. In the 1920s, Deed acted in a few small parts in French films. He finished his career working as a warehouseman at the Joinville studios.

Further reading

Gili, Jean A. (2004) "André Deed de Paris à Turin. Entre Pathé Frères et Itala Film," in Michel Marie and Laurent Le Forestier (eds.) *La firme Pathé Frères*, 293–310, Paris: AFRHC.

LAURENT LE FORESTIER

Del Colle, Ubaldo Maria

b. 1883; d. 1958

actor, director, Italy

After a brief stage career as an actor, beginning in 1903, Del Colle moved to moving pictures in 1905. He appeared in such classics as **Alberini** & Santoni's *La Presa di Roma* [The Capture of Rome] (1905) and **Comerio**'s *L'Inferno* [Dante's Inferno] (1909). Del Colle began directing first at **Pasquali** (1911–1913) and then at Savoia Film, before founding Del Colle Film in 1916. Appreciated as a prolific and eclectic director, he favored adaptations of popular novels, **serials**, and sensational love stories. From 1920 to 1928, he directed melodramas for Lombardo Film, a leading Neapolitan film company.

GIORGIO BERTELLINI

Delac, Charles

b. 1879; d. 1965

producer, distributor, France

Delac was born Chaloum ben Delak into a family of merchants in Mascara (Algeria). He received a degree from the Institut National Agronomique but, in 1907, became copy editor for **Phono-Ciné-Gazette** and general secretary of Edmond **Benoît-Lévy**'s exhibition company Omnia. Beginning in 1910, Delac headed Monofilm, the company in charge of distribution for **Film d'Art**, which he subsequently incorporated with Société générale de cinématographie, his own reorganized company, Delac et Cie, founded in 1910. After serving in the war, he attempted to duplicate the US model of vertical integration, linking Film d'Art (production), the **AGC** (distribution), and the Salle Marivaux in Paris (exhibition). He also founded a limited production partnership with Marcel Vandal, "Delac, Vandal et Cie," which they co-directed from 1919 to 1937. From 1928 to 1936, he headed the Chambre syndicale de la Cinématographie (the industry's employers' federation). Over his long career, Delac produced and distributed an extensive number of films.

JEAN-JACQUES MEUSY

Delmont, Joseph

b. 1873; d. 1935

actor, director, Germany

A globe-trotting circus artist and animal trainer, Delmont entered the moving picture business in 1906 with a series of animal and cowboy films for **Vitagraph**. In 1910, he returned to his native Austria and, early in 1911, went to Germany where he established himself as Eiko's leading actor-director of sensational **melodramas** and **crime films** by 1912. Delmont championed an alternative formula to the *Autorenfilm*, basing his films on narrative "linearity, logic, and psychology," which made *Der geheimnisvolle Klub* [The Mysterious Club] (1913) and *Der Desperado von Panama* [The Desperado of Panama] (1914) popular in many European countries, thanks to the use of stunt work, original locations, dynamic editing, and a mobile camera.

MICHAEL WEDEL

Demaria, Jules

b. ?; d. ?

manufacturer, France

In 1893, Jules Demaria took over the company his father had founded in 1858, which specialized in the manufacture and marketing of photographic accessories. Taking an interest in moving pictures, on June 29, 1898, he registered a patent for a film projector known as "Zoographe." He also commercialized Raoul **Grimoin-Sanson**'s equipment as well as other products by smaller manufacturers. In 1908, his company merged with the magic lantern manufacturer Lapierre and continued to manufacture film projectors. In 1912, Demaria became president of the film division of the national employers' federation, a position he held for fourteen years.

LAURENT MANNONI

Demenÿ, Georges

b. 1850; d. 1917

filmmaker, inventor, physiologist, educator, France

When Etienne-Jules **Marey** created the Station physiologique in Paris in 1882, he found an efficient collaborator in Demenÿ. Marey, who lived in Naples for half of the year, left Demenÿ to manage the Station, but also to make many **chronophotographs** (first on glass, then on film after 1889). In 1892, Demenÿ perfected the "Phonoscope," the first chronophotographic projector (featuring a transparent disc). Later that year he founded the "Société du Phonoscope," which finally ended his collaboration with Marey in 1894. Demenÿ set up his own workshop in Paris and started shooting films in a Levallois-Perret studio (1894–1895). His "Biographe" camera, with its 58mm unperforated film, was marketed at the end of 1895, along with the phonoscope projector (renamed "Bioscope"), but neither they nor a reversible camera using perforated 58mm film, were commercially successful. Under-financed and lacking a good business sense, in 1896 Demenÿ sold his rights to Léon **Gaumont**, who then succeeded in exploiting the film-driving mechanism for which Demenÿ had registered the original patent in 1894: a sprocket wheel, shortly thereafter used by projectionists all over the world. Demenÿ himself resumed his research on physical education and, in 1902, was appointed Professor of Applied Physiology at Joinville.

Further reading

Mannoni, Laurent, M. de Ferrière le Vayer, and P. Demeny (eds.) (1997) *Georges Demenÿ pionnier du cinéma*, Douai: Editions Pagine.

LAURENT MANNONI

DeMille, Cecil B.

b. 1881, Ashfield, Massachusetts; d. 1959, Hollywood, California

director, scriptwriter, USA

DeMille's father, Henry C. de Mille, was a successful Broadway playwright who often collaborated with producer David Belasco. Cecil graduated from the American Academy of Dramatic Arts in 1899 and began his career as an actor in 1900. Over the next dozen years he appeared in a number of plays, including *The Warrens of Virginia* (1907), which featured Mary Pickford and was written by his brother, William C. de Mille [de Mille was the family spelling, Cecil used DeMille as his professional name]. Cecil also wrote plays and helped manage the DeMille Play Agency, a literary brokerage established by his mother, Beatrice Samuel de Mille. A collaboration with vaudeville producer Jesse L. **Lasky** on several one-act operettas led to a lasting friendship.

In 1913, theatrical prospects were bleak for DeMille, and he planned to travel to Mexico as a war correspondent covering the revolution in that country. Lasky suggested, at the urging of his brother-in-law, Samuel Goldfish (later Goldwyn), that they try making movies instead. The result was the Jesse L. Lasky Feature Play Company (later merged with **Famous Players Motion Picture Company** and Paramount Pictures). DeMille and co-director Oscar Apfel journeyed to the west

coast with leading man Dustin **Farnum** to produce a feature-length film based on Edwin Milton Royle's play, *The Squaw Man*, and rented space at the Burns and Revier Studio in Hollywood. Shot in 18 days at a cost of $15,450.25, *The Squaw Man* was a success, and was followed by *Brewster's Millions*, *The Only Son* (both 1914), and several other collaborations with Apfel.

DeMille's first solo effort as a director was *The Virginian* (1914), based on the novel by Owen Wister, which showed a flair for the medium that was lacking in *The Squaw Man*. Here DeMille began to bring his camera closer to the actors and give greater attention to performances. He also dropped the convention of using **intertitles** to explain what was about to happen in the following scene, preferring instead to use dialogue **intertitles** to carry the necessary plot points. Joining forces with art director Wilfred Buckland and cinematographer Alvin Wyckoff, DeMille brought Belasco **lighting** (rechristened Lasky lighting) to the screen, giving the medium a new visual sophistication in films such as *Carmen* and *Maria Rosa* (both 1915). DeMille's greatest critical success in these early years was *The Cheat* (1915), although he had little regard for Hector Turnbul's script. *The Golden Chance* (1916) more closely reflected his dramatic and thematic interests and was perhaps his finest film of the period.

DeMille went on to a long and successful career in Hollywood. Although critics often dismissed his later work, he was an extraordinarily fine filmmaker in the 1910's.

Further reading

Birchard, Robert S. (2003) *Cecil B. DeMille's Hollywood*, Lexington: University of Kentucky Press.

Cherchi Usai, Paolo and Lorenzo Codelli (eds.) (1991) *The DeMille Legacy*, Pordenone: Edizioni Biblioteca dell'Immagine/Le Giornate del Cinema Muto.

Higashi, Sumiko (1994) *Cecil B. DeMille and American Culture: The Silent Era*, Berkeley: University of California Press.

ROBERT S. BIRCHARD

Denmark

The first moving pictures were shown in Denmark in 1896, and the first Danish-made films were shot the following year. Viable cinemas began opening in 1904, and in 1906 Ole **Olsen** founded **Nordisk Films Kompagni**, which soon grew into a major international company. On the home market, Nordisk began to face competition from **Fotorama** in 1909. The rapid growth in the number of cinemas attracted the attention of the authorities, and from 1907 film exhibition was subject to local censorship. From 1910 to 1914, Danish film production reached its peak. The well-crafted and often risqué Danish **multiple-reel/feature films** attracted a large international audience, and Nordisk made enormous profits. A number of new film companies were set up around 1913, but most of them proved short-lived. The outbreak of **World War I** had disastrous consequences for the Danish film industry: export markets closed, and the industry would never regain the strong international position it had enjoyed before the war.

Exhibition and distribution

In June 1896, an establishment called the Kjøbenhavns Panorama (Copenhagen Panorama) was opened by Vilhelm Pacht (1843–1912), a sometime artist who had previously worked at the Panoptikon, a **wax museum** founded in Copenhagen in 1885. Pacht would later present waxworks displays and peepshow boxes, but his initial attraction was a novelty: moving pictures. The first public presentation took place on 7 June 1896 (there was a press show the previous day).

Four days later, the **Skladanowsky** brothers presented their Bioskop at the famous Tivoli amusement park, but Pacht's establishment, renamed Panorama & Kinoptikon, remained one of the most important venues for moving pictures until it closed in 1899. A date of particular note was 25 December 1896, when Pacht presented the first show with Danish-made pictures, four brief films showing Copenhagen scenes shot by Peter **Elfelt**.

In the **music halls** or variety theaters of the largest Danish towns, moving pictures were included in the programs along with other acts, between chanteuses and acrobats. In 1898, moving pictures were one of the main attractions, but they quickly lost their novelty appeal. However, **itinerant exhibitors**, who put on film shows in **fairs/airgrounds** and in local meeting halls, could still attract an audience.

In 1900–1902, there were several attempts to set up permanent cinemas, but they all closed after a few months. The first viable cinema, the 158-seat Kosmorama, was opened in September 1904 by Constantin Philipsen (1859–1925), a former **magic lantern** operator, in a vacant store in central Copenhagen. A footman in a grand-looking blue uniform stood on the busy street outside and advertised the film shows. The venture was a success from the start, and Philipsen followed up on his success by opening a total of 26 Kosmoramas in towns across Denmark over the next few years. In most cases, however, he soon sold the cinemas to local operators.

Copenhagen's second cinema, Biograf-Theatret, was opened in 1905 by the experienced fairground showman and future tycoon Ole Olsen. In 1906, Elfelt also opened a new moving picture theater, the respectable Kinografen. Over the next few years, cinemas proliferated; by the end of 1909, there were 150 cinemas across the country, most of them so-called "storefront cinemas," set up in empty shops. Although some of these were in poorer neighborhoods, the more swankily-appointed downtown cinemas were really lucrative.

Moving picture shows were regulated by an 1861 ordinance that dealt with concerts, circuses, fireworks displays, and fairground attractions such as "menageries, panoramas, peepshow boxes, stereoscope collections and the like." These all required a license from the local chief of police. When permanent film exhibition venues were set up, they also were included under these regulations. In most places, only a few licenses were issued; only one town outside Copenhagen (Aalborg) had more than three cinemas. The authorities sought to inhibit aggressive competition by not allowing more cinemas than what the market would safely bear. The system was strongly supported by the exhibitors who had every interest in protecting their livelihood from competitors, and it remained in place until the 1970s. Unlike Sweden and Germany, where film exhibition was not controlled in this way, the Danish licensing system largely blocked the formation of cinema chains, which would turn out to be a significant handicap for the Danish film industry.

To some extent, it was possible to circumvent the licensing system. Fotorama, based in Aarhus, Denmark's second-largest city, managed to take control of a number of cinemas by renting licenses from those who held them or by entering into partnership deals with license holders. Led by the entrepreneurial Frede **Skaarup**, Fotorama was primarily a distribution company, but Skaarup worked dilligently to extend his control over as many cinemas as possible. When Fotorama began producing films in 1909, Skaarup was able to exploit the success of an unusually popular and lavish film, *Den lille Hornblæser* [The Little Bugler Boy], to gain influence over an even larger number of cinemas; if exhibitors wanted the film, they had to pay a percentage (typically 20% to 25%) of their earnings to Fotorama, rather than a fixed price.

In December 1908, *L'Assassinat du Duc de Guise* premiered at Kosmorama in Copenhagen. It was a considerable success and introduced the concept of *film d'art*. In Denmark, it was generally used to mean films made by "artists," that is, films with established stage actors in the leading roles, but the label also could be used by distributors to demand higher prices. In 1909, the Copenhagen chief of police, who was otherwise very reluctant to allow any new moving picture theaters to open, granted a license to an exhibitor who promised to devote his new venue to such films.

Two exhibitors' associations formed in 1910–1911 (one for Copenhagen, one for the rest of the country), and the trade paper *Filmen* began publication the following year. At the same time, the breakthrough of feature films changed exhibition practices. In the early years, varied programs of four, five, or more short films were common. Spectators were admitted at any time, except in the smallest theaters where the manager did double duty as ticket-seller and projectionist. Although continuous admittance remained widespread, feature film shows were increasingly held at fixed times. Two shows per evening, consisting of a feature and several shorts (typically a scenic film and a comedy), became the norm. In many small towns, however, moving picture theaters were open only a few days a week; moreover, the majority of Danish cinemas were closed during the summer.

Most moving picture theaters were tiny and modestly outfitted, and even the largest seated at most 300–400 people. This changed in October 1912, when a true **palace cinema**, supposedly the largest in Europe and aptly named Palads-Teatret (Palace Theater), opened in Copenhagen. It was housed in the old central station building, left vacant when the present central station building opened in 1911. It had 2500 seats and boasted a 30-piece orchestra. This splendid "temple of entertainment" had been conceived by Philipsen, with the intention of attracting a wealthy audience. Much like the legitimate theaters, Palads had only one show per evening, and there was usually an intermission, either between the shorts and the feature or during the latter, where the well-dressed cinema-goers could visit the tea room or stroll through the grand foyer. Palads was a success, and in the years after 1914, elegant and relatively large picture-houses (300–500 seats) opened in many provinial towns, often replacing the old storefront cinemas.

Censorship

Initially, the content of films was not monitored by the authorities. The situation changed in 1907 with the release of Doctor **Doyen**'s surgical films and of Nordisk's *Mordet paa Fyn* [The Murder in Funen], a film which closely followed the facts of a sensational sex murder case which had taken place only weeks before. The indignation aroused by these pictures led the Minister of Justice, P. A. Alberti, to institute film censorship. In Copenhagen, the responsibility was given to the theater censor (stage plays were then also subject to censorship); in the rest of the country, to the local chiefs of police.

The view of the cinema as a base and vulgar amusement was widespread, and it was easy to find parliamentary support in 1911 for the introduction of an amusement tax that added 20 per cent to the cost of a movie ticket. Attendance figures dropped noticeably, and exhibitors were furious. They also were annoyed by the great variation in the severity of censorship by local chiefs of police; some were sternly moralistic and banned many films, while others were much more indulgent. Many exhibitors were unhappy to see colleagues in neighboring towns make good money off scandalous films they themselves were banned from showing. Provincial exhibitors were therefore very much in favor of a national film censorship office whose rulings would apply across the country. National film censorship was indeed introduced in July 1913 and came fully into effect at the beginning of 1914, but exhibitors and distributors then were dismayed by the high cost of having films (and posters) censored.

The Danish censors were considered relatively lenient, and they often were compared favorably with the much stricter Swedish censors. Only one per cent of films submitted to the censors were banned outright, but many suffered cuts. The censors were particularly concerned about films that showed criminal acts such as safecracking or picking pockets in such detail that they might be imitated. They also sought to keep blasphemy and licentiousness away from the screen.

During **World War I**, there was a certain amount of political censorship as well. The preservation of Danish neutrality was of paramount importance, and the censors were diligent in their efforts to exclude films which had propagandistic content or might otherwise give offense to one of the belligerent powers.

Production

Until 1906, there were no film production companies in Denmark. Peter Elfelt was the only one to make films on a regular basis, but his practice remained small. Nordisk, the first and by far the most important company, only came into existence in 1906 because Ole Olsen began having problems getting a sufficient number of new films for his cinema. The proliferation of moving picture theaters across Europe increased the international demand for films so much that the existing production companies found it difficult to keep up. Olsen saw the commercial potential, and in January 1906, he began producing his own films. In many countries, cinema owners turned to film production for the same reasons as Olsen, but few of his competitors expanded as quickly and ventured as decisively into the international market.

Nordisk opened branches in four foreign countries in its first year and soon added more.

Three smaller but important production companies appeared several years later: **Biorama** and Fotorama both began producing films in 1909, and **Kinografen** followed in 1910. They originated in and were named after well-placed, plush cinemas, but had all concentrated on distribution and exhibition until **Pathé-Frères** opened a distribution office in Copenhagen in February 1909 and announced that it would henceforth deal directly with exhibitors (later that year, the French company began offering films with **intertitles** in Danish).

In terms of output, the new companies were insignificant next to Nordisk. By the end of 1909, Nordisk had produced and released more than 230 fiction films and a slightly larger number of non-fiction films, while the others had made only a few non-fiction films and five fiction films between them. The output of the smaller companies grew slightly in the following years, and more importantly, included some very influential pictures. In April 1910, Fotorama released the **white slavery** drama, *Den hvide Slavehandel* [The White Slave Trade], co-directed by the actor Alfred Cohn and the cinematographer Alfred **Lind**. At 706 meters, it was by far the longest film made in Denmark; internationally, it remains one of the earliest examples of the feature film.

The film was extremely successful. Within a few months, however, Nordisk released a plagiarized version, also entitled *Den hvide Slavehandel* (distributed in English-speaking countries as *In the Hands of Impostors*). Nordisk was able to market its scene-by-scene imitation internationally through its extensive distribution network. Fotorama threatened Nordisk with legal action, but the matter was settled out of court in December 1910.

The settlement obligated Nordisk to give Fotorama exclusive distribution rights for all of Nordisk's films in Denmark and Norway. At the time, however, the Danish and Norwegian distribution markets were of only marginal significance to Nordisk, and in return, Fotorama agreed to produce no more than eight films per year; indeed, the company stopped producing films altogether in 1913, concentrating on distribution instead: Fotorama's control of the most attractive Danish pictures now allowed it to dominate domestic film distribution.

A second, equally important feature film, *Afgrunden* [The Abyss], was released in September 1910. Alfred Lind again did the camerawork, but the director and star, Urban **Gad** and Asta **Nielsen**, were both newcomers, and the film was cheaply made with money put up by Hjalmar Davidsen, who had taken over the Kosmorama cinema in Copenhagen. Nielsen's intense and passionate performance brought her international stardom, and the film was tremendously successful; in Germany, its popularity led to an important change in distribution arrangements, helping to establish the so-called *Monopolfilm* system. Even though both these features had decidedly risqué stories, they could be promoted as "art films" because the leading roles were played by well-known stage actors.

From the beginning of 1911, Nordisk moved away from one-reelers. Instead, the company's mainstay became feature films, usually at least three reels in length. Costume pictures were almost completely abandoned; modern-day romantic dramas predominated. They gave actors like Valdemar **Psilander** strong, emotionally charged roles. The films depicted illicit desires—extramarital liaisons and love across class boundaries—that led to transgressions and misdeeds: unwanted pregnancies, jealousy, fraud, suicide, or attempted murder. These films are often referred to as "erotic melodramas" (although not a contemporary term, it describes them well).

Another important genre was the sensation film, action dramas with chases and dangerous stunts. Nordisk made numerous examples, but smaller companies such as Filmfabrikken Danmark and Kinografen specialized in this genre. The former (initially called Skandinavisk-Russisk Handelshus) was one of several new companies to appear.

Yet Nordisk still predominated: of the 160 or so fiction films released in 1912, 90 were made by Nordisk. Its success was phenomenal. In 1912, instead of paying dividends, the company was able to expand its stock capital from 450,000 crowns to 2 million—without issuing new stock. Then, in 1913, it paid out a 60 per cent dividend to its stockholders. This incredible success led to the

formation of a large number of new companies that wanted to share in the bonanza; **Dania Biofilm** is a good example. Most of them collapsed within a year, however, some without releasing a single film.

Nordisk sought to distinguish itself from its competitors by making high-class, ambitious films that would cater to a discerning audience. Karl Ludwig Schröder, a script supervisor at Nordisk's Berlin subsidiary, came up with the idea of the **Autorenfilm**: films based on works or original screenplays by famous authors. The most important and expensive was the impressive *Atlantis* (1913), based on a novel by 1912 Nobel Prize winner Gerhart Hauptmann, directed by August **Blom** and photographed by Johan **Ankerstjerne**. It was quite successful in Germany, but it did not become the international blockbuster Nordisk had hoped for, despite the spectacular scenes of the wreck of an ocean liner, evoking the Titanic disaster of the previous year.

Atlantis also displayed the high standard of Danish cinematography. Particularly at Nordisk, films were photographed with great flair, with many shots composed in depth, creating visually absorbing images with varying illumination in foreground and background, shots against the light, and large mirrors revealing off-screen space. Examples can be found in the films of Blom and **Holger-Madsen**, although the greatest visual stylist was Benjamin **Christensen**, who had his own company, **Dansk Biograf Kompagni**. Some films deliberately re-created famous paintings, seeking to claim some of the prestige of the fine arts: Vilhelm **Glückstadt**'s lost film, *De dødes Ø* [The Isle of the Dead] (1913), was a notable example. It was also one of the only Danish films to have an original score, by a well-known composer, Fini Henriques.

World War I was a disaster for the Danish film industry. The international markets became inaccessible. In 1915, Great Britain, France, and Italy banned the import of Danish films, and Russia followed suit in February 1916. These countries suspected (with reason) that Danish companies had sent them German films, falsely identified as Danish, thus circumventing the blockade of Germany. The loss of the Russian market was particularly unfortunate: it had been so lucrative that Nordisk made special unhappy endings for their films for Russian audiences.

As the war dragged on, film production declined precipitously, and all the smaller companies went out of business; only Filmfabrikken Danmark hung on, but made only nature documentaries after 1918. Nordisk invested heavily in an attempt to become the dominant film company in the German market, but this ended in failure. The golden age of Danish film was at an end.

See also: distribution: issues and debates; Germany: distribution; melodrama, sensational

Further reading

Engberg, Marguerite (1977) Dansk stumfilm: De store år (Danish Silent Cinema: The Great Years), 2 vols., Copenhagen: Rhodos.

Engberg, Marguerite (1977–1982) Registrant over danske film 1896–1930 (Filmography of Danish films 1896–1930), 5 vols., Copenhagen: Institut for Filmvidenskab/C. A. Reitzel.

Mottram, Ron (1988) The Danish Cinema Before Dreyer, Metuchen, N.J.: Scarecrow Press.

Neergaard, Ebbe (1963) The Story of Danish Film, Copenhagen: Det danske selskab.

Sandfeld, Gunnar (1966) Den stumme scene: Dansk biografteater indtil lydfilmens gennembrud (The Mute Stage: Danish Cinema until the Breakthrough of Sound), Copenhagen: Nyt Nordisk Forlag.

Tybjerg, Casper (forthcoming) An Art of Silence and Light: Cinema in Denmark 1896–1929, Copenhagen: Museum Tusculanum Press.

CASPER TYBJERG

Denola, Georges

b. 1880; d. 1944

filmmaker, editor, France

Denola was an actor at **Pathé-Frères** who "graduated" to directing in 1908, but soon moved to **SCAGL**, where his prolific output consisted mostly of dramatic and melodramatic subjects such as La Femme du saltimbanque [The Acrobat's Wife] (1911) and L'Enfant de la folle [The Madwoman's Child] (1913), but also of the **detective film**,

Rocambole (1913). In 1915, he introduced André Antoine to the craft of filmmaking and became his devoted assistant. Along with Louis Delluc, Denola later edited one of the first specialized film journals, Le Journal du ciné-club (1920–1921).

ALAIN CAROU

Dentler, Martin

b. 1861; d. 1933

exhibitor, distributor, producer, Germany

A trader in paintings and picture frames, Dentler entered the moving picture business as an **itinerant exhibitor** in **fairs/fairgrounds**. In 1905, he opened his first permanent cinema in his hometown of Brunswick, from which he built up a **cinema circuit/chain** across Germany. In 1908, he established one of the first distribution companies, Martin Dentler Ltd., which was instrumental in the transition from selling programs of films to renting separate, longer films, heavily advertised in advance with regard to their genre and **star** potential. From 1911, Dentler's company also produced its own films and in the mid-1910s (by then one of the leaders in distribution) published a monthly promotion magazine called Martin Dentlers Filmmarkt. It was turned into a joint-stock company and merged into Ufa in 1920.

MICHAEL WEDEL

department stores

The department store became a prominent urban phenomenon in the latter half of the 19th century. As a retail enterprise, it overtook the general store that had carried a little bit of everything, the outdoor market, and the small urban shop that specialized in a narrow line of merchandise. The department store sold items that traditionally had been made at home—clothing, canned and preserved food, household furnishings. After 1850, these goods were increasingly manufactured outside the home, and women of all classes had to purchase such items using cash or credit. By 1890, the department store offered all of these things in grand visual displays offset by majestic architecture, elegant facades, and alluring window displays.

All major cities in Europe and the USA had magnificent department stores, often covering a whole city block: Bon Marché in Paris, Self-ridge's in London, Macy's in New York City, Wanamaker's in Philadelphia, Marshall Field's in Chicago. These "commercial palaces" displayed consumer goods against backdrops of opulent chandeliers, glass cabinets, mirrors, and luxurious wood, draperies, and architectural details. They offered the enticing principle of free entry whereby one could entertain the right to look without having to make a purchase. They were so-called democratic domains for predominantly female shoppers that taught women the joys of "just looking." As one of the chief urban spaces in which women freely circulated in the late 19th century, they prepared women for the cinema by providing exemplary spectacles both inside the store and within the framed window displays set into the store's facades along the street.

Department stores also provided a subject for early films. *Bargain Day* (AM&B, 1903) and *Bargain Fiend, or Shopping a la Mode* (**Vitagraph**, 1907) comically portray the pandemonium of excited female shoppers at store sales. *A Busy Day for the Corset Models* (AM&B, 1904) offers the titillation of a well-dressed female shopper watching scantily-clad models try on and take off a series of corsets. Comedies such as *Shocking Stockings* (AM&B, 1904) and *Four Beautiful Pairs* (AM&B, 1904) are trick films that animate mannequins or exchange live models with mannequins as pranks on shoppers.

A few films even dealt with department store shoplifting, thievery increasingly understood as pathological or as a disease when engaged in by middle-class women. *Arrest of a Shoplifter* (AM&B, 1903) merely shows the crime and the woman's arrest by a plainclothes store detective, whereas Edwin S. **Porter**'s more elaborated narrative, *The Kleptomaniac* (**Edison**, 1905), ironically compares two felonies by women shoppers. The film alternates between a wealthy woman who shoplifts at the department store and an impoverished woman who steals a loaf of bread to feed her children. The court dismisses the wealthy woman and hands her back into the custody of her husband, whereas

the poor woman says a tearful good-by to her children and is carted off to jail. To underscore the irony, the film ends with Lady Justice, her blindfold askew, her scales tipped in favor of a bag of gold as against a loaf of bread.

See also: fashion; leisure time and space

Further reading

Leach, William (1993) *The Land of Desire: Merchants, Power, and the Rise of a New American Culture*, New York: Pantheon.

Williams, Rosalind (1982) *Dream Worlds: Mass Consumption in Late Nineteenth-Century France*, Berkeley: University of California Press.

LAUREN RABINOVITZ

Derba, Mimí [Herminia Pérez de León]

b. 1893; d. 1953

actress, scriptwriter, director, Mexico

Beginning her career as a stage actress at the age of nineteen, Derba starred in over seventy Mexican films between 1917 and 1953. Along with Enrique **Rosas**, Derba founded one of the first film production companies in Mexico, Azteca Film, in 1917. She wrote the script for its first film, *En defensa propia* [In Self-defense] (1917) and, later that year, became the first woman to direct a film in Mexico: *La Tigresa* [The Tiger]. Following the dissolution of Azteca Film, Derba took a twelve-year hiatus from the cinema, finally returning in 1931 with a major role in Mexico's first successful sound film, *Santa* [The Saint].

JOANNE HERSHFIELD

Desfontaines, Henri

b. 1878; d. 1931

actor, filmmaker, France

An actor in André Antoine's Théâtre libre, Desfontaines began his career in moving pictures in 1908, thanks apparently to Albert **Capellani**. He appeared in many **SCAGL** and **Film d'Art** films—including *L'Arlésienne* [The Girl from Arles] (1908) and *Peau de chagrin* [The Wild Ass's Skin] (1909)—before directing films for **Pathé-Frères** and **Éclipse**, where he directed many films himself, such as *Milton* (1911) and *Shylock* (1913), and co-directed others such as *Queen Elizabeth* (1912) with Louis **Mercanton**. During the war, while employed in the French Army's Photographic and Cinematographic Unit, he kept acting in and directing films. In the 1920s, Desfontaines became one of the masters of the Cinéromans **serials**.

THIERRY LEFEBVRE

Desmet, Jean

b. 1875; d. 1956

exhibitor, distributor, The Netherlands

After a decade on the Dutch **fairs/fairgrounds** with various attractions, Desmet established a touring moving picture theater in 1907: the Imperial Bio. Two years later, he opened his first permanent cinema in Rotterdam, followed by others, among which were two deluxe cinemas in Rotterdam and Amsterdam. In 1910, Desmet also became one of the first important Dutch distributors. While offering a wide range of films, he especially promoted Danish **multiple-reels/features** (1911–1912) and German features (1913–1914). His short films were mainly French, Italian, and American. During **World War I**, Desmet stopped purchasing films, sold most of his cinemas, and went on to a successful career in real estate and financing. Many of his rental prints survive and now make up the Desmet Collection at the Nederlands Filmmuseum.

See also: archives; distribution: Europe

IVO BLOM

detective films

Just as detectives appeared not only in popular fiction and dime novels, but also in **comic strips**, **vaudeville** sketches, and **advertisements**, as part of the turn-of-the-century mass culture from which early cinema drew its material, the detective inevitably appeared in early moving pictures. Thus, in 1900, **American Mutoscope and Biograph** (AM&B) shot a brief **trick film** of a disappearing burglar and entitled it *Sherlock Holmes Baffled*. Detectives (that is, plain-clothes men as opposed to uniformed police or gendarmes) also occur as characters in a number of early narrative films that show the processes and actions of criminals, such as **Pathé-Frères**' *Histoire d'une crime* [Story of a Crime] (1901), or its near replication by AM&B in *A Career in Crime* (1902).

But if we think of a detective film as not simply containing a detective character but as featuring the detection of a crime, then among the earliest films in the genre would be AM&B's "keyhole" film, *A Search for Evidence* (1903), in which a wife and a detective look through the keyholes of a series of hotel rooms (the interior of each room being shown through point of view shots framed within a keyhole-shaped mask) until they find the woman's husband entertaining a chorus girl. The film ends as the detective and wife break in on the carousing pair, having secured evidence for the woman's divorce. The relation between gathering clues and evidence and the visual devices of the cinema (point of view shots, close-ups) became central to the development of the genre.

Although the canonical histories of the detective story in literature privilege the process of ratiocination established by E. A. Poe, Emile Gaboriau, and Arthur Conan Doyle as the detective unravels a crime through reconstructing it based on clues, the detective also has strong roots in the action crime genre, and detectives are often action heroes as well, as adept at chasing and fighting criminals as at logical induction. Thus as the **chase film** format became more complex, the detective served as one of the chasers in pursuit of a criminal. Perhaps the most elaborate early film of this sort would be Pathé's *Tour du monde d'un policier* [Detective's Tour of the World] (1906), in which the chase literally encompasses the entire globe, as a detective follows the path of an apparent embezzler through various foreign nations, exotic cultures and dangerous situations.

The detective truly emerges as a generic character in the period of one-reel narratives, often referred to as cinema's "transitional period," approximately from 1907–1913, a period in which both increased narrative complexity and character development interacts with the development of action genres (such as the **western** or **crime film**). Although the detective film may be seen as a subgenre of the crime film, its emphasis on the figure of the detective and the detection/apprehension of the criminal gives it a distinct identity. Two aspects of the transitional period would seem to have special significance for this genre: characterization and analytical editing.

The increased emphasis on individualized character allowed the figure of the detective (and often his nemesis, the criminal) to gain a greater degree of recognizability and specificity. Vividly defined characters led the way to the symbiosis between the detective and the film series. Series films (a number of films linked by a recurring character, generally played by the same actor) began with comic characters (from cartoon characters like Happy Hooligan to Boireau or Cretinettti (André **Deed**) or Max (Max **Linder**), but the detective also offered a perfect role for a recurring dramatic character (although detectives often retained comic aspects, as in Pathé's *Nick Winter* series, or, somewhat later, in comic sidekicks). The popular literary genre of the dime novel and detective story supplied the model for such recurring characters in a nearly endless series of adventures. The internationally popular Nick Carter, hero of scores of widely translated dime novels, became one of the very first detective heroes with a film series: **Éclair** introduced a *Nick Carter* series in 1908 directed by Victorin **Jasset**, although other films with the Nick Carter character also appeared in the USA. Numerous detective series in almost every film-producing country then appeared: in France, Pathé's *Nick Winter*, **Eclipse**'s *Nat Pinkerton*; in Germany, Stuart Webb, Joe Deebs, Miss Nobody (one of many female detectives); in Denmark, **Nordisk** offered the first Sherlock Holmes series; in the USA **Kalem** produced "The Girl Detective" series.

The emerging stylistics of analytical editing also shaped the genre (or were exploited by it). Since detection frequently involves a visual discovery, the cinematic representation of the look of a character became important in many films of the genre. As already mentioned, AM&B's *A Search for Evidence* narrativized the point of view structure present in many early films as a comic or salacious attraction, in order to portray an investigation. Likewise, **Biograph**'s *The Boy Detective* (1908) ends with a medium shot in which it is revealed that the boy's pistol is in fact a cigarette lighter. The use of a closer view to reveal a significant aspect of the story became essential to the detective or mystery narrative with Biograph's film from slightly later in 1908, *Betrayed by a Handprint*, using a close-up of a handprint left by a lady burglar, which identified her as the criminal. Similar narratively significant closer shots pointing out clues can be found in a large number of early detective films in each country.

Since detective plots generally center on the visual identification of objects and of people, the possibilities of visual ambiguity (as well as gaining a final clarity) became essential to the genre, and was open to creative exploration by filmmakers. Early cinema detectives (as well as their doppelgangers, the master criminals) were almost always masters of disguise as much as detectors of clues or action heroes, and many films use disguise as an essential plot element. The theme of disguise also allows the genre to play with the uncertainty of modern identity as well as class and gender roles (rich men make up as tramps, women disguise themselves as men—and vice versa). Thus themes of doubles, mistaken identity, and uncanny resemblances appear frequently in early detective films.

Towards the end of the one-reel era, new patterns begin to emerge. Conan Doyle's brother-in-law, E. R. Hornung, had realized the pattern set by Doyle's stories could be re-vitalized by switching focus to a criminal and produced the series of "Raffles" stories dealing with a gentleman safe cracker—a character frequently appearing in early films, as in **Vitagraph**'s *The Society Raffles* (1905), and later in a female version, the *Lady Raffles* series (1913) for **Universal**, starring Grace **Cunard** and directed by Francis **Ford**. In the early 1910s, now in **multiple-reel films**, mysterious master criminals invaded the screen internationally, such as Zigomar (France), Doctor Gar El Hama (Denmark), Tigris (Italy), or Fantômas (France). Although a distinct genre of its own in one respect, the master criminal film tends to intertwine with the detective genre, since the clever criminal needs an equally clever opponent. Thus Éclair and Jasset's second Zigomar film interbred the two forms, as shown by its title, *Nick Carter versus Zigomar* (1912); similarly, the second of Louis **Feuillade**'s Fantômas films, *Juve vs. Fantômas* (1913) features his nemesis the inspector Juve. Not only do the master criminal series generally involve a detective character, the criminal in these films uses many of the detective's techniques: disguise, scientific processes, and careful observation.

The second major innovation occurred at the very end of the early cinema period: the move from the series to the **serial**. Although the two forms are distinct, they sometime tend to blur. The series consists of separate films with autonomous story-lines, but with a recurring character. The serial consists of interlinked episodes possessing not only recurring characters, but also an overarching narrative line. But when the detective has a recurring nemesis, this distinction could be blurred. Perhaps it is best defined in terms of the production and distribution arrangements: serials are produced as a single multiple-reel production with regular and rather closely spaced release dates (such as one episode every week), which emphasize the need to see the films in a regular manner.

Feuillade's five *Fantômas* films produced for **Gaumont** in 1913–1914 are best considered as a series, since each film was released separately with no consistent release pattern. However, there is a degree of overarching action between episodes and certain actions in one film are only clarified in a later one. By contrast, later Gaumont serials, not to mention Pathé's American serials with Pearl **White**, were produced and released as coordinated episodes of a single film, often with endings that suspended action at unresolved points (the famous "cliff hanger" device). Not all serials were detective films, but nearly all were sensational **melodramas**, and detectives and the detection of a crime was a central aspect to their form. American serials especially frequently featured heroines who, while rarely professional detectives, often undertook the investigation of crimes and the apprehension of criminals,

whether as potential victims of criminal plots (as in White's Pathé serials) or as female professionals (Helen **Holmes** as a girl telegrapher in Kalem's *Hazards of Helen* series, or Grace Cunard as a girl reporter in *The Broken Coin*. These "serial queens" exemplified the action hero amateur detectives, leaping on speeding trains or from racing automobiles as they chased murderers, thieves, and abducters.

Another form closely related to the detective genre exists throughout the period of early film, although its most elaborate forms come at the end of the period: the recreation of a famous crime and usually the capture of a criminal, often with devices that stress the fidelity of the film to actual events (filming on location, getting assistance from participants—occasionally even starring people who were actually involved). Examples of this genre appear very early, as in AM&B's *The Black Hand* (1906), whose publicity emphasized that its incidents "are for the most part identical with actual occurrences." Thus a 1910 United States production, *The Italian Sherlock Holmes*, relied on advice from the actual detective Petroni in production, while French production companies made a series of films based in varying degrees on the activities of the anarchist gang, the Bande à Bonnot. Early feature films from 1913–1914, following on the success of George Loan Tucker's *Traffic in Souls* (1913)—one of the first great urban thrillers, detailing prostitution rings and official corruption, supposedly based on testimony before New York's vice committees—frequently detailed either the processes of criminal syndicates or the procedures of police, such as *The Line-Up at Police Headquarters* (1914), directed by Frank Beal, who had also directed a prostitution expose, *The Inside of the White Slave Traffic* (1913), starring Deputy Police Commissioner of New York, George S. Dougherty, as himself. The popularity of the detective genre also led to parodies of the form, picking up on the strong relation the genre often showed to comedy. Comedians frequently played comic detectives. Gale Henry's *Lady Baffles and Detective Duck* (1915), for Universal, provides a delightful surviving example, burlesquing in particular the genre's love of disguise and hidden passages.

The detective genre contributed to early cinema's eventual synthesis of narration and sensation by bringing together narrative devices that greatly increased spectator involvement in the unfolding story. The genre honed techniques of suspense and characterization and developed a strong hermeneutic code of clues and foreshadowing that encouraged viewers to not only follow the action but also anticipate outcomes. At the same time, the genre highlighted numerous attractions, sensations and thrills in the course of development: from speeding trains and airplanes to the various stunts and acts of physical daring that particularly characterized the serials. Such emotionally exciting fare was frequently attacked by middle class reformers, censors, and/or clergy for either encouraging criminal activity or simply over-stimulating viewers (especially children). The very reactions against it, however, indicate its popularity and its power.

Figure 27 Poster for Éclair's *Nick Carter* series, 1908.

Further reading

Abel, Richard (1994) *The Ciné Goes to Town: French Cinema, 1896–1914*, Berkeley: University of California Press.

Bean, Jennifer M. (2002) "Technologies of Early Stardom and the Extraordinary Body," in Bean and Diane Negra (eds.) *A Feminist Reader in Early Cinema*, Durham: Duke University Press.

Lacassin, Francis (1972) *Pour une contre histoire du cinema*, Paris: Union Générale d'Editions.

Singer, Ben (2001) *Melodrama and Modernity: Early Sensational Cinema and its Contexts*, New York: Columbia University Press.

TOM GUNNING

Deutsche Mutoskop & Biograph (German Biograph)

exhibitor, producer, Germany

The Deutsche Mutoskop- & Biograph- Gesellschaft m. b. H. (German Biograph), the German affiliate of the **American Mutoscope and Biograph** Company, was one of the most important companies producing moving pictures in Germany during the first decade of the 20th century. It was founded on 14 March 1898, and based in Berlin, by Curt Harzer, who had signed a contract in London with the International Mutoscope and Biograph Syndicate, which was empowered to issue licenses by the US parent company and thus establish subsidiaries. German Biograph paid annual fees to the syndicate, but operated autonomously. In January 1906, German Biograph was taken over by the Automat A.-G. Hartwig & Vogel, which was owned in turn by the chocolate factory, Hartwig & Vogel (based in Dresden), and which produced vending machines.

According to the recollections of Karl A. Geyer (1956), who was hired as the technical director of German Biograph in February 1906, the company's most important economic branch until 1906–1907 was the distribution of the Mutoscope, a peephole moving-picture machine based on flip-card devices. At first, the Mutoscope was rented and operated by the company itself, but from 1899 onwards it was also sold. The Mutoscope was installed in

penny arcades, shopping arcades, and hotels. The company regularly serviced the machines, supplying the latest pictures on flip cards. Automat A.-G. Hartwig & Vogel became interested in the Mutoscope because it hoped to further its vending machine business—setting up a Mutoscope alongside a chocolate machine.

In 1900–1901, when the public screening of moving pictures had become a lasting success, German Biograph rented the **Biograph 70 mm projector** (which used film of 68 mm to 70 mm—the sources disagree), together with a projectionist and film program to the largest variety theaters (e.g., the Hansa-Theater in Hamburg, the Wintergarten in Berlin) and also to the German Navy League. The German *varieté* was a form of popular theatrical entertainment similar to American **vaudeville** and British **music halls**. While 44% of the Biograph syndicate's worldwide output in the years 1900 to 1906 was fictional films, German Biograph produced almost nothing but non-fiction films (about 200 in all by November 1902). Some were produced for the Navy League to promote the German Government's plans to expand the fleet. Others called *optische Berichterstattung*, or **news event films**, were especially popular in variety theaters. These showed military operations, Emperor Kaiser Wilhelm II, sports events, and new technological inventions. As early as 1900, German Biograph officially was appointed to film the Emperor and his family, e.g., *Die Ankunft Sr. Majestät Kaiser Wilhelm II. in Port Victoria am 8. November 1902* [H.I.M. the German Emperor—Arrival at Port Victoria] (1902). The company also accompanied the international troops to China to film their intervention in the Boxer rebellion (Alfred Graf von Waldersee, head of the international forces, was German); C. Fred Ackerman of American Biograph was the cameraman. Besides its own output, German Biograph also distributed films from its sister companies and their parent company—*Assault on the South Gate* (1901), *Star Theatre* (1901) and *Cake Walk* (1903)—and, in turn, it also supplied those companies with films, e.g., *S. M. Küstenpanzerschiff "Odin" im Gefecht* [Battleship "Odin" with All Her Guns in Action] (1900).

According to Geyer, the variety theater business initially was not very profitable, due to the high

operating costs; but it did serve to publicize the Mutoscope. In 1907–1908, however, the situation seems to have changed, because, in an advertisement in *Der Komet* (9 February 1908), German Biograph now recommended using the Mutoscope as an advertisement for the film programs: "Your cinematographic theater will become doubly attractive when you use our promotional Mutoscope to demonstrate the exhibition of living pictures in miniature with it."

Beginning in 1906–1907, German Biograph increasingly concentrated on the production of fiction films to meet the demand created by two forms of film exhibition which were rapidly expanding during this period: traveling film shows and permanent cinemas. Because these exhibitors used 35mm film, German Biograph converted its production to this standard. Before 1906, 35mm reduction prints were used (the earliest evidence for this can be found in October 1903). In order to ensure the supply of new films for the Mutoscopes, blow-up prints had to be produced after 1906.

To be able to meet the increased demand for fiction films, German Biograph needed a studio. After using a small one in the Wilhelmstrasse, Berlin, for less than a year, in 1907, the company moved to a new, larger studio in Lankwitz outside Berlin (its construction had begun in 1904), which was the first German studio to be used exclusively for film production. Comedies were produced in great numbers, e.g., *Die guten Hosen* [The Good Trousers] (1911), as were dramas, e.g., *Verirrte Seelen* [Lost Souls] (1911). In 1908, the company presented a gramophone, the Biographon, which could be synchronized with every standard projector, along with six new **Tonbilder** (sound pictures) every week. An example is *Daß nur für mich dein Herz erbebt* [May Your Heart Tremble Only For Me] (1908), an aria from Verdi's *Il trovatore* sung by Enrico Caruso and acted by Siegward Rolf of the Berliner Volksoper. In 1910, Charles **Decroix** became the artistic director, and in 1911, Paul **von Woringen** became the new general manager. Others working for the company during this period were Franz Porten, Joseph **Delmont** and Max **Mack**.

Because of its conversion to fiction films, German Biograph survived much longer than its European sister companies, all of which had been dissolved by 1908. However, during the second decade of the 20th century, the company lost its important economic position, because it was not flexible enough to adapt to new market developments. Perhaps most importantly, it did not adopt the *Monopolfilm* distribution system, in which films were given a special competitive advantage by limited booking, greater length, and stars. The last films by German Biograph that can be traced were produced in 1923. As co-owner of the studio in Lankwitz (together with Flora-Film GmbH, Fern Andra Film-Atelier Georg Bluen & Co, and Lixie Film-Atelier Weißensee GmbH), German Biograph existed at least until 1933.

See also: distribution: Europe; Germany; itinerant exhibitors

Further reading

Garncarz, Joseph (2001) "On the Origins of Cinema: Film Exhibition in Variety Theatres and Travelling Shows in Germany, 1895–1907," in Tim Bergfelder, Erica Carter and Deniz Göktürk (eds.) *German Cinema Book*, London: British Film Institute.

Geyer, Karl A. (1956) "Erinnerungen eines Film-technikers," *Kino-Technik*, 2: 64–66.

JOSEPH GARNCARZ

Di Doménico family

An Italian family that built an extensive exhibition, distribution, and production empire based in Bogotá, Colombia, but spanning Central America and the Antilles.

Originally from Castelnuovo di Conza, in Salerno, Italy, the Di Doménico brothers were orphaned at an early age. After traveling through the Antilles and Africa for their uncle's trading business, Francesco and Vincenzo decided to invest in the cinema and to immigrate permanently to the Americas circa 1910. Traveling with a partner, Benedetto Pugliesi, the brothers' equipment consisted of two **projectors**, a generator, and a lot of European films. They toured the Antilles, organizing screenings throughout the islands, calling

themselves the "Cinema Olympia." After stopping in Venezuela where they exhibited moving pictures in all the coastal cities and renewed their stock of films via Panama family contacts, they settled in Bogotá. The business prospered and the brothers sent for the other family members, cousins Giovanni and Donato Di Doménico and brothers-in-law Peppino and Erminico Di Ruggiero, who would end up managing the family interests in Panama which served as their distribution center.

In 1912, after a successful year in makeshift locales, the family inaugurated the Salón Olympia with other local investors. The Olympia was a luxurious theater, seating 3000 to 6000 spectators; the screen was in the middle of the hall and spectators seated behind it paid less and used mirrors to decipher the **intertitles**. The theater also standardized orchestral accompaniment, an innovation for the Bogotá market. The Di Doménicos always privileged European imports and were in intense competition with new exhibitors beginning to import films from the USA.

In 1913, the family created SICLA, Sociedad Industrial Cinematográfica Latino Americana, to venture into production and retain their competitive edge in the market; they also opened new theaters in Panama, Barranquilla, Medellín, and other locales. Eventually their distribution networks spanned the region and even reached Europe (with an agency in Barcelona). Locally, Francisco Di Doménico began a regular **newsreel**, *Diario colombiano* [Colombian Journal] and filmed civil events, culminating with *El drama del 15 de Octubre* [The Drama of October 15] (1915), the first Colombian feature-length film, reconstructing the notorious and violent assassination of a high-ranking general and starring the assassins themselves. The film was ambivalently received and even censored in some municipalities, which set back the family's commitment to nonfiction production. Eventually urged on by their competitive spirit, they embarked on fictional feature production with *Aura o las violetas* [Dawn or the Violets] (1923), an adaptation of a national literary classic directed by brother Vincenzo, and the first of four that he would direct in the 1920s.

Meanwhile, however, Francesco retired to Italy and Vincente followed him in 1927. Peppino took over the family business but, also eager to retire, arranged to sell it to Cine Colombia, a new exhibition company from Antioquia province. Although Donato and Giovanni remained in the exhibition business in Colombia, the reign of the family over Colombian exhibition had ended.

ANA M. LÓPEZ

dialogue accompaniment

An exhibition practice, prevalent primarily in North America between 1908 and 1910, that used performers hidden behind the **screen** to give voice to characters appearing in otherwise non-talking films.

Perhaps the first known practitioner of dialogue accompaniment for moving pictures was LeRoy Carleton, who from 1903 to 1910 worked as head **sound effects** specialist for **lecturer** Lyman H. **Howe**. By 1905, Carleton and his staff added vocal "impersonations" to the repertoire of sounds they routinely produced from behind the screen. In keeping with general sound effects strategies at the time, Carleton used voice not to describe and expand upon the action but to mimic delimited sounds associated with select persons depicted on screen. Because vocal performance (in terms of content and style of delivery) was guided by audience expectations for speech that culturally and naturalistically corresponded with on-screen characters, the practice initially was heralded for enhancing a film's "realism."

Carleton's efforts inspired imitation, as well as attempts to advance the technique beyond impersonation. In 1908, over a dozen companies emerged to provide dialogue accompaniment. These companies—Humanovo, Actologue, and Dramagraph were among the most prominent— promoted their services to exhibitors as a new kind of dramatic novelty, "talker pictures."

To produce such films, dialogue companies obtained silent films from film exchanges. War films, dramas, and melodramas were favored subjects, although comedies occasionally were adapted for dialogue as well. After removing any existing **intertitles**, a writer watched the selected picture

several times and developed a dialogue script that was sensitive to character psychology and story development. This script was rehearsed by a troupe of three to six actors who were sent on the road to perform the dialogue at contracted theaters. To add "realism," actors delivered their lines from positions directly behind the screen characters they were speaking, often with full bodily gestures as if performing in a play. Troupes sometimes prepared two films per engagement, allowing exhibitors to change talker pictures at midweek.

Some theaters also used homegrown talent, hiring local stage actors or untrained amateurs (including children) willing to work for low wages. Local "talkers" brought a stronger improvisational element to their performances than did traveling troupes, and a film could be spontaneously adapted to the language and milieu of the theater's audience. Performers could also play with audience expectations, adding humor by speaking dialogue that created a disconnect between voice and image.

Dialogue accompaniment emerged when competition for audiences was intense. Theater owners needed to differentiate themselves at a time when films were not yet generally distributed on a "first run" basis. There also was no **star system** to promote individual films and, by extension, individual theaters. Moreover, although films were becoming longer, new forms of visual storytelling did not always result in clear, coherent narratives. In this context, dialogue accompaniment was a novelty that attracted audiences and helped clarify sometimes confusing narratives. When performed by actors trained for the legitimate stage, film talk had

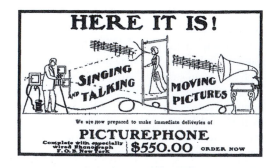

Figure 28 Miles Bros advertisement, 1908.

the added advantage of enhancing an exhibitor's cultural status.

Because it gave control over a film's presentation to talker troupes and individual exhibitors, the practice of dialogue accompaniment was unpredictable and expensive. Steps by film companies to standardize production, distribution, and exhibition, along with increased use of dialogue titles as films became longer after 1910, ensured that character voices would come from the screen rather than from behind it.

See also: acting styles; *filme cantante*; screenwriting; Zukor, Adolph.

Further reading

Klenotic, Jeffrey (2001) "'The Sensational Acme of Realism': 'Talker' Pictures as Early Cinema Sound Practice," in Richard Abel and Rick Altman (eds.) *The Sounds of Early Cinema*, 156–166, Bloomington: Indiana University Press.
Veronneau, Pierre (1999) "An Intermedia Practice: 'Talking Pictures' in Montreal, 1908–1910," *Film History*, 11.4: 426–432.

JEFFREY KLENOTIC

Díaz Quesada, Enrique

b. 1883, Havana; d. 1923, Havana

cameraman, director, Cuba

Considered the "father" of Cuban cinema, Díaz Quesada's interest in photography and panoramic exhibitions led him, in 1898, to assist José **Casasús** in producing the first Cuban film, *El brujo desapareciendo* [The Disappearing Magician]. He became the most significant filmmaker of early Cuban cinema, with the first documentary (*El parque de Palatino* [Palatino Park] (1906)), the first traveling shot (*Los festejos de la Caridad en la ciudad de Camagüey* [The St. Charity Festivities in the City of Camagüey] (1909)), the first film studio (on a Havana rooftop in 1913), and the first

feature-length fiction film (*Manuel García, o el rey de los campos de Cuba* [Manuel García, or the King of the Cuban Countryside] (1913)). He documented the key social and political events of the decade, including the presidential inaugurations of José Miguel Gómez and Mario García Menocal, the inauguration of the Maceo statue and park in Havana, the departure of Charles Magoon (US interventor), and the armed uprising of the party "Independientes de color" in eastern Cuba.

He was associated with entrepreneur Francisco Rodríguez and the Moving Picture Company, as well as with distributors, **Santos y Artigas**, with whom he had a long and productive relationship. He also was skilled at obtaining commercial backing for his early projects: *El parque de Palatino* was funded by the US amusement park company that owned the park; *El sueño de un estudiante de farmacía* [The Dream of a Pharmacy Student] (1910), by the millionaire Sarrá, owner of a prominent pharmacy in Havana; and *Festival Infantil de Bohemia* [Bohemia Children's Festival] (1912), by the newsweekly *Bohemia*. Díaz Quesada was also responsible for the only Cuban serial, the ten-episode *El genio del mal* [The Genius of Evil] (1910).

Although other Latin American film pioneers relied on the models of Italian melodramas or French **historical films** of the period, Díaz Quesada found inspiration in Cuban themes and developed them along historical-romantic lines in his subsequent feature films: *El capitán mambi* [The Rebel Captain] (1915), *La manigua o la mujer cubana* [The Manigua or Cuban Woman] (1915), *El poder de los ñáñigos* [The Power of the Ñáñigos] (1917), *Sangre y azúcar* [Blood and Sugar] (1919), among others. He directed 17 of the 40 fiction films produced in Cuba between 1907 and 1922. When he died unexpectedly from pneumonia, he left behind an unfinished script for what could have been his masterpiece, *El Titán de bronze*, about independence hero, Antonio Maceo.

Shortly after his early death, a fire destroyed the laboratories where his films were stored: only one minute of celluloid (the amazingly fresh and innovative *El parque de Palatino*) remains of his oeuvre.

ANA M. LÓPEZ

Dickson, William Kennedy Laurie

b. 3 August 1860, Le Minihic-sur-Rance, France;
d. 28 September 1935, Twickenham, England

inventor, filmmaker, studio executive, educator, writer, USA and UK

An Englishman born in France with family ties in the USA, W. K. L. Dickson's work in cinema was as international in scope as his background. He inherited skills in painting and music, was educated in the classics, and trained in the sciences. Hired by Thomas **Edison** as an electrical engineer, his strong interest in **photography** led Edison to assign him as the principal experimenter in the development of the **Edison Kinetograph** and **Kinetoscope**, the first commercially successful motion picture camera and viewing machine. Dickson also contributed to the development of two other early motion picture devices, the **Latham**'s Eidoloscope and the Mutoscope. In 1894, with his sister Antonia Dickson, he published a pamphlet describing Edison's devices, one of the earliest published works on the motion picture.

At Edison's laboratory, in 1891–1892, Dickson designed a camera that used 35mm filmstock with four perforations per frame. This format, devised by Dickson, became an international standard which has been, and still is, used in most commercial theaters. In order to manufacture films for Edison, he established a system consisting of a camera, a studio, a laboratory to develop and print the films, and a peep-show viewing machine, the Kinetoscope. His "Black Maria" studio in West Orange (New Jersey) was the earliest commercial film studio. Between 1893 and 1895, he produced about 125 films there.

In 1895, he left Edison and with a group friends, founded a rival film company, **American Mutoscope and Biograph** (AM&B). Dickson set up the company's film production, first in the USA and then in Europe. He designed studios in New York and London, established regular film production, and trained camera operators in both locations. He also was instrumental in establishing the company's branches in Paris, Amsterdam, and Berlin. As a filmmaker, he acted as producer and director,

making arrangements for the filming, planning the production, rehearsing the "take," and instructing the camera operator on how the film should be shot. Between 1896 and 1902, Dickson produced some 500 films. These were carefully planned moments of action and were often imitated. The films he made on moving trains influenced one of the most popular "genres" of early cinema, the **phantom train ride**. He also specialized in filming celebrities; among the prominent persons he recorded were: President McKinley, Queen Victoria, Prince Edward (later King Edward VII), the young Duke of Windsor (Edward VIII), Emperor Franz Joseph, Kaiser Wilhelm, Queen Wilhelmena, President Faure (France), General Kitchener, Cecil Rhodes, and several prominent stage personalities. He filmed in **South Africa** during the Boer War, and his films of Pope Leo XIII, the first made in the Vatican, were among the most prestigious films made before the turn of the century. Several prominent cameramen were trained by Dickson, among them were D. W. **Griffith**'s first cameramen, Billy **Bitzer** and Arthur **Marvin**.

Dickson retired from filmmaking around 1903 and opened an Edison-styled laboratory in London which he operated until about 1920.

Further reading

Dickson, W. K. L. and Antonia (1895) *History of the Kinetograph, Kinetoscope and Kineto-Phonograph*, New York: Albert Bunn—facsimile edition (2000) New York: Museum of Modern Art.

Dickson, W. K. L. (1901) *The Biograph in Battle*, London, T. Fisher Unwin—facsimile reprint edition (1995), with new introduction by Richard Brown, Trowbridge: Flick Books.

PAUL SPEHR

dime museums: USA

Dime museums were a significant venue for screen entertainment in the USA from the early 1800s into the early 1900s. In June 1804, at Boston's Columbian Museum, a Mr. Bates exhibited his phantasmagoria, which included a range of projections: a Female Spirit Rising from Her Tomb, the Ghost and Hamlet, and an Egyptian Pigmy Idol that Instantaneously Changes to a Human Skull. In May 1863, P. T. Barnum showed photographic lantern slides as the principal attraction at his American Museum in New York City. By the 1890s, an informal network of dime museums dotted the USA (they generally charged 10¢ admission), housing permanent exhibits of curios complemented by human and animal performers on a small stage. Attractions included boxing monkeys, fat ladies engaged in bicycle races, human lizards.

Given their interest in screen entertainment, dime museums often served as an important early venue for moving pictures. For three weeks in the late summer of 1895, Kohl & Middleton's Clark Street Dime Museum in Chicago was among the first entertainment venues to show projected moving pictures, featuring the **Lathams'** Eidoloscope. On 20 September 1896, after a one-week trial run, the Vitascope moved into Heck & Avery's Museum in Cincinnati, remaining there for many months. After impresario Harry **Davis** opened his six-round film **re-enactment**, *The Maher-Choynski Fight*, at his Pittsburgh museum on 1 February 1897, it subsequently was shown at Bradenburgh's 9th and Arch Dime Museum in Philadelphia, Huber's Museum in New York City, and similar metropolitan venues.

Huber's Museum initially hired various exhibitors for limited periods of time. During the Spanish-American War, Minnie Schult sang patriotic tunes illustrated with moving pictures, including "The Battleship Maine Song." In November 1899, after being sued by Thomas A. **Edison** for patent infringement, owner George Huber established a relationship with the Kinetograph Company, an Edison affiliate, which provided Huber's with films into the **nickelodeon** era. In Philadelphia, Sigmund **Lubin** developed a close relationship with Bradenburgh's Museum, which first showed moving pictures in September 1897. Two months later, Lubin constructed an open-air studio on the museum's rooftop, hiring many performers that appeared in Bradenburgh's theater. Bradenburgh's remained the premier venue for his films until Lubin opened his own theaters as the nickelodeon era began.

The Eden Musee in New York City became an especially important center for moving picture activities. Modeled after the Musée Grévin in Paris, the Musee catered to a more upscale audience, charging 25¢ admission. It featured wax works, orchestral concerts, and occasional special performances (marionettes, dancers, and so forth). The Musee began to show moving pictures in December 1896 and became the first venue in the USA to make them a regular part of its programs—that continued until it closed in 1918. Near the end of 1897, the Musee hired William **Paley** to film *The Passion Play of Oberammergau* and *The Opera Martha*. After being sued for patent infringement by Edison, the Eden Musee and Paley became Edison licensees. While Paley took films of the Spanish-American War for Edison, he seems to have shot others that were shown exclusively at the Musee. Its personnel sometimes structured these early one-shot films into complex narratives in "post-production," which was then under exhibitors' control. *Panorama of the War*, for instance, offered a narrative recounting of the Spanish–American War—contemporary history in the making.

The Musee's importance for early cinema faded once leading **vaudeville** theaters (Keith's, Proctor's, Pastor's) became regular venues for exhibiting films during the course of 1899.

See also: audiences: surveys and debates; dioramas and panoramas; magic lantern shows; museum life exhibits; wax museums: Europe.

Further reading

Dennett, Andrea Stulman (1997) *Weird & Wonderful: The Dime Museum in America*, New York: New York University Press.

Musser, Charles (1990) *The Emergence of Cinema: The American Screen to 1907*, New York: Scribners.

CHARLES MUSSER

Dintenfass, Mark M.

b. 1878?, Austria; d. 1953, Cliffside Park, New Jersey

producer, executive, USA

Dintenfass seems to have entered the film business by managing Actophone, a company involved briefly in talker pictures. In 1909, he founded an early independent production company,

Champion Film, in Fort Lee, New Jersey, which prospered enough by 1912 to join **Universal**, which Carl **Laemmle** and others had formed as a national distributor. Although never a major player in the industry, Dintenfass continued to produce films at Champion through the late 1910s.

RICHARD ABEL

dioramas and panoramas

The original panoramas were scenes painted on the interior of a cylindrical surface, with the viewer standing on a central platform and walking around to see all of the view. The intended effect was of being present at the actual location. Patentee Robert Barker exhibited the first, a view of Edinburgh, in that Scottish city in 1788. His larger panoramas, including Napoleonic battles, were a success in London.

John Vanderlyn painted *The Palace and Gardens of Versailles* (1816–1819)—which still survives—exhibiting it until 1829 in New York City. Panoramas were revived later in the century, with "news" scenes including the Franco-Prussian War and the Battle of Gettysburg. L. A. A. **Le Prince**'s experiments with photographic motion pictures were perhaps inspired by the idea of adding movement to the huge static panoramas he helped construct.

An early "moving picture" of modest dimensions but expensive admission prices, the Eidophusikon, opened in a London house in 1781, and subsequently at other venues. The small audience saw a framed illuminated picture with moving and changing effects, including a seascape with mechanical boats entering and leaving. Lighting was changed by using rear-lit translucent backgrounds, and complex scenes such as a storm at sea could be dramatized by thunderous sound effects and tumultuous music.

In 1822, before his success with photography, Louis Jacques Mandé Daguerre, with his partner Charles Marie Bouton, opened the Diorama in Paris. Seated audiences saw enormous paintings of famous places and historical events, the size of a modern Imax screen. Parts of a scene could be painted on the canvas back, only showing through when lit from behind. Controllable shutters in the walls and roof beamed daylight onto any part of the translucent linen, causing the scene to subtly change, from summer to winter, from day to night. Simple motion effects included drifting clouds, flowing water, and flickering flames. Sometimes actual objects or people would be placed in the foreground. A second Diorama opened in London and rival shows appeared in American and European cities. The Paris Diorama was destroyed by fire in 1839.

Moving panoramas were first popular in 1820s English pantomimes, eventually becoming attractions in themselves. A canvas painting wound onto a pole was slowly unrolled behind a proscenium and onto a second pole, with accompanying lecture and music. John Banvard's 1840s rolling panorama of the Mississippi River was deceptively advertised as three miles long. It was first shown in Boston and New York and then at London's Egyptian Hall, where Albert Smith was celebrated in the 1850s for his *Ascent of Mont Blanc* moving panorama.

In 1893, inventor and theater director Steel MacKaye patented the Spectatorium, with a cycloramic background over 400 feet long and movable dimensional scenery mounted on railway tracks. A huge water-filled reservoir was to simulate sea scenes. MacKaye planned to place real buildings, actual actors, and living plants within the perspectively aligned scenery. A giant building was constructed for the 1893 Chicago **World's Fair**, but his company went bankrupt before completion.

Circular panoramas continued to be built into the 20th century. From 1912, the long-established Poole's Myriorama toured Great Britain with a moving panorama of the Titanic disaster. After 1896, however, the photographic moving picture became the pre-eminent method for presenting "living" scenes of the world.

See also: news event films; travelogues

Further reading

Griffiths, Alison (2003) "'Shivers down your spine': panoramas and the origin of the cinematic reenactment," *Screen* 44.1: 1–37.

STEPHEN HERBERT

distribution: Europe

Before 1902, film distribution in Europe was relatively unstructured, although the **Lumière** operators functioned loosely within a European network, even if they often worked for separate companies. That changed when selling films became as profitable as selling apparatuses. Then new companies such as **Warwick Trading** made film distribution their primary business. Soon London became the center for both the distribution of American films in Europe and European films in the USA. American companies eventually would open agencies there, although **Vitagraph**—before 1914, the most active American production company in the European distribution market—made the unusual decision to establish a laboratory for its European prints in Paris. Germany, second only to Britain in the number of exhibition venues, would also become a second center for European distribution.

Between 1902 and 1907, **Pathé-Frères** dominated the distribution market in Europe—as in the rest of the world—especially in the **fairs/ fairgrounds**. Pathé opened up distribution agencies throughout the continent, increasing its control and making its network tighter and more efficient. By 1907, the firm had expanded exponentially: besides the head office in Paris, there were branches in most European capitals, in cities such as Barcelona, Milan, and Odessa, and, outside of Europe, in New York, Calcutta, and Singapore. This horizontal structure, combined with a vertical integration of production, distribution, and exhibition, made the company a near monopoly in the new industry, inspiring the later **Edison** trust or **Motion Picture Patents Company** (MPPC). Pathé standardized the market in the sense that it supplied a reliable, regularized output of new films in all available genres, enough to fill complete film programs, with the additional appeal of stencil-coloring, state-of-the-art equipment, and substantial **publicity** materials such as colorful posters. The company thus created loyal clients and satisfied customers in fairgrounds, **music halls** or **vaudeville** theaters, and early permanent cinemas. Most important were Pathé's low production costs and therefore acceptable purchase prices, which for several years discouraged competition.

Between 1907 and 1914, however, Pathé's closed distribution model was challenged by the open distribution model that developed in countries such as Great Britain, Germany, the Netherlands, Denmark, and Italy.

Although the fairgrounds were important clients to Pathé initially, they had several disadvantages: the company had little control over the circulation of films once they were purchased by **itinerant exhibitors**, so that old prints could be as useful as new prints, and—most important—the profit margin was low. Therefore, in 1907, Pathé introduced a system of renting films, for a designated period of time. Only after the 1909 Paris conference, however, did this system become more and more accepted among other production companies, distributors, and exhibitors in Europe. The related effort to establish uniform rental prices, also discussed at the Paris conference, was accepted in countries such as Belgium and France but not by others. Pathé's introduction of film rentals had the effect of boosting permanent cinemas throughout Europe but also of marginalizing fairground cinemas. The company provided its own example by opening Pathé cinemas throughout Europe.

Ironically, Pathé's attempt to establish a monopoly position stimulated competition, particularly in the sectors of distribution and production. After 1907, Pathé's domestic and foreign rivals also opened film rental offices in Paris, London, Berlin, and Brussels. Others put their film distribution in the hands of international companies such as **Raleigh & Robert**, **Aubert**, and the M. P. Sales Agency, or even in those of local resellers and renters. Moreover, Pathé's focus on producing and marketing short films became a disadvantage when Danish, German, and Italian companies began to promote **multiple-reel/feature films** and when audiences, exhibitors, and new independent distributors picked up on these. Aubert, for instance, became prominent because of its rental of Italian, Danish and, later, American features.

From early on, countries such as Great Britain and Germany had a more open-market system. In Great Britain, for instance, producers sold their films to renters, who in turn distributed them to as many theaters as they could. As there was seldom an exclusive contract with any one theater for a film, prints of the same film could be rented to a number of theaters in the same district. Any exhibitor who could not rent a desired film from one renter could turn to another who possessed more prints of the same film or could simply rent a different title. As long as short films were the mainstay of film exhibition, and **stars** played no significant role, renters had difficulty differentiating their products. A short film could easily be replaced by another. The flood of prints in circulation stimulated a second-hand trade, particularly in films bound for the Far East. London thus also became the center for the sale of second-hand prints, with Germany again second. Films of all nationalities and production companies were offered for sale or hire after their first run. The second-hand traders charged prices that were far below the prices charged by the production companies themselves, so that the latter often experienced difficulties in selling their new films. The producers faced competition not only from each other but also from their own past productions.

Germany's open market was even less centralized than Great Britain's. Film companies had representatives in Berlin, but agents would show films to local renters, who then bought prints outright and rented them to theaters. Germany also had the problem of over-circulation. Price wars, ever more frequent changes of program (sometimes thrice weekly), and a large second-hand trade threatened to ruin the business. This spiraling devaluation of the market reached a crisis point in 1907–1909. The solution turned out to be a specialized business sector that would be capable of guaranteeing a twice-weekly change of program, specifically with long films or features. It was only with the arrival of this sector that the rental of individual films got underway in Germany, bringing to an end the era of the autonomous short film.

To make the renting of individual films attractive, a system of sole rights for distributors was devised, under which a distributor might acquire exclusive rights in a given geographical area—a country or a province—for a stated period of time, which might be one or even several years. The distributor then might assign part of the rights on a film to a theater operator, conferring upon the latter the exclusive right of exhibition within a defined area—usually a city—for a specified exhibition period, which might be that of a film's very first screening. This was the origin of the film premiere. The growing popularity of these "sole-rights" or "monopoly" films owed much to their image of exclusiveness, which the publicity surrounding them carefully cultivated by foregrounding and mythologizing the main

actors—a prime example being Asta **Nielsen**—and by their (sometimes extreme) length.

Up to this point in time the unrestricted sale of films had been unproblematic because programs had consisted only of short films. The chances that someone might be showing exactly the same films as his competitor were slight. With the coming of the feature film, however, attention was focused on just a few titles that everyone wanted to screen. However, for years a sort of gray zone existed in which the old system continued to exist in parallel with the new practices. Short films continued to take up a quarter or a half of the program as a whole, and were not "protected" against screening by competitors. Even after the introduction of exclusive screening rights, many films were still being freely exchanged, since some film companies preferred to sell as many copies of their movies as possible. Moreover, short films and older films did not usually come under the exclusive system.

With the rise of independent distributors, exhibitors were forced to concede much of their power, in so far as they had any. Still, the power of exhibitors and distributors remained relative, and the fortunes of both were tied to a continually growing audience. Without that growing demand, the rise of exhibitors and distributors would never have taken on the dimensions it did. The desire to see moving pictures was a factor, consequently, in the willingness of audiences to accept the inconvenience of looking at reissued films or worn-out and damaged prints.

Figure 29 Jean Desmet's Cinema Royal, Rotterdam, with a poster of Cines' *La tutela* [Guardianship] (1913) in four languages. (Courtesy of Ivo Blom.)

Further reading

Abel, Richard (1994) *The Ciné Goes to Town: French Cinema 1896–1914*, Berkeley: University of California Press.

Blom, Ivo (2003) *Jean Desmet and the Early Dutch Film Trade*, Amsterdam: Amsterdam University Press.

Müller, Corinna (1994) *Frühe deutsche Kinematographie. Formale, wirtschaftliche und kulturelle Entwicklungen 1907–1912*, Stuttgart/Weimar: Metzlar.

Thompson, Kristin (1985) *Exporting Entertainment.America in the World Film Market*, London: British Film Institute.

Ulff-Møller, Jens (2001) *Hollywood's "Film Wars" with France: Film-Trade Diplomacy and the Emergence of the French Film Quota Policy*, Rochester: University of Rochester Press.

IVO BLOM

Donisthorpe, Wordsworth

b. 1847, Leeds; d. 1913, Hindhead

political activist, inventor, England

In 1876, Donisthorpe patented his Kinesigraph camera for sequence pictures taken on glass plates, based on a technology developed by his father for the wool industry. He suggested that the pictures could be projected in rapid sequence in conjunction with **Edison**'s new phonograph, to produce talking screen portraits. With cousin William Carr Crofts, he patented a second camera in 1889, using roll film, and shortly afterwards shot a test sequence of traffic in Trafalgar Square, London. Unable to make their projector work, however, they eventually abandoned the project.

STEPHEN HERBERT

Dora Film

Founded by Elvira and Nicola **Notari** in Naples in 1906, Dora Film initially specialized in hand-painted filmed advertisements, urban travelogues, and street views known as *films dal vero*. Subsequently, inspired by Italian sentimental novels and Neapolitan *sceneggiate* (stage dramatizations of dialect songs), Dora productions, often hand-painted and accompanied by live singing, alternated vernacular depictions of battered female lives with patriotic dramas of sentimental war heroism. As a leading exponent of Neapolitan vernacular realism, after **World War I**, Dora films regularly reached Southern Italian immigrants living in North and South America. The transition to sound, along with fascist censorship, which opposed depictions of misery, delinquency, and regional subcultures, caused Dora's commercial demise.

GIORGIO BERTELLINI

double-film-band projectors

Several inventors proposed projectors using two bands of film, to significantly decrease the wear on film prints by halving the speed at which they needed to stop and start, as well as producing a better ratio of light to darkness during projection. Derived from **magic lantern** dissolving view apparatuses, Robert Duncan Gray, Owen A. Eames, and William **Friese-Greene** all experimented with such machines, the most famous of which was the Bioskop of Max **Skladanowsky** that gave moving picture projections to a paying audience at the Wintergarten Theatre in Berlin throughout the month of November 1895.

DEAC ROSSELL

Doublier, Francis

b. 1878; d. 1948

projectionist, cameraman, France

An apprentice in the photographic factories by the age of 12, Doublier assisted Charles Moisson at the first public **Cinématographe Lumière** projections in Paris on 28 December 1895. The two filmed the Tzar's coronation in Russia on 26 May 1896, after which Doublier traveled worldwide for the **Lumière** company, projecting its films in Sofia, Bucharest, Athens, Constantinople, Cairo, Bombay, Shanghai, and Peking. After filming scenes from the 1900 Paris **World's Fair**, he opened a Lumière factory to manufacture photographic plates in Burlington, Vermont, and remained its director until 1911. He then served as technical director for **Éclair American** until 1914. A succession of posts as director of film laboratories followed, mostly in New Jersey, until Doublier ended his career as vice-president of Major Film Laboratories in New York in 1944.

GLENN MYRENT

Doyen, Eugène-Louis

b. 1859; d. 1916

surgeon, filmmaker, France

A renowned surgeon, Dr. Doyen took an interest in cinema as early as June 1898. With the assistance of two technicians, Ambroise-François **Parnaland** and **Clément-Maurice**, he assembled one of the world's first collections of surgical films. In February 1902, the film of an operation during which he separated conjoined sisters Doodica and Radica Neik triggered a heated controversy in the medical profession. In 1905, a court decided that Doyen was the "author" of the films Parnaland had been selling commercially, without permission. Doyen spent the last years of his life perfecting (with the support of Auguste Hulin) a trichromatic process aimed at filming his surgical procedures in **color**.

THIERRY LEFEBVRE

Dranem [Armand Ménard]

b. 1869, Paris; d. 1935, Paris

café-concert singer, film actor, France

With his grotesque silhouette, Parisian working-class accent, and silly songs charged with saucy innuendo, Dranem was one of the most popular singers of his time. He began his career in 1894 at the Concert de l'Epoque before moving to the Concert-Parisien. **Pathé-Frères** launched his film career with *Le Salut de Dranem* [Dranem's Salute] (1901). Thereafter, he acted in numerous short films: from *Histoire grivoise racontée par une concierge* [Saucy Story as Told by a Concierge] (1902), *Ma Tante* [My Aunt] (1903), *Le Mitron* [The Baker's Boy] (1904), and *Le rêve de Dranem* [Dranem's Dream] (1905) to *Le Tondeur galant* [The Gallant Shearer] (1912). He also performed in **Chronophone Gaumont** films from 1906 on: *Les P'tits pois* [The Green Pea], *Etre légume* [To Be Top Brass], *Le Trou de mon quai* [My Wharf's Hole], *V'la le rétameur* [Here's the Tinker], *Allumeur-Marche* [Torch-Walk], *Le Boléro cosmopolite*, and *Le vrai Jiu-Jitsu* [The Real Jiu-Jitsu]. He performed in films until his death in 1935.

LAURENT MANNONI

Drankov, Aleksandr

b. 1880; d. 1949

filmmaker, Russia

A self-proclaimed "court photographer" who had been working on the fringes of the film business since 1902, Drankov founded the first Russian-owned film production company in late 1907. Although held in contempt by many of his contemporaries for the "sensationalism" of his films, his allegedly unscrupulous business practices, and his general vulgarity, Drankov displayed an unerring sense for the tastes of the mass public. After the Bolshevik revolution in 1917, Drankov emigrated to Istanbul and attempted to set up a new production company there. He was last heard of running a photography studio in San Francisco, and his date of death remained unknown until 1999, when his grave was discovered in a San Francisco cemetery.

DENISE J. YOUNGBLOOD

Drankov

Founded in 1907 in St. Petersburg by the portrait photographer Aleksandr **Drankov**, the Drankov studio challenged the dominance of **Pathé-Frères** on the Russian market and remained a top producer for the next ten years. By the eve of 1917 Revolution, Drankov had released 85 titles, second only to the output of the **Khanzhonkov** studio. Drankov's inaugural production, *Stenka Razin* (1908), is usually considered the "first Russian film"—that is, made in Russia by Russians for a Russian audience. Drankov promoted the picture lavishly, commissioning a **musical score** from I. M. Ippolitov-Ivanov and a lurid poster, showing the peasant rebel about to hurl the captive princess into the Volga. The studio's hyper-melodramatic, "sensational" style thus was established quite early, as was criticism from the cultural elite whom Drankov so enjoyed shocking.

The studio soon learned that the horrors of contemporary urban life supplied better material for popular entertainment than did history—and churned out hit after hit. Especially successful commercially was Drankov's series of light-hearted **crime films** based on the exploits of well-known criminals. Most notable among these was the three-part serial about the adventuress and thief Sonia Bliuvshtein, *Sonka zolotaia ruchka* [Sonka the "Golden Hand," 1915]. Part three of *Sonka* played twelve of Moscow's leading **palace cinemas** simultaneously and was heavily advertised in the mass circulation daily *Russkoe slovo* [The Russian Word]. Dismissing the critical outcry that the studio was portraying life in crime too lightly, Drankov followed *Sonka* with a similar series, *Razboinik Vaska Churkin* [The Robber Vaska Churkin].

The Drankov company also introduced the screenplay contest to the Russian public in 1915. "Scenario famine"—the scramble for storylines—had become acute by then, as Russian production soared, due to the difficulties of importing foreign films during **World War I**. The 1,000 ruble first prize in these contests was quite a large sum of money since writers were ordinarily paid only 100 to 200 rubles for a script.

Despite a marked level of creativity, especially in promotion, Drankov did not seek artistic acclaim. The company never engaged in the battle for high-priced **stars**, **screenwriters**, and directors as did Khanzhonkov, **Thiemann & Reinhardt**, and **Yermolíev**. The studio continued to make films obviously designed to appeal to mass tastes, rather than those of the upwardly mobile. Whether this

strategy actually resulted in higher profits is not clear from the scanty evidence left behind. Drankov's contemporaries believed him to be a businessman with few scruples. In 1913, when the studio was recapitalized with funds from the respectable capitalist A. G. Taldykin (and renamed Drankov & Taldykin), Drankov's critics hoped Taldykin's influence would raise the firm's cultural profile, but there were no discernible changes.

Drankov's business sense did not translate into political sense in 1917. Among the studio's last films was a celebration of the Socialist Revolutionary Party leader Ekaterina Breshko-Breshkovskaia, *Babushka russkoi revoliutsii* [Grandmother of the Russian Revolution]. The SR's were archenemies of the Bolsheviks and would soon be outlawed. Drankov had to flee Russia, and his studio was disbanded.

See also: melodrama, sensational

Further reading

Leyda, Jay (1960) *Kino: A History of the Russian and Soviet Film*, London, George Allen & Unwin, Ltd.

Youngblood, Denise J. (1999) *The Magic Mirror: Moviemaking in Russia, 1908–1918*, Madison: University of Wisconsin Press.

DENISE J. YOUNGBLOOD

Duhamel, Sarah

b. ?; d. ?

actor, France

A child actress who performed at several Paris theaters for André Antoine as well as toured the provinces, Duhamel came to **Pathé-Frères** in 1911 to develop and star in one of the company's more successful **comic series**, *Rosalie* (1911–1913). Although she also was partnered with Little Moritz (Moritz Schwartz) in a linked series of comic shorts, the few surviving films—such as *Rosalie et sa phono* (1911)—reveal her skillful use of trick effects as well as broad physical comedy.

In 1913, she moved to **Éclair**, where she starred briefly in another series, *Petronille* (1913–1914).

RICHARD ABEL

Duncan, Francis Martin

b. 1873; d. ?

micro-cinematographer, Britain

F. Martin Duncan was the son of a noted scientist, and himself became a scientist and naturalist of note, specializing in microphotography. He had already experimented with **chronophotography** in the pre-cinema period, showing the results in motion on a Zoetrope. In 1904, Charles **Urban** encouraged him to adapt his techniques to cinema, and together they launched a long-running and popular film series entitled *The Unseen World*, advertised as being shown by the "Urban–Duncan Micro-Bioscope." Duncan later pursued a career as a zoologist and writer of popular books on nature.

See also: scientific films: Europe

LUKE McKERNAN

Durand, Jean

b. 1882; d. 1946

filmmaker, France

Durand started his career as a journalist before turning to the cinema and directing three films for **Pathé-Frères** in 1908. He joined **Lux** in 1909, then **Gaumont** late in 1910 to replace Roméo **Bosetti** and take over the *Calino* **comic series**, whose main actor was Clément **Migé**. With a group nicknamed "Les Pouittes" (The Bedbugs), Durand launched the careers of Lucien Bataille (*Zigoto*, 1911–1912) and Ernest **Bourbon** (*Onésime*, 1912–1914). His career, interrupted by **World War I**, continued until 1919 with such highlights as the *Serpentin* series (starring Marcel **Levesque**) and a few films starring his wife, Berthe Dagmar.

THIERRY LEFEBVRE

Dureau, Georges

b. ?; d. ?

editor, journalist, France

Dureau and Edmond **Benoît-Lévy** emerged as key players in the journalist/intellectual field supporting the young French film industry. Initially editor of *Argus-Phono-Cinéma* (1906–1908) and *Phono-Cinéma-Revue* (1908), Dureau founded **Ciné-Journal** in August 1908; it quickly became the leading trade paper, and its success soon generated others. Dureau served as editor until the journal merged with *Le Journal du Film* in 1923 (Mme Dureau sustained its publication during **World War I**). In his editorials, Dureau often identified issues bearing on central aspects of the new medium and thus set the agenda for pertinent debates, establishing an important base for French film theory and criticism. He continued to contribute to the journal until 1928.

MARINA DAHLQUIST

Duse, Eleonora

b. 1859; d. 1924

actor, Italy

The great star of the Italian stage, Duse performed in but one film, **Ambrosio**'s *Cenere* [Ashes] (1916), towards the end of her career. In a rural drama supposedly set in Sardinia, she plays a poor woman who abandons her illegitimate child and lives in solitude. Years later, she approaches her son, then leaves him for good and dies. Duse herself apparently selected the homonymously-titled novel by Grazia Deledda for her film debut. Yet reviewers criticized the fragmentary character of the story and the melodramatic gestures of the stage star, overlooking the much more unrestrained acting of her co-star Febo Mari. Although the film knew only a limited release, from the 1940s on it has been considered a precursor of Italian neorealism.

IVO BLOM

Duskes, Alfred

b. 1881; d. ?

producer, Germany

Duskes began his career in 1902 as operator of a self-built film **projector** touring the Berlin pub scene. In 1905, he founded Duskes Spezialfabrik für Kine-matographen, Films, etc., which primarily dealt with cinema equipment and was renamed Duskes Kinematographen- und Film-Fabriken Ltd. in 1907, by which time it had equipped over fifty storefront cinemas. From 1906, Duskes produced films on a regular basis in his own glass-house studio at Friedrichstrasse. He specialized in comic sketches (some featuring child actor Curt Bois) and **re-enactments** such as *Der Hauptmann von Köpenick* [The Captain of Köpenick] (1906), directed by Heinrich **Bolten-Baeckers**, the company's most prolific comedy director up to 1909. Between 1907 and 1909, the majority of Duskes' output, however, was comprised of *Tonbilder* based on famous operas and operettas and using his own *Cinephon* sound system, over which he carried on a heated patent-feud with Oskar **Messter** in 1908. After many of its films were destroyed in a fire in January 1912, the company was forced into liquidation, but immedi-ately re-opened as Duskes Ltd., which diversified its output to include *Autorenfilme* (through Literaria-Film, a joint venture with **Pathé-Frères**), melodramas, and **detective films**.

MICHAEL WEDEL

Dussaud, François

b. 1870; d. 1953

physicist, inventor, Switzerland, France

Born in Geneva, where he held a chair in physics and chemistry at the Ecole de mécanique, François (or Franz) Dussaud presented his microphonograph (developed in collaboration with Casimir **Sivan**) in Paris in December 1896. He used the invention to tackle the question of the synchronization of sound and image, in parallel to research by others such as F.-A. **Baron**, Henri **Joly**, and **Clément-Maurice**. After moving to Paris, he presented his Phonorama (an audiovisual show patented on

1 July 1897), using films made by Felix **Mesguich**, at the 1900 Exposition, where he also exhibited, at Chalet #9 in the Swiss village, a number of inventions designed for Pathé **phonographs**. The same year, as an engineering consultant for **Pathé-Frères**, he developed patents in color reproduction (Dussaudscope, April 1904), daylight projection (February 1908), and low-voltage projection (November 1910). In July 1907, he became head of the Dussaud company, which held a distribution monopoly for Pathé films in nine dis-tricts of northern France as well as in Switzerland.

ROLAND COSANDEY

Dutch Mutoscope & Biograph

In 1898, Daniel Louis Uittenboogaart founded the Nederlandsche Mutoscope & Biograph Maat-schappij, following a successful Netherlands tour of the spectacular **American Mutoscope and Bio-graph** films covering the coronation of Queen Wilhelmina, taken by William K. L. **Dickson**. The company's sharp 68mm projections of news events were of much better quality than the usual *actualités*. They not only functioned as a variety number in **music halls** and **fairs/fairgrounds**, but also were shown in mutoscopes installed in public places. Among the Dutch company's productions were the inserted filmed scenes in the revue, *De Nieuwe Prikkel* [The New Prickle], in 1899. After 35 mm **celluloid** film stock became standard, the company went bankrupt in 1902.

ANSJE VAN BEUSEKOM

Dwan, Allan

b. 1885; d. 1981

scriptwriter, director, USA

An engineer in the employ of the Peter Cooper Hewitt Company of Chicago, Allan Dwan entered the film industry in 1909 by selling stories to the **Essanay Film Manufacturing Company**, quickly becoming its scenario editor. When the **American Film Manufacturing Company** was established in Chicago in late 1910, Dwan and several of his Essanay colleagues jumped to the new studio. He was sent to Tucson, Arizona, in 1911 as the production manager for Frank Beal's western company and soon replaced Beal as director. The company moved to California, working out of San Juan Capistrano and La Mesa, before settling in Santa Barbara in the summer of 1912. Dwan remained with the "Flying A" as the company's brand was called, until May of 1913, when he left to work for **Universal**.

While at American, Dwan personally directed or supervised over 250 short films. In addition to those he directed himself, Dwan was responsible for overseeing the films of Wallace Reid and Marshall Neilan, both of whom went with him to Universal, where they repeated the "Flying A" pattern of alternating one-, two-, and three-reel productions. While at Universal, Dwan directed his first feature, *Richelieu* (1914), a six-reel film starring Pauline Bush and Lon Chaney. By mid-1914, Dwan was under contract to **Famous Players**, directing a diverse and successful series of feature films, culminating in the Mary **Pickford** vehicles, *A Girl of Yesterday* and *The Foundling* (both 1915).

With the creation of the Triangle Film Corporation in late 1915, Dwan went to work for Fine Arts, under the supervision of D. W. **Griffith**. While there, he was assigned such star vehicles as *Betty of Greystone* (Dorothy Gish) and *An Innocent Magdalene* (Lillian Gish). However, his greatest success at Triangle-Fine Arts was with Douglas Fairbanks, for whom he directed *The Good Bad Man*, *The Half-Breed*, and *Manhattan Madness* (all 1916). After Triangle, Dwan worked for a variety of independent companies, achieving his greatest success in the 1920s with Famous Players-Lasky-Paramount and Fox.

According to Dwan, he learned to direct films by watching Griffith's **Biograph** films, paying close attention to his camera placement, as well as his handling of actors. Dwan was an engineer by training and clearly enjoyed the challenge of technical problems, such as **lighting** a scene and moving the camera, but he also worked economically and never lost himself in such minutiae if other, better-qualified technicians were available. Above all, Dwan saw filmmaking as a logical, or "mathematical" process, in which every problem had a solution and most solutions involved simplification. The evidence of the comparatively few films of his that survive from his early years, such as *The Poisoned Flume* (1911), reveals a director of economical means, one who would willingly subsume ornament in the service of the story, to the point where such modesty of means became the hallmark of his style.

Further reading

Bogdanovich, Peter (1971) *Allan Dwan: The Last Pioneer*, New York: Praeger.

STEVEN HIGGINS

Dyer, Frank L.

b. 2 August 1870, Washington, D.C.;
d. 4 June 1941, New Jersey

lawyer, executive, USA

A patent attorney, Frank Dyer handled the patenting of the **Edison Kinetoscope** and **Kinetograph** and, in 1903, became Edison's General Counsel. From 1897 until 1914, he managed Edison's case in the legal battles known as the US **patents wars**. In 1908, he was made general manager of Edison's enterprises, including the motion picture business. When the protracted legal battle with **Biograph** was settled, he became president of the **Motion Picture Patents Company**, a position he held until December 1912, when he became president of the **General Film Company**. Dyer returned to private law practice in 1914.

PAUL SPEHR

E

Eastman, George

b. 1854; d. 1932

inventor, manufacturer, philanthropist,
USA

An amateur photographer in Rochester, Eastman
began producing gelatin dry plates in 1880, and,
four years later, paper roll film. He introduced the
first commercial transparent roll of film stock (made
of cellulose nitrate) in 1889, making possible two
years later the development of W. K. L. **Dickson**'s
motion picture camera, for Thomas A. **Edison**.
After the "Kodak" brand was patented (1888), he
established the Eastman Kodak Company in 1892,
which soon became the leading manufacturer of
motion picture stock worldwide, and a driving force
in photography's further development. Eastman's
private home is now a museum and an **archive**
holding a vast collection of early films.

See also: celluloid; film developing, printing, and
assembly

Further reading

Brayer, Elizabeth (1996) *George Eastman, A Biography*, Baltimore: Johns Hopkins University
Press.

PAOLO CHERCHI USAI

Eastman Kodak Company

Eastman Kodak Company, the world's leading
manufacturer of motion picture stock, was established by George **Eastman** in Rochester in 1892
and given the name "Kodak" after a 1888 patent for
a still camera (an earlier company, founded in 1881,
dealt with a revolutionary process of dry-plate
photography). The first transparent cellulose
nitrate film stock commercially distributed (1889)
helped W. K. L. **Dickson** in his experiments for
Thomas A. **Edison**. Kodak's early method for
manufacturing film was an improvement over those
previously devised by John Carbutt (Philadelphia)
and the Celluloid Company (Newark). However,
the company had problems with the chemistry of
the process and virtually discontinued making
cellulose film stock from late 1892 to mid-1895.
Consequently, Dickson began acquiring film from
the **Blair Camera Company** (Boston) in April
1893. The **Lumière** brothers started their experiments with cellulose stock bought from European
Blair Camera (London), where film was cut to
35 mm but not perforated (this was left to users),
and eventually set up their own manufacturing
plant in Lyon with the help of Victor Planchon. A
similar strategy was adopted in Great Britain by Birt
Acres; Blair Camera (until 1898) and Anthony &
Scovill (Ansco, after 1900) were among Kodak's
competitors in the early years of cinema.

Initially reluctant to enter the business (busy as
he was with the amateur photography market, and
sharing Edison and Lumière's belief that the interest for moving pictures would soon fade away),
Eastman was startled by the outburst of demand for

film stock after 1895, and was unprepared to satisfy the increasing volume of orders. It was only after Eastman bought Blair Camera and its technology for making longer strips of film (1899) that Kodak established its supremacy in the world market. In 1908, Kodak began producing a cellulose acetate base; in 1912, **Gaumont** commissioned a 35mm "safety" film stock with panchromatic emulsion (sensitive to all the colors of the visible spectrum) for **Chronochrome**, its additive **color** process. Kodak itself designed a two-color subtractive process in 1916 (Kodachrome), but would not manufacture "safety" stock on a commercial scale until the invention of 16mm for the non-theatrical market (1920).

Eastman's business principles were reflected in the organization of his company: mass production at low cost; a focus on the customer; extensive advertising; international distribution (several branches for manufacturing and sales soon were established all over the world). Integrating these principles was a flexible, dynamic approach to management which was highly innovative for its time. Fostering growth through continuing research, treating employees in a self-respecting way (staff received dividends from company profits), and reinvesting income to build and extend the business were distinguishing features of Eastman's philosophy as an entrepreneur, thus making Kodak a benchmark in the history of corporate industry of the early 20th century.

See also: celluloid; film developing, printing, and assembly; monopoly capitalism: USA

Further reading

Collins, Douglas (1990) *The Story of Kodak*, New York: Harry M. Abrams.

Spehr, Paul C. (2000) "Unaltered to Date: Developing 35mm Film," in John Fullerton and Astrid Söderbergh Widding (eds.) *Moving Images: From Edison to the Webcam*, 3–27, Sydney: John Libbey.

Theisen, Earl (1967) "The History of Nitrocellulose as a Film Base," *Journal of the SMPE*, 20 (March 1933), reproduced in Raymond Fielding (ed.) *Technological History of Motion Pictures and*

Television, 118–119, Berkeley: University of California Press.

PAOLO CHERCHI USAI

Éclair

Founded in March 1907, Éclair reached a production level on par with **Pathé-Frères** and **Gaumont** before inexorably declining during **World War I**. The signatures on the founding document of the Société française des films "L'Éclair" included Ambroise-François **Parnaland**, an inventor who had begun his career in cinema in 1895, and Charles **Jourjon**, a lawyer and skilled businessman. During the following months, a factory and studios were built in Épinay-sur-Seine and regular production began.

In the summer of 1908, Victorin **Jasset** was hired by Éclair to adapt the popular American dime novel series, *Nick Carter*, for the screen. Pierre Bressol played the detective and the series, which lasted for more than a year, met with a considerable success worldwide, establishing Éclair's reputation. Other series adaptations followed: *Morgan le pirate* (1909–1910), *Le Vautour de la Sierra* [The Vulture of the Sierra] (1910), and most notably *Zigomar* (1911–1913) and *Protéa* (1913–1917), starring Alexandre **Arquillière** and Josette **Andriot**, respectively.

Besides these popular films, Éclair created a subsidiary, ACAD (Association cinématographique des auteurs dramatiques), in November 1909, in response to **Film d'Art** and **SCAGL**. Supervised by Émile **Chautard**, the films produced by ACAD covered every genre: **historical films** (*La Dame de Montsoreau*, 1913), social dramas (*Gerval, le maître de forges* [Gerval, the Factory Manager], 1912), etc. Maurice **Tourneur** also directed his first films for Éclair, tapping into the repertory of the Grands Boulevards theaters (*Les Gaietés de l'escadron* [The Squadron at Play], 1913) and of the Grand Guignol (*Figures de cire* [Waxworks], 1914). In addition, Jean Méry and Léon Gillon manufactured excellent cinematographic apparatuses under the supervision of technical director Georges Maurice.

In 1912, Éclair stepped up its production and soon became a serious competitor to Pathé and Gaumont. In July the first installment of

Éclair-Journal appeared, a weekly **newsreel** designed to counter the hegemony of its rivals. At the same time, the *Scientia* series initiated an important production of **scientific films** directly inspired by the successes of Jean **Comandon** for Pathé. Éclair's famed **comic series** also began to appear, with title-characters such as *Willy* (1912–1914), played by young Willy Sanders, and especially *Gavroche* (1912–1914), with Paul Bertho, and *Casimir* (1913–1914), with Lucien Bataille.

Moreover, Éclair developed several subsidiaries abroad in order to increase the diffusion of its films and to diversify its production, with **Éclair American** clearly the most important. Beginning as a sales office in late 1909, this subsidiary became a full-fledged production company with a studio and laboratories in Fort Lee (New Jersey) by 1911. Under the direction of Étienne **Arnaud**, production steadily increased until March 1914, when a fire destroyed the Fort Lee premises. In the meantime, Émile **Cohl**, Chautard, and Tourneur had arrived in the USA to reinforce the local crew.

The Fort Lee fire and the beginning of World War I sealed Éclair's fate. After struggling for six years, the company was declared bankrupt in 1920.

See also: crime films; detective films

Further reading

Abel, Richard (ed.) (1993) "Lightning Images: The Éclair Film Company, 1907–1920," *Griffithiana*, 47.
Bousquet, Henri and Mannoni, Laurent (eds.) (1992) "Éclair 1907–1918," *1895*, 12.
Le Roy, Éric and Laurent Billia (eds.) (1995) *Éclair. Un siècle de cinéma à Épinay-sur-Seine*, Paris: Calmann-Lévy.

THIERRY LEFEBVRE

Éclair American

The French company **Éclair** established an American branch in 1911, with the construction of a state-of-the-art studio and laboratory complex in Fort Lee, New Jersey. While employing Americans in front of the camera, Éclair's front office and technical team in Fort Lee was at first primarily French, including Etienne **Arnaud**, Emile **Chautard**, Emile **Cohl**, and Benjamin Carré. Éclair briefly sent a production unit on location to Pawnee City, Oklahoma, in late 1912, and a year later established a second permanent studio in Tucson, Arizona. A devastating studio fire in Fort Lee on 19 March 1914 resulted in much of the staff moving to the **World Film Corporation**, and within a year Éclair sold its American operation.

Further reading

Higgins, Steven (1992) "American Éclair, 1911–1915," *Griffithiana*, 44/45: 89–129.

STEVEN HIGGINS

Eclipse

The société générale des cinématographes Eclipse, a public limited company with a capital of 600,000 francs, was founded by George Henri **Rogers** and Paul Joseph Roux in August 1906. Eclipse, which took over the **Charles Urban Trading Company**'s Paris franchise in November that same year, owned a shop in the passage de l'Opéra and a small studio in Courbevoie. In July 1908, a new increase in capital (1,500,000 francs) made it possible for the company to launch Charles **Urban** and Albert **Smith**'s kinemacolor films and to purchase a majority of shares in the Radios company, which had been created in 1907. By 1913, Eclipse was the fourth largest French film manufacturer, releasing 150 films per year, among them the *Arizona Bill* series, directed by Gaston Roudès and starring Joë **Hamman**. Ten years later, after suffering financially during **World War I**, the company was purchased by Omnium EEG.

See also: Desfontaines, Henri; Mercanton, Louis

LAURENT MANNONI

Edamasa Yoshiro

b. 1888; d. 1944

cameraman/director, Japan

Born in Hiroshima, Edamasa was hired by **Yoshizawa Shoten** in 1910 and learned the techniques of shooting motion picture film from Chiba

Yoshizo. After working as a cameraman at **Fukuhodo** and Toyo Shokai, he moved to **Tenkatsu** in 1914, when the company was founded. He displayed particular skill in filming trick effects, and he was keenly interested in modernizing Japanese cinema. In 1919, he finally directed his first film, *Ai no kyoku* [The Melody of Sorrow]. In the 1920s and 1930s, he directed more than twenty films.

HIROSHI KOMATSU

Edison Home Kinetoscope

Thomas **Edison**'s 1912 Home Kinetoscope projector, promoted for domestic, school, YMCA, and club use, was designed to show **Edison Company** moving pictures. This projector used 22mm safety film stock ingeniously featuring three rows of tiny pictures. No rewinding was necessary during a presentation: the first strip was shown by cranking the handle forward; the center strip (with images printed in reverse order), by simply cranking the handle backwards; the third strip, by turning the handle forward again. The projector could also show special slides. There was no camera for making amateur movies, however, and the system was short-lived.

STEPHEN HERBERT

Edison Kinetograph camera

Thomas **Edison**'s Kinetograph was the first commercially successful moving picture camera. Begun as a cylinder device, it was essentially completed by Edison's assistant, W. K. L. **Dickson**, in the spring of 1892, but was not used for commercial production until 1894. Designed to use strips of 35mm **celluloid** film stock with four sprocket holes on each side of an image one inch wide, it set the international standard which the industry has used since 1896. Edison delayed patenting the Kinetograph until 1897, but after it was accepted the patent was used to sue his major competitors.

PAUL SPEHR

Edison Manufacturing

Owned by Thomas A. **Edison** and formed in December 1889, Edison Manufacturing was based in Orange, New Jersey. It was part of Edison's high technology manufacturing complex: the Black Maria moving picture studio was located directly behind Edison's Laboratory. The company produced and marketed a variety of products including batteries, fans, and dental equipment. The inventor shifted his moving picture activities from his Laboratory accounts to Edison Manufacturing on 1 April 1894. The company sold both exhibition equipment (initially the peep-hole **Kinetoscope**, but later the projecting Kinetoscope) and film prints. Commercial filmmaking can be dated from Eugen **Sandow**'s appearance before the **Edison Kinetograph** (Edison's moving picture camera) on 6 March 1894. Although a handful of subjects shot in 1893 and early 1894 subsequently were offered for sale, Edison Manufacturing produced over 125 subjects for Kinetoscope exhibition between March 1894 and the end of 1895.

Under William **Gilmore**, vice-president and general manager of Edison Manufacturing, W. K. L. **Dickson** headed the Kinetograph Department while William **Heise** was chief cameraman. When Dickson departed in April 1895, eventually to join forces with **American Mutoscope and Biograph** (AM&B), Heise was left in charge of film production. Film subjects fell into two overlapping groups. Many were of the world of masculine blood sports: rat baiting, cock fighting, boxing, and even jousting. The second, larger group offered short visual excerpts of American performance culture: serpentine and skirt dancers, Annie Oakley and bronco busters from Buffalo Bill's Wild West, scenes from Broadway shows, trained animals acts, and so forth. Many of these were of risqué or even illegal performances (prize fights, dancing by underage children, cock fights) and presented in public, often refined (hetero-social) venues.

Edison's moving picture business had faded by late 1895 and was only revived with film projection. The company manufactured the Vitascope (often known as "Edison's Vitascope") for **Raff & Gammon**, and also resumed film production (under Raff & Gammon auspices), this time for the screen. The effort to quickly manufacture projectors and films for a national market was an impressive accomplishment, but it often was marred by start-up glitches. The Vitascope debuted at Koster & Bial's Music Hall in New York City on 23 April 1896; within the next few months, it opened in most US cities. Seventy-three Vitascopes eventually were manufactured, while more than eighty different moving picture subjects were shot in the spring and summer of 1896. Responding to the location shooting of both the Eidoloscope Company and the **Lumière** company, Edison developed a portable camera that was first used to shoot outdoor scenes of New York City on 11 May 1896.

Edison broke with Raff & Gammon in late October 1896, for the Vitascope by then was an outmoded machine, and many rivals had entered the field, selling projectors that used Edison films (with four rectangular perforations on each side of a single frame, a different format from that used by Lumière and others). Edison responded with its own machine, the Projectoscope or Projecting Kinetoscope, which debuted in Harrisburg, Pennsylvania, on November 30. Various prototypes were put into circulation during the next months, and the "perfected" projector was offered for sale at $100 on 16 February 1897. The Projecting Kinetoscope was a crucial part of Edison's business for the next fifteen years, with profits reaching a high of $220,622 in 1907–1908. Profits would average between 17% (in 1897–1898) and 64% (in 1907–1908) of Edison's film-related business.

Edison Manufacturing took firm control of its own filmmaking activities in late October 1896 and hired James H. **White** away from Raff & Gammon, making him the head of its Kinetograph Department. At this point, Edison himself began to **copyright** the most important subjects in his own name. White and his crew dashed about the eastern USA, taking films of heroic fire companies, mounted police charging the camera, the Buffalo horse market, and Niagara Falls. In August 1897, he and cameraman Frederick W. Blechynden toured various western states, Mexico, and the Far East, finally returning to San Francisco in May 1898, after the Spanish American War was well under way. They took over 130 films that were

eventually copyrighted. Heise remained based in Orange, taking films in the Black Maria while his boss was on the road.

In December 1897, Edison's lawyers launched a legal offensive against US producers and prominent exhibitors, suing them for infringing on Edison's patents. J. Stuart **Blackton**, Albert E. **Smith**, and William **Paley** were among those who accepted these claims (often after being sued) and became Edison licensees. They subsequently provided the company with numerous subjects to sell. Paley, for example, provided dozens of Spanish–American War films. AM&B, with its large format (68/70 mm) film, was Edison's chief remaining competitor; in fact, its challenge was so powerful that the inventor-businessman almost sold his moving picture interests to the company in 1900. Thus, when Edison Manufacturing was incorporated in early May 1900, Edison's film business was excluded from the process of incorporation.

After AM&B failed to make good on its option payment, Edison voided the contract and renewed his commitment to the film business. The company hired Edwin S. **Porter** in November 1900 to improve its film equipment and kept him on as it built a roof-top studio at 41 East 21st Street, New York City. The studio opened in February 1901, where Porter worked with actor and scenic designer George S. Fleming. Fleming left in 1903, to be replaced by a succession of collaborators, including G. M. **Anderson** (1903–1904), Wallace **McCutcheon** (1905–1907), and J. Searle **Dawley** (1907–1909). When White took charge of Edison's London sales office, he was replaced first by William Markgraf (1903–1904) and then Alex T. Moore (1904–1909).

The studio became an increasingly important part of Edison's business, as the company made story films the keystone of its production policy—e.g., *Jack and the Beanstalk* (1902), *Life of an American Fireman* (1902–1903), *The Great Train Robbery* (November 1903). Although staged films were more expensive to make than *actualités*, 85% of film sales from original Edison negatives were in this category by 1904. Edison story films were popular and highly regarded, although their number was comparatively modest and represented a steadily decreasing portion of films shown on US screens.

The moving picture boom that resulted from the rise in **nickelodeon** theaters hit Edison's film business particularly hard as it went through a series of inter-related crises in 1908–1909. In June 1908, Thomas Edison replaced Gilmore and made his lawyer Frank L. **Dyer** vice president and Charles Wilson general manager of Edison Manufacturing. To better meet demand for new subjects, the company increased its production units to two and soon to four. Unfortunately, the quality of films continued to decline. Porter proved inept at running the studio and failed to modernize his system of representation. By February 1909, he was demoted, and Horace Plimpton became studio manager. During this period, Edison was reorganizing the US industry around the Film Service Association and then the **Motion Picture Patents Company** (MPPC).

Under Plimpton, the quantity and quality of production gradually improved; by 1912 the company was releasing five reels of new subjects per week and its films were as highly regarded as those by any company except **Biograph**. In April 1911, the newly formed Thomas A. Edison, Inc. took over the commercial film business, and Edison invested considerable energy and money in two ventures that proved unsuccessful. The **Edison Home Kinetoscope**, launched in late 1911, sought to bring commercial movies into the home in a manner that looked toward the VCR revolution of the 1980s. The Kinetophone, which debuted in February 1913, attempted to show synchronous sound films and enjoyed a brief fad. Meanwhile, Edison and the MPPC were sued for anti-trust violations and ultimately lost in the courts. These problems all proved distracting as Edison lagged behind in one crucial area of business—the emergence of the **multiple-reel/feature film**. When faced with previous problems in the past, Edison had been able to play catch up; this time the scale of operations proved

Figure 30 Edison cameramen, *c.* 1910. (Courtesy of the Robert S. Birchard Collection.)

too large, and competitors such as **Famous Players Motion Picture Company** were too well entrenched. After the onset of **World War I**, which resulted in the loss of foreign markets, Edison's film business was only breaking even. It stopped marketing projectors in 1915, and its filmmaking business began to lose money by 1917. On 30 March 1918, Thomas A. Edison, Inc. sold its film business to the Lincoln & Parker Film Company for $150,000 in cash and $200,000 in stock.

See also: celluloid; US patent wars

Further reading

Bowser, Eileen (1990) *The Transformation of Cinema, 1907–1915*, New York: Scribner's.
Musser, Charles (1990) *Before the Nickelodeon: Edwin S. Porter and the Edison Manufacturing Company*, Berkeley: University of California Press.

CHARLES MUSSER

Edison, Thomas Alvin

b. 11 February 1847; d. 18 October 1931

inventor, business executive, USA

The "Wizard of Menlo Park" was already a popular idol when he announced, in 1888, that he was experimenting on an "an instrument which does for the Eye what the phonograph does for the Ear." He had become an international celebrity with the unexpected advent of the **phonograph**, and his work with electric illumination enhanced his image. In 1888, he opened a well-equipped, state-of-the art laboratory in Orange, New Jersey, where he supervised specialized experimenters with the support of carpenters, pattern makers, blacksmiths, machinists, and laborers. The creation of the **Edison Kinetograph** (camera) and **Kinetoscope** (viewing device) was one of several projects started in the new lab. Edison assigned these projects to W. K. L. **Dickson**, an electrical specialist who was also the lab's photographic specialist. With Charles Brown and, later, William **Heise**, experienced machinists, as his assistants and two machine shops to deal with mechanical issues, Dickson concentrated on resolving various photographic problems.

Because of numerous difficulties, primarily inadequate photo materials, progress was slow. By the end of 1891, experiments had resulted in a **celluloid** film with an image one inch wide, stabilized by four perforations on either side, a format still in use today as 35 mm. In the spring of 1892, the camera was ready, and that summer a prototype viewer was designed. The Black Maria studio and facilities to develop and print film followed. The introduction of the Kinetoscope was delayed, however, until April 1894.

Edison was skeptical about the commercial future of the Kinetoscope, and it proved to be a short-lived success. Its initial profits saved him during a severe economic crisis in 1894, but the Kinetoscope business was flat by 1896. After briefly marketing **Armat**'s Vitascope, Edison introduced his own projector and began selling machines and films himself. He faced stiff competition from a variety of projection systems and had no patent for a projector. In 1897, when the patent for the camera was issued, Edison used it in a series of lawsuits that eliminated much of his American competition. The well-financed **American Mutoscope and Biograph Company** resisted, however, and a decade of patent wars followed.

Edison was more interested in machines than film production, but it was the sale of films that made **Edison Manufacturing** the dominant American company in the US market through the first decade of the 20th century. The company managers, William **Gilmore** and Frank L. **Dyer**, focused more on controlling costs than on the quality of their films. So despite pioneering work by Edwin S. **Porter** and the quality direction of J. Searle **Dawley**, John H. Collins, and others, Edison films gained a reputation for stodginess.

Edison's company dominated the **Motion Picture Patents Company** when it was created in early 1909, but this effort to control the US market failed to prevent the growth of independent producers. The company was unable to overcome energetic competition and the advent of **multiple-reel/feature-length films**, and Edison's motion picture fortunes faded during the 1910s. His name disappeared from **screens** in 1918.

See also: electricity

Further reading

Israel, Paul (1998) *Edison: A Life of Invention*, New York: John Wiley.

Musser, Charles (1997) *Edison Motion Pictures, 1890–1900*, Washington/Gemona: Smithsonian Institution Press/Le Giornate del cinema muto.

PAUL SPEHR

editing: early practices and techniques

The **Kinetoscope** and **Cinematograph** were devices designed to produce a series of rigorously continuous images of an event. A careful and meticulous examination of the earliest reels of film, however, reveals that this procedure was quickly transgressed by the first operator-filmmakers, who were led to fragment the images on the film strip at an early date. This in turn put them on the trail of assembling and editing. Because these animated views were brief, the earliest exhibitors often had to assemble a single reel out of a series of separate films (whether similar in nature or not) in order to prepare a program. This led them too towards assembling and editing.

These operators were the first to carry out some form of film editing. At this initial stage the editing was done in-camera while they shot *actualités*. During shooting, they often were obliged to use a stop-camera technique, and in this way they could be said to have manipulated the film strip. Let's say the operator is filming some sort of procession. He starts to film, but after exposing only part of his reel he realizes, with the first group of people having passed his camera and exited the frame, that if he doesn't intervene the picture he is shooting might end on an empty frame. So he stops turning his crank for a moment and waits until the second group of people in the procession is within sight before resuming. Usually this is done without changing the framing. The reel will thus be composed of two spatio-temporal fragments, shot from the same camera angle and presenting a constant perspective. The result is a visible "jump" in the

image, as in **Lumière**'s *Paris: les souverains russes et le président de la République aux Champs-Elysées* [Paris: The Russian Sovereigns and the President of the Republic on the Champs-Elysées] (1896). This kind of resumption (**Gaumont** catalogues employ the term *reprise*, or resumption) is nothing more or less than a form of cutting. It is an *in-vivo* form of cutting, carried out on the site of shooting directly onto the negative before the film is developed.

This practice, which produced a temporal ellipsis in the event being filmed, has only recently been noticed, although it was quite common before the turn of the last century. There are a number of occurrences in Lumière films and an even greater proportion in **Edison** films. Cecil **Hepworth** even advised operators to employ this technique: "however promising the beginning may be, long before the end all interesting incident may have given out. In which case, perhaps the best thing to do is to at once leave off turning, without moving the instrument, and resume turning when suitable incidents recur" (*Animated Photography*, 127–128).

Since the act of stopping the camera and resuming shooting sometimes produced a certain number of defective (fogged) frames on the film strip, some operators did not hesitate to use scissors and glue, or mending devices (available commercially for the repair of broken film), in order to excise such imperfections. In this way they "matched" two fragments, as in Edison's *A Storm at Sea* (1900).

The same stop-camera technique can be found in the work of the first filmmakers of artificially arranged scenes (particularly **trick films**). The stop-camera technique made it possible to make people appear or disappear as if by magic, or to have one person or thing take the place of another. This was done by shooting two consecutive takes on the same strip of film with the same framing. The greatest practitioner of such tricks was Georges **Méliès**, who was meticulous enough to match shots by "cleaning them up" through cutting out frames in order to eliminate the imperfections that could arise in the passage from one shot to another. Such imperfections could result from the fact that the camera did not stop immediately, but only gradually, or from mistakes or slight shifts on the part of actors, as in *L'Impressionniste fin-de-siècle* [An Up-to-Date Conjurer] (1899).

With time these experiments in assembling films and fragments of films led operators and filmmakers, even in these early years, to extend this fragmentation further, to the point of shooting unequivocally pluri-punctual views. These consisted of two or more shots of the same space on the same film strip, but from different camera perspectives—as in G. A. **Smith**'s *As Seen Through a Telescope* (1901)—or of two or more segments of the same action, but taking place in different spaces—as in James **Williamson**'s *Stop Thief!* (1901)—or even,

finally, of two or more distinct episodes of the same story—as in Edison's *Love and War* (1899).

Shots were generally placed back-to-back through straight cuts, but some filmmakers, such as Méliès—as in his *féerie*, *Cendrillon* [Cinderella] (1899)—preferred to use a dissolve. The presence of dissolves so early in film history is not, however, an early use of what would later become a part of classic film language; it was an inheritance, rather, from the **magic lantern** show: lantern operators could move from one glass slide to another by means of a technique known as "dissolving views."

These diverse editing practices, all carried out by film producers, co-existed alongside numerous editing practices by film exhibitors. The latter owned their prints, purchasing rather than renting them, and had no choice, given the brevity of the first moving pictures, but to glue them end to end in order to put together a substantial program. From this assemblage of separate moving pictures to direct intervention within them was but a step, one that was even easier to take because exhibitors were encouraged to do so by the producers themselves. There are numerous invitations to do precisely that in the catalogues of the day. See, for example, this comment found in the Edison catalogue (July 1901) about *The Funeral Arriving at Hyde Park*: "This is a fine film and taken in connection with the other films makes a complete pictorial illustration of the obsequies of Queen Victoria"; or this one from the Lumière catalogue (1901) about *Panorama de Beaulieu à Monaco I, II, et III* [Panorama of Beaulieu in Monaco I, II, and III]: "These last three pictures may be added to one another."

(a)

(b)

Figure 31 35mm nitrate print of *Le chevalier mystère* [The Mysterious Knight] (George Méliès, 1899): (a) A cement splice on the positive copy is visible as a dark line between the frames; (b) A cement splice made on the negative source shows on the positive copy as a pale area near the top of the frame. (Courtesy of George Eastman House.)

See also: archaeology of cinema; cinema of attractions; editing: spatial relations; editing: tableau style; editing: temporal relations; itinerant exhibitors; news event films

Further reading

Bottomore, Stephen (1990) "Shots in the Dark: The Real Origins of Film Editing," in Thomas Elsaesser (ed.) *Early Cinema: Space, Frame, Narrative*, 104–113, London: British Film Institute.

Gaudreault, André (2001) "Fragmentation and Assemblage in the Lumière Animated Pictures," *Film History*, 13.1: 76–88.

Hepworth, Cecil M. (1970 [1900]) *Animated Photography: The ABC of the Cinematograph*, New York: Arno Press.

Musser, Charles (1991) *The Emergence of Cinema: The American Screen to 1907*, New York: Charles Scribner's Sons.

ANDRÉ GAUDREAULT

editing: spatial relations

Through editing filmmakers can build a synthetic space out of several shots or break a space down into partial views. In early cinema the predominance of single-shot films and the early aesthetic of display that marks the **cinema of attraction** placed emphasis more on semi-autonomous views than on creating a larger cohesive space through editing. However, narrative films that traced action over several shots, such as the popular **chase films**, which emerged around 1904, created a growing sense of spatial continuity achieved through editing. Spatial analysis—breaking a single space into several overlapping viewpoints—became common only toward the end of the era around 1913, when practices such as cutting-in to close-ups or reverse-angle cutting became common practice, reflecting a new emphasis on characters and their reactions.

Noel Burch first suggested a threefold schema of possible spatial relations between shots that (with slight modifications) are useful in describing the spatial aspects of editing in early cinema. *Alterity* denotes that the space in one shot is entirely different from the space in the following shot. These two spaces are mutually exclusive, and they are at some distance from each other. *Proximity* indicates that, although two successive shots do not share a common space, they are closely situated, often literally contiguous. *Overlap* indicates that the two successive shots share some common space: they literally overlap.

These somewhat abstract categories can be clarified with specific examples. Alterity consists in a cut from one space to an entirely different and distant space—from one location to another. When Edwin S. **Porter** cuts from the dance hall in *The Great Train Robbery* (1903) to the posse chasing the robbers in a landscape, we have an example of alterity. Proximity is a somewhat flexible concept, since it indicates a "close" relation, something inherently immeasurable. The clearest examples of proximity would be contiguity, such as cuts from one room to an adjacent one, or from inside a building to outside. In proximity, simple actions bridging shots—a look, a shout, or a simple physical action of crossing a threshold—indicate their close spatial relations. Overlap is a much more stable concept. By sharing some common space between successive shots, overlap allows spatial analysis, such as the breakdown of space into separate shots that characterizes the **classical Hollywood** construction of a scene. The clearest example of editing in this category would be the cut-in to a close-up from a long shot of the same scene. The second, closer shot enlarges a detail of the longer view. But while this sort of cut-in may be the most frequent, it remains only one example of overlap. In early cinema, a cut-back to a longer view from a close-up appears almost as frequently. Other possibilities of overlap also exist, such as cutting to a different angle of the space shown in the previous shot.

The types of spatial editing appeared in early cinema history more or less in the order listed. Alterity appeared first in films that often provided a series of separate views of an action or a place. This sort of spatial editing characterizes early multi-shot films such as Georges **Méliès**' *Barbe bleu* [Bluebeard] (1900) or Edison's *Love and War* (1899), all of whose cuts would be examples of alterity. But proximity editing appeared soon after, especially in early fiction films. The cutting between the inside and the outside of the burning house in Porter's *The Life of an American Fireman* (1903) or even the movement from room to room in the factory tour that opens Méliès' *Le Voyage à la lune* [A Trip to the Moon] (1902) could be seen as examples of proximity cutting.

The earliest examples of overlap thematize the act of enlargement. Especially frequent among early British filmmakers, cutting into a closer view seemed to provide a particularly enjoyable visual attraction. G. A. **Smith**'s *Grandma's Reading Glass* (1900) acts out the enlargement by showing a young boy using his grandmother's reading glass to enlarge a watch, a kitten, and his grandmother's eye. Smith's slightly later *The Sick Kitten* (1903) cut-in for a closer view of the kitten without any narrative motivation other than pleasure in seeing the kitten's reaction as it licks the spoon offered it by the boy playing doctor. Likewise, Smith's 1903 *Mary Jane's Mishap* cuts repeatedly to close-ups of Mary Jane's mugging for the camera. In contrast, Méliès generally avoids cutting–in. Barry Salt has speculated that the enlargement of the key to gargantuan dimensions in *Barbe bleu* served as a replacement for a close-up, magically magnifying a narratively important object. Difficulty in integrating closer views into a larger spatial whole is not restricted to continental examples. The famous close-up of the outlaw leader Barnes firing at the camera in Porter's *The Great Train Robbery* remains within an abstracted space not directly related to any other shots of the film. With the increasing emphasis on character-based narratives, overlap editing gradually increased, although it did not become a frequent device for storytelling until around 1912–1913.

The succession of predominant types of spatial relations allows us to sketch a morphology of editing in early cinema. The earliest dominant format for filmmaking seems to avoid editing entirely by restricting most films to a single shot. This reliance on single shots dominated filmmaking from the 1890's and remains common through 1904 or so. These single-shot films present a self-contained view, as in the **Lumière** films of everyday life—*Repas de bébé* [Baby's Breakfast], *Arrivée d'un train à La Ciotat* [Arrival of a Train at Ciotat Station]—or foreign travel—*Défilé de policemen* [Police Parade in Chicago], *Les Pyramides* [The Pyramides and the Sphinx]. André Gaudreault uses the term *unipunctual* to describe these films, indicating they are taken from a single spatial viewpoint. However, his in-depth examination of the early films of Lumière and **Edison** has revealed that even what has been described as "single shot" films often do not lack editing, of a sort. Although taken from a single viewpoint, *actualités* by Lumière, Edison, and other early filmmakers include brief ellipses in which the action seems to jump. These "jumps" were evidence that camera operators would frequently stop turning the crank briefly and then resume filming without changing camera position. Since stopping the camera often caused over-exposed flash frames, a splice could be made in the negative to eliminate them. Thus,

recording an event could be compressed, eliminating dead time, for instance, when filming a procession (therefore, this practice relates more to temporal than spatial articulation).

Thus the earliest stage of film editing could be said to maintain a single simple spatial orientation. The camera was involved in displaying space and the events it contained, rather than articulating, or reconstructing it. Spatial articulation in cinema's earliest era was more commonly achieved by **camera movement** (as in the shots from moving vehicles in **phantom train rides**) than editing. The dominant conception of film in its first few years is of a succession of views, more or less autonomous, although often linked together thematically, either by the manufacturer or by the exhibitor. A certain autonomy of shots marked cinema's first years, and this reflects the predominance of alterity as a spatial relation between shots in multi-shots films. Even within films of several shots, the conception of the film as a series of views, often exhibiting a certain discontinuity, still rules until about 1903 or 1904. This does not mean, of course, that there are no films involving spatial analysis even before 1900, such as Lumière's films of bullfights in Spain, which include views from different spatial positions. However, the succession of semi-independent views, or attractions, loosely linked together either by a theme of some elementary narrative action, predominates. Alterity serves as the obvious spatial equivalent to this conception of a film, including both *actualités* and loosely linked narrative forms, such as Porter's *Uncle Tom's Cabin* (1903), which presents this well known story in a serious of semi-autonomous tableaux.

Although the concept of proximity remains flexible, it takes on a new importance in the general move away from semi-autonomous views or dramatic tableaux and in the new fiction genres that begin to appear around 1904, which favor a greater degree of spatial continuity and continuous action. The enormous popularity of the **chase film**, which begins in 1904, provides the clearest example. Although the exact distance between successive shots may not be specified in a chase film, the continuous action and linear temporality of the action generally indicates a proximate spatial distance between the successive phases shown.

The greater unity of action and time that the chase format brings to narrative cinema after 1904 encourages the development of genres of closer spatial relations.

Another genre, never as popular as the chase film but in some ways pre-dating it, also encouraged spatial proximity or even overlap in editing. This would be the genre of mediated looks that alternates between a viewer and what this viewer sees, usually using some visual device (a telescope, a key hole, a microscope, a magnifying glass, opera glasses, etc.). Cutting between viewer and what that viewer sees, this kind of film conveys the earliest example of the figure of point-of-view cutting. British filmmakers again provide some of the best and earliest examples, such as Smith's *As Seen Through A Telescope* (1900), or the previously mentioned *Grandma's Looking Glass*, but the genre was international and continued through at least 1906, including such films as **Pathé-Frères**'s *Un Coup d'oeil par étage* [Scenes on Every Floor] (1904) and Cecil **Hepworth**'s *Inquisitive Boots* (1905). These films shade into others that make frequent use of proximate intercutting based on point of view editing without a mediating device, as in **Vitagraph**'s *The Boy the Bust and the Bath* (1906), which intercuts between male voyeurs peeping on what they believe to be a beautiful girl bathing (actually a bust placed in the tub by a mischievous boy).

Overlap editing in conjunction with proximity editing is standard practice at Pathé-Frères by 1906–1907. For the most part, overlap still involves cut-in close shots that enlarge a small object of narrative importance, as in Albert **Capellani**'s *Un Drame de Venise* [A Venetian Tragedy] (1906), where a beggar pieces together a torn-up letter that allows him to revenge himself on a pair of illicit lovers. The same film also presents the movement of characters through three contiguous spaces, as when the nobleman's wife leaves her small reading room, enters and crosses the adjacent bedroom to a window, and her lover, in a gondola on the canal outside, returns the kiss she blows at him. Within another year, both forms of spatial editing are joined with parallel editing, based on alterity, in such Pathé films as *A Narrow Escape* (1908), which tracks robbers moving through two pairs of adjacent spaces in and around

a doctor's house, intercuts his journey by car to care for a sick child in a distant house with the robbers' attack, and climaxes with matching cut-in close ups of the doctor and his wife as she telephones him for help.

More complicated forms of overlap cutting make their way into basic narrative technique rather late. Cutting between facial close ups of characters within the same space, for instance, can be found as early as **Essanay**'s *The Loafer* (1911), but they remain relatively uncommon until around 1912–1913, when both Vitagraph and **Biograph** begin to work with multi-shot sequences within a single space, as in Rollin S. Sturgeon's *The Greater Love* (1912) and D. W. **Griffith**'s *The Lady and The*

(a)

(b)

Figure 32 Sequential frame stills of a doctor and his threatened wife in spaces distant from one another but linked by telephone, in Pathé-Frères' *A Narrow Escape* (1908).

Mouse (1913). Although there are European films around this time that also introduce overlapping shots within a single space, there is a tendency in European films (but also in some early American features) to rely more on **staging in depth** within a single shot to emphasize narrative importance.

Thus the period of early cinema moves from a reliance on the single shot, to the stringing together of separate semi-autonomous shots, to the intertwining of shots in closer spatial relations. However, this should not be seen as a linear progression, but as an indication of the shifting role of cinema in the period. Moving from displaying an attraction to following a physical action, to constructing narratives that depended on greater insight into a character's emotions or motivations made these shifts necessary.

See also: editing: early practices and techniques; editing: temporal relations

Further reading

Abel, Richard (1994) *The Ciné Goes to Town: French Cinema, 1896–1914*, Berkeley: University of California Press.

Burch, Noel (1990) *Life to Those Shadows*, Berkeley: University of California Press.

Gaudreault, André (ed.) (1988) *Ce que je vois dans mon ciné*, Paris: Meridiens-Klincksieck.

Gunning, Tom (1990) *D. W. Griffith and the Origins of American Narrative Cinema*, Urbana: University of Illinois Press.

Keil, Charlie (2001) *Early American Cinema in Transition: Story, Style, and Filmmaking, 1907–1913*, Madison: University of Wisconsin Press.

Musser, Charles (1990) *The Emergence of Cinema: The American Screen to 1907*, New York: Scribner's.

Salt, Barry (1983) *Film Style and Technology: History and Analysis*, London: Starword.

Thompson, Kristin (1985) "From Primitive to Classical," in *The Classical Hollywood Cinema: Film Style and Mode of Production to 1960*, 157–173, New York: Columbia University Press.

TOM GUNNING

editing: tableau style

A survey of advertisements for the first programs of moving pictures reveals that each screening was the product of an assemblage of separate pictures. Until 1900 or so, moving pictures were in fact very short (often less than one minute long) and at least a dozen titles were needed to make up an attractive and minimally substantial program. The practice of exhibitors assembling the various components of a screening already constituted, in a sense, a form of editing. Most often, the constitutive elements of these assemblages were juxtaposed in an extremely haphazard way and had no real connection to each other. These assemblages could nevertheless occasionally involve creating a sequence of pictures having the same topic.

Soon, however, manufacturers of moving pictures began to offer for sale pluri-punctual pictures which already were "joined up" and which necessarily were longer in length (even if, around 1900, they rarely were longer than three or four minutes). These films used a series of "tableaux" to illustrate a story whose temporal and narrative scale would normally require an even longer length. The tableaux were placed end to end and thus presented actions unfolding in a somewhat loose manner. The result was moving pictures full of gaps (ellipses, in fact), whose comprehensibility often rested on spectators' prior knowledge of the story. In such films manufacturers thus gravitated to subjects already known, by and large, by the public. The canonical example of this, of course, is **Edison**'s *Uncle Tom's Cabin* (1903), a picture made up of fourteen tableaux. Spectators of the day, in the USA at least, were likely to know the story by heart. In many cases, the understanding of these more complex stories also was furthered by explanations provided by a **lecturer** or the lyrics of a song (two forms of accompaniment which were widespread during this period). Such was the case with Edison's *Love and War* (1899), an **illustrated song** in six tableaux which told the story of a young man returning home after serving in the army.

The presentation of a series of distinct images for narrative purposes was a widespread practice even before the appearance of moving pictures. It was, for example, one of the most common **magic lantern** techniques, in which the projection of images often was accompanied by a verbal commentary or song. The **wax museum** also may have served as a model for the construction of juxtaposed tableaux. Thus a film like **Pathé**'s *Histoire d'un crime* [The Story of a Crime] (1901), in six tableaux, is an adaptation to the screen of a tableaux series of wax figures on display at the time at the Musée Grévin.

As a general rule, the tableaux placed in series to recount the action of the first pluri-punctual films were more or less independent of each other. In fact, each of these pictures was a micro-story showing an autonomous segment of the action. This can readily be seen in the case of the numerous "Passion Plays." An early significant example was the **Lumière** series, *La Vie et la Passion de Jésus-Christ* (1898), composed of thirteen independent tableaux of 17 metres each (nos. 933–945 of the Lumière catalogue). Each of these tableaux was sold separately. This practice of selling series in sections, which persisted until around 1906, left it up to the exhibitor to compose his or her own unique program. Simply put, it allowed the exhibitor to devise his or her own version of the Passion Play "à la carte." The May 1903 Pathé catalogue says this about *The Life and Passion of Christ*: even if "this series comprises 32 pictures," "all these subjects are sold separately, too, but we have formed 2 smaller series of 20 and 12 pictures comprising the most interesting and necessary scenes." The same picture could thus be projected in different "cuts." The tableau aesthetic, which governed the assemblage of pictures at the time, allowed for such versatility, in so far as the autonomy of each scene created a narrative that proceeded by leaps and bounds, relying very little on the interaction between its diverse constituent elements.

At times the question of close communication between tableaux was not even an issue, especially when they were juxtaposed for illustrative rather than narrative purposes. This is the case of films such as AM&B's *The Four Seasons* (1904) and Edison's *The Seven Ages* (1905), two films whose purpose is not to follow the adventures of a character step by step but to illustrate, metaphorically, the various stages of life, from birth (thus the first

tableau in the Edison film is entitled "Infancy") to old age (the two final tableaux are entitled "Second Childhood" and "What Age?") via childhood ("Playmates" and "Schoolmates") and adulthood ("The Lovers," "The Soldier," "The Judge"), with a minimum of continuity between tableaux.

The tableau aesthetic, which was founded on the unity of action, space, and time, began to lose ground once filmmakers stopped assuming that the camera was a passive device for simply recording images and began to use it actively. This change in the camera's role took place in conjunction with a change in acting practices. Actors now came to transgress the centripetal frame of the camera's field of vision by walking out of frame to continue, in another spatial framing, an action they had begun in the earlier spatial framing. It was this truly centrifugal tendency that led filmmakers to represent a continuous action across several different tableaux, giving rise, most notably, to what would become so important for the development of editing, the **chase film**, which proliferated between 1904 and 1907.

Once the camera was set in motion, shots tended to become shorter and show only a fragment of a scene. This is the case in Georges **Méliès**' *Voyage dans la lune* [A Trip to the Moon] (1902), which is composed in large part of a series of relatively autonomous tableaux but which also contains a "sequence," that of the rocket's return to earth, in which four shots succeed each other in less than twenty seconds.

See also: cinema of attractions; editing: early practices and techniques; *féeries* or fairy plays

Further reading

Gaudreault, André (1984) "Temporality and Narrativity in Early Cinema, 1895–1908," in John L. Fell (ed.) *Film Before Griffith*, 311–329, Berkeley: University of California Press.

Gaudreault, André (1987) "Theatricality, Narrativity, and 'Trickality': Re-evaluating the Cinema of Georges Méliès," *Journal of Popular Film and Television*, 15.3: 110–119.

Gunning, Tom (1984) "Non-Continuity, Continuity, Discontinuity: A Theory of Genres in Early Films," *IRIS*, 21: 101–112.

ANDRÉ GAUDREAULT

editing: temporal relations

A close examination of early cinema reveals that editing takes the major role in temporal articulation. However, temporal articulations can appear even within a single shot (through time-lapse photography) or a single framing (camera stoppage). Early cinema also shows examples of a rather rare form of temporal articulation, temporal overlap, in which two views of simultaneous action are shown successively. For the most part, early narrative films use editing to create temporal ellipses, allowing narrative compression. These ellipses become shorter after 1904 and often move towards the creation of seemingly continuous time over cuts. The rise of parallel editing from 1906 to 1909 shows a new interest in specifying temporal relations, indicating not only simultaneity but also frequently moving towards a narrative deadline. For the most part temporality in early film narratives is linear and progressive, but flashbacks do play a role, especially by 1913–1914.

From a common sense point of view, a single shot not only records an action but also the time it takes to unfold. Whereas this may be true of *actualité* filmmaking, in fiction films the camera may record the "real time" of the action, but the time depicted could be indicated through other markers. For instance, in **American Mutoscope and Biograph**'s *Five Minutes to Train Time* (1902), the quickly moving hands of a clock and the hurried actions of the characters indicate time has been speeded up. Temporality can also be transformed within a single shot by adjusting the camera speed, as in fast motion or time-lapse photography. AM&B *Star Theater* (1902), for instance, portrays in minutes the destruction of a theater in Brooklyn, which took weeks to accomplish. The same company's *Down the Hudson* (1903) uses undercranking and time lapse to compress a river voyage lasting some hours into minutes. Effects of compressed or speeded-up motion also are found in early *actualités* that showed the growth of plants, which appeared as early as 1898 in Oskar **Messter**'s *Blumen Arrangement*, and in others by **Urban**, **Pathé-Frères**, and **Gaumont** between 1910 and 1912. Undercranking is used for comic effect in early **comedies** such as Biograph's *Mr. Hurry-up of New York* (1907), **Vitagraph**'s *Liquid Electricity* (1907), and Gaumont's *Onésime horlanger* (1912). Early farces are frequently undercranked a bit for the comic effect of unnatural motion— a device that is exaggerated and parodied in Vitagraph's delightful *Goodness Gracious* (1914). Reverse motion (achieved by positioning the camera upside down while filming and then inverting the film in printing) offered another temporal gag, particularly that of people leaping out of water in films such as Pathé's *D'ou vient-il?* [Whence Does He Come?] (1905). Such effects could also be achieved during projection by speeding up or reversing a normally shot film; during the **cinema of attractions** era, **projectionists** frequently amused audiences with such tricks.

Perhaps the earliest (and most elemental) form of temporal articulation involves stopping the camera for a period and then resuming cranking. This basic device remained unnoticed, or at least unanalyzed, until André Gaudreault and his researchers recently investigated it systematically. Careful examination of **Lumière** negatives and **Edison** paper prints reveal that operators frequently stopped the camera while filming an event and then resumed filming after a short period. This allowed them to cover long-lasting events (such as processions), compressing their screen time by eliminating the dead time between exciting moments. Technically, this may not be a form of editing (although indubitably a temporal articulation), since it occurs in camera and not through splicing (the practice by later filmmakers is sometimes called "in-camera editing"). Yet examination of negatives and paper prints often reveals splice marks at these points, indicating that the ellipsis was further refined through splicing (perhaps to eliminate the flash frames of overexposed film which occurred when the camera stopped cranking).

Similar splicing within a single spatial framing occurs in **trick films** and has been referred to as a "substitution splice." Here again, the splice is often used to refine footage achieved by stopping the camera; but in this case, rather than compressing time, the shot gives the impression of instantaneous transformation. The process eliminates production time (spent in rearranging actors or substituting objects so that they seem to magically appear or transform on the screen). Therefore, while manipulating real time, this editing does not really articulate temporal relations. Such substitution splicing occurs very early in Edison's *Execution of Mary Stuart* (1895) and forms the principal devices of Méliès and Pathé's trick films.

Until about 1904, single-shot films dominated film production, severely limiting temporal articulations. However, as soon as films included more than one shot, temporal relations between them were implied. Multiple-shot films of the 1890's, such as Edison's *Love and War* or Pathé's *Passion Play* presented separate scenes in each shot and therefore each cut represented a considerable temporal ellipsis. In Edison's film, the cut from the battlefield in which the soldier is wounded to the soldier recovering in hospital may represent an ellipsis of hours or a few days, while in Pathé's film the ellipsis could cover decades, such as cutting from Joseph and Mary's flight to Egypt to Jesus as a grown man chasing money changers from the temple. Marked ellipses thus characterize early narrative films, which tend to be constructed of semi-autonomous tableaux. This is equally true of early *actualités* that consist of several shots, but these often show a relatively unmarked temporality (the temporal relation between one view of Niagara Falls and another is not really indicated), creating an atemporal mode of description.

However, when a narrative film covered an action stretching over several shots, ellipses could become shorter, or even disappear. The **chase film**, with its continuous mobile action over multiple shots encouraged shorter ellipses. Shots involving movement through extremely close or contiguous spaces could even promote the illusion of time continuing over a cut without any gap. AM&B earliest chase film, *The Escaped Lunatic* (1904), gives an example of this as the maniac's action of throwing a guard off a bridge is carefully matched over two shots with no noticeable ellipse—the cut is replicated in Edison's close copy, *The Maniac Chase* (also 1904). Such match-cutting would become a staple of the continuity attained by the later **classical Hollywood** cinema, giving the sense of a seamless blending of shots portraying continuous action. Cutting with small ellipses and some impression of continuous action becomes fairly common internationally after 1904, including films such as Pathé's *Dix Femmes pour un mari* [Ten Women for One Husband] (1905), Gaumont's *Le Coup de vent* [A Gust of Wind] (1906), or **Hepworth**'s *Rescued by Rover* (1905). Yet cuts on action in which time continues without interruption remain rare, usually found in cut-ins to closer views.

Stretching an action over two shots, each from a somewhat different spatial view point, however, sometimes ran counter to later rules of temporal continuity and early cinema's predominant temporal linearity. Films such as Méliès's *Le Voyage à la lune* [A Trip to the Moon] (1902), AM&B *The Discordant Note* (1903), and Edison's *Life of an American Fireman* (1903) display a temporal overlap between shots. In these films we watch an action from one viewpoint (such as the interior of a house) then see the same action again from another (such as the exterior of a house). Thus, in *A Discordant Note* we see a man throw an irritating singer out of a parlor through a window. Then, in the following shot, we see an exterior view of the window, which breaks a second time as the songster comes hurdling through. Although on the story level the man has only been thrown out once, we see it twice, as if time stuttered and repeated itself. While certain historians proclaim this as an awkward moment of "primitive cinema," one should emphasize that continuity editing following strict linear temporality was not yet fully canonized, and temporal overlap was a possible alternative. Charles Musser has related this practice to **magic lantern** narrative, which, dealing with still images, would not encounter the temporal contradiction that moving images introduced. In addition, due to the long dominance of single-shot films, shots retained a certain autonomy; therefore, presenting an action completely in each shot might seem more natural than fragmenting it over several shots. With the emphasis on display entailed by the cinema of attractions, presenting a dramatic action twice might be seen as doubling the visual pleasure. Thus in *Le Voyage à la lune* we see the rocket landing on the moon twice, once as it hits the moon-face in the eye, then in the following shot from the perspective of the moon's surface. Such temporal repetition should not be viewed as an avant-garde practice, as it was when Eisenstein employed temporal overlap in the bridge-raising sequence of *October* (1927), years after the rules of continuity editing had been established.

Until around 1906, ellipses comprised the primary temporal relations found in editing, with occasional cuts matching action to give the impression of continuity, while other cuts occasionally created the impression of repeated action and temporal overlap. Around 1906–1907, the strong use of intermediate spaces in Pathé films (e.g., exits from doorways, movement through stairwells) increased the use of continuous time over cuts. Around the same time the figure of parallel editing appeared in **comedies** and thrillers released by Pathé, from *Chiens contrebandiers* [Dog Smugglers] (1906) to *The Physician of the Castle* (1908). This technique was systematically explored and exploited in the films D. W. **Griffith** then produced for **Biograph** from 1908 through 1913. Parallel editing consists of specific temporal and spatial relations between shots. Spatially these actions take place in separate (often distant) locations. Temporally we are made to understand that each thread of action is occurring simultaneously. Further, this form of editing displays a pattern of alternation (ABABABA), with shots alternating between two sets of actions. The situation in which Griffith most dramatically exploited this figure was the "last minute rescue" (although parallel editing served as a basic narrative structure in many of his films), in which suspense is generated through cuts from a victim in danger to rescuers making their way towards the site of peril. The converging lines of action, combined with very specific temporal relations between shots, signaled a new emphasis on temporality in narrative films of this period. Compared to early narrative films which consisted of loosely-linked tableaux, films making strong use of parallel editing—such as Griffith's *The Lonely Villa*

(1909)—made time a key issue in their plots, creating narrative deadlines and suspense.

Flashbacks are often considered an essential part of temporal relations in cinema. Curiously, up until around 1914, flashbacks appear fairly infrequently, but when they do sometimes dominate a film, providing its basic narrative structure. Flashbacks, for instance, appear in only one film, *The House of Darkness* (1913), among the hundreds Griffith directed for Biograph. However, films that consist almost entirely of flashbacks do appear from 1907 through 1912, and generally are organized around either a famous historical figure or an object. Vitagraph's *Napoleon Man of Destiny* (1909) provides an example of the first form, in which the key events of Napoleon's life are portrayed as flashbacks. It is not always necessary for these flashbacks to appear through editing; occasionally the events appear through double exposure or superimposition within the image. Derived undoubtedly from theatrical vision scenes and popular illustrations in which memories appear within the space surrounding a character, this form of flashback appears in Edwin S. **Porter**'s *Fireside Reminiscences* (1908), in which visions of a previously happy marriage appear superimposed within the fireplace as a husband muses before it. Many of the object-based flashback films survive only through their catalogue description, so it is difficult to tell exactly how they were managed. Biograph's *The Music Master* (1908), for instance, consists of a musician's memories evoked by his old violin. This format, which continued through at least 1913 with **Thanhouser**'s *Just a Shabby Doll*, usually consisted of characters recalling the course of their life. But after 1911, Charlie Keil locates a number of more punctual uses of flashbacks to supply a bit of important information, such as in **Selig**'s *One Hundred Years After* (1911) or Bison-101's *Blazing the Trail* (1912). Following the increased focus on character in narrative films, such brief flashbacks often explained a character's motivation. However, as Keil writes, flashbacks are not always primarily tied to character memory but sometimes indicate a narrative strategy revealing important information previously withheld.

See also: editing: spatial relations; editing: tableau style

Further reading

Abel, Richard (1994) *The Cine Goes to Town: French Cinema, 1896–1914*, Berkeley: University of California Press.

Burch, Noel (1990) *Life to Those Shadows*, Berkeley: University of California Press.

Gaudreault, André (2001) "Fragmentation and Assemblage in the Lumière Animated Pictures," *Film History*, 13.1: 76–88.

Jay, Ricky (2001) *Jay's Journal of Anomalies*, New York: Farrar Straus and Giroux.

Keil, Charlie (2001) *Early American Cinema in Transition*, Madison: University of Wisconsin Press.

Musser, Charles (1990) *Before the Nickelodeon: Edwin S. Porter and the Edison Manufacturing Company*, Berkeley: University of California Press.

Thompson, Kristin (1985) "The Continuity System," in David Bordwell, Janet Staiger, and Kristin Thompson, *The Classical Hollywood Cinema: Film Style and Mode of Production to 1960*, 194–213, London: Routledge & Kegan Paul.

TOM GUNNING

education

"Although animated photography is regarded popularly as an amusement, and the palace cinema is maintained to be the poor man's theatre, efforts are being made to lift the invention into a higher and more useful plane." F. A. Talbot's words, in his *Practical Cinematography* (1913), express what many felt on looking at how the motion picture medium had evolved: that it was missing its vocation. The notion that motion pictures could and should educate sometimes was mixed with not a little disdain for the popular tastes of the average cinema **audience**. Primarily, however, it was thought that, because moving pictures were such as great attraction to children, they could be used to occupy their minds with better things: so attractive a medium ought to be able to impart lessons to otherwise inattentive young minds.

Education in early cinema could be defined rather broadly. For some, it meant films of an informative character seen by the general public in commercial cinemas; for many, it meant films specifically designed for pedagogical use with children;

for others, it meant highly specialized **scientific** and medical films which could present evidence or demonstrate processes. As an extension of the **magic lantern** used as an instructional guide, film even was seen to have a missionary quality. The problem, however, was that increasingly the only place to see a film was in a commercial cinema, where it had to conform to the demands of entertainment. A number of manufacturers denied that any such problem existed, and declared that their *actualités*, **travelogues**, and scientific films were self-evidently educational, and the equal of fiction films in entertainment value.

Such altruism combined with hopes of an untapped market in the early projection service of the Catholic publisher, **Maison de la Bonne Presse**, in France, in the educational film catalogues of George **Kleine** in the USA (first published in 1910), and in the scientific series produced in France by **Pathé-Frères**, **Gaumont**, **Éclair**, and **Eclipse** in the early 1910s. In Great Britain, Charles **Urban** expressed the matter clearly with his slogan, "to amuse and entertain is good; to do both and instruct is better." Urban stressed the educational value of his films from 1903 onwards, publishing one of the earliest catalogues of educational films in 1909, and putting on "Urbanora" shows that espoused both educational and entertainment values. However, he recognized that for film to educate it had to be taken out of the **music halls** and cinemas. In 1907, he published *The Cinematograph in Science, Education and Matters of State*, a rallying cry to schools, hospitals, government agencies, and the military to take moving pictures to any institutions where a public waiting to learn could be found.

The cause of the educational film was given particular impetus by Thomas **Edison**. He made a number of pronouncements claiming that the motion picture would supplant the written word as a means of educating, among them this one from 1913: "Books will soon be obsolete in the schools. Scholars will soon be instructed through the eye. It is possible to teach every branch of human knowledge with the motion picture. Our school system will be completely changed in ten years." This statement became notorious when a number of teachers took him at his word, while others feared that film projectors might supplant them altogether. Moreover, by 1912, the **Edison Company** and its French competitor, Pathé, had introduced apparatuses for **amateur** filmmaking and projection—the **Edison Home Kinetoscope**, using 22 mm safety film, and the **Pathé Kok projector**, using 28 mm safety film—both of which also could be used in schools. But the equipment remained too expensive, the non-flammable film stock was not always reliable, and the range of films available simply did not match educational needs. Joseph **Joye**, the Swiss priest who amassed a collection of over a thousand films from commercial sources (1902–1914) for teaching children and adults, was an extraordinary exception.

Few in the pre-**World War I** era grasped the real demands of using films for education. For films to flourish in schools required a proper theoretical understanding of the pedagogical issues involved, and the availability of suitable films and equipment. It was a new enterprise, not an extension of that which already existed. Underpinning theories began to emerge in the USA during the 1910s, centered particularly at the University of Chicago, the home of not only Kleine but also John Dewey, a leading exponent of the "New Education," which rejected learning by rote and advocated a broader concept of learning through "activity," leading to "growth." Chicago was at the forefront of thinking in American education, and it was there that the "visual education" movement took root. Visual education shifted the issue from the materials available to the pedagogic need. In a key study done at the university (1922–1924), Frank N. Freeman looked beyond the insistent propaganda of the film manufacturers and applied a scientific method to determine what kinds of films, and under what circumstances, had pedagogical value. Moving pictures and other visual media were recognized as a unique stimulus to the imagination, but as visual aids, not substitutes. The teacher remained necessary after all.

At the same time as a theoretical understanding emerged, libraries of more suitable films became available to a growing non-theatrical market, stimulated by the introduction of safety film stock in gauges narrower than 35 mm. The development of 16 mm film stock by **Eastman Kodak Company** (1923) effectively established a new form of cinema, one not based on the imperatives of theatrical exhibition but directed at specific audiences that wanted or needed to learn. Although the educational film was a firm aspiration of some early cinema pioneers, it was slow in coming to full realization.

Further reading

Freeman, Frank N. (ed.) (1924) *Visual Education: A Comparative Study of Motion Pictures and Other Methods of Instruction*, Chicago: University of Chicago Press.

Krows, Arthur Edwin (1938–1944) "Motion Pictures—Not for Theaters," *Education Screen* (September 1938–June 1944).

Talbot, F. A. (1913) *Practical Cinematography and its Applications*, London: William Heinemann.

Urban, Charles (1907) *The Cinematograph in Science, Education and Matters of State*, London: Charles Urban Trading Company.

LUKE McKERNAN

Egypt and other Arab countries

Until the early 1920s in the Arab world, cinema existed primarily in Egypt and Palestine, *al-Sham* (that is, Syria and Lebanon), and the *Maghrib* [Maghreb], notably Tunisia, Algeria, and Morocco. What that meant, however, was the exhibition of moving pictures, for production was carried out either by foreign companies or foreign residents. Moreover, Egypt was the only Arab country in which this activity led to the development of a native industry during colonial times, firmly established after the foundation of the Studio Misr in 1934.

Exhibition began almost as early as in Europe. In November 1896, the **Cinématographe Lumière** projected films in Egypt to an exclusive audience, first in the Tousson stock exchange in Alexandria and then in the Hamam Schneider (Schneider Bath) in Cairo. Lumière projections also took place later that year in Algiers and Oran. In 1897, Albert Shamama, also known as Shemama Chickly, organized a similar event in Tunis; that same year Lumière films were projected at the Royal Palace in

Fez, Morocco. By 1900, Cinématographe programs were featured at the Europa Hotel in Jerusalem.

In 1897, a Cinématographe Lumière (theater) began to offer regular screenings in Alexandria. The construction of other permanent cinemas soon followed. In 1906, the French company **Pathé-Frères** opened a moving picture theater in Cairo, which joined three other cinemas then running in the capital and in Alexandria. In both cities, it became common to present moving pictures along with theater performances. By 1911, there were eleven moving picture theaters operating in several Egyptian cities; ten years later the number had increased to approximately fifty.

In Tunisia, the Omnia Pathé was inaugurated in 1907. One year later, Egyptian Jews opened a cinema in Jerusalem called the Oracle. In Oran and several other Algerian cities with a high concentration of Europeans, the first permanent cinemas opened in 1908. Although few Arab Algerians went to the movies, in Egypt, by 1912, cinemas were offering European films with the titles and **intertitles** translated into Arabic and usually projected on a smaller, adjacent screen. This helped to open up viewing to the poorer and less educated urban population. Syria provided a sharp contrast: the first screening, in Aleppo, did not take place until 1908 and a permanent cinema was not established until 1914.

Before the 1920s, the films distributed in Egypt were French, Italian, Danish, or German. American agents did not gain a foothold until 1925. At first, state censorship was absent; in 1911, however, the Cairo government charged police chiefs to strictly control whatever was screened in the movie theaters. In 1918, the first case of direct censorship occurred, prohibiting *al-Azhar al-mumita* (Mortal Flowers) for religious reasons. Eventually, in 1921, the General Security Department of the Ministry of Interior was charged with certifying imports before they could be released for exhibition.

As elsewhere in the European colonies, film production in the Arab world was initiated by foreign travelers, starting with Lumière cameramen. **Promio** shot the first film in Egypt, *Place des consuls à Alexandrie*, in 1897. Some years later, the French-Algerian (*pied-noir*) Felix **Mesguich** shot several short films in Algeria for Lumière, after which he seems to have traveled to Egypt to record

its monuments and returned to witness the French invasion of Morocco. In 1916, Pathé established **newsreel** production offices in Tunis, Algiers, and Casablanca.

The first "native" Egyptian **actualité**, *Ziyarat al-khidiwi li-masjid al-Mursi Abu al-'Abbas bi-l-Iskandariyya* (*The Khedive's Visit to the Mursi Abu al-'Abbas Mosque in Alexandria*), was shot in 1907 by two established photographers, 'Aziz Bandarli and Umberto Malfasi (alias Dorès), the proprietors of a studio in Alexandria. For the next decade, they not only continued to produce *actualités* but imported European films to be accompanied by phonographs at their "Cinémaphon" theater. Soon others joined in producing **news event films** of strong national interest, such as the funeral of the Egyptian leader and patriot, Mustafa Kamil, in 1909.

The first "native" short fiction films appeared in Egypt during and shortly after **World War I**. In 1917, with the financial backing of the Banca di Roma, Dorès established the SITCIA company in Alexandria and co-directed *Nahw al-hawiya* [Towards the Abyss]. In view of wartime restrictions, SITCIA intended to take advantage of a more open native market as well as local weather conditions. Yet, after the construction of a studio and the production of three short subjects, the company went bankrupt, due to the poor quality of the films and the producer's lack of cultural sensitivity. Its last production, *Mortal Flowers* (1918) was banned by the authorities because it showed Arabic Qur'anic verses upside down.

In 1918, SITCIA had already presented "native" performers. The actor-turned-director, Muhammad Karim, starred in its two last productions. Karim later trained in Germany and returned to become one of the most important filmmakers of the 1930s and the first director of today's public Higher Film Institute. However, it was the stars of theater who helped to establish local fiction films. Fawzi Gaz'irli and his troupe, for instance, starred in Léonardo La Ricci's *Madame Loretta* (1919), shot by Alvise Orfanelli, who had worked for SITCIA as a technical assistant. One year later, Amin Sidqi and the very popular comedian 'Ali al-Kassar performed in Bonvelli's short theater adaptation, *Al-Khala Al-Amirikaniyya* (The American Aunt). By 1922, Egypt was producing at least one fiction film a year, most of which—like

La Ricci's *Khatim Sulayman* [Sulayman's Ring], also shot by Orfanelli—addressed Egyptian audiences whose preferences were largely shaped by the flourishing popular comic and musical theater.

The most important person associated with the cinema of these years was Muhammad Bayyumi, who had traveled to Europe in search of training and equipment. In 1923, he shot the first Egyptian feature-length fiction film, Victor Rosito's *Fi Bilad Tut ʿAnkh Amun* [In the County of Tutankhamon], and founded his own newsreel, *Jaridat Amun*; later he directed several short fiction films and established a short-lived film school. Bayyumi also cooperated with Talʿat Harb's Sharikat Misr li-l-Sinima wa-l-Tamthil (Misr Company for Cinema and Performance), first established in 1925, which became the precursor of the Studio Misr.

Elsewhere in the region "native" production was decisively delayed except for Tunisia, where Shamama Chickly made the first short film, *Zuhra*, in 1922. Two years later, he directed one of the first Arab feature-length fiction films, *ʿAin Al-Ghazal*

[The Girl From Carthage]. Syria and Lebanon, however, had to wait until the late 1920s; Iraq, Palestine, Morocco and Algeria were delayed until the 1950s and 1960s, largely due to the political, social, and economic conditions generated by European **colonialism**.

See also: audiences: surveys and debates; law and the cinema; theater, legitimate

Further reading

Farid, S. (ed.) (1992) *Tarikh al-sinima al-ʿarabiyya al-samita, al-Ittihad al-ʿam li-l-fananin al-ʿarab*, Cairo: mihrajan al-Qahira al-sinima'i.

Leaman, O. (ed.) (2001) *Companion Encyclopaedia of Middle Eastern and North African Film*, London: Routledge.

Shafik, V. (1998) *Arab Cinema: History and Cultural Identity*, Cairo: AUC-Press.

Wassef, M. (ed.) (1995) *Egypte: 100 ans de cinéma*, Paris: Institut du Monde Arabe/Editions Plume.

VIOLA SHAFIK

Figure 33 Theatre des fleurs program, Beirut, Syria, c. 1911. From *Moving Picture World*, 1912.

electricity

The most important period of electricity's development, application and diffusion throughout the spheres of industry, domesticity, and commercialized leisure took place between 1880 and 1930, and thereby roughly coincided with that of silent cinema. The hallmarks of modernity—the annihilation of space and time, the disembodiment of **communication**, the acceleration of production, the mechanization of **leisure** and consumption, the rapid circulation of bodies and commodities, and the rise of the mass spectacle—are unthinkable without electricity.

An invisible force sensible only through touch, electricity was known and experienced primarily though its effects—light, heat, and motive force—and hence by whatever (signifying) machine completed its circuit. Between 1880 and 1900, electricity remained a public, urban phenomenon, and was easily incorporated into—and indeed accelerated the development and spread of—the burgeoning culture of commercialized leisure, commodity culture, and mechanized forms of production. Initially, electricity found its greatest audience at **world's fairs** and expositions, which featured popular displays of new electric technologies and spectacular nighttime light spectacles. These massive illumination displays served the multiple functions of creating crowd-pleasing attractions that doubled as advertisements for electric lighting, all the while demonstrating industrial capitalism's ability to manufacture the illusion of a "bright" future based on notions of technological progress. Notable displays included: the 1882 International Exhibition (London), which included a blinking sign that spelled out the name, "Edison"; the 1889 Exposition Universelle in Paris; the 1893 World Columbian Exposition (Chicago), which featured a dramatic illumination of the "White City" by arc lights; and the 1901 Pan-American Exposition's "City of Living Light" (Buffalo), which offered a nighttime illumination of 350,000 incandescent lights. The latter was designed by Edison employee, Luther Stieringer, and was filmed for **Edison Manufacturing** by Edwin S. **Porter**, who claimed that his films, *Panorama of Esplanade by Night* (1901) and *Pan-American Exposition by Night* (1901), were the first successfully shot at night using incandescent lighting. The relation between electricity displays at world's fairs and moving pictures was extended to exhibition in Paris in 1911 when **Gaumont** opened the Electric Palace cinema, modeled after the 1900 Paris Exposition's Palace of Electricity.

As well as providing a medium for the display of electric light, moving pictures also represented electricity's lethal power over the body. Following the assassination of President William F. McKinley at the Pan-American Exposition by Leon Czolgosz, Porter made the **re-enactment** film, *Execution of Czolgosz with Panorama of Auburn Prison* (1901), which represented the death of the assassin in a relatively new penal technology, the electric chair. In 1903, Edison produced *Electrocuting an Elephant* (1903), which showed the death of Luna Park's elephant, Topsy, by an electrocution device designed by the company itself. Later **Vitagraph** films such as *Liquid Electricity; or, The Inventor's Galvanic Fluid* (1907) and *Galvanic Fluid; or, More Fun with Liquid Electricity* (1908) traded upon early 20th-century notions of electricity as a life-giving force that animated the body (inspired, no doubt,

by Luigi Galvani's 1786 experiments in which he made a dead frog's leg move through the application of an electric current).

Electric illumination via the arc light first replaced gas lighting in theaters, on busy city streets, and in the workplace. Electric arc lighting was first used in the Paris Opera House in 1836, and was adopted in major urban centers in the USA and Europe to illuminate **department store** windows (Wanamakers installed lights in its Philadelphia store in 1878). Russian engineer Paul Jablochkov lit Paris boulevards with arc lights in 1867, sparking a drive to illuminate busy urban thoroughfares in the 1870s and 1880s (most famously on Broadway in New York City, where the dramatic urban nightscape was popularly called the "Great White Way"). When used indoors, electric illumination did not give off smoke or odor, or consume oxygen, and greatly reduced the risk of fire associated with gas lighting. Out of doors, it was impervious to bad weather and could be turned on with the flick of a switch, eliminating the need for lamplighters.

Unlike the arc lighting that it eventually replaced, incandescent light (invented by Thomas **Edison** in 1879) did not flicker or generate significant heat, and its even, bright illumination made work at night possible, thereby making possible the extension of the workday. As the Edison direct current system then was replaced by Westinghouse's alternating current system (invented and patented by the Croatian immigrant, Nikola Tesla, in 1888), the efficient transport of electricity across greater distances became feasible, allowing factories to be built farther from generating stations. The electrification of the factory also rationalized its organization into patterns of sequential production, making the assembly line possible. The electric landscape of a Westinghouse factory was the subject of a series of popular films made by **American Mutoscope and Biograph** in 1904. Films such as *Coil Winding Machines* and *Assembling and Testing Turbines* rather self-reflexively display the manufacture of electric machinery by electric machinery.

Electric modes of **transportation** helped mobilize workers and crowds to and through the electrified urban landscape. The electric streetcar, in particular, expanded the boundaries of the city, created commuter suburbs, integrated outlying rural areas and small towns into the economies of nearby cities, and generated new forms of mechanized leisure, particularly **amusement parks**, which were built at the ends of streetcar lines to generate traffic, and whose rides were modeled after streetcar technology. The electric streetcar influenced the location of **nickelodeons** and larger moving picture theaters in towns and cities, as venues for commercialized leisure tended to cluster around streetcar lines, especially stations for intersecting lines.

Electrification penetrated domestic space after 1910, first through incandescent lighting, then through electric companies' secondary yet profitable market of household appliances. As film historians have noted, domestic forms of electronic communication, such as the telephone, were used to create a sense of simultaneous action taking place in different spaces, as in **Pathé-Frères'** *A Narrow Escape* (1908) or **Biograph**'s *The Lonely Villa* (1909). Buster Keaton would lampoon the perils and pleasures of the electrified modern home in *The Electric House* (1924).

Further reading

Marvin, Caroline (1988) *When Old Technologies Were New: Thinking About Communications in the Late Nineteenth Century*, Oxford: Oxford University Press.

Nye, David (1990) *Electrifying America: Social Meanings of a New Technology, 1880–1940*, Cambridge, MA: MIT Press.

Platt, Harold (1991) *The Electric City: Energy and the Growth of the Chicago Area, 1880–1930*, Chicago: University of Chicago Press.

Schivelbusch, Wolfgang (1995) *Disenchanted Night: The Industrialization of Light in the Nineteenth Century*, Berkeley: University of California Press.

KRISTEN WHISSEL

Elfelt, Peter [Lars Peter Petersen]

b. 1866; d. 1931

photographer, filmmaker, exhibitor, Denmark

Lars Peter Petersen took the name Elfelt in 1901, when he had established himself as Denmark's most distinguished still photographer (he was named the Royal Court Photographer in 1900). From 1896 to 1907, he shot more than 100 short films. They were, with very few exceptions, scenic views and *actualités*, often showing public events such as fairs or parades, with Royal participation whenever possible. He also recorded performances by famous actors and ballet dancers. In the years before 1905, Elfelt showed his films as an **itinerant exhibitor**; in 1906, he opened his own moving picture theater in Copenhagen.

CASPAR TYBJERG

English pattern cameras

Several British manufacturers built cameras around two wooden 400-foot film magazines placed one above the other inside a wooden case, giving the apparatus a distinctive tall and thin appearance. Such English pattern cameras were made by John Arthur Prestwich, Alfred **Darling**, James **Williamson**, and Urban & Moy from about 1898. The design's advantage was a well-balanced, manoeuvrable camera with doubled light security for the quickly interchangeable film magazines. The form was gradually abandoned as additional accessories and lens turrets showed the advantage of a more cubic design with side-by-side or exterior film magazines.

DEAC ROSSELL

Ernemann Imperator projector

Founded in 1889 by the textile salesman Heinrich Ernemann, the Ernemann firm began making film apparatuses in 1903; although it merged with three other companies in 1926 to form Zeiss Ikon AG, the Ernemann brand was maintained through the 1980s. Introduced in 1909, the Imperator was an early all-steel (instead of iron) construction that continued to be manufactured until 1933. Some 15,000 were produced during that time, with 22 of 28 major cinemas in Paris in 1913 using the Dresden-made apparatus. Fully enclosed after

1914, the Imperator had a Maltese Cross (Geneva) **intermittent** sealed in an oil bath, front disk shutter, and centrifugal fire shutter.

DEAC ROSSELL

Esoofally, Abdulally

b. 1884; d. 1957

exhibitor, India

A pioneer of film exhibition in India along with F. B. Thanawalla and J. F. **Madan**, Esoofally started as an **itinerant exhibitor** in South East Asia; after 1908, he toured all over India with a fifty-by-hundred-foot tent that accommodated 1,000 spectators. His repertoire consisted of *actualités* such as the 1911 Durbar films and some of the earliest story films. In 1914, he set up permanent theaters in Bombay in partnership with Ardeshir Irani and eventually helped the latter run the Imperial Film Company that produced India's first talkie, *Alam Ara*, in 1931.

SURESH CHABRIA

Essanay Film Manufacturing Company

The Chicago-based Essanay Film Manufacturing Company was the result of a nervous alliance between a businessman, exchangeman George K. **Spoor**, and a popular artistic sensibility, G. M. "Broncho Billy" **Anderson**. Established in 1907, Essanay (the name derived from the initials of the partners, S & A) was a relatively weak firm and nearly collapsed when it was decided to exclude the company from **Edison**'s association of licensed film producers if **Biograph** elected to join. Biograph opted out, and Essanay received its license and retained its status when the **Motion Picture Patents Company** was formed in late 1908. Among Essanay's early players in its Chicago studio were J. Warren Kerrigan and Ben **Turpin**. Future director Allan **Dwan** joined the company in 1909 as an electrician and soon became Essanay's scenario editor. G. M. Anderson had long advocated making **western** films in real western locations, and he spent most of his time on the road in the west, making pictures in Colorado and various other locations. In 1909 he made *Broncho Billy and the Baby*, based on a story by western writer Peter B. Kyne, but it was only one of many varied western films.

In 1910, Essanay was severely crippled when a new independent rival, the **American Film Manufacturing Company**, raided virtually all of the Chicago studio's talent and technical employees. Rebuilding its staff, Essanay's roster of stars would eventually include Francis X. **Bushman**, Beverly Bayne, Ruth Stonehouse, Henry B. **Walthall**, and Bryant Washburn among others. Anderson eventually settled in Niles, California, near San Francisco, and built a permanent studio. His unit specialized in westerns, especially the *Broncho Billy* series that began regular production in 1911 (and in which Anderson himself starred) as well as the popular *Snakeville* **comic series** starring Augustus Carney as Alkali Ike, Margaret Joslin as Sophie Klutz, Harry Todd as Mustang Pete, and Victor Potel as Slippery Slim. In 1915, Anderson hired Charlie **Chaplin** away from the **Keystone Film Company**, and in the year Chaplin worked for Essanay he turned out fifteen one and two-reel comedies, including what is arguably his first classic, *The Tramp* (1916). Although Spoor was appalled at the $1,250 a week salary paid to Chaplin, he would reap a fortune from the Chaplin films.

While Anderson continued to turn out short films for the **General Film** program, Spoor launched a feature film program at the Chicago studio releasing through V-L-S-E (**Vitagraph-Lubin-Selig**-Essanay) and later K.E.S.E. (Kleine-Edison-Selig-Essanay) programs of George **Kleine** and General Film. Essanay features such as *Graustark* (1915) and *The Prince of Graustark* (1916) were well produced but lacked star power after the romantic team of Bushman and Bayne left to join Metro in 1915. Becoming increasingly disenchanted with Anderson's heavy spending and with the market for short films constricting, Spoor bought out Anderson's share in Essanay in 1916 and shuttered the Niles studio. His own operation in Chicago didn't last much longer, ceasing production in 1918.

Further reading

Kiehn, David (2003) *Broncho Billy and the Essanay Film Company*, Niles, CA: Farwell.

ROBERT S. BIRCHARD

ethnographic films

Early ethnographic films grew out of a range of 19th-century social, cultural, and scientific practices and are irreducible to a single site, personality, or institution. Exploiting an enduring fascination (in the West) with representing "native" peoples in pictorial form, ethnographic filmmakers followed in the footsteps of professional and amateur artists who had sketched, painted, and photographed native peoples the world over. Though the term "ethnographic film" was not coined until after World War II, early films featuring non-Western peoples were variously categorized as **travelogues** or scenics, manners and customs, **industrial films**, or **scientific films**, in the **trade press**, **newspapers**, and periodicals of the time and were shown in many venues, from **nickelodeons** to high-class **illustrated lectures**, natural history museums, private clubs, and other elite organizations. While the anthropological definition of "ethnography" as an immersive, long-term fieldwork experience among native peoples rarely figured in commercially-produced films, early promoters turned to the language of anthropology, especially discourses of accuracy and authenticity, as a way of shoring up the legitimacy and scientific status of their films.

Any understanding of ethnographic film must be informed by its pre-cinematic predecessors, for museums of natural history, native villages at **world's fairs**, and 19th-century scientific and commercial **photography** all supported the growth of a new visuality which heightened its popularity for turn-of-the-century **audiences**. In short, ethnographic cinema grew out of a modern form of seeing that drew upon a range of pre-cinematic institutions and signifying practices. Sharing the role of popular conveyor of ethnographic knowledge with museums, photographs, and world's fairs, ethnographic films competed with, and sometimes supplanted, these earlier entertainment forms, bringing distant images of native peoples to audiences in a cheap and transportable form.

Museums of natural history were important staging grounds for debates over the efficacy of visual modes of representing ethnographic knowledge and can be seen as mediators between the worlds of professional anthropology and popular culture. In negotiating the often competing demands of education and spectacle, such museums sparked debates over the possibility of popularized modes of ethnographic representation in ways that prefigured how cinema would later be discursively constructed by museum professionals. Similarly, native villages at world's fairs and expositions, where nations of the earth promoted their material wealth and cultural life in huge, ostentatious exhibits, crystallized a number of debates that were instrumental in shaping both scientific and popular perceptions of ethnographic film. The iconography and rhetorical form of much early ethnographic film likewise drew upon 19th-century photographs made by anthropologists and commercial photographers. Images of native peoples were produced in widely varying contexts, including missionary outposts, the colonial metropole, tourist centers, anthropological expeditions, permanent or peripatetic photographic studios, and world's fairs, and circulated freely across scientific and popular markets.

Given the antipathy towards moving pictures by most members of the nascent discipline of anthropology, the filmmaking efforts of British anthropologists such as Alfred Cort Haddon (1898) and Walter Baldwin Spencer (1901) stand out as exceptional, along with those of the Austrian Rudolf Pöch (1907), the American Pliny E. Goddard (1914), and the Norwegian Carl Lumholtz (1914–1917). Haddon's six brief films shot in the Torres Strait Islands off the Northeast coast of Australia were produced as salvage ethnography records of a culture believed to be on the brink of extinction. As a novice cinematographer, Haddon struggled with the new technology, complaining both about his inexperience as a filmmaker and the camera's tendency to jam. Haddon nevertheless recommended that his colleague Baldwin Spencer take a camera with him on his fieldwork expedition to Central Australia some three years later; an accomplished photographer, Spencer had both scientific and popular audiences in mind for his films and photographs and lectured extensively with the films and **magic lantern** slides in Australia and Great Britain. Working under extremely taxing conditions, including dealing with the climate and the interpersonal complexities of gaining access to the Arrernte people's ceremonial life, this first generation of anthropologist-filmmakers broke new ground in making a case for the usefulness of the moving picture camera as an anthropological tool. Surviving as some of the earliest moving picture records of indigenous peoples, these films are testimony to the pioneering spirit of early 20th-century anthropologists, who, against all odds, returned home from the field with both still and moving pictures of the peoples they had studied.

But films shot by anthropologists were vastly outnumbered by those made by commercial producers; from the moment **Edison** shot Native American performers appearing with Buffalo Bill's (William F. **Cody**'s) Wild West show in New Jersey in 1894, native peoples were the subject of countless films made by commercial manufacturers, including **Lumière, American Mutoscope and Biograph, Lubin, Selig, Kalem**, and **Pathé-Frères**, as well as traveling lecturers such as E. Burton **Holmes**, Lyman H. **Howe**, and Frederick Monsen. Even after the waning of interest in *actualités* after 1905, non-fiction films flourished in commercial programs well into the 1910s, with travelogues turning a regular profit in the rapidly consolidating industry. On a textual level, commercially-produced ethnographic films are often indistinguishable from films shot by anthropologists; close-ups are rarely, if ever, used in the pre-1915 films, with the long shot and medium long-shot and occasional medium-close up reflecting the preferred distance between filmmaker and subject. Commercial filmmakers exploited a great many of the visual tropes of anthropological filmmaking, including indigenous dance, pre-industrial production, and ceremonial life. Commercially-produced ethnographic films also competed for audiences with films made by filmmaker-adventurers such as Paul J. Rainey and Martin and Osa Johnson, who in the 1910s showed their films in both museums and moving picture theaters. Filmed as part of a hunting expedition, Rainey's *African Hunt* (1912) was hugely successful, a clear indication that audiences had not tired of images of native peoples by this time. In fact, scenes of ethnographic interest were interpolated into Hollywood adventure narratives in the 1930s, including *King Kong* (1933), drawing upon a tradition of ethnographic spectacle in western image-making that predates cinema.

While many of the commercially-produced and anthropological films have not survived or have lain unidentified in film archives around the world, some have been recuperated by native peoples as part of cultural regeneration movements; other films, such as those produced by Baldwin Spencer of Central Australian Aborigines have come under the curatorial tutelage of government museums, who, acting in the interests of indigenous groups, restrict access to films with sacred ceremonial content. Contemporary filmmakers have also turned to the early cinema archive for creative inspiration and to resignify the meanings of early *actualités*. In terms of the eclectic range of filmmaking that can be called ethnographic, the early cinema period was certainly a vibrant moment in the history of the genre, providing ample evidence of ethnographic filmmaking long before Robert Flaherty shot *Nanook of the North* in 1922.

See also: Aeroscope camera; animal pictures; colonialism: Europe; expedition/exploration films; imperialism: USA; museum life exhibits; newsreels

Further reading

Griffiths, Alison (2002) *Wondrous Difference: Cinema, Anthropology, and Turn-of- the-Century Visual Culture*, New York: Columbia University Press.

Peterson, Jennifer Lynn (2004) *World Pictures: Travelogue Films and the Lure of the Exotic*, Durham: Duke University Press.

Rony, Fatimah Tobing (1996) *The Third Eye: Race, Cinema, and Ethnographic Spectacle*, Durham: Duke University Press.

Russell, Catherine (2000) *Experimental Ethnography: The Work of Film in the Age of Video*, Durham: Duke University Press.

ALISON GRIFFITHS

Evans, Fred ("Pimple")

b. 1889; d. 1951

actor, Great Britain

Britain's most popular film comedian of the early cinema period, and a rival to **Chaplin** during **World War I**, Fred Evans (the nephew of Will

Evans) came from a **music hall** background. He entered films in 1910, developing the character of "Charley Smiler" at Cricks and Martin; but in 1912, he created "Pimple," with a white-painted face, cheeky grin, and love of absurdity best revealed in satires on contemporary issues (*Miss Pimple Suffragette* and *Pimple Anarchist*) and parodies of film and stage hits. *Pimple's Battle of Waterloo* (1913) spoofs the **British and Colonial** epic film, while the Pythonesque *Pimple in the Whip* gleefully ridicules the stage hit that was filmed straight by Maurice **Tourneur** in 1917. Several hundred Pimple films were made between 1912 and 1922, for Folly Films, Phoenix, Piccadilly and others, most of them co-written and directed by Evans and his brother Joe. Evans was an unsophisticated clown, whose own comic business tends to unfunny farce, but the best of his parodies are mischievous, high-spirited fun. He ended his film career in the 1930s, as an extra.

LUKE McKERNAN

Ewers, Hanns Heinz

b. 1871; d. 1943

author, scenario writer, Germany

While most famous as the scenario writer of *Der Student von Prag* [The Student of Prague] (1913 and 1926), Ewers was equally celebrated for his 1904 novel, *Alraune*, the story of a fatal love between a scientist and his female creation, which was adapted to film four times between 1919 and 1952. The mixture of fantastic and Romantic themes in both stories proved very popular before and (especially) after **World War I**. Ewers wrote the scenarios for eight films in 1913 alone, making him an important force behind the *Autorenfilm*'s artistic aspirations.

See also: screenwriting

SCOTT CURTIS

expedition/exploration films

By the late 19th century, **photography** had become an essential tool for European and American expeditions wanting to document their

work and discoveries, and when moving picture **cameras** became available these too were soon seized on by explorers and geographers. The first expeditions to make films of their work were anthropological: Alfred Cort Haddon in New Guinea and Walter Baldwin Spencer in Australia both made films of native peoples before 1901. But geographical explorers and travelers soon followed suit; in October 1910, *Moving Picture World* noted: "No exploring party to-day is complete without a moving picture outfit."

At the dawn of the 20th century the cinema public was widely ignorant of the sights of the wider world: even parts of Europe were little known and therefore of great curiosity value. The Alps attracted filmmakers from the earliest years, with Mrs. Main filming winter sports in 1902. Mountaineering expeditions became screen adventures when Frank Ormiston-Smith and then Frederick **Burlingham** released films of their climbs. Further east, when Harry De Windt explored the byways of the Balkans in 1906, he had a cameraman, John MacKenzie, record the scenes they saw for distribution by Charles **Urban**.

The remotest regions of the earth were soon being filmed, including parts of Asia. In 1907, a cameraman working for the Duc de Montpensier filmed scenes and customs of the local people in French Indochina. The Duc d'Abruzzi was another titled explorer, and he too decided to have his exploits filmed, as he ascended Himalayan peaks in 1910. Even further afield, Danish explorer Captain Mikkelson was in New Guinea in early 1909, where he recorded scenes for **Nordisk**; two years later Eric Marshall went further inland and filmed the elusive New Guinea pygmies for **Gaumont**. On neighboring Borneo, Carl Lumholtz was equipped with a moving picture camera during his long explorations beginning just before World War I; further south in Australia, Francis Birtles' journeys across the continent were also filmed.

South America was fertile territory for expeditions, soon equipped with movie cameras, such as Charles W. Fitzgerald's 1910 project to explore the Orinoco. Theodore Roosevelt organized an Amazon expedition in 1913–1914, and took along cameraman Carl von Hoffman as well as Anthony Fiala, who had previously filmed in the polar regions. At much the same time, explorer Captain

Besley was traveling through Brazil and Peru, and the resulting films of the journey were copyrighted in 1914.

But in this era it was Africa that attracted the most high-profile expeditions, which were motivated as much by hunting as by geographical exploration. Hunter and explorer Adam David went to southern Sudan in 1907 and returned there in 1910, on both occasions together with cameraman Alfred **Machin**. In 1911, Cherry **Kearton** filmed extraordinary scenes as Buffalo Jones lassoed wild animals in east Africa. Kearton took considerable risks in this work, for shooting films of wild animals could be highly dangerous: cameraman Octave Friere was killed while filming in Africa in 1911.

Perhaps the most famous safari of the era was led by Roosevelt in east Africa, and **Selig**'s re-enactment of the hunt was released to great success in 1910. Paul Rainey's *African Hunt* (1912) also created huge interest. The following year Sir Thomas Dewar's big game expedition departed for East Africa and was filmed by cameraman J. W. Parker: the resulting film shows Dewar wounding and then killing a lion.

See also: *actualités*; animal pictures; colonialism: Europe; ethnographic films; imperialism: USA; re-enactments; travelogues

Further reading

Brownlow, Kevin (1979) *The War, the West, and the Wilderness*, London: Secker and Warburg.

Jordan, Pierre-L. (1992) *Premier Contact, Premier Regard*, Marseille: Musé de Marseille.

STEPHEN BOTTOMORE

F

Fabre, Marcel

b. 1886; d. 1929

actor, Italy

Originally a circus clown from Spain, Marcel Fabre began his film career with short **comedies** at **Éclair** and **Pathé-Frères**. Hired in 1910 by **Ambrosio** as the answer to **Cines'** Tontolini (Ferdinando **Guillaume**) and **Itala**'s Cretinetti (André **Deed**), he became internationally known as Robinet (France, Spain), Nauke (Germany), and Tweedledum (Britain, USA). His companion in this **comic series** was Nilde Baracchi, known as Robinette. Robinet was a tall and clumsy type, a shameless libertine, a figure involved in wild and destructive chases often triggered by ill-use of modern means of transportation. In 1914, Fabre—who also directed at Ambrosio—made the grotesque feature, *Saturnino Farandola*, based on the science fiction novel by Robida.

IVO BLOM

facial expression films

The art of distorting facial features in a grotesque manner played an essential part in popular entertainments for centuries: e.g., **fair/fairground** farces and circus clown acts. Closely related to caricature, these live performances created effects from hilarity to terror. Talented performers or those endowed with naturally exaggerated features provided a mobile array of uncanny facial effects.

Early cinema offered a new dimension to such performances: the possibility of enlargement whereby facial expressions filled the screen. Such early "close-ups" magnified faces and concentrated attention. Therefore, facial expression films could be considered an early film genre that exploited the unique devices of the cinema.

Judging not only by surviving prints but also by their frequency in early film catalogues, facial expression films were very popular. Many early films fall into this category such as **Edison**'s *Facial Expressions* (1902), or *Goo-goo Eyes* (1903), which show performers making grotesque expressions or rolling their eyes in an unbelievable manner. However, we should also include in the category many less exaggerated films whose close framing (sometimes a "bust shot" framing the head and chest rather than just the face) show performers in typical actions, resembling character sketches. Edison's famous early close-up **Kinetoscope** films, *The May Irwin Kiss* (1896) and *Fred Ott's Sneeze* (1894), would provide examples, as would *A Dull Razor* (1900) or **Pathé-Frères**'s *Ma Tante* [My Aunt] (1903), with **Dranem** in "auntie drag." In the more grotesque facial expression films, the performer manipulates his or her face rather than creates a character portraying a type or typical action. In such films, the performer acknowledges the camera directly, usually staring and performing for it (in character sketches, this is not always true).

Most of these films consist of a single shot, so, although closely framed, they are not part of an edited sequence, as the term "close-up" might imply. However, the origin of the facial close-up as

Figure 34 Dranem in Pathé's *Ma Tante* [My Aunt] (1904).

an edited figure seems to come from facial expression films. Thus G. A. **Smith**'s *Mary Jane's Mishap* (1903) repeatedly cuts into close shots of Mary Jane as she mugs while doing her chores. These close-ups do not convey dramatic revelation or narrative empathy (common motivations for later close-ups), but rather display the grotesque expressions as attractions. Edwin S. **Porter**'s *The Whole Dam Family and the Dam Dog* (1905) consists of seven facial expression close-ups revealing the caricature-like physiognomies of family members, followed by two long shots in which the Dam Family dinner is interrupted by their dog. The famous shot of the moon face receiving the rocket in its eye in Georges **Méliès**' *Le Voyage à la lune* [A Trip to Moon] (1902), most likely takes its framing from facial expression films. Thus the genre became cannibalized by longer and sometimes more complex films that incorporated close framings of the face either making grimaces or presenting a physiognomic type.

Further reading

Gunning, Tom (1997) "In Your Face: Physiognomy, Photography and the Gnostic Mission of Early Film," *Modernism/Modernity*, 4.1: 1–29.

Jay, Ricky (2001) "Grinners, Gurners and Grimacies," *Jay's Journal of Anomalies*, 45–52, New York: Farrar Straus Giroux.

TOM GUNNING

fairs/fairgrounds: Europe

The exploitation and exhibition of moving pictures by traveling fairground showmen in Europe was a significant factor in the growth of cinema's popularity. Playing to a largely rural population at the great 19th-century fairs throughout Europe, and in cities such Nottingham, Bremen, Leipzig, Paris and Milan, the early showmen presented their wondrous exhibitions to audiences that ultimately would demand permanent venues.

Fairs were regulated and controlled by local authorities or landowners with final authority in the hands of the exhibitors. They occurred on dates fixed by the religious, agricultural, or new industrial calendar, lasted anywhere from several days to several weeks, and were protected by national legislation or the prescriptive right of landowners to hold a fair on a particular day of the year. By the late 1800s, the traveling fair was one of the most important popular venues for entertainment in Europe. The introduction of steam-powered roundabouts and merry-go-rounds in the 1860s in England and then throughout Europe, together with the new rail system of transportation, led to the transformation of what was perceived as an antiquated and dying tradition into centers of modernity, incorporating the latest innovations of the new industrial age. By 1900, for instance, over 200 fairs were held on a weekly basis throughout Great Britain, and this pattern was repeated in France, Belgium, the Netherlands, Italy, and Germany, where they were encouraged by everyone from wealthy industrialists to small shopkeepers eager to entice people and their money. This network of traveling fairs, many of which had their origins in the Middle Ages, provided a ready-made circuit for the fairground exhibitor to present a range of new attractions, including Ghost shows, X-ray **photography** and, in 1896, moving pictures.

The introduction of moving pictures into a vibrant and established mode of exhibition was an immediate success. Fairground showmen were quick to see its commercial possibilities. The necessary equipment for a basic show was cheap, could be purchased in most major cities and, more importantly, could be incorporated easily into existing exhibitions. Portable booths or theaters, which may have previously exhibited human oddities, wild animals or optical and illusion displays, also could be converted for showing moving pictures. Moreover, one of the characteristics of exhibition, as least on the continent, was the fluidity of movement across frontiers. The itineraries of the showmen were dictated by festival calendars and the state of the roads and railways much more than by borders. In the case of Trieste, which remained part of the Austro-Hungarian Empire until **World War I**, the ethnic and linguistic mix of the population ensured that a showman such as Ivan Bläser, born in Prussia, was known as Jean, Johann, Ivan or Giovanni Bläser, depending on the audience he was addressing. In fact, reflecting a dominant theme in modern Italian history, fairground exhibitors moved more easily between France, Austria, Switzerland, the Adriatic countries and northern Italy than between northern and southern Italy. Trieste also was a center from which moving pictures spread into Istria, Dalmatia, Slovenia, Croatia and Bosnia.

Countries with a historic network of trade and pleasure fairs such as France, Italy, Germany, the Netherlands, Switzerland, and Great Britain provided a dynamic and fluid circuit for the showmen to build on. In France, for instance, nine fairs were presenting moving picture shows as early as 1896; three years later, the number had increased to forty. By 1902, no fair was without at least one moving picture show, many of them supplied with apparatuses and films by **Pathé-Frères** (whose own origins lay in the Paris fairs), and certain showmen had established regional circuits: for instance, the Iunik family around Paris, the Dulaar family around Lyon. By 1905, some shows were beginning to settle permanently in town or city squares, becoming French versions of the **nickelodeons** in the USA. In northern Italy, the fairs included moving picture shows in increasing numbers from 1899 onwards. The potent mixture of sonorous names such as Cinematografo Gigante, l'Imperale Kinematographe, or the exotic American Bioscsope, together with the novelty of steam-generated electric lighting, drew large crowds in the provinces, yet rarely farther south than Tuscany. In 1902, at one Milan fair there were three moving picture shows among the forty-two amusements; the following year, the number had increased to

six; by 1906, at a neighbouring fair, to eight. The topics addressed by the shows were similar to those found elsewhere—the Boer War, the Chinese War, Royal ceremonies (coronations, weddings and funerals), and the ever popular local *actualités*. This pattern was repeated everywhere but in Scandinavian countries such as Sweden and Finland, where fairground shows were limited in their success and longevity.

Exhibition patterns in Great Britain were similar to those on the continent, with the caveat that fairgrounds shows remained uniquely a British affair. The first showman known to exhibit moving pictures on British fairgrounds was Randall **Williams**, who included them in his converted Ghost show at the World's Fair Christmas show in London in 1896. By 1900, nine moving picture booths were in operation at Hull Fair, one of oldest and largest traveling fairs in Europe. By 1906, at Nottingham Goose Fair, seven of fifteen amusement booths presented moving picture. Although no European showmen attended British fairs, organ manufacturers such as Marenghi and Gavioli in Paris supplied lavishly ornate organs for the fronts of the British shows. However, these soon were incorporated into purpose-built traveling moving picture booths by British manufacturers.

The rate of decline for fairground exhibition was different in each European country. For the most part, the emergence of distribution circuits based on renting rather selling film prints for exhibition in permanent cinemas was common throughout Europe. However, there were variations. In Italy, changes in legislation led to the development of permanent cinemas as early as 1905, whereas in Switzerland **itinerant exhibitors** such as Willy Leuzinger continued until the 1940s. A number of exhibitors—for instance, George **Green** in Scotland, Søren Nielsen in Denmark, and Jean **Desmet** in the Netherlands—went on to establish a circuit of cinemas in areas where they would have once exhibited their shows. However, the majority remained on the fairgrounds and invested in the next "latest wonder of the age," such as the electric Scenic Railway.

By 1914, moving picture exhibition had all but disappeared from the fairgrounds on the continent and in Great Britain. Yet the fairgrounds' importance as a venue for moving pictures, in both

Figure 35 From *Mitchell and Kenyon 772*: Sedgwick's bioscope showfront at Pendlebury Wakes, August 1901. James Kenyon of Mitchell and Kenyon is standing to the left of the poster. (Copyright British Film Institute.)

industrial cities and rural communities, should not be underestimated. For fairground showmen laid the foundations for the emergence of permanent moving picture theaters in villages, towns, and cities throughout Europe.

See also: distribution: Europe; electricity; transportation

Further reading

Bernadini, Aldo (2001) *Cinema Italiano delle Origini: Gli ambulanti*, Gemona: Le Cineteca del Friuli.

Convents, Guido (1994) "Motion picture exhibitors on Belgium fairgrounds," *Film History*, 6: 2: 238–249.

Deslandes, Jacques and Jacques Richards (1968) *Histoire comparée du cinéma II: Du cinématographe au cinéma, 1896–1906*, Paris: Castermann.

Kosanović, Dejan (1995) *Trieste al Cinema 1896–1918*, Gemona: La Cineteca del Friuli.

Rossell, Deac (2000) "A slippery job: travelling exhibitors in early cinema," in Simon Popple and Vanessa Toulmin (eds.) *Visual Delights: Essays on the Popular and Projected Image in the 19th Century*, 50–60, Trowbridge: Flicks Books.

VANESSA TOULMIN

Falena, Ugo

b. 1875; d. 1931

playwright, theater critic, film director and scriptwriter, Italy

An educated and ambitious man of the theater, Falena, in 1909, became artistic director of **Film d'Arte Italiana**. Aided by casting director

Gerolamo **Lo Savio,** he attracted prominent stage actors, from Ermete **Novelli** and Maria **Jacobini** to Francesca **Bertini**, to produce stylized adaptations of celebrated literary and theatrical works. At Film d'Arte Italiana, he directed and supervised, among others, *Salomé* [Salome] (1910) and *Francesca da Rimini* [Francesca di Rimini] (1910), before moving, in 1916, to smaller firms such as Tespi and Galatea.

GIORGIO BERTELLINI

Famous Players Motion Picture Company

From 1912–1919, the Famous Players Motion Picture Company (Famous Players-Lasky by 1916) innovated some of the most significant strategies of the period, from the **star system** and feature film programs to vertical integration.

Famous Players was formed on 1 June 1912 by Adolph **Zukor**, Daniel Frohman, and Edwin S. **Porter**. The company was founded to produce high-budget, **multiple-reel/feature films** adapted from successful stage plays. Its first venture was the co-financing and US release of *Queen Elizabeth* (with Sarah **Bernhardt**), which debuted in New York City in August 1912. Famous Players' first production was *The Prisoner of Zenda* (February 1913), a critically acclaimed film that made little profit, due to difficulties with the state rights system of feature distribution. **General Film** refused to distribute Famous Players' product, while most other distributors were unwilling to risk a potential lawsuit from the **MPPC** for the distribution rights to a single film.

To combat this, during July and August 1913, Famous Players joined with the Jesse L. **Lasky** Feature Play Company and Bosworth Film Company to release a yearly program of feature films. They also signed an agreement with five distributors, including W. W. **Hodkinson**'s Progressive Motion Picture Company. The agreement required Famous Players to release thirty features per year, which necessitated a change in production strategy. Rather than producing only expensive adaptations of successful plays, Famous Players divided its productions into Class A, B, and C features, which ranged from *Queen Elizabeth*-style adaptations to three-to-five reel films using Famous Player's stock company. Although Class C films were ostensibly the cheapest, the stock company included such stars as Mary **Pickford**, who soon would become one of the biggest movie stars in the world. Famous Players and its affiliate companies did not ignore Pickford's early success, as the firms began investing in the star system for both production and advertising purposes. By 1918, six of the top stars in Hollywood worked for Famous Players: Pickford, Marguerite Clark, Douglas Fairbanks, Harold Lockwood, William S. **Hart**, and Wallace Reid.

The eight companies that joined forces in 1913 would become the backbone of Paramount Pictures, which was formed on 8 August 1914. One month later, Paramount became the first distributor to offer a complete program of four- to six-reel features, releasing as many as two per week. In 1916, Famous Players, Lasky, and Paramount would combine into Famous Players-Lasky, with Zukor in charge, having ousted Hodkinson from his Paramount presidency. This made Famous Players-Lasky the largest producer–distributor in the USA.

Famous Players-Lasky would become a vertically integrated firm in 1919. As a response to the new theater chain, First National (led by the **Mastbaum** brothers), which lured Pickford away from Famous Players, Zukor began buying hundreds of first- and second-run theaters throughout the country. To accomplish this, Famous Players held a public stock offering, raising ten million dollars in cash. This marked neither the first instance of vertical integration nor of Wall Street influencing. However, the size of Famous Players' theater-buying spree transformed the film industry; after 1919, to be a "Major," a company had to become vertically integrated.

MICHAEL QUINN

Farnum, Dustin

b. 1874, Hampton Beach, New York;
d. 1929, New York City

actor, USA

A successful stage actor in several repertory companies from 1897, Farnum's feature film debut came in *Soldiers of Fortune* (1914) for the All Star

Feature Company. He next appeared in Cecil B. **DeMille**'s *The Squaw Man* (1914) for the **Lasky** Feature Play Company. Thereafter, he was known primarily as a rugged **western** hero, and worked for various producers until 1926, when he briefly tried vaudeville until a kidney ailment forced his retirement. Winifred Kingston, often his co-star, became his second wife in 1926. He was the brother of director Marshall Farnum and actor William Farnum, whose own career took off with *The Spoilers* (1914).

ROBERT S. BIRCHARD

fashion

Fashion, like early film, was international. Fashionable clothing played a variety of roles in films made between 1894 and 1915. It provided subject matter for nonfiction films and **costumes**, as an essential part of mise-en-scene, for narrative films. It functioned as a selling point for film producers and theater managers to prompt women to buy movie tickets, and they, in turn, watched the screen to learn the current styles.

In the 1890s, fashion emanated from Paris, and it is not surprising that both **Gaumont** and **Pathé-Frères**, first in *actualités* and then in **newsreels** documented the latest spring hats, evening gowns, and accessories, often enhanced by **color**. In addition, newsreels also included scenes of events where fashionable display was traditionally as important as the event itself, including horse races at Ascot (England) or Longchamps (France). Both the **World Film Corporation** and Pathé-Frères experimented with an "all-fashion" format, producing short films that featured gowns by prominent Paris designers including Worth, Paquin, Jenny, and Cheruit. In some American cities **department stores** created fashion films, for projection in either the store itself or local theaters, as **advertisements** of their wares to potential customers.

Fashion also played a crucial role in the mise-en-scene of those films with contemporary story lines, serving to enhance a character's traits or to function as motivation within the narrative chain of cause and effect. Initially actors brought their own clothes to wear in their roles, and autobiographies of

such **stars** as Lillian **Gish** and Mary **Pickford** attest to the importance of a versatile wardrobe as one of the tools of the actor's trade. Here film followed theatrical practice. The legitimate **theater** also set a precedent by using costumes created by haute couture designers in Paris, London, and New York. Plays would be reviewed as dramas in the theatrical journals and as fashion shows in the fashion trade press. Actresses functioned as both manikins and players, setting style trends for the women in the theater audience and for the women who read descriptions of the clothes in magazines. In the years before the costume designer became part of the film production team, this tradition was followed by the movies—especially in the films of prominent stars who enlisted their own designers to make their costumes. One of its consequences was that actresses became trend setters nationally and internationally—costumes worn by Italian divas like Lyda **Borelli** and Francesca **Bertini** in the early 1910s were published in fan magazines in Japan—and their public personas, as models of fashion, affected the roles they took on in their film work.

Fashion also served as the raw material for film narrative. In the USA, D. W. **Griffith** made *Those Awful Hats* (1909), about the "problem" of ladies wearing hats in a **nickelodeon**, as well as *The New York Hat* (1911), about a hat's potential to create scandal for Pickford's small town character. In 1913–1914, **Mutual Film Corporation** produced a popular **serial**, *Our Mutual Girl*, whose chief pleasures derived from its heroine's self-expression through fashion and just "shopping around." In 1915, American producer George **Kleine** released *The Fashion Shop* (1915), shot in the real Fifth Avenue couture shop of Madame Heller in New York City.

See also: leisure time and space: USA; spectatorship: issues and debates; trade press; women's movement, Europe; women's movement, USA

Further reading

Luckett, Moya (1999) "Advertising and feminity: the case of Our Mutual Girl," *Screen*, 40.4: 363–383.

Steele, Valerie (1999) *Paris Fashion: A Cultural History*, New York: Oxford University Press.

Turim, Maureen (1994) "Seduction and Elegance: The New Woman of Fashion in Silent Cinema," 140–158, in Shari Benstock and Suzanne Ferris (eds.) *On Fashion*, New Brunswick: Rutgers University Press.

LESLIE MIDKIFF DEBAUCHE

féeries or fairy plays

Féeries, or fairy plays, originally were a stage genre that became popular during the 19th century, especially in France. In other European countries there were similar kinds of magical plays, such as the *Märchenstücke* or *Zauberstücke* in Germany and Austria, or, within the tradition of popular culture, even the Pantomime in England. But contrary to the French *féeries* these did not develop a strong link to early cinema. Although stage *féeries* shared a number of features with other theatrical forms such as the *opéra comique* or operetta—in particular, the combination of music, ballets, songs, and stage action—in *féeries* these all were primarily conceived of as spectacular elements, while narrative (or dramatic conflict) played only a secondary role. The subject matter was generally fantastic or supernatural and included a number of miraculous or magical events. These were presented by means of sophisticated stage tricks, another important component of the genre. Very often the tricks were extremely complicated and had to be executed with the help of intricate machinery off stage. Visual splendor was achieved through luxurious staging, rich costumes and colorful dance scenes. In other words, stage *féeries* clearly foregrounded an aesthetic of spectacular display.

The first filmic *féeries* appeared quite early in French sales catalogues. In 1899 Georges **Méliès** announced his film, *Cendrillon* [Cinderella], as a "grand and extraordinary *féerie* in twenty tableaux." Among the nine categories listed in the **Pathé-Frères** sales catalogue of 1900, there was one heading grouping together *Féeries et contes* (distinguishing between fairy plays and fairy tales). Earlier still, in 1896, a hand-colored 58mm film,

photographed with a **Demenÿ** camera and produced for **Gaumont** by Alice **Guy**, was made to feature as a special attraction in a stage *féerie* called *La biche au bois* [The Hind in the Forest] which was given at the Châtelet theater in Paris.

The integration of filmic *féeries* into stage performances was not an uncommon practice. Stage producers apparently saw moving images as yet another spectacular trick or attraction that could be added to the show. Méliès repeatedly received orders from theaters for cinematographic interludes. He sometimes reworked these productions and released them as independent works to exhibitors of screen entertainment. Thus, in 1905, he created a film for the stage show, *Les 400 coups du diable* [The 400 Tricks of the Devil], which, one year later, he transformed into his own "grande féerie en 35 tableaux" with the slightly modified title, *Les quat'cents farces du diable* [The 400 Pranks of the Devil].

In other cases, filmic *féeries* were distributed under the same (or a similar) title as well-known stage plays, even though there were considerable differences in their plot lines. In 1875, for instance, the Théâtre de la Gaîté in Paris presented *Voyage dans la lune* [A Trip to the Moon], and in 1882 there was a stage production of *Voyage à travers l'impossible* [The Impossible Voyage], but neither had anything in common with the two famous films with similar titles made by Méliès in 1902 and 1904, respectively. And, in the case of *Voyage dans la lune*, neither the film nor the play were adaptations of the famous Jules Verne novel.

Even though filmic *féeries* appeared as a separate category in the catalogues of numerous French production companies and were recognized by the **trade press** as a distinct type of film, it is not easy to clearly define them as a genre. With regard to subject matter, they often were based on traditional fairy tales, but this was not always the case. Nor did every film based on a fairy tale appear in the catalogues as a *féerie* (hence the distinction between *féeries* and *contes* in the Pathé catalogue). In other respects they often had much in common with **trick films**. As in the stage genre, one of the most salient characteristics of filmic *féeries* lay in the quite systematic use of trick techniques. Thus, for example, Méliès claimed in his 1907 essay,

Figure 36 Production photo from *Le Voyage dans la lune* [Trip to the Moon] (Méliès, 1902).

"Les vues cinématographiques," that his (somewhat legendary) discovery of the substitution trick, because of a camera jam when filming at the Place de l'Opéra, almost immediately led him to create his first *féeries*. Even though stage technicians, too, were capable of producing an astounding range of trick effects, including pyrotechnics, multiple transformations, and sudden changes of scenery, the cinematic trick techniques obviously enabled filmmakers to achieve these effects without having to rely on complex mechanical devices.

In spite of the obvious difficulties in constructing an exact definition, *féeries* can be described in terms of generic coherence. Most of their distinctive features are clearly linked to the fact that *féeries* relied chiefly on spectacular display, and less on dramatic conflict or narrative logic. Accordingly, as a rule *féeries* were shot indoors, using a stage-like setting, painted backgrounds, studio-built scenery, and more or less frontal mise-en-scène. With regard to the concepts forged by Tom Gunning and André Gaudreault, one could say

that in their mode of spectatorial address they were much more deeply rooted in the **cinema of attractions** than in the cinema of narrative integration. Even in films based on well-known tales such as "Ali Baba and the Forty Thieves," the narrative mainly served as a framework within which visual attractions could be presented.

The two filmic versions of *Ali Baba et les quarante voleurs* produced by Pathé-Frères in 1902 (directed by Ferdinand **Zecca**) and 1907 are a case in point. The 1902 film consists of seven shots, each preceded by an **intertitle** announcing the main theme of the *tableau*, the narrative being presented in both an elliptic and a fragmentary way. Without prior knowledge of the tale, it is impossible to reconstruct the story as it is told in the *Arabian Nights*. But even though the 1907 version includes 23 shots (and 8 intertitles), it depicts more or less the same events, with each scene now broken down into several shots. In both cases, the narrative is reduced to a series of key moments. At the same time, both versions introduce a number of purely spectacular elements that do not serve any narrative function, namely elaborate dance scenes (absent from the original tale) and a "grand finale," the so-called "apotheosis," which is announced explicitly in the last intertitle. The term "apotheosis" stems from the stage tradition and refers to a splendidly arranged image (or *tableau*), where all the characters were grouped into ornaments and where a number of additional effects were displayed in order to produce a powerful and spectacular conclusion, presenting to the audience an overwhelming wealth of visual stimuli. The dance scenes and the apotheoses thus can be seen as strong elements of attraction.

In their sales catalogues, production companies such as Pathé Frères highlighted the spectacular elements of their *féeries* as well as the production value of these films, particularly the sets, costumes, ballets, and also the apotheoses. Occasionally even those responsible for the **set design** or **costumes** were credited, especially when their names, such as V. Lorent-Heilbronn, were well known in connection with their professional activities for the stage. The apotheoses in particular were presented as a major attractional feature. Thus, to quote but one example among many, the 1907 Pathé-Frères catalogue describes another *féerie* based on an *Arabian Nights* tale, *Aladdin ou la lampe merveilleuse* [Aladdin's Lamp] (shot by Segundo de **Chomón** and directed by Albert **Capellani**): "This scene ends with a magnificent apotheosis."

Besides the visual splendor of the mise-en-scène, there was yet another attractional feature in *féeries*, even though it was not always present, nor was it exclusive to the genre: namely, **color**. Many *féeries* in the Pathé sales catalogues were available in stencil-colored prints (and both of the *Ali Baba* films have been preserved in colored versions). In some cases it was only the apotheosis that was offered in colors. Coloring, of course, made *féeries* a more expensive type of film, as did their often quite considerable length. Some of Méliès's films belonging to this genre reached the then rather exceptional length of more than 400 meters. In the sales lists of other companies, *féeries* also generally were much longer than the rest of the titles that were advertised.

So, compared to fairy tale films, *féeries* privileged spectacular attractions over narrative; compared to trick films, they were more complex and longer, and their tricks were motivated by the fantastic and miraculous subject matter. This, of course, by no means constitutes a definitive definition, but both the trade press and catalogue descriptions suggest that such distinctions were made in production and distribution practices. Individual films might include features that would appear to make them *féeries*, and yet be categorized differently in a sales catalogue.

Given these relatively high production values, exhibitors would have to invest more money when acquiring a *féerie* than was the case with most of the other productions—and apparently they were willing to do so because of the visual attractions such a film could offer. Pathé-Frères, however, occasionally also tried to provide *féeries* for clients who did not have the means to purchase the more expensive versions. The company's 1907 catalogue offered *La fée printemps* [The Spring Fairy], which was only 80 meters long and available in either colored or uncolored copies. The catalogue description ran as follows: "This *féerie* is a very attractive act and particularly suited when a limited number of spectators does not allow the purchase of longer films." Quite obviously, *féeries* were seen as an important component to a program, and Pathé apparently wanted to ensure that it could offer a full range of products to all segments of the market.

In spite of the relative prominence accorded to *féeries*, evident even in contemporary discourses in the trade press, few companies were involved in their regular production. The two main producers clearly were Méliès's Star Film and Pathé-Frères. Other French companies such as **Lux** or Gaumont only occasionally advertised *féeries*. Outside France, *féeries* appeared irregularly. In fact, the term itself was used chiefly in France. The Méliès films that were sold in France as *féeries* were announced in the American sales catalogues as "spectacular productions" or "spectacular pantomimes." Likewise, Pathé's 1902 *Ali Baba* was advertised as a "New and Original Moving Picture Spectacular Production." Interestingly, the marketing of *féeries* in the USA highlighted their most characteristic feature, namely their attractional qualities, whereas the link to fairy tales, so prominent in the French term, was absent.

Figure 37 Poster for *La Poule aux Oeufs d' Or* [The Hen with Golden Eggs] (Pathé 1905).

For almost a decade *féeries* were highly prestigious. From 1908 or 1909 on, however, their importance gradually declined, and *féeries* appeared less and less frequently in sales catalogues, even though articles in the trade press continued to hold them in high esteem. Audience preferences shifted to other kinds of films where narrative logic and dramatic conflict played a more important role. In 1912 and 1913, there were only four titles categorized as *féeries* in the Pathé sales catalogues. One of them was a remake of an earlier title, and two others were produced by Méliès for the company. These marked the *féeries'* definitive decline.

See also: editing: early practices and techniques; editing: tableau style

Further reading

Abel, Richard (1994) *The Ciné Goes to Town: French Cinema, 1896–1914*, Berkeley: University of California Press.

Ginisty, Paul (1910) *La féerie*, Paris: Louis Michaud.

Kessler, Frank (2000) "In the Realm of the Fairies: Early Cinema between Attraction and Narration," *Iconics* (Japan Society of Image Arts and Sciences), 5: 7–26.

Singer Kovács, Katherine (1983) "Georges Méliès and the Féerie," in John L. Fell (ed.) *Film Before Griffith*, 244–257, Berkeley: University of California Press.

FRANK KESSLER

Fengtai Photography Studio

Founded by Ren Qingtai in 1892, Fengtai was the first **photography** studio and motion picture enterprise in Beijing, gaining fame for its theatrical studio pictures and group portraits. Starting in 1905, the Studio produced several of the first Chinese-made films, in particular filmed performances of famous Peking **opera** actors, including Tan Xinpei. Shooting was done in the Studio's courtyard in broad daylight, mostly by the photographer Liu Zhonglun. Shown at the Studio's own Daguanyuan theater and elsewhere, these films were popular among Chinese audiences. The Studio was destroyed in a fire in 1909.

ZHEN ZHANG

Ferrez, Julio

b. 1881, Rio de Janeiro; d. 1946, Rio de Janeiro

sales agent, exhibitor, cameraman, Brazil

The son of Brazil's most important turn-of-the-century photographer, Marc Ferrez, Julio became interested in the cinema early. He was **Pathé-Frères'** representative, selling the company's equipment and films and, from 1907, running the Pathé cinema in Rio de Janeiro. He was one of the most accomplished pioneer cameramen, with films such as Antonio **Leal**'s *A mala sinistra* [The Sinister Suitcase] (1908)—a reconstruction of a famous crime—and his own *Nhô Anastasio chegou de viagem* [Mr. Anastacio Arrived from a Trip]

(1908), the country's first known **comedy**. Through 1910 he worked with all of the principal filmmakers; afterwards he focused his energies on the family's exhibition circuit in Rio.

ANA M. LÓPEZ

Fescourt, Henri

b. 1880; d. 1966

journalist, scriptwriter, filmmaker, France

Coming from southern France, as did his mentor Louis **Feuillade**, Fescourt obtained a law degree and became a professional journalist in Paris before beginning to write scenarios for **Gaumont** in 1911. A year later, he began directing films for the company and soon demonstrated his skill at parallel editing in such films as *Jeux d'enfants* [Children at Play] (1913). After the war, Fescourt became a major French filmmaker, directing **serials** at Cinéromans and such historical epics as *Les Misérables* (1925–1926). His book, *La foi et les montagnes* (1959), remains one of the best firsthand accounts of French cinema history.

RICHARD ABEL

Feuillade, Louis

b. 1873; d. 1925.

scriptwriter, director, France

Raised in a devoutly Catholic, anti-republican family, Feuillade worked as a journalist in Languedoc until 1898, when he moved to Paris to write for *La Croix* and to assist in editing *Revue-mondiale*. Hired by Léon **Gaumont** in late 1905 as a scenario writer and assistant to Alice **Guy**, he advanced to head of film production by 1907, writing and directing all of the kinds of films produced at **Gaumont**, from **trick films**, *L'Homme aimanté* [The Magnetized Man] (1907), and **comedies**, *Thé chez le concierge* [Tea at the Concierge's] (1907), to sensational **melodramas**, *Légende des phares* [Legend of the Lighthouse]

(1909), and **historical films**, *Le Huguenot* [The Huguenot] (1909).

In 1910, Feuillade introduced the *Bébé* [Jimmy] **comic series**, starring Clément **Mary**, which ran to nearly seventy films over the next two years. Replacing *Bébé* was the *Bout-de-Zan* [Timmy] series, starring René **Poyen**, which eventually included some forty films. From 1911 to 1913, Feuillade wrote and directed the famous *Les Scènes de la vie telle qu'elle est* [Scenes of Life As It Is] series, stories of melodramatic pathos such as *Les Vipères* [A Village Gossip] (1911), *La Tare* [Shame] (1911), and *Le Destin des mères* [The Fate of Mothers] (1912) that were wrapped in a realist aesthetic and advertised as "slices of real life."

During these early years, Feuillade's films were marked by sober, restrained acting (for instance, Renée **Carl** and Suzanne **Grandais**), solid narrative construction, skillful composition and lighting, and a flexible editing style. A good example from this period is the stencil-colored historical romance, *La Fille de margrave* [The Margrave's Daughter] (1912), which even enjoyed a critical success in the USA.

In 1913 came the film for which Feuillade is best remembered, *Fantômas*, based on the serialized crime novels of Marcel Allain and Pierre Souvestre and starring René **Navarre**. The first of five feature-length films, *Fantômas* established the fantastic realism that was characteristic of this **crime** series before it was interrupted by the war. Throughout, this master of disguise moved freely through familiar landscapes and social milieux, especially in and around Paris, his incredible, often bloody exploits deftly masked by the reassuringly mundane façade of daily life.

During the war, Feuillade returned to the crime series with *Les Vampires* [The Vampires] (1915–1916), starring **Musidora** as Irma Vep, the film's most powerful, consistently deceptive criminal figure. Partly in response to provincial bannings of this film, Feuillade enlisted popular novelist Arthur **Bernède** to write more conventional adventure stories involving an updated chivalric hero for his first **serial**, the hugely successful *Judex* (1917).

Feuillade was a consistently popular filmmaker for Gaumont right up to his death in 1925.

See also: color; editing: spatial relations; editing: temporal relations; multiple-reel/feature films; staging in depth

Further reading

"Feuillade and the French Serial" (1996) *The Velvet Light Trap*, Spring, 37.

Lacassin, Francis (1995) *Maître des lions et des vampires*, Paris: Pierre Bordas & fils.

RICHARD ABEL

film d'art

Emerging in 1907–1908, *film d'art* referred to a certain kind of fiction film whose aim was to ennoble the cinema through an association with literature and theater, often through adaptations of historical drama. It is thought to begin with Edmond **Benoit-Lévy**'s initiative to record on film Michel **Carré**'s famous pantomime, *L'Enfant prodigue* [The Prodigal Child]. Directed by the author, the film was unsuccessful when presented in June 1907, but it did modify the prejudice many writers then held against cinema.

In February 1908, Paul **Laffitte** founded **Film d'Art**, from which the name for this kind of film derived. Henri Lavedan of the Académie Française was the company's artistic director, and its aim was to get famous authors to script films in which the most celebrated actors of the time (Charles **Le Bargy**, Mounet-Sully, Sarah **Bernhardt**) would peform. Heralded by a press campaign, the 17 November 1908 première of *L'assassinat du Duc de Guise* [The Assassination of the Duke de Guise], directed by André **Calmettes**, created a considerable stir. Due to the reputation of the Parisian theater world, this production's international success was to transform the industry in a profound way. In the USA, for instance, this and other *films d'art* encouraged companies such as **Vitagraph** and **Biograph** to take up similar filmmaking practices and led actors from the legitimate theater to agree to to be filmed. Contrary to historical myths, *The Duke de Guise* is characterized by a restrained **acting style** (in contrast to earlier styles of gesticulation), a cohesive narration, and a relatively complex psychology. D. W. **Griffith**, among others, took it as a lesson.

In March 1908, Eugène **Gugenheim** and Pierre **Decourcelle** founded **SCAGL**, which, like Film d'Art, was distributed by **Pathé-Frères**. Directed by André **Capellani**, this company's films specialized in adaptations of confirmed literary successes, from Alphonse Daudet's *L'Arlèsienne* (1908) to Victor Hugo's *Notre Dame de Paris* (1911) and *Les Misérables* (1912). Other companies soon followed: **Éclair** founded A.C.A.D.: **Gaumont**, Grand Films Artistiques; and **Eclipse**, Série d'art. For its part, Pathé-Frères launched **Film d'Arte Italiana** and Film d'art russe.

There are many reasons why *film d'art* came into being at this moment. In 1906–1908, certain authors took legal action against Pathé-Frères for forgery of their work. At that time also, moving pictures were beginning to attract an increasing percentage of theater-goers in France. Consequently, *film d'art* can be seen as a reaction on the part of the **legitimate theater** to take advantage of the cinema's growing success. Reciprocally, for film companies such as Pathé-Frères, which faced a crisis of overproduction

Figure 38 Poster for *L' Assassinat du duc de Guise* [Assassination of the Duke of Guise] (Film d' Art 1908).

(1907–1909), it provided more suitable subjects to lure a middle-class clientele into the new cinemas that were being built expressly for them.

Despite its allegedly theatrical aesthetic, the principal merits of *film d'art* were to introduce artistic preoccupations into the cinema and to faciliate the initial exchanges, soon to become so characteristic of cinema, between high and low culture.

Further reading

Abel, Richard (1994) *The Ciné Goes to Town: French Cinema, 1896–1914*, Berkeley: University of California Press.

Carou, Alain (2002) *Le cinéma français et les écrivains: histoire d'une rencontre, 1906–1914*, Paris: AFRHC/Ecoles de Chartes.

JEAN-PIERRE SIROIS-TRAHAN

Film d'Art

Film d' Art epitomizes efforts in French cinema from 1908 on to widen its audience and attract more educated segments of the population. In reaction to the bulk of earlier film production—mediocre playlets—Film d'Art offered the audience adaptations of famous classic and contemporary plays, with renowned stage actors.

Two academicians were the mainspring in the founding of Film d'Art: Charles **Le Bargy**, a famous member of the Comédie Française, and novelist and playwright Henri Lavedan. With their clout and the generous remuneration they offered, they managed to secure prestigious collaborations.

Founded by businessman Paul **Lafitte** in February 1908, Film d'Art was a public limited company (*société anonyme*) with an initial capital of 500,000 francs. Among its major subscribers were several shareholders of the Compagnie des **Cinéma-Halls**: the Formigé brothers, Émile Célerier, and the Laffitte brothers (Célerier and Laffitte also were administrators for **Théophile Pathé**). The investors in Film d'Art probably hoped to distribute their productions through the network of Cinéma-Halls, but the collapse of that company forced them to turn to **Pathé-Frères** not only for the technical infrastructure needed for production, but for exhibition as well.

The public launching of Film d'Art took place on 17 November, 1908 at the Charras theater (near the Paris Opera) with several films, the most famous being *L'Assassinat du duc de Guise* [The Assassination of the Duke de Guise], a series of "historical tableaux" running 340 meters, written by Henri Lavedan, directed by Le Bargy and André **Calmettes**, and accompanied by original music from Camille Saint-Saëns. For the first time, a moving picture event was widely commented on by the press. While some journalists (and a few authors) were indignant that renowned artists and writers had compromised themselves, others were more lenient, or even had favorable reactions. Other productions soon followed: *La Tosca, Le Baiser de Judas* [Judas' Kiss], *Le Retour d'Ulysse* [Ulysses's Return], all released in 1909.

Due to poor management and a lukewarm reception of its subsequent productions (on the part of both popular audiences and frequent theater-goers) Film d'Art went through a major financial crisis in 1909. Playwright Paul Gavault took over as director in June 1909, but failed to improve the situation of the company. In 1911, the board of directors had to resign, and Charles **Delac** (of Monofilm) purchased the company, soon naming Louis **Nalpas** as artistic director of production. In March 1910, the **AGC** (Agence Générale Cinématographique) took charge of distributing the company's output. Several of these films enjoyed a worldwide success: *Mme Sans-Gêne*, with Gabrielle Réjane (1911), *La Dame aux camélias* [Camille], with Sarah **Bernhardt** (1912), and Henri **Pouctal**'s 4,000-meter *Les Trois Mousquetaires* [The Three Musketeers] (1913).

A number of similar companies were created in the wake of Film d'Art, among which were the Société Cinématographique des Auteurs et Gens de Lettres (**SCAGL**), affiliated with Pathé-Frères, and the Association Cinématographique des Auteurs Dramatiques (ACAD), affiliated with **Éclair**. Moreover, others sought to copy them by creating "artistic series" whose films were rented at higher prices. The movement probably widened the audience for cinema in France, yet its close connection to the **legitimate theater** discouraged the development of a means of expression specific to cinema.

See also: staging in depth

JEAN-JACQUES MEUSY

Film d'Arte Italiana

Established in Rome in March 1909 by the Italian branch office of **Pathé-Frères** and modeled on the French company's own 1908 "artistic" subsidiary, **Film d'Art**, Film d'Arte Italiana specialized in bringing Italy's most celebrated theatrical figures to the screen. Headed by talent scout Gerolamo **Lo Savio** and with Ugo **Falena** as artistic director, Film d'Arte Italiana cast stars of the legitimate **theater**—most notably Ermete **Novelli**—but also of **opera**, dialect comedy, and melodrama for its artistically ambitious one- or two-reelers. Among these were *Otello* (1909) and *Il Trovatore* (1911), starring a young Francesca **Bertini**.

GIORGIO BERTELLINI

film developing, printing, and assembly

Early cinematography relied on a series of processes to make a finished product for projection. Both individual filmmakers and manufacturers purchased raw **celluloid** film stock coated with a light-sensitive emulsion, ordering it cut to their required width. All further operations in filmmaking were undertaken by a filmmaker or others within a company, including perforating the raw stock, prior to about 1905. When the unexposed stock was ready, the procedure was as follows:

(1) Shoot the film in the camera. (2) Process (develop and fix) the exposed negative. (3) Print the negative onto another strip of unexposed film in the camera or in a separate printing machine. (4) Process the exposed positive.

If comprising more than one shot, the final viewing print was compiled in one of two ways: (1) the sections of negative were spliced together in the required order, and this assembled negative was used to print any number of final positives; or (2) all the usable negative material was printed up in any order, and the resulting positive shots were assembled together for each finished print.

For development, the strip of film was wound onto a large drum which revolved, with the lower section passing through a trough of photographic developing solution. Alternatively, the film was wound around pegs on a flat cross-frame, the whole of which was submerged in developer. A red viewing light (early printing film was insensitive to red) was used to check the progress of the development. The film was then washed and the process repeated with a fixing solution, followed by further washing. The same procedure was used for both the negative and the positive.

In general, many of the techniques and technologies involved in film developing, printing, and assembly appeared earlier than most histories record, with the possible exception of the closely-studied and much-debated juxtaposition of two separate images in an "editing" process, either by joining two separate pieces of film or by stopping and then re-starting the camera.

There were no editing machines for viewing the negative or positive shots as they were being selected, trimmed, and assembled. Running the film from spool to spool on a rewinding bench, good eyesight and a magnifier helped to determine where to trim a shot. With the help of a small splicing block, film lengths were joined together by scraping the emulsion on the very end of one shot, applying film cement to soften the exposed celluloid base, and overlapping the next shot by one perforation.

In a film contact printer, separate reels of negative and positive film stock were threaded across an aperture, with the two strips of film in direct contact as they passed a light source. That Birt **Acres** could sketch the outline of such a printer in June 1895 was made easier because most early film production apparatus was inherited from existing technology. For four decades and beyond, his design would remain conceptually unchanged. Mechanical printing and developing apparatus had its origins in the early 1890s in equipment for the mass production of **postcards**, photographic prints, and **magic lantern** slides, as well as the centralized finishing of amateur roll-film prints by several firms. Notable apparatus was built for this purpose by the Automatic Photograph Company in the USA, Neue Photographische Gesellschaft in Germany, and Rotary Photographic Company in Great Britain.

An early frame counter (*c.* 1905) in the Barnes Collection, made by the Veeder Manufacturing Company of Hartford, Connecticut, exemplifies the initial importation of existing technology into moving picture work. From 1895, Veeder was a specialist in the production of mechanical counting and measuring apparatus, particularly odometers and tachometers for bicycles, automobiles, and machinery, and he simply transferred their patented technology to a new market.

Following the lead of the **Cinématographe Lumière**, many early **cameras** also were intended for both projection and printing, or could easily be adapted to these purposes. The first separate motion picture printers moved the film continuously, which could cause problems with slippage between the film strips as they were exposed. As a result, dedicated cameras were often preferred, printing the intermittently-moving film strip one frame at a time, or step by step.

In sharp contrast to the unsophisticated technology used for developing and printing by most early manufacturers, which resulted from a lack of capital investment rather than a lack of mechanical ingenuity, an elaborate step-printer incorporating feedback mechanisms to notify the operator of any errors was developed by the **American Mutoscope and Biograph Company** in 1897–1898 to make clear projection prints from the images placed randomly on unperforated film stock that was produced by its camera.

Certain early techniques, particularly the tinting and toning of projection prints and the insertion of **intertitles** in fiction films, both after 1901, encouraged the handling of individual shots at the printing and developing stages. Each release print was then assembled entirely by hand out of its component parts. As a result, basic printing machines and wooden developing racks serviced by young boys or women remained in use until **World War I**, after which fully mechanized printing and developing machinery for the mass production of complete prints finally became common.

Figure 39 Pathé-Frères' film splicing lab, Vincennes, *c.* 1910.

Figure 40 American Film Company editing room, Santa Barbara. (Courtesy of the Robert S. Birchard Collection.)

Cecil **Hepworth** built a continuous, linear developing machine as early as 1898, patented with Charles **Urban**, but it was never commercialized. In 1907, **Gaumont** began to use a continuous developing apparatus with the film strip running through a series of tubes holding the different developing chemicals, and Bell and Howell marketed a fully mechanized continuous printer in 1911. Only gradually were both technologies accepted across the industry, as inexpensive female labor for the assembly of finished prints (or for their stencil colouring) remained a viable alternative to capital investment in laboratory machinery. Not until the near-simultaneous diversion of women into war industries and the post-war consolidation of production and exhibition in the film industry did mass production by machine become economically preferable.

See also: color

Further reading

Marette, J. (1950) "Les procédés de coloriage mécanique des films," *Bulletin de l'association française des ingénieurs et techniciens du cinema*, 7: 3–8.

Rossell, Deac (2001) "The Biograph Large Format Technology," *Griffithiana*, 66–70: 78–115.

Salt, Barry (1992) *Film Style & Technology: History & Analysis*, 2nd ed., London: Starword.

STEPHEN HERBERT AND DEAC ROSSELL

film festivals and occasional events

Film festivals and other occasional or regular events have played an important part in heightening both the visibility of early moving pictures and our understanding of the silent film experience, which was largely forgotten for decades following the coming of sound. During that period silent films generally remained archaic artefacts, far removed from their original exhibition context as well as the **musical accompaniment** which—however ephemeral and varied—represented an integral element of the "silent" film experience. Before the 1960s, the only consistent attempts to preserve that experience were by New York's Museum of Modern Art Film Department, whose musical director from 1939 to 1967, Arthur Kleiner, provided highly intelligent piano accompaniments to public screenings (his collection of some 700 **musical scores** is now held by the University of Minnesota), and at London's National Film Theater which in the first years after its inception in 1952 employed distinguished veterans of the silent era—Arthur Dulay, Ena Baga, Florence de Jongh—to complement the silent screen image with a degree of authenticity. From the mid-1960s, international film festivals such as Venice and Berlin have presented side-bar retrospectives which frequently include silent films, generally accompanied by piano or electronic organ. And the practice continues.

The first festival wholly dedicated to silent films, Le Giornate del Cinema Muto, was established in 1982 by a group of enthusiasts in the small Italian town of Pordenone, and since then has grown in size and international reputation. Its presentations often have brought to light hitherto unexplored areas of early cinema history, including the cinemas of Tsarist Russia, Japan, and pre-Caligari Germany as well as complete retrospectives of **Vitagraph**'s output and the **Biograph** films of D. W. **Griffith**. Cinema Ritrovato, the annual festival presented by the Cineteca di Bologna, is by definition a presentation of newly restored films, and these generally include a high proportion of silent films. In England, the annual Nottingham Silent Weekend regularly offers important rediscoveries from early British cinema.

The 1978 Brighton Congress of the Fédération Internationale des Archives du Film (FIAF), which endeavored to bring together every known film surviving from the very first years of cinema, is now acknowledged as the watershed event that reinvigorated the study of early cinema. Subsequent FIAF presentations have included the memorable 1999 London Congress, which screened only films surviving in the form of original nitrate prints.

Moreover, individual **archives** have provided opportunities for important screenings of early films: in the 1990s, for instance, the Nederlands Filmmuseum has organized workshops on early nonfiction, color, and ethnographic films.

The occasional retrospectives sponsored by the Association française de recherché sur l'histoire du cinema (AFRHC) have included a memorable 1986 presentation of early French **comedies**. Domitor, an international society devoted to promoting the study of early cinema, organizes biennial conferences, always supplemented by film programs: among the most notable of these have been the 1994 New York conference on "cinema at the turn of the century," the 1996 Paris conference on **Pathé-Frères**, and the 1998 Washington conference on early sound practices.

Further reading

Holman, Roger (ed.) (1982) *Cinema 1900/1906: An Analytical Study*, 2 vols., Brussels: FIAF.

DAVID ROBINSON

filme cantante (sung films)

A cycle of films that appropriated theatrical spectacles such as operettas and musical revues and led to the first popular acceptance of locally made films in Brazil. Produced between 1908 and 1911, they were characterized by a peculiar form of sonorization: well-known singers positioned behind the screen provided live accompaniment. The first *filme cantante* ostensibly was invented by Francisco **Serrador** in São Paulo, but the genre thrived in Rio de Janeiro, where William **Auler** was the most significant producer. The cycle ended rather abruptly in 1911, as foreign films began to dominate the growing cinema business, and national producers closed their doors.

See also: dialogue accompaniment, *phonoscènes*

ANA M. LÓPEZ

Filmen

Filmen was the principal Danish trade paper (1912–1926), although its name changed to *Kinobladet* in 1918. Initially published by the distribution company **Kinografen**, it was taken over in 1913 by the Copenhagen Exhibitors' Association and co-edited by Jens Locher and Vilhelm **Glückstadt** until 1916, after which Locher became sole editor. Appearing biweekly, *Filmen* included advertisements and industry news as well as occasional articles on film aesthetics.

CASPAR TYBJERG

films sonores

Pathé-Frères generally left to **Gaumont** the—very costly—privilege of exploring new technologies, for instance, sound films. Early on, however, perhaps because of its strong **phonograph** division, the company ventured into the production of sound films, if only timidly. Its 1900 catalogue included Ferdinand **Zecca**'s *Le muet mélomane* [The Dumb Music Lover] with Charlus. In 1905, it marketed projecting equipment for "cine-phonographic scenes." In 1908, Pathé purchased the rights to Maurice Couade's synchronizing system linking cinematographic equipment and the phonograph, and dozens of sound films were shot with some celebrities (**Prince**, for instance). Yet Pathé never managed to compete in a French market dominated for the most part by Gaumont and Georges **Mendel**.

LAURENT MANNONI

Finch, Flora

b. 1869; d. 1940

actor, USA

Born in England, Finch's long film career began at **Biograph** with *Mrs. Jones Entertains* (1908). It was her role as "Mrs. Bunny," the bone-thin, ill-dressed, hen-pecking wife to portly John **Bunny**, however, that gained global attention. Produced at **Vitagraph** between 1910 and 1914, the **comic** series popularly dubbed "bunnyfinchgraphs" made the Finch-Bunny duo the first significant American comedy team. Following Bunny's death in 1915, Finch starred in a 1917 comic series as "Flora" and then, in the early 1920s, in a two-reel "Fun Frolics" series, before transitioning to secondary dramatic roles in films such as *The Cat and the Canary* (1927).

JENNIFER M. BEAN

Finland

Early cinema coincided with the most turbulent era in Finnish history. Finland became independent in 1917, having been an autonomous Duchy in the Russian Empire since 1809. This was also a Golden Age of Finnish art. Yet these epochal events and trends were but vaguely reflected in contemporary Finnish cinema.

Moving images had been screened before (the Electrotachyscope in 1892), but the beginning of cinema in Finland was marked by the premiere of the **Cinématographe Lumière** at the Café Seurahuone in Helsinki, on 28 June 1896, brought from Russia by Arthur Grünwaldt. This high society event gave immediate esteem to the medium.

During the next five years, moving pictures were shown in Finland through the tours of K. J. Ståhlberg, Oskar Alonen, and J. A. W. Grönroos. The circus impresario Grönroos founded Finland's first film distribution office, Pohjola, in 1899. The first permanent cinema, Kinematograf International, was opened in Helsinki in 1901. The business boomed, but standards of exhibition were poor until 1908. By the eve of **World War I**, however, Helsinki could boast a high standard of cinema exhibition, with **palace cinemas** such as Maxim (1911).

There was a rich culture of **musical accompaniment** especially from 1908 on. The best cinemas had 25-piece orchestras. **Intertitles** in Finnish and Swedish was introduced in 1910. Before that, **lecturers** were crucial, and some were even major attractions. After 1910, many cinemas presented variety acts as well.

The business grew phenomenally in popularity as moving pictures conveyed the excitement of

modernity, urbanity, technology, and internationalism. Children packed the cinemas, the queues jammed traffic. A vogue for **crime films** brought a demand for control by 1905. The police started to patrol cinemas, and it helped that there were film buffs among their ranks. Censorship was a dirty word, especially under Finland's new liberal Constitution of 1906. However, preventive film control had to be established in 1911: films were to be approved in advance by local police departments.

Lumière cameramen Félix **Mesguich** and Francis **Doublier** had shot *hors catalogue* views in Finland in 1898. The first film both shot and screened in Finland was *Nikolainkadun koulun koulunuorisoa välitunnilla* [Nikolainkatu School-children at Play] (1904) by American Bioscope. The Finnish film production was to be dominated thereafter by **Atelier Apollo**, **Finlandia Film**, and **Lyyra Filmi**. A fourth company, Pohjoismaiden Biografi Komppania, produced 47 shorts and a few features, including Konrad Tallroth's directing debut, *Kun onni pettää* [When Luck Fails] (1913).

A wide variety of moving pictures from other countries quickly reached Finnish screens. **World War I** brought a ban on German films; after which Russian art films reaped success. The prohibition of cinematography during the war halted Finnish fiction film production in 1916 for three years. By 1915, there were 105 cinemas in Finland and 1.85 attendances yearly per capita. By 1917, at least 28 fiction films and at least 350 nonfiction films had been produced in Finland. Some two hours of Finnish early cinema survive: all of it nonfiction except for some footage from *Sylvi* (1913).

Further reading

Hirn, Sven (1981) *Kuvat kulkevat. Kuvallisten esi-tysten perinne ja elävien kuvien 12 ensimmäistä vuotta Suomessa* (Moving Images. The Tradition of Visual Entertainment and the First 12 Years of Cinema in Finland), Helsinki: Suomen elokuvasäätiö.

Hirn, Sven (1991) *Kuvat elävät. Elokuvatoimintaa Suomessa 1908–1918* (Living Images. The Development of Cinema in Finland 1908–1918), Helsinki: VAPK-Kustannus/Suomen elokuva-arkisto.

ANTTI ALANEN

Finlandia Film

In 1912, engineer Erik Estlander (1871–1945), distributor of **Pathé-Frères** films in Finland, established a film production company called Ab Finlandia Film. For the next four years he produced 60 shorts, most of them *actualités*. In 1915, Estlander built Finland's first film studio, a glass atelier, in which two feature fiction films were shot before the Russian ban on cinematography stopped production. Estlander produced Finland's last fiction film before independence: *Eräs elämän murhenäytelmä* [A Tragedy of Life] (1916). It was confiscated, and the director, Konrad Tallroth, moved briefly to **Svenska Biografteatern** in Sweden.

ANTTI ALANEN

Fitzhamon, Lewin

b. 1869; d. 1961

filmmaker, Great Britain

Lewin "Fitz" Fitzhamon was Cecil **Hepworth**'s principal director, making literally hundreds of one-reelers between 1904 and 1912.

Originally a **music hall** performer, he first turned to film in 1900 with Robert **Paul**, directing some films and acting in others, including *Briton vs Boer*. In 1904 he joined Hepworth as "stage manager," replacing Percy **Stow**, where he wrote, directed, and frequently acted in two films a week for the next eight years. Fitzhamon was naturally inventive, but he also brought the discipline of his music hall sketch background to the art of the one-reeler, never more so than in *Rescued by Rover* (1905), enormously popular in its day, and admired ever since for its skill in creating spatial and temporal continuity through editing. A countryman at heart, he loved working with animals, which he frequently showed performing heroic deeds of rescue, as in *Dog Outwits the Kidnappers* and *Dumb Sagacity*; he also shared Hepworth's love of effects in such **trick films** as *Sister Mary Jane's Top Note* (1907) and *The Man and his Bottle* (1908). He developed several **comic series** for Hepworth, such as *Poorlucks* and the anarchic *Tilly* series with the young Alma **Taylor** and Chrissie **White**. In addition, he turned out topicals or *actualités*, fantasy films such as *Prehistoric Peeps*, **westerns** such as *The Squatter's Daughter*, domestic **melodramas** such as *Falsely Accused*, and **chase films** such as *A New Hat for Nothing*.

In 1912, Fitzhamon left Hepworth to form his own company, Fitz Films, before ending his career as a director for hire with various producers, in 1913–1914. He also was an occasional writer, publishing two novels, in 1904 and 1915. Fitzhamon's films were unsophisticated fare, with no concern except to get the central trick effect or plot idea across, but their very lack of pretension makes for pleasurable viewing now. The best of them—*What the Curate Really Did*, *That Fatal Sneeze*, *Tilly and the Fire Engines*—display an original imagination and an innocent delight in the basic possibilities of film.

See also: editing: spatial relations; editing: temporal relations

LUKE McKERNAN

Floury, Edmond Louis

b. 1862; d. 1923

filmmaker, producer, critic, France

For fifteen years Edmond Floury was general secretary of the Châtelet theater in Paris (after his father's death, his mother officially became director, while his brother Félix was the administrator). It is in this role that Floury commissioned a **color** film sequence from **Gaumont** (directed by Jacques Ducom), for *La Biche au bois*, a *féerie*/**fairy play** spectacle that opened at the Châtelet on 14 November 1896.

In December 1912, after working at **Pathé-Frères** as a filmmaker and artistic director, Floury created a short-lived production company, Sélecta Film, whose films were distributed by Pathé. In June 1914, he became a film critic for *Le Courrier cinématographique*.

His son, also named Edmond (1887–1959), was Jean Benoît-Lévy's cameraman and directed educational shorts.

JEAN-JACQUES MEUSY

Foersterling, Hermann

b. ?; d. ?

manufacturer/exhibitor, Germany

An electrical novelty entrepreneur who tested the **Kinetoscope** for Ludwig **Stollwerck**, Foersterling was selling counterfeit copies of **projectors** by May 1896 (possibly Birt **Acres**'s); from July 1896, his quality copy of a **Continsouza** apparatus was widely used across northern and central Europe under the name, Edison's Ideal. He also provided customers with a clever advertising and promotional campaign, associating his counterfeit machines with the names of both **Edison** and **Lumière**. In 1897, he lost a court cast to Oskar **Messter** for infringing one of his trademarks, fell ill, and retired soon after.

DEAC ROSSELL

Ford [O'Fearna or Feeney], Francis

b. 1882; d. 1953

actor/director, USA

Francis Ford entered the film industry as an actor/director hired by Gaston Méliès around 1908. In 1912, he went to work for the **New York Motion Picture Corporation**, acting in and then directing Bison-101 **westerns** as well as Broncho Civil War subjects for Thomas **Ince**. After meeting actor/writer Grace **Cunard**, he moved to **Universal** in 1913, where the two launched a six-year cycle of adventure and **detective films**, among them **serials** such as *Lucille Love, Girl of Mystery* (1914),

The Broken Coin (1915), and *The Purple Mask* (1917). After directing several low-budget independent serials and melodramas in the 1920s, he continued acting in small roles, mostly for his younger brother John Ford.

JENNIFER M. BEAN

Foster, William

b. 1860; d. 1940

filmmaker, writer, theatrical manager, USA

The first African American film producer, Foster began his show business career as a **vaudeville** publicist and booking agent. After serving as Business Representative of the legendary black-owned Pekin Theater in Chicago, he founded the Foster Photoplay Company, specializing in non-degrading, black-cast **comedies**. In the first of at least eleven films, *The Railroad Porter* (1913), Foster highlighted black middle-class urban life. Foster also wrote extensively about the black entertainment world for **newspapers** like the *Defender* (Chicago) and *Freeman* (Indianapolis) under the pen name, Juli Jones.

See also: black cinema, USA

JACQUELINE STEWART

Fotorama

Founded in 1908 by photographer Thomas Hermansen (1867–1930), this film company was based in Arhus, Denmark's second-largest city, and carried his name until it was changed to Fotorama in 1910. Led by Frede **Skaarup**, the company became a powerful distributor and, in 1909, began making commercially attractive films so as to extend its influence over exhibitors. Among them was the first Danish feature, the **white slave film** *Den hvide Slavehandel* [In the Hands of Impostors] (1910), photographed by Alfred **Lind**. After **Nordisk** made a pirated copy, an out-of-court settlement gave Fotorama Danish distribution rights to Nordisk's productions. Although it ceased production in

1913, Fotorama remained the principal Danish distributor until the 1930s.

CASPER TYBJERG

Fox, William

b. 1 January 1879; d. 8 May 1952

exhibitor, distributor, producer, USA

William Fox was an important pioneering exhibitor who built the foundation of a movie empire that would eventually include his name: Twentieth Century-Fox. After he lost control of his company in 1930, however, this industry innovator—who early on realized the advantages of controlling the production and distribution of the films he presented in his theaters—was reduced, inappropriately, to a question: who was the Fox in Twentieth Century-Fox?

His family had brought him to the USA nine months after his birth as Wilhelm Fried of Tulchva, Hungary. Before the 19th century ended, the newly named "William Fox" struggled mightily to find his place in his new country. He had quit school in 1890 at age 11, and tried numerous occupations, principally in and around New York's garment trade. He was still searching when he noticed the lines in front of a penny arcade, and in 1905 he entered the then emerging **nickelodeon** industry.

Fox opened his first **penny arcade** in Brooklyn, steadily opened more arcades and then nickelodeons, established the **Greater New York Film Rental Company** in 1907, and later began to take over existing far larger theaters such as the Dewey on Fourteenth Street. Ever a conservative businessman, Fox leased and operated theaters showing not moving pictures exclusively, but "small time vaudeville," which Marcus **Loew** and others had pioneered with success. He leased space so that he could see if his booking ideas could and would make a go at that location. Only then did he commit.

In 1910, he purchased the 2,000-seat Academy of Music on Union Square, where, for three years, he tried a live stock company, produced a play a week, and charged 10, 20 or 30 cents. By the end of

1912, he had lost a reported $380,000. Only then did he turn to moving pictures exclusively, and made profits. In time he had 25 theaters in and around New York City.

Dissatisfied with the demands of the **Motion Picture Patents Company** on Greater New York Rental, by 1912, Fox sued. As the case dragged on, he finally decided to produce his own feature films in 1914. That initial season his Box Office Attractions Company created eight titles. In 1915, the Fox Film Company and allied subsidiaries produced 40 films, reportedly accumulated more than a $500,000 in profit, and signaled the end of "early cinema."

By then, Fox was a fully integrated, pioneering vertical power, able to deliver his own films to his own theaters. Thereafter, Fox expanded on all fronts, opening a Hollywood studio in 1917. But he overextended, was forced out, and spent the last 22 years of his life a bitter outsider, barely remembered as "half" of Twentieth Century-Fox, a company he never ran.

Further reading

Allvine, Gelndon (1969) *The Greatest Fox of Them All*, New York: Lyle Stuart.

Gomery, Douglas (1992) *Shared Pleasures: A History of Movie Presentation in the United States*, Madison: University of Wisconsin Press.

DOUGLAS GOMERY

framing: camera distance and angle

Cinematography implies selecting a certain partial view of the world: that is, including some things within the film frame and excluding others. The camera is set up at a certain distance from the subject and at a certain angle to it, showing more or less of what might be shown.

The distance depends in part on the lens used. Although longer lenses seem to have been used at the very beginnings of the cinema (3-inch, or 75mm ones are often recommended in manuals of cinematography), for most of the period covered by this encyclopedia, the standard lens for studio filmmaking was a 50mm one. Longer lenses were occasionally used, especially in *actualité* shooting, to enlarge a distant object, and shorter lenses were very occasionally used also, to capture the entirety of a big set—e.g., **Gloria**'s *Ma l'amor mio non muore!*/Love Everlasting (1913)—but most scenes in most films were shot with a 50mm lens. Taking the lens as given, however, distance and angle were primarily determined by the choice of framing.

The basic principle governing framing in early cinema was to include all the significant aspects of the subject in the film picture. There are a very few early exceptions to this, such as R. W. **Paul**'s *A Chess Dispute* (1903), in which two quarreling chess players disappear below the bottom frame line, limbs and weapons appearing momentarily to signify the off-screen fight, and thus flaunting off-screen space in a way characteristic of the exposure of devices in the **cinema of attractions**. And it can be argued that in POV (point of view) editing and inter-cutting, each shot evokes part of the action that is visible only in the other shots, and hence is off-screen. But the function of these editing patterns seems basically inclusive, being to show as much of the significant action as possible in the shortest time. Although in most *actualités* it was often impossible to conform to this principle, in "composed views"—that is, fiction films and **re-enactments**—the principle of inclusiveness ruled.

This demand for inclusiveness governed the typical framing of composed films until about 1905. The camera was set up with the lens at eye level and horizontal, and at a distance which would include the characters' feet (about 15 meters with the standard 50mm lens). The resultant image has the characters' heads in the middle of the frame, with a lot of the backdrop or setting visible above them. Between 1905 and 1909, the camera was gradually brought closer (to about 5 meters with the standard lens), without excluding any part of the actors' bodies, so that their heads were close to the top frame line, their feet near the bottom. In order to maintain the full length of the figure within the frame, the closer camera had either to be tilted down, or lowered, or a combination of the two. In France, cameramen working for **Pathé Frères** lowered the camera to waist height. This is adumbrated as early as 1906 in such films as

Un Drame à Venise [A Venetian Tragedy], but its adoption as a constant norm seems to derive from **Film d'Art**'s *L'Assassinat du duc de Guise* [Assassination of the Duke de Guise] (1908); by 1909 almost every shot in a Pathé film uses this low horizontal camera. An example is the Max **Linder** film, *Les Débuts de Max au cinématographe* [Max Linder's Debut as a Cinematograph Artist] (1910), which is not only shot entirely in this way, but shows Pathé cameras set up at this low height in its scenes of the filming of a Pathé **comedy**. The result is an image where, as characters recede from the camera their heads get lower and their feet higher in the frame. **Gaumont** filmmakers, by contrast, continued to use an eye-level camera, but tilted it down, the result being an image in which all the characters' heads are near the top of the frame, while their feet are higher the further away from the camera they are, and a lot of the ground is visible. In the USA, cameramen combined the two approaches, and also varied camera height and angle from shot to shot, with the result that American films have less of a "studio look" than French ones.

Such framings were used for the main scenes in a film; indeed, many films consisted solely of one or a series of such inclusive scenes, perhaps with intervening **intertitles**. However, there were closer framings than this. **Magic lantern shows** often included portraits of famous figures, usually as bust-length pictures, and some early films continued this tradition, particularly those featuring a performer who did quick-change impressions of current notables, or simply made funny faces—e.g., **Vitagraph**'s *Oh! You Dirty Boy!* (1905). From around 1900, closer views were also inserted into fiction films otherwise consisting of inclusive scenes. These closer shots can be further classified. In the "emblematic shot," a closer view of a principal character (sometimes still a full-figure shot, sometimes a waist-up shot or bust shot) or significant object at the beginning and/or end of the film functions as a kind of punctuation point—e.g., **Lubin**'s *Bold Bank Robbery* (1904). In the "magnified view," a closer shot of a detail is inserted into an inclusive scene shot—e.g., G. A. **Smith**'s *Mary Jane's Mishap* (1903). And certain actions seem to have allowed free-standing closer shots in a sequence of full scenes (although similar shots can

also occur as cut-ins to a magnified view): in the fragments deposited by the Vitagraph Company at the Copyright Office in Washington, D.C., between 1905 and 1909, waist-up shots or bust shots of characters talking on a telephone—as in *A Night Out* (1908)—and shins-up shots of courting couples—as in *Francesca di Rimini* (1907)—or couples getting married at the altar—as in *Mine at Last* (1909)—are often found without any frames from a surrounding full shot.

At the beginning of the 1910s, the full-length shot begins to be replaced as the basic scene shot by a closer view, one which cuts off the feet of the principal characters at the front of the playing area. In the USA, this gives rise to what the French called the *plan américain*, a shot which frames the characters from the thighs upwards, achieved by placing the camera about 3 meters from the subject. In Europe, this closer view was usually slightly longer, framing characters from the shins upwards (dubbed in the USA "French foreground"). All interiors in many films were shot at this distance. With a 50mm lens, the front of the playing area is only 1.5 meters broad in such a framing, so a scene in a room set carves out a very long and narrow sliver from the imaginary space of the full room (in fact, if such shots are examined closely, it is often clear that no real room would ever have the arrangement of walls and furniture visible in the frame). With the low Pathé camera, such framings usually result in no floor being visible either, and in at least one Vitagraph film, *The First Violin* (1912), the filmmakers had to build a ceilinged set to avoid discovery of the studio fixtures above the walls. Despite the fact that such eccentric framings would seem to expose the invisible presence of off-screen space, they still continue to function as the arena in which all the significant action occurs.

Despite the deviation from strict horizontality implied by the "Gaumont angle," all the views so far discussed are close to the horizontal. Vertical cameras were used early for **trick films**, to create the illusion that characters lying on a painted floor were flying or walking up walls—as in Pathé's *La Soubrette ingénieuse* [The Ingenious Soubrette] (1902)—and in dramatic films slightly higher and lower angles are used where settings, usually locations, demand it—e.g., for shots from street level to the raised porch of a house, or from the sides of canyons to action in their depths in **westerns**. Only at the very end of the period covered here are more deviant angles found. Sometimes these are motivated by POV—as in the high-angle shots of the crowd greeting the returned Captain de Valen in Léonce **Perret**'s *L'Enfant de Paris* (1913); sometimes they are completely unmotivated—as in the wedding reception scene in Evgenii **Bauer**'s *Nemye svideteli* [Silent Witnesses] (1914).

Everything so far has assumed that the camera was static during the shooting of a scene. Of course, from the beginnings of the cinema, cameras also moved. Such shots, however, almost never transgressed the principle of inclusion. Most movements were reframing ones, with the significant action kept at the same point in the frame, even when they were tracks with a moving vehicle or long pans, such as those accompanying the main characters walking from their homes to the mine in Pathé's *Au pays noir* [The Miner] (1905). Towards the end of the period covered here, especially in Germany, pans that reframe one significant character in a scene may exclude a second for part of that scene. In Urban **Gad**'s *Das Mädchen ohne Vaterland* [The Girl without a Country] (1912), when gipsy girl Zidra (Asta **Nielsen**) visits the rooms of Lieutenant Ipanoff in a Central European fortress, the camera is positioned so that it has to show either the area near the door left or an alcove rear right. When a visitor knocks, Zidra hides behind curtains near the door, and Ipanoff shows the visitor to the alcove; thenceforth the camera pans back and forth between the door area and the alcove as Zidra emerges and leaves the room in search of secret plans, Ipanoff comes momentarily to the door and finds her gone, she returns to her hiding place while he is in the alcove, he shows the visitor out, and Zidra emerges, pretending to have been behind the curtains all along. And in Viggø **Larsen**'s *Die Sumpfblume* [The Swamp Flower] (1913), in a scene in Edgar von Schmetting's Paris apartment, the camera first pans with von Schmetting and his model Sandra (Wanda Treumann) as they move to the dining room further right; von Schmetting then exits left back into the studio as Sandra explores the dining room; she opens some curtains on the right side of the dining room and discovers the bedroom in an alcove behind them; she exits into the alcove closing the curtains behind her; pan left off the dining room to show von Schmetting at his desk in the studio; pan right with him as he rises and goes into the dining room; he looks around for Sandra, then advances towards the curtained doorway right. These virtuoso pans begin to assume the functions that André Bazin later attributed to Jean Renoir's moving camera in such films as *La Règle du jeu* [Rules of the Game] (1939).

See also: acting styles; camera movement; editing: spatial relations; editing: tableau style; facial expression films; set design; staging in depth

Further reading

Brewster, Ben (1990) "Deep Staging in French Films 1900–1914," in Thomas Elsaesser and Adam Barker (eds.) *Early Cinema: Space, Frame, Narrative*, 45–55, London: British Film Institute.

Brewster, Ben and Lea Jacobs (1997) *Theater to Cinema: Stage Pictorialism and the Early Feature Film*, Oxford: Oxford University Press.

Salt, Barry (1992) *Film Style and Technology: History and Analysis*, 2nd ed., London: Starword.

BEN BREWSTER

France

Production

Film production in France went through several stages during the early cinema period. Initially, the chief purpose in producing and selling film prints was to promote the sales of moving picture **cameras** and **celluloid** film stock. As projected moving pictures became a profitable form of entertainment in **fairs/fairgrounds** and **music halls**, manufacturing film prints for sale in and of itself assumed an importance in the emerging industry. This quickly reached the level of mass production, largely through the efforts of **Pathé-Frères** which, by 1906–1907, was manufacturing a half dozen to a dozen subjects a week and selling hundreds of prints of each title through a worldwide network of sales agencies. Indeed, for a short time, French firms were the largest suppliers of moving pictures across the globe. Through an early form of vertical integration—linking regularized film production to distribution (a regional circuit of rental exchanges) and exhibition (a chain of permanent cinemas)— Pathé-Frères even sought something like a monopoly in the industry within France, but the ever-expanding market for moving pictures outpaced its plans, and its dominance was brief. Other companies successfully took up manufacturing films as their principal line (or one of their principal lines) of business, and, by 1911–1914, film production was dispersed among a "cottage industry" of large, medium, and small firms, a condition which would more or less characterize the industry in France for the rest of the century.

As the largest French manufacturer of photographic plates and roll film in the late 19th century, **Lumière** was the first to invest in film production by training scores of photographers and sending them around the world, in 1896–1897, to publicize the Lyon company and its products. After producing nearly a thousand short film subjects, many of them *actualités*, and establishing a market for the **Cinématographe Lumière** and film stock, however, the company took no interest in the commercial exhibition of films and soon abandoned production altogether. **Gaumont**, another important manufacturer of optical equipment, shared Lumière's interest in designing and marketing apparatuses, so that Léon **Gaumont**'s secretary, Alice **Guy**, was given the task of producing short films of all kinds, also initially for promotional purposes. The **magician** and illusionist, Georges **Méliès**, who had witnessed the first public screening of the Cinématographe, however, saw moving pictures as an extension of the performances given at his Paris theater and soon, through his company Star-Film, was producing scores of short **trick films** and longer *féeries* **or fairy plays** from the 120-meter *Cendrillon* (Cinderella) (1899) to the 260-meter *Le voyage dans la lune* [Trip to the Moon] (1902), the latter often made available in hand-colored prints. As a fairground entrepreneur and owner of a **phonographic** supply shop just outside Paris, Charles **Pathé** quickly saw an opportunity to exploit moving pictures as entertainment by manufacturing them as consumables like canned goods. Rather than specialize in *actualités*, trick films, or

féeries, Pathé-Frères set out to produce a wide range of subjects (especially fiction films) to supply the needs of the fairgrounds and music halls, with Ferdinand **Zecca** directing many early titles, from *Par le trou de la serrure* [Peeping Tom] (1901) to *Histoire d'un crime* [The Story of a Crime] (1901) and *Ali Baba et les quarantes voleurs* [Ali Baba and the Forty Thieves] (1902). By 1902, the company's annual output had surpassed that of Méliès, and Pathé was constructing a "glass house" studio (the first of several) in Vincennes to further increase production.

Méliès' Star-Film reached its apogee around 1903–1904, producing forty-five films—among them the 335-meter *Le Royaume des fées* [Kingdom of the Fairies] (1903)—using two side-by-side cameras to record a second negative that could be shipped to the USA for making positive prints. Because Star-Film remained a family firm (without outside investment) and Méliès himself proudly maintained his status as an independent artist, the company lost its competitive edge as Pathé began to industrialize production. Gaumont, by contrast, following Pathé's lead, sought outside investors to augment the range, number, and frequency of its fiction film releases. By late 1905, it had a huge "glass cathedral" studio in Paris (the first to use mercury vapor lamps) and an adjacent factory printing 10,000 meters of positive film stock a day. At the same time, Guy was training newly hired Louis **Feuillade** and others as scriptwriters and filmmakers. For its part, Pathé-Frères expanded its physical plant with three more studios and a maze of laboratories that, by late 1906 (with 1,200 employees) was developing, splicing, and printing (and sometimes stencil-coloring) up to 40,000 meters of positive film stock a day—much of it headed for its largest market, the USA. To achieve that output level, the company instituted a "director-unit" system, supervised by Zecca, in which each of a half-dozen filmmakers—Lucien **Nonguet**, Gaston **Velle**, Georges **Hatot**, Segundo de **Chomón**, and André **Capellani**—regularly worked with a small unit (cameraman and cast) to produce at least one fiction film title a week. Although Pathé's trick films, *féeries*, **chase films**, **comedies**, and sensational **melodramas** were particularly popular, its 950-meter *La Vie et la Passion de N. S. Jésus Christ* [Passion Play] (1907) probably was seen by more people worldwide, and more often, than any other film during the period.

Pathé and Gaumont's success prompted other French companies to set up shop producing films. Several of these instituted in early 1907— **Théophile Pathé**, Le Lion—although well capitalized, remained small and did not last long. Launched at the same time, **Lux** was soon producing several films a week, directed by Gérard **Bourgeois**, and scoring consistent hits. Although founded in 1906, as the Paris branch of **Charles Urban Trading Company**, **Eclipse** did not become a serious competitor until it was reorganized in 1908, renovated a "glass house" studio in Boulogne-sur-Seine, and began producing such films as Joë **Hamman**'s early **westerns** and Henri **Desfontaines**' dramas under the "Radios" label. Formed in 1907 by two Paris lawyers, Charles **Jourjon** and Marcel **Vandal**, **Éclair** also took nearly a year to amass a studio and sufficient laboratories in Epinay-sur-Seine and develop into a major producer. Victorin **Jasset** led this effort for Éclair, exploiting the formula of producing a series of sensational films built around a single character, in the *Nick Carter* **detective films** (1908–1910), *Riffle Bill* westerns (1909), and *Morgan le pirate* adventure films (1909). The most ambitious of these new companies undoubtedly was **Film d'Art**, founded in early 1908 (with Pathé's financial support), whose aim was to produce quality films or *films d'art*, most from original scenarios. Engaging Comédie française actors and playwrights to work in its "glass house" studio in Neuilly, Film d'Art produced a number of influential films, from *L'Assassinat de duc de Guise* [The Assassination of the Duke de Guise] (1908) to *La Tosca* (1909). Yet, despite their impact, receipts failed to match expenses, and the company had to be sold by 1911. One reason was that Pathé's terms for distributing Film d'Art's titles were less favorable than those for its own affiliate, **SCAGL**, also founded in 1908, with exclusive rights to adapt works by authors of the Société des gens de lettres. Capellani headed SCAGL's production at one of the studios within Pathé's complex at Vincennes, directing some subjects himself and supervising others such as Georges **Monca** and René **Leprince**. So successful was SCAGL that Gaumont, Éclair, and Eclipse all soon launched their own special lines of "artistic" films.

Up until 1911, French films generally were released in single reels (averaging 300 meters) or in split reels (in which two subjects shared a single reel). Within this limited format, French firms developed the standardized production strategy of the series, in which individual titles having the same subject could be released on a regular basis. Pathé first introduced the concept in 1908 with its **newsreel** *Pathé-Journal*, different versions of which soon spread around the world. Pathé, along with Gaumont, also used the strategy to create unusually popular **comic series** around a central character/actor: the one with *Boireau*/André **Deed** (1907–1909, 1912–1914), *Max*/Max **Linder** (1910–1914), *Rigadin*/Charles **Prince** (1910–1914), *Little Moritz*/Maurice Schwartz (1910–1912), and *Rosalie*/Sarah **Duhamel** (1911–1912); the other with *Calino*/Clément **Migé** (1909–1913) and *Bébé*/Clément **Mary** (1910–1912). Éclair followed suit with *Gontran*/René Gréhan (1910–1914), *Willy*/Willy Sanders (1911–1914), and *Pétronille*/Duhamel (1912–1914); as did Lux with *Patouillard*/Paul Bertho (1910–1912), and Eclipse with *Arthème*/Ernest Servaes (1911–1914). As a further sign of the comic series's success, Gaumont added three more in 1912: *Onésime*/Ernest **Bourbon** (1912–1914), *Bout-de-zan*/René **Poyen** (1912–1914), and *Léonce*/Léonce **Perret** (1912–1914). Moreover, Gaumont used the series format to highlight its irregular production of chiefly single-reel "realist" films, released generally as *Scènes de la vie telle qu'elle est* (1911–1913). Most French firms also continued to use the single-reel and split-reel format for their nonfiction production—especially **travelogues**—and Pathé and Éclair in particular developed respected series of **scientific films**.

In 1911, in concert with Danish, Italian, and German companies, the French launched a concerted attempt to produce **multiple-reel films** on a regular basis. At SCAGL, Capellani led this effort with prestigious literary adaptations: *Le Courrier de Lyon* [The Orleans Coach] (1911), *Notre Dame de Paris* (1911), *Les Mystères de Paris* [The Mysteries of Paris] (1912), *Les Misérables*, in four parts of three reels each (1912), and *Germinal* (1913). For Film d'Art (now owned by Charles **Delac** and headed by Louis **Nalpas**), Gabriele Réjane and Sarah **Bernhardt** starred in adaptations of their stage successes, respectively, *Madame*

Sans-Gêne (1911) and *La Dame aux camellias* [Camille] (1912); even greater acclaim then came to Bernhardt in the independently-produced *Queen Elizabeth* (1912). For Pathé and then his own company, **Valetta** Films, Camille **de Morlhon** contributed "modern dramas" such as *La Broyeuse des coeurs* [Heart Breaker] (1913) that paralleled current boulevard melodramas in Paris. At Éclair, Jasset devoted his efforts to **crime films**, beginning with the pulp adaptation, *Zigomar* (1911), which was hugely successful worldwide, followed by other sensational melodramas, and to "social dramas" such as *Au pays des ténèbras* [Land of Darkness] (1912). At Gaumont, Perret and Feuillade worked in a similar vein, culminating in *Le Mystère des roches de Kador* [In the Grip of the Vampire] (1912), the series of five *Fantômas* features (1913–1914), and the "blockbuster" melodrama, *L'Enfant*

de Paris [In the Clutch of the Paris Apaches] (1913).

As the costs of making films rose and the French found it increasingly difficult to export their films for the profitable US market, Pathé provoked a kind of decentralization in the industry by pulling back from direct investment in production and committing its resources to distributing the work of its growing affiliates (each of which secured much of its own financing): among others, these now included **Film d'Arte Italiana** (Italy), **Pathé russe** (Russia), **Pathé Cinematograph** (USA), as well as **Comica** and its comic series directed by Roméo **Bosetti**, headquartered in Nice. Other Pathé personnel such as André **Andréani** and André **Heuzé** left to form the nucleus of Georges **Lordier**'s Les Grand Films Populaires, which took over the bankrupt Lux studio and produced box office

Figure 41 Pathé-Frères' Vincennes studio.

hits such as *Le Bossu* [The Hunchback] (1913). Charles **Burguet** also successfully located his Films Azur in Nice, and two of the most popular French stars, Suzanne **Grandais** and Yvette **Andreyor** (both at Gaumont), independently tried to spin off their own series of films in Paris. Although Gaumont itself, by contrast, took on more and more filmmakers (supervised loosely by Feuillade), it also dispersed its director units by constructing a new "Victorine" studio near Nice. Éclair did likewise, developing its own production affiliate in the USA, to which Maurice **Tourneur** was sent not long before a fire destroyed its facilities in early 1914. Although it could only make a limited number of feature films each year, Film d'Art enjoyed a measure of profitablility with classic adaptations such as Henri Pouctal's *Les Trois Mousquetaires* [The Three Musketeers] (1913).

Although this "cottage industry" of decentralized production may have inversely mirrored the consolidation and departmentalization then going on in the US film industry, France's average annual output of films, measured in meters of positive film stock, held relatively steady (between 300,000 and 350,000 meters) up to beginning of **World War I**.

RICHARD ABEL

Sales, rentals and exhibition

When the **Lumière brothers** launched their Cinématographe in 1895, they intended to exploit their invention as a whole, assuming that the company would handle everything that much later would become distinct activities. This integral exploitation of moving pictures was epitomized in the Lumière apparatus itself, as it was capable of performing all these functions: shooting (production/direction), printing (publishing), projection (exhibition). Within 18 months, as competitors appeared on the market, the Lumière brothers had to commercialize their apparatus (two new versions of which were designed exclusively for public projections) as well as their films.

Whenever they did not constitute the marginal activity of a large company (Pathé-Frères, Lumière,

Figure 42 Modern Palast fairground cinema.

Gaumont), moving pictures were only the business of small-scale shopkeepers. Georges William **de Bedts**, A.-F. **Parnaland**, Georges **Mendel**, and others sold a little of everything: cameras, unexposed or exposed celluloid film stock, punches, projector stands, and often **photography** supplies as well. Many were more or less inventors and ran low-capital businesses as simple or general partnerships.

Exhibition very quickly became a branch of the industry in its own right. Whichever of the various entertainment venues in which they worked, from the fairs/fairgrounds to music halls or **cafés-concerts**, early exhibitors tried to accommodate their moving pictures to pre-existing frameworks while the first owners of small cinemas were appearing in major cities. For many years, the only way for any of them to get films was to purchase them. They would then resell them to their poorer, less demanding peers in the profession. **Itinerant exhibitors** had the advantage of an ever-changing audience as they moved from one location to the next: they could thus screen the same films for a long time and maximize their profits. By contrast, sedentary exhibitors and exhibition services working with just a few regular music hall or café-concert customers had a more difficult time amortizing their films since the programs had to be changed often. With a price of about 2 francs per meter in the early years (3 francs for films in **color**), a half-hour show, including interruptions, cost from 600 to 800 francs, with an entrance price of about half a franc. Around 1906–1907, as programs became longer and audiences began asking for a new program each week, the money the exhibitor had to disburse ranged from 2,500 to 3,000 francs a week, or 125,000 to 150,000 francs a year (according to the trade journal, *Phono-Ciné-Gazette*). Even if one includes the resale of films on the secondhand market, usually at half price, the financial burden remained high for the permanent cinema exhibitor. Exhibition in fixed sites was thus conceivable on a large scale only with the institutionalization of a rental system.

The rental system, which required some organization, debuted later than the secondhand market, which for a long time relied on mutual agreement. According to Charles Pathé, who did not provide precise information, the first ventures

into renting films dated back to 1904. In Paris, exhibition services, which had to renew their programs frequently in order to get contracts with prestigious companies, resorted to rentals very early. In the Paris area, Booston Vio owner Georges **Petit** began as early as 1904. A. Davignon (National Bioscope) and Georges **Froissart** (American Vitograph) also followed suit, as probably did small shopkeepers already involved in secondhand sales. The trend became clearer in 1906. In August of that year, the Pathé representative in Berlin (where the rental system was already developed) wrote to Charles Pathé to encourage him to get involved. In Paris a new company, the Société du Cinématographe Automobile, offered to rent exhibitors complete programs in return for a fee equal to 25% of the receipts with a minimum of 1,000 francs a month. Until then, Pathé had carefully followed the different small-scale experiments with rental so that his company could eventually benefit from them. There now was a serious risk that a powerful rental corporation could constitute itself outside Pathé's orbit and reap major profits from the company's films. Although Pathé did not find a satisfactory rental option straightaway, he was able to modify his strategy very swiftly. He first put Froissart & Sons (a family business his company had taken over) in charge of the new rental department in early 1907. In May, facing difficulties, Pathé and his administrators acknowledged that "the project of supervising our own rentals throughout French territory as a whole is inapplicable." They decided to promote the formation, thanks to their personal

Figure 43 Poster for the Cinéma Pathé, *c.* 1907.

connections, of five regional concessionary companies that contractually would have *exclusive* rights over the exhibition of Pathé-Frères films in their own network of cinemas and would not, of course, be allowed to show any other films.

The termination of film sales by Pathé, announced through an official notice in July 1907, elicited heated reactions from exhibitors, especially the fairground showmen, who would from then on have to get their supplies elsewhere. Pathé justified the measure as a means to prevent prints in poor condition from continued exhibition because of the bad publicity they brought to the business. In fact, his central concern was that old films resold or rented at low prices might saturate the market and represent competition for new releases.

The concessionary companies, which had been hastily put together in the second half of 1907, were not able to set up a network of cinemas extensive enough to provide Pathé films with a substantial enough outlet. Pathé put an end to this monopolistic endeavor early in 1908, when it decided that the companies also would be allowed to rent films to independent exhibitors in their respective regions. The decision much improved their situation but not for long. A year later, Pathé decided to buy back their exclusive rental rights and set up its own rental services. First Omnia (early in 1909) and then Cinéma-Exploitation (August 1909) successively lost this privilege.

In most foreign countries, Pathé continued selling its films for a few more years as it had done in the past, but it was careful to affix along print edges this warning: "Introduction in France and Switzerland prohibited" (and, after the company **Belge Cinéma** was created, "Exhibition in France, Switzerland and Belgium prohibited"). Thus French or Swiss exhibitors (and shortly thereafter their Belgian or Dutch peers) who were tempted to circumvent the new rules and purchase Pathé films in countries where they were still being sold were immediately taken to court.

Gaumont, which in commercial matters had always followed the strategies initiated by Pathé, gradually set up a rental system and halted the sale of films completely and definitively only in February 1910. Independent rental businesses, no longer having access to Pathé and Gaumont films, now got their films (with or without exclusive rights) from companies that did not engage in rentals as well as from foreign companies which were beginning to set up shop in Paris. They constituted a free film market which was flourishing even prior to World War I. Etablissements L. **Aubert** and **AGC** (Agence Générale Cinématographique), to mention the most important ones, soon were the leaders of this new branch of the business.

In 1909, Georges Méliès organized the first Congrès international des Editeurs de Films (International Conference of Film Publishers), which opened on February 2 in Paris. A crisis of overproduction had been rampant since the previous year and had been particularly hard on French manufacturers. It was mostly due to the arrival on the national market of new French and foreign companies. Charles Pathé, George **Eastman**, Léon Gaumont, Charles **Urban**, and generally the representatives of the main companies took part in the conference. For lack of an intervening power to force the manufacturers to curb their production, the Conference attacked the rental businesses on the free market, accusing them of triggering the crisis: "... the rental businessman is a terrible enemy of the manufacturer; ... the purchase of a single film is enough to cater to a whole population of patrons ...; after a few rentals, his purchase has been amortized and any subsequent rental is all profit to him. ... In the meantime, the manufacturer has received no money other than that from the sale of his film and has to wait, for any further profit, until the last pieces of junk have disappeared" (*Ciné-Journal*, 11–18 March 1909). One of the most radical measures, agreed to by the 32 companies adhering to the "Consortium," had the effect of targeting rental businesses: beginning on March 15, it provided for the compulsory return of film prints to manufacturers no later than four months after purchase. A sale thus became a four-month rental, and the renting trade lost its raison d'être. Small exhibitors, who would usually rent old films at low cost, saw their future seriously threatened. Yet on the scheduled date, most manufacturers, afraid of losing their customers, did not implement the measure, which therefore went unheeded. After this failure, a more limited second Conference took place on 16–18 April 1909. Foreseeing the turn events were going to take, Charles Pathé decided not to attend. Indeed, the main measures previously taken (particularly those related to the return of films to publishers) ended up being repealed, and only a few consensual decisions were made. At the end of 1909, Éclair and the Union des Grands Editeurs tried to reach an agreement with a few other manufacturers on the basis of the decisions made at the first Conference. As encouragement, Éclair and **Lux** invited the press to auto-da-fés of films, but no one followed their example. On 1 October 1912, Éclair finally stopped selling films and organized its own rental service.

After these initial tentative steps, common rules did emerge. Film rentals were charged by the meter, as was the case with sales before. At a time when a system of first-run cinemas with exclusive rights did not exist, moving pictures usually did not run for more than a week in many cinemas, regardless of their reception by audiences. The rental fees, therefore, were calculated by the week and along a sliding scale after the first week of release, when they usually were 0.30 franc a meter (films belonging to an "artistic series," as well as those tinted or colored, were charged a slightly higher rate). After the fifth or sixth week, films were added to the pool from which the poorest exhibitors could select. The rental fee was then reduced to 0.08 franc per meter, sometimes even less, but the condition of the film was not guaranteed. By comparison, when films were sold to exhibitors by manufacturers, they cost on average 1 to 1.25 franc per meter. It was only after the war that a new price scale for film rentals (based on the exhibitors' receipts) appeared.

Until 1911, Paris exhibitors had to make the rounds of the rental businesses in order to choose their films. That year, the Syndicat des Exploitants du Cinématographe (Trade Association of Film Exhibitors) managed to organize the projection of new films for the free market at a single location once a week (the Consortium cinema in the 11th arrondissement of Paris), while Pathé and Gaumont organized separate screenings in their own facilities. Exhibitors filed their orders at these corporative screenings, which allowed publishers and rental businesses to know exactly how many prints would be needed at release time, two or three weeks later. Such screenings later would be organized by the Chambre syndicale de la Cinématographie (Employers' Federation of the Film Industry).

At that point, the French film industry was comprised of three links in a chain: manufacturing, renting, and exhibiting, a trinity which prefigured (without quite exactly corresponding to) what would emerge in the course of the interwar period: production, distribution, and exhibition.

Figure 44 Poster for the Kinema Gab-Ka, Paris, December 1910.

Audiences

From December 1895 through much of 1896, the Cinématographe Lumière, quickly joined by competitors, set up shop in the central Paris neighborhoods, mainly in the Grands Boulevards area, where people from various social backgrounds (residents of other neighborhoods, as well as foreign visitors) would mix. The first location where the Cinématographe was exploited, the Salon indien of the Grand Café, while a modest basement room, was situated in the most elegant

Figure 45 Poster for the Gaumont-Palace, 1913.

section of the Grands Boulevards, the boulevard des Capucines near the Opéra. The entrance fee (one franc for a screening lasting under half an hour) was relatively high, but not to the extent that it would have been an obstacle for a less well-off audience (it would later be reduced to a half franc in order to match the competition's rates).

At a time of strong interest in scientific and technical inventions, moving pictures aroused curiosity among all social classes. "Never before has a new spectacle become so conspicuous and fashionable more swiftly. Are you interested in the Cinématographe? You can find it everywhere, in the basements of the large cafés on the boulevards and in the outbuildings of music halls, in theaters, where it is featured in variety shows, in salons, where hosts offer this fashionable pastime to their guests through private screenings," Dr. Regnault wrote in *l'Illustration* on 30 May 1896. In fact, he

was slightly anticipating, as moving pictures were just starting to expand.

The account Pauline de Broglie (who was to marry Count Jean de Pange) gave of the Salon indien screening (her father had brought her along in an elegant coupé) has become well known. In May 1897, a moving picture machine (Henri Joseph **Joly**'s, this time around) was set up at the Bazar de la Charité, a charity bazaar organized by the Paris nobility that ended in a tragedy. Its organizers had likely been concerned more with the amusement of children than with the satisfaction of adults who probably already had seen "moving photographs." In any case, as this tragedy suggests, moving pictures were not yet considered an amusement unworthy of respectable families.

Around 1897, and particularly after the fire at the Bazar de la Charité, moving pictures entered a second period that lasted until 1906. The first few years were chaotic. At the Salon indien receipts fell considerably, from 65,671 francs in 1896 to 46,411 francs in 1897 and to 32,501 francs in 1899. Others of Lumière's Cinématographe located in the working-class neighborhoods of Paris (those of the Porte Saint-Martin or of the Grands Magasins Dufayel, for instance) more or less kept their turnover at the same level but did not experience actual growth. Moving pictures, however, were then beginning to be accommodated in a variety of locations, and the receipts of a few small, fixed cinemas located in metropolitan centers do not truly reflect exhibition as a whole. It is revealing, then, to look at the yearly turnover for the film branch of the largest French company, Pathé-Frères. For the 1898–1899 fiscal year (which, exceptionally, spanned a period of 18 months), it was 161,800 francs. It increased over the following fiscal year, which spanned only 12 months, to reach 163,900 francs. In 1900–1901, it was boosted by the Paris Exposition and doubled (322,300 francs). It grew rapidly over the following years: by 50% in 1901–1902 and 1902–1903 (464,300 francs and 685,600 francs, respectively), then by about 100% on average (1,249,200 francs in 1903–1904; 2,194,500 francs in 1904–1905; 4,934,900 francs in 1905–1906; 12,162,100 francs in 1906–1907; 25,600,000 in 1907–1908). Until 1906, growth was essentially due to itinerant exhibitors operating on the fairs/fairgrounds and others showing moving pictures in cafés-concerts and similar entertainment businesses in large cities. In the latter businesses, where moving pictures were part of a longer program, there is no evidence that the audience make up was altered. For instance, the public of the Folies Bergère, with or without moving pictures, was not the same as the more working-class audiences of the Eldorado. What essentially characterized audiences during this second phase was that they were not yet movie-goers. They saw moving pictures when given the occasion, but the pictures alone rarely motivated their attendance.

Turning urban audiences into loyal patrons required that moving pictures first settle in permanent cinemas, in city centers as well as outlying neighborhoods. This third period, whose first indications can be observed in 1906, started early in 1907 in Paris and almost immediately afterwards in major provincial cities. Attempts now were made to widen the range of audiences and attract more consistently the educated segments of the population. Not only did some cinemas emulate the bourgeois opulence of legitimate **theaters**, but the narrativity of films was also gaining in development and complexity. Film d'Art and SCAGL, soon followed by others, sought to bring classical or contemporary works of the stage to moving pictures and to attract famous performers of the day in front of the camera. Were these efforts successful? Undoubtedly so, since the broadening of cinema audiences and their increasing loyalty can be dated to this period. Was the intelligentsia as a whole seduced by this new form of spectacle sometimes described as art? Did the well-off bourgeoisie, accustomed to prestigious theaters, regularly attend the new cinemas? Absolutely not. Despite their enhanced reputation, moving pictures remained a second-rate spectacle for many. That Anatole France, then at the height of his fame, would dare to appear in a cinema on the Grands Boulevards owed more to the fact that he was not averse to provocations directed at his own readership. Many among the educated classes (a good example was René Doumic) would acknowledge that the only moving pictures that had any worth were nonfiction: scientific films, travelogues, newsreels, etc. Only in 1917–1918 would new attitudes towards

moving pictures begin to appear among the French intellectual and artistic elite.

Regulation

When the Cinématographe Lumière became a public entertainment in December 1895, it was not subject to any specific status, and uncertainty as to its future did not warrant particular attention on the part of authorities. It was one of many novelties that Parisians enjoyed and initially was often included in the programs of **wax museums**, cafés-concerts, and other recreational venues.

As with other kinds of shows, moving pictures were subject to the poverty tax (*droit des pauvres*), besides the taxes all businesses already had to pay. The poverty tax, which was levied by the health and social security services to finance hospitals, represented a 10% addition to the price of tickets and was levied directly by a controller assigned to the business or according to a set fee. The poverty tax, which exhibitors fiercely fought, was not repealed until 1941. Moreover, exhibitors paid the wages of police agents whose presence in their theaters during screenings was required by law, as in theaters, cafés-concerts, etc.

Concern for audience safety in places where moving pictures were shown did not result initially in specific measures. Only with the catastrophe of the Bazar de la Charité (a charity bazaar organized by members of high Paris society, in which 120 people were burned alive on 4 May 1897) did the authorities become aware of the danger posed by moving pictures, especially when a non-electric source of light was used. Measures specific to cinema were made official, on 1 September 1898, by an order of the Paris chief of police (article 108). Several of these had applied as early as the days following the disaster: **projectors** had to be put in an incombustible, airtight booth; oxyetheric lamps were prohibited; a tank containing water mixed with alum had to be placed between the condenser and the strip of film; the film had to be unwound into a slitted metal case; smoking was prohibited; two buckets of water had to be close at hand, etc. These directives, however, applied only to Paris since in other French towns regulations involving entertainment businesses were in the mayors' hands. On 10 August 1908, police regulation specified and complemented the measures taken in 1898. As Pathé-Frères had started manufacturing a cellulose acetate nonflammable film stock, the Paris chief of police promulgated an order to prohibit nitrate film stock that would take effect on 1 July 1915. Yet World War I and the realization that this type of film stock was of a lesser quality postponed implementation of the measure through successive delays until the 1950s.

Censorship

When moving pictures emerged, the only existing official censorship applied to theaters, and it was very unobtrusive. Mayors and prefects, however, retained police powers that allowed them to ban an amusement or a show if they considered that it threatened the maintenance of law and order.

Early cinema was a marginal attraction which seemed quite harmless; although **pornographic** films appeared almost immediately, they remained within the walls of brothels and private clubs. In 1906, theater censorship disappeared *de facto* when Parliament withdrew funding for the board in charge of it. From then on, plays were no longer examined prior to the performances, and censorship could be exercised only after opening performances, on the initiative of local authorities. In 1907, voices were raised in favor of a ban on the Pathé-Frères film, *À Biribi* (directed by Lucien Nonguet), which denounced the inhumane conditions of detention in the famous military penal colony, and a few mayors prohibited it in their city.

In August 1908, a police regulation stated that the opening of a theater required preliminary application and inspection. Its article 214 included a thinly veiled threat: "The authorization granted to a theater will be withdrawn in the event of an offence against public decency or a disruption of law and order."

In 1909, the issue of censorship became topical again with the quadruple capital execution that was to take place in Béthune. The police were to prevent its filming but allegedly failed to do so. The Ministry of the Interior then enjoined mayors to prohibit the exhibition of any films related to capital executions in their towns and declared that cinema should be considered "alongside other attractions or curiosity shows."

A new affair took place in 1912. For Éclair, Victorin Jasset had produced a fiction film, *L'Auto grise* [The Grey Automobile] based on the "bande

à Bonnot" (Bonnot gang) even before the famous gangster was arrested. Then, just after Bonnot had died in the house besieged by police, Éclair announced that production was starting on a sequel, *Hors la loi* [Beyond the law]. Both films were released without incident in Paris but were banned in many provincial towns. The following year, the new chief of police of the Seine district (which included Paris) prohibited "without exception the exhibition of any film representing recent crimes."

As World War I drew near, committees for the defense of "morality" intensified their activism and proponents of "moral order" gained ground. As soon as war was declared, a preliminary censorship was put in place by military commandment and implemented in the Seine district by police headquarters. All theaters now had to submit a copy of their programs for approval. In December 1915, the chief of police established a system by which visas were granted to films after a reading of their scripts, given the fact that time constraints made it impossible to screen all films. In June 1916, the Minister of the Interior charged a national control committee with the power to grant the visas, but did not repeal municipal and prefectoral prerogatives. Moving pictures thus had become subject to both local and national censorship.

The preliminary control of films, which was established during World War I, was to undergo several changes before it was repealed in 1974.

JEAN-JACQUES MEUSY

See also: distribution: Europe; law and the cinema: regulating exhibition

Further reading

Abel, Richard (1990) "The Blank Screen of Reception in Early French Cinema," *Iris*, 11:27–47.

Abel, Richard (1994) *The Ciné Goes to Town: French Cinema, 1896–1914*, Berkeley: University of California Press.

Abel, Richard (1996) "Booming the Film Business: The Historical Specificity of Early French Cinema," in Richard Abel, *Silent Film*, 109–124, New Brunswick: Rutgers University Press.

Coissac, G.-Michel (1925) *Histoire du cinématographe: de ses origines à nos jours*, Paris: Cinéopse.

Maugras, Emile and Maurice Guegan (1908) *Le Cinématographe devant le droit*, Paris: V. Giard et F. Brière.

Meusy, Jean-Jacques (1995) *Paris-Palaces ou le temps des cinémas, 1894–1918*, Paris, CNRS Editions.

Meusy, Jean-Jacques (2001) "La stratégie des Sociétés concessionnaires Pathé et la location des films en France (1907–1908)," in Michel Marie (ed.) *Pathé, le retour de l'Empire*, Paris: AFRHC.

Pathé, Charles (1970) *De Pathé Frères à Pathé Cinéma*, Lyon: SERDOC, Premier Plan.

Sadoul, Georges (1948) *Histoire générale du cinema II: les pionniers du cinéma, 1897–1909*, Paris: Denoël.

Sadoul, Georges (1951) *Histoire générale du cinema III: Le cinéma devient un art (l'avant-guerre), 1909–1920*, Paris: Denoël.

Frau, Raymond

b. 1887; d. 1953

actor, Italy

Frau was as a circus clown and acrobat in France, performing in the **music hall** and **café-concert**. In 1912, he was hired as a comic actor by **Cines**, and created the internationally popular character of Kri Kri, known abroad as Bloomer (Britain), Patachon (France, Holland), Kri-Kri (Spain, Portugal) and Mucki/Krikri/Bliemchen (Germany). The Kri Kri farces are memorable because of their special effects and surreal scenes that establish a world in which people decapitate themselves, gravity no longer counts, and nasty doubles walk through mirrors and pester their "originals." Frau returned to France in early 1916, creating the character of Dandy in a comic series for **Éclair**.

IVO BLOM

Freer, James Simmons

b. 1855; d. 1925

filmmaker, Canada

In the fall of 1897, Freer, a Manitoba farmer, purchased a camera from the **Edison Company** and began filming harvest scenes, the first domestically produced moving pictures in Canada. He expanded his subjects to include the Canadian Pacific Railway, which then sponsored a tour of his films in an effort to spur immigration. Accompanied by lectures, his show, "Ten Years in Manitoba," met sufficient success in Great Britain in 1898 that the Canadian government sponsored a second tour in 1902. By that time, however, Freer had ceased filming original material, and his subsequent exhibition efforts garnered little interest.

CHARLIE KEIL

Fregoli, Leopoldo

b. 1867; d. 1936

comic stage actor, filmmaker, Italy

Celebrated for his humorous imitations and rapid costume changes, throughout the 1890s Fregoli played the theaters and **cafès-concerts** of Europe as well as North and South America. In 1897, while on tour, he acquired a **Cinematographe** at the **Lumières**' factory in Lyon. Shooting and later assembling a few 20-meter shorts of his stage performances, he created an original show called *Fregoligraph*, which he exhibited until 1904, and which exposed several **Méliès**-like tricks (i.e., substitute splices and stop-motion cinematography). Behind the screen he uttered the lines of his own characters with impressive and unprecedented synchronism.

GIORGIO BERTELLINI

Frenkel [Bouwmeester], Theo

b. 1871; d. 1956

filmmaker, actor, Britain/Netherlands, the

Frenkel began his career in 1908 at Cecil **Hepworth**'s studio in England. A very productive filmmaker, he moved to **Charles Urban Trading Company** in 1910, where he eventually specialized in Kinemacolor films. His spectacular dramas, often featuring his wife and himself in glamorous costumes and monumental landscapes, however, were not successful. Frenkel returned to the Netherlands during **World War I**, becoming the most experienced filmmaker of that neutral country. *Het wrak van de noordzee* (The Wreck of the North Sea) (1915) and *Genie tegen geweld* (Genius Against Violence) (1916) proved his skills with action films.

ANSJE VAN BEUSEKOM

Freuler, John L.

b. 1872; d. 1958

distributor, producer, USA

Freuler was a Milwaukee exchange man whose **Motion Picture Patents Company** licenses were revoked in 1910. To provide films for his customers, he partnered with Samuel S. **Hutchinson** in forming the Chicago-based **American Film Manufacturing Company**, of which he was the chief executive until its closure in 1921. In 1912, he also joined Hutchinson, Charles Hite, and Harry **Aitken** in founding the **Mutual Film Corporation** which, with **General Film** and **Universal**, soon controlled the market for short-film programs in the USA. Freuler headed Mutual until its receivership in 1918.

BEN BREWSTER

Friberg, C. A. (Carl August)

b. 1868; d. 1915

exhibitor, distributor, Sweden

C. A. Friberg, a bricklayer turned building contractor, invested heavily in moving picture theaters around 1906 in his home town of Karlskrona and adjacent cities (Växjö, Ronneby, Kristianstad, among others), in addition to starting a film exchange in his own name. Surviving catalogues evidence the scope of the enterprise: numerous titles were offered from major European producers as well as from American manufacturers. In the early 1910s, the exchange moved to Stockholm and was later incorporated as a part of AB Svensk filmindustri (SF). The Friberg trademark became a fixture at SF, predominantly used as a production brand for popular, non-prestige films.

JAN OLSSON

Friese-Greene, William [William Edward Green]

b. 1855; d. 1921

photographer/inventor, England

The owner of several portrait studios in England, Friese-Greene was inspired by J. A. R. Rudge's glass-plate moving images to patent two sequence cameras: one in 1889, with engineer Mortimer Evans; another (stereoscopic) in 1893, from a design by Frederick Varley. "Films" taken with his cameras, including a view of Kings Road, Chelsea, were taken at a slow rate and projection proved unsuccessful. He also devised, with John Alfred Prestwich, a flickerless projector (1896) and patented a **color** motion picture process (1905), later challenging **Urban**'s Kinemacolor patent. Poor financial control, however, led to two bankruptcies. Posthumously championed as "The Inventor of Kinematography," Friese-Greene was the subject of an unreliable biography, and a romantic biopic, *The Magic Box* (1951).

STEPHEN HERBERT

Froelich, Carl

b. 1875; d. 1953

cameraman, director, Germany

Froelich entered **Messter**'s technical department in 1903 and quickly became one of the principal cameramen for *actualités*, **scientific films**, *Tonbilder*, and, increasingly from 1911 onwards, melodramas starring Germany's biggest star Henny **Porten**. As co-director with William Wauer, Froelich created the special effects for *Richard Wagner* (1913), perhaps the best surviving testimony to his expertise in trick cinematography and his flair for visual brilliance. During **World War I**, he was one of only eight licensed cameramen at the German front, shooting rare combat material for Messter's weekly **newsreel**, *Messter-Woche*.

MICHAEL WEDEL

Froissart, Georges

b. 1856, Roubaix; d. 1913, Paris

exhibitor, distributor, France

Froissart began projecting moving pictures in Paris **music halls** and **cafés-concerts** in 1899. His company generally appeared in programs under the name *American Vitograph Froissart* or *Vitographe américain du professeur Froissart*, which linked his activity to that of **magicians**. For many years Froissart managed film screenings (using **Pathé-Frères** equipment and films) in such venues as the Fauvette, Eldorado, and Folies Bergère, and the popularity of American Vitograph also extended throughout the French provinces and into neighboring countries, including the Maghreb. Early on the company also rented films, but when Pathé decided to institute a rental system, in April 1907, it absorbed American Vitograph and hired Froissart and his son to set up a nationwide rental service. Within a month, however, Pathé abandoned the project and established regional concessionaries that would be responsible for renting and exhibiting its films, one of which, Cinéma-Exploitation, bought back American Vitograph in June 1907. By mid-1908, Froissart had returned to his independent activity. When he died in 1913, his son took over the business, but music hall and café-concert screenings already were declining.

JEAN-JACQUES MEUSY

Frusta, Arrigo

b. 1875; d. 1965

scenarist, Italy

Frusta was the penname of Augusto Sebastiano Ferraris, a lawyer, journalist, poet, and, from 1908, head of **Ambrosio** Film's Scriptwriting Department—the first one in the Italian film industry. Rarely a director, he scripted hundreds of films of all genres, including *La fucina* [The Iron Foundry] (1910), from a Friedrich Schiller poem, and the patriotic *Nozze d'oro* [The Golden Wedding] (1911), winner of the first prize at the International Exhibition in Turin. Appreciated for his literary taste, Frusta helped Ambrosio Film move from a pioneering firm offering lowbrow entertainments to a culturally ambitious film company.

GIORGIO BERTELLINI

Fukuhodo

Taking advantage of the moving-picture boom in Japan, Tabata Kenzo established a chain of theaters in 1910. In Tokyo alone, he opened no less than eight theaters, all of them built by the Endo-gumi guild under the supervision of **Kobayashi Kisaburo**. Constructed of concrete, each theater was a modern building containing about 350 seats. Founding the theater chain then led Tabata to establish his own film production company. He launched filmmaking at Fukuhodo's Nippori studio in July 1910, and it soon became one of the major film companies in Japan.

HIROSHI KOMATSU

Fuller, Loïe

b. 1862; d. 1928

dancer, filmmaker, USA

Although Fuller later directed a number of "art films," her importance for early cinema lies in the "serpentine" dance she introduced in 1892. This had Fuller swirling large billowing cloth sheets into a variety of constantly transforming shapes, bathed in changing colored electric light. A spectacle based on motion, light, and **electricity**, the serpentine paralleled the fascination of early cinema. Scores of early **dance films** were made of the serpentine and by nearly every production company, usually hand-colored to convey the lighting effects. Fuller supposedly appeared in one or more early films: a 1907 **Pathé-Frères** film claims to feature her, although the identification remains uncertain. Most filmed serpentine dancers were Fuller imitators.

TOM GUNNING

Fuller, Mary

b. 1888; d. 1973

actor, USA

First appearing before the camera at **Vitagraph** in 1908, Mary Fuller's career accelerated at **Edison** where she performed in numerous one-reel subjects, from **opera** adaptations such as *Aida* (1911) to **western** shorts such as *The Luck of Roarin' Camp* (1910). In 1912, Fuller starred in the first American **serial**, *What Happened to Mary?*, as well as its 1913 sequel, *Who Will Marry Mary?*. By 1914, Fuller was rated among the top female stars by US audiences, and made a third serial with Edison, *The Active Life of Dollie of the Dailies*. To the surprise of many, she retired from the screen in 1916–1917.

JENNIFER M. BEAN

Furniss, Harry

b. 1854; d. 1925

graphic artist, lantern lecturer, filmmaker, Great Britain

Born in Ireland, Furniss established himself as a successful illustrator and caricaturist through his work for *The Illustrated London News* and *Punch*. An active self-publicist, he became an international "pictorial entertainer" in the 1890s, touring Great Britain, the USA, and Australia in a variety of shows with **magic lantern slides** of his popular cartoons. In 1912, he visited the **Edison Company** and soon turned to film as a new medium for representing his interests. From his house at Hastings, he produced a number of **animation films** in 1914, two of which featured his "lightning-sketching for the cinematograph."

FRANK GRAY

Fynes, J. (James) Austin

b. 1859; d. 1928

vaudeville manager, exhibitor, USA

In 1893, **vaudeville** entrepreneur B. F. **Keith** hired fellow Bostonian J. Austin Fynes, the *New York Clipper*'s managing editor, to run his Union Square Theater in New York City. To compete with Keith's rival, F. F. Proctor, Fynes initiated the trend of presenting well-known dramatic actors in playlets to attract middle-class audiences to vaudeville. He helped bring moving pictures to Keith theaters in 1896 and, after quitting Keith, then to Proctor's theaters as well. In 1906, Fynes left Proctor to open one of the first **nickelodeons** in Manhattan, and later arranged a Keith–Proctor alliance that led eventually to a vaudeville oligopoly.

ALAN GEVINSON

G

Gabet, (Baron) Francisque [François Marie]

b. 1846; d. 1930

businessman, France

Baron Gabet was the tutelary figure on the board of directors of the Compagnie générale de Phonographes et Cinématographes et Appareils de précision (**Pathé-Frères**), which he headed from 1900 until his death. A former Lyon stockbroker, Gabet represented the business and financial world of the city on the company's board of directors. He also was president of the board of directors of Cinématographe Monopole (one of six Pathé concessionary companies for exhibiting and renting films), founded in 1907. Finding it impossible to support the two companies' often contradictory interests, he resigned from the latter in 1909. Gabet served on the boards of directors of many important industrial companies. An advocate of alpine sports and tourism, he headed the Club Alpin Français from 1919 to 1922.

JEAN-JACQUES MEUSY

Gad, Urban

b. 1879; d. 1947

filmmaker, Denmark

Gad's mother was a leading Danish playwright, which led him to begin his career as a stage designer. In 1910, he directed the independently produced *Afgrunden* [The Abyss], which gave Asta **Nielsen** her international breakthrough. This "art film in two acts" was not only of an unusual length for its time (850 meters), but also dramatically well structured. Gad directed most of Nielsen's films until 1914, in Denmark and Germany. In 1919, he published *Filmen-dens Midler og Maal* [Film: Purpose and Practice] (translated into German in 1921), the first major book in Danish on filmmaking.

CASPER TYBJERG

Gallo, Mario

b. 1874; d. 1945

director, producer, Argentina

Gallo emigrated from Italy to Argentina in 1905. He had the distinction of making the country's first fiction film, *La revolución de Mayo* [The May Revolution] (1909), as well as *El fusilamiento de Dorrego* [The Execution of Dorrego] (1910), for the centenary celebrations of Argentine independence. Credited with directing several important **historical films**, he also founded a film laboratory, film studio, and production company, Actualidades Gallo Film, which released a **newsreel** beginning in 1920. As early as 1908, he experimented with synchronizing **phonographs** and moving pictures, and later he often filmed adaptations of **operas** and, during exhibition, had singers perform behind the **screen**.

KATHLEEN NEWMAN

Ganguly, Dhirendranath

b. 1893; d. 1978

painter, photographer, filmmaker, actor, India

A painter and art teacher, Ganguly turned to **photography** and filmmaking when he set up Indo-British Film in Calcutta in 1918. Its first production, *Bilet Pherat* [England Returned] (1921), directed by Nitish C. Lahiri and starring Ganguly himself, is considered a landmark: the first Indian film set in a contemporary setting, a genre later called "social." After a brief stint as producer in Hyderabad, Ganguly returned to Calcutta to establish British Dominion Films (1929) with famous actor-director P. C. Barua. Ganguly continued to direct and act in films well into the sound era.

SURESH CHABRIA

Gardin, Vladimir

b. 1877; d. 1965

filmmaker, Russia

The "black sheep" of a respectable military family, Gardin abandoned an army career in 1898 for the theater. In 1912, he joined the **Khanzhonkov** studio as an actor. Gardin quickly moved on to a lucrative career at **Thiemann & Reinhardt**, co-directing (with Iakov **Protazanov**) the biggest box office hit of Russian cinema, *Kliuchi schastia* [The Keys to Happiness] (1913). Gardin left Thiemann in 1915 over a contract dispute, becoming co-owner of a new studio, Vengerov & Gardin, part of the wartime boom in the Russian film business. Gardin remained in Russia after 1917 and continued to direct in the Soviet cinema through the late 1920s, making the same elaborate melodramas and costume dramas he had excelled in before the revolution. He returned to acting in the 1930s, playing his last role in 1950.

Further reading

Gardin, V. R. (1949) *Vospominaniia* (Memoirs), vol. 1, 1912–1921, Moscow: Iskusstvo.

DENISE J. YOUNGBLOOD

Gardner, Helen

b. 1884; d. 1968

actor, producer, director, scenarist, costume designer, USA

A beautiful, convention-defying woman with a prosperous, aristocratic background, Helen Gardner studied acting and pantomime at the predecessor of the American Academy of Dramatic Arts. She began her film career at **Vitagraph** in *How She Won Him* (1910) and achieved critical praise and popularity as Becky Sharp in *Vanity Fair* (1911).

In early 1912, Gardner formed her own production company, Helen Gardner Picture Players, the first American company established by a **star** and with the purpose of making **multiple-reel/feature films**. In addition to producing and starring in her own films, made at her Old Tappan (New Jersey) studio, she also worked as editor and **costume** designer. Her first film, *Cleopatra* (1912), is considered the first six-reel feature produced in the USA. The steamy roles she created for herself led critics to call Gardner the screen's first vamp.

In 1914, after producing eleven features, Gardner closed her company and was hired by Vitagraph and other companies to act, direct and write scenarios. In 1918, she founded another company and produced a remake of *Cleopatra*. In all, she appeared in more than fifty films from 1910 to 1924.

DORIN GARDNER SCHUMACHER

Gärtner, Adolf

b. 1870; d. ?

director, writer, Germany

A stage actor and director, Gärtner was brought into the film business by Oskar **Messter** in 1910. Only occasionally working in comedy, as with the country-bumpkin subject, *Mericke aus Neu-Ruppin kommt nach Berlin* [Mericke from Neu-Ruppin Comes to Berlin] (1911), he soon became the regular director of the company's popular **star**, Henny **Porten**. Gärtner's dramatic treatment of cinematic space and narrative conflict in melodramas such as *Tragödie eines Streiks* [Tragedy of a Strike] (1911) or *Des Pfarrers Töchterlein* [The Priest's Daughter] (1912) decisively shaped Porten's star image, before he was replaced by Curt A. Stark in 1912. Gärtner, who co-authored some of his films, left Messter in 1913 and turned to work for Ernst **Reicher**'s *Stuart Webbs-Film Company*, where he directed some of the most remarkable of its popular **detective films**, including *Die Toten erwachen* [The Dead Awaken] (1915) and *Der gestreifte Domino* [The Striped Domino] (1915).

MICHAEL WEDEL

Gasnier, Louis

b. 1882; d. 1963

filmmaker, producer, France, USA

Hired at **Pathé-Frères** in 1905, Gasnier specialized in **comic films** such as *Le Cheval emballé* [The Runaway Horse] (1908) and directed several installments in the *Boireau* series as well as the first films featuring Max **Linder**. Beginning in 1909, he helped Charles **Pathé** establish foreign subsidiaries, including **Film d'Arte Italiana** and, more important, **Pathé-American**, whose new studio was located in Bound Brook (New Jersey). Gasnier served as artistic director of the American company and also made films, most notably the famous **serial**, *The Perils of Pauline* (1914). Its success enabled him to create his own company, Astra Film, which supplied Pathé with detective serials well into the 1920s. He then settled in the USA permanently.

LAURENT LE FORESTIER

Gaumont

At the start of **World War I**, Gaumont was France's second largest producer, distributor, and exhibitor. It released six globally distributed films a week; it operated the world's largest movie theater; and its directors contributed to the emerging conception of films as engrossing narratives. With its rival, **Pathé-Frères**, Gaumont was instrumental in creating a middle-class mass audience.

Léon **Gaumont** acquired a photographic and portable camera business and named it L. Gaumont & Cie in August 1895. He hired Georges **Demenÿ**, an engineer who had developed a moving picture **projector** while working in Etienne-Jules **Marey**'s laboratory, to compete with the **Cinematograph Lumière**. The Demenÿ-Gaumont Chronoscope used 60 mm film stock (actually, it was 58 mm wide) until 1897, when Gaumont adopted the **Edison** 35 mm gauge. About two hundred *actualités* and **travelogues** shot by licensed cameramen were available for purchase by owners of the machines. Gaumont's manufacturing shop on a site next to the Buttes Chaumont park in Paris, built in 1896, would in ten years become "Cité Elgé" (punning on Gaumont's initials). According to an 1899 document, a "terrace" was set aside for shooting scenes, and Gaumont's private secretary, Alice **Guy**, seems to have been the first to make films there.

Gaumont aspired to gain international clients. In 1898, he appointed Alfred Claude Bromhead as his London agent to market the company's **cameras** and projectors. **British Gaumont** was formed in 1906 to manage the growing export business. Gaumont reincorporated in 1906 as Société Etablissements Gaumont, capitalized at 2.5 million French francs. By 1908, there were 14 foreign agencies, including one in New York, headed by Bromhead. When the **Motion Picture Patents Company** excluded Gaumont in 1909, he relied on the importer George **Kleine** to handle the limited number of Gaumont releases that the Trust allowed to be shown in the States. Gaumont persevered and set up a lab and studio in Flushing, a New York suburb, to produce **Chronophone** films. This was a **sound** system for synchronizing records and films headed by Guy and Herbert Blaché, whom she had married. (After the demise of Chronophone, Guy-Blaché founded **Solax**.)

Louis **Feuillade** became head of production in 1907. He directed films himself, but also supervised a stable of writers, directors, and actors who, although independent, frequently collaborated and made films that crossed genres. The **comedy** farce, as in *Le matelas alcoolique* [The Alcoholic Mattress] (1906), and the **chase film**, as in

La course aux potirons [The Pumpkin Race] (1908), were early Gaumont hallmarks. Roméo **Bosetti** directed and starred in several **comic series**. Many *féeries/fairy plays* as well as **animation films** were made by Emile **Cohl**. Other successful genres included **biblical films**, **historical films**, domestic **melodramas**, and kid comedies featuring child actors, Anatole Clément **Mary** (a.k.a. René Dary) and René **Poyen**. Jean **Durand** directed films with a troupe of erstwhile **music hall** performers and a menagerie of animals. Later he created a rollicking *Onésime* comic series and some *Arizona Bill* **westerns**. Léonce **Perret**, an established stage personality, directed and acted in sophisticated comedies. Among the most prominent repertoire actors were Yvette **Andreyor**, Renée **Carl**, Suzanne **Grandais**, and René **Navarre**.

After 1909, Gaumont films as a whole grew more serious in tone. Feuillade was consciously distancing himself from the old chase formulas. Other influences were: audiences' interest in the sophisticated stories of **Film d'Art** and spectacles from Italy; **Vitagraph**'s two- and three-reel melodramas; Pathé's dark social realist films; and D. W. **Griffith**'s exported works. Perret and Feuillade became adept at melodrama in subjects such as *Gardien de la Camargue* [The Camargue Ranger] (1910) and *Le Coeur et l'argent* [Love vs. Money] (1912). In 1911, Gaumont released Feuillade's social problem films under the series title *La vie telle qu'elle est* [Life As It Is]. He also directed the studio's most ambitious **crime film** series, starting with *Fantômas*, released in five feature films (1913–1914).

The Gaumont program mixed challenging films with lighthearted fare and novelties to attract an urban, educated audiences. American films, especially multiple reelers beginning around 1910, increasingly used **editing** strategies and dramatic POV structures to tell their stories. Gaumont directors, however, continued to prefer **staging in depth** and long takes. Some historians do not see this as a lag in stylistic development, but rather, as a mode of production intended to differentiate the European style from the American.

Gaumont's expansion tracked Pathé's. The company launched a weekly **newsreel**, *Gaumont Actualités*, in 1910. To take advantage of the southern climate, Gaumont built a studio in Cimiez, a suburb of Nice, in 1912. Throughout the period Léon Gaumont experimented with **color** and sound processes.

As for distribution, Gaumont's original clients were the showmen who worked the **fairs/ fairgrounds**, music halls, and **cafés-concerts**. When Pathé abandoned direct sales of prints in favor of rentals in 1907, Gaumont briefly profited by servicing Pathé's former customers. In 1910, however, Gaumont also adopted the rental circuit system and established the Comptoir Ciné-Location.

Gaumont's entry into exhibition began with the lease of legitimate **theaters** during the "dark" periods between plays and in summer. In 1908, the company began converting storefronts into moving picture theaters in Paris, and slowly expanded into the provinces. The pre-1914 pinnacle of exhibition was the Gaumont-Palace, formerly the Hippodrome on the Place Clichy. It opened in September 1911, and accommodated 3400 patrons. The programs were carefully selected subjects, presented with full orchestras and choirs.

Gaumont's capital in 1914 was more than 4 million francs, and it was vertically integrated: that is, every aspect from production through

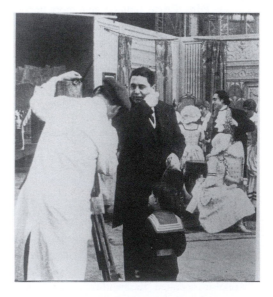

Figure 46 Georges Specht, Léonce Perret, and René Poyen in the Gaumont studio, *c.* 1913.

exhibition was controlled in-house. With the war's onset, Gaumont relocated its base of production to the Nice studios and struggled to continue making films, until it was taken over by MGM for several years in the late 1920s.

Although Gaumont still operates, it never regained the strength or influence it enjoyed before the devastating Great War.

Further reading

Abel, Richard (1994) *The Ciné Goes to Town*, Berkeley: University of California Press.

Corcy, Marie-Sophie *et al.* (eds.) (1998) *Les premières années de la société L. Gaumont & Cie*, Paris: AFHRC.

Hugues, Phillippe d' and Muller, Dominique (1986) *Gaumont, 90 ans de cinéma*, Paris: Ramsay/Cinémathèque Française.

DONALD CRAFTON

Gaumont, Léon-Ernest

b. 1864; d. 1946

manufacturer, producer, France

Léon Gaumont was the son of Auguste Ferdinand Gaumont, who among other occupations was a cabman in Paris, and Marguerite Gaumont née Dupenloup, a maid. In October 1876 he entered the Collège Sainte-Barbe, probably with the financial assistance of his mother's employer, the countess of Beaumont, and showed himself more gifted in mathematics, geography, and physics than in French. As the material situation of his parents deteriorated, he was forced to leave school at the age of 16.

He continued educating himself by attending the Institut populaire du Progrès at the Palais du Trocadéro, where he took courses in physics, biology, and astronomy, as well as the Observatoire populaire du Trocadéro. Léon Jaubert, the founder and director of both institutions, recommended him to Jules **Carpentier**, then head of a precision engineering and optics workshop (where the **Cinématographe Lumière** would later be manufactured). He was employed there as a ledger

clerk, which had the advantage of familiarizing him with company management techniques.

Discharged from the military service in November 1886, Gaumont resumed his job with Carpentier and, in June 1888, married Camille Maillard, who brought an important dowry to the household. He left Carpentier to work briefly for an electric bulb manufacturer and, in March 1894, was hired by the Comptoir général de Photographie, then headed by Félix-Max Richard. When a serious conflict opposed Richard to his brother, the company had to be sold and Gaumont, helped by personal connections, took advantage of the opportunity. In August 1895, aged 31, he negotiated its transformation into L. **Gaumont** et Cie, a limited partnership company, with a capital of 200,000 francs, mostly provided by Gustave Eiffel, the architect of the 1889 tower, Louis Vallot, the director of the Observatoire du Mont-Blanc (both these contacts he had made through his former employer), and Alfred Besnier, a stockbroker.

Besides the **photography** supplies previously sold by Comptoir, the company exploited Georges **Demenÿ**'s patents and thus made its entrance into the history of cinema. Gaumont, who was keenly aware of technical questions without being himself a first-rate inventor, invested in long-term research into **color** and **synchronized sound**, which brought the company renown but little profit. In December 1906 and January 1907, after realizing that the future development of his enterprise required its transformation into a public limited company (société anonyme), he replaced the former partnership with the Société des Établissements Gaumont (SEG), with a capital of 2.5 million francs. Gaumont, the principal shareholder, was backed by the Banque Suisse et Française (later the Crédit Industriel et Commercial) whose representative Pierre Azaria was named president of the board of directors (a position he held until 1927).

Adept at establishing useful connections and relying on the tradition of mutual aid among Sainte-Barbe alumni, Gaumont managed, despite his social background and his initial level of education, to gain access to influential scientific and financial circles. In 1894, he was invited to join the Société française de photographie, where, year after year, he presented the innovations of his company. In 1898, Jules Carpentier sponsored his admission to the Société des ingénieurs civils. In 1919, he was named an administrator of the newly created Institut d'Optique.

As a boss, Gaumont had the temperament of a fighter. A tough businessman, he occasionally proved sly and wily. His hardworking habits also made him time-conscious, and he did not hesitate to turn away those he deemed importunate. He was particular about punctuality with his employees and often treated them unpleasantly. He did not like to delegate power and did it only when the company's expansion forced him to (for instance, when Louis **Feuillade** was named head of film production). A highly cautious administrator, he did not innovate commercially and would usually await the results of decisions made by **Pathé-Frères** to take action himself. It is to Gaumont's credit that, after France entered **World War I**, he rapidly went back into production despite the difficulties of the period. He

was able to bring Gaumont to the second rank among French companies and to maintain that position.

Further reading

Corcy, Marie-Sophie, Jacques Malthête, Laurent Mannoni, and Jean-Jacques Meusy (eds.) (1999) *Les premières années de la société L. Gaumont et Cie. Correspondance commerciale de Léon Gaumont 1895–1899*, Paris: AFRHC/Bibliothèque du Film/Gaumont.

Garçon, François (1995) *Gaumont, un siècle de cinéma*, Paris: Gallimard/La Découverte.

Mannoni, Laurent (1994) *Le grand art de l'ombre et de la lumière, archéologie du cinéma*, Paris, Nathan.

JEAN-JACQUES MEUSY

Figure 47 Léon Gaumont. (Copyright Musée Gaumont.)

Gaumont projectors

In 1895, **Gaumont** marketed Georges **Demenÿ**'s "phonoscope" projector and its chronophotographic discs as the "Bioscope," but without success. Engineer Léopold Decaux then supervised the production of the company's subsequent projectors: the 1896 reversible "Chronophotographe," using perforated 58 mm film (with which the Châtelet theater projected *La Biche au bois* [The Doe in the Wood] in 1896); the 1897 reversible "Chronophotographe," now using 35 mm film; the 1899 "Chronophotographe projecteur," (which became the "Série V" in 1901, with a double projection capacity); the 1900 amateur "Chrono de poche," using 15 mm film; the 1900 "Chrono de précision"; the 1904 "Chrono de précision série VII"; and the 1908 "Chrono série VII b." It was only then that Gaumont launched its own production of Maltese-cross projectors: the "Chrono CM" was patented on April 14, 1908; an updated "Chrono projecteur série X" also was ready by 1910. All of the Gaumont machines, and especially early ones, were recognized for the care that went into their manufacture.

LAURENT MANNONI

Gauntier, Gene [Genevieve Liggett]

b. 1880 (?); d. 1966

actor, scriptwriter, director, USA

Daring and adventurous, the popular "Kalem Girl" literally leaped into the movies in AM&B's *The Paymaster* (1906), then joined **Kalem** in 1907. Filming on-location worldwide, she wrote, starred in, co-directed/directed, and did stunts in hundreds of films during a ten-year career. She created brave Irish colleens, a resourceful cross-dressing Civil War spy named Nan (prototype for the **serial** queens), and the Virgin Mary in the first American feature-length life of Christ filmed abroad. After founding Gene Gauntier Feature Players with Sidney **Olcott** in 1912, she went on to sign with **Universal** in 1915 and retired three years later to become a journalist/novelist.

GRETCHEN BISPLINGHOFF

Gauvreau, Georges

b. 1866; d. 1949

exhibitor, Quebec

A theater producer, Gavreau in 1900 became head of the Théâtre National, the first Francophone theater in Quebec, where he rapidly turned moving pictures into a popular, regular attraction. In 1907, noting that their popularity rivaled that of the theater, Gauvreau built the Nationoscope in Montreal. In this luxurious theater, the first designed specifically for the screening of moving pictures, Gauvreau even experimented with talker pictures. Its immediate success led other Montreal exhibitors to replace their rather humble "scopes" with more adequate venues. In 1910, Gauvreau sold the Nationoscope and devoted himself solely to theater, but his important activity as an exhibitor fostered enduring exchanges between both media.

GERMAIN LACASSE

Gavin, John

b. 1875; d. 1938

actor/director, Australia

A stage actor before appearing in his first film, *Thunderbolt*, in 1910, John Gavin worked as a producer/director, in partnership with his actor/writer wife Agnes, specializing in outback adventure films. In 1911, he directed six of these for other producers (Southern Cross Productions, and Crick and Finlay), then set up his own company and made two more. In 1916, he made two shorts and his most important film, *The Martyrdom of Nurse Cavell*. Beginning in 1918, the couple spent several years in Hollywood, then returned to act and produce in Australia until 1928.

INA BERTRAND

Gelabert, Fructuoso

b. 1874; d. 1955

filmmaker, Spain

A pioneer of Spanish cinema who constructed his own **camera** and, between 1897 and 1902, shot several *actualités* in the city of Barcelona. Gelabert probably was the author of *Riña en un café* [Argument in a Café] (1897), considered Spain's first fictional film. From 1903 to 1910, he worked as director and cameraman with Diorama, later called Films Barcelona. His most important film from this period was *Los guapos de la Vaquería del parque* [The Handsome Men of the Dairy] (1905). After 1910, he continued working as a documentary filmmaker and technical director.

JOAN M. MINGUET

General Film Company

General Film was formed on 18 May 1910 by the **Motion Pictures Patents Corporation** (MPPC) to be its national distribution arm. It acted as the sole distributor of the MPPC's programs of short films until the latter firm's dissolution in 1915.

General Film innovated a number of distribution practices: a pricing strategy based on each film's age, an early form of block booking, and a run-clearance-zone system. Although General Film attempted to distribute longer and more expensive films by 1912, the single-reel distribution strategy it had developed—with limited advertising and daily changes of films—eventually proved inadequate as **multiple-reel/feature films** became dominant.

See also: monopoly capitalism: USA

MICHAEL QUINN

Germany

Production

Germany had, in the fields of film technology, optics and photographic instruments, its share of inventors and pioneers. Simon Stampfer, Ottomar **Anschütz**, the **Skladanowsky** brothers, Oskar **Messter**, Hermann O. **Foersterling**, Guido **Seeber**, the **Stollwerck** and **AGFA** factories all were innovators of international stature, and also offered a solid manufacturing and engineering basis. The city of Hamburg hosted the first International Cinematographic Industry Exhibition as early as June 1908. Yet Wilhelmine Germany was not a major film-producing country. Cultural and economic conservatism caused film production to remain at a pre-industrial stage up to about 1912, mostly because production failed to adjust to rapidly changing patterns in distribution and exhibition practice. The Skladanowsky brothers' public presentation of their "Bioscop" projector in November 1895 at the Berlin Wintergarten may have preceded by a one month the first public demonstration of the **Cinématographe Lumière**, but exhibition remained in the hands of "Wanderkinos" showmen or **itinerant exhibitors** longer than elsewhere. Permanent cinemas did not become the rule until around 1911 (growing from 40 in 1905 to almost 3000 by 1914).

Of the companies that established themselves during the early years mainly in Berlin, Hamburg, and Munich, **Deutsche Mutoskop & Biograph** (1898), Messter-Projection/-Film (1901), Jules Greenbaum's Deutsche Bioscop (1902), and Duskes (1901/1905) stand out. Most were family businesses, manufacturing optical and photographic equipment, entering into film production mainly as a way of selling **cameras** and **projectors**. Such an approach to filmmaking may have delayed the development of an indigenous film industry, for even the largest and most successful among them, **Messter**, had a production policy diversified across more genres (and uses) of moving pictures than was appropriate for creating a market and consolidating a brand identity in the first decade. Oskar Messter's **Tonbilder** (sound pictures) indicated his interest in synchronization along the lines of **Edison**'s experiments, but they were too technically complex for mass exhibition. While Messter was as interested in the scientific and military uses of moving pictures as he was in their entertainment potential, the strategy of Paul **Davidson**, the other important German producer of the early period, was entirely entertainment-oriented. A success in the Frankfurt fashion business, Davidson built up his Allgemeine Kinematographen-Theater Gesellschaft (**PAGU**/AKGT) in 1906, by first establishing a chain of cinemas. In 1910, he took up production in Berlin, to complement his supply of films from abroad, notably **Pathé-Frères** (France) and **Nordisk** (Denmark). Crucially, Davidson took under contract one of Nordisk's major assets, the husband-and-wife-team of Urban **Gad** and Asta **Nielsen**, whose first Davidson-produced film was *Heisses Blut* [Hot Blood] (1911). Other major production firms established during what became a shift to longer films were **Vitascope** (1909), Komet-Film (1911), **Continental-Kunstfilm** (f 1911), Eiko-Film (1911) and Luna-Film (1913).

The German film industry adapted slowly to feature films as the standard product, hesitating between the alternatives of horizontally-diversified (Messter) or vertically-integrated (PAGU) companies, with the result that until 1913–1914, no more than 14% of the total number of films shown in German cinemas were German-produced. Although the figures are difficult to verify, estimates indicate that between 1905 and 1910 French (30%), American (25%), Italian (20%), and Scandinavian (15%) film imports made up 90% of the films shown in Germany. According to Emilie **Altenloh**, whose case study of cinema-going in one industrial location broke down the films' countries of origin by genres, German production did better in dramas (12% of the total) than in **comedies** (only 3%).

Much German production was confined to one- or two-act films (from 300 to 500 meters in length), confirming that the major structural move in early cinema, the transition to the **multiple-reel/feature film**, did not impose itself in Germany until 1912. An exception were the Asta Nielsen films, all three-reelers (from 700 to 1200 meters), whose success is further evidence of how the combination of **star** and feature length became the "norm" of popular and profitable cinema. Other companies copied PAGU, and Henny **Porten** (discovered by Messter and often directed by Carl **Froelich**) soon rivalled Nielsen as Germany's major female star of the pre-war period, although less well-known internationally. Messter proved adept at taking actors from stage and **vaudeville** under contract, giving many later stars their debut, among them Emil Jannings, Lil Dagover, and Conrad Veidt.

Messter also proved to be a pioneer in production facilities, erecting a studio that could be operated exclusively by artificial light as early as 1896. Other purpose-built studios, emerging at the same time as permanent cinemas around 1905–1906, combined natural and artificial light. The first glass-house studios were built near Berlin in Neubabelsberg (by Deutsche Bioscop), Tempelhof (by PAGU) and Weissensee (by Vitascope) in 1912/13.

This was the period when Germany began to develop a number of genres that would become typical for its reputation as a distinct national cinema. Vitality and wit emanated, for instance, from the films of Joseph **Delmont**, whose feeling for the excitement of the metropolis made him depict Berlin, in *Das Recht aufs Dasein* [The Right to Exist] (1913), gripped by a construction and housing boom. While the surreal slapstick comedies of Karl **Valentin** have often been noted, comedies like Franz **Hofer**'s *Hurrah! Einquartierung* [Hurrah! We're being Billeted] (1913) and *Das rosa Pantöffelchen* [The Pink Slipper] (1913) anticipate Ernst **Lubitsch**'s frantic farces from the mid-teens. Outstanding among other genres were sensational **melodramas** and **detective films**, featuring a star detective with an Anglicised name. These films cast a fascinated eye on modern technology, on the mechanics of crime and detection, with protagonists revelling in disguises and engaging in spectacular stunts, especially for frequent chase scenes, as in Max **Mack**'s *Wo ist Coletti?* [Where is Coletti?] (1913) and the films of Heinrich **Bolten-Baeckers**. Some films—for instance, Paul **von Worringen**'s *Die Landstrasse* [The Country Road] (1913), Bolten-Baeckers' *Hands of Justice* (1913), or Joe **May**'s *Der Mann im Keller* [The Man in the Cellar] (1913)—show considerable cinematic sophistication, combined with an adventurous use of outdoor locations and detailed period interiors. Here **lighting, camera movement,** and **editing** began to be deployed as part of a stylistic system, which compares well with the handling of space and narration in American, Russian or French films of the time.

These popular genres and their stars have been eclipsed, perhaps unfairly, by the most commented-on aspect of 1913, namely, the emergence of the so-called *Autorenfilm*. Nordisk was a prime force behind the *Autorenfilm*, producing two of the most costly ventures: *Atlantis* (1913), based on a Gerhart Hauptmann novel, and *Das fremde Mädchen* [The Strange Girl] (1913), a "dream play" written for the screen by Hugo von Hofmannsthal. German firms also specialized in such adaptations: Literaria, founded as a joint venture with Pathé, in order to exploit the latter's literary rights in Germany. The *Autorenfilm* underscores the international character of German film production in 1913, with actors and directors from Denmark undoubtedly exercising the strongest influence on domestic production.

The expansion of German production was well under way when war broke out. The hostilities further stimulated demand for films from domestic producers, once the import embargo was in force. Some firms, such as Davidson's PAGU, dependent on Pathé, at first suffered substantial losses. But there were also winners: the confiscation of property from foreign firms operating in Germany gave a new generation of producers their breakthrough. A young sales representative for **Gaumont** and **Éclair**, Erich Pommer, seized his chance and formed Decla ("Deutsche Éclair"), which was to become the key production company of German quality cinema after the war. In 1914, 25 German firms competed with 47 foreign ones; by 1918, the ratio was 130 to 10, not only a dramatic inversion, but an unsustainable increase in small, but vulnerable companies.

THOMAS ELSAESSER

Distribution

As in many other countries, it was the Lumière Cinématographe that originally brought moving pictures to Germany and secured their popular success. A noted chocolate manufacturer and slot machine operator, Ludwig Stollwerck showed an early interest in commercially exploiting the Lumière invention in Germany. Lumière operators also toured Germany from 1896 onwards, and in their wake a number of showmen successfully set up business with tent-theaters and *Wanderkinos*, making the new medium familiar to the public.

Film companies such as Messter, Deutsche Mutoskop & Biograph and Duskes all distributed films, in order initially to market their own projectors and other technical equipment by providing suitable "software." This also was the case with Hermann O. Foersterling, Philipp **Wolff**, and A. Hesekiel. Prior to 1906, however, Messter was the only serious German competitor to the predominantly French imports of films and apparatuses. For Messter, the Cinématographe presumed different distribution and exhibition contexts. The basic elements of cinema—as technology, as commodity, as public space—were developed separately by Messter, consequently, making him the first to commercially exploit its non-entertainment applications in a systematic manner: **newsreels**, aerial photography, **scientific films** featured in his activities alongside comedies, dramas, staged **operas** and *Tonbilder* (films mechanically synchronized with a sound source). Films for Messter had exchange value that commanded different use-values, rather than vice versa. He was also one of the first to supply non-commercial exhibition circuits and to apply the principle of value addition that came from restriction of access, for the purposes of exclusivity, to attract a better-paying public.

Non-commercial distribution networks existed already around the turn of the century, set up by scientific, educational, religious or (para-)military organisations. The German Navy League, for instance, built up tightly regulated circuits at the national, regional and local level throughout the country between 1900 and 1907, propagating its strategic aims. The Colonial League did the same for overseas trade, showing films for free to schoolchildren and apprentices. From 1907 onwards, mainly non-fiction films were financed, distributed and exhibited via alternative networks by members of the *Kinoreformbewegung* (cinema reform movement) all over Germany.

Given that Germany was a net importer of films, one key to understanding the transformations of German cinema before 1914 lies in the way films were traded—that is, bought, sold, exchanged. It makes patterns of distribution the dominant factor in the developments affecting both production and exhibition. With the establishment of permanent cinemas, aggressively competitive practices quickly arose in the commercial sector. As a consequence of over-ambitious cinema building projects, price wars on admission, and the accelerated turnover of frequent program changes, the German film industry ended up in a deep crisis that lasted from 1906 to 1909. A feverish second-hand trade in complete programs among cinema owners was both a precondition for and an inevitable product of the attendance boom. But the insatiable demand for films only sucked in cheap imports and choked domestic production, unable to compete on cost. Because of this trade and barter system among exhibitors, the few existing distribution companies (only five in 1907) could not consolidate into an autonomous branch of the film industry or serve as the pivotal link between production companies and theater owners. Instead, exhibitors themselves set up local or regional distribution networks, which, from 1908 onwards, were structured around a film rental system priced according to the running times of a complete program, the so-called *Staffelmieten-System*, with the consequence that older films were recycled and new ones suffered rapid devaluation. The first attempt to break up this system was the (short-lived) marketing ploy of the *Terminfilm*: single films with limited release dates, heavily advertised in the trade press in advance. Introduced in 1909 in the hope of cashing in on the legitimate theaters' thirst for novelty attractions and exclusivity, it failed to establish itself as a profitable practice, because an undeveloped production sector could not deliver quality product under such time pressure.

However, the *Terminfilm* did encourage the rapid rise of specialized distribution companies (22 in early 1910). Following the lead of Pathé-Frères and its push towards vertical integration, the German distribution and exhibition sector stabilized around 1909/10 with the introduction of the twice-weekly program change and the transition from selling to renting. Only then did the trade of single films gain a foothold in the German market, and the variety program of short films, as a distinct historical period of cinema, came to an end.

Late in 1910, the unexpected success of the **boxing film**, *Jack Johnson vs. Jim Jeffries* (1880 meters), exclusively distributed by PAGU, as well as the Danish production *Afgrunden* [The Abyss] (850 meters), exclusively distributed by Ludwig **Gottschalk**'s Düsseldorfer Film-Manufaktur, pointed to the financial potential of the single feature-length film, when marketed under conditions of restricted access and sole distribution rights. What in other countries became the zoning and clearance agreements, guaranteeing an exhibitor exclusivity of a film for a specific period in a specific geographical area, was known in Germany as the *Monopolfilm* (monopoly film). As elsewhere, it proved the single most important factor in changing the film business of the early period, leading to a revolution in virtually every aspect of the industry. A local monopoly enabled the exhibitor to charge higher admission prices at the box office, which, in turn, allowed distributors to advance capital to producers, who in turn could invest in higher production values and allocate more competitive budgets. The feature film as a commodity traded under monopoly conditions improved profits in all three areas of the film business, giving a boost to domestic production and allowing the German industry to consolidate itself from within. The *Monopolfilm* also created the first star-system, with actresses like Asta Nielsen and Henny Porten achieving fame solely on the basis of their work in the cinema, boosted by advertising campaigns targeting the single film, instead of promoting a mixed program.

Once the distribution practice of the *Monopolfilm* was established as the norm around 1911, the domestic production sector began to expand substantially. Typically, it had by then passed into the hands of exhibitors such as Paul Davidson or distributors such as Gottschalk and Martin **Dentler**. Due to their buying power and investment, the German film business gradually attained international standards, which it reached with a flourishing star-and-genre-cinema as well as an art cinema—the *Autorenfilm*—by 1913, well before the beginning of the war and the closing of the borders to French imports.

THOMAS ELSAESSER AND MICHAEL WEDEL

Exhibition

The first moving picture was shown in Germany by the Skladanowsky brothers in the Berlin "Wintergarten" on 1 November 1895. Initially costly, and hence coveted by early film entrepreneurs, moving picture demonstrations were booked only by the largest **music halls** or variety theaters, and usually for a single short run during the season. By 1900, however, moving pictures were being used regularly as the final act on a program because audiences would stay especially to see the films. Many second-rate variety theaters began showing films after 1905, and weekly **newsreels** continued to be shown in such venues well into the 1920s.

The Cinématographe exhibitions of the Lumière company also helped to popularize moving pictures. Organized by the chocolate manufacturer Ludwig Stollwerck in 1896–1897, these exhibitions were vigorously promoted at trade fairs, exhibits, and large fairs such as the Munich Oktoberfest. Offered every half-hour, Lumière exhibitions usually comprised ten one-minute films, showing interesting subjects from around the world.

Itinerant exhibitors, who had purchased projection equipment and a repertoire of film prints, arranged similar programs for exhibition on the road. In the tradition of **magic lantern** and panorama shows, they began traveling the **fair/fairground** circuit in 1896. By 1900, moving pictures had become a popular attraction at fairs. By

1908, such showmen were presenting grandiose film exhibitions in large tents equipped with boxes and bleachers.

During this period, audiences especially were attracted by entertaining, informative films providing "trouble-free travel." In "optical reports" or *actualités* shown in variety theaters, early audiences saw footage of the German fleet (1898) and the Boxer Uprising in China (1900). In the fairground cinemas, fiction films were well received, particularly *féeries/fairy plays* aimed at children and family audiences.

Initial attempts to establish permanent cinemas were made as early as 1896–1897. One of these, owned by Oskar Messter, was located at Unter den Linden 21 in Berlin; but it closed in 1897 after changing hands several times. Current research suggests that just one of these early urban "cinemas" endured, at the Stollwerck branch office, Kaiser-Wilhelmstrasse 11–15 in Hamburg, where presentations of the Cinématographe became part of an extensive permanent sales exhibit of assorted automatic devices directed at international customers. It was here that moving pictures found a home until 1899. Its lasting appeal also was attributed to the foresight of the **Lumière brothers**, who dispatched cameramen throughout the world to shoot 1,000 short films prior to 1898.

Berlin and Hamburg established the first permanent cinemas in 1905. New cinemas then proliferated between 1906 and 1909; in Berlin alone, the number fluctuated between 300 and 400 from 1907 to 1912. Initially, most of these were small, simply furnished "storefront cinemas," much like **nickelodeons**. While cinemas first appeared in large and mid-sized cities, by 1908 many smaller cities had three or four cinemas each. Permanent cinema programs were modeled on those in variety theaters, with short films taking the place of the numbered live acts. In contrast to the USA, German cinemas did not alternate films with live acts.

At first, the cinema boom was fed by an overabundance of used projectors and films left over from the days of the traveling showmen, which were traded on a cheap second-hand market. Soon a distribution system was set up for supplying new programs, and many cinema owners bought these weekly and then redistributed them. In 1906, the first cinema chains were established for the purposes of amortization: local ones such as James Henschel, in Hamburg, and national circuits such as Allgemeine Kinematographengesellschaft (later PAGU), in Frankfurt/Main, and **Weltkinematograph**, in Freiburg/Breisgau. In addition, cinema owners formed cooperatives that offered program exchanges on a subscription basis.

The number of cinemas rapidly exceeded demand, resulting in fierce competition. Obliged to surpass existing operations, new cinemas were more comfortably furnished. This in turn prompted the older cinemas to make renovations. Automatic devices providing **musical accompaniment** increasingly were replaced by live musicians. The **program format** changed as well, as the length of cinema programs reached 90 minutes as early as 1908–1909. In time, programs at second-rate cinemas lasted up to two or three hours. Moreover, cinema owners had to change their program more frequently to attract a loyal audience of regulars several times a week. By 1907–1908 weekly program changes were well established; by 1909, two and even three changes per week were commonplace.

At the same time, competition forced cinemas to keep undercutting one other's ticket prices, encouraging them to demand cheaper film rental fees and purchase prices. Most German cinemas showed foreign films, particularly French films from Pathé-Frères, which offered an incomparably inexpensive and convenient system for acquiring films. Around 1910 Pathé held from one-fourth to one-third of the German cinema market. Nevertheless, cinemas normally did not show programs consisting exclusively of Pathé films.

While the cinema boom hastened film's advancement as a mass medium, it also created an unsavory atmosphere of unscrupulous profiteering and cultural deficiency. In order to improve the reputation of the cinema business, and as a competitive strategy, many large, luxurious **palace cinemas** were built from 1910 on. These establishments clearly contrasted with the notion of cinema as a cheap amusement.

The transition to feature-length films and a "monopoly"-distribution system, which developed near the end of 1910, resulted in changes to program formats and to the cinema business itself.

By the mid-1910s, many programs consisted of two feature films along with a weekly newsreel, although some included three features as well as several short films. Feature-length films and the "monopoly" system also resulted in greater distinctions among cinemas. Elegant movie theaters were built for accommodating film premieres; in Germany, these were concentrated in Berlin, the undisputed center of the German film industry ever since the short film era.

In the early 1910s, consequently, the cinema business experienced a general upswing. From roughly 1,000 cinemas around 1910, the number rose to 2,371 by 1913. This rapid rise continued into **World War I**, finally being halted by the crisis of 1917–1918.

Audiences

From the start, people from all walks of life gained access to moving pictures. Well-to-do, intellectual audiences frequented the large, luxurious music halls or variety theaters, while middle- and lower-class people attended less expensive performances of itinerant exhibitors on fairgrounds and at carnivals or those in second-rate music halls, bars, and rented halls. The new medium was inaccessible only to such people as day laborers or agricultural workers and their families, since their extremely low incomes generally did not allow them to partake in commercial amusements. This economic distinction also applied to the early permanent cinemas. From the very beginning there were always two categories: well-furnished cinemas for the well-to-do and family audiences, and inferior, cheaper cinemas for less-well-to-do and especially young audiences.

The cinema was the first mass medium in Germany to solicit children as consumers of amusements by offering half-price admission. A relatively new practice, it had been a tradition only among itinerant show people and at certain municipal exhibitions, such as panoramas. The cinema met with an extraordinarily strong response among young people; unconfirmed accounts claim that they represented the majority of early filmgoers. Children, even from rural areas, went to the cinema on their own, and urban youth were often very selective in their viewing choices. The cinema gave children and young people freedom from

adult control; they could snack, smoke, and read trashy literature during the intermissions. Young couples found an enclave for fondling, and older girls a place to leave younger siblings they were supposed to be minding.

In 1907, anti-cinema protests were mounted, primarily by teachers, citing concerns about child protection. As a result, between 1908 and 1914, local and regional restrictions were enacted which limited children's access to the cinema. The edicts were not uniform, but were generally repressive. As an exception, Hamburg arranged regular special children's presentations in 1908.

Particularly during the child protection debate, some contributors brought forth reactionary, nationalistic arguments against the cinema, opposing the predominance of foreign films and denouncing the cinema as a public health hazard. While these attacks did not completely disappear, by 1912 the views of Hermann Lemke, a teacher active in journalism, generally prevailed. Lemke viewed film as a means of **education**. At his suggestion, Pathé-Frères and other, mostly foreign, companies produced films for classroom use and arranged special public showings of cultural films. As a result, the nationalistic discussion among child protectors eventually waned. Further initiatives advocated the use of film for educational purposes. In 1911, the *Lichtbilderei* society was founded by a Catholic organization in München-Gladbach; the society published the magazine *Bild und Film* [Image and Film] (1911–1915) and operated its own film distribution company. This initiative was directed not only at young people and teachers, but also at educated and cultured audiences from rural as well as urban areas.

While the interest of the public and other media (press, theater, literature) in the cinema had remained quite low as long as child protection was at issue, the transition to feature-length films after 1910 sparked a broad-based discussion. In 1913–1914, the cinema was the third most discussed topic of the day (a rank it lost abruptly due to the outbreak of World War I). This second cinema debate focused on film as a possible new art form. The advent of feature films placed the cinema in direct competition with the legitimate **theater** in presenting staged fictional narratives, a development which was viewed as presumptuous and indicative of intellectual decline. Led by the cultural elite (writers, artists, critics, the culturally-interested educated class), the debate generally repudiated film as an art form. At the same time, many writers and artists actively turned to film, which incited vehement criticism, but also won them overwhelming popularity and success. In addition, competition among cinemas spurred the building of large, luxurious and relatively expensive palace cinemas, which met with excellent audience response. As early as 1912–1913, there was a differentiation among these urban cinemas. Some focused on modern, young, open-minded moviegoers (Marmorhaus, Berlin), while others targeted older or family audiences. Still other cinemas catered to the less-privileged. In pre-World War I Germany, even though the cinema was not culturally acknowledged, it had widely established itself as the new mass medium for all sectors of society.

Hence the transition to feature films gave great impetus to the success of the cinema, which wooed adult audiences more resolutely than ever before. The variety offered by the short film program had provided unpretentious entertainment, gripping and surprising viewers of all ages. By contrast, the feature film required the audience to willingly accept the illusions of its fictitious worlds and, as in live theater, to immerse themselves reflectively in the portrayed events. Audiences accustomed to traditional culture encountered a familiar means of reception in the cinema, and culturally inexperienced audiences gained practice in being exposed to fictional presentations. In Germany, the feature films of the 1910s lasted approximately one hour, remaining substantially shorter than evening-long plays. Hence cinema programs usually comprised more than one film and continued to offer a combination of reflection and surprise. For culturally unpracticed audiences, the cinema of the 1910s played a decisive role in broadening exposure to fictional portrayals and in helping subsequent movie audiences devote their attention to films that would last two or three hours.

The early cinema of the 1910s offered both children and adults of all classes an informal retreat beyond the behavioral norms that applied at venues of traditional culture. There was no dress code; one could come and go at will; and eating, drinking and smoking were permitted in second-rate cinemas, prompting even the upper classes to frequent them. Yet the cinema's greatest advantage was its direct emotional appeal and the freedom of the spectators to surrender to their feelings. In contrast to the theater, which demanded decorum, concentration and emotional control, the cinema allowed moviegoers not only to chat and laugh freely, but also to cry, a benefit that even men appreciated.

CORINNA MÜLLER

Regulation

As moving picture theaters "sprouted like mushrooms" between 1904 and 1914, various civic groups became increasingly alarmed. Dank, dark storefront theaters were considered to be physically and morally offensive. The medium's incessant temporal and visceral rush was thought to be highly suggestive and thus influential on young and undeveloped minds. Specific films were often shocking or titillating, or both. The outcry to regulate theaters and moving pictures rose from these complaints, but must also be considered against imperial Germany's rising crime rate, which by 1914 had increased 20 percent above its 1880 level, with juvenile crime rising the highest. Moving pictures, the very emblem of **modernity**, was a convenient scapegoat.

Police in Germany's largest cities were the first to act. In 1906, Berlin authorities decreed that, much like legitimate theater shows, moving pictures should be approved by the police before public projection. Other cities were not as strict as the capital, but local authorities still imposed various ordinances to regulate picture theaters, especially by restricting school-age children from attending without an accompanying adult.

Local standards varied considerably, however, and the mechanism for censoring films was cumbersome and costly for both police and exhibitors. Between 1912 and 1914, consequently, state governments centralized censorship procedures. The Interior Minister encouraged states to follow Berlin's lead. Berlin also held the most prominent position economically in the fledgling film industry, so as state governments deferred to its judgment, the Berlin censorship office became the de facto clearinghouse for the nation. The Berlin office banned any film that might endanger the general welfare, that might be physically or psychologically harmful, or that might threaten moral values. Crime and detective stories, scenes of adultery or prostitution, politically or religiously inflammatory material, violent or gruesome scenes, or those deemed inappropriate for children were most commonly subject to censorship.

Theater lobbyists were especially appalled at the spread of moving picture theaters. Not only did they encroach on the legitimate theater's economic turf, but unlike the latter, picture theaters were not subject to the German commercial code and therefore did not need a license to open. Around 1911 several theater associations demanded that moving picture venues be subject to the same regulations and that their daily operations be more tightly regulated. Film exhibitors fought this, of course, but before legislation was considered, several sympathetic city governments took matters into their own hands by instituting a 5 to 20 percent amusement tax on tickets for moving picture theaters in order to stem their spread. By 1914, the imperial government had introduced a bill to regulate such theaters through licensing, a bill that surely would have passed, but was shelved by the outbreak of war.

See also: audiences: surveys and debates; distribution: Europe; law and the cinema: regulating exhibiton

Further reading

Cherchi Usai, P. and Codelli, L. (eds.) (1990) *Before Caligari: German Cinema, 1895–1920*, Pordenone: Edizioni Biblioteca dell'Immagine.

Curtis, Scott (1994) "The Taste of a Nation: Training the Senses and Sensibility of Cinema Audiences in Imperial Germany," *Film History*, 6: 445–469.

Elsaesser, T. and Wedel, M. (eds.) (1996) *A Second Life: German Cinema's First Decades*, Amsterdam: Amsterdam University Press.

Hellwig, Albert (1913) *Rechtsquellen des öffentlichen Kinematographenrechts*, M. Gladbach: Volksvereins-Verlag.

Müller, Corinna (1994) *Frühe deutsche Kinematographie: Formale, wirtschaftliche und kulturelle Entwicklungen 1907–1912*, Stuttgart/Weimar: Metzler.

Paech, Anne and Joachim (2000) *Menschen im Kino*, Stuttgart/Weimar: Metzler.

Stark, Gary D. (1982) "Cinema, Society, and the State: Policing the Film Industry in Imperial Germany," in Gary D. Stark and Bede Karl Lackner (eds.) *Essays on Culture and Society in Modern Germany*, 122–166, College Station, TX.: Texas A & M University Press.

SCOTT CURTIS

Ghione, Emilio

b. 1879; d. 1930

actor, Italy

Born in Turin, Emilio Ghione began his film career as a stunt-man and extra to round out his meager income as a painter of miniatures. In 1911, he was hired by **Cines** to act in in *S. Francesco, Poverello d'Assisi* [Saint Francis, the Poor of Assisi] (1911), directed by Enrico **Guazzoni**. Between 1912 and 1914, Ghione appeared in many films directed by Baldassare **Negroni** and starring Francesca **Bertini**, among them *L'Histoire d'un Pierrot* (1914). Thereafter, he turned to the adventure **serial** of apaches and gigolettes, where he repeatedly played the ambiguous Za la Mort, characterized by an anguished, emaciated mask of a face. With serials such as *Il Triangolo Giallo* [The Yellow Triangle] (1917) and *I Topi Grigi* [The Grey Mice] (1918), Ghione became the best-paid male star of the silent period in Italy. Despite this, he became sick and poor during his last years.

ANGELA DALLE VACCHE

Giambastiani, Salvador

b. ?, Italy; d. 1921, Santiago

photographer, producer, Chile

An experienced photographer, when he arrived in Chile from Italy in 1915—via Buenos Aires— Giambastiani became the most significant producer of Chilean silent cinema. From a production studio in Santiago, he initiated a steady output of fiction as well as nonfiction features, especially after teaming with fellow pioneer Luis Larraín Lecarios and entrepreneur George Bidwell as "Chile Films." He was skilled at obtaining commercial funding, notably for *Recuerdos del Mineral El Teniente* [Remembrances of the El Teniente Mine] (1918), Chile's first socially conscious documentary, ironically financed by the mine's owners, the U.S. Braden Copper Company.

Surprisingly, given the era and its cultural mores, he also actively collaborated with his common-law wife, 17-year-old Gabriella von Bussenius, who wrote the script for and directed *La agonía de Arauco* (The Arauco Agony) (1917), which focused on the indigenous *mapuche* population, albeit as a backdrop for a melodramatic love story. Giambastiani's unexpected death in 1921, after the premiere of *Los payasos se van* [The Clowns Are Leaving] directed by Pedro **Sienna**, was a blow to the incipient industry.

ANA M. LÓPEZ

Giampietro, Josef

b. 1866; d. 1913

actor, Germany

A Viennese stage actor, folk comedian, and operetta singer who rose to unequalled popularity in the mid-1880s, Giampietro went to Berlin in 1904 to become the celebrated star of the Metropol variety theater. With his gaunt body, bald head, monocle, and walking stick (the perfect example of Viennese nonchalance), he also appeared on screen in 1907, reciting his most famous couplets in **Messter**'s *Tonbilder*. In *Don Juan heiratet* [Don Juan is Getting Married] (1909), a **comedy** directed by Heinrich **Bolten-Baeckers** and still the most memorable role of his short career in moving pictures, Giampietro plays the converted lady-killer with foppish noblesse. In 1912, a year before his untimely death, his salary for one film amounted to 10.000 Reichsmark, a figure no other German film actor could claim at the time. His influence on male acting styles in German popular

cinema was still felt in 1916, when, as director Max **Mack** observed, the elegantly flapping movements of the typical "Giampietro gesture" were omnipresent in studios and talent scouting locations.

MICHAEL WEDEL

Gildemijer, Johan Hendrik

b. 1871; d. 1945

distributor, exhibitor, producer, scriptwriter, filmmaker, Netherlands

In 1911, Gildemijer became a film distributor and owner of an Amsterdam-based cinema in the German Union circuit. He was the exclusive distributor for Asta **Nielsen**'s German films produced by **PAGU**/Union and, together with Jean **Desmet**, was the most important renter of German and Danish films in the early 1910s. During **World War I**, he went into production, writing his own scripts. The first film, *Fatum* (1915), was directed by Theo **Frenkel**, but the subsequent ones he directed himself. *Gloria Transita* (1917) was his principal success: this story of the rise and fall of an opera star had the live accompaniment of singers who synchronized their voices to the actors on screen.

ANSJE VAN BEUSEKOM

Gilmore, William E.

b. 5 June 1863, New York; d. 17 January 1928, Orange, New Jersey

executive, USA

A former secretary to Samuel Insull of the General Electric Co., William Gilmore became **Edison**'s business manager on 1 April 1894, two weeks before the first **Kinetoscope** parlor opened. He continued in that capacity until 1908, when he retired and went into private business. Edison charged Gilmore with making his business affairs more orderly, and the latter's management style was tough and hard-nosed. Gilmore negotiated the first contracts for distributing Edison's films with

Raff & Gammon and **Maguire & Baucus**. From 1897 until he retired, he directed Edison's patent suits, sent detectives to harass competitors, and built Edison's reputation for ruthlessness.

PAUL SPEHR

Gish, Lillian

b. 1893; d. 1993

actor, USA

Renowned for her roles in D. W. **Griffith**'s films, Gish played sentimental parts with originality and grace. Touring as a stage child actress from 1902, she and her sister Dorothy joined the **Biograph** stock company in 1912. Her notable one-reel films include *The Lady and the Mouse* (1913) and *The Mothering Heart* (1913). She followed Griffith to **Mutual**, appearing in **multiple-reel films** such as *Home, Sweet Home* (1914) and, as Elsie Stoneman, in *The Birth of a Nation* (1915). Her reputation was secured with his later features, especially *Broken Blossoms* (1919) and *Way Down East* (1920). She parted from Griffith in 1921 and continued to act.

LEA JACOBS

Gladtvet, Ottar

b. 1890; d. 1962

filmmaker, Norway

Gladtvet began his career in 1906, as a projectionist in his father's cinema, and made his debut as a **newsreel** cameraman in 1912. Not satisfied with making *actualités* or working as a cameraman on fiction films by Peter **Lykke-Seest**, he tried his luck as a director. *Overfaldet paa Postaapnerens Datter* [The Assault on the Mailman's Daughter] (1913) was a **western**-inspired melodrama; and *Revolutionens Datter* [Daughter of the Revolution] (1918), a contemporary action film. In the 1920s, he established his own company, Gladtvet Film, which produced *actualités*, **animated advertising films**, and **industrial films**.

GUNNAR IVERSEN

glass-plate projectors

Relying on the wide experience of late-19th-century photographers in working with glass plate negatives and positives, several inventors and manufacturers proposed projectors using glass plates with thumbnail images arranged in rows or in a spiral, which gave about 20–30 seconds of moving pictures at about one-sixtieth of the cost of **celluloid** without any fire danger. Early designs were sketched by Pierre-Victor **Continsouza** and René **Bünzli** (1896), the Bettini brothers (1897), Robert Krayn (1897), and others. At least two had some success: Leonard Ulrich **Kamm**'s Kamma-tograph, holding 550 frames in a spiral on a 12-inch disk sold widely from about 1900, and Theodore **Brown**'s Spirograph developed by Charles **Urban**, from 1907 to 1922.

DEAC ROSSELL

Gliewe, Max

b. ?; d. ?

engineer, Germany

An experienced engineer and manufacturing pioneer who designed most of Oskar **Messter**'s apparatuses from late 1896 through 1900. Before signing on with Messter he produced and sold his own Maltese Cross (Geneva) projection machines in both Germany and Great Britain, and his former partner and brother-in-law, Karl Grahner, designed very similar projection apparatus for Philipp **Wolff** in late 1896. The European origins of the three-bladed shutter, the solution to screen flicker, also came from Gliewe in 1902, when he applied an improvisation from travelling showman Theodore Pätzold to Messter's line of equipment.

DEAC ROSSELL

Gloria Films

Also known as Film Artistica Gloria, the company was established in Turin by Mario **Caserini** and exhibitor Domenico Cazzulino, acting respectively as artistic director and head administrator. For brief periods, Gloria attracted directors Giuseppe **De Liguoro** and Amleto Palermi and actors Mario **Bonnard** and Lyda **Borelli**, the latter protagonists of an exemplary modern melodrama, *Ma l'amore mio non muore!* [Love Everlasting] (1913). Ambitiously oriented toward feature-length modern dramas and **historical films** such as *Nerone e Agrippina* [Nero and Agrippina] (1914), Gloria also produced numerous **comedies** after 1914.

Further reading

Bernardini, Aldo (1999) "Film Artistica 'Gloria'," *Bianco & Nero*, 60: 6.

GIORGIO BERTELLINI

Glücksmann, Max

b. 1875?; d. 1946

producer, distributor, exhibitor, Argentina

After emigrating from Austria in 1890, Glücksmann became one of Argentina's major film producers and distributors of the early period, an important producer of **newsreels** in the later silent period, owner of the record label Nacional Odeón, and an active public figure in the Jewish community of Buenos Aires. As the manager of Casa Lepage, a photographic supplies company which imported film equipment, he produced *actualités* with Eugenio **Py**. In 1908, he purchased Casa Lepage and transformed the company into a major film exhibitor. By the 1920s, Glücksmann owned some 100 cinemas in Argentina, Chile, Uruguay, and Paraguay.

KATHLEEN NEWMAN

Glückstadt, Vilhelm

b. 1885; d. 1939

filmmaker, Denmark

Glückstadt was responsible for the more artistically ambitious productions of **Filmfabrikken Danmark**. In *De dødes Ø* [Isle of the Dead] (1913), a lost film, Glückstadt was inspired by the Swiss symbolist painter, Arnold Böcklin, recreating more

than twenty paintings as tableaux within the film. Also in the symbolist vein are two extant films: *Den Fremmede* [The Stranger] (1914) has a bearded, Christ-like figure who rights wrongs; *Enhver* [Everyman] (1915) is a modern-dress version of the medieval morality play. Because of their supernatural subject matter, these films mistakenly have been claimed as precursors of German Expressionist filmmaking.

CASPER TYBJERG

Goncharov, Vasilii

b. 1861; d. 1915

filmmaker, Russia

The oldest member of the first generation of Russian filmmakers, Goncharov followed an unusual path to the movies. A career civil servant in the imperial **transportation** ministry, he resigned his position in the bureaucracy after his wife's death to fulfill his dream of becoming a writer. Facing the fact that he had little talent, he joined **Pathé-Frères** as a director in 1909 and **Gaumont** in 1910, before being wooed to the **Khanzhonkov** studio. Goncharov specialized in historical spectacles; his most important film was Russia's first "full-length" feature film, the 2,000 meter *Oborona Sevastopolia* [The Defense of Sevastopol] (1912), about the Crimean War siege.

DENISE J. YOUNGBLOOD

Gottschalk, Ludwig

b. 1876; d. ?

distributor, producer, exhibitor, Germany

Gottschalk founded his distribution company, *Düsseldorfer Film-Manufaktur*, in 1906 and specialized in **Messter's Tonbilder**. When distribution in Germany shifted from complete programs to single films in 1909, he reorganized the company and was the first to rent individual titles, initially popular *actualités*, but soon also fiction films with distinctive qualities such as French *films d'art* in **color** prints. With the German release of Asta **Nielsen** and Urban **Gad**'s *Afgrunden* [The Abyss]

(1910), for which Gottschalk acquired the sole distribution rights, extraordinary length became a decisive factor for creating a new commodity, the monopoly film. In 1911, Gottschalk, who also owned a number of cinemas, founded the *Frankfurter Film-Compagnie* and ventured into production with a strong bias towards **crime films** and heavy melodramas.

MICHAEL WEDEL

Grandais [Gueudret], Suzanne

b. 1893; d. 1920

actor, France

A striking Parisian blonde, with some stage experience, Grandais first appeared regularly in Louis **Feuillade**'s *Scènes de la vie telle qu'elle est* (Life As It Is) series at **Gaumont** and soon became a **star** for Léonce **Perret** in sensational **melodramas** such as *Main de fer* [International Conspiracy] (1912) and in the refined *Léonce* **comic series** (1912–1913). Arguably the most popular French actress of the early 1910s, Grandais was equally adept at playing subtly pathetic figures, deceptive partners in crime, or witty wives who deftly outsmarted their husbands. She was killed in an auto accident, while filming the **serial** *L'Essor*, in 1920.

RICHARD ABEL

Grau, Robert

b. 1858; d. 1916

businessman, critic, USA

Robert Grau was born into a family of theater impressarios whose specialty was **opera**. Grau devoted almost four decades to the amusement business and was thus in an ideal position to chronicle its vicissitudes and changes, especially the breakthrough of **vaudeville** in the 1880s and 1890s. His many publications, such as *Forty Years Observation of Music and the Drama* (1909), have a biographical slant in their focus on thespians; and *The Theatre of Science* (1914) takes up the emerging crowd of picture personalities in front of and behind the camera, and not least the inventors.

The latter book, dedicated to D. W. **Griffith**, was one of the first attempts to provide an overview of the pre-history and early days of the new amusement, and consequently has been addressed by scholars of all kinds from pioneers like Lewis Jacobs to the latter-day revisionists.

JAN OLSSON

Grauman, Sid(ney)

b. 17 March 1879; d. 5 March 1950

exhibitor, USA

In 1905, Sid Grauman and his father opened the Unique and Lyceum theaters in San Francisco as small-time **vaudeville** houses. Destroyed by the 1906 earthquake, the Graumans rebuilt the National on the site of the Unique. In 1908, Sid wanted to expand, his father did not; so Sid moved to New York City, and then Los Angeles, but failed in both. Only with the 1918 opening of his ornate **palace cinema**, the Million Dollar theater, and later with the Chinese, in Los Angeles, did he became rich and famous.

DOUGLAS GOMERY

Great Britain

The early years: exhibition and audiences

Film production and distribution are dependent upon exhibition, and the early years of British film exhibition were dominated by temporary shows and traveling showmen, who used their profits to buy short films from British production companies. However, after 1908 the shift of exhibition into permanent cinemas created a demand for larger numbers of longer films, which British producers could not satisfy. Domestic production continued, but from 1909 onwards the British film industry increasingly revolved around the importation and exhibition of American films.

In Great Britain, moving pictures were first adopted by showmen, who used them to increase the appeal of **penny arcades**, **magic lantern shows**, **music halls**, and **fairs/fairgrounds**. For a decade after the opening of the first **Kinetoscope** parlor in London in 1894, moving pictures remained an extension of established forms of entertainment.

Exhibitions of projected film, which began in 1896, were regarded as sophisticated magic lantern shows. Early **projectors** could show both film and slides, and, in 1901, P. N. Hasluck's *Optical Lanterns and Accessories* noted that the introduction of moving pictures "has given lantern work a new lease of life, and has revived the great popularity it enjoyed many years back." The "town hall showmen" who adopted them were often traveling lanternists, whose audiences followed the established "Lantern Season," from October to March.

Initial audiences were composed of casual visitors to town centers and fairgrounds, who paid to be shown ten, twenty, or thirty minutes of moving pictures. Showmen were equally mobile, and seldom remained in one town for more than a fortnight. As late as 1907, the principal market for new films remained the fairground, and the immense painted and gilded show fronts built that year for William Taylor's Premiere Show of the Universe and Pat Collins' Wonderland Show were the most magnificent buildings ever constructed for touring moving picture exhibition.

The early years: production and distribution

Early British producers were self-financed, and as much constrained by the British weather as by the size of the market. Production was seasonal, for the early studios were either open-air, as with Cecil **Hepworth**'s 1898 studio at Walton-on-Thames, or glass-roofed, as with Robert **Paul's** 1899 New Southgate studio. The autumn and winter were too dull for daylight filming, so fictional production mainly took place in the summer months. However, exhibition was concentrated in the autumn and winter, and thus, as A.C. Bromhead of **British Gaumont** explained in 1904, "the summer is a slack selling time, but a busy time getting stock ready for the winter's demand."

In 1903 Hepworth built himself an indoor studio with ten supplementary arc lamps, to try to overcome these problems, but the seasonality of film production did not begin to disappear until 1907. As late as 1908 British production and distribution

were still following "the season," which covered the dark evenings from October to March each year, and brought the largest audiences.

Early film distribution showed strong regional differences on top of this seasonality. In 1904, Lancashire and Yorkshire, the counties of the industrial north, were considered to be the best markets for films, whereas "Scotland and Ireland do not count for much." The principal method of distribution was by the sale of prints to exhibitors, and popular films sold in large numbers—four hundred copies in the case of Hepworth's *Rescued by Rover* (1905). Showmen like William **Jury** built up large stocks of films, and began hiring them to other exhibitors; but in 1906 there were only four rental companies in Britain.

British producers valued films according to the cost of production, and in 1905 they still priced their prints "according to the subject and the expense incurred." The usual price was 6d a foot, but in 1906 **Pathé-Frères** shocked the British industry by introducing a standard rate of 4d a foot. British producers combined to resist a general change, but early in 1907 Charles **Urban** broke ranks, and the price dropped to 4d. a foot. Domestic production companies could still flourish, and the profits of the **Charles Urban Trading Company** rose from £1,500 in 1904 to £7,600 in 1907. But the British market absorbed increasing numbers of foreign films: when the Kinematograph Manufacturers Association (KMA) was formed in 1906, the majority of its members were not domestic filmmakers but rather the agents of foreign production companies.

Film distribution also began to change through the rapid growth of rental companies, and in 1907 it was claimed that much of the recent expansion of the market had been driven by a shift from buying to hiring films. However, rental prices were still effectively fixed by producers, as they were related to the price of film and the life of a print. In 1908 the working life of a print was put at sixteen weeks, which, at 4d a foot, meant that it was impossible for renters to profit if their average weekly charge fell below £1 per 1,000 feet.

1909–1914: exhibition, audiences, and regulation

Around 1908, British exhibition practices began to change, as projected film broke away from its magic lantern past. As that year's **Wrench** company catalogue observed, there was a growing demand from showmen for film-only **projectors**, due to "the present custom amongst film makers to print the title with each film." But film exhibition was still rooted in 19th-century showmanship, and it was estimated that fewer than 900 people were employed in exhibiting moving pictures throughout the country.

Another influence on exhibition practice came from the danger of fire. Nitrate film stock could easily catch fire, especially since many showmen still used limelight projectors, with compressed oxygen and highly-inflammable hydrogen gas. In 1907, the KMA began pressing for safety legislation, arguing that it was "to protect ourselves, just as much as the public." The result was the Cinematograph Act 1909, which introduced a system of licensing designed to control exhibition of inflammable film.

The 1909 Act led to the closure of many temporary shows and encouraged the shift of exhibition into permanent venues with film-only performances. Although the construction of permanent cinemas only began in earnest in 1909, returns collected for the *Bioscope Annual* indicate that by the end of 1910 Great Britain had some 2,900 permanent cinemas, which rose to 3,800 by 1912, and 5,000 by 1914. For the first time moving pictures came to be associated with a single type of venue, and a single set of exhibition practices.

Projection equipment also changed rapidly after 1909, as older portable lanterns were replaced by heavy film projectors installed in special projection booths well away from the audience. These projectors used electric arc illumination rather than limelight, and many cinemas adopted the name "Electric Theater" to remind patrons how much brighter and bigger their pictures were. Yet their exteriors were still based on the fairground show, with bright lights, garish posters, and uniformed barkers.

Most British cinemas were relatively small and drew their audience from the surrounding area. In 1914, half of all cinemas had between 400 and 800 seats, and their audiences retained a sense of community and familiarity. They clapped, shouted, and booed during performances, although the management could still assert its authority if necessary. The new cinemas employed large numbers of staff, from doormen and ticket collectors to **projectionists** and musicians. By 1914, it

was estimated that some 75,000 people were employed in exhibition.

Permanent cinemas served a well-defined audience that was largely poor but remarkably regular in its attendance. Low ticket prices encouraged frequent visits, and it was claimed, in 1910, that a typical cinema "is often visited by the same people several times in a week." Exhibitors undercut the legitimate **theaters** and music halls, encouraging working-class attendance. "We are catering for the masses," acknowledged one exhibitor in 1914, "and for those who cannot afford . . . to go to ordinary theatres."

In 1912, many cinemas still ran a "continuous show" of short programs throughout the afternoon and evening. However, audiences were inclined to stay longer in the new venues, and, by 1914, the dominant pattern was a three-hour program, incorporating longer films, presented only twice a day. The slower turnover of audiences suited the larger cinemas, which were able to impose such a program on the industry, for although the majority of auditoriums held fewer than 800 seats, the majority of seats overall were in cinemas of larger capacity.

Film exhibition also was affected by legislation. The 1909 Act introduced annual licences for film shows, but these were intended only as a supplementary licence for theaters and music halls whose general safety was controlled by earlier legislation. The shift of exhibition into permanent cinemas revealed a loophole, for these venues did not require other licences. From 1910 on, local authorities thus began adding unexpected conditions to the new film licences, in an effort to guarantee audience safety.

Free to exercise their prejudices, local authorities also began to add censorship clauses, in an effort to control the content of films. In 1911, realizing the danger, the KMA set about constructing a trade censorship that would reduce their interference, and protect the profitable mainstream of the industry. The result was the British Board of Film Censors (BBFC), run by the KMA; in January 1913, the Board began suppressing all films "in any way opposed to the better feelings of the general public." The BBFC was remarkably successful. During 1913 and 1914, its examiners viewed 13,770 films, but its President—a KMA nominee—signed rejection certificates for only 35 of them. The Cinematograph Exhibitors Association complained in private that he "passed everything that was at all possible, in the interests of manufacturers," but the BBFC's public image helped protect the industry from interference.

The BBFC was of great assistance to exhibitors, whose audience was growing far more slowly than predicted. By 1913, British cities seemed swamped with cinemas: "when . . . a single suburb of London has nine picture theatres, it is surely time to pause." Returns collected for the *Kinematograph Year Book* indicate that, by 1914, Britain's 5,000 cinemas held 4.25 million seats, although ticket sales were estimated at only 7,000,000 or 8,000,000 a week. With two or more shows a day, many performances must have been largely empty.

In 1914, film exhibition still seemed precarious. Moving pictures were an established form of entertainment, but competition between venues was so intense that exhibitors were forced to subdivide the market, using strategies based on genre, price, music, and **advertising** to attract different audiences. Attempts to move the audience upmarket proved futile, until the outbreak of war raised general attendance levels and boosted middle-class patronage.

1909–1914: production and distribution

The rapid growth of permanent cinemas from 1909 onwards had, in turn, four important effects on British film production and distribution.

The first was a rapid increase in the demand for new films, which was principally met by increasing imports. In 1909, British studios provided only 15% of domestic releases, by comparison with 30% from the USA and 40% from France, and they proved unable to increase their market share. By 1910, domestic producers were unable to supply more than a fraction of the 4,100 films released onto the British market. They increased output from 370 fiction films in 1910 to 830 by 1914, but were still outstripped by demand. As was admitted in 1915, in British cinemas "most programmes are entirely American, with the exception of a scenic (French or Italian), and the topicals and gazette (**newsreel**)."

The second impact of permanent cinemas was on film length. Audiences stayed longer in the new auditoria, and the owners of larger halls realized that longer films were also a useful economic strategy against their smaller rivals. Small auditoria required a higher turnover of audiences, and simply could not function with longer films. From 1909 onwards, a sharp drop in the output of fiction films under ten minutes long thus coincided with the gradual closure of the smaller venues. In 1909 only 3% of all British fiction films ran for more than fifteen minutes at the standard projection speed, but this rose to 31% by 1912, and to 48% by 1914.

A whole new class of long fiction films, running for more than twenty-five minutes, was also created to satisfy the larger venues. In 1914, British studios released some 230 of these long films—**multiple-reel/feature films**—accounting for 28% of all production. It is likely that fewer prints were made of these longer productions, but it is obvious that British audiences were now prepared to spend a whole evening in the cinema, where they expected to see longer dramatic films. In July 1914, 20% of all new fiction releases on the British market, both domestic and imported, ran for more than twenty-five minutes.

The third impact of permanent cinemas was on film renting. The travelling showman changed his audience more frequently than his films, but permanent exhibition demanded a different approach. By 1912, rental practices worked on a sliding scale based on the age of the print, and although a "first-run" program might cost over £20 a week, a small hall could pay just £7 a week for "4,000 to 5,000 ft. of film of about six weeks old." By 1914, there were 260 rental companies in Britain, with a third of them based in London, by comparison with only 43 production companies, or representatives of foreign production companies.

The growing length and expense of feature films also led to a division between the "exclusive" release and rentals on the "open market." Exhibitors risked losing money if the market was saturated with prints of a popular film, and "exclusives" guaranteed them exclusive local rights for a premium fee. In 1911 Barker Motion Photography made only twenty prints of its *Henry VIII*, ten for exclusive release in London and ten for the provinces, with the promise that they would be publicly burned after six weeks of exhibition—and the promise was kept. This was exceptional, but in 1913 **British and Colonial** sold the exclusive British rights for *The Battle of Waterloo* to one renter for £5,000. By 1914 some 1,000 "exclusives" had been released onto the British market.

The fourth major effect of permanent cinemas lay in the creation of newsreels, for regular news bulletins required regular attendance. The ground was prepared by the so-called "Topical War" of 1910, a burst of price-cutting that saw **news event film** drop to $2\frac{1}{2}$d a foot. It was now economic to release regular bulletins of news event film to permanent cinemas, and the industry responded with the *Pathé Gazette* and *Gaumont Graphic*. However, the small profit margins remained a constant inhibitor to the production and distribution of factual film in Britain. As the editor of the *Éclair Journal* noted in 1914, "the exhibitor will not pay for more than 500–600 feet, and he wants it at a rock-bottom price."

One problem in combating foreign imports was that British film production remained under-capitalized. Capital was hard to find, and in 1912 it was estimated that only £2.5 million was invested in British film production, by comparison with some £10.3 million in film exhibition. British studios increased in size, but the production sector remained small. In 1913 it was estimated that although the thirty British studios drew on a pool of 2,000 film actors, not more than fifty of them were full-time. There were also few writers for films, which is not surprising when only £5–£10 was paid for the synopsis to a single-reel film, and many British producers still regarded £1 as sufficient "for a good plot". By 1914, £3.2 million allegedly was invested in British production, but British cinemas were said to employ 75,000 people, with an investment of £13.9 million.

World War I further weakened British production, and left the market open to American manufacturers. By 1917 British producers were releasing a hundred and fifty fiction films a year, but it was estimated that British exhibitors needed ten times that number to survive. As a result 95% of the films shown in Britain cinemas were imported, 75–80% of them from the USA. As the chairman of the Cinematograph Exhibitors' Association explained, some moviegoers might object to so many imported films, but "British films are so

Figure 48 "Inside a picture palace," *The Sphere*, April 1913.

few and far between that (you) would wear (your) boots out trying to find them."

By 1914, whereas film production had become an art as well as an industry, exhibition still remained a branch of showmanship. People went to be shown moving pictures, not to see a film for itself, and they were always conscious of their presence in the auditorium. Film was an urban phenomenon, and being in the cinema was part of being in the city. The history of exhibition was the history of the "night out"; moviegoers did not pay for imaginative access to a particular film or film **star**, but for time spent as part of the cinema audience.

See also: audiences: research and projects; audiences: surveys and debates; cinema and the law: regulating exhibition; distribution: Europe

Further reading

Barnes, John (1983) *The Rise of the Cinema in Great Britain*, London: Bishopsgate Press.

Burton, Alan and Laraine Porter (eds.) (2000) *Pimple, Pranks & Pratfalls: British Film Comedy before 1930*, Trowbridge: Flicks Books.

Burton, Alan and Laraine Porter (eds.) (2003) *Scene-Stealing: Sources for British Cinema Before 1930*, London: Flicks Books.

Burton, Alan and Laraine Porter (eds.) (2001) *The Showman, the Spectacle and the Two-Minute Silence: Performing British Cinema before 1930*, Trowbridge: Flicks Books.

Hiley, Nicholas (1995) "The British Cinema Auditorium," in Karel Dibbets and Bert Hogenkamp (eds.) *Film and the First World War*, 160–170, Amsterdam: Amsterdam University Press.

Hiley, Nicholas (1997) "Fifteen Questions About the Early Film Audience," in Daan Hertogs and Nicolas de Klerk (eds.) *Uncharted Territory: Essays on Early Nonfiction Film*, 105–118, Amsterdam: Stichting Nederlands Filmmuseum.

Hiley, Nicholas (1998) "'At the Picture Palace': The British Cinema Audience, 1895–1920," in John Fullerton (ed.) *Celebrating 1895: The Centenary of Cinema*, 96–103, Sydney: John Libbey.

Hiley, Nicholas (2002) "'Nothing More than a "Craze"': Cinema Building in Britain from 1909 to 1914," in Andrew Higson (ed.) *Young and Innocent?: The Cinema in Britain, 1896–1930*, 111–117, Exeter: University of Exeter Press.

Low, Rachael (1948–1979) *The History of British Film*, 6 vols., London: George Allen & Unwin.

Toulmin, Vanessa (2002) "The Importance of the Programme in Early Film Presentation," *KINtop*, 11: 19–33.

NICHOLAS HILEY

Greater New York Film Rental Company

A film exchange organized by **nickelodeon** owner William **Fox** around 1906. In 1909, the **Motion Picture Patents Company** started buying up the most successful exchanges in order to consolidate and control film distribution. Fox refused to sell and his MPPC. license was revoked. He filed suit under the Sherman Anti-Trust Act for illegal restraint of trade and eventually prevailed, but in the meantime he started distributing independent product and producing his own films. Greater New York became known as Box Office Attractions in 1914 and was reorganized as the Fox Film Corporation in 1915.

ROBERT S. BIRCHARD

Greece

Compared with some of its Balkan or Mediterranean neighbors, Greece was slow to welcome moving pictures, perhaps due to the stifling effect of Turkish rule in some regions. The first projections seem not to have taken place until 1897. Although films were being shown in some variety theaters in Athens in 1903, permanent cinemas too were slow in arriving, and even as late as 1913 there were only seven or eight year-round cinemas in the entire country—by contrast, tiny Malta, two years earlier, had at least half a dozen shows in the capital city alone. There were some cinema "hot-spots": notably Saloniki which in 1910 had four booming moving picture shows, according to the US consul there. French films were popular, and even as late as 1920 Wids was reporting that French and Italian films dominated Greek screens.

Film production in Greece was equally slow to start. **Lumière** operators did not film in the country, and the first person to do so was probably Frederic Villiers, who shot some Greco-Turkish war incidents in Thessaly in the spring of 1897. Dimitris Meravidis may have filmed *actualités* in Greece around 1903, and the 1906 Olympic events were certainly filmed by **Gaumont** and **Pathé-Frères**. From 1907, the Manaki brothers were shooting scenes in Macedonia and its surroundings, and Joseph Hepp was filming in Greece from around 1910. The first Greek production company, Athina Films, may date from this year, although a 1913 source claims the first was the "Fabrique panhellénique de films S. Léonce." These companies made *actualités*, a genre that boomed during the Balkan Wars of 1912–1913, with foreign and local cameramen recording military incidents. The most famous film from the Greek front was Robert Schwobthaler's *Sous la mitraille* [Underfire] (1913).

In 1914, the first Greek feature film was produced, an adaptation by Kostas Bahatoris of *Golfo*. At this time renters such as Gaytis and Mosco were doing good business, importing from **Selig** and other foreign companies.

See also: the Balkans; Turkey/Ottoman Empire

Further reading

Démopoulos, M. and Aktsoglou, B. (1995) *Le Cinéma grec*, Paris: Centre Georges Pompidou.
Chambre de Commerce française en Grèce (1913) "The cinematograph in Greece," *Bioscope*, 4 December: 978.

STEPHEN BOTTOMORE

Green, George

b. 1861; d. 1915

exhibitor, distributor, Scotland/England

Green first exhibited moving pictures at the Carnival, Glasgow, in December 1896, after purchasing a Theatrograph from R. W. **Paul**. Between 1898 and 1914, he operated roundabouts and up to four moving picture booths in the **fairs/fairgrounds** throughout England and Scotland. In 1902, after purchasing the rights to the fairground and moving picture concessions for the Cork Exhibition, he commissioned **Mitchell & Kenyon** to film factory gate scenes and other topicals or *actualités* to show in the evenings. By the time Green died in 1915 (and was succeeded by his son Herbert), he had amassed a chain of thirteen picture theaters in Glasgow, Dundee and Ayr, established a film rental and production company known as Greens of Glasgow, and started a cinema construction company.

VANESSA TOULMIN

Green, John C.

b. 1866; d. 1951

showman, Canada

A month after Canada's first public exhibition of moving pictures in Montreal, Green debuted the Vitascope in Ottawa. Promoted by the Holland Brothers, this screening ostensibly involved a **lecture**, commentary, and **magic lantern show**, although Green's involvement may have been limited to the latter, as other acts replaced him after the first two weeks. Nonetheless, out of this beginning Green purchased an **Edison projector** and developed a two-hour show, complete with **illustrated song** slides and magic, which he toured across Eastern Canada and the USA. Working at various **amusement parks** and fairs, Green's career as an **itinerant exhibitor** is typical of the era.

CHARLIE KEIL

Gregory, Carl Louis

b. 1882 d. 1951

Photographer, cinematographer, USA

Born in Walnut, Kansas, Gregory completed a chemistry degree at Ohio State University and became an official photographer at the 1904 Louisiana Purchase Exposition. From 1907 to 1908, he made photographs and films for the US Reclamation Service. After working briefly for Burr McIntosh as a stage manager and photographer, he joined the **Edison** Company in June 1908. Two years later he became chief photographer for **Thanhauser**, overseeing construction of its California studio. Eventually, he left to become chief photographer on **Williamson**'s submarine expedition in the West Indies: *Thirty Leagues Under the Sea*, 1914. In 1915 he signed with Metro as cinematographer; during World War I he served as a lieutenant in the US Signal Corps. In 1936 he was hired by the National Archives, where he became the first person to successfully copy materials from the Library of Congress Paper Print Collection onto celluloid stock.

CHARLES MUSSER

Griffin, John J.

b. 1855; d. 1931

exhibitor, Canada

Involved in a variety of theatrical entertainments, including the circus, Griffin decided to convert a Toronto storefront into a moving picture theater in March 1906. His first attraction was Edison's *The Train Wreckers*. Called the Theatorium, this 5¢ theater may lay claim to being Canada's first permanent **nickelodeon**-styled establishment devoted to films, although Ernest **Ouimet**'s initial Ouimetoscope began operations a few months earlier. Blending film and **vaudeville**, Griffin opened over a dozen more theaters in Toronto and across southern Ontario. In addition to this circuit, Griffin also supplied over 150 houses with vaudeville entertainment in both Canada and the USA.

CHARLIE KEIL

Griffith, D. W. (David Wark)

b. 1875; d. 1948

actor, scriptwriter, filmmaker, USA

More exaggerated claims have been made for this American director than any other figure in film history, but hyperbole should not cause us to underestimate Griffith's very real contributions. After a modest career as a theatrical actor and playwright, Griffith came to moving pictures in early 1908, contributing scenarios for and acting in films produced by both **Edison** and **Biograph**. By 1908, the **nickelodeon** boom had

created a voracious demand for new product, and American companies were seeking to break the deadlock of production caused by Edison's patent claims and legal actions. The new regularized mode of production that ensued, especially through the **Motion Picture Patents Company's** formation, and the increased emphasis on story films that this promoted greatly influenced Griffith's career.

Griffith took over directing at Biograph in the summer of 1908. Although Biograph had long employed a partnership of cameramen and directors to make its fiction films, Griffith modeled himself on new theater directors such as David Belasco who crafted individual styles for each stage production, paying close attention to new naturalistic styles in performance and **set design** and the potential of new technologies, such as electrical light. Griffith did not merely coach actors and prepare scenarios, as had previous Biograph directors, but rather constructed the narrative style of each film.

The era of Griffith's filmmaking for Biograph (1908–1913) saw a shift in the models for fiction film, from a focus on physical action (as in the **chase film** or slapstick farce) to an increased attention to psychological characters and realistic contexts. Griffith absorbed the chase film into new scenarios of suspenseful action and generally shifted farce production to the company's second unit. His work with actors yielded nuanced performances from, among others, Mary **Pickford**, Mae **Marsh**, Lillian **Gish** and Bobby Harron. Griffith based his narrative style primarily on editing, increasing the average number of shots per one reel of film from under twenty to more than eighty by 1913. This increase (which also can be found to a lesser extent in other companies) derives primarily from his use of parallel editing, cutting between different locations in patterns of alternation. Griffith did not restrict such editing to creating suspense but also used it to reveal a character's thinking and create moral contrasts—or even political argument, as in *The Corner in Wheat* (1909). The more than 400 films Griffith directed at Biograph were in the forefront of the move toward narrative integration in American cinema, and include many mini-masterpieces: *After Many Years* (1908), *The Country Doctor* (1910), *Rose of Salem Town* (1910), *The Lonedale Operator* (1911), *The Informer* (1912), and *The Mothering Heart* (1913).

Figure 49   D. W. Griffith directs *Death's Marathon* (1913), with Henry Walthall. (Courtesy of Charles Musser.)

In his last year at Biograph, Griffith chaffed at being restricted to single-reel films, with occasional exceptions such as *Judith of Bethulia*, which ran four reels. Biograph shelved the film and removed Griffith from direction, which led to his leaving the company, taking Billy **Bitzer** and many actors with him. Joining **Mutual Film**, he produced a series of four-reel feature films in 1914, including the extraordinary Edgar Allen Poe adaptation, *The Avenging Conscience*, bringing his psychological editing to a climax. He then began work on his historical epic, *The Birth of a Nation*, which helped to inaugurate a new era of film history.

See also: acting styles; editing: spatial relations; editing: temporal relations; lighting

Further reading

Gunning, Tom (1990) *D. W. Griffith and the Origins of American Narrative Film*, Urbana: University of Illinois Press.

Jessonowski, Joyce (1987) *Thinking in Pictures: Dramatic Structure in D. W. Griffith's Biograph Films*, Berkeley: University of California Press.

TOM GUNNING

Grimoin-Sanson, Raoul (Grimoin, Raoul Adrien)

b. 1860; d. 1941

photographer, inventor, exhibitor, industrialist, France

Born in Elbeuf, the son of a weaver and a mender of clothing, Grimoin (he later added Sanson to his name) initially had a career making anthropometric **photographs** for the Brussels police department (1892) and photomicrographs for the city's university.

On 5 March 1896, he registered a patent in France for his "Phototachygraph," a film projector using an exhaust system. He also created the Cinéorama, a system of 360° film projection comprising ten **projectors** arranged according to a star-shaped pattern and which he vainly attempted to operate at the 1900 Paris Exposition.

He later invested in industrial applications for cork (for instance, waterproof cork cloth used for gas masks) and made a fortune supplying the French army during **World War I**. He cast himself as a pioneer of cinema through his memoirs, *Le Film de ma vie* (1926), his film, *L'Histoire du cinéma par le cinéma* (1927), and his arguments with Henri René **Bünzli** and P. Victor **Continsouza** over the paternity of the Maltese cross (1928).

Further reading

Meusy, Jean-Jacques (1991) "L'énigme du Cinéorama," *Archives*, 37.

JEAN-JACQUES MEUSY

Gual, Adrià

b. 1872; d. 1920

filmmaker, Spain

Early 20th-century Modernist dramatist. In 1904 Gual participated in "spoken projects" at the Sala Mercè, a Barcelona theater designed by Antoni Gaudí. For a brief period in 1914, he became artistic director for **Barcinógrafo**. Influenced by **Film d'Art**, he adapted several literary works to the cinema: *El alcalde de Zalamea* [The Mayor of Zalamea] (1914), by Calderón de la Barca; *Fridolín* (1914), by Schiller; *La gitanilla* [The Little Gypsy] (1914), by Cervantes; *Los cabellos blancos* [The White Hair] (1914), by Tolstoi; and *Misteri de dolor* [Mystery of Pain] (1914), an adaptation of one of his own plays.

JOAN M. MINGUET

Guazzoni, Enrico

b. 1876; d. 1949

director, art director, Italy

Educated as a painter and decorator, Guazzoni first worked as an art director at Alberini & Santoni. During his golden period at **Cines** (1909–1917) he directed **historical films** of exceptional worldwide success. In 1913, after *Bruto* [Brutus] (1911) and before *Cajus Julius Caesar* [Julius Caesar] (1914), he completed the eight-reel blockbuster, *Quo Vadis?*, adapted from Henry Sienkewicz's popular novel and employing more than 2000 extras. His talent for rich pictorial compositions and an unusual depth of perspective turned the historical epic into a highbrow cosmopolitan entertainment, affecting the production and marketing strategies of most Italian film companies.

GIORGIO BERTELLINI

Gugenheim, Eugène

b. 1857; d. 1923

playwright, financier, executive, France

Gugenheim served as the administrator of several Parisian theaters and authored several hit plays before co-founding the Société cinématographique des auteurs et gens de lettres (**SCAGL**) with Pierre **Decourcelle** in 1908. According to Decourcelle, Gugenheim had the original idea for the project and involved the **Merzbach** bankers, then major shareholders in **Pathé-Frères**. Although his activity was less visible than Decourcelle's in the management of SCAGL prior to 1914, it was no less significant.

ALAIN CAROU

Guillaume, Ferdinando

b. 1887; d. 1977

actor, director, Italy

Guillaume and his entire well-bred circus family were hired by **Cines** in 1910. Soon he was launched in a **comic series** as the character of Tontolini, or Jenkins in Britain and the USA. This series made an international reputation for Cines and Italy in the field of comic films. After the success of his first feature-length film, *Pinocchio* (1911), Guillaume moved to **Pasquali**, where he created the character of Polidor, continuing his double profession of leading actor and director. At his peak in 1912–1913, he was shooting up to four films a month; thereafter, the number of his films shrunk considerably. Guillaume managed to pursue a career in cinema until the early 1920s and had occasional comebacks, as in several Federico Fellini films.

IVO BLOM

Gundersen, Jens Christian

b. 1868; d. 1945

exihibitor, distributor, filmmaker, Norway

A solicitor and amateur actor, Gundersen became the most influential cinema owner and film importer in Norway from 1907 to 1919. Setting up business in Kristiana in 1907, he acquired cinemas in several cities and established several film distribution companies. He had exclusive rights for **Vitagraph** in the Scandinavian market and for other companies such as **Nordisk**, **Ambrosio**, **Edison** and **Éclair** in the Norwegian market. In 1911, he directed *Dæmonen* [The Demon], a sensational **melodrama**, photographed by Alfred **Lind** in Denmark. In 1926, Gundersen became the first director of the municipal cinemas in Oslo.

GUNNAR IVERSEN

Guy Blaché, Alice

b. 1873; d. 1968

filmmaker, France/USA

The first woman filmmaker and among the first to direct a fiction film. The nearly one thousand films she produced had a significant impact on the development of filmic storytelling. She trained the best of the second generation of French filmmakers, including Victorin **Jasset**, Emile **Arnaud**, Romeo **Bosetti**, and Louis **Feuillade**.

She began her film career as office manager to Léon **Gaumont** in 1895 and was present at the March 1895 demonstration of the **Cinématographe Lumière**. She probably began making films herself in the spring of 1896 and was quickly put in charge of the **Gaumont** company's film production. Her specific goal was to apply literary narrative techniques to film. Those she made before 1900, such as *La Concierge* (1899) show the

possibilities of pre-montage filmic narration and a use of off-screen space at its most sophisticated. In addition, she directed over one hundred *phonoscènes* for the Gaumont **Chronophone** between 1902–1906. Significant films from this period include *Madame a des Envies* [Madame Has Her Cravings] (1906) with an early dramatic use of the close-up, and *La Passion*, (The Life of Christ) (1906), with Jasset as an assistant.

In 1907 she married Gaumont manager Herbert Blaché. Blaché was transferred to the USA and eventually became manager of Gaumont's Flushing studio in New York. In 1910, Guy founded her own company, **Solax**, using the Flushing studio to produce films that then were distributed through Gaumont's licensed connections. Solax was critically and financially successful enough for Guy to build her own studio in Fort Lee in 1912; she became perhaps the only woman in the world to have owned her own studio plant. The steady output of one-reelers she directed at Solax best represent her satirical, feminist style, especially *Cupid and the Comet* (1911), *House Divided* (1913), *Matrimony's Speed Limit* (1913), and *Officer Henderson*, (1913); of special interest is *A Fool and His Money* (1912), with an all-black cast. In addition to these early "screwball" **comedies**, she produced stirring melodramas and elaborate fantasy films such as the three-reel *Dick Whitington and his Cat* (1913).

The Solax Company floundered when Gaumont's access to licensed distribution was cut off, and from 1915 Guy worked for her husband's company, Blaché Features, and as a director for hire. She produced and directed a series of features starring Olga Petrova and another series starring Claire Whitney, all unfortunately lost. Her feature for Hearst, *The Ocean Waif* (1916), shows that working as a director for hire forced her to compromise her vision, but her penultimate film, *Her Great Adventure* (1918), starring Bessie Love, shows that she had adapted with the times and could still produce a deft and biting feminist satire. After Blaché Features went bankrupt and her marriage ended in 1920, she returned to France and never made another film.

See also: black cinema, USA; dance films; editing: early practices and techniques; women's movement: USA

Further reading

McMahan, Alison (2002) *Alice Guy Blaché: Lost Visionary of the Cinema*, New York: Continuum.

ALISON McMAHAN

Gys, Leda

b. 1892; d. 1957

actor, Italy

Thanks to an introduction by the Roman poet Trilussa, Leda Gys (Giselda Lombardi) was hired by **Cines** in 1913 to appear in three short films directed by Baldassarre **Negroni**. Working for both Cines and its branch Celio, between 1913 and 1914, she sharpened her skills in some two dozen short- or medium-length films directed by Enrico **Guazzoni** and others. It was then that Gys began to develop a personal screen type based on American stars, combining the girl-next-door innocence of Mary **Pickford** and the suffering pathos of Lilian **Gish**. After appearing in a number of dark melodramas, she triumphed in *Christus* (1916), a religious epic shot on location in Egypt and Palestine. She then married producer Gustavo Lombardo and settled in Naples, where she switched to doing light-hearted romantic comedies directed by Eugenio Perego throughout the 1920s. Thanks to her versatile acting, Gys was the only Italian diva who never played vamp roles and the only one whose career lasted until the advent of sound films.

ANGELA DALLE VACCHE

Häfker, Hermann

b. 1873; d. 1939

reformer, theorist, Germany

Häfker was the most visible leader and theorist of the loosely organized film reform movement in Germany. His articles and monographs dating from 1908 are among the earliest serious considerations of cinema's cultural significance and aesthetic potential. Offended by the seediness of storefront theaters and the general lack of "taste" in commercial film production, film reformers sought to "uplift" cinema by offering films that reflected middle-class sensibilities in "tasteful" alternative venues. Häfker's own specially organized screenings emphasized explicit rules of attentive **spectatorship** and careful, aesthetic presentation, thus anticipating most current film exhibition standards.

SCOTT CURTIS

Haggar, William

b. 1856; d. 1925

exhibitor, filmmaker, Great Britain

Born of a **fairground** family, and a prominent showman, William Haggar became one of the most distinguished of pre-1910 British filmmakers. Four of the 35 films he made between 1902 and 1908 are extant, including the influential **chase film** *A Desperate Poaching Affray* (1903) and *The Life of Charles Peace* (1905), a fictional version of a real criminal's exploits. Noted for their energy, resourceful editing, and **staging in depth**, Haggar's films spanned **comedy**, chase and **trick films** as well as truncated versions of his own stage melodramas. They were mainly released by **British Gaumont** and **Charles Urban Trading Company** in Britain; at least seven were distributed in the USA.

DAVE BERRY

Hale's Tours

George C. Hale introduced Hale's Tours and Scenes of the World at the 1904 Saint Louis exposition. His success led to a 1905 summer season at the Kansas City Electric Park. With partner Fred Gifford, Hale took out two patents and licensed the illusion railroad ride to exhibitors. In 1906, Hale and Gifford sold the rights east of Pittsburgh to William A. **Brady** of New York and Edward B. Grossmann of Chicago and the southern states rights to Wells, Dunne & Harlan of New York. They sold additional licenses to C. W. Parker Co. of Abilene, Kansas, for traveling carnival companies, and the Pacific-Northwest state rights to a group of men who incorporated as "The Northwest Hale's Tourist Amusement Company" in Portland, Oregon. Licenses were sold abroad as well for several years until the increased systematization and consolidation of the cinema industry forced the partners out of business sometime after 1910. Between 1906 and 1911, there were more than 500 installations at **amusement parks** and storefront theaters in North America as well as in Havana, Melbourne,

Paris, London, Berlin, Bremen, Hamburg, Hong Kong, and Johannesburg.

Hale's Tours consisted of one or more theater cars, each seating 72 "passengers." The moving pictures that showed out the front end of the car offered a filmed point of view from the front or rear of a moving train. The goal was to create the sensory illusion of movement into or away from a scene, accentuated by mechanical apparatuses and levers that simultaneously vibrated, rocked, and tilted the car. Representative film titles included: *A Trip on the Catskill Mt. Railway* (**American Mutoscope and Biograph**, 1906), *The Hold-Up of the Rocky Mountain Express* (American Mutoscope and Biograph, 1906), *Trip Through Utah* (**Selig**, 1906), and *Trip Through the Black Hills* (Selig, 1906). While steam whistles tooted and wheels clattered, air was blown into the travelers' faces.

Imitators and variants capitalized on Hale's and Gifford's success: Palace Touring Cars, Hurst's Touring New York, Cessna's Sightseeing Auto Tours, Citron's Overland Flyer, Auto Tours of the World and Sightseeing in the Principal Cities, White & Langever's Steamboat Tours of the World, and Hruby & Plummer's Tours and Scenes of the World. Even Philadelphia film manufacturer Sigmund **Lubin** took out a patent in 1906 for an illusion ride that simulated hot air balloon travel.

Hale's Tours capitalized on and extended the popular **phantom train ride** films made from the late 1890s on (some films even were used in Hale's Tours installations). The films specially manufactured for Hale's Tours, however, did not always maintain a strict cowcatcher point of view: they employed various kinds of editing and **camera movement**, although usually only after an initial one- to two-minute travelling shot. Moreover, they often expanded the travel format with views of tourist attractions or with comic and dramatic scenes that typically featured mingling between men and women, one class and another, farmers and urbanites, train employees and civilians, ordinary citizens and outlaws, etc. Even an early film classic such as **Edison**'s *The Great Train Robbery* (1903) sometimes could be found in Hale's Tours cars.

See also: transportation; travelogues

Figure 50 Interior of Hale's Tours train car. (Courtesy of Charles Musser.)

Further reading

Rabinovitz, Lauren (2001) " 'Bells and Whistles': The Sound of Meaning in Train Travel Film Rides," in Richard Abel and Rick Altman (eds.) *The Sounds of Early Cinema*, 167–180, Bloomington: Indiana University Press.

LAUREN RABINOVITZ

Hamman, Joë (Jean)

b. 1885; d. 1974

actor, filmmaker, France

Inspired by a trip to the American Far West, Hamman changed his first name to Joë (pronounced Joey) and began acting in French **westerns** for **Lux**, beginning with *Le Desperado* [The Desperado] (1908). After working at **Gaumont** in such westerns as *Le Railway de la mort* [Their Lives for Gold] (1912) and *La Prairie en feu* [The Plains Afire] (1912), mostly filmed in the Carmague region near Marseille, Hamman directed and starred in **Eclipse**'s popular *Arizona Bill* series (1912–1913). Throughout the 1920s, he continued to act in films, especially historical dramas such as Jean Kemm's *L'Enfant Roi* [The Boy King] (1923) but also comedies such as Henri **Desfontaines**' *Le capitaine Rascasse* (1927). With the dawn of sound, Hamman directed more westerns as well as French versions of German films.

GLENN MYRENT

Hansen, Kai

b. ?; d. ?

director, Russia

Probably of Danish origin, Hansen joined the **Pathé-Frères** company in Moscow around 1910. Together with Maurice André **Maître**, he made *films d'art* such as *Princess Tarakanova* (1910), a Russian variation on the *Assassination of the Duke of Guise* (1908): a historical subject starring a known stage actor and using a strongly codified **acting style**. After Maître's departure in 1911, Hansen was put in charge of Pathé's Russian production. When the company curtailed its foreign production, Hansen launched his own (short-lived) filmmaking business in Moscow. In 1914, he left for Norway, planning to shoot an adaptation of an Ibsen play on location.

YURI TSIVIAN

Harrison, Louis Reeves

b. 1857; d. 1921

journalist, critic, scriptwriter, author, USA

From 1908 to 1920, Harrison was a prolific, influential staff writer for *Moving Picture World*. He wrote most of its film reviews as well as editorials that exhorted scriptwriters to be sensitive to the moods of the public, encouraged cooperation between producer and exhibitor, advised producers to draw on current events for screen material, urged honesty in film criticism, condemned salacious films as pernicious, and celebrated the merits of **color** photography and **sound effects**. Along with interviewing many contemporary directors and producers; he toured studios in New York and New Jersey, depicting them in his column, "Studio Saunterings." A scriptwriter of original material, he also wrote film adaptations and predicted that, with the lengthening of feature films, more literary works would be adapted for the screen. In 1916, he

published *Screencraft*, a notable volume of essays on film production and **screenwriting**.

MADELINE F. MATZ

Hart, William S.

b. 1865; d. 1946

actor, director, USA

A stage actor who had starred in the original production of *Ben-Hur* but then specialized in western plays such as *The Squaw Man* and *The Virginian*, Hart switched to moving pictures in 1914 through Thomas H. **Ince**. Playing exclusively in **westerns** such as Reginald Barker's *The Bargain* (1914) or his own *Hell's Hinges* (1916), Hart quickly became a movie **star**: tall, lean, and with a ruggedly beautiful face. Although often uncredited, Hart directed many of his own films, emphasizing authenticity based on his childhood experiences of the West. Typically he played the "Good-Badman," a frontier reprobate redeemed by the spread of civilization. By 1920, his popularity was waning, and he retired in 1925.

KRISTIN THOMPSON

Hartlooper, Louis

b. 1864; d. 1922

actor, lecturer, Netherlands

As a former **music hall** actor, Hartlooper worked as a **lecturer** with the **itinerant exhibitor** Alex Benner until 1905. After becoming a popular local star in several cinemas in Utrecht by the early 1910s, he was hired by the city's prestigious moving picture theater, Rembrandt Bioscoop, in 1913. There he performed with **Éclair**'s *Les enfants du capitaine Grant* [The Children of Captain Grant] (1914), which he once had directed on stage. His style was emotive and empathized the melodramatic, using elaborate gestures and many different voices. From 1913 on, Hartlooper also was active in the first Dutch union for film lecturers.

ANSJE VAN BEUSEKOM

Hatot, Georges

b. 1876; d. ?

filmmaker, France

Beginning in 1897–1898, Hatot directed historical reconstructions for **Lumière**, including a *Passion*. From 1905 to 1907, he worked for **Pathé-Frères**, essentially shooting scripts written by André **Heuzé** such as *Les Chiens contrebandiers* [Dog Smugglers] (1906). A conflict with Ferdinand **Zecca** hastened his departure from the company, after which he may have been employed briefly by **Éclair**. In 1907, he definitely became the administrator for a small production company, Le Lion. During this period, he shot films in the company's studio in Montreuil, and he also owned a theater in Paris, Cinéma de l'Univers (1909). In November 1912, when Le Lion was liquidated, Hatot still was one of its shareholders.

LAURENT LE FORESTIER

Heise, William

b. ?; d. 14 February, 1910

engineer, cameraman, USA

A veteran machinist at **Edison**'s laboratory, Heise was assigned to assist W. K. L. **Dickson** in the **Kinetoscope** experiment in October 1890. He learned **photography** and became the principal operator of the **Edison Kinetograph** camera which he ran during most of the tests. When production was moved to the **Edison Manufacturing Company** in 1894, he operated the camera and developed and printed the films. Dickson resigned in April 1895, leaving Heise as Edison's only experienced filmmaker. When James **White** took over production in October 1896, Heise stayed on as camera operator and technician but apparently left Edison in late 1898.

PAUL SPEHR

Hepworth

There were three main production companies that bore the Hepworth name. Hepworth & Co. was founded by Cecil **Hepworth** and his cousin Monty Wicks (hence their trademark name, "Hepwix") in 1899. The Hepworth Manufacturing Company was incoporated in 1903, and was responsible for most of the classic titles under the Hepworth banner. A further incorporation resulted in Hepworth Picture Plays, created in 1919, which were marketed in the USA by the non-producing Hepworth Animated Film Corporation.

Hepworth was from the outset based at Walton-on-Thames, outside London, and gradually built up a community of producers and performers who gave a unifying quality to the company's output. Initially producing **travelogues** and comic **trick films**, Hepworth came to prominence with the arrival of Lewin **Fitzhamon** as its chief film director in 1905. Creative **chase films** such as the enormously popular *Rescued by Rover* (1905) matched the best of the American and French producers, and the distinctive use of local scenery (including films shot in Dorset's Lulworth Cove) began to mark Hepworth's product as worthily British.

Hepworth's greatest strength was its company of actors, who were both genuinely popular and more astutely marketed than was the case for any other British film company of the period. Hepworth actors (who could be seen playing the lead in one production and then lurking in a crowd scene for the next) included Jack Hulcup, Gladys Sylvani, Hay Plumb, Harry Royston, Alec Worcester, May Clark, and especially Alma **Taylor** and Chrissie **White**, young stars of the *Tilly the Tomboy* series and loyal to Hepworth for many years.

Hepworth films were lauded as the best of British production, and the company made a successful transition to the production of **multiple-reel films**. Thomas Bentley directed the Charles Dickens adaptations, *Oliver Twist* (1912) and *David Copperfield* (1913), and much prestige was gained by the filming of Sir Johnston Forbes-Robertson in *Hamlet* (1913). The onset of **World War I** saw the loss of many key staff, with Cecil Hepworth himself taking over some of the directorial duties, but new stars were uncovered in Henry Edwards, Violet Hopson and Stewart Rome, and the company enjoyed a notable success with *Comin' Thro' the Rye* (1916).

The company expanded after the war and continued feature film production, with Taylor as the leading player, but the general slump in British production at this time, and an increasingly antiquated approach, led to its demise in 1924.

Throughout the twenty years or so that Hepworth concentrated on fiction film production, its output was notably consistent in theme and quality. Technical excellence, attention to detail and a modest but certain commitment to quality production combined with a sustained sentimental outlook and a scenic national identity. In the early cinema period, this craftsmanship was greatly prized.

See also: Shakespeare films

Further reading

Hepworth, Cecil (1951) *Came the Dawn: Memories of a Film Pioneer*, London: Phoenix House.

Low, Rachael (1949) *The History of the British Film: 1906–1914*, London: George Allen & Unwin.

LUKE McKERNAN

Hepworth, Cecil

b. 1874; d. 1953

filmmaker, Britain

The son of T. C. Hepworth, a leading **magic lantern** showman and lecturer, Cecil Hepworth from early on showed a considerable knowledge of the photographic business, combined with notable mechanical ability and an inquiring mind. He was closely involved with the arrival of moving pictures in Great Britain, first as a skeptical correspondent for *Photographic News*, but he changed his ideas quickly enough to produce the first British film book, *The ABC of the Cinematograph* (1898). He encountered motion pictures for the first time at Robert **Paul**'s Kinetoscope exhibit at Earl's Court in May 1895, and the following year worked as Birt **Acres**' assistant at the first royal command film performance, at Marlborough House, in July.

In 1898 he was hired by Charles **Urban** at **Maguire & Baucus** (shortly to become **Warwick Trading**) after Urban witnessed how Hepworth had made improvements to his **Warwick Bioscope projector**. Hepworth devised an automatic printing plant for Urban and took Warwick's first film (the 1898 university Boat Race); after being unceremoniously sacked, he went into business on his own in 1899. Situated at Walton-on-Thames, the various **Hepworth** companies progressed from *actualités* and **trick films**, which he directed

himself, to fiction films directed by Percy **Stow** and then Lewin **Fitzhamon**, whose **animal pictures** proved popular. A stock company of players, of whom the particular favorites were Alma **Taylor** and Chrissie **White**, coupled with a gentle outlook and a belief in quality of production, gave Hepworth films a distinctive style. From 1911, when the players began to be strongly marketed through posters, **postcards** and newspaper articles, Hepworth films were the leading force in British film production, characterized by sentimental sweetness, naturalistic performances and a particular "English" atmosphere that Hepworth consistently sought. Cecil Hepworth himself devised the Vivaphone system of **synchronized sound** films in 1910, leading to the production of a large number of sound shorts and even some "interviews" with politicians such as F. E. Smith and Bonar Law.

Hepworth and his company were guiding lights for the continually beleaguered British film industry, and he successfully pioneered the production of British **multiple-reel films** with *Oliver Twist* in 1912. With the onset of **World War I**, Hepworth increasingly took over the direction of films for himself, and despite several key members of the company being called up, Hepworth films prospered for the duration of the war. In 1919, however, he unwisely spent £100,000 on new plant and premises, just as the slump in British film production began. His films also were looking increasingly antiquated, an effect exacerbated by his belief in fades to black rather than cuts for changes of shot (which he believed were jarring on the eyes). His company ended up in receivership in 1924.

Hepworth's latter years were spent lecturing on film history and producing trailers and **advertising films**, including governmental "food flashes" during World War II (in some of which he appears as an elderly grocer). His autobiography, *Came the Dawn*, is an evocative and informative account of the early cinema period.

Further reading

Hepworth, Cecil (1951) *Came the Dawn: Memories of a Film Pioneer*, London: Phoenix House.

Low, Rachael (1949) *The History of the British Film: 1906–1914*, London: George Allen & Unwin.

LUKE McKERNAN

Heuzé, André

b. 1880; d. 1942

scriptwriter, filmmaker, France

From 1904 on, Heuzé was one of the main script-writers working for **Pathé-Frères**. He tackled all kinds of films, but had a partiality for comic **chase films** such as *La Course à la perruque* [The Wig Chase] (1906) or the *Boireau* **comic series**. In 1912, he became a director for Les Grands Films Populaires: his *Le Bossu* [The Hunchback], which featured Henry **Krauss** in its cast, was one of the most successful films of 1913. In 1914, Heuzé briefly served as editor-in-chief of a new trade journal, *Le Film*. During **World War I**, he worked in the Service Photographique et Cinémato-graphique des Armées.

LAURENT LE FORESTIER

Higgins, Ernest

b. 1871; d. 1945

cameraman, Australia

Higgins began his film career as a **projectionist** in 1903, then moved to Sydney in 1908 as a cam-eraman on *actualités*, **news event films**, and features for Cozens **Spencer**, working with direc-tors Alfred **Rolfe** and Raymond **Longford**. His film of the December 1908 Johnson-Burns boxing match was distributed world-wide. After shooting one film for **Australasian Films**, from 1914 on, he worked mainly on the nonfiction and compilation films of the company set up with his two brothers, though he sometimes photographed for other directors. In later years his career was over-shadowed by that of his brother Arthur.

INA BERTRAND

Hindustan Cinema Films Company

Established in Nasik by D. G. **Phalke** in 1918, Hindustan Cinema Films Company replaced **Phalke Films** company through which he had made his earliest films. The new company had shareholding partners, the first of its kind in India, which put its studio on sounder financial footing. Phalke himself resigned from the company's board in 1919, returning four years later to direct almost half of its 96 films made up to 1933. Most of these were mythological tales, including the famous *Kaliya Mardan* [The Conquest of Kaliya] (1919) and the first of his two sound films, *Setu Bandhan* [Bridging the Ocean] (1932).

SURESH CHABRIA

Hintner, Cornelius

b. 1875; d. 1922

filmmaker, art director, poster painter, Austria

Born in Bozen, Tyrol, to a family of painters and sculptors, Hintner studied art and later became an airplane pilot. In November 1912, he began wor-king as a cameraman for **Pathé-Frères'** branch office in Vienna, especially during the Balkan war. His own dramatic film, *Unter Palmen und ewigem eis* [Under the Palms and the Eternal Ice] (1914), produced by Hilda Film (Vienna) and set amid the mesmerizing Tyrolean glaciers, seems to anticipate the later genre of German *Bergfilm*. Between 1916 and 1919, Hintner worked as a filmmaker for the Hungarian companies, Star and Astra, directing among others, Bela Lugosi.

PAOLO CANEPPELE

Hirtz, Eduardo

b. 1878, Duisburg, Germany; d. 1951, Porto Alegre, Brazil

graphic designer, exhibitor, filmmaker, Brazil

A pioneer of *gaucho* (from the state of Rio Grande do Sul), Hirtz was in the graphic design business when, in 1905, he opened the Cinema Coliseu in Porto Alegre. He began making films in 1907, after purchasing two **cameras** and setting up a complete laboratory in the city. He traveled throughout the state, shooting many *actualités* as well as the first locally produced fiction film, *Ranchinho do sertão* [Small Country House] (1909).

ANA M. LÓPEZ

Hispano Films

Production company founded in Barcelona (Spain) in 1907, mainly under the management of Albert **Marro** and Ricardo de Baños. Between 1907 and 1909, they made more than thirty nonfiction films. In 1908, they filmed an adaptation of *Don Juan Tenorio*, and, in 1909, they began to specialize in romantic adventure films: *Don Juan de Serrallonga* (1910), *Carmen o la hija del bandido* [Carmen or the Bandit's Daughter] (1911). The outstanding work of the company's second period, up to 1918, was the seven-episode *Barcelona y sus misterios* [Barcelona and its Mysteries] (1916), co-directed by Marro and J. M. Codina.

JOAN M. MINGUET

historical films

A historical film can be defined several ways: (1) a film that chronicles an historical event and takes its primary characters from history, such as **Pathé-Frères**' *L'Epopée Napoléonienne* [Napoleon] (1903–1904) or **Selig**'s *Christopher Columbus* (1912); (2) a film that chronicles an historical event and features fictional characters, as in D. W. **Griffith**'s *The Birth of a Nation* (1915); (3) a film set in an historical period and featuring fictional characters, as in **Gaumont**'s *La Fille du Margrave* [The Margrave's Daughter] (1912); and (4) adaptations of literary works which conform to one of the above definitions, such as **Vitagraph**'s *A Tale of Two Cities* (1911) and Co-operative Films' *Richard III* (1911), adaptations of a Dickens novel and Shakespeare play, respectively. This entry will discuss the characteristics of historical films in early cinema's three most important film-producing countries (France, Italy, and the USA), their significance to the emergence of **multiple-reel/feature films**, and the ways in which historical films related to their intertextual and social context.

Italian producers had a distinct advantage over their French and American competitors when it came to screening their national history, for they could shoot in the oldest historical locations. They augmented this natural advantage with hundreds of extras and elaborate sets recreating classical architecture, all shot in depth, the combination giving Italian historical films a reputation for surpassing spectacle. The first version of *Gli Ultimi Giorni di Pompeii* [The Last Days of Pompei] (**Ambrosio**, 1908) inaugurated a cycle of spectacular history films set in antiquity. **Italia**'s *La Caduta di Troia* [The Fall of Troy] (1910) was a great success both in other European countries and in the USA. But **Cines**' *Quo Vadis?* (1913) and Italia's *Cabiria* (1914) were undoubtedly the most important of the spectacular histories in terms of the Italian industry's foreign reputation. Adapted from the best-seller by Polish novelist, Henryk Sienkiewicz, and set in the Rome of the mad Emperor Nero, *Quo Vadis?* boasted location exteriors along the Appian Way, five thousand extras, a chariot race and real lions, as well as detailed **set designs**, clever **lighting**, and **staging in depth**. The twelve-reel *Cabiria*, depicting the second Punic War between Rome and Carthage, brought the history cycle to a striking conclusion just before the onset of **World War I**. The film featured visually stunning scenes such as the burning of the Roman fleet and Hannibal's troops crossing the Alps; director Giovanni **Pastrone** then enhanced the spectacle through extended **camera movement** (unusually long, slow dollies) that created a sense of depth through movement rather than set design alone.

Like the Italians, French producers seemed generally to prefer filming their own history. *L'Epopée napoléonienne* was typical, relating as it did the life story of a French national icon, and the film's success inspired Pathé-Frères to produce several other history films in 1903–1904, including *Ghuillaume Tell*, *Marie Antoinette* and *Christophe Colomb*. Film d'Art's *L'Assassinat du Duc de Guise* [Assassination of the Duke de Guise] (1908)—in which the titular Duke, a leading Catholic in the religious disputes of the 16th century, was killed at the instigation of Henri III—is arguably the most important history film produced in France during the silent era.

Figure 51 Production photo for *Napoleon* (Pathé, 1903).

Figure 52 Production photo for *Notre Dame de Paris* (SCAGL, 1911).

The film's literate script, written by Henri Lavedan, a member of the Académie Française, together with its authentic décor and furnishings, staging in depth, **acting**, and editing that presage those of a later period, distinguished it from the French industry's ordinary output. *L'Assassinat du Duc de Guise* established the template for subsequent historical dramas filmed by Pathé, **Gaumont**, and particularly **SCAGL**. By 1911, the historical film was among the most prominent genres of the French film industry, and producers like SCAGL began turning out multiple-reel films such as *Le Courier de Lyon* [The Orleans Coach] (1911) and *Notre Dame de Paris* (1911). But it was the Franco/Anglo/American co-production of *Queen Elizabeth* (1912), starring Sarah **Bernhardt**, that rivalled *L'Assassinat du Duc de Guise* in terms of its impact upon subsequent production. Filmed in London and premiering in Chicago, it proved pivotal in the transition to the feature film.

While the Italians and the French on the whole preferred to record their own history, American producers, as befitted such a polyglot nation, indiscriminately filmed the full range of Western history: three 1895 **Edison Kinetescope** films, *The Execution of Mary Queen of Scots, Joan of Arc*, and *The Rescue of Capt. John Smith by Pocahontas*, well illustrate the American industry's early inclusiveness. Of course, American filmmakers, some as jingoistically patriotic then as they are now, also filmed American history, as in **Edison**'s Revolutionary War films that featured George Washington: *Battle of Bunker Hill* (1911), *The Death of*

Nathan Hale (1911), *How Washington Crossed the Delaware* (1911), and *Church and Country: An Episode of the Winter at Valley Forge* (1912). Since the transitional period of the early 1910s coincided with the Civil War's sesquicentennial, this conflict came to constitute an important subject of American historical films—and of the spectacular action scenes characteristic of sensational **melodrama**—with companies such as **Kalem**, Kay-Bee, Broncho, and 101-Bison turning out more than three hundred such films between 1908 and 1913. Among the most important of these was Thomas **Ince**'s five-reel *The Battle of Gettysburg* (1913), whose release coincided with a fiftieth-anniversary reunion celebration held on the actual battlefield, and, of course, Griffith's *The Birth of a Nation*.

History films, along with **biblical films**, played a major role in the American film industry's bid for respectability as it attempted to establish itself as a mainstream mass entertainment appealing to men, women, and children of all classes. That the *New York Daily Tribune* reviewed the Paris premiere of *L'Assassinat du Duc de Guise* at a time when US newspapers did not review films certainly boosted the industry's quest for respectability. The George **Kleine** papers at the Library of Congress contain voluminous files of endorsements from educators and other opinion leaders for *Quo Vadis?*. But it was home-grown product that would most effectively persuade social elites such as state officials and educators of the new medium's *bona fides*. In 1909, Vitagraph Company, one of the leading

American producers and a member of the **Motion Picture Patents Company**, released two separate reels titled *Washington Under the British Flag* and *Washington Under the American Flag*. The first reel depicts the young George Washington as a surveyor and an army officer, chronologically presenting a series of major battles and life events, then segues into his courtship of and marriage to Martha Curtis. The second deals with his career from the beginning of the revolution to his retirement from the Presidency.

With this as with its other history films, Vitagraph sought to make its representation of the central character and the historical era conform to widely circulating texts that would be familiar to both social elites and a significant percentage of nickelodeon audiences. The company's **publicity** stressed its commitment to an historical authenticity that consisted of (1) correct period detail, (2) key events, (3) key images, and (4) iconographic consistency. In the case of the *Washington* films, correct period detail meant the proper colonial mansions and Revolutionary War uniforms well-known to audiences from **illustrated magazines** and/or school textbooks. The film's narrative was structured around the key events—important battles, political incidents, and personal milestones—central to popular recountings of Washington's life and the Revolutionary War. The second reel, for instance, shows Patrick Henry delivering his "liberty or death" speech, the Battle of Bunker Hill, Washington crossing the Delaware, the winter in Valley Forge, the surrender at Yorktown, and Washington's inauguration as the first President. Its key images include "realizations" of two famous **paintings** that hung in classrooms around the country: Emmanuel Leutze's *Washington Crossing the Delaware* and the *Spirit of '76*, depicting a man bearing the Star and Stripes, flanked by a fife player and a drummer. The film's iconographic consistency derived from its actor's resemblance to the bewigged character of countless paintings, statues, and commercial ephemera (such as cigar **advertisements** and stationery) that were part of spectators' everyday lives. These four guarantors of historical authenticity set the template for historical films ever after.

In dealing with the Civil War and Reconstruction, *The Birth of a Nation* may have deviated from historical accuracy, but it certainly helped to establish the feature film as the norm rather than the exception in the USA. Prior to the film's January 1915 release, Griffith's publicity department had hyped its expense, huge cast, and historical accuracy, creating great public anticipation for the famous director's most ambitious project. When it premiered at the largest **palace cinemas** in Los Angeles and New York, the admission price was $2, the same as that charged for Broadway plays, which ensured that the film would be taken seriously—as indeed it was, widely advertised and reviewed in the general press rather than the **trade press**. All these factors demonstrated that the cinema had come of age as a legitimate mass medium. Of course, the film attracted attention for other reasons as well, its reprehensible racism eliciting outrage from the African-American community and their supporters and revealing the detrimental social impact that the new mass medium could have.

By contrast to *The Birth of a Nation*, which proved controversial despite deriving authority from no less a person than President Woodrow Wilson, who had penned one of the histories from which Griffith claimed to have drawn the script, the majority of American historical films produced during this period were designed to offend as few people as possible, neutral enough for screening in all sections of the vast country. The hundreds of Civil War films preceding Griffith's epic, for instance, tended to stress the heroism and self-sacrifice of both North and South rather than espouse the justice of one side's cause over the other's. Overall, the companies producing historical films sought legitimacy and respectability, not controversy.

Further reading

Abel, Richard (1994) *The Ciné Goes to Town: French Cinema, 1896–1914*, Berkeley: University of California Press.

Bertellini, Giorgio (ed.) (2000) Special issue on early Italian cinema, *Film History*, 12.3.

Uricchio, William and Pearson, Roberta E. (1993) *Reframing Culture: The Case of the Vitagraph Quality Films*, Princeton: Princeton University Press.

ROBERTA E. PEARSON

Hodkinson, W. W.

b. 1881; d. 1971

exhibitor, distributor, USA

Born in Colorado, Hodkinson entered the moving picture industry in 1907, opening a theater in Ogden, Utah. In 1910, he moved into distribution by forming the Progressive Motion Picture Company in California. After selling Progressive to the **General Film Company** in 1911, he bought it back when General Film refused to allow his demands that his theaters charge higher-than-average admission prices. Hodkinson became the first president of Paramount Pictures Corporation in 1914, implementing many of its early feature film distribution strategies. He was deposed by Adolph **Zukor** in 1916.

MICHAEL QUINN

Hofer, Franz

b. 1882; d. 1945

actor, scriptwriter, director, Germany

Born Franz Wygand Wüstenhöfer in Malstatt (Saarland), Hofer began his career as a stage actor and playwright in 1909. A year later he began working as a **screenwriter** for **Messter**'s Henny **Porten** series and for directors such as Viggo **Larsen**—*Die schwarze Katze* [The Black Cat] (1910)—and Walter Schmidthässler—*Das Weib ohne Herz* [The Woman Without a Heart] and *Der Zug des Herzens* [The Pull of the Heart] (both 1912).

After directing his first film, *Des Alters erste Spuren* [First Traces of Age] (1912–13), for the newly founded Luna-Film, Hofer directed a total of 25 films for the company during a three-year period, the most productive and commercially successful phase of his career. Combining the roles of scriptwriter and director, Hofer exercised complete control over the style and content of his films, whose generic provenance ranged from early sophisticated **comedies**—e.g., *Hurra! Einquartierung* [Hurrah! Quartering!] (1913) and *Das rosa Pantöffelchen* [The Pink Slipper] (1913)—and **detective films**—e.g., *Der Steckbrief* [The "Wanted" Poster] (1913) and

Vampyre der Großstadt [Vampires of the City] (1914)—to melodramas—e.g., *Kammermusik* [Chamber Music] (1915))—often set against the background of **World War I**, as in *Weihnachtsglocken 1914* [Christmas Bells 1914] (1914). Although his films repeatedly had been exposed to radical censorship measures from early on, *Die schwarze Natter* [The Black Viper] and *Die schwarze Kugel oder Die geheimnisvollen Schwestern* [The Black Bowl, or, The Mysterious Sisters] (both 1913) greatly contributed to the *Sensationsfilm*, a genre based on fast-paced physical action, heavy eroticism, and explicit violence, which became the primary target of the conservative cinema reform movement.

Because Hofer wrote his own scripts, the **trade press**, however, honored his films as *Autorenfilme* and thereby acknowledged an unmistakable stylistic signature marking his work at least from 1913 on. Judging from eleven surviving films (1912–1916), Hofer's main formal qualities consisted of unforeseeable, bizarre twists of plot; extravagant decors and **lighting** patterns, often emphasizing ornamental shadows and picturesque silhouettes; a complex use of symmetrical compositions, masked shots, and internal montage through superimposed views; and, finally, a strong emotional charge produced by keyhole shots and point-of-view editing, frontal staging, and direct address. Navigating his protagonists through such intricate cinematic terrain, Hofer also drew memorable performances from (predominantly female) actors whose names are long forgotten. The most notable was the young Dorrit Weixler, who became a star with *Das rosa Pantöffelchen*. She appeared in ten more of his films before she split from Hofer and committed suicide in December 1916 at the age of 24.

Only recently rediscovered, Hofer now is regarded as one of the most fascinating German directors of the transitional period. His unique construction of narrative reveals a dynamic stylistic paradigm radically different from either the **classical Hollywood cinema** or the often static theatricality of European "quality" productions. But the elegance and originality with which Hofer integrated into the narrative process devices linked to a **cinema of attractions** also points to the intertextual pertinence of several 19th-century forms of popular culture such as the variety theater, **shadow** plays, **stereoscopy**, and **magic lantern shows**.

See also: melodrama, sensational; staging in depth.

McHAEL WDEL

Holger-Madsen

b. 1878; d. 1943

actor, filmmaker, Denmark

A stage actor known for his mastery of the art of make-up, Holger-Madsen was first hired by **Nordisk** in 1907 and assigned to direct films in 1912. One of the company's most respected film-makers, he was put in charge of several large-scale projects, including the anti-war epic, *Ned med Vaabnene* [Lay Down Your Arms!] (1915), adapted by Carl Dreyer from a novel by the pacifist writer Bertha von Suttner. A gifted stylist, Hoger-Madsen embellished his sometimes stiffly moving films with striking **lighting** effects, using shadows and **staging in depth**, notably in *Evangeliemandens Liv* [Life of the Evangelist] (1914).

CASPER TYBJERG

Holland, Annie (née Payne)

b. 1844; d. ?

exhibitor, Great Britain

Annie Holland toured the British **fairs/fair-grounds** with her six sons (after her husband died in 1893), operating a small sideshow and set of swingboats. Her brothers included the Fat Boy of Peckham and Captain Thomas Payne, one of the most influential showmen in the United Kingdom. From 1901 to 1914, she turned to exhibiting moving pictures on the same fairgrounds. Holland's "Palace of Light" was one of the largest and most extravagant of fairground shows and reputedly held up to 1000 people. In 1915, the show was converted for use as a shanty cinema in Measham, until a permanent building was erected in the 1920s.

VANESSA TOULMIN

Hollandia

The production company, Hollandia, resulted from a merger in 1913 between the N.V. Maatschappij voor Wetenschappelijke Cinematografie and the N.V. Maatschappij voor Artistieke Cinematografie, both founded by Maurits H. **Binger** in 1912. He engaged former stage director Louis Crispijn Sr. to direct films starring Annie **Bos.** Typical Dutch settings were filmed on location: long stretches of beach, countryside windmills, and the Volendam or Amsterdam canals became Crispijns' trademarks. In 1915, Binger himself began directing, with Jan van Dommelen replacing him on weekends. Hollandia's financial situation deteriorated in 1919. The nonfiction branch reorganized as Polygoon, and the hybrid "boring British" fiction films, produced by Anglo-Hollandia, lost their appeal. When Binger died in 1923, Hollandia ceased to exist.

ANSJE VAN BEUSEKOM

Hollandsche Film

After making a series of nonfiction films in the Netherlands in 1909 for **Pathé-Frères**, Alfred **Machin** returned in 1911 to found Hollandsche Film, Pathé's Dutch production company. In the early 1910s, it co-produced more than a dozen Dutch films, half of which were directed by Machin himself in and around the picturesque village of Volendam. Although *Het vervloekte geld/L'or qui brûle* [Cursed Money] (1912), the first released Hollandsche Film, starred Dutch actor Louis Bouwmeester, all other films had Franco-Belgian casts and crews. Paradoxically, this foreign production company was the first in making uniquely Dutch films, exploiting a folkloristic representation of the Netherlands as a country of fishermen, windmills, tulips, and clogs.

IVO BLOM

Holmes, Elias Burton

b. 8 January 1870; d. 22 July 1958

lecturer, USA

The son of a Chicago banker, who traveled with his family while in his teens, Holmes gave his first travel lecture at the Chicago Camera Club in 1891. Two years later he turned professional. In 1897, John Stoddard designated him as his successor, and that fall Holmes added moving pictures at the end of his **illustrated lecture**. For the 1899–1900 season, he integrated films into his programs, alternating them with slides—a practice that he continued for many years. He lectured over the slides, often hand-colored, but would generally let the films "speak for themselves." Catering to societal elites, Holmes gave an annual series of five lectures at Carnegie Hall, the Brooklyn Institute of Arts and Sciences, and other prestigious venues across the country. In the 1910s, he provided Paramount with **travelogues** for distribution to regular moving picture theaters. Holmes continued to give lectures until retiring in 1950, although his organization remained active even after his death.

CHARLES MUSSER

Holmes, Helen

b. 1892; d. 1950

actor, USA

Helen Holmes was the most celebrated of early railway-action stunt stars, vying at times with Pearl **White** for the title of American cinema's most daring female player. Beginning at **Keystone** in 1912, Holmes soon relocated to **Kalem** where she appeared in numerous short railway and **western** subjects, ultimately starring as the gutsy girl telegrapher in the initial 48 episodes of *The Hazards of Helen* (1914–1917) series. Along with J. P. McGowan, her husband/director, Holmes left Kalem for a brief stint at **Universal** before signing with McGowan's independently formed Signal Corporation to star in a string of railway-oriented **serials** popular throughout the late 1910s.

JENNIFER M. BEAN

Hopwood, Henry Vaux

b. 1866; d. 1919

technical writer, England

An employee of the Patent Office library in London, Hopwood was the author of *Living Pictures*, the first comprehensive technical review of cinematography; a thoroughly researched and careful account. In September 1899, *The Optician* published an article by Hopwood concerning **trick films**, and a supplement updating his book. A revised edition was entrusted to a colleague, R. B. Foster, and eventually published in 1915.

Further reading

Hopwood, Henry V. (1899) *Living Pictures, Their History, Photo-Production and Practical Working*, London: Optician and Photographic Trades Review.

STEPHEN HERBERT

Horsley, David

b. 1873, West Stanley, England; d. 1933, Los Angeles, California.

producer, executive, USA

In 1907, Horsley first began producing films in the backyard of his Ideal Billiard Parlor in Bayonne, New Jersey. In 1908, when his brother William joined the business, Horsley Manufacturing became **Centaur** Film. Denied membership in the **Motion Picture Patents Company**, Centaur became the first independent manufacturer, with Al Christie as chief filmmaker. Relocating their company west in 1911, the Horsleys set up Nestor Film, the first Hollywood studio, where cameraman Charles Rosher got his start. Active in the formation of **Universal**, David withdrew to produce pictures for release through **Mutual** and William became involved in constructing Universal City. In the 1920s, the brothers were partners in the William Horsley Laboratory, later called Hollywood Film Enterprises, which is still in business today as Hollywood Film and Video.

ROBERT S. BIRCHARD

Howe, Lyman H.

b. 1856; d. 1922

lecturer, exhibitor, USA

As a phonograph exhibitor, Howe began touring northeastern states in 1890. Unable to acquire territorial rights for **Edison**'s Vitascope, he had his own animatoscope **projector** built and began showing films in conjunction with **phonographs** on 8 December 1896. Early in his career, Howe often showed films in **churches** and/or for local civic organizations—for people opposed to mainstream commercial entertainment. His evening-length programs grew in popularity as he developed an array of audio accompaniments—including elaborate **sound effects** and actors speaking behind the screen (endowing characters with dialogue). Although he himself stopped traveling in 1901, by 1907 he had four or five companies constantly on the road, often playing prominent legitimate **theaters**. His circuit reached a high-point in the 1909–1911 period, then gradually contracted. In the end, he was a casualty of Hollywood, the influenza epidemic of 1919, and an outmoded cultural sensibility.

See also: dialogue accompaniment

CHARLES MUSSER

Hulfish, David S. (Sherrill)

b. 1873; d. ?

journalist, writer, USA

A versatile Chicago journalist, primarily focusing on technical matters, Hulfish was a recurrent contributor to *Nickelodeon/Motography* (beginning in 1909), mainly as editor of a column for exhibitors and others, "Some Questions Answered." In 1910, he became the magazine's patent expert, outlining the more important US motion picture patents. He also advertised as a solicitor of patents specializing in motion pictures.

Hulfish published a number of influential works of reference and instruction, among them: *The Motion Picture, Its Making and Its Theater* (1909), *Cyclopedia of Motion-Picture Work* (1911), *Motion-Picture Work* (1913, reprinted in 1970). Along with in-depth technical descriptions, Hulfish thoroughly discussed all aspects of the new industry.

MARINA DAHLQUIST

Hutchinson, Samuel S.

b. 1869, Wyoming; d. ?

distributor, executive, USA

After a career as a pharmacist or banker (sources differ), Hutchinson established Theatre Film Service in 1905, an early film exchange with offices in Chicago and San Francisco. In 1906 he joined Charles J. Hite in H & H Film Service; in 1910 he helped establish the **American Film Manufacturing Company** with John R. **Freuler**; in 1912, all three became associated with Harry **Aitken** in founding **Mutual**. Later Hutchinson also headed the affiliated Signal Film Company and Vogue Comedy Company. Although production ended at American in 1921, Hutchinson continued to operate its Chicago film laboratory for several years thereafter.

ROBERT S. BIRCHARD

illustrated lectures

Illustrated lecture was the popular term for the numerous documentary-like, audio-visual programs that flourished before 1920. Indeed, they were perhaps the dominant form of screen practice before moving pictures. Travel lectures were particularly popular, but the range of topics was extremely broad, from scientific subjects, exemplified by Abbé François Moigno's influential work in France, to social-issue programs such as Jacob Riis's "How the Other Half Lives and Dies" (1888) in the USA.

Soon after the emergence of moving pictures, **magic lantern** showmen began to intergrate them into their lectures. In late 1896, at the Brooklyn Institute of Arts and Science, Alexander Black organized a program that included films and a lecture on glaciers using colored photographic slides. In March 1897, Henry Evans Northrop delivered a full-length illustrated lecture, "A Bicycle Tour Through Europe," that integrated slides and films, using four or five hand-tinted photographic slides for each **Lumière** film that was shown. Slides were cheaper, more plentiful, and avoided the flicker effect that was hard on spectators' eyes. This method of alternating slides and film became popular with such titles as "The Horitz Passion Play" (1897) and "The Passion Play of Oberammergau" (1898). It was common in England as well, where Robert W. **Paul** presented the two-hour illustrated lecture "Army Life, or How Soldiers Are Made" (1900) and G. West & Sons had several touring companies showing "Our Navy," a highly popular illustrated lecture that began in the 1890s and ran for many years.

Prominent lecturers such as E. Burton **Holmes** and Dwight Elmendorf integrated slides and films for their 1898–99 season; and this approach was adopted by others such as Edward Curtis, Frederick Monsen, and Garret P. Serviss by the 1906–07 season. About the same time, similar forms of integration were developed by "educational" groups such as the **Maison de la Bonne Presse** and Société populaire des beaux-arts in France.

Many of the early **multiple-reel/feature films** appearing after 1912 were documentary-like versions of illustrated lectures. These represented an important shift for two reasons. First, they consisted entirely of moving pictures. Second, they were also multi-unit enterprises, in some cases with an international reach. Popular subjects such as *Rainy's African Hunt* (1912), *The Durbar in Kinemacolor* (1912) and *Sir Douglas Mawson's Marvelous Views of the Frozen North* (1915) were shown in different countries with locally selected narrators who, although of varied ability, tended to write their own scripts and so humanize and personalize their subjects.

After 1915–16, documentary-like programming moved increasingly in two different directions. One was the illustrated lecture using films (or slides and films); the other was the multi-unit program of the same subject that came increasingly to rely on intertitles rather than a lecture. The latter was often the version designed for broad release. Thus, former President Theodore Roosevelt's 1914 illustrated lecture, "The Exploration of a Great River," was reworked with **intertitles** and released as *Colonel Theodore Roosevelt's Expedition into the Wilds* (1916). The need for a reliable and

Figure 53 Lyman Howe program, 1906. (Courtesy of Charles Musser.)

consistent message with broad distribution at low cost was undoubtedly one reason why, during **World War I**, the US government used intertitles rather than lectures for such films as *Pershing's Crusaders* (1918) and *America's Answer* (1918). These films were what became known as the *documentary*.

The documentary program (with intertitles) emerged as the dominant form after World War I, but the illustrated lecture still remained popular, at least in selected circles, throughout the silent period and beyond.

See also: biblical films; color; education; religious filmmaking; travalogues

Further reading

Musser, Charles and Carol Nelson (1990) *High-Class Moving Pictures: Lyman H. Howe and the Forgotten Era of Traveling Exhibition, 1880–1920*, Princeton: Princeton University Press.

CHARLES MUSSER

illustrated magazines

The illustrated magazine was one of many cultural contexts within which moving pictures emerged, and some parallels can be drawn between the content of the magazine medium and moving picture production and exhibition. In particular the proportions of different subject matter categories in both suggest related concerns with representing aspects of everyday life recognizable to consumers as well as extraordinary events or foreign cultures presented as exotic aspects of a wider world.

From the early days of commercial printing, periodical publications often included some kind of illustration, although this mainly consisted of generic decorative motifs rather than realistic representations tied to written texts. In the 18th century, in parallel with the beginnings of **newspaper** publication, magazines discussing political and general issues began to appear, and this trend continued into the early 19th century, particularly through general-interest titles with a broadly educational mission. Illustrated magazines of all types became widespread in Europe and the USA from the middle decades of the 19th century onwards. Three main genres can be distinguished: (1) weekly news magazines such as *Illustrated London News* (London, 1842), or *L'Illustration* (Paris, 1843) and their satirical counterparts such as *Charivari* (Paris, 1832) and *Punch* (London, 1841); (2) ever-increasing numbers of special interest monthlies such as trade papers, hobby magazines, and the publications of political or religious pressure groups; and (3) monthly miscellanies such as *Harper's Magazine* (New York, 1847), *Cornhill Magazine* and *Temple Bar* (both London, 1860).

The monthly miscellany offers perhaps the closest comparison to early moving pictures. Initially its content was a mixture of serialized fiction and general-interest articles, including some social commentary, with a relatively low proportion of illustration dictated by the cost of wood engraving. However, changes in printing technology, and other economic factors such as increasing **leisure time** and disposable income among a middle-class readership, gradually made mass circulation possible and allowed cheaper, easier, and more prolific illustration. A new generation of illustrated monthly general-interest magazines appeared in most markets from the late 1880s, in which the amount of illustration increased and the contents became more "popular" through inclusion of elements such as celebrity profiles, stories for children, and "curiosity" pictures and puzzles. The first such titles included *Scribner's Magazine* (New York,

1887) and *Strand Magazine* (London, 1891), and numerous other titles followed the same format in the 1890s, especially mass magazines in the USA, from *Munsey's* and *McClure's* to *Ladies' Home Journal* and *Saturday Evening Post*.

The staple of these magazines continued to be fictional stories (self-contained short stories, series of unconnected stories involving the same characters, or serialized novels), and factual articles on contemporary life, in almost equal proportions. All sections of the magazines exhibited a large number of illustrations: *Strand* claimed to include at least one picture at every double-page opening, and rarely if ever failed in this ambition. One important feature was the adoption of **photography** for illustration: previously photographs had been reproduced by means of woodcut engravings, but the development of the halftone process in the 1880s allowed magazines to carry an increasing number of direct photographic reproductions. With very few exceptions, photographic illustrations were used only in factual articles, with the fictional items using line drawings or watercolor paintings; but in most other respects factual and fictional content were indistinguishable in presentation.

The mixture of different types of text in a general-interest magazine like *Strand* offers a parallel to the mixed content of a typical early moving picture show, with factual, comic, and fictional views assembled into a hybrid format of short elements which were more or less interchangeable. The similar presentation styles of factual and fictional items in the magazines also were echoed in the presentation of many early fictional films, which depended for some of their effect on a willingness to believe that the events portrayed "really happened" in the same way as the street scenes or other *actualités* which usually accompanied them. The magazines' high proportion of illustration, particularly the use of photography or pseudo-photographic detail in drawings, made a further bid towards visual representation of the "real" world, an aspiration that the magazines then tended to see as finally achieved by the moving picture.

Most of the illustrated monthlies included coverage of moving pictures. The earliest accounts, from the mid-1890s onwards, were factual, giving more or less accurate descriptions of the effects of the new technology. Discussion of the moving picture in this context tended to align it with other technological "marvels of the age" such as the X-Ray photograph, the automobile, and the flying machine, all of which were celebrated by magazine articles at one time or another in the 1890s and 1900s. From as early as 1896, until well into the 20th century, another feature of the magazines' treatment of the cinema was the inclusion of fictional stories which often served a plot function, revealing information which led to the denouement of the story. At a later stage, in the 1910s, the magazines began to feature moving picture personalities among the celebrities they covered, although at this time specialist magazines aimed at movie-goers were also beginning to appear, such as *The Pictures* (London, 1911) and *Motion Picture Story Magazine* (New York, 1912).

See also: department stores; magic lantern shows; moving picture fiction; music halls; program formats; serials; trade press; vaudeville.

Further reading

Crangle, Richard (1999) "Astounding Actuality and Life: Early Film and the Illustrated Magazine in Britain," in Claire Dupré la Tour, André Gaudreault, and Roberta Pearson (eds.) *Le Cinéma au tournant du siècle/Cinema at the Turn of the Century*, 93–102, Québec/Lausanne: Éditions Nota Bene/Payot.

Ohmann, Richard (1996) *Selling Culture: Magazines, Markets, and Class at the Turn of the Century*, London: Verso.

Vann, J. Don, and VanArsdel, Rosemary T. (eds.) (1994) *Victorian Periodicals and Victorian Society*, Toronto: University of Toronto Press.

RICHARD CRANGLE

Figure 54 Cover of *Le Petit Journal*, illustrated supplement, 16 May 1897.

illustrated songs

At least in the USA, the illustrated song was a live act closely linked with moving pictures in many exhibition formats during the cinema's first two decades. Attempts to export illustrated songs to countries such as Great Britain and Sweden, around 1909–1910, proved unsuccessful. Indeed, some picture theaters in the USA—not only small neighborhood houses, but even the best and largest ones located downtown—promoted singers and songs as much as films, and as late as 1913.

Originating in the mid-1890s, most likely as a means of publicizing the latest popular songs from Tin Pan Alley publishers in New York City (and generating more sales of sheet music), the "song illustrator" (a vocalist, accompanied by a pianist and projected colored glass slides) became a common **vaudeville** act during the decade prior to the first **nickelodeons**. This was especially true of family vaudeville, characterized by smaller houses and fewer acts (from five to eight) than high-class vaudeville, where illustrated songs and moving pictures usually came in tandem at the end of the program, probably because they initially used the same projecting apparatus.

The nickelodeons that emerged in 1905–1906 built their short programs around these popular tandem acts, alternating a reel of film with a single song. The illustrated song typically involved a vocalist and pianist performing a popular song, backed by a projected set of twelve to sixteen colored glass slides that, in sequence, "illustrated" the lyrics. "Behind the scenes," the act had to have a stereoptican mounted alongside one or more projecting machines (and the requisite number of **projectionists**) in the projection booth. Since many picture theaters already had a stereoptican for making announcements, promoting upcoming films, and advertising local businesses, and since their payrolls already included a pianist and stereoptican operator, the theater owner's only added expense came from hiring one or more local singers (or using a song publisher's "plugger") and renting the slide sets (which cost far less than the films).

To meet the escalating demand for song slides, major manufacturers emerged by 1910, primarily in New York: Scott & Van Altena, praised for the quality of its slides; DeWitt C. Wheeler, known for the quantity of its offerings; and Henry B. Ingram, a company that specialized in older ballads. Surviving song slide sets reveal not only vivid displays of **color** but also surprising effects: in Scott & Van Altena's "Just to Live the Old Days Over" (1909), a memory image of a young woman appears in a close up of a hand-held mirror; in Wheeler's "What a Funny Little World This Is" (1911), a man perches on the crescent moon and croons to a smiling globe, surrounded by clouds and stars.

A program of illustrated songs and moving pictures created a unique mix of national mass culture and local popular culture. Both were cultural commodities that could circulate throughout the country, almost simultaneously; yet both became "finished products" only in performance. Unlike the films, whose distribution grew increasingly centralized and regularized, the songs depended more and more on a decentralized pool of local performers: vocalists, pianists, or even small orchestras, and audiences willing to engage in sing-alongs (the chorus of a song usually was printed on the last slide of a set). In short, they sustained the notion, first established in nickelodeons, that picture theaters could serve as "social centers" in many communities. At the same time, however, the songs

still could function differently in different regions, cities, and even neighborhoods. In metropolitan areas, they may have helped the masses of new immigrants from eastern and southern Europe to learn English. In other cities from St. Louis to Des Moines, where earlier German immigrants had developed a strong musical tradition, they could be exploited as a form of cultural capital that served to uplift and legitimate the new "cheap amusement."

Yet, overall, both the songs and slides evoked a kind of "innovative nostalgia" that could appeal to a wide variety of audiences. Whereas the sentimental or patriotic lyrics often were set to the new rhythm of ragtime, the figures in the slides—mostly "lower middle class whites"—seemed to exist in a "world in between," particularly marked by their tendency not to sport the current fashions advertised in the mass magazines but to dress slightly behind the times. Not yet successful or comfortably well off, they seemed less drawn to the future than to a past simpler life, whether that of

Figure 55 Sheet music cover for "Beautiful Eyes," 1909. (Courtesy of the Marnan Collection.)

the "old country" (Ireland was a particular favorite) or that of a rural area or small town.

Illustrated songs began to lose their allure by 1913–1914, for several reasons. Song slide manufacturers never reached a level of industrialization and economic clout anywhere near that of the film industry by the early 1910s. Feature films also had an impact, transforming the **program format** of many picture theaters and changing them from places where people could learn the latest songs to "refined" spaces where they could hear orchestras "toning the picture" with special **musical scores**. Finally, as a form of popular culture dependent on local musical talent, illustrated songs were a casualty of theater managers' growing loss of control over exhibition. Still, the business provided work for a good number of people who would later become well known in the film industry, from Roscoe "Fatty" **Arbuckle** and Abe **Balaban** (singers) and Sam **Katz** (pianist) to Alice **Joyce**, Anita Stewart, Norma **Talmadge**, and Florence **Lawrence** (models for song slides).

See also: fashion; illustrated magazines; magic lantern shows; migration/immigration; projectors; star system

Further reading

Abel, Richard (2001) "That Most American of Attractions, the Illustrated Song," in Richard Abel and Rick Altman (eds.) *The Sounds of Early Cinema*, 143–155, Bloomington: Indiana University Press.

Abel, Richard (2001) "Reframing the Vaudeville/ Moving Picture Debate with Illustrated Songs," in Leonardo Quaresima and Laura Vichi (eds.) *The Tenth Muse: Cinema and Other Arts*, 473–484, Udine: Forum.

RICHARD ABEL

IMP

One of the more enterprising of exchange operators to emerge in the **nickelodeon** era, Carl **Laemmle** entered into production after falling out with the **Motion Picture Patents Company** in 1909. The company he created, the Independent Motion Picture Company, was better known by its acronym IMP. Employing the **advertising** acumen of his chief associate, Robert Cochrane, Laemmle created strong brand-name recognition for his company in a series of ads featuring a devilish character who promised "IMPish fun" and "pictures of IMPortance" as an alternative to less compelling MPPC fare. In truth, most IMP films initially were markedly inferior to the bulk of MPPC productions, but this did not deter Laemmle from engaging in numerous promotional stunts to keep his company's name at the forefront of the industry.

While Laemmle launched IMP with a high-profile adaptation of Longfellow's poem, *Hiawatha*, the company's typical productions tended toward low-brow **comedy** and action-filled drama. Laemmle's strongly populist bent helped keep IMP films popular, though few of the surviving titles compare with the best offerings from company leaders of the day, such as **Biograph** and **Vitagraph**. Despite this relative lack of quality, IMP proved an industry innovator in its business practices. The company's growth led to the leasing of a 15,000 square foot lot in New York City in mid-1910, reportedly the largest piece of land in Manhattan acquired by a motion picture company up to that time; construction of a Hollywood studio followed a year later. In 1911, led by produc- tion head C. A. Willett, the IMP stock company (which then included Mary **Pickford**, Owen **Moore**, and King **Baggot**, director Thomas **Ince**, and cameraman Tony Gaudio) travelled to Cuba. Although presumably a means of circumventing MPPC prohibitions against the Independent company filming in the USA, the trip also represents an early example of American motion picture producers exploiting other countries' locales for scenic interest, resulting in numerous "Spanish-flavored" Pickford vehicles.

Perhaps most famously, Laemmle perfected the strategy of stealing high-profile talent from established companies. One of Laemmle's major coups involved luring Florence **Lawrence** from Biograph in late 1909 and publicizing her debut at IMP by generating falsified news stories about her death. Some credit this stunt, which culminated in a celebrated appearance by Lawrence in St. Louis to verify that she was alive, with creating the first bona fide movie **star**. While this is debatable, Laemmle's efforts placed actors at the center of marketing strategies in the years following. In 1910, IMP successfully enticed Pickford from

Biograph as well, promoting her subsequent films as "the Little Mary Imps." Although neither of these casting coups resulted in memorable films, they proved Laemmle's talent in keeping his company's name in the spotlight.

By 1912, IMP had become a pre-eminent Independent producing concern, and convincingly challenged the MPPC's attempted control of the industry by consolidating a number of companies under the umbrella distribution label **Universal**. Laemmle's influence only grew as Universal became a major force in the feature-era, post-MPPC American film industry.

See also: publicity: issues and debates

Further reading

deCordova, Richard (1990) *Picture Personalities: The Emergence of the Star System in America*, Urbana: University of Illinois Press.
Drinkwater, John (1931) *The Life and Adventures of Carl Laemmle*, New York: G. P. Putnam's Sons.

CHARLIE KEIL

imperialism: USA

The United States' search for and acquisition of a new overseas empire in the late 1890s provided a crucial context for the emergence of early cinema during the same decade. Both moving pictures and the "new" extra-continental imperialism were culturally, socially, and economically significant by-products of rapid, wide-scale industrialization and **urbanization** following the Civil War.

Between 1870 and 1900, the USA experienced a 97% increase in its population. This was coupled with a rapid industrial expansion that transformed a country of self-sufficient farmers into a nation of industrial wage laborers and middle-class managers increasingly dependent upon industry. The intensification of industrialization and urbanization led to an increase in production output with which domestic consumption could not keep pace. Hence, the USA was rocked by a series of devastating depressions, the worst of which took place in the years 1873–1878, 1882–1885, and 1893–1897.

During these boom-and-bust cycles, droughts, bad winters, and a resurgence in the strength of the European wheat markets also placed a great deal of pressure on agriculture, forcing farmers to sell crops at steadily decreasing prices. The last of the depressions coincided with what was regarded by some alarmists as another worrying watershed: as Frederick Jackson Turner announced at the 1893 World's Columbian Exposition in Chicago, the vast American frontier had officially closed, thereby shutting off a "safety valve" that had helped the nation deal with social problems such as the settlement and self-sufficiency of new immigrants, the "overpopulation" of urban centers, as well as the cultivation of new natural resources and new markets. A series of violent labor strikes seemed to confirm suspicions that only a radical solution could solve the nation's manifold economic and social problems.

By the 1890s, numerous politicians, intellectuals, industrialists, and military officials agreed that an overseas commercial empire that linked US production to Asia (especially China) would provide a cure for the nation's ills by providing new markets for surplus production. The influential naval theorist, Alfred Thayer Mahan, urged that this empire be built through the establishment of a web-like network of naval bases in the Pacific and the Caribbean, joined together by new **communication** and **transportation** technologies and an isthmian canal. With the establishment of this empire, he promised, would come strengthened commercial and political power in the international arena. To this end, the US government built a new fleet of modern armored battleships in the early 1890s and stepped up enforcement of the Monroe Doctrine. The USA's expansionist outlook found ideological support in the doctrines of Social Darwinism, eugenics, and racial theories, which cast cultures and nations into a drama of violent struggle for the "survival of the fittest." Perceiving the world in these terms provided dubious justification for the domination of one people by another, as imperial violence was explained away as a necessary corollary to the uplift and "civilization" of less advanced populations by ostensibly more advanced Anglo-Saxon nations.

The USA acquired its overseas empire through military conflict with and triumph over an

"Old World" colonial power, Spain. In the 1890s, Spain was involved in the ongoing violent suppression of independence movements in Cuba and the Philippines. The US government regarded Cuba's instability in particular as a liability to its own economic and political well being, for it led to a steady loss of US investments and trade and thereby contributed to the nation's economic woes. Moreover, "yellow" **newspapers** such as the *New York World* and *New York Journal* frequently reported on atrocities resulting from a brutal policy of re-concentration that displaced rural Cubans to camps in towns and cities where they suffered from starvation and disease. In early 1898, after Spain failed to put into place reforms for Cuban self-determination, resistance turned into revolution; President William McKinley responded by sending the battleship "Maine" to Havana Harbor as a symbol of US resolve to protect its "interests" in Cuba. When a massive explosion ripped the battleship apart on February 15, killing 260 sailors on board, war with Spain seemed inevitable. Although the cause of the explosion was never determined, the theory of a Spanish mine gripped the public imagination and intensified calls for war. The USA declared war on Spain, which it swiftly defeated, thanks primarily to its new navy. On May 1, Admiral George Dewey's Asiatic Squadron defeated Admiral Montojo's fleet near Manila and on July 3, Admiral Sampson's North Atlantic Squadron, led by Commodore Schley, defeated Admiral Cervera's fleet near Santiago (an ensuing controversy over who was responsible for this victory was later represented in Edison's 1901 film, *The Sampson-Schley Controversy*). Although the leader of the Filipino independence movement, Emilio Aguinaldo, had worked with the US military to defeat Spain, he was betrayed when the USA annexed the Philippines and then prosecuted a bloody three-year military campaign to suppress Filipino resistance to its own imperial rule, killing 200,000 Filipino civilians in the process. Spain ceded Puerto Rico, the Philippines, and Guam to the USA, and Cuba was occupied until 1902. Having also annexed the Hawaiian Islands in 1898, the USA now had its commercial-territorial overseas empire.

The ideology of empire was popularized in the sphere of commercialized leisure on the midways of **world's fairs**, in museums of natural history, "wild west" shows, and moving pictures shows, which featured displays that contrasted the USA's industrial, social, and political "progress" with the ostensible "savagery" of less industrialized, often non-white populations living in areas deemed desirable for commercial expansion and exploitation. Just as it did for other industries, imperialism gave the fledgling film industry a much-needed boost in 1898. Early cinema was well-suited to represent the global mobilizations of overseas imperialism, for it could bring "living pictures" of Theodore Roosevelt's famous Rough Riders, massive new battleships, military camps, and troops embarking for the Philippines to curious audiences who clamored for spectacular representations of the nation's high-tech bid for power. Hence **Edison** Manufacturing sent William **Paley** to Tampa and Cuba, while **American Mutoscope and Biograph** (AM&B) sent Billy **Bitzer** and Arthur **Marvin** to Cuba, and later, C. Fred Ackerman to the Philippines. Manufacturers renamed **cameras** and **projectors** "wargraphs" and "warscopes," and moving pictures were organized by exhibitors at venues such as New York's **Eden Musee** into thematically coherent twenty-minute programs interspersed with **magic lantern** slides and **illustrated songs**. Audiences cheered the Rough Riders charging towards the camera in *Roosevelt's Rough Riders* (AM&B, 1898), observed a supply train being unloaded in *US Cavalry Unloading Supplies at Tampa* (Edison, 1898), watched soldiers marching in formation in *10th US Infantry 2nd Battalion, Leaving Cars* (Edison, 1898), and even witnessed the initiation of a new volunteer in *Blanket Tossing a New Recruit* (Edison, 1898). Edison's *Love and War* (1899) told delighted audiences the story of a US private who is heroically injured on the battlefield, meets his true love—a Red Cross nurse—while in a camp hospital, and returns home a hero.

Although cameramen were able to film camp activities, coaling battleships, and preparatory troop movements, they were unable to capture moving pictures of battle. Harsh and dangerous conditions on the war front, the use of guerilla warfare, the extended trajectories of modern military technologies, the blinding smoke from gunpowder, and the weight and bulk of moving picture cameras made shooting films of battles nearly impossible, so companies resorted to staging **re-enactments**. Hence, many of Edison's films representing battles fought during the Spanish–American War and the ensuing Philippine–American War were shot in West Orange, New Jersey, and featured members of the New Jersey National Guard. Among others, such films include *The Battle of San Juan Hill* (1899), *Advance of the Kansas Volunteers at Caloocan* (1899), and *US Troops and Red Cross in Trenches at Candaba* (1899). These films tended to place the camera in trenches alongside charging soldiers or in the direct line of enemy fire, thereby visually positioning the spectator in the midst of the depicted battle and increasing the "reality effect." This strategy of producing re-enactments in the absence of *actualité* footage was continued in later representations of imperial conflicts, such as the Boxer Rebellion. Extending this mutually beneficial relationship between early cinema and imperial culture were films of the victory and homecoming parades that followed the end of the war. Although many of these films can seem opaque to contemporary viewers, their catalogue descriptions provide scholars of early cinema with crucial interpretive insight to the kinds of meanings such films had for turn-of-the-last-century audiences.

In sharp contrast with the extensive cinematic representation of imperialism in European films, the *actualité* and re-enactment films produced during and shortly after the war constitute the large majority of films that engage directly with the overseas American imperialism during the silent era. Although the war with Spain was itself popular and found extensive representation—for example, in Frederic Remington's **paintings**, in Stephen Crane's newspaper stories, and in Roosevelt's popular war memoir, *The Rough Riders*—the new overseas empire largely faded from moving picture screens within a few years. In 1903, AM&B *The American Soldier in Love and War* told the story of an injured soldier taken captive by Filipinos, only to be found and rescued by his fiancée. A few years later, a handful of fiction films emerged with the surge of interest in Civil War films and **westerns** following the **nickelodeon** boom: these include **Kalem**'s *A Soldier of the U.S. Army*

(1909) and **Selig**'s *Up San Juan Hill* (1909) and *Under the Stars and Stripes* (1910). Another series released by **Universal** followed in 1913, with these now being **multiple-reel films** such as *The Battle of Manilla*, *The Battle of San Jan Hill*, and *The Grand Old Flag*.

There are political, cultural and ideological explanations for the later erasure of the overseas empire from the popular imagination. In many respects, the national mythology articulated by the western (from historical novels to moving pictures to Buffalo Bill's (William F. **Cody**'s) "Wild West") presented a more credible framework for extolling the virtues of American republicanism in popular culture. In fact, pro-imperialists initially framed the conflict with Spain and the later subordination of the Philippine insurgency as a mere continuation of westward expansion, yet the analogy was not sustainable. In contrast to westward continental expansion, which could be associated with democracy, agrarianism and pioneer self-reliance, US overseas imperialism seemed to contradict many of the nation's prevailing ideas about itself. Not only did the "new" imperialism foster dependence in its subject populations and deny them the rights enjoyed by US citizens, it also ultimately resulted in the United States' transformation into the very image of tyrannical colonial rule it had once perceived in Spain. Rather than rescuing Spain's former colonies, the US simply subjected them to further exploitation and violence. The ongoing "pacification" of the Philippines (which lasted until 1903), along with regular newspaper reports of horrifying atrocities committed by the US military against civilians there (most notoriously, their deployment of the "water cure"), cast a shadow over the image of US heroism and benevolence projected at the war's beginning in 1898. The vociferous and culturally influential Anti-Imperialist League (whose founding members included Mark Twain and Jane **Addams**) publicly called into question the legitimacy of American imperial rule. By contrast, the Supreme Court decided in Downes vs. Bidwell that the new possessions would not be protected by the Constitution, and so were made politically, socially, and culturally extraneous to the continental USA.

Although of a different order, the US cinema's cultural empire was well established by the mid-1910s, partly through the immense popularity of westerns. The outbreak of **World War I** sharply reduced film production in France and Italy, the US industry's greatest competitors at home and abroad. Thereafter, the USA's huge and highly profitable domestic market generated the capital required to maintain Hollywood's grip on overseas markets.

See also: colonialism: Europe; migration/immigration: USA; museum life exhibits; news event films; propaganda films

Further reading

Hoganson, Kristin (1998) *Fighting for American Manhood: How Gender Provoked the Spanish–American and Philippine–American Wars*, New Haven: Yale University Press.

LaFeber, Walter (1963) *The New Empire: An Interpretation of American Expansion 1860–1898*, Ithaca: Cornell University Press.

Kaplan, Amy and Donald E. Pease (eds.) (1993) *Cultures of US Imperialism*, Durham: Duke University Press.

Musser, Charles (1997) *Edison Motion Pictures, 1890–1900: An Annotated Filmography*, Washington, D.C.: Smithsonian Institution Press.

KRISTEN WHISSEL

Ince, Ralph

b. 1887, Boston; d. 1937, Kensington, London

actor, director, USA

Born to a theatrical family, Ralph Ince appeared on stage as a youngster. He studied art, however, and became a **newspaper** cartoonist. Joining **Vitagraph** around 1906, Ince gained attention playing Abraham Lincoln in the studio's "Lincoln cycle" of one-reelers in the early 1910s. He discovered and later married actress Anita Stewart and directed several of her films. Ince worked as an actor in early talkies, but moved to Great Britain in 1934 and returned to directing. He was the brother of director-producer Thomas H. **Ince** and actor-director John Ince.

ROBERT S. BIRCHARD

Ince, Thomas H.

b. 1880; d. 1924

actor, director, scriptwriter, producer, USA

The second of three sons born to an immigrant English stage actor and his wife, Thomas Harper Ince spent his youth traveling across the USA in various theatrical stock companies and **vaudeville** troupes. He entered movies in 1910, acting in *His New Lid*, a one-reel **Biograph comedy** directed by Frank Powell. Drawn to Carl **Laemmle**'s New York-based **IMP** Company by Joseph Smiley, a former vaudeville partner, Ince was hired as an actor but was quickly made director of the Mary **Pickford** unit, traveling to Cuba for a season of filming.

In late 1911, Ince secured the position of chief director for Adam **Kessel**, Charles O. **Baumann**, and Fred J. **Balshofer**'s **New York Motion Picture Company** (NYMP), replacing Balshofer as the head of production at the company's Bison studio in California and bringing cameraman Ray Smallwood and actress Ethel Grandin with him from IMP. Within weeks of their arrival, NYMP secured the services of the Miller Brothers 101 Real Wild West Show. The Bison brand was changed to Bison-101, and Ince was soon producing a series of two- and three-reel **westerns**, such as *Indian Massacre* and *The Invaders* (both 1912), that had a visual authenticity and narrative energy that was the envy of the industry. A second unit for one reel releases, with actor Francis **Ford** in charge, was soon established, and by mid-1913, after completing his first feature film, *The Battle of Gettysburg*, Ince had turned over all directorial duties to subordinates, controlling the studio's output from the producer's chair.

Ince assumed a financial interest in the **Keystone** brand when Kessel and Baumann hired Mack **Sennett** from **Biograph** in 1912. Production expanded to such an extent that over time several new brands—Kay-Bee, Broncho, Domino—were created, giving the illusion of

Figure 56 Thomas Ince seated with his Bison-101 Indian actors, *c.* 1912. (Courtesy of the Robert S. Birchard Collection.)

a differentiated product, even though all NYMP releases came from the same factory. By mid-1915, Kessel and Baumann joined forces with Harry **Aitken** to form the Triangle Film Corporation, employing the talents of Ince, Sennett and D. W. **Griffith** to release a pre-packaged feature program to theaters every week. With Triangle's demise in 1917, Ince established himself as an independent producer, releasing through Paramount-Artcraft. He maintained his independence until his death in 1924.

If Ince is remembered for anything (besides his untimely, and decidedly un-scandalous death), it is for the production system he established at "Inceville," the NYMP studio in Santa Monica. While not the first American producer to utilize an assembly-line process of filmmaking, he was certainly the first to exploit fully its enormous potential for streamlining production and increasing profits; in addition, he recognized early on that such

a system could be an effective means of putting a personal stamp on an industrial product. Within months of his arrival on the west coast, he had asserted his primacy at the studio, and the press and public were referring to, and praising, NYMP releases as "Ince" films.

Further reading

Abel, Richard (2004) "The 'Imagined Community' of the Western, 1910–1913," in Charlie Keil and Shelley Stamp (eds.) *Cinema's Transitional Era: Audiences, Institutions, Practices*, 131–170, Berkeley: University of California Press.

Higgins, Steven (1984) "I film di Thomas H. Ince," *Griffithiana*, 18–21.

Wing, W. E. (1913) "Tom Ince, of Inceville," *The New York Dramatic Mirror*, 24 December: 34.

STEVEN HIGGINS

India

Although modest in scale, early Indian cinema was nevertheless a culturally important phenomenon that significantly shaped the emerging mass culture of modern India. The context of colonial rule and rapid social and technological change interacted with indigenous traditions of spectacle to create a unique expression of the modern that articulated India's response to the industrial-capitalist culture of the West.

Alongside the traditional theatrical folk forms that toured urban areas of British India during festivals, nascent moving picture audiences already were exposed to proscenium theater performances, mass-produced printed images, gramophone recordings, and **magic lantern shows**. For instance, the Indian version of the magic lantern—called *shambarik kharolika* and created by Mahadeo Gopal Patwardhan in Bombay—traveled to different parts of India with stories from the Hindu epics that anticipated the **mythological** genre by more than a decade. Visiting showmen brought a succession of moving picture shows after the **Lumière** Brothers' agent, Marius Sestier, first presented their **Cinématographe** at Bombay's Watson's Hotel in July 1896. Among these were Stewart's "Vitagraph," Hughes' "Moto-Photoscope," and Prof. Anderson's "Andersonoscograph," shown in theaters or tent cinemas set up in playgrounds in Bombay, Calcutta, and Madras. The first audiences consisted of Europeans and the local elite, but they soon expanded to include other strata of the urban and semi-urban population.

By 1898, footage shot in India by foreign operators became a popular attraction—"exotic" views of monuments and bazaars, religious processions, and filmed theater scenes. Prof. Anderson's *Train Arriving at Bombay Station* and *Poona Races '98* are the earliest "local scenes" known to have been screened throughout India.

In the same year, professional photographers H. S. **Bhatavdekar** in Bombay and Hiralal **Sen** in Calcutta entered the film exhibition trade and soon began making and distributing their own films. These were mostly *actualités* and photographed plays shown between theater performances, variety acts, and imported European films.

Bhatavdekar was among the cameramen who shot the pageantry of the 1902 Delhi Durbar, perhaps the most popular attraction of the period along with other colonial-historical subjects such as the Boer War and Queen Victoria's funeral.

Within a few years, exhibitors such as J. F. **Madan** and Abdullaly **Esoofally** had mobilized sufficient resources to make moving pictures available in more distant parts of India. Equipped with films for two or three programs, they traveled from city to city and throughout the countryside, following the trail established by theater companies with their popular folk plays. After 1907, touring and permanent cinemas multiplied, showing mostly imported films from virtually every major film company distributed in Europe: **Pathé-Frères**, **Gaumont**, **Éclair**, **Ambrosio**, **Lubin**, **Warwick**, **Vitagraph**, **Nordisk**, **Messter**, and **Urban**.

While two previous story films were made in Bombay in 1912—*Pundalik* and *Savitri*, both with religious and mythological subjects—it was D. G. **Phalke**'s *Raja Harishchandra* (1913) that marks the true beginning of Indian cinema. Phalke consciously gave his work a political complexion by placing it in the context of the *swadeshi* movement (the nationalist program of self-reliance). He saw himself as the founder of the Indian cinema industry because previous pioneers had mainly produced *actualités* or distributed and exhibited imported films.

Phalke's subsequent films also transposed mythological stories from oral tradition and theatrical spaces to cinematic forms of narration. Combining trick photography, tableau-style **editing**, and shooting from a distance, with multi-shot construction and even parallel editing, *Kaliya Mardan* [The Conquest of Kaliya] (1919), for instance, aroused a strong religious and quasi-nationalist response from audiences which identified the serpent-demon Kaliya with oppressive British rule.

Others followed Phalke's example in the other two major filmmaking centers of Calcutta and Madras. After early efforts by Madan, S. N. **Patankar**, N. **Mudaliar**, and Suchet **Singh**, the artisanal methods of the pre-studio era were gradually replaced in the early 1920s by more professional studio-based productions, from Phalke's **Hindustan Cinema Films Company**,

Madan Theatres Limited, Painter's **Maharashtra Film Company**, and others. A greater variety of subjects was introduced with social dramas such as Dhirendranath **Ganguly**'s *Bilet Pherat* [England Returned] (1921), **historical films** such as Painter's *Sinhagad* (1923), and costume films such as **Kohinoor**'s *Indrasabha* (1925). Other subjects included **religious films**, stunt films, **crime films**, literary adaptations, and **comedies**.

While the demand for Indian films steadily increased, foreign films still dominated exhibition. They were cheaper to rent, and they also were immensely popular, especially the American **serials** and the American **stars** such as Pearl **White**, Eddie Polo, Douglas Fairbanks, and the silent comedians. In fact, Indian stars were often publicized with epithets like the "Indian Mary **Pickford**" (Ermeline) and "Indian Eddie Polo" (Nandram).

But the Hollywood influence did not extend to Indian film style, for the popular folk theater forms remained stylistically dominant. Frontal staging, direct address to the camera, familiar plots, indigenous décor and **costumes**, narration provided by a **lecturer**, and traditional **musical accompaniment** all gave Indian films a distinctive character.

The Report of the Indian Cinematograph Committee (1927–1928) gives most of the basic information available about the 1910s and 1920s. The studios were crudely equipped, and the use of artificial lights was rare. All the equipment and raw stock was imported, and budgets were generally low. The studios maintained a permanent staff of technicians and stars, but heroines were largely drawn from among dancing girls and Anglo-Indians, as women from the "respectable" classes were reluctant to have anything to do with filmmaking.

Films were exhibited with multi-lingual titles, in English and in one or more of the major Indian languages, depending on the linguistic composition of the audience. Bombay releases, for instance, had titles in four languages: English, Hindi, Gujarati, and Urdu. Lecturers often were hired to read the **intertitles** for illiterate spectators, and sometimes also "dubbed" actors' dialogue.

After 1918, touring and permanent cinemas came under fire safety laws, and the British

Figure 57 D. S. Phalke. (Courtesy of National Film Archive of India.)

colonial government became sensitive to the depiction of white society (and women, in particular) in imported films and to the potentially volatile expressions of communal or nationalist sentiments in Indian productions. Censorship was enforced on all exhibition sites from 1920 under the Indian Cinematograph Act, and certification became an effective instrument of state control.

It is tragic that tropical climatic conditions, the apathy of both government and producers, and the inevitable process of nitrate decomposition have virtually wiped out India's silent film heritage. But the handful of surviving fragments and the more numerous stills, booklets, posters, and press **publicity** help to recreate a part of the vibrant chapter of early Indian cinema and its culture.

See also: colonialism: Europe

Further reading

Chabria, Suresh (ed.) (1994) *Light of Asia: Indian Silent Cinema, 1912–1934*, New Delhi: Wiley Eastern Limited.

Rajadhyaksha, Ashish and Paul Willemen (1994) *Encyclopaedia of Indian Cinema*, New Delhi: Oxford University Press.

Rangoonwalla, Firoze (1975) *75 Years of Indian Cinema*, New Delhi: Indian Book Company.

SURESH CHABRIA

Indonesia

The first screening of moving pictures in Indonesia (then known as the Dutch East Indies or Nederlandsch Indie) took place in Batavia (now Jakarta) on 5 December 1900. Ticket prices ranged from two guilders for first class, down to half a guilder (50 sen) for third class, a price equivalent to the cost of 10 liters of rice. For the city's indigenous inhabitants, such prices were prohibitive, so audiences exclusively were comprised of Dutch, other Europeans, and Chinese expatriates. Even when the cheapest tickets dropped to 25 sen the following year, movie-going remained out of reach for the local population until 1905, when the cheapest tickets fell to 10 sen—for indigenous people only.

Early screenings took place in rented buildings or by means of **itinerant exhibitors** who toured the islands. The Dutch authorities began to apply censorship quite early (revising the rules in 1916, 1925, and 1926) in order to limit scenes showing brutality or immodest and unlawful behavior. By the 1920s, most film exhibition was controlled by Chinese-owned companies. Initially, films were imported from Europe (especially **Pathé-Frères** films from France) and the USA. The earliest hits appeared in 1905: **Edison**'s *Uncle Tom's Cabin* (1903) and Pathé's *Le petit poucet* [Tom Thumb] (1905). By the 1920s, the cinema was popular everywhere in the islands and dominated by fare from Hollywood—e.g., *The Young Rajah* (1924), starring Rudolph Valentino—and from China—e.g., *Li Ting Lang* (1924) and *The Grandson* (1925).

The Dutch Colonial Government initiated film production in 1910, importing filmmakers from Europe to make local nonfiction films. Later, Eurasian filmmakers—Dutch and other expatriate Europeans—also joined in. In 1925, the Eurasian 'Flip' Carli planned to make a documentary film on the opening of the Night Fair of Bandung (a city in West Java) called *Pasar Malam Bandung*; at the last minute his permit was revoked, however, and the Government gave the project to a filmmaker from abroad.

The first local feature fiction film, *Loetoeng Kasaroeng* [The Disguised Monkey], was made in 1926 by Eurasian filmmakers G. Kruger and L. Heuveldorp. The Chinese entered production in 1928 when the Wong Brothers made *Lily van Java* [Lily of Java], while Carli made *Njai Siti* [The Sound of Blood] in 1930. But these and subsequent films had primitive production values and could hardly compete against imported product. When the Wong Brothers, Tan Brothers, and The Teng Chun pioneered local sound film production in 1931, success likewise was not immediate.

It would take the Great Depression, the Japanese occupation during World War II, and then the achievement of national independence before Usmar Ismail could make *Darah dan Doa* [The Long March] in 1950, marking the advent of a truly indigenous film production.

See also: colonialism: Europe

S. M. ARDAN (TRANSLATED BY
RAYMOND EDMONDSON)

industrial films

Films depicting industrial processes were commonplace in early cinema. With titles such as **Pathé-Frères**' *Comment se fait le fromage de Holland* [How They Make Cheese in Holland] (1909), Powers' *The Japanese Silk Industry* (1914), and **Selig**'s *Harvesting Alfalfa in New Mexico* (1912), industrial films documented all manner of production processes, from traditional handicrafts to mechanized modern manufacturing. Like other early nonfiction films, industrials were shown in both commercial and non-commercial venues. What sets this kind of film apart is its explicit concern to document labor and the production of goods and raw materials. This fascination with new and old production technologies is characteristic of early cinema's historical moment of origin just after the industrial revolution. Industrial films helped a modernizing culture come to terms with the changing nature of labor, technology, and commercial production in the newly industrialized world.

Unlike another prominent kind of early non-fiction film, **travelogues** or travel films, which drew upon a tradition of picturesque landscape representation over a century old, industrial films did not have a long-standing aesthetic tradition to contend with. This is not to say that they lacked pre-cinema traditions, for in fact, like most other early films, industrials poached upon previous representations that had appeared in **newspapers**, **illustrated magazines**, scientific and technical exhibitions, and **world fairs**. These other media had been documenting production processes since the mid-19th century, satisfying a growing curiosity to see how things worked as machinery became more complex with the onset of industrialization. Even descriptions of simple processes were of interest, as evidenced by the many how-to manuals that emerged in mid-century, which covered topics such as soap making or how to make a rocking chair. Yet this taste for technical description did not have the same aspiration to represent beauty as did the so-called high-class travelogue genre. Instead, the goal seems to have been to educate audiences about technology and to demystify industrial production through the observation of process. Industrials were never as popular as travel films, yet for the first two decades of cinema history they appeared frequently on **screens**, exemplifying what historian Neil Harris has called the "operational aesthetic": a fascination with technology and mechanical description.

Single-shot industrial films were made during the *actualité* film period in the 1890s and sometimes sold in groups. **Edison** made a few films on the Chicago stockyards in 1897, for example, with titles such as *Sheep Run*, *Chicago Stockyards*, and *Cattle Driven to Slaughter*. It was common for different companies to release films on the same subject. Selig also made a group of films in 1901 on the Chicago stockyards; this series was relatively cheap and convenient for Selig to produce, since at the time the company was still based in Chicago.

The extensive series included almost sixty subjects, with titles such as *Entrance to Union Stock Yards*, *Dumping and Lifting Cattle*, *Sticking Cattle*, and *Dressing Beef*. Exhibitors could selectively choose which of the films in the series to project. Although the order in which they would appear was by and large dictated by the films—one probably would show the stockyard entrance before showing the dressing of beef, for example—the exhibitor could still choose which films to omit and the order in which to show them.

As the *actualité* period drew to a close and film structure grew more complicated, industrial films expanded into a self-contained multi-shot structure. They continued to be shown in the variety programs of the earliest permanent moving picture theaters alongside **comedies**, dramas, **news event films**, and **illustrated song** slides. To understand the industrial film's place in this transitional period of film history (the **nickelodeon** era in the USA), it is helpful to understand nonfiction genres in general at this time. One of the more striking aspects of early cinema is how numerous the nonfiction genres were, in comparison with the story films that were divided simply into comedies and dramas. The trade journals in the USA, which listed new releases on a weekly basis beginning around 1907, typically divided nonfiction films into categories such as scenic, industrial, **scientific**, **sports**, news events, acrobatic, and nature films. The concept of "nonfiction" did not yet exist as a generic boundary in early cinema. Instead, films were organized by subject in a manner that today seems based on rather minute and arbitrary distinctions. If part of the project of early cinema was to produce knowledge about the world and to educate its audience, it seems that the logic employed by the medium was that of the inventory: early nonfiction genres produce a kind of inventory of what exists in the world. As a subset of the large categorical distinctions made by individual film genres, industrial films inventoried the variety of goods produced around the world.

Industrial films frequently were sponsored by the commercial companies whose production was being documented, and the films served a promotional as well as an informational function. However, industrial films were not simply advertisements. Early **advertising** films such as

International Film's *Dewars Scotch Whisky* (1897) were designed to sell a product. This film shows three men in kilts dancing around boisterously, presumably filled with Dewars scotch. In contrast to this obviously staged commercial film, industrial films were concerned to realistically document a production process. Likewise, this genre was not about the circulation of goods—fiction films were there to dramatize consumption. Instead of encouraging commercial exchange or dramatizing commercial circulation, then, industrial films were about production in the most material sense.

Although they were not simply commercials, then, industrial films did have an important relation to the industrial economy that produced them. At the turn of the 20th century, people had become dissociated from the production methods that brought consumer goods to them. The everyday presence of craftsmanship had begun to disappear with the onset of mass production and the importation of goods. Industrial films demystified the process by which products arrived in front of the consumer fully formed. In doing so, they implicitly celebrated the commodity culture that produced the items being showcased. The goods and raw materials we see produced in these films are of a great variety: tobacco, rubber, lumber, steel, pottery, straw hats, and wine are just some of the many items whose production was documented. These, by and large, are not luxury goods but the materials and products necessary for everyday life. A high percentage of industrial films documented the cultivation and processing of food items, for example. The audience's curiosity may have been piqued by the familiarity of the objects produced. Likewise, many in the audience were workers, some of whom would have labored in the trades or factories shown in these films. The common experience of labor and consumer goods was one of the appeals of this genre.

Industrial films are like other early nonfiction film genres in that they do not follow the techniques of continuity editing that were being developed during this period in story films. And yet industrial films do follow a simple narrative structure: that of production. Industrial films tell the story of the birth of a consumer product. We see each product go through a series of processes, each one following from the previous in an inviolable order. Cricks & Martin's *A Visit to Peek Frean and Co.'s Biscuit Works* (1906), for example, follows the narrative logic of production through a modern factory assembly line. Running slightly more than eleven minutes, the film documents modern factory production in Great Britain, the nation that pioneered industrial manufacturing. The film begins at the very start of the production process, as the factory's steam power is fired up. We see milk and flour arriving in a long shot taken outside the factory, and then the camera moves inside to document the manufacturing of the biscuits. After an **intertitle** announcing "Making biscuits, general view," we see an extreme long shot of machinery and workers wearing white caps and aprons. The film continues to show biscuit dough being rolled out, formed, put through the ovens for baking, and then the biscuits being packed for sale. In the film's concluding shots, we see a series of horse-drawn carriages and a few automobiles driving away to deliver the biscuits around the city.

The detailed steps of this production process—from the beginning of production to distribution—are carried out by a series of humans interfacing with machines. This is a highly mechanized factory, and yet some production duties are still performed manually. This film is careful to show the factory's working conditions in a favorable light—the Peek Frean factory looks relatively clean and orderly—yet the repetitiveness of the labor and boredom of the laborers is everywhere apparent. Some of the workers glance up from their duties to look curiously at the camera, but they remain as anonymous as the machines they are working on. A man who appears to be an inspector wanders into many of the shots, officiously pawing over the biscuits moving through the production line, probably for the benefit of the camera. In this film we see value being imbued into the commodity via the labor (both human and mechanical) that goes into producing it: industrials demonstrate that the product shown has value. By simply presenting a vision of what this production process looks like, rather than providing any interpretation of that process, the film also mitigates any suspicion that the labor we are viewing might be exploitative. Such an interpretation would be valid, of course, but it would require drawing upon ideas from outside the world of the film.

This example, as well as the very term "industrial," would seem to indicate that these films only documented modern factory production, but, in fact, films showing traditional handicrafts were also part of the industrial film genre. **Eclipse**'s *Making Bamboo Hats in Java* (1911), for example, was sold as an industrial, even though the objects being produced are not emblematic of modern industrialism. Also, *Making Bamboo Hats in Java* may have included Javanese scenery worthy of a travelogue, but the production process was the more important element by which to assign generic classification in this case. The fact that industrial films were so frequently concerned to document handmade labor indicates that the genre appealed to a nostalgia for the production methods of the pre-modern world. The moment of the traditional craft industry's destruction also became the moment at which it seemed important to picture it, as a kind of foil to the new methods of mechanical production.

By about 1912, the term "industrial" appears with less and less frequency in the trade press and manufacturers' catalogs. By this time almost all nonfiction genres, with the exception of travelogues, were becoming subsumed under one or more all-encompassing categories. What had been a proliferation of nonfiction genres in the decade before was reduced to simply **newsreels** and **scientific** or educational films. This was in part an attempt to consolidate the commercial appeal of nonfiction films, but it also was an indication of how the industry had changed, from nonfiction to fiction films being predominant. Industrial films were still made (indeed they still exist today), but they were rarely exhibited commercially once the feature film era had begun.

See also: audiences: surveys and debates; cinema of attractions; education; ethnographic films; Kleine, George; labor movement: Europe; labor movement: USA; lecturer; program formats

Further reading

Gunning, Tom (1995) " 'Those Drawn with a Very Fine Camel's Hair Brush': The Origins of Film Genres," *Iris*, 20: 49–62.

Harris, Neil (1973) "The Operational Aesthetic," in *Humbug: The Art of P. T. Barnum*, 61–89, Boston: Little, Brown and Co.

Hertogs, Daan, and Nico de Klerk (eds.) (1997) *Uncharted Territory: Essays on Early Nonfiction Film*, Amsterdam: Stichting Nederlands Filmmuseum.

Lefebvre, Thierry (1993) "The Scientia Production (1911–1914): Scientific Popularization Through Pictures," *Griffithiana*, 47: 137–155.

Meusy, Jean-Jacques (1995) "La diffusion des films de 'non-fiction' dans les établissements Parisiens," *1895*, 18: 169–199.

Musser, Charles (1990) *The Emergence of Cinema: The American Screen to 1907*, New York: Scribners.

JENNIFER LYNN PETERSON

Figure 58 Frame still from *A Visit to Peak Fraen and Co.'s Biscuit Works* (Cricks and Martin, 1906).

Inoue Masao

b. 1881; d. 1950

actor, director, Japan

Inoue began his career as a stage actor in Osaka in 1897, after which he moved to Tokyo to join the troupe of the famous actor Ii Yoho—and soon became its chief actor. Whereas many renowned actors of this period ignored moving pictures, Inoue had a strong desire to perform in films. In 1915, he played the leading role in the *rensageki* (a drama combining live stage action and film footage), *Tojo no himitsu* [The Secret of the Tower]. In 1916, he directed the first of three films, *Nasanu naka* [No Blood Relation], for a newly established company,

Kobayashi Shokai. He even founded a private institute of motion picture study at his own home in Tokyo. Inoue was one of the most intelligent and ambitious actors in the 1910s and 1920s in Japan.

HIROSHI KOMATSU

intermediality and modes of reception

Recent theories of literature and art have emphasized the importance of reception for the understanding of an artwork. However, as a historical phenomenon, reception must always be reconstructed. Our richest sources, of course, are essays and reviews, but these generally were written by professional writers or intellectuals and so may not reflect the response of an average audience member, which ultimately may be beyond our reach as historians. However, the way works are targeted at specific audiences may well tell us a great deal about the intended or envisioned reception.

Early cinema developed within an atmosphere of intermediality and could be seen as the culmination of several different media; therefore, its earliest reception was partly determined by the context within which it was viewed. **Lumière** first premiered its **Cinématographe** before specialists in **photography**, alongside experiments in **color** photography. Thus these groups saw moving pictures as a "peculiar development of instantaneous photography." The operation of moving pictures also were featured in Albert A. Hopkins' book, *Magic: Stage Illusion and Scientific Diversions* (1898), which placed them in a long tradition of visual illusions, a frequent context for the reception of early films, which often were exhibited by stage magicians (e.g., Leopoldo **Fregoli**, Albert **Smith**, Felicien Trewey, David Devant). Thomas **Edison** premiered his **Kinetoscope** before the Brooklyn Institute of Art and Sciences in 1893, one of many scientific demonstrations of the new invention of moving pictures that saw the apparatus primarily as an example of new advances in technology, parallel to the developments in air travel, wireless telegraphy, the telephone, or the X-ray. This reception context placed moving pictures as a direct development of the scientific **chronophotography** of Edwaerd **Muybridge**, Etienne-Jules **Marey**, and Alfred

Londe. Kinetoscope films soon featured **vaudeville** performers—strongmen, acrobats, and serpentine dancers—and the commercial premiere of projected films in New York City took place in vaudeville theaters, so that moving pictures perhaps ultimately were seen as part of the entertainment world. Within the vaudeville circuit films often were most popular when they showed current events and **British Mutoscope and Biograph** especially, under the leadership of William Kennedy Laurie **Dickson**, promoted the idea of the weekly Biograph offerings as a "Living Illustrated Newspaper," a model that other companies also followed. Moving photographs, the latest visual illusion, the latest scientific development of technology, canned vaudeville, or a living **newspaper**—all these were reception contexts for early cinema, shaping audiences' expectations and experiences of the new medium.

If one turns to written reports of first viewings of cinema, we can distinguish two basic modes of reception that sometimes fused. The first is a reception that stressed the scientific, technological aspect of the films and their means of production and frequently invoked their realism. The second reception I will call "uncanny," because it stressed the strange effect of moving pictures, their ghostly or bizarre quality. Interestingly, these two modes relate dialectically rather than as opposites, and sometimes occurred in the same review. Although the uncanny mode would seem to deny the realism of moving pictures, in fact, it often located their uncanny effects in an excess of realism. In noting the novel perceptual aspects of moving pictures, the uncanny mode also supplied some of the earliest phenomenological accounts of cinema.

The scientific/technological receptions of early projections stressed the processes by which moving pictures were made. The earliest newspaper reports on Edison's kinetoscope, for instance, emphasized that they comprised hundreds of separate photographs on flexible film. Projected moving pictures usually were described (more or less correctly) as a combination of the kinetoscope and the **magic lantern**, occasionally invoking such devices as the zoetrope or phenakistoscope, relating the new invention to previously known ones and providing it with a scientific pedigree. Such accounts also offered explanations of the phenomenon of persistence of vision, discussed the rates of speed of photography and projection, and often related the innovation to other recent inventions, frequently citing Edison. These articles often speculated on the future of the nascent industry, announcing the possibilities of combining the invention with the **phonograph**, and filming both stage plays and **operas**. Film was seen as a triumph of realism and even proclaimed a hedge against mortality, since films would preserve the living appearance of people long after they were dead.

This concept of cinema as a pathway to immortality relates directly to the uncanny reception. Articles written by Maxim Gorky on first viewing the Lumière films in 1896 typify this mode of reception when he described cinema as "the kingdom of shadows." Perhaps the most detailed and thoughtful appreciation of first screenings, Gorky's and another appearing in London's *New Review* (February 1897) under the name O. Winter both emphasized that while moving pictures were realistic in some respects they were unreal in others, lacking especially both color and sound. Winter claimed, "It is all true and all false." He also felt that the Cinématographe was inartistic because it was not selective, and compared it to the avant-garde movements of the era, the Pre-Raphaelites in **painting** and Emile Zola in literature, both of which he considered similarly "unselective" in their realism.

A number of commentators stressed the strange power that moving pictures seemed to exert over viewers, especially when representing rapidly moving objects such as trains. One New York reviewer declared, "attention is held almost with the vice of a fate," while Gorky mused, "You forget where you are. Strange imaginings invade your mind. Your consciousness begins to wane and grow dim." The novel formal effects of moving pictures frequently were noted, such as the sudden disappearance of a view when it came to an end or the strange fact that people disappeared as they walked past the edge of the screen. Almost universally, early commentators focused on the dynamic effect of a train coming towards the camera (although no authentic record of audience panic from first showings in metropolitan areas has been located) as well as the subtlety of motion shown in capturing the effects of wisps of smoke and the spray of water.

See also: archaeology of cinema/pre-cinema; communication; electricity; transportation

Further reading

Harding, Colin and Simon Popple (eds.) (1996) *In the Kingdom of Shadows: A Companion to Early Cinema*, Cranbury: Fairleigh Dickinson University Press.

Niver Kemp R. (ed.) (1971) *Biograph Bulletins, 1896–1908*, Los Angeles: Locare Research Group.

Tsivian, Yuri (1994) *Early Cinema in Russia and its Cultural Reception*, trans. Alan Bodger, London: Routledge.

TOM GUNNING

intermittent movements

The intermittent presentation or recording of sequential photographs was a key element of moving picture systems. The necessary intermittency, 12 to 16 images per second or above, could be achieved either mechanically, by starting and stopping the image-carrying **celluloid** band, or optically, by combining a number of mirrors or lenses with a continuously moving image carrier. Mechanical systems quickly predominated due to their ease of construction, while optical intermittents remained largely one-off designs needing expensive and delicately adjusted precision components, as in the intermittent illumination of the **Anschütz** Schnellseher, the moving lenses of the Maskelyne camera/projector, or the revolving mirrors of the Leiz projector.

Mechanical intermittent movements converted the constant motion of a hand crank, spring winding, or electric motor into discontinuous motion at the aperture of a camera or projection device. In the beater, or dog, movement first applied by Georges **Demenÿ** to a **Marey**-style chronophotographic camera in 1893, a short rod mounted at the edge of a revolving disk struck the film band so that one frame of film was pulled forward at each revolution. Many times improved, the beater was considered the most reliable early design, and was available from many manufacturers until about 1910. The claw movement used first in the **Cinématographe Lumière** of 1895 featured two small hooks at the end of an oscillating arm, also attached at the edge of a revolving disk, to pull down single frames to its working aperture.

Ultimately inadequate for projection apparatuses, the claw movement is still frequently used in sophisticated form in moving picture **cameras**. The Maltese Cross, or Geneva, movement incorporated a pin at the edge of a disk that ran in the slot of a four- or five-sided scalloped star which therefore moved intermittently; the deeply concave sides of the star ran against a raised platform on the disk when the pin was not active in its slot so that a frame of film was held positively still at the aperture. At first considered noisy, expensive, and subject to wear, after about 1905 the Maltese Cross movement became an essential component in both cameras and **projectors** because it kept the image precisely steady at the aperture when projecting large images in theaters. **American Mutoscope and Biograph** (AM&B) developed a unique gripper intermittent for its apparatus, where two counter rotating disks, each with a raised section on its rim, advanced the film band by friction. Other infrequently used mechanical intermittents, developed in part from manufacturing considerations and in part to avoid patent conflicts,

include: the drunken screw, where an eccentric thread sporadically moved a toothed gear; the ratchet, where a sprung hook was released by a curved incline acting on a cam; and the snail, where a disk with multiple pins intermittently engaged another disk set perpendicularly to it. The many variations of intermittent movements are frequently discussed in early moving picture reports and are a valuable aid to tracing the activity of inventors, pioneers, exhibitors, and manufacturers.

Further reading

Herbert, Stephen (1996) "Technical Essay," in Stephen Herbert and Luke McKernan (eds.) *Who's Who of Victorian Cinema*, 3–7, London: British Film Institute.

Hulfish, David S. (1913) *Motion Picture Work. A general treatise on picture taking, picture making, photo-plays, and theatre management and operation*, Chicago: American School of Correspondence.

Rossell, Deac (1998) *Living Pictures. The Origins of the Movies*, Albany: State University of New York Press.

Rossell, Deac (1999) "Die soziale Konstruktion früher technischer Systeme der Filmprojektion," *KINtop*, 8: 53–82.

DEAC ROSSELL

intertitles and titles

Intertitles are shots of texts printed on material that does not belong to the diegesis of a film and, therefore, are distinct from textual inserts such as calling cards, letters, posters, etc. First used artisanally by exhibitors, by 1907–08 they were the subject of discussions as to their usefulness, visual and linguistic form, frequency and length. By 1910, they came into general use and during the following decade became the norm in the industry. With the advent of sound cinema, intertitles were rejected as non-cinematic and obsolete palliatives to the absence of sound, an attitude initially accepted by **archives**. Yet their importance cannot be denied, for intertitles contributed decisively to the emergence of **editing**, the autonomy of film narrative independent of a **lecturer**, and even the development of the feature fiction film.

As a term, intertitle appeared in the early 1930s to differentiate the practice from the then new process

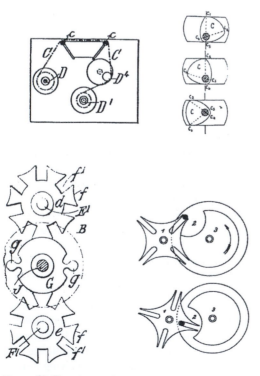

Figure 59 Four intermittent movements.

of subtitling which provided, at the bottom of the image, a translation for speech in foreign-language sound films. The terms in currency during the silent era itself were mainly "title" and "sub-title," although "captions," "headings," or "leaders" also were used. "Title cards" referred to the material on which the texts were inscribed in order to be filmed.

The appearance of the first intertitles in film screenings is better understood when one considers cinema's emergence within the context of contemporary spectacles—particularly the tradition of **magic lantern shows**. The first exhibitors presented a variety of moving pictures (which generally lasted a minute or less and consisted of a single shot), **illustrated songs**, magic tricks, comic acts, tableaux vivants, and lantern shows. Whether in **fairs/fairgrounds**, in **vaudeville** houses or **music halls**, or later in **nickelodeons**, most of the time they were equipped with a **projector** and a lantern (or combined apparatus) and could therefore project both films and glass slides—the latter often to announce features on the program. Thus, a slide could be projected with the title of the next film while the reel was being changed. The spectator would then see a succession of moving pictures and titles on the screen, as was already the case in magic lantern projections illustrating fairy tales, for instance, or tableaux vivants and mime shows that presented Passion plays on the fairgrounds, with a lecturer and signs bearing titles. This system allowed for fluid, uninterrupted projection and, accordingly, for the succession of narrative and thematic sequences—a far cry from later criticisms about the disruption created by intertitles.

Early on, some manufacturers began to put titles on films for sale. In France, the first **Gaumont** catalog read: "We are pleased to provide our customers with printed titles on film for all the films in our Collection. Titles on film for all the listed films of our collection, approximate length 5 ft. In French, in a foreign language." Purchase was optional, and titles could be ordered by providing a specific text, including for international distribution.

What the dominant modes of projection were at the time is still difficult to assess; practices differed. From its beginnings in 1896, **American Mutoscope and Biograph** would project a slide announcement before each film, whether an

actualité, a **re-enactment** of events, or a recreated scene from the legitimate **theater**. In these early years, each shot could be **copyrighted**, giving the insertion of intertitles some legitimacy in exhibition prints. Exhibitors also often made titles themselves, on slides or on film. After purchasing films, they could transform or adapt them to their audiences, according to the principles of novelty, diversity, and entertainment. There was no editing in the sense that we understand today. A more appropriate term would be "program montage," with the projection of films preceded by titles, or not. Indeed, films could be announced by a lecturer, without titles, especially when audiences were not literate enough, shows had small budgets, or films privileged the attraction of the moving image, its "magical" or spectacular aspects, beginning with **trick films** and comic gags.

In those screenings that involved a similar theme or episodes of a narrative, logic determined the succession. As in lantern shows, images could call to mind famous episodes already familiar to audiences. These series could do without titles: the lecturer would fill in potential gaps. Thus **biblical films** and Passion plays could be projected without titles, as could well-known *féeries*/**fairy plays** and **historical films**.

Initially, even for films that included more than one shot, scenes could be purchased separately, which made their presentation with titles easier. Around 1902–03, some films that included a series of several shots edited as a whole with titles became available for sale. These alternated texts and "tableaux-shots"—title/shot/title/shot—in a form of tableau style editing. Such films could be found in France: **Pathé-Frères**' *Ali Baba et les quarante voleurs* [Ali Baba and the Forty Thieves] (7 shots, 7 intertitles) and *Les Victimes de l'alcoolisme* (Victims of Alchoholism) (5 shots, 5 intertitles), both directed by Ferdinand **Zecca** in 1902; in Great Britain: G. A. **Smith**'s *Dorothy's Dream* (1903); and in the USA: **Edison**'s *Uncle Tom's Cabin* (14 shots, 14 intertitles) directed by Edwin S. **Porter** in 1903.

The Edison catalog heralded this practice as innovative: "In this film we have made a departure from the old method of dissolving one scene into another by inserting announcements with brief descriptions as they appear in succession. Sold in one length only." From then on, plausibly, intertitles also were called "sub-titles" to distinguish them from the main title.

This mutation had important consequences. The purchase or creation of separate titles and intertitles was no longer the prerogative of the exhibitor; rather, manufacturers provided a film ready for use. The history of the practice is not linear, however: American Mutoscope and Biograph used slides until 1904, some exhibitors continued to edit films artisanally, and **Vitagraph** apparently dispensed with intertitles until *Francesca di Rimini* (1907). The diversity of practices makes it difficult to trace how titles and intertitles actually were projected. Their fragile chemical composition, which often accelerated the deterioration of exhibition prints, has added to the difficulty. Hence, other sources than the films themselves—such as catalogs, the **trade press**, music **scores**, etc.—can help identify important landmarks in the history of the practice.

The first intertitles looked like main titles: their bold capital letters take up much of the screen space (which in turn explains their conciseness). They could also present very short sentences summarizing the action. Certain films such as Edison's *The Kleptomaniac* (1905) showed a systematic economy of words, with each intertitle consisting of one word.

Around 1905, whole sentences became more frequent and could introduce a cluster of shots, but short expressions would endure, most notably to provide indications of time and place. When films started lengthening around 1907, a simultaneous increase in the number of shots, intertitles, and words occurred. Longer texts in smaller capitals filled the screen. In order to hierarchize statements within the same intertitle, different sizes of capital letters were used, and the written word itself became a visual element, as in D. W. **Griffith**'s *The Light That Came* (1909).

As the industry grew more organized, the practice of intertitling became conventional. In the USA, in 1909–10, some companies even used ready-made intertitles such as "THE NEXT DAY," "FORGIVEN," or "WEDDING BELLS" for very different films. The first forms of credits also appeared: as early as 1911, characters and actors were introduced in the same intertitle, thus marking the beginnings of the **star system**, and the film's main title often appeared in large capital letters at the top of each intertitle. Whereas 25% of 1907–1909 films preserved today include intertitles, 70% of 1912 films do.

Around 1913, as **multiple-reel films** and features running five reels or more became the norm, the frequency of short intertitles decreased. Capital letters gradually disappeared, as lower case letters and punctuation came into use.

While intertitles could still serve to introduce new narrative segments, they no longer named a key moment in the story that images would illustrate, nor did they designate only one entity (a shot or a scene). Titles and images fused so as to unfold the narrative together. The terms "title" and "sub-title" no longer were used in their literal sense and came to refer to any text, including the characters' dialogue. The case of characters' speech neatly illustrates this process. Between 1910 and 1914, as **acting styles** became more restrained and close shots more frequent, speech moved from discourse reported in capital letters (and always preceding the shot in which words were being spoken) to direct discourse in lower case letters and framed by quotation marks (inserted within the shot where words were being spoken). This "dialogic intertitle" appeared only gradually. Reactions to such experimentation were prompt: while it allowed speech to be adjusted to the moment of utterance, it also raised objections, mainly for disrupting the unity of the shot.

As intertitles became widespread, the trade press debated their usefulness and limits. The main criticisms were that they (1) spoiled suspense by giving in advance a summary of the action, (2) had an adverse impact on the "reality effect," (3) were too frequent or too lengthy, and (4) lacked explicitness and readability. Yet there was consensus on certain points. Intertitles were considered indispensable to understanding a film and made possible a more supple narration, as long as they aroused curiosity without giving away too much information and remained as inconspicuous as possible. They also had to be legible: that is, projected according to the readerly rate of one word per second, with five seconds overall added for the slowest spectators.

The development of intertitles also had other effects, beginning with transforming the environment in which moving pictures were exhibited. Specifically, they conveyed information formerly provided by live speech, whether from a lecturer or from actors behind the screen, as in talker pictures. The disembodied discourse they created allowed audiences to identify both with the point of view of the camera and that of the texts as they were reading them. By eliciting audience participation in the succession and articulation of elements, they maintained a discursive coherence. They addressed each spectator individually, much like the reader of a book, and participated in the construction of a spectator-subject and thus a radical change in the reception of films. Whereas during the early years, spectators would talk to one another and make comments about the films, now they became increasingly silent. Indeed, one of the problems with the advent of sound films was their low volume (only the closest spectators could hear anything); by contrast, intertitles could be read from a distance even in large theaters.

They also made films more acceptable, which proved particularly helpful for those experimenting with new practices. The intertitle's function as anchor (in the Barthesian sense) allowed it to fix the meaning of the image and reassure the audience as to what was being shown. An omniscient scriptural voice was being asserted, similar to that of the all-knowing narrator in novels. It gave characters speech, formulated their intentions, feelings, knowledge, social status, and history, the social relations that bound them together, the causality of events, and spatio-temporal cues. The characters' motivations (not action alone) would henceforth move the narrative forward: the story could unfold as though the diegetic world actually existed.

This omniscient scriptural voice widened the range of possibilities for complex, original narratives. Intertitles made it possible to explain a less familiar or more elaborate narrative and to modulate suspense through the selective delivery of information. As the cinema gained in self-sufficiency, it proved able to tell a story on its own as well as invent its own stories.

Finally, the development of intertitles coincided with a newfound legitimacy for the cinema around 1910—the opening of large theaters, the accompaniment of symphonic orchestras, and the increase in artistic or literary adaptations through such companies as **Film d'Art**, **SCAGL**, and Vitagraph—all of which aimed to attract middle- and upper-class audiences and to affirm cinema's autonomy as an art.

Around 1915, the quality of writing in intertitles gained new emphasis. In *Cabiria* (1914), for instance, Giovanni **Pastrone** asked Gabriele **D'Annunzio** to write the intertitles, as a guarantee of quality, in order to attract a learned audience. In *Intolerance* (1916), Griffith exploited the discursive value of writing with footnotes, citations, moral and political commentaries, etc. This film actually presented the texts in superimposition on different backgrounds for each of the historical periods represented.

After 1916, the usual white lettering on a dark background, complete with a company's logo, increasingly gave way to specific typography accompanied by symbolic backgrounds and emblematic illustrations. This so-called art-title (in the USA) considerably reinforced the symbolic iconicity of films, but it also granted the intertitle a privileged status vis-à-vis the images and risked disrupting a film's reading.

Anita Loos popularized the idea that intertitles could contribute to a film's success. She launched the trend of intertitles ripe with plays on words and witticisms, as in the famous intertitle of *Intolerance* ("When women cease to attract men they often turn to reform as a second choice") and in the films she wrote with John Emerson for Douglas

Figure 60 Thanhouser title card set up. (Courtesy of the Robert S. Birchard Collection.)

Figure 61 Marking for editing or title insertion, Pathé, 1912. (Courtesy of George Eastman House.)

Fairbanks. In the 1920s, the profession of inter-titling flourished. Some Hollywood craftsmen, legend has it, could even rewrite all the intertitles of a film that had failed in order to give it a new lease on life. By contrast, following a purely iconic conception of cinema, the French avant-garde of the 1920s rejected the conventions of intertitling established during the previous decade.

Until 1903, intertitling was mostly artisanal; from 1903 to 1909, it became part of the business of manufacturers. After 1910, as production increasingly became specialized, the task of **screen-writing** could include the writing of intertitles at the end of the production process. Indeed, in 1912, Vitagraph reportedly created the earliest specialized department of intertitle writers. During the projection of dailies during the early 1910s, the director (sometimes with the help of a script) would indicate the order of shots and where to place intertitles. Photograms would then be inserted in the film negative to indicate their placement. These "flash titles" could be photographs of small glass plates bearing a number, a cue, or a few temporary, often handwritten words (it could also be a random photograph). This saved wasting negative film stock and made it easier to produce positive prints for use abroad.

Intertitles generally were produced after the negative had been edited but before positive prints were made. They were traced on pieces of cardboard and filmed separately, so as to allow for adjustments in contrast or legibility. Only at the end of this process would they be inserted into prints by either the producer or distributor, in the language needed.

This practice makes it difficult today to locate intertitles and to make definitive assertions about their history prior to 1915. Preserved negatives include mostly "flash titles" or cues, all of which can be precious elements in their restoration. Yet positive prints are often devoid of intertitles. Either their material has undergone alterations or the boxes containing intertitles, which were supposed to come with the reels, have been lost. They also may have been removed from the prints: re-releases in the past sometimes suppressed or modified the intertitles. Finally, surviving prints of the same film can feature intertitles that differ greatly in number and kind. Thus, although considered until recently as an obsolete, non-cinematic device, and despite being a particularly unstable component of silent films, the intertitle is now an object of research and reconstruction as well as a subject of serious study.

See also: authentication; preservation; spectatorship: issues and debates

Further reading

Bordwell, David, Janet Staiger and Kristin Thompson (1985) *The Classical Hollywood Cinema*, New York: Columbia University Press.

Bowser, Eileen (1990) *The Transformation of Cinema, 1907–1915*, New York: Scribner's.

Cherchi Usai, Paolo (2000) *Silent Cinema: An Introduction*, London: British Film Institute.

Dupré la Tour, Claire (ed.) (2003) *Intertitle and Film. History, Theory, Restoration/Intertitre et film. Histoire, théorie, restauration* (Proceedings of the Cinémathèque Française International Conference, Paris, March 1999), *Iris*, 31–32.

Musser, Charles (1990) *The Emergence of Cinema: The American Screen to 1907*, New York: Scribner's.

Pitassio, Francesco and Leonardo Quaresima (eds.) (1998) *Scrittura e immagine: La didascalia nel cinema muto/Writing and Image: Titles in Silent Cinema*, Udine: Forum.

CLAIRE DUPRÉ LA TOUR

Iran (Persia)

Until 1930 only nonfiction films were made in Iran. Up to then, cinema remained artisanal, driven by a few key entrepreneurs, who engaged in both exhibition and production (in that order) and were supported in an ad hoc manner by the royal court, the local elite, or the era's superpowers (Imperial Britain and Czarist Russia). Later, several commercial exhibitors and cameramen emerged who relied generally on market forces. These pioneers were trained in Europe and exhibited European nonfiction and fiction films. They also filmed and exhibited original *actualités* and performance films. The lion's share of production and exhibition was in Tehran.

The travel diary of Muzzafared-Din Shah Qajar clearly specifies the circumstances of the first Iranian nonfiction film, *Jang-e Golha* [Battle of Flowers]. The date was 18 August 1900; the location was Ostend, Belgium; the occasion was the Shah's review of a "flower parade," during which fifty floats laden with women threw flowers to the Shah who joyously returned them; the cinematographer was Ebrahim Khan Akkasbashi Sani al-Saltaneh, the court photographer, using a **Gaumont** camera. Later in Iran, Sani al-Saltaneh filmed spectacles such as *Shirha-ye Baghvahsh-e Farahabad* [Lions in Farahabad Zoo] (1900) and *Marasem-e Moharram va Qamehzani* [Moharram Processions and Head-Cutting] (1901), which shows an annual Shii Muslim procession that includes men who cut and beat their foreheads with swords. Sani al-Saltaneh also shot performance films (apparently using court comedians and jesters), some of which were comic and colored by

Iranian ethnocentrism, such as *Moshajereh ba Arab* (Argument with an Arab) and *Savari Geraftan-e Kutuleh az Arab* [The Dwarf Rides the Arab]. He showed these, along with French and Russian **news event films**, at the houses of the elite and at the royal palace during celebrations such as weddings and birth and circumcision ceremonies.

Also in 1900, French Roman Catholic missionaries set up in Tabriz a non-commercial public venue, Soleil Cinema, whose films were so popular that patrons were turned away due to a lack of space. It was Ebrahim Khan Sahhafbashi-e Tehrani, an entrepreneur reformist, who first showed moving pictures publicly in the backyard of his antique shop and, in November—December 1904, opened the first commercial cinema, screening films purchased in Europe, and in whose entrance he installed three **Edison Kinetoscopes**. Apparently, he also employed a **lecturer** who explained what was on the screen to audiences unaccustomed to film viewing. This continued an earlier, pre-cinema performance practice called *pardehkhani*, or "reading of the curtain" (the Persian word for movie screen is curtain). However, this pioneering cinema did not last beyond a month, due both to a religious proscription by the leading Muslim cleric Shaikh Fazllolah Nuri, which forbid showing unveiled women on the screen, and to royal displeasure at Terhani's pro-constitutional reform activities.

Ethnic, religious, and national minorities were instrumental in developing cinema, and most of the film pioneers were educated abroad. Mehdi Rusi Khan, who was of a mixed English and Russian background and also was politically conservative, showed **Pathé-Frères** nonfiction films and **comedies** in the Shah's harem, in the homes of the elite and, beginning in 1908, on a regular basis in two commercial theaters in Tehran. For his Naseri Avenue Cinema he hired a pianist and a violin player to provide live music for the films. His Farus Cinema had such modern amenities as an electric generator, electric fans, a restaurant, and a bar. Rusi Khan may have been the first exhibitor to offer a student discount at half price, and he certainly was the first to build a theater chain. Because of his innovations as well as his politics and ethnicity, the Farus Cinema became an arena for political struggle. On the one hand, it was a favorite spot for the right-wing upper class and foreigners, particularly Russian and British diplomats, who afterwards drank and carried on loudly in the bar. On the other, pro-constitution Mojahedin fighters at one point seized the theater at gunpoint to view and discuss films.

Another key pioneer was Khanbabakhan Motazedi, trained at Gaumont in Paris, who set up the first film laboratory. In 1916, he also opened the Korshid (Sun) Cinema, the first commercial venue that accepted women, but it took another decade before they became an integral part of audiences. Significantly, Motazedi was also the cameraman who filmed **newsreels** of Reza Shah Pahlavi's activities. These were the first local newsreels, shown regularly in theaters before imported feature films well into the 1920s.

See also: audiences: surveys and debates; law and the cinema; colonialism: Europe

Further reading

Naficy, Hamid (1996) "Iranian Cinema," in Geoffrey Nowell-Smith (ed.) *The Oxford History of World Cinema*, 672–678, London: Oxford University Press.

Naficy, Hamid (2000) "Self-Othering: A Postcolonial Discourse on Cinematic First Contact," in Fawzia Afzal-Khan and Kalpana Seshadri-Crooks (eds.) *The Pre-Occupation of Post-Colonial Studies*, 292–310, Durham: Duke University Press.

HAMID NAFICY

Ireland

As befits a colonized country, Ireland's experience of cinema during its first twenty years was primarily of other countries' films and of being represented by foreign filmmakers. These representations by French, British, and later American filmmakers began with the **Lumieres**' screening of moving pictures in Dublin on 20 April 1896, exactly two months after a similar screening in London. Indeed, the oldest surviving moving picture images

of Ireland (Belfast and Dublin, September 1897) were made by a Lumiere cameraman, although earlier films were produced. Unsurprisingly, it was British filmmakers as they expanded their markets and subjects (followed by Americans) who mostly filmed Ireland during the cinema's first decade, representing the country as a quaint rural backwater with visually dramatic scenery designed to attract cosmopolitan tourists.

It was this image of predominantly rural Ireland which was central to the activities of Sidney **Olcott** (of Irish-Canadian extraction), Gene **Gauntier**, and the **Kalem** Company when they visited Ireland for the first time in June 1910. Their only fiction film that year, and Ireland's first such film, was the one-reel *The Lad From Old Ireland*, a tale of how an impoverished agricultural laborer travels to New York, makes his fortune, and returns to Ireland with his American wealth to save his sweetheart from eviction. This was the first of more than twenty films Olcott and Gauntier made in Ireland before **World War I**, the later ones either made under the banner of the Gene Gauntier Feature Players or, in 1914, released by **Lubin**. The most controversial subject of these films, Irish history of the revolutionary 1798–1803 period, became the iconic template for American cinema's representations of the Irish prior to the 1916 Rising, the event which not only heralded the final phase of the struggle against British **colonialism**, but changed how Ireland was cinematically represented, leading as it did to a retreat from sensitive historical subjects towards the safer territory of comedy or the experience of Irish migrants in America. 1916 also saw the establishment of the Film Company of Ireland, the most important film production company of the silent period, which went on to produce a range of films not emulated by indigenous Irish film-makers until the 1970s.

Film exhibition remained largely under the control of Irish entrepreneurs until the 1910s, when the market had developed sufficiently for British companies to enter. The first permanent moving picture theater, established in Dublin in 1909, was promoted by writer James Joyce, a resident of Trieste at the time, who convinced local businessmen of the venture with his access to Italian financing. Within six months, however, the premises was acquired by a prominent English exhibition company which quickly expanded its interests in central Dublin, opening the first prestigious cinema in 1910. Due to the depressed economic conditions of Dublin's working classes at the time, perhaps unlike elsewhere, Ireland's early cinema **audience** disproportionately depended on a well-off clientele that could afford such upscale movie-going.

Further reading

Rockett, Kevin (2001) "Representations of Irish History in Fiction Films Made Prior to the 1916 Rising," in Lawrence Geary (ed.) *Rebellion and Remembrance in Modern Ireland*, 214–228, Dublin: Four Courts Press.

Rockett, Kevin, Luke Gibbons, and John Hill (1988) *Cinema and Ireland*, rev. ed., London: Routledge.

KEVIN ROCKETT

Isola, Emile and Vincent

b. 1860/1862; d. 1945/1947

exhibitors, France

The Théâtre Isola, located at 39 boulevard des Capucines in Paris, in front of the Grand Café where **Lumière** had presented the **Cinématographe**, initiated screenings of "living photographs," accompanied by magic tricks, on April 2, 1896. The two owners, who had been born in Algeria, were (like Georges **Méliès**) professional **magicians**. For their screenings they purchased a copy of the latter's "Kinétographe" (which they renamed "Isolatographe") from George William **de Bedts**. In 1896, they purchased another (also renamed the Isolatographe) so as to present screenings in a Berlin theater. In 1897, the Isola brothers bought the Parisiana theater in Paris, thereby establishing their position in the film exhibition business. They also managed the Olympia and the Folies-Bergère cabarets, where films were shown.

LAURENT MANNONI

Itala

Itala was founded in Turin in 1907 as Carlo Rossi & C., but changed its name in 1908, under the management of Carlo Sciamengo and Giovanni **Pastrone**. Thanks to the latter, a former administrator turned producer and filmmaker, the company rapidly expanded and soon became—after **Cines** and **Ambrosio**—the third most important film company of Italian early cinema. Pastrone managed to lure away from **Pathé-Frères** the comedian André **Deed**, whom he considered to be even better than Max **Linder**. Soon Pastrone had a regular troupe formed by comic actors Deed, Ernesto Vaser, and Emile Vardannes and dramatic actors Dante Testa, Alexandre Bernard, Lydia Quaranta, Edouard Davesnes and Italia **Almirante Manzini**. Direction at Itala was not done by Pastrone alone, but often too by Vincenzo Denizot and Romano Borgnetto.

Thanks to Deed's success as the comical character of Cretinetti, Pastrone was able to stage larger productions and invest in **historical films**, which was rewarded by the international success of *La caduta di Troia* [The Fall of Troy] (1911). Whereas *La caduta di Troia* was 600 meters long, Itala's subsequent historical and contemporary films were produced in ever increasing lengths: the drama *La figlia perduta* [The Lost Daughter] (1912) measured 1007 meters; the **crime films**, *Vittoria o morte* [Victory or Death] (1913) and *Tigris* (1913), 1300 meters and more. In 1911, Pastrone also lured Spanish cameraman Segundo de **Chomón** away from Pathé-Frères. Chomón's skill in trick photography and special effects soon became visible in Itala films such as the sensational **melodrama**, *Padre* [Father] (1913). This film also was praised for the dramatic acting of the famous theater actor Ermete **Zacconi**, leading to other vehicles for Zacconi such as *Lo scomparso* [The Dread of Doom] (1913) and *L'Emigrante* [The Emigrant] (1915). Itala also produced non-fiction films on such subjects as the Italian army, natural landscapes, and animal life.

Pastrone's own ambitions culminated in the super-production *Cabiria* (1914). It displayed "grandeur" through gigantic three-dimensional sets, spatially enhanced by long, slow, often arcing tracking shots. It combined mass spectacle and choreography with an intimate love story and thrilling adventures. Pastrone also gave the film grandeur in a literary sense, by releasing it in the unheard length of 18 reels, later reduced to 14. He added prestige by procuring an original score by Ildebrando Pizzetti and Manlio Mazza and intertitles written by Gabriele **D'Annunzio** and even marketing the film as a D'Annunzio creation. *Cabiria* was launched with a massive worldwide **publicity** campaign and was an instant success, although the film's release was delayed in some countries because of the outbreak of **World War I**. *Cabiria* marked the apogee of the historical film within early Italian cinema but foreshadowed the genre's downfall at the same time.

With the rise of the diva during the war, rather than boost Italia Almirante Manzini, the leading actress of *Cabiria*, Pastrone transformed former Cines star, Pina **Menichelli**, into the ultimate femme fatale of the Italian silent screen. He also launched the career of the real discovery of *Cabiria*, the former dockworker Bartolomeo **Pagano**, alias the good-hearted muscleman Maciste, as a **serial** character. In 1919 Itala merged into the Unione Cinematografica Italiana.

See also: camera movement; comic series

Further reading

Alovisio, Silvio (2000) "The 'Pastrone System': Itala Film from the Origins to World War I," *Film History*, 12.3: 250–61.

Bertetto, Paolo and Gianni Rondolino (1998) (eds.) *Cabiria e il suo tempo*, Turin: Museo Nazionale del Cinema/Il Castoro.

IVO BLOM

Italy

For Italy, the cinema began slowly but developed rapidly from 1905 on, culminating in the early 1910s. Between 1896 and 1904, cinema was defined by exhibition, with programs consisting mainly of foreign film titles. The emergence of permanent cinemas, the beginnings of (short) film production, and the expansion of distribution marked the period between 1905 and 1910. Overproduction led to a crisis in 1908–1909 that was overcome by a reorganization of the industry. A new generation of wealthy aristocrats and industrials replaced the pioneers and made film-making a matter of cultural and national prestige as well as commercial entrepreneurship. The rise of the feature film, which culminated in the world-wide success of several historical films, marked the period between 1910 and 1914. During this era, the industry sought to attract new bourgeois audiences, especially through the diva films.

1895–1904: Italy as an exhibition country

The first film showings already announced the rivalry between Turin and Rome as early centers of the new industry. An **Edison Kinetoscope** opened in Turin on 21 April 1895, followed by other Kinetoscopes in cities such as Palermo, Messina, and Bologna. The first **Cinématographe Lumière**, however, was shown in Rome on 12 March 1896, by the French photographer, Henri Le Lieure. Cinématographe shows soon followed in Milan and Naples and in other cities a few months later. On 10 September 10 1896, Lumière operator Pierre Chapuis showed the Cinématographe to an invited audience in Monza, at the Villa Reale, the royal residence, and on 20 November he filmed the king and queen there. Other competing apparatuses also appeared, such as Georges **Demenÿ**'s Chronophotographe, Robert **Paul**'s Theatrograph, and Edison's Vitascope. Even prior to the first Lumière shows in Italy, Filoteo **Alberini** had patented his own Kinetografo Alberini, a combined **camera**, **projector**, and printer, on 11 November 1895. Characteristically, Alberini lacked the industrial structure and finances of the Lumières and had to work as an exhibitor, waiting a decade before starting film production.

The Lumière operators were probably the first Italians who produced their own films. These were *actualités* of sports events, public ceremonies, monuments, panoramas, and street scenes. Early in 1896, Vittorio **Calcina**, who held the Lumière concession for northern Italy, and his assistant Giuseppe Filippi were trained at the Lumière factory in Lyon and obtained the first camera-projector, plus twelve film titles which they projected at the Photographic Circle in Milan on 29 March 1896. Filippi shot new scenes at Milan such as *Bagni di Diana* [Baths of Diana] and *I pompieri* [The Fire Brigade] that were shown on 5 September 1896 at the Teatro Milanese. Francesco Felicetti, a photographer with a shop in Rome who held the Lumière concession for southern Italy, promoted screenings at the café-chantant Olympia in Rome and the Salone Margherita in Naples. Just as in the rest of Europe the Lumière Cinématographe rapidly conquered Italy in 1896.

Next to the Lumière operators were the pioneers Italo Pacchioni and Roberto Troncone. In Milan in 1896, Pacchioni constructed his own camera with his brother Enrico, with which he shot *Arrivo del treno nella stazione di Milano* [Arrival of a Train in the Station of Milan] and fiction films such as *Il finto storpio al castello Sforzesco* [The Fake Cripple at the Sforza Castle]. Troncone, who would become one of the leading men of Neapolitan film production, obtained a camera in 1897 in Paris and projected his first film publicly in 1900 at the Salone Margherita in Naples: *Il ritorno delle carrozze da Montevergine* [The Return of the Carriages from Montevergine].

Although Cinématographe shows continued into the 20th century, the Lumière's moment of glory in Italy was over by the second half of 1897. Two circuits guaranteed some kind of continuity in moving picture exhibition: **vaudeville** theaters and **cafés-concerts** in the major cities and **fairground** shows in northern Italy. Pioneers within these circuits were often operators initially associated with the Cinématographe such as Filippi. In the Italian vaudeville and café-chantant theaters, film was inserted in programs as a variety act. The famous vaudeville artist Leopoldo **Fregoli** played an important role in this difficult period after 1897. He used a Cinématographe, rebaptized the "Fregoligraph," to shoot and project the transformation tricks and comical scenes which he performed all over Europe.

In the northern cities, moving pictures were shown in theaters by touring vaudeville companies as part of their programs and by **itinerant exhibitors** such as Pacchioni and Giuseppe Boaro. The latter continued a long and rich Italian tradition of touring showmen in the 18th and 19th century. They had showed images of the world via popular prints, the 'vedute' of the Mondo Nuovo, magic lantern slides, panoramas, **dioramas**, and stereographic photos and had made sense of these through their commentary. The French films of **Pathé-Frères**, **Gaumont**, and Georges **Méliès** dominated Italian screens throughout the fairground cinema period.

The "golden age" of the fairground cinema occurred when moving picture shows became longer in duration. Both the vaudeville and fairground circuits were international in nature, so that foreign companies and traveling showmen could show their films in Italian theaters. The brothers Kühlmann, for instance, were the leading traveling showmen in northern Italy in the years after 1900. Eventually, the two circuits merged. Whereas numerous touring showmen opened permanent cinemas, some early permanent cinema owners also ran traveling shows that performed in theaters and vaudeville houses. Itinerant exhibitors gradually disappeared from Italy between 1907 and 1912, yet a handful continued into the 1920s and 1930s in sparsely populated regions lacking an infrastructure of permanent cinemas.

1905–1910: Emergence of the cinema industry

Expansion and dispersion

The three fundamental sectors in the film industry were established around 1905: production, distribution and exhibition. Between 1904 and 1907, permanent cinemas began to appear, first in Rome and Naples, then in the northern cities; new openings peaked, in 1907, at 27 in Naples, 33 in Milan, and over 40 in Rome. By 1908, however, Milan had become the capital of Italian cinema exhibition with approximately 80 cinemas in all.

Thanks to low prices, longer films, and better projection, managers attracted a growing working class and lower middle class audience to their cinemas. Local institutions decreed laws to impose hygiene in the halls and to re-educate spectator behavior, but were powerless against a perceived increase in illicit affairs. By attending cinemas, women became ever more present in the public sphere. The expanding market, together with the increasing demand for new films, led to the foundation in Rome and Turin of the first "film factories." At the same time film distribution expanded from a local to a national level, satisfying the increasing number of cinemas all over Italy. The Giolitti government stimulated investments in new affairs, creating a favorable climate for the emergence of an Italian cinema industry.

Characteristic of early Italian film production was its lack of centralization. Although production was most active in Turin and Rome, it generally was so dispersed and localized that, between 1905 and 1910, some 500 production companies were active. The most important were: in Rome, the Alberini & Santoni company (1905) which, in 1906, turned into **Cines**; in Turin, the **Ambrosio** company (1906) founded by Arturo **Ambrosio**, the Carlo Rossi & C. company (1908) which soon became **Itala**, and **Pasquali** e Tempo (1909). Other less important firms appeared in cities such as Genova, Naples, Venice, Pisa, and Milan, notably that of Luca **Comerio**, which became **Milano Films** in 1909. All these companies distributed their short films throughout Italy and even exported abroad.

Literature and art

From 1907 on, a flood of specialized trade journals such as La **Cine-Fono** and La **Vita Cinematografica** started to appear, and totaled some 90 in all by 1914. From 1908 on, regular columns on moving pictures were published in major daily **newspapers**, and writers connected with the *verismo* movement began to sell their works for film adaptation. The industry used their names extensively to gain cultural respectability. This eventually led, in 1914, to the anti-Futurist biweekly *Odiernismo* launching a campaign for cinema literature and promoting the scenario as an autonomous literary work.

Avant-garde futurists also appropriated the new medium. Movement, dynamism and visuality obsessed the Futurists, leading them to discover the cinema as a source of inspiration for poetry, theater, **painting** and **photography**. Its value as an autonomous modern art form—anti-realist, dynamic and visually powerful—was recognized in many Futurist publications and manifestos. Ricciotto **Canudo**, the first film aesthetician and a tireless promoter of cinema, published an important essay, "Il trionfo del cinematografo," as early

as 1908, followed by his influential *Manifesto of the Seventh Art* (1911). In 1910–1912, Arnaldo Ginna and the painter, Bruno Corra, produced synaesthetic abstract films entitled *Musica cromatica* [Chromatic music], experimenting with moving colors inspired by poetry and music. Ginna went on to make the futurist film, *Vita futurista* [Futurist Life] (1916), now considered lost. Yet indirect futurist influences can be traced in mainstream production—for instance, in Bragaglia's war-time dramas, containing sets designed by Enrico Prampolini.

The era of the short film

The kinds of films made by French film companies originally influenced Italian fiction production. Moreover, directors, actors, and technicians were lured away from France to work for the Italian companies. After the crisis of 1908–09, however, Italian directors discovered the benefits of using their own historical traditions and landscapes. Italian film production began to focus on the historical drama as a reconstruction of tableaux and characters from Italy's own past, whether Roman Antiquity, the Renaissance, or the Risorgimento. Filmmakers based their works on 19th century-novels, mainly French and Italian, since they contained well-known and easily comprehensible stories for a general audience. The first international successes of Italian cinema were the Ambrosio historical films, *Gli ultimi giorni di Pompei* [The Last Days of Pompei] (1908) and *Nerone* [Nero] (1909). Indeed, one of the production units that Pathé-Frères set up in various European countries, in 1909, was **Film d'Arte Italiana**, whose principal subjects were historical films produced by actors and directors drawn from the theater.

Next to the historical film, the Italians focused on two other genres: comedy and non-fiction. Itala copied the French format of the **comic series** with recurring recognizable characters, often former acrobats and clowns. In 1909, Itala producer Giovanni **Pastrone** lured away Pathé's star comedian André **Deed** to act and direct in a series called *Cretinetti*, providing the company with commercial and critical success. Other companies soon followed: Cines with Tontolini (Ferdinando

Guillaume), Kri Kri (Raymond **Frau**), and Lea (Lea Giunchi); Ambrosio with Robinet (Marcel **Fabre**), Fricot (Ernesto Vaser), and Gigetta (Gigetta **Morano**). These actors formed a virtual school of film comedy that enabled directors to experiment with film language, special effects, and editing, and with marketing and branding. Actualité films maintained their importance, building on the experience of the Lumière operators and developing with fine results thanks to independent cameramen like Comerio and companies such as Ambrosio, where Roberto **Omegna** and Giovanni **Vitrotti** shot **travelogues** and **scientific films** that sometimes gained international renown.

Between 1909 and 1910, Italy's biggest and best-organized companies (Cines, Film d'arte italiana, Ambrosio, Itala, Pasquali, and Milano) all released a regular weekly schedule of films. They expanded into the most attractive foreign markets in Europe and the USA, through local agencies or even their own subsidiaries. In the USA, where foreign imports were blocked by the **Motion Picture Patents Company**, the obstacle was gradually overcome thanks to such independent distributors as George **Kleine**. This expansion revitalized the Italian companies, allowing them to surpass the limitations of the national market and launch even more ambitious projects in 1911.

1911–1914: the "golden age" of early Italian cinema

The revolution of the **multiple-reel/feature film**

The most significant event for Italian early cinema in 1911–1914 was its contribution to the launching and success of the feature film on the international market: a major revolution in cinema history which provoked a series of changes, transformations and adaptations in all systems and uses in all sectors.

Production companies enlarged and modernized their studios. Distributors introduced a system of exclusive rental rights, with a range of prices tailored to zones of exhibition and to the importance and anticipated success of each film. Feature films caused programs to lengthen, which led to fewer shows; they also required larger auditoriums in order to accommodate more spectators per show. As a consequence, new cinemas containing 1000 to 1500 seats and offering more luxury and

convenience opened in the major cities. In raising their ticket prices, these new **palace cinemas** tended to exclude the lower classes, and their success threatened the viability of older cinemas. As the cinema became increasingly similar to the theater, its audience became primarily the middle classes, which the most fashionable genres could well address.

A new generation of filmmaker-entrepreneurs came from the financial world, the liberal professions, and the aristocracy to partly replace the pioneers of the two preceding generations. Between 1910 and 1912 these newcomers established themselves either within existing structures or founded new ones. Thanks to their network of associations, they could provide the capital necessary to impose their business mentality and ideology onto the film world.

The chief protagonists were baron Alberto Fassini, who bought Cines; count Giuseppe **De Liguoro** at Milano Films (who also became the leading director); lawyer Giovanni Meccheri and baron Baldassarre **Negroni** who founded the Celio Film company in Rome. Several others such as Savoia and **Gloria** sprang up in Turin; Caesar, in Rome, and Napoli in Naples. Their production agenda also was backed in the distribution sector by two major newcomers: the lawyer Giovanni Barattolo, unusually active in opening movie palaces all over Italy, and Gustavo Lombardo, of Neapolitan noble origins and founder of the trade journal *Lux*. Thanks to these men, film production improved overall. Every company initiated an "artistic series" of films. Initiatives to attract intellectuals, journalists, and dramatic authors multiplied. Film was no longer seen merely as a commercial affair, but equally as a sign of prestige and affirmation of cultural superiority. The new generation launched Italian cinema in risky productive enterprises without an assured national market. It focused on monumental and expensive historical reconstructions that encouraged a rapid and appropriate growth in film length. This policy paid off commercially and helped Italian producers to profile themselves on the international market.

The rapid development of the feature film was marked in 1911 by three films: Milano's *L'inferno* [The Inferno], directed by Francesco Bertolini and

Adolfo Padovan in collaboration with De Liguoro; Cines' *La Gerusalemme liberata* [Jerusalem Delivered] directed by Enrico **Guazzoni**; and finally Itala's *La caduta di Troia* [The Fall of Troy] directed by Pastrone and Romano Borgnetto. After their international success, other companies strove to make similar productions. This led, in 1913, to Cines' monumental *Quo vadis?* (2,250 meters), directed by Guazzoni, and, in 1914, to Itala's *Cabiria* (over 4,000 meters), directed by Pastrone. Together with Denmark and France, Italy was the European trendsetter in the establishment of the feature film. On the American market these long Italian films were crucial in making feature films a new factor in programming.

The Italian State now began to recognize cinema's importance, its social function and moral and educational influence. Its principal actions were to institute centralized censorship (more political and ideological than moral), in 1913, and impose a tax, in 1914, on every cinema ticket, thus adding to the numerous taxes already mandated by local authorities. Censorship was encouraged by producers, distributors, and exhibitors who believed an official body would guarantee wide circulation for their ever more expensive products.

The diffusion of the feature film accelerated the process of dispersing and multiplying production activity, shifting the industrial center from Turin to Rome and Naples and giving rise to a myriad of local initiatives. Competition flourished and prevented the consolidation of the few companies equipped with an industrial infrastructure sufficient to produce feature films with any kind of regularity during the second half of the 1910s. This carelessness about industrial organization combined with wild spending had negative effects in the long run and may explain the continual upsurges and declines in the Italian cinema. It had the positive effect, however, of assuring Italian filmmakers the space to experiment in different directions.

Producers, directors, and genres

The emergence of the feature film also had consequences for directors and actors. In order to make their names known for **publicity** purposes, they now had to demonstrate superior qualities. Among those who met the challenge and became the first *auteurs* of Italian cinema were, after Pastrone and De Liguoro, Luigi **Maggi**, Ernesto Maria **Pasquali**, Mario **Caserini**, Baldassarre Negroni, Ugo **Falena**, Gerolamo **Lo Savio**, Enrico Novelli **Vidali**, and Nino **Martoglio**.

These men can be compared to Hollywood producers in that they often supervised other directors such as Guazzoni or Nino **Oxilia**. The "quality" genres they helped to establish were adapted to the new possibilities the feature offered, including adaptations of classic novels and dramatic works from the 19th century. Yet literary and theatrical influence was not limited to content alone. It also affected the language, style, and rhythm of films, as well as the performance of actors and even in some cases—Ermete **Zacconi**, Lyda **Borelli**, Eleonora **Duse**—from where they came. The new conditions created by the feature film led to a devaluation of the genres previously most popular, from farce to nonfiction. Usually of shorter length, they were reduced to a complementary, if still essential, role in the program.

The "quality" genres: the historical film and diva film

The first of these "quality" genres was the historical film. It perfectly matched the artistic ambitions as well as the nationalism of the new generation of

Figure 62 Frame still of Nero singing to Rome burning, in *Quo Vadis?* (Cines, 1913). (Courtesy of Ivo Blom.)

cinema entrepreneurs, who shared the political and colonial aspirations of the Italian government. The gigantic sets, the masses of extras, and the well-structured, ample narratives, were also meant to make ordinary people forget any difficulties of the moment. Evoking the values and glories of the past compensated for the unsatisfactory everyday reality of a relatively young nation afflicted by social upheaval, corruption, and political instability.

Guazzoni was a specialist in the genre. In films subsequent to *Quo vadis?*, he confirmed his talent for elaborate, three-dimensional sets, choreographed mass movements of people, and rich and well-composed images. Guazzoni's films were well received worldwide and contributed to the recognition of Italian cinema. Pastrone's *Cabiria*, a source of inspiration for D. W. **Griffith**'s *Intolerance*, with its enormous three-dimensional sets, accentuated by arcing tracking shots, its action and battle scenes, and its trick photography, would form the apex of the genre—and initiate its decline.

The second of these "quality" genres owed a debt to Gabriele **D'Annunzio**, whose work and lifestyle so inspired Italian cinema that it could be called "D'Annunzian." The exalting and aestheticizing trends launched by D'Annunzio generated a kind of film that, together with the historical film, well suited the new filmmakers. The most characteristic genre of the Italian cinema from 1913 on, this was the salon drama or diva film. Its charm lay above all in the extreme expression of emotion, the body language, the ecstatic, dominant performances of leading actresses, whether "femmes fatales" or "femmes fragiles." Here, melodramatic stories culminating in death and loss, are set against—at least for the average moviegoer—the escapist milieu of the elite and the world of the arts. Stylistically, these films encouraged a tableau-like style that favored mise-en-scène over montage and discontinuity over continuity.

It was within the framework of the diva film that the **star system** developed. Inspired by the success Asta **Nielsen**'s first films, Italian companies began to design films with narratives centered on the physical presence of an actress. The diva film turned actors into stars, recognizable beyond the variety of characters performed. The success of Gloria's *Ma l'amor mio non muore!*

Figure 63 Frame still of Lyda Borelli in *Ma l'amore mio non muore* [Love Everlasting] (Gloria, 1913). (Courtesy of Ivo Blom.)

[Love Everlasting] (1913) made Lyda Borelli the most representative of the first generation of divas. Others included Francesca **Bertini**, whose career as a diva began with *Sangue bleu* [Blue Blood] (1914), and Pina **Menichelli**, the filmic "femme fatale" par excellence. The genre peaked during **World War I**, after which the diva actresses either withdrew from the cinema or pursued careers in other European countries.

The **crime film**, *comedy, and "realist film"*

Although unsuited to the culture of D'Annunzio, some genres maintained their hold on popular audiences. Here, foreign models from the French, German, Danish, and American cinema influenced the Italian adventure film or crime thriller. An archetypal villain in adventure films opposite Bertini, Emilio **Ghione** introduced the character of Za la Mort in Caesar Film's *Nelly la Gigolette* [Nelly the Dancer] (1914). This would eventually lead to a number of Za la Mort **serials**, the Italian answer to the popular French and American crime serials. By contrast, *Cabiria* introduced the character of the good-humored strongman Maciste (Bartolomeo **Pagano**), who then starred in a series of adventure films, sometimes released as serials. Also quite distant from the decadent atmosphere of D'Annunzio were the delightfully fresh comedies with uncomplicated actors and actresses such as Camillo **De Riso**, Eleuterio **Rodolfi**, Leda **Gys**, and Morano.

Realist films remained marginal in Italy, but some excellent results were achieved from 1911 on. This genre was tied to local and regional culture and mores, often Sicilian and Neapolitan, and depended on location shooting outside of the studios. Two significant works were Morgana's *Sperduti nel buio* [Lost in Darkness] (1914), directed by Nino Martoglio from a play by Roberto Bracco (who also wrote the script), still acclaimed well into the 1940s; and Caesar's *Assunta Spina* (1915) starring Bertini and Gustavo **Serena**, who also directed. Although based on a play by Salvatore di Giacomo, *Assunta Spina* was shot in and around Naples and displayed a rather restrained acting by the otherwise often eccentric Bertini. In the late 1910s, this regionalist, realist genre would lead to modest but important Neapolitan productions by such companies as **Dora Film** (with director Elvira **Notari**) and Lombardo Film (with Gys).

Nonfiction: **travelogues** *or scenics*

The extensive imports of French nonfiction films into Italy and reciprocal export of Italian nonfiction films mutually influenced both cinemas. Cines or Ambrosio travelogues, consequently, can look stylistically much like those of Gaumont or Pathé-Frères, in their use of lateral pans, for instance, or their use of natural sources for framing, **lighting** and movement: natural contours, silhouettes at sunsets, and lateral or diagonal movements of water currents. Similarly, split-screen effects and circular or semicircular masks enhanced picturesque, **postcard**-like effects, as did the intensive use of **color** in tinting, toning, and stenciling.

Famous cities and antique locations were the subject of Italian nonfiction films, just as were those of foreign companies that filmed in Italy, but not exclusively. What is most remarkable in Italian non fiction, however, is the high number of films of less familiar locations and extant titles without any indication of location or without identifiable subjects, thus only hinting at a rather vague atmosphere, a romantic and picturesque sensation of nature, or simply a feeling of nostalgia.

See also: audiences; distribution: Europe.

Further reading

Bernardini, Aldo (1980–1982), *Cinema muto italiano I–III*, Rome/Bari: Laterza.

Bernardini, Aldo (1999) "L'epopea del cinema ambulante," in Gian Piero Brunetta (ed.) *Storia del cinema mondiale. I. L'Europa. I. Miti, luoghi, divi*, 109–146, Turin: Einaudi.

Bernardini, Aldo (2002) *Cinema muto italiano: I film "dal vero," 1895–1914*, Gemona: La Cineteca de Friuli.

Bertellini, Giorgio (ed.) (2000) *Film History*, 12.3—special issued devoted to early Italian cinema.

Blom, Ivo (2001) "Travelogues italiani: un genere da riscoprire," in Michele Canosa (ed.) *A Nuova Luce. Cinema muto italiano I/ Italian Silent Cinema I*, 63–74, Bologna: Clueb.

Brunetta, Gian Piero (1993 [1979]) *Storia del cinema italiano. Il cinema muto 1895–1929*, Rome: Editori Riuniti.

Brunetta, Gian Piero (1997) *Il viaggio dell'icononauta. Dalla camera oscura di Leonardo alla luce dei Lumière*, Venice: Marsilio.

Nowell-Smith, Geoffrey (1996) *The Companion to Italian Cinema*, London: British Film Institute.

IVO BLOM

itinerant exhibitors

Itinerant exhibition was one of the most common methods of film distribution and screening in the pre-**World War I** period. Since exhibitors generally owned their own films until approximately 1903 (at least in the USA, when film exchanges emerged), they faced two basic choices. Those that stayed in one place had to find ways to change their films with considerable frequency. Relatively large companies such as **American Mutoscope and Biograph**, American **Vitagraph**, or R. W. **Paul** had multiple exhibition units, so they could rotate films among the fixed venues (e.g., **vaudeville** houses) they served. Others, typically smaller entrepreneurs, showed the same repertoire of films for a much longer period of time by traveling from town to town. They built on a tradition of traveling shows that preceded the cinema. In many parts of Europe, showmen toured the **fairs/fairgrounds**, filling long-standing dates as they offered a variety of live entertainments. Many—from Randall **Williams** or Annie **Holland** to Jean **Desmet** or Frédéric **Krüger**—added films to their repertoire and prospered. Although circuses such as Ringling Brothers showed films on their midways and small-time showmen screened films at carnivals and country fairs in the USA, this tradition was far less vital there.

In the USA, traveling exhibitors were the principal purveyors of films in towns and small cities where there were no vaudeville houses. Many showed films in **churches** and opera houses (often for only one evening but, if the town was big enough, for two or three days). Lyman H. **Howe** had toured the northeast giving **phonograph** concerts in the early 1890s and added films to his repertoire by the end of 1896. Soon he dropped the phonograph, and his program consisted primarily of films. Some of the more successful traveling showmen in North America such as John Dibble, D. W. **Robertson**, and Archie L. **Shepard** developed circuits that they would cover two or more times during the course of a theatrical season: Howe, for example, established a pattern of fall and spring visits. Before the onset of **nickelodeons** in 1905–1906, these exhibitors generally showed the same kinds of films as vaudeville houses.

Some of the most popular traveling shows in the USA in the 1890s toured with **boxing films**. At least ten companies were on the road showing Veriscope films of *The Corbett–Fitzsimmons Fight* (1897). When the Veriscope's commercial potential was exhausted, they closed and the personnel looked for new work. Before the introduction of the three-blade shutter for **projectors** in 1903, traveling exhibition was logistically challenging and often of limited profitability. If showmen had the "right" program—Spanish-American War or Boer War films or McKinley funeral subjects—they could make good money. A run of bad luck could leave even an experienced exhibitor such as Edwin Hadley broke—and forced to hire himself out as a **projectionist**. The years between 1903 and 1906 were the boom years for traveling exhibition in the USA. Lower film costs, improved projection, and the availability of longer story films made success far easier to achieve. Numerous single-unit companies toured the country playing small

town opera houses, churches, schoolrooms, and vacant storefronts. Established showmen put multiple units in the field: Howe had three by the fall of 1904; Robertson had five during the 1905–1906 season. Vitagraph had several units on the road in 1904–1905, returning to cities on a frequent basis. Increased patronage also meant increased competition, and in some towns and circuits exhibitors developed intense rivalries.

Many traveling exhibitors in Europe became involved in production. Welsh showman William **Haggar** shot many films, including such early story films such as *A Desperate Poaching Affray* (1903). In northern England, **Mitchell and Kenyon** catered to numerous traveling showmen from the late 1890s into the early 1910s, providing them with local *actualités* for a fee. In the USA, **Edison**'s patents claims made filmmaking far riskier, and there was less small-time production. Nonetheless, to boost patronage, some showmen arranged to take local views, including such scenes as students leaving the local high school, fire runs, and local officials. Howe took films of special news events and his filmmaking efforts became more ambitious after 1911–1912, once legal risks receded. Huntley Entertainers, operating in the Wisconsin area, shot scenes in various towns that they could then edit into a longer fiction films, ensuring larger patronage on their circuit.

The proliferation of specialized motion picture theaters after 1906 in the USA and shortly thereafter in most of Europe reconfigured the field. Traveling exhibitors could not compete with movie houses even though they charged roughly the same amount (or even less) in terms of units of screen time. Theaters running on a daily basis were able to show films first and were more convenient. In the USA and elsewhere, many traveling showmen settled down and opened storefront theaters, including Shepard, Thomas L. **Tally**, and George Green (in Scotland). Others, such as William **Swanson** and William **Steiner** opened film exchanges. In general, exhibitors who remained on the road had to offer films that differed from nickelodeon fare. Howe and many other exhibitors featured "talking pictures" in the 1907–1909 period: for each touring company, they hired a few actors to perform from behind the screen, adlibbing sync dialogue for screen characters. With a rich assortment of **sound effects**, these showmen provided a more elaborate show than the nickelodeons. As movie theaters focused more and more on fiction films, Howe emphasized **travelogues**, military subjects, and news events, enlivened with early **animation** films and sanitized **comedies** that middle-class parents found acceptable for viewing by children. Companies seeking to exploit new, expensive technology often relied on traveling shows. Kinemacolor used this method to introduce its **color** films, while the Edison **Kinetophone** Company employed sixteen road-show units to exhibit mechanically synchronized motion pictures in the summer of 1913. Early **multiple-reel/feature films** also were often shown by traveling showmen who acquired the exclusive rights for a particular territory.

Traveling exhibitors survived in the USA, Europe, and elsewhere by playing small villages and rural areas that could not support regular theaters. After 1911–1912, some showmen began to travel using automobiles, which opened up new territory, swelling their ranks. Automobiles could also provide a reliable source of power to run projectors and lights. Frank H. Thompson, for instance, started Thompson Pictures in Wisconsin in 1911 and thrived into the 1920s. Traveling

Figure 64 American Entertainment Co. poster, c. 1900.

exhibitors thus provided a means to present moving pictures under a wide range of circumstances when regularized, permanent venues for these activities had not been established.

Further reading

Rossel, Deac (2000) "A slippery job: Travelling exhibitors in early cinema," in Simon Popple and Vanessa Toulmin (eds.) *Visual Delights: Essays on the Popular and Projected Image in the 19th Century*, 50–60, Trowbridge: Flicks Books.

Swartz, Mark E. (1985) "An Overview of Cinema on the Fairgrounds," *Film Reader*, 6: 65–77.

CHARLES MUSSER

Ivens, Cees A. P.

b. 1870; d. 1941

photographer, Netherlands

Father of the Dutch documentary filmmaker Joris Ivens, Cees Ivens was an entrepreneur in photographic devices. After he took over the **photography** business from his father in Nijmegen in 1894, he opened C.A.P.I. stores in Groningen, Amsterdam, and The Hague. Always interested in new technologies, he wrote about the **Edison Kinetoscope**, the **Cinématographe Lumiére**, and other **cameras** and **projectors** in the local Nijmegen newspaper up to 1898. Thereafter, he regularly showed moving picture experiments for the members of a club of amateur photographers. In 1912, he produced and—together with the rest of the Ivens family—participated in Joris Ivens' first film, *De wigwam* [The Wigwam], a **western** involving the rescue of whites captured by Indians.

ANSJE VAN BEUSEKOM

J

Jacobini, Maria

b. 1892; d. ?

actor, Italy

Born to an upper-middle-class family in Rome, Jacobini began her acting career with **Savoia**. Despite her family's opposition, Maria as well as her sister Diomira, who also became a lesser-known actress, prevailed. In her early films, Jacobini played dangerous and alluring vamps, as in *Zingara* [Gipsy] (1912). By 1916, however, it was clear that she excelled in somewhat melancholic, delicate roles that demanded a sober, understated acting style. Hence the success of *Come Le Foglie* (1916) directed by Gennaro Righelli—who later became her husband—and *Addio Giovinezza* (1918) directed by Augusto Genina, in commemoration of Nino **Oxilia**. After working in Italy, Germany, and France during the 1920s, Jacobini's career ended with the advent of sound. From 1937 on, she taught acting at the Centro Sperimentale di Cinematografia; among her pupils was Alida Valli.

ANGELA DALLE VACCHE

Janssen, Pierre-Jules-César

b. 1824; d. 1907

astronomer, France

Venus passes between the Sun and the Earth only twice in a century. In 1849, Hervé Faye had suggested that **photography** could be used to record this phenomenon and so determine, scientifically, the parallax of the Sun and its distance to the Earth. Janssen advanced this idea by exploiting the principle of Plateau's stroboscopic disc as well as the photography of movement advocated before him by Ducos du Hauron, Du Mont, Cook and Bonelli. Thus, in 1873, he devised his "photographic gun": thanks to a rotating obdurator, the machine was able to shoot 48 successive images in about 72 seconds on a mobile daguerreotype disc 7.28 inches in diameter. The "gun" was to influence Etienne-Jules **Marey** who, in turn, developed a more sophisticated "photographic gun" in order to record movement in 1882.

LAURENT MANNONI

Japan

In film histories, Japan has garnered attention as a vibrant film-producing nation that created works different from those of America and Europe and retained aspects of early cinema longer than others.

When the **Edison Kinetoscope** arrived in Japan in November 1896 and the **Cinématographe Lumière** and Vitascope in early 1897, the technology was foreign, but such pre-cinematic entertainments as the **magic lantern** were so developed that some commentators failed to see the invention's novelty. Moving pictures were thus inserted into such existing practices as sideshow entertainment. The Japanese who first imported the technology, businessmen such as Inabata Katsutaro and Araki Kazuichi, eventually left commercial exploitation to experienced showmen like **Yokota Einosuke** and **Komada Koyo**. In their hands, films toured the country in traveling shows centered as much around the *benshi*'s linguistic flourishes as the Western scientific marvel of moving images.

The first films shot in Japan were by **Lumière** cameramen such as François Girel and Gabriel **Veyre** in 1897 and 1898. In 1897, the **Konishi** Photographic Store imported a **Gaumont** camera and one of its assistants, Asano Shiro, became the first to use it, creating picturesque *actualités* of Tokyo streets and dancing geisha. Shibata Tsunekichi began filming staged performances in works such as *Inazuma goto* [Lightning Burglar] (1899), a sensational recreation of a real thief's exploits. His *Momijigari* [Viewing Scarlet Maple Leaves] (1899) recorded the performance of two famous Kabuki actors and thus doubled as both a document and a theatrical event. Such multivalency left definition of these works up to the space of exhibition, especially to the words of the *benshi*, some of whom apparently presented *Inazuma goto* as an *actualité*. Exhibition itself could become a mimetic event when Tsuchiya Tsunekichi, for instance, presented sumo wrestling films in 1900 with all the pageantry of the real thing.

There were initially few domestically produced films—foreign product (first from France and then the USA) would continue to dominate the industry until the mid-1920s. Supply was unreliable and **itinerant exhibitors** lived a mercurial life of playing in tents and rented halls. **Yoshizawa Shoten**, one of the initial exhibitors of the Cinématographe, was the most stable of the companies, regularly importing films, occasionally producing its own, and ultimately opening Japan's first permanent moving picture theater, the Denki-kan, in Tokyo's entertainment district of Asakusa in 1903. That the second theater did not appear until 1907 is testimony to the fact that the industry was not yet stable and capitalized enough to regularly supply multiple theaters.

The Russo-Japanese War in 1904–1905 produced the industry's first economic boom. Almost any war film, including even foreign pictures of other wars and "faked" battle scenes, could attract audiences to patriotic shows if articulated as movies from the front. Japanese producers competed to send cameramen to the battleground, but it was the shortage of authentic footage, and the resulting usage of **re-enactments**, that raised suspicions in Japanese audiences and led, in the spheres of both production and reception, to discourses distinguishing fiction and non-fiction, the staged and the actual.

The popularity of war films greatly expanded the industry and its audience base. Theater construction boomed in 1908 as movie houses began to push out older **vaudeville** and sideshow entertainments. Police restrictions greatly limited the number of theaters—which had relatively large capacities as a result—yet their elaborate Western-style facades symbolized the cinema's central role in the spectacular world of such urban playgrounds as Asakusa or Osaka's Sennichimae. In 1910, Yoshizawa even opened an **amusement park** entitled Luna Park which included cinematic rides resembling **Hale's Tours**.

Regularization of production helped enable this theatrical expansion. Yoshizawa opened Japan's first studio in Tokyo in January 1908, **M. Pathé** followed with another in 1909, and **Yokota Shokai** built one in Kyoto in 1910. The latter two had limited facilities, but, with contract players starting to replace temporary hires, they were ultimately producing at least two films a month. Since former traveling exhibitors built these studios to feed their own theaters, the industry was vertically integrated from early on, albeit with exhibition forces in control. Often only one print of a film was made, then released at the company's flagship house, and passed down the hierarchy of theaters either directly owned by the company or through block-booking contracts. This arrangement would remain intact until the early 1920s, with some elements lasting even longer.

It was in this period that the cinematic practices that would dominate the industry until the late 1910s were established. The success from 1909 of Yokota's films starring **Onoe Matsunosuke** and filmed by **Makino Shozo** helped make such excerpts from Kabuki plays, called *kyuha* or old school, a theatrical mainstay. Pictures with modern settings, termed *shinpa* or new school, were also often based on theatrical productions, although it was in this genre that the influences of foreign films, especially **Pathé-Frères comedies** and **chase films**, was felt. For instance, Chiba Yoshizo's films for Yoshizawa such as *Ono ga tsumi* [One's Sin] (1908) featured location shooting and variable camera distance. Theatrical codes dominated, however, as framing imitated the proscenium arch and male *onnagata* played female parts. Stories were portions of longer plots that audiences already knew, so narratives in these mostly one-reel films neither were self-contained nor, with few intertitles or visual means of narration, generated exclusively through the text. Although audiences usually watched Japanese and foreign films together in the same program, the latter had initially only limited influence on the former.

With spectators calling out the names of their favorite *benshi* and actors, the attraction of cinema was less in the film's world than in the exhibition space. After the success, in 1908, of exhibiting *Soga kyodai kariba no akebono* [Dawn at the Soga Brother's Hunting Grounds] with dialogue accompaniment, *kowairo* (voice imitation) narration would be the *benshi*'s choice for narrating Japanese films until the early 1920s. If this offered the spectacle of imitated theater for less than the cost of the legitimate stage, films were also used, from around 1909, as an attraction in theatrical plays called *rensageki* (chain drama) in which scenes on film alternated with those on stage. This form, which would hit its peak in the mid-1910s, epitomized cinema's articulation as a unique, live performance in a local space.

In 1910, film production topped 300 as such new players as **Fukuhodo** entered the field, program lengths increased, and runs at theaters were shortened. The popularity of the movies was also prompting fears among social leaders: in 1912, one major newspaper, the *Asahi*, declared that the cinema was all harm and no benefit. Such "cinemaphobia" would plague the medium for much of its early years in Japan. Film companies attempted to present a respectable image: Yoshizawa founded the high-class film magazine *Katsudo shashinkai* [Moving Picture World] in 1909, and M. Pathé's **Umeya Shokichi**, courting politicians, managed to attach his cameraman to Japan's first expedition to the South Pole in 1910. The enormous popularity of **Éclair**'s *Zigomar* (released in late 1911), however, sparked fears of movie-led criminality.

With the *Asahi* fanning the flames, Tokyo police banned the film and its Japanese imitators in October 1912.

The decision of Yoshizawa, Yokota, M. Pathe, and Fukuhodo to emulate the **Motion Picture Patents Company** and form in late 1912 a monopoly, **Nikkatsu**, headed by respectable social figures, was part of their effort to legitimize the business. Yet the dubiousness of their financing soon scared the elites away. Nikkatsu would dominate production in the 1910s with studios in Kyoto and Tokyo's Mukojima, but refugees from the merger rallied at **Komatsu Shokai**, Toyo Shokai, M. Kashii, and eventually **Tenkatsu**, breaking the monopoly.

By 1914, Nikkatsu was producing four three- to four-reel films at each of its studios a month, including such hits as *Kachusha* [Katusha] (1914), starring the *onnagata* **Tachibana Teijiro**. Yet longer and lesser-known stories were being supported not so much by complex visual techniques but by the *benshi*. This and other factors sparked intellectual fans such as **Kaeriyama Norimasa** to launch criticism of Japanese films in journals such as *Kinema Record* and *Katsudo no Sekai* (Movie World). Taking their examples from foreign cinema, especially American films, which came into prominence in Japan with the start of **World War I**, these reformers called for the elimination of such theatrical conventions as the *onnagata*, inclusion of **intertitles** and visual techniques like the close-up, and increased stress on **screenwriting**. Their Pure Film Movement proposed a modern industry centered on production not exhibition and a definition of cinema that excluded such mixed texts as *rensageki*. Dreaming of exporting Japanese films, they envisioned a cinema that could speak for itself without a *benshi*, a text that was a self-contained, diegetic world. Their aspirations expressed both hopes about **modernity** and elite fears about the culture of Japanese cinema's low-class audience. That this embodied a cultural power struggle over meaning production and **spectatorship** is evident in the fact that police crackdowns on cinema had some of the same targets. Tokyo's landmark film regulations of 1917 finally shifted censorship from local precincts to city hall, but they also essentially eliminated *rensageki*, licensed *benshi*, enabled police surveillance of the audience, and in general suppressed the live aspects of cinematic entertainment that might modify a text after censorship. The determination of meaning would begin to shift from exhibition to production.

Tenkatsu gave Kaeriyama the opportunity to put his ideals into practice, starting with *Sei no kagayaki* [A Glow of Life] (released 1919), but cinematic form was already changing in 1917–1918, prompted by the influence of foreign films, pressure from authorities, and wartime prosperity. At Mukojima, **Tanaka Eizo** helped introduce the naturalism of *shingeki* (new drama) theater into *shinpa*, and **Inoue Masao** at Kobayashi Shokai and **Edamasa Yoshiro** at Tenkatsu experimented with cinematic form. Tenkatsu's *kyuha* films starring **Sawamura Shirogoro** and even those of Onoe Matsunosuke were showing the influence of foreign **serials** and **trick films**.

By the early 1920s, especially after the great quake of 1923 that leveled the Tokyo industry, Japanese cinema had changed considerably. With two studios founded in 1920, Shochiku and Taikatsu, adding wind to reform's sails, female actors eventually replaced *onnagata*, intertitles and scriptwriting became central, modernized *jidaigeki* superseded *kyuha*, and many elements of **classical Hollywood cinema** were adopted. Even *kowairo* for domestic cinema was supplanted by the unobtrusive narration epitomized by foreign film *benshi* like **Tokugawa Musei**. Yet the Pure Film Movement was not wholly victorious. *Benshi*, for instance, would remain popular until sound arrived in the mid-1930s, but their attraction faded in light of a **star system** for actors.

Debates over how much of early cinema remained in Japanese films of the 1920s and 1930s continue, although they can be clouded by Western desires for alternatives to Hollywood or by Japanese aspirations for national uniqueness. What is certain is that Japanese film in its first four decades was a divided, if not hybrid cinema, as various forces in society used cinema to battle over and negotiate with modernity, Westernization, social class and power, and the construction of the nation. That "mixture" itself became the object of conflict—a bane to some, a pleasure to others—underlines how the specificity of Japanese early cinema must be understood not by contrasting

Figure 65 Frame still from *Momijigari* [Viewing Scarlet Maple Leaves] (1899). (Courtesy of the Kawakita Memorial Film Institute.)

a pure Japan with the West, but by locating it in a complex of differences inside and outside Japan.

See also: law and the cinema; lecturers

Further reading

Bernardi, Joanne (2001) *Writing in Light: The Silent Scenario and the Japanese Pure Film Movement*, Detroit: Wayne State University Press.

Burch, Noël (1979) *To the Distant Observer: Form and Meaning in the Japanese Cinema*, Berkeley: University of California Press.

Gerow, A. (2000) "One Print in the Age of Mechanical Reproduction," *Screening the Past*, 11: http://www.latrobe.edu.au/screeningthepast/

Hase M. (1998) "The Origins of Censorship: Police and Motion Pictures in the Taisho Period," *Review of Japanese Culture and Society*, 10: 14–23.

Komatsu, H. (1992) "Some Characteristics of Japanese Cinema Before World War I," in A. Noletti, Jr. and D. Desser (eds.) *Reframing Japanese Cinema*, 229–258, Bloomington: Indiana University Press.

Tanaka Junichiro (1975–1976) *Nihon eiga hattatsushi*, 5 vols., Tokyo: Chuo Koron.

AARON GEROW

Jasset, Victorin-Hippolyte

b. 1862, Saint-Joseph (Fumay), France;
d. 1913, Paris, France

filmmaker, France

Although relatively unknown, Jasset is one of the finest French filmmakers from the 1907–1914 period, along with Louis **Feuillade** and Léonce **Perret**. Nothing is known of his childhood, except that his parents were innkeepers. After studying sculpture in Paris with Etienne-Jules Dalou, he designed theatrical costumes and decors. His reputation was made in 1900, when he directed *Vercingétorix*, an epic-scaled pantomime, for the opening of the Hippodrome. There he met stage manager Georges **Hatot**, with whom he would later co-direct a number of films, but it is now impossible to know who did what in their production.

From 1905 to 1910, he and Hatot worked for a variety of film companies: **Gaumont**, **Eclipse**, **Éclair**, Editions du film négatif, **Raleigh & Robert**, and possibly **Pathé-Frères**, Le Lion, and Le Soleil. He definitely worked for Gaumont in 1906, and has since been erroneously credited as the author of several Alice **Guy** films, including her masterpiece, *La Vie du Christ* [The Life of Christ] (1906). Although he and Hatot worked for Eclipse about the same time, in 1907 Jasset was hired by Éclair, where he got the idea for a series of films centered around one main character, the detective *Nick Carter* (1908), based on an American dime novel. It was a great success and more series followed: the **western** *Riffle Bill* (1908–1909), *Morgan le pirate* (1909), *Meskal le contrebandier* [Meskal the Smuggler] (1909), and *Docteur Phantom* (1909) for Raleigh & Robert.

Separating from Hatot in 1910, Jasset became artistic director for the Éclair studios in Epiney, where he made **films d'art** such as *Hérodiade* (1910), based on the Gustave Flaubert novel. In 1911, he went back to making a crime series, but this time with the novelty of a **multiple-reel film** depicting Léon Sazie's evil genius *Zigomar* (1911). The film was a huge international success, inspiring two encores, *Zigomar contre Nick Carter* (1912) and *Zigomar, le peu d'anguille* [Zigomar the Eel-Skin] (1913). In 1911, he published a major article in several issues of **Ciné-Journal**, perhaps the first text

on the history of film style. He also worked in other genres, directing a Zola adaptation, *Au pays des ténèbres* [The Land of Darkness] (1912), a realist melodrama, *Rédemption* (1912), and a science fantasy, Gaston Leroux's *Balaoo* (1912). His last film proposed yet another innovation: the hero of *Protéa* (1913) is a female spy, an acrobatic Mata-Hari, played by his favorite actress, Josette **Andriot**. This final masterpiece reflects Jasset's popular style: rhythmic action, fantastic realism, rich visuals, an anarchistic philosophy, a disdain for psychology, and an attention to **lighting** that earned him the nickname "the Rembrandt of the cinema."

A refined dandy and the author of more than 100 films, many difficult to credit with certitude and most lost today, Jasset died suddenly in June 1913 after a medical operation.

See also: crime films; melodrama, sensational

Further reading

Abel, Richard (1994) *The Ciné Goes to Town: French Cinema, 1896–1914*, Berkeley: University of California Press.
Deslandes, Jacques (1975) "Victorin-Hippolyte Jasset," *L'Avant-Scène Cinéma*, 163: 241–296.

JEAN-PIERRE SIROIS-TRAHAN

Jeffs, Waller (Osmund)

b. 1861; d. 1941

exhibitor, Great Britain

Waller Jeffs was an **itinerant exhibitor** in the early 1900s who worked primarily as an agent for the first British touring moving picture companies, including A. D. **Thomas**, Ralph **Pringle**, and Sydney Carter of New Century Pictures. In 1901, Jeffs established the Curzon Hall in Birmingham, one of the earliest continuous venues for showing moving pictures, and commissioned **Mitchell and Kenyon** to shoot local scenes that could be shown the same evening of their filming. Throughout the 1900s, he presented his travelling shows as Waller Jeffs Pictures; a farewell tour in 1912 was done in association with Alfred **West** of *Our Navy* fame.

One of the founder members of the Cinema Veterans' Association, Jeffs served as President in 1932–1933.

VANESSA TOULMIN

Jenkins, C. Francis

b. 1867; d. 1934

inventor, USA

Inspired by figures like Thomas **Edison** and Cyrus McCormick to become a professional inventor, Jenkins began working on moving pictures in 1891 and, with Thomas **Armat**, produced a **projector** for **Kinetoscope** films that was demonstrated publicly in September 1895. Bitter over Armat's sale of their **Phantoscope** apparatus to **Raff & Gammon**, he turned to work on television and was selling home receivers for his system by 1931. He was a founder of the Society of Motion Picture Engineers (now SMPTE), received the medal of the Franklin Institute, and held over 400 patents.

DEAC ROSSELL

Johnson and Gibson

Chemists Millard Johnson and W. A. Gibson began producing **news event** and **industrial films** from 1902, establishing facilities for developing and printing film at their headquarters in the Melbourne suburb of St. Kilda (Australia) and running an exhibition service that rented out **projectors** with moving picture programs. The outstanding success of *Living London* (1904), which they distributed in association with theatrical entrepreneurs, J. & N. Tait, encouraged them to embark on producing Australia's longest fictional narrative film to that date, *The Story of the Kelly Gang* (1906). In March 1911, they and the Taits formed Amalgamated Films, later merged into **Australasian Films**.

INA BERTRAND

Johnson, Arthur

b. 1876; d. 17 January 1916

actor, USA

A tall, dark and handsome stage actor whom D. W. **Griffith** enlisted for the first film he directed at **Biograph**, *The Adventures of Dollie* (1908). Johnson continued with Biograph as a romantic leading man until the spring of 1910, when he joined the newly-formed **Reliance** company, which he soon left for **Lubin**. There he was teamed with the former Biograph actress, Florence **Lawrence**, and after she left Lubin in 1912, with Lottie Briscoe. He was among the first actors to be recognized by the **trade press** as having **star** power.

EILEEN BOWSER

Johnson, Jack

b. 1878; d. 1946

boxer, celebrity, USA

As the first black heavyweight boxing champion (1908–1915), John Arthur Johnson achieved unprecedented celebrity and power for an African American. Motion picture coverage of his six title bouts and other screen appearances contributed to his notoriety. Although censored by authorities, films of Johnson's victories drew large audiences worldwide. African-American theaters in the USA often made the screenings into celebratory events, for Johnson's **star** presence offered a rare counter-stereotype to the prevalent racist imagery.

Motion pictures of Johnson defeating "white hopes" appeared almost annually. In 1908, **Gaumont** filmed him taking the title from Tommy Burns in Australia. The **Motion Picture Patents Company** distributed **Kalem**'s *Johnson–Ketchel Fight* (1909) and invested $100,000 in **Vitagraph**'s *Johnson–Jeffries Fight* (1910). The latter elicited more public commentary than any single film prior to D. W. **Griffith**'s *The Birth of a Nation* (1915) and was censored in many locales. In fact, the film motivated a 1912 ban on the distribution of all fight films in the USA.

A flamboyant, photogenic, brash figure, Johnson was prosecuted for his relations with white women, forcing him into exile. Yet he continued to fight in remote locations, where independent producers filmed his bouts versus Flynn (New Mexico, 1912), Moran (Paris, 1914) and Willard (Havana, 1915).

See also: black cinema, USA; boxing films; law and the cinema

DAN STREIBLE

Johnson, Noble M.

b. 1881; d. 1978

actor, filmmaker, USA

Son of a Colorado racehorse trainer, Johnson made his screen debut in **Lubin**'s *The Eagle's Nest* (1909). During the 1910s, he appeared in numerous **Universal westerns**. In 1916, Johnson (an African-American) co-founded the Lincoln Motion Picture Company, a pioneering **black cinema** enterprise. Though the handsome and imposing Johnson starred as a black hero in Lincoln productions such as *Realization of a Negro's Ambition* (1916), he also played various racial roles in Hollywood films (Native Americans, Mexicans, Arabs, whites) through the 1950s. His brother, George P. Johnson, maintained an extensive black film history collection.

JACQUELINE STEWART

Joly, Henri Joseph

b. 1866; d. 1945

inventor, manufacturer, France

In May 1895, Charles **Pathé** started selling counterfeit **Edison Kinetoscopes** made by R. W. **Paul**. In order to renew the choice of moving pictures then available, Joly proposed to him to produce new 35 mm films. On August 25, 1895, Joly registered a patent for a reversible camera operating with 35 mm perforated film. The first films,

including *Le Bain d'une mondaine* [The Bath of a Society Lady] were shot in September 1895. After Pathé suddenly broke their relation early in 1896, Joly became an associate of Ernest Normandin. Their "Cinématographe Joly-Normandin" was being used at the Bazar de la Charité during the disastrous fire of May 4, 1897, after which the machine was rebaptized "Royal Biograph." Later Joly sold his patents to Georges **Mendel** and other manufacturers. A new patent bearing his name (dated April 13, 1905) described a revolutionary process that made it possible to record sounds on film thanks to a mirror reflecting the vibrations of the membrane of a **phonograph**. In October 1906, Joly founded **Lux**, a company he was forced to leave two years later. In the early 1920s, he was still registering patents, but ended his life destitute.

Further reading

Mannoni, Laurent (December 1996) "Repères biographiques sur Henri Joly, l'initiateur technique de Charles Pathé," *1895*, 21: 16–34.

LAURENT MANNONI

Jones, Aaron J.

b. 1876?; d. 1944

exhibitor, USA

Jones entered the film business in Chicago by running **penny arcades**, some of which he began turning into downtown **nickelodeons** in late 1905. By 1907, he was known as the "Napoleon of Chicago amusements," head of Jones, Linick, & Schaefer, a company that operated a half dozen theaters in The Loop (led by the Orpheum and Bijou Dream), numerous arcades, and most of the concessions at White City **amusement park**. At the height of his career, the company operated thirty-two theaters in downtown Chicago and its suburbs.

RICHARD ABEL

Jourjon, Charles

b. 1876; d. 1934

producer, industrialist, France

A successful lawyer, Jourjon created **Éclair** (Société française des films l'éclair) in April 1907 with Ambroise-François **Parnaland**. Excluding Parnaland from decision-making in 1908, Jourjon (assisted by Marcel Vandal) took charge of the company's expansion. A studio and laboratories were built in Epinay-sur-Seine; sales offices were opened worldwide (notably in New York and Fort Lee, New Jersey, where another studio was built); A.C.A.D. (Association cinématographique des auteurs dramatiques) was founded in 1911; *Éclair-Journal* and Scientia films began to appear in 1912. In September 1911, Jourjon also founded the Union des grands éditeurs, a public limited company designed to sell and rent films produced by Éclair, **Vitagraph**, **Lux**, and **Itala**. Jourjon remained at the company's helm until 1934, despite the economic difficulties Éclair met with after **World War I** (it went bankrupt in 1920). His son-in-law, Jacques Mathot, took over after his death.

LAURENT MANNONI

Joyce, Alice

b. 1890, Kansas City; d. 1955, Los Angeles

actor, USA

"Kalem Girl" Alice Joyce brought great beauty and a cool reserve to her screen appearances. She was a telephone operator and model (including posing for **illustrated song** slides) before working in moving pictures. Joyce was a major **star** and widely publicized favorite of fans for **Kalem** from 1910 until the company was absorbed by **Vitagraph** in 1917. She continued with Vitagraph, later worked for others, retired briefly in 1923, but returned in character roles before quitting for good in 1933. She was married three times: actor Tom Moore was her first husband; director Clarence Brown, her third.

ROBERT S. BIRCHARD

Joye, Joseph-Alexis

b. 1852; d. 1919

Catholic priest, educator, Switzerland

Father Joye, a Jesuit priest trained in **photography** and slide projection in England, initially used the **magic lantern** as a tool for entertaining and educating both children and adults in a parish of Basel (Switzerland). In 1902–1903, he began to introduce moving pictures into his repertoire. His initiative eventually resulted in a collection of films representing all genres and from nearly every major manufacturer, most of them made between 1905 and 1914 and purchased on the secondhand market. The 1,300 prints which survive were deposited at the National Film and Television Archive (NFTVA) in London in 1976. They now comprise one of the richest homogeneous **collections** of pre-1914 films for researchers.

See also: archives

Further reading

Cosandey, Roland (1993) *Welcome Home, Joye! Film um 1900. Aus der Sammlung Joseph Joye*, London/Frankfurt/Basel: NFTVA/Stroemfeld/ Roter Stern.

ROLAND COSANDEY

Jury, Sir William Frederick

b. 1870; d. 1944

exhibitor, distributor, businessman, Great Britain

William Jury had little formal education and worked at a number of jobs before entering the film business in 1897 as an **itinerant exhibitor**. His company, Jury's Imperial Pictures, came to dominate British film renting, but he also had a major interest in exhibition as director of the Weisker Brothers cinema chain. In 1915, Jury helped create and then chaired the British Topical Committee for War Films. In 1916, he became trade representative on the War Office Cinematograph

Committee, which took over official filming of the war; in 1918, he was appointed head of the new Cinematograph Department of the Ministry of Information. Jury was knighted for his war work, and remained a major figure in the industry through shareholdings in rental and exhibition companies, including Provincial Cinematograph Theaters.

NICHOLAS HILEY

K

Kaeriyama Norimasa

b. 1893; d. 1964

critic, filmmaker, Japan

Educated in mechanical engineering, Kaeriyama's criticism of contemporary Japanese films and his ideas on the true "photoplay," published in *Kinema Record* and *Katsudo shashingeki no sosaku to satsueiho* (The Production and Photography of Motion Picture Drama) (1917), made him the leader of the Pure Film Movement. Hired by **Tenkatsu** in 1917, Kaeriyama first put his ideas into practice directing *Sei no kagayaki* [The Glow of Life] (released in 1919), but while his films encouraged reformist tendencies, they were rarely successful. After 1924, he turned to working on film technology.

AARON GEROW

Kalem

Founded in 1907 in New York City by experienced moving picture businessmen George **Kleine** of **Kleine Optical** and Samuel **Long** and Frank **Marion** from **Biograph**, **Kalem** (named for the owners' last initials), was an early member of the **Motion Picture Patents Company**. The company was known for high quality productions (often accompanied by "special music" or **musical scores** specifically prepared for the films), innovative use of stock companies and on-location shooting, and controversies surrounding the first filmed version of *Ben Hur* (1907) and *From the Manger to the Cross* (1912). From the outset economic necessity as well as aesthetic decisions dictated the almost exclusive use of outdoor filming. Kalem became one of the first American companies to regularly send its production units outside the city; first to locations in New Jersey and Connecticut, then to Jacksonville (Florida) in order to take advantage of picturesque locales and weather for year-round filming. Eventually permanent studios were established in New York/New Jersey, Florida, and California.

These years provided the training ground for directors Sidney **Olcott**, Kenean Buell, Marshall Neilan, and Carlyle Blackwell and actors Gene **Gauntier** (the first "Kalem Girl" and a major **screenwriter**), Alice **Joyce**, Ruth **Roland**, Mae **Marsh**, Miriam Cooper, Helen **Holmes** and Helen Gibson (stars of popular **serials**), Robert Vignola, Jack Clarke, Tom Moore, and Lloyd Hamilton and Bud Duncan (stars of the "Ham and Bud" **comic series**). The company produced socially conscious story films in historically accurate settings as well as sensational **melodramas** (from railroad films to **westerns** and Civil War films), **comedies**, **travelogues**, and serials such as the *Hazards of Helen*. In 1907, Gauntier scripted an unauthorized adaptation of *Ben Hur*, and Harper Brothers and the General Lew Wallace Estate brought suit for infringement of **copyright**. The Supreme Court eventually ruled against Kalem, levying heavy fines and establishing precedent law concerning the necessity of obtaining the rights to artistic properties before filming.

Olcott and Gauntier became central figures in, arguably, the first traveling stock company. In 1910, Olcott, adept at using local history and

Figure 66 Kalem Company exterior set, with Alice Joyce, *c.* 1912. (Courtesy of the Robert S. Birchard Collection.)

atmosphere, took the touring stock company to Ireland for the first on-location shooting abroad. "The O'Kalems" returned often to record films such as *The Colleen Bawn* (1911), which received popular and critical acclaim for its beautiful scenery and authenticity of detail. Noting the extensive coverage of their adventures, the attraction of familiar stories, and their advertising potential, Marion suggested in 1911 that they film Bible stories in the Middle East. This resulted in *From the Manger to the Cross*, the first American feature-length story of the life of Christ shot on location. Although its release caused a heated controversy, the film received support from religious organizations for its reverent attitude and careful treatment. Despite being a financial gamble, it was a tremendous success.

Kalem resisted making a complete changeover to features, however, and the company eventually ceased production and was sold to **Vitagraph** in 1919.

See also: biblical films; law and the cinema

Further reading

Gauntier, Gene (n. d.) "Blazing the Trail," memoirs in the Museum of Modern Art (New York);

edited version published in installments in *Woman's Home Companion* (October 1928–March 1929).

Harner, Gary (1998) "The Kalem Company, travel and on-location filming," *Film History*, 10: 188–207.

GRETCHEN BISPLINGHOFF

Kamm, Leonard Ulrich

b. ?; d. ?

engineer/inventor, England

The most successful "filmless" motion picture apparatus was the Kammatograph, named for its inventor, Leonard Kamm. Kamm's ingenious domestic camera/projector, which used 12-inch glass discs, was patented in 1898, and sold from 1900 on. There were two models: the first with 350 pictures for a duration of approximately 30 seconds, the second with 550 smaller pictures with a duration of 45 seconds. Kamm and his son continued in the projection business, making professional **projectors** (using motion picture film) with patented improvements as well as other optical equipment.

STEPHEN HERBERT

Katz, Sam(uel)

b. 3 April 1892; d. 12 January 1961

exhibitor, USA

An immigrant from Poland who settled in Chicago, Sam Katz, while still in high school, opened his own nickelodeon in an abandoned grocery store. Four years later, he and his father acquired a second theater, the Wallace. Before 1915, Katz remained a small player in Chicago. But that year, teamed with the **Balaban** brothers, he would begin to build the largest chain of moving picture theaters in the world—the Paramount-Publix circuit.

Further reading

Gomery, Douglas (1985) "Sam Katz," *Marquee*, 17.3: 5–9.

DOUGLAS GOMERY

Kearton, Cherry

b. 1871; d. 1940

filmmaker, Britain

Kearton was a pioneering wildlife still photographer, often working with his brother Richard, and published many popular guides. He started making wildlife films in 1907. Theodore Roosevelt was an admirer, and chose Kearton to accompany him on an African big game hunting expedition in 1909, the films of which started a trend for **expedition/exploration** and hunting films. Kearton increased his film interests, marketing Proszinski's **Aeroscope camera** and taking over the **Warwick Trading Company** in 1913. He created the wartime **newsreel**, *The Whirlpool of War*, and filmed in Belgium in 1914–1915, then German East Africa in 1916. After the war he continued to publish widely, but his films now featured too much fabrication and sentimentality. The Royal Geographical Society gives an annual Cherry Kearton medal for achievements in wildlife photography.

See also: scientific films

LUKE McKERNAN

Keith, B(enjamin) F(ranklin)

b. 1846; d. 1914

vaudeville entrepreneur, exhibitor, USA

Founder of the most powerful circuit in **vaudeville**, Keith debuted "continuous vaudeville" at his Boston **dime museum** in 1885. With an emphasis on "clean entertainment," Keith built palatial theaters and headed a booking syndicate that by 1907 had monopolized big-time vaudeville in the East. Keith's company exhibited **American Mutoscope and Biograph** films for more than eight years beginning in 1896, operated **nickelodeons** in New England and Canada beginning in 1906, and financed the **Edison Kinetophone** in 1913. At his death, Keith himself controlled 20 theaters with some 400 additional theaters booked by the syndicate. His associate, Edward F. Albee,

continued to run the Keith empire—and nearly all of big-time vaudeville—until 1928.

ALAN GEVINSON

Kennedy, Jeremiah J.

b.?; d?.

producer, distributor, executive, USA

In 1907, Kennedy was put in charge of **American Mutoscope and Biograph** (AM&B) by the company's financial backer, the Empire Trust. Rather than liquidate the company, Kennedy decided to oppose **Edison**'s attempt to control the US film industry. His aggressive negotiations led to the formation of the **Motion Picture Patents Company** (MPPC) in 1908, in which **Biograph** (AM&B reorganized) united with Edison as an equal partner. Under Kennedy, with D. W. **Griffith** as principal director, Biograph achieved a quality of product that made it a recognized leader among US manufacturers. In 1911, Kennedy agreed to manage **General Film Company** (the distributor for MPPC films), the first American attempt to integrate film production and distribution. Kennedy's role in acquiring exchanges for General Film was central to the US Government suit against the MPPC as an illegal trust in 1913.

TOM GUNNING

Kessel, Adam

b. 1866, Keeseville, New York; d. 1946, Keeseville, New York

executive, USA

Kessel first entered the film business in 1908, when he took half interest in a film exchange to settle a gambling debt. With partner Charles O. **Baumann**, he founded **New York Motion Picture Company** to produce moving pictures in 1909 when the **Motion Picture Patents Company** threatened to cut off his film supply. New York Motion Picture first specialized in Bison and then Bison-101 **westerns**; after an acrimonious struggle with **Universal**, it became an umbrella company for **Keystone**, Kay-Bee, Broncho, and

Domino brands. In 1915, Kessel and Baumann joined with Harry **Aitkin** to form the Triangle Film Corporation. Kessel sold out to Aitkin in 1917.

ROBERT S. BIRCHARD

Keystone Film Company

One of several studios owned by the **New York Motion Picture Company**, Keystone was founded in 1912 to produce **comedies** for the **Mutual** organization. Headed by managing director Mack **Sennett**, Keystone became the most popular and influential US comedy studio of the 1910s. In addition to launching the careers of several notable performers, the studio also pioneered the **multiple-reel** comic feature, with the six-reel *Tillie's Punctured Romance* (1914). The following year, Keystone joined Thomas **Ince**'s Kay Bee and D. W. **Griffith**'s Fine Arts companies as members of Harry **Aitken**'s short-lived Triangle Film Corporation. Upon leaving Triangle for Paramount in 1917, Sennett relinquished the Keystone trademark, renaming the company "Mack Sennett Comedies."

See also: Arbuckle, Roscoe; Chaplin, Charles; Mace, Fred; Normand, Mabel; Sterling, Ford; Turpin, Ben

Further reading

Lahue, Kalton and Terry, Brewer (1967) *Kops and Custards: The Legend of Keystone Films*, Norman, OK: University of Oklahoma Press.

ROB KING

Khanzhonkov, Aleksandr

b. 1877; d. 1945

sales agent, producer, exhibitor, publisher, Russia

Khanzhonkov, scion of a well-to-do Don Cossack family, served in the imperial army for ten years before working as a sales agent for several European and American manufacturers and then

establishing the production company that bore his name in 1907. Unlike his arch-rival Aleksandr **Drankov**, who catered to the urban petty-bourgeoisie's taste for sensational **melodrama**, Khanzhonkov was determined to make cinema a respected art in Russia. He succeeded in making his name and his Pegasus **trademark** synonyms for high quality. To this end, he invested lavishly in historical epics, such as the 1912 hit, *Oborona Sevastopolia* [The Defense of Sevastopol], for which tsar Nicholas II awarded him the St. Stanislav Cross. Khanzhonkov also worked tirelessly to attract first-rate talent to his firm and promoted and paid them handsomely. He built Russia's grandest **palace cinema**, seating 2,000, in Moscow in 1913 and published two first-rate film journals, *Kinematograficheskii vestnik* (The Cinematographic Herald) and *Pegas* (Pegasus). After the revolution, Khanzhonkov remained in Soviet Russia, where the term *khanzhonkovshchina* (Khanzhonkov-ism) became an epithet for decadence in cinema.

Further reading

Khanzhonkov, A. A. (1937) *Pervye gody russkoi kinematografii* (The First Years of Russian Cinematography), Moscow/Leningrad: Iskusstvo.

DENISE J. YOUNGBLOOD

Khanzhonkov & Co.

Launched in 1906 to retail **Charles Urban Trading Company** films and **projectors** and **Hepworth** pictures in Russia, by 1908 Khanzhonkov & Co. had become the Moscow representative for such companies as **Deutsche Bioscop**, **Éclair**, **Vitagraph**, and **Itala**. 1908 was also the year when Russian films first appeared in the market, five of them directed by Vasilii **Goncharov** for Khanzhonkov—among them, *Song About Kalashnikov the Merchant*, *Selecting the Tsar's Bride*, and *16th Century Wedding in Russia*—all marked by owner Aleksandr **Khanzhonkov**'s interest in Russian history and Russian literary classics. Although the company's main rival for the Russian market, **Pathé-Frères**, was at that time

(1908–1911) exploiting many of the same subjects, Russian trade reviews would typically credit the Khanzhonkov & Co. with fidelity and authenticity, finding these qualities lacking in the Russian fiction films released by Pathé. Remembered as Russia's pioneering production company, Khanzhonkov & Co. never ceased to distribute foreign films through a half dozen branch offices across the empire, which gave its business the financial stability lacking in its Russian rivals such as **Drankov**.

With the advent of **multiple-reel** and feature films, Khanzhonkov & Co.'s stake in history and classics remained strong—its seven-reel *Oborona Sevastopolia* [Defense of Sebastopol] arguably was one of the longest films released in 1911, as was the five-reel *1812* in 1912—but in the 1910s, it was complimented by a new interest in other areas. First, Khanzhonkov & Co. was the only production company in Russia that had a Scientific Department (1911–1916), whose **travelogues** and **ethnographic films** as well as occasional **scientific films** (on agricultural, medical, and zoological subjects) filled low-priced matinee shows at Khanzhonkov-owned **palace cinema** in Moscow. Secondly, the company lent its premises to **animation**, financing the pioneer filmmaker, Wladyslaw **Starewicz**. Thirdly, Khanzhonkov was active in his efforts to involve writers and playwrights of fashion and fame, such as Mikhail Artsybashev, Leonid Andreyev, and Aleksandr Voznesensky, in **screenwriting**, as a result of which the center of gravity in the company's repertoire shifted from the past to the present, from historical epics to salon melodramas. Among other factors, this shift was connected with the rapid rise (1913–1917) of the studio's new director, Yevgeni **Bauer** (soon to become, along with Khanzhonkov, one of the company's principal stockholders), who would gradually upstage the veteran Pyotr **Chardynin**. Khanzhonkov's company also was the first in Russia to recognize and take advantage of the drawing power of the actor as **star**—e.g., Ivan **Mosjoukine**, Vera Karalli, Vera **Kholodnaia**.

Khanzhonkov emigrated in 1920, but, unlike his younger rival Iosif **Yermoliev**, he was not able to either take his former employees with him or open a new film business abroad.

YURI TSIVIAN

Kholodnaia, Vera (née Levchenko)

b. 1893; d. 1919

actor, Russia

The daughter of a provincial teacher, Kholodnaia was sent to Moscow by relatives, after her father's death, to study ballet at the Bolshoi school. She was "discovered" by director/producer Vladimir **Gardin** in 1914 and introduced to Evgenii **Bauer**, for whom she starred in a number of important films, notably *Deti veka* [Children of the Age] (1915) and *Zhizn za zhizn* [A Life for a Life] (1916). Her work in Petr **Chardynin**'s *Molchi, grust, molchi* [Be Still, Sadness, Be Still] (1918) is also memorable. Of the 40 films she made in her short career, only 5 survive. When she died in Odessa during the Spanish influenza pandemic, Kholodnaia was mourned as the greatest **star** of Russian cinema.

Further reading

Ziukov, B. B. (ed.) (1995) *Vera Kholodnaia: K 100-letiiu so dnia rozhdeniia* (Vera Kholodnaia: For the 100th Anniversary of Her Birth), Moscow: Iskusstvo.

DENISE J. YOUNGBLOOD

Kinematograph and Lantern Weekly

This important British trade journal had its origins in the monthly *Optical Magic Lantern Journal and Photographic Enlarger*, which ran from 1889 to 1903, under editors J. Hay Taylor and briefly Alfred **Saunders**. Re-launched as *Optical Lantern and Cinematograph Journal* in 1904 under a new editor, Theodore Brown, the journal two years later began using the more "correct" spelling of "kinematograph" (from the Greek). In 1907, it became *Kinematograph and Lantern Weekly*, soon the most authoritative and substantial of British early trade journals, going from less than a score of pages in its first issues to some 200 by **World War I**.

Under the influential Edward Thomas Heron's ownership, Brown continued briefly as editor; subsequent editors included Low Warren (1912 to 1917). Regular features included a news column by "Stroller," articles by writers such as technical editor Colin N. Bennett, and film criticism (which remained tame compared to its American counterparts). Odhams acquired the journal in 1917 and dropped "lantern" from the title two years later.

See also: *Bioscope, The*; trade press

STEPHEN BOTTOMORE

Kinematograph, Der (1907–1935)

The first trade journal devoted to moving pictures in Germany, *Der Kinematograph* immediately trumpeted the cause of *Kinoreform* (cinema reform) from its Düsseldorf headquarters. With a preponderance of articles exploring and encouraging the possibility of cinema's artistic legitimacy, the journal was an important voice in Germany's debates about cinema's aesthetic value. As cinema's role in Germany's cultural life became more secure, the journal shifted its attention to such practical matters for the industry as taxes and censorship. But solutions to or defenses against such encroachments were always cast in terms of "reform" or "Art" in its pages.

SCOTT CURTIS

Kinetophone

Borrowing its name from a sound version of his 1890s peep-show **Kinetoscope**, **Edison** and his associates worked intensively from 1908 to 1913 to develop the **synchronized sound system** that finally debuted in 1913 as the Kinetophone. The Kinetophone solved many technical problems that had stymied previous systems (amplification, synchronization, simultaneous recording of image and sound), but it failed because of a faulty exhibition strategy and an outdated conception of film subject and format. Exclusively licensed to a single

vaudeville theater circuit, the Kinetophone's circulation was limited; restricted to films that replicated vaudeville turns in an era of **multiple-reel/fiction films** narratives, its usefulness was compromised.

RICK ALTMAN

Kinetoscope

The Kinetoscope, one of the first devices designed to show moving pictures, was a peep-hole viewing machine that was run by **electricity** (direct current, sometimes using batteries). The machine had a relatively short commercial life (April 1894 through 1900) and was a profitable venture for only the first year and a half. The standard model exhibited films that were 1.5 inches in width (close to today's 35mm format) and about 42 feet in length. Since Kinetoscope films were shot and exhibited at approximately 30–36 frames per second, they lasted less than 20 seconds. When placed in the machine, films were joined end-to-end so as to form a continuous loop and threaded on a bank of rollers. The film moved continuously (there was no intermittent mechanism), and the illusion of movement depended on a shutter mechanism. The image was illuminated by light from behind the filmstrip, whose **celluloid** base was translucent. When the spectator looked into the machine, s/he saw the entire picture approximately one time, although the exhibition might not begin with the film's beginning. At least during its initial exploitation, patrons were charged 5¢ to look at each film. Various methods were used to activate the machine, eventually including a nickel-in-the-slot device.

Developed at the Edison Laboratory by Thomas A. **Edison** and his staff (including W. K. L. **Dickson** and William **Heise**), the Kinetoscope was part of Edison's initial motion picture system. A prototype, using a horizontal-feed system and a 1/2-inch film strip, was first shown to members of the National Federation of Women's Clubs, who visited Edison's Laboratory on 20 May 1891. The commercial prototype, which used a vertical feed system, was demonstrated at the Brooklyn Institute of Arts and Sciences on 9 May 1893. Two films were shown: *Blacksmithing Scene* and *Horse Shoeing*. Edison announced his intention to show the

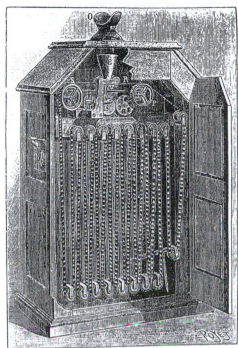

Figure 67 Engraving of a Kinetoscope, 1894.

Kinetoscope at the Columbian World Exposition in Chicago in 1893. **Publicity** was released to this effect, but the promised exhibition never took place.

Through the **Edison Manufacturing Company**, Edison conducted much of his motion picture business in coordination with three separate groups or companies. The first was the Kinetoscope Company, owned by Edison's former secretary Alfred O. Tate, Andrew Holland, Norman Raff and Frank Gammon. With an initial order of 25 machines, they opened the first Kinetoscope parlors: one in New York City at 1155 Broadway (near Herald Square) with ten machines on 14 April 1894, another in Chicago with ten more in mid-May, and a third in San Francisco with the last five on June 1. The second company, headed by Franz Z. Maguire and Joseph D. Baucus, was incorporated as the Continental Commerce Company in September and acquired the exclusive rights to sell and exhibit the Kinetoscope overseas. The third was the Kinetoscope Exhibition Company, which was committed to showing **boxing films** in an enlarged Kinetoscope that accepted 150-foot film loads: these were usually arranged in banks of six, with each machine showing a different match round. Edison sold Kinetoscopes for $200 to $225 each, and the three companies then resold them for approximately $350—although the price soon fell to $250.

See also: Maguire and Baucus; Raff and Gammon; projectors

Further reading

Musser, Charles (1990) *The Emergence of Cinema to 1907*, New York: Scribner's.

CHARLES MUSSER

Kinografen

Originally the name of a Copenhagen moving picture theater, founded in 1906 by Peter **Elfelt**, this company soon became an important distributor in Denmark. In 1910, Kinografen turned to production and quickly had an international hit with *De fire Djaevle* [The Four Devils], directed by Alfred **Lind**. This success allowed the company to expand production and construct a large studio. Until 1914, its leading performer and director was daredevil Ejnar Zangenberg (1885–1918), who specialized in sensational **melodramas**. Although Kinografen produced some films for the international market up to 1914, its primary business remained domestic distribution within Denmark.

CASPER TYBJERG

Kinora

Devised by the **Lumières** in France, and acknowledging a patent by an American, Herman Casler, the 1896 Kinora was a miniature domestic clockwork mutoscope viewer, later manufactured by **Gaumont**. From 1902, hand-cranked versions were sold by various companies in England where the system became very popular. Motion portraits were taken at London studios, and catalogs included American and English films for sale or rent. An amateur camera, using paper rolls, also was available for several years. The Kinora disappeared *c.* 1913.

Further reading

Anthony, Barry (1996) *The Kinora: Motion Pictures for the Home 1896–1914*, London: The Projection Box.

STEPHEN HERBERT

Kirchner, Albert (a.k.a. Léar)

b. ?; d. ?

filmmaker, manufacturer, exhibitor, France

A photographer working for Eugène **Pirou**, Albert Kirchner made several **pornographic** films, including *Le Coucher de la mariée* (1896), with Louise Willy. In 1897–1898, he registered three patents for the "Biographe français Léar," which

then was manufactured and marketed in two models, one for 35 mm film, the other for 60 mm film, by a company he founded with Antelme and Pacon. He also organized screenings with the "Biographe" at the Oller museum and at the café Frontin in Paris in 1897. At the same time, he directed a *Passion du Christ* (in twelve scenes) for **Maison de la Bonne Presse**. In 1898, Kirchner sold all his negatives to Gaumont and died soon after.

LAURENT MANNONI

Klaw & Erlanger

In 1896, theater owner-producers Marc Klaw and Abraham Erlanger agreed to produce a "multimedia" *Passion Play*, portions of which were filmed at Horitz, Bohemia, the following year. This hour-and-a-half program combining moving pictures, lantern slides, and a lecture played for several weeks each in major cities such as Philadelphia, Boston, Baltimore, Rochester, and New York. Much later, in 1913, Klaw & Erlanger joined with **Biograph** to film theatrical properties that they controlled. Produced by the Protective Amusement Company (a subsidiary of Klaw & Erlanger), these **multiple-reel films** (featuring prominent Biograph players) did not open in Klaw & Erlanger theaters, however, until well into 1914. The joint enterprise was not successful.

PAUL SPEHR

Kleine, George

b. 1864, New York City; d. 1931,
New York City

sales agent, distributor, executive USA

George Kleine served as a peacemaker who brought some measure of order to the early motion picture industry. His father manufactured stereopticons and other optical supplies and, after graduating from New York City College in 1882, George joined the family business in Chicago. He was quick to embrace the new novelty of moving pictures and soon became the major retailer for projectors, **cameras**, and films in the Midwest. He placed the first known ad for a moving picture in the 19 September 1896 issue of *The Clipper*, a theatrical trade paper based in New York. In 1903, he began importing European films to the USA, and in 1906 he established a film exchange. The following year he bankrolled Frank **Marion** and Samuel **Long** to establish the **Kalem** Company, the name derived from the initials of Kleine-Long-Marion.

Kleine sided with **American Mutascope and Biograph** in the **patents wars** and resisted **Edison**'s efforts to put an end to the production, distribution, and exhibition of unlicensed films. However, the chaotic mushrooming of film exchanges and the resulting decline in business pushed him to seek a truce between the rival Edison and **Biograph** interests. His efforts bore fruit in late 1908 with the establishment of the **Motion Picture Patents Company**. When the MPPC established the **General Film Company** as its distribution arm in 1910, Kleine sold his exchanges to the new entity for $2 million. He served as vice-president of General Film from 1910 to 1913 and was made president in 1916.

In 1913, he imported the Italian spectacle *Quo Vadis?*, which was booked in legitimate theaters at advanced prices. The film created a sensation and set the stage for the feature era in the USA. This success led Kleine to establish the Photodrama Producing Company of Italy and commission Italian productions of *The Last Days of Pompeii* and *Othello*, and demand that "one or more scenes are to be spectacular in the full extent of the word." He built a studio in Turin, but it was completed just days before the outbreak of **World War I**, and Kleine gave up his efforts to produce in Europe. He was no more successful producing films in the USA. Based on the surviving evidence, his American efforts had little to offer in dramatic values or production polish. In an effort to service the growing feature market, Kleine established K. E. S. E. (Kleine-Edison-**Selig**-**Essanay**) and later the Kleine-Edison Feature Service, but the product of these old line producers could not compete with the productions from **Famous Players**-Lasky, Metro, or even the reorganized Greater **Vitagraph**. Kleine's last production was a **serial**, *The Hope Diamond Mystery* (1921). He

became treasurer and chairman of Ritz-Carlton Pictures in 1923.

With the death of his wife in 1924, Kleine closed his Chicago office and moved to New York, where he dabbled in non-theatrical distribution until shortly before his death.

ROBERT S. BIRCHARD

Kleine Optical Company

Formally incorporated in 1897 after several years in business, the Chicago-based Kleine Optical Company was the earliest non-producing enterprise to sell motion picture equipment and films. Operated by George **Kleine**, the company was an early importer of European pictures. Kleine Optical gave up selling films directly to exhibitors and established its own film exchanges in 1906. After joining the **Motion Picture Patents Company**, it then sold its exchange interests to the **General Film Company** in 1910. George Kleine retained the company name and used it for his other motion picture activities up to the time of his death in 1931.

ROBERT S. BIRCHARD

Klercker, Georg af

b. 1877; d. 1951

filmmaker, actor, Sweden

The rediscovery of 22 preserved films directed by Klercker has led to his re-emergence in the history of early cinema, as the most important Swedish director besides Victor **Sjöström** and Mauritz **Stiller**.

After having abandoned a military career for the theater, thereby causing a scandal in his aristocratic family, Klercker was hired by producer Charles **Magnusson** in 1911 to head the **Svenska Biografteatern** studios in Stockholm. His first film, *Två bröder* [Two Brothers] (1912), produced by Swedish **Pathé**, was banned by the censors. During his Svenska Bio period, from 1911 to 1913, he wrote and directed several film dramas and

comedies, of which one is preserved: *Ringvall på äventyr* [Ringvall in Search of Adventure] (1913).

Klercker left Svenska Bio for Swedish Pathé in 1913, directing one film, *För fäderneslandet* [For the Fatherland] (1914), which also brought him to Copenhagen for a period.

In 1915, he was hired as director by Hasselblad, a camera company in Gothenburg, which had gone into film production and built a new studio at Otterhällan. The company produced 30 feature films during three summer seasons, 1915–1917. Klercker is credited as director for all but one, and many of the scripts were written directly for the screen by outside authors. Among the Hasselblad productions were several Danish style sensational **melodramas**, such as *Mysteriet natten till den 25:e* [The Mystery of the Night Before the 25th] (1917) which was banned by the censors, and comedies, *I kronans kläder* [In Uniform] (1915). The company also produced dramas exploring different social milieux, some with a realist or critical tendency—such as *Aktiebolaget Hälsans gåva* ["Gift of Health" Ltd.] (1916), a satire on medical quackery written by the director of the national Board of Censors, Gustaf Berg—as well as the only Swedish war film produced during **World War I**, *För hem och härd* [For Home and Hearth] (1917), which promoted the national emergency service.

The films directed by Klercker at Hasselblad have generally been considered conventional in their storytelling. On the other hand, they are characterized by a remarkable cinematography, experimenting with natural **lighting** and using advanced deep-focus lens. Stylistically, most of the melodramas remain pre-classical in their rather consistent use of static shots and **staging in depth**, whereas a late comedy like *Löjtnant Galenpanna* [Lieutenant Madcap] (1917) contains sequences of fully elaborated continuity cutting.

Hasselblad merged into the Skandia company in 1918, and Klercker disappeared completely from film production, only to make an unsuccessful comeback in 1926 with the film *Flickorna på Solvik* [The Girls of Solvik].

See also: editing: spatial relations; editing: tableau style; editing: temporal relations

Further reading

Söderbergh Widding, Astrid (1999) "Towards Classical Narration? Georg af Klercker in Context," in John Fullerton and Jan Olsson (eds.) *Nordic Explorations: Film Before 1930*, 187–203, London/Sydney: John Libbey.

ASTRID SÖDERBERGH WIDDING

Kobayashi Kisaburo

b. 1880; d. 1961

exhibitor, producer, Japan

Starting out as a traveling showman for **Yokota Shokai**, Kobayashi became an executive at **Fukuhodo** and **Nikkatsu** before helping found **Tenkatsu** in 1914. His control over several major theaters epitomized the influence exhibitors had over the industry. His importation of such films as **Éclair**'s *Zigomar*, **Itala**'s *Cabiria*, D. W. **Griffith**'s *Intolerance*, and **Universal**'s *Bluebird* films, as well as his support of film journalism, had a profound impact on Japanese film culture. He founded Kobayashi Shokai in 1916 and Kokkatsu in 1919, but lost his position in 1921 after a scandal.

AARON GEROW

Kohinoor Film Company

Established by Dwarkadas Sampat in 1919, Kohinoor Film was perhaps the first Indian studio to decisively move away from the artisanal production practices of D. G. **Phalke**, S. N. Patankar, and others. Early documentaries and the feature-length *Bhakta Vidur* [Saint Vidur] (1921) reflected Sampat's nationalist leanings. But with directors like Homi Master, Kanjibai Rathod, and Mohan Bhavnani making some of the most popular films of the silent era, Sampat transformed Kohinoor into an American-style studio that could produce several films simultaneously. These featured some of the most famous stars of the 1920's: Raja Sandow, Khalil, Gohar, Sulochana, Fatma Begum, Sultana and Zubeida.

SURESH CHABRIA

Kolm, Louise Veltée

b. 1873; d. 1950

producer, filmmaker, Austria

Born in Vienna, Louise Veltée, wife of Anton Gustav Kolm, was a co-founder, in 1910, of First Austrian Kinofilms Industries and then, in 1911, of **Wiener Kunstfilm**. In these companies she served in several capacities: editor, set designer, producer, and director. Among her films are *Die Glückspuppe* [The Lucky Doll] (1911), *Trilby* [Three Tales of Terror] (1912), *Der Meineidbauer* [The Farmer Forsworn] (1915), and *Der Traum eines österreichischen Reservisten*, (An Austrian Reservist's Dream) (1915). Once a widower, she married another co-founder, filmmaker Jacob Fleck, with whom she directed numerous silent features and then talkies, in Germany and Austria.

PAOLO CANEPPELE

Kolowrat-Krakowsky, Alexander "Sascha" Joseph

b. 1886; d. 1927

producer, Austria

Born in Glenridge, New York, but of an old, noble, and rich Bohemian family, Count "Sascha" Kolowrat-Krakowsky was a pilot and racer who, in 1909, became fascinated by moving pictures. In 1910, he founded Sascha-Filmfabrik in Vienna, initially producing nonfiction films. During **World War I**, the Count served as the War Ministry's chief of film production. After the war, he produced the most important Austrian films, casting the best-known actors (Fern Andra, Marlene Dietrich, Lucy Dorraine, Willi Forst) in conjunction with the best directors (Michael Kertesz, Gustav Ucicky).

PAOLO CANEPPELE

Komada Koyo

b. 1877; d. 1935

benshi, Japan

Born in Osaka, Komada was one of the first professional **benshi**. Employed by Hiromeya, an advertisement agency in Tokyo, Komada became involved in the company's production of the first Kabuki film, *Momijigari* [Maple Viewing] (1899). Subsequently, he became interested in film exhibition and organized a traveling company, to tour throughout Japan with a set of **projectors** and repertory of films. In contrast to the ordinary *benshi* employed by a movie theater, Komada remained independent, showing his films at rented public halls and schools. In the later years of his life, he founded his own company called Sekai Film, which manufactured educational films.

HIROSHI KOMATSU

Komatsu Shokai

This company was founded by Saito Kotaro in 1903. Komatsu organized **fair/fairground** attractions, including moving pictures. Originally Komatsu bought its films from other companies and showed them on the fairgrounds. Although the company soon began to produce its own films, these remained chiefly fairground entertainment. In 1914, Komatsu Shokai revitalized its filmmaking branch, founding its own studio in Takadanobaba, Tokyo. Yet its films were hardly seen in major cities because in the mid-1910s the large urban movie theaters were almost totally dominated by two other companies, **Nikkatsu** and **Tenkatsu**. Still, Komatsu Shokai continued to make films until the early 1920s.

HIROSHI KOMATSU

Konishi Photographic Store

Founded by Sugiura Rokuemon in 1876, the Konishi Photographic Store imported diverse photographic materials from abroad. The first motion picture **camera** the company imported was a British camera called the Baxter & Wray Cinematograph. With this camera, store employee Asano Shiro shot an *actualité* of Tokyo street scenes in 1897. The second imported motion picture camera was from **Gaumont**, which Shibata Tsunekichi shot the first kabuki film, *Momijigari* [Maple Viewing], in 1899. Konishi Photographic

Store also assisted Gabriel **Veyre** from France in presenting a motion picture show for a Japanese prince at the French embassy in Tokyo in December 1898.

HIROSHI KOMATSU

Kosmofilm

The Polish production company, Kosmofilm, was established by Henryk Finkelstein and Samuel Ginzburg in Warsaw in 1913. Run by Finkelstein, it had its own studio and laboratory on Rymarska Street. Along with films based on Yiddish plays such as *Dem chazons tochter* [The Cantor's Daughter] (1913) and *Di sztifmuter* [The Step-mother] (1914), which drew on acting talent from the city's Jewish Theater, Kosmofilm produced a three-act adaptation of the Polish national opera, *Halka*, in 1913. In its two years of existence, the company produced nearly twenty fiction films and documentaries, quickly becoming Poland's main producer until its merger with **Sfinks** in 1915.

SHEILA SKAFF

Krauss, Henry (a.k.a. Kraus, Henri)

b. 1866; d. 1935

actor, filmmaker, France

Originally a theater actor, Krauss first brought his compelling power and photogenic figure to the cinema in **SCAGL**'s *Marie Stuart* (1908). His acting, which steered clear of bombast, turned many lead parts into memorable roles, in literary adaptations and **historical films** produced usually for SCAGL: *Notre-Dame de Paris* (1911), *Les Misérables* (1912) and *Germinal* (1913), all directed by Albert **Capellani**. Krauss also directed several films for SCAGL between 1915 and 1918, and he kept acting under the direction of other filmmakers such as André Antoine in *Les Frères corses* [The Corsican Brothers] (1917).

LAURENT LE FORESTIER

Krüger, Fréderic

b. ?; d. ?

exhibitioner, producer, Germany/Belgium

In 1902, the German entrepreneur Krüger bought an itinerant moving picture theater from Henri Opitz, a fairground showman in Belgium. By 1907, he had become the first Belgian tycoon in exhibition with more than a dozen film projection teams active in the **music halls** and on the **fairs/fairgrounds**. In early 1908, Krüger opened several permanent theaters in Antwerp and also began to produce *actualités*. In trying to compete with **Pathé-Frères**, however, he went bankrupt. La **Belge Cinéma** took over his business office and personnel and used them to quickly establish its own presence in Belgium.

GUIDO CONVENTS

L

labor movement: Europe

Two tendencies in the West European labor movement can be discerned (further research is still needed on other parts of Europe). One saw the cinema largely in a negative light: it offered workers only vulgar entertainment instead of culturally uplifting them, and at the same time kept them away from political or trade union meetings. Only by showing educational films could the medium be put to good use. The other, by contrast, welcomed the opportunity that moving pictures offered to reach mass audiences with an explicit political message. Well aware that film was an expensive medium, it looked for ways to overcome this obstacle. German social democracy offers a good example of the former attitude; the French "anarcho-communist" movement, the latter.

A few early examples are known of labor organizations showing moving pictures at meetings. The Manchester and Salford branch of the Independent Labor Party, for instance, enlivened its "Greatest Social on Earth" in February 1898 with "living pictures," augmenting the lantern slide pictures that long had been a common feature of its programs. In his novel *The Ragged Trousered Philanthropists* (1914), Robert Tressell gives a vivid description of such a **magic lantern slide show**. On the continent, labor propagandists also were making use of lantern slides: for example, during the Dreyfus campaign in France. But the transition to moving pictures turned out to be more difficult. Reflections on the nature and function of the cinema did not begin until around 1908, after moving pictures had become a regular part of everyday life, as evidenced by the growing number of theaters.

It was the popularity of the Kintops that prompted German social democrats to express their concern, adapting arguments used in earlier campaigns against "Schundliteratur" (vulgar literature). Thus Franz Förster wrote in April 1912, in *Die neue Zeit*: "The most stupid nonsense is presented as humor, the most impossible backstairs novels are undergoing here their resurrection.... [T]he inner lives of hundreds of thousands of our fellow citizens are being poisoned by the so-called moral dramas that are dripping with false sentimentality." This dismissive attitude led to such extremes as a resolution adopted in 1910 by the Socialist Free Youth in Cologne, in which working class youth were urged to avoid the movie theaters and other despicable forms of entertainment and join the movement instead.

Within several years, however, other voices were calling for a more thoughtful approach. They warned that opponents of social democracy were making successful use of moving pictures. Ironically, it was the bourgeois cinema reform movement, which had become a powerful force in Germany, that offered a useful framework or model. This movement sought to enlighten people by publishing film reviews, opened reform movie theaters (possibly sponsored by local councils), programmed "carefully selected films" at competitive prices, and promoted educational and cultural films ("Kulturfilme").

In December 1913, Franz Förster now appealed, again in *Die neue Zeit*, to trade unions to equip their halls with a film **projector** and start trade union cinemas. Yet only a handful of these actually opened for business. Figures given by another organizaiton of social democracy, the National Committee for Workers' Education, were just as telling about the lack of enthusiasm: during the 1913–1914 season, only 27 of its branches organized moving shows, which totalled a meager 62. Nor was the labor press particularly anxious to develop a kind of film criticism that acknowledged what attracted spectators to the movie theaters in the first place. Illustrative is the attitude of the *Hamburger Echo* with regard to a screening of Albert **Capellani**'s *Germinal* (1913) in Breslau (Wroclaw), in October 1913, especially organized by the local Workers' Education Committee. While hailing the film as a successful attempt "to put the cinematograph in the service of the labor movement," the newspaper also wrote that it demonstrated "an extraordinary lack of taste," for the film version of Zola's novel was "a brutality against literature and a crime against the people." The *Hamburger Echo* continued: "to us it looks more like the Trade Union House competing against the cinema enterprises rather than the cinema competing against vulgar literature. For literature in film form is vulgar, even when it is derived from the works of Zola, Schiller, or Goethe." The fact that the organisers of the film show in Breslau had urged spectators to turn to the book itself, as the censor had stripped *Germinal* of its most poignant captions, made no difference to the *Hamburger Echo*.

Given such attitudes prevailing, it is no surprise that despite its strength German social democracy refrained from attempts to make its own films. With regard to visual propaganda and education, the emphasis remained entirely on producing lantern slides. Surprisingly, given the intensity of the theoretical debates within the German movement, hardly any reference was made to the Marxist dogma of base determining superstructure, which would logically preclude any form of proletarian film production under capitalist conditions.

Equivalents of the German trade union cinemas also could be found in Prague and Vienna as well as elsewhere. In the South Wales coal fields, a few miners' institutes fitted their main halls with projection equipment in the early 1910s. Around the same time, the first cinemas owned by local cooperative societies in the North of England opened their doors. In Belgium, regular moving picture shows were given by People's Houses in Brussels, Ghent, Louvain, and Liège, while a number of cooperative societies and Bourses du Travail in France did likewise. But all of these movie theaters had in common the fact that they relied on films produced and distributed by companies that had little affinity with the labor movement or, worse, were squarely opposed to it.

In 1913, a group in France decided that it was time to change this. In October 1913, they founded the cooperative society, Le **Cinéma du peuple** (People's Cinema) with a capital of 20,000 Francs, comprising 800 shares. The aim of the society was: "the production, the reproduction, sale, and rental of cinematograph films as well as all their accessories." In addition, "the Society will make efforts to raise the intellectual level of the people. It will continually exchange with various groups of the Proletariat ideas that are based on the class struggle and that have the aim of suppressing wage labor by a social (and) economic transformation." The founding members, which included the writer and propagandist for Proletarian Culture, Marcel Martinet, had various and often lengthy left-wing antecedents. They might be described as "anarcho-communists." In January 1914, the new society was able to premiere its first production, *Les Misères de l'aiguille* [The Miseries of the Needle], which featured **Musidora** in the role of an exploited seamstress, shortly before her appearance as Irma Vep in Louis **Feuillade**'s *Les Vampires* (1915) would make her famous. Within two weeks this film was followed by **newsreel** footage of the funeral of the prominent Socialist Jean Jaurès and others films such as *L'Hiver! Plaisir de riches! Souffrances de pauvres!* The latter was a good example of a "deadly parallel" that labor propagandists found so effective filmmaking, in which the pleasures enjoyed by the rich during wintertime were contrasted with the sufferings of the poor.

Further productions included *La Commune! Du 18 au 28 mars 1871*, a film on the Paris Commune, and the social drama, *Le vieux docker* [The Old Dockworker]. There were plans for a film about the Spanish anarchist and freethinker, Francisco Ferrer, and a regular workers' newsreel, but the outbreak of **World War I** put an end to the activities of the Le Cinéma du peuple.

While commercial premieres in Paris were attended by audiences of up to 5,000 (for instance, at the Gaumont-Palace), it is unclear how effective was the national (and international) distribution network of Le Cinéma de Peuple. After overcoming problems such as the non-arrival of a print from Brussels and a ban by the Mayor of Amsterdam, for instance, Dutch revolutionary socialists—political friends of the French anarcho-communists—managed to show a film on the Paris Commune in May 1914. It is highly likely that this title was produced by Le Cinéma du peuple. Already prior to this screening, the revolutionary socialists had shown a keen interest in the cinema. In September 1913, for their loyal following in Amsterdam, they had opened their own Roode Bioscoop (Red Cinema) in the Dutch capital. In a movie theater whose previous owners had gone bankrupt, social dramas on such topics as the misery caused by alcohol were given a left-wing interpretation by a comrade in the role of **lecturer**. Once it proved impossible to break even financially, the theater had to close before the end of the year. Efforts to open another Red Cinema, in the province of Friesland, another stronghold of revolutionary socialism, also failed.

With the growing number of workers employed in the cinema trade the question of trade union organization inevitably made itself felt. The unionization of technicians working in the film studios and labs would only emerge later (in Great Britain and France, as late as the 1930s), but cinema **projectionists** were aware of the need for organization early on. In Great Britain, the National Association of Cinematograph Operators (NACO), affiliated with the National Association of Theatrical Employees, was founded in 1906. In Germany, two associations were set up: the International Cinematograph Operators Lodge and the Free Association of Cinematograph Operators of Germany. These unions were essentially craft-oriented, but there were also projectionists who held a broader view on unionization and therefore joined larger "modern" unions which organized across craft barriers, such as the Electrical Trades Union in the United Kingdom or the Steelworkers' Union in Germany. Actors and musicians working in the cinema also could join existing unions, if they were not already members because of their previous occupation.

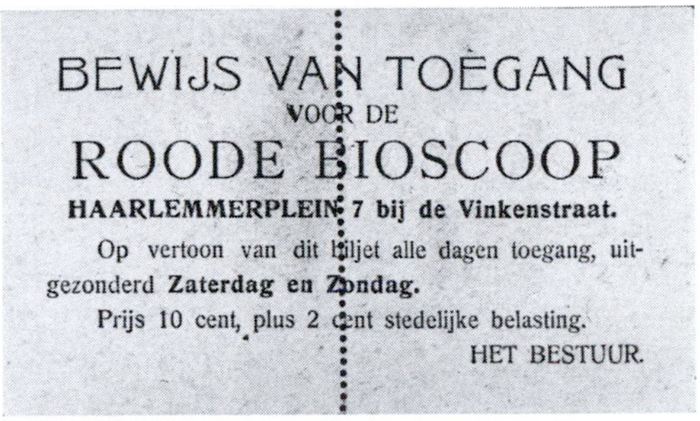
BEWIJS VAN TOEGANG
VOOR DE
ROODE BIOSCOOP
HAARLEMMERPLEIN 7 bij de Vinkenstraat.
Op vertoon van dit biljet alle dagen toegang, uitgezonderd Zaterdag en Zondag.
Prijs 10 cent, plus 2 cent stedelijke belasting.
HET BESTUUR.

Figure 68 Ticket for the Red Cinema, Amsterdam, *c.* 1912. (Courtesy of Bert Hogenkamp.)

See also: consumer cooperatives: Europe; labor movement: USA; women's movement: Europe; women's movement: USA

Further reading

Chanan, Michael (1976) *Labour Power in the British Film Industry*, London: British Film Institute.

Hogenkamp, Bert (1984) "De Roode Bioscoop" *Skrien*, 136: 33–35.

Hogenkamp, Bert (1986) *Deadly Parallels: Film and the Left in Britain, 1929–1939*, London: Lawrence & Wishart.

Kinter, Jürgen (1985) *Arbeiterbewegung und Film: Ein Beitrag zur Geschichte der Arbeiter- und Alltagskultur und der gewerkschaftlichen und sozialdemokratischen Kultur- und Medienarbeit*, Hamburg: Medienpädagogik-Zentrum.

Kinter, Jürgen (1992) "'Durch Nacht zum Licht': Vom Guckkasten zum Filmpalast. Die Anfänge des Kinos und das Verhältnis der Arbeiterbewegung zum Film," in Dagmar Kift (ed.) *Kirmes–Kneipe–Kino: Arbeiterkultur im Ruhrgebiet zwischen Kommerz und Kontrolle (1850–1914)*, 119–146, Paderborn: Ferdinand Schöningh.

Mannoni, Laurent (1993) "28 octobre 1913: création de la Société 'Le Cinéma du peuple'," *1895* (numéro hors série "l'année 1913 en France"), 101–107.

Perron, Tangui (1995) "'Le contrepoison est entre vos mains, camarades': CGT et cinéma au début du siècle," *Le mouvement social*, 172: 21–36.

BERT HOGENKAMP

labor movement: USA

From their inception, moving pictures were vehicles of propaganda and persuasion as well as education and entertainment. Some were even made by groups that today we would not usually associate with the cinema industry, including labor unions and others concerned with the conditions of working-class life. Among those that dominated the labor movement during the period of early cinema were the reformist American Federation of Labor (AFL), whose ranks tripled between 1900 and 1910, and the more radical Western Federation of Miners (WFM) and International Workers of the World (IWW). For more than a decade after the emergence of **nickelodeons**, moving pictures and the working class were intertwined, as Steven Ross puts it so succinctly, in three important ways: working-class people were the industry's main **audience**; they were the frequent subjects of films; and they were makers of movies—both as employees who labored for manufacturers and as independent producers who turned out their own. As early as 1907, in fact, workers, radicals, and labor organizations were making movies that challenged the dominant ideology of individualism and portrayed collective action as the most effective way to improve the working-class lives. Arguably, labor and the left forged an oppositional cinema that used film as a medium of hope to educate, entertain, and mobilize millions of Americans.

The film industry assumed a rather ambivalent attitude toward labor issues during the early cinema era. Scores of conservative films depicted capitalists and businessmen in a positive light and denigrated labor leaders and unions, often conflating the AFL and others with the IWW as typical of labor activism and tarring them all by association with anarchists and socialists. In films such as **Biograph**'s *The Iconoclast* (1910) and **IMP**'s *The Dynamiter* (1911), labor troubles were even ascribed to foreign-born malcontents, unshaven and slovenly in appearance, and allegedly prone to violence. The majority of films, however, promoted the cliché that labor and capital needed each other to prosper, epitomized in the final tableau of *The Right to Labor* (1909), whose **intertitle** read: "Capital and Labor grasp hands and the angel of prosperity waves the olive branch above them." In such films, as well as a rare pro-labor film like Reliance's *Locked Out* (1911), union leaders and strikers were given legitimacy; although most were men (reflecting the gender bias of unions themselves), female activists were prominent in films such as **Thanhouser**'s *The Girl Strike Leader* (1910). Improving the conditions of working-class life, however, usually depended on the benefice of a "good capitalist." A good example is **Edison**'s *Children Who Labor* (1912), produced in cooperation with the National Child Labor Committee and released during a national debate over child-labor legislation. Here, the solution to individualized capitalist greed came not from the workers themselves or even government intervention but a factory owner who realizes and remedies his "mistakes." The dire consequences of failing to remedy such "mistakes" were revealed in **Éclair**'s sensational **melodrama**, *Why?* (1913), in which frightened capitalists shoot at angry workers who then take revenge by burning down the Woolworth Building and setting fire to much of Manhattan. Almost alone among these films was All-Star Feature's *The Jungle* (1914), adapted from the Upton Sinclair novel, whose main character is a Lithuanian immigrant hired by a Chicago packing house. Crushed by the working conditions, police violence, and a foreman's lack of scruples, the man finds some measure of hope when he wanders into a socialist meeting and is transfixed by a speaker modeled on Eugene V. Debs.

That labor unions and strikes could be tolerated and even sometimes honored during this period was due in part to the fact that the industry itself faced few major labor problems before 1916. Workers were slow to organize on studio lots and often were bitterly divided by jurisdictional disputes over who should exert some control over their labor in production. Unionization campaigns remained sporadic and largely unsuccessful until the creation of Actors' Equity and the more radical Photoplayers' Union in 1916. The IWW was involved in many of those campaigns from as early as March 1911, when it chartered the Motion Picture Theater Workers of New York City. Two years later, Maude Thompson organized five hundred workers at the Edison Company (Orange, New Jersey) into an IWW local that protested poor wages and working conditions. In 1914, the IWW also organized movie extras at the **Universal Film Manufacturing Company** in Los Angeles, demanded a wage increase, and led a strike when the company refused. **Projectionists** provided the one significant exception. Faced with the threat of deskilling practices and, as a consequence, declining wages as well as sometimes appalling working conditions, they launched the industry's first successful unionization drive in 1910. Yet, tellingly, they affiliated with actors' and theatrical unions rather than those of industrial workers.

Recognition of moving pictures' powers of persuasion, along with anger over so many anti-labor, anti-union films, led to a slowly but steadily increasing grass-roots working-class film movement. As early as 1907, for instance, a Cleveland man shot and exhibited films of the strike-ravaged Cripple Creek mining area of Colorado. In 1908, the Boot and Shoe Workers' Union produced a short film "depicting industrial scenes," which it then used in unionization drives throughout New England. By the early 1910s, several corporations were using movies to promote their interests. Especially aggressive was the National Association of Manufacturers (NAM), which, after the disastrous 1911 Triangle fire (which killed more than a hundred female garment workers), produced two films depicting employers' heightened concern for workplace safety: *The Workman's Lesson* and *The Crime of Carelessness* (both 1912). Provoked by these propaganda efforts, labor activists countered with their own films. In 1911, the AFL sponsored *A Martyr to His Cause*, which recounted the life and career of John McNamara (indicted for dynamiting the *Los Angeles Times* building a year earlier) in order to demonstrate that trade unionists were the true upholders of democratic institutions. This film played to big audiences in "leading theaters and moving picture houses" across the country for several months that fall, until McNamara's brother confessed to the crime. More successful were those films that presented their political messages in the guise of popular sensational melodrama stories. A good example was *From Dusk to Dawn* (1913), a feature film produced at Occidental Film (a small studio in Los Angeles) by Frank Wolfe, a former reporter who had worked with Clarence Darrow on the AFL's McNamara defense team and was an expert photographer. This innovative docudrama used the romance between an iron molder and laundress to focus on a successful fight against factory exploitation and the election of a Socialist governor (the iron molder) who signs into law a "right to work" bill guaranteeing jobs for all wage earners. Darrow himself often appeared with the film in exhibition, and audience demand was so great that Marcus **Loew** booked the film into his New York **cinema circuit/chain**. Inspired by *From Dust to Dawn*, New York socialist actor Joseph Leon Weiss wrote and directed *What Is To Be Done?* (1914), which dramatized the lessons of the recent Ludlow (Colorado) massacre through the story of a love affair between a factory owner's son and a stenographer who not only organizes his father's factory workers but also educates and politicizes him.

For the most part, labor organizations in the USA, unlike in Europe, tended to be involved more directly in film production and distribution than in film exhibition. There were a few attempts to establish "worker" cinemas, but only one seems to have proved all that successful. In 1909, for instance, Chicago radicals briefly ran a theater with the explicit aim of spreading "Socialist propaganda." Two years later, militants opened the Socialist Movie Theater in downtown Los Angeles to mount daily programs of pro-labor features and locally produced **newsreels** (perhaps shot by Wolfe). This theater developed into a multipurpose political space where labor, socialist, and suffragist organizations showed films, gave talks, and held rallies. More typically, labor activists showed films in order to increase attendance at meetings and rented or were granted permission to use existing moving picture theaters for special occasions, especially on Sundays in cities where "blue laws" prohibited public entertainments. In early 1912, for instance, the violent strike in the textile mill town of Lawrence (Massachusetts) prompted mass meetings at theaters in several New England cities. In Pawtucket (Rhode Island), the Socialist Labor Party held a "meeting in aid of Lawrence strikers" at the 1,200-seat Bijou Theatre. In Lawrence itself, the manager of the Colonial Theatre, which had suspended its Keith **vaudeville** and moving picture programs during the strike, booked James K Hackett's company for a week's performances of the pro-labor play, *The Grain of*

Dust. Later that summer, Bronx socialists rented the Rose Theater for a Sunday evening of films that included socialist-produced newsreels of the Lawrence strike and recent May Day parades along with *The Cry of the Children.* Indeed, as Ross concludes, unions and socialists throughout the country regularly "used films to publicize strikes, raise funds, and attract large crowds to rallies and gatherings" up until the USA entered **World War I** in 1917.

See also: migration/immigration: USA; labor movement: Europe.

Further reading

Brownlow, Kevin (1990) *Behind the Mask of Innocence: Sex, Violence, Prejudice, Crime: Films of Social Conscience in the Silent Era,* Berkeley: University of California Press.

Enstad, Nan (1999) *Ladies of Labor, Girls of Adventure: Working Women, Popular Culture, and Labor Politics at the Turn of the Twentieth Century,* New York: Columbia University Press.

Ross, Steven J. (1998) *Working-Class Hollywood: Silent Film and the Shaping of Class in America,* Princeton: Princeton University Press.

Sloan, Kay (1988) *The Loud Silents: Origins of the Social Problem Film,* Urbana: University of Illinois Press.

RICHARD ABEL

Laemmle, Carl

b. 1867; d. 1939

exhibitor, distributor, producer, USA

Carl Laemmle (originally Lammle, pronounced Lemly) was born in Laupheim, Wurttemberg, Germany, the tenth of thirteen children. At age 13, he left school and apprenticed to a dealer in stationery goods and novelties. In 1884, he set sail for America to join his older brother Louis in Chicago. Here he continued to work in the retail business, eventually settling in Oshkosh (Wisconsin), where he worked as manager of a dry goods store owned by Samuel Stern (whose niece, Recha, he married in 1898).

In early 1906, Laemmle returned to Chicago, intending to enter the chain store business. Instead, he was captivated by one of the city's first **nickelodeons**: "the basic idea of motion pictures and Mr. Woolworth's innovation," he realized, "were identical." For Laemmle, the nickelodeon was a cheap new form of dry goods emporium, but one which could be started up without inventory costs.

Backed by Stern, Laemmle opened the "White Front," in February 1906, and another theater, the "Family," two months later. Dissatisfied with George **Spoor**'s local film rental exchange, he established his own, the Laemmle Film Service, by year's end. Laemmle drew on his retail experience in emphasizing personal service and customer satisfaction in both exhibition and rental businesses. His partners were his brother and Robert H. Cochrane, an advertising man with whom he had worked in Oshkosh. Instead of their product, Cochrane's campaigns promoted Laemmle himself as an honest, "straight from the shoulder" businessman not unlike his customers. "I am the moving picture man," Laemmle's smiling face announced from these ads, claiming to have better taste, experience, and judgment than anyone else in the industry. This first-person style of **advertising** would continue throughout his career.

Within two years, Laemmle Film Service had expanded to ten offices in the Midwest and Canada, and claimed to be the largest such operation in the country. In early 1909, Laemmle agreed to license films from the **Motion Picture Patents Company**, but withdrew in April because of disagreements involving royalty payments and business management. When the MPPC cut off his supply of films, he was forced to become a producer through his new company, **IMP** (Independent Moving Pictures). To protect itself from the MPPC's legal assaults, IMP joined with **New York Motion Picture Company** and other independent producers to form the **Motion Picture Distributing Sales Company** in 1910. The Sales Company (which Laemmle headed) was not just an alternative to the **General Film Company** (set up to handle licensed releases) but also a vehicle for coordinating the independents' eventually successful legal defense.

The Sales Company eventually broke up, with half of its members reorganizing as the **Universal Film Manufacturing Company** on 20 April 1912.

Figure 69 Carl Laemmle. (Courtesy of Richard Koszarski.)

Of the original incorporators, Jules **Brulator**, Charles **Baumann**, and William **Swanson** soon left, and Pat **Powers** began a lengthy battle with Laemmle over corporate control. In 1915, Universal consolidated its inherited production facilities, building a large new studio in Fort Lee (New Jersey), and an even larger Universal City north of Hollywood. Soon all production was concentrated at Universal City, where Laemmle could perfect his notion of the mass production of inexpensive films. After buying out Powers in 1920, Laemmle moved his home from New York to California in 1924, purchasing Thomas **Ince**'s Beverly Hills estate.

Although one of the first to heavily promote his **stars**, notably Florence **Lawrence** in 1910 and Mary **Pickford** in 1911, Laemmle later decried the increased costs of star salaries. The economics of feature film production also disturbed him, and he maintained a full program of short film releases longer than any of his rivals. During the 1920s, Laemmle continued to focus on small exhibitors, while his competitors built large theater chains which shut Universal out of the best markets.

Not especially interested in production, Laemmle never developed an efficient system of studio management, and became a target of humor for staffing the studio with members of the Stern and Laemmle

families (including a nephew, William Wyler). The appointment of his 21-year-old secretary, Irving Thalberg, as head of production in 1920 was a typically capricious gesture. Laemmle sold his interest in Universal in 1936 and devoted his last years to assisting Jewish emigration from Nazi Germany.

Further reading

Drinkwater, John (1931) *The Life and Adventures of Carl Laemmle*, New York & London: G. P. Putnam's Sons.
Laemmle, Carl (1989) "This Business of Motion Pictures," *Film History*, 3.1: 47–71.

RICHARD KOSZARSKI

Laffitte, Paul

b. 1864; d. 1949

writer, executive, France

Laffitte, a former newspaper theater columnist, founded the **Compagnie des Cinéma-Halls** with his brother Léon in 1907. Cinéma-Halls transformed the place Clichy racetrack in Paris into a moving picture theater, yet Lafitte remains best known as the founder of **Film d'Art** in February 1908. With Film d'Art, the new industry put on a cultivated, affable face in order to attract writers to the cinema. However, Lafitte's poor management of the company disqualified him in the eyes of its board of directors in June 1909. After the collapse of Cinémas-Halls, he maintained a foothold in the industry as director of an **advertising** company, La Publicité animée.

ALAIN CAROU

Lamster, Johann Christian

b. 1872; d. ?

army officer, filmmaker, curator, the Netherlands

In 1912, the Dutch Colonial Institute commissioned Lamster, a captain in the Dutch army in the former Dutch East Indies, to film the beneficial effects of colonization in the Indies and to create a better understanding of those effects among Dutch audiences. First Lamster went to Paris to learn the trade at **Pathé-Frères**, well known for its **travelogues**. The fifty-six short films he then made between 1912 and 1913 dealt with such subjects as industry, agriculture, education, tourism, ethnography, and the army. In 1924, he would begin a new career as curator at the Colonial Institute.

See also: colonialism: Europe

IVO BLOM

Lange, Konrad

b. 1855; d. 1921

reformer, Germany

A prominent art historian at the University of Tübingen, Lange devoted the last decade of his life to film reform, an unlikely cause for a man of his stature and position. He was not at the vanguard of the movement, having entered the fray in 1912, but his name lent it considerable rhetorical weight. Much more interested in warning the nation about the dangers of movie-going than actually reforming film production and exhibition (*contra* Hermann **Häfker**), Lange and his proclamations had a considerable legacy in later, sociologically-oriented media-effects research.

SCOTT CURTIS

Larsen, Viggo

b. 1880; d. 1957

actor, filmmaker, Denmark, Germany

Hired by Ole **Olsen** as an attendant at his Copenhagen cinema, the ex-soldier Larsen was put in charge of film production at **Nordisk** soon after the company began operation. Larsen directed most of the company's films until 1909, including the famous *Løvejagten* [The Lion Hunt] (1907–1908), a Sherlock Holmes **detective film** series, and several Napoleon pictures—Larsen, who supposedly resembled the emperor, took the

lead role. In 1910, he settled in Germany where he was very successful, working in nearly every genre, from **comedies** to **westerns** to social dramas such as the impressive *Die Sumpfblume* (1913).

CASPER TYBJERG

Lasky, Jesse

b. 1880; d. 1958

producer, USA

Born in California, Lasky had a successful career in **vaudeville** and the legitimate **theater** before entering the moving picture business. In 1913, he formed the Jesse L. Lasky Feature Play Company with Samuel Goldfish (later Goldwyn) and famed theatrical producer Cecil B. **DeMille**. Its first film, *The Squaw Man* (1914), was one of the first feature films produced in Hollywood. The Lasky Company distributed through Paramount from its inception in 1914, merging with Adolph **Zukor**'s **Famous Players** to form Famous-Players Lasky in 1916. Lasky was one of the thirty-six founders of the Academy of Motion Picture Arts and Sciences.

MICHAEL QUINN

Latham, Gray and Otway

inventors/filmmakers/exhibitors, USA

Gray (1867–1907) and Otway (1868–1906) Latham founded the Kinetoscope Exhibition Company with Samuel J. Tilden and Enoch J. Rector to exploit their **boxing films**. After exhibiting fights between Michael Leonard/Jack Cushing and James **Corbett**/Peter Courtney, they formed the Lambda Company with their father Woodville (1837–1911), employing Eugene **Lauste** to develop a **projector**, with advice from W. K. L. **Dickson**. Their Panopticon used 2-inch-wide film and opened publicly on 20 May 1895. Improved as the Eidoloscope, using a loose loop of film that reduced wear on the celluloid, it was again exhibited more successfully, and the

"Latham Loop" became a key element in the formation of the **Motion Picture Patents Company**, although Lambda was inactive by 1898.

DEAC ROSSELL

Lauste, Eugene

b. 17 January 1857, Montmartre district, Paris, France; d. 27 June 1935, Bloomfield, New Jersey, USA

inventor, USA, UK

In London in the early 1900's, Eugene Lauste designed one of the earliest systems to record sound on film but was unable to market it. A former **Edison** employee and friend of W. K. L. **Dickson**, Lauste was hired by the **Latham** family in the fall of 1894 to help design a **camera** and a **projector**. The extent to which Lauste contributed to the design of their Eidoloscope is controversial. In 1897, Lauste was sent to Europe by **American Mutoscope and Biograph** company, where he briefly managed the **American Biograph** company studio outside Paris. In 1930, Western Electric bought Lauste's patents for sound.

PAUL SPEHR

Lautensack, Heinrich

b. 1881; d. 1919

writer, Germany

A playwright, poet, and cabaret artist constantly running into censorship problems, Lautensack was employed by Deutsche Bioscop until May 1912, when he became script editor and public relations manager at the newly founded **Continental-Kunstfilm**. He wrote a string of melodramas, often using parallel plot construction and strong psychological conflicts, as in *Zweimal gelebt* [Living Twice] (1912), *Entsagungen* [Renunciations] (1913), and *Zwischen Himmel und Erde* [Between Heaven and Earth] (1913). In 1918, Lautensack scripted the funeral of his mentor Frank Wedekind and produced it as a film. He died shortly afterwards, mentally deranged, in a sanatorium.

MICHAEL WEDEL

Lavanchy-Clarke, François-Henri

b. 1848; d. 1922

businessman, Lumière concessionary, Switzerland

Lavanchy-Clarke, the Swiss importer of Sunlight soap (manufactured by Lever Brothers, Liverpool), also had interests in automatic dispensers and **advertising** innovations. He was one of the founders of Georges **Demenÿ**'s Société générale du Phonoscope (1892–1895) with, among others, German industrialist Ludwig **Stollwerck**. Serving as an intermediary between the latter and the **Lumières**, he obtained the rights to exploit the **Cinématographe Lumière** in Switzerland and, in May 1896, presented the novelty of "moving photographs" as a means to promote Sunlight products, on the fringes of the Swiss national fair in Geneva. The Swiss subjects of the Lumière catalog, filmed for the most part by cameraman Constant Girel (1873–1952), derive from this concession. The Lavanchy deposit of original prints, whether listed in the Lyons catalog or not, constitutes one of the richest ensembles in the Lumière collection preserved at the Archives du Film in France.

See also: archives; collections

Further reading

Cosandey, Roland (1992) "Lavanchy-Clarke: Sunlight & Lumière, ou les débuts du cinématographe en Suisse," *Equinoxe* (Lausanne), 7: 9–27.

ROLAND COSANDEY

law and the cinema

The legal history of moving pictures reflects the challenges of a new medium entering an established discursive framework: existing regulatory and protective principles seem clear enough, but the devil is in the detail. The very contours of the medium were at stake, its technology, social interactions, production practices, and vulnerability to any number of concerned (and opportunistic) constituencies. The process of legal integration, as a look at any of the major sites of juridical and legislative activity reveals, entailed a process of social rationalization with very real implications for the shape and practice of the medium.

The patent process sparked the first legal battles, as competing claimants struggled to define and control the technological platform that would give the medium substance. **Edison**'s premature patents for the **Kinetoscope** and **Kinetograph** (1891) would take two decades to resolve, in the process driving out some competition and stimulating others to develop creative alternatives. The fact that his patents were limited to the USA stimulated very different developments in Europe, which also had the benefit of alternate technological solutions.

The medium's legal identity also took form relatively early, but its changing cultural status would sometimes result in pressures to rewrite the law. In New York City, for example, the medium's mechanical platform caused it to be categorized as a "common show" along with merry-go-rounds and roller coasters. But film's growing popularity after 1906 and the fact that common shows could operate on Sundays when "entertainments of the stage" were banned, led to growing pressure to rethink this definition (something that formally occurred in 1913).

Legal protection for the creative labor of filmmakers through the **copyright** process also took time to develop. In the USA, for example, film was retrofitted to take advantage of the protections finally afforded the photographic image in 1884. Edison learned the hard way in his 1902 struggle with **Lubin** that this meant *every* image or frame; only a decade later were motion pictures as such finally protected by international copyright. In many European countries, the issue of creative authorship and moral rights solved the new medium's problems in far more elegant fashion—a distinction in protection with implications for contemporary trans-Atlantic market battles (and with them, issues of tariffs and film's status as commercial product or cultural good). Film's relations with other expressive media were also tested,

as for example in the 1907 *Ben Hur* case where Harper and Brothers and the General Lew Wallace Estate brought suit against the **Kalem** Company (and won). Cinematic content was additionally impinged upon through censorship provisions, whether enacted on the local or national level.

The site of moving picture exhibition also opened up a range of legal issues. Licensing (of businesses, of **projectionists**), safety (electrical, health, fire), and architectural codes (seating, construction materials), in addition to regulations regarding the age, race, and gender of patrons, all offered opportunities for legislation and litigation. Although most frequently played out in a local arena, these issues would leave lasting impressions on the physical and social space of the cinema.

The history of the cinema's *pas de deux* with the various agencies of the law, whether proscriptive or judgmental, whether local or national, whether in one national legal tradition or another, would be determining of subsequent cultural practices.

See also: audiences: surveys and debates; trade marks; US patent wars

WILLIAM URICCHIO

law and the cinema: regulating exhibition

The moving picture entered a world already organized around various cultural practices and forms of social control. Its institutionalization owed much to interactions with existing regulatory frameworks and to the development of new, more medium-specific social guidelines. The processes by which a new technological constellation became a widespread cultural practice, while multiple and complex, tended to be centered on that aspect of the medium most visible in the public's eye—exhibition. This is not to minimize the importance of the struggles over patents, **copyrights**, tariffs, and various forms of contract law, but rather to suggest that the regulatory battle over the sites of film exhibition were fierce, visible, and highly revealing in terms of the cultural landscape that the medium would inhabit. Moreover, since the regulatory process and the debates that surrounded it often were inscribed as public record, they produced significant residue helping to shape subsequent efforts of researchers concerned with the medium's history.

Regulatory efforts initially consisted of simple extensions of existing municipal licensing categories for public entertainments or for the operation of mechanical devices. The regulatory environment remained relatively stable until (depending on the national context) ca. 1906–1909, when the cinema began to attract mass audiences and permanent moving picture theaters began to multiply. Any number of constituencies perceived this development as a threat to the status quo and pressed the case for containment of the new medium. The groups calling for regulation were as varied as their motives, and included existing theatrical interests, religious leaders, progressive uplift organizations, the insurance industry, selected film companies, together with municipal agencies of all sorts, from the police and fire departments to building, electrical, and health departments. Motives ranged from either outright suppression or progressive notions of civic improvement to the maximization of profit, whether in the form of graft or legitimate business opportunities. More often than not, legislation—whether municipal, state, or national—was the preferred mode of regulation; but regulation also appeared in the form of trade association policy (for example, in the USA, the efforts of the **Motion Picture Patents Corporation** (MMPC) and **National Board of Censorship** (NBC)), fire insurance guidelines, and professional norms (for example, for **projectionists**).

Regulatory efforts took many forms and affected nearly every aspect of film exhibition. Those regulations dealing with moving picture content are better known as censorship; but other sets of regulations were imposed regarding film stock, whether nitrate or safety. Sometimes they even specified the topics that could be shown: for example, **religious films** only, on Sundays. Licensing guidelines sometimes also determined how films would be accompanied and whether or not live acts could be included (or whether other more expensive categories such as theatrical licensing would be more appropriate). Extensive

regulations specified the physical environment of the hall and projection booth, including building materials, aisle width, exit door locations, maximum numbers of seats, air circulation, and even lighting levels. Still other regulations limited the locations of moving picture theaters (zoning ordinances), and the exterior uses of electric signs and music. Moving picture operators, too, were subject to regulations regarding age, training, and, in some cases, even citizenship. And **audiences** were not exempt from regulatory guidelines. Some cities barred under-16 year olds from admission, imposed **racial segregation**, and on occasion banned women and certain ethnic minorities from the cinema. Some localities even required the presence of firemen or a policeman to assure physical safety or matrons to assure the moral safety of vulnerable audience members. Still other municipalities barred the showing of films on Sundays. Whether legislative act or *de facto* police intervention, these restrictions were often tested in the courts, resulting in protracted negotiations between the interests of cinema owners and the varied interests of the community. In many cases, regulatory efforts supported badly needed improvements for the fast-growing medium; but in others, they provided opportunities for suppression or excuses for bribery and extortion. And in some instances, regulations were even used by the dominant faction of the industry to pressure the competition out of existence.

Although the specific motives and strategies for motion picture regulation depended heavily on local circumstances, a detailed example offers an opportunity to explore the complications and lasting implications of early regulatory efforts. New York City, home to several major film studios (**Edison**, **Vitagraph**, **Biograph**) and trade publications (*Moving Picture World, New York Dramatic Mirror*), although not necessarily typical of exhibition in other American cities or locales elsewhere in the world, nevertheless, exemplifies some of the key conditions that film exhibitors and regulators faced. In the American scene, New York City emblematized the political, social and cultural contestation attendant to rapid **urbanization**, growing immigrant populations, and labor unrest. Particularly after 1907, cinema and its audiences were increasingly associated with these developments, triggering a number of attempts to contain if not eradicate them. Between 1908, when New York's Mayor George B. McClellan, Jr. summarily revoked 550 **nickelodeon** licenses, and 1913, when the Board of Alderman, the city's legislative body, passed a long-contested ordinance regulating the construction of new moving picture venues, a multiplicity of players advocated various approaches to regulating exhibition sites and disciplining their audiences.

The backstory to this development helps to explain the array of sometimes-contradictory motives in the regulatory effort. First, material conditions at a number of nickelodeons were indeed poor, reflecting the limited means and scruples of some exhibitors who were drawn to the medium as something of a "get rich quick" scheme. Particularly in tenement districts such as the city's Lower East Side, where space and financial resources were at a premium, police reports documented nickelodeon fire exits that led to blind walls, badly constructed balconies, and projection booths with exposed wiring. Although such conditions may have existed in only a minority of cinemas, their extremity was such that they posed very real hazards both for their patrons as well as for the tenement blocks within which they were located. Such venues were seized upon as exemplary not only by the cinema's enemies but also by its supporters, such as progressive reformers who sought to improve the conditions of tenement life. They were used by organizations such as the MPPC and NBC that sought to standardize a higher quality exhibition experience.

A second background factor relates to the significant losses encountered by the insurance industry in the early years of the 20th century. The 1906 San Francisco fire had shown the devastation that an urban conflagration could bring to bear upon lives and, perhaps more importantly, property. The 1908 Boyertown, Pennsylvania, opera house fire served as the primary exemplar of the dangers of moving pictures even though the film equipment had not, in fact, caused the fire. These events formed key components of the perceptual framework through which elites, particularly, of course, those in the fire insurance business, perceived nickelodeons. Crowded urban conditions in conjunction with the dangerously volatile films could spell

disaster for the nation's largest metropolis. A National Board of Fire Underwriters (NFBU) expert reported that "After such a conflagration, there would not be a fire-insurance company left in the world." The NFBU sponsored systematic surveys of such factors as building construction materials, commercial property uses, population densities, and fire department effectiveness, all as ways of evaluating the fire hazard in a given locality. Their recommendations, enforced by city-wide insurance rates, gained the immediate attention of municipal governments and often appeared re-written as thinly disguised city ordinances.

A third and more complex explanatory background can be found in the various constituencies that shaped municipal governments and that more often than not responded to perceptions of national developments on a local level. Secular and clerical conservatives alike seized upon the moving picture as an embodiment of all that was wrong with the rapidly changing social scene. The medium's ability to mobilize the masses together with the uncertain but nevertheless suspect nature of what happened in darkened nickelodeons led to calls for total suppression. The film industry, meanwhile, instrumentally supported any suggestion that might lessen its perceived threat to the status quo, frequently allying itself with progressive reformers and "professionals" and their formulation of policy proposals for dealing with the problems of sanitation, fire, and so forth. The situation was complicated by an array of political actors representing different constituencies and pressures and by licensing distinctions that encouraged circuitous action. For example, since New York City's nickelodeons were licensed as "common shows" (and not "entertainments of the stage"), an issue such as Sunday closings could take the form of investigations into fire safety rather than outright Sabbath violation, as it did in the 1908 closings. Although the motives and viewpoints of these various constituencies differed, they played out in the contentious arena of urban politics.

Lurking beneath these various positions are a number of not so apparent issues such as whether a mono-cultural or multi-cultural environment would prevail, or indeed, how culture itself would be defined and by whom. On the one hand, we can see how certain assumptions about working class and immigrant audiences helped to fuel regulatory concerns. Described in the case of New York City as "excitable foreigners," "foreign, low-grade and ignorant communities," and "panicky crowds", the nickelodeon's audiences were constructed as in dire need of control. Yet, on the other hand, the uplifting vision of the progressive era was growing in importance, and with it the notion that squalid living conditions, political corruption, and social despair (all, as played out in the city and its synecdoche, the cinema) could all be bettered through a process of rationalization and regulation. While stoked by the fears of nativists and repressive clerics, the engine of reform was driven by progressives working on a number of different fronts to regulate and improve society and with it, moving pictures.

Notable among these progressive groups was the NBC, an organization discretely funded in part by the MPPC and run by prominent social reformers. Although best known for its recommendations regarding film content, the NBC encouraged regulation of cinemas using a variety of tactics. They developed a model cinema, offering an example of how things ought to be; they proposed site regulations, guidelines for safe and clean cinemas; and finally they conducted studies of exhibition conditions making sure that the data reached those involved in framing new ordinances. A rather different approach to regulation was advocated by the professional classes of heating and ventilating engineers, architects, electrical engineers, medical doctors, and fire insurance underwriters. The engineers of middle-class norms, they embraced regulation as an extension of the Enlightenment project of rationalization, providing the micro-technologies of control that would leave a lasting imprint on the physical conditions of moving picture exhibition.

Ironically, the municipal organs empowered to regulate moving picture exhibition and to enforce those guidelines were often in need of regulation themselves. Again, the specifics are highly local, but New York City's Police and Fire Departments in the years leading up to the **World War I** were prone to corruption, as was the Bureau of Licenses which handled nickelodeon permits. Enforcement of building codes or the efforts of the Department of Water Supply, Gas and Electricity to train and license projectionists, while well-intended, often

broke down at the level of execution. In a sense, these organizations took their lead from the progressive reformers and from the just-mentioned professionals, the sources in most cases of regulatory code. Their enforcement efforts were, in turn, controlled by those reformers and professionals, as the role of insurers (and in particular, the NBFU) demonstrates. National and indeed multi-national in scope, the insurance industry and the professional societies with which it was intertwined dwarfed the power of any particular municipality, ultimately determining both regulatory frameworks and assuring their reasonable enforcement.

See also: migration/immigration

Further reading

Bowser, Eileen (1990) *The Transformation of Cinema, 1907–1915*, New York: Scribners.

Grieveson, Lee (2004) *Policing Cinema: Movies and Censorship in Early Twentieth-Century America*, Berkeley, University of California Press.

Uricchio, William and Pearson, Roberta E. (1994) "Constructing the Mass Audience: Competing Discourses of Morality and Rationalization in the Nickelodeon Period," *Iris*, 17: 43–54.

Waller, Gregory (1995) *Main Street Amusements: Movies and Commercial Entertainment in a Southern City, 1896–1930*, Washington, D.C.: Smithsonian Institution Press.

WILLIAM URICCHIO

Lawrence, Florence (Florence Annie Bridgwood)

b. 1886, Hamilton, Ontario; d. 1938, Los Angeles

actor, USA

"Biograph Girl" Florence Lawrence was the screen's first star before producers revealed actors' names. She entered films in 1907 with **Edison**, joining **Biograph** the following year. Her acting style was broad, but she charmed audiences. After signing her with **IMP**, Carl **Laemmle** confirmed her **star** status with a **publicity** stunt in early 1910; a year later, she joined **Lubin**. **Universal**'s Victor brand was established to feature the still popular Lawrence in 1912. She quit the movies in 1914, and a later comeback was short-lived. She ended her career as an extra; death was by suicide.

Further reading

Brown, Kelly R. (1999) *Florence Lawrence, The Biograph Girl*, Jefferson: McFarland.

ROBERT S. BIRCHARD

Le Bargy, Charles

b. 1858; d. 1936

actor, producer, France

A colorful but unruly member of the Comédie-Française, Le Bargy was the first artistic director of **Film d'Art**, founded in 1908. He supervised the shooting of *L'Assassinat du duc de Guise* [The Assassination of the Duke de Guise] (1908), in which he also played the title role. His subdued **acting style**, which was original for the period, did not fail to attract attention from the critics. He also acted as baron Scarpia in the second version of *La Tosca*, the one eventually released in 1909. Although Le Bargy left Film d'Art along with Paul **Laffitte**, his influence apparently was crucial in the company's preference for studio over location shooting.

ALAIN CAROU

Le Blond, Elizabeth Alice Frances

b. 1861; d. 1934

mountaineer, writer, Great Britain

From 1883 on, Elizabeth Le Blond (née Hawkins-Whitshed, twice married before wedding Francis Bernard Aubrey Le Blond in 1900) published many books on mountaineering that drew on her experience of the Alps, particularly in winter ascents. An English aristocrat and non-conformist sportswoman, she presided over the Ladies Alpine Club from 1907 to 1934 and long lived in the Engadine (Switzerland). She used a moving picture **camera** at least once: the September 1902 **Williamson** catalog featured a series of ten "views" of "Winter Sports in the Engadine" made by her or under her direction in Saint-Moritz around 1899–1900. Cecil **Hepworth** brought attention to these films in *Animated Photography* (1900). Although Le Blond's interest in moving pictures was more ephemeral than her practice of **photography** (see the plates in E. F. Benson, *Winter Sports in Switzerland*, 1913), it does evince the close ties between cinema, tourism, and sports during these early years.

Further reading

Frischknecht, Jürg *et al.* (2002) *Filmlandschaft: Engadin, Bergell, Puschlav, Münstertal*, Chur: Bündner Monatsblatt.

ROLAND COSANDEY

Le Prince, Louis Aimé Augustin

b. 1841, Metz, France; d. 1890 (?)

inventor, France, England, USA

The French subject of cinema's earliest tragedy. Experienced in **photography** on metal and ceramics, Le Prince also managed several large circular panoramas in the USA. From 1886, he experimented with moving picture machines. In various countries, he patented a **camera** with from one to sixteen lenses (the one- and two-lens versions were disallowed in the USA), testing a 16-lens machine in Paris in 1887. In England, his single-lens camera took paper negative sequences around October 1888: a garden scene, his son playing the melodion, and traffic on Leeds bridge. Financially burdened and despairing of projection success, Le Prince disappeared on a train journey in France on 16 September 1890.

Further reading

Rawlence, Christopher (1990) *The Missing Reel*, London: Collins.

STEPHEN HERBERT

Leal, Antônio

b. 1876, Viana do Castelo, Portugal;
d. 1946, Rio de Janeiro, Brazil

cameraman, filmmaker, Brazil

Among the most successful pioneers, Leal began filming *actualités* in 1905, after working as a photographer. In 1908, he and a business partner established a production company, Fotocinematográfica Brasileira, and opened the Cinema Palace (both centrally located in Rio). Although continuing to make actualités, Leal also produced a variety of *filmes posados* (fiction films). One of his earliest suggests the complicated **modernity** embodied by the medium: *O comprador de ratos* [The Rat Buyer] (1908) exploited the government's efforts to eradicate yellow fever by buying dead rats, whose inadvertent consequence was a thriving rodent industry. Indeed, Leal was a crucial figure in developing the popular genre of **crime films**: he shot Francisco Marzullo's *Os estranguladores* [The Stranglers] (1906) and directed *A mala sinistra* [The Sinister Suitcase] (1908). After 1910–1911, he was forced by market pressures to focus on **newsreel** production with only occasional forays into fiction.

ANA M. LÓPEZ

lecturer

Before cinema's arrival, **magic lantern shows** were generally accompanied by commentary by the lanternist, who could thereby announce or explain the views he was presenting or provide verbal narration for the images. An analogous situation prevailed for the projection of the first moving pictures, a practice which continued into the 1910s. In fact, in early cinema it was relatively common for a lecturer to provide the viewer with commentary on the images as they unfolded on the screen. In addition to this role as a "voice-over narrator," the lecturer could also elect to personify the characters on screen (by acting out their dialogue) or provide the film with **sound effects**. He might also read the film's **intertitles** out loud, which, given the high degree of illiteracy among

some poorer audiences, would have been extremely useful if not essential.

Itinerant exhibitors often performed a dual role as **projectionist** and lecturer, punctuating their screenings with random commentary. In **fairground** shows and the first **nickelodeons** or storefront theaters, the lecturer was often an employee of the exhibitor. His first task was to act as a barker at the entrance to attract an audience and entice them to enter the show, which he would then comment on. In **vaudeville**, the lecturer might also be the master of ceremonies, whose patter would link the moving pictures with acts.

The lecturer was always an intermittent presence, never an essential part of a moving picture show. Nevertheless, he enjoyed a certain popularity, especially during the years 1904–1908, when his presence seems to have become quite widespread, with the apparent collaboration of the film manufacturers themselves, who provided exhibitors with texts which could be read out during projection.

Only in the past twenty years has this "live film commentator" begun to emerge from the shadows. He reappeared in the wake of the growth of research into early cinema that arose out of the Brighton Conference of 1978, and also as a consequence of Noël Burch's study of Japanese cinema. In Japan, the **benshi** lasted longer and remained much more well-known to their public than did their Western counterparts.

Except in the case of Japan, commenting on a film was never a stable practice with well-established norms. We still don't know the extent of the practice from one continent or country to another. Recent research, however, indicates that the lecturer was considerably more common than formerly had been believed. It is hard not to conclude that his almost complete disappearance from the "collective memory" of the pioneer film historians was the result of some sort of repression. For these historians (from the 1920s through the 1960s), the lecturer may have appeared to be negligible, despite his ubiquity, because he cast the cinema into the "realm of the circus" at a time when it was important to establish cinema's pedigree.

Since then, the lecturer's presence has been demonstrated convincingly in **Canada** (and particularly **Quebec**, where close scrutiny of daily newspapers of the period has recently made it possible to describe his work in relative detail), the Netherlands, Spain, France, and the USA. Traces of his passage can also be found in countries such as Russia, China, Korea, and Iran, as well as throughout South America. Oddly enough, there are few traces of his presence in Italy, unlike that country's barker or *imbonitore*.

Before 1900, the lecturer's role was primarily to endow the images on the screen with a "human element." Views of the day were simple, short, and relatively easy to understand. Most often they sought to provide little more than sheer visual pleasure, and by all appearances no "explanation" was required to understand them. During this period, the lecturer's role was to provide entertainment and to embellish the apparatus' performance by compensating for its inherent "mutism."

We can suppose that over time the lecturer's role was gradually transformed into that of an accessory to the narrative. Films began to get longer as stories became more complex, especially as the number of shots increased. Narrative continuity, which was relatively easy to maintain when films consisted of a single shot, came to be seriously threatened. Each interruption in the filming gave rise to a spatial or temporal interruption in the story being told and poked holes in the narrative fabric. The narrative thread was constantly at risk of being broken, leaving the spectator with too great an interpretive role and constantly on the verge of incomprehension. Unequivocal language was called to the rescue of the equivocal image. But between written language and spoken language, the choice was not easy. "If some film manufacturer would make every one of his film subjects explain themselves as they pass through the machine, he would soon have all the business he could attend to," wrote W. M. Rhoads in a letter to *Moving Picture World* (22 February 1908). "If instead of having a few words of explanation on his films about every 100 feet, as most of them do, [he] would have these explanations come in at every 20 or 30 feet (or at every place in the film where an explanation was necessary), then the theater manager would have no use for a lecturer." And so it became necessary to choose between two "evils": either to resort to intertitles, which significantly increased the cost of the film (sold by the

meter or foot) and interrupted the flow of images, or to turn to the lecturer, whose comments were local in nature and could thus contradict the story told by the images, a story devised by the film's producer. The industry would soon decide in favor of an internally developed narration, through the images (using **editing** in particular), at the expense of that external figure, the lecturer (soon to be kicked out of the hall), and at the expense also of intertitles, whose excessive use began to be curtailed.

See also: cinema of attractions; classic Hollywood cinema; dialogue accompaniment

Further reading

Burch, Noël (1979) *To the Distant Observer: Form and Meaning in the Japanese Cinema*, Berkeley: University of California Press.

Gaudreault, André and Germain Lacasse (ed.) (1996) "Le bonimenteur de vues animées/The Moving Picture Lecturer," *Iris*, 22 (special issue).

Lacasse, Germain (2000) *Le bonimenteur de vues animées. Le cinema "muet" entre tradition et modernité*, Quebec City/Paris: Nota Bene/ Méridiens Klincksieck.

Musser, Charles and Carol Nelson (1991) *High-Class Moving Pictures: Lyman H. Howe and the Forgotten Era of Travelling Exhibition 1880–1920*, Princeton: Princeton University Press.

ANDRÉ GAUDREAULT

leisure time and space: USA

Leisure during the late 19th and early 20th centuries consisted of myriad activities ranging from respectable to licentious, pastoral to urban, instructive to entertaining, and homosocial to heterosocial. A key phenomenon during this period was the development of inexpensive commercialized leisure such as midway side shows at world and pan-American expositions (see **world's fairs**), **amusement parks**, **vaudeville** theaters, dance halls, and **nickelodeons**. Business enterprises in this category were characterized by low admission costs, and a clientele that was largely heterosocial and heterogeneous in ethnic and, in some cases, class terms, and vast in number. In 1904, most rides at Coney Island cost 10 cents; in 1909, a dance hall "affair" in Manhattan cost 25 cents per couple and 10 cents for a single woman. Reformer Michael Davis reported in 1911 that moving picture shows in Manhattan were charging 10 cents for adults and 5 cents for children. Business men and reformers alike cited high attendance numbers: five million visitors at Coney Island's Luna Park in 1907; and in 1909, daily audiences at picture shows of from a quarter to a half million on Sundays in New York City alone and a daily national audience of 4,000,000 people in almost 2,000 picture theaters in 118 cities. In 1911, an estimated four to five million young men and women attended over 100 dance halls in Manhattan.

These commercial activities were distinct, on the one hand, from ethnic, home, church, and community based activities such as religious festivals, neighborly socializing on tenement steps, and parades on public holidays, and, on the other hand, from didactic and improving activities such as lectures on thrift and working conditions in working girls' associations and settlement houses, strolls in landscaped public parks, and work or club sponsored summer vacations. In the context of this variety of ways of spending time, commercialized recreation was a paradigmatic marker of a modern urban Americanized lifestyle. The spaces of commercialized leisure were subject to the scrutiny of middle class reform organizations, which sent investigators into the field to amass data on the safety of buildings and to uncover details on the behavior of customers. At the same time, subcultural groups such as single female wage earners or black urban movie-goers (see **black cinema: USA**) used the locales of dance hall, nickel theater, and the like to recast leisure for their own purposes. This dual sense of the meaning of leisure—as regulation and as pleasure—was a striking characteristic of the period from the 1890s to the mid-1910s in the USA.

The social and political implications of leisure as a context for assessing the role of early cinema can be analyzed in relation to this tension around commercialized recreation and to other historical developments: shifts in the meaning of work and leisure as a result of monopoly **capitalism**;

modernity and **urbanization**, especially a restructuring of space and time associated with an urban sensibility attuned to the experience of shock; the related phenomenon of *flânerie*, involving new modes of perception or subjectivity invested in literal and imaginary mobility; the emergence of consumer culture as a realm for expressing individual autonomy; and, especially from the 1910s, mass production linked to mass consumption associated with Henry Ford's use of moving assembly lines in car manufacturing and his high $5 per day wage. In the context of these developments, the physical spaces of urban streets, **department stores**, amusement parks, nickelodeons, and factories became emblematic spaces of modern life with its attendant changes in the structure of experience. During this period, women's increased presence in heterosocial public spaces and concentrations in urban centers both of immigrants from Eastern and Southern Europe and of African-Americans also posed the potential of leisure as a realm for articulating alternative public spheres. That is, public spaces such as moving picture theaters were also discursive sites which could provide the occasion for imagining identity and community in ways that went beyond reformers' assessments or commercial imperatives and that held out the potential for negotiating in a public manner the contradictory experiences associated with **modernity**.

This era often is referred to as the Progressive period because of the reformist political sensibility of the time, and one area of reformers' activity, budget studies, contextualized leisure in relation to the material constraints on working class families. Reported expenditure on recreation was a small percentage of overall household budgets. In one study of two hundred workingmen's families living in New York's Greenwich Village, average annual income from all sources for a family averaging 5.6 members was $851 annually with average allocations of 43.4% on food, 19.4% on rent, 10.6% on clothing, and 1.5% on recreation. Families living on $820 annually (within the range of $800–$900 recommended as a reasonable living wage, including $15 for savings), spent $9.34 or about 18 cents per week on recreation. Almost half of the sample had annual incomes of $800 or below, and just under half reported no expenditures on recreation.

While the dynamics in the interview situation may have led to under-reporting of perceived inappropriate expenditures (in this case, additional money for leisure probably came from the 3.3% allocation for "spending money"), budget studies, nevertheless, foregrounded the struggles with finances on the part of working class and immigrant groups. The constraint of low wages particularly affected single female wage earners, and as a result, young women's relationship to commercialized leisure was often filtered through a heterosexual dating culture in which women accepted "treats" from men, including meals, gifts, or tickets for shows or amusement park rides.

The term, "cheap," was frequently attached to low-priced commercial recreations and, for reformers, carried the additional connotation of dubious moral worth. Within this designation, however, reformers also made distinctions with regard to respectability. John **Collier** in 1908 assessed various "cheap amusements" and contrasted the improved nickelodeon, which had reached the status of "family theater," to the less reputable melodrama **theater**, cheap vaudeville, and **penny arcade**. Davis in 1911 similarly viewed penny arcades and two-thirds of dance halls as undesirable, but moving pictures as "wholesome." Positive assessments were often associated with a family or middle class presence.

The meaning of leisure for historical agents, however, went beyond reformers' frames of reference. Social historians, in particular, eschew top down models of historical influence and suggest the importance of the diverse perspectives of class, race, ethnicity, gender, sexual orientation, age, and locality. In the subculture of young female wage earners in New York City, going to the heterosocial leisure spaces of amusement parks, dance halls and nickelodeons, promenading unsupervised on city thoroughfares, wearing fashionable (gaudy to reformers) clothing, hats, and shoes, and experimenting with sexual assertiveness in "tough" dancing produced subcultural milieus for negotiating identity. Treating also suggested a divergence of views. For reformers, it was implicated in the sexual temptation of the weak-willed girl. For young female wage earners, treating involved a more fluid continuum of heterosexual sexual behaviors and personal styles. Within subcultures

race also mattered. When black women were visible on the streets, their behavior was more likely to be pathologized and institutional solutions involving surveillance proposed. For working-class men in the industrial town of Worcester, Massachusetts, an alternative **saloon** culture challenged individualistic and competitive values associated with industrial capitalism, fostering instead an ethos of mutuality and collectivity with other men through treating companions to rounds of drinks. "Occupational saloons" also provided free lunches and cashed checks, while "ethnic saloons" served as meeting places for fraternal organizations and gangs.

Struggles over leisure were also related to attempts to regularize and control the work day associated with capitalist industrialization, for example, through time sheets and time clocks. E. P. Thompson argues that such work practices in England (from the 1700s) resulted in an inculcation of time efficiency into workers' sensibilities and in a distinction between workers' time and employers' time, and the segregation of work from "everyday life"' and social intercourse. Notwithstanding the importance of work subcultures as spaces of social exchange, Thompson's analysis also holds true for the period of 1880–1920 in the USA when both reformers and workers viewed leisure time as a necessary respite from the monotony and increasing regimentation of work. During the same period, moreover, a shift in dominant values from a 19th-century producer ethos (hard work, self-denial, saving, and male workers as independent producers) to a consumerist ethos (spending, immediate gratification, waged labor as the norm, and the male wage linked to an "American standard of living") prioritized consumer culture. Merchandising, which transformed urban environments into a world of commodities, was the response of corporate business to the plethora of goods resulting from industrialization, and a purported democratization of access to goods was enhanced by turning urban spaces into zones of fantastic visual effects, electrical lighting and signs, billboards, and cinematic images projected on the sides of buildings. The department store with its spectacular displays of commodities behind plate glass show windows, like moving pictures, linked vision to consumer desire.

These phantasmatic spaces also invited a mode of consumer-**spectatorship** invested in mobility or *flanérie*, a term indebted to Walter Benjamin's study of 19th-century modernity through the sensibility of Charles Baudelaire and the male flaneur as social observer strolling in early-mid 19th century Parisian arcades and later as a figure "parrying" the shocks of urban modernity. With some revision, *flanérie* has been extended to the activities of woman as "flaneuse" and to turn-of-the-century mass culture. Whether this peripatetic sensibility is refigured as a new mode of subjectivity with liberatory potential or as a training ground in a new sexual politics of geography, vision structured through mobility characterized the experience of department stores, expositions, amusement parks, tourist attractions, and cinema.

In the late 19th and early 20th centuries, cities such as New York and Chicago, with their mass transit, vehicular traffic, and crowds, were characterized by sensory over- stimulation and a dislocated and fleeting sense of space and time, resulting in the contemporary malady of "neurasthenia" or nervousness. The kinesthetic thrills of amusement park rides rehearsed this urban experience in the name of leisure. For Benjamin, walking in city traffic was akin to illumination by **electricity**, **photography** as a technology of mechanical reproduction, the movement of goods on an assembly line, and the "rhythm of reception" of moving pictures, all of which replayed the assaultive experience of sense perception permeated by the shock experience and, in doing so, provided a training ground for consciousness akin to the protective stimulus shield in Freud's economy of the psyche. During the 1920s, the hegemony of a Fordist mentality ("Fordize or die!"), the affiliation between mass production, mass consumption and Americanization, and the problem of the individual in relation to the anonymous mass (even more than neurasthenia) preoccupied social observers. Leisure during the period of early cinema stands at the crossroads of various transformations.

See also: advertising; audiences: surveys and debates; cinema of attractions; fashion; migration/immigration: USA; palace cinemas; transportation; women's movement: USA

Further reading

Benjamin, Walter (1983) *Charles Baudelaire: A Lyric Poet in the Era of High Capitalism*, trans. Harry Zone, London: Verso.

Charney, Leo and Vanessa R. Schwartz (eds.) (1995) *Cinema and the Invention of Modern Life*, Berkeley: University of California Press.

Friedberg, Anne (1993) *Window Shopping: Cinema and the Postmodern*, Berkeley: University of California Press.

Hansen, Miriam (1991) *Babel and Babylon: Spectatorship in American Silent Cinema*, Cambridge: Harvard University Press.

Leach, William (1993) *Land of Desire: Merchants, Power and the Rise of a New American Culture*, New York: Vintage Books.

More, Louise Boland (1907) *Wage-Earners' Budgets: A Study of Standards and Cost of Living in New York City*, New York: Henry Holt and Company.

Peiss, Kathy (1986) *Cheap Amusements: Working Women and Leisure in Turn-of-the-Century New York*, Philadelphia: Temple University Press.

Rabinovitz, Lauren (1998) *For the Love of Pleasure: Women, Movies and Culture in Turn-of-the-Century Chicago*, New Brunswick: Rutgers University Press.

Thompson, E. P. (1967) "Time, Work-Discipline, and Industrial Capitalism," *Past and Present*, 38: 56–97.

CONSTANCE BALIDES

Leonard, Marion

b. 1880; d. 1956

actor, USA

A striking, dark-eyed actress, Leonard first appeared in **Biograph** productions just prior to D. W. **Griffith**'s directorial debut in 1908. She became one of the most notable early Griffith heroines, particularly effective in melodramas such as *Lines of White on a Sullen Sea* (1909) and *The Sealed Room* (1909). In 1910, she defected to **Reliance**, along with a number of other high-profile actors, including Henry **Walthall** and

Arthur **Johnson**. Although her husband, Stanner E. V. Taylor, remained associated with Biograph, she never returned. By the mid-teens, she had established her own production company, but she faded from public view before the decade's end.

CHARLIE KEIL

Lépine, Charles-Lucien

b. 1859; d. 1941

cameraman, filmmaker, France, Italy

According to **Pathé-Frères**' accounting records, Lépine began working for the company as an outdoor cameraman. In 1904, he was promoted to directing films whose action required on-location shooting, such as *Vot'permis? Viens l'chercher!* [The Gun License] (1905) or *Odyssée d'un paysan à Paris* [The Odyssey of a Peasant in Paris] (1905). In 1906, he and his technicians went to work in Italy for the Carlo **Rossi** company. Following his departure, in July 1906, Charles **Pathé** had him sentenced to 10 months in prison. This condemnation dealt his career a fatal blow.

LAURENT LE FORESTIER

Leprince, René

b. 1875; d. 1929

actor, filmmaker, France

Leprince began acting for **Pathé-Frères** around 1909, before swiftly moving to making films. Between 1912 and 1914, he and Ferdinand **Zecca** jointly directed many of Pathé's most ambitious productions in the *Scènes de la vie moderne* and *Scènes de la vie cruelle* series, some of which paired Gabrielle **Robinne** and René Alexandre: *La Lutte pour la vie* [Fight for Life], *Cœur de femme* [A Woman's Heart], etc. Max **Linder** also regularly asked him to direct his films between 1912 and 1916. During the 1920s, Leprince remained loyal to Pathé and made a few successful feature films for the company.

LAURENT LE FORESTIER

Levesque, Marcel

b. 1877; d. 1962

actor, filmmaker, France

Levesque, who came from the theater, was one of the few well-known actors to be hired by **Gaumont**. His lanky physical appearance marked him out for comic parts, best exploited in the *La Vie drôle* series: *L'Illustre Mâchefer* [Marvelous Mâchefer] (1914). He soon became one of the central figures of Louis **Feuillade**'s universe thanks to the roles of Mazamette in *Les Vampires* (1915–1916) and Cocantin in *Judex* (1917). After the war, he unsuccessfully attempted to return to film comedy with the *Serpentin* series. One of his last roles was in Jean Renoir's *Le Crime de M. Lange* (1936).

LAURENT LE FORESTIER

Lichtbild-Bühne, Die (1908–1939)

Paul Lenz-Levy, the founder, editor, and publisher of *Die Lichtbild-Bühne*, quickly established himself as a tireless supporter of the exhibitor in Germany. The journal's pages are filled with news of threats to the theater owner's livelihood (e.g., higher film prices, police regulations, entertainment taxes), against which it served as an important organizing force. While not overtly reformist, "LBB" was explicit about the financial and patriotic benefits of artistic legitimacy. Ultimately, however, Lenz-Levy's journal was concerned with the adverse effects of industry trends (such as **multiple-reel/feature films**) on the small-time exhibitor.

SCOTT CURTIS

lighting

The development of lighting may be seen as the result of two concurrent trends in the early period: the move from natural to artificial light sources, and the elaboration of techniques for selectively lighting actors and areas of the set. These trends are related, since it is much easier to achieve differentiated light levels on a set when all of the variables can be manipulated, and one does not have to compete with the relatively powerful and fixed light of the sun. Barry Salt, whose *Film Style and Technology* is indispensable for any consideration of this topic, has noted that early film lighting is quite distinct from both still **photography** and theatrical lighting. By 1898 it was standard practice for still photographers to achieve a "soft" look by manipulating lenses, diffusing hard light sources and softening shadows with reflected light. This look would not become a norm in cinema until the 1920s. While the theater provided models for dramatic and pictorial uses of light, theatrical lighting techniques were not directly applied by moving picture cameramen due to differences in the playing area between the cinema and the stage (see **staging in depth**): in the cinema, it is much easier to place lights at eye-level and immediately to the side of the actors, and as soon as they began to use artificial light, film-makers exploited these possibilities.

Artificial lighting devices for film derived from commercial applications, street lighting, and the stage. Mercury vapor lamps, called "Cooper-Hewitts" in the USA after the company that produced them, were relatively low-powered tubes deployed in multiple banks. **American Muta-scope Biograph** used them in its "dark" studio, constructed in 1904. Carbon arcs, in which the light came from an electrical discharge between two carbon rods, were the basis for several, quite distinct, **lighting apparatuses**. Enclosed arcs similar to street lights, "Aristos," were typically hung in rows above the sets, although they could also be set on floor stands. Like Cooper-Hewitts, multiples of arc floods acted as a diffuse source, for general illumination. **Vitagraph** used them in this manner in its Brooklyn studio built in 1906. But, unlike Cooper-Hewitts, individual arc lamps were a point source, and hence could be used for precise directional lighting. Floor stand arcs, "Klieg lights," made by Kliegl Brothers, a company that also produced units for theatrical lighting, consisted of two pairs of carbon rods in an encased housing (they produced a characteristic double shadow sometimes visible in early films). Employed from about 1908, floor stand arcs allowed for selectively lighting the set, and for some of the earliest low-key lighting effects. Spotlights, already in use in the theater and

absorbed into filmmaking around 1914, consisted of a carbon arc with a focused beam, which provided much less rapid fall-off than a floor stand arc, and a narrower, more intense beam. In addition to floor stand arcs and spotlights, small carbon arc lamps could be disguised and placed around the set to simulate firelight, lantern light, candles, etc.

Incandescent lights were the commonest form of illumination in the theater in this period, because they were not as hot as carbon arcs, required less power to run, and, unlike carbon arcs, could be wired through a resistor so that they could be dimmed, allowing for gradual lighting changes. However, the orthochromatic film stock employed in this period required light of a higher color temperature (toward the blue end of the spectrum) than incandescents could provide, so that filmmakers did not experiment with them until 1928, after the widespread adoption of panchromatic stock.

In the beginning, films were shot on open air stages with undiffused sunlight coming from above and behind the camera to give harsh, sharply defined shadows (unless the day was cloudy, a rather haphazard way of securing a diffused light source). The Black Maria, the studio in which the first **Edison** films were shot, had a panel which opened in the roof and rotated to follow the sun. Much early work on film lighting consisted in attempts to mitigate the effects of harsh natural light and to achieve a softer and more consistent form of general illumination. In 1897, Georges **Méliès** built a studio with glass roof and walls which, on the model of photographic studios, had cotton diffusers that could be stretched over the set. Specially prepared prismatic glass eventually replaced cloth diffusers as, for example, in Vitagraph's 1906 studio. By 1902, the most advanced manufacturers had stopped shooting in the open air: in its glass studio, **Pathé-Frères** supplemented diffused daylight with arc lights, as did **Gaumont**. In 1904, AM&B's deployment of Cooper-Hewitts suspended from the ceiling and on vertical floor stands meant that the harsh qualities of sunlight had been dispensed with entirely. By 1908, the stylistic norm for shooting in interiors was to have diffused general light from above, from either natural or artificial sources, supplemented by floor stand units. One refinement in this style occurs in 1910, when filmmakers shooting in exteriors begin to use the sun as a back light, behind the actors, and ease the shadows on their faces with reflector fill, bouncing the sunlight onto the actors' faces.

Selective lighting grew out of an interest in effects lighting, relatively easy to trace, and, more difficult, subtle changes in methods for general illumination which provided for a key-to-fill ratio—a differentiation between the main light for a subject and the subsidiary light which produces modeling and washes out the strongest shadows.

In the earliest films, spectacular lighting effects were painted on sets otherwise lit by diffused sunlight, as in Méliès's *Entretien de Dreyfus et de sa femme à Rennes* [Dreyfus Meets His Wife at Rennes], part of his 1899 Dreyfus affair series, in which paint mimics the effect of light coming through the prison window. Filmmakers rapidly began to exploit arc lights to provide singular effects: the tableau of old age in Edwin S. **Porter**'s *The Seven Ages* (1905) has a fire-effect done with an arc floodlight in the fireplace, as does **Griffith**'s *The Drunkard's Reformation* (1908). A more complex set-up provides the effect of dawn light coming into Pippa's bedroom in Griffith's *Pippa Passes* (1909). In 1909, filmmakers begin to experiment with silhouette and contre-jour effects in which the subject, often illuminated by natural light entering through a background window or a door, appears only in shadowy outline. Exterior contre-jour effects were also possible, as when characters were framed against a lighted sky, or light was reflected off a body of water in the background. Isolated instances may be found in Griffith's films of 1909, but the device is developed more extensively in Italian films such as **Cines**' *Patrizia e schiava* [Patrician and Slave] (1909) and *Il Cid* (1910), or **Milano**'s *L'Inferno* [Dante's Inferno] (1911). By 1913, it becomes a standard pictorial flourish for European filmmakers such as Léonce **Perret**, and also for American filmmakers in the European tradition, such as Maurice **Tourneur**.

Mood lighting, usually more extended sequences of low-key lighting to evoke an atmosphere of mystery or despair or dread, seems to begin in 1911. Salt cites the examples of the robbery scene in Albert **Capellani**'s *Le Courrier de Lyon* [The Orleans Coach] (1911) and the ending of Louis **Feuillade**'s *La Tare* [The Taint] (1911) among other similarly lit films from Gaumont's *La Vie telle*

quelle l'est [Life As It Is] series. Filmmakers in Denmark and Sweden also led the way, using practical light sources to provide extended sequences of atmospheric low-key illumination in such films as Victor **Sjöström**'s *Ingeborg Holm* (1913) or Benjamin **Christensen**'s *Det Hemmelighedsfulde* X [The Mysterious X] (1913). Salt documents other techniques perfected by Danish cameramen between 1911–1913, including lighting a scene from a single source off camera, apparent light changes within the duration of the shot (as characters turn lights on and off), and low-key effects with controlled daylight. Although there are earlier American examples, such as Vitagraph's *Conscience* (1912), the Americans initiate prolonged experiments with low-key lighting in 1915–1916. Salt describes two films, Ralph **Ince**'s *His Phantom Sweetheart* (Vitagraph, 1915) and J. Searle **Dawley**'s *Silks and Satins* (**Famous Players**, 1916) shot on the East coast, apparently almost entirely with artificial light. Better known are a series of films made in Hollywood between 1915 and 1916 for Jesse **Lasky** by Cecil B. **DeMille**, his cameraman Alvin Wyckoff and art director Wilfred Buckland, including *The Cheat*, *The Golden Chance*, *Trail of the Lonesome Pine*, and *The Heart of Nora Flynn*. What came to be known as "Lasky lighting" or "Rembrandt lighting" in the trade press consisted of one or two floor stand arcs placed extremely close to the actors or, more rarely, spotlights used as the primary source of illumination of a scene. The rapid fall-off of Klieg lights meant that only one or two planes of the image would be illuminated, and the placement of the lights favored the production of strong, dark shadows and a palpable sense of directionality. DeMille was particularly adept at exploiting the dramatic potential of these pictorial effects: at climactic moments characters turn lights on and off, or move in and out of inky shadows.

Effects lighting as it developed in both Europe and the USA was meant to be spectacular: keyed to the progress of the drama, and notable as an effect. However, this is quite far removed from the functions normally fulfilled by lighting in the **classical Hollywood cinema**. Although there are later instances of effects lighting, most of the time classical lighting is important for its spatial rather than dramatic qualities: it creates a sense of depth and volume, helps to separate figure from background, and shows off the actors to advantage. This is achieved through so-called "three point lighting" using key, fill, and back light (in fact, in any given shot there are probably many more lights than three, but any particular light can be assigned to at least one of these three functions). Three point lighting does not becomes standard in American filmmaking until around 1919, but a number of developments in the early cinema tend in this direction. The bigger East coast studios had moved largely to artificial light by 1912 (although in California most filming was done with diffused sunlight boosted by front arcs until perhaps as late as 1916), and by 1915 companies such as Vitagraph were lighting some scenes entirely with floor stand arcs. The arcs were sometimes placed on one side of the actors (rather than from above, as was the norm), a set-up which produces some figure modeling and, due to the rapid fall-off of the arc lights, differential lighting of figure and background. In other instances, such as *Silks and Satins*, when the arcs were lined up on either side of the camera, the relative intensities of the lights were varied so as to give a stronger (hence "key") light from one side, and a weaker (hence "fill") light from the other. Another option, one relying on natural light, is evident in the films of Tourneur, who, evidently following lighting practices in use in Italy and Scandinavia, preferred natural light coming in from only one side of the set, seconded by small amounts of artificial fill light on the actors. As Patrick Keating has noted, this provided for a very soft key light, and a subtle key to fill ratio.

Back lighting in interiors is not consistently employed until 1918, although it sometimes appears earlier as a variant of effects lighting, with arc floods placed to simulate light coming through a doorway or window (again, *Silks and Satins* provides an example) or as a result of arcs placed in what Salt calls the "three-quarters back" position, to the side and slightly to the rear of the actors. But spots above and behind the actor to provide a rim of light around the figure do not come into use until 1916; they figure prominently in subsequent films starring Mary **Pickford** shot by cinematographer Charles Rosher.

See also: set design

Further reading

Bordwell, David, and Janet Staiger and Kristin Thompson (1985) *The Classical Hollywood Cinema: Film Style and Mode of Production to 1960*, London: Routledge & Kegan Paul.

Jacobs, Lea (1993) "Belasco, DeMille and the Development of Lasky Lighting," *Film History*, 5.4: 405–418.

Keating, Patrick (2000) "The Birth of Backlighting in the Classical Cinema," *Aura Film Studies Journal*, 6.2.

Salt, Barry (1992) *Film Style and Technology: History and Analysis*, 2nd ed., London: Starword.

LEA JACOBS

lighting apparatus

Apparatus to manipulate natural light or provide artificial illumination for moving picture work was initially taken over wholesale from existing 19th-century photographic practice. Early film studio architecture was often remarkably similar to the physical premises used by the more elaborately outfitted photographic portrait studios and identical with those used for taking life model lantern slides, such as the studios at **Bamforth** in England, or Krüss in Germany, with good access to sunlight by means of at least one glass wall and a large skylight, using elaborately rigged muslin curtains to diffuse the light falling on the subject to be photographed. A moving picture variant for intensive production allowed the stage to pivot and follow the sun during the day, as in the experimental **Edison** studio (the "Black Maria") or the later installation of the **American Mutoscope and Biograph** company. In both studio and open air work a variety of reflectors were used to highlight details; these could be as simple as a white sheet thrown over a screen or even a newspaper held at the proper angle but commonly were made of canvas stretched over a wooden frame or a large piece of bristol board. The main illumination issue for moving picture photography was a severe constraint on exposure times, which could not be varied over a wide range to accommodate differing light conditions as in still **photography**; until about 1915 moving picture exposure times were fixed roughly between 1/32 second and 1/15 second for a camera with a two-bladed shutter running at 16fps (frames per second), depending on the type and construction of the **intermittent movement** employed. As a result, moving picture photography demanded intense illumination and both the capital costs and operational expenses were significant, even in open sunlight where extra personnel were needed to hold or position reflectors or adjust the shades of glass studios.

Distinct from still photographic work, the demand for powerful illumination in moving picture photography precluded the use of gaslight, which was too weak, or magnesium strips, which were too rapidly exhausted, and promoted the use of the electric arc lights that had been one of several options for studio photographers since the mid-1860s. This electrically-efficient lamp with a direct current source produced a bright white light that in the 1890s was considered a positive necessity, since there was no alternative that would provide sufficient illumination for the exacting conditions demanded by moving picture photography. Arc lamps were bright enough that they were sometimes used to supplement daylight in glass studios, and carbon-arc lights with a variety of improvements continued to have a substantial place in filmmaking well into the 1980s. From the beginning, the carbon-arc light source was usually placed in the focus of a parabolic reflector shaded by a screen of opal (milk) glass or a linen screen to diffuse its output, and either hung from the studio ceiling or mounted on a tall floor stand. To keep the burning carbons properly adjusted the arcs were often tended by young boys of 10–13 or so perched at the top of ladders who suffered heat, sparks, and bits of spitting metal as they tinkered with feed screws to maintain the illumination. After about 1905, arc lamps initially designed for lighting city streets, characteristically providing a generally unfocussed white light from a beehive-shaped glass container backed by a metal reflecting collar, were sometimes used for studio illumination in densely packed overhead banks, and specialist arc lamps of all sizes, such as those designed as theatrical spotlights, were used for special lighting effects.

A year or two after their introduction in 1901 for the illumination of large offices, the Hewitt low-pressure mercury vapor lamp began to provide an alternative to electric arc lighting. With three-foot-long tubes about three inches in diameter often arranged in banks of four in shallow wooden trays either hung directly overhead or mounted on floor stands, this lamp provided general illumination with decidedly less heat and less constant attention than the arc light. The monochromatic blue light produced by mercury vapor lamps was well suited to early orthochromatic film stocks which were principally sensitive only to blue and green light, and this combination, together with racial theories of the period, encouraged the development of flat white make-up so that "white" performer's naturally reddish skin tones did not completely disappear when photographed and thus appear "dark" or "non-white."

At the turn of the century, Nernst lamps were also briefly used for studio lighting, since they provided an intense white light without either the noise and sparks of an arc lamp or its need for constant adjustment, and could be used in situations where alternating current was available. This unusual lamp, made obsolete for general lighting purposes by the development of long-lasting tungsten filaments after about 1907, was particularly efficient and produced a daylight-balanced light from a bi-metal filament of zirconium and hafnium that was an insulator at room temperature and needed to be heated to become conductive. Because a Nernst bulb produced its bright light from a small, concentrated filament it was also suitable for projection apparatus, and units of typically four bulbs mounted horizontally were applied to film projectors as late as 1912. In the USA, the electrical and lighting pioneer George Westinghouse was involved in establishing both a company for the manufacture of Nernst lamps and the Cooper-Hewitt company for the manufacture of mercury vapor lamps; the Aristo Lamp Company (no relation to the present firm in Connecticut) was a principal manufacturer of overhead arc lamps used both in studio production and for urban street lighting.

Figure 70 Cooper-Hewitt mercury vapor lamps, Biograph studio. (Courtesy of Charles Musser.)

See also: celluloid film stock; electricity; lighting; racial segregation: USA

Further reading

Beebe, Murray C. (1902) "Nernst Lamp," *The National Engineer*, VI, 8: 1–4.

Hepworth, Cecil M. (1897) *Animated Photography. The ABC of the Cinematograph*, London: Hazell, Watson & Viney, Ltd.

Salt, Barry (1992) *Film Style & Technology: History & Analysis*, 2nd ed., London: Starword.

DEAC ROSSELL

Lincoln, W. J.

b. 1870; d. 1917

writer, exhibitor, director, producer, Australia

William Joseph Lincoln had an established reputation as a fiction writer and theatrical manager before entering the film industry as manager of J. C. Williamson's touring Bio-Tableau company in 1904. After managing moving picture theaters in Melbourne, he began to write and later to direct films for Amalgamated Pictures between 1911 and 1915. The partnership he formed in 1913 with actor Godfrey Cass (the Lincoln-Cass Company) made nine feature films in 1913, but failed financially. From 1915 he returned to **screenwriting**, but alcoholism cut his career short.

See also: Australasian films

INA BERTRAND

Lind, Alfred

b. 1879; d. 1959

exhibitor, cameraman, director, Denmark, Germany

A Danish carpenter turned moving picture exhibitor in Iceland (1905), Lind first was affiliated with the Danish company, **Nordisk**, as a cameraman and director. In 1909, he worked for **Fotorama** in Aarhus, but returned to Copenhagen and was hired for even shorter stints by practically every studio there: **Kinografen**, *De fire Djævle* [The Four Devils] (1911); Kosmorama, *Afgrunden* [The Abyss] (1911); **Filmfabriken Danmark**, *Den flyvende Cirkus* [The Flying Circus] (1912). Lind formed his own company in 1912, yet with limited success. Moving to Germany in 1913, he worked for Eiko and others. Beginning in the mid-teens, he directed films in Italy and then in Switzerland. He had a predilection for circus films and favored sensational **melodramas**. Lind returned to his old occupation as a carpenter in the 1930s.

JAN OLSSON

Linder, Max (Gabriel-Maximilien Leuvielle)

b. 1883, Caverne; d. 1925, Paris

actor, filmmaker, France, USA

Max Linder committed suicide with his young wife at age 42. This tragic destiny, added to the fact that his films long remained unseen, made him one of the first accursed filmmakers. Between 1910 and 1914, however, he was immensely popular. His daughter Maud reclaimed his place in cinema history with her 1983 book and accompanying video, *L'Homme au chapeau de soie* [The Man with the Silk Hat].

He was born near Bordeaux and discovered early that his vocation was acting. He made his debut in theaters in Bordeaux and Paris, where he took the pseudonym Max Linder. Louis **Gasnier**, then supervising walk-on parts at the Théâtre de l'Ambigu in Paris, probably brought Linder to **Pathé-Frères**, where he appeared in many comic films between 1905 and 1908.

The decisive idea of creating the Max character came in 1910. Linder had to carve out a place for himself among the recurring figures of the French **comic series**: *Boireau*, *Gontran*, *Roméo*, and *Calino*. Their comic style was still largely gestural, and Linder's direct rival, **Prince**-Rigadin, was reorienting the comic series towards **vaudeville** and light comedy.

Linder's idea was to impersonate a normal man in situations whose comic force arose from annoyances. The situation, not gestures or acrobatic feats, became the source of laughter. This kind of comedy was meant to please the bourgeois audiences for **Film d'Art**. His character was short, dark-haired, with a moustache covering an upper lip that opened onto a toothy smile. He wore a costume consisting of top hat, tails, vest, striped pants, polished shoes, and soft-yellow gloves. These features made him a somewhat pretentious dandy, that is, an idle bourgeois living beyond his means. Max also spent most of his time courting young women, not always successfully. The social status to which he aspired (he often tried to get married) kept eluding him. The laughter thus elicited appealed both to feelings of superiority (mocking Max's pretentions as a parvenu unaware of certain codes) and an impulse to sarcasm (deriding the society he was attempting to enter). This laughter was often tinged with a slight bitterness symptomatic of the social status of a whole class of bachelors to which he belonged and which would disappear with the war.

Linder often was compared to **Chaplin**. The two men admired each other and met during the Frenchman's trip to the USA in 1916–1917 (where he had a brief stint at **Essanay**). However, Max was not as disenfranchised as Chaplin's tramp, and Linder's mise-en-scène was more static, drawing its inspiration from a more traditional comic style. He remained close to popular

Figure 71 Production photo of *Max Linder contre Nick Winter* (Pathé, 1911).

European culture, in films based on songs, such as *Le Pendu* [The Hanged Man] (1906), or fabliaus such as *Max amoureux de la teinturière* [Max in Love with the Dye-Maker] (1912). Yet Linder's filmic style was not as archaic as is often thought: his static framing, medium shots, and waist-level camera work simply suited his kind of comedy.

Further reading

Mitry, Jean (1967) "Max Linder," *Anthologie du cinema*, 2: 289–348.

Engelbert, Manfred (1994) "Max, Kind der Belle Epoque, Die französische Filmkomödie im Zeitalter ihrer Weltgeltung," in Faulstisch/Korte (eds.) *Fischer Filmgeschichte 1 (1895–1924)*, 201–215, Frankfurt/Main: Fischer Tachenbuch Verlag.

FRANÇOIS DE LA BRETÈQUE

Lindsay, Vachel

b. 1879; d. 1931

poet, critic, USA

An important poet, Lindsay was one of the first American intelligentsia to take moving pictures seriously, writing reviews for *The New Republic* and, in 1915, publishing the first serious American book on film aesthetics, *The Art of the Moving Picture* (revised in 1922). Both the reviews and book pioneered a "hieroglyphic" theory of American popular culture, whose new picture language, Lindsay believed, had nearly millennial implications. Although published in 1915, the book contains many detailed and insightful discussions of single-reel films and early film **audiences**. Lindsay also wrote poems to a number of American film **stars** (Mary **Pickford**, Blanche **Sweet**, John **Bunny**).

TOM GUNNING

Lo Savio, Gerolamo

b. 1865; d. 1931

director, Italy

Employed as director at **Film d'Arte Italiana** between 1909 and 1914, like his colleague Ugo **Falena**, Lo Savio worked on ambitious literary adaptations. Contributing to the career of actors both young and established, he directed **Shakespeare** films such as *Otello* [Othello] (1909) and *Il mercante di Venezia* [The Merchant of Venice] (1910), starring Francesca **Bertini** and Ermete **Novelli**, but also the two-reel *Lucrezia Borgia* [Lucretia Borgia] (1912), with Gustavo **Serena**. Apparently his career did not extend past **World War I**.

GIORGIO BERTELLINI

Loew, Marcus

b. 8 May 1870; d. 5 September 1927

exhibitor, USA

Marcus Loew was an important pioneering exhibitor in New York City who would build a movie empire that would eventually include MGM. Marcus Loew died before MGM was reaching its apex as a studio, and sadly the head of his subsidiary, Louis B. Mayer, is far more—yet inappropriately—celebrated.

Born of immigrant parents on Manhattan's Lower East Side, Loew was unsuccessful at various occupations until 1903, when (at age 33) he invested in a **penny arcade**. Soon Loew opened more arcades across New York City. He then invested in two **Hale's Tours** shows, looking for some combination of entertainment to secure his market niche.

In 1906, Loew decided to offer a combination of **vaudeville** and moving pictures at low prices. He took over a 2,000-seat house in Brooklyn that had been home to a burlesque troupe, refurbished it, and named it the Royal. Next he leased the legitimate theatrical power Shubert company's excess theaters, refurbished them, and ran what he called "small-time vaudeville." In October 1909, he took over on his own a legitimate **theater**, and renamed it the Lincoln Square; a year later he opened the spectacular National theater in the Bronx. The very next day he premiered Loew's Seventh Avenue theater, in upper Manhattan. By 1910, Loew had made his mark as perhaps the most important movie presenter in New York City.

As his company expanded, he needed skilled managers, and found them in the **Schenck** brothers. In 1910, "Nick" and "Joe" joined Marcus Loew to form Loew's Theatrical Enterprises. Thereafter Nicholas moved up the executive ranks of the theatrical chain as Loew's right hand man, and upon Loew's death succeeded him. In 1911, Loew's Theatrical Enterprises was valued at $5 million. Two years later, Loew's was able to take over a twenty-year-old legitimate theater, the American, and made this Times Square theater its New York City flagship. As the decade of the 1910s progressed, Loew's Theatrical Enterprises grew to dominate "small-time vaudeville" in the largest city in the USA. Indeed, Loew considered himself a vaudeville entrepreneur who also showed moving pictures.

Thereafter, however, he and Schenck reversed the formula, featuring the movies with an added stage show. To create a guaranteed supply of films, they merged with Metro-Goldwyn-Mayer, and created the most famous studio of the 1920s and 1930s. But Loew's Theatrical Enterprises would always be run—even after its founder's death—as a theater chain which used MGM as a means to guarantee control over the films for its the theaters. Symbolically, Loew never lived in Hollywood, but ran his theatrical business from New York City.

See also: cinema chains or circuits; palace cinemas

Further reading

Crowther, Bosley (1957) *The Lion's Share: The Story of an Entertainment Empire*, New York: E. P. Dutton.

Gomery, Douglas (1992) *Shared Pleasures: A History of Movie Presentation in the United States*, Madison: University of Wisconsin Press.

DOUGLAS GOMERY

Londe, Albert

b. 1858; d. 1917

photographer, France

Londe was the photographer of Doctor Charcot at the hospice de la Salpêtrière in Paris and the author of several books: *La photographie instantanée* (1886); *La photographie moderne* (1888 and 1896); and *La photographie médicale* (1893). In 1883, he developed an electrical machine equipped with nine lenses which he used to photograph the movements of pathological cases. The same year he also demonstrated a more sophisticated 12-lens machine. The many photographs he achieved are of excellent quality but create problems when the negatives are examined: images have to be read from right to left and top to bottom. In 1898, Londe purchased a **Demenÿ** camera from **Gaumont** and made a few 35mm films which now are preserved at the Archives du Film, in Bois d'Arcy.

Further reading

Bernard, Denis and André Gunthert (1993) *L'Instant rêvé Albert Londe*, Nîmes/Laval: Jacqueline Chambon/Trois.

LAURENT MANNONI

Long, Samuel

b. 1875; d. 14 August 1915

engineer, executive, USA

Superintendent of the **American Mutoscope and Biograph** laboratory in Hoboken, New Jersey, from 1898 to 1907, and one of three founders of **Kalem**. Long joined AM&B at the age of 23, and was soon put in charge of the manufacture and assembly of film prints and Mutoscopes. During the struggles that led to the establishment of the **Motion Picture Patents Company**, Long and Frank **Marion** bought out George **Kleine**'s interest in Kalem, and Long became president. He also served as director and treasurer of the **General**

Film Company, and remained Kalem's president until his early death of typhoid.

EILEEN BOWSER

Longford, Raymond

b. 1878; d. 1959

actor, director, Australia

Longford was a stage actor who began his film career in two melodramas in 1911. Though he continued to act occasionally throughout his life, it was in directing that he made his mark, becoming the most prolific and significant Australian director of silent feature films. He was partnered in his personal and professional life by Australia's first movie **star**, Lottie Lyell, and her early death from tuberculosis in 1925 marked the end of Longford's most productive period. His most famous and brilliant achievement is *The Sentimental Bloke* (1918).

INA BERTRAND

Lordier (Lévy), Georges

b. 1884; d. 1922

exhibitor, filmmaker, publisher, producer, France

The son of an orchestra conductor, Lordier managed theaters in Douai, Lens, and Valenciennes at age 18. In 1904, he was hired by **Pathé-Frères** as a filmmaker. In 1907–1908, as Pathé established a **cinema circuit**, he moved into exhibition, opening theaters in the northern and western regions of France for Omnia, a Pathé affiliate. During the early 1910s, he opened or bought seven theaters in Paris. In 1912, he created the trade weekly *Le Cinéma* and began a career as a producer with the series "Les Grands Films Populaires," which were shot in the studio he had acquired from **Lux** when it went bankrupt. Early successes included *Le Bossu* [The Hunchback] (1913), *Les Cinq Sous de Lavarède* [Lavarède's Five Sous] (1913), and *Jacques L'Honneur* (1914).

JEAN-JACQUES MEUSY

Lowenstein, Hans Otto (a.k.a. Hans Otto)

b. 1881; d. 1931

filmmaker, Austria

Born in Oderfurth, Moravia, Lowenstein become an **opera** singer in Vienna. In 1913, for Phillipp & Preßburger, he directed *König Menelaus im Kino* [King Menelaus at the Movies], which combined filmed scenes with live performed scenes on stage. In the same year, for Sascha Film, he directed an **advertising** film for detergents, *Wie Ninette zu ihrem Ausgang kam* [How Ninette Got A Free Evening]. During **World War I**, he worked for the military film production unit and organized mobile picture theaters for soldiers. Using his own sound system, he later shot the first Austrian talkie.

PAOLO CANEPPELE

Lubin Manufacturing Company

A film production corporation and member of the **Motion Picture Patents Company** (MPPC), the Lubin Manufacturing Company was founded by Siegmund **Lubin** when he reorganized his original moving picture business in 1909. To meet the production quotas of the MPPC, the company left its small electric studio in Philadelphia's business district in 1910 and moved to a larger studio and processing facility in the industrial neighborhoods of North Philadelphia. Lacking space for outdoor sets, the company expanded again in 1912, establishing another studio on a 350-acre estate in nearby Betzwood, Pennsylvania. Further growth followed with studios at Jacksonville, Florida (1912–1915), Los Angeles (1913–1916), and Coronado, California (1915–1916). A large stock company, led by popular Lubin director, Romaine Fielding, worked on permanent location in the Southwest (1912–1915). All raw footage from the branch studios went to the Betzwood studio for processing and distribution.

One and two-reel films produced at these studios included sensational **melodramas, westerns,** **comedies**, **serials**, and educational films. Among the notable film personalities who found work at the various Lubin studios were Florence **Lawrence**, Pearl **White**, Arthur **Johnson**, Marie Dressler, Oliver Hardy, Alan Hale, L. C. Shumway, Edward Sloman, and Henry King. Writer Epes Winthrop **Sargent** authored many Lubin scenarios.

In 1912, Lubin purchased the rights to several sensational plays and borrowed heavily from Philadelphia's Drexel Bank to finance their production as **multiple-reel films**. During the years 1913–1916, the company made forty-four feature-length films. In addition to the appeal of successful stage dramas with their original casts, Lubin features relied heavily on spectacles like Civil War battles, earthquakes, and train wrecks to draw audiences. However, the writing, acting, and photography were often mediocre and failed to keep up with rapidly changing industry standards. As the first member of the MPPC to produce features, Lubin suffered financial losses when the **General Film Company**'s distribution system proved inadequate to handling them. Unable to recover even the expense of production, Lubin joined with **Vitagraph**, **Selig**, and **Essanay** in 1915 to form VLSE, a feature film distribution company, but this proved too little, too late.

A disastrous fire at the Philadelphia studio in 1914, combined with the outbreak of **World War I**, and the subsequent loss of overseas markets, further damaged the company's financial stability. The expensive legal problems of the MPPC, the dwindling market for shorter films, and overwhelming competition combined to bring the firm to the verge of bankruptcy in 1915. The branch studios were phased out. Hoping to shield some assets, the company created a shadow corporation, the Lubin Film Company, to which the Betzwood facilities were attached. Nevertheless, both Lubin corporations were seized by creditors in 1916. In 1917, the Philadelphia studio was sold at auction, and the Lubin Manufacturing Company was dissolved. The Lubin Film Company was purchased by Wolf Brothers, Inc. of Philadelphia and became the basis for the Betzwood Film Company, which operated until 1921.

Figure 72 Lubin studio interior, Philadelphia, Pennsylvania. (Courtesy of Charles Musser.)

Further reading

Eckhardt, Joseph (1997) *The King of the Movies; Film Pioneer, Siegmund Lubin*, Cranbury, NJ: Fairleigh Dickinson University Press.

JOSEPH ECKHARDT

Lubin, Siegmund

b. 1851; d. 1923

manufacturer, filmmaker, producer, exhibitor, USA

One of the original film pioneers, Lubin is best remembered for his skillful commercial exploitation of every facet of the early moving picture industry. A skilled optician, Lubin left his native Germany for the USA in 1876. In addition to the optical shop he established in Philadelphia in 1885, he opened **penny arcades** and produced **magic lantern** slides. After purchasing a moving picture **camera** from C. Francis **Jenkins** in 1896, Lubin made his first films and devised his own Cineograph **projector**. Convinced of the profit potential of motion pictures, Lubin embarked on an ambitious mass marketing campaign in 1897. Through ads in the *New York Clipper*, and widely distributed free catalogs, Lubin offered **vaudeville** managers and **itinerant exhibitors** projectors, films, slides, **screens**, spotlights, theater fronts, phonographs, tickets and tents. In 1899, he expanded his marketing campaign to Germany as well.

Lubin's first studios were in his backyard or on rooftops in Philadelphia's Tenderloin, but by 1907 his facilities occupied an entire building in the business district. When his seasonal film exhibitions at **amusement parks** proved profitable in 1899–1901, Lubin opened Philadelphia's first permanent **nickelodeon** in 1902. By 1909, when he sold them, his chain of moving picture theaters and film rental exchanges numbered sixteen establishments in six states.

Unable at first to meet his customers' increasing demand for new films, Lubin frequently copied the films of his competitors and offered "every known film" at bargain prices. Lubin's pragmatic business policies resulted in frequent lawsuits for **copyright** and patent infringement. **Edison** pursued Lubin in court for ten years before forcing him, in 1908, to accept a license as the terms of his inclusion in the **Motion Picture Patents Company** (MPPC). As the only immigrant Jew in the MPPC, Lubin was viewed with some suspicion and often found himself in awkward situations. His market projections (most of which would prove to be accurate) were frequently ignored, and he balanced his loyalty to the MPPC with clandestine help to Jewish independents like Mark **Dintenfass**, Harry **Warner** and his brothers, Samuel Goldwyn, Jesse **Lasky** and Cecil B. **DeMille**.

The success of his **Lubin** Manufacturing Company was undermined by Lubin's indifference to the artistic and narrative development of the motion picture. Altthough some of his early *actualités*, **comedies**, and **chase films** showed promise, Lubin ultimately—and ironically—proved ambivalent toward changes taking place on screen.

"Pop" Lubin was a favorite subject for reporters from the **trade press**. His colorful personality, his experiments (some dubious) with sound films, medical films, and home movies, the amenities he provided his employees, and his sweeping predictions for the industry's future, all made for good press. His patriarchal attitude and lavish lifestyle made him the prototype of the Jewish movie mogul long before that term was used.

See also: cinema circuits or chains

Further reading

Eckhardt, Joseph (1997) *The King of the Movies; Film Pioneer, Siegmund Lubin*, Cranbury, NJ: Fairleigh Dickinson University Press.

Eckhardt, Joseph (1999) "The Effect Is Quite Startling: Siegmund Lubin's Attempt to Commercially Exploit Sound Motion Pictures, 1903–1914," *Film History*, 11.4: 408–417.

JOSEPH ECKHARDT

Lubitsch, Ernst

b. 1892; d. 1947

actor, director, Germany

Best-known as the director of American comedies in the 1920s and 1930s, Lubitsch began his career in 1911 as a walk-on for Max **Reinhardt**'s theater in Berlin and acted in Reinhardt's troupe regularly during the war years. By 1914, he was starring in and directing films that featured his Yiddish characterization of a "Schusterjungewitz," an impish, opportunistic apprentice, whose rude humor struck a chord with audiences. The success of such comedies as *Schuhpalast Pinkus* [Shoe Salon Pinkus] (1916), brought the opportunity to direct grander productions, especially historical epics, such as *Madame Dubarry* (1919) featuring Pola Negri, which eventually earned them both an invitation to Hollywood.

SCOTT CURTIS

Lumière et fils

In 1883, in Lyons, Antoine Lumière and his sons began manufacturing gelatin silver-bromide photographic plates (a process Louis **Lumière** had developed). The first factory, which was poorly equipped and employed a dozen workers, produced 216,000 plates the first year. By 1890 there were more than 200 workers, and the annual output was 4 million plates. In order to diversify its activity with the manufacture of bromide paper, in 1892, the family business was transformed into the "Société Anonyme des Plaques et Papiers Photographiques Antoine Lumière et ses Fils" (Antoine Lumière and Sons: Public Limited Company for Photographic Plates and Paper), with a capital of 3 million francs.

Given these favorable conditions, it took Louis Lumière only a few months in 1895 to solve the problem of projecting moving photographic images, moving from the experimental stage to that of practical application. His unusual ability to improve on ideas or preexisting techniques, preserving the best elements already established and innovating others so as to optimize their usefulness and industrial production, also extended to the infrastructure of the company, where he put into place the means necessary for exploiting his research.

This concentrated research resulted in a demonstration to a group of industrialists and financiers in Paris on 22 March 1895, in which Louis used a prototype **Cinématographe** to project a film, "Sortie d'usine" (Workers Leaving the Factory). The apparatus had another eleven private demonstrations in France and Belgium between April and December, while a commercial version of the Cinématographe was being developed for public exhibition, the first of which his father Antoine organized on 28 December 1895 at the Salon indien of the Grand Café in Paris. Thereafter, his brother Auguste organized many of the others.

The publication of numerous articles on the Cinématographe resulted in purchase requests as early as 1895. However, the Lumière company chose to control exhibition by setting up a system whereby concessionaries would receive a Cinématographe equipped for projection and the personnel needed to install it in exchange for 60% of the receipts. Without any significant competition from others, the Cinématographe was established simultaneously in France and abroad, with private presentations preceding regular exhibition: London (February 1896), Rome (March), Cologne (April), Geneva, Madrid and Saint-Petersburg (May), New York (June), Mexico City (August), Melbourne (September), and Japan (January 1897). Only cameramen employed by the company were authorized to use the equipment and material necessary for shooting the films that allowed for a renewal of exhibition programs, films (representing a total of thirty-one countries) that were later featured in the company's catalogues.

By July 1896, the gross receipts for exhibitions of the Cinématographe already had reached more than a million francs, but the concession system was abandoned by the end of the year, due in part to difficulties in managing so many cameramen/projectionists but also to competing manufacturers that increasingly contested the company's initial monopoly. The Cinématographe as well as the films were now offered for sale through catalogs, first to concessionaries and cameramen wanting to set up their own business and then to the public, from May 1897 on. A production peak of 508 films

was reached in 1897, up from 298 in 1896. In 1898, the numbers declined to 205 films and kept dropping thereafter in the face of competition, with only 136 films made between 1901 and 1905, when production stopped. Exhibitions of the Cinématographe ended in Lyons in 1902, and in 1907 the last Lumière catalog appeared—a simple reprint of the 1905 catalog, featuring only two thirds of the total of 1422 titles (none more than sixty meters in length) produced between 1895 and 1905.

The adventure of the Cinématographe lasted only ten years. Louis Lumière explained at the end of his life that the company's raison d'être was primarily the manufacture of photographic products, not films. Indeed, the gross receipts for the Cinématographe from 1896 to 1900, while far from negligible, represented only 15% of the company's profits. It also seems that Louis lost interest in the future of his invention after its development phase was over. As early as June 1896, he turned over to the company the profits arising from the patent he had registered with his brother, without compensation, and immediately directed his research interests along other paths, most notably trichromatic **photography**. No further developments were made in the Cinématographe. Consequently, as its technical and aesthetic advantage waned, the Lumière company gradually lost its domination in the increasingly competitive sector of film production.

Beyond its contribution to moving picture exhibition, the Cinématographe indeed revolutionized the content of moving images. The first **Edison** films were limited to scenes staged for the **Kinetograph** in the Black Maria studio, most often with a black backdrop so as to make human figures and objects stand out. The Cinématographe, a machine weighing barely over twenty pounds (making it easy to handle) and providing an excellent depth of field and a good sensitivity thanks (among other things) to the slower speed at which the film ran through the mechanism, by contrast, was highly mobile and could engage with everyday life. Lumière cameramen shot outdoors and on location, and their films quickly won audiences over. Thanks to this freedom, they established many of the categories of nonfiction and short fiction that were accepted by most other manufacturers during the first few years of cinema, at least until longer fiction films became more and more dominant.

The Lumière company, whose core business was not the production of spectacle entertainment, then went back to its original activity, but its influence over early cinema had been sealed. Its one link to the film industry remained the manufacturing of 35mm **celluloid** film stock through its subsidiary, the Société des Pellicules Françaises. Initiated in Monplaisir in 1896 in association with Victor Planchon to meet the needs of production, this activity continued until the early 1940s, thanks to a new factory built in the early 1900s in Feyzin, a few miles away from Lyons.

See also: Doublier, Francis; Hatot, Georges; Mesguich, Félix; Promio, Alexandre; Velle, Gaston; Veyre, Gabriel.

Further reading

Aubert, Michelle and Jean-Claude Seguin (eds.) (1996) *La production cinématographique des frères Lumière*, Paris: BiFi.

Chardère, Bernard (1987) *Lumières sur Lumière*, Lyons: Institut Lumière/Presses Universitaires de Lyon.

Chardère, Bernard (1995) *Le roman des Lumière*, Paris: Gallimard.

Meusy, Jean-Jacques (1996) *Cinquante ans d'industrie cinématographique 1906–1956*, Paris: Fondation Crédit Lyonnais/Le Monde Editions.

JEAN-MARC LAMOTTE

Lumière, Auguste and Louis

Auguste: b. 1862, Besançon, France; d. 1954, Lyons, France

industrialist, biologist, chemist, inventor, France

Louis: b. 1864, Besançon, France; d. 1948, Bandol, France

industrialist, physicist, chemist, inventor, filmmaker, France

Auguste and Louis Lumière came to Lyons in 1871, when their father Antoine set up a photography shop in the city center. The brothers learned **photography** at an early age and studied physics and chemistry at the highly selective La Martinière vocational high school. At the age of 17, Louis developed a dry-plate gelatin silver bromide emulsion that would contribute to the reputation and financial success of the factory his father founded in 1883 to manufacture and commercialize photographic plates. Thanks to the increasing industrial clout of the **Lumière** company, the brothers were able to conduct research in a variety of fields, as their many papers and patents indicate.

When the **Edison Kinetoscope** was introduced in Paris in September 1894, Antoine asked his sons to explore the possibilities of recording and projecting moving images. Although Auguste worked on several designs, these proved unsuccessful until Louis added a mechanism similar to that of a sewing machine that would allow a strip of film to run through the apparatus intermittently. Late in 1894, the principle of Louis's design was confirmed through experiments with an initial prototype of the machine using 35mm paper film. On 13 February 1895, the two brothers registered a patent application for the **Cinématographe**, and Louis had a second prototype built by Charles Moisson, the Lumière's head mechanic. On 22 March, he and Moisson gave a public presentation of the machine in Paris to the Société d'Encouragement pour l'Industrie Nationale, projecting the "sortie des ouvriers et ouvrières de l'usine Lumière" (male and female workers leaving the Lumière factory) recorded on **celluloid** film stock. It was the first time that moving images were presented on a large screen, following a protocol still in currency today: a single-sprocketed strip of film featuring a number of photographic images shot at regular intervals was run intermittently through a projector at the same image-per-second ratio as the shooting ratio, resulting in the synthesis and enlargement of these images for an audience.

Louis supervised the development and manufacture of the apparatus with Parisian engineer, Jules **Carpentier**, and that of the celluloid film stock with Victor Planchon, while Auguste organized the apparatus's commercial exhibition, beginning on 28 December 1895, at the Salon Indien of the Grand Café in Paris.

Figure 73 Louis and Auguste Lumière, 1895.

Louis also was the first Lumière cameraman, shooting all of the 1895 films and thus establishing the range of subjects and aesthetic style of the films featured in the Lumière catalogues between 1896 and 1905. He claimed to have made a total of fifty films, shot mostly in Lyons and La Ciotat; Auguste, his wife, and daughter appeared in at least one of them, *Repas de bébé* [Breakfast with Baby].

Auguste later devoted most of his work to chemistry and medical research: he was responsible for the first working X-ray machine in France. By contrast, Louis pursued his research on still as well as moving images with such endeavors as a photographic panorama (Photorama, 1902), the Autochromatic process for color photography (launched commercially in 1907), 3-D portraits using photostereosynthesis (a forerunner of holograms), and a stereoscopic film process using anaglyphs, in the 1930s.

Further reading

Chardère, Bernard (1995) *Le roman des Lumière*, Paris: Gallimard.

Pinel, Vincent (1994) *Louis Lumière inventeur et cinéaste*, Paris: Editions Nathan.

JEAN-MARC LAMOTTE

Lundberg, Frans

b. 1851; d. 1922

exhibitor, distributor, producer, Denmark, Sweden

Frans Lundberg was a former wine merchant when he invested in a Copenhagen moving picture theater in 1905, Nørrebro Filmtheater (by proxy due to the legal ramifications for securing permission to exhibit films in Denmark). Later, Lundberg bought a theater in Malmö, Stora Biografteatern, and organized an exchange for selling and renting films. After producing a few *actualités*, he launched his two first features in 1910, in addition to several sync-sound films. In 1911 and 1912, Lundberg had the leading studio in Sweden, producing around ten features per year (in the main with Danish actors), which then were marketed internationally by Robert Glombeck in Berlin. Lundberg retired after the 1912–1913 season, partly due to conflicts with the newly established national censorship board.

JAN OLSSON

Lux

The public limited company Lux, which manufactured phonographs, **cameras**, and films was established in Paris by engineer Henri **Joly**, on October 4, 1906, with a capital of 1,100,000 francs. In 1908, Joly left after a change in the majority of shareholders. Thereafter managed by several administrators (including Chalupt and Bernheim), the company produced cameras (developed by Léopold Löbel) and films, many directed by Gérard **Bourgeois**. A studio was established on boulevard Jourdan in Paris and a laboratory opened nearby in Gentilly. Despite the production of two or three films per week by 1913 and distribution agreements outside France with **Aquila** (Italy) and **Kinografen** (Germany), Lux had to be dissolved in October 1913.

LAURENT MANNONI

Luxemburg, Grand Duché

In October 1896, the photographer Jacques-Marie Bellwald (1871–1945) organized the first film screening with a **Joly** apparatus in an Echternach hotel and then several weeks later in the capital. Shortly thereafter, another **itinerant exhibitor**, Adolphe Amberg, began giving public film screenings, along with a special one for the family of the Grand Duke. In 1899, the **Lumière** company produced an *actualité* of the way Mercier champagne was made in the village of Epernay in Luxemburg. Shown at the **world's fair** in Paris in 1900, this film probably was the first film shot in Luxemburg.

For several years, a number of travelling showmen from neighbouring countries operated in Luxemburg. Among them was the German family of Marzen, which became a regular visitor in theaters and hotels between 1899 and 1906. They also filmed scenes in the capital city and interesting events such as *Rosenfest in Luxemburg* (1905). In 1907, the Marzen family opened the first moving picture theater in the German city of Trier and, four years later, a second one named Cinema Parisiana in the city of Luxemburg. Several other travelling showmen who worked the hotels, cafés and theaters came from France, among them the Megemont's Cinemato français and the Bio Royal (Grand Ciné-Théâtre).

At the important **fair/fairground** held annually in Luxemburg, showmen (mostly from Germany) appeared with canvas tent theaters as early as 1898. One of the first was Bläser with his Bläser'schen Kinematographen. In 1902 he even produced local films such as *Auf dem Paradeplatz in Luxemburg am Sonntagmittag*. Soon he had competitors from other fairground showmen such as Philipp Leilich (1905), Hirdt (1907) and W. Kling (1907–1909). There also were entrepreneurs who toured the small country with their canvas theaters outside the normal fair period. The Oceanic Vio Company (1908–1909) was one such enterprise with a tent that seated 2,500 spectators. The German showman, Alexandre Flaschenträger, who operated mainly in the Netherlands, Belgium, and northern France, also worked the fairs in Luxemburg. There, he even opened a moving picture theater in 1910; when it failed, he went back to the fairgrounds with a canvas Luna Park.

In December 1907, the first moving picture theater opened in Luxemburg as the Cinéma Modern. Two years later the second opened its doors, the Cinéma Pathé. The Swiss company Elektrische

Lichtbühne A.G., based in Zürich, opened the fourteenth theater in its **cinema chain** in Luxemburg in 1910. Before 1914, most of the films shown in the cinemas came from Germany, France, the USA, and Scandinavia. In 1910, **Pathé-Frères** offered its clients in Luxemburg the first four fiction films ever made in this small country: *Le séducteur*, *L'arbre creux*, *Le guide*, and *La conversion du braconnier*. Film exhibitors generally showed **newsreels** either from **Gaumont** or Pathé, but some filmed local events such as the funeral of the Grand Duke in 1912.

Further reading

Etringer, Norbert (1983) *Lebende Bilder. Aus Luxemburgs guter alter Kinozeit*, Luxemburg: Imprimerie St-Paul.

GUIDO CONVENTS

Lykke-Seest, Peter

b. 1868; d. 1948

scriptwriter, filmmaker, Norway

A prolific author of popular novels, Lykke-Seest began his career as a **screenwriter** in 1912 at **Nordisk** in Denmark and **Svenska Biografteatern** in Sweden, where he wrote most of the early films of Victor **Sjöström** and Mauritz **Stiller**. Returning to Norway in 1916, he established his own production company, Christiania Film Compagni, writing and directing six features between 1917 and 1919. Most popular was his last feature, *Historien om en gut* [The Story of a Boy] (1919). This company represented a promising start to extensive and professional film production in Norway.

GUNNAR IVERSEN

Lyyra Filmi

Hjalmar V. Pohjanheimo (1867–1936), a successful sawmill industrialist, founded the Lyyra **cinema chain** in Finalnd in 1910, and soon expanded into importing and distributing films. Also employed in this family company were Elina Pohjanheimo and their four sons, Adolf, Hilarius, Asser, and Birger. In 1913, the company distributed the first feature-length Finnish fiction film, the tragic *Sylvi*. Encouraged by its success, Lyyra went into production, making 14 fiction films before 1917 (the majority of Finnish fiction films). Their line of serious "domestic picture plays" began with *Verettömät* [The Bloodless] (1913). For its ambitious projects Lyyra employed talent like the theater director Kaarle Halme, the playwright Yrjö Veijola, and even the national poet Eino Leino.

Simultaneously, Lyyra produced light entertainment: farces such as *Kosto on suloista* [Revenge is Sweet] (1913) and thrillers like *Salainen perintömääräys* [The Secret Testament] (1914).

ANTTI ALANEN

M. Pathe

This Japanese film company, established by **Umeya Shokichi** in 1906, had no connection with the French company of **Pathé-Frères**, although Umeya imported and showed many French Pathé films as an exhibitor in Malaysia and Singapore, and then in Japan. The first film produced by M. Pathe was *Soga kyodai kariba no akatsuki* [Soga Brothers—Dawn of the Hunting Field], released in 1908. M. Pathe constructed a studio in Tokyo in 1909, where it produced both new-school and old-school films.

HIROSHI KOMATSU

Mace, Fred

b. 1878; d. 1917

actor, director, USA

After a successful stage career in musical comedy, Mace joined Mack **Sennett**'s **Biograph** unit in 1911 and then became one of the founding members of the **Keystone Film Company** the following year. Although he never developed a consistent comic persona, Mace was the first of Sennett's comedians to achieve great popularity, noted in particular for his Biograph performances as "One-Round O'Brien." In 1913, Mace quit Keystone to produce **comedies** for Harry **Aitken**'s **Majestic** label. When these proved unsuccessful, Mace briefly returned to Keystone in 1915, before departing yet again in a failed attempt to resuscitate his stage career. His death in a New York hotel room was recorded as a heart attack.

ROB KING

Machin, Alfred

b. 1877; d. 1929

filmmaker, France, Belgium, Netherlands

Based on his experience as a French photographer-reporter, Machin was hired in 1907 to work for **Pathé-Frères**. In 1908 and 1909, he filmed along the Nile River in Africa, which resulted in almost twenty film titles. These were first released world wide by Pathé as short **travelogues** such as *Chasse au marabout en abyssinie* (1911) and then put together in longer "documentaries" such as *Comme une lettre nous parvient des grands lacs de l'Afrique Centrale* (1911). Between 1909 and 1914, Machin produced dozens of films in Belgium for La **Belge Cinema**—for instance, *Maudite soit la guerre* [Cursed Be War], 1914—and in Holland for **Hollandsche Film**—for instance, *Het vervloekte geld* [Arson at Sea], 1912. During **World War I**, he shot news footage at the French front. In the 1920s, Machin directed fifteen dramatic films with his own production company, Niza.

Further reading

de Kuyper, Eric (1995) *Alfred Machin: Cinéaste, Film-Maker*, Brussels: Royal Belgian Film Archive.

Lacassin, Francis (2001) *Alfred Machin. De la jungle à l'écran*, Paris: Dreamland.

GUIDO CONVENTS

Mack, Max

b. 1884; d. 1973

director, Germany

Coming from the stage, Mack entered the cinema industry as an actor in 1910, but soon turned to writing and directing two-reel **comedies** and melodramas for **Vitascope**, **Continental-Kunstfilm**, and Eiko. With *Der Andere* [The Other One] (1912/13), he directed the first **Autorenfilm**, introducing Albert **Bassermann** to the screen. In 1913–1914, Mack continued his collaboration with Bassermann for three more prestige literary adaptations, but above all established himself as a prolific and highly profitable filmmaker of urban comedies such as *Wo ist Coletti?* [Where is Coletti?] (1913) and *Die blaue Maus* [The Blue Mouse] (1913).

MICHAEL WEDEL

Madan, Jamshedji Framji

b. 1856; d.1923

exhibitor, distributor, producer, India

Madan came from Bombay's thriving Parsee Theatre district in the late 19th century where he owned two theater companies. An enterprising businessman, he shifted to Calcutta in 1902. Three years later, he established the Elphinstone Bioscope Company, which produced and exhibited nonfiction films in urban theaters and on the traveling cinema circuit—the most famous being Jyotish Sarkar's *Bengal Partition Movement* (1905). After acquiring sales and distribution rights for **Pathé-Frères** films, Madan's empire expanded greatly, and he eventually established **Madan Theatres Limited** in 1919, which dominated production, distribution, and exhibition in India throughout the 1920s and into the 1930s.

SURESH CHABRIA

Madan Theatres Limited

The second of two companies founded by J. F. **Madan** that dominated Indian exhibition, distribution and production during the silent era. The first, in 1905, was Elphinstone Bioscope, which soon became the leading producer and distributor of indigenous and foreign films in permanent and traveling cinemas in British India. Later, Elphinstone produced two of the earliest feature films in Bengal: *Satyawadi Raja Harishchandra* [Truthful Raja Harishchandra] (1917) and *Bilwamangal* (1919). Madan Theatres, established in 1919, consolidated Madan's activities even further. Many Madan productions were filmed plays, and the company regularly hired foreign talent and adapted major Bengali literary works. After Madan's death, his third son kept expanding the empire until its decline in the late 1930s.

SURESH CHABRIA

Maggi, Luigi

b. 1867; d. 1946

actor, director, Italy

Hired in 1906 by Arturo **Ambrosio** as an actor and casting manager, Maggi soon moved to direction, displaying an inventive and self-confident talent for **historical films**. He authored such crucial works as *Gli ultimi giorni di Pompei* [The Last Days of Pompeii] (1908) and *Nerone* [Nero, or the Burning of Rome] (1909), notable for their combination of antique calamity and archeological realism. He also directed *Satana* [Satan] (1912), whose complex metahistorical narrative foreshadowed, D. W. **Griffith**'s *Intolerance* (1916). At **Ambrosio** Film until 1914, he also later worked for Leonardo, **Film d'Arte Italiana** and **Milano** Films.

GIORGIO BERTELLINI

magic lantern shows

Contemporary researchers often expend much time and effort in trying to establish the exact moment of the "birth of moving pictures." For the showmen and spectators of the late 19th century there was no such moment: moving pictures were not "born" but represented a stage in the natural evolution of the **magic lantern**. Most of the first film **projectors**, including the **Lumière Ciné-matographe**, were small mechanisms that, in place of the regular slide, could fit in front of the lens of a conventional magic lantern. In the 1890s, films were introduced into shows as a fancy new style of mechanical slide; and writers of the time did not always think they were an improvement, comparing their flickering black-and-white images unfavorably with the bright colors and exquisite hand-painted detail of "dissolving views."

The magic lantern had had more than two centuries to develop highly sophisticated techniques and a wide range of uses for entertainment and instruction prior to the emergence of moving pictures. Its invention, around 1660, is now generally credited to the Dutch scientist Christian Huygens, although some claims are made for the Danish mathematician Thomas Rasmussen Walgensten. Huygens clearly regarded the lantern as a strictly scientific demonstration of dioptrics, not as a diversion, and he and his brother resorted to all sorts of ruses to prevent their father from showing off the magic lantern (as no more than a puppet show) at the Louvre in Paris. Walgensten had no such inhibitions, and the shows of "the learned Dane" were celebrated throughout Europe. The Jesuit polymath Athanasius Kircher, to whom the invention is often erroneously attributed, also was clearly a showman as well as savant. His *Ars Magna Lucis et Umbrae* (1671), containing the first printed illustrations of lanterns, show them using slides with images of saints, devils, and sinners burning in hell. This potent mixture of sanctity, terror, and comedy that had once characterized the old Mystery Plays would remain a staple of lantern entertainment.

The magic lantern quickly passed into general circulation, and by the end of the 17th century was as indispensable to the cultivated European gentleman's "cabinet" as the telescope, microscope, and astrolabe. In such circumstances, the pedagogical uses of the lantern were early recognized. In his *Oculus artificialis teledioptrics sive telscopium* (1685), Johannes Zahn proposed that anatomical drawings could be made on glass or mica to be viewed by a number of people at the same time,

and also suggested enclosing small living specimens in box slides which might be projected with the aid of sunlight—an early version of the solar projection microscope.

The magic of the lantern was too appealing, however, to remain the preserve of scientists and scholars. The first half of the 18th century saw the rise of a breed of humble itinerant showmen, often referred to as "Savoyards," who adopted the lantern as their own. They and their families roamed the roads of Europe with their lanterns and boxes of slides on their back, and with some musical instrument—a drum or hurdy-gurdy or "orgue de Barbarie"—to attract the crowd. They set up their shows wherever they could, in barns or taverns or, on lucky days, in gentlemen's houses. Their repertory was very small (contained in one traveling box) and seems to have consisted of a medley of moral tales, little farces, and portraits of the celebrities of the day.

In the late 18th century came conscious efforts to reclaim the magic lantern as a medium for "rational" instruction. Benjamin Martin, in *The Young Gentleman and Lady's Philosophy* (1772), for example, pleads for this "noble optical Instrument, whose Nature and use have been but little considered, and those applied to serve the lowest Purposes, by which Means this Instrument has been brought into Disgrace, and acquired the vile name of *Magic Lanthorn*." Martin proposes to "discard the Infamous Appelation of *Magic*, and substitute in its Room the true and deserved, Epithet of *Megalographic* Lanthorn, by which the Nature of the Instrument is . . . nothing more than the *producing of a very large and magnified Picture of a small Object*."

At the same time it was being reclaimed for scholarship, the lantern saw a dramatic renascence as a medium for spectacular and sophisticated entertainment. In the early 1790s, Paul Philidor (Paul de Philipsthal) exhibited his newly-named "Phantasmagoria," a complex production using a variety of lantern effects to present a "Gothick" spectacle, replete with specters and monsters. The most characteristic element was the technique of moving the lantern towards or away from the screen to give the impression that the image, perhaps a ghastly head or a monstrous form, always maintained in exact focus, seemed to diminish or grow magically. The idea was swiftly adopted (or stolen) and developed by a Belgian artist and showman, Etienne Gaspard Robertson, whose phantasmagoria performances achieved fame throughout Europe and were widely imitated in the first decade of the new century.

Heralded by the Phantasmagoria, the 19th century saw the magic lantern reach the peak of its technical excellence, and discover the greatest variety of uses. It passed now from the preserve of showmen and scientists to become established as a home entertainment. In the first years of the century, John Scott, an artists' colorman in the Strand, marketed outfits of lanterns and slides with the precocious advertising slogan, "A cheerful house should never be without one." True industrial production and systematic marketing of the magic lantern—both for home or professional use—was instituted by Philip Carpenter, an optician who moved from Birmingham to London in 1827. Carpenter standardized lanterns of the highest optical quality and developed a method of transfer-printing slides from copper plates. He was, moreover, the first to issue printed lecture notes to accompany his scientific slide series.

Carpenter's innovations suited the 19th century's energy for popular **education**, which combined instruction with amusement for the edification of adults as well as children. This was the age of the **lecturer**, and charismatic scientific platform performers like Humphry Davy, Michael Faraday, and John Tyndall were stars in their own right. Whereas his predecessors made occasional use of the lantern, for Tyndall it was an indispensable accessory, essential to his famous lectures on "Light." While London society flocked to such fashionable lecture-performances, the working people of England sought instruction and improvement in the Mechanics' Institutes, centers of popular adult education which proliferated throughout Great Britain and the USA in the mid-century. A magic lantern was essential to the equipment of every such self-respecting organization.

Another uniquely 19th-century phenomenon was metropolitan institutions dedicated to popular education and the diffusion of knowledge of applied science—in their way, super-mechanics' institutes. In London the most important of these were the Royal Adelaide Gallery (1834), Royal Polytechnic Institution (1838), and Royal

Panopticon of Science (1854). The Adelaide Gallery exhibited some of the earliest and most advanced "dissolving views" and "a Grand Oxy-Hydrogen Microscope, by Carey, with many fine objects for exhibition on a disk seventeen feet in diameter." The most elaborate and sophisticated lantern shows ever exhibited, however, were those of the Royal Polytechnic during its years under the direction of Professor John Henry Pepper—generally if questionably credited with inventing the stage illusion of "Pepper's Ghost." The Polytechnic employed a team of highly skilled painters to create slides of exceptional size for its elaborate, multi-lantern installations. Apart from its scientific lantern lectures, the Polytechnic was a magnet for London society for its Christmas spectacles, which rivaled the "live" seasonable pantomimes of the London theaters, employing music, narration, and **sound effects** alongside elaborately mechanized slides.

The latter half of the century saw the development of lanterns of ever-increasing technical elaboration—superb Victorian structures in mahogany and brass—and a repertory of complex mechanical slides to produce the illusion of movement. With the advent of photographic slides, the lecture phenomenon flourished, as more and more professional lecturers made themselves available to educational organizations throughout Great Britain, the USA, and much of Europe. The most active proponent of visual education was the Abbé François Moigno in France, who earned the title, "the Apostle of Projection," with the vast collection of slides he formed for teaching purposes at his Salle de Progrès, established in 1872. By the 1880s, serious users of the instrument now styled it the "Optical Lantern." A number of technical manuals on its use appeared: the most widely read, T. C. Hepworth's *Book of the Lantern* (1888), ran to several editions. Optical lantern societies in Britain and America published regular journals dedicated to the technique and uses of the instrument.

By 1914, the leading London supplier of this market, Newton & Co, asserted: "Lantern Slides are now used so largely and successfully in all the best and most progressive of our Schools and Colleges that no educational institution of any pretension to modern methods of teaching can afford to do without them." Newton offered around 100,000 different slides for sale or hire, on every conceivable subject, listed in a multi-volume catalogue of more than 900 pages. As well as for regular education, lantern slides were an important tool for religious organizations (notably the Church Army and the **Salvation Army**), temperance organizations, and missionary societies, who often set up their own distribution systems.

Into this self-confident world, in 1896, erupted the moving pictures. A clairvoyant few foresaw that the old lantern's days were numbered, but most shared the optimism of a veteran of the Royal Polytechnic, Edmund H. Wilkie, who reassured readers of the 1897–1898 *Optical Magic Lantern Journal Almanac* that "so far from superceding general lantern work, it will most likely act in the contrary manner, and by directing the public attention to optical exhibitions give a powerful

Figure 74 "Bob the Fireman" set of four magic lantern slides. (Courtesy of Charles Musser.)

impetus to dissolving view entertainments generally." But moving pictures already were taking their place in the **music hall** and **vaudeville** house, to which the magic lantern had never aspired, and becoming a major **fair/fairground** attraction. The lantern still served well for instructional purposes, but in terms of entertainment it was soon clear that it could not compete with the newcomer.

The home market also boomed in the late 19th and early 20th centuries as toy manufacturers like Plank and Bing in Germany and Lapierre and Aubert in France mass-produced tin-plate lanterns in models ranging from basic toys selling for a few pence to more elaborate models that might serve the more modest professional. Slides in varying sizes were printed by chromolithography. From the late 1890s, toy lantern makers also began marketing elementary film projectors.

The magic lantern survived well into the 20th century. Even after the Second World War, a few schools and churches still kept and occasionally used their lanterns, and survivors of the old slide distributors maintained ever-diminishing catalogues. In fact, the lantern never really died. Although its purely entertainment functions were altogether superceded by the cinema, the diapositive slide projector, a direct stage in the evolution of the apparatus, continued to serve for lectures, demonstrations, and domestic photographic shows into the 21st century.

See also: biblical films; illustrated lectures; illustrated songs; religious filmmaking

Further reading

Mannoni, Laurent (2000) *The Great Art of Light and Shadow: Archaeology of the Cinema*, trans. Richard Crangle, Exeter: University of Exeter Press.

Mannoni, Laurent, Donata Pesenti, and David Robinson (1995) *Light and Movement: Incunabula of the Motion Picture 1420–1896*, Pordenone/Paris/ Turin: Le Giornate del cinema muto/Le Cinémathèque française/Museo Nazionale del Cinema.

Robinson, David, Stephen Herbert, and Richard Crangle (2001) *Encyclopedia of the Magic Lantern*, London: Magic Lantern Society.

DAVID ROBINSON

magic lanterns and stereopticons

Image projection began in ancient times with metal mirrors. From the 15th century, lanterns came into use: a drawing (c. 1420) shows a projection lantern with a devil slide or puppet attached but no focusing (objective) lens, so projected image detail would have been limited. Projection lanterns with reflector, oil illuminant, condenser lens (to concentrate the light), slide stage, and objective lens date from the 1650s, using glass slides with simple painted pictures.

Late 18th-century fantascopes/phantascopes used for rear-projection phantasmagoria shows had wheeled stands. As the lanternist or operator pulled the hidden machine away from the screen the image grew in size, with focus sometimes adjusting automatically by a cam attached to the wheels that activated levers fitted to the lens. Mechanical slides provided simple animation. Small working models and puppets with graveyard and skeleton themes were also shown, using opaque projection techniques.

From around 1800, the Argand lamp provided brighter oil illumination. With the 1830s introduction of limelight—a mixed hydrogen/oxygen gas jet flame heated a block of lime until it glowed a fierce white—images could fill huge theater screens. Later, electric arc lamps appeared. For those still using oil, multi-wick burners reduced flicker. Improved lenses benefited projection, important for the detailed photographic and finely-painted slides marketed from 1850 on. Other slide production techniques included black printed outlines colored in by hand, and chromolithographic transfer slides.

Side-by-side double lanterns with "dissolving" shutters were popular by the 1850s, making possible gradually changing views. For easier operation, a biunial arrangement with one lantern above the other was introduced. Most impressive was the triunial. Some had a removable top lantern, giving the choice of single, double, or triple projection.

In Europe, a simplified metal "phantasmagoria" lantern with crooked conical chimney, sometimes hand-held in use, was popular mid-century. Magic lantern construction after 1850 commonly switched to a mahogany or Russian-iron box, with external fittings in brass. In the USA, magic lanterns were often called stereopticons (a term sometimes used for home **stereoscope** viewers). A popular design had two rails forming a base, on which nickel-plated parts could be moved independently.

Globe-shaped lampascopes, popular in France, could be placed on an ordinary domestic oil lamp. The same manufacturers specialized in toy projectors, including one shaped like the Eiffel Tower. Toy lanterns also were made in the USA and Great Britain, but the most prolific manufacturers were in the Nuremberg region of Germany. From 1800 until the 1920s, vast numbers in many shapes and sizes were exported.

Slipper slides, lever slides, and chromotropes added movement to projected lantern images. More sophisticated sequential-image devices included the choreutoscope and "wheel of life" slide. From 1896, some lanternists incorporated motion pictures. Their outfits had lamphouses designed to swing or slide across from slide-lens to film mechanism. The motion picture **projector** eventually developed independently. Slide lanterns were used extensively in motion picture theaters until the 1970s.

The magic lantern/stereopticon continued to evolve into bulb-illuminated 35 mm slide and filmstrip projectors. Today's video and data projectors—with illuminant, image carrier, and objective lens—are direct technical descendants of the magic lantern.

Figure 75 Docwra triple lantern.

Further reading

Robinson, David, Stephen Herbert and Richard Crangle (eds.) (2001) *Encyclopaedia of the Magic Lantern*, London: Magic Lantern Society.

STEPHEN HERBERT

magicians

Parallel with **magic lantern** showmen and photographers, magicians were amongst the first identifiable groups of practitioners to take up the new medium of moving pictures in 1896. Innovative and highly skilled in mechanics, optics, and the construction of elaborate illusions, apart from the digital manipulations involved in prestidigitation, established magicians recognized the entertainment potential of the new medium and quickly became active in exhibition, filmmaking, and the manufacture and sale of apparatus.

The magicians Georges **Méliès** and the **Isola** brothers (Emile and Vincent) were in the invited audience at the public premiere of the **Cinématographe Lumière** at the Grand Café in Paris on 28 December 1895, and both parties tried to buy a machine from the **Lumières** but were rebuffed by their early policy of not selling the apparatus. Méliès quickly acquired a Robert **Paul** **projector** from Great Britain, and began showing moving pictures at his Théâtre Robert-Houdin on 5 April 1896. Three days later, the Isola brothers, at the time the principal competitors of Méliès, began exhibiting films at their own theater across the street from the Grand Café. They acquired the rights to a projector designed by Louis Charles and not only began producing films but from mid-April 1896 also sold the machines across Europe to exhibitors in Berlin, Vienna, Brussels, and elsewhere. By late 1896, Georges Méliès, now well-established as a filmmaker and exhibitor, began to sell his own cinematographic apparatus developed with Lucien Korsten and Lucien **Reulos**, again closely based on the Louis Charles design.

Both of these Paris magicians were probably encouraged by the experience of David Devant, a leading British magician and partner to the legendary John Nevill Maskelyne in the Egyptian Theatre, "England's Home of Mystery," in London's Piccadilly. Devant persuaded a reluctant Maskelyne to add moving picture projections on a Robert Paul Theatrograph in March 1896, a few days before the machine's inventor opened his own exhibition at the Olympia Theatre. Devant became an agent for Paul's apparatus, selling one to Méliès in Paris and to other magicians such as Carl Herz, simultaneously becoming the sole agent for Méliès's films in Great Britain until 1900. Meanwhile, Devant starred in several Paul films, including *The Mysterious Rabbit* and *The Egg-Laying Man*, and with Maskelyne set up a touring exhibition service that was active in London and several provincial British cities. In 1897, Maskelyne's son John Nevil Maskelyne junior developed an unusual **camera** and projector using an optical intermittent and continuously moving film band that operated at the Egyptian Theatre for several years and remained in use for high-speed **photography** at the Woolwich Arsenal as late as 1905.

Although a number of American film pioneers were also neophyte magicians before beginning substantial film careers—including Billy **Bitzer**, J. Stuart **Blackton** (co-founder of the **Vitagraph** Company), and **amateur films** pioneer Alexander Victor—it was the acceptance of moving pictures from the very beginning by long-established magicians such as Méliès, Isola, Devant, and Herz that contributed greatly to turning an illusion that many people thought of as a passing novelty into a lasting medium of entertainment.

Further reading

Barnouw, Erik (1981) *The Magician and the Cinema*, New York/Oxford: Oxford University Press.

DEAC ROSSELL

Magnusson, Charles

b. 1878; d. 1949

exhibitor, producer, Sweden

Charles Magnusson entered the industry as a Gothenburg-based cameraman in addition to owning a moving picture theater. After several spectacular successes, Magnusson was hired as an executive at **Svenska Biografteatern** (SB) in 1909, a company that he was instrumental in moving from small-town Kristianstad to Stockholm, in 1912, and merging into AB Svensk filmindustri, in 1919. He was the impetus behind the production emphasis that took SB from popular genres to films based on literary masterpieces, often authored by Selma Lagerlöf, and directed by either Victor **Sjöström** or Mauritz **Stiller**. Ivar Kreuger, the Match King, who later gained control of the company, maneuvered him out of Svensk filmindustri in the late 1920s.

JAN OLSSON

Maguire & Baucus

In 1894, through the Continental Commerce Company, **phonograph** speculator F. Z. (Franck Zeveley) Maguire (c. 1860–1910) and lawyer Thomas Baucus became **Edison**'s agents for marketing the **Kinetoscope** in countries outside North America. Focusing on Europe, Maguire went to London, while Baucus handled affairs in the USA. When the Kinetoscope business declined, Maguire & Baucus sold projectors, films, and phonographs in both Britain and the USA and for a short while were the leading marketers of Edison and **Lumière** films. In 1897 Charles **Urban** was sent to manage the London office, and changed the name of the British firm to **Warwick Trading Company**. Although Maguire and Baucus remained officers in Warwick Trading, they gave more attention to their phonograph business.

PAUL SPEHR

Maharashtra Film Company

A set painter before D. G. **Phalke**'s *Raja Harishchandra* inspired him to make films, Baburao Painter (1890–1954) established the Maharashtra Film Company in Kolhapur in 1918, with the help of local ruler Shahu Maharaj. With films such as *Sairandhri* (1920), *Sinhagad* (1923),

and *Savkari Pash* (1925), Maharashtra Film broke new ground in all three major genres of early Indian cinema: **mythological** tales, **historical films**, and socials. Perhaps the only comparable work at that time came from Phalke's **Hindustan Cinema Films Company**. After important personnel left to establish Prabhat Film Company in 1929, the company declined and closed down in 1932.

SURESH CHABRIA

Maison de la Bonne Presse

The Maison de la Bonne Presse, the Paris publisher of major Catholic newspapers headed by Paul Feron-Vrau, created a "visual education" department in May 1896. Created by Vincent de Paul Bailly, the department was managed by G.-Michel **Coissac**. Its purpose was to counter secular propaganda by means of the **magic lantern** and the film **projector**. In 1897, Bonne Presse made its debut in film production with a *Passion du Christ* (in twelve scenes) directed by **Kircher**, which was followed by other religious films during the 1900s and 1910s. Bonne Press also published specialized periodicals, including *Les Conférences* (starting in 1901) and especially *Le Fascinateur* (from 1903 on).

LAURENT MANNONI

Maître, Maurice André

b. ?; d. ?

director, France, Russia

An associate of Ferdinand **Zecca**, Maître was sent to Moscow in 1908 to help establish **Pathé-Frères'** film production in Russia. He first shot *actualités* and short **travelogues** and then directed film adaptations of literary classics or *films d'art*, often jointly with Kai **Hansen**: for instance, *Princess Tarakanova* (1910). Pathé's commitment to local color filled Maître's films with peasants, samovars, and other trappings of the folk. His greatest commercial success was *Lekhaim* (1910), based on a Jewish folk theme. In 1911, he returned to France and continued working for Pathé, directing a new version of the *Passion Play* (1913).

YURI TSIVIAN

Majestic

Harry **Aitken** launched Majestic Films by enticing Mary **Pickford** away from **IMP** with a higher salary in 1911. Although Pickford eventually returned to **Biograph**, Majestic remained in business until it merged with **Reliance** in 1914. Another former Biograph employee, D. W. **Griffith**, was hired to oversee production at Reliance-Majestic that year, and directed four features himself, most notably *The Avenging Conscience*. Aitken also became president of the **Mutual Film Corporation**, the umbrella distributing organization which handled the films of Reliance-Majestic, among others. In 1915, he then joined with Reliance's founders to set up the Triangle Picture Company, a temporary home for Griffith, Thomas **Ince** and Mack **Sennett**.

CHARLIE KEIL

Makino Shozo

b. 1878; d. 1929

director, producer, Japan

Born in Kyoto. After a career as a theatrical player, Makino entered the motion picture business as a director for **Yokota Shokai** in 1908. After his first film, *Honnoji Kassen* [The Battle at the Honnoji Temple] (1908), he made many *kyugeki* (old-drama) films starring **Onoe Matsunosuke**. After Yokota Shokai merged into **Nikkatsu** in 1912, he stayed on and became chief director at Nikkatsu's Kyoto unit. In 1921 he founded his own independent company and invited young, talented directors to make quality films there. As a producer, he gave directors relatively free rein in their filmmaking, and as a result, many artistic period dramas originated at his company in the 1920s.

HIROSHI KOMATSU

Malaya

The territories of Malaya were colonies of Great Britain from the late 19th century, and had a mixed population of Europeans, Chinese, and Malays. This racial division was to be reflected in the peninsula's experience of cinema throughout the 20th century. The first appearance of moving pictures in Malaya was in Kuala Lumpur in 1898 when film of Queen Victoria's Diamond Jubilee was shown, and the next recorded screening was of Russo-Japanese war films in 1906. By 1909 the southernmost territory, Singapore, was host to three establishments showing films: the Alhambra, the Marlborough, and Harima Hall. While the first attracted Chinese audiences, the last was well patronized by Europeans, and showed *films d'art* as part of a live variety program featuring London acts.

By 1911, the US Consul reported that in addition to these venues, there were some six others throughout the rest of the peninsula. **Pathé-Frères** supplied most of the **projectors** and films for these shows, although American movies were making inroads by the following year. With its own local office, Pathé had an advantage over others: Italian films, for instance, had to be ordered direct from the manufacturers; other films, from London agents.

The cinema advanced rapidly, and the value of film-related goods imported into Singapore rose from $140,000 in 1910 to $383,000 in 1911. By 1913 there were 12 to 14 film venues across Malaya, and the following year Singapore alone had five cinemas with more in the offing. The new Alhambra of 1914 was the most ostentatious cinema yet, and large, seating up to 4,000, although most of the other cinemas were more basic wooden buildings with thatched roofs. The racial division came into play here, with the poorer native Malays (up to a thousand persons in some venues) restricted to viewing from behind the **screens**, therefore seeing everything reversed left to right. This racial separation was maintained in succeeding years, with natives occupying the downstairs of cinemas, whereas the higher classes (mainly Europeans) occupied the balconies. It might be added, however, that cinemas were among the few social spaces in Malaya where the races came together at all.

A concentration of theater ownership in Chinese hands, which has since characterized cinema in Malaya, began in this period. In 1913, most cinemas were reported to be owned by just one man (possibly Tan Cheng Kee), and the following year the Chinese-owned "Cinematograph Français" group had theaters in Selangor, Malacca, and Perak, along with several touring shows.

In 1912, film censorship was proposed for the colony, requiring that written descriptions of all films be furnished to the chief police officer. It is not clear to what extent this scheme was enacted, and it was only in the 1920s that a systematic censorship was imposed, after the colonial government became alarmed that the "loose" behavior of white women in Hollywood melodramas was diminishing respect for the colonial masters.

See also: Cambodia; colonialism: Europe; Thailand (Siam); Vietnam

Further reading

Stevenson, Rex (1974) "Cinemas and Censorship in Colonial Malaya," *Journal of Southeast Asian Studies*, 5.2: 209–224.

STEPHEN BOTTOMORE

Marey, Etienne-Jules

b. 1830; d. 1904

physiologist, chronophotographer, France

A professor of physiology at the College de France in Paris, Marey originated a "graphic method" of recording human and animal movement, for which he developed various electrical and mechanical devices. After encountering Eadweard **Muybridge**'s serial photographs of moving figures, Marey turned to **chronophotography** as a more precise method of recording. Once his Paris-funded center, the Station physiologique, opened in 1882, Marey constructed the first of several "photographic guns" or fixed-plate **cameras** to advance his research. In 1888, he designed a camera that

substituted **Eastman** paper roll film for glass plates, and his first series of chronophotographs were presented to the Académie des sciences later that year. Within another year, he was using transparent **celluloid** film. During his career, Marey amassed thousands of glass plates and nearly 800 short chronographic films, many images from which were reproduced in his encyclopedic work, *Le Mouvement* (1894). Committed to analytical research, Marey left it to others such as his young collaborator, Georges **Demenÿ**, to exploit the optical systhesis of movement in projection.

RICHARD ABEL

Marion, Frank J.

b. 1870; d. March 1963

producer, director, scriptwriter, USA

Marion produced and directed films for **American Mutoscope and Biograph** (AM&B) through the end of 1906, when he organized **Kalem** with Samuel **Long**, head of the AM&B laboratory in New Jersey, and George **Kleine**, an important Chicago importer and distributor. While at AM&B, Marion worked in collaboration with Wallace **McCutcheon** until the latter left for **Edison** in 1905, and then became responsible for AM&B's output, hiring an occasional director for specific films. As Kalem's production expanded, Marion gave up directing and managed the production units led by other directors.

EILEEN BOWSER

Mark, Mitchell H.

b. ?; d. 1918

entrepreneur, exhibitor, USA

Mark was first known for developing **penny arcades** in Buffalo, New York, and then in other cities in the Northeast, one of which in New York City inspired Adolph **Zukor** to enter the business. Mark was a pioneer exhibitor, locating his first theater, the Comique, on fashionable Scollay Square in Boston in 1906. After Zukor bought the theater in 1907, Mark opened another Comique in the nearby shoe factory town of Lynn, built up a small chain of theaters in the Northeast, and soon headed an important real estate firm. In 1914, Mitchell H. Mark Realty financed the construction or remodeling of several major **palace cinemas**: the Strand (New York City), the Park (Boston), and the New Victoria (Buffalo).

RICHARD ABEL

Marro, Albert

b. 1878; d.1956

filmmaker, Spain

A pioneer of Spanish cinema, Marro first worked as an **intinerant exhibitor**. In 1901, he filmed "Panoramic views" with Segundo de **Chomón** and, in 1902, founded the Macaya y Marro production and distribution company. With a solid cultural background, he soon was making films that aimed to connect with audiences through a mastery of cinematic language: *Locura de amor* [Madness of Love] (1909), *Don Pedro el cruel* [The Cruel Don Pedro] (1911). In 1916, with J. M. Codina, he co-directed the successful series, *Barcelona y sus misterios* [Barcelona and its Mysteries] for **Hispano Films**.

JOAN M. MINGUET

Martoglio, Nino

b. 1870; d. 1921

poet, playwright, film director, Italy

Promoter of dialect theater in his native Catania (Sicily), Martoglio launched vernacular stage performers Giovanni Grasso, Angelo Musco, and Mimì Aguglia. After a stint at **Cines** in 1913, he founded Morgana Film and directed three films, including the now lost *Sperduti nel buio* [Lost in Darkness] (1914). Adapted from a play by Neapolitan writer Roberto Bracco and starring Giovanni Grasso, *Sperduti* was a key instance of plebeian realism. Hailed with the extant *Assunta Spina* (1915) as a forerunner of Italian neorealism, it uniquely combined Neapolitan dialect melodrama with Sicilian vernacular performances.

GIORGIO BERTELLINI

Marvin, Arthur

b. 1861; d. 1911

cameraman, USA

Brother of the **American Mutoscope and Biograph** company's co-founder Henry **Marvin**, Arthur Marvin was one of America's first professional motion picture cameramen. Marvin had already been working for AM&B twelve years, sharing studio and location camera duties with G. W. "Billy" **Bitzer**, when he photographed D. W. **Griffith**'s first film, *The Adventures of Dollie* in June of 1908. Both worked with Griffith until late 1909, when Marvin began photographing second-unit **comedies** for Frank Powell. Arthur Marvin died in California in January 1911.

STEVEN HIGGINS

Marvin, Harry

b. 6 September 1862, Jordan, New York; d. 12 January 1941, Venice, Florida

inventor, studio executive, USA

One of the partners who founded the **American Mutoscope and Biograph Company** at the end of 1895, Marvin was the company's Vice President, President, or General Manager through most of its history. He provided the impetus for the design of the company's **cameras**, **projectors**, and mutoscopes or peep show machines, which were manufactured at his Marvin Rock Drill Co. in Canastota, New York. He also served as President of the **Motion Picture Patents Company**. In the

1880s Marvin patented a mining drill which was a predecessor of the modern pneumatic drill, and in the 1920's he designed an automatic radio tuning system.

PAUL SPEHR

Mary, Clément (a.k.a. "Bébé," "le petit Abélard," "Dary, René")

b. 1905; d. 1974

actor, France

The son of Abélard Mary, Clément Mary was hired by **Gaumont** at the age of five to star in the **comic series**, *Bébé* (74 films between 1910 and 1912), directed by Louis **Feuillade**. A typical idea driving the series' films was to place him in the situation of a grown-up: for instance, *Bébé jardinier* [Bébé as Gardener], *Bébé juge* [Bébé as Judge], *Bébé agent d'assurances* [Bébé as Insurance Broker].

In 1912, preparing for a successor, Feuillade introduced a toddler nicknamed Bout-de-Zan (René **Poyen**) into the series in *Bébé adopte un petit frère* [Bébé Adopts a Little Brother]. Mary's father balked at the competition, and Gaumont took the matter to court, which ruled in favor of terminating Bébé's contract in December 1912 but rejected Gaumont's claim of copyright to the name "Bébé" and its refusal to allow the young star to appear in any film until 1 June 1913. Gaumont later took the precaution to register "Bout-de-Zan" as a **trademark**.

Bébé went to Eclectic Films (initially named Cosmopolitan Films), controlled by **Pathé-Frères**, and began a new comic series with *Bébé n'aime pas sa concierge* [Bébé Doesn't Like His Concierge]—16 films were made until January 1916, most of them directed by Henry Gambart. In 1913, his parents owned a small theater in the 20th arrondissement of Paris that they called "Bébé cinéma."

As an adult, Clément Mary went on to work in cinema and television under the name of René Dary, from 1934 to 1968.

JEAN-JACQUES MEUSY

Mason, Bert

b. 1880; d. 1960

cameraman, Quebec

Mason was the first professional cameraman in Quebec. Born in England, he arrived in Quebec in 1905 and was hired by Léo-Ernest **Ouimet** to sing along with **illustrated song** slides. Ouimet taught him to operate a **camera** and then made him his regular cameraman. After Ouimet temporarily left the film business in 1912, Mason offered his services to producers of local *actualités*. He quickly built up a network of buyers, including Fox News, and until the 1930s he shot much **newsreel** footage throughout Canada. At the end of his career he returned to work in exhibition.

GERMAIN LACASSE

Mastbaum, Jules and Stanley

b. 1872/1880; d. 7 December 1926/7 March 1918

exhibitors, USA

These brothers, while not the pioneers of moving picture exhibition in Philadelphia, by 1915 dominated exhibition in the third largest city in the USA. Not poor immigrants, but college graduates, they entered the cinema business through their well-established real estate company. They purchased their first theater in 1911, and by 1914 had opened the 1,500 seat Stanley, which established the **palace cinema** era in Philadelphia. Early untimely deaths meant Warner Bros. would run their **cinema circuit/chain** for most of its existence.

DOUGLAS GOMERY

Matuszewski, Bóleslaw

b. 1856; d. 1941 (?)

photographer, cameraman, writer, Poland, Russia, France

Bóleslaw Matuszewski is a myth that should be returned to history. The myth rests on an uneven historical reception: on the one hand, the fabricated interpretation of *Une nouvelle source de l'histoire* [A New Source of History], a 12-page pamphlet published in Paris by the author and widely circulated throughout Europe as early as late March 1898, and reprinted in various translations since 1955; on the other hand, the persistent neglect that met a second work, also printed in Paris and dated "August-October 1898," *La photographie animée, ce qu'elle est, ce qu'elle doit être* (Moving Photography, What It Is, What It Should Be), although it has been reprinted in 1980 and 1995 and its importance long recognized by Polish scholars. A rich compilation of statements appears in an appendix to this latter text, which testifies to the positive reaction of French public opinion to the idea of a "dépôt de cinématographie historique" (archive of historical films) put forward in the initial pamphlet and which never materialized.

These writings and the appended statements comprise a fundamental ensemble of sources on the natural continuity between the photographic museum of the 19th century and the notion of a cinematographic museum of the 20th—not as an ancestor to our current film **archives** but to those devoted to nonfiction films. The principal assumption was that an irrefutable historical value could be ascribed to film because of the supposedly intrinsic objectivity of its recording system. In a later pamphlet, *Une innovation en graphologie et dans l'expertise en écriture* (1899), Matuszewski made the point that cinema could be used to denounce or expose fraudulent claims.

Matuszewski's project, founded on a notion of cinema widely shared by his contemporaries, went beyond the mere collection of documents. It contemplated their systematic organization from a national and encyclopedic as well as preservationist and didactic perspective. Moreover, it introduced the notion of a legal deposit and expressed an early concern for film access and care.

What little is known about Matuszewski's career (he was born in that part of Poland annexed by Russia) falls in line with this project. He was a photographer in Warsaw in 1895 and perhaps a cameraman (or simply a photographer) at the court of Nicolas II around 1896. Temporarily establishing himself in Paris at the turn of the last century, he was an active Francophile throughout his life. Between 1895 and 1900, he belonged to that cohort of first "men with a movie camera." Because none of his films seems to have survived, filmographers are still struggling to identify specific films from secondary sources and available statements by the filmmaker himself.

See also: *actualités*; news event films; re-enactments

Further reading

Matuszewski, Bóleslaw (1995) *Nowe zrodlo historii* (Une nouvelle source de l'histoire, 1898), *Ozywiona fotografia, czy jest czym powinna* (La photographie animée, ce qu'elle est, ce qu'elle doit être, 1898), 2nd ed., Warsaw: Filmoteka Narodowa. (reprint of Matuszewski's writings in French, with a Polish translation).
Matuszewski, Bóleslaw (1999) *A New Source of History. Animated Photography: What It Is, What It Should Be*, Warsaw: Filmoteka Narodowa.

ROLAND COSANDEY

May, Joe

b. 1880; d. 1954

filmmaker, producer, Germany

One of Weimar Germany's most prominent filmmakers—and a director of routine studio films after his emigration to Hollywood—May established himself in the 1910s as director and producer of the most successful **serials** and **crime films** of early German cinema—for instance, *Hilde Warren und der Tod* [Death and Hilde Warren] (1917)—many of which starred his wife, Mia May. He discovered and promoted such new talent as Thea von Harbou, E. A. Dupont, and Fritz Lang, whose early work very much bears the imprint of May's mysteries and melodramas.

SCOTT CURTIS

McCay, Winsor

b. 1870?; d. 1934

animator, USA

McCay was a **comic strip** artist renowned for such series as "Dreams of the Rarebit Fiend." After his friend, J. Stuart **Blackton**, introduced him to film animation, he completed a moving picture adaptation of *Little Nemo* (1911). Of his ten cartoons, the most influential was *Gertie* (1914), presenting a loveable trained dinosaur who lumbers from a cave and obeys, rather peevishly, McCay's commands. McCay's films were intended to accompany his **vaudeville** act as well as be shown in moving picture theaters.

Further reading

Canemaker, John (1987) *Winsor McCay: His Life and Art*, New York: Abbeville Press.

DONALD CRAFTON

McCutcheon, Wallace

b. November 3, 1861, New York City; d. ?

studio executive, filmmaker, USA

A former theater manager, Wallace McCutcheon was hired by **American Mutoscope and Biograph** after W. K. L. **Dickson** went to Europe. He supervised AM&B productions from about 1897 until 1905, when he was hired by **Edison**. Returning to **Biograph** in 1907, he hired D. W. **Griffith** as an actor, and Griffith got a chance to direct when McCutcheon fell ill. McCutcheon is credited with directing some of AM&B's best-known early productions, particularly *The Escaped Lunatic* (1904) and *Personal* (1904), films that popularized **chase films**. He finished his career with the Gaston **Méliès**'s American company. His son, actor Wallace McCutcheon, Jr., also worked for Biograph and their careers are sometimes confused.

PAUL SPEHR

McDowell, John Benjamin

b. 1878; d. 1954

cameraman, producer, Great Britain

"Mac" McDowell trained as an engineer at Woolwich Arsenal in London, before joining **British Mutoscope and Biograph** in 1898, as cameraman and projectionist. In 1906, he joined the **Warwick Trading Company** as a news film cameraman and, one year later, became chief cameraman of the **Walturdaw** company. In 1908, McDowell joined the newly-created **British and Colonial Kinematograph Company** and soon was its managing director, producing both **news event films** and dramas. In 1915, he helped to create the British Topical Committee for War Films, which handled official filming of the war. In 1916, he volunteered as cameraman for the official documentary *Battle of the Somme*, remaining at the front until the end of the war, and winning the Military Medal. McDowell subsequently worked for companies supplying film stock.

NICHOLAS HILEY

McRae, V(irginia) H.

b. ?; d. ?

journalist, USA

V. H. McRae was one of the first women to play an active role in the emerging motion picture business. From 1891 until 1893, she was editor and general manager of *The Phonogram*, the first trade magazine of the North American **phonograph** industry. Her magazine reported on the as yet un-marketed motion picture, and she anticipated that the evolving phonograph business would be a promising market for **Edison**'s motion picture devices. After the magazine ceased publication, she conducted a class to train women as stenographers, a profession previously dominated by men.

PAUL SPEHR

Medina, José

b. 1894, Sorocaba, São Paulo; d. 1980,
São Paulo

filmmaker, Brazil

Medina became interested in the cinema when he
saw films projected for workers at the Votorantim
cement factory in Sorocaba. He moved to São
Paulo, studied **painting** and **photography**, and
worked with amateur theatrical companies. In 1919
he met Gilberto **Rossi** and began a long and productive association in fiction and **newsreel** production: Rossi provided technical know-how and
Medina artistic control. Their *Exemplo regenerador*
[Regenerative Example] (1919), produced over a
long weekend as an exercise in continuity editing,
proved successful with local audiences and was followed by *Perversidade* [Perversity] (1920) and others. Although he abandoned the cinema in the
1930s for radio, where he had a productive career for
26 years, Medina also led the Foto-Cine club Ban-
deirantes, which had great cultural significance in
the 1950s–1960s.

ANA M. LÓPEZ

Méliès, Gaston

b. 1852; d. 1915

businessman, filmmaker, France, USA

The elder brother of Georges **Méliès**, Gaston had
his start in the film business in 1903, when he
opened a New York sales office for Star Films. He
proved an able manager, and he himself became
interested in production. With the declining
appeal of Georges' **trick films** and *féeries*, in 1909
Gaston determined to make films more in the
American style. He set up in Texas to produce
westerns, with director William Haddock and
cameraman William **Paley**. In 1911, he shifted
operations to California, but eventually could not
compete. Gaston's swansong as a filmmaker was a
trip to the Pacific and East Asia with a company of
actors and technicians in 1912–1913.

See also: Chicago Film Exchange; Oceania/South
Pacific

Further reading

Malthête, Jacques (1990) "Biographie de Gaston
Méliès," *1895*, 7: 85–90.

STEPHEN BOTTOMORE

Méliès, Georges

b. 1861; d. 1938

filmmaker, producer, France

Born the third son of a Parisian shoe manufacturer,
Georges Méliès worked in his father's enterprise
only for a short time. In 1884, during a professional
stay in London, he frequently attended **magicians'**
shows at the Egyptian Hall and befriended John
Nevil Maskelyne, who taught him the art of illu-
sionism. After his return to France, Méliès performed at the Musée Grevin and the Galérie
Vivienne in Paris. In 1888, when his father retired,
Georges's two brothers, Henri and **Gaston**, took
over the factory, while he used his share of the
family fortune to begin a career as director of
the Théâtre Robert-Houdin, specializing in magic
shows. Simultaneously, in 1889–1890, he also drew
caricatures for a political weekly edited by his cousin, Adolphe Méliès, under the alias of Geo Smile.

On 28 December 1895, Méliès was one of the
spectators witnessing the Paris première of the
Cinématographe Lumière. A few months later,
in April 1896, he began to show moving pictures at
the Robert-Houdin with a Theatrograph, a machine manufactured by Robert William **Paul**, presented by Méliès under the name *Kinétograph(e)*:
according to recent research, a machine copyrighted and put on the market under this name in
September 1896 by Méliès, together with Lucien
Reulos and the mechanic Lucien Korsten, seems
to have been identical to one copyrighted by Louis
Henri Charles in April that year. In May/June
1896, Méliès started shooting his own films with a
modified Theatrograph.

In 1897, Méliès erected his first studio in his
garden in Montreuil-sous-Bois, where a second was
built in 1907. From 1896 to 1909, he produced
films of various genres under his own name and for
his own company, Star Film, registered as a **trade**

mark in 1902. In order to protect his business interests in the USA, in 1903 Méliès sent Gaston to New York to open a sales office. Although the G. Méliès Manufacturing Company joined the **Motion Picture Patents Company** in early 1909, Méliès was unable to meet production demands, and, in December 1909, Gaston began shooting his own films in the USA. By 1910, Méliès had abandoned film production and returned to the stage, touring Europe with a magic show. Between 1911 and 1913, now financed by Charles **Pathé**, he produced the last six of his more than 500 films.

In 1923, financial failure forced Méliès to sell his Montreuil property, including all of his remaining positive and negative film stock, representing several hundreds of films. The same year, a project extending the Boulevard Haussmann destroyed the Théâtre Robert-Houdin and the Passage de l'Opéra. In December 1925, Méliès was married to his second wife, the actress Charlotte Faes, who, under the name of Jehanne d'Alcy, had played in a number of his early films. She was the concessionaire of a candy and toy boutique in the Gare Montparnasse, where both worked during the following years. When Léon Druhot, editor of *Ciné-Journal*, as well as other writers became interested in the "pioneers" of cinema, their recognition of Méliès's merits led to a gala evening at the Salle Pleyel in Paris, December 1929, where nine of his films, which had been rediscovered, were screened. In 1931, Méliès received the Croix de la Légion d'Honneur, handed to him by Louis **Lumière**. One year later, he, his wife, and his granddaughter Madeleine were given an apartment at the Château d'Orly, owned by the Mutuelle du Cinéma, where he lived until his death on 21 January 1938.

The name of Georges Méliès is above all associated with **trick films** and *féeries*, which, indeed, form a major part of his production. After allegedly having discovered stop motion or the substitution edit/splice because of a camera jam while he was filming at the Place de l'Opéra (the device in fact had already been used by others before), Méliès used it widely in his films. They appear as crucial tricks in recreations of magical illusions such as *Escamotage d'une dame chez Robert-Houdin* [Conjuring a Woman at the Robert-Houdin] (1896), but also in a more narrativized form as, for example, in *Voyage dans la lune* [A Trip to the Moon] (1902) with its "exploding" Selenites. In many cases, substitution splices were combined with other trick effects such as double exposure, pyrotechnics, or multiple exposures. Some of these films were made initially to be shown as interludes in stage shows. Méliès's *féeries* and trick films were visually spectacular productions, many of them distributed in **color** versions.

However, Méliès's filmography features many different genres: his first films often were Lumière-like "views," such as his "remake" of *Une partie de cartes* [A Card Game] (1896). Other examples include a series of films shot during the Paris Universal Exposition in 1900. Méliès also produced a number of staged **actualités**, among others his famous film, *Affaire Dreyfus* (1899), and *Le sacre d'Edouard VII* [The Crowning of Edward VII] (1902), commissioned by Charles **Urban**. Other genres found in Méliès's catalogues are comical scenes, melodramas, and numerous films based on literary or legendary stories such as *Jeanne d'Arc* (1900), *Les aventures de Robinson Crusoé* [The Adventures of Robinson Crusoe] (1902), or *Le Juif errant* [The Wandering Jew] (1904).

Despite a number of exceptions, the typical Méliès film is a studio production in a tableau style, with the filmmaker controlling every phase of the process: **screenwriting**, **set design**, *mise-en-scène*, camera work, tricks, and editing. In most cases, he also appears as the main actor. Contrary to **Pathé-Frères**, which quickly embarked on an industrialized mode of production, Méliès continued to see himself first of all as an artist and craftsman. Film historians, therefore, often regard him as an early *auteur*. This mode of production, however, proved disadvantageous in the rapidly evolving market which led to cinema's industrialization. In addition, demand for the fantastic genres in which Méliès excelled and for which this mode of production was particularly suited declined from 1908 on.

Today Méliès is one of the best documented early filmmakers, thanks to the ongoing efforts of the Méliès family to collect and present his work. They have recovered a large number of his films,

Figure 76 Georges Méliès (left) in his Montreuil studio.

many of them from the families of **fair/fairground** exhibitors, who once formed a large part of Méliès' clientele.

See also: editing: early practices and techniques; editing: tableau style

Further reading

Cherchi Usai, Paolo (1991) (ed.), *Lo schermo incantato/A Trip to the Movies. Georges Méliès (1861–1938)*, Pordenone/Rochester: Biblioteca dell'Immagine/George Eastman House International Museum of Photography.

Malthête, Jacques (1996) *Méliès. Images et Illusions*, Paris: Exporégie.

Malthête, Jacques and Michel Marie (1997) (eds.) *Georges Méliès, l'illusionniste fin de siècle?*, Paris: Presses de l'Université de la Sorbonne Nouvelle/ Colloque de Cerisy.

Malthête, Jacques and Laurent Mannoni (2002) (eds.), *Méliès, magie et cinéma*, Paris: Paris-Musées.

FRANK KESSLER

melodrama, domestic

As a cultural form, melodrama dates from the end of the 18th century, or the French Revolutionary period. Associated with a new class, the bourgeoisie, melodrama defined itself against a decaying and decadent aristocracy, long aligned with tragedy. The term has its origins in *mélo-drame* (music-drama) and refers to a kind of theater in which expression through speech, bodily gesture, and mise-en-scène can be understood by analogy with musical orchestration. Yet equally important is the shift from the allegorical of tragedy to the personal of melodrama. Since the social is represented as the personal, the setting is predominantly the home and the situations both familiar and familial.

Early cinema, as it imported its situations from theatrical melodrama, was similarly preoccupied with the emotional ties of family relations, the feelings that bound family members together and the conflicts that broke those bonds. Examples abound in early **Pathé-Frères** films: in *La Loi du pardon* [The Law of Pardon] (1906), a young daughter reconciles her father and wayward mother; in *Ecole du malheur* [Distress] (1907), a young girl whose "rehabilitated" father dies in an accident is taken into a kindly gendarme's family. Melodrama has been popularly understood in terms of contrasts, often characterized as nothing more than polar opposites in battle: virtue against villainy, justice against criminality, innocence against corruption. In many early films, the drama can be abbreviated, exaggerating these polarities. But it also can be worked out rather subtly, as in Pathé's *Les Deux soeurs* [Two Sisters] (1907), where an older sister saves a younger (both orphaned) from the temptation of her rich, philandering lover. When film melodrama took advantage of editing for contrast, moreover, alternation between scenes of rich and poor could produce a powerful single-reel morality play. In D. W. **Griffith**'s *A Corner in Wheat* (1909) and *Gold is Not All* (1910), dramatic contrast is produced by pairing scenes of exploiters and exploited, back to back. Here, an invisible storyteller seems to intervene, to hold back and give out parts of the story in such a way that the viewer is directed to empathize with as well as to pass judgment on the characters and situations.

While the one-reel contrast drama may have accentuated melodrama's stark oppositions, the move to **multiple-reel/feature films** meant that the more complex aspect of melodrama could organize these narratives. Rather than by rigid polarity, melodrama could be structured by reversals, most often the reversal of fate experienced by the protagonist whose virtue is first persecuted and later recognized. This pattern often is worked out in narratives where the hero is falsely accused or the heroine is thought to be promiscuous or untrue, that is, in stories about misrecognition that gives way to recognition—or does not, as in many of Louis **Feuillade**'s *Scènes de la vie qu'elle est* [Life As It Is] (1911–1913). Here the domestic melodrama specializes in situations in which identities are disguised and relationships masked in such a way that the characters (unknowingly) flirt with disastrous consequence. In Gloria's *Ma l'amor mio non muore!* [Everlasting Love] (1913), neither lover is aware of the true identity of the other. Elsa (Lyda **Borelli**) is known to her lover by her stage name, and she knows him only as Max, not the heir to the Duchy of Wallenstein. She is, in fact, the daughter

of one of the Duke's generals who fell out of favor when he committed suicide.

Although melodrama structures its reversals in such a way that the audience is surprised, often just at the denouement, one thing is always known: which characters will be favored in the end. For the most important principle of melodrama is the miraculous reversal of hierarchies. Paradoxically, the weak and powerless are elevated by the very virtue that is reviled by evil-doers, although rewards may not come in the world's terms, which is why the sainted innocent in domestic melodrama may triumph but not necessarily live. Women and children are thus privileged over men in the melodramatic scheme of things. This moral reversal is most dramatic in the classic domestic melodrama, Harriet Beecher Stowe's *Uncle Tom's Cabin; or, Life Among the Lowly*, the best-selling novel which was reproduced in thousands of stage versions after its appearance in 1852. At least three film versions appeared before 1915 produced by **Edison** (1903), **Vitagraph**, (1910), and **World Film Corporation** (1914). In all three, Little Eva and Uncle Tom, the one weakened by childhood disease and the other by the brutality of slavery, aligned as they are with purity and goodness, are elevated above the rest, even in death.

Out of moral confusion and ambiguity, melodrama strives to produce, in Peter Brooks's terms, "moral legibility." In melodrama, audiences can find the means of managing the most difficult of moral dilemmas raised by the occurrence of unspeakable acts: adultery, incest, patricide, and slavery. Of American race melodrama, exemplified by *Uncle Tom's Cabin*, Linda Williams has argued that "since the mid-nineteenth century, melodrama has been…the primary way in which mainstream American culture has dealt with the moral dilemma of having first enslaved and then withheld equal rights to generations of African Americans."

In order to render the moral scheme legible both theater and film melodrama perfected devices for the production of on-stage and on-screen effects, devices designed to produce the optimum desired feelings in spectators: astonishment, anxiety, or pity. Just as important as **acting styles** were modes of staging and editing. According to Ben Brewster and Lea Jacobs, early film melodrama took a "situational and pictorial" approach in which the tableau, a frozen moment, allowed for a prolongation of the pictorial as well as emotional values in a scene. Such tableaux were more likely to be found in films adapted from the theater, but in the cinema they were not likely to be held as long. Instead, a kind of tableau effect governed the overall framing, staging, and structuring. An exceedingly efficient moralizing device, the tableau was able to visualize the oppression of the powerless in summary form. For instance, Edwin S. **Porter**'s *Uncle Tom's Cabin* (1903) is organized into fourteen single-shot scenes, each proceeded by an **intertitle**, as in scene fourteen's "Tableau: Death of Uncle Tom." Here the action within a tableau may appear as flat and two-dimensional as the cardboard sets against which the actors gesticulate. See Scene 3. The Escape of Eliza, in which the lawyer Marks shakes his umbrella at Eliza and her child as the slave flees across the ice-covered river.

One of the more significant changes in film melodrama was the shift from a restricted flatness or two-dimensionality to the broader possibilities of **staging in depth**. Most pronounced in European melodrama, but also seen in American films, staging in depth allowed the action to unfold within several spatial planes, from background to foreground, often using the possibilities of specially constructed **set designs** and/or selective **lighting**. Long flights of steps, platforms, windows, pillars, or rooms within rooms structured the more complex dramatic movement. Examples of this can be seen

Figure 77 Frame still from Edison's *Uncle Tom's Cabin* (1903).

in Feuillade's *La Tare* [The Taint] (1911) or Pathé's *La Coupable* [The Anonymous Letter] (1912) and in the elegant and passionate moves of *Ma l'amour mio non muore!*, in which Lyda Borelli, in response to the revelation of her lover's identity, choreographs a series of elaborate bodily poses, orchestrated against the interior steps of his lavish villa.

Inspired by Italian but also Danish cinema, Russian melodrama went even further with the possibilities of spatial pictorialism, the enlarged space of the set harmonizing with an acting style developed from the Moscow Art Theatre and associated with playwright Anton Chekhov. As Yuri Tsivian describes it, the Russian "aesthetics of immobility" derives from a tradition of the long or "full" scene, which encouraged the artistic freedom of the actor, combined with the influence of minimalism, a reduction of movement. In order to achieve this effect, Yakov **Protazanov** allegedly orchestrated the movements of his actors by periodically yelling "Pause." The immobility of the Russian acting style combined with an intricacy of staging developed into moralizing devices capable of carrying the great weight of expression necessary to melodrama, the form in which the unspeakable must somehow be "spoken."

A great deal is at stake in European and especially East European melodrama since familial strife is conveyed by characters who represent royalty and aristocracy. Vast inheritances and the fates of nations hang in the balance. Class difference explains the distance characters can rise and fall. In American melodrama, this class dichotomy tends to get transposed into a country versus city opposition. In addition, American melodrama is more hurried, particularly in Griffith's films, where fast cutting becomes an important melodramatic device. Not only are the American shot lengths generally shorter than the European, but in Griffith there also is a pronounced pattern of alternation between scenes, edited in incrementally shorter lengths toward the narrative climax in such a way as to produce a heightened visual effect. First seen in films from *The Lonely Villa* (1909) to *The Lonedale Operator* (1911), this effect is suggestive of the rapidly beating heart, an effect straining for audience involvement in the outcome of the scene. Again and again in the cross-cut scene, the victim is first put in danger and then miraculously rescued. Yet the rescue that comes "in the nick of time," the stock and trade of sensational **melodrama**, is underwritten by deeper principles: the rescue of innocence restores the melodramatic order in which the powerless will triumph.

Russian melodrama, however, represents an important exception to the American rule of the triumphant happy ending. Knowing well that audiences in Russia preferred sad to happy endings, when Protazanov remade *The Lonely Villa*, he changed the ending, in accord with the original French stage and film versions, so that the rescue of the family besieged by robbers in their home fails. The husband in *Drama po telefonu* [Drama on the Telephone] (1914) arrives too late and finds his wife already dead. Articulated in the Russian press as "All's well that ends badly," this principle of domestic melodrama held that the ending should follow from the inevitable. The Russian parlor dramas, so despised by the 1917 revolutionaries as decadent Czarist cinema, best exemplify this tendency. As seen in the pre-revolutionary work of Evgenii **Bauer**, these Russian versions of family life present domestic turmoil as interminable as well as inevitable. Preferring to pictorialize the grim side of human relations, Bauer consistently chooses narratives that lead to suffering. Victimized women are never rescued, the estranged are never reunited, and the dead refuse to stay dead. Describing the Russian moral scheme in general and Bauer's films in particular, Maya Turovskaya summarizes the pattern of hopelessness as "sin, reckoning, suffering." The hero of *Grezy* [Daydreams] (1915), unable to forget his first wife after her death, is driven to strangling his mistress when she taunts him about his unnatural fixation. In *Ditya Bol'Shogo Goroda* [Child of the Big City] (1914), Manka rises from the gutter to heights of power and a life of dissipation. Meanwhile, her former suitor, Viktor, suffers from her rejection, finally dropping dead on the steps outside the restaurant where she dances on into the night. The next morning, exiting with her entourage, she steps decorously over his corpse. The unwillingness to put a "false" happy ending on domestic melodrama makes it clear that love does not conquer all and that home is not the happiest place on earth.

See also: editing: early practices and techniques; editing: tableau style; theater, melodrama; spectatorship: issues and debates

Further reading

Abel, Richard (1994) *The Ciné Goes to Town: French Cinema, 1896–1914*, Berkeley: University of California Press.

Brooks, Peter (1976) *The Melodramatic Imagination: Balzac, Henry James, Melodrama and the Mode of Excess*, New Haven: Yale University Press.

Brewster, Ben and Lea Jacobs (1997) *Theatre to Cinema: Stage Pictorialism and the Early Feature Film*, Oxford: Oxford University Press.

Gaines, Jane (1995) "Revolutionary Theory/Pre-revolutionary Melodrama," *Discourse*, 17.3: 101–118.

Gunning, Tom (1990) *D. W. Griffith and the Origins of American Narrative Film*, Urbana: University of Illinois Press.

Tsivian, Yuri (1989) "Some Preparatory Remarks on Russian Cinema," in Paolo Cherchi Usai, Lorenzo Codelli, Carlo Montanaro, and David Robinson (eds.) *Silent Witnesses: Russian Films 1908–1919*, London: British Film Institute.

Williams, Linda (2001) *Playing the Race Card: Melodramas of Black and White from Uncle Tom to O. J. Simpson*, Princeton: Princeton University Press.

JANE GAINES

melodrama, sensational

A major genre of early cinema, sensational melodrama drew directly upon conventions already well established in adjacent amusements catering to popular audiences, particularly dime novels and "10–20–30" (i.e., popular-priced) stage melodrama. A defining ingredient was what, in theater, were known as "sensation scenes"—scenes of high action, suspense, violence, and hazard, usually set in extraordinary, visually-arresting locales. Protagonists faced life-threatening dangers posed by forces of nature (floods, fires, volcano eruptions, earthquakes, quicksand, lightning, precipices, waterfalls, etc.) and technology (runaway locomotives, buzz-saws, dynamite explosions, sinking battleships, etc., along with all sorts of "infernal machines"—i.e.,

intricate death-delaying contraptions used to pro-
long suspense). For critics in the decades around the
turn of the century, the term sensational melodrama immediately conjured up a familiar iconography: one 1908 writer pointed to, "Trap-doors,
bridges to be blown up, walls to be scaled, instruments of torture for the persecuted heroines, freight
elevators to crush out the lives of the deserving
characters, elevated trains to rush upon the pros-
trate forms of gagged and insensible girls;" a 1919
essayist evoked, "Dire distresses, hazardous situations, thrilling rescues, theatrical and sensational
clap-trap, suspense and surprise."

This "blood and thunder" strain of sensational
melodrama might be regarded as a predecessor of
what today we usually label "action-adventure" or
"thriller." Its narratives presupposed a dualistic or
"Manichaean" world in which virtue and villainy
were sharply delineated, with no ambiguity or
ambivalence. The underlying dynamics of melodramatic stories were thus very simple—unmitigated good versus unmitigated evil—but their
narrative structures tended to be rather complex,
hinging on convoluted causality, extraordinary
coincidences, sudden revelations and twists of circumstance. Critics habitually complained that the
genre was more concerned with generating exciting
spectacle and "situation" than with attending to
narrative continuity or communicating nuances of
character psychology.

One might also delineate a second (sometimes
overlapping) strain of sensational melodrama based
on a broader sense of the term "sensational"—i.e.,
sensational as it functions in phrases like "sensational journalism" and the "sensational novel."
This kind of sensationalism involved the arousal of
curiosity and excitement by "incidents intended to
move either compassion or a sense of horror-struck
surprise" (as a critic of sensational journalism put
it in 1893). A feeling of thrill was still the
crucial effect, but it was prompted not so much by
spectacles of physical peril, wild action, and suspense than by riveting incidents of immorality—
various acts of malice, deviance, deception, cruel-
ty, and illicit desire, along with corollary states of
tribulation, torment, and abjection in those suffering the consequences. Adultery, jealous obsession, blackmail, rape, murder, suicide, venality,
viciousness, false accusation, mock marriage,

seduction-and-abandonment, prostitution, shocking
confessions and recognition scenes: elements such
as these distinguished this broader strain of sensational melodrama. Such narratives relied less on
grand spectacle, death-defying stunts, and frantic
races to the rescue than on situations of moral/
social transgression and emotional duress akin to
those in scandal tabloids and sensation novels.

The earliest film melodramas emulated popular-
priced stage melodrama both in their motifs and in
their use of artificial stagecraft to render sensation
scenes. **Pathé-Frères'** *Un Drame au fond de la mer*
[Drama Beneath the Sea] (1901), for example, used
a background of painted flats to depict an under-
water view of a sunken ship and the descent of two
divers to the ocean floor scattered with bodies and
treasure. The film consists of a single incident of
melodramatic violence: motivated by greed, one
diver attacks the other from behind, cuts his air
hose, and grabs the treasure. The victim staggers
around and collapses as the murderer ascends.
Edison's *Life of an American Fireman* (1901),
directed by Edwin S. **Porter**, was built around two
sensation scenes—a thrilling race of fire trucks and
a treacherous rescue of a woman and child trapped
in a burning building. *The Great Train Robbery*
(1903) expanded on the characteristic motifs by
showing a violent binding-and-gagging, a daring
robbery, three shocking murders, a racing locomotive, a hot pursuit on horseback, and a final gunfight
killing all the bandits. Porter's *The Trainer's
Daughter; or, A Race for Love* (1906) moved even
closer to the classic sensational-melodramatic form,
employing the conventional triangle of ingenue,
favored beau, and jealous villain, and climaxing in a
thrilling horse race in which the young woman
(who has promised to wed the owner of he winning
horse) rides fearlessly in place of the beau's jockey
(beaten badly by the villain) and defeats the villain's horse by a nose. Such racetrack melodramas
were a common subgenre of the sensational melodrama **theater** on both sides of the Atlantic around
the turn of the last century. The plot of Porter's
film closely resembles that of Theodore Kremer's
A Race for Life, a 10–20–30 melodrama that toured
for several years beginning in 1904. An identical
narrative was used later in *The Girl and the
Motor Boat* (1911), the only difference being that
the race involved speedboats instead of horses.

During cinema's great expansion as a story-telling medium during the period of the **nick-elodeon** boom, filmmakers and critics frequently noted that moving pictures had a natural proclivity toward sensational melodrama, not just because cinema appealed to the same popular audience that had sustained 10–20–30 stage melodrama, but also because of properties specific to the medium. Film had an inherent capacity for spectacular realism (allowing real explosions instead of stagy approx-imations), and editing techniques such as cross-cutting facilitated the rapid alternation and suspenseful protraction of actions taking place simultaneously in different places. In race-to-the-rescue sequences that formed the climax of so many such films, shots alternated, with escalating tempo, between the space of the victim (e.g., barricaded in a room), the contiguous space of the villain (trying to break in), and the distant space of the hero rushing frantically toward the point of intersection.

D. W. **Griffith**, while not the inventor of such editing techniques, certainly exploited them with great finesse. His early films for **Biograph** gravi-tated heavily towards blood-and-thunder melo-drama (at least during the first seven months of his career, before he shifted focus to sentimental, domestic **melodramas** about noble sacrifice and moral reawakening and other dramas better suited to the "uplift" campaign prompted by the forma-tion of the **Motion Picture Patents Company**). In this initial phase, the majority of Griffith's output contained some combination of extreme moral polarity, abduction, assault, brawling, bru-tality, binding-and-gagging, murder, and infernal machines. A typical example is *The Fatal Hour* (1908), which studio **publicity** described as an "exceedingly thrilling and stirring incident of the Chinese White Slave Traffic." It contains two vio-lent abductions of women by a Chinese villain and his henchman, the binding and gagging of a female detective, an infernal machine (the pistol in front of which the detective is tied will fire when the hands of a clock reach twelve), and a "wild ride" to the rescue. In typical melodramatic fashion, the story hinges on a chance occurrence: the police apprehend the henchman and learn the location of the imperiled detective after the henchman is injured in a streetcar accident.

The **Kalem** Company was notable (although not unique) in that its production policy centered almost exclusively on sensational melodrama. Films like *Saved By the Telephone* (1912), *A Sawmill Hazard* (1912), and *The Wheel of Death* (1913), in which villains strap the hero to the mas-sive paddle wheel of a Mississipi Riverboat, trans-lated into film some of the most classic chestnuts of 10–20–30 melodrama. Beginning with its *Girl Spy* series in 1909 (starring Gene **Gauntier**), Kalem built many films around the heroics of courageous young female protagonists—"girl spies," "girl detec-tives," "girl reporters," "girl telegraphers," and so on. The studio's most famous implementation of the plucky girl formula was the *Hazards of Helen* series of railroad thrillers, which ran for 119 weekly episodes between November 1914 and March 1917. Each episode offered some permutation of simple moral polarity, graphic action, and female agency.

By the mid-1910s, the films most immediately associated with sensational melodrama were **seri-als**. With few, if any, exceptions, all serials fell within this genre. They covered a range of sub-genres (such as **detective films**, **westerns**, gothic films, patriotic films, and working-girl melo-dramas), but they all concentrated on violence and intense action—abductions, entrapments, brawls, hazardous chase sequences and last minute res-cues—in narratively stark conflicts between a heroine or hero-heroine team and a villain and his criminal accomplices. Film serials were an imme-diately recognizable and iconographically faithful descendant of 10–20–30 melodrama and its liter-ary cousins. As titles like *The Perils of Pauline* (1914), *The Exploits of Elaine* (1915), *The Yellow Menace* (1916), *The House of Hate* (1918), *The Lurking Peril* (1920), and *The Screaming Shadow* (1920) convey, serials promised superabundant thrills.

European cinemas also found success with sen-sational melodramas in the form of series and serial thrillers, as well as stand-alone features. In France, **Éclair** was probably the first to draw directly upon the dime-novel detective tradition with its extre-mely popular series, *Nick Carter* (1908), followed by *Zigomar* (1911) and various sequels, all directed by Victorin **Jasset**. Louis **Feuillade** directed a number of celebrated **crime films** for **Gaumont**, including *Fantômas* (1913–1914) and *Les Vampires* (1915–1916). The Danish studio **Nordisk** produced at least five features focusing on the criminal exploits of evil Dr. Gar-el-Hama, running from 1911 to 1916. German studios were especially fond of series based on gentleman investigators with Anglo-Saxon names like Joe Deebs, Harry Higgs, and Joe Jenkins. The *Stuart Webbs* series of features was the most successful, or at least enduring, totaling some fifty-odd films between 1914 and 1926, all starring (and most also scripted and produced by) Ernst **Reicher**. The importance of German sensational melodrama in the early 1910s recently has come to light through the rediscovery of dynamic crime thrillers such as Heinrich **Bolten-Baecker**s' *The Hand of Justice* (1912) and Joseph **Delmont**'s *Das Recht auf das Dasein* [The Right to Exist] (1913).

It was in Europe, however, that the second strain of sensational melodrama, exploiting situations of moral/social transgression and emotional duress, found particular favor. The label "erotic melodrama" is useful in underscoring the fact that sex (understood broadly to encompass both passions and gendered power relationships) was at the heart of virtually every situation generating this form of sensationalism. A Russian feature film from 1913 well illustrates this point. In *Za Gostinoi Dveriami* [Behind the Drawing Room Doors] (directed by Evan Lazarev and Petr **Chardynin**), a beautiful young woman and an older man visit the studio of a handsome young artist. The artist, assuming that the older man is the woman's father, falls in love with her, and the affection is reciprocated with passionate kisses once the older man is out of sight. Meanwhile, the artist's mistress, seeing all this transpire in the studio, fumes with jealousy. Later, she tries to slash the portrait that the artist is painting of his new fiancée, but cuts the artist's hand instead. He rebuffs her and storms off to a café. There, he encounters several seedy characters, including a brazen demimonde who strikes up a conversation with him. His world is shattered when he learns from her that his fiancée is actually a prostitute, and the older man is her pimp. After confronting his fiancée and threatening her with a pistol, the artist slashes the portrait, puts the pistol to his head and commits suicide.

This Russian film may be more extreme and tragic than most, but many European cinemas in the early 1910s produced such highly-charged narratives of passion and distress. Most notable were Danish productions such as *Afgrunden* [The Abyss] (1910), starring Asta **Nielsen**, and luxurious Italian films showcasing the heightened **acting style** of "divas" like Lyda **Borelli** and Francesca **Bertini**. With their emphasis on displays of aristocratic grandeur, psychological conflict and emotional nuance, many erotic melodramas involved a mode of stately pacing and character depth that earned them some degree of legitimacy as bourgeois art cinema. In this, they differed quite markedly from the blood-and-thunder tradition stemming from popular-priced theater.

Not surprisingly, many critics and guardians of culture disdained sensational melodrama as a worthless and sometimes even degenerate form of cinema. Pennsylvania's head censor was especially averse to serial thrillers: "In the main (they are) made up of shooting, knifing, binding and gagging,

Figure 78 Poster for Pathé-Frères' *Nuit de noël* [Christmas Eve Tragedy] (1908).

drowning, wrecking and fighting. . . . It is crime, violence, blood-and-thunder, and always obtruding and outstanding is the idea of sex. . . . (They are) the most hurtful and the most noxious and altogether objectionable kind of a crime picture that we have. The serial is the old dime novel made into a picture. There is nothing more deplorable than those crime serials, and yet I do not know how to get rid of them."

The same sort of objections tainted the reputation of certain sensational feature films, especially **white slave films** such as Universal's *Traffic in Souls* (1913). Yet most sensational melodrama was unobjectionable. As the movie-going public expanded into a mass audience, mainstream studios and filmmakers found ways to deliver "punch" without provoking charges of luridness or vulgarity. Griffith's feature films, for example, found a palatable middlebrow register of modulated sensational melodrama through a number of strategies, such as embedding spectacular action within ostensibly educational historical epics, using **intertitles** to underscore moral lessons, inserting passages of droll humor (more characteristic of Feuillade), highlighting picturesque motifs and tableaux, and, perhaps most important, creating fully rounded sympathetic protagonists displaying charm, charisma, and humility, thereby obviating the routine complaint that characters in sensational melodramas were nothing but superficial puppets to be yanked through a series of assaults.

Figure 79 Frame still from *The Black Hand* (American Mutoscope and Biograph, 1906).

See also: editing: spatial relations; Machin, Alfred; Mack, Max; Perret, Léonce

Further reading

Abel, Richard (1994) *The Ciné Goes to Town: French Cinema, 1896–1914*, Berkeley: University of California Press.

Rahill, Frank (1967) *The World of Melodrama*, University Park: Pennsylvania State University Press.

Singer, Ben (2001) *Melodrama and Modernity: Early Sensational Cinema and Its Contexts*, New York: Columbia University Press.

Youngblood, Denise J. (1999) *The Magic Mirror: Moviemaking in Russia, 1908–1918*, Madison: University of Wisconsin Press.

BEN SINGER

Mendel, Georges

b. 1871; d. ?

filmmaker, inventor, France

In 1895, Mendel was selling photographic cameras when he met Charles **Pathé** and became interested in his counterfeit **Kinetoscopes**. In December 1896, he registered a patent for a reversible **camera** called the "Cinématographe parisien." Two years later, he opened his own factory in Paris and began making films primarily for **fair/fairground** exhibitors (his 1897 catalog listed 134 titles) while also marketing British films. Perhaps most interesting, as early as 1901, he was producing sound films for his "Cinémato-gramo-théâtre," a process of **synchronized sound** involving the **phonograph** developed by Henri **Joly**. Mendel prospered enough to build a glass-structure theater in Bagnolet in 1910. By 1914, his catalog of "Films artistiques chantants" (Artistic Films with Songs) included more than 300 sound films.

See also: *phonoscènes*

Further reading

Mannoni, Laurent (April 1993) "Du cinématographe parisien au Cinémato-gramo-théâtre: Georges

Mendel, pionnier du cinéma muet et sonore," *Archives*, 53.

LAURENT MANNONI

Menichelli, Pina

b. 1890; d. 1984

actor, Italy

Menichelli joined the **Cines** company in 1912, performing in numerous short **comedies** and dramatic films such as the epic feature, *Scuola d'eroi* [How Heroes Are Made] (1914). Giovanni **Pastrone** launched her career as a diva in *Il Fuoco* [The Fire] (1915), which earned her the nickname, "Our Lady of Spasms," because of her abrupt gestures. Yet posed, she resembled an aggressive bird of prey, with owl-like hats and long dark robes framing her serpentinean neck and face, with its kohl-outlined eyes. *Il Fuoco* was an instant popular and critical hit throughout Europe. After a series of dramatic diva films, Menichelli ended her film career in 1924.

IVO BLOM

Mercanton, Louis

b. 1879; d. 1932

filmmaker, France

After an international career on the stage, Mercanton joined **Eclipse** in 1911 and became its artistic director. He co-directed his films with Henri **Desfontaines**, and from 1916 on with René Hervil. Mercanton was Sarah **Bernhardt**'s director of choice: he directed her in *Adrienne Lecouvreur* (1912), *La Reine Elisabeth* [Queen Elizabeth] (1912), a resounding success in the USA, *Jeanne Doré* (1916), and *Mères françaises* [French Mothers] (1917). He produced the *Suzanne* series of films starring Suzanne **Grandais** (1916–1917), before directing Marcel L'Herbier's first scripts for *Le Torrent* (1917) and *Bouclette* (1918). After the war he founded his own company, Les Films Louis Mercanton.

THIERRY LEFEBVRE

Merzbach, Saül and Georges

b. 1868/1874; d. 1915/?

bankers, France

Saül and Georges Merzbach headed Les fils de Bernard Merzbach (Bernard Merzbach's Sons), a private bank formed as a general partnership in 1900. Their company had taken part, albeit on a limited scale, in increasing the capital of **Pathé-Frères** in 1905, 1906 and 1908.

Early in 1906, as the Pathé company was trying to gain some measure of autonomy from **Eastman**, it asked them to negotiate the purchase of the European **Blair Camera** factory in Foots-Gray near London.

The brothers contributed capital to several new companies created in the sphere of Pathé-Frères. In June 1907, they provided almost a third of the initial capital of a Pathé concessionary company, Cinéma-Exploitation. In June 1908, they became the second largest stockholders in **SCAGL**, which Saül had founded and on whose board of directors both brothers sat, along with Charles **Pathé**, Pierre **Decourcelle** and Eugène **Gugenheim**. In June 1910, their bank (and both brothers personally) provided more than a fourth of the capital for another of Pathé's concessionary companies, the Cinémas Modernes.

As associate director (1907–1913), Saül had rescued the Banque Commerciale et Industrielle from collapse. He was also the main partner in a theater journal, *Le Gil Blas*.

JEAN-JACQUES MEUSY

Mesguich, Félix

b. 1871; d. 1949

projectionist, cameraman, France

Mesguich was one of the **Lumière** brothers' most active cameramen, in reality as well as in his own imagination. If one believes his 1933 autobiography, *Tours de Manivelle* [Cranking the Handle], he was responsible for shooting hundreds of Lumière films between 1896 and 1898, in the USA, Russia, France, and North Africa (he had been born in Algiers). Upon his return to Paris from Saint Petersburg in 1898, he left the **Lumière** company and worked as a cameraman for the **Charles Urban Trading Company** in London. He credits himself with later filming Wilbur Wright in flight with a handheld **camera** and with producing some of the first **advertising films** for Ripolin and the Wagon-Lits companies in France.

GLENN MYRENT

Messter Biophon

In August 1903, Oskar **Messter** began marketing a **synchronized sound system** for films at first using a mechanically linked gramophone and **projector**; in 1906 he began using the gramophone to control the speed of the projector. Some 500 theaters in Germany installed the Biophon, plus others in Denmark, Austria, and Bohemia, all of which drew on the approximately 450 short sound films that Messter produced between 1907 and 1910. Messter had an "understanding" with **Gaumont** that he would not sell his apparatus in France, as long as Gaumont agreed not to sell its **Chronophone** in Germany; his plans for a formal worldwide monopoly, however, were rejected by the larger French firm.

DEAC ROSSELL

Messter consortium

German film pioneer Oskar **Messter** founded several companies during his film business activities from 1896 to 1917. After taking over his father's optical and mechanical workshop, Ed. (uard) Messter, in Berlin and then acquiring the workshops of Max **Gliewe** and Georg Betz, Messter began manufacturing film **projectors** and **cameras** in late 1896. In four years, the company's profits increased nearly tenfold. After trying in vain to set up a joint-stock company in order to accelerate his expanding business ventures, in 1901 Messter reorganized his cinema activities into a consortium of three companies: Messter's Projection for production and distribution, Vereinigte Mechanische Werkstätten for manufacturing

projectors and cameras, and Kosmograph Compagnie for exhibition in variety theaters. Between 1903 and 1909, nearly 80% of the consortium's profits resulted from the *Tonbild* (synchronous sound films) part of the business. When the *Tonbild* market collapsed in 1909, the consortium went through a difficult period before leading the transition from short films to **multiple-reel films**, distributed through the "Monopolfilm" system. After successfully launching Henny **Porten** as a film **star** in 1912, Messter restructured the consortium in 1913: Kosmograph Compagnie became a production company called Messter-Film; Autor Film was founded to produce Porten's feature films; and Hansa-Filmverleih took over distribution of all Messter films (Porten's films sold on average 130 prints each all over the world). During **World War I**, German film manufacturers expanded their business as the dominant French companies were closed down. Although Porten remained the most popular German star, the Messter consortium now profited even more from its weekly **newsreel**, *Messter-Woche*, than from its feature films. Messter himself urged the German government to expand its commitment to the film sector, and in late 1917 the consortium was sold to Ufa, thus contributing the basic stock for building up the greatest German film company.

Further reading

Kessler, Frank, Sabine Lenk, and Martin Loiperdinger (eds.) (1994) "Oskar Messter— Erfinder und Geschäftsmann," *KINtop*, 3.

Koerber, Martin (1996) "Oskar Messter, Film Pioneer: Early Cinema between Science, Spectacle, and Commerce," in Thomas Elsaesser and Michael Wedel (eds.) *A Second Life: German Cinema's First Decades*, 51–61, Amsterdam: Amsterdam University Press.

Loiperdinger, Martin (ed.) (1994) *Oskar Messter— Filmpionier der Kaiserzeit*, Frankfurt am Main/ Basel: Stroemfeld Verlag.

Loiperdinger, Martin (ed.) (1995) *Special-Catalog No. 32 über Projections—und Aufnahm—Apparate für lebende Photographie Films, Graphophons, Nebelbilder-Apparate, Scheinwerfer etc. der Fabrik für optisch-mechanische Präcisions-Instrumente von*

Ed. Messter, Berlin 1898 (reprint), Frankfurt am Main/Basel: Stroemfeld Verlag.

MARTIN LOIPERDINGER

Messter, Oskar

b. 1866; d. 1943

inventor, cameraman, producer, distributor, exhibitor, Germany

Messter was a formative figure for the first twenty years of German cinema. After training in mechanics, he took over his father's microscope manufacturing business in 1892 and started making film **projectors** by the summer of 1896. Of major importance to the technology of film projection was his 4-slotted Maltese Cross construction, patented in 1900, which is still an essential device in film projectors today. Messter published his first catalogue of films and cinematographic devices as early as 1898 and shot hundreds of single-shot films before launching the first era of sound film in Germany (ca. 1903–1913) with his Biophon process. From 1909 on, he concentrated on producing **multiple-reel films** and soon made Henny **Porten** the only **star** who could rival Asta **Nielsen** in popularity in Germany. During **World War I**, he was a film censorship officer, and he designed special **cameras** for aircraft reconnaissance, with the result that his weekly *Messter-Woche* **newsreel** set the standard for film reporting from the front. At the end of 1917, Messter sold his companies to Ufa, thus contributing the basic stock for building up the greatest German film company. In order to secure his place in the pantheon of world film pioneers, he became a film historian of sorts and published his autobiography in 1936.

Further reading

Kessler, Frank, Sabine Lenk, and Martin Loiperdinger (eds.) (1994) *KINtop 3: Oskar Messter—Erfinder und Geschäftsmann*, Frankfurt am Main/Basel: Stroemfeld Verlag.

Loiperdinger, Martin (ed.) (1994) *Oskar Messter—Filmpionier der Kaiserzeit*, Frankfurt am Main/Basel: Stroemfeld Verlag.
Loiperdinger, Martin (ed.) (1998) *Special-Catalog No. 32 über Projections- und Aufnahme-Apparate für lebende Photographie Films, Graphophons, Nebelbilder-Apparate, Scheinwerfer etc. der Fabrik für optisch-mechanische Präcisions-Instrumente von Ed. Messter Berlin* (1995 reprint), Frankfurt am Main/Basel: Stroemfeld Verlag.
Messter, Oskar (1936) *Mein Weg mit dem Film*, Berlin: Max Hesses Verlag.

MARTIN LOIPERDINGER

Mexico

Ferdinand "Bon" **Bernard** and Gabriel **Veyre**, licensees of the **Lumière** company, arrived in Mexico City on 25 July 1896. Their first exhibition for General Porfirio Díaz, then president of Mexico, took place on 6 August 1896, in the Chapultepec Castle. One week later, they held a second performance for invited guests in the mezzanine of the Plateros Drug Store; the following day they offered a third to the general public for 50 cents, the same price for an opera ticket on the floor level of the National Theater. Despite the fact that it was a rainy day, people came to see the show in droves, and instead of one performance there were five. Bothered by the heterogeneity of the crowd, the country's elite asked for a special performance each Thursday at one peso per ticket, double the normal price; however, the **Cinématographe Lumière** soon was no longer a novelty because another entrepreneur appeared with **Edison**'s Vitascope.

That same weekend, Veyre became the country's first filmmaker with a moving picture of General Porfirio Díaz riding on horseback through the Forest of Chapultepec. In Mexico City and Guadalajara, Veyre eventually made nearly forty films: among them *The Pane Baths*, *Bayonet Practice*, *Students of the Military College*, *Indian Market at the Viga Canal*, and *The Horses' Bath*.

The public quickly accepted moving pictures, and within four years, twenty-two theaters had opened in Mexico City, despite the fact that a new film was only shown every three weeks. Entrepreneurs, in order to compete, alternated variety or **vaudeville** programs with the few new moving pictures that they received. The municipal authorities were not prepared to handle this unexpected number of new theaters, and civil order soon was out of their control. The press in Mexico City and Guadalajara jointly published the crime rates in the neighborhoods surrounding the theaters. Because of protests from the press, due to constant scandals, the authorities closed the theaters in 1900, and for the next six years entrepreneurs traveled the country showing films by Lumière, Edison, **Joly**, **Méliès**, **Pathé-Frères**, and others. In 1906, with the promise of a consistent supply of many more new films, the distributors of European and North American films sponsored thirty-four new theaters in Mexico City. When the Revolution began in 1910, moving picture theaters increased their capacity from 300 to 800 seats (on average), as more and more soldiers arrived in the capital from the countryside. French films continued to be most popular until 1913, when Italian divas such as Lyda **Borelli** began to appear on the screens and touched the amorous sentiments of the public.

The production side of the new industry was characterized by the Lumière model. Due to high costs, entrepreneurs preferred to record gathering places, such as promenades in the plazas and cities, crowds exiting buildings, workers leaving the workplace, and bull fight arenas, in order that the public might come to see themselves on the screen. They also recorded floods, railroad accidents, and the president's trips throughout the country. The cinema of those years was characterized, therefore, by the portrayal of real events in *actualités*, which allowed the Revolution of 1910—for the very reason that it was an actual event—to become the primary subject or "star." The structure of Mexican films was unique for the way that they developed their narratives: they respected the spatial and temporal sequence of events, as was done in Salvador **Toscano**'s film of Porfirio Díaz's trip to the Yucatán and the **Alva** brothers' 1908 film of Díaz's interviews in Cuidad Juarez, on the northern border, with US President Taft. In this way, single-shot views led to lengthy films of three hours in duration, as for example in the Alva's 1911 film about the taking of Ciudad

Juarez by the Revolutionaries. Until 1914, the industry rarely made fiction films; instead, historical events served as the basis for early Mexican film production.

See also: editing: spatial relations; editing: temporal relations; itinerant exhibitors

Further reading

Almoina, Elena (1975) *Notas para la historia del cine mudo en México*, 2 vols., México City: UNAM.

de los Reyes, Aurelio (1972) *Los orígenes del cine en México*, México: UNAM.

de los Reyes, Aurelio (1979) *Vivir de sueños, el cine mudo en México de 1896 a 1920*, México City: UNAM.

de los Reyes, Aurelio (1986) *Filmografía del cine mudo mexicano, 1896–1920*, vol. I., México City: UNAM.

Ramírez, Gabriel (1988) *Crónica del cine mudo mexicano*, México City: Cineteca Nacional.

Reyes de la Maza, Luis (1971) *Salón Rojo*, México City: UNAM.

Toscano, Salvador (1996) *Cartas a su madre*, México City: UNAM.

Veyre, Gabriel (1996) *Correspondencia con su madre*, México City: UNAM.

AURELIO DE LOS REYES

Migé, Clément

b. ?; d. ?

actor, France

Formerly a clown, Migé starred in one of **Gaumont**'s first **comic series**, *Calino* (1909–1910). After Roméo **Bosetti**, its director, left the company, Migé continued the series under Jean **Durand**'s direction and became part of the Pouites burlesque troupe. Surviving the competition of a homonymous **Pathé-Frères** series (1911), Migé's adventures as Calino lasted until 1913 and occasionally crossed paths with Ernest **Bourbon**'s Onésime, as in *Onésime se marie, Calino aussi* (Onésime Gets Married, So Does Calino) (1913). The two comics shared a resolutely unreal universe characterized by constant pratfalls and incessant destruction.

LAURENT LE FORESTIER

migration/immigration: USA

Although ostensibly acknowledged, the emergence of early cinema and the phenomena of turn-of-the-20th-century migrations are profoundly interrelated: their threads span from social and economic history to racial politics and film aesthetics. The historical appearance of moving pictures coincided, in fact, with an increasing network of commercial transactions and movement of goods and peoples connecting industrially developed countries with each other and with underdeveloped ones. Whereas the international circulation of films influenced the development of most national cinemas, migrations had their most significant cultural impact in the USA. Here the influx of new populations deeply affected every cultural realm, including popular entertainments. From its inception, then, early cinema constantly and variously interpellated the multinational and multiracial fabric of American society. And it did so by asserting the moral and cultural superiority of American culture and lifestyle through more or less overt displays of racialized nationalism.

Traditional scholarship on early American cinema has dealt with "migrants" mainly as European immigrants. In the USA, however, migration was a historically broader and more complex affair, inclusive of domestic dimensions. Between 1890 and 1915, a staggering fourteen million southern and eastern Europeans arrived in the USA; from 1850 to **World War I**, approximately one million Asians (Japanese, Chinese, Koreans, Filipinos, and Indians), despite numerous restrictions, landed on the West Coast; through the imposition of a border, more than a million Mexicans and Mexican-Americans found themselves to be "migrants" in a new country. Furthermore, thousands of African-Americans (the figure reached approximately a half million after 1916) had begun moving northbound to urban environments away from the rural South.

At the turn of the 20th century, the USA was thus a nation of migrants facing racial and cultural diversity at home and abroad. Domestically engaged in nativist debates over eugenic taxonomies, post-slavery interracial relationships, and compatibility between foreign nationalities and American citizenship, the country was also proudly conducting imperialistic wars in Asia and the Caribbean. The public emphasis of an all-American identity, indeed an Anglo-Saxon one, was both enhanced and threatened by the increased domestic visibility of foreigners and former slaves. Early cinema was closely imbricated in these charged public debates. In brief, migrants to and within the USA inflected early American cinema's ideological, aesthetic, and social fabric, by patterning films' subject matter, genres, representational patterns, styles, and **stars**' identity—both on- and off-screen. In addition, movie-going among foreigners, blacks, and their descendents contributed to defining the public nature of cinema during its decisive formative years and its establishment as the most affordable national pastime.

From early on the film industry's own ideological self-posturing praised the new medium for its "universal" appeal and intelligibility in the face of former slaves' and newcomers' striking cultural and linguistic diversity. Yet, both film industry and traditional historiography have constantly hailed cinema as a visual *esperanto* precisely for, and not in spite of, its *American* character. Consequently, American film history has claimed that from its origins American cinema welcomed, addressed and, ultimately, encouraged the integration of foreign and unassimilated constituencies. This has often hindered the radical methodological challenges presented by migrations, as it has undermined the resilient diversity of people's movements and cultural exchanges.

Specifically, film historiography has focused on three primary realms: production, reception, and representation. Firstly, film accounts have regularly underscored the non-American origins of most early film producers and distributors. Carl **Laemmle**, William **Fox**, Adolph **Zukor**, Sam Goldwyn, Louis B. Mayer, and others were mostly Jewish entrepreneurs from eastern Europe and Russia who found themselves excluded from established lines of business. They shaped early cinema's business practices, before and after the industry moved to Hollywood; even more significantly, they contributed to the development of film narratives centered on a proud all-American identity.

Secondly, both early and recent film historiography has emphasized the extraordinary diversity of early film audiences, crowding **nickelodeons** of large urban centers, where cinema emerged and consolidated itself as prime popular entertainment. Quite detrimentally, however, the lack of proper consideration for African-American film commentaries and for forms of evidence produced in languages other than English has prevented many scholars from reading American films against the grain of audiences' multicultural loyalties and multinational origins. For instance, disregarding such sources as the black and the ethnic press, monocultural and monoglottistic studies of film reception, coupled with a persistent methodological privilege of films' semiotic significance, have supported the notion that American cinema amalgamated the reception of most, if not all its spectators. Recent works on Jewish, Italian, and African-American spectators and on such diverse reception venues from neighborhood halls and variety shows to foreign and multilingual stages and ghetto theaters have openly questioned this common interpretation. From a spectatorial viewpoint, American cinema elicited what, with reference to African-American reception, Anna Everett has called "processes of transcoding." Among immigrants and former slaves, these modern and communal dynamics of acculturation supported new forms of cultural and racial identity, through mongrelizing operations of re-positioning, complicity, and self-expression.

Thirdly, cinema studies recently has begun to examine how early film narratives represented national and racial *others*—from immigrants to former slaves to native Americans—in stories of economic misery, criminal inclinations, moral dilemmas, and problematic adaptation to American civic and ethical values. In the midst of domestic Anglo-Saxonist crusades against migrations and in support of overseas expansionist campaigns, US culture at large addressed the potential loyalty of these "dissonant" groups. For

decades, American theater, **vaudeville**, literature, and music had engaged in such racist practices as racial impersonations, whether in comedies or crime stories, stage black minstrelsy, and even slave narratives (often composed by former masters and white authors). Moving pictures continued these controversial practices, and this persistence determined the *racialness*, or intrinsic racial quality, of the American filmic image. Because turn-of-the-20th-century discourses and theorizations of race were connected inextricably to the phenomena of international and domestic resettlements, the critical trope of "migrations" may bridge the long established divide opposing discussions of film representations of white vs. non-white populations.

In the heat of the post-1880s waves of immigration from Southern and Eastern Europe, in fact, scientific and political arguments converged in a common preoccupation about the biological effects of this exodus for the American republic. Cosmopolitan in scope, but jingoistic in purpose, these research enterprises compared world races throughout history with the presumed Anglo-American distinctiveness. The resulting eugenic program produced a multitude of racial taxonomies and hierarchies rather than a simple white/non-white juxtaposition, as it correlated racial stocks with inherent national and cultural qualities and scales of human development and worth. European, but also Asian, Mexican, and African-American populations were thus divided in terms of outer physical traits, from craniology to hair type and skin color, but also in terms of national and community predispositions, such as criminal attitudes, literacy, and civic stance toward Anglo-Saxon Americanism.

After the mid-1910s, the growing migration of blacks from the South and the arrival of populations of African descent from the Caribbean supported the emergence of the New Negro Movement, with its race riots, labor strife, and visible protests, which engendered, in historian Matthew Pratt Guterl's words, "a national mass culture obsessed with the 'Negro' as the foremost social threat." Up until that point, however, the composite power of the aforementioned racial distinctions was not at all subservient to color-based paranoid fears and legalized civic discriminations. Writing at the height of this cultural phase, in his influential *The Passing of the Great Race* (1916), Madison Grant argued: "the term 'Caucasian race' has ceased to have any meaning," except when it is used to contrast Europeans with "Negroes," "Indians," or "Mongols."

In the years before 1915, then, the cultural discourse of race in the USA encompassed more than color distinctions. Predictably, in this period American films presented a vast array of racialized depictions, exhibited through strict hierarchical arrangements. Caucasian or not, however, they all stemmed from a white, Anglo-Saxon entitlement. Such supremacist cinematic racialness was an aesthetic dimension that, operating as a racial unconscious, inflected even the countless films where no foreigners or African-Americans, Asians, and Native Americans ever appeared. Still, in pre-1915 US cinema the distinction between whiteness and non-whiteness was a powerfully discriminatory trope, on- and off-screen, as it defined, in legal, social, and representational terms, civil entitlements that certain individuals enjoyed, while others did not.

Within the contours of American racial discourse, the imbricated tropes of "migrations" and "cinematic racialness" may help to explain a wider series of aesthetic practices adopted by American films to tell stories about new and old Americans. In general, early American cinema portrayed African-Americans, Asian-Americans, and Native Americans as subjects *extraneous* to the realm of American polity, ostensibly "unfit," from a racial standpoint, to adapt to and assimilate with American mainstream society. By contrast, the ambivalent status enjoyed by racialized white European immigrants was determined by the fact that adaptation and assimilation were not denied in principle, but simply questioned and problematized with variable results. In other words, for European ethnics in general, unlike non-white subjects, allegations of racial inadequacy, were difficult, but not impossible to overcome.

The most blatant example of cinematic racialness engaged in "processing" migration and its characters was silent comedy. Indebted to the irreverent physical routines of circus and vaudeville theater, **comedies** and **comic series** cast immigrants, and outsiders generally, by showcasing

their incapacity to master the challenges of modern technology and urban life, from **transportation** to commercial artifacts, and thus to adapt to an American lifestyle inflected by the Protestant work ethic and Anglo-Saxon puritanism. Another instance was represented by the **western**. Mimicking and further visualizing dime novels, Remingtonesque **paintings**, and popular stage plays, the genre equated the conquest of the frontier and its social and natural landscapes—including the romanticized, but doomed "savage" Indians—with a quintessentially American national geneaology. Western films displayed a racially discriminating ideal of American identity and citizenship and thus represented an ideological move toward the *Americanization* of American cinema. This patriotic move also had commercial value as it aggressively pitted a national production against competing film traditions—most notably that of France.

A further example is offered by the many racial and interracial dramas of crime and love, where "migrants" were protagonists of stories of emotional disfunction, resilient (self)marginalization, and difficult, if not impossible assimilation. Their racial status, and specifically their color and eugenic attributions—from violent inclinations to self-control or lack thereof—determined how they featured side by side with Anglo-Saxon characters and what kind of Caucasian empathy could result. Countless sensational **melodramas** cast racialized

Figure 80 The Pests of our Pacific and Atlantic Coasts: Uncle Sam: "There shall be no discrimination. I will shut you both out." *Judge*, 23 (17 December 1892).

European immigrants in nativist narratives displaying their questionable assimilative qualifications for citizenship or, in Matthew Frye Jacobson's words, their "probatory whiteness," a status that was constantly denied to African-Americans, Latinos, Asian-Americans, and Native Americans. Recent work on female stars' white ethnicities has shown how Euro-American actors could differently activate assimilation myths and enable forms of characterization, spectatorial identification, and moral closure denied to other racialized groups.

When read through the broad lens of migrations, the **modernity** of early American cinema appears to be defined by the encounters, exchanges, and conflicts of people of allegedly different racial background, on- and off-screen. Namely, this modernity is constituted by the heavily commercialized imbrications between national and racial difference on the one side and the so-called mainstream culture on the other. "Migrant communities" were visibly coded and differentiated in narrative, representational, and socio-spectatorial terms by the very American power game of racial identities and national loyalties as well as racial loyalties and national identities.

See also: audiences: surveys and debates; black cinema, USA; colonialism: Europe; ethnographic films; imperialism: USA; Pathé Cinematograph; racial segregation: USA; white slave films

Further reading

Abel, Richard (1999) *The Red Rooster Scare: Making Cinema American, 1900–1910*, Berkeley: University of California Press.

Bertellini, Giorgio (2001) *Southern Crossings: Italians, Cinema, and Modernity: Italy, 1861– New York, 1920*, Ph.D. dissertation, New York University.

Brownlow, Kevin (1990) *Behind the Mask of Innocence*, London: Jonathan Cape.

Everett, Anna (2001) *Returning the Gaze. A Genealogy of Black Film Criticism, 1909–1949*, Durham: Duke University Press.

Gevinson, Alan (ed.) (1997) *Within Our Gates: Ethnicity in American Feature Films, 1911–1960*, Berkeley: American Film Institute Catalog/ University of California Press.

Guterl, Matthew Pratt (2001) *The Color of Race in America, 1900–1940*, Cambridge: Harvard University Press.

Haenni, Sabine (1998) *The Immigrant Scene: The Commercialization of Ethnicity and the Production of Publics in Fiction, Theater, and the Cinema, 1890–1915 (German-American, Yiddish, Italian-American, New York City)*, Ph.D. dissertation, University of Chicago.

Negra, Diane (2001) *Off-White Hollywood: American Culture and Ethnic Female Stardom*, New York: Routledge.

Stewart, Jaqueline Najuma (1999) *Migrating to the Movies: The Emergence of Black Urban Film Culture, 1893–1920*, Ph.D. dissertation, University of Chicago.

Stokes, Melvyn and Richard Maltby (eds.) (1999) *American Movie Audiences: From the Turn of the Century to the Early Sound Film*, London: British Film Institute.

Thissen, Judith (2001) *Moyshe Goes to the Movies: Jewish Immigrants, Popular Entertainment, and Ethnic Identity in New York City (1880–1914)*, Ph.D. dissertation, Utrecht University.

GIORGIO BERTELLINI

Milano Films

Milano Films emerged on December 1909 from the financially troubled SAFFI-Comerio (formerly **Comerio Films**). A national market crisis and SAFFI-Comerio's own ambitious projects, particularly a spectacular adaptation of Italy's quintessential literary classic, Dante's *Divine Comedy*, had proved fatal. By contrast, Milano became a most exemplary Italian company, defined by great financial possibilities and grand plans of cultural uplift.

Backed by capital of the local aristocracy and not just the emerging Milanese industrial bourgeoisie, Milano Films had the most modern and well-equipped film studios in Italy. Its owners and administrators shared a common didactic aspiration to establish a national cultural hegemony and foster a sense of national identity.

Thus Milano engaged in the production of *actualités* of national, and not just local, interest and adaptations of classics of world and national literature. In this spirit, in 1909, it attempted, unsuccessfully, to obtain Gabriele **D'Annunzio**'s collaboration.

In a few years, Milano Films successfully released highbrow **historical films** onto the national and international markets, including *San Paolo* [The Life of St. Paul] and *Sardanapalo, re dell'Assiria* [Sardanapolus, King of Assyria], directed, respectively, in 1910, by Giuseppe **De Liguoro**, then the company's artistic director, and Ubaldo Maria **Del Colle**. Proudly resuming the Dante project, Milano went on to produce the four-reel *L'Inferno* [Dante's Inferno] (1911), directed by Francesco Bertolini and Adolfo Padovan. Marketing it worldwide as a unique cultural event, the company distributed the film with enormous success in the USA through Monopol Film, in an agreement with the **General Film Company**. Overall, Milano's profits there, however, never reached the level of those of **Ambrosio**, **Itala**, and **Cines**.

Because of the enthusiastic reception of *L'Inferno*, Milano Films immediately capitalized on the historical epic by releasing *L'Odissea* [Odyssey; or Homer's Odyssey] (1911) and De Liguoro's *San Giorgio cavaliere* [St. George and the Dragon] (1912). After 1912, Milano Films diversified its output by including gripping love melodramas such as *La smorfia del destino* [Playthings of Fate] (1912) as well as successful **comic series** such as *Cocciutelli* (1911–1912) and *Bonifacio* (1912–1913), both known in the USA as "Kelly."

On the eve of **World War I**, Milano Films reduced its foreign exports and focused on the domestic market with a series of dramatic-adventure productions directed by the talented Baldassarre **Negroni** and Augusto Genina. One of the few titles exported abroad was *Il Rubino del destino* [Rubies of Destiny] (1914). From an average of 90 productions released per year from 1910 to 1914, beginning in the mid-1910s, the annual output decreased to 30 titles. Milano's films acquired a progressively decadent look, especially with the casting of such divas as Lina Millefleurs, Pina **Menichelli**, and Mercedes Brignone. By 1915, the days of profitless

patronage were over. A new revenue-oriented administration tried to survive the wartime financial difficulties. Although it succeeded until 1920, the overall crisis of Italian cinema forced the company to fold in 1927.

Further reading

De Berti, Raffaele (2000) "Milano Films: An Exemplary Story of a 1910s Film Company," *Film History*, 12.3: 276–287.

GIORGIO BERTELLINI

Miles Brothers

Herbert and Harry Miles were traveling photographers from Cincinnati, Ohio. Becoming interested in moving pictures, they joined the Alaska gold rush in 1900 and shot films in the area, which they later sold to the **American Mutoscope and Biograph Company**. In 1901, they began showing films in Alaska. Herbert became associated with AM&B in New York as a sales agent, while Harry established what is believed to be the first film exchange, Miles Brothers, renting films to **vaudeville** houses, in San Francisco in 1902. The business expanded to include **amusement parks** and **nickelodeons** by 1905–1906, and the company started its own nickelodeon circuit in New York. An attempt to move into film production was stymied by the San Francisco earthquake in 1906. After serving as secretary of the Film Service Association, Herbert became manager of the **Motion Picture Distributing and Sales Company** in 1910 but left to found the short-lived Republic Film Company.

ROBERT S. BIRCHARD

Miller, Arthur C.

b. 1895, Roslyn, Long Island; d.1970, Hollywood

cameraman, USA

Three-time Oscar-winner, Arthur C. Miller was a prominent cinematographer whose career was cut short by illness. He first worked as an assistant to

Fred **Balshofer** with the **New York Motion Picture Company** in 1909, and photographed his first film, *A Heroine of '76*, for **Rex** in 1910. He worked for director Louis **Gasnier** at the American branch of **Pathé-Frères** and photographed *The Perils of Pauline* (1914). Miller contracted tuberculosis in 1950, and retired from active camera work soon after. A recurrence of the disease led to his suicide.

ROBERT S. BIRCHARD

Minier, Louis

b. 1870; d. 1910

exhibitor, Quebec

A pharmacist in the French army, Louis Minier became a representative for the **Lumière** company in 1896 and left for Montreal with an assistant named Louis Pupier. They presented the first moving picture demonstration in Canada on 27 June 1896, in Montreal, for an audience of notables. The **Cinématographe Lumière** was featured for several weeks at the Théâtre Palace before Minier took the invention to the National Fair in Toronto and then toured the main cities of Quebec during the winter of 1896–1897. Shortly thereafter, he abandoned the cinema and became a pharmacist in Montreal. After a few years he left for St-Pierre-et-Miquelon, where he reportedly died around 1910.

GERMAIN LACASSE

Mistinguett (Jeanne-Marie Bourgeois)

b. 1872; d. 1956

singer, dancer, actor, France

Entering show business as an "eccentric singer" billed as "Miss Tinguette" (hence her stage name), Mistinguett quickly became a lead performer at the Eldorado **music hall** in Paris and then broadened her repertoire with major roles in stage plays, dance revues, and moving pictures. In 1907, she partnered with Max Dearly in a popular acrobatic dance, "La Valse Chaloupée" (her legs were christened a "national treasure"); five years later she created another dance sensation at the Folies-Bergère with young Maurice Chevalier. In 1908, she joined **SCAGL** and then **Pathé-Frères**, sometimes playing opposite **Prince** in the *Rigadin* **comic series** but also taking on dramatic roles such as Eponine in *Les Misérables* (1912) and an actress much like herself in the "terrifying cinemadrama," *L'Epouvante* [Terror-Stricken] (1911). Although she would star in a series of **detective films** during **World War I**, Mistinguett's continuing fame came from performing in the Paris music halls, often with Chevalier, well into the 1930s.

RICHARD ABEL

Misu, Mime

b. 1888; d. ?

director, Germany

A Romanian-born ballet dancer and pantomime artist, Misu worked for **Lux** and **Pathé-Frères** in France, but directed his first films in Germany for **Continental-Kunstfilm** in 1912: *Das Gespenst von Clyde* [The Ghost of Clyde], *Titanic—In Nacht und Eis* [Titanic—In Night and Ice] and *Mirakel* [Miracle]. Misu mixed melodrama with thematic topicality, a concept which made *Titanic* an international hit and earned him a contract with **PAGU**, for which he made another sea-drama, *Excentric Club* (1913). In 1914, Misu, who also scripted and starred in his films, went to the USA, but seems to have made only one more film, *The Money God*.

MICHAEL WEDEL

Mitchell and Kenyon

The firm of Mitchell and Kenyon was founded by Sagar J. Mitchell (1866–1952) with partner James Kenyon (1850–1925) in Blackburn in November 1897. It produced and released *actualités*, fiction films, and fake war films under the trade name of Norden and became one of the largest companies in Great Britain in the 1900s.

Mitchell and Kenyon's first film, *Blackburn Market on a Saturday Afternoon*, was shown above its Blackburn premises on 27 November 1897. By September 1899, the company had come to national prominence with the release of three Norden film titles: *The Tramp's Surprise*, *The Tramps and The Artist*, and *Kidnapping by Indians*.

With the outbreak of the Boer War in October 1899, the company turned to the production of fake war films of events in the Transvaal as well as the Boxer rebellion in China. These were shot in the countryside around Blackburn and consisted of fictionalized scenes based on the battle-fronts. Titles were available directly from the manufacturers but also were distributed by **Gaumont**, **Walturdaw**, and Charles **Urban**, the latter of which advertised *A Tragic Elopement* in November 1903.

Until recently Mitchell and Kenyon was most known for its fake war films, ten of which survive, including titles such as *The Dispatch Bearers* (1900), *Winning the VC* (1900), and *Attack on a Mission Station* (1900). However, the discovery of approximately 850 negatives in the original premises in the early 1990s has led to a major revaluation of the company's contribution to film-making in the United Kingdom. 65 fiction titles now are preserved in the Cinema Museum (London), including *Diving Lucy* (1903), billed in the USA as the "biggest English comedy hit of the year," and 780 actualités form the Peter Worden Mitchell and Kenyon Collection at the British Film Institute.

This material reveals a clear pattern of commissioning and exhibition in Great Britain between film companies and early **itinerant exhibitors**. The showmen were largely based in the North of England, although the geographical spread of their activities encompassed Scotland and Ireland. Exhibitors associated with Mitchell and Kenyon included A. D. **Thomas**, who presented films under the banner of Edison-Thomas Pictures, Ralph **Pringle** of the North American Animated Photo Company, and George **Green**. Mitchell and Kenyon's association with travelling

showmen first occurred in April 1899, when Green commissioned films of workers leaving local factories in Blackburn that could be shown at the Easter fair. The company went on to film scenes of local interest, including factory gate films, sporting events, processions and phantom rides, throughout town centers in the North of England. Throughout the 1900s, Mitchell and Kenyon continued to film local scenes but also to produce dramas such as *Black Diamonds or the Collier's Daily Life* (1904) and **comedies** such as *The Interrupted Picnic* (1906). Although commissioned to film events in Glasgow in 1906 and Yorkshire in 1908, Mitchell and Kenyon seem to have restricted their activities to Blackburn and its surrounding locality by 1909. The latest surviving films date from 1913, when it appears that the firm ceased production. The partnership did not dissolve, however, until 1922.

See also: fairs/fairgrounds; re-enactmanets

Further reading

Toulmin, Vanessa (2001) "'Local films for local people': Travelling showmen and the commissioning of local films in Great Britain, 1900–1902," *Film History*, 13.2: 118–137.

Toulmin, Vanessa (2002) *Mitchell and Kenyon*, London: British Film Institute.

Whalley, Robin and Peter Worden (1998) "Forgotten firm: A short chronological account of Mitchell and Kenyon, cinematographers," *Film History*, 10.1: 35–51.

VANESSA TOULMIN

Mix, Tom (Thomas Hezekiah Mix)

b. 1880, Mix Run, Pennsylvania; d. 1940, Florence, Arizona

actor, USA

Mix appeared in his first credited film in 1910, performing a rodeo stunt in **Selig**'s *Ranch Life in the Great Southwest*. Although he starred in several jungle pictures, Mix became famous at Selig for his westerns, especially beginning with *The Law and the Outlaw* (1913). Next to G. M. **Anderson** and William S. **Hart**, Mix became a wildly popular, flamboyant cowboy star. Yet like Buffalo Bill **Cody**, many of his legendary deeds were in fact fables he himself had invented. Although never a cowboy in real life, he was an outstanding marksman and rodeo stuntman in his numerous movies.

Further reading

Birchard, Robert S. (1993) *King Cowboy: Tom Mix and the Movies*, Burbank: Riverwood Press.

NANNA VERHOEFF

modernity and early cinema

Modernity refers to the conditions of the modern world; while this can indicate the whole of western history since the Renaissance (or the Enlightenment, or the French Revolution), in the context of early cinema the term most often refers more narrowly to the period since the industrial revolution, and specifically the changes in **transportation**, **communication**, and **urbanization** occasioned by such new inventions/innovations as: the railway, telegraph, telephone, **electricity**, **photography**, **imperialism** and worldwide markets, mass marketing and the rise of a consumer culture, as well as the new importance of scientific research for industry and society. In other words, it refers to "the second industrial revolution" in the latter part of the 19th century, and the innovations on which the emergence of early cinema was dependent.

Consideration of early cinema and modernity attempts to place cinema as an industry and form of entertainment, as well as a narrative and aesthetic form, in relation to the historical and cultural context in which it developed, especially fitting it into the novel patterns of modern life. As an aspect of a cultural history of cinema, the relation between modernity and early cinema would seem to be an obvious topic, unless one maintains a strict formalist position that art as an autonomous form cannot be subjected to social analysis. Clearly, patterns of early cinema exhibition in cities must be looked at in terms of urbanization, reform legislation, and class tensions. Even the non-urban **fair/fairground** exhibitions that formed the most frequent venue for cinema in Western Europe before the 1910s changed in relation to the industrialization of the fair, the introduction of electricity as a marvel, and the display of modern devices (including X-rays and electrical generators) as attractions in themselves. Early film production, especially by international companies (such as the various branches of the **American Mutoscope and Biograph Company** in the USA, Great Britain, and continental Europe at the turn of the century, or **Pathé-Frères** after 1904), must be approached in terms of new international systems of trade. The technology of the cinema itself depends on modern production of precision machinery and innovations in photographic chemistry, not to mention cinema's origin in scientific research via **chronophotography**. In terms of technology, distribution, production and exhibition, early cinema makes constant use of the new conditions of modernity; indeed it could be said to exemplify them as a new means of mechanical art and entertainment.

Short of abandoning (or radically narrowing) the project of film history, it would seem that early cinema must be investigated in terms of modernity. While certainly some issues in film history may not relate directly to the themes of modernity, nonetheless issues of imperialism, gender, and race or ethnicity all take specific forms in the period of early cinema and are dependent on the economic, technical, and social transformations of the era. Work in investigating cinema and modernity has made use of a Germanic tradition closely associated with the term, including works by Max Weber, Georg Simmel, Georg Lukacs, Siegfried Kracauer, Walter Benjamin, and Theodore Adorno. More recent theorists such as Linda Dalrymple Henderson, Stephen Kern, Anson Rabinbach, Jonathan Crary, and Wolfgang Schivelbusch also have been influential in defining modernity for film history. Although there is considerable overlap in the themes and even some of the conclusions of these authors, there also are enough differences that it should not be assumed that everyone dealing with the issue of modernity and early cinema necessarily share all the same assumptions.

For the earliest period of film production and exhibition, reception of the new marvel almost universally invoked not only the wonders of modern technology, but also new experiences of unfamiliar and even uncanny effects this new technology spawned. Further, many early films featured aspects of modern life: the movement of crowds in big city streets, workers emerging from factory gates, trains arriving at stations. Images of speeding locomotives stimulated perhaps the greatest excitement from commentators on the first film programs. Thus they saw such programs as offering a view of a new life as well as a new invention. Although scenes of modern life did not exhaust the repertory of early films, which included **vaudeville** acts, scenes of everyday life, and picturesque images of nature (ocean surf, Niagara Falls), modern images undeniably characterized early film programs.

Early films, consequently, represented aspects of modern experience in both themes and forms. Approaches to defining "experience" vary from theorist to theorist, from the more phenomenological claims of Tom Gunning to the cognitivist investigations of Ben Singer or the more psychoanalytically shaped theories of some of the feminist historians (Miriam Hansen, to a degree). However, these differences do not interfere with a shared assumption that films reflect changes in historical experience as well as relying on basic cognitive consistencies. Historical experience appears in the way films are received (understood and discussed) by **audiences** as well as in the way they are made. Thus Hansen's work emphasizes cinema's role as an "alternative public sphere" for early audiences, especially the women and recent immigrants who made up a significant proportion of the **nickelodeon** audience in urban theaters. Movies, due to low ticket prices, created working-class audiences mixed in gender, ethnicity, and age. And working-class audiences, as social historians such as Ralph Rosenzweig have shown, treated the nickelodeon as a social club as much as a place to view films. Film provided food for discussion and a reference point for processing new experiences.

More controversial, perhaps, is Gunning's argument that the format of cinema's first decade, which he terms the **cinema of attractions** (brief non-narrative doses of visual pleasure—unusual scenes, gags, acts, tricks, or scenic views), can be related to the experience of modernity. Gunning claims the presentational modes of attractions paralleled the shocks that Benjamin saw as typical of modern experience (and of cinema). A great proportion of early films took confrontational and exhibitionistic stances towards their viewers, as opposed to the more traditional absorption and contemplation called for in the traditional arts. Thus, the brevity of these films and their frequent use of surprise (explosions, tricks appearances and transformations, or display of visual curiosities) created a fast-paced, unpredictable, and even nerve-shaking experience. The direct address to the audience found in many early films (either through actors addressing the camera—as in the outlaw firing at the audience in **Edison**'s *The Great Train Robbery* (1903)—or through the **phantom train rides** which, as Charles Musser puts it, position the "spectator as a passenger") aggressively seized audience attention with a sensation more closely related to the attractions of **fairgrounds** and carnivals than the traditional aesthetic experience offered by legitimate **theater**, the classic novel, or the art museum.

While hardly a modernist or avant-garde technique, the cinema of attractions exemplified the confrontational and often absurdist energy that avant-garde artists in the 1910s appropriated from the popular arts—the **music hall**, the circus, the **comic strip**—as well as the cinema. The specific forms of the cinema that attracted many modernist artists—especially their fast pace and compression of time—also repelled many middle-class reformers of the era who very specifically related these aspects to the effects of modernity that they found pernicious.

Thus, in 1911, Hermann Kienzl, a German theater critic, launched an attack on cinema saying:

> The psychology of the triumph of cinema equals the psychology of the metropolis [. . .] because the metropolitan spirit—constantly rushed, staggering from fleeting impressions, curious and impenetrable—is exactly the soul of the cinema [. . .] And because the city dweller is as accustomed to nervous stimulation as an arsenic eater to his poison, he is especially thankful when

a film gives him an exciting cops and robbers story in about a minute.

Likewise, a Brazilian journalist writing in 1909 used cinema as the emblem for this speeded-up pace of modern life brought on by new technology:

> The great symbols of our era, the automobile, our delight, and the phonograph, our torment, collapse distances and preserve voices just to avoid wasting time. In the future, if our planet does not hurry to its finish and end up carried off on the tail of a comet, the man of our era, I speedily declare, will be classified as the "*homo cinematographicus*."

Examples of such reactions to cinema as the epitome of modernity could be multiplied and, as the examples cited show, are international.

Two points should be stressed. Although the modern forms of technology and commerce clearly shaped the processes of early film production, the claim that cinema had an intense relation to the experience of modernity was repeatedly articulated as a theme in the reception of early cinema. Critics (and, putatively, audiences) understood cinema as an essential part of the novelty of modern life. Its images, its principle icons, and its forms, especially its temporal structure, presented scenarios that seemed tailored to people attempting to inhabit this brave new world. Secondly, although cinema's first decade corresponds to certain aspects of the experience of modernity (brevity, confrontation, shock), the more narrativized cinema of its second decade just as obviously inhabits and reflects upon this modern world. Indeed, the greater expansion of cinema after 1906 arguably heightened its association with modern life.

Some critics, doubting the value of relating early cinema to modernity, have claimed that such a relation cannot in itself explain stylistic change, especially given the strong transformation of cinema from the attractions mode of the first decade to the greater reliance on narrative structures and psychological characters after 1906. Yet no one has claimed that modernity supplies the total explanation for film style. Indeed in his work on D. W. **Griffith** at **Biograph**, Gunning emphasized the role such factors as changing audiences, industry re-organization, pressure from censorship boards and reformers, and attempts to regularize production contributed to the increased narrativization of cinema and the stylistic forms that took in the period around 1909. However, this is not to say that modernity cannot be related to different styles and their success with audiences. Aspects of film style in 1903 as well as 1911 can be related to modernity, although often to different aspects. From 1903 to 1910, the fast-paced aspect of early cinema, so often compared to the tempo of modern life, moved from the brevity of individual films, the rapid succession of attractions, and the variety of the early film program, to a new use of fast-paced editing, a quick succession of gags within slapstick films, and the thrilling death-defying stunts in **serials**. The desire articulated after 1908 to attract "respectable, middle class audiences" does lead in some instances to films which seem to reflect more traditional cultural values, especially as opposed to the ribald humor and outright anarchy of certain films of the first decade. But the popularity of slapstick comedies, action serials, and sensational **melodramas** into the early feature era shows that film audiences still demanded the new dramaturgy based in shocks, one which can be related to modernity in terms of temporality, technology, new concepts of gender, and the ongoing pursuit of thrills and excitement.

Further reading

Bordwell, David (1997) *On The History of Film Style*, Cambridge, MA: Harvard University Press.

Charney, Leo and Vanessa Schwartz (eds.) (1995) *Cinema and the Invention of Modern Life*, Berkeley: University of California Press.

Crary, Jonathan (1990) *Techniques of the Observer: On Vision and Modernity in the Nineteenth Century*, Cambridge, MA: MIT Press.

Gunning, Tom (1994) "An Aesthetic of Astonishment: Early Film and the (In) Credulous Spectator" in Linda Williams (ed.) *Viewing Positions: Ways of Seeing Film*, 114–133, New Brunswick: Rutgers University Press.

Gunning, Tom (1994) "'The Whole Town's Gawking': Early Cinema and the Visual Experience of Modernity" *Yale Journal of Criticism*, 7.2: 189–201.

Hansen, Miriam (1991) *Babel and Babylon: Spectatorship in American Silent Film*, Cambridge, MA: Harvard University Press.

Kern, Stephen (1983) *The Culture of Space and Time, 1880–1918*, Cambridge, MA: Harvard University Press.

Rabinovitz, Lauren (1998) *For the Love of Pleasure: Women, Movies and Culture in Turn-of-the-Century Chicago*, New Brunswick: Rutgers University Press.

Singer, Ben (2001) *Melodrama and Modernity: Early Sensational Cinema and its Contexts*, New York: Columbia University Press.

TOM GUNNING

modes of production: issues and debates

Marx used the term "mode of production" to analyze different economic systems with respect to methods of organizing labor, allocating power, controlling material and financial resources, distributing profit, and so on. In general, the modes of production Marx examined were very broad and distinct economic structures such as slavery, feudalism, capitalism, and socialism. More than just an issue of material or economic activity, Marx saw modes of production as intimately tied to larger social and ideological manifestations, whereby, as he wrote in *A Contribution to the Critique of Political Economy* (1859), "The mode of production in material life determines the general character of the social, political and spiritual processes of life."

In cinema studies, the term has been used rather more narrowly, generally sidestepping the social-reflectionist implications of Marx's base/superstructure paradigm and focusing not on broadest-level economic structures but rather on different ways of organizing the film-production process with respect to divisions of labor and authority. For cinema historians, a "mode of production" refers to a particular set of production practices—a particular system by which financial and material resources are mobilized, decisions are made, and work functions are divided in the manufacture of films. Technically speaking, a distinction can be made between a "mode" and

a "system" of production—the latter being a specific configuration or articulation of the former. So, for example, recent scholars can discuss *the* "Hollywood mode of production" (as a mode based on the detailed division of labor) while describing historical shifts in the specific systems of divided labor constituting that mode. In practice, however, the terms "mode" and "system" are generally used interchangeably.

The most fully elaborated analysis of modes of production in silent cinema has concentrated on the US industry. Janet Staiger's groundbreaking work in *The Classical Hollywood Cinema* mapped out four dominant production systems that developed more or less sequentially in the silent era: the "cameraman" system (1896–1907); the "director" system (1907–1909); the "director-unit" system (1909–1914); and the "central producer" system (1914–1930).

In Staiger's breakdown, the initial "cameraman" system was a mode with little or no division of labor. The filmmaker was a Jack-of-all-trades craftsman, conceiving and executing virtually all parts of the production process. The same person selected subject matter, decided upon technological and photographic options (cameras, lenses, raw stock, etc.), handled staging (manipulating lighting, setting, people), photographed scenes, developed and edited the film. The cameraman may or may not also have been the owner/manager in charge of capital direction, but in any case he was a "unified" artisan exercising broad knowledge and control over the endeavor. In all subsequent systems, there would be increasingly distinct and fine subdivisions of labor, with strong functional segregation between decision-makers and order-followers.

The cameraman system faded away, at least in the USA and much of Europe, because its output capacity was inadequate and because it was economically inefficient (since it paid a skilled craftsman for tasks that could be done by cheaper, less-skilled workers). The subsequent "director" system (dominant in 1907–1909, but evident in some studios a few years earlier) increased specialization by shifting primary authority from the cameraman to a separate director. The cameraman became a more limited technician, in charge of cinematography and developing, while the director assumed responsibility for producing (budgeting and planning), research, location scouting, stage design, casting, performance coaching, editing, and various other decisions. Scenarios or plot sketches now usually were written by another person, but directors had authority to modify stories at will.

With escalating demand following the **nickelodeon** boom, and with the **Motion Picture Patents Company**'s rationalization of manufacture and distribution, output had to be greatly stepped up and regularized for fixed-schedule releasing. In the "director-unit" system that prevailed for about five years after 1909, Staiger argues, studios boosted output by creating multiple production units operating concurrently, either in different locales (enhancing scenic quality and permitting year-round shooting) or, after the early 1910s migration to Hollywood, at the same facility. Although there was some sharing of mid-level workers among units (cameramen, prop-men, etc), each "stock company" remained largely autonomous, headed by its own director. The director's purview and authority was comparable to the prior system, but the pattern of task specialization and vertical hierarchization continued as work functions solidified into more clearly delineated departments.

In the early 1910s, with the emergence of the **multiple-reel/feature film** and the general dissemination of "scientific management" models of industrial efficiency, the "central producer" system of production became prevalent. The shift toward longer, more complicated and capital-intensive productions demanded greater planning and logistical coordination among units and departments. The director's job became much more narrowly focused, as a producer took charge of all pre- and post-shooting decisions (including script selection), and a production manager typically took responsibility for day-to-day financial oversight and facility planning. The detailed (usually shot-by-shot) continuity script became the crucial tool facilitating a new level of centralized managerial control (while also aiding production efficiency by allowing scenes to be shot out of chronological sequence).

Charles Musser has contested key components of Staiger's schematization. He argues that a "collaborative" system, and not the "cameraman"

system, was the primary mode of production before 1908. While the cameraman system was commonly employed for making *actualités* (especially by firms like **Lumière** which had developed light-weight, user-friendly equipment), most fiction filmmaking (as, for example, at **Edison** Manufacturing) involved a collaborative pairing of two essentially equal partners with complementary skills. One might handle cinematography, developing, and editing, while the other might construct sets and direct actors, with subject selection and general planning performed by both. Where Staiger posits a phase of unified artisinal labor during the first decade of film production, Musser sees a division of labor from the start—however, involving a "horizontal" division of tasks rather than the "vertical" hierarchization of power instituted in the production systems that followed.

Musser and Staiger also disagreed on how best to describe those subsequent systems, beyond recognizing the overall trajectory of increased specialization and vertical organization. Whereas Staiger proposes three distinct and sequential dominant systems—the director, director-unit, and central-producer systems—Musser considers only the third of these historically valid. Studio records, he argues, indicate that central management (owners, producers, studio managers) exercised substantial control over individual productions and studio staff from at least 1908 on. While there were certainly variations and fluctuations in the relationships between directors and producers, directors were seldom practically autonomous or responsible for the full spectrum of preplanning, shooting, and post-production. Moreover, describing a separate system based on the emergence of multiple production units is problematic, Musser points out, since "multiple or single units were not characteristic of any period" in particular. Musser therefore affirms only one crucial transformation in American production systems: a shift around 1908 from a mode of production dominated by collaboration to one governed by hierarchy and centralization.

Further research into industry records is needed to help adjudicate such questions of classification and periodization, and to determine how closely the European situation (or situations) corresponded to the American. Richard Abel, for instance, observes relatively less of an impetus toward the centralization of management control in the French industry before **World War I**. There, an abundance of small companies employed either the director system or the director unit system, affiliated with parent distributors, who nevertheless retained primary dominion over scenario development, production planning, and financing. This suggests that second and third stages of Staiger's model might better describe circumstances in the French industry in the early 1910s, but much more work would be needed to support any such conclusion.

See also: screenwriting

Further reading

Abel, Richard (1994) *The Ciné Goes to Town: French Cinema, 1896–1914*, Berkeley: University of California Press.

Jessop, R. (1987) "Mode of Production" in John Eatwell *et al.* (eds.) *The New Palgrave: A Dictionary of Economics*, Vol. 3, 489–492, London: Macmillan.

Musser, Charles (1996) "Pre-Classical American Cinema: Changing Modes of Film Production," in Richard Abel (ed.) *Silent Film*, 85–108, New Brunswick: Rutgers University Press.

Staiger, Janet (1985) "The Hollywood Mode of Production to 1930," in David Bordwell, Janet Staiger, and Kristin Thompson, *The Classical Hollywood Cinema: Film Style and Modes of Production to 1960*, 87–153, London/New York: Routledge & Kegan Paul/Columbia University Press.

BEN SINGER

Modot, Gaston

b. 1887, Paris; d. 1970, Paris

actor, France

Modot had one of the longest acting careers in the history of French cinema. Between 1905 and 1907, he was a painter and frequented Montmartre cabarets. In 1910, **Gaumont** hired him as an extra for a film shot by Jean **Durand**. From then on, he became part of the troupe led by Lucien Bataille, the Pouites, who improvised frenzied chases and

wild fights to be captured on film. He appeared in most episodes of the *Onésime* and *Calino* series (150 films between 1911 and 1914). In 1911, he also acted in a series of **westerns** directed by Joë **Hamman** in the Camargue. Although restricted to character parts, Modot was very popular, thanks to his athleticism, proletarian looks, and sober, modern acting style. Yet the best was still to come, once he would meet and work with Luis Buñuel, René Clair, Jacques Feyder, and Jean Renoir.

FRANÇOIS DE LA BRETÈQUE

Monca, Georges

b. 1888; d. 1939

actor, filmmaker, France

Monca came from a theater background, which led Louis **Feuillade** to hire him as an actor for **Gaumont** in 1906. Lucien **Nonguet** then hired him as a filmmaker for **Pathé-Frères**, and he soon moved to **SCAGL** in 1909. At SCAGL, Monca directed a wide range of films, including *Le petit chose* [Little What's-His-Name] (1912) and *Sans famille* [Homeless] (1913), but specialized in **comedies** and later vaudevilles. He was best known, however, for directing most of the *Rigadin* **comic series**, starring Charles **Prince** (they made approximately 200 films together).

ALAIN CAROU

monopoly capitalism: USA

The era of early cinema saw the formation of an industrial system of capitalism applied to film production, distribution, and presentation. Typically, as new technologies offer the possibilities of new industries, at first entry is open, firms are small, and competition vigorous and ever changing. Then as a few companies grow—based on their skills of assuming control of production, distribution, and/or exhibition—they seek to gain a measure of market power through some means of monopoly power.

Thus from the innovation of moving pictures until 1908, all kinds and types of producers, distributors (sales agents), and exhibitors flourished, all seeking profits and means of protecting them in the long run. The consolidation of such power would not come until the formation of the Hollywood studio system—just after the period of early cinema—but the struggles of moving from an open system towards monopoly capitalist consolidation would define the cinema's initial decades.

The moving picture business during the final years of the 19th century can be best understood as one of economic freedom and independence—with no one dominant firm or set of firms. At first many entrepreneurs tried to make films, in locations across the USA. Many bet that northern New Jersey, near the entertainment capital of New York City, or Florida, where one could film 365 days a year, would become production centers, just as Detroit was becoming the center of automobile production. No one initially even considered Southern California as a possible locus of industry production.

Moreover, films could be imported with relative ease to the USA, and many came from France. Indeed, early sales agents such as George **Kleine** and rental exchange men such as Carl **Laemmle** and William **Fox** built their business in part as importers (especially of **Pathé-Frères** subjects), able to distribute films to a growing number of presentation outlets. Distribution was by-and-large regional, as sales agents distributed films to big cities and their surrounding states. **Itinerant exhibitors** simply purchased films, and then ran them as they made their circuits. National distribution would come only later.

Finally, presentation, which started with peep shows, turned to projection in a variety of theatrical settings—**vaudeville** theaters, local "opera" houses, **amusement parks**, and then early **nickelodeons**—with companies such as **Vitagraph** emerging to offer exhibition services, also on a regional basis. No one imagined until at least 1910 that theaters presenting moving pictures exclusively would eventually define exhibition.

There were no specific constraints dampening this open competition. Sources of financing varied across the board. There was a lack of unionization. Censorship by cities and states would not come until later. This was a period when operations remained relatively small, at least for US companies, and everyone did a little bit of everything.

But as with capitalism in general, the wide-open competition of the moving picture business in the late 1890s and early 1900s would prove short-lived. The possibility of using patents to fashion a monopoly offered the first means for well-financed capitalists such as Thomas **Edison** to consolidate power, set up barriers to entry to possible competitors, and thereby also increase their profits. Taking their cue from mergers and monopoly practices in other well-established industries—such as the **electricity** and **communication** (specifically, the telephone) businesses—in 1908 ten motion picture companies put aside their differences, accepted Edison's patents, and formed the **Motion Picture Patents Company** (MPPC).

The MPPC drew inspiration from far larger industries where patent pooling was a common practice. This was particularly the case in the oil industry under the control of the Standard Oil Corporation run by John D. Rockefeller. Pooling patents in such expanding businesses kept rivals at bay, and permitted monopoly capitalists a means to secure their profits. The lone risk—as Rockefeller and Edison would experience—was government anti-trust suits under the Sherman Act to break up trusts. At this point in U.S. history, both the Republican and Democrat parties in the Progressive era preached and to some degree practiced liberal anti-trust policies. No symbol marked this more than the break-up of Rockefeller's Standard Oil.

The MPPC patent collusion monopoly would also fail, eventually ruled illegal by the U.S. Supreme Court. But in the process of seeking monopoly economic power, the Trust would redefine the motion picture industry, and leave it open to innovations in business practices which would lead to the Hollywood studio system.

The central problem for any collusive set of companies is how to enforce, supervise, and maintain control. To monitor middlemen who now rented films, the MPPC Trust went into the business of film distribution with its **General Film Company**. General Film became the first national distributor of moving pictures across the whole of the USA. But the Trust could not find a way to control the huge number of exhibitors and exhibition venues. Nickelodeons opened at an exponential rate for several years after 1905 and may have reached 10,000 by 1910; that so many of these remained or became independent attested to the Trust's difficulty and eventually led to its failure in this sector of the business.

The MPPC also failed because its members, as in many a cartel before and after, chafed under the terms of the crude (indeed forced) marriage of companies, and their different corporate strategies. For example, some members wanted to produce longer, **multiple-reel films**, while others seemed content making their profits with short subjects or one-reelers. Collusion proved impossible, and simply permitted the rise of the best of the independents (all initially exhibitors and then distributors)—Laemmle and **Universal**, Adolph **Zukor** and Paramount, Marcus **Loew**, and Fox.

Zukor and company learned their lessons well from the Trust. Between 1910 to 1915, for example, General Film innovated and standardized relations between distributors and exhibitors in terms of the run-zone-clearance system that Paramount would later use to enforce its monopoly practices. That is, a film was booked exclusively within an area (a zone) for its "first-run" presentation. Then there would be a period of time (the "clearance") in which the motion picture would not be shown before it appeared for its "second-run." Exhibitors liked this run-zone-clearance system because they felt protected in booking a film, knowing that the same subject would not appear across the street. Distributors liked the system because it milked the top dollar from customers who knew they would have to wait for their audience's favorite moving picture unless they paid top prices to see it in first-run. By the 1920s, Zukor would extend this run-zone-clearance system around the world.

In short, the capitalists who fought the MPPC, would—as the era of early cinema came to an end—accomplish what the Trust had attempted: control of the production, distribution, and exhibition of moving pictures through a system of vertical integration. In the process, they took over the world of cinema and created a Hollywood hegemony. They accomplished a collusion only a Rockefeller or J. P. Morgan could really appreciate.

See also: law and the cinema: regulating exhibition; US patent wars

Further reading

Cassady, Ralph Jr. (1982) "Monopoly in Motion Picture Production and Distribution: 1908–1915," in Gorham Kindem, *The American Movie Industry*, 25–68, Carbondale, IL: Southern Illinois University Press.

Gomery, Douglas (1992) *Shared Pleasures: A History of Movie Presentation in the United States*, Madison: University of Wisconsin Press.

Hampton, Benjamin B. (1931) *A History of the Movies*, New York: Covici Friede.

McCaw, Thomas K. (ed.) (1997) *Creating Modern Capitalism*, Cambridge: Harvard University Press.

DOUGLAS GOMERY

Moore, Annabelle

b. *c.* 1878; d. November 1961

dancer, stage performer, USA

Born Annabelle Whitford, Moore debuted at the 1893 Columbian Exposition in Chicago and, as Peerless Annabelle, was a featured performer when she danced for **Edison**'s **Kinetoscope** in the summer of 1894, the first of four times she appeared in the Black Maria. She also was one of the first performers filmed by the **American Mutoscope and Biograph Company**. Of her various dances, the best known was her serpentine dance à la Loïe **Fuller**. She played the Gibson Girl in the first *Ziegfeld's Follies* (1907) and remained in the company until 1912, when she retired and later remarried, becoming Annabelle Buchanan.

PAUL SPEHR

Moore, Owen

b. 1886, County Meath, Ireland; d. 1939, Beverly Hills

actor, USA

A handsome, but quirky leading man, Moore (his family settled in Toledo in 1898) played juvenile leads on stage before joining **Biograph** in 1908. After performing a variety of roles for

D. W. **Griffith**, he followed Mary **Pickford** in her brief alliance with **Majestic**, and they were married in 1911. Moore also followed Pickford in joining **Famous Players**, playing opposite her in *Caprice* (1913), but the couple had a stormy relationship, in part due to Moore's alcoholism, and divorced in 1920. Moore's brothers, Tom, Matt, and Joe, also had acting careers in the movies.

ROBERT S. BIRCHARD

Morano, Gigetta

b. 1886; d. 1986

actor, Italy

After training in Turin's amateur theater, Morano began working at **Ambrosio** in 1909, performing in a wide variety of genres: drama, comedy, romance, and crime stories. She had a major success with her role as Mam'zelle Nitouche in *Santarellina* (1912), which made her a leading actress in Italian cinema. In 1913–1916, she appeared in a series of piquant bourgeois **comedies** such as *Acque miracolose* [Miraculous Wells] (1914). Well known as the character of "Gigetta," Morano often was coupled with actors Eleuterio **Rodolfi** and Camillo **De Riso**. Her last parts were in Federico Fellini's *I Vitelloni* [Overgrown Calves] (1953) and *Otto e mezzo* [8½] (1963).

IVO BLOM

Mosjoukine (Mozzhukhin), Ivan

b. 1890; d. 1939

actor, Russia

After a brief career on stage, in 1911 Mosjoukine became a full-time actor for **Khanzhonkov**, first in **comedies** and then in dramas. His performance as an inconsolable widower in Yevgeni **Bauer**'s *Life in Death* (1914) is remembered for a close shot in which a slow tear trickles down his dispassionate face. Moving to **Yermoliev** in 1916, Mosjoukine became famous as a neurasthenic lead: steely eyes and a doleful brow were his trademark

image. In 1920, along with other Russians in the industry, Mosjoukine emigrated to France and became a major **star** during the 1920s. Outliving his fame and fortune, he died of consumption in France in 1939.

YURI TSIVIAN

Motion Picture Distributing and Sales Company (Sales)

Founded in 1910 by the leading Independent film producers, Carl **Laemmle** of **IMP** and Adam **Kessel** and Charles **Bauman** of the **New York Motion Picture Company**, the Motion Picture Distributing and Sales Company (Sales) attempted to introduce a measure of regularity and control into the distribution of Independent films. Although some Independent producers initially viewed it with suspicion, denouncing it as a trust, the Sales Company soon supplied nearly all non-MPPC films to Independent exchanges, setting release dates and rental schedules. In 1912, Harry **Aitken**'s **Mutual Film Corporation** triggered a split in the Independent field, and Sales was reorganized as **Universal Film Manufacturing Company**, a powerful Independent faction, but no longer the exclusive source of Independent films.

TOM GUNNING

Motion Picture Patents Company (MPPC)

The Motion Picture Patents Company (MPPC) was established at end of 1908 after more than a year of negotiation to reconcile film producers on the US market, bringing to an end more than a decade of legal wrangling, primarily over Edison's patent claims to motion picture **cameras**, film stock, and **projectors**. Often referred to as the "Trust," the MPPC sought to limit competition and exert control over all areas of the industry (production, distribution and exhibition). Such restraint of free competition had been attacked by legislation such as the Sherman Anti-Trust Act; however, it was believed that patents holders were exempt from anti-trust legislation.

The MPPC was a patent-pooling organization, a holding company separate from its member companies. Edison held a number of key patents through which he had long tried to control the industry. However, the camera of the **American Mutoscope and Biograph Company** avoided the specificities of Edison's patents. After a 1907 court decision found cameras other than the Biograph infringed Edison's patents, the US industry split into Edison and Biograph camps. The recent enormous expansion of **nickelodeons** caused a demand for new product that neither the Edison group (which included **Vitagraph Selig**, **Lubin**, and newly formed **Essanay** and **Kalem**, as well French companies, **Pathé-Frères** and Georges **Méliès**) nor Biograph (which also included imports from France, England, and Italy through George **Kleine**) could separately supply, although each side substantially increased production. With Kleine as principle mediator, the opposing sides finally negotiated a compromise.

The MPPC was comprised of the previously mentioned American companies, along with Pathé, Méliès, and Kleine, who imported films from **Gaumont** and **Eclipse**. It was believed the MPPC could dominate domestic production and that no films could be made without violating its combined patents. Further, the MPPC sought to control distribution and exhibition through its patents on film stock and projectors (although economic clout was the true weapon). Exhibitors and distributors (or "film exchanges") were issued licenses by the MPPC, which not only entailed the payment of royalties in recognition of the patents but also strictly regulated their business. Distributors had to obey release dates, retire prints after a certain period (films were now leased rather than sold), and accept other regulations. Exhibitors were committed to show only "Licensed" films (those of MPPC members) and to pay a regular royalty acknowledging the MPPC's projector patents (exchanges were to collect this unpopular fee). The MPPC portrayed its control of the industry as a reform, addressing the content of films (submitting films to the **National Board of Censorship**) and maintaining theater safety and cleanliness, as well as curbing the dubious practices of early exchangemen.

Opposition to the MPPC began almost immediately. Exchanges and exhibitors chaffed at the regulations and fees and sought new production sources, initially foreign imports and gradually new "Independent" production companies. Although attempts to create a non-infringing camera were largely unsuccessful, the MPPC patents proved difficult to enforce and eventually did not hold up in court. By 1911, through the **Motion Picture Distributing and Sales Company**, the Independent faction was holding its own, even after the MPPC set up its own distribution system, **General Film**, which bought up exchanges and eliminated those not willing to be absorbed. The popularity of many independent films and the apparently more exhibitor-friendly policies of the Sales Company gave them an edge. Allegedly, the Independents were more progressive in pursuing such new policies as advertising **stars** and producing longer films. However, MPPC companies did promote stars (Edison) and release **multiple-reel films** (Vitagraph especially). More detailed economic analysis is needed to explain the MPPC's decline, but it would seem it was simply not able to accommodate new practices quickly enough.

The US government took action against the MPPC under anti-trust legislation beginning in 1912. However, the final judgment did not come until 1915, which officially dissolved the already-failing company.

See also: law and the cinema; US patent wars

TOM GUNNING

moving picture fiction

The idea of moving pictures drew literary attention well before their appearance in public demonstrations. Two French novels are especially notable in this regard. In Villiers de l'Isle-Adam's *L'Eve future* [Tomorrow's Eve] (1886), an inventor named Thomas Alva Edison, the Wizard of Menlo Park, commissioned to create an artificial woman, devises a means of photosculpturing a beautiful but intellectually inadequate model into a figure unsurprisingly called Eve. This philosophical tale explores the epistemological implications of not only capturing the material world but also of projecting inner life by way of new technologies. In Jules Verne's *Carpathian Castle* (1892), a similar inventor develops technologies for storing and disseminating sound over telephone wires, and, more importantly, for projecting moving pictures on a glass screen in a painterly rather than photographic fashion.

Initial interest during the first decades after early cinema's emergence was expressed predominantly on the level of similes and metaphors, and in at least four categories. As Wolfgang Schivelbusch suggests, writers for some time had needed projected moving images to succinctly express (1) *the panoramic flow of impressions from inside means of transportation.* In a 1909 short story, "Järnvägsresan" (The Railroad Trip), for example, Hjalmar Bergman explicitly related impressions apprehended through the compartment window to moving picture shows, thus bypassing analogies to **painting** or theater. In a 1908 novel, Octave Mirbeau more critically described **modernity**'s automotive speed mania in moving picture terms: "life disappears cinematographically like the trees, walls, and shadow silhouettes flanking the road." Filmic metaphors also were elicited from fixed vantage points, primarily (2) *for framing lively street scenes* and bustling traffic situations. For a **magic lantern** enthusiast such as August Strindberg, filmic analogies are to be expected. In his Parisian fragment, "Jakob brottas" (Jacob Wrestles), from *Legender* (1898), the narrator remarks, apropos a teeming traffic panorama, that the streetlight illuminates "a most lively cinematographic picture." (3) *Interior scenes detachedly observed* from a distance, or through exterior windows, offered yet another stock situation calling for similes invoking cinematic spectatorship. In *Stella Dallas* (1923), Olive Higgins Prouty labeled such a situation "a scene at the movies," thus summing up a convention harking back at least to E. W. Hornung's "An Old Flame," in *The Black Mask* (1901), where a prying character describes what he sees: "It was like a lantern-picture thrown upon a screen." (4) *Analogies between the mental apparatus and the filmic apparatus* were commonplace. "The brain has become a cinematographe," wrote Bo Bergman in *Drömmen och andra noveller* [The Dream and Other Short Stories] (1904). By contrast, Henning Berger

described memory as a "horrible combination of phonograph and cinematographe," in "Brefvet" [The Letter] (1906).

The third category soon led writers to explore the implications or consequences of this new form of spectatorship more thoroughly. In Maurice Normand's short story, "Avant le cinémaographe" (In Front of the Cinematographe) (1900), ***actualité*** footage from a faraway battlefield gives rise to an intense encounter one evening in the Alhambra Variety Theater in Paris. An Irish chambermaid working for an aristocratic family sees her fiancé on screen, an Irish soldier fighting in the Boer War, and later believes that he is shot fatally in front of her eyes. Normand weaves together observations on the vicissitudes of **spectatorship** as well as documentary authenticity before offering a happy, yet mystifying resolution. In Herman Babson's "Jim: A Christmas Motion Picture Story" (1903), an old man loses his mind, during a War-graph show that includes footage from the Spanish-American War, after seeing his beloved son on screen. Eventually, the reader learns what the old man already knows—that the son has died in battle. In Rudyard Kipling's "Mrs. Bathurst" (1904), an enigmatic and evocative story about sexual obsession patched together by means of four narrating voices, a character named Vickery (one of the four voices) repeatedly visits a cinema to watch a film sequence featuring the mysterious Mrs. Bathurst. Vickery's fatal attraction to the woman's screen image, his desire and irrevocable despair, is confirmed again and again through the powerless gaze he fixes on the screen. In all three stories, spectatorship involves seeing the phantasmatic image of a loved one, which, much as in l'Isle-Adam and Verne's earlier novels, produces a profound, multi-faceted sense of loss.

In later fiction, apprehending a familiar face on the screen happened more often by chance, and did not necessarily involve a loved one. In the first novel set in Hollywood (at least partly), B. M. Bower's **western**, *Jean of the Lazy A* (1915), a missing person is detected in a **newsreel** from Mexico. Indeed, the ghostly storage function of the film medium made human presence transportable and retrievable, as evidence, in contexts far removed from the time and place of shooting. In James S. Barcus' novel, *The Governor's Boss*

(1914), much as in Universal's *Traffic in Souls* (1913), dictograph recordings expose a crooked politician, but in this case, the sound recording is combined with surreptitious filming in order to document criminal transactions.

The inability to read the source and meaning of images on the screen with assurance provided impetus for scores of scenes in fictional stories. Henning Berger's "Spegeln" (The Mirror) (1914) offered a complex visual embedding of exterior shooting. The protagonist of the story is startled to see inexplicable actions in a mirror reflecting the street through a window behind him. The explanation for this soon emerges when a film crew enters the restaurant in which he is sitting. Less complicated misreadings were more common. Bower's first film story, "Like A Knight of Old" (1910), offers a **western** example of uncalled-for-gallantry in a shooting situation mistakenly taken for the real thing. Filming on location sometimes could be used as a cover for criminal operations, as in Robert Hughes' story, "The Great Cinematographic Crime" (1910). The French poet Guillaume Apollinaire wrote one of the more troubling variations on this in his 1909 story, "Un beau film" (A Great Film), about the cold-blooded shooting of what we would now call a "snuff film" and its subsequent success with the Parisian public.

By the 1910s, American authors regularly, if only in passing remarks, either snubbed the melodramatic aspect of moving pictures or belittled cinema audiences. Yet this became a running theme in Rupert Hughes' *We Can't Have Everything* (1917). Bower's western novels, including *The Phantom Herd* (1916), *The Heritage of the Sioux* (1916), and *The Quirt* (1917), by contrast, were as enthusiastically promotional of the industry as were the juvenile series pioneered by the Stratemeyer Syndicate. Paralleling Bower's endeavors, William Almon Wolff's *Behind the Screen* (1916) depicted activities, often in poignant detail, in the film colony of Fort Lee, New Jersey. Here, reforming the industry by fighting the Edison Trust is the central concern of a young man who has inherited some stock in a film company and wholeheartedly embraces the enterprise. Much like Bower's heroes, he decides to produce a moving picture and thereby transform the industry. Charles

E. Van Loan's collection of short stories, *Buck Parvin and the Movies* (1915), which later were filmed, sought to balance irony and idealism in a more playful manner.

European authors were usually less sanguine in their criticism of the movies. In Danish writer Albert Dam's novel, *Mellem De To Seer* [Between Two Lakes] (1906), in a chapter called "Living Pictures," a gruesome duel between two film rivals runs parallel to the romantic love affair being shown on a primitive screen in a tent show. Luigi Pirandello's novel, *Si gira* [Shoot!] (1914), presents a harsh, multi-faceted critique of modernity. Here, moving pictures are depicted as a kind of virus that desensitizes its audience and contributes to an undesirable cultural transformation. The first-person narrator, a cameraman, is a victim of his own apparatus and ends up wrecked and totally enslaved by his shooting.

Figure 81 Moving Picture Boys book cover. (Courtesy of Jan Olsson.)

In the late 1910s and early 1920s, would-be film actors starred in many of the new novels about moving pictures: Harry Leon Wilson's *Merton of the Movies* (1922) is the most prototypical example. Paralleling this trend, tinsel town scandals were chronicled in dark strokes, in such novels as Edgar Rice Burroughs' *The Girl from Hollywood* (1923). Exhibiting a change of heart, Hughes tried to rehabilitate the industry's and its stars' reputation in *Souls for Sale* (1922). But the first actual movie **star** in a novel could be Fredegonde Perlenblick in Carl Einstein's *Bebuquin* (1912). Her chauffeur cruises the streets in an eccentric car sporting a flashing film marquee on the roof, a gimmick more Hollywood than Hollywood.

See also: travelogues

JAN OLSSON

moving picture fiction: juvenile series

The New York-based Stratemeyer Syndicate pioneered juvenile series on moving picture topics by introducing three more or less parallel series in the early 1910s. Two were penned by the nom de plume Victor Appleton: the ten-volume *Moving Picture Boys* (1913–1919) and seven-volume *Motion Picture Chums* (1913–1916); the other, by Laura Lee Hope: the seven-volume *Moving Picture Girls* (1914–1916). The five-volume *Motion Picture Comrades* (from 1917), published by The New York Book Company, was a less sophisticated spin-off from the Stratemeyer series. The most lasting series, *Ruth Fielding* (1913–1934), was authored by Alice B. Emerson. It did not start out as a moving picture series proper, but turned into one when young Ruth became introduced to the film world (in volume 9) and soon was its most stellar member with a company of her own. Moving picture installments figured in several series without serving as the focal point for an entire run, for instance, the *Rover Boys* and *Dave Dashaway*.

JAN OLSSON

Moving Picture News

Published in New York, beginning in 1908, and edited by Alfred **Saunders** (the original editor of *Moving Picture World*), *Moving Picture News* soon became the most important trade paper supporting the Independents. Unlike the *World*, the *News* tended not to give by-lines to the writers of its columns and reviews, and, after Saunders left in 1912, its interest in exhibition eventually led to its consolidation with *Exhibitors' Times* in September 1913, and its rechristening as *Motion Picture News* (which lasted until 1930). The merger expanded both the length of each issue and its circulation, which reportedly reached 16,000 by 1914.

RICHARD ABEL

Moving Picture World

Published in New York, beginning in March 1907, *Moving Picture World* quickly surpassed *Views and Films Index* (which it bought out in 1911) as the most important trade weekly in the industry. The *World* staked out a middle ground between the **Motion Picture Patents Company** and the Independents, and editor J. P. Chalmers (who died in an accident in 1912) recruited writers such as W. Stephen **Bush**, Louis Reeves **Harrison**, Epes Winthrop **Sargent**, Thomas **Bedding**, and others to contribute influential columns, reviews, and special articles. By 1914, its circulation reportedly had reached 15,000. Although it continued to be published until the 1930s, its influence had waned by the 1920s.

RICHARD ABEL

Mudaliar, R. Nataraja

b. 1885; d.1972

filmmaker, India

Mudaliar single-handedly founded the cinema industry in South India. A prosperous automobile dealer before switching to moving pictures (apparently inspired by D. G. **Phalke**'s pioneering efforts), he learnt filmmaking in Poona from a Mr. Stewart, who was the official cinematographer at the Delhi Durbar of 1902. Back in Madras, Mudaliar set up the Indian Film Company to make *Keechaka Vadham* [The Slaying of Keechaka] (1917) in a makeshift studio. Widely released, this film was followed by five more **mythological** tales before the twin disasters of his studio burning down and the death of his only son prompted him to retire in 1923.

SURESH CHABRIA

Mullens, Bernard (Albert) and Willy (a.k.a. Alberts Frères)

b. 1879/1880; d. 1941/1952

exhibitors, filmmakers, the Netherlands.

In their years as **itinerant exhibitors**, the Mullens brothers regularly filmed local and national *actualités*. They also experimented with **synchronized sound** films and produced short **comedies** such as *Ah! Ah! die Oscar!* [Ha! Ha! That Oscar!] (1905), inspired by **Edison**'s *Personal* (1904), and *De mésavontures van een Fransch heertje zonder pantalon aan het strand te Zandvoort* [A Dandy without Trousers] (1905), an international success. From 1910 on, they opened up permanent cinemas while continuing **fair/fairground** shows until the outbreak of the war. Willy Mullens would become the most prolific Dutch nonfiction cameraman from the mid-1910s on.

IVO BLOM

Müller-Lincke, Anna

b. 1869; d. 1935

actor, Germany

Wilhelmine Germany's archetypical comedienne of Berlin-style humor, from 1902 Müller-Lincke was the female star of the Metropol variety theater. In 1907, she made her most successful operetta songs, largely written by her then husband Paul Lincke, into a series of *Tonbilder* for Deutsche Bioscop. Early on in her career, Müller-Lincke specialized in comical old lady roles, which shaped

her screen image after 1910. In numerous films for Heinrich **Bolten-Baeckers**, she played the figure of the comic mother or severe mother-in-law. In Max **Mack**'s fast-paced Berlin comedy *Wo ist Coletti?* [Where is Coletti?] (1913) she appears briefly as the resolute old lady confronting the fake detective. Due to her immense popularity, she also made **advertising films** and, after 1914, **propaganda films** for War Bond Drives.

MICHAEL WEDEL

multiple-reel/feature films: Europe

The multiple-reel feature film became an important production and exhibition format for European cinema in the years 1910–1914. The leading innovators were studios in Denmark, France, and Italy, with others quickly following suit in countries such as Germany, Sweden, Russia, and Great Britain. The successful niche-marketing of the longer formats in turn exerted pressure on American studios to turn to multiple-reel films. By the start of the **World War I**, the long feature film was clearly established and in some countries was beginning to supplant the variety format of short films.

A basic characteristic of the feature film is length: one can define a feature film as consisting of more than one reel. The single-reel format (a maximum of about 350 meters, or 15 minutes screened) dominated early cinema before 1910 and had somewhat arbitrarily come to be regarded as an upper limit, perhaps due to its convenience for exhibitors. Short films allowed for varied programming with little financial risk resting on any particular title, required only one projector and no reel change, and allowed a regular turnover of audience in the relatively small theaters.

Films before 1910 rarely exceeded this limit, especially in the early years, but when they did, the presentation generally was spread across several screenings. Two early examples from **Pathé-Frères** in 1903 were *Epopée napoléonienne* [Life of Napoleon] (430 meters) and *La Vie et la Passion de Jésus-Christ* [The Life and Passion of Jesus Christ] (1,425 meters), both of which were distributed and shown as episodic **historical** or biblical films that could be split up and adapted to the needs of exhibitors. Serials in the 1910s used the same strategy to reduce the length of any particular screening. Feature films, by contrast, can be defined as multi-reel films shown in a single screening. The idea of the feature thus depends as much on the way films were delivered to audiences as it does on formal textual characteristics like length. Including exhibition criteria in the definition also reminds us that the phenomenon was a part of spectator experience even in countries that had little national feature film production of their own.

A third characteristic of the feature—the original, fictional scenario—is not as essential to the definition, but reveals some interesting tension in the category. Historical re-enactments and literary adaptations lent themselves to multiple-reel exposition in obvious ways, because small episodes could be strung out across a long narrative like pearls on a string. Previous attempts to depict familiar cultural material of this sort in short films had often attracted criticism for the elisions of historical detail, plot, and characterization forced upon the material by the format. The multiple-reel film enabled more sustained exposition, and thus allowed adaptations and recreations to expand to a more suitable length. Original fiction films, by contrast, were more narratively challenging in the feature format, since they required filmmakers to develop new storytelling strategies in order to ensure that audiences could orient themselves over longer screening times without the crutch of previously familiar texts.

The reasons for the emergence of the multiple-reel feature film in Europe in 1910–1911 are several. Spectator-oriented explanations locate the cause in growing consumer appetite for longer narrative and over-familiarity with the one-reel format. From an industrial perspective, the feature film allowed companies to concentrate resources and attach cultural prestige to their titles. It was also a way of differentiating product; the flood of American single-reel films by 1909–1910 gave longer films a competitive edge as an attractive alternative product from European studios.

The timing and scope of initial feature film production is revealing of particular national studios and their genre strategies. Denmark, for example, was especially early in producing multiple-reel fiction features, emphasizing white slave films and the so-called "erotic melodramas." *Den hvide Slavehandel* [The White Slave Trade] (706 meters), which premiered successfully in the spring of 1910 in Denmark, drew equal comment for its risqué subject matter and its length, even though its total screening time was just over thirty minutes. Later that fall came the premiere of an even more influential film internationally, Urban Gad's *Afgrunden* [The Abyss] (750 meters), starring Asta Nielsen in her first film role. Nielsen's performance etched itself, along with the feature format, into the consciousness of much of Europe during the film's widespread distribution in 1910–1911. As early as mid-1911, single-reel production already was the exception at Nordisk, as at most of the other Danish studios. In all, the Danish film industry produced forty-nine multiple-reel fiction films in 1911 alone.

The influence of the Danish feature was especially strong in Germany, where Ole Olsen's extensive distribution network provided a ready outlet for erotic melodramas. Equally important, however, was the speedy emigration of both Nielsen and Gad to the German film industry, where they continued making similar multiple-reel films from 1911 on. Two of their films there that year, *Heisses Blut* [Hot Blood] (830 meters) and *Der fremde Vogel* [The Foreigner] (974 meters), were landmark Bioscope features. The Messter studio's first long-format film, *Das gefährliche Alter* [The Dangerous Age] (760 meters), was also filmed in early 1911. In Germany the enthusiasm for long films among exhibitors was immediate due to the resounding financial triumph of the white slave films, but their success was probably more a result of the coincident establishment of the monopoly rental system. At any rate, the terms *Monopolfilm* and feature film became interchangeable in Germany in the early 1910s.

Between 1907 and 1910, Pathé Frères was an international leader in the single-reel film market. Yet, in conjunction with SCAGL, the company was beginning to produce and distribute literary adaptations and series films to be shown over several screenings, already demonstrating an interest in increased length. In early 1911, Albert Capellani produced the first multiple-reel French historical feature to be shown in a single screening: *Le Courrier de Lyon* [The Orleans Coach]

(750 meters) debuted in March of that year, the same month the Danish films first made their way into the French market. By early fall, Pathé had further success with a Victor Hugo adaptation, *Notre Dame de Paris* (810 meters). This line of production culminated in Capellani's ambitious 1912 version of *Les Misérables* (3,400 meters), which was divided into several showings, but now in four long, feature-length parts.

A **Gaumont** production from the fall of 1911, Louis **Feuillade**'s *La Tare* [The Taint] (803 meters), exemplifies a second line of specialization in the French feature film industry, namely the realistic urban melodrama. This film, Gaumont's first three-reeler, also had its roots in the series format, in this case Feuillade's *Scènes de la vie telle qu'elle est* [Scenes of Life as It Is]. Using bourgeois milieus, location shooting, and **staging in depth** strategies, the French urban melodramas provided well-crafted feature-length narratives about contemporary society.

A third line of development, the **crime** or **detective films**, further underscores the lines of continuity between the early French feature and its series predecessors, as in **Éclair**'s *Nick Carter* (1908–1910). Victorin **Jasset**'s influential feature from September 1911, *Zigomar* (935 meters), adapted the existing detective series to the new feature exhibition format by tying over the action from reel to reel through a series of climaxes. This genre reached its fullest form in Feuillade's *Fantômas* series (1913–1914), which eventually consisted of five films, each feature-length in its own right.

The French feature, unlike the Danish, did not immediately supplant the single-reel film within its national production context. Rather like the coexistence of novels and short stories, the mixed production of features and one-reelers continued in France up to **World War I**. Likewise, the French industry demonstrated more continuity with its pre-feature period by extending and building on existing formats like the serial and the historical drama.

In Italy, the turn to literary and historical material prefigured the rise of the feature-length film, as it had in France. Many single-reel films before 1911 dealt with material taken from classical history and mythology, cherished Italian writers, and other prestigious European authors. This prepared the way for the premiere of the first long-format feature (again in March of 1911), **Milano**'s *Inferno* (1,300 meters). Here too the given episodic structure of the material allowed for length to simply accumulate, but the visual interest of the subject matter also points to what would become a signature of the Italian feature film, namely an unusually powerful balance of both spectacle and narrative elements.

Although the earlier Italian costume dramas had relatively modest lengths, the exceptional features after 1912 were strikingly ambitious in scope. *Quo vadis?* (2,250 meters) from 1912 and *Gli ultima giorni di Pompei* (The Last Days of Pompei) (1,958 meters) from 1913 gave indications of what was to come in the culmination of the Italian historical spectacle in 1914, *Cabiria* (4,500 meters). (The average length of the Italian feature film was somewhat shorter than these, having stabilized at around 1000–1500 meters by 1914.) Less concerned with continuity and plot probability, the Italian costume features nevertheless excelled at special effects, sumptuous sets, and intricate crowd choreography.

A second specialty of the Italian feature that began just before World War I, the *diva* films, featured strong performances by female actors such as Lyda **Borelli** and Francesca **Bertini**. The first of these was Borelli's debut film, *Ma l'amor mio non muore!* [But my love does not die!] (2,600 meters), from 1913. Taken together, the *diva* films suggest an important connection, as with the Asta Nielsen films in Demark and Germany, between the rise of the feature film and the development of a **star system** within the film industries of Europe. Just as the feature film allowed exhibition to be organized around a single title, the emergence of a star system allowed titles to be attached to a specific performer's name.

The consequences of the feature film's emergence in Europe before the war were far-reaching. The particulars were different in each country, but in general the feature played a prominent role in the systematization of the cinema industry. With the rise of the feature format, the value of the single film title increased along with its financial risk. The consolidation of production capital necessary for the longer films put pressure on smaller companies, many of which went under financially or were bought up by the larger ones.

Figure 82 Frame enlargement of Asta Nielsen and Poul Reumert in the "Gaucho Dance" scene from *Afgrunden* [The Abyss] (Nordisk, 1910). (Courtesy of the Danish Film Museum.)

Exhibitors betting on a single title instead of many shorter ones likewise sought the protection of the monopoly rental system and introduced new **palace cinemas** that could accommodate more customers at once in the longer screenings. A resulting rise in ticket prices also changed the demographics of the cinema audience, tilting it more heavily toward the middle class. Film genres that had thrived in the variety exhibition format, such as *actualités* and **comedies** (which did not play a significant role in the development of the European feature film), now faced pressure from the newly overcrowded cinema programs, and in some countries (such as Germany and Denmark) fell off in production. Finally, film criticism emerged as a dedicated journalistic endeavor in the wake of feature titles and their extended runs in the cinemas, adding to the predictability of the

cinematic product. In short, by the start of World War I, many of our current assumptions about the feature film format were already in place.

See also: audiences: surveys and debates; *autorenfilme*; film distribution: Europe; theater, legitimate; melodrama, sensational; multiple-reel/feature films: USA; program formats; spectatorship: issues and debates; trade press

Further reading

Abel, Richard (1994) *The Ciné Goes to Town: French Cinema, 1896–1914*, Berkeley: University of California Press.

Bernardini, Aldo and Jean A. Gili (1986) *Le cinema italien: De La Prise de Rome (1905) à Rome ville ouverte* (1945), Paris: Centre Georges Pompidou.

Engberg, Marguerite (1977) *Dansk Stumfilm—De Store År*, Copenhagen: Rhodos.

Müller, Corinna (1994) *Frühe Deutsche Kinematographie: Formale, wirtschaftliche und kulturelle Entwicklungen*, Stuttgart: Verlag J.B. Metzler.

Sandberg, Mark B. (2001) "Pocket Movies: Souvenir Cinema Programmes and the Danish Silent Cinema," *Film History*, 13.1: 6–22.

MARK B. SANDBERG

multiple-reel/feature films: USA

Distribution in the American cinema in the 1910s was dominated by a small number of cartels—by 1912, there were four, **General Film**, **Mutual**, **Universal**, and Film Supply—which required the theaters they supplied to rent film from one distributor exclusively, in exchange for the guarantee of a rapidly changing program of high-quality films. They supplied this program by contracting with producers, also on an exclusive basis. The demand for product was high because novelty was the only premium a film could command, so moving picture theaters needed ever more new films, and the program often changed daily or every other day. The system was built around the constant module of the 1,000-foot reel. In 1909, most films were shorter than this, so producers supplied "split reels," two films making up the 1,000-foot unit. By 1912, most films were a single reel, within a few feet of the modular length.

As early as 1909, films of more than one reel were introduced into the program, by dividing them into reel-long units and issuing each on a different day. Late in 1909, **Vitagraph** issued its four-reel *Les Misérables* and its five-reel *Life of Moses* over several weeks. In June 1910, the company offered its *Uncle Tom's Cabin* on three consecutive days; in November 1911, it released its first two-reel film on a single day, *Auld Lang Syne*, and a month later a three-reel film on a single day, *Vanity Fair*. Most of the other quality producers began to issue two- and three-reel pictures on a single day by 1912 (either by adding to the footage in their regular weekly schedule, or by dropping

one or two of their regular one-reel slots); films up to 1,000 meters from European producers were handled in the same way.

By 1912, most theaters had multiple projectors and could therefore screen multiple reels continuously, but by no means all did so. In general, they treated multiple-reel films as they treated the multiple reels of the program of one-reel films they regularly showed, whether with or without a shorter or longer break between the reels. Multiple-reel films issued over several days were naturally enough divided into parts that would stand on their own, since all patrons would not necessarily be able to attend all the sessions; the same structure usually characterized the simultaneously released multiple-reel films as well, both because some theatres did not screen continuously and because this became a standard principle of scenario construction, recommended in script-writing manuals until the late 1910s.

This system had no place for films longer than three reels, the films that later came to be called "feature films" (the standard program was usually only an hour or so, i.e., four reels), but the entertainment industry had a ready-made alternative in the state-rights system, in which exclusive rights to an act were granted to a regional franchise holder, who would then book it into theaters in his or her territory, guaranteeing the theater owner exclusive exhibition for a negotiable period, thus allowing long runs and a run-up period for an **advertising** campaign. The much longer films being made in Europe from 1910 on were imported into the USA and exhibited in this state-rights market: a famous example being the 1912 Anglo-French four-reel production *Queen Elizabeth* which provided Adolph **Zukor** with his entrée to film distribution. Many of these films were very successful, both commercially and in prestige terms, so American producers soon began to make their own. Most of these came from new companies, e.g., Helen Gardner Picture Plays, built round the husband-and-wife team of Helen **Gardner** and Charles Gaskill, which released its first film, *Cleopatra*, in six reels, in late 1912. Most of the established production companies were too hard pressed supplying the short-film market to venture into features, and open moves in this direction by those with the capacity to do so were inhibited by the threat this represented to the cartels they depended on. However, Gardner and Gaskill were contracted to Vitagraph both before and after their experiment with features, and it may well be that Vitagraph supported if it did not initiate Helen Gardner Picture Plays. Moreover, in 1913, **IMP** made Universal's first feature, the six-reel *Traffic in Souls*, supposedly without the knowledge of its president, Carl **Laemmle**.

Although the state-rights system could be very profitable for an importer or producer film by film, it provided too uncertain a cash flow for the continuous production of long and expensive films (feature films were usually four or more times as expensive per foot as regularly produced one-reelers). William **Hodkinson** saw early that it was necessary to establish for features the equivalent of the distribution cartels dominating the short-film industry, and in 1914 he founded Paramount Pictures as a national distributor offering a full annual program of features to theaters that

committed themselves to Paramount's offerings, and contracted with producers, notably Zukor's **Famous Players** and Jesse L. **Lasky** Feature Plays to supply the films. Other, similar distributors of a program of features soon followed, notably **World** (soon backed by the Shubert theatrical empire), Box Office Attractions (founded by William **Fox**), VLSE (see Vitagraph), and Triangle.

Some of the feature-length multiple reel films held to the principle of organizing their narratives into four or more reel-length units—World's *Uncle Tom's Cabin* (1914) and most of the features directed for the company by Maurice **Tourneur** would be examples. Yet some writers and directors seem to have set themselves deliberately against this practice, making features with few pauses in their stories, and those not at the reel end, most notably Walter Macnamara and George Loane Tucker in *Traffic in Souls*.

See also: multiple-reel/feature films: Europe; program formats

Further reading

Bowser, Eileen (1990) *The Transformation of Cinema 1907–1915*, New York: Scribner's.

Brewster, Ben (Fall 1991) "*Traffic in Souls*: An Experiment in Feature-Length Narrative Construction," *Cinema Journal*, 31.1: 37–56.

Gevinson, Alan (1988) "The Birth of the American Feature Film," in Paolo Cherchi Usai and Lorenzo Codelli (eds.) *The Path to Hollywood, 1911–1920*, 132–154, Pordenone: Edizioni Biblioteca dell'Immagine.

Quinn, Michael (2001) "Distribution, the Transient Audience and the Transition to the Feature Film," *Cinema Journal*, 40.2: 35–56.

BEN BREWSTER

Figure 83 Poster for *Traffic in Souls* (Universal, 1913).

Munsterberg, Hugo

b. 1863, Germany; d. 1916, USA

psychologist, USA

A German émigré, Munsterberg was a prominent psychologist (Harvard University) who often popularized his ideas in leading **illustrated magazines** such as *Munsey's*. His *The Photoplay: A Psychological Study* (1916) was arguably the first major work of film theory. Anticipating later classical formalist currents, he affirmed film's legitimacy and independence as a fine art by stressing the unique ways in which cinematic devices transform the world recorded on film. He was particularly interested, however, in exploring a film/mind analogy, highlighting correspondences between cinematic processes like flashbacks and close-ups and mental processes like memory and attention. With this conception of film as an objectification of the inner workings of the mind, Munsterberg situated cinema within the prevailing framework of idealist aesthetics derived from Kant and Schopenhauer. Cinema, he argued, could be built on the same foundation as all genuine art—namely, harmonious isolation from practical interests, connections, and strivings of the will.

Further reading

Langdale, Allan (ed.) (2002) *Hugo Munsterberg on Film—The Photoplay: A Psychological Study and Other Writings*, New York: Routledge.

BEN SINGER

Murdock, J(ohn) J.

b. *c.* 1860; d. 1948

vaudeville manager, executive, USA

A "power behind the throne" of the **Keith vaudeville** oligopoly, Murdock managed Chicago's Masonic Temple Roof in the late 1890s and led the Western Vaudeville Managers' Association. In 1909, Murdock formed the International Projecting and Producing Company (IPPC) to organize independent film distributors challenging the **Motion Picture Patents Company**. Although the IPPC failed, Murdock successfully lobbied Congress to lower tariffs on imported film. In 1911, Murdock became general manager of the Kinemacolor Company of America, and in 1912 managing director of the American Talking Picture Company formed to release **Edison**'s **Kinetophone** films. In 1927, Murdock engineered the

merger of the Keith theaters with Pathé-Exchange and Producers Distributing Corporation, then served as the new company's president until his retirement in 1929.

ALAN GEVINSON

museum life exhibits

Museum life exhibits were the offspring of 19th-century entertainment and display forms that sought to re-create scenes from life through the blending of two-dimensional and three-dimensional elements. Heavily influenced by the *trompe l'oeil* effects of the Daguerrean **diorama**, in which semi-transparent illusionist **paintings** were subjected to dramatic **lighting** effects, creating the illusion of movement and times of day, and by early 19th-century circular panoramas which often integrated props and scenic elements into the foreground of flat painted backgrounds, museum groups sought to give spectators the sensation that they were looking out through a window onto a scene from nature. But museum life exhibits also were indebted to other 19th-century amusements, including theatrical tableaux (where actors froze the dramatic action in poses encapsulating or heightening a narrative situation), *tableaux vivants* or "living picture" parlor games (where individuals struck poses imitating dramatic scenes from painting or literature), and Madame Tussaud's **wax museum**.

American artist and museum curator Charles Willson Peale was among the first to paint artificial backgrounds for his zoological specimens in the 1780s, thus creating a prototype for the enormously popular habitat group (a group illustrating the fauna and flora of a particular geographical region) that would become a fixture in late 19th-century museums of natural history. Unlike museum life groups (which contained wax, papier mache, or, more commonly, plaster cast mannequins of indigenous peoples in their native surroundings), habitat groups dramatically illustrated scenes from nature, sometimes synthesizing large numbers of species in a single exhibit in order to illustrate the range of mammals that could be found on a single continent.

As examples of popularized modes of representing scientific knowledge that had first appeared at the Crystal Palace Exposition in 1851, museum life exhibits groups can be seen as attempts by curators to modernize and popularize museums, to make science and natural history more accessible to popular audiences through visual spectacle. Symptomatic of how the visual rhetoric of **advertising**—eye-catching displays and easily assimilable visual messages—inflected museum design, museum life exhibits offer evidence of how new modes of visual consumption associated with **world's fairs**, **department stores**, and popular amusements left their mark on museum exhibition. Situated as the central attraction in a gallery, the feature that would instantly catch the wandering gaze of the museum-goer, life exhibits also were designed to serve a loftier pedagogical goal, by encouraging visitors to closely examine related objects in glass cases once they had finished looking at the life exhibit. However, the extent to which museum life exhibits were successful in eliciting a more intellectual response to the objects on display in glass cases (or even encouraging museum-goers to walk over to the glass cases) was uncertain; instead, the groups may have functioned as beacons for tired, aimless spectators, luring them from one gallery to another.

Museum life exhibits shared a number of phenomenological qualities with early **ethnographic films** as a result of their rectangular frames, dramatic lighting, and heightened verisimilitude. Moving from group to group, spectators may have experienced scenes representing native peoples in similar ways to such films, which staged equally emblematic moments of indigenous life, such as basket-making, pottery-making, or food preparation for the camera. Retaining to this day a strong proto-cinematic feel, museum life exhibits continue to be enormously popular with visitors, especially children; blending illusionist artistry with scientific accuracy, museum life exhibits straddle high and low culture and remain fascinating legacies of 19th-century visuality.

See also: education; expedition/exploration films; scientific films; travelogues

Further reading

Griffiths, Alison (2002) *Wondrous Difference: Cinema, Anthropology, and Turn-of-the-Century Visual Culture*, New York: Columbia University Press.

Wonders, Karen (1993) *Habitat Dioramas: Illusion of Wilderness in Museums of Natural History*, Uppsala: Acta Universitatis Upsaliensis, Figura Nova Series 24.

ALISON GRIFFITHS

music hall

The introduction of moving pictures coincided with the industrialization of music hall. Originating in Britain as a tavern-based, comedy-oriented entertainment in the 1840s, music hall remained loosely organized and modestly presented until the 1890s, when a number of large syndicates established chains of new theaters throughout Europe. Variety acts were provided with long-term bookings for music hall circuits, their travel aided by an extensive railway network. As the exchange of performers across Europe proliferated, the increasing size of theatrical buildings strengthened the demand for visually-oriented, spectacular shows. When, during the period of 1895–1897, moving pictures were first exhibited in Berlin at the Wintergarten and Apollo; in London at the Empire, Alhambra, and Palace; and in Paris at the Olympia, Eldorado, and Casino de Paris, they joined ballets, animal acts, and elaborate sketches as components of lengthy variety programs. Until the construction of the first permanent cinemas, music halls provided a ready-made distribution service for moving pictures of all kinds. Music hall performers, keen at first to exploit the new medium in a theatrical context, became filmmakers and actors, some eventually founding their own production companies.

Music hall **audiences** varied widely across Europe. Generally, however, sophisticated metropolitan halls were aimed at a predominantly male clientele, while women and children were more likely to attend **fairs/fairgrounds** and the smaller theaters in poorer and suburban areas. By 1904, two gigantic London halls, the Hippodrome and Coliseum, had broken new ground by providing carefully vetted entertainment for middle-class, family audiences. Requiring multiple **projectors** and a continuous supply of subjects, music hall syndicates began to promote the films of major manufacturers such as **Lumière**, R. W. **Paul**, and the **American Mutoscope and Biograph Company**, leaving smaller halls to **itinerant exhibitors**. Music hall audiences were often volatile and voluble: in 1899, coverage of the Dreyfus court martial caused anti-French demonstrations in Britain, while films taken during the Boer War of 1899–1902 resulted in condemnation of Britain when shown in continental theatres. Selections of films initially were presented as one element of the music hall program, their variety resembling the mixture of acts around them. From the time of the earliest exhibitions attempts were made to bring an element of collective significance to the moving pictures shown, with complimentary or juxtaposing subjects grouped together. The constrictions of the music hall program discouraged the making of longer films, although multi-scene fiction films, particularly those of Georges **Méliès**, were exhibited by the early 1900s.

Many of the earliest moving pictures were transcriptions of music hall acts. **Edison**'s use of variety performers as **Kinetoscope** subjects from 1894 on was followed by Paul and Birt **Acres** in their counterfeit Kinetoscope of 1895 and by the **Skladanowsky** Bioscop at the Wintergarten during the same year. Although Paul accepted the advice of the Alhambra's manager by producing a made-up scene, *The Soldier's Courtship*, in April 1896, many of his early films depicted performers in abbreviated versions of their already well-known stage acts. Familiarity with the on-screen performers proved popular with audiences, and for the artists themselves the films acted as valuable **publicity**. In France, Félicien Trewey, one of the most popular European variety entertainers, appeared in Lumière films, before introducing the **Cinématographe Lumière** into Britain in 1896. The veteran French performer Paulus commissioned Méliès to make films of his act which were exhibited at the Ba-ta-clan Theatre, Paris, in 1897. The following year the Italian quick-change artist Leopoldo **Fregoli** renamed a Lumière Cinématographe the Fregoligraph, integrating films of himself into his stage act. Britain's leading music hall comedian Dan Leno

appeared in several films, as did the internationally famous Little Tich (Harry **Relph**), but neither had the opportunity to develop a distinct screen personality. In continental Europe stage comedians increasingly began to appear in **comic series** of films. **Dranem** was already a major **star** when he first appeared for **Pathé-Frères** in 1901, but other performers enjoyed more modest careers before becoming well known and popular, if only by nickname, on screen. Ferdinando **Guillaume** and Enesto Vaser from Italy; Marcel **Fabre** from Spain/Italy; and Charles **Prince** and André **Deed** from France had all been variety performers before appearing in moving pictures.

Given the brevity of early moving pictures, an easily recognized context helped amplify simple narratives. The Brighton pioneer George Albert **Smith**'s productions of 1897–1903 were guided and informed by the collective expertise of his wife Laura Bayley, an accomplished stage comedienne, and two popular local comedians, John Danby Hunter and Tom Green. Similarly, James **Williamson**'s films used the talents of M. D. Phillippe, an international mime artist and two music hall performers Sam Dalton and Dave Aylott. Many filmmakers drew on their background in various forms of variety entertainment, notably Ferdinand **Zecca** and Roméo **Bosetti** for Pathé; William **Haggar** and Alf **Collins**, whose films were issued by **British Gaumont**; and Lewin **Fitzhamon,** for **Hepworth**. Visually, moving pictures borrowed heavily from music hall and pantomime. The knockabout skills developed in Fred Karno's mime troupes were much in demand, and several Karno comedians appeared in moving pictures before Charles **Chaplin** and Stan Laurel achieved international fame. Chases, funny walks and falls, the standardized comic **costume** of Chaplin and other screen performers all derived to a large extent from a music hall background.

As the moving picture industry developed, music hall performers sought to gain autonomy from the syndicates who controlled their industry. In 1912, a group of British music hall performers belonging to a self-help association, the "J's", financed the Ec-Ko film company, employing Fred **Evans** (1889–1951) as director and comedian. Evans had toured European music halls with his family troupe in the 1890s and 1900s. As the clown-like Pimple he appeared in over a hundred films, many reflecting his music hall background in the use of jokey **intertitles**, the burlesquing of contemporary events, and a slapstick approach to comedy. Other companies founded by music hall performers were Sunny South (1914), created to exploit the popularity of Fred's uncle Will Evans, and Homeland (1915), which produced several ambitious two- and three-reel comedies starring Billy Merson.

Music hall had fostered and informed moving pictures, but increasingly its impersonality and restrictive practices caused both audiences and performers to transfer their allegiance to cinema.

See also: cafés-concerts; chase films; comedies; *féeries*/fairy plays; trick films; vaudeville

BARRY ANTHONY

musical accompaniment

It is useful to recognize four distinct practices and periods of silent film accompaniment, if one focuses primarily on the USA.

(1) Although inaugural celebrations of moving picture projection present a special case, during cinema's first decade the process of accompanying a film was most often assimilated to the theatrical pit orchestra tradition of furnishing the sounds implied by on-stage action. At the time, this was called "cue music," meaning music provided in response to a visible cue. Nineteenth-century stage versions of *Uncle Tom's Cabin* and *The Great Train Robbery* had required musical accompaniment for songs and dances, and a stage melodrama like *Monte Cristo* called on the orchestra to provide a waltz for a society ball and a march to synchronize soldiers' on-stage steps. Contemporary film catalogues recommended a similar accompaniment logic for films: "Music can be very appropriately and effectively rendered simultaneously with the exhibition of many Vitascope subjects. All subjects made up of dancing, marching, or other acts and scenes where musical selections in time with the movement are in place, can be made more interesting and remarkable by the addition of music." (March 1896 Vitascope catalogue) **Phonograph** catalogues proposed a similar practice: "By the use of the [Graphophone Grand], in connection with the Cineograph, musical records, harmonized to the films of dancers or of marching, can be reproduced so that the audience may see the dancing or the marching and hear the music to the steps at the same time." (1899 Prescott catalogue) Many early films—including those emulating **illustrated song** slides—were thus sprinkled with visible music cues. Because source music was normally required in specified situations only, early film accompaniment was usually discontinuous.

(2) The first half of the nickelodeon period (1905–1910) was characterized by intermittent accompaniment, with regular juxtaposition of radically divergent practices. Music was often employed as ballyhoo, to attract passersby. Mechanical pianos were thus often placed at the rear of the projection space or in the entryway; alternately, a phonograph might be placed in the projection booth, directed toward the street. Whether outside or inside, an automatic piano would sometimes continue to play during the screening. Since nickelodeons regularly featured illustrated songs, the film portion of the program would often be screened in silence, while fans were turned on and the pianist or orchestra rested. Recalling earlier practice, films would at times be accompanied by source music only. More often, the choice would fall on popular tunes; sometimes randomly chosen, with no attempt to match the film, these were frequently tied to on-screen action by title or lyrics. A departure scene might thus be accompanied by the popular song, "I'm Going Away"; party preparation, by "It Looks Like a Big Night To-night"; or **Vitagraph**'s *Chew Chew Land* (1910), by "Oh You Spearmint Kiddo, With the Wriggley Eyes." Only occasionally during this period was accompaniment music chosen according to a logic that would later become familiar—for its emotional match to a particular film character or event. Around 1907–1908, the development of musical accompaniment was interrupted by several short-lived experiments popular for a season or two: synchronized sound films, "talking pictures" with live voices behind the screen providing dialogue,

and informal lectures explaining on-screen action. There was also at this time an upsurge of sound effects, often provided by the "trap" drummer, named after the theatrical term for visual and **sound effects**.

(3) At the start of the new decade (1910–1915), several loosely coordinated efforts sought to improve and standardize film accompaniment. While sound practices continued to exhibit substantial variety, they benefited from the new prestige associated with cinema. Whereas earlier theaters often treated film as just another **vaudeville** act, as filler between illustrated songs, or as one among several novelties, moving pictures progressively took over the program. A new approach to accompaniment coincided with this enhanced status. Columns by Clyde Martin (*Film Index*), Clarence E. Sinn (*Moving Picture World*), and Ernst J. Luz (*Moving Picture News*) regularly argued for continuous piano or orchestral accompaniment, using appropriate musical selections chosen during a preliminary viewing of the film. During this period, previously favored popular music increasingly was shunted toward comic situations, while light classical music now was preferred for dramatic films. Musical suggestions appeared with increasing regularity in the **trade press**. Interest in offering special music with prestige film releases at times led to original compositions destined for film accompaniment. Several manufacturers even sponsored piano accompaniment demonstration tours. Thanks to the success of the first **musical scores** and music compilations categorized according to appropriate film applications, the music publishing industry began to recognize cinema as a potential source of income. Organs were installed in many theaters, and there was a substantial increase in the number and size of orchestras accompanying films. Though standardization was not yet achieved, the ideal of carefully selected, artistically played, continuous musical accompaniment was clearly established.

(4) Thanks to the film's notoriety, national visibility, and phenomenal success, Joseph Carl Breil's score for D. W. **Griffith**'s *The Birth of a Nation* (1915) achieved an extraordinary level of popularity and prestige, helping to enforce accompaniment standards built around careful selection and quality execution. For over a decade, the

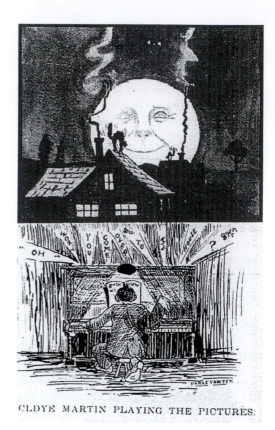

Figure 84 Clyde Martin Plays the Pictures, *Film Index*, 27 June 1911.

Figure 85 "A rare moment of silence from an effects set-up and the pianist too," from "Jackass Music," *Moving Picture World*, 1911.

standards proposed in the 1910–1915 period and stabilized during the mid-1910s thus continued to reign. Continuous accompaniment was the rule, with a strong preference for emotionally motivated light classical instrumental music (avoiding the title orientation associated with popular songs). Sound effects were produced by the orchestra rather than by specialized effects personnel as in the theater, and as a rule reserved for comedy or narratively important special cases. Influential manuals by Edith Lang and George West (1920) and George W. Beynon (1921) reinforced the desirability of smooth transitions, careful modulations, and thematic development. Indexed compilations of existing compositions, such as Erno Rapée's 1924 *Motion Picture Moods*, helped to propagate and standardize these practices. During the twenties, the popular Wagnerian leitmotif technique progressively slid toward the use of full songs as themes.

See also: dialogue accompaniment

Further reading

Abel, Richard and Altman, Rick (2001) (eds.) *The Sounds of Early Cinema*, Bloomington: Indiana University Press.

Altman, Rick (1996) "The Silence of the Silents," *Musical Quarterly*, 80. 4: 648–718.

Marks, Martin M. (1997) *Music and Silent Film*, New York: Oxford University Press.

RICK ALTMAN

musical scores

It is useful to distinguish among three types of film score: collections of short original pieces to be used by musicians as needed, compilation scores, and original scores.

During the late 19th century, music publishers commissioned hundreds of short pieces. Destined for theatrical use, these were sold in sets and identified by tempo (andante, agitato tremolo, hurry), dance type (waltz, two-step, jig), or appropriate application (farewell, battle, melancholy). Similar compositions were eventually published for film accompanists: Gregg A. Frelinger's 1909 *Motion Picture Piano Music*, Clarence E. Sinn's 1910

Orpheum Collection of Moving Picture Music, the anonymous 1910 *Emerson Moving Picture Music Folio*, Eugene Platzman's 1911 *F. B. Haviland's Moving Picture Pianist's Album*, and J. S. Zamecnik's 1913 *Sam Fox Moving Picture Music*. By 1914, Carl Fischer alone offered three such collections: *Carl Fischer Moving Picture Folio*, *Carl Fischer Loose Leaf Motion Picture Collection for Orchestra*, *Carl Fischer Dramatic Music*. In Europe, the several volumes of Giuseppe **Becce**'s 1919 *Kinothek. Neue Filmmusik von Giuseppe Becce* served a similar function.

The written record of compilation scores—fully written-out scores combining existing and original music—does not begin until after 1910. The success of special arrangements for such prestige films as **Pathé-Frères**'s *Il Trovatore* (1911) spurred the development of scores at least partially based on existing material. The most important American compilation score composer was Joseph Carl Breil, whose leitmotif-oriented scores for *Queen Elizabeth* (1912) and *Cabiria* (1913) paved the way for his immensely influential score for *The Birth of a Nation* (1915). Incorporating selections drawn from contemporary popular music, traditional folk music, and classics from Beethoven to Weber, Breil's score received full orchestral rendering in upscale road shows. It influenced future film accompaniment in two complementary manners. Along with other high profile film scores of the mid-1910s, the music for *The Birth of a Nation* demonstrated the usefulness of providing either a full score or a list of carefully chosen music selections for every feature film released. Additionally, the popularity of a portion of Breil's score as a popular song ("The Perfect Song") led to increased interest in building theme songs into silent scores, thus cementing the symbiotic relationship tying music publishers to the film industry.

Original music for film accompaniment was improvised by pianists from the earliest days of cinema. Fully developed orchestral scores were introduced in the USA only in the 1910s (earlier European scores such as Saint-Saëns' 1908 music for *L'Assassinat du Duc de Guise* were not used for American projections). From 1911 to 1913, Walter Cleveland Simon composed scores for *The Confederate Ironclad* (1912), *From the Manger to the Cross* (1913), and over a dozen other **Kalem** films. Between 1912 and 1914, Modeste Altschuler wrote music for several films, including *Pilgrim's Progress* and *Spartacus*. George **Kleine** sponsored a 1913 score by Palmer Clark for *The Last Days of Pompeii*. The success of Breil's compilation score for *The Birth of a Nation* rapidly led to original scores commissioned for other mid-1910s super-productions such as *Civilization* (Victor L. Schertzinger) and *The Fall of a Nation* (Victor Herbert). From then on, prestige production became synonymous with original score. Many of the most important films of the 1920s were projected to orchestral scores by William Axt, David Mendoza, Victor Schertzinger, or Mortimer Wilson. Others had music composed by the musical director for the studio's most prestigious theater, including Erno Rapée and Hugo Riesenfeld. As compared to Europe, where film scores were regularly written by "serious" composers (Paul Hindemith, Arthur Honegger, Darius Milhaud, Camille Saint-Saëns, Erik Satie, Dmitri Shostakovich), American film scores repeatedly arose from the world of music publishing or film exhibition.

See also: musical accompaniment

Further reading

Marks, Martin M. (1997) *Music and Silent Film*, New York: Oxford University Press.

RICK ALTMAN

Musidora (Jeanne Roques)

b. 1889; d. 1957

actor, writer, filmmaker, France

Musidora won fame with two parts: the female cat-burglar Irma Vep in Louis **Feuillade**'s **crime film**, *Les Vampires* [The Vampires] (1915–1916), and the equally deceptive Diana Monti in the crime **serial**, *Judex* (1917). During Musidora's affiliation with **Gaumont** between 1914 and 1917, Feuillade also employed her versatile and candid acting style in fifteen popular farces featuring Marcel **Levesque**. Previous to and parallel with her work in cinema, Musidora was a successful comic stage performer. By 1920, she would write and direct four films for her own company, Musidora Film.

ANNETTE FÖRSTER

Mutual Film Corporation

In July 1906, in Milwaukee, John Freuler and Harry **Aitken** opened the Western Film Exchange, a distributor dealing primarily with theaters in the Midwest. Western Film had moderate success until the formation of the **Motion Picture Patents Company** in 1908, as the MPPC's licensing rules limited its ability to acquire films from producers. To combat the MPPC's interference, Aitken and Freuler moved into production, starting the **American Film Manufacturing Company** in 1910, and the **Majestic Motion Picture Company** in 1911. Majestic was notable for its acting talent, which initially included Mary **Pickford** and Owen **Moore**, and, eventually, Gloria Swanson, Douglas Fairbanks, and Mabel **Normand**.

American and Majestic distributed through the **Motion Picture Sales and Distributing Company**, one of the first and largest competitors to the **General Film Company** (the MPPC's distribution arm). Founded in April 1910, by Carl **Laemmle**, Adam **Kessel**, and Charles **Baumann**, the Sales Company aimed to control independent (non-MPPC) distribution in the USA. When Majestic joined the Sales Company in 1911, it was charged a greater distribution percentage than its founding producers, **IMP** and the **New York Motion Picture Company** (NYMPC). Shortly after the fee increase, Freuler and Aitken left Sales, forming the Mutual Film Corporation in March 1912.

One of the first motion picture firms to receive significant Wall Street investment, Mutual was capitalized at $2.5 million dollars; by comparison, Paramount Pictures Corporation was capitalized at a mere $100,000 in 1914. This led to much of Mutual's early success, enabling the firm to steal a number of producers away from the Sales Company, including American, **Reliance**, and **Thanhouser**. Along with Majestic, these companies immediately placed Mutual as one of the top distributors of short films in the USA. Most of the other Sales members then reorganized into the **Universal Film Manufacturing Company** in June 1912.

Although very successful in distributing weekly short film programs, by 1914 Mutual included two of the most important **multiple-reel/feature film** producers in the USA: NYMPC, the home of Thomas **Ince**, and D. W. **Griffith** Films. In the

1913–1914 season, Mutual would release several major early features, including Ince's *The Battle of Gettysburg* (June 1913) and Griffith's *The Avenging Conscience* (August 1914).

Aitken would leave Mutual in 1915 to form Triangle, taking with him Ince and Griffith. Aitken and Griffith abandoned the distributor because of its refusal to finance the latter's *Birth of a Nation*. Aitken was forced to cover much of Mutual's initial investment in the film, while Griffith risked bankruptcy over the remaining financing.

Mutual would quickly return to its roots as a short-film distributor, which was cemented by signing Charlie **Chaplin** in 1916. Some of Chaplin's most famous shorts were made at Mutual, including *The Pawnshop* and *One A.M* (both 1916). Despite an offer of one million dollars to stay, Chaplin moved to First National in 1917, and Mutual's fortunes rapidly declined. Freuler resigned as president in 1918, and shortly thereafter Mutual was absorbed into the Affiliated Distributors Corporation. Mutual's films eventually became part of RKO.

MICHAEL QUINN

Muybridge, Eadweard

b. 1830, England; d. 1904, England

photographer, USA

An immigrant to the USA in 1851, Muybridge gradually became skilled at **photography**, recording Far West landscapes for exhibition as **stereographs** and panoramas. In 1872, railroad magnate Leland Stanford hired him to answer this question: could a trotting horse have all four hooves off the ground at once? After several experiments, Muybridge got a convincing result by setting up twelve cameras in a row aimed across a racetrack at a white wall (marked off with vertical numbered lines), each camera triggered by a trip wire. After sequences of these and other images

were published in scientific and photographic journals, from 1880 on, Muybridge lectured in the USA and Europe, presenting his images on a projecting phenakistiscope and influencing others such as Etienne-Jules **Marey**. In 1884–1885, using an improved apparatus, he produced more than 100,000 sequence photographs of animals and humans in a variety of activities, many of which were reproduced in *Animal Locomotion* (1887). In 1893, his motion sequences were projected in the Zoöpraxographic Hall at the Chicago **world's fair**.

RICHARD ABEL

mythologicals

Mythologicals retold popular stories and legends from the *puranas* or ancient tales collected in the great Hindu epics, *Mahabharata* and *Ramayana*. In the first decade of early Indian cinema (1913–1923), mythologicals comprised more than 70 percent of the output and included D. G. **Phalke**'s *Raja Harishchandra* (1913) and **Lanka Dahan** (1917) and the earliest films made in Calcutta and southern India. Phalke deliberately chose such subjects for two reasons: (1) to appeal to the largest Indian—and even international— audiences, and (2) reflecting his *swadeshi* orientation, to make "Indian" films about Indian gods and saints to counteract the **biblical films** then being imported. As a narrative form, mythologicals drew their inspiration from indigenous folk performances adapted to the mode of the European proscenium theater. Unlike biblical films, they did not promote any one religion; instead, they grew directly out of popular traditions in response to both nationalist and commercial impulses. The typical mythological combined cinema's photographic realism with the special effects techniques of **trick films** to narrate stories of Hindu gods, goddesses and saints with conviction and naiveté which won over a large **audience** to movie-going.

SURESH CHABRIA

N

Nalpas, Louis

b. 1884; d. 1948

distributor, producer, France

Born in the Greek community of Smyrna (Turkey), Nalpas arrived in Paris in 1909 to deal in film exports for **AGC**. In 1911, he began working for **Film d'Art** and became its director when Charles **Delac** was drafted in 1914. His most notable productions included Henri Pouctal's *Alsace* (1916) and Abel Gance's early films. After he left Film d'Art early in 1918, Nalpas settled in Nice and produced René Le Somptier's *La Sultane de l'amour* (1919) and the *Serpentin* **comic series** with Marcel **Lévesque**. Dreaming of a Hollywood on the Riviera, he built the Victorine studios in 1919, with the financial backing of Serge **Sandberg**. Nalpas is best known, however, as head of **serials** production at Cinéromans during the 1920s.

THIERRY LEFEBVRE

Napierkowska, Stacia

b. 1886; d. 1945

dancer, actor, France, Italy

Originally trained as a dancer, Napierkowska (Rene Claire Angele Napierkowski) performed at various Parisian **music halls**, where she was noticed by André Antoine, the Théâtre Libre director who had just fired Mata Hari (who soon entered history as a spy). Antoine hired Napierkowska for an arabesque in *Anthar*, an "orientalist" production that had an amazing success. **Mistinguett** saw her performance and got her a role in **Film d'Art**'s *L'Empreinte* [Imprint] (1908). Napierkowska's film roles tended to exploit her fame as a dancer, as in André **Capellani**'s *Notre Dame de Paris* (1911), Louis **Feuillade**'s *Les Vampires* (1915), and Germaine Dulac's *Venus Victrix* (1918). During **World War I**, however, she acted in at least twenty Italian films. Aging and overweight, her last role as Antinea in Jacques Feyder's *L'Atlantide* (1921) was far from successful.

ANGELA DALLE VACCHE

Natan, Bernard (previously Tanenzapf, Nathan, and Natan, Théodore)

b. 1886; d. 1942, Auschwitz, Poland

manufacturer, producer, France

In 1909, three years after arriving in Paris from Romania, Bernard Natan and two associates founded Ciné-Actualités, a small general partnership company involved in a variety of moving picture work. In January 1911, he was sentenced to four months in prison for an "outrage to public decency," an incident that was to serve as an excuse for a violent anti-Semitic campaign against him in the 1930s. In 1913, he set up the Rapid-Film laboratory in Paris; in 1914, he launched a **newsreel**, *Ciné-Gazette*.

A volunteer during the war, later decorated with the Military Cross, Natan saw his name cleared in late 1919 and became a French citizen in 1921. In 1924, he transformed Rapid-Film into a public limited company (société anonyme) and set up Rapid-Publicité; two years later he built Studios Réunis in conjunction with Productions Natan, the producer notably of Marco de Gastyne's *La Merveilleuse Vie de Jeanne d'Arc* [The Marvelous Life of Joan of Arc] (1929). By 1929, the Natan group had merged with Pathé Cinéma, and Natan became the head of the new entity.

JEAN-JACQUES MEUSY

National Board of Censorship

The National Board of Censorship was the chief self-regulatory body of the US film industry in the early 1910s. Concerned about increasing governmental control over film exhibition, industry leaders agreed to submit their films to a Board of Censorship formed in March 1909 by the People's Institute, a respected Progressive organization. **Boxing films**, **white slave films**, and birth control films received particular scrutiny from the Board. But with no legal authority, the Board struggled for jurisdiction with police agencies as well as state and local censorship commissions. Changing its name to the National Board of Review in 1916, the organization ultimately turned its energies towards classifying films.

SHELLEY STAMP

Natural Color Kinematograph

Charles **Urban** established Natural Color Kinematograph in London, in March 1909, to exploit the Kinemacolor process in Great Britain. Owing to the particular nature of its **color** process, the company mostly produced *actualités*, **news films** and **travelogues**, often of a spectacular nature, such as the coronation of George V or the subsequent Delhi Durbar ceremonies in India. Fiction film production, with F. Martin Thornton and Theo Bouwmeester as directors, was hampered by the difficulties of using Kinemacolor in a studio,

but still more by poor filmmaking. The company went into voluntary liquidation in 1914, following a court case which invalidated the Kinemacolor patent, and its business for a short while was taken over by another Urban company, Colorfilms.

LUKE McKERNAN

Navarre, René

b. 1883, Paris; d. 1968, Paris

actor, producer, France

René Navarre became famous for his starring role in Louis **Feuillade**'s **crime film**, *Fantômas* (1913). He started his acting career with **Gaumont** in 1910, where his collaboration with Feuillade soon earned him an annual contract. After accompanying Feuillade to Spain in August 1914, Navarre left Gaumont to found his own production company in 1916. In October 1919, he created the Société des Ciné-Romans, in partnership with Serge **Sandberg** and Jean Sapène, to produce a regular schedule of **serials**. A popular actor in the 1910s, Navarre embodied a successful instance of the career change from actor and **star** to film producer.

FRANÇOIS DE LA BRETÈQUE

Negroni, Baldassarre

b. 1877; d. 1945

director, Italy

Beginning in 1911 at **Cines** as a cameraman and scriptwriter, Negroni soon developed into an important and imaginative director at Celio Film. To enforce a perfect sound synchronism during exhibition, he shot the French pantomime, *Histoire d'un Pierrot* [Pierrot the Prodigal] (1914), starring Francesca **Bertini** and Emilio **Ghione**, at the rhythm of the accompanying music. While at **Milano Films** between 1914 and 1915, Negroni completed a dozen films, mostly aristocratic love melodramas and adventure stories, featuring the diva Hesperia, his soon-to-be wife. She later followed him to Tiber Films (1915–1921).

GIORGIO BERTELLINI

Nepoti, Alberto

b. 1876; d. 1937

actor, director, Italy

Nepoti began his acting career in 1909 at **Film d'Arte Italiana**, working with Gerolamo **Lo Savio** and Ugo **Falena**. At Savoia Film in 1912, and under the direction of Nino **Oxilia**, he starred with Maria **Jacobini** in *Il cadavere vivente* [The Living Cadaver] (1913) and *Il focolare domestico* [Family Life] (1914). At Savoia he also co-directed *Satanella* [Mephisto-phelia] (1913), with Ubaldo Maria **Del Colle**. Typecast as the "rival lover," he achieved celebrity through such aristocratic melodramas as Giovanni **Pastrone**'s *Tigre Reale* [Royal Tigress] (1916) and *La Trilogia di Dorina* [Dorina] (1917), both starring diva Pina **Menichelli**.

GIORGIO BERTELLINI

Netherlands, the

Soon after 1896, when Dutch audiences first encountered them, moving pictures became a regular variety act in **music hall** programs and the principal attraction of **itinerant exhibitors** in the **fairs/fairgrounds**. Permanent theaters appeared in city centers beginning in 1907, the same year **Pathé-Frères** transformed the market by shifting from selling to renting films. Exhibition and distribution dominated Dutch film activity from the start. Film production remained a gentleman's hobby and did not become a widespread profession as in France, Denmark, Italy, or Germany.

The early years

Although **Edison Kinetoscopes** had been exhibited in several Dutch locations as early as 1894, the first public showing of moving pictures was given by a Belgium representative of the **Lumière** company, Camille Cerf, with a **Cinématographe** operated by Francis **Doublier,** on 12 March, 1896, in Amsterdam's most important shopping street, the Kalverstraat. This program contained the same Lumière films as in many other European cities; lacking the appropriate license, however, Cerf

showed them without **musical accompaniment**. After six weeks in Amsterdam, he organized film screenings during the summer season at the luxurious Kurhaus beach hotel at Scheveningen. In 1896, the **Skladanowsky** brothers from Germany and Robert **Paul** from England toured the Netherlands with their apparatuses, showing their programs in music halls. Madame Olinka also gave shows at the Amsterdam Flora Theater, using the Kinematograph projector of **Försterling** & Co. The following year, Oskar **Messter** would give shows at the Flora. In 1896, the first Dutch itinerant exhibitor, George Christiaan **Slieker**, toured the fairgrounds with his "Grand Théâtre Edison."

Film production began in the usual contexts of fairgrounds and music halls or variety theaters. The first films included self-made *actualités* such as those recording events related to the Royal Family or the visits of Paul Kruger, **re-enactments** such as those on the Boer War, and a handful of short **comedies**. In December 1898, a Dutch branch of the **American Mutoscope and Biograph** (AM&B), the Nederlandsche Biograaf & Mutoscope Maatschappij (**Dutch Mutoscope & Biograph**), was founded, focusing on exhibition and distribution but occasionally producing *actualités* and inserts for stage revues. Franz Anton **Nöggerath** Sr., owner of the Amsterdam Flora theater, was the first theater owner to take up film production, distribution and exhibition in 1897. At the Flora, his films had a fixed position as a closing act, before the final musical number played by the orchestra. **Program** conventions ruling in variety theaters are likely to be responsible for this positioning as a follow up to the *tableaux vivants* numbers depicting current *fait divers* and historical events copied from **paintings**. Newspapers wrote in astonishment that the "Kinomatograaf" was able to attract an audience for years, while other popular acts constantly were replaced.

The fairground years

From 1902 to 1907, the films circulating in the Netherlands were largely those of Pathé-Frères, especially on the fairgrounds. In December 1905, Pathé established an agency in Amsterdam that sold, and later rented, programs of its films directly to exhibitors. From 1911 on, after opening the first

Pathé cinema in Amsterdam, the company filmed local *actualités*, mostly shot by cameraman Herman van Luijnen.

Because there was no **nickelodeon** period in the Netherlands and the music halls showing films were restricted to the three major cities of Amsterdam, Rotterdam, and The Hague, the fairgrounds shaped the development of a cinema culture. The most important itinerant showmen were Willy and Albert **Mullens** (aka Alberts Frères), who called themselves "les rois du bioscope" and traveled through Belgium, France, and Germany as well as the Netherlands. They set the tone in the accommodation and style of fairground shows, with programs presented with accompanying music and lecturing by Willy Mullens. Apart from their own local productions, they rented films from Pathé and introduced these in city venues outside the fairground season, advertising their programs in king-size format in the local newspapers. From 1911 on, most of the leading Dutch fairground exhibitors such as the Mullens brothers, Alex Benner, and Jean **Desmet** shifted to constructing and managing permanent cinemas. Others switched to other fairground attractions or traveled to towns without permanent cinemas. Some, such as Carmine Riozzi and the Welte family, would even continue until the World War II.

Exhibition and distribution after 1907

The permanent theaters that first appeared in cities in 1907 included other acts as well as films on their programs. Theaters were responsible for the presentation of a particular film—with musical accompaniment by a trio or a big orchestra, with or without a **lecturer**, and with live stage acts preceding and alternating with the films. Their most important objective was to make a foreign film familiar to their Dutch audiences. Films were imported from different countries, and the distributors and exhibitors were responsible for the translation of **intertitles/titles** and intertitles and for hiring a lecturer and musicians. Translations either emphasized the exotic aspect, as often happened with the Italian diva films, or replaced foreign specificities with Dutch alternatives.

After 1908, Pathé lost its dominance as a generation of film distributors arose. Some such as

Johan **Gildemeijer** promoted certain national cinemas; others such as Franz Anton **Nöggerath** Jr. and Jean Desmet offered a wider range of films. The emergence of permanent cinemas, which boomed first in Rotterdam in 1911 and then one year later in Amsterdam, and the introduction of **multiple-reel/feature films** led to a rental system of exclusive rights that boosted independent film distribution. Around the outbreak of **World War I**, these distributors would encounter fierce competition from a new generation led by Loet C. Barnstijn, and exhibitors would fight a battle over film selection and hierarchization, with future cinema "king" Abraham Tuschinski as the winner.

Especially after the introduction of feature films and the emergence of **stars**, theater owners competed with each other in the presentation of films according to a system of differentiation that extended from first run to sixth run houses. The most important deluxe cinemas were located in the main shopping streets and entertainment areas of the big cities. In the early 1910s, the major cinemas in Amsterdam were owned by the principal distributors who thus premiered their films in their own theaters. The institution in 1916 of a weekly film exchange in Amsterdam forced cinema owners and distributors across the country to come to the city to negotiate and enforce their contracts. This would lead in 1921 to the organization of the Nederlandse Bioscoopbond (NBB), an association of distributors and cinema owners founded to protect their business and to close the market to outsiders.

Production in the 1910s

After the limited national output of the early years, film production increased in the 1910s. As Franz Anton Nöggerath Jr. developed into one of the most important Dutch distributors, he also managed to establish a modest, if short-lived, film production company. More stable was the **Hollandia** company, founded in Haarlem in 1912. Elaborating the clichéd representation of Holland introduced by Pathé's Dutch production affiliate, **Hollandsche Film**, Hollandia's director and producer Maurits **Binger** tried to lure foreign audiences with Dutch "exotic folklore." Former theater director Louis H. Chrispijn was mainly in charge of directing films with popular Dutch themes and characters. Most players at Hollandia were former theater actors, such as leading actress Annie **Bos**; the major cameraman was Feiko Boersma.

The outbreak of World War I and the diminishing of foreign imports would boost national film production as well as stimulate more popular acclaim for Dutch films. Films now exploited national subjects such as the struggle against the sea, were based on well-known plays, novels and paintings, and were intended for the home market—with the expectation that they would reach an international market after the war. All Dutch directors, from Binger and Gildemeijer to Theo **Frenkel** Sr., had high hopes for the future of the Dutch film industry once the war would be over. The domestic market was too small to cover expenses, however, and foreign investments did not return the expected profits. Moreover, the competition from abroad became too fierce.

Stylistic changes appeared: although Dutch filmmakers adopted the new norm of constructing sequences of alternating shots that varied in framing, they remained committed to an **acting style** of grand explanatory gestures, which had been abandoned in most other countries. After the war was over, the Dutch "adventure" in fiction films would fizzle out, and nonfiction production would become the industry's major focus, pioneered by Willy Mullens and Hollandia documentarist Jules Stoop.

See also: distribution: Europe

Further reading

Beusekom, Ansje van (1996) "The Rise and Fall of the Lecturer as Entertainer in the Netherlands. Cinema Exhibition Practises in Transition Related to Local Circumstances," *Iris*, 22: 131–144.

Beusekom, Ansje van (1997) "Written Images/ Spoken Words: Modified Images in Early Cinema Exhibition," *Scrittura e imagine. La didascalia nel cinema muto*, 283–293, Udine: Forum.

Blom, Ivo (1999) "Chapters from the Life of a Camera-Operator. The Recollections of Anton Nöggerath: filming news and non-fiction, 1897–1908," *Film History*, 3: 262–281.

Blom, Ivo (2003) *Jean Desmet and the Early Dutch Film Trade*, Amsterdam: Amsterdam University Press.

Dibbets, Karel, and Frank van der Maden (eds.) (1996) *Geschiedenis van de Nederlandse film en bioscoop tot 1940*, Houten: Wereldvenster.

Donaldson, Geoffrey N. (1997) *Of Joy and Sorrow. A Filmography of Dutch Silent Fiction*, Amsterdam: Stichting Nederlands Filmmuseum.

Klerk, Nico de (1999) "A Few Remaining Hours. New films and the interest in technology in Amsterdam film shows, 1896–1910," *Film History*, 2: 5–17.

Tempel, Mark van den (1997) "'Als Daguerre dat eens kon aanschouwen . . .' The Mutoscope & Biograph Company als voorloper van het bioscoopjournaal in Nederland," *Jaarboek Mediageschiedenis*, 8: 51–72.

ANSJE VAN BEUSEKOM AND IVO BLOM

Figure 86 Studio of Anton Nöggerath Jr., at Sloterdijk (now Amsterdam), 1911, from *De Kunst*, 193, p. 8. (Courtesy of Ivo Blom.)

New York Dramatic Mirror

The *New York Dramatic Mirror* was an important theatrical trade weekly that introduced a page on the "moving picture field" in May 1908, when it asked Frank **Woods** to solicit advertisers and begin writing copy. The section quickly increased to as many as eight pages as Woods instituted a systematic weekly "Review of Late Films," which included "special features" by April 1912, and began writing an influential column of commentary (especially on film aesthetics), signed "Spectator." Although Woods left the paper in August 1912, the "Motion Picture" section remained significant, especially in its reviews of feature films. By 1914, the circulation of the *Dramatic Mirror* reportedly was 17,500.

RICHARD ABEL

New York Morning Telegraph

The first daily newspaper in the USA to publish a page devoted to moving pictures in its Sunday edition, beginning at least as early as January 1910. Initially, **vaudeville** and moving pictures were covered together in one section of the paper, but in early 1912, under editor George Terwilliger, moving pictures were given their own section, which eventually ran six to eight pages (including reviews, articles, small news items, and extensive ads) and was sold separately as a weekly supplement. The *Morning Telegraph* strongly supported the Independents, and with a reported circulation of 70,000 by 1914, its Sunday supplement probably was the most widely read trade paper, certainly by its core readership of exhibitors.

RICHARD ABEL

New York Motion Picture Company

Organized by Adam **Kessel**, Charles O. **Baumann**, and Fred J. **Balshofer**, the New York Motion Picture Company (NYMP) released its first film, *Disinherited Son's Loyalty*, on 21 May 1909 under the Bison brand. Kessel and Baumann had been partners in the International Film Exchange, while Balshofer had been a cameraman for the **Lubin** company, as well as forming his own short-lived studio, Crescent, in 1908. Operating without a license from the **Motion Picture Patents Company** (MPPC), the three men positioned their company's product as an independent alternative to the films distributed by **General film**. NYMP soon became the American distributor for Italian producers **Ambrosio** and **Itala**, establishing their headquarters on Union Square in New York City.

Like most early film studios, NYMP filmed its western subjects in New Jersey. Balshofer, the company's director and cameraman, soon became dissatisfied with the look of his films and determined that the Bison brand needed to distinguish itself from the competition by filming its stories against a real western backdrop. Thus, in late 1909, he and a troupe of actors traveled to Los Angeles and established a base of operations in Edendale; from there, they roamed over southern and central California, scouting locations and filming western scenarios. While Balshofer and his troupe were working in California, Kessel and Baumann formed the **Reliance** Moving Picture Company, releasing its first film, *In the Gray of Dawn*, on 22 October 1910.

In November of 1911, NYMP hired Thomas H. **Ince** to take charge of the Bison brand and Balshofer returned east, leaving the company soon after. Within weeks of his arrival, Ince significantly expanded the studio and moved it to Santa Monica, on the Pacific Ocean. Within the year, the company's releases lengthened to two and three reels (mostly **westerns** and Civil War films), and the production staff grew to include such new directors as Francis **Ford**, Charles Giblyn, and Jay Hunt. In the summer of 1912, NYMP hired Mack **Sennett**, Ford **Sterling**, and Mabel **Normand** away from **Biograph** and formed the **Keystone Film Company**, which took up residence in the old Edendale studio. Its first release was a split reel, *Cohen Collects a Debt* and *The Water Nymph* (23 September 1912). On 1 June 1913, NYMP released its first feature film, Ince's five-reel *The Battle of Gettysburg*.

In 1910, NYMP had joined with Carl **Laemmle** and other independent producers to create the **Motion Picture Distributing and Sales**

Company. By early 1912, that company had fractured into the **Universal Film Manufacturing Company**, **Mutual Film Company**, and Film Supply Company. At first, Kessel and Baumann aligned themselves with Laemmle and Universal, but within six weeks they had defected to Mutual. As a result, they lost the use of the 101 Bison brand to Universal, creating in its place the Broncho, Kay-Bee, and Domino brands.

By mid-1913, NYMP reorganized with Kessel as its president, Baumann as vice-president, and Harry **Aitken** as assistant treasurer. Two years later, the three reorganized yet again as the Triangle Film Corporation, combining the talents of Ince, Sennett, and D. W. **Griffith** into a formidable independent production company and putting NYMP out of business.

STEVEN HIGGINS

New Zealand

From its earliest days filmmaking in Aotearoa New Zealand was local, personal, and irregular. In 1895, travelling showman A. H. Whitehouse became the first person to exhibit moving pictures in New Zealand, by means of the **Kinetoscope**. The first public screening took place the next year when a popular imported program was presented during a **vaudeville** performance. **Newspapers** were soon reporting enthusiastically on the wonder and intense curiosity aroused by this new device and the infinite possibilities of which it appeared capable. Two years later, on 1 December 1898, Whitehouse filmed the first scenes to be taken locally, recording the opening of the Auckland Exhibition. A day or so later, several short films of Maori were taken by Major Joseph **Perry** for the **Salvation Army**. The Limelight Department of the Salvation Army (Melbourne, Australia) recognised with alacrity the potential of this new medium, making many regular and successful tours of the country, often shooting films locally to supplement their programs. By 1901, the government was sufficiently convinced of film's usefulness to officially commission them to record a Royal visit.

Actualités of local events and people gave local **audiences** a sense of their own images on the screen, personalizing the excitement of going to the moving pictures. Anything from picnics to parades was filmed, usually by an enterprising operator from the nearest picture theater, squeezing in as many people, shops, or street scenes as possible. Completed quickly, printed and processed in makeshift backyard laboratories, they were shown within days and consistently proved a big draw. Official **news event films**, **travelogues** or scenics (both the landscape and the Maori were regarded as especially photogenic), and anything of a grand or pompous nature particularly involving visiting dignitaries (especially royalty) and including processions, parades, or large crowds were also popular with the participants, the filmmakers, and the public.

In 1905, West's Pictures and the Brescians (a musical troupe managed by Henry Hayward) made the first of their three hugely profitable tours of New Zealand and Australia. Both T. J. **West** and Hayward went on to play major roles in the development of film exhibition in New Zealand. The country's first permanent picture show was established in 1908, the same year the first film exchange began renting and importing films, and the first purpose-built picture theater opened two years later. By 1913, the three major film distribution and theater-owning companies—John Fuller and Sons, Hayward's Pictures, and J. D. Williams—amalgamated to form New Zealand Picture Supplies.

In 1912, in search of novel settings for photoplays, Gaston **Méliès** and seventeen members of his company from the USA spent several months in New Zealand, making five scenics as well as three dramatic shorts. The first fiction feature film made locally, *Hinemoa*, was produced by George Tarr and photographed by Charles Newhan; it premièred in the early weeks of **World War I** to big business.

Further reading

Dennis, Jonathan (1993) *Aotearoa and the Sentimental Strine*, Wellington: Moa Films.

Dennis, Jonathan and Jan Bieringa (eds.) (1996) *Film in Aotearoa New Zealand*, Wellington: Victoria University Press.

JONATHAN DENNIS

Newman & Sinclair Reflex camera

Longstanding British manufacturers Newman & Sinclair introduced an early reflex moving picture camera in 1911, where through-the-lens viewing of the scene to be shot was accomplished by moving a 45° mirror into place behind the lens at the aperture, which diverted the image into a viewfinder for proper framing. Also featuring side-by-side 400-foot magazines and a quality lens system, the camera was housed originally in a wood frame (later made of aluminum) with a distinctive milled pattern, and was in use for many years.

DEAC ROSSELL

Newman, Arthur Samuel

b. 1861; d. 1943

inventor, manufacturer, Great Britain

Arthur Newman was a camera designer who in 1890, with Julio Guardia, formed the manufacturing firm of Newman and Guardia. In 1896, inspired by a **Lumière** show, Newman began designing his own moving picture camera; in 1897, he launched the "N and G" Kinematograph Camera, selling one immediately to Sir George Newnes's Antarctic expedition. The company gained a reputation for its film equipment, and, after Guardia's death in 1906, Newman left to specialize in lightweight cameras, forming Newman and Sinclair with James A. Sinclair in 1909. Newman designed the **Newman & Sinclair Reflex camera** that Herbert **Ponting** took on Scott's 1910 Antarctic expedition; he also helped to perfect the compressed-air-driven **Aeroscope** camera, which his firm began manufacturing in 1912. Newman's cameras were reliable and well-constructed, and remained popular with explorers and war cameramen until the 1940s.

NICHOLAS HILEY

news event films

The first news event films were partly about the phenomenon of moving pictures. The fleeting performances shown on the **Edison Kinetoscope** in New York in April 1894 or on the **Cinématographe Lumière** in Paris in December 1895 announced the arrival of a startling new medium. The ability of that medium not only to record reality, but through appropriate exhibition to report on it, was swiftly grasped by the early filmmakers. Films of news events were common from the earliest years and among the proudest achievements of the young industry.

The first news event to be filmed, arguably, was the Epsom Derby in March 1895, done by Birt **Acres**. Since this kind of film has to be delivered to a screen with rapidity, and to be presented as news, however, Robert **Paul**'s film of the 1896 Derby is a better candidate for the "first" news event film, as it was rushed onto the **music hall** screens within twenty-four hours of the race finishing. Thereafter, news events, whether presented as "hot" news or not, were among the most noted of the earliest film subjects, including **Lumière**'s Coronation of the Czar of Russia series (1896), the numerous films taken of Queen Victoria's Diamond Jubilee procession (1897), and the **American Mutoscope and Biograph** and Edison films of Admiral Dewey's victory celebrations (1899).

Wars gave exhibitors the opportunity to present regular film reports, which served a rudimentary news function. W. K. L. **Dickson**'s copious films for **British Mutoscope and Biograph** of the Anglo-Boer War (filmed in 1899–1900, though the war continued until 1902) were shown nightly at the Palace Theatre, London, and the regular audience looked upon the screenings as a means to catch up on the war, albeit four weeks or more later. An alternative means of giving the audience the news it wanted to see was supplied by **Mitchell & Kenyon**, which recreated scenes of British military heroism on the hills outside Blackburn. **Pathé-Frères** and Edison filmed similar dramatizations (often misleadingly referred to as "fake newsreels"), with Edison filming action from both the British and Boer point of view, according to audience taste. A similar division in the news function of moving pictures was illustrated by films of the Dreyfus trial, where AM&B's painstakingly achieved *actualités* (including *paparazzi*-style shots of Alfred and Lucie Dreyfus) vied with the meticulous studio **re-enactments** of Georges **Méliès**.

News event films developed in the early 1900s into a form commonly referred to, in Britain, as topicals. Most film companies understood that a part of their business included the topical trade, covering state ceremonies, royal visits, sports events, or disasters such as the San Francisco earthquake of 1906 or the eruption of Vesuvius in the same year. The skills and production set-up required to produce studio dramas was clearly not the same as that required for the rapid production of news event films, and growing sophistication within the cinema industry inevitably led to specialization. By the end of the decade, particular companies were becoming known for their topical work, just as others were for **travelogues** or **industrial films**. Larger firms such as Pathé and **Gaumont** even created separate production units to deal exclusively with fiction or *actualités*. In Britain in particular, firms such as **Jury's**, **Warwick**, and the various **Urban** companies dealt almost entirely in news and *actualité* film.

News event films followed the simple premise of giving illustration to events that another medium, **newspapers**, already had made into news. This was the guiding principle behind the logical next step in news film production, **newsreels**, which created a package of short items with some degree of topicality, which could be exhibited regularly. Newsreels first appeared in France with *Pathé Fait-Divers* in 1908, and soon spread to cinema programs the world over, gradually ousting the longer, single-story topical form.

The 1910–1914 period was a productive one for the newsreels and the producers of topicals. An event such as the sinking of the Titanic created an avid demand for any kind of pictures representing the tragedy, something that led almost inevitably to much fake news footage being circulated. News event films of this period illustrated rather than analyzed, and particularly popular was the pageantry of the coronation of King George V (1910), the Investiture of the Prince of Wales (1911) and the Delhi Durbar (1911), all filmed in Kinemacolor by Charles **Urban**. War provided potentially the richest subject, although the travels and discomforts undergone by the cameramen in filming the Balkan Wars of 1910–1913 seldom resulted in footage of abiding interest or news value, as the mistrust of military officials, the limitations of

Figure 87 From *Le Petit Journal*, 1911.

camera technology, and not least danger kept the operators from the front.

The outstanding news story of the early cinema period came at its close, namely **World War I**. Despite the hazards, censorious officialdom, and the impossibility of getting to the battlefront, numerous British, French, and American cameramen entered Belgium in the early months of the war, and such was the plethora of footage that news companies were able to produce additional war news topicals, such as Cherry **Kearton**'s *The Whirlpool of War* (1914–1915). It was the war that saw the topical fade and the newsreels develop into a more sophisticated and popular medium; by the war's end, a newsreel was an essential part of every cinema program.

See also: boxing films; colonialism: Europe; expedition/exploration films; imperialism: USA; labor movement: Europe; labor movement: USA; program formats; sports films; women's movement: Europe; women's movement: USA

Further reading

Brown, Richard and Barry Anthony (1999) *A Victorian Film Enterprise: The History of the British*

Mutoscope and Biograph Company, 1897–1915, Trowbridge: Flicks Books.

Fielding, Raymond (1972) *The American Newsreel 1911–1967*, Norman: University of Oklahoma Press, 1972.

Huret, Marcel (1984) *Ciné actualités: histoire de la press filmée*, Paris: Henri Veyrier.

Mesguich, Félix (1933) *Tours de manivelle*, Paris: Editions Bernard Grasset.

LUKE McKERNAN

newspapers

The principal news medium throughout the period of early cinema, the newspaper shared some content material with the new medium but also evidenced important differences. Although a large proportion of the subject matter of the early moving picture was factual, in the shape of **actualités**, these were often generic scenes of contemporary life rather than reportage of specific events. In setting out to describe and illustrate current events as they occurred, by contrast, both media faced technological and **communication** limitations that often made it necessary to resort to fictional images, rather than first-hand images taken on the spot.

The daily newspaper emerged in Europe in the 18th century, evolving from a business culture in which merchants needed up-to-date intelligence of commodity shipments, prices, and other current events affecting their trade. But it was only with 19th-century technological advances and social changes that the newspaper began to assume major importance as a social force. The telegraph, especially on an international scale, allowed rapid gathering of news from remote locations; steam-powered and rotary printing presses made mass production possible; the development of halftone printing in the 1880s and 1890s allowed a great increase in illustration; and growing railway networks made widespread distribution possible in European countries and regions of the USA. Equally important were the general spread of literacy and increasing **leisure time** and disposable income, as well as the abolition of political controls such as the British Stamp Tax (a tax on newspaper publication).

The free dissemination of news always had a political dimension, in which control of information was just as important as technical aspects of its distribution. With the increasing growth and liberalization of the newspaper market, a number of powerful individuals emerged as controllers of large sections of the market in their respective countries. Many of these "press barons" used their publications overtly to promote their own political agenda: for example the British liberal W. T. Stead ran a number of high-profile social reform campaigns in his *Pall Mall Gazette* in the 1880s; others, like William Randolph Hearst in the USA and Alfred Harmsworth (Lord Northcliffe) in Great Britain, took a more conservative line while increasing their own wealth and political influence. The common factor of many newspapers of the 1880s and 1890s was a populist approach that earned them the blanket title of "the new journalism" in some circles.

In the second half of the 19th century, international transmission of news became very efficient, allowing next-day publication of reports transmitted by telegraph or telephone; moreover, nationwide daily distribution of newspapers became a sophisticated operation. Yet the illustration of news remained problematic until the end of the century: the time required for producing wood engravings meant that next-day publication of images was impractical, with the result that illustration of the news was almost exclusively the province of weekly **illustrated magazines**, summarizing the week's events with engravings from drawings. Although the illustrations carried by these papers were increasingly engraved from photographic originals, a significant proportion of them remained artists' impressions of events that had only been reported verbally. This was particularly the case in reporting foreign wars, in which events occurred and changed rapidly, and in any case had to be presented in a generally heroic light for home consumption. Daily newspapers did not make large-scale use of illustration until the early 1900s: the first to use **color** extensively, in Sunday supplements, was the *New York World* (1895); the first to use only halftone photographs, Harmsworth's *Daily Mirror* (London, 1903).

The dependence on essentially fictional illustration to represent remote news events offers a direct parallel with some of the content of early moving pictures. John Barnes' definition of the "news film" as recording "a particular historic event, happening . . . irrespective of the camera's presence" is useful; on this basis Barnes judges that roughly 40% of British film production to 1900 was news-based (with another 40% "non-fiction" and 20% "fiction"). However, the need to produce images of remote events to which the camera had no access, or from which exposed film could not be returned rapidly for developing, meant that a small but significant proportion of the "news" titles were actually staged films or **re-enactments**. Examples are **Vitagraph**'s model-based films of naval battles in the Spanish–American War (1898), battlefield scenes from the Anglo-Boer War (1899–1902) produced on English locations using actors by British manufacturers such as **Mitchell & Kenyon**, and Georges **Méliès**' film series of the Dreyfus trial (1899). Most genuine "news" films tended to show public events whose timing and location were predictable, such as processions, ship launches, Royal occasions, etc.; the same was true of the illustrated newsweeklies and illustrated daily newspapers.

The 1900s saw the **news event film** begin to emerge as a self-contained genre distinct from the dramatic or comic entertainment film. In some ways this was related to the development of fixed projection venues: one of the earliest sites in Britain was the "Daily Bioscope" opened in London in May 1906 with the aim "to portray important events from day to day." However, the time taken to make and distribute copies of a film meant that for several years moving pictures lagged behind the newspaper in portraying the latest events, although on occasion films of an event could be projected on the same day. The **newsreel** format, comprising a short digest of recent events inserted into an entertainment program, was initiated by **Pathé-Frères** in 1908 (versions of its *Pathé-Journal* then spread to other countries), and remained an integral part of cinema programming until the 1960s. Still, the daily newspaper would remain the most immediate source of image-based news until the development of electronic news-gathering and transmission systems in the 1970s.

See also: photography; transportation

Further reading

Abel, Richard (2002) "A Marriage of Ephemeral Discourses: Newspapers and Moving Pictures," *CINEMA et Cie*, 1: 59–83.

Barnes, John (1996–1998) *The Beginnings of the Cinema in England 1894–1901*, 5 vols., Exeter: University of Exeter Press.

Brown, Lucy (1985) *Victorian News and Newspapers*, Oxford: Clarendon Press.

RICHARD CRANGLE

newsreels

Newsreels differ from the **news event films** or topicals of the early cinema period. The term "newsreel" is too often loosely used to describe all films of news events, hence **Lumière** *actualités* are sometimes called "newsreels," which is wholly inaccurate. A newsreel was a specific means of packaging and exhibiting news on film, a collection of disparate topical stories, generally each of no more than a minute's length, on a single reel of film, exhibited regularly. Although a convenient label, the term "newsreel" did not become common until 1917; prior to that the reels were variously called topicals, animated newspapers, etc. **Pathé-Frères** created the first newsreel in France in 1908—*Pathé Fait-Divers*, soon to become *Pathé Journal*—and it was followed by newsreels from **Gaumont** (*Gaumont Actualités*), **Éclair** (*Éclair-Journal*) and **Eclipse** (*Eclipse-Journal*). The first British newsreel was an offshoot of the French, *Pathé's Animated Gazette* (1910), swiftly followed by *Warwick Bioscope Chronicle* (1910), *Gaumont Graphic* (1910) and *Topical Budget* (1911). Germany had *Eiko-Woche* and *Messter-Woche*. In the USA, the first newsreel was *Pathé's Weekly* (1911), followed by **Vitagraph**'s short-lived *Monthly of Current Events* (1911), Gaumont's *Animated Weekly* (1912), *Mutual Weekly* (1912) and **Universal**'s *Animated Weekly* (1912).

The newsreels emerged, not coincidentally, at the time of a boom in cinema construction, for a regular news service was dependent on a regular audience, loyal to a theater and likely to pay repeated visits. Newsreels in European countries generally settled into a bi-weekly release pattern; in the USA, the distances involved meant that most were weekly, although Pathé achieved a bi-weekly release pattern for more than a year just before **World War I**. Their inspiration was **newspapers**, which supplied their choice of names and their news agenda. The newsreels seldom broke a news story, although they could produce sensational scoops such as the trapped anarchist gangs in London's Siege of Sidney Street (1911), the capture of Paris' Bonnot Gang (1912), and the suffragette Emily Davison killed by a horse at the 1913 Epsom Derby. The co-operation of Pancho Villa with **Mutual** in filming the Mexican revolution became notorious, but was not typical. Mostly they were content to provide illustration to news events the public was already familiar with through newspaper coverage, and they quickly became reliant upon the safe subjects of civic ceremonies, military displays, ship launchings, royal visits, **travel**, **sports** and **fashion** items (which Pathé and Gaumont illustrated with stencil

color), for which the newsreels would become best known. Commentary, in the form of introductory **intertitles**, was minimal and largely descriptive. It was only during World War I that the newsreels started to place intertitles within a story and to develop the informal, facetious, and popular style that would characterize their period of great success in the 1920s.

See also: program formats

Further reading

Fielding, Raymond (1972) *The American Newsreel 1911–1967*, Norman: University of Oklahoma Press.
McKernan, Luke (1992) *Topical Budget: The Great British News Film*, London: British Film Institute.

LUKE McKERNAN

Figure 88 Poster for *Pathé Journal*, 1908.

nickelodeons

One of the terms—others included nickel theater, electric theater, theatorium—used to refer to the small storefront theaters that became so popular for presenting short, continuous programs of moving pictures in the USA beginning around 1905. Such theaters had existed before then, but most had been operated as temporary venues by traveling showmen—an exception was T. L. **Tally**'s Electric Theatre in Los Angeles. Nickelodeon became the accepted term for these partly because that was what Harry **Davis** called the storefront theater he opened in Pittsburgh in June 1905, whose immediate success, legend has it, inspired others that opened throughout that fall and winter, from New York to Chicago.

By the spring of 1906, a dozen or more nickelodeons were operating profitably in each of several metropolitan areas—New York, Philadelphia, Pittsburgh, Cleveland, and Chicago. Within a year, their numbers increased exponentially to include hundreds in New York and Chicago, and **Moving Picture World** estimated that there were between 2,500 and 3,000 throughout the country. Within another year, the overall figure had more than doubled, and both the **trade press** and moral reform organizations agreed that New York City nickelodeons "entertained three to four hundred thousand people daily" or nearly three million a week.

Typically, the nickelodeon was housed in a long, narrow room seating several hundred people, sometimes on wooden chairs, with a raised projection booth at one end and a nine-by-twelve-foot **screen** hung in a small stage space or attached to the back wall at the other. A piano and drum set were placed to one side of and below the screen. The street front, made of wood and/or pressed metal, was designed to attract passersby day or night as a modern marvel of **electricity**. A ticket seller's booth was centered within an entrance and exit area set back several feet from the sidewalk, all ringed by hundreds of electric lights often in a multitude of colors, some of which spelled out the name of the theater in huge letters. In its 1908 catalog, Sears Roebuck even offered a prepackaged nickelodeon front, which suggested the low costs, at least initially, of equipping a nickelodeon.

The size and design of the nickelodeon were shaped by pre-existing as well as new city ordinances. Building codes and fire laws, for instance, meant that licensing fees were different for legitimate theaters and "common shows" or cheap amusements, and the latter, accordingly, often had restricted seating arrangements: the maximum was 299 in cities from New York City to Youngstown (Ohio). Other regulations governing public safety and health led to a certain number of required exits, overhead fans, low levels of lighting, and lead-lined projection booths—to protect against accidents involving the highly flammable nitrate film stock.

The nickelodeon drew on and combined several features of other, earlier venues for showing moving pictures. From **vaudeville**, for instance, it took the idea of offering continuous entertainment in short, discrete, repeatable acts, specifically pairing moving pictures with **illustrated songs**, which usually had worked in tandem at the end of programs. From the **penny arcade**, it took the idea of inviting passersby to drop in for a short visit, as a kind of window shopping. The length and number of programs in any one nickelodeon depended on its location and clientele: some ran no more than fifteen or twenty minutes, with forty or more shows a day, if the theater was open from morning to midnight; others ran close to an hour, much like

family vaudeville, with far fewer shows. By 1907, many theaters were changing their programs daily, while the great majority changed theirs from one to three times a week.

The **audience** for the nickelodeon was hardly homogeneous or unchanging, but most commentators at the time agreed that women and children were particularly important and so were new immigrants from eastern and southern Europe (whose numbers peaked at one million in 1907), especially in metropolitan areas of the Northeast and Midwest. More specifically, they included shoppers (both middle class and working class), off-work employees (particularly young, single, white-collar women and men), out-of-school children, and neighborhood residents. By 1908, certain moral reformers were hailing the nickelodeon as a new "family resort," a "true theater of the people," that addressed a genuine need of communities for respectable commercialized leisure. Indeed, as the nickelodeon competed with and sometimes displaced the **saloon**, a crucial late 19th-century institution of leisure for working-class men, the trade press joined in promoting it as the principal social center in many working-class (especially immigrant) residential areas.

By the end of the decade, as the total number of moving picture theaters reached perhaps 10,000, larger cinemas began to emerge alongside nickelodeons. Many of these were part of what were now circuits of theaters controlled not only by Davis, who again had initiated the trend and given his circuit the evocative name of Bijou Dream, but other entrepreneurs: William **Fox** and Marcus **Loew** (New York), Aaron **Jones** and William **Swanson** (Chicago), William Bullock (Cleveland), Siegmund **Lubin** and Stanley **Mastbaum** (Philadelphia), O. T. Crawford (Saint Louis), the **Saxe** brothers (Milwaukee), and Archie **Shepard** (New England). Not only had the nickelodeon established a permanent base for movie exhibition in the USA, it also attracted many men into the business—Fox, Loew, Carl **Laemmle**, Adolph **Zukor**, Harry **Warner** and his brothers— who would soon go on to create the Hollywood production system.

See also: cinema and the law; cinema circuits or chains; migration/immigration: USA; leisure time

Figure 89 Exterior of the Normal Theater, Chicago, 1909.

Figure 90 Interior of the Keith Bijou theater, Boston, *c.* 1910.

Figure 91 Interior of the Wonderland Theater, Troy, New York, *c.* 1908.

and space: USA; musical accompaniment; projectionists; sound effects; transportation; urbanization

Further reading

Abel, Richard (1999) *The Red Rooster Scare: Making Cinema American, 1900–1910*, Berkeley: University of California Press.

Bowser, Eileen (1990) *The Transformation of Cinema, 1907–1915*, New York: Scribner's.

Gomery, Douglas (1992) *Shared Pleasures: A History of Movie Presentation in the United States*, Madison: University of Wisconsin Press.

Musser, Charles (1990) *The Emergence of Cinema: The American Screen to 1907*, New York: Scribner's.

RICHARD ABEL

Nielsen, Asta

b. 11 September 1881, Copenhagen; d. 25 May 1972, Copenhagen

actor, Denmark, Germany

Born to a working-class family, Nielsen managed to begin the career in the theater she hoped for, but she could not rise above secondary roles. In 1910, she took a chance on moving pictures with Urban **Gad**, a set painter in her theater, who wrote, directed and produced their first film, *Afgrunden* [The Abyss] (1911), which was an explosive success. It launched Nielsen as one of the first truly international film **stars**. Her personal appearances would draw crowds throughout Europe and beyond.

The subject of *Afgrunden* is a female revenge plot that turns to tragedy. The key scene was the "gaucho dance." Nielsen, a respectable young woman led astray by a circus dancer, wraps a whip around her partner in their provocative stage act as she twists her body around his, exciting, dominating, and finally immobilizing him. No one missed her cinematic chemistry. Gad and Nielsen soon accepted a movie offer in Berlin, where Nielsen would appear in nearly seventy-five films over two decades.

Between 1911 and 1915, Nielsen and Gad, who were married in 1912, made over thirty films for Paul **Davidson's** **PAGU**. Some 16 of these were shot by cameraman Guido **Seeber**. Over an eight-month season, Nielsen might become a society lady, a circus performer, a scrub woman, an artist's model, a suffragette, a gypsy, a newspaper reporter, a film star and filmmaker in *Die Filmprimadonna* [The Film Star] (1913), a child in *Engelein* (1913), a male bandit in *Zapatas Bande* [Zapata's Gang] (1914) or, later, the title character in *Hamlet* (1920). Nielsen was brilliant in tragic or comic roles, her sensuality matched by her intelligence, resourcefulness and physical agility. She excelled at playing unconventional personalities resisting traditional class and sex roles, often doomed to failure. She expressed inner conflict in a uniquely cinematic, understated manner. She was immediate, natural, and modern. Her slim figure accentuated by suggestive costumes, from rags to exquisite fashions, she crossed class and gender lines convincingly from one film to the next.

Nielsen brought to the cinema people who had never taken it seriously. She wrote in her autobiography (1945–1946) that, from the beginning, she and Gad worked toward artistic excellence. Her naturalness was the result of careful study of her image magnified on the screen. Contemporary writers such as Belá Balász celebrated Nielsen in essays defining cinema as an art form. Her own writings on film were published in 1928.

Many of Nielsen's films after she separated from Gad in 1916 have disappeared or exist only in fragments. She is perhaps best known today for her role in Pabst's *Die freudlose Gasse* [Joyless Street] (1925), long after her famous spontaneity had become a stylized, mask-like expressivity that had great influence on **acting styles** in Weimar cinema. She made one sound film in 1932. Nielsen was active in many public arenas after she returned to Copenhagen in the mid-1930s.

See also: multiple-reel/feature films: Europe; melodrama, sensational

Further reading

Bergstrom, Janet (1990) "Asta Nielsen's Early Films," in Paolo Cherchi Usai and Lorenzo Codelli (eds.) *Before Caligari*, Pordenone: Biblioteca dell'Immagine.

JANET BERGSTROM

Nikkatsu

The Nikkatsu film trust came about in 1912 with the merger of four major film companies in Japan: **M. Pathe**, **Yoshizawa Shoten**, **Fukuhodo**, and **Yokota Shokai**. Originally it had two units for producing films. In the Kyoto unit, old-school dramas were made under the direction of **Makino Shozo**, while in Tokyo new-school dramas were made at the Mukojima studio. The formation of Nikkatsu prompted the emergence of independent film companies. Conservative and repetitious, Nikkatsu films became a target of attack by sophisticated film fans who wanted to revitalize Japanese cinema. As a result of their demands for modernized forms of cinema, Nikkatsu sought to transform its production in the late 1910s and early 1920s. From such efforts came such excellent directors of the later period as Mizoguchi Kenji.

HIROSHI KOMATSU

Nilsson, N. P.

b. 1842; d. 1912

exhibitor, producer, Sweden

N. P. Nilsson, a former horse-dealer, changed his business interests in 1904 when he opened his first moving picture theater in Stockholm, the London. Soon he was operating a handful of the most important theaters in the capital, and simultaneously managing an exchange. In 1911, Nilsson and his son Axel began producing feature films: of two titles based on texts by August Strindberg, *Miss Julie* (1912) and *The Father* (1912), the latter has survived. The renowned variety star, Anna Hofman-Uddgren, directed these films. N. P. Nilsson's premature death in 1912 curtailed this production initiative, and the exchange and theaters were later sold; Axel Nilsson, however, continued to work in the industry.

JAN OLSSON

Nöggerath, Franz Anton Jr.

b. 1880; d. 1947

cameraman, exhibitor, distributor,
producer, The Netherlands

The son of F. A. **Nöggerath** Sr. worked in Great
Britain from 1897 to 1908 as a cameraman and laboratory employee, filming Queen Victoria's 80th birth-
day and recording the first moving pictures of Iceland.
After his father's death, he took over the business,
expanding distribution with French and Italian films
and constructing a studio outside Amsterdam in 1911
for producing fiction films. Despite the presence of
renowned stage actors such as Louis Bouwmeester
(**Frenkel**) and Caroline van Dommelen, this fiction
production—largely **historical** and theatrical films
such as *De Greep* [The Grip] (1909), *De Banneling*
[The Exiled] (1912), and *Onschuldig veroordeeld*
[Guileless Condemned] (1912)—was commercially
unsuccessful and halted in 1913.

ANSJE VAN BEUSEKOM

Nöggerath, Franz Anton Sr.

b. 1859; d. 1908

exhibitor, distributor, filmmaker,
the Netherlands

In 1896, Anton Nöggerath Sr. began to include
moving pictures in his variety theater, the Flora, in
Amsterdam. In 1897, he became the first and
most important Dutch film distributor during the first
decade of Dutch cinema history, importing apparatuses and films from the **Warwick Trading Company** for distribution in the Netherlands and abroad.
He also produced local *actualités* and short fiction
films, selling his product throughout Europe. In 1907,
he opened the Bioscope-Theater in Amsterdam, the
first Dutch purpose-built permanent cinema.

ANSJE VAN BEUSEKOM

Noguès, Pierre

b. 1878; d. 1971

scientific filmmaker, France

Noguès entered the Institut Marey in 1900 and
devoted himself (like Lucien **Bull**) to fast-motion

shooting. Whereas Bull obtained very high fre-
quencies by immobilizing the film and using sparks as
well as a rotating prism, Noguès managed to drive
35mm film through a camera at a very high speed
without breakage. From 1904 on, he developed several **cameras** equipped with claw mechanisms and
later sprocket wheels and safety catches. In 1920, he
reached a maximum frequency of 380 images/second.

Much like **Marey**, his mentor, Noguès focused
on rapid movements in human and animal locomotion, which slow motion made it possible to
analyze. Among his films are *Le lancer du disque de
l'athlète Jean Bouin* [The Throw of the Discus by
Athlete Jean Bouin], which he directed sometime
before 1914, and several on the flight of birds.

See also: scientific films: Europe

LAURENT MANNONI

Nonguet, Lucien

b. ?; d. ?

set designer, filmmaker, France

Nonguet initially recruited casts for **Pathé-Frères**
and soon became Ferdinand **Zecca**'s main collaborator, in charge of set decors, especially for major
féeries/**fairy plays** such as *La Belle au bois
dormant* (Sleeping Beauty) (1902). His work as a
filmmaker first involved **historical films** and
re-enactments such as *L'Assassinat du Grand
Duc Serge* [Assasination of the Grand Duke Serge]
(1905). After directing several dramas such as
A Biribi (1907), Longuet moved on to **comic series**, directing a few of the *Boireau* films, with André
Deed, as well as those starring Max **Linder**. He is
said to have left for Italy around 1911.

LAURENT LE FORESTIER

Nordisk Films Kompagni

The principal Danish production company,
founded in 1906 by Ole **Olsen**. During its first year,
the company opened sales agencies in Sweden,
Norway, Germany, and Italy. In 1907, Great

Britain and Austria-Hungary were added. An American subsidiary, the Great Northern Film Company in New York, was opened in 1908; despite considerable efforts, however, it was not allowed to join the **Motion Picture Patents Company**, and Great Northern became one of the independents' most important suppliers.

Films were shot on open-air stages until the first enclosed studio with glass walls and roof was ready in 1908. Before 1910, almost all of Nordisk's fiction films were one-reelers directed by Viggo **Larsen**. Nordisk produced all kinds of films: **comedies**, costume dramas, and **detective films** (including several Sherlock Holmes pictures). Most successful of all was *Løvejagten* [The Lion Hunt] (1907), which showed actual lions being shot dead on camera—as various Danish locations stood in for Africa.

Nordisk sold its films ready-made to distributors, tinted and with **intertitles** in different languages. Its large manufacturing facility stood in the excise-free zone of Copenhagen's port, allowing raw film stock to be imported and finished films to be exported free of customs duties. The photographic standard of the films was very high: the company was awarded a gold medal for technical quality at the International Cinematographic Industry Exhibition in Hamburg in 1908.

Nordisk's international standing was further enhanced by the decision to emphasize feature film production from the beginning of 1911, following the success of *Den hvide Slavehandel* [In the Hands of Impostors] (1910). Outstanding directors such as August **Blom** and **Holger-Madsen** ensured high standards, and actor Valdemar **Psilander** became an international **star**. To gain even more prestige, the company emphasized the production of *Autorenfilme*.

By 1912, Nordisk was one of Europe's leading film companies. The Danish market was far too small to serve as a secure home base for a major international company. In order to ensure continued growth, Olsen sought to attain a dominant position in the German distribution and exhibition markets, achieving what has later been called vertical integration. Nordisk's stock capital was doubled to finance the expansion, which included acquiring distribution rights for the films of **PAGU** and other companies. By 1916, one in four films released in Germany was distributed by Nordisk's subsidiary.

At the same time, the company kept up a very high level of production (from 1914 to 1916, it produced 120 to 130 fiction films per year, of which most were features), gambling that it could flood the market with its stock of unsold films as soon as **World War I** ended. This proved to be a grave mistake, and Nordisk's troubles were exacerbated by Germany's growing hostility to having a large section of its film industry in foreign hands. Eventually, the UFA conglomerate was set up, and Nordisk was forced to hand over its German assets. Although it never recovered international pre-eminence, Nordisk does still exist today as an active film production company.

See also: distribution: Europe; multiple-reel/feature films

CASPAR TYBJERG

Normand, Mabel

b. 1892; d. 1930

actor, director, USA

A spirited and vivacious comedienne, Normand first found regular film work in 1911 in John **Bunny**'s **Vitagraph comedies**. After joining **Biograph** later that year, she entered a personal/professional relationship with Mack **Sennett** and became the leading lady at his newly established **Keystone Film Company** in 1912. Normand was the first Keystone performer to be promoted to director: in 1914, she helmed several slapstick shorts, including *Mabel's Strange Predicament* and *Caught in a Cabaret*. Dissatisfied with short comedies, Normand founded the Mabel Normand Feature Film Company in 1916, starring in its only production, the six-reel *Mickey* (1918). During the 1920's, her career was damaged by ill health and public scandal.

See also: Arbuckle, Roscoe

Further reading

Fussell, Betty Harper (1982) *Mabel*, New Haven: Ticknor and Fields.

ROB KING

North American Phonograph

A company established in 1888 by Jesse Lippincott, a wealthy drinking glass manufacturer, to market **Edison**'s **phonograph** and Alexander Graham Bell's Graphophone. North American Phonograph's business practices established a pattern for marketing Edison's **Kinetoscope** in 1894. Agents with concessions from North American Phonograph made the first substantial investments and hence were the first distributors of motion pictures in North America. Among them were **Raff & Gammon**, Thomas Lombard, Andrew and George Holland, **Maguire & Bancus**, Peter Bacigalupi, and Charles **Urban**. A maverick phonograph company, Columbia Phonograph of Washington, D.C., helped popularize projection by manufacturing and marketing C. Francis **Jenkins' Phantoscope** projector.

PAUL SPEHR

Norton, Charles Goodwin

b. 1856; d. 1940

businessman, writer, filmmaker, Great Britain

For most of his working life, Norton ran a stationery business in London and, around 1900, he began to take an active interest in the **magic lantern** and moving pictures. His well-informed guide to the magic lantern was published in 1895, with revised editions continuing to appear until 1912. Norton himself specialized in screen presentations for both public and private consumption, entertaining the Royal family on a number of occasions, and his films of London, such as *Tram Ride* (1898), processed by G. A. **Smith**, are some of the finest early moving images of the city. Arguably, his multi-shot non-fiction films, *Foundling Hospital Sports Day* (1899) and *A Country Cattle Show* (1899), contributed to the development of continuity **editing**.

FRANK GRAY

Norway

The first exhibition of moving images in Scandinavia took place in Kristiana, Norway's capital, on 6 April 1896. Between 6 April and 5 May 1896, Max and Emil **Skladanowsky** showed their Wintergarten-programme at the city's Circus Variété. After leaving Norway, the German brothers traveled to Denmark and Sweden.

For the next ten years **itinerant exhibitors** roamed Norway, setting up their equipment in **fairs/fairgrounds** or in **music halls**. On 1 November 1904, the first permanent cinema, Kinematograf-Theatret, opened in Kristiania. Before the year ended four more cinemas had opened; by 1915, Kristiania had twenty-one cinemas. A "**nickelodeon** boom" swept across Norway, and cinema-going became a popular urban form of entertainment that attracted all classes. The largest groups, however, were woman and children.

Audiences in Norway loved French **comedies**, American **westerns**, and all kinds of *actualités*. Although cinema-going became a major popular entertainment form, domestic film production remained small, mainly taking the form of **actualités**. Between 1906 and 1919, only seventeen fiction films were made. Most seem to have taken their strongest inspiration from the Danish erotic or "social" melodramas, showing either flirtation among the rich or the temptations and dangers of lower-class city life. These Norwegian fiction films were made by a variety of production companies and filmmakers, including Peter **Lykke-Seest**, Jens Christian **Gundersen**, and Ottar **Gladtvet**. They were not widely distributed, however, and did not receive the best of reception.

By 1910 many voices were raised in Norway against the new and powerful medium. The most influential came from teachers' organizations, complaining about the cinema's supposed harmful effect on the younger generation. This led to The Film Theatres' Act, passed in 1913 by Parliament. This Act stipulated that municipal councils were to license all public showings of films within the area of their jurisdiction, and thus control the rapidly growing interest in cinema; it also established a Central Board of Film Censors.

Shortly after the Film Theatres' Act was passed, local municipalities began taking the initiative to buy local cinemas from their private owners. In 1917, a National Association of Municipal Cinemas was formed, and, by 1925, municipal cinemas were well established in the capital, now named Oslo, spelling the end of private cinema ownership in the big cities, or on a large scale, throughout Norway.

Developed through both national legislation and local initiative, the municipal cinema system was—and still is—a Norwegian peculiarity, a unique break with the predominant Western capitalist paradigm of the cinema.

The municipal system may have operated for the common good of the local community, but it had one serious flaw: it did not generate production capital. Before 1913, film producers had been cinema owners, like Gundersen; the new system made it harder to produce feature films in Norway. Only in 1920 did a few, more nationally-oriented features begin to be produced.

See also: law and the cinema; melodrama, sensational

Further reading

Soila, Tytti, Astrid Söderbergh Widding and Gunnar Iversen (1999) *Nordic National Cinemas*, London: Routledge.

GUNNAR IVERSEN

Notari, Elvira Coda

b. 1875; d. 1946

scriptwriter, director, producer, Italy

Neapolitan Elvira Coda was Italy's earliest and most prolific woman filmmaker. Founder of **Dora Film** with her husband Nicola Notari, between 1906 and 1930 she scripted, directed, and produced about sixty **multiple-reel/feature films**, one hundred *actualités*, and countless other shorts. Drawing upon Naples' rich popular culture and Italian romantic literature, Notari's silent urban melodramas cast female protagonists in the largely unseen world of the underclass, displaying law-transgressing behaviors and dark love stories of jealousy and revenge. Filming on location with non-professional actors decades before neorealism and synchronizing her films' exhibition with "live" singing and music, Notari's personal authorship and dense regional poetics have long been neglected by Italian cinema history.

Further reading

Bruno, Giuliana (1993) *Streetwalking on a Ruined Map: Cultural Theory and the City Films of Elvira Notari*, Princeton: Princeton University Press.

GIORGIO BERTELLINI

Novelli, Amleto

b. 1881; d. 1924

actor, Italy

Born in Bolgna, Novelli was one of the most famous male **stars** in diva films. He worked extensively with Pina **Menichelli**, as in *Scuola d'Eroi* [School for Heroes] (1913) and Lyda **Borelli**, as in *La Marcia Nuziale* [The Wedding March] (1915). His performance as the writer-dandy Corrado Silva in Carmine Gallone's *Malombra* (1918), opposite Borelli, is especially memorable. Less effeminate than Alberto **Collo** and less bohemian than Febo Mari, Novelli produced an interesting character in *Malombra* by oscillating between the sinister and the passionate, the transgressive and the oppressive. He died in 1924, as a result of an accident during the making of *Il Corsaro* (1923).

ANGELA DALLE VACCHE

Numa Peterson's Trading Company

In spite of short exhibition stints in 1896, the breakthrough for moving pictures in Sweden came at the Stockholm Exhibition in 1897, where Numa Peterson's company, in conjunction with the **Lumière** company, operated a moving picture show. Alexandre **Promio** even shot films in Sweden and took on apprentices from Peterson's firm. After operating a theater for nine months in 1898, Peterson settled on selling equipment and films to exhibitors and soon became **Pathé-Frères'** initial Swedish representative. In 1903, the company shot a handful of sync-sound films under the French-inspired heading, Swedish Immortal Theater, showcasing theatrical luminaries in their signature material. After 1906, the Peterson venture gradually disappeared from the film business.

JAN OLSSON

Nuremberg toy projectors

Toy cinematograph projectors, usually combined with a toy **magic lantern**, appeared for Christmas, 1898, in the catalogue of Gebrüder Bing in Nuremberg, a product quickly imitated by the other optical toy manufacturers in the city, including Johann Falk, Georges Carette, and Ernst Plank. A simple stamped 5-sided Maltese Cross (Geneva) **intermittent** was standard, with films either short lengths cut from 35mm copies or lithographed tracings from theatrical productions. From the worldwide center of metal toy manufacture, Nuremberg goods were delivered in mass quantities to retailers such as Gamages in Great Britain and Sears, Roebuck in the USA.

DEAC ROSSELL

Oceania/South Pacific

Moving pictures first arrived in the islands of the Pacific through film production rather than exhibition, and Hawaii, which had been annexed by the USA in 1898, was the first island group to greet filmmakers. E. Burton **Holmes** and Oscar Depue shot scenic views and local agriculture in 1899, and they were followed by cameraman Robert K. **Bonine** who later established himself permanently in Hawaii as a filmmaker. By 1907, Leopold Sutto (traveling on the same boat as writer Jack London) was filming the Solomons and other islands for **Pathé-Frères**. In 1912, a local Tahiti photographer, Maxime Bopp du Pont, began shooting films, and early in 1913 an expedition under Gaston **Méliès** (brother of Georges **Méliès**), with a company of actors and two cameramen, spent a month filming on the island.

The Méliès company found film exhibition flourishing in Tahiti, with two large cinemas in the capital, Papeete, and another seven elsewhere on the island. Moving pictures had caught the public's fancy in French Polynesia, and by 1914 there were four cinemas in Papeete (largely financed by the Vicomte de Giron). Moving pictures also prospered on other islands in the Pacific, and Hawaii was again in the vanguard. As early as 1908 there were five **nickelodeons** in Honolulu, and five or six more on other islands of the group by the following year. In 1915 *Photoplay* reported that there were no fewer than 35 moving picture theaters in Honolulu alone.

While some audience segmentation was occurring by the end of this period, generally the **audiences** who attended Hawaiian shows were mixed—American (white), Hawaiian, Chinese, Japanese. A comparable audience diversity seems to have been the case on some other Pacific islands. The British protectorate of Fiji first enjoyed film shows in 1909, and by 1910 an Australian showman, Arthur Guest, was touring films to mixed Fijian and Hindu audiences. By 1913, there were three modern cinemas on the island, running T. J. **West**, Cozens **Spencer**, and **Gaumont** programs respectively, with the films distributed from Sydney. In Samoa, too, film prints came from Australia; by 1912, a local company was giving three shows a week there.

All kinds of films were screened, but the island peoples evinced particular interest in nonfiction films, especially those of impressive foreign technology, such as huge locomotives and other machines. Cinemas in Tahiti were so popular by 1913 that the authorities kept them closed three nights of the week so they would not take over island life completely. Some accounts, from Guam, for example, say that moving pictures even acted as a spur for local people to earn extra money to pay for cinema tickets. But in certain regions the colonial authorities considered films which showed fighting and shooting to be demoralizing for the population, and by 1914 there was talk of censorship.

See also: colonialism: Europe; imperialism: USA

Further reading

"Hawaiian shows" (1909) *Film Index*, 23 January: 12.
"Weekly Notes" [report from Fiji] (1910) *Kinematograph and Lantern Weekly*, 1 September: 1065.

STEPHEN BOTTOMORE

Olcott, Sidney (John Alcott)

b. 1872; d. 1949

actor, scriptwriter, director, USA

Initially an actor at **Biograph**, Olcott gained prominence as **Kalem**'s first filmmaker (1907–1912), directing the original *Ben Hur* (1907). He was an energetic, prolific pioneer of on-location shooting abroad, in Ireland (with popular, often political films), the European continent, and the Middle East—e.g., *From the Manger to the Cross* (1912). A dispute over *Manger* led to formation of the Gene **Gauntier** Feature Players (1912–1914). After releasing films independently ("Sidfilms"), he signed with **Famous Players** in 1915; later he worked for Goldwyn and Paramount. A recognized talent, he directed major silent stars such as Mary **Pickford** and Rudolph Valentino until his retirement in 1927.

GRETCHEN BISPLINGHOFF

Oliver, David

b. ?; d. ?

exhibitor, distributor, producer, Germany

An émigré from Galicia and an exhibitor since 1905, Oliver became co-director of **Nordisk**'s German subsidiary, Nordische Films, in 1906, which he built into one of the country's largest distribution companies before 1917. After the outbreak of **World War I**, Oliver restructured Nordische into a horizontal group of production and distribution companies, including his own Oliver Films (established in April 1915), all feeding into Nordische's distribution network. At the same time, operating independently with his own capital, he pushed the company's vertical integration by acquiring the Union Theater chain from **PAGU** and merging it with his own theaters to form Union-Theater Ltd. Due to its Danish origins, Nordische frequently was the target of hostile nationalist rhetoric and, in 1918, finally was merged into uFA, whose theater and distribution division Oliver then managed. After serving as a board member of Decla-Bioscop, he began working as a real estate agent and became involved in financing and supervising some of the most prestigious cinema construction projects in 1920's Germany.

MICHAEL WEDEL

Olsen, Ole

b. 1863; d. 1943

producer, Denmark

Olsen, who came from a very poor rural background, became a successful **fair/fairground** showman in the late 1880s. In 1905, he opened a moving picture theater in Copenhagen; the following year, he founded the production company **Nordisk** and quickly led it to international prominence. He became famous as Denmark's only real film tycoon and pulled off various Barnum-like **publicity** stunts, as when he turned the shooting of the shipwreck scenes for August **Blom**'s *Atlantis* (1913) into a major media event. He sold his Nordisk stock in 1914, but remained head of the company until 1922, when stockholders, concerned by Nordisk's financial difficulties, finally pushed him aside.

CASPAR TYBJERG

Omegna, Roberto

b. 1876; d. 1948

cameraman, director, Italy

A cousin of Guido Gozzano, one of Italy's major poets and a part-time scriptwriter, Omegna was a successful film exhibitor in Turin by 1901.

Three years later, he was making *actualités* with Arturo **Ambrosio** and soon was made the head technician and nonfiction filmmaker at **Ambrosio Film**, where he worked until 1923. The director and technical supervisor for more than sixty fiction films, Omegna gained real fame for his **ethnographic films** of Asia, Africa, and Latin America (often completed with Giovanni **Vitrotti**) and his **scientific films** about insects, plants, and minerals.

GIORGIO BERTELLINI

Onoe Matsunosuke

b. 1875; d. 1926

actor, Japan

After joining a touring theatrical troupe in 1889, Onoe became acquainted with **Makino Shozo** and played on the stage of the Senbonza theater in Kyoto, where Makino directed. Together with Makino, he entered **Yokota Shokai** in 1909. As a star of the old-school drama, he appeared on average in one film per week. His **acting style** and his patented facial expressions often were imitated in children's plays. Because of their status as children's entertainment, Onoe's films were always regarded as a form of lowbrow spectacle by the cultural elite.

HIROSHI KOMATSU

opera

Opera and moving pictures quickly established a fruitful relationship that, by 1915, had produced several hundred films of opera subjects. The moving picture had the same ability to paint dynamically in broad brush strokes on a grand canvas as did opera: the essentially "semaphore" nature of operatic acting of the period adapted easily to the "pantomimic" acting required of early film performers. These similarities were quickly recognized by a number of filmmakers worldwide, and the early industry adopted both operatic plots as subject matter and operatic stars as performers to add the desired respectability and legitimacy to

a form still viewed by many as novelty light entertainment.

Early subjects shared with opera included Goethe's *Faust* (**Lumière**, 1898; **Méliès**, 1898, 1903, 1904; **Edison**, 1900), Beaumarchais' *The Barber of Seville* (Méliès, 1904), Dumas' *La Dame aux Camelias* (**Nordisk**, 1908), Schiller's *Louisa Miller* (**Itala**, 1910) and Prevost's *Manon* (**Pathé-Frères**, 1910). During the especially rich period of 1907–1911, and in conjunction with productions of *films d'art*, specific opera adaptations included Auber's *Fra Diavolo* (**Walturdaw**, 1907), Mascagni's *Cavalleria Rusticana* (**Éclair**, 1909), Strauss's *Elektra* (**Vitagraph**, 1910), Verdi's *Il Trovatore* (**Lubin**, 1909; Pathé-Frères, 1911), and Lehar's *The Merry Widow* (Nordisk, 1907, **Kalem**, 1907). In Russia, Shuvalov's *Boris Godunov* (1907), featuring scenes from the play on which Mussorgsky's opera is based, was one of the earliest Russian fiction subjects; in 1911, Vasili **Goncharov** filmed scenes from Glinka's opera, *A Life for the Tsar* and directed the first film based on a Tchaikovsky opera, *Eugene Onegin*. No less than five versions of Sardou's *Tosca*, the source of Puccini's opera, appeared prior to 1915, including two versions for **Film d'Art**, the less successful of which (1908) starred Sarah **Bernhardt**. Edwin S. **Porter** first brought Wagner's great sacred music drama *Parsifal* to the screen, serialized in twelve parts, for Edison in 1904, scarcely a year after the work's American premiere.

Opera films were often accompanied by **musical scores** arranged from the original works and sometimes featured live singers performing either next to or behind the screen. Subjects shared with opera also provided ideal material for experiments in **synchronized sound** film, for which a gramophone record often featuring a distinguished operatic singer supplied the soundtrack. **Clément-Maurice** exhibited a selection of these at the 1900 Paris Exposition, including a scene from Gounod's *Romeo et Juliette*. Leading exponents included Oskar **Messter** who produced his first **Tonbild** in 1903, and later released abridged versions of Lehar's *The Count of Luxemburg* (1909) and Strauss's *Die Fledermaus*. In France, Georges **Mendel** produced a series of *films chantants* (singing films) which, by 1906, included scenes from *La Boheme*, *Rigoletto*, *Mignon*, *Lakme*,

Herodiade, and *Guillaume Tell*. One of the earliest women directors, Alice **Guy**, made numerous *phonoscènes* for **Gaumont** between 1905 and 1907, featuring artists from the Paris Opera; she even attempted, unsuccessfully, to film the most well known opera star of the time, Enrico Caruso.

Mendel used Caruso's recording of the "Sextet" from Donizetti's *Lucia Di Lammermoor* as the soundtrack for his 1908 film version of the scene. The American pioneer George R. Webb first demonstrated his "singing pictures" in 1914, and three years later screened scenes from *Pagliacci* and *Rigoletto* that also used Caruso's recorded voice. Caruso himself, who initially had a poor opinion of the cinema and screen acting, eventually would make two features for **Famous Players**-Lasky: *My Cousin* (1918) and *A Splendid Romance* (1918).

Early film appearances by **stars** from the opera stage included Emmy Destinn in *Die Macht des Gesanges* (1913), Berta Kalich in *Marta of the Lowlands* (1914), based on D'Albert's opera *Tiefland*, and Fritzi Scheff in *Pretty Mrs. Smith* (1915). The Italian soprano, Lina Cavalieri, renowned as "The Most Beautiful Woman in the World," appeared in Playgoers Film Company's *Manon Lescaut* (1914), accompanied by the French tenor Lucien Muratore. The following year Cavalieri made *Sposa Nella Morte* [The Bride of Death] for Tiber Film in Rome, and appeared in a further six features. In Russia, the tenor Dmitri Smirnov starred in the **Drankov**'s **detective film**, *The Secret of Box Letter A* (1915), and the phenomenal bass, Feodor Chaliapin, repeated his stage role as Tsar Ivan from Rimsky-Korsakov's opera *The Maid of Pskov*, in a screen version of Sharez's *Tsar Ivan Vasilyevich Groznyi* [Ivan The Terrible] (1915).

Cecil B. **DeMille**, whose early theatrical experiences included working for a touring opera company, appreciated the operatic scope and potential of the moving picture. Amongst his earliest successes, in 1915, was a screen version, for the Jesse **Lasky** Feature Play Company, of David Belasco's play *The Girl of the Golden West*, upon which Puccini had based his opera, which had premiered at New York's Metropolitan in 1910. DeMille also directed one of America's most widely-loved opera stars, Geraldine Farrar, in

her debut features, *Carmen*, *Maria Rosa*, and *Temptation*, all made for Lasky in 1915. Farrar, who would make fourteen silent films in all, scored a notable personal success repeating her popular stage characterization of Bizet's heroine, although DeMille engaged his brother William to provide a scenario in order to avoid paying royalties to the estate of the original author, Prosper Merimée.

Opera stories were also selected as vehicles for established non-operatic stars: Pauline Frederick appeared in Famous Players' *Zaza* (1915) based on Belasco's adaptation of a popular French play, set by Leoncavallo for an operatic version the following year. Even Mary **Pickford** appeared in the title role of another Puccini opera subject, *Madam Butterfly* (1915), opposite Marshall Neilan as Pinkerton.

See also: acting styles; law and the cinema

Further reading

Citron, Marcia J. (2000) *Opera on Screen*, New Haven: Yale University Press.

Fawkes, Richard (2000) *Opera on Film*, London: Duckworth.

Franklin, Peter (1994) "Movies as Opera," in Jeremy Tambling (ed.) *A Night in at the Opera*, 77–110, London: John Libbey.

Wlaschin, Ken (1997) *Opera on Screen*, Los Angeles: Beachwood Press.

PAUL FRYER

optical intermittent projectors

Technically, projection using moving mirrors, prisms or lenses and continuously running film was superior to intermittently moving the celluloid itself, which invariably damaged expensive prints. Such apparatuses were designed by John Nevil Maskelyne (1896), Paul Mortier (1897), and many others: over 200 optical projection patents were granted between 1896 and 1910. But the expense of their engineering, especially given the reliable **magic lantern** equipment that was easily adapted for films, inhibited commercial success apart from the Mechau projector of 1912 (called Arcadia in Great Britain), with over 500 manufactured through 1934. The principle was revived for the Imax system in 1967.

DEAC ROSSELL

Orientaliska teatern

Founded in 1907, Orientaliska teatern was the principal cinema in N. P. **Nilsson**'s chain of Stockholm cinemas. Frequently criticized for the sensational nature of the Danish and French films which the cinema exhibited, Nilsson established a modest production unit headed by Anna Hofmann-Uddgren that produced six films between 1911 and 1912. Capitalizing on local promotions or topical events such as the visit of William Booth to Stockholm in 1911, Orientaliska teatern also produced screen adaptations of August Strindberg: *Fröken Julie* [Miss Julie] (1912) and *Fadren* [The Father] (1912), neither of which were well received.

JOHN FULLERTON

Ors, Eugeni d'

b. 1881; d. 1954

writer, Spain

Art critic and philosopher. Between 1906 and 1915, Ors published several articles on moving pictures in Barcelona. He considered moving pictures to be a lesser art, acceptable for the working classes but not at all for the bourgeoisie. Between 1910 and 1911, together with Ramón Rucabado, he organised anti-cinema campaigns all over Spain, criticizing moving pictures for flaunting immoral behavior and having little artistic merit. He argued that censorship served to defend ethical and aesthetic standards. He fervently believed that cinema should concentrate specifically on educational nonfiction.

See also: law and the cinema

JOAN M. MINGUET

Ouimet, Léo-Ernest

b. 1877; d. 1972

exhibitor, distributor, producer, Quebec

Léo-Ernest Ouimet was the first and foremost film exhibitor, distributor, and producer in Quebec during the silent period. Initially a theater electrician, he opened Montreal's first moving picture theater, the Ouimetoscope, in 1906, and met with a phenomenal success. He quickly moved into distribution, as well as the production of *actualités* on local events: *Incendie de la rue Notre-Dame* [Fire in Notre-Dame Street] (1906), *Effondrement du pont de Québec* [Collapse of the Québec bridge] (1907), *Tricentenaire de Québec* [Tricentennial of Quebec] (1908). After becoming a nationwide distributor in Canada and a producer of medium-length films, Ouimet left for Hollywood in 1920, but failed in his venture to produce feature-length films. He returned to Montreal to work as a distributor and exhibitor (1930–1934) and finished his career as a liquor store manager.

GERMAIN LACASSE

Oxilia, Nino

b. 1889; d. 1917

playwright, director, scriptwiter, Italy

In 1912, young playwright Nino Oxilia became interested in moving pictures. He learned filmmaking under Ubaldo Maria **Del Colle** at **Pasquali** and then Luigi **Maggi** and Mario **Caserini** at **Ambrosio**. In 1913, he directed sophisticated melodramas starring Alberto **Nepoti** and Maria **Jacobini**, his fiancè, for Savoia Film. At Celio Film, in 1914, he completed *Sangue blue* [Blue Blood], with Francesca **Bertini**. In 1915, for **Cines**, he created his masterpiece, the musical poem *Rapsodia Satanica* [Satanic Rapsody] (not released until 1917), featuring Lyda **Borelli** and an original symphonic score by Pietro Mascagni. He died in combat during **World War I**.

GIORGIO BERTELLINI

P

Pagano, Bartolomeo or Maciste

b. 1878; d. 1947

actor, Italy

Born in the region of Liguria, Bartolomeo Pagano was working in the docks of Genoa's harbor when Giovanni **Pastrone**, impressed with his muscular physiognomy, chose him for the leading role of Maciste in *Cabiria* (1914), the ground-breaking spectacular film which so influenced D. W. **Griffith** in making *Intolerance* (1916). After such a successful beginning, Maciste became the protagonist of a series of films, from *Maciste* (1915) and *Maciste Alpino* [Maciste in the Mountains] (1916) to *Maciste all'Inferno* [Maciste in Hell] (1926), throughout which he played a good giant who protects and helps those who are weak or downtrodden, while keeping himself out of trouble and embodying the best patriotic values.

ANGELA DALLE VACCHE

PAGU/AKGT

The Allgemeine Kinematographen-Theater Gesellschaft (AKGT), founded in Frankfurt/Main in 1906 by Paul **Davidson**, ran the biggest **cinema chain** in Germany by 1910. Profits from its Union-Theater (U.T.), sited in prime locations in Berlin and other regional industrial centers, allowed it to expand into theater equipment supply, production, and distribution under the new name, Projektions-AG "Union" (PAGU) in 1910. Between 1910 and 1912, when AKTG was liquidated, attendance in U.T. cinemas rose from 2.5 million to 6 million, proof of PAGU's success in widening its **audience** appeal to include upper middle-class tastes with luxury theater design and feature films. In 1913, PAGU moved operations to Berlin and opened new production facilities in Berlin-Tempelhof, specifically to produce films starring Asta **Nielsen**, which it had distributed exclusively since 1911. In 1914, PAGU bought **Vitascope** and hired Ernst **Lubitsch**, eventually its most successful director.

THOMAS ELSAESSER

painting and the visual arts

The complex relationship of painting to early cinema can be summarized under three main headings. First, and most generally, paintings served as important sources for **costumes**, **set design**, and the overall style of many historical subjects, as they had long done in the theater. Then, more specifically, a number of early films can be interpreted as "realizations" of well-known or generic paintings. Finally, a third relationship arose from the changing representation of the artist as protagonist. Beyond these, there are also broader questions of how moving pictures found their place within a culture already saturated with visual images, where painting still occupied a pre-eminent place; and the related issue of how painters and the audience for the visual arts related to the new medium during its first two decades.

A first response to the moving image for some commentators was to compare it to recent styles of painting, although not as a compliment. The

Russian writer Maxim Gorky evoked the "soundless shadow of movement" in a famous article of 1896, before joking that he might be suspected of Symbolism, in a reference to the newly fashionable school of poetry and painting, popularly believed to specialize in morbid and supernatural subjects. In the same year, an English art critic compared moving pictures with the distinctive painting of a Victorian group: "both the cinematograph and the Pre-Raphaelite suffer from the same vice . . . [both] are incapable of selection." However derisory, these references convey the sense of a new way of picturing the world and also of the modishness of moving pictures that offended some. The reference to the Pre-Raphaelite group of painters that included Dante Gabriel Rossetti, William Holman Hunt, and John Everett Millais also serves to recall how central a certain kind of moralizing narrative painting had become during the 19th century. A painting such as Hunt's *The Awakening Conscience* (1854), in which a woman rises from sitting on a man's lap as if inspired, could provoke extended public discussion as to the moral and dramatic meaning contained in this emblematic moment. Even more relevant to early moving pictures were the picture series, such as George Cruickshank's *The Drunkard's Children* (1848) or William Frith's *The Road to Ruin* (1878), widely available as prints and **magic lantern** slides, which taught viewers to "read" narrative across the individual pictures that marked its decisive stages.

Such habits of interpretation were well ingrained by the time moving picture producers started to consider what subjects would interest their patrons. Many early films were derived indirectly from famous paintings that already had passed through the Victorian chain of reproduction. Millais's chivalric fireman in *The Rescue* (1855) had become "Bob the fireman" in a lantern slide set before emerging as the rescuer hero of James **Williamson**'s *Fire!* (1901). Similarly, the various "Life of Christ" films produced in the USA and France between 1897 and 1906 all drew directly or indirectly on the painterly tradition of depicting Biblical episodes. Leonardo da Vinci's *Last Supper* (1498) inevitably influenced the realization of this scene, along with many classic crucifixion paintings; but the most consistently used source was undoubtedly Jacques Joseph Tissot's comprehensive illustration of the Bible, published between 1896 and 1904 on both sides of the Atlantic. This curious combination of evocative first-hand observation and maudlin religiosity would leave its mark on later "religious" and **biblical films**. Another widely popular subject was the Faust story, and in particular the figure of Mephistopheles, which appears in the catalogues of **Edison**, **Lumière**, Robert **Paul** and Georges **Méliès**. Here the cultural impetus may well have come initially from the popularity of Charles Gounod's **opera**, or from Henry Irving's long-running stage production, but the main iconographic source for the central characters' costumes and appearance seems to have been Eugène Delacroix's illustrations of Johann Wolfgang von Goethe's *Faust*, made in 1828–1839 (and approved by the author).

By 1909, when Vitagraph launched its very successful *Life of Moses*, it had become sound business practice to advertise the range of painterly sources, which in this case were said to include: "Tissot, Gérôme, Gustav-Doré [*sic*], Edwin Austin Abbey, Briton Reviere, Sir Lawrence Alma-Tadema, R. A. Joseph Israel and Benjamin Constant." The mere mention of names that were both resonant and approved (even if many are now forgotten by art historians) became an index of the "quality," and in this case propriety, that Vitagraph sought. Of these artists, Jean-Léon Gérôme's two Roman amphitheatre paintings, *The Christian Martyr's Last Prayer* (1863) and *Pollice Verso* (1874), and Alma-Tadema's intimate scenes of Roman high life, such as *Silver Favorites* (1903) and *Her Eyes Are with Her Thoughts* (1907), would remain highly influential among all filmmakers engaged in re-creating the ancient world, from the Italians to Cecil B. **DeMille**. Similarly, Doré's illustrated books and the Mediterranean and Middle Eastern landscapes of David Roberts became pervasive, if often unacknowledged, sources for atmospheric settings and **lighting** schemes.

Painting could also play a more central role in early cinema. At the beginning, when moving pictures were brief and often shown in mixed programs with lantern slides, it is clear that some subjects were, effectively, "realizations," or extrapolations into motion from originally painted images, which had become widely known through engravings, lithographs, and, increasingly, photographic reproduction. So, for instance, of the **Kinetoscope** productions made by Alfred Clark for

Figure 92 Pollice verso, by Jean-Léon Gérôme (1859). (Phoenix Art Museum.)

Edison in 1895, *The Execution of Mary Queen of Scots* approximated the grouping of figures in an anonymous painting of the event from 1587, while *The Burning of Joan of Arc* related quite closely to the composition of Jules Eugène Lenepveu's much-reproduced painting of the same title. Lumières' *Mort de Marat* [Death of Marat] (1897), like most of the "historic views" supervised by Georges **Hatot** around 1897–1898 to supplement the *actualités* that comprised most of the company's catalogue, almost inevitably drew its central image of the assassination in a bath from Jean Louis David's famous 1793 painting. For historical subjects that were more modern, yet prior to the invention of **photography**, paintings (and their subsequent reproduction) were a crucial means of lodging decisive images in the popular memory; and in the case of the French Revolution's most famous episodes, the near-contemporary record-cum celebration provided by David and others was crucial. Among the Vitagraph quality productions of 1908–1810, a film such as *Napoleon, the Man of Destiny*

(1909) drew on more than a decade of rising interest in Napoleon and various dramatizations, but also crucially on the realization of David's *Coronation of Napoleon and Josephine* (1807) and Horace Vernet's *Napoleon's Farewell to the Old Guard* (1825).

However, as films became longer, and began to develop distinctive editing patterns, direct allusion to a painting would interrupt the pattern, creating a new version of the frozen tableau of the Victorian stage. In Vitagraph's *Washington Under the American Flag* (1909), for instance, the inauguration is staged to match Felix Darley's painting, except that the tableau is disrupted by a three-quarter view of Washington and the other characters on the balcony, as if, in the middle of a public event, the viewer is granted a private moment. Realizing famous moments as they were painted would continue for another decade, but the practice already had begun to seem archaic in relation to cinema's developing narrative structures. A relatively late example of the direct influence of painting would seem to be Elwin Neame's *The Lady of Shalott* (1912), although this lost film is known only from reviews. One of these makes clear the film's commitment to realizing the central motif of Tennyson's original poem—that the bewitched Lady can only see the outside world reflected in a mirror—and its success in creating a "mystical effect," as well as a highly praised "almost stereoscopic" river scene. Tennyson had provided many subjects for English Pre-Raphaelite painters, and the Lady of Shalott was a favorite, with major works by Holman Hunt and several by John Waterhouse being among the most popular of all English paintings. Neame is unlikely to have tackled this essentially Symbolist subject without the support of the painterly tradition, although we cannot judge if the film was modeled on any specific works.

Turning to the image of painters and other artists on screen, there is a clear evolution across the first twenty years of moving pictures from conventional stereotypes towards representations that did engage, to some degree, with the revolution in visual arts actually underway in this period. In 1898, for instance, the pioneers Méliès and Paul both included in their output a number of "art" subjects. Méliès's *Pygmalion et Galathée* (1898) realized the classical story of the sculptor whose love for the statue he has made miraculously brings her to life, following Gérôme's sentimental painting of the subject, while *Rêve d'artiste* [An Artist's Dream] (1898) promised a fantasy with "transparent women" and *L'atelier d'artiste* [The Artist's Studio] (1898) was described as a "farce about models." In Paul's *Come Along, Do* (1898), an elderly man visiting an art exhibition is distracted by a nude female statue, until his wife hurries him away; and the catalogue account which is all that survives of Paul's *The Artist and the Flower Girl* (c.1901) describes a struggling artist offering shelter on a cold night to a flower girl, who later "creeps off unobserved" after hearing the banter of his friends—this soon after Giacomo Puccini's *La Bohème* (1896). Several years later, the Pygmalion theme again appeared in two of Edwin S. **Porter**'s films for Edison, *An Artist's Dream* (1900) and *The Artist's Dilemma* (1901), which involve variations on the theme of female images becoming "real" through the actions or desires of a stereotypical artist. Here the artist is little more than a conventional device who sanctions a new form of Victorian theater's "transformation" scene, with stop-action allowing figures to appear and

QUO VADIS ? - La morte del Gladiatore

Figure 93 Frame still from *Quo Vadis?* (Cines, 1913). (Courtesy of Ivo Blom.)

disappear easily. He is also licensed to consort with women, often in states of undress; and in the *fin de siècle* climate typified by Oscar Wilde's *Picture of Dorian Gray* (1890) and George Du Maurier's *Trilby* (1894), he may be associated with occult powers, as in Paul's *The Devil in the Studio* (1901).

The early years of the new century saw a series of radical challenges both to traditional salon painting and to the various Symbolist movements that had consolidated the idea of an "avant-garde" in art in the 1890s. It has often seemed surprising that Cubists such as Pablo Picasso or Futurists such as Umberto Boccioni in Italy and Mikhail Larionov in Russia did not pursue their experiments in representing multiple points of view and simultaneity by means of film— and indeed their work is often explained by reference to the emergence of cinema. But while many of these modernist artists were undoubtedly filmgoers, there were as yet few obvious ways for them to enter the world of film production. Wassily Kandinsky, shortly before he began to paint abstractly, considered the possibility of making a film of his "light play," *Der gelbe Klang* [The Yellow Noise], around 1912; and the Russian-born painter Léopold Survage produced a series of abstract pictures in Paris in 1913 which he hoped, vainly, to animate on film. The Russian avant-garde was the first, in 1914, to appear in a film that reflected their iconoclastic stance: *Drama v kabare futuristov* [Drama in the Futurists' Cabaret No. 13]. A surviving still from this lost film shows the painters who acted themselves, Larionov and Natalia Goncharova, blazoned with the distinctive images that they habitually wore. However, the one major artist of the period who did abandon painting for cinema was not an avant-gardist, but the respected British Academician, Sir Hubert **von Herkomer**, a former social realist who set out to make apparently conventional narrative films in 1913, although in his own studio and under his control. If moving pictures had effectively taken over the traditional role of history painting by 1912, with major commemorative films appearing in many countries, the place of the oppositional artist in cinema would remain problematic until the 1920s.

Further reading

Christie, Ian (2001) "Before the Avant-Gardes: Artists and Cinema, 1910–1914," in Leonardo Quaresima and Laura Vichi (eds.) *La Decima Musa/The Tenth Muse: il cinema e le alter arti/ cinema and other arts*, Udine: Forum.

Meisel, Martin (1983) *Realizations: Narrative, Pictorial, and Theatrical Arts in Nineteenth-Century England*, Princeton: Princeton University Press.

Uricchio, William and Roberta E. Pearson (1993) *Reframing Culture: The Case of the Vitagraph Quality Films*, Princeton: Princeton University Press.

Winter, O. (1896) "Ain't It Lifelike," *The New Review*, February, reprinted in *Sight and Sound*, 51.4 (Autumn 1982): 294–296.

IAN CHRISTIE

palace cinemas

A palace cinema was an ornate theater of more than 1,000 seats—typically 2,000 to 5,000—staffed by a corps of ushers and an orchestra, showing both feature-length films and live stage entertainment, and air conditioned. The image of the 5,000-seat Radio City Music Hall still glows as an example at the beginning of the 21st century, but the concept was little more than nascent during the early cinema period.

At first, entrepreneurs converted existing theaters to show moving pictures along with **vaudeville**. For example, in November 1907, impresario William A. **Brady** refurbished the 1,200-seat Alhambra, located on New York City's Union Square, to present moving pictures, but with an emphasis still on live entertainment. Marcus **Loew** built his empire on taking over large legitimate theaters and presenting "small time vaudeville" shows which included moving pictures.

It was actually far from New York City where pioneering exhibitors first built palace cinemas, and then the concept finally made it to New York where many of its finest examples were constructed after the middle 1910s. An early example was the 900-seat Princess, which the **Saxe** brothers opened in Milwaukee, in December, 1909. Costing $50,000, the Princess represented Milwaukee's first theater built for moving pictures, not adapted to show them. While not quite a palace, it was ornate in a European style. Four ushers in cadet grey uniforms assisted "guests" to their "elegant" seats. Cut flowers lined the lobby. Twelve hundred incandescent lamps ensured that the Princess' facade would not be missed during a nighttime visit downtown. The Princess contained Milwaukee's first theater organ and a seven-piece orchestra. That is, save for size, lack of feature films, and air conditioning, the Princess possessed most of the traits of a palace cinema.

S. L. (Roxy) **Rothapfel** had worked for the Saxe brothers in Milwaukee, and is usually credited as the father of the palace cinema with his October 1913 opening of the Regent on the corner of 116th Street and Seventh Avenue in New York City. At nearly 2,000 seats, it was twice the size of the Princess and other mini-palaces then dotting the larger cities of the USA. Roxy had learned his lessons well; although the Regent was located nine miles north of Times Square, by April 1914 he was managing the brand new 3,000-seat Strand in Times Square, placing him squarely in the forefront of the movement toward palace cinemas.

The first planned palace cinema, the Central Park, was opened in Chicago by **Balaban** & **Katz**, on Saturday 27 October 1917. With its Rapp & Rapp design, 2,000 seats, corps of uniformed ushers, and air conditioning, the success of the Central Park set off a wave of palace cinema building in the USA.

Figure 94 Saxe Theatre, Minneapolis, 1912.

See also: audiences: surveys and debates

Further reading

Gomery, Douglas (1992) *Shared Pleasures: A History of Movie Presentation in the United States*, Madison: University of Wisconsin Press.

Hall, Ben M. (1961) *The Best Remaining Seats: The Story of the Golden Age of the Movie Palace*, New York, Bramhall House.

DOUGLAS GOMERY

Palestine

Early cinema production in Palestine, which was under Turkish Ottoman rule until 1917, consisted chiefly of biblically-oriented **travelogues** shot by American and European cameramen, as well as the initial efforts of several Zionist filmmakers.

During cinema's first decade, both **Lumière** and **Edison** operators visited Palestine, as did pioneers including Henry Howse. A landmark biblical epic filmed on location by Sidney **Olcott** was **Kalem**'s *From the Manger to the Cross* (1912).

Zionist cinema sprang from other media used in propaganda, such as pamphlets and lectures, the latter of which accompanied **magic lantern shows** from the 1890s on. Lantern slides were gradually augmented and then largely supplanted by motion pictures fulfilling the same purposes: promoting the Zionist cause among both Jewish and non-Jewish audiences throughout the world and raising funds for Zionist activity.

The founder of modern political Zionism, Theodor Herzl, initiated filming in Palestine in 1900, based on proposals made by a Warsaw-born Viennese student, Adolf Neufeld; this earliest attempt was abortive and no further activity apparently took place for the remainder of the decade. The immediate pre-war years saw successful accounts of Zionist progress produced by Englishman Murray Rosenberg (in 1911) and Noah Sokolovsky's Odessa-based Misrach Company (in 1913). One of the founding fathers of the city of Tel Aviv, Akiva Arieh Weiss, has been claimed as the first locally-based Jewish filmmaker, although substantiating evidence is lacking.

The most active Jewish film pioneer in Palestine was Ukrainian-born Yaakov Ben Dov (1882–1968), originally a still photographer, whose motion picture career began with the British conquest of the country in 1917. Most of his films were produced or sponsored by official Zionist organizations and, though at times they endeavored poetically to stir nationalistic fervor, they almost totally eschewed the use of actors or fictitious plots or characters. The lack of local facilities resulted in post-production being carried out largely in either Germany or Great Britain.

Feature film production seems scarcely to have been envisioned until the earliest known scripts were authored by Zionist official, Joseph Gal-Ezer, in 1920, and very few commenced shooting in the silent era, towards the end of which Ben Dov's most prominent successors, Natan Axelrod and Baruch Agadati, entered the field.

By contrast to Palestine's meager production activity, film-going was extremely popular, with the earliest documented screening taking place at a Jerusalem hotel in June, 1900. It was not until 1913, however, that the country's first permanent cinema, the Eden, was opened in Tel Aviv. The proprietors had been granted exclusive rights of operation in the city for a thirteen-year period, which resulted in a plethora of cinemas along the Tel Aviv-Jaffa municipal boundary by 1926.

In the absence of a local **trade press**, few details are known of distribution patterns, but one known circuit of the early 1920s began in **Egypt** and continued through Palestine, Lebanon and Syria to Turkey.

See also: biblical films; propaganda films

Further reading

Tryster, Hillel (1995) *Israel Before Israel: Silent Cinema in the Holy Land*, Jerusalem: Steven Spielberg Jewish Film Archive.

HILLEL TRYSTER

Paley, William ("Daddy")

b. 1857; d. 1924

cameraman, USA

Born in Lincolnshire, England, Paley emigrated to the USA where he became an X-Ray exhibitor.

Attracted by the film industry, in 1897 he built a **projector** which he named the "Kalatechnoscope," and also undertook filming assignments. In March 1898, Paley contracted with **Edison** to film Spanish-American war incidents, and traveling to Cuba was soon known among war correspondents as "the Kinetoscope Man," distinctive both for the camera he operated and for his own size. Following recovery from a near fatal fever, Paley formed a partnership with William F. **Steiner** in 1904 to manufacture short **comedies**. When that venture eventually failed, he returned to working as a cameraman, and from 1910 to 1911 was shooting **westerns** for Gaston **Méliès**. In March 1912, filming for Nestor, he suffered a fall, and as a result lost a leg, which finished his career.

STEPHEN BOTTOMORE

Parnaland, Ambroise-François

b. 1854; d. 1913

film equipment manufacturer, industrialist, France

After founding "Parnaland Frères" in April 1895, Ambroise-François registered his first patent for a **chronophotographic** machine on February 25, 1896. Two other patents followed for reversible **cameras**, including the "Cinépar," which was mareketed in France and Britain. After opening a store in Paris, Parnaland started producing films as well as selling his apparatuses to other companies. In 1898, he recorded Dr. **Doyen**'s surgical operations with **Clément-Maurice**, but he was taken to court for selling the films to exhibitors. By 1907, Parnaland was marketing several kinds of excellent apparatuses and offering a catalog of 480 films that he had directed since 1896. This enabled him, in association with lawyer and financier Charles **Jourjon**, to form the Société des films et cinématographes **Éclair** in April 1907. He left the company around 1909.

Further reading

Mannoni, Laurent (May 1993) "Ambroise-François Parnaland, pioniere del cinema e co-fondatore della società Éclair," in Richard Abel and Lorenzo Codelli (eds.) "Lightning Images: the Éclair Company, 1907–1920," *Griffithiana*, 47: 10–30.

LAURENT MANNONI

Pasquali & C. (1908–1921)

Founded as Pasquali & Tempo in 1908 by accountant, journalist, director, and producer Ernesto Maria **Pasquali** and a few Turinese businessmen, Pasquali was to become one of the most aggressive and ambitious Italian film companies. Initially, the company released a number of quality films without owning studios. In July 1910, however, through administrative restructuring and refinancing, Pasquali & Tempo became Pasquali & C. It immediately built its own studios—three, all at once, equipped with artificial lighting—and began turning known and unknown actors and directors into household names.

First it created an outstanding screen couple by luring away Alberto **Capozzi** and Lydia De Roberti from **Ambrosio** Film, protagonists of *Gli ultimi giorni di Pompei* [The Last Days of Pompeii] (1908). Pasquali also hired other notable actors such as Mary Cleo Tarlarini, Gustavo **Serena**, Maria **Jacobini**, and Ubaldo Maria **Del Colle**, the last of which soon also worked as a director. The films released in this period include the poignant modern drama, *Calvario* [The Ordeal] (1911), possibly one of the company's first **multiple-reel films**, as well as the romantic adventure, *La prigione infuocata* [The Flery Prison], and the vengeful melodrama, *L'Uragano* [The Uragan], both directed in 1911 by Del Colle.

Between 1911 and 1914, Pasquali had its most productive period. In 1912, Ferdinand **Guillaume** was hired away from **Cines**, where he had become famous as Tontolini, to launch the **comic series**, *Polidor* (1912–1915), and become Italian cinema's most celebrated film comedian. The shift to feature films increased rather than reduced the company's average output, which amounted to 78 films per year, with a maximum of 100 titles in 1912. Although only 70 of a total of 400 films produced survive, and 50 of these are *Polidor* comedies, it is possible to argue that Pasquali's dramatic production comprised mostly **historical films** rather than modern romances or adventure films.

In 1913, Pasquali opened a branch in Rome and hired Enrico **Vidali** as artistic director. Vidali distinguished himself by directing two of the company's most remarkable international hits, the six-reel *Spartaco* [Spartacus] (1913) and, aided by Del Colle, the nine-reel *Jone o gli Ultimi Giorni di Pompei* [The Last Days of Pompeii] (1913), produced in only 26 days in open competition with Ambrosio's much-publicized production of the same title. Pasquali slightly altered the film title to avoid, in vain, a lawsuit from Ambrosio. The success of both films in the world market, where they often competed with the same title, showcased the winning equation of highbrow entertainment and spectacular feature-length productions.

The war took a toll on Pasquali: a most ambitious adaptation from the Bible had to be cancelled. Fourteen fiction films were released in 1915, eleven the year after, seven in 1917, and only four in 1918. In 1919, Ernesto Maria **Pasquali** died. Within a year, the company became part of the Italian trust of film firms, UCI (Unione Cinematografica Italiana), whose production strategies accentuated, rather than solved, Italian cinema's crisis throughout the 1920s.

GIORGIO BERTELLINI

Pasquali, Ernesto Maria

b. 1883; d. 1919

journalist, scriptwriter, director, producer, Italy

A scriptwriter and director at **Ambrosio** Film, Pasquali founded Pasquali & Tempo (later **Pasquali** Films) in Turin in 1908. Director of second-rate **historical films**, as a producer he challenged competitors with an aggressive micromanaging style similar to Giovanni **Pastrone**'s. In 1912, he became president of the *Unione Italiana Cinematografisti*, Italy's first trade association. That year, he lured from **Cines** comedian Ferdinand **Guillaume** and launched him in the *Polidor* comic series; he also produced **crime films** and achieved international fame with historical epics, *Spartaco* [Spartacus] (1913) and *Jone* [The Last Days of Pompeii] (1913). **World War I** curtailed his activities.

GIORGIO BERTELLINI

Pastrone, Giovanni

b. 1883; d. 1959

producer, director, Italy

Pastrone's reputation largely derives from the historical epic, *Cabiria* (1914), made with the collaboration of poet Gabriele **D'Annunzio**; however, his contribution to the art of cinema goes beyond the technical achievements of that film, the most profitable ever until the release of *The Birth of a Nation* (1915).

The strategy implemented by Pastrone in the early 1910s through **Itala** Film, the third largest company in Italy after **Ambrosio** and **Cines**, was threefold. As a manager, he reformed the production process by applying a tightly organized procedure to shooting and editing, anticipating similar methods later employed by Thomas **Ince** and Mack **Sennett**. As a producer, he exploited one of the main assets of Italian cinema (**comedies**, hugely successful and exported worldwide) by luring from **Pathé** the comedian André **Deed**, whose **comic series**—based on the character "Cretinetti" ("Foolshead" in English) and marked by a distinctive flair for mayhem—became a box office phenomenon. From a technical standpoint, Itala productions were blessed by the expertise of Spanish special effects wizard Segundo de **Chomón**, also from Pathé.

Drawing upon a tradition inaugurated by Pathé and **Gaumont**, Pastrone garnered another commercial triumph with *La caduta di Troia* [The Fall of Troy] (1910), notable for its three-dimensional sets (a striking departure from the painted backdrops of earlier films) and a bold approach to depth of field. His bourgeois melodramas were enhanced by spectacle (buildings on fire became an Itala Film visual trademark), mystery—as in the virtuoso set pieces for *Tigris* (1913)—and a compact narrative

structure. At a time when most theater performers regarded moving pictures with contempt, Pastrone persuaded stage celebrity Ermete **Zacconi** to take the leading role for the two-reel *Padre* [Father] (1912).

It was with his most ambitious project, the three-hour *Cabiria*, that Pastrone brought early Italian cinema to its zenith. An astounding feat of technique and mise-en-scène, this dramatized rendition of the war between ancient Rome and Carthage displays his directorial talent at its best. Multiple exposures were employed for the sequence where the eruption of Mount Etna (staged by Chomón) brings destruction and grief; elaborate tracking shots (such as in the scene dedicated to a ceremony in the temple of the pagan god Moloch) drew the audience into the scene; and the supporting role of Numidian slave Maciste (Bartolomeo **Pagano**) gave birth to a **star** phenomenon and to a new kind of action film (the "strong men" genre) which was destined to grow throughout the silent era and continue well into the 1960s.

D'Annunzio's influence can be detected in Pastrone's two other major works, *Il fuoco* [Fire] (1915) and *Tigre reale* [Royal Tigress] (1916). Their decadent symbolism is controlled by an intimate, chamber-piece form, finding its full expression in the flamboyant performances of Pina **Menichelli**, one of the most gifted representatives of the diva phenomenon which preceded the collapse of Italian cinema in the aftermath of **World War I**.

See also: camera movement; historical films; multiple-reel/feature films: Europe; staging in depth; trick films

Further reading

Bertetto, Paolo and Gianni Rondolino (eds.) (1998) *Cabiria e il suo tempo*, Turin: Museo Nazionale del Cinema/Milan: Il Castoro.

Cherchi Usai, Paolo (1985) *Giovanni Pastrone*, Florence: La Nuova Italia.

Pastrone, Giovanni (1977) *Cabiria*, Turin: Museo Nazionale del Cinema.

PAOLO CHERCHI USAI

Patankar Friends & Company

Among the founding institutions of Indian cinema, with **Phalke Films**. Although its first film, *King Shriyal*, was not released until 1918, the company grew out of cameraman-director S. N. Patankar's association with V. P. Divekar and A. P. Karandikar on an abortive 1912 project, *Savitri*. Their *Death of Narayanrao Peshwa* (1915) is almost certainly India's first **historical film**, and the **mythological** tale, *Ram Vanvas* (The Exile of Rama) (1918), the first **serial**. The company briefly included Dwarkadas Sampat and Mohanlal G Dave, who established the influential **Kohinoor Film Company**. It had to shut down in 1922, when Patankar left to form the National Film Company.

SURESH CHABRIA

Pathé (Australia)

This branch opened in Melbourne in July 1909, and grew to be the largest film distributor and producer (but not exhibitor) in the country. Pathé introduced the weekly **newsreel** to Australian audiences, at first with imported issues, then with local material added, and in November 1910 with a fully local version (incorporated into *Australasian Gazette* issued by **Australasian Films** in 1916). Several local camera operators who went on to careers in feature film production began working on Pathé newsreels, and the company also produced its own series of **multiple-reel feature films** in 1911. It joined Australasian Films in 1913.

INA BERTRAND

Pathé, Charles

b. 1863, Chevry-Cossigny, France; d. 1957, Monaco

businessman, manufacturer, producer, France

After several unsuccessful ventures, Charles Pathé began his career exploiting **Edison**'s Phonograph in the **fairs/fairgrounds** around Paris in 1894. The profits he made enabled him to open a store in Vincennes where he also sold counterfeit **Kinetoscopes** before he had Henri **Joly** manufacture his own **chronophotographic** equipment.

In 1896, Charles and his brother Émile became partners in founding **Pathé Frères**. After a merger with the **Contisouza** and **Bünzli** precision tool factory, mediated by Claude Grivolas, the company became the Compagnie générale, de phonographes, cinématographes et appareils de précision (1900). Charles and Émile were its salaried directors, in charge of the cinematograph and the **phonograph** divisions, respectively.

Charles's day-to-day responsibilities mainly involved the supervision of the Vincennes facilities and their production capacity in relation to the company's objectives. In 1902, he decided that the workshops in Vincennes would be expanded and a studio would be built on a plot of land that he owned on the rue du Bois. There he oversaw film production, either in its early stages (through preparation meetings with Ferdinand **Zecca**, directors and set decorators) or after shooting, through the projection of filmed scenes which he would accept, refuse, or have remade.

Charles enjoyed great freedom of action, often making decisions on his own and reporting them to the company's administrators after the fact (he himself was appointed an administrator only in October 1911). No strategic decision eluded his control, from opening sales offices around the world or shifting the company's policy from selling to renting films to establishing a subsidiary such as **SCAGL** or taking over European **Blair**, a film stock manufacturer (in that purchase he used the **Merzbach** brothers as frontmen). After the international conference of film manufacturers, held in Paris in 1909, his policy of renting films became general practice. A key figure in the French film industry, he made Pathé-Frères into the first vertically integrated film corporation and even got involved in the creation of several of its franchise holders, such as Cinéma-Exploitation (1907).

Yet his apparent omnipotence was not without drawbacks. The company's administrators seriously questioned his competence during the financial crisis of 1908–1909. Bursting with commercially innovative ideas (creating cinematographic apparatuses for amateurs, developing non-flammable

Figure 95 Ferdinand Zecca and Charles Pathé in the latter's office.

film, etc.), he quickly reversed the situation. During **World War I**, his efforts focused on the management of Pathé Exchange in the USA and some of his responsibilities in France devolved upon his assistant, Léon Madieu.

By the war's end, his power was beginning to decline: in 1919, the company was split in two, one of which now was devoted solely to producing film stock, and many subsidiaries were sold off. Charles himself eventually retired in 1927, when the Kodak Pathé company was created.

Further reading

Kermabon, Jacques (ed.) (1995) *Pathé, premier empire du cinema*, Paris: Centre Georges Pompidou.
Pathé, Charles (1970) *De Pathé-Frères à Pathé-Cinéma*, Lyon: SERDOC.

LAURENT LE FORESTIER

Pathé Cinematograph

For a brief period, between 1905 and 1908, Pathé Cinematograph sold a larger quantity of moving pictures weekly than any other manufacturer in the USA.

Established as a sales agency in New York City in August 1904, with J. A. **Berst** as manager, the company was the second of a vast network of such agencies that **Pathé-Frères** created worldwide over the next four years. So successful was the New York agency, especially in supplying imported film prints to B. F. **Keith**'s **vaudeville** circuit, that a branch office was opened in Chicago in September 1905, with E. H. Montagu as manager.

Within another year, Pathé Cinematograph almost single-handedly created crucial conditions for the **nickelodeon** boom by releasing from three to six new film subjects per week.

The apogee of Pathé's dominance on the US market came in 1907–1908. A factory for printing positive film stock (from negative prints shipped from France) was constructed in Bound Brook, New Jersey, in the summer of 1907, and within months the company's volume of business doubled. A third sales agency opened in Birmingham (Alabama) and later relocated to New Orleans. **Laemmle**'s Film Service, one of the largest rental exchanges in the country, boasted that its "cracking good business" was almost "completely supplied with Pathé films." One of those, a four-reel, stencil-color version of the *Passion Play* (1907), probably was seen by more people (and more than once) than any other single film at the time. Having financed the first US trade journal devoted to moving pictures, *Views and Film Index*, in early 1906 (in partnership with **Vitagraph**), Pathé began offering, direct to nickelodeon managers, a "Weekly Bulletin" of information on its new releases, which now amounted to five reels of eight to ten titles that sold, on average, two hundred copies each.

Yet, faced with aggressive competition from both established and newly created manufacturers, financial strains that forced the company not to risk setting up its own rental exchange system, and a persistent (sometimes openly hostile) perception of its "foreignness," Pathé eventually acquiesced to **Edison**'s legal maneuvers that resulted in the formation of the **Motion Picture Patents Company** in late 1908. After reducing the number of weekly releases imported from France and promoting its "art films" (made by **Film d'Art** and **SCAGL**), the company capitulated in 1910 by constructing a studio in Jersey City to produce and market "American" films, under the supervision of Louis **Gasnier**.

During the early 1910s, as its distribution of French imports shifted largely to affiliates, Pathé became one of a dozen important US film manufacturers, even adding a second studio in Los Angeles, headed by James **Young Deer**, for the production of **westerns**. In July 1911, it also introduced the first, highly successful **newsreel**, *Pathé Weekly*. Undoubtedly its most famous production, financed jointly by Hearst newspapers,

Figure 96 Pathé advertisement, *Views and Films Index*, 1906.

was *The Perils of Pauline* (1914), the influential **serial** starring Pearl **White**.

With the beginning of **World War I**, Pathé Cinematograph was transformed into Pathé-Exchange, which supplied Pathé-Frères with much of its profits through 1918.

Further reading

Abel, Richard (1999) *The Red Rooster Scare: Making Cinema American, 1900–1910*, Berkeley: University of California Press.

RICHARD ABEL

Pathé Film (Sweden)

In the summer of 1910, **Pathé-Frères** opened a branch in Stockholm, and subsequently offices in Malmö (1912) and Gothenburg (1914). Siegmund **Popert** (1874–1935), a company veteran, was at the helm. Pathé Film helped **Svenska**

Biografteatern (SB) finance a new studio at Lidingö, and French writer-director Paul Garbagni even directed a film there, while Victor **Sjöström** served as a Pathé-Frères apprentice in Paris. Later the two companies formed a joint enterprise, Phoenix, primarily for distributing SB films through Pathé-Frères's international network. Pathé Film also embarked on film production in Sweden by enlisting SB's stage manager, Georg af **Klercker**; however, its first production was banned by the newly formed national censorship body. Soon the ties to SB were severed, and Pathé Film concentrated on distribution and a limited non-fiction production until it became part of Skandia in 1918.

JAN OLSSON

Pathé KOK projector

The flammability of nitrate film stock encouraged sales of **Pathé-Frères'** 1912 hand-cranked KOK projector—named for the Pathé cockerel trade mark—which was limited to the use of "safety" film. A built-in dynamo provided **electricity** for the lamp, and patented asymmetrical perforations made showing the 28 mm film out-of-frame or back-to-front next to impossible. Nonfiction films, short fiction films, and **serials** were released on this format. Although Alexander Victor introduced an adapted projector in the USA, the KOK was particularly popular in European educational and domestic markets before the introduction of 16 mm and 9.5 mm formats in the 1920s. Cameras were marketed in France and North America, but 28 mm remained primarily a projection gauge.

STEPHEN HERBERT

Pathé russe

Pathé-Frères's presence on the Russian scene was felt in every area of the film industry, from film stock and equipment sales and lab services to film production and distribution. The first (as of 1900) Pathé representative in Russia was Richard Jacob, whose mission was to sell **phonographs** and gramophones; in 1904, a Pathé store opened in Moscow (followed by others in Saint-Petersburg, in 1905, and in Odessa, in 1906), with the inventor of the Pathéphone, Guillaume Kemmler (1856–1917), serving as manager. The store included a moving picture section (headed by Maurice Gachet), which dealt in **projectors** and film stock. In March 1907, Pathé established a distribution branch agency in Rostov, which later that year expanded into a network of regional agencies. Film production began early in 1908, when Pathé sent Maurice **Maître** and cameraman Joseph Mundviller (Meyer) to shoot *actualités* in Russia with an eye to distributing them there, in France, and in the rest of the world (including the USA). Among them were *Cossacks of the Don, Moscow Clad in Snow,* and *Astrakhan Fish Factory*; later actualités were presented as a series called *Picturesque Russia*.

In 1909, Pathé russe was founded in Moscow, with Gachet as its head and Maître and Kai **Hansen** as filmmakers. Their task was to produce fiction films that would combine cultural specificity with an international appeal and would thus be distributable both at home and abroad. Aided by Russian-born stage designer Czeslaw Sabinski and a cast of Russian actors, Maitre and/or Hansen began by producing ethnically marked films—the folk-like *The Dashing Merchant* (1909), the pagan/pastoral *Mara* (1910), or the Jewish *Lekhaim* (1911)— **historical films** such as *An Episode from the Life of Dmitri Donskoi* (1909), *Peter the Great* (1910), or *Princess Tarakanova* (1910), and literary adaptations such as *The Duel* (1910) and *Lieutenant Ergunov* (1910), both after Aleksandr Kuprin. It was this dual strategy that was responsible for the twofold reputation of Pathé films in Russia: on the one hand, the company was praised for having established a "quality film" standard; on the other, most of its films were criticized for perpetrating bloopers and stereotypes of Russian life, past or present.

In 1912, Pathé russe constructed a state-of-the-art enclosed studio in Moscow in order to produce not only quality films, but now also sensational **melodramas** such as *The Mystery of House # 5* (1912) or Evgenii **Bauer**'s *Gory Glory* (1913). This period also included co-productions such as *1812* (1912), involving Pathé and its main rival **Khanzhonkov**, and Bauer's *Twilight of a Woman's Soul* (1913). In 1913, Pathé curtailed its production in Russia but continued to play a significant role in distribution.

Further reading

Abel, Richard (1990) "Pathé's Stake in Early Russian Cinema," *Griffithiana*, 38/39: 242–247.

YURI TSIVIAN

Pathécolor

As early as 1906, the **Pathé-Frères** film stock coloring factory employed 200 female workers in Vincennes. The coloring was still done by hand at the time: stencils were cut out of positives by trained workers. The application of some seven different colors (with an aniline base) was also manual. In late 1906, the company introduced a mechanical process to the factory, which was patented on October 22, 1906. Jean Méry, however, came up with an even better system that was patented in two stages: the stencil cutting on January 15, 1907 and the coloring machine on February 28, 1908. An electric pantograph made it possible to cut stencils quickly and with high precision, enabling the company to deliver "Pathécolor" film prints with **color**s impeccably applied. The Pathécolor process was in operation until 1928. Pathé-Méry cutting and coloring machines are preserved at the Cinémathèque française.

Further reading

Marette, J. (1950) "Les procédés de coloriage mécanique des films," *Bulletin de l'AFITEC* 7: 3–8.

LAURENT MANNONI

Pathé-Frères

Pathé-Frères was not only the largest, most influential French film company before **World War I** but also the first acknowledged global *empire* in cinema history.

The company originated in 1895 in the **fairs/ fairgrounds** of Paris where Emile and Charles **Pathé** exhibited **Edison** phonographic cylinders. Within a year, the brothers opened a shop in Vincennes to supply their fairground clientele with phonographic merchandise and counterfeit **Kinetoscopes** (Edison had no patent protection in Europe). By late 1897, they had attracted a major investor, Claude-Agricol-Louis Grivolas, and turned Pathé-Frères into a joint-stock corporation with one million francs of capital.

Until 1900, the **phonograph** division, run by Emile, contributed 90 percent of its revenue. Charles worked on the technical and marketing problems involving **cameras**, **projectors**, and **celluloid** film stock, which led to **Continsouza** and **Bünzli** being contracted to design apparatuses and material for the company. With those problems solved, he soon realized that films had great commercial value and set about mass producing them like canned goods, hiring Ferdinand **Zecca** to handle their production. By 1902, Pathé-Frères was constructing a glass house studio in Vincennes, producing 8,000 meters of negative film stock per year, and launching a drive to make its **trademark** red rooster films the chief moving picture attraction in France.

Within four years, the moving picture division was double the size of the phonograph division and dedicated to proving that cinema would be "the schoolhouse, newspaper, and theater of tomorrow." In 1904, Charles added a second studio in Vincennes and a third in Montreuil. At Joinville-le-pont, a maze of factories grew up for manufacturing cameras and projectors and developing film stock, with a department for producing stencil-**color** positive film prints. By 1905, Pathé-Frères was selling 200 cameras and projectors per month—far more than any competitor—and 12,000 meters of positive film stock per day, most of it now fiction films. By late 1906, positive film stock production had tripled to 40,000 meters or 100,000 feet per day; the moving picture division alone had 1,200 employees, many of them women hired to do the repetitive detail work of splicing and coloring prints.

Zecca now supervised a growing number of filmmakers, each of whom specialized in one or more film subjects. Lucien **Nonguet** handled *actualités* and **historical films** such as *L'Epopée*

napoléonienne [Napoleon] (1903); Gaston **Velle**, **trick films** and *féeries*/**fairy plays** like *La Poule aux oeufs d'or* [The Hen with the Golden Eggs] (1905); Zecca himself, sensational **melodramas** like *L'Honneur d'un père* [A Father's Honor] (1905); Georges **Hatot**, comic **chase films** such as *Dix Femmes pour un mari* [Ten Women for a Husband] (1905); and Albert **Capellani**, domestic **melodramas** like *La Loi du pardon* [The Law of Pardon] (1906). Scenarios initially were written by G. Rollini, Zecca's brother-in-law, and André **Heuzé**; and troupes of actors were recruited from the **music halls**, circuses, and other popular entertainments. By the late summer of 1905, these filmmakers could turn out four or five film titles per week, making the French company the first to achieve such a high level of regularized mass production.

This achievement also arose from a global network of film distribution that Charles, with the aid of Serge **Sandberg**, **Popert**, and others, set up between 1904 and 1906. Pathé-Frères agencies spread out first through the developed nations and French client states: Moscow, New York, and Brussels (1904); Berlin, Vienna, Chicago, and St. Petersburg (1905); Amsterdam, Barcelona, Milan, and London (1906). Within another year, its offices had monopolized Central Europe as well as the colonized areas of India, Southeast Asia, Central and South America, and Africa. In the USA, Edison threatened to curtail the French company's expansion with a patent suit; Charles retaliated by marketing his films several weeks prior to their release in Europe and by underselling his competitor. By October 1906, Pathé-Frères's film sales averaged 75 copies each of sometimes a dozen film titles per week, constituting from one-third to one-half of the growing American market. The company could rightly boast that it had "boomed the film business" in the USA and that, for both quality and quantity, Pathé films were "tops in the world."

Within France, Pathé films were shown in a variety of established spectacle attractions. In Paris, there were **cafés-concerts** and music halls such as the El Dorado, Olympia, and Folies-Bergère, the Musée Grevin which was promoted as "a newspaper in waxwork," or the Dufayel **department store** which exhibited films for children. The principal markets for Pathé-Frères, however, were the fairgrounds or *fêtes foraines* in the provinces and city *faubourgs*. Fairground cinemas worked within regional circuits, traveling by train and encamping in designated public spaces for several weeks. By 1902, nearly every fair had one or two cinemas, mixing short films with live acts and **magic lantern** shows in more or less continuous programs. By 1906, business was so profitable that some were settling permanently in town squares, much like French versions of the **nickelodeons** springing up in the USA. By then, Pathé films made up at least 75 percent of the fairground cinema programs and sometimes monopolized them completely.

In 1907, Charles sought to secure the company's position by systemically industrializing every sector of the new industry. In association with Edmond **Benoît-Lévy** and others, Pathé constructed one cinema after another in Paris and other cities, beginning with the Omnia-Pathé in late 1906, taking control of the shift in exhibition from the fairgrounds to permanent sites in urban shopping and entertainment districts. By 1909, Pathé-Frères had a circuit of 200 cinemas throughout France and Belgium, probably the largest in Europe. In order to better regulate film distribution, in 1907–1908, he and his associates also created six regional agencies to rent, rather than sell, a weekly program of films. Although the production of positive and negative film stock continued to rise, Charles now saw that the company's future security depended much more on distribution and exhibition than on production.

That decision came after Charles realized that Pathé-Frères's could not sustain its position in the USA, even though, by 1908, up to 200 copies of each film title were being shipped there. The emergence of new production companies, the Film Service Association, **Motion Picture Patents Company** (MPPC), **National Board of Censorship**, and an often virulent discourse of Americanization in the press—all served to curtail the circulation of Pathé films in what clearly had been its principal market. To make up for that loss, the company turned to augment its market share in Central and Eastern Europe. Charles also initiated plans to manufacture negative film stock so as to reduce his company's dependence on **Eastman**

Kodak. Most tellingly, he adopted the strategy of shifting film production onto affiliate companies, beginning with **Film d'Art** and **SCAGL** in France. Soon that strategy was extended to affiliates outside France—including Italy, Russia, Spain, Belgium, Germany, and even the USA—in an effort to make the company's films more distinctive and attractive on the international market.

Nevertheless, Pathé-Frères played a crucial role in standardizing and upgrading film production in France, initially through domestic melodramas like *Les Deux Soeurs* [Two Sisters] (1907) and *grand guignol* or sensational **melodramas** like *Pour un collier!* [All for a Necklace] (1907). Within such films there coalesced a system of representation and narration that relied not only on long-take tableaux recorded by a waist-level camera, bold red **intertitles**, inserted letters, and accompanying **sound effects** but on changes in framing through **camera movement**, cut-in close shots, POV shots, reverse-angle cutting, and alternation in editing. This system achieved remarkable effects in melodramas as diverse as *Les Forbains* [The Pirates] (1907), *A Narrow Escape* (1908), or *L'Homme aux gants blancs* [The Man in White Gloves] (1908) and in comic films like *Le Ruse de mari* [Artful Husband] (1907) or *Le Cheval emballé* [Runaway Horse] (1908). In short, Pathé films deployed most of the elements so basic to the system of narrative continuity that historians still often celebrate in slightly later **Biograph** films.

Another instance of standardization was the continuing series, in which one film after another was made and marketed around a single, named character/actor. As early as 1907, Pathé-Frères began releasing a **comic series** called *Boireau* (Jim), named after a recurring character played by André **Deed**. *Boireau*'s success led to a half-dozen other comic series, especially after Deed left to work in Italy. Among those regularly distributed, two stood out. One was *Rigadin*, starring Charles **Prince** as a parodic white-collar Don Juan; *Le Nez de Rigadin* [Rigadin's Nose] (1911), for instance, ruthlessly mocks his large upturned nose, one of the comic's singular assets. The other starred Max **Linder** as a young bourgeois dandy. Skillful, cleverly structured gags distinguish Linder's work from *La Petite Rosse* [The Little Vixen] (1909) through *Victime du quinquina* [Max Takes Tonics] (1911) to *Max pédicure* (1914). Yet another innovative form of the continuing series was *Pathé Journal*, the world's first weekly **newsreel**, released in slightly different versions from one country to another.

With this standardization came a parallel effort to legitimate the cinema as a respectable cultural form. Supported by the **trade press**, this effort was first visible in the distribution of literary adaptations or *films d'art*, produced by SCAGL and Film d'Art, both with close ties to prestigious Paris theatres. The best known was *L'Assassinat du Duc de Guise* [The Assassination of the Duke of Guise] (1908), whose deep-space *mise-en-scène*, economical **acting style**, and succinct editing influenced subsequent **historical films**, many based on 19th-century plays and **operas**. Most evident in those dealing with French history, such as SCAGL's *La Mort du Duc d'Enghien* [The Death of the Duke of Enghien] (1909), it was also apparent in others such as Film d'Art's *La Tosca* (1909). Generally, the only subjects not following this pattern were "oriental" films such as *Cléopatre* [Cleopatra] (1910), whose moments of tableau spectacle, accentuated by stencil color, and exotic characters indirectly reinforced the mandate for France's colonial empire.

In early 1911, Pathé-Frères introduced several films of three or more reels: Capellani's *Le Courrier de Lyon* [The Orleans Coach] and Gérard Bourgeois's *Victimes d'alcool* [Victims of Alcohol]. After it became clear that such lengthy films would prove acceptable, every major company invested in the new format, with subjects spanning the spectrum, but SCAGL drew especially on familiar literary adaptations in films such as Capellani's *Notre Dame de Paris* (1911), starring Henry **Krauss** and Stacia **Napierkowska**. Over the next few years, multiple-reel films became the principal weekly attraction on French cinema programs. Perhaps the best historical film was Capellani's twelve-reel *Les Misérables* (1912), also starring Krauss. Yet by then most multiple-reel films distributed by Pathé-Frères were contemporary subjects: Camille **de Morlhon**, for instance, proved adept at imitating boulevard melodramas in **Valetta** productions such as *La Broyeuse des coeurs* [Heart Breaker] (1913).

By the time of World War I, no other film company was as large as Pathé-Frères. Its camera

and projector were the industry standard. Its circuit of cinemas had increased with the construction in Paris of new **palace cinemas** such as the Pathé-Palace (1911), the renovated Omnia-Palace (1912), and the Lutetia-Wagram (1913). The positive film stock it distributed worldwide had risen to nearly 100,000 meters per day. Its capital stock had reached 30 million francs, and its workforce, scattered among a dozen or more affiliates, included 5,000 employees in France and 1,500 abroad. The company also was producing negative film stock on a scale that was competitive with both Eastman Kodak and the German company **AGFA**. That production of film negative would become "the principal and most vital component" of Pathé's business by the war's end.

See also: colonialism: Europe; editing: spatial relations; editing: temporal relations; multiple-reel/feature films: Europe; set design

Further reading

Abel, Richard (1994) *The Ciné Goes to Town: French Cinema, 1896–1914*, Los Angeles: University of California Press.

Bousquet, Henri (ed.) (1993–1996) *Catalogue Pathé des années 1896 à 1914*, Bassac: Henri Bousquet.

Kermabon, Jacques (ed.) (1994) *Pathé, premier empire du cinema*, Paris: Centre Georges Pompidou.

Meusy, Jean-Jacques (1995) *Paris-Palaces, ou le temps des cinémas (1894–1918)*, Paris: CNRS.

Pathé, Charles (1970) *De Pathé-Frères à Pathé-Cinéma*, Lyon: SERDOC.

Sadoul, Georges (1948) *Histoire générale du cinéma II: les pionniers du cinéma, 1897–1909*, Paris: Denoël.

RICHARD ABEL

Pathé-Frères cameras

In contrast to Léon **Gaumont**, Charles **Pathé** was not a technician. In 1897, however, he became associates with **Bünzli** and **Continsouza**, who provided him with excellent cameras and projectors. The company he and his brother Emile transformed into **Pathé-Frères** in 1900 then absorbed Bünzli and Continsouza's workshops. Several kinds of claw-mechanism cameras were developed and sold under Pathé's name: ones encased in walnut (1903), in mahogany (1905), and in black leather (1909), followed by an enhanced version (1911); and a portable camera (1913). Yet the most popular camera in the world for many years to come was the Pathé Professional, which first appeared in 1908. Also covered with black leather and equipped with two exterior magazines that could accommodate up to 120 m of film, a 51mm Voigtländer lens that made it possible to operate in overcast weather, and an automatic dissolve device, the camera was still in use in the 1920s.

LAURENT MANNONI

Pathé-Frères (Great Britain)

After establishing a sales agency in London in 1902, Pathé-Frères soon was responsible for over 20% of the films shown in Great Britain. In 1906, Pathé jolted its rivals by reducing its prices from 6d to 4d a foot, forcing a reluctant industry to do likewise. Production began in 1910 with *Pathé's Animated Gazette*, the first British **newsreel**. In 1911, a studio was constructed at Great Portland Street (London) to release fiction films through the "Britannia" brand, beginning with *David Copperfield* (1912). George Pearson was hired as a director, and a subsidiary, Union Film Publishing, was created in 1913, filming at Alexandra Palace and issuing films under the "Big Ben" brand. **World War I** thwarted Pathé's ambitions, but its newsreel flourished to become a mainstay in British cinemas for decades to follow.

LUKE MCKERNAN

Pathé-Frères projectors

Charles **Pathé** was fortunate to associate with excellent technicians very early on: first Henri **Joly**, then René **Bünzli** and Victor **Continsouza**.

Figure 97 Poster for Pathé-Frères, *c.* 1906.

Figure 98 Omnia-Pathé program, 1913.

Bunzli and Continsouza's company, which was taken over by Grivolas and merged into **Pathé-Frères**, in 1900, manufactured excellent Maltese-cross projectors, which were exported worldwide under the Pathé brand name. The first sold by Pathé was developed in 1897; the next, the "Robuste," appeared in the 1899 catalog. After reaching an agreement with Jules **Carpentier**, Pathé also marketed a transformed **Lumière** projector equipped with a sprocket system (several versions were sold until 1908). Yet Continsouza provided Pathé with what shortly would become an industry standard, a Maltese-cross "Cinématographe Pathé no 2" (1903). It underwent several modifications between 1905 and the late 1910s, resulting in the oil-lubricated A. B. R. projector, one of the best-selling projectors at the time. Also worthy of notice was the elegant 1908 "projecteur Pathé modèle anglais," intended mostly for clients familiar with Bioscope-type projectors.

LAURENT MANNONI

Paul, Robert William

b. 1869; d. 1943

inventor, manufacturer, producer, Great Britain

The leading English pioneer of moving pictures was already a successful London instrument maker, when in 1894 he was asked to manufacture replicas of the **Edison Kinetoscope**. An early partnership with Birt **Acres** produced a **camera** with which the first English films were taken, including the Oxford and Cambridge Boat Race and the Derby, as well as several short dramas and **music-hall** performances. After these were shown on kinetoscopes during the summer of 1895, Paul and Acres parted company acrimoniously, and Paul produced no new films for months. However, he conceived a special auditorium which would give the impression of time travel, similar to that of H. G. Wells' *The Time Machine*; and he managed to develop his own **projector** in time to give public demonstrations at almost exactly the same time as the

Cinématographe Lumière appeared in Great Britain, in February 1896.

With a new camera design, he became the main supplier of moving picture equipment in Europe, selling to many showmen and **magicians**, including David Devant and Georges **Méliès**, and establishing regular shows at many London venues. For a short period, he was busy as both cameraman and projectionist, filming the 1896 Derby and showing it the next evening to acclaim, along with other subjects, at London's Alhambra music hall. But he soon managed to train operators and began to commission films, including a successful series taken in Spain and Portugal by Harry Short. Although Paul proposed that the British Museum act to preserve moving pictures, his idea was not accepted. The pageantry of Queen Victoria's Jubilee in 1897 offered a spectacular and lucrative new subject, yet within a year Paul felt that interest in moving pictures was waning, and so planned a studio and laboratory in the London suburb of Muswell Hill which would make possible more elaborate productions. The studio's **trick films**, using multiple exposures for supernatural effect and elaborate scenery, were popular for some years, competing with those of Méliès and **Pathé-Frères**. So were his "sensational" subjects using models, such as *A Railway Collision* (1898), and **comedies** with risqué themes, one of which, *Come Along, Do!* (1898), was among the first narrative films to consist of two separate shots.

The Boer War of 1899–1902 provided new opportunities, both for *actualités* filmed in South Africa and for dramatic **re-enactments** of typical scenes filmed at a golf course near the studio, as well as a major nonfiction series, *Army Life* (1900). Paul pioneered literary adaptations, moving from a single tableau of *The Last Days of Pompeii* (1899) to the multi-scene *Scrooge, or Marley's Ghost* (1901), and his technical interests led to experiments in **scientific films**. At least one of his most elaborate later productions, *The ? Motorist*, directed by Walter Booth in 1905, was widely shown, with a viewing recorded by the Russian writer Andrei Bely. However, as the demand for longer dramatic films grew, Paul's share of the market declined. In 1910, he closed down his film business, bizarrely destroying all his negatives, and concentrated on scientific instrument making for the rest of his career.

Further reading

Barnes, John (1976–1995) *The Beginnings of the Cinema in England*, vols. 1–5, Exeter: Exeter University Press.

Paul, R. W. *et al.* (1936) "Before 1910: Kinematograph Experiences," *Proceedings of the British Kinematograph Society*, no. 38, London: BKS.

IAN CHRISTIE

penny arcades

Penny arcades provided inexpensive amusement, often using coin-operated attractions—machines that told fortunes, measured strength (hand grip or lungs), punched out name plates, took pictures automatically, and so forth. Located along commercial urban thoroughfares, arcades depended on walk-in pedestrian traffic—people with free time and money that could be spent in a casual fashion. Penny arcades were thus often seen as places that attracted idle and disreputable elements of society—those lacking a puritanical work ethic and penny-pinching outlook. Moreover, many arcades relied on suggestive **advertising** and a fast-talking street barker to bring in patrons off the streets. Many arcades were in entertainment districts and often affiliated with theaters—places to spend time and money before or after a show (or instead of going to a show). Among the arcades' most popular attractions was the peep-hole machine showing moving pictures. **Kinetoscopes** occasionally appeared in arcades in the mid to late 1890s, but they were quickly replaced by mutoscopes, which were much less expensive to run (the mutoscope used a reel of cards rather than a film loop and was hand-cranked rather than powered by **electricity**). **The American Mutoscope and Biograph Company** launched a network of mutoscope parlors early in 1898, and had set up regional companies to exploit the device by 1899. After the initial novelty passed, however, mutoscopes were placed in penny arcades.

Arcades and early storefront moving pictures theaters were closely connected. In Pittsburgh, Harry **Davis** had a penny arcade affiliated with his Avenue Theater (featuring **vaudeville**). By late 1904, it included a small room, accommodating about thirty standing patrons, where moving pictures were projected. The pictures were heavily patronized and when the theater and the arcade burned down, he opened what many consider the nation's first **nickelodeon** in June 1905. The following year, New York boasted over twenty nickelodeons and as many arcades on Park Row and the Bowery. According to *Views and Films Index* (October 1906)**,** "these moving picture shows and arcades are supported by the residents of the vicinity, the great Italian settlement on the one side and the great Jewish settlement on the other. Proof of this is that on Saturdays, which is the Jewish Sabbath, great holiday crowds from the East Side throng the Bowery, peeking into the slot machines, looking at the pictures and testing their powers on other devices, and this is the best day of the week."

In general, the amusement industry shifted from arcades to moving picture theaters, as the early careers of Mitchell **Mark**, Marcus **Loew**, and Adolph **Zukor** demonstrate. Zukor's Automatic Vaudeville Company, which owned a string of high-class arcades in New York City, opened the Crystal Theater above his Fourteenth Street Arcade in 1906 and bought Mark's Theatre Comique, Boston's first picture theater, in 1907. Some entrepreneurs opened a nickelodeon with an adjacent arcade, and when the one proved a success and room was needed for expansion, the arcade provided the likely space.

Penny arcades were among the favorite targets of reformers. Peep-hole viewing was suggestive of transgressive voyeurism. Mutoscope pictures were often risqué by turn-of-the century standards (though not as risqué as their titles would often suggest). Reformers were particularly concerned because young women and children had easy access to mutoscope pictures. Both before and after the nickelodeon era, reformers sought to shut down or tightly regulate these alleged breeding grounds of vice.

Further reading

Bueschel, Richard M. and Steve Gronowski (1993) *Arcade 1: Illustrated Historical Guide to Arcade Machines*, New York: Hoflin Publishing.

CHARLES MUSSER

Peón, Ramón

b. 1897, Havana; d. 1971, San Juan, Puerto Rico

cameraman, director, journalist, Cuba

In 1916, Peón abandoned a secure job as a chemist in the sugar industry to travel to Hollywood as a laboratory assistant and, eventually, worked as a **newsreel** cameraman for **Gaumont**. Upon his return to Cuba in 1919, he established a commercial production company, edited the periodical *Guía Social de Cines* [Society Guide to Theaters], and made his directorial debut with *Realidad* [Reality] (1921). Peón was relentless in his cinematic endeavors: he filmed the first aerial shots of Havana (the plane crashed) (1920), co-founded several production companies (Golden Sun Pictures, BBP, and others), and directed eleven fiction films between 1920 and 1930 (out of a total of 39 films produced in all). *La virgen de la Caridad* [The Virgin of Charity] (1930) capped the silent era in Cuba and was characterized by Georges Sadoul as a precursor of neorealism. Peón also must be credited with vastly improving the technical quality of Cuban cinema in the 1920s and with introducing elements inspired by popular theater into his narratives.

With the advent of sound, Peón participated in the "Hispanic" film boom in the USA, and moved to Mexico in 1931, where he had a long and prolific career, returning to Cuba regularly to film co-productions.

ANA M. LÓPEZ

Perret, Léonce

b. 1880, Niort, France; d. 1935, Paris, France

actor, scriptwriter, filmmaker, France

Léonce Perret began his career in the theater and took advantage of a 1909 tour in Berlin to act in several films produced by **Gaumont**'s local production unit. In early 1910, he returned to Paris (and the Elgé studios) as an employee of that German subsidiary. Louis **Feuillade** noticed him among the onlookers on the set of *Esther* (1910) and hired him to replace René Alexandre in the role of King Assuerus. After directing him in

several more films, Feuillade encouraged him to move into directing.

Perret soon proved himself the company's second major director. Much like Feuillade, he tackled very different subjects, moving from **comedies** such as *La Grève des domestiques* [The Servants' Strike] (1912) and the *Léonce* **comic series** (1912–1914), in which he also played the lead role, to **detective films** such as *Main de fer* [The Iron Hand] (1912) and melodramas such as *Les Deux chemineaux* [The Two Vagabonds] (1913). Also like Feuillade, he constituted an almost unchanging production crew, often working with the same cameraman (Georges Specht) and actors (including Suzanne **Grandais**, Suzanne Le Bret, and his wife Valentine Petit). Similarly, he made as many films from scripts written by others as from his own: *Le Crime du grand-père* [The Grandfather's Crime] (1910) came from a scenario by Abel Gance; *Léonce et Poupette* and *La Belle-mère* [The Mother-in-Law], both came from Marcel **Levesque** in 1914.

His films are characterized by a strand of realism quite rare at the time. Perret often used both indoor and outdoor locations, favored the movement of actors in depth, and framed his characters more closely than usual. He also favored natural **lighting** effects, even shooting into the light in *Léonce à la campagne* [Léonce Goes to the Country] (1913). He developed a modern conception of **set design** that enriched the narrative rather than served as a cosmetic adornment and even led him to experiment with off-screen space.

Unlike most directors at Gaumont (most notably Feuillade), Perret was not mobilized during the war because of his health. In 1915, he had moved to Nice in order to continue making films, and at a salary higher than Feuillade's. Still, on the strength of the international success of such **multiple-reel/ feature films** as *L'Enfant de Paris* [A Child of Paris] (1913), which sold 350 prints worldwide, he left Gaumont in 1917 to work in the USA. He was to stay there until 1921, making a total of 18 feature films. He then moved back to France where he continued a distinguished and highly successful filmmaking career.

See also: editing: spatial relations; staging in depth

Further reading

Fescourt, Henri (1959) *La foi et les montagnes ou le 7ème art au passé*, Paris: Paul Montel.

LAURENT LE FORESTIER

Perry, Joseph

b. 1862; d. 1943

director, Australia

As chief technician of the Limelight Department of the **Salvation Army**, Joseph Perry produced the visual component (slides and short motion pictures) for lantern lectures and Commandant Booth's multi-media presentations, including *Soldiers of the Cross* (1900), and *Salvation Army International Congress Cosmorama* (filmed in London, in 1904). After that, the production program was curtailed, but revived long enough for Perry to make *Heroes of the Cross* and *The Scottish Covenanters* (1909). When the Limelight Department was disbanded in 1910, Perry left the Salvation Army, but continued working in commercial film distribution in Asia.

INA BERTRAND

Peru

The first screening in Peru took place in Lima, on 2 January 1897, organized for the president and other government officials by two **Edison** cameramen using the Vitascope. The first public screening occurred two days later in the Estrasburgo Gardens. The **Lumière Cinématographe** arrived one month later: the first public screening took place on 2 February 1897, also in the Estrasburgo Gardens.

The audience for these screenings was the Limeña elite, the enfranchised citizens of what historians call the "Aristocratic Republic," a nation in which only 5% of the population had the right to vote and in which that 5% governed and suppressed all peasant protests and urban popular movements. Lima looked above all to Europe, and was beginning to undergo a modern transformation financed by the rubber boom.

Once the appeal of moving pictures was confirmed, other entrepreneurs emerged, although the lack of **electricity**, geographical isolation, and cultural differences between cities and countryside impeded their diffusion. An unknown operator filmed the first indigenous images, including *La Catedral de Lima* [The Lima Cathedral], which were shown on 23 April 1899, at the Teatro Politeama. Five years later, Juan José Pont, an entrepreneur, returned from a trip through Brazil, Argentina, and Chile with a "Biógrafo Automático" and, on 23 February 1904, showed a series of views of Lima shot five days earlier. In 1904 he also filmed a presidential trip to Arequipa, during which the president died unexpectedly; Pont filmed his funeral, which he exhibited in the port city of Callao in May 1904.

The first Lima movie theater, seating 600, the Empresa del Cinema Teatro was built in 1909. It was immediately successful, and another company, Compañía Internacional Cinematográfica, opened the Cine Teatro in 1912. The competition between the two was intense. Both imported films from Europe and the USA and expanded rapidly, moving into neighboring countries and into production.

Working for the Empresa del Cinema Teatro, Jorge Enrique Goitizolo shot *actualités* between 1909 and 1915 as well as the first Peruvian fiction film, a **comedy** entitled *Negocio al agua* [Business to the Water] (1913). Meanwhile, the Compañía Internacional Cinematográfica joined the competition with its own fictional production, *Del manicomio al matrimonio* [From Madhouse to Matrimony] (1913), a "tragicomedy" directed by Fernand Lund. This was the last fiction film produced until 1922.

Filmmaking in Peru initially was conceived as a documentary activity, and the films exhibited demonstrate a desire to capture events of socio-political significance (e.g., the centenary celebrations of 1921) as well as the characteristics of urban life in Lima (among them, the yearly carnival celebrations). Fictional filmmaking—more expensive, difficult to produce, and in direct competition with the more appealing European films, with their recognized **stars** and *auteurs*—was simply too much of a risk. Thus, as was the case in Chile, the cinema in Peru did not develop beyond its first documentary impulses until the 1920s. An early example was *Caminos de la venganza* [Roads to Revenge] (1922) by Luis Uguarte, a melodrama stressing the contradictions between rural and urban life, a theme that would become standard in later Peruvian cinema. The first fiction film to become a *succès d'estime* was *La Perricholi* (1928), a large-scale historical drama which was the only Peruvian fiction film to address the colonial past until the 1980s. The film participated in the 1928 Seville Exposition in Spain and acquired a good deal of prestige.

Alberto Santana, a Chilean, was perhaps the country's most important filmmaker of the period, certainly the only one able to sustain ongoing production and to engage with the genres of comedy and melodrama that imported films had made popular. His *Los abismos de la vida* [The Abysses of Life] (1929) exploited the melodramatic figure of the naive provincial girl tricked into prostitution but saved from her fate by an honest man. On the eve of sound cinema, the Peruvian cinema went into a profound crisis.

Further reading

Bedoya, Ricardo (1992) *100 Años de cine en el Perú: una historia crítica*, Lima: Universidad de Lima/ Instituto de Cooperación Iberoamerica.
Carbone, Giancarlo (1992) *El cine en el Perú: 1897–1950, testimonios*, Lima: Universidad de Lima.

ANA M. LÓPEZ

Phalke Films

Phalke Films was the launching pad of D. G. **Phalke**'s ambition to make "Indian images" for the "sons of India." Established in 1912 in Bombay, its first production, *Raja Harishchandra*, was successfully released as part of a variety program at the Coronation Cinematograph on 3 May 1913. Phalke then shifted the studio to his native Nasik because of easier access to locations and shrines associated with the **mythological** tales he was putting on film. Virtually the only active studio between 1913 and 1915, this essentially family enterprise was replaced by a partnership firm, **Hindustan Cinema Films Company**, in 1918.

SURESH CHABRIA

Phalke, Dhundiraj Govind
b. 1870; d. 1944
filmmaker, India

Born in an orthodox brahmin family, Phalke printed oleographs of Hindu gods until 1908. Inspired by a **biblical film** that he saw in Bombay, he made the first true Indian story films, mainly **mythological** tales. The first was *Raja Harishchandra* (1913), for which he went to England to purchase film equipment. His films featured a combination of traditional narratives with inventive special effects typical of the mythological genre that dominated early Indian cinema. He also made **advertising films** and *actualités*, one of which featured the famous surviving footage of himself at work.

SURESH CHABRIA

phantom train rides

Phantom train rides were films that presented a view from the front or (more rarely) the back of a moving train in order to create the overall impression of the viewer as a railway passenger. In most cases, a camera was mounted at a slightly tipped angle on the cowcatcher of a moving train in order to produce the effect of continuous movement into the landscape. The scenery included the tracks in the foreground as parallel lines that converged at the horizon. Telephone poles, bridges, tunnels, and other man-made or natural objects within the frame also functioned as markers of flow. All these elements contributed to the perceptual experience of the moving camera as a recreation of the flow of the environment. Such **travelogues**, made almost from the inception of moving pictures, were among the first to convey a sense of spatial continuity through continuous motion.

Phantom train rides featured not only rail travel in picturesque landscapes—for instance, **American Mutoscope & Biograph**'s *The Haverstraw Tunnel* (1897); **Edison**'s *Going Through the Tunnel* (1898); AM&B *Frazer Canon* (1902)— but also urban subway and trolley trips—for instance, AM&B's *Interior N.Y. Subway, 14th Street to 42nd Street* (1905). Perhaps the most unusual phantom train ride was the film of the *Schwebebahn* (or suspended train) at Wuppertal, Germany. Built in 1901, the *Schwebebahn* was an urban rail line that consisted of cars supported by iron arches spanning the Wupper river bed. In 1903, AM&B filmed a phantom train ride on the Schwebebahn and released the film as *Flying Train*.

After 1905, phantom train rides became a staple of **Hale's Tours** and Scenes of the World installations, and many were made specifically for use in those installations.

See also: cinema of attraction

LAUREN RABINOVITZ

Phantoscope

Washington, D. C. inventor C. Francis **Jenkins** applied the name Phantoscope to three motion picture devices he designed: an 1894 version of the **Edison Kinetoscope**; a **projector** co-designed with Thomas **Armat** in 1895, and his own revised version of that **projector** made after parting company with Armat. Jenkins sold rights to the third Phantoscope to Columbia Phonograph Co. of Washington, D. C., which manufactured the inexpensive 35mm projectors at their factory in Bridgeport, Connecticut. Sold to showmen across the USA, the Phantoscope gave many Americans their first glimpse of moving pictures. It made an important contribution to establishing 35mm **celluloid** film stock as a standard format.

PAUL SPEHR

Philippines, the

Moving pictures were introduced into the Philippines against the backdrop of war and revolution. Two days after the Filipino martyr, Dr Jose Rizal, was shot and killed (his death ignited Filipinos to take up arms against Spain), moving pictures were screened in the business district of Escolta in Manila: the date was 1 January 1897.

A Spanish businessman, Francisco Pertierra, organized the screening, using a *cronofotografo* (Georges **Demenÿ**'s chronophotographe). Although the event was met with enthusiasm, his business lasted only three weeks. Seven months later, two Swiss, Leibman and Peritz, opened another show using the **Cinématographe Lumière**, acquired by a Spanish soldier-turned-film operator, Antonio Ramos. It ran for three months.

By then the revolution was gaining strength, and Spanish rule in the Philippines, as it was in other Spanish colonies, was nearing its end, hastened by the outbreak of the Spanish–American War that was provoked by the sinking of the US battleship "Maine" near Havana, Cuba, in 1898. Commander George Dewey found it opportune to invade the Philippine Islands, resulting in the Battle of Manila Bay on 1 May 1898. The short-lived war and the ensuing Philippine–American War in 1899 nipped the growth of the moving picture business in the bud.

The social havoc that halted activities in the islands, however, had an inverse effect in the USA. Manufacturers such as **Edison** produced film **re-enactments** that supported American **imperialism**. Other companies sent cameramen to the war-torn islands—e.g., C. Fred Ackerman of the **American Mutoscope and Biograph Company**.

It took the cessation of war in 1902 for the film business to resume on a regular basis. Manila then was generally dependent on Europe for its supply of moving pictures. **Pathe-Frères'** establishment of a sales agency in 1909 assured a steady stream of European films until the outbreak of **World War I** crippled European control of film distribution. The war allowed American companies to assume supremacy on the local market, starting with a **Lubin** agent stationed in Manila in 1911 and a **Universal** rental exchange office founded in 1918.

Despite the fact that Americans owned and managed most moving picture theaters, films had Spanish titles and **intertitles** in both Spanish and English until the 1920s. Hispanic practices only diminished when the American regime took firm control of native society. Outside Manila, early film reception was steeped in wonder and even superstition: some even described moving pictures as "the work of the devil."

In 1911, censorship was imposed, ostensibly to protect Philippine society, with an American, George Seaver, in charge. In 1912, American businessmen began to expand into film production. Edward Meyer Gross competed with Albert Yearsley in producing the first film on Dr Rizal, by now hailed as a national hero. Although both films were successfully screened, native writers criticized them as **propaganda**.

As American control became more pronounced in the film business, only elite Filipinos shared in the profits. Even the first all-Filipino film, *Dalagang Bukid* [Country Maiden] (1919), produced by Malayan Movies and directed by Jose Nepomuceno, could not escape the shadow of American influence—nor could other early native films thereafter.

Further reading

Deocampo, Nick (2003) *Cine: Spanish Influences on Early Cinema in the Philippines*, Manila: National Commission for Culture and the Arts.

NICK DEOCAMPO

Phono-Ciné-Gazette

The bimonthly *Phono-Gazette* was first published in Paris on 1 April 1 1905. Edited by Edmond **Benoît-Lévy** (legal counsel for **Pathé-Frères**), its initial subject was "issues involving the phonograph," but it soon developed a strong interest in moving pictures and, on 1 October 1905, became *Phono-Ciné-Gazette*, "the magazine of talking machines and cinematographs." *Phono-Ciné-Gazette* devoted extensive space to legal and economic questions surrounding cinema and also presented information on the most recent technical innovations and the latest films. Influenced by Charles **Pathé** behind the scenes, *Phono-Ciné-Gazette* supported the shift from a system of selling to renting films in 1907. As the first journal devoted to the French film industry (it disappeared in December 1909), *Phono-Ciné-Gazette* is a precious resource for historical research.

Further reading

Toulet, Emmanuelle (1989) "Aux sources de l'histoire du cinéma … Naissance d'une presse sous influences," *Restaurations et tirages de la Cinémathèque française* 4 (14–25), Paris: Cinémathèque française.

LAURENT MANNONI

Phono-Cinéma-Théâtre

The Phono-Cinéma-Théâtre, which opened on April 28, 1900 at the Paris Exposition, offered screenings of sound films. The synchronism between projector and **phonograph** was set manually by **Clément-Maurice** and his brother Georges, and the films had been directed by Clément-Maurice with a **Parnaland camera**. Marguerite Vrignault, an actress from the Comédie-Française, and Paul Decauville were the financial backers. Great actors were featured in its repertory: Félicia Mallet acted in *L'Enfant prodigue* [The Prodigal], Sarah **Bernhardt**, in *Hamlet*, Gabrielle Réjane, in *Ma Cousine* [My Cousin], Victor Maurel, in *Les précieuses ridicule* [Preening Preciosities]. Although the Phono-Cinéma-Théâtre was not very successful at the Exposition, tours were organized in Europe shortly afterwards.

LAURENT MANNONI

Phonogram, The

Established in 1891 and published by the National Phonograph Publishing Co. (World Building, New York City), *The Phonogram* styled itself as "The Official Organ of the Phonograph Companies of the U. S." It was one of the first journals in the USA to cover motion picture activities. Closely tied to **Edison**'s **phonograph** business, its editor-general manager, V. (Virginia) H. **McRae**, encouraged phonograph investors to consider the yet-to-be-marketed motion picture a potentially allied business. *The Phonogram* ceased publication in 1893, but its brief publication spanned the transition of the phonograph from an unsuccessful business tool to an entertainment device with great potential.

PAUL SPEHR

phonography

Efforts to capture speech and environmental sounds in symbolic form date to ancient times. Literally meaning "sound writing," phonography formally emerged as a term for the general field of discourse with the publication of John Jones's *Practical Phonography* (1701), which proposed a system of symbols recorded by hand on paper to document phonetic representations of human speech. Prior shorthand systems in England date to at least the 16th century. In the traditional study of the evolution of writing systems, phonography is one of three main types, along with semasiograpy and metagraphy.

Until the mid-19th century, phonographic investigations were pursued mainly by philologists and linguists within specialized areas of study: e.g., orthography, phonetics, phonology, and stenography. The latter discipline developed into the most widely recognized derivation of phonography principally through the work of Isaac Pitman and John Gregg, who perfected proprietary stenographic systems for creating business and legal transcriptions that remain in worldwide use to this day.

The landscape of phonography changed radically when experimenters, inspired by successes in the field of **photography**, reconceived the challenge of "writing sound" from that of perfecting representational symbols to the fundamentally different problem of creating technologies for fixing the literal facsimile of a sound to an enduring intervening storage medium. The elegant technological breakthrough came with Thomas **Edison**'s phonograph in 1877, which showed that one device could both record and play back literal transcriptions of the human voice and other sounds. Thereafter, improvements to Edison's concept by Chichester Bell, Charles Tainter, Emile Berliner, and others before the end of the 19th century initiated a progression of advancements throughout the next century, in acoustical, electrical, analog, and digital sound technologies, that has proceeded unabated to the present.

The impact of phonographic technologies on world culture has been profound. Edison initially believed the principle application of his invention would be in the world of business as a stenographic device. However, the future was foreshadowed within a year when a German manufacturer licensed the phonograph to produce a line of talking dolls. From that point on experimental applications of sound recording proliferated freely in the worlds of commerce, science, **education**, **leisure**, and the arts. For example, in the USA educational reforms were formulated in the 1880s based on the use of phonographic machines to teach English and speech to ex-slaves, recent immigrants, and the hearing impaired. The social acceptance of single women in the industrial urban workforce began with their employment as secretaries, typists, and stenographers to transcribe recordings and manage the resulting increase in correspondence and office workflow. In the 1890s, ethnographers recorded for posterity on wax cylinders the languages and songs of North American Indian populations that were then rapidly disappearing. Music publishers embraced sound recordings as a means of selling sheet music, and **vaudeville** and **opera** performers, to increase their popularity. Politicians recorded speeches for delayed broadcast at party meetings, and **magic lantern** showmen projected illustrated comic and melodramatic narratives against a background of suitably atmospheric recorded music.

The fusion of commerce with the insatiable appetite for popular entertainment in the industrial world of the late 19th century created the cultural dynamo that pushed the development of sound recording on a path of its own, and also in parallel to its perhaps inevitable synchronization with moving images. Edison turned his attention in the late 1880s to perfecting the technology of motion pictures. From the beginning, his ambition was to produce simultaneously recorded sounds and moving images. Although no commercially viable sound movie system was perfected until the 1920s, Edison's laboratory staff, led by W. K. L. **Dickson**, did produce a successful prototype **synchronized sound** movie in late 1894.

Two paths of technological phonography evolved after the 1890s. One was theoretically consistent with its pre-technology focus on speech and sound, which can be traced through topical areas as diverse as the recording and music industries, the science of acoustics, radio broadcasting, personal recording and listening devices, and public audio research archives. The other became inextricably linked with moving images, leading to sound movies, broadcast television, satellite communications, home video recorders, picture phones, and the proliferation of portable entertainment devices today.

Further reading

Chanan, Michael (1995) *Repeated Takes—A Short History of Recording and Its Effects on Music*, London: Verso.

Lastra, James (2001) *Sound Technology and the American Cinema*, New York: Columbia University Press.

Sterne, Jonathan (2003) *The Audible Past*, Durham: Duke University Press.

PATRICK LOUGHNEY

phonoscènes

On November 7, 1902, Léon **Gaumont**, with the assistance of engineer Léopold Decaux, presented three **chronophone** sound films or *phonoscènes* at the Société française de photographie. The first featured Gaumont himself talking about a photographic system; the other two represented dances accompanied by music. According to Gaumont's own testimony, almost no one could hear distinctly the words he uttered because of the poor quality of the **phonograph**. Initially limited because of this technical problem, the **Gaumont** company's production of *phonoscènes* increased substantially in 1906 thanks to the development of a powerful compressed-air phonograph system, the Elgéphone, and the construction of a special studio at Buttes-Chaumont in Paris. There Alice **Guy** directed the performers as they lip-synced the songs or words of their own playback recordings. Many famous music-hall artists collaborated on these *phonoscènes*: Charlus in *Viens Poupoule* [Come Here, Chick], Polin in *La belle cuisinière* [The Lovely Cook] and *La Vénus du Luxembourg* [The Luxemburg Venus], Mayol in *La Paimpolaise* [The Girl from Paimpol] and *La Mattchiche*, **Dranem** in *Le trou de mon quai* [My Wharf's Hole], *Le vrai Jiu-Jitsu* [The Real Jiu-Jitsu] and *Five o'clock Tea*. Opera solos and duets also were available—from *Carmen*, *Mireille*, *Mignon*, *Faust*, *La Tosca*, *Le Barbier de Séville*—as were patriotic tunes—"La Marseillaise," "Le Père la Victoire"—popular songs—"La Tonkinoise," "Au clair de la lune," "La Krakette 'par le cochon monda'," "O Sole Mio"—and musical dances—"Ballet égyptien," "Cake-Walk du Nouveau-Cirque," "Ballet d'Hamlet." Most of these "singing" films had to be recorded in long shot so that mismatches between sound and image (the music of the phonograph and the lips of the singers) would not be conspicuous.

Fairground showmen and theater directors valued this kind of attraction, and Gaumont *phonoscènes* attracted a curious audience to major Paris theaters such as the Olympia, Parisiana, and Antoine. The Gaumont company itself also presented regular chronophone shows of *phonoscènes* at the London Hippodrome (1906), at the Paris Moulin-Rouge and Théâtre du Gymnase (1907), at the Gaumont-Palace (1911), as well as in several New York theaters in June 1913 (these were produced in a New York studio with actors lip-syncing to commercial phonographs). Charles Proust, an **itinerant exhibitor**, even took a program of *phonoscènes* on a successful tour of South America. When Gaumont improved the electrical synchronizing system again in 1911, a few audible speeches and monologues were recorded for projection, such as *Communication téléphonique* with Galipaux. In February 1910, *Ciné-Journal* claimed that 700 Gaumont *phonoscène* titles were in stock, but a company catalog published two years later listed approximately 460 for purchase, along with their respective discs. Unfortunately, little of this fascinating material has survived.

See also: cafés-concerts, music halls; sound machines

LAURENT MANNONI

Phonoscope, The

The Phonoscope, "A Monthly Journal Devoted to Scientific and Amusement Inventions Appertaining to Sound and Sight," began publication in New York on 15 November 1896. With reports on the moving picture business in the USA and advertisements from prominent and not so prominent moving picture companies, it was and still is an important record of the beginnings of the US industry. There were brief notes and longer articles about production, exhibition, censorship, legal affairs, and personnel matters as well as occasional reports of activities in Canada, England, and the rest of Europe. It ceased publication in December 1898.

PAUL SPEHR

photography

Film theorists such as André Bazin and Siegfried Kracauer have based their understanding of the film medium on its derivation from photography. Yet it could be claimed that cinema derived from a number of media of which photography was only one. Still, the importance of photography for not only the theory but the history of early cinema should not be downplayed. The photographic process distinguishes cinema from such pre-cinematic moving illusions as Emile **Reynauld**'s Pantomime Lumineuse.

A fixed photographic image was achieved by the 1840's by Neipce, Daguerre and Talbot. The initial exposure time for images ranged from several hours for the first experiment to close to a minute for some exposures until the 1860's. Therefore, early photography was very much *still* photography, quite at antipodes to motion photography. Throughout the latter part of the 19th-century, photographers sought shorter exposures, aiming at an instantaneous photography that could actually freeze action in full motion. Some success was achieved by the early 1870's: Eadweard **Muybridge**, for instance, claimed successful shots of a trotter in mid-stride. But the innovation of dry plate photography in the next decade made instantaneous photography widely possible. A leading commercial innovator in the dry plate process, the

Lumière Company in France, saw a direct connection between instantaneous photography and the possibility of motion pictures. In inventing the **Cinématographe**, one of the first motion picture camera and projection systems, the Lumières brought together lessons in the analysis of motion from Muybridge, French chronophotographers such as Albert **Londe**, Etienne-Jules **Marey** (and his assistant Georges **Demenÿ**), and the German Ottomar **Anschütz**. Marey and Muybridge were also influential on Thomas **Edison**'s slightly earlier peep show motion picture device, the **Kinetoscope**, which was engineered largely by William Kennedy Laurie **Dickson** whom Edison hired partly because of his mastery of photography. Both the Edison and Lumière devices (as well as that pioneered in the USA by Thomas **Armat** and Frances **Jenkins**) departed from earlier devices used by Anschutz and Demenÿ by adopting flexible roll film on **celluloid** in place of glass plates.

Initially, motion pictures were widely seen as a new photographic device. However, unlike the **Eastman Kodak** camera, which revolutionized photography through its ease of use and placed cameras in the hands of millions, motion picture **cameras** were complex and needed highly-trained operators. Motion picture projection initially was equally complex. Thus motion pictures became associated with show business rather than the practice of amateurs or artistic still photography. Nonetheless, *actualités* produced in cinema's first decade reflected many of the genres of still photography: exotic views, views of every day life, images of celebrities, and picturesque scenes. Early actualité filmmakers, such as the cameramen that Lumière sent around the world in the 1890s (e.g., Alexandre **Promio**, Félix **Mesguich**, Gabriel **Veyre**) thought of themselves as photographers of a specialized sort. Motion picture "operators" (as they were commonly called) dealt with lenses and film stocks, as did other photographers, although exposure rates were determined by the cranking speed of the camera. Many aspects featured in art photography especially, such as manipulation of focus, exposure and the processes of printing, played little role in motion picture photography, which may have seemed a more mechanical process—until experiments in **lighting** and composition began to appear after 1907.

See also: archaeology of cinema/pre-cinema; chronophotography

Further reading

Frizot, Michel (ed.) (1998) *A New History of Photography*, Koln: Konemann.
Rossell, Deac (1998) *Living Pictures: The Origins of the Movies*, Albany: SUNY Press.

TOM GUNNING

Pickford, Mary

b. 1892; d. 1979

actor, USA

Mary Pickford began her acting career in Toronto, Canada, when she was eight years old. Working under her real name of Gladys Smith, she, her mother Charlotte, sister Lottie, and brother Jack made their living playing small roles for local theater companies. From 1901 through 1907, she toured Canada and the USA, performing in melodramas including *Uncle Tom's Cabin* and *East Lynne*. In 1907, she impressed New York theatrical producer David Belasco and won a role in *The Warrens of Virginia*. Belasco renamed her Mary Pickford. As an adult, she would become especially well known for her portrayal of children: *The Poor Little Rich Girl* (1917), *Rebecca of Sunnybrook Farm* (1917), *Pollyanna* (1920).

In 1909, seeking to earn more money, she went to the **Biograph** studio, in New York City, where D. W. **Griffith** hired her for five dollars a day. Despite her initial scorn for the movies, she would return to the stage only once, to star in *Good Little Devil* (1913) for Belasco. Under Griffith's direction, Pickford played a variety of roles, and her talent was quickly recognized and rapidly honed. She first appeared playing a minor part in *Two Memories* (May 1909); one month later, she played the romantic heroine in *The Violin Maker of Cremona*. In July 1909, teamed with Billy Quirk, Pickford was the featured player in a series of romantic **comedies**. By the end of 1909, her acting style had become more natural, devoid of large,

melodramatic gestures, and she showed a gift for comedy. Throughout the 1910s, she would exhibit the same versatility in her feature-length film roles as she showed in the repertory environment of Biograph.

Between 1909 when she began her movie career working for Biograph and 1919—when she, Douglas Fairbanks (whom she would marry in 1920, after divorcing Owen **Moore**), Charlie **Chaplin**, and Griffith formed United Artists—Pickford acted for Independent Motion Picture or **IMP** (1911), **Majestic** (1911–1912), **Famous Players**-Lasky (1913–1914), Paramount (1914–1916), Artcraft (1916–1919), and First National. Each move granted her both higher salary and greater creative control over her work, evidence of an astute business woman as well as talented actress.

The **trade press** published articles praising her performances as early as 1910, noting that her fans called her "Little Mary." By 1912, **illustrated magazines** such as *McClures*, as well as **newspapers**, spread the word of her high salary. Noted for her small size, golden curls, and large expressive eyes, her popularity also was manifested by her appearance in advertisements for Red Cross Shoes and later Pompeian Face Cream (1916). An advice column called "Daily Talks" signed by Pickford was carried in newspapers such as the *Cleveland Leader* and *Philadelphia Telegraph* (1916). She was the subject of sheet music, as in "Sweet Little Mary Pickford" (1914). In fact, her sobriquet, "America's Sweetheart," was coined as early as 1914. In 1915, *Ladies World* magazine christened Pickford, "The Most Popular Girl in the World."

See also: acting styles; advertising; fashion; publicity; star system; theater, legitimate; theater, melodrama

Further reading

Brownlow, Kevin (1999) *Mary Pickford Rediscovered, Rare Pictures of a Hollywood Legend*, New York: Harry N. Abrams, Inc.
Whitfield, Eileen (1997) *Pickford The Woman Who Made Hollywood*, Kentucky: University of Kentucky Press.

LESLIE MIDKIFF DEBAUCHE

Piel, Harry

b. 1892; d. 1963

director, Germany

Trained by Léonce **Perret** at **Gaumont**, Piel made his first film, *Schwarzes Blut* [Black Blood], after his return to Germany in 1912, and gained immediate success by deftly combining modern technology and crime detection with romance, drama and suspense. His sensational **melodramas** and **detective films**, including the two-part *Menschen und Masken* [Men and Masks] (1913), were notorious for their often bizarre subjects and exotic flavor, their breakneck speed and audacious stunt work. Known to his audience as the "dynamite director," Piel began to appear in his own films only after **World War I**.

MICHAEL WEDEL

Pike, Oliver

b. 1877; d. 1963

cameraman, Great Britain

A well-known nature photographer, Pike took up filming in 1907 when quieter **camera** models allowed him to film wild animals from a camouflaged blind. He initially released films such as *St. Kilda, Its People and Birds* (1908) through James **Williamson**. In 1909, he switched to **Pathé-Frères**, perhaps because of their expertise in **color**, releasing such titles as *Glimpses of Bird Life* (1910). One of the first nature filmmakers to realize the importance of narrative, Pike continued making successful natural history films until the 1940s. His work continued the tradition of other nature filmmakers from before **World War I**, including W. Pfeffer (in 1898), F. Martin **Duncan**, Cherry **Kearton**, F. Percy **Smith**, C. R. Kellogg, Frank Chapman, Raymond L. Ditmars, and J. C. Bee Mason.

See also: expedition/exploration films; scientific films: Europe

STEPHEN BOTTOMORE

Pinschewer, Julius

b. 1883; d. 1961

producer, Germany

Berlin-born Julius Pinschewer's career began in 1910 and ended in 1959, covering a German period until 1934, and a Swiss period thereafter. From early on, Pinschewer devoted himself to commissioned films, more specifically **advertising films**. He worked mainly as a producer, building up and rationalizing an advertising business which considered the medium of film as a "living poster" better suited than others for commercial and institutional persuasion. This accounts for the diversity of genres (**trick films**, **travelogues**, short fiction films) and collaborators (including Guido **Seeber**) that he engaged in the service of a variety of products: condiments, alcohol, pharmaceutical products, snap fasteners, corsets, war bonds. It also explains his willingness to promote national **propaganda** through moving pictures during **World War I**, a period crucial in the development of the ideological uses of cinema.

Further reading

Amsler, André (1997) *"Wer dem Webefilm verfällt, ist verloren für die Welt": Das Werk von Julius Pinschewer, 1883–1961*, Zurich: Chronos.

ROLAND COSANDEY

Pinthus, Kurt

b. 1886; d. 1975

critic, Germany

Pinthus' essay in the *Leipziger Tageblatt* on *Quo Vadis?* (1913), perhaps the most successful early European feature film, was among the first extended newspaper film reviews in Germany and may be counted as the first step toward serious German film criticism. Well-connected to the Expressionist movement in literature before **World War I**, Pinthus commissioned a group of idealistic young authors to write film scenarios for publication; the resulting anthology, *Das Kinobuch* [The Film Book] (1913), stands as a unique literary experiment and a testament to the cine-matic—as opposed to theatrical—potential of the medium.

See also: screenwriting

SCOTT CURTIS

Pirou, Eugène Louis

b. 1841; d. 1909

photographer, filmmaker, France

Pirou was official photographer to the Presidency of the French Republic and to many celebrities. In early 1896, he tried to buy an **Edison** Vitascope, but his request was ignored, so he came to an agreement with Henri Joseph **Joly**, who had developed a camera-projector. In October 1896, Pirou organized a moving picture program at the Grand Café de la Paix (close to where the **Ciné-matographe Lumière** was featured). It included scenes from the Czar's recent visit to Paris and *Le Coucher de la mariée* [The Bride Goes to Bed], a risqué sequence that was widely imitated by oth-ers. Louise Willy, an Olympia **music hall** star, played the bride in the film, which was directed by Albert **Kirchner**, a.k.a. Léar. On 11 February 1897, Pirou deposited photograms of the 77 films he had produced at the Bibliothèque nationale (Paris).

The Pirou-Normandin **projector** (Joly and Normandin became partners) was exploited in several other venues in Paris as well as at the Nice casino, but seems to have disappeared towards the end of 1900. Pirou was made a Knight of the Legion of Honor in 1903.

JEAN-JACQUES MEUSY

Poland

Early cinema in Poland is inseparable from that of the Austro-Hungarian, Russian, and Prussian Empires, each of which controlled a section of the country until 1918. Yet an independent, characteristically Polish and Yiddish-speaking cultural life existed that included moving pictures. Although cinema devel-oped mainly in Warsaw, **itinerant exhibitors** brought moving pictures to smaller towns such as Cracow, Lodz, Poznan and Lvov.

The first public demonstrations of **Edison**'s **Kinetoscope** occured in Warsaw in early 1896. The first demonstration of the **Cinématographe Lumière**, brought from Vienna by Eugene Dupont, took place in Cracow in November 1896, before an audience of workers, trades people and small business owners. Moving pictures soon became a means of **education** and enjoyment in all sections of the country, as **audiences** crowded into make-shift theaters to see *actualités*, **news event films**, and **travelogues**.

Soon Polish businessmen began to invest in the cinema. Engineer and photochemical factory owner Piotr Lebiedziski developed and sold **camera** equipment and **celluloid**. The Popawski brothers, Jan and Józef, working with Lebiedziski, built a Zooskop Uniwersalny (Zooscope), with which they recorded scenes on glass plates in the mid-1890's. Pleograph inventor Kazimierz **Prószynski** established the first production com-pany in 1901–1902, making the first single-shot story film, *Powrót birbanta* [The Return of the Merry Fellow] (1902). Boleslaw **Matuszewski**, working in Warsaw and Paris, wrote early theore-tical essays and tried to work on production. In 1899, the first distribution firms were established to buy, sell, and eventually rent foreign films. From that date through 1908, exhibitors enlisted popular local **magicians** to perform magic shows, puppet shows, and pantomimes alongside moving pictures. Brothers Wadysaw and Antoni Krzemiski orga-nized well-attended shows in rented theaters and storefronts throughout the Russian section, adver-tising widely in flyers and **newspapers**.

Interest and attendance increased between 1908 and 1914. Accordingly, the number of picture theaters rose, and businesses such as G. Kemmler (representing **Pathé-Frères**) and Roll and Sia grew up to manage exhibition. Production compa-nies were formed, including Mordka Towbin's Kantor Sia, the artist-run Kooperatywa Artystycy-na, Henryk Finkelstein's **Kosmofilm**, and Alek-sander Hertz' **Sfinks**, with varying degrees of success. A small cadre of cameramen, directors and stage-and-screen actors was established: among the most successful were cameraman Stanisaw Sebel, directors Wiktor Biegaski and Andrzej Marek (aka Mark Arenstein), and actors Antoni Fertner, Ester Rachel Kamiska, Samuel Landau, and Maria Mirska. A **trade press** dedicated to moving pictures began to appear in 1909, although only one journal, the trilingual *Organ*, survived until 1914. As the length of film projections increased dramatically during this period, the practice of including live entertainment in exhibitions was eliminated.

While more abundant, higher-quality foreign films remained a popular choice for spectators and exhibitors, aided by the addition of Polish **intertitles** in 1908, Polish and Yiddish-speaking filmmakers made approximately one dozen fiction films each year between 1911 and 1914. The most successful were adaptations of Yiddish stage plays, Polish canonical novels, and historical narratives. A new era in cinema began with the restoration of Poland's independence in 1918.

Further reading

Banaszkiewicz, Wadysaw and Witold Witczak (1966) *Historia filmu polskiego, tom I: 1895–1929* (The History of Polish Film, volume I: 1895–1929), Warszawa: Wydawnictwa Artystyczne i Filmowe.

Manicki, Jerzy and Kamil Stepan (1996) *Pleograf: słownik biograficzny filmu polskiego 1896–1939* (Pleograph: A Biographical Dictionary of Polish Film, 1896–1939), Kraków: Staromiejska Oficyna Wydawnicza.

SHEILA SAFF

polar expedition films

By historical accident the culmination of polar expeditions coincided almost exactly with the early years of cinema. From the 1890s, explorers were taking moving picture **cameras** to both the Arctic and Antarctic, and increasingly so after the turn of the century.

The Arctic attracted the greatest numbers of would-be filmmakers. Already in mid-1898, Robert K. **Bonine** and Thomas Crahan were en route to the Klondike where they filmed for the **Edison** company. Three years later the Baldwin-Ziegler expedition included a cameraman who filmed its activities, and the Wellman airship expeditions of 1906 and of 1907 were also filmed, the former for **Warwick Trading**. In 1908, Sandon Perkins screened films of his Arctic travels, and the following year cameraman Anthony Fiala's film of an expedition was released as *A Dash for the North Pole*. This was a year of great controversy in the polar field, with Frederick Cook and Robert Peary arguing about who had discovered the North Pole: several films related to the dispute were released, including *The Truth About the Pole* (1911).

From 1911 to 1913 a number of others made films in north latitudes, including Henry Howse, W. Bool, Geo Boruss, Conrad Luperti (of the Emerson Hough expedition), William **Harbeck**, Walter Winans, Albert E. Cawood, and Fred Granville. In 1913, three major films about the North were heavily promoted as featured attractions: Beverly B. Dobbs' *Atop of the World in Motion*; the Carnegie Museum Expedition film; and *Big Game Hunting in the North Pole Icefields*. These films featured scenes of northern native peoples and wildlife such as walruses and polar bears. In May 1914, a film of the Lerner expedition, *Mit der Kamera in Ewigen Eis*, was also heavily promoted in Germany. Early Arctic filmmaking culminated with George H. Wilkins' appointment as cinematographer of the Stefansson expedition (1913–1916).

The Antarctic region also was extensively filmed. In mid-1898, the Borchgrevink expedition left for the Antarctic carrying a Newman and Guardia film camera, though it is not clear if any films were ever made and shown of this venture. But Ernest Shackleton's first expedition was shot successfully by either Claude McDonnell or E. M. Marshall; in 1909, the resulting film was being booked in exclusive venues all over Great Britain. Dr. Charcot's expedition (1910–1912) was also filmed, and on his return he lectured with his footage in France. Films survive from two south polar ventures of 1912: cameraman Yasunao Taizumi's scenes of a Japanese expedition, and Robert Cushman Murphy's films of whaling and wildlife in South Georgia (for the American Museum of Natural History). Several thousand meters of film were shot during Roald Amundsen's

Figure 99 Poster for Herbert Ponting, *Bioscope*, 1912.

successful run to the South Pole, and it was edited as *La Decouverte du Pôle Sud* for its French release in late 1912.

Amundsen had beaten Robert F. Scott to the Pole by days, but the film of the latter's tragic expedition shot by Herbert G. **Ponting** was the greatest achievement of polar filmmaking. Landing in the Antarctic in 1910, Ponting spent sixteen months shooting, and after his return gave numerous lectures in Great Britain with his film. At about the same time cameraman Frank Hurley was starting to film the Shackleton expedition (1914–1917), and his resulting work is of almost as much interest as Ponting's.

See also: ethnographic films; expedition/exploration films; scientific films: Europe; travelogues

Further reading

Arnold, H. J. P. (1969) *Photographer of the World: the Biography of Herbert Ponting*, Rutherford: Fairleigh Dickinson University Press.

"The Canadian Arctic Expedition" (1913) *Bioscope*, 5 June: 717.

"Shackleton film a drawing card" (1909) *Kinematograph and Lantern Weekly*, 21 October: 1173.

STEPHEN BOTTOMORE

Poli, Sylvester

b. 1859; d. 1937

vaudeville entrepreneur, USA

A rival of **vaudeville** magnate B. F. **Keith**, Poli opened his first theater in 1892 in New Haven, Connecticut, and built primarily in New England a circuit of theaters known for "clean entertainment" and low salaries to performers. Poli brought the **Cinématographe Lumière** to New Haven in 1896, then booked the **Biograph** 70mm projection service for his theater circuit (1896–1903), followed by **Vitagraph**'s exhibition service from 1903 on. After intense pressure, he joined Keith's booking syndicate in 1906, a capitulation crucial to the creation of a vaudeville oligopoly. Between 1915 and 1919, Poli's theater in New Haven screened a series of Italian feature films.

ALAN GEVINSON

Ponting, Herbert

b. 1870; d. 1935

photographer, cinematographer, lecturer, Great Britain

Already a famous photographer, specializing in the Far East, Ponting learned cinematography to join Captain Robert Scott's ill-fated 1910 British Antarctic expedition. On board ship and at the base camp, he produced what remain the most famous still and moving images of explorers in this awesome landscape. His first film compilation was playing in 1911, ironically as Scott and his companions met their lonely death. Ponting devoted the rest of his life to lecturing about their heroic example, and trying to safeguard the film record. He produced a full-length version, *The Great White Silence* (1924), and added sound for *90° South* (1933).

IAN CHRISTIE

Popert, Siegmund

b. 1874; d. 1935

sales agent, distributor, France, Sweden

A German Jew born in Hamburg, Popert became the top salesman for the **phonograph** division of **Pathé-Frères** throughout Europe. As a crucial advance man, he was sent into England and Germany to begin marketing the French company's films and moving picture apparatuses, and his success then prompted other forays into the USA, Russia, Austria, Italy, Spain, and elsewhere in central and eastern Europe. In 1910, he established **Pathé Film**, the French company's branch office in Stockholm, and served as its manager during the rest of the decade.

RICHARD ABEL, JAN OLSSON

pornography

Subjects depicting sexual situations were produced and distributed as soon as moving pictures came to exist; in fact, scenes of explicit sexuality for the screen had been manufactured in large supply through most of the techniques developed prior to cinema, from animated silhouettes to zoetrope strips and magic lantern slides. However, the conditions under which these images were made and presented, the objections raised against their collective consumption, and the social stigma attached to them ensured their virtual disappearance from official cinema history. To talk about "public" screenings in relation to the display of these images is somehow inadequate, as they were shown in secluded areas such as brothels, or in other locations—known in English-speaking countries as "smoking parlors"— where attendance was reserved to a male **audience**.

The first official announcements of films restricted to adult viewers were made by **Pathé-Frères**, whose 1902 catalogue includes a section dedicated to *scènes grivoises à caractère piquant* (scenes of erotic character) and whose 1904 titles included *Le Bain des dames de la cour* [Courtesans' Bath], *La puce* [The Flea], and *Le Coucher de la parisienne* [A Parisian Lady Goes to Bed]. No sexual intercourse was actually visible in these films, whose appeal to male spectators was based on the French theatrical tradition of the *pochade* (a farce of salacious theme), voyeurism, and female nudity, very much in the vein of erotic **postcards** then widely distributed in kiosks and barber shops. A more explicit variation on this genre, beginning in 1906, was promoted by the Austrian company, **Saturn** Film, the first corporate firm specializing in films for adult viewers.

In all likelihood, however, the Pathé and Saturn productions represent only a small minority of a much larger corpus of amateur shorts of which very little, if anything, is extant; together with a few scenes of unknown origin and rare fragments of animated views, these are the only films of this kind which defied the predictable process of destruction after their clandestine life. However, given the wide array of extant images portraying sexual acts for the **magic lantern** (ranging from conventional intercourses to sado-masochism, group sex, and bestiality), it is fair to assume that the consumption of similar items for the moving picture apparatus was equally widespread, although no examples of such variety are documented until the late 1910s: for instance, the first film of homosexual intercourse known to survive, *Cast Ashore*, is dated after 1920; a short farce incorrectly attributed to Gabriele **D'Annunzio**, *Saffo and Priapo*, in which two women sodomize a priest with a wooden phallus was probably shot between 1921 and 1922. The most important collections held by public archives are at the Cinemathèque de Toulouse in France and in the Jugoslovenska Kinoteka in Belgrade; a largely unknown corpus of works from the period are in the hands of private collectors. One of the most famous in the connoisseur world, allegedly assembled by King Farouk of Egypt, was circulated in the underground market.

See also: law and the cinema

Further reading

Achenbach, Michael, Paolo Caneppele and Ernst Kieninger (1999) *Projectionen der Sehnsucht. Saturn: Die erotischen Anfänge der österreichischen Kinematografie*, Wien: Filmarchiv Austria.

Borde, Raymond (1986) *L'Enfer des cinémathèques*, Avignon: Rencontres Cinématographiques du Festival d'Avignon.

POLO CERCHI UAI

Porten, Henny

b. 1890; d. 1960

actor, Germany

Porten first appeared in the 1906 *Tonbild*, *Meissner Porzellan* [China from Meissen], which was directed by her father, an **opera** singer and director, for Oskar **Messter**. After completing school in 1907, she became a film actor, working for various companies before being placed under contract by Messter in 1910. Initially given no billing, she made an immediate impression with her striking appearance, her presence, and her seemingly direct, yet precisely calculated, additive **acting style**. In the 1910s, Porten became Germany's most popular movie **star**, her name synonymous with the rise of the film medium.

Historians later attributed Porten's popularity to her personification of the image of German femininity: a voluptuous yet pointedly non-erotic blonde who embodied values such as self-sacrifice, forbearance, and subordination. Yet, in the early 1910s, she had been labeled "German" to distinguish her from the Danish movie star Asta **Nielsen**. In intellectual circles she was persistently censured as a "star of the common people." In contrast to Nielsen, known as the "**Duse** of cinematic art," Porten represented everything that intellectuals despised about the *Volk*.

Much like Nielsen, however, Porten supported the cause of women's liberation in nearly all of her films, albeit not in the area of erotic libertinism. Instead, she pointed out the societal repression to which women living in patriarchy were subjected. Her heroines suffered the social ostracism of extramarital relationships and unwed motherhood; the drawbacks of a male, military code of honor; marital rape; and inequitable rivalry with men at work. The only German actress to advocate women choosing a career over marriage, she was also committed to international reconciliation and opposed to the war. At the same time, she appeared not only in **comedies** but stylistically experimental films. She also discovered and fostered other actors (Emil Jannings, Franz Lederer, Willi Forst) and directors (Robert Wiene, E. A. Dupont, Wilhelm Dieterle).

In 1921, she set up her own production company, which soon foundered; turning to a production partnership with director Carl **Froelich**, she increasingly pursued success. During this period she developed an unusual profile, playing double and multiple roles modeled on Ernst **Lubitsch**'s *Kohlhiesels Töchter* [Kohlhiesel's Daughters] (1920): two female characters, one of them beautiful, weak and stupid, and the other ugly, strong and clever, with the latter developing a subversive independent existence beside the attractive star.

Despite her fame as the "mother of German film," borne out in the National-Socialist- oriented *Mutter und Kind* [Mother and Child] (1933), she was discredited by the Nazis for refusing to divorce her second husband, who was considered Jewish. Spurned by the postwar West German film industry, she acted in her last two films at Defa in East Berlin in 1953–1954.

See also: women's movement: Europe

Further reading

Belach, Helga (1986) *Henny Porten. Der erste deutsche Filmstar 1890–1960*, Berlin (West): Haude & Spener.

CORINNA MÜLLER

Porter, Edwin S(tanton)

b. 21 April 1870; d. 30 April 1940

exhibitor, director, producer, USA

Porter left his hometown (Connellsville, Pennsylvania) to join the Navy in 1893. During his service, he became interested in moving pictures and, in 1896, convinced family friends to acquire exhibition rights to **Edison**'s Vitascope for California and Indiana. Thereafter, he traveled as an exhibitor through the USA, Canada, and the Caribbean. From 1898 until early 1900, he also showed moving pictures at the Eden Musee, New York City's famous **wax museum**. Although he used variety formats to present single-shot films, he also sequenced them into elaborate, multi-shot narratives.

Edison Manufacturing hired Porter in November 1900 to improve its **projector** and to outfit its new rooftop studio in Manhattan. Porter stayed on to become chief cameraman and studio head. From the outset, he worked collaboratively with men trained in the theater: George Fleming (1901–1903), William Martinetti (1903–1904), G. M. **Anderson** (1903–1904), Wallace **McCutcheon** (1905–1907), and J. Searle **Dawley** (1907–1908). Porter managed all aspects of film production (including editing) and, between 1901 and 1903, applied his skills as an exhibitor in structuring short films into sequences. Partially inspired by Georges **Méliès**, he developed more elaborate continuities between shots (not just narrative, but spatial, temporal, and visual relations). His progress can be traced from *Terrible Teddy the Grizzly King* (1901) and *The Execution of Czolgosz* (1901) to *Jack and the Beanstalk* (1902), *How They Do Things on the Bowery* (1902), and *Life of An American Fireman* (1902–1903). Within the broad, diffuse system of representation characteristic of the pre-nickelodeon era, Porter embraced techniques of overlapping action and temporal repetition that marked the leading edge of cinematic practice.

With his collaborators, Porter made a variety of fiction films 500 to 1,000 feet in length: e.g., *Uncle Tom's Cabin* (1903), *The Great Train Robbery* (1903), *The Ex-Convict* (1904), *The Miller's Daughter* (1905), *The "White" Caps* (1905), *Dream of a Rarebit Fiend* (1906), *Cohen's Fire Sale* (1907). In the summer of 1907, he and Dawley moved to a new studio in the Bronx, where they made such titles as *College Chums* (1907) and *Rescued from an Eagle's Nest* (1908). By 1908, at the height of the **nickelodeon** boom, exhibitors were demanding more films—and films that told a clear, readily understood story. While **Pathé-Frères** and D. W. **Griffith** did much to address these demands, Porter resisted. As

his working methods became antiquated, he was demoted and, by late 1909, fired.

At Edison, Porter increasingly resisted corporate, hierarchical organizations of labor, favored stories that expressed an old-middle-class ideology alienated from the new economic order, and opposed storytelling methods that enabled cinema to function effectively as mass entertainment. Although never abandoning these values, after leaving Edison he did compromise: his storytelling was simplified, stripped of its most extreme and engaging qualities. As a business partner in subsequent ventures, Porter was able to continue working, but only with a co-filmmaker. Indeed, he frustrated some associates: Adolph **Zukor** later dismissed him as an artistic mechanic, not a dramatic artist.

Between 1910 and 1912, Porter was a key figure in forming the New York-based Defender and **Rex** film companies. In October 1912, he sold his shares in Rex and become production head for **Famous Players**, where he made feature films with well-known stage stars: *The Count of Monte Cristo* (1912) with James O'Neill, *The Prisoner of Zenda* (1913) with James Hackett, and *In the Bishop's Carriage* (1913) with Mary **Pickford**. In 1915, he sold his interests in Famous Players to become president of the Precision Machine Company. Under his supervision, its **Simplex projector** became the industry standard. In 1925, Porter slid quietly into retirement, and reclusion in Manhattan.

See also: editing: early practices and techniques; editing: spatial relations; editing: tableau style; editing: temporal relations

Further reading

Musser, Charles (1990) *Before the Nickelodeon: Edwin S. Porter and the Edison Manufacturing Company*, Berkeley: University of California Press.

CHARLES MUSSER

Portugal

In June 1896, the first films were shown in Portugal by Erwin Rousby, who came from Madrid with the Animatografo bought from R. W. **Paul** in London.

Three months later Rousby included in his programs a number of films shot in Portugal by Paul's cameraman Henry Short. Among them were *Lisbon, the Fish Market* and *A Portuguese Railway Train*. In November 1896, the Porto-born photographer Aurélio Paz dos Reis (1862–1931) organized screenings in Lisbon with the Kinématographo Português **projector**, a **Méliès–Reulos** apparatus bought in Paris. He produced many films by himself and probably the first Portuguese film, *Saída do pessoal Operarario da fabrica Confiança*. In January 1897, he took his shows to Rio de Janeiro (Brazil) for a few weeks, but they failed due to technical difficulties. On his return to Portugal, he left the moving picture business.

During the next ten years, many foreign **itinerant exhibitors** operated in Portugal, working mainly in theaters in Porto and Lisbon with a range of apparatuses: i.e., **Biograph**, Bioscope, Cosmograph, **Lumière**, or **Pathé-Frères**. Elsewhere film projections in the open air, as in Cascais in 1897, became a regular event. An important exhibitor and producer was Manuel Maria da Costa Veiga. From 1899, he shot scenes of the royal family and various events in Lisbon and its surroundings. In 1905 his company, Cinematográfica de Film, sold films such as *Visita do imperador Guilherme II da Alemanha* to Oskar **Messter**.

The first moving picture theater, the Salao Ideal, opened in Lisbon in 1904. The owner, Júlio Costa, included in his programs **Gaumont** films using a **synchronized sound** apparatus. As the founder of the Empresa Portuguesa Cinematografica (1908), Costa is considered the first Portuguese industrialist of cinema. In 1909, two other companies, Lusitania Filme and Portugália Filme (founded by Joao Freire Correia), began regular production. Portugália Filme built a film studio where fiction films such as *Os crimes de Diogo Alves* were made. About the same time, colonial documentaries were shot in Sao Tomé: *A cultura do Cacau em Sao Tomé* by Ernesto de Albuquerque (1883–1940) and *Serviçal e Senhor* by Cardoso Furtado. In 1910, Invicta Filme also began producing films in Porto, which then were distributed by Pathé and Gaumont throughout the world.

As the country's own production was rather small, most films on Portuguese screens came from abroad, mainly from France before 1908. Thereafter, as distributors settled in Lisbon, other films, especially from Italy and the USA, found their way to Portuguese audiences.

Further reading

Duarto, Fernando (1983) *Joao Tavares e o primitivo cinema português*, Lisbon: Cinemateca Portuguesa.

Matos-Cruz, José de (1989) *Prontuário do cinema Português 1896–1989*, Lisbon: Cinemateca Portuguesa.

Ribeiro, Félix (1983) *Filmes, Figuras e Factos da história do cinema Português 1896–1949*, Lisbon: Cinemateca Portuguesa.

GUIDO CONVENTS

postcards

Simultaneous with the development of moving pictures, postcards became a new popular form of visual representation in Europe and North America in the early 20th century. Postcards frequently drew on the same subject matter as did early films, and the two forms may have had some reciprocal influence in terms of genre, point of view, and style.

The first official postcard was printed by the Austrian government in 1869, and soon after printers began making cards that could be sent through the mail bearing a message or advertisement. Commercially printed and hand-tinted souvenir cards that featured aesthetically appealing views only became widespread, however, when two **world's fairs** popularized them. The 1893 Chicago World's Columbian Exposition and the 1900 Paris Exposition both sold cards as souvenirs to be saved or given to friends. Postcards then became an industry when: (1) governments authorized private manufacture of the cards and their circulation through the mail, (2) new technologies made **color** printing cheap enough for cards to be easily affordable, and (3) governments allowed space on the backside of cards to be divided, so that personal messages could be imprinted (1902 in England, 1903 in France, 1908 in the USA). By the early 1910s, the postcard industry employed over 30,000 people worldwide. As in the cinema industry, women laborers initially were hired to color postcards by hand.

The postcard was as much a new mass, commercialized way of seeing as were moving pictures. Between 1900 and 1910, for instance, 10,000 views of Paris alone were manufactured. Millions of cards annually circulated through the world's postal systems. As in early moving pictures, postcards provided a photographic means of access to sites and events—both local and distant. They generally relied on the conventions of commercial **photography** for portraiture and urban advertisement. They used perspective, for instance, positioning the camera above ground level so that the camera's eye, and thus the spectator's eye, dominated the viewed space. Many early *actualités* of panoramic views duplicated those of postcards.

As in early moving pictures, postcards also depicted other subjects, from ethnic stereotypes to fantastic views. Some postcards even featured a series or sequence of views, providing a simple narrative. Similar narrative depictions of disrobing women, jokes or comic tricks, and stolen kisses can be found in both early moving pictures and postcard series. Magazine critics in Britain, France, and the United States all fretted over the popularity of the phenomenon—not so much because of the content of some genres but because buying and sending postcards, they feared, would replace the art of letter writing.

See also: advertising; comic films; framing: camera distance and angle; dioramas/panoramas; pornography; travelogues; trick films

Further reading

Bowers, Q. David (1989) "Souvenir Postcards and the Development of the Star System, 1912–1914," *Film History*, 3: 39–45.

Stevens, Norman D. (ed.) (1995) *Postcards in the Library: Invaluable Visual Resources*, New York: Haworth Press.

LAUREN RABINOVITZ

Pouctal, Henri

b. 1856; d. 1922

filmmaker, France

Trained as a stage actor (Odeon Theatre), Henri Pouctal became a film actor for **Film d'Art** in 1908 and soon graduated to directing such films as *Werther* (1910) and *Camille Desmoulins* (1911). Eventually he advanced to become head of film production in 1913. As the scriptwriter and director of approximately fifty Film d'Art productions before **World War I**, Pouctal was considered by Louis Delluc as one of the best French filmmakers. During the war, he specialized in patriotic epics such as *Alsace* (1916), starring Gabrielle Réjane. He is perhaps best known for his later adaptations of French literary classics such as Emile Zola's *Travail* (Labor) (1919–1920), as well as *Gigolette* (1920) and *Le Crime du Bouif* (1921).

GLENN MYRENT

Power, Nicholas

b. 1854, New York City; d. 1921, Palm Beach, Florida

inventor, manufacturer, USA

Founder of a company bearing his name, Power worked tirelessly to develop a "flickerless" moving picture **projector** in the early 1900s. The **Power's Cameragraph** established his reputation for high quality, and by 1906, his company's forty technicians were manufacturing around 700 projectors a year. The Cameragraph No. 5 (first introduced in 1907) and the Cameragraph No. 6 (in 1916) were among the most respected in the industry, partly because equipment for the machines constantly was being updated. On his retirement, the Nicholas Power Company merged with the International Projector Company.

RICHARD ABEL

Power's Cameragraph No. 5 projector

Introduced in 1907, the Cameragraph No. 5 made by pioneer Nicholas **Power** proved widely popular in both Europe and the USA for its precision manufacture, featuring a four slot Maltese Cross (Geneva) **intermittent** balanced by a heavy fly-wheel, internal two-bladed shutter, and a heavy "cooling" plate that acted as a heat sink to protect the film. The No. 6 Cameragraph of 1916 introduced an unusual Maltese Cross movement where a four-pin gear ran through an "x" shaped slot, increasing the speed of movement between frames and giving a brighter image with less flicker, continuing Power's reputation for quality design.

DEAC ROSSELL

Powers, Patrick A.

b. waterford, Ireland, 1870;
d. New York City, 1948

distributor, producer, executive, USA

After a varied early career, Powers became a distributor of **Edison** and Victor **phonographs**; in 1909, he gravitated into film production, forming Powers Film. In 1910, he joined Carl **Laemmle** in establishing the **Motion Picture Distributing and Sales Company**, and when the Sales Company split into **Mutual**, **Universal**, and Film Supply in 1912, Powers joined Laemmle at Universal, as its treasurer. Despite constant friction between the two men (for a time, Powers headed **Warner's Features**), Powers remained indispensible to Universal thanks to his control, through outright ownership and reliable proxy votes, of the company's exchanges in the Northeast. Powers eventually resigned from Universal in 1920.

BEN BREWSTER

Poyen, René-Georges

b. 1908; d. 1968.

actor, France

Poyen joined Louis **Feuillade**'s crew at **Gaumont** in late 1912 and was cast in *Bébé adopte un petit frère* [Bébé adopts a younger brother] (1912). Feuillade then created a new **comic series** for him called *Bout-de-Zan*, whose main character was recognizable by his adult clothing (a derby hat and suit). This series lasted until 1916, and totaled 52 films. The cast also included Marguerite Lavigne (the mother), Edmond Bréon (the father), and Jeanne Saint-Bonnet (the maid). Poyen's collaboration with Feuillade continued in many other films, most notably in *Les Vampires* (1915–1916), *Judex* (1917), and *L'Orphelin de Paris* [The Orphan of Paris] (1924).

LAURENT LE FORESTIER

preservation

In order to ensure the physical integrity of films and their **access** for present and future generations, moving image **archives** have designed a set of methods and techniques in answer to different goals. The term "preservation" refers to all procedures necessary for protecting, restoring the content, and organizing the intellectual experience of a film on a permanent basis. This definition fulfills three basic requirements: making sure that the object is not further damaged; bringing it back to a condition as close as possible to its original state; providing access to it, in a manner consistent with the way the artifact was meant to be exhibited. Various actions are taken in order to meet these objectives: (a) conservation, all the activities necessary to prevent or minimize the process of physical degradation of the material, with the minimum intervention or interference with the object (storing a nitrate print in a vault equipped with temperature and humidity control systems is part of this process); (b) duplication, the set of practices related to the creation of a replica of the moving image, either as a backup of existing original or preservation components, or as a means to give access to the moving image; (c) restoration, the set of technical and intellectual procedures aimed at compensating for the loss or degradation of portions of the moving image; (d) reconstruction, the editing process through which a print whose appearance is as similar as possible to a desired version considered as authoritative is created by interpolating, replacing, or reassembling sections within the copy and with footage retrieved from other copies (some segments—such as **intertitles**—may be newly created by the archive); (e) recreation, a strategy for presenting an imaginary account of what the film would have been if some or all of its missing parts had survived. The latter course of action is taken when material directly or indirectly related to the film is used in order to give an idea of its original concept.

It is worth pointing out that the term "restoration" in moving picture preservation is different from its equivalent in most other disciplines, in the sense that it necessarily involves the reproduction of a source print. We clean a painting, treat the canvas, adjust the frame, and fix unstable pigments, then we exhibit the painting itself. A nitrate film (and, for that matter, any moving image carrier known today) may be cleaned, repaired, edited, or otherwise treated. However, as long as it is the object of a preservation process (that is, if a decision has been made concerning its archival status), the artifact as such cannot be exhibited. Another distinctive feature of photographic moving images—comparable only to analog phonographic recordings on disc or tape—is that they cannot be experienced without progressively damaging them. Consequently, they must be duplicated onto another carrier whose eventual decay through wear and tear will not affect the possibility of providing access to their content through a new copy. If the print found is a positive, the laboratory creates a preservation negative from it and one positive print ("answer print") in order to verify the quality of the negative, makes corrections if necessary, then produces one or more prints for access. Terminology is not uniform: "viewing print," "projection print," "reference copy," "distribution print," "access copy," "release print," and "show print" may mean slightly different things, but what they have in common is the fact that they can be viewed because their gradual loss of quality or accidental damage will not endanger the survival of the archival master and the negative.

Contrary to common belief, digital technology is a useful but limited tool in the preservation work. It can be of great help in the restoration process by reducing or eliminating damage to the moving image (such as scratches, tears, or pieces of missing emulsion) and by compensating for alterations in contrast or color balance; however, it is not an adequate solution for the purpose of long-term conservation of the moving image itself, due to the extreme instability of the carriers and the quick obsolescence of the formats. Prints struck on 35 mm film are by far the most stable elements available today, and it is in this form that archives continue to preserve them as long as motion picture film stock is manufactured.

It must also be stressed that any preservation activity involving the duplication of an early film onto a new carrier involves a loss of information. No viewing print (whether photomechanical or digital) struck from an original is currently able to imitate the full range of the visual qualities of the source. The unique texture of the orthochromatic emulsion used in most early films finds no equivalent in modern copies; the same applies to the nitrate base, whose effect on the projected image cannot be adequately rendered in the acetate or polyester base of film stock produced at present, let alone in any reproduction with electronic means. The extent of the loss takes dramatic proportions in relation to the **color**: neither tinting or toning, nor other more sophisticated techniques such as hand-coloring, stencil, and the various systems involving the use of non-standard printing and projection devices (**Chronochrome**, Kinemacolor, early Technicolor) have been replicated in a way that may be considered as authentic, despite all attempts to resuscitate the systems that made them possible.

At its best, preservation of early cinema succeeds in bringing the viewer an experience which resembles but is not identical to moving images whose actual look is either lost forever, or remains visible in the surviving original prints. To enhance this approximation, archives recommend that early films are shown under conditions similar to those of the time of their release: prints are screened with **projectors** allowing variable speed (16 frames per second was the standard rate during the first two decades of cinema) and equipped with three-blade shutters, thus reducing the flickering effect on the screen. Finally, early films are shown at the "silent" aspect ratio (ca. 1:1.28 to 1:1.31) on **screens** of proper size and material, with the accompaniment of live **music**, **sound effects** or **lecturers**, as was

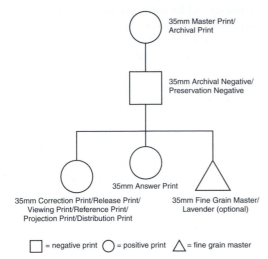

= negative print ◯ = positive print △ = fine grain master

Figure 100 Preservation pattern of a 35 mm silent positive print. (Paolo Cherchi Usai.)

common practice throughout the world. In doing so, archives recognize that a crucial moment of the preservation process takes place away from the laboratory and outside the vaults, in the architectural space where early films are exhibited, and in the cultural context in which their presentation is revived for a new audience.

See also: authentication; collections

Further reading

Bowser, Eileen (October 1990) "Some Principles of Film Restoration," *Griffithiana*, 38–39: 170–173.

Cherchi Usai, Paolo (2000) "The Ethics of Film Preservation," in *Silent Cinema: An Introduction*, 44–76, London: BFI Publishing.

McGreevey, Tom and Joanne L. Yeck (1997) *Our Movie Heritage*, New Brunswick: Rutgers University Press.

Sargent, Ralph N. (1974) *Preserving the Moving Image*, Washington, D.C.: Corporation for Public Broadcasting/National Endowment for the Arts.

PAOLO CHERCHI USAI

Prince, Charles

b. 1872; d. 1933

actor, scriptwriter, France

Born Petitdemange, on the southwestern outskirts of Paris, Charles took the stage name of Prince and became a Boulevard theater star, celebrated especially for his comic roles at the Variétés. Hired by Charles **Pathé** in late 1908, he initially worked with Georges **Monca** and **Mistinguett** on some of **SCAGL**'s films but soon developed a **comic series** around a character named Rigadin, whose popularity rivaled that of Max **Linder**, at least in France. The series often gently parodied the serious bourgeois drama of the pre-war period and its principal subject of *amour*, for Rigadin usually was either shyly courting, timidly involved in a love affair, or having marital problems. Prince starred in more than 200 *Rigadin* films (for which he wrote most of the scenarios) through 1920 (with a hiatus of several years during **World War I**), after which he played minor film roles in the late 1920s and early 1930s.

RICHARD ABEL

Pringle, Ralph

b. ?; d. ?

exhibitor, Great Britain, Ireland

Originally an agent for A. D. **Thomas**, Ralph Pringle in 1901 set up his own travelling exhibition company, North American Animated Photo, which presented moving pictures shows in town halls and theaters throughout Great Britain and Ireland. Between 1901 and 1907, he commissioned **Mitchell & Kenyon** to make non-fiction films of local scenes that were shown in the same evening. His circuit eventually included Edinburgh, Glasgow, Sunderland, Newcastle, Bristol, Huddersfield, Liverpool, Birmingham and Dublin. From 1908 onwards, Pringle opened permanent cinemas in Bristol, Leyland, Edinburgh, and Glasgow.

See also: itinerant exhibitors

VANESSA TOULMIN

program formats

The term *program* applies to the presentation format of a range of performative and—later—broadcast entertainments. The program is a container format: i.e., it consists of a number of discrete attractions sequenced by an organizing agent with the design to regulate audience involvement, usually for the duration of a single visit. Individual attractions, moreover, can themselves be a program (for example, a series of films embedded in a **vaudeville** show). *Program formats* refers to the ways these presentations are put together. In terms of its constituent elements, a program can be a line-up of either homogeneous or heterogeneous items. In either case multiple channels may be employed (for example, films accompanied by **music** or **lecturers**). In terms of coherence, the format introduces functional and content relations: the former concerns matters of arrangement, rhythm, variation, contrast, and balance; the latter concerns the ways in which a program's composition can be overlaid with meaning (artistic, thematic, symbolic, narrative).

Given such a broad (although weak, for lack of substantial, worldwide research) perspective, one finds film programs in many contexts, reflecting various ways in which early cinema was positioned, depending on purpose, venue, location, period, or audience composition. But it also excludes certain ways of film presentation. **Kinetoscopes**, for instance, offered a single film for individual viewing; but even when an establishment boasted a number of such machines, the viewer, not the management, decided on the number and order of items viewed. And full-length projections of **boxing films** based their coherence not on the program format, but on the course of the recorded fight. Nevertheless, the program became the dominant format of film presentation.

After the turn of the century, with the rise of more elaborate traveling shows and permanent moving picture theaters, the film program extended its span to become a mainstream, full-length entertainment, either as a homogeneous attraction or interspersed with **illustrated songs** or other lantern slide projections and/or with live acts. Before this development, the adaptability of the film program to existing performances was all-important. Because of early cinema's conceptual indeterminacy—as science, entertainment, **education**—the occurrence of independent (that is, non-embedded), homogeneous film programs was limited. Most were intended primarily as technical demonstrations, such as programs by the **Lumière** company, R. W. **Paul**, and other pioneer manufacturers. These typically were set in (sometimes makeshift) non-entertainment venues. As entertainment, on the other hand, film programs were added to or extended the repertoire of existing attractions, notably in **fairs/fairgrounds** and other itinerant shows. Yet, the vocal introductions that often framed pioneers' showcase screenings as science or the acts that often punctuated or sandwiched fairground screenings point up the ease with which films could be combined in a mixed format. In heterogeneous programs, the predominant category prior to permanent theaters, moving pictures were fitted in with other performances: within larger narratives (for example, **travelogues** and other **illustrated lectures**) or in modular formats (for example, vaudeville, **music halls**, **cafés-concerts**, **chautauquas**).

Initially, film programs tended to be relatively short. As scientific demonstrations, programs would often not exceed 15 minutes. When these demonstrations were targeted at mass audiences, rather than at restricted peer group spectators, the frequency of projections rather than program length was increased. A well-documented case is the Lumière programs at the **world's fair** in Montpellier, from April to November 1896, which were screened forty to fifty times a day. But as entertainment the film program would really spread its wings. In fairground shows, particularly in Europe, high-frequency projections of short programs gave way to lengthier shows, in bigger, often elaborately embellished tents. In vaudeville, film programs at first did not last significantly longer than most other acts. But their continuing popularity, particularly because of the contrast newsworthy, nonfiction subjects created with the rest of the bill, often merited an increase in length. Surviving program bills of the Palace Theatre of Varieties in London reveal that within a year after their introduction, in the spring of 1897, the length of the **British Mutoscope and Biograph** Company's screenings had doubled to half an hour, the longest act by far on the bill. This extension coincided with the growing predominance of filmed *actualités*. Fairground and other traveling programs, incidentally, typically had a pronounced version of **actualités** material, such as local films featuring people and events of the locale in which the program was shown.

Independent film shows, whether on fairgrounds or in **nickelodeons**, initially relied on a relatively high audience turnover with screenings throughout the day; these continuous shows allowed people to "drop in" at any time. The very autonomy of these programs meant, however, that an individual film's contribution became more important. In a sense, local films can be seen as doing just that, yet they functioned primarily as a special attraction to draw crowds. The independent film show's development into a full evening's entertainment was the result of longer, rather than more, films, and with higher production values—especially in the case of the **multiple-reel/feature film**. All this was a reflection of developments in production, **distribution**, and exhibition practices: on the one hand, processes of rationalization, standardization, and increase in scale and, on the other, a process of "gentrification" in terms of ownership, film subjects, and target audiences. Despite these developments, programs would not have looked the same in terms of make-up, structure, or length: the presence and quality of live acts, lecturing or music as well as the number, order, or novelty of films appear to have differed widely, although it is difficult to attribute such differences to a single factor or circumstance. Yet, surely, the resistance of theater managers to the encroachments of other sections of the industry would have played a part. Within limits, even individual theaters (an example would be those managed by S. L. **Rothapfel** in the USA) could develop a distinctive style of programming. The feature film, in particular, appears to have been central in the struggle for control of the audience's attention (and money). Its varying length, its "narrative elasticity," strongly suggests that by the early 1910s control over the program was as yet undecided. But the fact that in surviving bills it was not uncommon to find a longer film divided into numbered acts, as if with each new act another film began, does reveal that the program format and its contents could, in a sense, be at odds.

Audience involvement was regulated by various ways of sequencing. In larger content-related programs, narrative was primarily responsible for the sequencing. In functionally organized programs, sequencing principles were invariable, regardless of whether a film program was embedded or independent, although embedded films also were affected by strategies governing the entire line-up (determining position, "tone"). Common principles were: variation (of mood, of subject, particularly the alternation of familiar or local with novel or exotic scenes), separation (of mood, of subject, particularly in terms of a hierarchy of taste), and build up (crescendoing or delaying in terms of spectacle or notoriety, descending in terms of newsworthiness, or both in terms of length). Given these principles, the program progressed through a series of recommencements, with each individual item ideally being different from its predecessor. Thus, each film would be presented in the most favorable or appropriate way. However, repetition and "unfortunate proximity" could not always be avoided, not in the least because of the simultaneous application of these principles. Moreover, as sequencing often involved a mixture of functional and content relations (for example, an event depicted by a series of films), measures to either prevent or encourage the creation of links between successive films were crucial. Particularly in programs of very short films, such sequencing measures can be seen as the exhibitors' equivalent of editing: in the Mutoscope & Biograph Company's programs in London, for instance, sequencing sometimes was used to create "invisible," symbolic meanings.

Even though programming principles were endorsed, if not prescribed, by all sections of the industry, there also was a good deal of contingency. It was not uncommon to speed up, cut or drop a film altogether in order to squeeze in another show. Also, in moving picture theaters well into the 1910s, a show's starting time and the time of a spectator's entry did not always coincide: on the handbills for Jean **Desmet**'s theaters in the Netherlands, for instance, the announcement that patrons could enter the show at any time was removed only in 1912. Continuous shows that allowed movie-goers to enter the film show at any given moment undermined careful program

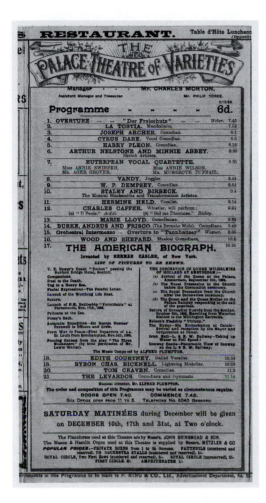

Figure 101 Palace Theatre of Varieties program, London, December 1897.

comic, the documentary fictional, the functional meaningful, or vice versa. After all, the cognitive processes activated by the program format were as much a risk as an asset.

See also: editing: early practices and techniques; itinerant exhibitors; magic lantern shows; palace cinemas; spectatorship: issues and debates

Further reading

Allen, Robert C. (1980) *Vaudeville and Film 1895–1915: A Study in Media Interaction*, New York: Arno Press.

Altman, Rick (1996) "The Silence of the Silents," *Musical Quarterly*, 80.4: 648–718.

André, Jacques et Marie (1987) *Une saison Lumière à Montpellier*, Perpignan: Institut Jean Vigo.

de Klerk, Nico (2000) "'Pictures to be shewn': programming the American Biograph," in Simon Popple and Vanessa Toulmin (eds.) *Visual Delights: Essays on the Popular and Projected Image in the 19th Century*, Trowbridge: Flicks Books.

Müller, Corinna (1994) *Frühe deutsche Kinematografie. Formale, wirtschaftliche und kulturelle Entwicklungen 1907–1912*, Stuttgart/Weimar: J.B. Metzler.

Toulmin, Vanessa (1994) "Telling the tale: the story of the fairground bioscope shows and the showmen who operated them," *Film History*, 6.2: 219–237.

NICO DE KLERK

composition (although the relatively high number of comic numbers in many programs may at least have enabled latecomers to settle in more easily). Furthermore, audience involvement did not necessarily always follow the leads provided by titles, **color**, lecturers, or music; spectators could pick up on any element in a series of films to create links unforeseen, quite literally, by exhibitors and producers. With the increase of film length in multiple-reel and feature films, the "contagiousness" of contiguous films probably decreased. Still, because of its very format, the program could potentially—and "parasitically"—render the tragic

projectionists

The **Cinematographe Lumière** doubled as its own projector, and early Lumière operator-filmmakers as projectionists. But, like Plato's hermaphrodites, moving picture projection was soon divorced from production *per se*. With few exceptions, early cinema scholars, however, unlike the beings in Plato's fable, have shown little interest in "reuniting" production and projection. Institutional, narrative, and even spectatorial accounts of early cinema all neglect projection and see it merely as a neutral conveyance. But beyond its own history—of technological change, trade unionism, working-class culture, social regulation, and the export of **modernity** to the cultural periphery—projection also exists as early cinema's lost hermaphrodite, combining the poles of "production" and "consumption." Projection allows us to see early cinema as being "produced" along a continuum which ended only at the point of consumption.

It is hazardous to generalize, but two principal projection periods and paradigms in early cinema seem to exist. The first is the "showman" era (*c*. 1896–1905), when **projectors** were primitive, cantankerous affairs that gave a poor quality image and the projectionist, visible to the audience, was often an **itinerant exhibitor** (both performer and entrepreneur) who owned his own equipment and stock of films. The second is the "storefront" or **nickelodeon** era (*c*. 1905–1910), which saw rapid improvement in projector technology (but not to the point of standardizing construction, completely eliminating flicker, or making it possible for "anyone" to operate and maintain the equipment safely and competently). Here the projectionist was transformed into something of an industrial laborer (as his new name the "machine operator" suggests), an invisible employee confined to a cramped and insalubrious booth for long periods of time, enduring the worst working conditions ever found in the film industry.

The importance of the showman projectionist—women did not enter the trade until **World War I** in England—to a **cinema of attractions**, although still unexplored, is implicit in this theory's notion of cinema's appeal as apparatus and event. His role became more complex, however, during the storefront period. This period saw the first systematic state regulation of film exhibition, around public safety—fire was a constant worry—and "morality." Here, professional operators urged mandatory examination and licensing to complement the regulation of projector and booth design (and as a way to rid the trade of unskilled workers, who drove down wages). Despite the obvious logic of such a proposal and the important public safety issues at stake, in France and England, for example, they were completely ignored. Yet the principal image of the machine operator that has come down to us is that of the unskilled rogue whom

professional operators were trying to eliminate. Faced with rapid proletarianization, declining wages (at a time of windfall exhibition profits), and appalling working conditions, machine operators launched the film industry's first unionization drive, a decade before the Hollywood studios. But the very issue of which union to join was itself a dilemma: were they industrial workers, or performing artists? It is significant that, in both England and the USA, they eventually joined actors' and theatrical unions.

As part of their drive for recognition, operators launched an unprecedented debate on the quality of exhibition and the proper treatment of films. Again, they were ignored, except by the industry's nascent **trade press**, which editorialized in favor of operators and in some cases freely declared themselves the "official organs" of operator interests. Trade press technical columns, especially by the machine operators' most ardent supporter, F. H. **Richardson**, in the pages of *Moving Picture World*, led to the publication of a score of projection manuals in the early 1910s—perhaps the first body of early commentary on the new art.

Projection played an essential role in defining early cinema's modernity, most intriguingly in its mediation between cultural metropolis and periphery. Early projectors were hand-cranked—the first motor-driven projectors appeared in 1908, but did not come into widespread use for a number of years—and this constant cranking was part of the drudgery of projecting. In Russia, as Yuri Tsivian has shown, hand-cranking became the means whereby the lowly operator initially corrupted and then helped compel revision of the traditionally slow and "theatrical" Russian **acting style**, simply by speeding up the action on the screen. Tsivian describes this procedure as an "aesthetic of reception," but in fact it was a narrative intervention—acting codes were an important narrative device of the period—and therefore an aesthetic of *production*. Herein lies projection's greatest importance in the storefront period.

Early films, as Kevin Brownlow has documented, were shot at an astonishing variety of speeds, even within a single film. Sometimes this was mere carelessness, but often, in the absence of narrative conventions (later codified in the **classical Hollywood cinema**), it was a deliberate and indispensable narrative device. But operators went one step further, arguing that this technique was often neglected or improperly executed. A good machine operator would constantly monitor the film he was projecting and spontaneously alter the speed of projection from one scene to the next (later, this activity was institutionalized in the form of cue sheets). This, they argued, made of them artists indispensable to the production of film narrative. In this view, narrative was not constructed in the studio alone but also in thousands of individual projection booths: a film's production began with the turning of the camera crank and was completed only with the turning of the projector crank. This claim has wide-ranging implications for institutional, narrative and spectatorial accounts of early cinema which have not yet been fully explored.

See also: law and the cinema; labor movement, Europe; labor movement, USA; spectatorship: issues and debates

Further reading

Barnard, Timothy (2002) "The 'Machine Operator': *Deus ex Machina* of the Storefront Cinema," *Framework*, 43.1: 40–75.

Brownlow, Kevin (1990) "Silent Films—What was the Right Speed?" in Thomas Elsaesser (ed.) *Early Cinema: Space, Frame, Narrative*, 282–290, London: British Film Institute.

Malkames, Don (1967) "Early Projector Mechanisms," in Raymond Fielding (ed.) *A Technological History of Motion Pictures*, 97–104, Berkeley: University of California Press.

Musser, Charles (1990) *The Emergence of Cinema: The American Screen to 1907*, New York: Scribner's.

Richardson, F. H. (1912) *Motion Picture Handbook, A Guide for Managers and Operators of Motion Picture Theatres*, 2nd ed., New York: Moving Picture World.

Tsivian, Yuri (1994) *Early Cinema in Russia and its Cultural Reception*, trans. Alan Bodger, ed. Richard Taylor, London: Routledge.

TIMOTHY BARNARD

Figure 102 Keith Bijou projection room, Boston, 1910.

Figure 103 Pre-fabricated Gaumont projection booth, c. 1906. (From J. Rosen, *L'Histoire d'une industrie. Le Cinematographe*, Paris: Société des editions, 1906.)

projectors

A variety of moving picture projectors were produced by numerous manufacturers, beginning in 1896. Because there was no dominant mode of film exhibition until the emergence of purpose-built theaters and the establishment of film rental patterns, projector manufacture remained both diversified and hotly competitive through the end of the early cinema period, with the repeated introduction of radical technological options like **glass-plate projectors** and **optical intermittent projectors** complimenting a plethora of devices with mechanical **intermittent movements** made across a wide range of both quality and price.

From 1896 to the turn of the century, film projectors were often considered a new type of mechanical lantern slide, and were intended for attachment to an existing **magic lantern** or produced in a combination lantern/cinematograph. The Riley Kineoptoscope designed by Cecil Wray (1896) was fitted wholly within a standard lantern slide stage, and manufacturers like Watson And Sons (UK), Ed. Liesegang Co. (Germany), the Enterprise Optical Manufacturing Co. (USA), and others all offered moving picture projection accessories for existing magic lanterns. Some early manufacturers, such as Philipp **Wolff** in Germany, **Pathé-Frères** in France, and Siegmund **Lubin** in the USA, offered projection apparatuses principally as an encouragement to exhibitors while their core business remained the production and sale of film subjects. Engineering-driven firms like Oskar **Messter** in Germany or Robert **Paul** in Great Britain saw apparatus manufacture as a leading component of their firms, integrated with film production and sales. By the time the **Cinémato-graphe Lumière** was offered for public sale in early 1897, the field they had pioneered was crowded and their lack of either experience or interest in apparatus manufacture doomed the firm to an early exit from the moving picture world.

Early projectors used a variety of mechanical designs to translate the steady rotation of a crank or an electrically driven shaft into the intermittent stopping of each frame at the projection aperture. At the time, projector designs were divided into two general categories with many contending variations in each basic type: (1) "continuous" intermittents, where the mechanical parts were in steady motion, as in the beater, gripper, claw and epicycloidal movements; and (2) "intermittent" designs, where the parts themselves stopped and started for each change of frame, as in the Maltese Cross (Geneva), ratchet and pawl, broken gear, and drunken screw movements. Until about 1904, the "continuous" intermittents, especially the beater movement that continued to be made until about 1910, were considered superior because of their smooth operation, resistance to wear, and economy of construction. The Maltese Cross (Geneva) intermittent, which had the advantage of holding each frame of film steady during projection before moving the film forward to the next frame, appeared early in projector construction, in apparatuses designed by Robert Paul, Pierre-Victor **Continsouza** and Messter, among others, but became the dominant technology only after about 1905, with the increased demand for larger pictures in substantial halls, when the advantages of its steady picture overcame the expense of a precision-machined apparatus. Alternatively, the Maltese Cross intermittent could also be made very cheaply from stamped tin: it was the standard movement in **toy projectors** made largely in Nuremberg from 1898 and produced in the hundreds of thousands through the 1920s.

Influential early projectors included apparatuses made by Paul in Great Britain, who sold machines even before his own premiere engagement as an exhibitor in late February 1896; Paul's Theatrograph design, at first with a double and then a single Maltese Cross intermittent, was sold to **magicians** and **itinerant exhibitors** (including Georges **Méliès** and Carl Herz) and copied by at least two pirate manufacturers in Germany before the end of the year. The French magic lantern firm of Clément & Gilmer made an inexpensive, sturdy design also using a Maltese Cross intermittent called the Vitagraphe that was quickly copied by Hermann **Foersterling** in Germany and R. J. Appleton & Co. in Britain, amongst others. The **Edison** Vitascope, initially developed by Thomas **Armat** and C. Francis **Jenkins**, was a beater intermittent machine of mid-1896 that found rapid success through its association with the "Wizard of Orange." By 1897, proprietary technologies began to appear: the **Gaumont** Chronophotographe, a beater intermittent machine using 60mm wide film; the **Joly**-Normandin Cinématographe with a broken-gear intermittent and five perforations per frame; and the most successful proprietary system, the **American Mutoscope and Biograph**'s apparatus with a gripper inter-mittent using 68mm wide film running at 30 frames per second, which was widely used in large **vau-deville** theaters in the USA and **music halls** in Europe.

After the turn of the century, a number of improvements were gradually added. The three-blade shutter, a counter-intuitive solution to flicker on the screen where two narrow blades interrupted the projection beam while a frame was being shown on the screen, arrived simultaneously early in 1903, in the Biograph apparatus in the USA and the Messter projector in Germany. Fire shutters, introduced in simple form in 1897, were automated as in the **Power's Cameragraph No. 5** of 1907. By 1909 the Maltese Cross intermittent was fully enclosed in an oil bath to reduce both wear and noise, as in the Motiograph and Powers No. 6 machines. Although beater movement projectors were still on the market, the Maltese Cross inter-mittent came to dominate professional projection as exhibition and distribution patterns changed. The arrival of the wholly new **Simplex projector** in 1911, featuring precision manufacture and innovative design of its gate and frame, produced a sturdy machine that would be in wide use for nearly four decades. By this time, projector manufacture was in the hands of specialist precision optical and mechanical firms (some also surviving film pio-neers) such as Messter, **Ernemann** and Bauer in Germany; Pathé, Gaumont and **Debrie** in France; Kalee (A. Kershaw & Sons) and Ross in Great Britain; Simplex (International Projector Co.), Nicholas **Power** Co., and the Enterprise Optical Co. in America.

See also: cameras

Further reading

Hulfish, David S. (1913) *Motion Picture Work. A general treatise on picture taking, picture making, photo-plays, and theatre management and operation*, Chicago: American School of Correspondence.

Mannoni, Laurent (1996) *Le Mouvement continué. Catalogue illustré de la collection des appareils de la*

Figure 104 Powers Cameragraph, 1906.

Figure 105 Cinématographe Lumière in use as a projector, from *La Nature*, 1896.

Cinémathèque française, Milan/Paris: Mazzotta/Cinèmathèque française, Musée du cinéma.

Rossell, Deac (1998) *Living Pictures: The Origins of the Movies*, Albany: State University Press of New York.

Tümmel, Herbert (1986) *Deutsche Laufbildprojektoren. Ein Katalog,* Berlin: Stiftung Deutsche Kinemathek.

DEAC ROSSELL

Promio, Alexandre

b. 1868; d. 1926

projectionist, cameraman, France

Designated by the **Lumière** company as its head cameraman in 1896, after projecting many of their films in France, Promio trained most of the Lumière cameramen then sent around the globe. Among Promio's contributions to the company's catalogues—nearly 500 short films—were the first films from Canada (Niagara Falls), the USA (Boston, Chicago, New York), the Middle East (Palestine, Turkey, Egypt) and North Africa (Algeria, Tunisia). Promio established a visual style based on the dynamics of movement within the frame, seen in the first recorded moving camera shot from a vaporetto on the Grand Canal in Venice (1896). He later headed Théophile **Pathé**'s film production company (1907–1910) and, after **World War I**, served as head of the government's cinematographic and photographic service in Algeria.

GENN MRENT

propaganda films

In 1898, the visionary writer Boleslaw **Matuszewski** prophesied that films could truly "move men's souls." It was soon realized that spectators might even be "moved" in political directions: cinema could be powerful propaganda. In the USA, during the 1896 Presidential election, backers of William McKinley who were associated with **American Mutoscope and Biograph** screened films at political meetings which showed their candidate in a favorable light. In the 1900 election, films again were released of McKinley, but also of the other candidates, William Jennings Bryan and Theodore Roosevelt. The former was depicted in agricultural pursuits, the latter leading a military group, and Roosevelt increasingly promoted himself in moving pictures in subsequent years. In both the 1908 and 1912 elections, presidential candidates also appeared in campaigning films.

The political value of film also was appreciated elsewhere in the world. In Great Britain, from 1896 on, showmen David Devant and Douglas Beaufort projected films at gatherings of the Primrose League, connected with the Conservative party. During the 1906 and 1910 elections, the issues of import tariff reform and "alien" immigration were the subjects of politically charged films, such as Lewin **Fitzhamon**'s *Free Trade Versus Fair Trade* (1905).

Moving pictures also were used for wider political ends. In France during the Dreyfus affair there were strong political opinions on both sides, and the pro-Dreyfusard position found expression in Georges **Méliès**' *L'Affaire Dreyfus* (1899). The early cinema period coincided with the Progressive era in the USA, and many films with biting political and social messages were made: by suffragettes, labor unions, socialists, and a wide array of reformers. **Edison**'s *Children Who Labor* (1912), for example, was part of a campaign against child labor, while *A Martyr to His Cause* (1911) was made for the union cause by the American Federation of Labor. Meanwhile, in some European countries worker's cinemas were being planned and established from 1912, notably the **Cinéma du peuple** in France.

But propaganda from the conservative side was also appearing at this time in the form of numerous commercially released movies with an anti-union message. Films also were made as colonial propaganda, showing the work of overseas industries and missionaries and promoting emigration to the colonies.

Images of the military were widely circulated in this era as implicit or explicit propaganda. Moving pictures of the Spanish–American war of 1898 were shown throughout the USA and helped to sustain a new expansionist mood in the country. During Italy's colonial adventure in North Africa, from 1911 on, films played a similar role on the home front. But war films could have different messages for different sides in a conflict. In Great Britain, the patriotic flame was fed by films of the Boer war (1899–1902), but the same images elicited hostility when shown in countries such as Belgium and Ireland. For this reason, films of the Russo-Japanese war (1904–1905) could be ordered from manufacturers with either pro-Russian or pro-Japanese **intertitles**.

See also: advertising films; colonialism: Europe; imperialsm: USA; labor movement: Europe; labor movement: USA; re-enactments; religious filmmaking; women's movement: Europe; women's movement: USA

Further reading

"The Kinematograph and the Election" (1910) *Kinematograph and Lantern Weekly*, 20 January: 618–619.

Ross, Steven J. (1998) *Working-Class Hollywood: Silent Film and the Shaping of Class in America*, Princeton: Princeton University Press.

STEPHEN BOTTOMORE

Prószynski, Kazimierz

b. 1875; d. 1945

inventor, filmmaker, Poland

The first model of Kazimierz Prószynski's Pleograph (Pleograf/Biopleograf) **camera** was created between 1894 and 1896. Public demonstrations of his consistently malfunctioning immobile and hand-held cameras took place in Warsaw in 1898 and 1899. Two years later, Prószynski established the country's first production company, Pleograph, on Nowogrodzka Street. He made a dozen *actualités* before shooting a one-shot fiction film, *Powrót birbanta* [The Return of the Merry Fellow] (1902). In *Walkirie* [Valkyries] (1903), he filmed part of a live performance of Richard Wagner's **opera**. Although Pleograf folded in 1903,

PrószyNski continued to work on his inventions in Belgium, France, and England from 1906 on.

SHEILA SKAFF

Protazanov, Jakov

b. 1881 ; d. 1945

filmmaker, Russia

Protazanov had the longest career of a filmmaker in Russian/Soviet film history. After graduating from the Moscow School of Commerce, in 1909 he was hired by the Gloria company in Moscow to write scripts and direct films; three years later he advanced to do similar work for **Thiemann & Reinhardt**. Protazanov was a versatile director of **comedies**, sensational **melodramas**—such as a 1912 film biography of Lev Tolstoy and *Drama by the Telephone* (1914), a Russian adaptation of a famous play by André de Lorde—and especially "cultured" films and Russian classics. After all, his first script was a screen version of a poem by Pushkin, to whom he would return in A *House in Kolomna* (1914) and *The Queen of Spades* (1916), both starring Ivan **Mosjoukine**. His box-office hit for Thiemann & Reinhardt, *Keys of Happiness* (1913), defined the "pause-pause" manner of **acting** and directing that would become the trademark of Russian pre-Revolutionary cinema. After agreeing to work for the **Yermoliev** studio in 1914, over the next five years Protazanov developed a distinctive filmmaking style associated with his regular star Mosjoukine. For the most part, they created morbid, visually exquisite films with a decadent, satanic, or mystical tinge. The threat of insanity lurking in Mosjoukine's steely eyes made such otherwise different films as *The Queen of Spades, Satan Triumphant* (1917), *Little Ellie* (1918), and *Father Sergius* (1918)—stories, respectively, about a gambler, the Devil, a murderous pedophile, and a self-mutilating monk—appear to be of the same cycle. Occasionally, however, Protazanov could turn out a more conventional melodrama such as *Jenny the Maid* (1918), at the end of which an aristocrat is pleasantly surprised to discover that the maid he is in love with is an impoverished member of his own class.

In the end, what made Protazanov's work unique was not so much a consistency of style, but rather his ability to modify his stylistic choices, depending on when and where he was making films. After a period of working for émigré film companies in France and Germany (1920–1923), Protazanov returned to the Soviet Union where he became a leading director, equally successful in science fiction, comedy, and political films; his last film was made in 1943.

Further reading

Christie, Ian and Julian Graffy (1993) (eds.) *Protazanov and the Continuity of Russian Cinema*, London: British Film Institute.

Tsivian, Yuri (1999) *Immaterial Bodies: Cultural Anatomy of Early Russian Films*, CD- ROM, Los Angeles: Annenberg Center of Communication, University of Southern California.

YURI TSIVIAN

Psilander, Valdemar

b. 1884; d. 1917

actor, Denmark

Psilander was the greatest **star** of the Danish silent cinema, chiefly in melodramatic roles. He had his stage debut in 1901 and entered moving pictures in 1910. After *Ved Faengslets Port* [Temptations of a Great City] (1911), Psilander became a star at **Nordisk** and won international fame. With a handsome, open face and courteous manner, he often played dashing, urbane, but weak-willed characters who let themselves be tempted to commit immoral acts. He left Nordisk in 1916 to become his own producer, but he died soon afterwards, apparently of heart failure.

CASPER TYBJERG

publicity: issues and debates

The formative years of cinema overlap with the modernization of the **advertising** and public relations industries, which provided models for promotional theory and practice, including a shift from advertising as merely announcing the availability of products to creating and shaping demand for them. By the 1890s, women had become a key consumer group, brand names and **trade marks** were commonly used, and ads in **newspapers** and **illustrated magazines** reached mass audiences—all techniques that would become important to the film industry, if unevenly over time. Nonetheless, before the **nickelodeon** era, film promotion was shaped by many of the same factors that limited the industry more generally, including inconsistent film production, distribution, exhibition, and demand.

The promotion of comparable entertainment forms including **vaudeville**, **amusement parks**, and circuses or traveling tent shows also provided models for the emerging film industry, with their emphasis on novelty and spectacle. While early films were shown at such venues, they were rarely identified in promotion as individual works, partly because they were short and usually combined into larger variety programs. Indeed, the earliest film promotion generally was directed more toward exhibitors than the public, since the former had to be convinced to buy films and equipment, a precondition for the actual projection of films to **audiences**. Catalogues provided by film manufacturers from **Edison** and **American Mutoscope and Biograph** to **Lumière** and **Pathé-Frères** thus became essential for informing exhibitors of the availability and basic content of films. During the early years of cinema's existence, the novel experience of seeing a moving image was privileged over film content. For that reason, the mechanisms used to promote cinema, such as posters or barkers, concentrated on film technologies, production company names, and content as it related to spectacle. Increased production of story films led to a shift in marketing strategies wherein more attention was devoted to individual titles, although the emphasis continued to tend toward spectacle and sensation over narrative *per se*. Individual films also could serve as promotion for the companies that made them, resulting in the increased importance of the trademark as a form of artistic authorization; in other instances, early genres could cultivate promotional associations for other commercial interests, as when kinesthetic **travelogues** set aboard trains promoted the railroad industry.

The rapid mass popularization of cinema that began around 1905 in the USA, and slightly later elsewhere, created the conditions for intensified promotional strategies rather than being a product of them. The nickelodeon boom of 1905–1908 forced the industry to tailor its marketing to huge new audiences increasingly drawn to single-reel narrative entertainments. Developments in distribution, including the advent of film rentals and predictable delivery dates of new titles, meant that exhibitors could vary their offerings and screen their programs of one-reelers according to reliable release schedules. Some production companies became associated with certain genres, such as the Bison **westerns** produced by **New York Motion Picture**, the **crime films** by **Éclair**, or literary adaptations from **Film d'Art**, **SCAGL**, or **Thanhouser**. The film industry established new media channels for the distribution of advertising and publicity, key among these being the **trade press**. Entertainment industry trade weeklies like *New York Dramatic Mirror* gave more attention to film, and new film industry papers like *Moving Picture World* and *Ciné-Journal* catered specifically to exhibitors with ads and information about various aspects of theater management, including promotion. Trade journals devoted extensive photo-based layouts to upcoming releases, and production companies paid for full-page ads touting their new films. Another key media channel was the fan magazine, first appearing in the early 1910s to promote films, actors, and film culture generally to mass audiences. In addition to these, film promotion incorporated "exploitation" gimmicks—common in circus promotion—such as parades, contests, and giveaways that could attract attention to local movie theaters and cinema generally.

As the film industry expanded and standardized in the 1910s, so too did the scope of its marketing strategies. The emerging Hollywood studios increasingly made and distributed promotion for use in various contexts, thus assuming greater control over their images, which expanded to include lantern slides, trailers, and press books describing whole ad campaigns for individual films. The constituent elements of films became the basis for promotional efforts, so that the developing narrative and stylistic armature of the cinema was enlisted to sell the screen: storylines, characters, spectacle, and realism all became grist for the marketing mill. The advent of the **star system** around 1910 assumed primary importance, providing identifiable personalities—from youngsters like Mary **Pickford** to divas like Lyda **Borelli** and famous stage performers like Sarah **Bernhardt**—whose appeal transcended that of individual films, thus lending a degree of stability to the industry. As with films that could be promoted via tie-ins to other products, the star system provided readily identifiable images for circulation through various consumer goods and collectibles, including pennants, spoons, and publicity photos. More generally, stars could promote consumerism through their endorsement of films, other products, and modern lifestyles.

While films and actors became objects of promotion, the industry also increasingly promoted itself as a respectable form of entertainment, partly by cultivating associations with middle-class and women movie-goers, both of whom had economic and culturally legitimizing value. During **World War I**, for example, US movie theaters often provided civic-minded fare along with their film offerings, such as the "four-minute" men who would give patriotic speeches during reel changes. Although movie theatres could tailor promotional campaigns to local interests, increasingly film publicity became centralized within the

Figure 106 Cartoon from *Motion Picture Story Magazine* (September 1912).

advertising departments of studios that were moving toward a model of vertically integration. Their intricately devised promotional repertoire of cut-sheets, lobby cards, posters, tie-ins and personal appearances demonstrates that the maturation of the film industry by the end of the war produced an approach to marketing that ensured the widespread and long-term acceptance of motion pictures as the pre-eminent form of popular entertainment.

See also: leisure time and space; transportation

Further reading

De Bauche, Leslie Midkiff (1985) "Advertising and the Movies, 1908–1915," *Film Reader*, 6: 115–125.

Fuller, Kathryn (1999) "Viewing the Viewers: Representations of the Audience in Early Cinema Advertising," in Richard Maltby and Melvyn Stokes (eds.) *American Movie Audiences*, 112–128, London: British Film Institute.

Gaines, Jane (1990) "From Elephants to Lux Soap: The Programming and 'Flow' of Early Motion Picture Exploitation," *Velvet Light Trap*, 25: 29–43.

Norris, James D. (1990) *Advertising and the Transformation of American Society, 1865– 1920*, New York: Greenwood Press.

Staiger, Janet (1990) "Announcing Wares, Winning Patrons, Voicing Ideals: Thinking About the History and Theory of Film Advertising," *Cinema Journal*, 29.3: 3–31.

CHARLIE KEIL AND JAMES LATHAM

Py, Eugenio

b. 1859; d. ?

cameraman, filmmaker, Argentina

An immigrant to Argentina from France in 1888, Py became a major cameraman and laboratory expert through working for Casa Lepage, a photographic supplies company in Buenos Aires, which imported film equipment. As early as 1897, he filmed *actualités* using an imported **Gaumont** camera. His footage of the Brazilian president-elect, *El viaje del Doctor Campos Salles*, visiting Buenos Aires in 1900, was shown the same evening to visiting dignitaries. Primarily noted for *actualités*, Py also is credited with synchronizing a moving picture to a **phonograph** in *Tango criollo* (1906) and then filming thirty-one other *phonoscènes* for Casa Lepage between 1907 and 1911.

KATHLEEN NEWMAN

Pyke, Montague Alexander

b. 1874; d. 1935

entrepreneur, exhibitor, Great Britain

Born in London, "Monty" Pyke worked as a commercial traveller before his expensive lifestyle, gambling, and stock market losses sent him to jail for bankruptcy in 1905. Discharged in 1908, and deciding to try his luck in film exhibition, Pyke formed "Recreations Limited." Although, he later admitted, his assets were simply "a very nice name plate on the door, and some office furniture on the hire purchase," Pyke raised £10,000 from eager investors and opened the "Recreations Theatre" (one of the first permanent London cinemas) in 1909. Its success led him to establish another fourteen companies over the next three years, all designed to add cinemas to the "Pyke Circuit." As his income rose to £10,000 in 1911, he returned to an opulent lifestyle—until competition cut into his profits. By 1914, all but two of Pyke's companies were closed down; by 1915, he was again bankrupt.

NICHOLAS HILEY

R

racial segregation: USA

The practice of separating the races (specifically, the barring of blacks from social interaction with whites) dominated American racial relations from the late-19th to the mid-20th century.

After the abolition of slavery in 1865, white Americans became increasingly concerned about how to monitor and control a newly freed black population. Paranoid rumors spread among white Southerners that emancipated blacks would attempt to take violent retribution against their former masters, including the rape of white women and the theft of white property (themes dramatized in D. W. **Griffith**'s *The Birth of a Nation*, 1915).

In a vehement backlash against Reconstruction–the federal program designed to reorganize the civic and economic life of the post-Civil War South–white Southerners blocked efforts to bring about the social equality of the races. Beginning in the 1870s, and particularly during the 1890s, Southern state legislatures enforced the segregation of public accommodations (e.g., trains, hotels, theaters, restaurants, schools), prohibited interracial marriage, and revoked black voting rights. Yet segregation was not limited to the South; in many Northern states blacks were denied access to places of employment and amusement. As the 19th century drew to a close, white supremacists worked to draw and redraw the "color line," while blacks expressed an increasing unwillingness to accept circumscription and second-class citizenship.

In 1891, a group of blacks in New Orleans organized to challenge the constitutionality of a Louisiana law mandating "equal but separate accommodations for the white and colored races" on passenger trains. The Supreme Court responded on May 18, 1896 with its (in)famous *Plessy v. Ferguson* decision, allowing states to maintain separate (and, many argued, patently unequal) social arrangements along racial lines.

Throughout the following decades, civil rights groups such as the National Association for the Advancement of Colored People (NAACP), founded in 1909, worked to dismantle "Jim Crow" segregation. Jim Crow, a popular blackface caricature from the 19th-century minstrel stage, became a widely used metaphor for segregationist practices (e.g., the Jim Crow car of a train or balcony of a theater). In many parts of the North, where segregation was not enforceable by law (*de jure*), it was common in practice (*de facto*).

During the early 20th century, numerous thriving African American communities developed under segregation. Among them, New York's Harlem and Chicago's South Side "Black Belt" flourished as centers for black business, religious, entertainment, and political institutions (e.g., black **newspapers**, Negro League baseball and **black cinema**). Still, the forced exclusion of blacks from mainstream society, and persistent racist restrictions in housing, employment, education, and recreation contributed to interracial antagonisms and often violence (e.g., riots in New York City, 1900; Atlanta, Georgia, and Brownsville, Texas, 1906; Springfield, Illinois, 1908).

The Supreme Court finally outlawed state-mandated segregation in its 1954 *Brown v. Board of Education* decision.

See also: law and the cinema; migration/immigration

Further reading

Franklin, John Hope and Alfred A. Moss (2000) *From Slavery to Freedom: A History of Negro Americans*, 8th ed., New York: Knopf.

Lofgren, Charles A. (1987) *The Plessy Case: A Legal-Historical Interpretation*, New York: Oxford University Press.

JACQUELINE STEWART

Raff & Gammon

In 1894, mining and oil speculator Norman Raff and his brother-in-law Frank Gammon were given a concession to market **Edison's Kinetoscope** and films in North America; operating as the Kinetoscope Company, they established a network of regional concessionaires throughout the continent. In 1896, when the Kinetoscope business faltered, they persuaded Edison to manufacture Thomas **Armat**'s **Phantoscope** as his own Vitascope projector, which they premiered at Koster & Bial's Music Hall in New York on 23 April 1896 and then marketed through the Vitascope Company. Competition from other projectors and Edison's decision to sell films and **projectors** through **Edison Manufacturing** forced the pair out of business, and, by the end of 1897, they had returned to their homes in Ohio.

PAUL SPEHR

Raleigh & Robert

In 1903, Charles Raleigh and Robert Schwobthaler opened a sales agency in Paris to sell the films of **Warwick Trading** and **American Mutoscope and Biograph**. By 1907, Raleigh & Robert also was producing French films in small numbers. Eventually, the company distributed French, Danish, and British films not only in France and England but also in Germany (where it specialized in non-fiction), perhaps because Schwobthaler had been born near Freiburg. In 1909, the company's small Paris studio was destroyed by fire, which halted production. In 1912, after Louis

Aubert had taken over many of its distribution contracts in France, Raleigh & Robert bought the rights to exhibit Kinemacolor films in Paris; when that venture failed, the company disappeared in 1913.

RICHARD ABEL, MARTIN LOIPERDINGER

Ramos, Antonio

b. ?; d. ?

exhibitor, producer, China

Spanish-born Antonio Ramos was the most prominent showman in Shanghai from the early 1900s on. He first began exhibiting films at the city's teahouses and then within his own **cinema circuit**, including the 250-seat Hongkew Theater, built in 1908. In 1923, he established the Ramos Amusement Corporation and, as an agent for **Famous Players**-Lasky, produced several features. Before retiring to Spain in 1926, Ramos sold his theaters, many of which were acquired by the Zhongyang Film Company led by, among others, **Zhang Shichuan**, for the exhibition of domestic films.

ZHEN ZHANG

Raymond, Matt

b. 1874; d. 1941

technician, exhibitor, England

An electrician at London's Royal Polytechnic Institution, Raymond overcame serious technical problems installing the **Cinématographe Lumière** for showman Felicien Trewey, who then engaged him to set up other **Lumière** shows. He probably also shot the first English Lumière films. After installng a Chard & Co. projector at the Shakespeare Theatre, Liverpool, for showing films during the pantomime, *Babes in the Wood* (1896), Raymond joined **Maguire & Baucus** selling **Edison** projectors. In 1898, he toured with a **Warwick Bioscope**, eventually installing these machines in **music halls** in several European countries. His Raymond Animated Picture Company (1905–25) established an early English **cinema chain**. Raymond served as treasurer of the Cinema Trade Protection Society (1907–1920), and later the Cinematograph Exhibitors' Association. From 1921, he was master of the "Anima" masonic lodge for film industry members.

STEPHEN HERBERT

Redfern, Henry Jasper

b. 1872; d. 1928

exhibitor, filmmaker, Great Britain

Jasper Redfern was a Sheffield optician, photographer, and photographic supplier who also provided Rontgen X-Rays for medical use. In June 1896, he became a **Lumière** agent, presenting the **Cinématographe** at the Empire Theatre, Sheffield, followed by shows in Rotherham, Liverpool, Manchester, and Chesterfield. In 1898, he toured with his local football team Sheffield United and filmed *Sheffield United vs. Liverpool* and additional cup matches, including the Football Association Cup Final, *Sheffield United vs. Derby* (1899). By 1903, he was touring a portable exhibition booth called Jasper Redfern's Palace by the Sea, appearing at Southsea and Westcliffe. In 1908, he retired from the moving picture business and devoted himself to optical and medical work at the Christie Hospital in Manchester.

VANESSA TOULMIN

re-enactments

The **Cinématographe Lumière**'s ability to reproduce reality was of course one of this apparatus' principal features. It is thus not surprising that *actualités* and **news event films** were among the most popular early genres. Nor is it surprising, in this context, that the major film manufacturers quickly developed the practice of sending operators (and sometimes entire teams of operators) to carry out what today we would call news stories on site, where the news event was unfolding. They even had their operators reconstruct, from scratch, various aspects of an event that had taken place out of the camera's view. For news events, whether because of their sudden and unexpected nature or their geographical distance, could escape the camera's notice. There were events, therefore, of which no image existed, leading manufacturers to treat them the way they already treated historical events: by re-constituting, reproducing, and re-enacting them.

The re-enactment is thus a category of moving pictures that can include both past and current events. A re-enactment pertains to the realm of the event, and more generally to that of history, whether distant or in the making. Should an event already be completed and thus seemingly beyond the camera's grasp, the filmmaker was at liberty to call upon all the resources of mise en scène (**set designs**, actors, **costumes**, etc.) in order to bring the past event to life. Early examples of such historical re-enactments are **Edison**'s *The Execution of Mary, Queen of Scots* (1895) and **Lumière**'s *Mort de Marat* [The Death of Marat] (1897). Should a current event, which would someday be viewed as a historical event, also be beyond the reach of the camera, here too the filmmaker would use these resources to make it possible for the spectator to be a witness. Examples of this kind of re-enactment are **Méliès**' *Divers at Work on the Wreck of the "Maine"* (1898) and Edison's *Bombardment of Taku Forts* (1900). In this way the filming of events was transformed, for the supposed requirements of history, into a process that turned operators into *metteurs en scène*, resulting in these somewhat peculiar artificially arranged scenes. The **camera**, that device for creating unparalleled reproductions of reality, thus could be involved in "reproducing" the event in both senses of the term: to re-produce, to make occur a "second time"; and to present a reproduction, a representation.

The most singular kind of re-enactment produced during these early years was that known as the "fake newsreel" (in French, *actualités reconstituées* or even *actualités postiches*—"artificial newsreels"). This was a cross between the **actualités** and the news event film and consisted of "recapturing" on film an event which had initially escaped the camera's penetrating eye. The most famous fake newsreel was in fact an anticipated newsreel, *Reproduction, Coronation Ceremonies–King Edward VII*, made in June 1902 by Georges Méliès for Charles **Urban**. Produced even before the coronation itself took place, this film was planned to be shown the evening of the event so it could enjoy the greatest possible news value. Méliès paid considerable attention to detail and undertook diligent research in order to prepare the decors in his suburban Paris studio, which reconstructed the nave in Westminster Abbey. The strange thing is, because the king was ill, the real coronation was postponed until 9 August, but the **copyright** on the American version of the film, a whole continent away, still was dated 8 August! Other fake newsreels included famous re-enacted **boxing films** and war films.

See also: cinema of attractions

Further reading

Gaudreault, André (1993) "The Cinematograph: A Historiographical Machine," in David E. Klemm and William Schweiker (eds.) *Meanings in Texts and Actions: Questioning Paul Ricoeur*, 90–97, Charlottesville: University of Virginia Press.

Levy, David (1982) "Re-constituted Newsreels, Re-enactments and the American Narrative Film," in Roger Holman (ed.), *Cinema 1900–1906: An Analytical Study I*, 243–260, Brussels: International Federation of Film Archives.

ANDRÉ GAUDREAULT

Reicher, Ernst

b. 1885; d. 1936

actor, director, Germany

The son of famous stage actor Emanuel Reicher, Ernst began acting in theaters in Munich and Frankfurt before settling in Berlin in 1912, where he happened to meet future film director Joe **May**. Their friendship and collaboration resulted in a series of **detective films** featuring the gentleman sleuth Stuart Webbs, the first of which was *Die geheimnisvolle Villa* [The Mysterious Villa] (1914). Even after breaking with May later that year, Reicher played Webbs in some 30 films over the next twelve years, providing the model for countless screen detectives of the silent era.

SCOTT CURTIS

Reinhardt, Max

b. 1873; d. 1943

director, Germany

As Germany's leading theater director, who revolutionized stagecraft in **lighting**, crowd direction, and scene change, Reinhardt was not only a major stylistic influence on the German cinema, but also crucial in training the elite of German actors entering the cinema in the early 1910s, including Albert **Bassermann**, Paul **Wegener**, and Ernst **Lubitsch**. His personal involvement in the cinema is difficult to assess. In 1909, his stage production of *Sumurun* was filmed in the USA, and in 1913/14 he lent his name to two **PAGU** films, the literary fantasies *Insel der Seligen* [Island of the Happy Ones] and *Eine venezianische Nacht* [A Venetian Night], commissioned to promote the *Autorenfilm* movement.

MICHAEL WEDEL

Reis, Luís Tomás

b. 1878, Alagoinhas, Bahia; d. 1940, Rio de Janeiro

filmmaker, Brazil

Although a military man, Reis developed a unique documentary practice in Mato Grosso and Amazonas while producing visual records of the expeditions of the national telegraph commission. In 1914 he directed *Expedição Roosevelt a Mato Grosso* [The Roosevelt Expedition to Mato Grosso], a chronicle of the ex-president's journey through the region. In 1916 he produced one of his most significant films, *Rituais e festas bororo* [Bororo Rituals and Celebrations], a beautiful record of an indigenous tribe now extinct. Reis worked outside the industry and apart from other filmmakers, which makes him all that much more extraordinary.

See also: ethnographic films; expedition/exploration films

ANA M. LÓPEZ

Reliance

One of several Independent companies to surface in 1910 as the **Motion Picture Patents Company**'s attempted control of the American market proved futile. Started by Charles **Baumann** and Adam **Kessel**, who also had founded the **New York Motion Picture Company**, Reliance depended upon **star** power to launch its new films. It lured a host of **Biograph** players at its inception, although few stayed with the company for long. Despite its changing talent pool, Reliance established a reputation as a dependable producer of dramatic films marked by innovative **lighting**. Sold in 1911 to Harry **Aitken**, Reliance was incorporated for one million dollars in 1913, at which time it had grown to encompass three studios.

CHARLIE KEIL

religious filmmaking

During the period of early cinema religious films were made almost exclusively for the Christian religion. Other religions did not make propaganda films, partly because these faiths were mainly centered in less developed parts of the world, where filmmaking began later, and because the other proselytizing religion, Islam, was reluctant to use imagery. As for Judaism, while Jewish participation in early cinema was manifold (Jewish film pioneers, films about Jewish life, Zionist films), their involvement was as an ethnic rather than a religious community. A rare example of early film being used to promote a non-Christian religion

would be **Phalke**'s films which were made from an ostensibly Hindu (and nationalistic) point of view.

Films were produced for the Christian faith for a number of reasons by various organizations. Some of the first were made by commercial production companies, in the form of Passion Play films, one of the most important "genres" of the early era. The first of these was made by Kirchner in 1897: in twelve scenes it depicted the life of Christ from birth to crucifixion. **Lumière** had Georges **Hatot** make the second in 1898; **Gaumont** had Alice **Guy** make another in 1899; and other companies soon followed. In addition, the genuine Horitz Passion Play was filmed in 1897 in Bohemia, though fake versions also were circulated. Some showmen would combine shots of different versions of the Passion Play, along with magic lantern slides on the same theme.

The **magic lantern** had been used for years by several religious organizations. The founder of the (Anglican) Church Army, Wilson Carlisle, hit upon this visual tool in the 1880s as a means to attract working people to his sermons, and when moving pictures became available he added them to the "attractions" offered by his church, St. Mary at Hill in the City of London. His "modern" practices attracted much criticism at the time on the grounds of poor taste.

Some Catholic clergy had used the lantern for propaganda since the late 19th century. In France *projections lumineuses* were widespread, and an organization which strongly supported them, **Maison de la Bonne Press** (run by Georges-Michel **Coissac**), promoted the use of moving pictures for the Catholic faith, and was itself making films by 1903. The Catholic Church elsewhere in Europe also engaged with the cinema. In early 1909, the company Unitas was formed in Italy to make Catholic films; by 1912 there was a chain of Catholic cinemas in Belgium; in Switzerland the Abbé **Joye** was showing his flock a wide variety of films—his surviving **collection** includes almost as many fiction as non-fiction titles. But while there was broad acceptance of the new media in these countries, in Spain and **Canada: Quebec** the Catholic hierarchy was opposed to using moving pictures for religious purposes. The Papacy too was ambivalent. Although the Pope himself was filmed (by W. K. L. **Dickson**) in 1898, in subsequent years the Vatican had a decidedly less sympathetic attitude to the cinema; before **World War I**, it issued edicts controlling, for example, the showing of films in church buildings. Among other Christian denominations the combination of religion and film proved equally controversial, and in Russia religious themes were censored from commercially released films.

Perhaps the most pro-film Christian organization was the **Salvation Army**. As early as 1897, the Australian branch of this organization was making films, and *Soldiers of the Cross* (1900) combined films and lantern slides in a show lasting two hours. The Salvation Army continued to be major force in the Australian film industry, and the British branch of the organization also used film and lantern projection for propaganda purposes, establishing a cinematograph department in 1903 under Frederick Cox. The department sent a cameraman, Henry Howse, to film the tour of the Holy Land by General Booth, leader of the Salvation Army, in 1905.

Church organizations that worked in the foreign mission field also were interested in the cinema. They generally used moving pictures to show the success of overseas missions to their supporters at home (rather than as a tool of control, to impress their foreign congregations). The Church Missionary Society (the largest Anglican missionary organization) sponsored a cameraman, Edward Cash, to travel through India and Ceylon in 1904 to 1905, filming CMS missionary projects, and he also filmed scenes "showing the hold which heathenism still has upon the people." The Methodists also used the new medium: Reverend J. Gregory Mantle traveled to India in 1902 and filmed the Delhi Durbar for Charles **Urban**, also recording scenes related to his church's missions in the country. In 1907, Mantle went to China, again filming mission scenes. By this time his church at Deptford in east London had a large complement of film and lantern equipment, and his staff of projectionists frequently appeared at religious meetings.

Religious themes continued to appear in commercially produced films, notably in Biblical tales, such as **Kalem**'s *From the Manger to the Cross* (1912), and in temperance stories. A religious element often marks the work of D. W. **Griffith** in

particular. Perhaps the culmination of early religious filmmaking was the *Photo-Drama of Creation* (1914) a hugely costly production, consisting of slides and films, and even some **synchronized sound**. The full version lasted eight hours, and the makers claimed it was shown in the USA and Europe no less than 20,000 times.

But exhibition was always the main focus in the religious use of moving pictures, and numerous priests and ministers of many denominations showed films, either in actual church services or in related activities such as Sunday School classes.

See also: biblical films; propaganda films

Further reading

"The Biograph in the Vatican" (1899) *Scientific American*, 14 January: 24.

Cosandey, Roland, André Gaudreault, and Tom Gunning (eds.) (1992) *Une invention du diable? Cinéma des premiers temps et religion*, Sainte-Foy/Lausanne: Presses de l'Universite Laval/Editions Payot.

Rapp, Dean (1997) "The British Salvation Army, the Early Film Industry and Urban Working-class Adolescents, 1897–1918," *Twentieth Century British History*, 7.2: 157–288.

STEPHEN BOTTOMORE

Relph, Harry ("Little Tich")

b. 1867, Cudham; d. 1928, Hendon

music hall and pantomime entertainer, England.

"Little Tich", only 4 feet 6 inches tall, was famous in Great Britain and France for over 40 years. An inspired comedian and parody dancer, Tich was so successful as a laughter-maker that showman Charles B. Cochrane later claimed that he had been unequaled in Paris. Little Tich was featured in a short **Phono-Cinéma-Théâtre** film for the 1900 Paris Exposition, performing his famous act involving balancing on 28-inch wooden boots, with accompanying music and effects. He appeared in only two other films, for Georges **Méliès** in 1905, and **Pathé-Frères** in 1907.

STEPHEN HERBERT

Requião, Aníbal Rocha

b. 1875, Curitiba, Paraná, Brazil; d. 1929

filmmaker, exhibitor, Brazil

One of the few pioneers of the Brazilian cinema to have been a native-born Brazilian, Requião operated exclusively in the province of Paraná. A small businessman and amateur photographer, he quickly gravitated to the new medium. His first film was *Desfile militar de 15 de novembro de 1907* [Military Parade on 15 November 1907]. In June 1908, he opened Curitiba's first exhibition venue, the Smart Cinema, where he exhibited European films as well as his own *actualités* capturing daily life. He shot more than 300 films between 1907 and 1912, when he suffered a heart attack and retired from the field. Two of these films have been preserved: *Panorama de Curytiba* [Panorama of Curitiba] (1909) and *Carnaval en Curityba* (Carnival in Curitiba) (1910).

ANA M. LÓPEZ

Reulos, Lucien

b. ?; d. ?

inventor, manufacturer, France

On September 4, 1896, Reulos registered a patent with Lucien Korsten and Georges **Méliès** for the "Kinétographe," a "machine for recording and projecting animated photographs." The principle on which the machine worked—a sprocket wheel activated intermittently by a screw mechanism and a pegged disc—was in fact the work of Louis Charles, whose patent was dated April 20, 1896. Whether Reulos and Méliès plagiarized Charles' design or signed an agreement with him remains unclear. Although the Kinétographe was offered for sale, it was used primarily at Méliès' Robert-Houdin theater. On November 20, 1896,

Reulos registered the **trademark**, a black star, for the future Star-Film company, but he would part from Méliès shortly thereafter to begin developing a **projector** for amateurs, the "Mirographe" (1900).

LAURENT MANNONI

Rex

An independent production company organized by Edwin S. **Porter**, Joseph Engel and William **Swanson** in 1909, with a jeweled crown for its **trademark**. Porter served as director; the first release was *Heroine of '76*; and the stock company included Phillips **Smalley** and Lois **Weber**. Rex joined the **Motion Picture Distributing and Sales Company** in the spring of 1910 and was absorbed into **Universal** in June 1912. Because Porter was already involved with **Famous Players** by the summer of 1912, Smalley and Weber took over directing films, but by September 1912, they too left. Rex remained a production unit within Universal up to 1918.

EILEEN BOWSER

Reynaud, Emile

b. 1844; d. 1918

inventor, exhibitor, France

A disciple of abbot Moigno, Reynaud taught courses illustrated with lantern slides in Paris in 1873. On August 30, 1877, he registered a patent for the "praxinoscope," an optical toy derived from the zootrope, but whose shutter system depended on rotating prismatic mirrors. A year later, he was marketing the machine successfully. Reynaud then came up with ingenious variations: the praxinoscope-théâtre, the vanishing spinning top, and the stereoscopic praxinoscope equipped for projections (1880). The most complex version, the "Théâtre optique" (patented on December 1, 1888), was able to project sprocketed bands of hand-painted transparent images, varying in length from 22 to 45 meters. It was this machine that Reynaud used to present his popular "Pantomimes lumineuses" at the Musée Grévin, from October 28, 1892, to February 28, 1900. During those eight years, Reynauld gave 12,800 performances to a half million museum visitors. Of the seven "playlets" that he created, only the first two survive: *Pauvre Pierrot!* [Poor Peter!] and *Autour d'une cabine* [Around a Cabin].

Further reading

Noverre, Maurice (1926) *La Vérité sur l'Invention de la Projection animée, Emile Reynaud, sa Vie et ses Travaux*, Brest: printed for the author.

LAURENT MANNONI

Richardson, Frank Herbert

b. 1867; d. 1943

journalist, USA

A long-time contributor to ***Moving Picture World***, Richardson tirelessly championed what he called "high class, expert work in the projection room." Richardson's columns and his lecture tours around the USA provided practical advice and inspiration to countless **projectionists** from the **nickelodeon** era onwards. He helped to raise and regularize industry standards by insisting on safe working conditions, correct speed of projection, and careful handling of prints. His *Handbook of Projection* first appeared in 1910 and went through several revised editions before his death.

GREGORY A. WALLER

Riche, Daniel

b. ?; d. ?

scriptwriter, filmmaker, France

A popular novelist, Daniel Riche sold his first scripts to **Pathé-Frères** in 1907. His fame enabled him to require high fees, which prompted Ferdinand **Zecca** to let him direct many of his own subjects such as *La Vengeance de Jean le loup* [The Vengeance of John the Wolf] (1910).

From 1909 to 1914, he worked regularly for **SCAGL**, effortlessly moving from dramas such as *Les Millions de l'orpheline* [The Orphan Girl's Millions] (1912) to **comedies** such as *Le Cœur n'a pas d'âge* [The Heart Does Not Age] (1913), and from original scripts to adaptations such as *Philémon et Baucis* (1911), after Jean de La Fontaine. In 1918, Riche became vice-president of the Société des Auteurs de Films.

LAURENT LE FORESTIER

Roberti, Roberto (a.k.a. Vincenzo Leone)

b. 1879; d. 1959

director, Italy

A stage actor in Naples in the late 1900s, Roberti was hired as a director at **Aquila Films** in 1912, and specialized in modern adventures and melo-dramas of morbid love such as *Tenebre* [Darkness] (1916). At Caesar Film in 1917, he worked with Francesca **Bertini**. After a brief stint at **Itala** Film, between 1918 and 1921, Roberti became Bertini's principal director in eighteen films, including *La contessa Sara* [Countess Sarah] (1919) and *La serpe* [The Snake] (1920).

Further reading

Bernardini, Aldo and Vittorio Martinelli (1985) *Roberto Roberti: direttore artistico*, Pordenone: Le Giornate del Cinema muto.

GIORGIO BERTELLINI

Robertson, D. W.

b. 1858; d. 1939

exhibitor, USA

Brooklyn-born Robertson began his career as a musician who used sleighbells and other novel instruments. He soon became a booking agent, providing wholesome talent for church groups and small opera houses. After purchasing an **Edison** projecting kinetoscope in 1897, Robertson had considerable success as an **itinerant exhibitor** over the next decade. Offering moving pictures and musical performances, "D. W. Robertson's Famous Moving Picture Company" was a headline attraction at **chautauqua** assemblies across the Midwest. Robertson's agency, the American Entertainment Bureau, remained in business into the 1920s.

GREGORY A. WALLER

Robinne, Gabrielle

b. 1886; d. 1980

actor, France

Alongside a prestigious career in the theater, Gabrielle Robinne worked in the cinema, where she made her debut in *L'Assassinat du Duc de Guise* (1908). After several more productions for **Film d'Art**, she appeared in a number of society dramas for the **SCAGL** between 1910 and 1913. Her legendary beauty became popular thanks to Ferdinand **Zecca** and René **Leprince**'s **multiple-reel/feature films**. At the time films such as *La Jolie Bretonne* [The Pretty Girl from Brittany] (1914) were known as part of a "Robinne–Alexandre series" (René Alexandre was her partner). In 1914, her box office success prompted Comédie-Française administrator Albert Carré to bar his performers from appearing in films–to no avail.

LAURENT LE FORESTIER

Rock, William T. ("Pop")

b. 31 December 1853; d. 27 July 1916

exhibitor, businessman, USA

In 1896, British-born "Pop" Rock and Walter J. Wainwright opened the Vitascope Theater in New Orleans, one of the first theaters showing moving pictures exclusively. In 1899, Rock joined J. Stuart **Blackton** and Albert E. **Smith** who were producing and exhibiting films through the **Vitagraph** Company. In 1900, he became the company's president and continued as principal

executive officer until shortly before his death. As an astute business manager, the brusque but likable Rock was responsible for making Vitagraph one of the most economically successful American film companies during the period before **World War I**.

PAUL SPEHR

Rodolfi, Eleuterio

b. 1876; d. 1935

actor, Italy

Rodolfi had long training as a theater actor before being hired by **Ambrosio** in 1912. He played in numerous comical films, performing as a witty and sometimes unfortunate gentleman, as in *Un successo diplomatico* [A Diplomatic Success] (1913). He was often coupled with Gigetta **Morano** in **comedies** that were the Italian equivalent of **Gaumont**'s restrained and situational *Léonce comic series* (directed by Léonce **Perret**) in France and **Vitagraph** comedies in the USA. From late 1913 on, Rodolfi began directing films as well, initially focusing on comedy. In the mid-1910s, he expanded his range to include **historical films** and theatrical adaptations, enlisting various "monstres sacrés" of the Italian theater. In 1917, he left Ambrosio and founded his own company.

IVO BLOM

Rogers, George H(enry?)

b. 1874?; d. 1912

cameraman, producer

An American, Rogers came to Paris at the turn of the century and worked for E. Burton **Holmes** and then Charles **Urban**, soon becoming Urban's Paris manager. When the Russo-Japanese war (1904–1905) broke out, Rogers had the ideal qualifications (speaking several languages including Russian) to film from the Russian side. Traveling across Siberia to the Far East, he recorded scenes of the Russian army as it faced defeat. In later years, with Paul Joseph Roux, he co-founded and successfully managed the **Eclipse** film company in Paris, but his career was cut short by his death following a serious illness.

STEPHEN BOTTOMORE

Roland, Ruth

b. 1892; d. 1937

actor, USA

Although remembered most for her robust action **serials** of the early 1920s, Ruth Roland's career began at **Kalem** in 1909, where she starred in multiple **western** and comedy shorts as well as eight episodes of *The Girl Detective* series. In 1915, Roland moved to the Balboa Feature Film Company, playing opposite Henry King in the morality drama series, *Who Pays?*, before accepting her first **serial** role as a girl reformer struggling with a genetic disposition for crime in *The Red Circle* (1916). In 1923, Roland chose not to renew her contract with Pathé-Exchange, turning to real estate investing and becoming a businesswoman of much acclaim.

JENNIFER M. BEAN

Rolfe, Alfred

b. 1862; d. 1943

actor, director, Australia

Alfred Rolfe and his wife Lily Dampier were actors before he became a prolific and influential filmmaker, directing at least thirteen **multiple-reel/feature films** in 1911 and eight in 1912, for the Australian Photo-Play Company. These were mainly bushranger films, in which he himself starred, and they were noted for their naturalistic locations and performance style. During **World War I**, he directed shorts and features for **Australasian Films**, specializing in patriotic films, but after the war his career waned, and he left the industry in the early twenties.

INA BERTRAND

Rosas, Enrique

b. ?; d. ?

producer, cameraman, showman, Mexico

A native of the city of Puebla, Rosas left tailoring to become a filmmaker and showman, traveling through Mexico either alone or with others. In competition with Salvador **Toscano**, for instance, he filmed a presidential trip to the Yucatán. In 1908, he opened a theater called the Paris Salon in Mexico City; later he emigrated to Havana, but returned to Mexico in 1913. In Veracruz he recorded Félix Díaz's uprising against the Francisco Madero government, for a film that he titled *Felicitous Rebellion*. He also documented the events that brought General Victoriano Huerta to power and the death of President Madero, in *The Tragic Tenth*. His most important film was *The Gray Automobile* (1919), a documentary eulogizing the Mexican Revolution.

AURELIO DE LOS REYES

Rosenthal, Joseph

b. 1864; d. 1946

cameraman, Great Britain

A colorful pioneer of the British film industry, Rosenthal started working for Charles **Urban** around 1897, and rapidly became a trusted cameraman. When the Boer war broke out in October 1899, he was sent to film in South Africa and later that year traveled to the Boxer Rebellion and then the Philippine–American war. His course was now set as a globetrotting filmmaker, and over the following few years he shot *actualité* and news footage in Australia, Canada, and India. In 1904, he filmed with the Japanese forces in the Russo-Japanese war. After being dismissed by Urban, in 1908 he set up his own company, Rosie Films, and continued shooting nonfiction films for the rest of his career.

See also: news event films

STEPHEN BOTTOMORE

Rossi, Carlo

b. ?; d. ?

pioneer, producer, Italy

With industrialist Guglielmo Remmert, chemist Carlo Rossi founded Carlo Rossi & C. in Turin in 1907. After hiring technicians from **Pathè-Frères**, Rossi's firm soon reached international markets through alliances with **Hepworth** Manufacturing and **Kleine Optical**. That year, Rossi employed a young accountant, soon-to-be chief executive, Giovanni **Pastrone**. On February 1908, however, Rossi liquidated the company over disagreements with Remmert, who went on to co-found **Itala** Film. Afterward, Rossi patented a few cinematic devices, became an administrator at **Cines**, hired on as a director at **Pathè-Frères**, and ended his career as an exhibitor in Turin.

GIORGIO BERTELLINI

Rossi, Gilberto

b. 1882, Livorno, Italy; d. 29 July 1971, São Paulo

producer, cameraman, Brazil

Initially a photographer, Rossi learned the film trade in Italy; then immigrated to São Paulo in 1911. He developed a brisk business with **advertising films** and commissioned documentaries (*filmes de cavação*). His first non-commissioned film was a crime **re-enactment**, *O crime de Cravinhos* [The Crime of Cravinhos] (1919), which he shot and directed. With José **Medina**, he experimented with continuity editing à la D. W. **Griffith** and produced *O exemplo regenerador* [The Regenerative Example] (1919) with much success. Together they made fiction films throughout the 1920s, although Rossi always depended on documentary production, especially the state financing he obtained for *Rossi Actualidades* (1921–1931), the longest running **newsreel** in the silent period. The coming of sound interrupted Rossi's progress; he produced several newsreels and two fiction films before retiring in 1962.

ANA M. LÓPEZ

Rothapfel, S. L. ("Roxy")

b. 9 July 1882; d. 13 January 1936

exhibitor, USA

Rothapfel served in the U.S. Marine Corps until 1908 when he and his father-in-law opened a **nickelodeon** in Forest City, Pennsylvania. His success led to a series of positions managing theaters around the USA, most notably for the **Saxe** brothers in Minneapolis and Milwaukee. In October 1913, now nicknamed "Roxy," he moved to New York City to manage the Regent; six months later, he was managing the Strand in Times Square, placing him squarely in the forefront of the movement toward **palace cinemas**. Indeed, his 1920s Roxy theater would become Times Square's most famous palace cinema.

DOUGLAS GOMERY

Royal Bioscope

India's earliest indigenous production and exhibition concern was established by Hiralal **Sen** and his brother Motilal in 1899. Besides showing imported European films at Calcutta's Classic Theater, they filmed and exhibited versions of classic stage performances such as *Alibaba and the Forty Thieves* (1904), supposedly of feature length, and several *actualités*, including the Durbars of 1902 and 1911. Royal Bioscope catered to the local elite, and, unlike its chief competitor, **Madan Theatres**, did not venture into large-scale exhibition and distribution. The Sen brothers split temporarily in 1912 and a fire destroyed all their films shortly before Hiralal's death in 1917.

SURESH CHABRIA

Russia

The era of moving pictures began in Russia on 6 May 1896 in St. Petersburg's Aquarium **amusement park**, with a screening arranged by **Lumière**. Three weeks later, the new attraction had its Moscow debut in the Hermitage Operetta Theatre, with a program from **Edison**. By the summer, the novelty was featured at the large provincial trading fairs of European Russia. The empire's unstable political situation did not augur well for the development of a new industry, and over the next decade, Russia was racked by famine, strikes, rebellion, war, and revolution. Although American and British entrepreneurs moved in early, the French companies of Lumière, **Pathé-Frères**, and **Gaumont** persevered in the face of daunting obstacles to lay the foundations for the Russian film industry.

In Russia, as elsewhere, moving pictures were a summertime "attraction," one of many entertainments on the **fair/fairground** and **vaudeville** circuits. Although Lumière immediately opened a theater in St. Petersburg, and others followed suit with storefront operations or arcade stalls, until 1904, there seemed to be more money to be made from travelling shows that could move on after the novelty had worn off. Russia's vast expanses, poor roads, and inhospitable climate made this a doubtful proposition, but one that attracted European (and Russian) adventurers.

Production and distribution

In 1907, Aleksandr **Drankov**, a "photo-journalist" and portrait photographer in St. Petersburg, opened his own studio to challenge French control. After the triumph of his first film, *Stenka Razin*, native-owned production and distribution companies proliferated, often run by Russians who had worked previously for French firms, especially Gaumont and Pathè. The balance of power began slowly to shift, stimulated by the rise of nationalist sentiments. The center of the Russian film business was the empire's second largest city, Moscow, which was home to major studios—**Khanzhonkov**, **Thiemann & Reinhardt**, **Yermoliev**, Kharitonov, Perskii, and Vengerov & Gardin—as well as lesser known ones such as Frenkel, Taldykin, and Trofimov. The most important provincial companies were Libken (Iaroslavl), which owned a chain of theaters as well as a studio and distribution offices, and Mintus (Riga), which featured the production of "Jewish" films. At the industry's height in 1916, Russia boasted 47 studios.

The number of pictures produced by Russian companies grew rapidly, from 19 (1909) to 129 (1913), an impressive increase considering the strong competition from well-financed foreign manufacturers. Foreign films continued to dominate Russian screens before **World War I**, but the French now had to compete not only with Russian films but also with those from Germany, Sweden, Denmark, and Italy, often imported by Russian-owned distribution companies.

Native Russian production skyrocketed after the outbreak of the war in 1914. German imports were entirely cut off, and other foreign films became increasingly rare as the war deepened and land routes became more difficult to traverse. As a result, Russian production nearly doubled from 1913 to 1914, from 129 to 230 titles; by 1916, to 500 titles. The majority of these were full-length feature films, as opposed to the dominance of one- and two-reelers only a few years earlier.

Exhibition

By 1913, the empire counted 1,400 to 1,500 moving picture theaters. St. Petersburg, with a population of about two million, numbered 130; Moscow, half the size of the capital, had 67. Typical capacity ranged from 300 to 800 seats. St. Petersburg and Moscow boasted a few 2,000-seat **palace cinemas**, but the smaller the town the more likely the "theater" was to be a storefront operation with a few dozen hard-backed "Viennese" chairs and a **projector** placed in front of the audience.

Given the explosion of the film industry after the war began, it is not surprising that exhibition sites increased as well. By 1916, there were about 4,000 movie theaters in Russia serving two million viewers daily. Petrograd (as St. Petersburg was renamed, 1914–24) now had 229 movie theaters, with 15 on its central boulevard, Nevskii Prospekt. According to one Soviet film historian, by this time the cinema outsold the stage 10 to 1, a significant shift.

The moving picture theater business saw considerable turnover, especially in the early years. Many budding entrepreneurs had little capital and less business experience. Finding qualified **projectionists** and competent improvisational pianists was a continuing source of difficulty. The **trade press** railed against theater owners who economized by turning off the heat or lights in the lobby, making patrons wait in the cold and dark. The press also published allegations about false **advertising**, the poor condition of prints, and incorrect projection speed.

The most serious problem facing theater owners and moviegoers alike was the ever-present threat of fire from projectors. The worst disaster occurred in 1910 at a social club on the railway line between Moscow and St. Peterburg. Ninety-three people died, with 45 seriously injured. This catastrophe, widely reported in the Russian press, led to much-needed safety rules as well as regular inspections of theaters.

With the growth of a "respectable" urban **audience** (willing to pay well for the privilege of watching films in comfortable surroundings), theater owners realized the importance of investing in amenities. By 1914, the number of large newly-constructed theaters, seating at least 900–1000 (with fire exits), was on the rise. These theaters advertised their ability to separate social classes on the basis of space and ticket price. For example, loge boxes, which afforded the most separation and privacy, cost 4–6 rubles, well beyond the means of the shopgirls and clerks who were a mainstay of the movie-going audience and occupied the 20 kopek back-of-the-hall seats.

Other amenities were important, too—especially music. As competition among big city theaters increased during the war, orchestras became more common, both to accompany the films and entertain during intermission. Despite the growing popularity of stringed instrument accompaniment, the pianist A. Levin remained the acknowledged master of film music. His performances at Moscow's Forum Theater received as much applause as the films. Heating, ventilation, and electrical lights were also promoted in theater advertisements, along with the quality of food and drink at the buffet, cafe, or restaurant connected to the theater.

Before the war, programs followed a format laid out in the trade journals. One prescription for success, dating from 1911, consisted of a 1,240 meter program with five titles: one sensational **melodrama** (600 meters), one long **comedy** (300 meters), one *actualité* (100 meters), and two short comedies (120 meters each). The program ran continuously, and it was considered perfectly normal to drop in at any point. Owners were advised to change the entire program at least twice a week; those with heavy regular patronage changed them more often, so that their clients would not be tempted to check out another theater. After the astonishing success of Thiemann & Reinhardt's 5,000 meter blockbuster, *Kliuchi schastia* [The Keys to Happiness], in 1913, the five-film format was gradually abandoned in favor of one full-length contemporary melodrama, accompanied by a couple of short films. The main attraction's title appeared in a theater's advertisements, and theater managers were judged by their ability to select and book a "hit" before their competitors did.

Advertising became an increasingly important part of the moving picture theater budget. Studios conducted extensive advertising campaigns in the trade press and supplied theaters with ever more elaborate posters, **publicity** stills, and **postcards** of **stars**. But theaters also produced their own flyers and programs (which often elaborated the film's plot).

Audiences

The imperial census of 1897 put Russia's population at 125 million; by the time war broke out in 1914, it was about 140 million. Concrete sales and attendance figures for the cinema are hard to come by. One 1914 account, looking back at the previous year, reported 108 million tickets sold and estimated that regular patrons numbered some 12 million. This seems a minuscule figure until one considers that it represents nearly *half* of Russia's urban population.

Unlike their counterparts in many European countries, Russia's influential intelligentsia did not snub the movies. Even though Tsar Nicholas II had initially proclaimed moving pictures "harmful rubbish," the imperial family (whose passion for **photography** was well-known) arranged for private screenings. Despite this demonstrated interest from the "better classes," moving pictures were considered primarily an entertainment for the petty bourgeoisie and the literate proletariat, for students and young lovers, and for children. The trade press characterized theaters by the social class that frequented them, a fact indicating that despite the ability of the largest theaters to keep classes separated through seating arrangements, most people preferred to attend a theater where they felt welcome.

Bad behavior in theaters was a constant source of worry in the business. Some critics of manners at the movies saw the practice of coming and going whenever one desired as disrupting the pleasure of those who wanted to see an entire picture. Other admonitions concerned the visual obstruction of ladies' elaborate headgear and intrusive noises like loud talking and coughing during the show.

Young people were believed to go to the movies mainly to "kill time" and to escape the vigilance of their parents. Theaters provided a public space to see friends—and to be seen. Lovers snuggled in the back rows, to the discomfiture of traditional patrons. Hooligans and rowdies were also known to congregate around moving picture theaters, occasionally roughing up a cashier to let them in without paying. And on at least one occasion, a teenage revolutionary was arrested outside a theater handing out Marxist leaflets to patrons before the show.

Children's fascination with movies was particularly alarming. Russian films, especially during the war years, were undeniably sensational—violent and erotic with few, if any, moral messages. Theater owners occasionally attempted to organize children's programs, but it was difficult to find suitable films from the Russian repertory. Foreign pictures were considered unsuitable for children merely because they were foreign. In 1914, the leading liberal journal, *Vestnik Evropy* [The European Herald], conducted a survey of nearly 1,500 school children and found that an alarming 38 percent would rather go to the movies than read a book. A later study explored the relationship between the movies and juvenile delinquency. But these same movies inspired important Soviet directors, like Lev Kuleshov (who got his start working with Evgenii **Bauer**) and Fridrikh Ermler, who fondly remembered skipping school in his native Latvia to catch the latest picture.

The "Canon"

Despite the rapid growth of the Russian industry, the vast majority of pictures appearing on Russian screens before 1914 were still foreign—more than 1,000 titles in the period 1912–1914 alone. German, Swedish, and Danish melodramas found particular favor among Russian audiences, as did the lavish Italian historical costume epics. French **comedies** reigned supreme, and the French *Fantômas* **detective** series inspired Russian imitators.

In the first period of Russian production, 1908–1912, only 85 of 226 films were fiction, the rest being *actualités*, **newsreels**, and **travelogues**. Of these early fiction films, 53 percent were adaptations of literary classics, and 26 percent were historical tales. By 1913, however, there was a marked shift toward full-length pictures of at least 1,000 meters drawn from the sensational melodramas of best-selling authors such as Leonid Andreev, Mikhail Artsybashev, and Anastasiia Verbitskaia. Adaptations from Pushkin, Chekhov, Gogol, and Tolstoi continued to enjoy favor, but "low-brow" sex and suicide sold well at the box office, too.

The 1913 sensational melodrama, *Kliuchi schastia* [The Keys to Happiness], directed by Vladimir **Gardin** and Iakov **Protazanov**, was the biggest commercial success of Russian cinema. Other major hits were Protazanov's adaptation of Pushkin's *Pikovaia dama* [The Queen of Spades] (1916) for Yermoliev, and Pëtr **Chardynin's** *Molchi, grust, molchi* [Be Still, Sadness, Be Still] (1918), starring Vera **Kholodnaia**, for Kharitonov. The Khanzhonkov studio's *Voina i mir* [War and Peace] (1915) and *Stenka Razin* (1915) also were hits, along with two adventure **serials**: Drankov's *Sonka zolotaia ruchka* [Sonka the "Golden Hand"] (1914) and Yermoliev's *Sashka seminarist* [Sashka the Seminary Student] (1914).

Of the empire's many directors, five have earned an enduring place in the history of early Russian cinema. Vasilii **Goncharov** was the first director to establish a name for himself, but his early death limited his contributions. Pëtr Chardynin, Vladimir Gardin, and Iakov Protazanov were versatile and reliable directors of high-quality films who enjoyed the rare privilege of seeing their names on the billboards for their pictures—and exerted a major influence on Soviet cinema. Wladyslaw **Starewicz** was the Russian master of the **trick film**. But certainly the Russian director with the most memorable and original cinematic style was Evgenii Bauer, who excelled in the darkly erotic melodrama Russian audiences adored, raising the genre to new levels of artistry.

Because of Russian cinema's relatively late start, the industry had a difficult time developing native stars who could compete with their glamorous, well-established European counterparts. Among European stars, Max **Linder** was in a class by himself, as was Asta **Nielsen**. But Valdemar **Psilander**, known in Russia as "Garrison," came in a very close third. Francesca **Bertini**, Lyda **Borelli**, Suzanne **Grandais**, and Henny **Porten** also had their share of Russian admirers. During World War I, however, a number of Russian actors achieved sufficient name recognition to receive star billing: Vladimir Maksimov (1880–1937), Vitold Polonskii (1879–1919), and the fabled Ivan Mozzhukhin, who worked in France after the Russian Revolution as "Mosjoukine." All three men distinguished themselves portraying the brooding anti-hero of the contemporary melodrama, but Mozzhukhin displayed a comic gift as well. Among the many fine actresses of Russian cinema, the queens of the screen were former ballerinas, Vera Karalli (1888/89–1972) and Vera Kholodnaia. Kholodnaia's untimely death in 1919, when she was at the height of her beauty and fame, symbolized the end of an era.

Censorship and the Press

Russian imperial censorship, the most stringent in Europe, was primarily political; censors rarely concerned themselves with issues of morality, sexuality, or violence in the arts. It was reported in the earliest day of the "illusion" that the police would occasionally visit a moving picture operator to ascertain that the show did not offend public morals, which sometimes resulted in seizure of offensive material, but more often in a bit of money changing hands. After the Revolution of 1905, with the establishment of the putative constitutional monarchy, state censorship relaxed considerably and became even more narrowly political, focused on preventing the spread of socialist ideas. In the cultural community, the practice of self-censorship was long ingrained.

In any case, no one in the Russian film industry was interested in fomenting a socialist revolution that would jeopardize their business interests, so they did not find it particularly difficult to avoid running afoul of political regulations. Practically speaking, there were two ways for a film to get into censorship

trouble. The first was that the Romanovs claimed a monopoly on the production and distribution of their own image; until the dynasty's tricentennary celebration in 1913, studios had to subject their *actualités* and newsreels to stringent evaluation. Since it was highly unlikely that any fictionalized story about the Romanovs (or their immediate ancestors) could be approved, studios played it safe by situating their historical melodramas no later than the age of Catherine II (1762–1796).

The second dictate prohibited depiction of religious issues offensive to the Russian Orthodox Church, which had been coopted by the state in 1721. Problems centered mainly on screen adaptations of the works of Lev Tolstoi. From the 1880s to his death in 1910, the great writer was engaged in a constant battle with Church authorities over their spiritual monopoly. So formidable was Tolstoi's moral authority in Russian society that the Church even forbade showing newsreel footage of his funeral. Protazanov tried for years to bring Tolstoi's *Otets Sergii* [Father Sergius], the story of a young nobleman's tortured path to faith, to the screen. Not only did *Otets Sergii* raise the Church's ire, it also showed the tsar's great-great grandfather and namesake, Nicholas I, in a most unfavorable light. Only in 1917 did he finally make the film, with Mozzhukhin in the title role.

Mostly the industry preferred to police itself, through guidelines published in the trade press. This press survives remarkably intact in the Russian State Library in Moscow and is an excellent source for the early development of the industry. The only independent journal was *Sine-fono* (Cine-phono), published by S. V. Lure (its independence was compromised in 1914 when Lure founded his own distribution company). The other major journals were published by the studios: *Kine-zhurnal* (Cine-Journal) (Perskii), *Vestnik kinematografii* (The Cinematographic Herald) (Khanzhonkov), *Pegas* (Pegasus) (Khanzhonkov), *Proektor* (Projector) (Yermoliev), and *Ekran Rossii* (The Russian Screen) (Skobelev Committee). Although all reviewed films from the other studios (as well as their own), commercial rivalries were obvious and reviews were far from "objective." The main focus of the trade press at this point, however, was to establish cinema as a respectable form of culture and entertainment and to raise its artistic standards.

The final years

Because Russian cinema began late and ended abruptly, its "early" period may be defined as 1908–1918, rather than 1895–1914. Russia's wartime movie business was an island of prosperity in the midst of a national economy in collapse. During the war, taxes on moving pictures increased dramatically as the government frantically searched for new sources of revenue. Commercial studios now faced competition from the state-financed Skobelev Committee, which was supposed to produce patriotic films to support the flagging war effort (after 1914, the number of commercially produced movies on war themes plummeted, due to flagging audience interest).

After the February 1917 revolution, only Yermoliev seemed to recognize the danger the mounting chaos presented to the film industry. He formed the first producers' association in March, and distributors, filmworkers, theater owners, and the trade press quickly followed, all forming their own associations in the spring and summer. But by the fall of 1917, shortages of **electricity** left theaters dark most of the week, and the Bolsheviks closed them altogether in November and December. When the capital moved from Petrograd to Moscow in March 1918, production companies in Moscow began evacuating their studios and personnel to the Crimea, a stronghold of counterrevolutionary forces. By 1919, most of the Russian film industry was in exile, primarily in Paris, Berlin, and Prague. A few even made their way to Hollywood.

See also: distribution: Europe; multiple-reel/feature films: Europe; law and the cinema; program formats

Further reading

Ginzburg, S. (1963) *Kinematografiia dorevoliutsionnoi Rossii* (Cinema in Prerevolutionary Russia), Moscow: Iskusstvo.

Likhachev, B. S. (1927) *Kino v Rossii (1896–1926): Materialy k istorii russkogo kino* (Cinema in Russia (1896–1926) Materials toward a History of Russian Cinema), vol. 1: 1896–1913, Leningrad: Academia.

Tsivian, Yuri with Paolo Cherchi Usai, Lorenzo Codelli, Carlo Montaro, and David Robinson (eds.) (1989) *Silent Witnesses: Russian Films, 1908–1919*, London: British Film Institute.

Tsivian, Yuri (1994) *Early Cinema in Russia and Its Cultural Reception*, Alan Bodger (trans.), London: Routledge.

Vishnevskii, Veniamin (1945) *Khudozhestvennye fil'my dorevoliutsionnoi Rossii: Fil'mograficheskie opisanie* (Feature Films in Prerevolutionary Russia: An Annotated Filmography), Moscow: Iskusstvo.

Youngblood, Denise J. (1999) *The Magic Mirror: Moviemaking in Russia, 1908–1918*, Madison: University of Wisconsin Press.

DENISE J. YOUNGBLOOD

Rye, Stellan

b. 1880; d. 1914

filmmaker, Denmark, Germany

Although of a military family, Rye became a successful stage director and playwright in Denmark. In 1911, he was jailed briefly for homosexual acts (then illegal). Moving to Berlin, he became a filmmaker in 1913. His most important work was the **Autorenfilm**, *Der Student von Prag* [The Student of Prague] (1913), from an original screenplay by horror writer Hanns Heinz **Ewers**. Paul **Wegener** plays a student who sells his mirror image (special effects by Guido **Seeber**) to a Mephistopheles-like figure, only to have his life ruined by this spectral double. In 1914, Rye enlisted in the German army and was killed on the Western front.

CASPER TYBJERG

S

saloons

Located on street corners, on the ground floor of tenements, close to factories and businesses, saloons were the most common "poor man's clubs" before the emergence of moving pictures. They provided an inexpensive space for informal socialization and homosocial, even rowdy, camaraderie. In addition, in contrast to other working-class social venues (fraternal societies, mutual benefit associations, and barber shops), saloons offered much-sought alcoholic indulgences, the favorite medicine among low-wage earners against the frustrations of poverty, toil, and life's insecurities. For immigrants, they also constituted a space to gather information to find jobs or to better their adjustment in the New World. For other Americans, however, saloons were vice resorts, a repository for addiction, crime, gambling, and prostitution.

In the 1890s, civic groups, moral reformers and religious organizations formed the Anti-Saloon League and mounted fierce anti-drink campaigns. What these crusades indeed displayed were broader anxieties over the rising commercialization of working-class' leisure time, occurring in such public venues as melodrama **theaters**, **vaudeville** houses, dance halls, **amusement parks**, and eventually **nickelodeons**. With the progressive rationalization of industrial labor, drinking (on and off the job) was to be banished. The saloon became a designated target. Furthermore, population changes and the continued increase in movie houses undermined the traditional neighborhood barroom. Moving picture theaters could draw the casual passerby and provide a gender-blind form of entertainment that suited the temperance-inspired middle-class preference for family amusements. In reaction, a few older establishments turned into cabarets, employing scantily dressed female dancers, while others opened dance floors or added live entertainment on small stages. In a few cases, barkeeps bought nickelodeons in adjoining building to control both businesses. For instance, in Chicago, writes Perry Duis, in 1910 "saloonkeeping was the largest occupational group of those entering the theater business."

Following a long but recently revamped tradition of songs and plays praising abstinence, moving pictures sought to persuade the anti-drink movement that movie-going was respectable and edifying. In so doing, the film industry, aided by the **trade press**, could achieve various goals. It could present itself publicly as the "substitute for the saloon"—Vachel **Lindsay**'s famous phrase—and sponsor middle-class values of work efficiency and home-centered family life, while also defeating the contemporary and just as morally righteous anti-film factions. D. W. **Griffith**'s *A Drunkard Reformation* (1909), symptomatically among the first films to pass the **National Board of Censorship** review, neatly illustrates this prohibitionist agenda. Furthermore, Griffith's film and others contributed to the emerging genre of realist, didactic melodramas regularly reviewed as "sermons in film." The combination of moral lesson and narrative advancements, specifically the rendering of characters' psychological growth and moral reformation through **editing** practices, was for cinema ideologically rewarding and aesthetically self-conscious.

Moving pictures could be differentiated from the debauchery of saloons and beer halls and at the same time gain narrative texture and aesthetic legitimacy.

Further reading

Cumbler, John T. (1979) *Working-Class Community in Industrial America: Work, Leisure, and Struggle in Two Industrial Cities, 1880–1930*, Westport, CT: Greenwood Press.

Duis, Perry R. (1983) *The Saloon: Public Drinking in Chicago and Boston, 1880–1920*, Urbana: University of Illinois Press.

Jon M. Kingsdale (October 1973) "The 'Poor Man's Club': Social Functions of the Urban Working Class Saloon," *American Quarterly*, 25: 472–489.

Peiss, Kathy (1986) *Cheap Amusements: Working Women and Leisure in Turn-of- the-Century New York*, Philadelphia: Temple University Press.

Rosenzweig, Roy (1983) *Eight Hours For What We Will: Workers and Leisure in an Industrial City, 1870–1920*, Cambridge: Cambridge University Press.

GIORGIO BERTELLINI

Salvation Army

From 1891, the Limelight Department of the Salvation Army (based in Melbourne) presented lectures illustrated by lantern slides and then, from 1897, by moving pictures. A studio was built in 1898, with Joseph **Perry** as chief technician. The Department produced mainly non-fiction films including government commissions for productions such as *The Inauguration of the Commonwealth* and *Royal Visit to Victoria* (both 1901). For a decade, it was the largest film producer in the country. Although a new studio was built in 1908, the Salvation Army decided to curtail production, and the Department disbanded in 1910.

INA BERTRAND

Sandberg, Serge

b. 1879; d. 1981

distributor, exhibitor, entrepreneur, France

A Lithuanian Jew who emigrated to France in 1900, Sandberg managed many of the sales agencies that **Pathé-Frères** opened in central and eastern Europe. In 1907, he founded one of a half dozen Pathé affiliates set up to rent and exhibit the company's films and made a fortune in the new cinemas of the Loire region. Becoming a French citizen in 1912, Sandberg served in the army's cinematographic unit during **World War I**. After the war, he and Louis **Nalpas** attempted to build a consortium of companies, including the Société des Cinéromans (for producing **serials**), La Victorine studios (constructed near Nice), SIC Éclair (for distribution), and his chain of cinemas. Compromised by the 1921 financial crisis, Sandberg was forced to sell his interest in Cinéromans to Jean Sapène in 1922.

RICHARD ABEL

Sandow, Eugen(e) [Friedrich Müller]

b. 1867; d. 1925

performer, Germany, USA

A German strongman promoted as "the perfect man" and "the strongest man in the world." After establishing himself in Europe, he came to the USA under the management of Oscar Hammerstein in June 1893. Following a stint at the Chicago **world's fair**, he performed at Koster & Bial's Music Hall from 11 December 1893 to 17 March 1894. On March 6, near the end of his long engagement, he visited the **Edison** Laboratory in Orange, New Jersey, and posed for several films in its Black Maria studio. This much publicized visit effectively launched serious commercial motion picture production. Two years later, Sandow posed for the rival **American Mutoscope and Biograph Company**. In the fall of 1896, he also toured the USA with an all-star **vaudeville** troupe, which included the **Biograph** projector as one of its features. Expenses proved too costly, however, and the show soon closed—ending Sandow's involvement in motion pictures.

CHARLES MUSSER

Santos, Francisco

b. 1873, Porto, Portugal; d. 1937, Pelotas, Rio Grande do Sul, Brazil

filmmaker, Brazil

A regional film pioneer, Santos learned the trade filming throughout the Mediterranean region. Once in Brazil, he entered the theatrical world and toured widely. He settled in Rio Grande do Sul and founded Guarany Films in 1912. The company produced *actualités*, **news event films**, and short fiction films, most notably, the charming **comedy**, *Os óculos do vovô* [Grandfather's Glasses] (1913), the earliest extant Brazilian fiction film. Its feature-length **re-enactment**, *O crime dos banhados* [The Crime of the Bathers] (1913), was extraordinarily successful. Unable to sustain production, however, Guarany Films focused on the exhibition sector, where it was a regional leader until the 1940s.

ANA M. LÓPEZ

Santos, Silvino

b. 1886, Sernache do Bonjardim, Portugal; d. 14 May 1970, Manaus, Brazil

filmmaker, Brazil

A photographer by trade, Santos settled in Manaus at the peak of the Amazonian rubber boom in the early 1900s. Commissioned by various "rubber barons," he photographed and, after 1913, filmed extensively throughout the entire Amazonian region. Working under arduous conditions (and using chemical formulas developed while studying with the **Lumières** in Paris), Santos shot and developed his films in the forest; unfortunately, this early footage is lost. Later, he produced three feature-length documentaries which obtained national and international distribution, most notably, *No país das amazonas* [In the Country of the Amazons] (1921).

ANA M. LÓPEZ

Santos y Artigas

A distribution consortium founded in Cuba in 1905 by two businessmen, Pablo Santos and Jesús Artigas, who shared a love of popular entertainment and a sharp business sense. The company grew into a sizable exhibition circuit encompassing Havana and other provincial capitals—the Compañía Cinematográfica Habanera—and dominated the distribution of the ever-popular European films through the 1910s. Santos y Artigas also sponsored Cuban productions and, in collaboration with Enrique **Díaz Quesada**, financed and produced the most significant films of the era. They were, without doubt, the most successful and solvent film business in the island.

In 1913 and again in 1915, the company sponsored national scriptwriting contests. The winning scripts—by Horacio de la Paz y Paz and Andrés Estévez, respectively— were filmed by Díaz Quesada as *El capitán mambi o los libertadores y guerrilleros* [The Mambi Captain or the Freedom Fighters and Guerrillas] (1914) and *La manigua o la mujer cubana* [The Manigua or the Cuban Woman] (1915): both mined Cuban history in order to create a sense of national identity via the cinema.

Diversifying their business interests in 1916, Santos and Artigas formed a circus company. In 1919, they severed their association with Díaz Quesada and gave up their film production business. Allied to US companies, they continued their distribution and exhibitions activities until 1929, when they focused exclusively on their ever more popular circus, which toured extensively throughout the island until the early 1960s.

ANA M. LÓPEZ

Sargent, Epes Winthrop

b. 1872; d. 1938

critic, screenwriter, USA

After working as a music and **vaudeville** reviewer, Sargent helped found *Variety* in 1905. Based on the magazine fiction he had been writing since 1898, he sold story ideas to film manufacturers until, in 1909, he became story editor at **Lubin**, where in just over a year hundreds of his scenarios, mostly for split-reel comedies, were produced. From 1911 to 1919, he wrote a **screenwriting** advice column for *Moving Picture World*. His *Technique of the Photoplay*, a highly influential screenwriting manual, went through three editions (1912, 1913, 1916). From 1928 to 1938, he wrote film reviews for *Variety* under the pseudonym Chic.

KRISTIN THOMPSON

Saturn

In the Austrian Empire, many movie theaters regularly offered *Herrenabende* or "Men Only Evenings." Their success induced Johann Schwarzer, a professional photographer, to establish Saturn, the first Austrian film company, in 1906. Over several years, Saturn produced at least 52 known erotic films, which were sold throughout the world. Each had an actress, completely nude, acting out a short comic or dramatic scene, as in *Baden verboten* [No Bathing] (1906–1907) and *Modelle* [Models] (1908–1910). Although these films achieved a huge success, complaints increasingly were registered in Germany, France, Great Britain, Italy, Japan, and the USA. In 1911, a court order put an end to Saturn's activity.

PAOLO CANEPPELE

Saunders, Alfred Henry

b. 1866; d. ?

editor, Great Britain, USA

Born in the west Midlands, as a young man Saunders joined the temperance movement, which led to lantern work. He acquired his first lantern in 1883, thereafter touring Great Britain giving **magic lantern shows**, and in October 1902 was appointed editor of the *Optical Magic Lantern Journal*. When the journal failed the following year, Saunders decided to emigrate to the USA. He continued his lantern work, but by late 1906 was editing *Views and Film Index*. In March 1907, he became founding editor of *Moving Picture World*, which was to become the leading US trade journal. But Saunders disagreed with the editorial policy of implicit support for the **Motion Picture Patents Company**, and in May 1908 he founded *Moving Picture News* (he was editor until 1913), where he campaigned for a free market in films, and for the educational uplift of the industry, publishing a book on the latter subject in 1914. A maverick in some ways—a vegetarian, Freemason, and associate of **Friese-Greene**—Saunders is surely unique in the early era in having edited four major trade journals in two countries.

STEPHEN BOTTOMORE

Sawamura Shirogoro

b. 1877; d. 1932

actor, Japan

Born in Tokyo and trained as a *kabuki* actor, Sawamura sometimes performed in films produced by **Yoshizawa Shoten**. Upon its founding in 1914, **Tenkatsu** hired him in order to compete with **Nikkatsu**'s star, **Onoe Matsunosuke**. At Tenkatsu, Sawamura became a **star** of the old-school drama. After the company's dissolution, he moved to Kokkatsu and then Shochiku. Although he acted until 1924, he never adapted to the **acting style** of the 1920s.

HIROSHI KOMATSU

Saxe, John and Thomas

b. 14 November 1871/1 November 1874;
d. 3 November 1939/16 December 1938

exhibitors, USA

Born in Ireland, the Saxes came to rural Wisconsin during the 1880s, to urban Milwaukee a decade later. In 1906, the brothers opened the Theatorium, one of the city's first **nickelodeons**. Their fifth theater, the Princess, opened in December

1909, and set a new standard for movie-going elegance in Milwaukee. By 1915 the Saxes dominated movie exhibition in Milwaukee, the rest of Wisconsin, and also owned theaters in Minneapolis and Chicago.

Further reading

Gomery, Douglas (1979) "Saxe Amusement Enterprises," *Milwaukee History*, 2.1: 18–28.

DOUGLAS GOMERY

SCAGL

Along with **Film d'Art**, SCAGL (Société cinématographique des auteurs et gens de lettres) was the first company to produce *films d'art* in order to promote a theatrical and literary aesthetic. It was founded on 23 March 1908 by two members of the Paris intelligentsia, Eugène **Gugenheim** and Pierre **Decourcelle**, with the backing of the **Merzbach** brothers (financiers and **Pathé-Frères** stockholders) as well as, to a lesser extent, Charles **Pathé**. Contrary to what is usually assumed, SCAGL did not originate from the Société des gens de lettres (SDGL) or any other organization controlling **copyrights**. According to Jean-Jacques Meusy, the confusion may in fact have been fostered by Decourcelle to tap into the prestige of the SGDL. From the very beginning, however, SCAGL's stated goal was to constitute a monopoly over film adaptations in order to diversify the activities of Pathé-Frères, its "editor" and distributor.

The company made its debut, in late September 1908, with Albert **Capellani**'s *L'Arlésienne* [The Girl from Arles], more than a month earlier than the famous première of Film d'Art, albeit without the same **publicity**. Besides, SCAGL differed in three ways from its direct competitor: (1) it specialized in the adaptation of prestigious novels, while Film d'Art sought original scripts; (2) it produced dramatic and comic films in equal numbers; and (3) it did not aim to make cinema an elite art but, on the contrary, strove to make an "artistic" cinema available to all classes of society. Another difference came from artistic director

Capellani's background as a former actor in André Antoine's Théâtre Libre, which clearly influenced SCAGL's output. Antoine himself even became the company's artistic director when Capellani left for the USA in 1914.

Early in 1909, SCAGL's own studios were unveiled on Pathé's factory lot in Vincennes, sealing the close ties with the company. Capellani shot prestigious adaptations such as Zola's *L'Assommoir* (Drink) (1909), the first French **multiple-reel** fiction film. He was assisted initially by other directors: Georges **Monca**, who specialized in **comedies**, and Michel **Carré** for **historical films**. They were joined by Georges **Denola** in 1910 and Adrien Caillard in 1912. Famous stage performers were contracted on a film-by-film basis: **Mistinguett**, Stacia **Napierkowska**, Gabrielle **Robinne**, Jeanne Delvair; Henry **Krauss**, Claude Garry, and Charles **Prince**. Capellani's own historical adaptations met with great success: *Notre-Dame-de-Paris* (1911), a four-part *Les Misérables* (1912), an equally ambitious *Les Mystères de Paris* (1912), and *Germinal* (1913). Carré directed *Athalie* (1910), based on Racine's famous play, while Monca shot the *Rigadin* **comic series** featuring Prince (1910–1912), and Denola made the *Rocambole* **detective** series (1914).

SCAGL films were often more popular than Film d'Art films; they also frequently moved beyond "canned theater" to engage with genuine aesthetic questions. Their significance makes the absence of a monograph on the company all the more glaring.

Further reading

Abel, Richard (1994) *The Ciné Goes to Town: French Cinema, 1896–1914*, Berkeley: University of California Press.

Azoury, Philippe (1995) "Les Miroirs de la dispersion: la S.C.A.G.L., exemple pour une archéologie du vocable 'film d'art'," DEA thesis, Université de Paris III.

Meusy, Jean-Jacques (1995) "Aux origines de la Société cinématographiques des auteurs et gens de lettres (Scagl): le bluff de Pierre Decourcelle et Eugène Gugenheim," *1895*, 19: 7–16.

JEAN-PIERRE SIROIS-TRAHAN

Schenck, Nicholas and Joseph

b. 14 November 1882/25 December 1878;
d. 4 March 1969/20 October 1961

exhibitors, USA

The Schenck brothers entered show business through **penny arcades** and **amusement parks**, first in Fort George, New York, and then in Palisades Park, New Jersey—both accessible to New Yorkers by ferry boat. In 1910, "Nick" and "Joe" joined Marcus **Loew** to form Loew's Theatrical Enterprises. Thereafter, Nicholas moved up the executive ranks of Loew's and, upon Loew's death in 1927, succeeded him. Joe left Loew's to become an independent producer, and later ran United Artists.

DOUGLAS GOMERY

Schneider, Eberhard

b. ?; d. ?

showman, manufacturer, distributor, USA

Schneider's claim to have worked on moving picture apparatuses at the Krupp factory in Essen in the early 1890s is lent some credence by his 1888 German patent (DRP 46 561) for an automatic viewer for stereoscopic lantern slides. Emigrating to the USA, he established an exhibition service active from early 1897 on the East Coast with an apparatus of Henri **Joly**. An able engineer, after 1900 he manufactured both **cameras** and **projectors** in New York City, and in 1904 was duly sued by **Edison**. In 1906, he established an early film rental exchange, which disappeared shortly after the formation of the **Motion Picture Patents Company**.

DEAC ROSSELL

Schuberg, John

b. 1875; d. 1958

exhibitor, Canada

Known professionally as Johnny Nash, the Swedish-born Schuberg brought moving pictures to Vancouver in 1898. Using an **Edison projector**, Schuberg travelled along the Canadian Pacific Railway line until he was able to purchase a black-top tent, with which he initiated a tour in 1899, and continued as an **itinerant exhibitor** for several years. In 1902, he rented a storefront in Vancouver and named it the Electric Theater, charging ten cents admission. He continued to open theaters in various locales over the years, until the Nash Circuit incorporated eight theaters. He eventually sold his interests to **Famous Players** in the 1920s.

CHARLIE KEIL

scientific films: Europe

The sciences worked in tandem with moving pictures from very early on. Their mutual attraction was first embodied in the unconventional figure of French physiologist, Etienne-Jules **Marey**. Beginning in 1882, Marey perfected several devices which anticipated the moving picture **camera**: the photographic gun and soon thereafter **chronophotography** on fixed plates and on a moving filmstrip. The series of images thus obtained (in Naples as well as in the Station physiologique in Paris, with Georges **Demenÿ** as a collaborator) greatly contributed to advances in the physiology of movement and in the understanding of dynamic phenomena. Marey's founding work was later carried on at the Institute that he opened in Paris in 1901 and to which he gave his name. As employees of the institution, Lucien **Bull**, Pierre **Noguès**, and the Spaniard, Joachim-Léon Carvallo, were Marey's main spiritual heirs. Their work in the areas of slow motion and radio-cinematography would have a considerable impact.

Undeniably, however, the advent of the **Cinématographe Lumière** in December 1895 aroused suspicion among the scientific community. Seen primarily as a form of entertainment, this new invention became suspect in the eyes of a profession little inclined to follow the fads of the day. The re-emergence of scientific cinematography was therefore very slow and came from brilliant innovators attracted by the technological novelty and its unexplored applications.

The first advocates of a post-Marey scientific cinematography were physicians and surgeons. Their profession quite naturally brought them in contact with a wide audience of peers and patients, and moving pictures seemed to them an appropriate medium, as would radio and television later. From June 1898 on, the Parisian surgeon Eugène-Louis **Doyen** had several of his operations filmed, including a famous *Séparation des soeurs xyphopages Doodica and Radica* [Separation of the Siamese Twins Doodica and Radica], which created a scandal in 1902. His considerable body of work (close to one hundred films, most of which have disappeared), while controversial, was emulated by others: Ernst von Bergmann, a German friend of Doyen's and a professor emeritus who produced several films with the technical assistance of Oskar **Messter**; Bodeslaw **Matuszewski**, whose cutting-edge innovations in Switzerland directly rivaled Doyen's; Medlinskij in Russia; and professors Auguste Broca and Jean-Louis Faure, also in France. All of these films were intended exclusively for use in teaching, but some occasionally circulated outside schools of medicine and medical conferences. Driven by an insatiable curiosity, many uninitiated audiences saw these brutal images in commercial venues as early as the beginning of the 20th century.

Neurology represented a second area where cinematography could find an application. The way had been shown, from the 1880s on, by Albert **Londe** and Dr. Paul Richer in Jean-Martin Charcot's unit at the Salpêtrière hospital. In 1898, George Marinescu shot an important series of films on the pathologies of human locomotion with a moving picture camera at the Pantelimon hospital in Bucharest, Romania. Similarly, in 1900, Belgian neurologist Arthur van Gehuchten began recording many sequences foregrounding the consequences of spinal cord traumas and myopathies. Several of his films, which have been restored, served to illustrate his famous posthumous book, *Les Maladies nerveuses* [Nervous Pathologies] (1920). In Italy, between 1905 and 1908, Osvaldo Polimanti, director of the Institute of Physiology at the University of Perugia, produced several cinematographic studies on the neuro-motor system of dogs. In a more conventional manner, also in 1908, Camillo Negro staged a typical case of hysteria

with the collaboration of cameraman Roberto **Omegna** in Turin, following in Charcot's footsteps.

The idea of coupling a moving picture camera with a microscope apparently came from the renowned British science educator, F. Martin **Duncan**, who had previously published a technical manual of microphotography. In 1903, he made a series of short films entitled "The Unseen World" for producer Charles **Urban**. These films, with their evocative titles—*Anatomy of the Water Flea*, *Circulation of the Blood in the Frog's Foot*, etc.—met with success when they were presented at the Alhambra Theater in London before being parodied by **Hepworth** (*The Unclean World*, 1903) and **Pathé-Frères** (*Le Déjeuner du savant* [The Scientist's Lunch], 1905, among others. At about the same time, Dr. François-Franck, a former substitute for Marey at the Collège de France, and his collaborator and future wife, Lucienne Chevroton, tried to improve the then still rudimentary techniques of micro-cinematography first developed by Marey, Bull, and Georges Weiss. Their device made it possible to record many phenomena unseen until then, as in the *Étude des mouvements browniens* [Study of Brownian Movements] made by his colleague Victor Henri in 1907.

Ultra-microscopy (also called black-backdrop microscopy), created within the German optical company Zeiss, in 1903, by Siedentopf and Zsigmondy, also soon found applications in cinematography. Starting in July 1903, Dr. Karl Reicher, a medical doctor in Berlin's Second Royal Clinic, presented several films made with Messter using this method. Black-backdrop micro-cinematography was then perfected and systematized by French physician Jean **Comandon**, first at the Hôpital Saint-Louis in Paris, then for Pathé-Frères which patented the technique in November 1909. An important series of films designed to make this knowledge accessible to a general public followed—the first was *La Cinématographie des microbes* [The Cinematography of Germs] in January 1910—and propelled the French company to first rank in Europe in terms of scientific **education**.

The discovery of X-rays by Germany's Wilhelm Röntgen in December 1895 was made possible by photographic plates which revealed the indiscreet images they could produce: the bone structure of Mrs. Röentgen's hand, the bone structure of small animals, etc. Two difficulties delayed an application in cinematography, however. First of all, X-rays were irrefrangible—that is, they were propagated in a straight line and could not be refracted as regular light rays could. Second, the exposure time required was very long, which apparently made single-frame shooting impossible.

The first radio-cinematographic images actually came from a Scottish physician, Dr. John Macintyre. A screening was organized in 1897 at the Glasgow Philosophical Society on the occasion of a "Ladies' Night." It consisted of a succession of X-ray photographs representing the movements of a frog's leg that had been transferred onto a filmstrip. The sequence was looped and the resulting film met with much success.

From 1906 on, Carvallo (a secretary, and later vice-president of the Institut Marey) worked on the development of a claw-mechanism for radio-chronophotography. Once successful, his device could record the unrefracted outlines of the digestive tract of small animals on film strips 60mm wide.

In 1910, Comandon and the Parisian radiologist André Lomon overcame the problems presented by X-rays through an experiment in filming the intensifying radioscopy screen (calcium tungstate made fluorescent by the impact of radiation). "Indirect" radio-cinematography then became the norm, and was later perfected in Germany, specifically by Robert Janker in the 1930s.

Among the other scientific uses of moving pictures, two original techniques endured the test of time more than others: stop-motion shooting, which makes it possible to accelerate the unfolding of observed phenomena during projection; and fast-motion shooting, which by contrast produces a slow-motion effect during projection.

The idea of stop-motion was first elaborated by Germany's Ernst Mach a few years before the advent of cinematography. It was taken up again by Marey who, in his work *Le Mouvement* (1894), touched on the "strange and marvelous" miracle of accelerated images. As early as 1898, thanks to a shooting technique based on regular, long intervals, Wilhelm Pfeffer, in Leipzig, studied the minuscule movements of plants and the effects of heliotropism on mimosas and tulips. The technique of stop-motion was also coupled with

micro-cinematography: in 1903 Antoine Pizon and Bull used this technique to analyze the development of a colony of botryllus, shooting at the rate of one image per 15 minutes. In 1908, Julius Ries, in Switzerland, and Lucienne Chevroton and Fred Vlès, in France, almost simultaneously managed to film the kinematics of the segmentation and growth of an urchin's egg.

The beauty of these various experiments attracted audiences in commercial venues throughout Europe in the early 1910s. Many botanical films regularly presented on theater programs resorted to this technique, as did numerous comic films—for instance, **Gaumont**'s *Onésime horloger* [Onésime Becomes a Clockmaker] (1912). Germaine Dulac's later fascination for these slow-motion images is well known, as is that of the 1920s theoreticians of pure cinema.

By contrast, fast-motion shooting, with which Marey also experimented, became his students' specialty after his death. Noguès, who had entered the Institut Marey in 1900, worked his whole life on developing a claw-mechanism chronophotograph. His device reached a rate of recording 140 frames per second as early as 1904. Although its speed was restricted (past 200 frames per second, there was a risk that the film might break), his camera earned him major successes: in June 1914, many of his films on birds' flight and human locomotion were presented personally to Raymond Poincaré, then President of the French Republic.

Bull, who had entered the Institut Marey in 1902, chose a radically different path. In March 1904, he presented a thesis on the "application of the electric spark to the chronophotography of rapid movements" at the Paris Academy of Sciences. The film strip did not have sprocket holes but instead was carried along in a continuous and extremely fast motion and was exposed thanks to brief magnesium sparks. The shooting rate increased from 1,500 frames per second, in 1904, to 80,000, in 1919, which made it possible to analyze the flight of many insects. In 1904, using a similar method, Germany's von Lendenfeld had recorded a dragonfly's flight at a rate of 2,000 frames per second. In 1909, Dr. Carl Cranz also led remarkable ballistic studies at Berlin's Military Academy, thereby contributing to improvements in German artillery.

Besides these many uses and a few others on which little documentation is presently available—for instance, the films of animated mathematics and geometry directed by Germany's Ludwig Münch from 1903 on—scientific cinematography also found an application in the domain of social hygiene propaganda. Edifying fiction films generally exposing the ill effects of alcohol, for instance, appeared at the very beginning of the century: Ferdinand **Zecca**'s *Les Victimes de l'alcoolisme* [Alcoholism's Victims] (1901), Robert William **Paul**'s *Buy Your Own Cherries* (1905), Gérard **Bourgeois**'s *Les Victimes de l'alcool* [Victims of Alcohol] (1911). What could be called a hygienist cinema developed mainly during **World War I** in response to the three main scourges of society: alcoholism, tuberculosis, and syphilis. It had as its model the films produced in the USA between 1910 and 1914 by the **Edison Manufacturing Company** for the National Association for the Study and Preservation of Tuberculosis. The many short films directed (among others) by Comandon during the war and distributed by the American Committee for the Prevention of Tuberculosis (the "Rockefeller Mission") exploited images

that had originated in scientific research and often dated back to earlier years. Thus the first images of the spirochete, which Comandon had obtained in 1909, were reused in the form of inserts as a means to legitimate the new discourse. Abstracted from the context of laboratory research for the purpose in hand, scientific images had become but mere illustrations for a then prevalent scientism.

See also: cameras; ethnographic films; expedition/exploration films; scientific films: USA

Further reading

Lefebvre, Thierry (ed.) (1995) "Images du réel. La non-fiction en France (1890–1930)," *1895*, 18.

Lefebvre, Thierry, Jacques Malthête and Laurent Mannoni (eds.) (1999) *Lettres d'Étienne-Jules Marey à Georges Demenÿ. 1880–1894*, Paris: Association française de recherche sur l'histoire du cinéma/Bibliothèque du film.

Mannoni, Laurent (1999) *Étienne-Jules Marey. La mémoire de l'œil*, Paris: Milano/Mazzotta/Cinémathèque française.

Martinet, Alexis (ed.) (1994) *Le Cinéma et la Science*, Paris: CNRS Éditions.

Thévenard, Pierre and Guy, Tassel (1948) *Le Cinéma scientifique français*, Paris: La Jeune Parque.

Tosi, Virgilio (1984) *Il Cinema prima di Lumière*, Turin: Edizioni Rai Radiotelevisione Italiana.

THIERRY LEFEBVRE

Figure 107 Poster for Urban's *Unseen World*, 1903.

scientific films: USA

If scientific filmmaking in Europe begins with Etienne-Jules **Marey**, then in the USA it must begin with Eadweard **Muybridge**. Muybridge's serial photographs of Leland Stanford's horse, published in 1878, were greeted enthusiastically by artists and scientists alike for their potential to chart the trajectory of human and animal movement. When Muybridge accompanied Stanford to Europe in 1881, artists fawned over his work.

Marey, however, was disappointed in the ultimate scientific value of the photographs: the 24-camera, trip-wire method of recording was prone to inaccuracy and incapable of the exact time intervals required for careful scientific research. Nevertheless, artists such as Thomas Eakins and Jean-Louis Meissonier encouraged Muybridge to continue his motion studies. It is in this light that Muybridge's major achievement, his 1887 collection of 781 plates called *Animal Locomotion*, must be considered. While there is little in these photographs that can be counted as rigorous scientific inquiry, Muybridge's work prompted Marey and **Edison** each to improve on his methods.

Physicians and scientists immediately recognized the potential of moving pictures for serious research. They appealed to the researcher for a number of reasons. Most obviously, film created a permanent record of movement; consequently, most scientific and medical films made in the early years attempted to build an archive of movement, thereby implicitly indicating the range of the normal and the pathological, the ideal and the substandard. Also, moving pictures were temporally manipulable; researchers could not only slow down or speed up the action and view it at their leisure, but they could also breakdown and reconstitute time and use the (ideally) steady frame rate of the camera to quantify speed and distance. Finally, moving pictures could be projected and shared, making them useful as an illustration, as an educational tool, and as evidence in the scientific community.

Despite these advantages, however, American scientists and physicians of the pre-**World War I** era did not adopt motion picture technology for their research as readily or as frequently as their European counterparts, primarily because state- and university-supported research in the USA was still embryonic at this point. For example, Johns Hopkins University's efforts to connect science and research to clinical practice were considered avant-garde when it opened the first four-year, post-graduate medical school in 1893. As late as 1911, the president of the Southern Surgical and Gynecological Association, Dr. Rudolph Matas of New Orleans, surveyed the range of medical and scientific filmmaking in Europe with the hope that "it will not be long before our own enterprising

teachers and operators, on this side of the Atlantic, will adopt this method of recording." Medical and scientific filmmaking remained confined to isolated cases in the USA until World War I, prompting the U.S. Army to support experimentation with motion picture technology in medicine.

As in Europe, neurologists were among the first to capitalize on film's many benefits. Dr. Walter Greenough Chase of Boston published his report on "The Use of the Biograph in Medicine" in 1905. Chase enlisted the services of **American Mutoscope and Biograph** (AM&B) to record the pathological movements of epileptics. But knowing that such seizures are by nature transient and ephemeral, Chase also obtained help from the Craig Colony for epileptics in New York: on a summer day he and the staff assembled 125 male patients on the lawn of the Colony and covered them with blankets, so that when a seizure occurred, the camera could be set up quickly and the blanket removed. Chase touted *Epileptic Seizure* (1905) as a diagnostic aid, an educational tool, and as a means of "studying and analyzing the muscular action" of epileptics.

Similarly, in 1912, Dr. Theodore Weisenburg of Philadelphia released a report of his five-year study of mental and nervous diseases. Following a long tradition of drawing and photographing mental patients in order to read surface symptoms and thereby connect them with deeper trauma, Weisenburg focused his **Lubin** camera on "the gaits, tremors, convulsions and different types of tics and spasms" common to some mental and nervous diseases. Weisenburg intended the films to be an archive of rare and exotic pathological movement that could be used to educate future physicians, but he also recognized that the films could provide new means of detection and diagnosis.

This potential for diagnosis coincided with the discovery of another potentially crucial diagnostic tool: X rays. Both moving pictures and X rays captured the public imagination at the turn of the last century, and many researchers worked hard to combine the two. Yet the efforts during the early years can only be considered experimental. First, X-ray technology itself was not immediately incorporated into medical practice. For the first five or ten years, the X ray was more symbolic than useful for diagnosis and research. Even as late as

1912, doctors did not routinely take X-ray films of patients undergoing surgery to repair fractures. Add to this reluctance moving picture film technology—cumbersome at best—and it immediately becomes clear that only the most determined researchers had the stamina required to link these technologies. Second, although by 1906 exposure times for X-ray film were down to a few seconds, these were not nearly fast enough for successful direct radiographic exposure of moving X-ray film. Even in 1910, when Dr. Lewis Cole of New York made his breakthrough films of the peristaltic movement of the stomach, the best he could achieve was two frames per second.

Further, in the direct method, the size of the film had to match the size of the section of the patient to be exposed, making for a very unwieldy apparatus. More promising was the "indirect" method: cinematographic recording of the fluoroscopic image. Edison's laboratory invented the fluoroscope only two months after the January 1896 publication of the discovery of X rays; this produced a simultaneous, real-time image of the patient on a translucent screen, which was coated with a material that fluoresced when exposed to X rays. The fluoroscopic image was dim and not nearly as detailed, but, theoretically at least, the exposure rate for filming was unlimited. Jean **Comandon** and André Lomon of France led the field in this method, but it wasn't until the development of image intensifiers in the 1950s that indirect X-ray cinematography could be considered practical for everyday use.

Researchers at the Yale Psychological Laboratory had much more modest and attainable goals. In 1905, they borrowed a **Kinetograph** camera from Edison in order to photograph and measure eye movements. By placing a small yet visible particle on the cornea and filming its movements, they could determine reaction patterns and the relation between the eyes during vision. Psychology in the USA at this point was very much interested in the relation between the mind and the body; motion picture technology promised to help determine such difficult-to-measure phenomena as reaction times. In psychiatry, there also were reports of cinema's therapeutic potential. In 1910, St. Elizabeths in Washington, D.C.—the nation's largest publicly funded institution for the mentally ill—praised the curative effects of cinema and claimed that moving pictures had become the most important means of amusing their patients, surpassing even live theatrical presentations. The use of therapeutic moving images in psychiatry and psychology continues today.

If St. Elizabeths found moving pictures helpful for controlling patients, Frank Gilbreth—a disciple of American industrial engineer Frederick W. Taylor—soon discovered that film could be a useful tool for keeping the worker in line as well. Taylor and Gilbreth were advocates of "scientific management," the application of scientific principles and measurement to the work process. Gilbreth, who is credited with developing "motion studies," felt that there was "one best way" to do a job. In order to find that way, he timed and analyzed the worker's movements, decided which were essential, and eliminated those that weren't. Moving picture technology was ideal for this time-and-motion study because it could record and break down movement and provide an accurate time base. Between 1905 and 1924, in the name of efficiency, Gilbreth made many films studying the minute movements of bricklayers, office clerks, and factory workers, thus laying the foundation for modern industrial psychology.

Europeans such as Marey (and members of the Marey Institute) and Comandon dominated the field of scientific cinematography in the early years. Even though their exploits were well publicized, records of similar efforts in the USA to harness high-speed cinematography, microcinematography, or other techniques are spotty. In 1909, Frank M. Chapman, the Curator of Birds for the American Museum of Natural History in New York, recorded a series of nature films at Pelican Island in Florida in order to study animal behavior and the mechanics of flight. In his announcement, Chapman states that "as yet only three or four men have attempted to do this in America." In 1906 the U. S. Department of Agriculture investigated time-lapse photography of plant growth in order to satisfy the demand in farming communities for more information about plant breeding.

Films such as these were intended primarily for educational purposes; the Department of Agriculture films, for example, were combined with others about new varieties of wheat on that year's touring "education train," a kind of "agri-prop" train for the masses. If Edison improved on Muybridge's methods, unlike Marey he did not seek to use his inventions for strictly scientific purposes. Instead, like Muybridge, he would continue to popularize science through the cinema, and "this form of science destined for the public at large" (in Comandon's words) dominated early scientific cinema in the USA. Most of the titles circulating for popular audiences were produced with an "edutainment" goal in mind: Raymond L. Ditmars' *The Book of Nature* (George R. Meeker, 1914), for example, featured animals from the Bronx Zoological Park (where Ditmars was Curator of Reptiles) performing circus acts as a finale. In 1913, Edison launched his own series of scientific films for educational purposes, which were designed "to utilize the motion pictures to teach all sorts of elementary facts" to school-age children. With such subjects as *The House Fly* (1912), *Magnetism* (1912), and *Ostrich Farming, South Africa* (1914), Edison hoped to cater to educators and reformers, who were also at the vanguard of the movement to "uplift" cinema to middle-class standards.

Of course, by 1913 scientific films in educational or entertainment venues were commonplace; with their unusual spectacle and educational veneer, they were both popular and easily justifiable. The **Kleine Optical Company**, for example, devoted a significant part of its catalog to educational subjects; indeed, the Edison films only supplemented the growing number of titles from such international producers as Charles **Urban**, **Éclair**, **Gaumont**, and **Pathé-Frères**. Yet, if the frequent exhibition of foreign scientific films spurred in 1912 the teaching-film movement in the United States—a bandwagon Edison tried to join—within two years that movement had come to a standstill because of a lack of pattern and completeness in available films. Producers made scientific films on a variety of subjects, but made no attempt to cover any one topic thoroughly, leaving educators with a collection of single films that did not meet curricular needs. The remedy would be found only when state agencies and university departments had the infrastructure and resources to make their own films, and thereby establish a thriving, native tradition of scientific cinematography. This would happen only in the 1920s and 1930s.

See also: education; ethnographic films; expedition/exploration films; scientific films: Europe

Further reading

Cartwright, Lisa. (1995) *Screening the Body: Tracing Medicine's Visual Culture*, Minneapolis: University of Minnesota Press.

Chase, Walter Greenough (1905) "The Use of the Biograph in Medicine," *Boston Medical and Surgical Journal*, 153: 21.

Cole, Lewis Gregory (1912) "The Gastric Motor Phenomena Demonstrated with the Projecting Kinetoscope," *The American Journal of Roentgenology*, 3:4.

Gilbreth, Frank B. (1911) *Motion Study: A Method for Increasing the Efficiency of the Workman*, New York: D. Van Nostrand Company.

Matas, Rudolph (1912) "The Cinematograph as an Aid to Medical Education and Research," *Transactions of the Southern Surgical and Gynecological Association*, 24.

Michaelis, Anthony R. (1955) *Research Films in Biology, Anthropology, Psychology, and Medicine*, New York: Academic Press.

Weisenburg, T. H. (1912) "Moving Picture Illustrations in Medicine, with Special Reference to Nervous and Mental Diseases," *Journal of the American Medical Association*, 59: 26.

SCOTT CURTIS

Scotland

Early cinema in Scotland was founded on the production of topical films or *actualités* for local exhibitors.

The spectacle of the moving image made its appearance in Scotland, to the delight of communities urban and rural, from 1896, courtesy of touring fairground showmen such as George **Green** and President Kemp, entrepreneurs such as Prince Bendon and J. J. Bennell, and optical lantern dealers such as William **Walker** and Lizars. These pioneers bought films from the emerging producers in England but augmented their programs with locally produced topical films, inviting audiences to come and see themselves on the screen. Green and Kemp even commissioned the English company **Mitchell & Kenyon** to make films for their **fairground** moving picture theaters. The first home-based production unit established in Scotland was Walker's Royal Cinematograph, making and showing local subjects in the Aberdeenshire area from 1897 to 1911.

This early use of local footage evolved into a tradition of filmmaking that was to mature when, prior to the Great War, exhibitors began to settle on permanent sites, as ice rinks, churches, and **music halls** were converted for the showing of moving pictures on a nightly basis. This production of local topical films for targeted audiences was widespread, promoted with gimmicks such as "Come and see yourself as others see you" and was to provide a core of work for the early production industry in Scotland. The Green family business set up its own in-house production studio, Green's Film Service, and from this was to come Green's Topical Productions and the short-lived *Scottish Moving Picture News* (1917–1922). Indeed, with its burgeoning circuit of cinemas, a film renting business, and film production studio facility all in place by the middle of the 1910s, Green's could claim to be one of the first vertically integrated companies in British cinema.

Less successful was the production of **multiple-reel/feature** films which never achieved any significant or sustained role in Scottish cinema history. The first known Scottish feature film was *Rob Roy* (1911) made by United Films in Glasgow. The earliest surviving native fiction film is *Mairi, Romance of a Highland Maiden* (1913), made by an established stills photographer, Andrew Paterson of Inverness. Scotland's principal screen contribution to fictional cinema has been as a source of landscapes and characters in historical dramas.

Perhaps a singular contribution to early scientific cinema was the recording of Dr. John Macintyre's successful X ray of a frog's leg at Glasgow Royal Infirmary; in March 1896; the film itself was presented to the London Royal Society the following year.

See also: itinerant exhibitors; scientific films: Europe

JANET McBAIN

screens

In early writings on moving picture exhibition in the USA, "curtain" was synonymous with "screen." The term offers a vivid evocation of how the film image was situated in **vaudeville** theaters, the dominant American exhibition space at the turn of the last century. In this venue, the screen was treated like a drop curtain, brought onto the stage, apparently in a downstage position, in order to present moving pictures as a vaudeville act and possibly conceal preparations for the next act. The screen assumed its position and its role within a pre-existing space and so took over the vocabulary of that space.

With the advent of the **nickelodeon**, the screen expressly assumed its dual role as both the final link in the chain of film technology as well as an element of architecture, defining—and being defined by—the space it inhabited. If the screen in vaudeville was indeed like a curtain, in the nickelodeon it could literally become part of the architecture, the only defining element at the front of the auditorium. In the simplest storefront venues, a white cloth on a stretcher might serve (hence, "sheet," another term for screen in this period), but in fancier venues it was not uncommon to plaster over an area of the front wall and paint it with calcimine to increase reflectance. The screen might then be set off from the wall by a gilded frame.

A 1911 **Moving Picture World** article noted the use of a gilded frame as the most common method of situating the screen in an auditorium. The gilded frame appears to be the one element common to both vaudeville and nickelodeon settings, and it remained a standard exhibition practice until the introduction of the **multiple-reel film**. The framed image invoked a kind of pictorialism in its presentation that explicitly tied the moving picture screen to its predecessor, the **magic lantern show**. Although the narrative film would establish its dominance as the primary form of moving picture entertainment in the nickelodeon period, the nickelodeon design with the framed image continued into the early 1910s, even in large theaters. When the American Theater opened in Salt Lake City, Utah on July 8, 1913, it was the largest theater showing moving pictures exclusively in

Figure 108 Interior of the American Theater, Salt
  Lake City, 1913.

the USA, holding 3,000 seats. While fairly elaborate stages would become *de rigeur* for all large
theaters through the rest of the decade, the
American Theater had an orchestra pit, but no
stage. Instead, there was a frame around the screen
and a shadow box to set the screen off from the
surrounding wall.

Throughout this period, screens remained relatively small. Technical writing on theater design
during the nickelodeon era recommended that
screen size be kept between twelve and fifteen feet
wide in order to preserve the illusion of what were
generally referred to as "life-size pictures." A predictable screen size producing a predictable size of
human subject depended on filmmakers generally
keeping the constant distance of the "12-foot line"
in production. However, as theatrical spaces grew
larger and the camera got closer to the actors
(especially in the USA), screens grew in size as
well. The most extreme example of this came with
the brief attempt to show films in the vast Madison
Square Garden in New York City in 1915. The
34-foot screen was billed as the largest in the
world, but there continued to be a strong sense that
the objects in the image should not appear too
large: as a consequence, the first row of seats was
placed 88 feet away from the screen. There was
another limitation on screen size: the belief that
any screen larger than 20–24 feet would make
evident flaws in **photography**, resolution, grain,
the limited brightness of carbon arcs at the time,
and the vibration of image. This restriction in

screen size would have some consequence for how
screens would be situated in the exclusive moving
picture theaters of the 1910s.

The closer camera **framing** in American
production was very much a response to the
emergence of moving pictures as primarily a dramatic art, since the enlarged human figure could
increase the range and intensity of expression.
Complementing this shift was the fact that
moving pictures were being shown more and more
frequently in melodrama **theaters** and then legitimate **theaters**, which had seen declining attendance for live performances. But in the context of
such theaters, the film image encountered an
exhibition problem defined in a 1909 *Moving Picture World* article: "To our mind, something in the
nature of a compromise between the ordinary and a
moving picture stage is desirable. Let us imagine
the ordinary stage opening. It may be forty or fifty
feet across and proportionately deep. But you do
not want a picture that size. It seems to us that the
best plan in such a case is to set the moving picture
screen well back on the stage and to connect
the sides of the house by suitably painted cloths or
side pieces so that when the house is darkened
and the picture is shown the audience have the
impression that they are looking at the enactment
of a scene set a little way back on the stage. They
look at it, as it were, through an aperture or tunnel,
at the side of which there is nothing to distract
their attention, but rather something in the nature
of a design complementary to the picture which
shall concentrate their attention on the latter."

Whereas an "ordinary stage opening" was
described as "forty or fifty feet across," screens in
this period were never more than half that width
and generally a good deal less. On such a stage,
black masking or even a gilded frame would only
emphasize the smallness of the image and decisively
set it apart from the dramatic space of the stage. The
solution of the set surrounding the picture would
make the space of the image continuous with that
of the stage: there would be a setting across the
entire stage as in any live performance, but in effect
all the action would take place upstage. The upstage
location would have the further benefit of creating
a light trap that would alleviate problems of screen
illumination that were not uncommon at the time.
As an element of a theatricalized stage, the film

image could rightfully take its place as a true competitor with live theater. In 1909, this could be presented as a novel idea, but by the middle of the next decade what would come to be called the "picture setting" became a standard practice in American motion picture exhibition.

When multiple-reel films began to appear in the USA in 1909–1910, distribution and exhibition practices determined that they be shown as separate reels on consecutive days. But subsequent "features" imported from Italy and France and even some "specials" that began to be produced in the USA signaled their special status by being shown as a single performance in legitimate theaters and exhibited with picture settings based on visual motifs from the films themselves. By the 1920s, many deluxe houses would institute the practice of changing picture settings with every change of a feature film, while some would limit changes to visual motifs in the settings related to the seasons. In the 1910s, however, the most common practice for the new **palace cinemas** was a standing set that would help define the distinctiveness of the theater.

In this period, Samuel **Rothapfel**, who would become famous as "Roxy," became the most influential exhibitor in the USA, setting standards for screen presentation that were imitated throughout the country. When he took over Regent Theater in New York City in 1913 to make it into a moving picture theater, working with the architect Thomas Lamb he had the stage radically redesigned to make it an appropriate setting for the screen. The stage was effectively divided into two different areas, with downstage taken over by an orchestra that would remain visible throughout the film performance. The on-stage orchestra became a familiar feature of such theaters in this period, not only to emphasize music as a key feature of moving picture performances but also to enhance the film image. Lamb and Roxy's design offered three advantages. In addition to the light trap it created, the upstage placement made the front row seats more usable. Furthermore, the tripartite design, with smaller stages for live performers on either side of the screen, made the screen itself seem less narrow.

The tripartite design would become the most commonplace strategy of picture settings in the 1910s. It was featured in two significant theaters that opened on Broadway in New York City in 1914, which also established two motifs that would become familiar elements in picture settings throughout the decade. When **Vitagraph** took over the Criterion in Times Square, previously a legitimate theater, it was renamed the Vitagraph and remodeled for film showings chiefly by building a stage set to surround the screen. The set, representing an artist's studio in lower New York, positioned at its center a large window that J. Stuart **Blackton**, Vitagraph's co-founder, dubbed the "Window on the World." Whereas the setting was used for stage presentations, films were shown on a screen dropped behind the large window, to suggest that the audience was viewing a real world *through* the window.

Further up on Broadway, the Strand, generally considered the first palace cinema, also opened in 1914, under Roxy's management, with a different standing set: "The setting suggested the interior of a Greek temple, marble-like pillars supported an airy graceful roof, while to the right and to the left, one looked out from the sides of the temple upon hazy landscapes which made one think of woodland and of meadows. The green garlands wound about the top of the pillars, the profusion of flowers in front of the temple, the harmony of the Greek type of architecture suggests even in its ruins—all combined to make a noble and striking habitation for the screen." The setting added two important elements to the Vitagraph setting: classical architecture and nature.

All three elements—the window, classicism, and nature—may be found in the window-in-the-garden setting for the Strand Theater in Newark, New Jersey, 1914, something of a template for picture settings in the 1910s. Together, these elements point to a common understanding of the film image. The use of classical architecture was an element of uplift, making claims for the status of the new art form. The window suggested that within the artificial confines of a stage setting, the filmed image looked out onto the real world, or, as Roxy would put it, the picture setting should be contrived so that the covered screen "ought [. . .] to represent a window [. . .] through which the audience may gaze upon the everlasting human procession and all the wonders of the world." Complementing the window were the elements of

Figure 109 Stage of the Strand Theater, Newark, 1914.

nature because, as writing in this period repeatedly points out, the direct presentation of nature was the one clear advantage film had over the stage. Whereas the film image could present the real world of nature as if seen through a window, conventional stage settings had to make do with *trompe l'oeil* evocations. In the context of a theatrically constructed nature, then, the moving picture image could demonstrate its superiority to the stage thanks to the way a creative theater manager might use stage art to set off the "natural" realism of the film image.

Further reading

Belton, John (1992) *Widescreen Cinema*, Cambridge: Harvard University Press.

Brewster, Ben and Lea Jacobs (1997) *Theater to Cinema*, Oxford: Oxford University Press.

Paul, William (1996) "Screening Space: Architecture, Technology, and the Motion Picture Screen," *Michigan Quarterly Review*, 35.1: 143–173.

Paul, William (1997) "Uncanny Theater: The Twin Inheritances of the Movies," *Paradoxa*, 3.3–4: 321–347.

Schoenbaum, M. H. (1914) "Screens," *Motion Picture News*, 2 May, 21–22, 42.

WILLIAM PAUL

screenwriting

The practice of screenwriting and the standardization of screenwriting rules developed rapidly and stabilized almost as quickly. In less than twenty years—from 1896 to 1914—when feature films had become an established format, the screenplay evolved from a few written lines describing the action and characters involved in the story to become a lengthy script of fifteen pages or more per reel of film.

In early cinema, screenwriting went hand in hand with the desire to tell stories. The practice of writing scripts intended for film production began as early as 1896, with the creation of the first *sujets composés* written by Georges **Méliès**. He probably was the first to have written stories destined specifically for moving pictures. One of his early films, *Le manoir du diable* (October 1896), tells of the struggle between Mephistopheles and Satan in a medieval cave.

The expression, *scénario cinématographique*, was first used in French by Méliès as a subtitle for his *Le voyage dans la lune* [A Trip to the Moon] (1902). The surviving script is three pages long, divides into thirty scenes, and details very clearly the action to be shot and the characters' roles in the story. According to Jean Giraud's dictionary of film terms (1958), the word *scénario* dates only from 1907. Yet original screenplays that survive in manuscript show otherwise. The first American script legally to be termed a scenario (or dramatic composition), for instance, was **American-Mutoscope and Biograph**'s *Tom, Tom the Piper's Son* (1904).

From 1896 to 1901, scenarios were written in synopsis form and rarely were longer than one paragraph. Many, in fact, were even shorter: they included a title and a one-line description of the action to be seen. Perhaps the most famous was **Lumière**'s *L'arroseur arrosé* [The Gardener and the Bad Boy] (1895). However concise these short descriptive titles may have been, their brevity mirrored the films' length: less than sixty seconds.

Indeed, these short early descriptions contain the essential and most fundamental screenwriting elements: characters and a story with a beginning, middle, and end (but not always). Not yet long enough to be considered screenplays, these evocative titles are nonetheless the first texts written in reference to a cinematographic moving image. They can be found in the catalogues of film companies such as Lumière (1901), **Lubin** (1903), and many others. These catalogues contain extremely interesting information for the study of early cinema.

For example, it was a common practice to print the screenplays in full (long mistakenly considered to be merely summaries) in company catalogues. In fact, early scripts were not only used as publicity material but also helped exhibitors explain the story to new, inexperienced spectators. For the first ten years or so, exhibitors would often hire a **lecturer** or *bonimenteur* to comment on and clarify the story during the projection of the film. Concerned about the spectator's inability to grasp emerging cinematographic modes of representation, Méliès later blamed himself for having presented elaborate stories too quickly, before the gradual education of the neophyte film spectator was completed.

Yet Méliès' self-doubt was unfounded. By 1902, his storytelling style was popular enough to inspire Edwin S. **Porter** at **Edison** to direct story films such as *Jack and the Beanstalk* (1902). As stories became more elaborate, so did the editing principles. Both techniques—screenwriting and editing—relied on one another to achieve narrative clarity and cinematographic storytelling fluidity. It was only when Porter gained some knowledge and control of editing that he interested himself in story films with more complex narrative structures, such as *The Life of an American Fireman* (1902–1903) and *The Great Train Robbery* (1903). Early stories rarely were original, however, because the first manufacturers required subjects that satisfied public understanding and demands. The first decades, therefore, were years of adaptations (in all the meanings of that term). In fact, the practice of writing screenplays evolved directly from 18th- and 19th-century literary and theatrical traditions.

Not only did the screenplay share common subjects with the stage play, for instance, but both were texts that conveyed a written story to a future spectator by the use of sequential scenes, a clear description of the action to be seen and of the characters' motives to be represented. In fact, the screenplay form (a text divided into numbered tableaux or scenes) and content (story sources) owed much to previous texts and spectacles. Méliès's *Le voyage dans la lune* was adapted from an 1891 stage attraction, *L'Astre des nuits*; Edison's *The Life of an American Fireman* was inspired by the lantern slide story, *Bob the Fireman: or Life in the Red Brigade* (1880); *Histoire d'un crime*, written and filmed by Ferdinand **Zecca** for **Pathé-Frères**, was first seen in wax tableaux at the Musée Grévin **wax museum** (1880) in Paris.

In 1902–1903, it became standard screenwriting practice to divide the story into scenes. Ambitious writers such as Zecca became experts in synthesizing such long stories as *Les aventures de Don Quichotte de la Manche* [Adventures of Don Quixote] (1903, 430 meters) into a minimal number of scenes. However striking an example, the majority of screenplays before 1906–1907 were still only two to four pages long, corresponding to the length of the films themselves. As for narrative developments, the screenplays produced after 1902 reveal a desire to help the story unfold in a continuous manner by better sequencing the main story points, as is evident in Méliès's script for *Voyage à travers l'impossible* [The Impossible Voyage] (1904). Notions of time, space, cutting and continuity came to the forefront of many scenario writer's preoccupations.

As editing techniques gained momentum, screenwriters took more and more liberty in writing stories that would, for example, occur simultaneously in two different locales or that would, by moving from one scene to the next, integrate time and space ellipses. For example, **Gaumont**'s *L'acrobate* [The Acrobat] (1907) has a mother caring for her children at home while the father is performing as an acrobat at the theater, and the story alternates between the two situations. Pathé screenplays were even more complicated, often using flash-backs, parallel actions, and off-screen events, as in *Pauvres gosses* [Poor Children] and *La policière* [Police] (both 1907). They confirm that screenplays were written with an awareness that the spectator participated in constructing the story; they did not simply rely on showing events in a consecutive, less dramatic way.

After 1907, narratives typically grew more elaborate and detailed as the public's demand for better stories was met by screenwriters with a more literary background. Having a name became important. Previously, writers preferred to use pseudonyms, unsure about the artistic validity of this new popular amusement. From then on, well-known writers such as Henri Lavedan in France offered their talent and reputation to the practice of screenwriting, most notably in **Film d'Art**'s *L'assassinat du duc de Guise* [The Assassination of the Duke de Guise] (1908). By specializing in adaptations of classical literary and theatrical pieces, companies such as Film d'Art gave stature to the cinema.

If moving pictures never had seemed so silent as when famous plays were being adapted to the screen, from the perspective of screenwriting this was hardly alarming. For, the screenplays of this period were rarely silent. They regularly gave precise instructions about the content of the **intertitles** and offered dialogue lines to be spoken by the characters. They also often used sound as a dramatic element in the storytelling, clearly establishing moving pictures as an audio-visual medium well before the advent of the technology of **synchronous sound** itself. For example, a great number of screenplays—from Edison's *Appointment by Telephone* (1902) to Pathé's *Deux voleurs qui n'ont pas de chance* [Two Luckless Thieves] (1907) or *Rigadin, garçon de banque* [Rigadin, the Bank Teller] (1912)—have characters listening behind closed doors or talking on the telephone, robbers getting caught because they make too much noise, or characters unexpectedly overhearing crucial information.

As the practice of writing screenplays grew indispensable, so did screenwriting rules to establish a cinematographic way to tell stories. Companies began to advertise the do's and don'ts of screenwriting to save time in reformatting the amateur screenplays they now were soliciting. The increasing need for original ideas reached an all-time peak in 1911, and coincided with two transforming events: the advent of the feature film and the U.S. Supreme Court Ruling about **copyright** law restricting the use of theatrical and literary material. Both helped institutionalize the craft of filmmaking.

Thus, not surprisingly, the first general screenwriting rules appeared in the USA in 1911, in articles written by Epes Winthrop **Sargent** and published in **Moving Picture World**. In France,

screenwriting rules first appeared in journals such as **Ciné-Journal** (1909) and *Cinéma-Revue* (1912), written, respectively, by Edmond Claris and Eugène Kress. Between 1912 and 1923, no less than 109 screenwriting manuals were published in English alone. The first to appear, Sargent's *The Technique of the Photoplay* (1911), is very detailed, and its precision about what can and cannot work in a screenplay confirmed screenwriting as a specialized practice. Screenwriters clearly were encouraged to master cinematographic language in order to avoid audio-visual redundancy and unrealistic production costs and to use the new medium to its maximum dramatic potential. With this newfound knowledge came a certain degree of renown for screenwriters—and that year Edison decided to give screen credit to scenario writers.

But the most important change came with the introduction of the **multiple-reel film** (of two to three reels) and the feature film (of four reels or more). The Europeans led the way, most notably the Italians, Danish, and French, moving quickly to features between 1911 and 1912. In the USA, the introduction of the multiple-reel format was established between fall 1911 and spring 1912, whereas that of the feature film format took longer. With the introduction of multiple-reel and feature films, screenplays lengthened to a minimum of fifteen pages per reel, finally offering narrative space to explore subjects in depth. This gave writers space to create a coherent fictional universe, develop the psychology of characters, and freed them from condensing a Jules Verne novel or a Shakespeare play into a few scenes of key moments.

The lengthening of the stories had yet another long-term transformative effect: in the USA, in particular, it led to the development of scenario departments that would, for efficiency's sake, break up the creative process of writing into standardized steps. In fact, the studios gave precedence to economic considerations over the creative aspect of inventing stories. Riding the wave of Taylorism, the studios applied the principle of division of labor to film production. Around 1912, scenario departments started replicating factory production work by subdividing the screenwriting process into individual and near autonomous tasks. At the head of the line were readers paid to recognize potential ideas; writers would then adapt promising suggestions into synopsis form, followed by a scene-by-scene scenario that would be further expanded and dialogued to become a shooting script. Not only did this new management style transform forever the modes of production, but screenplays were thus consecrated as indispensable blueprints of future films. However, far from being read as original pieces of writing, scripts primarily were used by producers to evaluate their risks and control the costs of each film. In a system developed most clearly by Thomas **Ince**, cost efficiency overruled most creative endeavors. From then on, screenwriting would be considered a "technique" and not be construed as an art.

By 1914, a standard form of the feature-length screenplay was recognized and used in Europe as well as the USA. Writers no longer used pseudonyms; instead they insisted on having their names listed in the screen credits. The craft of screenwriting was now recognized and well paid: even an unknown writer could get $20US for writing an unsolicited scenario. In many ways, the screenplay format and creative constraints developed for early cinema are still the norm in screenwriting practices today.

Note: between 1907 and 1923, more than fifteen thousand screenplays were deposited for copyright purposes at the Bibliothèque nationale in France.

See also: editing: spatial relations; editing: temporal relations

Further reading

Abel, Richard (1994) *The Ciné Goes to Town: French Cinema, 1896–1914*, Berkeley: University of California Press.

Azlant, Edward (1997) "Screenwriting for the Early Silent Film: Forgotten Pioneers, 1897–1911," *Film History*, 9.3: 228–256.

Bordwell, David, Staiger, Janet, and Thompson, Kristin (1985) *The Classical Hollywood Cinema: Film Style and Mode of Production to 1960*, New York: Columbia University Press.

Loughney, Patrick (1997) "From Rip Van Winkle to Jesus of Nazareth: thoughts on the origins of the American screenplay," *Film History*, 9.3: 277–289.

Raynauld, Isabelle (1997) "Original Screenplays, Collections and Writing Practices in France Between 1896 and 1918," *Film History*, 9.3: 257–268.

Raynauld, Isabelle (2001) "Dialogues in Silent Screenplays—What Actors Really Said," in Richard Abel and Rick Altman (eds.) *The Sounds of Early Cinema*, 69–78, Bloomington: Indiana University Press.

ISABELLE RAYNAULD

Seeber, Guido

b. 1879; d. 1940

cameraman, inventor, Germany

Originally a still photographer, Seeber was won over to moving pictures in 1895–1896, after seeing **Edison**'s **Kinetoscope** and **Lumière**'s **Cinématographe** in action. He obtained his first camera from Oskar **Messter**, but immediately began to develop and patent his own "Seeberograph," with which he shot hundreds of street scenes and other *actualités* from 1897 onwards. In 1904, Seeber devised a sound picture system under the name "Seeberophon." Head of the technical department at Deutsche Bioscop from 1909, he oversaw the building of the Babelsberg studios in 1911–1912, and was principal cameraman for Bisocop's Asta **Nielsen** series (1911–1913). With *Der Student von Prag* [The Student of Prague] (1913) and *Der Golem* [The Golem] (1914), Seeber earned his lasting reputation as Germany's leading pioneer of trick cinematography.

MICHAEL WEDEL

Segreto, Afonso

b. 1875, Italy; d. ?

filmmaker, Brazil

Guided by his brother Paschoal Segreto, Afonso was the first Brazilian filmmaker, shooting nearly

60 films between 1898 and 1901. After purchasing equipment in New York, he may have shot the first Brazilian film as his ship entered Guanabara Bay on 19 July 1898 (no evidence of the film exists).

Segreto shot many *actualités* of the power elites and visitors—*Chegada do Dr. Campos Salles a Petrópolis* [Arrival of Dr. Campos Salles to Petrópolis] (1898)—and picturesque cityscapes. Later, he filmed artists and comedians: *Un careca* [A Bald Man] (1899). *Dança de um baiano* [Dance of a Man from Bahia] (1899) was the first Brazilian film record of a dance, while *Quadrilla no Moulin Rouge* [The Moulin Rouge Corps] (1901) was the first using artificial light.

His sympathy with the radical Italian **labor movement**—*Círculo Operário italiano en São Paulo* [Italian Workers Circle in São Paulo] (1899)—caused problems for his family, given their allegiance to the power elites. In late 1901, the family sent Afonso back to Italy, and anonymity.

ANA M. LÓPEZ

Segreto, Paschoal

b. 1868, San Martino di Cileno, Salerno, Italy; d. 22 February 1920, Rio de Janeiro

entrepreneur, producer, Brazil

In 1883, Paschoal and older brother Gaetano left Italy for Brazil, where they began selling lottery tickets and thrived on gambling. Noting the popularity of the occasional film screenings, they opened the first moving picture theater, the Salão de Novidades Paris, in Rio in July 1897. Their success encouraged Paschoal to send his younger brother, Afonso **Segreto**, to New York to purchase filmmaking equipment. The *actualités* then shot by Afonso cleansed the company of its ignoble gambling origins, and Paschoal cannily expanded his entertainment empire with venues featuring films and other diversions.

In 1900, Paschoal established a studio and laboratory in Rio. Even after banishing Afonso to Italy, he supported local filmmaking, most notably in *Inauguração da Avenida Central* [Inauguration of Central Avenue] (1905) and *O Carnaval na Avenida Central* [Carnival on Central Avenue] (1906).

He remained the only regular producer/ exhibitor in Brazil until the boom of 1907, followed by Francisco **Serrador**'s alliances with USA distributors which introduced imported feature-length films.

Although Paschoal continued as a small exhibitor until his death, he expanded the rest of his business and left a lasting legacy of promoting low-cost multi-skit comical and musical entertainment.

ANA M. LÓPEZ

Selig Polyscope Company

Incorporated in 1900 by William N. **Selig**, the Selig Polyscope Company dominated early filmmaking in Chicago, along with the **Essanay Film Manufacturing Company** and **George Kleine Optical Company**. Selig Polyscope started with 50-foot slapstick **comedies**, **travelogues** from the Southwest, and **industrial films** for Armour & Company, which later proved fortuitous when the giant meatpacking company—in return for duplicate prints of the industrial films—provided Selig with free legal assistance in his patents battle with **Edison**. After losing that lawsuit in 1908, Selig Polyscope became a founding member of the **Motion Picture Patents Company** (MPPC). Freed from these legal troubles, the company prospered and moved to larger studio facilities in Chicago, supplemented by location filming in the South (Jacksonville, Florida), Southwest (Prescott, Arizona), and the West (Los Angeles, California). As early as 1903, Selig Polyscope began releasing **westerns** filmed in the West, first in Colorado by H. H. **Buckwalter**, then in Montana by G. M. **Anderson**, and, after 1910, in California with Tom **Mix**, who made over 100 one- and two-reel westerns under the Selig banner. Indeed, soon after dispatching a crew to Los Angeles in 1909, Selif opened a branch studio there (under the direction of Francis **Boggs**), becoming one of the first companies to settle in California.

Selig Polyscope's first big box office hit also came in 1909: *Hunting Big Game in Africa* (aka *Roosevelt in Africa*) re-enacted Roosevelt's African safari and coincided with headlines about the trip. It was an instant success and prompted the

Figure 110 Selig Polyscope West Coast Studio, Los Angeles. (Courtesy of the Robert S. Birchard Collection.)

company, in 1911, to invest in wild animals and establish Selig's Jungle Zoo opposite Eastlake Park in Los Angeles. Soon **animal pictures** and "jungle films" became a major part of the company's production, including the first film **serial**, Selig's *The Adventures of Kathlyn* (1914), starring Kathlyn **Williams**: the title of episode three gives an enticing flavor of the series, "The Temple of the Lion, or Kathlyn on a Runaway Elephant Becomes a High Priestess." The film's success was guaranteed by the serialization of episodes in dozens of **newspapers**, led by the *Chicago Tribune*. Selig then joined forces with the Hearst newspaper chain to produce the **newsreel**, *Hearst-Selig News Pictorial* (1914).

Troubled relations with exhibitors and a pesky anti-trust suit made the transition to features difficult for the MPPC. Still, Selig Polyscope invested in long films and did well by them. *The Coming of Columbus* (1912), an early **multiple-reel film**, was very successful, as was the nine-reel adaptation of Rex Beach's *The Spoilers* (1914). In 1915 Selig Polyscope teamed with **Vitagraph**, **Lubin**, and Essanay to form V-L-S-E, a company to distribute feature films, which the MPPC's **General Film Company** could not handle. V-L-S-E dissolved in 1916 and reformed briefly as K-E-S-E (Kleine-Edison-Selig-Essanay). Despite these efforts to accommodate the feature market, the financial pressure of the anti-trust suit was too much to bear. After the final appeals were lost in 1918, Selig Polyscope—like several other MPPC firms—closed its doors.

See also: US patent wars

Further reading

Lahue, Kalton C. (1973) *Motion Picture Pioneer: The Selig Polyscope Company*, New York: A. S. Barnes and Company.

Musser, Charles (1990) *The Emergence of Cinema: The American Screen to 1907*, New York: Scribner's.

SCOTT CURTIS

Selig, William Nicholas

b. 1864; d. 1948

showman, manufacturer, producer, USA

The son of a Chicago shoemaker, Selig flirted with upholstery before dubbing himself "Colonel" and embarking on a career as an itinerant showman. During a tour with his minstrel troupe, Selig encountered the **Edison Kinetoscope** and soon developed his own Polyscope **camera** and **projector**, modeled on the **Lumière** design. After manufacturing these machines, operating an exhibition service, and producing films for several years, he incorporated **Selig Polyscope** in Chicago in 1900. The principal defendant in Edison's many patent lawsuits, Selig nevertheless became one of the founding members of the **Motion Picture Patents Company** (MPPC) in 1909. He prospered until the MPPC lost its final appeals in 1918; after Selig Polyscope closed its doors, he led a retired life.

SCOTT CURTIS

Sen, Hiralal

b. 1866; d. 1917

photographer, filmmaker, India

Recognized as one of India's first filmmakers, along with H. S. **Bhatavdekar**. A successful photographer, Sen collaborated with visiting moving picture showman, Prof. Stevenson, to make his first films in 1898. One year later, he established the **Royal Bioscope** Company with his brother Motilal, and they exhibited imported European films at Calcutta's Classic Theater. They also filmed scenes from the theater's repertoire of stage plays, among them *Alibaba and the Forty Thieves* (1904). Sen ontinued to make *actualités* such as *Delhi Coronation Durbar* and *Royal Visit to Calcutta* (1912). He died soon after all his films were destroyed in a fire in 1917.

SURESH CHABRIA

Sennett, Mack

b. 1880; d. 1960

actor, director, producer, USA

A former musical comedy chorus boy, Sennett joined **Biograph** as an actor in 1908, becoming head of its comedy unit in 1911. The following year, Sennett established the **Keystone Film Company**, an all-comedy studio affiliated with Harry **Aitken**'s **Mutual** label. During the studio's first year, Sennett acted in and directed many Keystone releases, often parodying D. W. **Griffith**'s sensational **melodramas** in films such as *At Twelve O'Clock* (1913). From 1914, Sennett restricted his duties to those of production head, shaping a studio style distinguished by fast-paced editing and the breakneck antics of the "Keystone Cops." After an acrimonious split with Aitken in 1917, Sennett abandoned the Keystone **trademark** to produce "Mack Sennett Comedies" for, successively, Paramount, First National, and Pathé-Exchange.

Further reading

Lahue, Kalton (1971), *Mack Sennett's Keystone: The Man, the Myth, the Comedies*, South Brunswick: A. S. Barnes.

ROB KING

Serena, Gustavo

b. 1882; d. 1941

actor, director, Italy

A Neapolitan marquis and stage actor since 1899, Serena began acting in moving pictures for **Film** **D'Arte Italiana** in 1911. He later worked at Roma Film, **Cines**, and **Pasquali**, for which in 1914 he directed his first film. At Caesar Film in 1915, he starred in and directed modern love melodramas with Francesca **Bertini**, Olga Benetti, and Leda **Gys**. Most notably, Serena acted in and directed *Assunta Spina* (1915), a masterpiece of Neapolitan realism which transformed **Bertini**'s career. He directed the diva in her best works, including *La signora dalle camelie* [Lady of the Camelias] (1915).

GIORGIO BERTELLINI

serials

Serials were a prominent form of popular film in the later years of early cinema. While they remained a staple commodity for many decades (until television usurped their niche), their heyday was the novelty period between 1912 and around 1915 or 1916, when they enjoyed a number of remarkable box-office hits, massive **publicity**, and broad market saturation. By the end of the decade, with the domination of the **multiple-reel/feature film**, along with **palace cinemas** which emphasized middlebrow fare aimed at broader multi-class audiences, serials became peripheral offerings associated with cheap neighborhood theaters.

Series films, featuring the same protagonist and milieu from story to story (on the model of **comic strips** and adventure-tale "dime novels"), had become fairly common by 1910. They provided a profitable standardized format for producing, distributing, and exhibiting a variety of one-reel or split-reel subjects on a regular basis: **comic series**, **crime films**, **detective films**, and **westerns**. The serial films that appeared several years later added the element of a single overarching narrative conflict. In **Edison**'s *What Happened to Mary* (released in twelve monthly "chapters," beginning in July 1912 and generally considered the first serial) most episodes ended with more or less complete situational closure, but the battle over the heroine's inheritance continued throughout. By 1914, the narrative links between episodes had grown much stronger, as suspenseful cliffhanger endings—leaving melodramatic crises unresolved until the beginning of the next installment—became a crucial convention of the form.

With few, if any, exceptions, serial films exploited the genre of sensational **melodrama**, highlighting action, stunt-based thrills, violence, suspense, and spectacle. Stories typically centered, at least in the USA, around a young, unmarried "plucky" heroine who, with the help of a boyfriend, fights a villain and his henchmen who repeatedly abduct or try to kill the heroine in order to gain possession of an object promising wealth and power—a treasure map, plans for a new weapon, a jewel endowing supernatural powers, etc. The serial unfolds as a back-and-forth struggle for the physical possession of both the heroine and the "weenie" (as Pearl **White**, the leading serial **star** before 1920, dubbed the coveted object).

The commercial rationale behind serialization was straightforward: the goal was to entice spectators to return to the theater each week to follow the continuing story. The practice of parceling out a narrative to encourage repeat consumption was already familiar in popular literature. In the USA in this period, for instance, almost sixty mass-market magazines, and many hundreds of **newspapers**, routinely published works of fiction, the majority employing serialization. The pervasiveness of prose serials was both a precondition and an incentive for the creation of film equivalents. The close connection between prose serials and film serials is underscored by the fact that before around 1916, virtually every film serial was accompanied by prose-version "tie-ins" published in major magazines and newspapers—*What Happened to Mary*, after all, was serialized in *The Ladies' World*, the most popular working-class women's magazine. Hundreds, often thousands, of newspapers across the country exhorted consumers to "Read It Here in the Morning; See It On the Screen Tonight!" Another factor motivating studios to produce serials had to do with the vagaries of the transitional era. The first wave of serial production was precisely concurrent with the "feature craze." In the USA, the rise of the feature wreaked havoc on the prevailing organization of the industry built around the financing, production, distribution, and exhibition of one- and two-reel shorts. The industry mainstream was reluctant to complicate ensconced systems that had been highly profitable

for almost a decade, but at the same time it recognized the strong commercial demand for feature films. Serial films represented a compromise of sorts: they were "big" multi-reel narratives that could be ballyhooed like features, but they were less expensive to produce and rent, and they did not disrupt the longstanding practices of "variety program" distribution.

The most direct impetus for the first wave of serial-film production was simply the fact that a number of early productions were phenomenal hits enhanced by massive publicity from newspaper tie-ins. After the success of **Selig Polyscope**'s *The Adventures of Kathlyn* (1913–1914), **Thanhouser**'s *The Million Dollar Mystery* (1914), and **Pathé-Frères**'s *The Perils of Pauline* (1914) and *The Exploits of Elaine* (1915), many firms experimented with serials. Pathé, **Vitagraph**, **Universal**, and **Mutual** invested most heavily in the form. Although American serials dominated the world market, France, Germany, and other countries also produced them. Yet the Europeans tended to employ a somewhat different model: episodes were usually the length of feature films, rather than just one or two reels; they were released less frequently and less regularly; and, although there were some European "serial queens" (one prominent exception was Josephine **Andriot** in **Éclair**'s *Protéa* (1913)), the main focus was often on mastercriminals and shrewd detectives. Indeed, these films initially came in series, beginning with the three *Zigomar* films that Victorin **Jasset** produced for **Éclair** (1911–1913), the three *Main de fer* [The Iron Hand] films that Léonce **Perret** directed for **Gaumont** (1912–1913), and the five *Fantômas* features that Louis **Feuillade** made for Gaumont (1913–1914). Only with Feuillade's *Judex* (1917) did the Europeans begin their own long commitment to serials.

See also: audiences: surveys and debates; spectatorship: issues and debates

Further reading

Lahue, Kalton C. (1964) *Continued Next Week: A History of the Moving Picture Serial*, Norman: University of Oklahoma Press.

Singer, Ben. (2002) *Melodrama and Modernity: Early Sensational Cinema and Its Contexts*, New York: Columbia University Press.

BEN SINGER

Serrador, Francisco

b. 1878, Valencia, Spain;
d. 22 March 1941, Rio de Janeiro

exhibitor, producer, Brazil

Serrador built Brazil's most extensive and long-lasting exhibition and distribution empire. He began with sports and gambling; in 1906, he became an **itinerant exhibitor** in São Paulo; a year later, he inaugurated the city's first permanent cinema. With Alberto **Botelho**, he produced a series of popular **news event films** chronicling urban events. As the cinema became more popular, Serrador's business grew exponentially: he built several new cinemas and expanded into Rio de Janeiro, where he competed with William **Auler** and produced *filmes cantantes* (sung films). In 1911, he established the Companhia Cinematográfica Brasileira, the first well-financed and non-family-based film company with capital of $1.28 million; it quickly abandoned production to focus on exhibition and distribution, with its main product being American films.

Serrador traveled to Hollywood several times to study the industry and then introduce innovations: **palace cinemas**, sound films, city-like studio installations. His company maintained its dominance over the exhibition market in Brazil until 1978, decades after his death.

ANA M. LÓPEZ

set design

The earliest moving pictures are often thought to have required no design, since they were mainly open-air subjects shot on location, while theatrical décor is widely believed to have invaded the screen, with mostly unfortunate results, after 1908. Both of these assumptions can usefully be questioned by looking at a wider range of films than those normally considered landmarks. Early design is also inextricably linked with the growth of studio production and the introduction of artificial **lighting**. But the fact remains that film design remained a largely invisible profession until the early 1910s, apparently left to studio craftsmen, who may or may not have followed the instructions of directors and cameramen. Yet it was the visible impact of design between 1908 and 1914 that helped bring vast new **audiences** to the cinema, attracted by a new "educational" authenticity in recreating the past, and by the sheer scale of spectacle on offer.

Were even the early **Lumière** subjects innocent of design? *Les Forgerons* [The Blacksmiths] (June 1895) shows two men at work, with a brazier and anvil, and the water tub that produces the steam that early spectators admired. It was certainly filmed out of doors, but the backdrop looks as if it has been arranged to simulate a smithy interior. In the Lumières' *Charcuterie mécanique* [Mechanical Butchering] (1895), a live pig is driven into a long box labeled "charcuterie mécanique" from which sausages quickly emerge in an early example of a prop introduced into an otherwise natural setting. Six months earlier, theatrical resources already were being employed when W. K. L. **Dickson** filmed Robetta and Doretto in **Edison**'s *Chinese Laundry Scene* (1894), with a set that had two "practical" windows and a door for the duo's acrobatic comedy routine—presumably the same that they used in their stage act, although here set up in the Black Maria studio. Two years later, Georges **Méliès** produced the first of his **trick films**, setting these against the elaborate painted décor that usually appeared on the stage of his Théâtre Robert-Houdin, only now erected in the open air. And for his increasingly complex *féeries/* **fairy plays** and burlesques, he would continue to use essentially the machinery of 19th century theater, with its sprung trapdoors and optical magic effects.

Even the most elementary kinds of anecdotal film needed some degree of control over what would actually appear on screen. A transitional form of studio used by several pioneer filmmakers was the city-center rooftop, which offered seclusion, uninterrupted natural light, and potential access to nearby theatrical scenery. In Great Britain, Robert **Paul** filmed *A Soldier's Courtship* (1896) on the roof of the Alhambra Theater in central London, for which he required a park seat for the lovers, and as little background detail as was compatible with suggesting a park setting, to ensure the action remained legible. He may also have used one of the Alhambra's stock of painted backdrops for this (lost) first attempt at a "made-up" film, as he did for another, more dramatic subject, *The Arrest of a Bookmaker* (1896). However, Paul's 1898 "re-make," *Tommy Atkins in the Park*, was filmed in a natural setting, presumably near his new base on the outskirts of London: an early example of the studio "backlot." Other rooftop filmmakers included **Vitagraph**, with its "Happy Hooligan" series (1897), and the Eden Musée's *Passion Play of Oberammergau* (1898), shot on the roof of the Grand Central Palace in New York, with painted backdrops which evoked the long tradition of religious paintings.

The need for daylight, even when this began to be boosted by artificial lighting, would continue to govern the options available for films' settings until at least 1905, and much later in some countries. Sets would consist of backdrops or theatrical flats behind an open-air stage, or in the glass-house studios that began to appear after 1897. Generally these followed prevailing stage scenery traditions, with *trompe-l'oeil* painting techniques used for detail and decoration, and distance suggested through forced perspective. An important modification arose from the need to compensate for orthochromatic emulsion's **color** distortion. Most sets were therefore painted in shades of gray, with exaggerated black and white detail to register outlines and modeling. Since many of the subjects that required such settings were fairy tales or fantasies, often vaguely medieval or gothic, they operated with a repertoire of genre elements— castle dungeons, attics and battlements, the underworld or fairyland—which could be permutated and re-dressed for different productions. Other, more unusual, settings required major props, such as the large rocket shell seen in Méliès' *Le Voyage dans la lune* [A Trip to the Moon] (1902) or large-scale cyclorama painting, as seen in Pathé's *Un Drame au fond de la mer* [A Drama Under the Sea] (1901).

Another noteworthy feature of early Pathé practice in set design was the temporary adaptation of an established 19th-century stage device, the "vision scene," a typical example of which could be seen in *Oliver Twist*: visions appeared at the back disclosing pictures of his mother's reception at the workhouse and her death. In one of Ferdinand **Zecca**'s first realist productions for Pathé, *Histoire d'un crime* [Story of a Crime] (1901), three such "visions" appear, as dreams during the condemned man's last night before execution, on a small enclosed stage behind and above the foreground cell set. Although this device revealed the character's inner life, it conflicted with the general move towards an integral realism. However, it would reappear as a cinematic device after 1908, with a tendency in France and Scandinavia especially, to frame action at a distance by means of a doorway for interiors, or a gate for exteriors. In August **Blom**'s *Ekspeditrisen* (1911), for instance, two women by a window are seen from a darkened room; in André **Andréani**'s *Le Siege de Calais* (1911), two lines of soldiers stretch from the foreground to a distant gateway as the main characters approach. Such examples, noted by Barry Salt, indicate how design was beginning to move beyond merely providing décor towards planning sets for narrative purposes.

For the burgeoning studio-based companies, it made economic sense to build standing sets, of which the forerunner was Pathé's staircase and landing, first seen in *Peeping Tom* (1901), then in a series of "keyhole" films up to at least 1905, and in many **comedies** and melodramas thereafter. But with the increasing industrialization of film production, rooms were also becoming standing sets that could be rapidly redressed for different plot requirements and variety. A good example of the standard set by Pathé around 1906 would be *Effets d'un coup de rasoir* (Brown's Duel), a comedy about an irascible man who provokes fights with his family and everyone he meets as he goes about town. The five room sets through which he moves are all differentiated, although a striking Art Nouveau painting of a woman with naked shoulders first seen in his bedroom also appears in the restaurant scene. The bedroom and office sets have a screen and a wall, making a corner that gives these rooms greater depth. An open window in the drawing room set shows a (painted) window opposite, again adding depth; and the staircase set which, like the bedroom and restaurant, has elaborate painted shadows, is re-dressed with a concierge doorway to imply different levels. Careful attention to furniture and props gives the film's studio interiors considerable authenticity, helping them match the Paris street and park exterior; and all of this appears to have been achieved through the coordination of studio construction and property departments, without any specialist art director.

This term was probably first applied to Wilfred Buckland, who had been stage designer for the great New York producer of sensational **melodrama**, David Belasco, before he joined the latter's protégé, Cecil B. **DeMille** in Los Angeles in 1914. But six years earlier, the elaborate architecture of realist stage design that had become a feature of theater in the late 19th century finally reached the screen. The occasion was **Film d'Art**'s production of *L'Assassinat du Duc de Guise* [The Assassination of the Duke of Guise] (1908), which featured elaborately authentic **costume** and set design for its 16th-century story of royal perfidy. This and other Film d'Art productions were distributed by Pathé, which also developed its own competing artistic series through **SCAGL**. Although the legacy of the Film d'Art series was long dismissed by film historians as theatrical, hence "uncinematic," its impact on standards of décor and costume is undeniable, and its international influence was immediate, helped by Pathé's global distribution network. In 1909, **Pathé russe** appointed Czeslaw Sabinski, who had been working as a designer at the Moscow Art Theater, to head its décor department.

In the USA, favorable reviews of imported "artistic" productions encouraged companies seeking ways of differentiating their output to embark on historical subjects that placed a high premium on authentic décor and costume. The Vitagraph "quality" films of 1908–1913 offered a mixture of subjects drawn from classic literature (Shakespeare, Dante, Dickens), the Bible, and popular history (Washington, Lincoln, Napoleon). In many of these, familiar images from **painting** and graphic illustration dictated the overall visual style, with the set consisting essentially of painted flats, given depth by the strategic use of decorated pillars and drapes. Good **publicity** value could be had from such efforts, as Vitagraph reported of the preparations for its *Life of Moses* (1909–1910) that "scenic staff has been increased to permit the proper handling of the heavy and unusual scenery required"; while press comment was duly appreciative of the authenticity considered lacking in many films.

The early *film d'art* style was essentially on a chamber scale, filling the frame with unusually rich and suggestive detail, and adapting the scenic conventions of Henry Irving's "pictorial" theater and its equivalents in other countries. But in Italy it began to be applied to much larger and more spectacular subjects, notably those set in the ancient world. **Ambrosio**'s *Nerone* [Nero, or the Burning of Rome] (1909), **Itala**'s *La Caduta di Troia*, (The Fall of Troy) (1910), Ambrosio's second version of *Gli ultimi giorni de Pompei* [The Last Days of Pompeii] (1913), and **Cines**'s *Quo Vadis?* (1913) traced a rising graph of scenic and spectacular ambition, typically involving a combination of interior and exterior sets, with model shots for fire and volcano effects. History painting remained a crucial reference source, as did the 19th-century stage traditions of representing Ancient Rome, supplemented by the evidence of new archaeological findings. Finally, all these elements fused in the worldwide success of Itala's *Cabiria* (1914), a Punic War adventure epic which contrasted Roman Sicily with the exotic landscape and décor of Carthage, and featured as two massive set-piece constructions the pagan idol Moloch and the siege of Carthage. It also introduced the slowly tracking camera as a novel way of displaying Camillo Innocenti's extensive sets. The scale of *Cabiria*'s sets and crowd scenes would leave an indelible mark on all subsequent spectacle cinema, from D. W. **Griffith** to DeMille and Fritz Lang. Significantly, Griffith built his first major standing sets, a western town for *The Battle of Elderbush Gulch* and a walled city for *Judith of Bethulia*, in 1913, at the height of American enthusiasm for Italian spectacle.

Although the *film d'art* movement favored historical subjects, its influence began to be felt in the treatment of contemporary stories from about 1912. The *autorenfilm* movement in Germany and Denmark brought more sophisticated scripts, requiring greater scenic invention and variety, as in Blom's *Atlantis* (1913). In Russia, Evgenii **Bauer** came to cinema in 1912 after a varied career in stage design and **photography**; as the designer of all the films he directed for **Khanzhonkov** from 1913 to 1917, he brought a new sense of filmic space to the elegant interiors of his society dramas. Columns were used to give perspective as well as conceal side lighting, and Bauer pioneered the use of tulle sheets in place of painted flats to create lightness. Bauer's rediscovery at the end of the 1980s literally shed new light on the origins of modern film design.

See also: camera movement; historical films

Further reading

Abel, Richard (1994) *The Ciné Goes to Town: French Cinema, 1896–1914*, Berkeley: University of California Press.

Brewster, Ben and Lea Jacobs (1997) *Theater to Cinema: Stage Pictorialism and the Early Feature Film*, Oxford: Oxford University Press.

Musser, Charles (1990) *The Emergence of Cinema: The American Screen to 1907*, New York: Scribner's.

Salt, Barry (1983) *Film Style and Technology: History and Analysis*, London: Starword.

Uricchio, William and Roberta E. Pearson (1993) *Reframing Culture: The Case of the Vitagraph Quality Films*, Princeton: Princeton University Press.

Vardac, A. Nicholas (1949) *Stage to Screen: Theatrical Origins of Early Film*, Cambridge: Harvard University Press

IAN CHRISTIE

Sfinks

The Polish production company, Sfinks, was established by Aleksander Hertz in Warsaw in 1909 and continued to exist until 1936. Sfinks' initial production comprised *actualités* and **news event films**, beginning probably with *Wzlot aeroplanu w Warszawie* [An Airplane's Ascent in Warsaw] (1909). Its early **multiple-reel** fiction films included *Meir Ezofowicz* (1911), *Wykolejeni* [Aszantka/Human Wrecks] (1913), and Pola Negri's acting debut, *Niewolnica zymysłów* [The Slave of Sin] (1914). **Kosmofilm** merged with Sfinks in 1915, creating Poland's largest and most enduring production company. Sfinks documented the war through cooperation with German companies and produced patriotic films and melodramas through Hertz's death in 1928.

SHEILA SKAFF

shadow theater

The first moving images to be shown on a screen were shadows. Hand shadows were no doubt universal from the earliest times, but formal shadow theater with perforated leather puppets painted in translucent colors, appears to have originated in China or India before the second millennium.

The centuries-old *wayang kulit* shadow plays of Java are set in mythological times, some relating to local festivals and spirits, others dramatizing episodes from the *Ramayana* and *Mahabharata* epics of India. Performances extend through the night, with a single puppeteer manipulating the figures and providing the narration and voices, accompanied by a *gamelan* orchestra of three to five musicians. Stylized puppets and movements are used within a traditional scenario, with contemporary jokes for the clowns. Similar methods have been adopted in Bali and Malaysia. Alternative traditions developed in Turkey, Egypt, North Africa, and Greece, all featuring versions of the Turkish clown Karagoz or Black Eye.

The influence of these shows eventually spread to Europe. Italian shadow showmen performed in Germany and England from the late seventeenth century. France hosted several venues. François Dominique Seraphin opened a show in Versailles in 1784, featuring the traditional shadow play, *The Broken Bridge*; his family continued with shadow puppets until 1879. Eccentric showman Rodolphe Salis's *Le Chat Noir* shadow theater of 1882–1897 delighted Parisian intellectuals and bohemians with elaborate shadow playlets featuring zinc figures designed by Caran D'Ache and other well-known artists. Scenes incorporated clever perspective effects, with **magic lantern** slide projections providing painted backgrounds.

Elsewhere in Paris the animated stories of Emile **Reynaud**'s Théâtre Optique enchanted the public, and from 1895 the **Lumière Cinématographe** and its rivals brought a new form of projected shadows, photographic moving pictures, to the screen. A famous hand-shadow artist and friend of the **Lumières**', Felicien Trewey, took the Cinématographe to London in 1896.

With the introduction of moving pictures in the USA, at least one travelling puppet family, the Lanos, switched from marionettes to shadow figures cut from tar paper as an alternative to the expensive film projector. They revived a century-old show featuring a seascape with burning ship, flashing lighthouse beacon, and lifeboat. Few had seen real moving pictures, and for a while, in 1897, their audiences apparently were satisfied with this folk-art alternative.

English **magician** David Devant's own ingenious hand-shadow caricatures were filmed c. 1903, but otherwise there is little evidence of shadow theater being used as a theme in early moving pictures. Later silent cinema paid occasional homage to the medium, in such films as the German *Warning Shadows* (1923), which featured a traveling showman with a portable shadow theater, and especially in the exquisite series of silhouette films by Lotte Reiniger, including the cinema's first animated feature, *The Adventures of Prince Achmed* (1926).

In 20th-century Thailand, the cinema became known as *Nang* (leather), an allusion to its precursor of leather shadow puppets.

Further reading

Cook, Olive (1963) *Movement in Two Dimensions*, London: Hutchinson.

McPharlin, Paul (1949) *The Puppet Theater in America: A History, 1524–1948*, Boston: Plays, Inc.

STEPHEN HERBERT

Shakespeare films

Shakespeare was probably the literary figure most exploited by the new film industry in Europe and the USA prior to **World War I**. The appeal of Shakespearean material was twofold. First, for an industry hungry for narratives, Shakespeare provided a ready-made pool of well-known stories that could be freely appropriated and made potentially intelligible, even in highly compressed form. Second, Shakespeare's name was culturally weighty and (by association) morally respectable. Presenting Shakespearean subjects enabled the film industry to appropriate this kudos for itself. The moral outrage that films with salacious subjects often provoked made the redeeming effect repeatedly claimed for Shakespeare more desirable. Economic and cultural ambition, therefore, prompted the new medium to stake an early claim on the Bard.

The first film with a Shakespearean subject, shot in 1899 by the **British Mutoscope and Biograph Company**, comprised several short scenes from Sir Herbert Beerbohm Tree's stage production of *King John*. In its London exhibition, it served as an **advertising film**, promoting the stage production, whereas in its exhibition abroad, through the extensive Biograph network, its principal interest was as record of a celebrated English production. The one surviving tableau shows Tree as King John dying with histrionic ceremony in the grounds of Swinstead Abbey. As Tree himself later suggested, these brief scenes, like most early Shakespeare films, assumed an **audience** already familiar with the play.

Within ten years, however, the emphasis had changed. Ads now predicted that spectators who did not know Shakespeare could not fail to be delighted by the latest releases. Shakespeare films, no longer conceived primarily as mute recordings of acclaimed theatrical performances, were becoming more or less autonomous. There were, of course, exceptions. Frank Benson's Shakespeare films with the British Co-operative Cinematograph Company (of which the 1911 *Richard III* survives) deliberately identified themselves as records of particular performances at the Stratford Memorial Theatre and of Benson's own hyper-physical, emphatically gestural **acting style**. Films such as Georges **Méliès**' *Hamlet* (1907), the **Clarendon** *Tempest* (1908), and the many Shakespeare films produced from 1908 on by the American **Vitagraph** Company, however, were more of their moment in having no genesis in a stage production.

They simplified the action and presented whistle-stop narratives, punctuated by explanatory **inter-titles**, explicitly conceived for the cinema. Some were even linked to seasonally festive holidays: although shot in the summer of 1909, Vitagraph's frolicsome *Midsummer Night's Dream* was not released until Christmas Day. The same company's *Macbeth* (1909), by contrast, courted controversy, and its three goriest scenes had to be cut for the film's Chicago exhibition. Indeed, such censoring called into question contemporary claims made about Shakespeare's "improving" influence.

In the USA, **Thanhouser** followed Vitagraph in regularly including Shakespearean subjects amongst its output of prestige films, from A *Winter's Tale* (1910) to *Cymbeline* (1913) and *Two Little Dromios* (1914). Their real triumph, however, came in 1916 with a feature-length *King Lear* starring the eminent Shakespearean stage actor, Frederick Warde. Warde had already made a **multiple-reel** *Richard III* with the Broadway Film Company in 1912 (recently discovered and restored), and was the most well known of the entrepreneurial performers who gave lectures and live recitations as educative accompaniment to Shakespeare screenings in the more prestigious venues.

In Great Britain, the apparent permanence of a film performance was dramatically defied when William George Barker, in accordance with a curious business arrangement made with exhibitors ahead of time, recalled all prints of Tree's *Henry VIII* (1911) and staged a public burning. By contrast, Sir Johnston Forbes-Robertson's grave, unhurried, princely Hamlet was assured a lasting audience by the prestigious 1913 **British Gaumont–Hepworth** release. Within two years of its British release, this *Hamlet* had also been exhibited in Germany, India, and the USA.

In France, **Pathé-Frères**, **Lux** and **Eclipse**'s cultural aspirations were confirmed by films such as *Macbeth* (1909), *Hamlet* (1910), and *The Taming of the Shrew* (1911). In **Gaumont**'s *Le Roi au village* [A Village King Lear] (1911), Louis **Feuillade** imaginatively updated *Lear* to a peasant community in rural France. Other updatings were done more freely. Throughout the period titles were skittishly appropriated for material that bore little resemblance to Shakespeare. Examples include **Edison**'s *Burlesque on Romeo and Juliet*

(1902), Vitagraph's A *Midwinter Night's Dream* (1906), Pathé-Frères' *Roméo se fait bandit* (Romeo as Bandit, with Max **Linder**) (1909), **Selig**'s *The Cowboy and the Shrew* (1911), and **Essanay**'s *When Macbeth Came to Snakeville* (1914).

The Danish company **Nordisk** identified a market for a *Hamlet* (1910) made in Helsingör (Elsinore). Similarly, Italian companies capitalised on the authenticity of Italian settings for films of *The Merchant of Venice*, *Romeo and Juliet*, and *Othello*. Francesca **Bertini** appeared in several **Film d'Arte Italiana** adaptations, including a stencil-colored, tableau-style *Re Lear* (1910) and a cinematically more imaginative, two-reel *Romeo e Giulietta* (1911). **Cines** released a fast-paced but fascinating one-reel *Amleto* (Hamlet), in two versions (1908 and 1910), and a two-reel *Macbeth* (1909), which illustrated well the Italian power to narrate a story visually, free from an over-dependence on wordy intertitles. Paulo Azzuri's *Midsummer Night's Dream* (1913) provided an aura of shimmering, retrospective romance that the **Reinhardt**/Dieterle 1935 *Dream* would later imitate. Although Germany would produce the most memorable Shakespeare films in the later silent period, their most notable pre-war release was Film Industrie Gesellschaft's *Macbeth* (1913), starring the English actor Arthur Bourchier and partly shot in England.

In all approximately a hundred and fifty silent Shakespeare films were made before World War I. Their popularity was not as extraordinary in their own moment as it might now seem. That actors as prestigious and/or popular as Tree, Benson, Warde, Forbes-Robertson, Bertini, Sarah **Bernhardt**, Jean Mounet-Sully, Ermete **Novelli**, Dante Capelli, Rose Coghlan, Julia Swayne Gordon, "Biograph Girl" Florence **Lawrence**, "Vitagraph Girl" Florence **Turner**, Paul Panzer, Charles Kent, and Maurice **Costello** appeared in them was in itself a form of validation. Moreover, Victorian engagements with Shakespeare had prepared the ground. Moving pictures constituted a natural continuation, and stylised exaggeration, of the direction in which 19th-century theatrical productions had long tended. Where theater had been diluting its concentration on language—many productions replacing large sections of poetry with interpolated dialogue-free sequences of pantomimic action—film dispensed with spoken language almost completely. Indeed, American films in particular seemed to adopt the "key phrase, key image" approach that characterized many US stage productions. Where theater had demonstrated a hunger for increasingly elaborate and visually arresting effects, film was able to offer them in new and, in many cases, less labored ways. Where theater had a desire for realistic settings, film was able to supply them effortlessly. And where Victorians had been drawn, through Charles and Mary Lamb, towards an interest in Shakespearean narrative at the expense of the poetry, film's attention to plot offered a culmination of the trend.

Far from being oxymoronic, early Shakespeare films provide striking evidence of how Shakespeare plays were often presented and understood in the late Victorian period.

See also: color; editing: tableau-style; law and the cinema; lecturers; theater, legitimate

Further reading

Ball, Robert Hamilton (1968) *Shakespeare on Silent Film*, New York: Theater Arts Books.
Buchanan, Judith (2003) *Shakespeare on Film*, London: Longman.
Rothwell, Kenneth S. (1999) *Shakespeare on Screen*, Cambridge: Cambridge University Press.
Uricchio, William and Pearson, Roberta E. (1993) *Reframing Culture: The Case of the Vitagraph Quality Films*, Princeton: Princeton University Press.

JUDITH BUCHANAN

Sheffield Photo Co.

Established in 1882 by Frank Mottershaw, the Sheffield Photo & Fine Art Publishing Company began to exhibit moving pictures in 1897. In 1901, Frank Storm Mottershaw was appointed manager of the cinematograph department by his father, and within two years the company was transformed into Sheffield Photo. Important films included *A Daring Daylight Burglary* (1903) *Robbery of the*

Mail Coach (1903), *The Coronation of King Peter of Serbia* (1904) and *The Life of Charles Peace, The Notorious Burglar* (1905). The company's distribution agents were **Butcher's Film Service** in the United Kingdom and **Miles Brothers** in the U.S.A. The last fiction film produced was *Mad Musician* (1909).

VANESSA TOULMIN

Shepard, Archibald

b. 1876?; d. 1925

promoter, exhibitor, USA

Shepard was a traveling tent showman who quickly saw how to exploit moving pictures. As early as 1903–1904, he was presenting Sunday programs of moving pictures and **illustrated songs**, first in the mill town of Lowell, Massachusetts, and then throughout New England. Unlike Lyman **Howe**, he frequently renewed his stock of films and repeatedly revisited cities on his circuit during the year. In 1906, financed by Philadelphia developer, Felix Isman, he began taking long-term leases on theaters to program moving pictures exclusively. Within a year, he had a **cinema chain** of thirty from Atlantic City to Maine and soon was managing the Manhattan Theater on Herald Square, New York City. Although he eventually lost control of the chain, Shepard continued to manage the Standard Theater on Herald Square throughout the 1910s.

RICHARD ABEL

Shipman, Nell (Helen)

b. 1892; d. 1970

actor, scriptwriter, filmmaker, USA

After five years of stage acting with travelling companies and four years of free-lance **screenwriting**, Canadian-born Nell Shipman took to screen acting. *God's Country and the Woman* (1915) made her a **Vitagraph** stock actress until she quit in 1918. This film drew Shipman's attention to the popular fiction writer James Oliver Curwood, with whom she made *Back to God's Country* (1919), and established her screen persona—the outdoor girl living in harmony with nature and wild animals—which she upheld throughout her independent productions in the early 1920s.

ANNETTE FÖRSTER

Sienna, Pedro (Pedro Pérez Cordero)

b. 13 May 1893, San Fernando;
d. 10 March 1972, Santiago

actor, director, Chile

Sienna began his career as a theatrical actor, and premiered in moving pictures with Salvador **Giambatiani**'s company in *El hombre de acero* [The Man of Steel] (1917). His first directorial effort was *Los payasos se van* [The Clowns are Leaving] (1921). He is best remembered for his work as actor, director, and scriptwriter in the most significant Chilean silent film, *El húsar de la muerte* [The Hussar of Death] (1925), declared a national "monument" in 1978. The only Chilean film of this period to survive, *El húsar* is a visually compelling retelling of the exploits of national independence patriot Manuel Rodríguez. In 1966, Sienna was awarded the Premio Nacional del Arte in honor of his contributions to the national theater and cinema.

ANA M. LÓPEZ

Silvio, Alexandre

b. 1872; d. 1935

lecturer, exhibitor, Quebec

Alexandre-Silvio Jobin, known as Alex Silvio (his stage name), was an influential **lecturer** for twenty years in Montreal. At first a comedian and **vaudeville** artist, he became a lecturer around 1907 in the first Montreal moving picture theaters. His mastery of the art of lecturing foreign films in French made him so popular that soon he was

working simultaneously for several theaters. He went on to manage several of his own theaters where he and others he had trained lectured the films featured on vaudeville programs. He had to abandon this work around 1930 because of health problems and died shortly thereafter.

GERMAIN LACASSE

Simplex projector

Designed by Frank Cannock, an experienced maker of **projectors**, and Edwin S. **Porter**, **Edison**'s production chief, the Simplex projector was introduced in 1911 by the Precision Machine Company of New York. An exemplary machine, it would become the American standard, with various improvements, through the 1960s, and be widely used in larger theaters in Europe. Finely made to the highest standards, Model 1 had a fully-enclosed mechanism, adjustable shutter, a revolutionary sliding gate, fire shutter, and precision focussing and lens mounting.

DEAC ROSSELL

Singh, Suchet

b. ?; d.1920

filmmaker, India

Among India's earliest filmmakers, Singh studied filmmaking in the USA at **Vitagraph**. On his return, he started the Oriental Film Manufacturing Company in 1919 and made *Shakuntala* (1920) with the American actress Dorothy Kingdom and cameraman Baron Van Rayvon. However, **Patankar Friends & Company** quickly released its own more indigenous version of the Sanskrit classic, and like many subsequent films with foreign actors and crews, *Shakuntala* was not successful. Singh succeeded in making five more films, including a **newsreel** on the death of Tilak (a leading nationalist leader), before his untimely death in a car crash.

SURESH CHABRIA

Sivan, Casimir

b. 1850; d. 1916

clockmaker, inventor, collector, Switzerland

A Frenchman who settled in Geneva in 1888, Sivan played an important role in the clockmaking trade and may have been the first to showcase the **Edison Kinetoscope** in Switzerland, in March 1895. A year later, he registered the first Swiss patent for a combination camera-projector (now preserved at the George Eastman House). Only a few units must have circulated, and only three films made with them have survived, suggesting a production which remained limited, if not strictly experimental. These films from 1896 constitute, along with **Lavanchy-Clarke's Lumière** films, the incunabula of Swiss cinema. Their subject matter (a modern steam-powered streetcar, divers at the Bains des Pâquis, the entrance to the 1896 National Swiss Fair) displays an iconographic continuity with the photographic snapshot and an emphasis on movement made visible. Sivan also was interested in sound reproduction and collaborated with François **Dussaud**, but apparently did not pursue this research further.

ROLAND COSANDEY

Sjöström, Victor

b. 1879; d. 1960

filmmaker, actor, Sweden

Generally considered the most important filmmaker of the Swedish silent era, Sjöström began and ended his career as an actor, both on stage and on screen.

Born in Sweden, Sjöström moved in 1880 with his family to the USA, where he stayed until 1893. Back in Sweden, he trained as an actor and started working first in Finland and then in provincial Swedish theaters. In 1912, shortly after Mauritz **Stiller**, he was hired by Charles **Magnusson** at **Svenska Biografteatern**, the leading Swedish company. That same year, Paul Garbagni from **Pathé-Frères** was engaged as a tutor for Sjöström, Stiller, and Georg af **Klercker**; then Sjöström

accompanied him on a visit to the Pathé studios in Paris. The close collaboration between Sjöström, Stiller, and cinematographers Julius and Henrik Jaenzon also began in 1912.

Sjöström directed and acted in his first film in 1912, *Trädgårdsmästaren* [The Broken Springrose], from a scenario by Stiller; but the film was banned by the recently-founded Swedish censorship. In 1913, he wrote and directed *Ingeborg Holm*, a social melodrama (based on a theatrical piece by Nils Krok) that caused a general debate on the Swedish welfare system and led to a change in social legislation. Stylistically, the film is pre-classical in its use of filmic space, the omission of off-screen space, and the static deep-stage shooting combined with complex character movements. Still, *Ingeborg Holm* has generally been considered as groundbreaking both aesthetically and thematically, not least for its **staging in depth** and the qualities of the **acting**.

The collaboration between Svenska Bio and Pathé-Frères came to an end in 1913, and the company's attention turned towards Danish cinema. Sjöström made a trip to Copenhagen to study **Nordisk** Films, and inspiration from Danish melodramas came to govern Swedish production policies for several years.

Of the 30 films that Sjöström directed at Svenska Bio before 1917, only three survive. Apart from *Trädgårdsmästaren* and *Ingeborg Holm*, there is *Havsgamar* [Sea Vultures] (1916), written by Danish scriptwriter and director Fritz Magnussen, a history of smuggling and revenge. This film, like *Ingeborg Holm*, is characterised by a staging in depth style, where the movements of the actors articulate the drama.

The 27 lost films, many of them also written and acted by Sjöström, were mostly melodramas, a few of them with a twist of social realism. Towards 1917, a new change in Svenska Bio's production policy towards quality films and literary adaptations led to the so-called "golden age" of Swedish film, with Sjöström's *Terje Vigen* often considered the point of departure.

After a successful stay in Hollywood from 1923 to 1930, Sjöström returned to Sweden as an actor and producer, and made his last performance in Ingmar Bergman's *Smultronstället* [Wild Strawberries] (1957).

See also: editing: spatial relations; editing: temporal relations

Further reading

Fullerton, John (1990) "Spatial and Temporal Articulation in Pre-classical Swedish Film," in Thomas Elsaesser (ed.), *Early Cinema*, 375–388, London: British Film Institute.

Olsson, Jan (1994) "'Classical' vs. 'Pre-classical': *Ingeborg Holm* and Swedish Cinema in 1913," *Griffithiana*, 50: 113–123.

BO FLORIN

Skaarup, Frede

b. 1881; d. 1942

producer, Denmark

A brilliant entertainment entrepreneur, Skaarup was hired as **Fotorama**'s manager in 1908. He ruthlessly built up the company to become the top film distributor in Denmark. As a producer, he sought (within limited budgets) to maximize production values; successful films such as *Den lille Hornblaeser* [The Little Bugle Boy] (1909) allowed him to force exhibitors to pay a percentage of their profits as rental fees rather than a fixed sum—a forerunner of the "monopoly" system. In 1912, Skaarup became a theatrical producer, pouring vast amounts of money into extravagant musical revues during and after **World War I**.

CASPER TYBJERG

Skladanowsky, Max and Emil

b. 1863/1866; d. 1939/1945

inventors, exhibitors, Germany

The sons of a **magic lantern** showman, the Skladanowskys developed a projection device between 1892 and 1895 and named it the Bioscope. Inspired by magic-lantern technology, this two-lens system ran two bands of film simultaneously and projected them alternately at eight frames per second. On 1 November 1895, they projected a 15-minute program to a public audience at the Wintergarden in Berlin. They took their show on a European tour, but the simplicity of the **Lumière** design and the proliferation of **Edison**'s technology soon made the Bioscope obsolete.

SCOTT CURTIS

Skouras, Spyros

b. 1893; d. 16 August 1971

exhibitor, USA

Along with his younger brother George and his older brother Charles, Spyros Skouras came to St. Louis from Greece, around 1911. Two years later, the brothers acquired their first theater, the Olympia. By 1915, they owned but a handful of theaters; by the middle 1920s, however, they held most of St. Louis' **palace cinemas**. Later Spyros would run Twentieth Century Fox, while Charles ran the Fox theater chain, and George the United Artists theater chain.

Further reading

Gomery, Douglas (1984) "The Skouras Brothers," *Marquee*, 16.1: 18–20.

DOUGLAS GOMERY

Slieker, George Christiaan

b. 1861; d. 1945

showman, exhibitor, the Netherlands

On 16 July 1896, the Frisian-born Slieker showed his Grand Théâtre Edison at the annual fair in the Frisian capital of Leeuwarden, becoming one of the first Dutch **itinerant exhibitors**. Later that year Slieker's programs included three films shot by the Amsterdam photographer Machiel Hendricus Laddé, among which was one of the first Dutch fiction films, the comedy *Gestoorde hengelaar* [Disturbed Angler] (1896). Slieker's apparatus was bought from the German **Foersterling** & Co. and called "Edison's Ideal," hence the name of his attraction. After the cinema crisis of 1901–1902, Slieker was surpassed by other **fair/fairground** exhibitors such as the **Mullens** brothers, and he withdrew from the business in 1907.

IVO BLOM

Smalley, Phillips

b. 1875; d. 1939

actor, filmmaker, USA

Smalley's most frequent collaborator was his wife, director, screenwriter and actress, Lois **Weber**. They began working at **Gaumont**'s New York office in 1908. Weber wrote scripts for the company, and the couple both directed and acted in short films there. After working at **Reliance** and **Rex**, the two joined **Universal** in 1912, briefly left to work for Bosworth Productions in 1914, then returned to Universal where Smalley played leading roles in several features directed by Weber. The couple was first known professionally as "The Smalleys," but Weber quickly assumed most of the creative control.

SHELLEY STAMP

Smith, Albert E.

b. 4 June 1875; d. 1 August 1958

exhibitor, producer, executive, USA

The **Vitagraph** Company of America grew out of a partnership between two English-born vaudevillians, Albert E. Smith and J. Stuart **Blackton**. Smith performed as a **magician** and had the technical skill to convert an **Edison projector** into a movie camera. Beginning in 1896, the partners made moving pictures, which they included in their **vaudeville** act. Producing and exhibiting films soon became their primary business. Smith's experience as an entertainer, his technical know-how, and his business ability contributed greatly to the company's success. He was Vitagraph's president from 1916 until it was sold to Warners in 1925.

PAUL SPEHR

Smith, F. Percy

b. 1880; d. 1944/1945

filmmaker, Great Britain

Smith started his working life as a clerk at the Board of Education, while nurturing an interest in microscopy and nature **photography**. He made his first film for Charles **Urban** in 1908, and those that followed combined technical innovation with enormous care (they sometimes took more than a year to make). They also displayed a certain quirkiness, which makes his work stand out from that of other early nature filmmakers such as F. Martin **Duncan** or Oliver **Pike**. Smith's films gained much attention, especially his stop-motion reel, *The Birth of a Flower* (1910), and his films of insects' feats. He filmed in Kinemacolor as well as monochrome and, after working on official films during **World War I**, in the early 1920s gained yet greater acclaim with his "Secrets of Nature" series.

STEPHEN BOTTOMORE

Smith, George Albert

b. 1864; d. 1959

hypnotist, filmmaker, entrepreneur, Great Britain

Born in London, G. Albert Smith first came to public attention as a popular hypnotist in Brighton in the early 1880s. Indeed, he was recognized by the newly founded Society for Psychical Research (SPR) and appointed the Society's private secretary to its Honorary Secretary, Edmund Gurney. In 1887, Gurney carried out a number of "hypnotic experiments" in Brighton, with Smith as the "hypnotiser."

In 1892, by which time he had left the SPR, Smith acquired the lease to St. Ann's Well Garden in Hove. It was here that he developed his interests in the **magic lantern** and, in 1896, acquired his first moving picture **camera**. By the late 1890s, he had developed a successful film production and processing business with the assistance of engineer Alfred **Darling**. Smith's largest customer became the **Warwick Trading Company**, and through this relationship he established a partnership with its managing director, Charles **Urban**.

Smith himself made only the studio shot of the train carriage in *The Kiss in the Tunnel* (1899), but by inserting it into Cecil **Hepworth**'s **phantom rain ride** film, *View From an Engine Front—Train Leaving Tunnel*, he created a new film that demonstrated a clear sense of continuity and simultaneity across three shots. His filmic imagination continued to develop throughout 1900. *As Seen Through the Telescope*, *Grandma's Reading Glass*, *The House That Jack Built*, and *Let Me Dream Again* were remarkable for their interpolative use of close-ups, subjective and objective point-of-view shots, and reverse motion. Through these "experimental" films, Smith was instrumental in the development of continuity **editing**.

Smith's films in the years 1897–1903 were largely **comedies** and adaptations of popular *féeries*/**fairy plays** and tales. This work was influenced by his wife, Laura Bayley, whose career in the popular theater, particularly in pantomime and comic revues, helped Smith better understand visual comedy and the interests of seaside **audiences**. Laura would "star" in many of his most important films, including *Let Me Dream Again* and *Mary Jane's Mishap* (1903).

The two-**color** additive process known as Kinemacolor would dominate the rest of his career. It was launched in Paris and London in 1908 and transformed by Urban into a new enterprise: **Natural Color Kinematograph** Company. The company had success in the period of 1910–1913, producing over 100 short films from its studios in Hove and Nice. However, a patent suit brought against Kinemacolor by William **Friese-Greene** in 1914 led to its collapse and ended Smith's life in the film business.

In the late 1940s, Smith was "discovered" by Georges Sadoul, the French film historian, who invented the concept of the Brighton School to describe the contributions made by Smith and James **Williamson** to the development of film editing.

Further reading

Barnes, John (1996–1998) *The Beginnings of the Cinema in England 1894–1901*, vols. 2–5, Exeter: University of Exeter Press.

Bottomore, Stephen (2002) "Smith versus Melbourne Cooper: An End to the Dispute," *Film History*, 14.1: 57–73.

Gray, Frank (2000) "George Albert Smith's Visions and Transformations: the Films of 1898," in Simon Popple and Vanessa Toulmin (eds.) *Visual Delights: Essays on the Popular and Projected Image in the 19th Century*, 170–180, Trowbridge: Flicks Books.

Sadoul, Georges (1948) *British Creators of Film Technique*, London: British Film Institute.

FRANK GRAY

Smith, John William

b. 1877; d. 1948

cameraman, filmmaker, technician, Great Britain

"Jack" Smith was an optical lanternist who moved into the new field of cinematography in 1899 and soon was shooting **news event films** for Robert **Paul**. In 1907, he became general manager of the **Warwick Trading Company**, run by William **Barker**, and he shot many of the films in *London Day by Day*, its news film show at London's Empire Theater. In 1909, Barker founded **Barker Motion Photography**, and two years later Smith joined him as general manager. He worked on both news events films and dramas, such as the epic reconstruction of Queen Victoria's life, *Sixty Years a Queen* (1913). After Barker's company became involved with official war filming, Smith took personal charge of developing all official film for the Canadian Expeditionary Force. After the war, he remained the company's general manager until 1921, when he transferred to the Williamson Film Printing Company.

NICHOLAS HILEY

Solax

An "independent" film production company established by Alice **Guy** and Herbert Blaché in 1911, initially based in **Gaumont**'s abandoned studio in Flushing (New Jersey). By early 1912, through the **Motion Picture Distributing and Sales Company** (Sales), Solax was releasing two one-reel films per week, nearly all directed by Guy, and investing in construction of a new studio in nearby Fort Lee. The break up of Sales forced Solax to release its films through Film Supply, hastily set up by Blaché, rather than **Universal** or **Mutual**, and the association proved unprofitable, especially as the company began producing **multiple-reel films**. Between 1913 and 1914, Solax gradually was absorbed by Blaché Features, a pale imitation of **Famous Players**, which collapsed with the outbreak of **World War I**.

RICHARD ABEL

sound effects

The majority of moving picture programs in the early years probably had some kind of sound accompaniment, including sound effects that were quite common in Europe and North America. These effects were produced either by individual "traps" or by special **sound machines**, which incorporated a wide array of "noise-makers." Many spectators appreciated the addition of these sound effects to film shows, but antagonism to the practice also developed: some people simply criticized the inappropriateness of effects or the operators' lack of skill, while others suggested that sound effects had no place at all accompanying films. The widespread use of effects seems to have lasted less than half a dozen years, and the high water mark may have passed by the coming of **World War I**.

When the earliest films were presented in the 1890s, they often were shown either in silence or with only **musical accompaniment** or a **lecturer**, but more enterprising showmen soon provided sound effects accompaniment. The practice was inherited from the melodrama **theater** as well as **magic lantern shows** (whether held in halls or on **fairgrounds**), both of which had employed effects for many years. Whatever their venue, many early **Lumière** and **Biograph** shows had accompanying sound effects; in 1906, *Views and Film Index* suggested that **nickelodeon** patrons ought to enjoy effects in such films as those that showed objects

being smashed. Sound effects also were widely used by such showmen as Lyman **Howe**; one touring company (from Louisville, Kentucky) employed fifteen people to produce sounds, music, and vocal accompaniment for its moving pictures.

The standard British guide to cinema music of 1914, *Playing to Pictures*, included a section on sound effects, and described how specific effects could be made using such home-made apparatus as canisters filled with dried peas (for imitating rain falling or trains in motion). Standard noisemakers like bells, sirens, and whistles were soon available through companies like Tress, Yerkes and Co., and Hawkes and Son.

Sound effects could be intentionally quite funny, using some of the comic effects on sale individually or incorporated in effect machines. One of these was a baby cry, apparently used by some drummers whenever they saw a baby in a scene, provoking a big laugh from the audience. Another effect "trap," recommended by one writer, was even more hilarious: costing a mere 10 cents, the "Nose-Blo" was a ridiculously true-to-life imitation of a man blowing his nose.

A heated debate soon developed about the use of sound effects. William **Selig**, on a trip to London in the summer of 1909, told his interviewer that effects ". . . are overdone, and the tendency is to spoil the pictures." Over the next few years frequent criticisms of sound effects appeared in the British and American **trade press**. The complaints were on several different grounds. For one, there were objections that effects were out of sync with the picture. For another, there was the question of whether the *created* sound effect was a true representation of the sound that one would expect from the *real* scene. If sometimes the inaccuracy was merely annoying, the effect also could be quite ludicrously inappropriate: one critic complained of the "continuous use of a motor horn" in a screening of *The Last Days of Pompeii* (1913).

Another objection was that effects were too loud. At its premiere in Melbourne in December 1906, *The Story of the Kelly Gang* was accompanied by elaborate sound effects, but this was not to everyone's taste, one journalist complaining: ". . . there is a deal too much racket in connection with the show." In March 1913, one writer in the *Kine Weekly* was so annoyed at this kind of accompaniment that he described the sounds as "perverted effects" and "cacaphonic embroidery." This also pointed to another more general **problem**: that effects were being used in an unthinking manner, added willy-nilly to anything in the image. Clearly the immediate culprits for this aesthetic quagmire were the operators, frequently unskilled youths—"effects boys"—who could be employed for very low wages. And yet one could not blame them alone; sometimes managers demanded a regime of constant effects.

If many believed that sound effects were getting out of hand, and some even thought that they should be dispensed with altogether, others took a more neutral approach. Neither entirely pro nor entirely con, they argued that one should not just have effects but more *subtle* effects. In 1911, the American critic W. Stephen **Bush** opined that effects could improve a film show, but only if rehearsed and performed carefully. He also suggested that effects should only be introduced that had a "psychological bearing" on the situation as depicted on the screen.

This idea of a "psychological bearing" was an important one. The problem was that sound men were taking their job too literally and supplying sounds for anything that they saw on screen. Using the Bush approach would transform this practice in two ways: first, by not making sounds for some things that *were* within the frame and, second, by making sounds for some things that were not necessarily visible within the frame: for example, a bell tolling off screen that motivates a character.

But there was another question: if one omitted *some* sounds, why not eliminate them all? And, if sound effects were banished, what sound accompaniment would take their place? Some writers suggested that the piano alone was sufficient accompaniment for films, for this instrument could produce many kinds of sound effects. It is clear that this idea of "effect music"—that is, of imitating certain sounds using the piano's keys alone—was to become very important. It became a standard technique for musicians, especially in smaller theaters. In one of the earliest published guide books for cinema musicians, from 1913, Eugene Aherne devoted an entire section to this technique of "effect playing."

Figure 111 Group of technicians performing sound effects behind the screen, 1908. (Courtesy of George Eastman House.)

Apparently, from the 1910s on, effects were used less promiscuously in cinemas of all sizes. But they did not vanish entirely. In the later silent era, live sound effects were to be heard, most often it seems to accompany films which suggested loud noises, especially military films. And pre-recorded sound effects, of course, have been widely used in sound films since the 1930s. The intense debate of these issues in the early period may well have had an impact on the aesthetics of later sound effects practice.

Further reading

Bottomore, Stephen (1999) "An International Survey of Sound Effects in Early Cinema," *Film History*, 11.4, 485–498.

Bottomore, Stephen (2001) "The Story of Percy Peashaker: Debates about Sound Effects in the Early Cinema," in Richard Abel and Rick Altman (eds.) *The Sounds of Early Cinema*, 129–142, Bloomington: Indiana University Press.

Bush, W. Stephen (1911) "When 'effects' are unnecessary noises," *Moving Picture World*, 9 September: 690.

Hall, Emmett Campbell (1911) "Those sound effects," *Moving Picture World*, 23 September: 873–874.

Serk, S. de (1914) *Les Bruits de coulisses au cinema*, Paris: Bibliothèque générale du cinématographie.

STEPHEN BOTTOMORE

sound machines

Sound accompaniment was widely practised in early film shows, including that produced by mechanical devices. These ranged from phonographs to various kinds of player pianos and organs, while effects devices ran from individual "traps" to special machines incorporating a broad spectrum of sound effects.

Phonographs had been around before moving pictures arrived, and were sometimes used to accompany film shows or as an attraction in their own right, especially in the **fairs/fairgrounds**. Megaphones attached to phonographs also were used to attract the public into **nickelodeons**. Automatic pianos too were quite popular with early exhibitors because they would save the cost of the skilled pianist. The Harper Electric Piano Company in North London specifically targeted film exhibitors in its advertising by 1910, and its instruments were priced quite low, at £20.

The first sound effects machine, the "Ciné Multiphone Rousselot," was patented in France in 1907, and concentrated all noisemaking devices in one compact cabinet, including everything from the sounds of cars to the bangs of guns, plus noises of anvils and saws, birds and bells, thunder and horses' hooves. By 1908, **Pathé-Frères** was manufacturing its own multi-noise cabinet; by 1909, in Great Britain, the Allefex machine, invented by A. H. Moorhouse, was being marketed with the claim that it could generate over 50 different noises. One advantage of these devices was that they could be operated by one person, thus reducing the exhibitor's wage costs.

Such machines were made even more comprehensive by combining the effects component with a musical function. The Fotoplayer, manufactured in the USA from around 1912, was a player piano incorporating a small organ and a sound effects chest.

See also: phonography; sound effects

Further reading

"Effect Machines" (1909) *Bioscope*, 8 November: 4.
Meusy, Jean-Jacques (1995) *Paris Palaces, ou le temps des cinémas, 1894–1918*, Paris: AFRHC/ CNRS Editions.

STEPHEN BOTTOMORE

South Africa

Moving pictures first came to South Africa in early 1895 by way of **Edison**'s **Kinetoscope**. These apparatuses were sold to Lingard's Waxworks, which then displayed them in the cities of Durban, Johannesburg, and Cape Town. Because South African **music-hall** impresarios went to look for new acts in Great Britain, it was the international variety artist-illusionist Carl Hertz who first brought a **projector** (made by Robert **Paul**) to show moving pictures as part of his act, which opened at the Empire Palace of Varieties in Johannesburg, on 11 May 1896, and then toured widely. Other apparatuses soon followed, including the Vitagraph in Johannesburg in September, and the Theatergraph in Cape Town in December. Only in early 1897 did the **Cinématographe Lumière** arrive, and its programs initially were not shown in a music hall but in the Grand National Hotel's billiard room in Johannesburg. It was not as successful, however, as other projection systems, which came the following year. The Zenomettascope (a modified Cinématographe), for instance, toured the country, and one of the pioneers in South African cinema, J. B. Fitts, introduced projected moving pictures (from Great Britain) to his variety acts in the Good Hope Hall in Cape Town and then toured other big cities in the interior. Early in 1898, Frank Fillis used new Lumière and **Joly**–Normandin projectors to program moving pictures exclusively in Cape Town. One of his films, Georges **Méliès'** *The Temptation of St. Anthony* (1898) created a scandal, and for the first time critical articles were written about moving pictures in South African **newspapers**.

Before the turn of the century, films were imported from Europe and the USA. In 1898, after buying a **camera** from **Warwick Trading**, Edgar Hyman became the first South African to shoot scenes of Johannesburg and its surroundings as well as of Cape Town: *Kaapstad, van een trem-ker gezien* [Cape Town Seen from a Tram-Car] and *Scena op de Kaapsche Spoorweg* [Scenes on the Cape Railway]. He also filmed Paul Kruger, President of the Boeren, and, in January 1899, showed his film to Kruger, along with a number of Warwick films. The South African Biograph and

Mutoscope Company was one of the first film companies to emerge, premiering the large-format **Biograph** moving pictures to the Johannesburg public on 24 May 1899. With the outbreak of the Boer War, the company distributed films made by British as well as South African filmmakers, all of which made a prestigious tour of the country's important cities.

The war and the presence of thousands of British soldiers led to a sudden increase in film exhibition in the large British cities on the coast. By 1902, however, **itinerant exhibitors** had spread moving pictures throughout the country. In 1908, the first theaters showing moving pictures exclusively opened in Johannesburg, Durban, and Cape Town. Yet South Africans had to wait until 1910 to see the first indigenous fiction film, *The Great Kimberley Diamond Robbery* or *The Star of the South*, produced by the Springbok Film Company. One of the most successful companies, African Film Productions, in 1913, introduced its own **newsreel** called *African Mirror*, which lasted until 1984. One of the company's directors, Harold Show, then made the first South African **multiple-reel/feature** film, *De Voortrekkers* [Winning a Continent] (1916)—perhaps influenced by D. W. **Griffith**'s *The Birth of a Nation* (1915)—with the racist aim of bringing the Boers and British together in one country against one enemy: black South Africans.

Further reading

Barnes, John (1983) *Pioneers of the British Film*, III, London: Bishopsgate.
Berry, Donald (1947) "South Africa and the Cinema," *Sight and Sound* 16: 93–95.
Gutsche, Thelma (1972) *The History and Social Significance of Motion Pictures in South Africa 1895–1940*, Cape Town: Howard Timmins.

GUIDO CONVENTS

Spain

The **Cinématographe Lumière** was first presented in Madrid on 13–14 May 1896, then in Barcelona in December, at the Napoléon photographers center. Even earlier, there had been presentations of other shows of "animated photographs," such as the "Animatograph" and the "kinetograph." In June 1896, Alexandre **Promio**, a Lumière operator, arrived in Spain to make several films (in Barcelona, Madrid, etc.) which were added to the company's general catalogue in Lyon.

Moving pictures attracted the interest of businessmen and photographers. The pioneers of Spanish cinema included Antonio Tramullas (who worked at the Napoléon center in Barcelona and for the Coiné company in Zaragoza), Fructuoso **Gelabert**, Louis Josep Sellier (a Frenchman living in Galicia), Albert **Marro**, Eduardo Jimeno (who shot what was considered the first Spanish film, *Leaving Mass at the Pilar in Zaragoza*), Segundo de **Chomón**, and Angel García Cardona (who worked for the **Cuesta** company in Valencia).

The first theaters devoted to showing moving pictures were established between 1898 and 1901. National production increased, but the films were largely nonfiction: city views, bullfights, folk dances, military parades, and musical performances. By 1905, Barcelona and Valencia had become the centers for film production and distribution to the whole of Spain. As the market for moving pictures expanded, **Pathé-Frères** and **Gaumont** opened branches in Barcelona, managed by Louis **Garnier** and M. Huet, respectively. In Barcelona, moving pictures were so popular that, by 1911, the city had 139 picture theaters for a population of 500,000 people.

Imported films quickly filled Spanish screens and were well received, as French and Italian melodramas became the basic references for Spanish **audiences**. Spanish production lacked a strong industrial infrastructure, and many companies closed after making very few films. Consequently, theaters preferred to show foreign films rather than risk relying on Spanish products. The few production companies that survived for long were Cuesta, in the Valencia, and Films Barcelona, **Hispano Films**, **Barcinógrafo**, and Chomón & Fuster in Barcelona.

Between 1910 and 1915, Spanish filmmakers worked on very different artistic levels. In Madrid, Benito Perojo directed and starred in films centered on the "Peladilla" character, modeled on Charlie **Chaplin**. In Valencia, Angel García Cardona and Joan M. Codina made films drawing on Spanish folk traditions. In Barcelona, the capital of Spanish cinema up until 1918, the outstanding figure was Chomón, who, in 1901, already was specializing in coloring Pathé films for distribution and making *actualités*. In 1910, Chomón tried, unsuccessfully, to apply the industrial system of Pathé to the Chomón & Fuster company. Magí Muriá and Adrià **Gual** opted for a cultural cinema, adapting literary works featuring prestigious stage actors, such as Margarita Xirgu, and taking great care over the composition of shots or tableaux. Albert **Marro** and Joan M. Codina specialized in themes related to traditional festivals (bullfighting) and folk theater, highly popular with audiences. Codina also worked for Films Barcelona, where he demonstrated his technical mastery in films such as *Lucha de corazones* [The Battle of Hearts] (1913). He later directed two films for Condal Films, starring the dancer Tórtola Valencia: *Pasionaria* (1915) and *Pacto de lágrimas* [Pact of Tears] (1915).

From 1908, especially in Catalonia, there were anti-cinema campaigns, instigated by the church and intellectuals such as Eugeni d'**Ors** and Ramon Rucabado. Moving pictures were accused of encouraging immoral behavior, causing eye sicknesses, and having little artistic merit. Only nonfiction films were defended as valuable or useful. All these anti-cinema campaigns originated from the announcement of the first legal documents that implanted censorship in Spain. In late 1912, the first Royal Decree (28/XI/1912) was issued, outlining measures to regulate the production and exhibition of moving pictures in Spain. The reason behind the government's decision to issue the decree was a fire at a theater in Bilbao in which forty-five people died. In 1913, two more Royal Decrees (19/X/1913 and 31/XII/1913) were published, making the earlier censorship measures more precise and covering other social issues related to cinema. In 1915, the magazine *España*, edited by the philosopher Ortega y Gasset, included a section for film reviews written by Alfonso Reyes and Martín Luis Guzmán under the pseudonym "Fósforo" (the match). From then on, cinema was gradually more accepted by writers and intellectuals as a symbol of modern life.

See also: law and the cinema; distribution: Europe

Further reading

González López, P. (1987) *Els anys daurats del cinema clàssic a Barcelona (1906–1923)*, Barcelona: Institut del Teatre/Edicions 62.

Minguet Batllori, J. M. (1992) "L'Eglise et les intellectuels espagnols contre le cinéma," in Roland Cosandey, André Gaudreault, and Tom Gunning (eds.) *Une invention du diable? Cinéma des premiers temps et religion*, 12–20, Sainte-Foy/Lausanne: Les Presses de l'Université Laval/Editions Payot.

Minguet Batllori, J. M. (2004) "Early Spanish cinema and the problem of modernity," Film History, 16.1: 92–107.

Pérez Perucha, J. (1995) "Narración de un aciago destino (1896–1930)," in *Historia del cine español*, 19–121, Madrid: Ed. Cátedra.

JOAN M. MINGUET

spectatorship: issues and debates

Strictly speaking, "the spectator" names the abstract, hypothetical entity addressed by films. It should be distinguished conceptually both from concrete individual viewers and from the **audience** they compose, but it ought not be opposed to either. There could be no spectatorship without viewers, and it would make little sense to talk about moviegoers as such if films failed to enlist their interest. When and if viewers respond as though films address them personally, they effectively adopt the interests that films expect spectators to have. By this reasoning, "spectatorship" designates an ideological process. During the final quarter of the 20th century, cinema studies worried this logic to the point of exhaustion—without rejecting it. Early cinema studies made a particularly decisive contribution when it identified an historical shift from the addressee imagined by the first decade or so of movies to that imagined by the emerging feature film. Scholars initially strove to distinguish early cinema's addressee from the spectator presumed to be absorbed, pacified, or deluded by the **classical Hollywood cinema**. Inevitably, however, that distinction began to revise accounts of the latter addressee as well. The need to specify the various ways in which cinema has worked ideologically displaced the imperative to establish that dominant cinema was inherently ideological. Through attention to the histories of film form, exhibition, reception, and contemporary social life, early cinema studies reoriented field-wide arguments about what it means to watch a film.

In nearly all its variations, "spectatorship" focuses attention on the textual aspect of reception: what viewers share because they experience similar information in a relatively consistent manner, regardless of other characteristics that may serve to identify and group them—e.g., demographic distinctions, fandom, and consumption practices. For this reason, it is misleading to oppose the spectator to "real" viewers. Films necessarily address an imaginary entity, but not a "fake" one. Social consequences follow when a form of address succeeds on a mass scale. Because it differentiates that aspect of moviegoing dictated by movies themselves from the innumerable other ways audience members might be described, the spectator-viewer couplet allows—indeed compels—us to ask: How does cinema enlist the desire of so many different viewers? To what extent and in what ways do films control how viewers make sense of them? To what extent and in what ways have films defined the identities of those who watch them? What difference did it make, historically, for millions of persons to be addressed in a relatively consistent manner as members of a movie audience?

Possible answers range widely, and it bears emphasizing that it takes more than empirical research and textual interpretation to secure them. The concept of spectatorship requires scholars to commit, implicitly or explicitly, to one or another theory of film form (what the significant traits of "the movies" are), of the human subject (how I come to think of myself as an "I"), of culture (how a group's way of life relates to the information it shares), and of mass mediation (what it means that widely disseminated information is mass produced for profit by relatively few). Not every argument about spectatorship can be expected to give an exhaustive account of its conceptual underpinnings. Nonetheless, one should acknowledge

that such arguments occur in inherently difficult conceptual territory. The stakes are high, and the debaters do not always agree on premises.

When told in brief, the history of concern with spectatorship begins in the legendary 1970s—a lost moment of intellectual foment to which cinema studies feels ever compelled to return. As the story goes, "the spectator" arrived when Jean-Louis Baudry, Stephen Health, Christian Metz, Laura Mulvey, and their contemporaries appropriated and synthesized the account of semiotic structure pioneered by linguist Ferdinand de Saussure, the model of ideology proposed by Marxist Louis Althusser, the theory of subjectivity developed by revisionist psychoanalyst Jacques Lacan, and the accounts of realism and narrative developed by semiologist Roland Barthes. Although several surveys of "the spectator's" career are available, most significantly complicate the legend by emphasizing the rich political, intellectual, and institutional histories that formed the key figures and established their importance for others.

Regardless of what produced and privileged the spectator as an object of study, 1970s scholarship endowed it with four traits that proved decisive for its subsequent development. First, the "ordinary" (Hollywood) film was identified as a species of the "classical realist text," with prototypes in *quatrocento* painting and the 19th-century novel (e.g., Balzac). Accordingly, its spectator was a version of the bourgeois individual. Second, spectatorship was described as a "position" or "point-of-view" defined by twofold analogy with the camera's "look" and with the looks of characters on screen. Third, this position was said to offer an illusion of mastery over the visual field, an illusion at once psychologically satisfying to the spectator and ideologically beneficial to cinema as a capitalist institution. Fourth, by paying attention to who looked at whom on screen, Mulvey described the spectator position as implicitly masculine. This last contention proved stunningly productive; the disjuncture between a male spectator and the obvious fact of women viewers impelled what became the definitive spectator-viewer dialectic.

In a sense, the subfield of early cinema studies begins with the argument that the first three of the above-mentioned traits, and possibly the fourth, simply do not characterize the earliest films.

In a 1979 lecture, later published as "Primitivism and the Avant-Gardes: A Dialectical Approach," Noël Burch proposed that an historical break separates a "Primitive Mode of Representation" (PMR) from an "Institutional Mode of Representation" (IMR) by arguing that the two modes imply entirely different kinds of spectators.

Historians had already challenged the notion that film form evolved swiftly and logically towards its telos in the Hollywood feature. Burch took particular advantage of the discovery that Edwin S. **Porter**'s *Life of an American Fireman* (1903) did not include the breakthrough editing attributed to it in later histories. Rather than cross-cutting to produce the impression of continuous action, Porter showed interior and exterior shots of the fireman's rescue in series. In this way and others, Burch claimed, the film was consistent with the practices of the PMR, which addressed a spectator who remained "external" to the film's world. Neither absorbed in a fantasy of seeing this world from the superior perspective of a ubiquitous camera nor encouraged to identify with the thoughts and feelings of the characters, this spectator received minimal help in constructing the narrative and encountered spatio-temporal relations at odds with the legacy of novelistic realism.

That Porter's editing had apparently been considered a mistake and later "corrected," Burch argued, indicates a fundamental incompatibility between the norms of early spectatorship and viewers habituated to the IMR. What later viewers saw as an errant, alternative, or immature practice was, for the film's first audiences, a dominant practice. Yet the PMR did include harbingers of the IMR within in it. Burch identified a genre of early films in which someone (often a man) peers through a keyhole at someone else (usually a woman). These keyhole films, he proposed, offered early lessons in the sort of voyeuristic identification with the camera that would later prevail. This provoked argument over whether or not early cinema's gender arrangements generally differed from those of classical Hollywood. Overall, then, the PMR-IMR distinction reproduced and strengthened the account of the spectator developed by the 1970s synthesis. By locating this normative spectator on one side of a major historical divide, however, it significantly complicated the proposition that cinematic spectatorship could be traced directly to realist novels and paintings.

In the mid-1980s, Tom Gunning and André Guadreault worked to banish the evolutionary metaphor that lingered in descriptions of early cinema as "primitive." They recast the PMR as a **cinema of attractions**. Gunning particularly contradicted Burch's contention that identification with the camera does not occur in the earlier period. The appeal of the cinema of attractions, he argued, derived precisely from the camera's unified viewpoint, which allowed movies to address a curious spectator directly. Gunning also placed greater emphasis on narrative than did Burch, specifically opposing the spectacular appeal of early films to the narrative absorption cultivated by the feature. In this way, he defined early cinema spectatorship in positive terms (it was more than what the IMR was not) and suggested that classical Hollywood movies might encourage a permutation of the spectatorship of attractions whenever they interrupt their narratives to shock and thrill.

The intersection of a number of research concerns allowed Miriam Hansen to reframe the problem of early cinema spectatorship decisively in 1991. Perhaps most importantly, new histories of exhibition practices had emphasized the locally variable character of moviegoing before and during the **nickelodeon** period. Accordingly, Hansen identified the rise of the Hollywood feature as "the elaboration of a mode of narration that makes it possible to anticipate a viewer through particular textual strategies, and thus to standardize empirically diverse and to some extent unpredictable acts of reception" (16). Hansen accepted the notion of a cinema of attractions, but her formulation called into question the degree to which it could be thought of as uniformly addressing a spectator. Before 1910 or so, Hansen noted, no one wrote about a motion picture "spectator." Instead, commentators characterized audiences as different sorts of groups. By this logic, the spectator was less a discovery of 1970s theorists than an abstraction generated by filmmaking practice in the 1910s. When Hansen emphasized standardization as the feat accomplished by the emergent feature film's address, moreover, she defined the relationship between films and diverse viewers as an inherently contentious one. If she continued to characterize as dominant the male spectator of earlier criticism, for instance, she also argued that movies generated an "alternative public sphere" for women, a claim she supported through readings of later Rudolph Valentino films and their fan culture.

Hansen's methods and models informed a great deal of subsequent work, especially in the way she used a variety of social histories to situate the emergence of spectatorship in a turn-of-the-century USA roiled by **migration/immigration**, rampant consumerism, and changing gender roles. In the wake of her work, it became increasingly important to understand the information on screen as addressing the concerns of particular audiences at specific historical moments, even after 1910. The idea of a single position generated through identification with the camera lost some of its clout. The "ordinary film" was fractured into an ensemble of overlapping genres with more or less distinct addressees (e.g., sensational **melodramas**, slapstick **comedies**, moral uplift films, suffrage films, **serials**,). Similarly, the shift from one historical "mode" of spectatorship to another looked less like a sharp break than a prolonged and ragged tear. The spectator's implied gender remained a central concern, but questions of racial, ethnic, and national identity became equally urgent. Women moviegoers appeared as a new demographic entity

structurally included in cinema's address rather than as—or in addition to being—alienated inhabitants of a male spectator position. No longer a synonym for the confident subject of bourgeois realism, "the spectator" looked more like the disoriented masses of **modernity**, its subjectivity shaped by **urbanization**, rapid **transportation**, commodification, and shifting definitions of private and public spheres. It became common to disagree over how spectatorship managed differences among various sorts of viewers rather than whether or not it absorbed a singular subject. Although hardly the only subfield to reconsider spectatorship in these ways, early cinema studies has left an indelible mark on the field as a whole by requiring concrete attention to its history.

See also: editing: spatial relations; editing: temporal relations; multiple-reel/feature films

Further reading

Burch, Noël (1986) "Primitivism and the Avant-Gardes: A Dialectical Approach," in Philip Rosen (ed.) *Narrative, Apparatus, Ideology*, 483–506, New York: Columbia University Press.

Charney, Leo and Schwartz, Vanessa R. (eds.) (1995) *Cinema and the Invention of Modern Life*, Berkeley, University of California Press.

Gunning, Tom (1990) "The Cinema of Attractions: Early Film, its Spectator and the Avant-Garde" and "'Primitive' Cinema: A Frame-Up? Or, The Trick's on Us," in Thomas Elsaesser and Adam Barker (eds.) *Early Cinema: Space, Frame, Narrative*, 56–62, 95–103, London, British Film Institute.

Hansen, Miriam (1991) *Babel and Babylon: Spectatorship in American Silent Film*, Cambridge: Harvard University Press.

Mayne, Judith (1993) *Cinema and Spectatorship*, New York: Routledge.

Rabinovitz, Lauren (1998) *For the Love of Pleasure: Women, Movies, and Culture in Turn-of-the-Century Chicago*, New Brunswick: Rutgers University Press.

Williams, Linda (ed.) (1995) *Viewing Positions: Ways of Seeing Film*, New Brunswick: Rutgers University Press.

Figure 112 Wladyslaw T. Benda "They were permitted to drink deep of oblivion of all the trouble in the world"—illustration for Mary Heaton Vorse, "Some Moving Picture Audiences," *Outlook*, 24 June 1911.

MARK GARRETT COOPER

Spencer, Cozens

b. ?; d. 1930

exhibitor, producer, director, Australia

Charles Cozens Spencer arrived in Australia from New York in 1903, touring with the "Great American Wonderscope" (later "Theaterscope") and investing in some of the earliest permanent cinemas. Forming a production company, he made both nonfiction films, including the very successful Burns-**Johnson** fight (1908), and fiction films (from 1910), until his company was incorporated into **Australasian Films**. Just before that merger, he opened Australia's largest film studio in the Sydney suburb of Rushcutter's Bay in 1912, where Raymond **Longford** served as production supervisor and Ernest **Higgins** as chief cameraman. When Australasian Films withdrew from feature production, Spencer retired from the industry.

INA BERTRAND

Spoor, George K.

b. 1872, Chicago; d. 1953, Chicago

exhibitor, producer, investor, USA

Spoor first became interested in moving pictures in the late 1890's when he opened his Kinodrome service in Chicago, supplying films and projectors to **vaudeville** houses and **amusement parks** throughout the Midwest. He also sponsored the **projector** and **camera** inventions of Edward H. Amet and later Donald Bell and Bert Howell. In 1904, he founded National Film Renting, which then became an important rental exchange for the growing **nickelodeons**. In 1907, with G. M. **Anderson**, Spoor co-founded **Essanay Film Manufacturing Company**, soon one of the major firms making up the **Motion Picture Patents Company**. After Essanay ceased production in 1918, Spoor devoted much of his energy and money in a wide film process he called Naturalvision.

ROBERT S. BIRCHARD

sports films

Sport and film were intimately connected from the very inception of moving pictures, and sport and the demands of sports **audiences** created some of the most significant of early film productions.

Eadweard **Muybridge**'s first photographic sequences were of Leland Stanford's trotting horses, and many of his subsequent **chronophotographic** studies employed athletes from the San Francisco Athletic Club. Etienne-Jules **Marey** worked with the pioneer of French gymnastics, Georges **Demenÿ**, on his studies of human locomotion. Boxers were among the first subjects of the **Edison Kinetoscope**, and the first commercial sports film was Edison's *The Leonard-Cushing Fight* (1894), followed later that year by *Corbett and Courtney Before the Kinetograph*. The urge to show **boxing films** on a big **screen** (attracting a greater paying audience), led the **Latham** brothers to develop their Eidoloscope projector, which debuted in May 1895 with a boxing match. The film took advantage of the "Latham Loop" projection device to extend the film's duration, and by 1897 Enoch Rector was able to film the world heavyweight bout between James **Corbett** and Bob Fitzsimmons in its ninety-minute entirety, employing three **cameras** positioned in parallel.

In Great Britain, the first commercial film production was Birt **Acres** and Robert **Paul**'s film of the Oxford v Cambridge boat race in March 1895. Paul's film of the 1896 Derby was shown in **music halls** within a day of the race having been run, and its ecstatic reception announced the arrival of moving pictures in Great Britain. Soccer matches were filmed in Britain from the 1890s, and exclusive rights to film major games were soon hotly contested. Regional filmmakers would film local games with regularity, notably **Mitchell & Kenyon** in the north of England. Cricket challenged the ingenuity of filmmakers with its games lasting for days, but descriptive shots of stars such as Prince Ranjitsinhji and W. G. Grace in practice were gradually followed by necessarily compressed reports on Test matches. The emerging art of **editing** was as evident in the reduced reports of soccer, cricket and baseball games as it was in the fiction film. Only in boxing were special films covering entire bouts screened, with shortened versions made for wider exhibition.

In the USA, **American Mutoscope and Biograph** and Edison covered football, baseball, basketball, motor racing, athletics and the America's Cup yacht race. Films of baseball's World Series were especially popular, and **Essanay**'s films of the 1908, 1909, and 1910 World Series demonstrated increasing camera coverage and editing prowess to produce films of dramatic tension and evident sporting prowess.

Moving pictures and the modern Olympic Games emerged in the same year, 1896, although those first Games were not filmed. Marey and his associates produced chronophotographic studies of American athletes at the Paris 1900 Games, but it was not until the intermediate Games of 1906 that the industry took an interest. **Pathé-Frères**' coverage of the 1908 and 1912 Games (in London and Stockholm) employed increasing camera coverage and a movement away from the ritual and ceremony to engaging records of individual sports and athletes.

The most significant sports film of the early cinema period was that of the Jack **Johnson** v Jim Jeffries world heavyweight boxing match in 1910. The mere fact of its existence shocked white America, since the winner, the black Johnson, could now be imported into every neighborhood. Censorious authorities worldwide were similarly alarmed at the film's message of black superiority. The subsequent USA ban on the transportation of all **boxing films** (enacted in 1912) reflected not only the shock at Johnson's victory, but the growing power and influence of cinema itself.

See also: news event films

Further reading

McKernan, Luke (1996) "Sport and the First Films," in Christopher Williams (ed.) *Cinema: The Beginnings and the Future*, 107–116, London: University of Westminster Press.

McKernan, Luke (1998) "Lo Sport Nel Cinema Muto/Sport and the Silent Screen," *Griffithiana*, 64: 81–141 .

LUKE McKERNAN

staging in depth

In the earliest fiction films, the characters and significant actions were usually arranged across the screen, at a more or less equal distance from the camera. In the 1910s, especially in Europe, filmmakers began to organize long scenes by placing some characters and actions behind one another, and moving them from place to place in a deep set.

Staging in depth should not be confused with a great depth of field, as scenes can be deeply staged with some of the objects and characters in sharp focus while others are blurred. In the period covered by this encyclopedia, commentators suggest that everything visible in the frame should be kept in sharp focus. In practice, scenes with slightly soft foregrounds and backgrounds are not uncommon, but these seem to be tolerated accidents or defects rather than deliberate attempts at a shallow style, although the persistence of soft backgrounds in films shot in 1913 by G. W. **Bitzer** for **Biograph** in California (where conditions should not have forced the cameraman to open the diaphragm and thus lose depth of field) suggests that he may have been deliberately following a still-**photography** prescription, occasionally cited in cinematography manuals, which called for such a distinction in focus to make the foreground objects stand out. With film stocks of this period and the standard 50mm lens used in fiction film making, it was not difficult to maintain sharp focus from the rear to the front of even the most deeply staged setups in full scene shots, using artificial **lighting** in Northern climes, or unassisted daylight in Southern ones. Thus staging in depth as practiced in this period is more or less unaffected by technical problems of depth of field, and these will be ignored in the rest of this entry.

From the beginning, *actualité* cameramen had set up their cameras so that people, animals, and vehicles moved on a line relatively close to the lens axis, simply so that such moving subjects stayed in view for most of the two to three minutes of the films. Such compositions persisted in **actualité** films, reaching an apogee in the **phantom train ride** films shot from the front of a moving vehicle, where parallax effects produce a hallucinatory stereoscopic impression of depth. But in "composed views," most available models encouraged lateral compositions, with all significant elements along a line perpendicular to the lens axis. In still photography, "wide angularism" was condemned for the grotesque contrast in size of close and distant subjects in deep-staged wide-angle shots; and, while the live theater promoted a sense of depth in scenic vistas, often using false perspective to achieve it, the need to create a similar picture for spectators seated at a wide range of positions in front of the stage, and the false perspective itself, forced actors to keep to a single front plane, that of their "true size." In studio shooting, early fiction filmmakers followed this model, although Georges **Méliès** occasionally allowed entering and exiting characters to pass close to the camera—as in *Bagarre entre journalists* [The Fight in the Courtroom at Rennes] in the 1899 *Dreyfus* series. With the development of the **chase film**, action on location exteriors began to be staged in depth, for the same reasons that encouraged such compositions in *actualités*, but studio-shot chases continued to use lateral staging—as in the pursuit of the astronauts by the Selenites in Méliès' *Le Voyage dans la lune* [Trip to the Moon] (1902).

The impetus to deeper staging came from the tendency to film basic scene shots (ignoring cut-ins to "magnified views" and certain special closer views like opening and closing emblematic shots) from closer and closer to the action. The narrower playing area implied by such closer shots (2.5 meters at the front of a shot framing characters from head to toe, assuming use of the 50 mm lens standard for studio shooting in this period, 1.5 meters in the even closer shots that became the norm in the USA by 1911) forced filmmakers to place players one behind another, so the action had to be staged with a certain amount of depth. Once this happened, perhaps first evident in such **Film d'Art** productions as *L'Assassinat du Duc de Guise* [The Assassination of the Duke de Guise] (1908) and *La Tosca* (1909), filmmakers grasped a difference in principle between staging for the camera and live staging, that all the spectators are seated in the same imaginary place in relation to a projected image, and so one of the main barriers to deep staging in the theater did not exist for film: the whole audience would see every character in the frame visible through the camera lens, no matter how small the angular separation of those characters might have been. This allowed for elaborate blocking of different objects and characters on different planes of the picture, encouraging and even requiring a much more precise *mise-en-scène* than had ever prevailed on the live stage.

How staging in depth was used, and its overall significance as a stylistic option, changed in different ways in different filmmaking traditions as the 1910s progressed, and these different evolutions depended on differences in the development of the film scene. So long as this was conceived as a single visual unit (though occasionally interrupted by cut-ins), the long shot would be used for the high points of the action, and that action would characteristically be staged in depth, with lighting and **set design** emphasizing a single complex playing area, and the characters moving around the set and blocking one another on occasion to emphasize the significant elements of the action at each moment. This is how, for example, Mario **Caserini** staged General Holbein's dinner-party in **Gloria**'s *Ma l'amor mio non muore!* [Love Everlasting] (1913)—here the cameraman emphasized the depth in the scene by using a shorter lens, around 35 mm. Guests arrive and introductions are made at a table and chairs front right; later, the guests eat dinner in a rear left alcove; after dinner, while Holbein and his fellow officers drink their *digestifs* at the table front right, Elsa Holbein (Lyda **Borelli**) plays the piano midground left for her special guest, the adventurer Moïse Sthar; the officers then go off to a rear right alcove to look at secret plans, observed by Sthar from his place by the piano (here, too, there are cut-ins to isolate Sthar and the alcove). Later, when Elsa and Holbein have left front right to see out the other guests, Sthar goes to the rear right alcove, and, in a cut-in, steals the plans, returning to his place at the piano to take his leave before Elsa and her father return in the full framing. Lighting is fairly uniform in this scene (except in the right alcove, which is dark except for a practical arc in a table lamp in the cut-ins), but in Léonce **Perret**'s *Le Roman d'un mousse* [The Curse of Greed] (1914), the sets representing rooms in the house of the Comtesse de Ker-Amor and the Tango-Palace nightclub have split levels, drapes, and practical arcs in the lighting fixtures to create sub-arenas of action in a largely chiaroscuro visual field. Similar effects of such blocking in scenes can be found in Louis **Feuillade**'s *Juve contre Fantômas* (1913) and, more subtly, in Victor **Sjöström**'s *Ingeborg Holm* (1913). Other directors who favor deep-staged scenes fill them with furniture and drapes to create a complex arena for the action, notably Evgenii **Bauer**, as in *Child of the Big City* (1914), and Franz **Hofer**, as in *Die schwarze Kugel* [The Black Ball] (1913).

Not all filmmakers treated the scene in this way. Although for a short period in 1909, in the films he directed for Biograph, D. W. **Griffith** experimented with arranging an ensemble of actors in depth, probably under the influence of Film d'Art—as in the recognition scene in *A Baby's Shoe*—by the end of the same year, alternation between different actions and cutting in and out of doors in continuous actions gave rise to series of shots showing only fractions of the scene which are generally shallow-staged, though sometimes, especially in **western** exteriors, this shallow action is set up in front of a distant spectacular background, as in *Ramona* (1910). For others, although this treatment of the scene did not reach its full development until after the period considered here, long shots became "establishing shots," and most of the action in a scene would be in closer shots framing one or two characters, often both at the same distance from the camera. In either case, what depth there was became a matter of a spectacular setting for the action (as it had been for 19th-century spectacular theater), while the action itself was relatively shallow.

Broadly speaking, then, this means that staging the action in depth tended to be a European phenomenon because more European filmmakers stuck to the integral notion of a scene, while editing replaced its function of articulating the action for an audience in American films. However, European films which rely heavily on editing, such as Benjamin **Christensen**'s *Hævnens nat* [The Night of Vengeance] (1915) and Giovanni **Pastrone**'s *Tigre reale* [The Royal Tiger] (1916)—in contrast with the same director's *Cabiria*, (1914)—tend towards a shallower staging of the action. And not all American filmmakers adopted the shallow-staged style. Whereas the films produced by the **Vitagraph** Company of America in

that early 1910s do not have the uniformity that Griffith imposed on Biograph films, and some Vitagraph directors, notably Ralph **Ince**, favor highly edited and hence shallow-staged scenes, other directors such as Van Dyke Brooke, while their scenes are relatively short (as compared with those in *Ma l'amor mio non muore!*), do not break them up by either alternating editing or scene dissection, and use a low camera close to a scene in which some characters near the front have their backs to the camera—as in *A Friendly Marriage* (1911) and *The First Violin* (1912)—creating a space much more tightly packed than that of the party scene in *Ma l'amor mio non muore!*, but still a deep-staged one. Later, some directors of feature films in the USA, notably Maurice **Tourneur** in *The Whip* (1917), continue to stage climactic action in deep-staged long shots, even while using many shots in a scene.

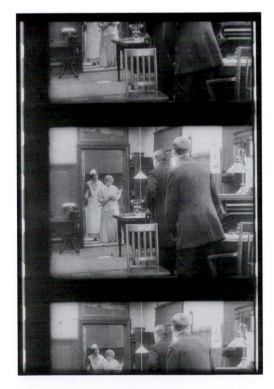

Figure 113 Frame enlargement from *Ingeborg Holm*, (Victor Sjöström, 1913). (Courtesy of John Fullerton.)

See also: editing: spatial relations; editing: temporal relations; framing: camera distance and angle

Further reading

Abel, Richard (1994) *The Ciné Goes to Town: French Cinema, 1896–1914*, Berkeley: University of California Press.

Bordwell, David (1995) *On the History of Film Style*, Cambridge: Harvard University Press.

Brewster, Ben (1990) "Deep Staging in French Films 1900–1914," in Thomas Elsaesser and Adam Barker (eds.) *Early Cinema: Space, Frame, Narrative*, 45–55, London: British Film Institute.

Brewster, Ben and Jacobs, Lea (1997) *Theater to Cinema: Stage Pictorialism and the Early Feature Film*, Oxford: Oxford University Press.

Salt, Barry (1992) *Film Style and Technology: History and Analysis*, 2nd ed., London: Starword.

BEN BREWSTER

star system

Although a star system in the legitimate **theater** and **vaudeville** or **music hall** existed before the advent of moving pictures in both Europe and the USA, this system was not immediately imported into the new industry. Film actors remained relatively anonymous until around 1910. The test of the existence of a star system is the ascendance of the player over the picture as a vehicle of promotion. The consequent financial considerations had their effect on casting and photoplay story choices and ultimately on the organizational structure of the early companies.

Perhaps the earliest example of promotion by means of personality was **Pathé-Frères**'s support of **Film d'Art**, the premise of which was that the public would want to see famous French actors in filmed versions of theatrical classics. A successful test of this premise came when Sarah **Bernhardt**, the most famous actress in the world, appeared in the Film d'Art version of *La Dame aux camélias* [Camille] (1912). A slightly different tradition of stardom predated the Italian film diva, focused on the primadonna or principal female singer in

opera. Here, too, Pathé-Frères exploited the connection between film and opera in the **Film d'Arte Italiana** adaptations which featured Francesca **Bertini**, who would become one of the great Italian divas. Generally, however, it is Lyda **Borelli**'s appearance in *Ma l'amor mio non muore!* [Everlasting Love!] (1913) that is accepted as the "birth of the diva."

Divismo, the Italian star system, differed in some significant ways from the system in the rest of Europe and the USA where stardom was more closely linked to competing companies. Whereas the Italian diva was a goddess who eclipsed male actors, other star systems featured both male and female actors who were portrayed as more secular. The first French star was the cultivated gentleman comic, Max **Linder**, whose popularity was cultivated by Pathé-Frères. In 1911, Pathé took out an ad in the trade papers wishing him recovery after his appendectomy operation, thus shoring up their investment. The company soon followed with full-page ads, the earliest **publicity** photos of all of their players including Rigadin (Charles **Prince**) and **Mistinguett**. In Germany, two companies moved to put potentially competing stars under contract around the same time. In 1910, Henny **Porten** signed with **Messter**-Projection/Film, and Paul **Davidson** put the **Nordisk** company asset, Asta **Nielsen**, under contract to his Allgemeine Kinematographen-Theater Gesellschaft (**PAGU/AKGT**).

In the USA, the association between stars and companies was the most pronounced, which is clear from the way actresses were identified by studio name, even before their stage names were released to the public: Florence **Lawrence** was the "IMP Girl"; Gene **Gauntier**, "The Kalem Girl"; Florence **Turner**, "The Vitagraph Girl." The history of film stars is often said to begin with Carl **Laemmle**'s March 1910 publicity stunt, which promoted Lawrence as a movie star in an effort to launch his new **IMP** (Independent Moving Picture Company) venture. But the appearance of these company stars around 1910 is actually more coincidental. Perhaps the most elaborate **advertising** campaign launched Marion **Leonard** as the star of the independent Gem company which no longer existed by the time the **Rex** company bought and released her first films. In December

1910, Mary **Pickford** left **Biograph** (the company that would refrain from star promotion until 1913) for IMP, and her new studio used the occasion to highlight her photograph in a full-page spread in *Moving Picture World*.

After the establishment of a commercial star system between 1910 and 1913, the international trade in films made it increasingly necessary for stars to be distinctive, which meant that they often defined themselves in relation to or against other national stars. The Dutch star Annie **Bos**, for instance, studied the performances of Italian divas Borelli, Bertini, and Pina **Menichelli**. Bertini in turn was inspired by Nielsen in *The Abyss* (1910), and Nielsen herself was contrasted with the Italian stage legend Eleonora **Duse**. Although Germany was always a relatively international industry, it was important locally that Porten be distinguished as "German" from the Danish star Neilsen who, although working in Germany, seemed to lose her national identity as she transcended national boundaries. Another test of the earliest cultural cross-over phenomenon was Ivan **Mosjoukine** who, beginning in 1911, became a major Russian star and then had a successful second career as a French star in the 1920s.

Although the star system is most often explained in terms of promotion, the phenomenon also depended upon technological changes and directing practices. The distance between camera and players was relatively great in early cinema, and conventions of shooting did not necessarily frame the face. It would not be until 1912 that the face itself would become the subject of close-up attention in the American cinema. In Italy, the camera did not move from long shot to close up until 1914, which implies that fans were able to identify their favorite players in long shots in an era before the existence of motion picture credits. It was not until the **Edison Manufacturing Company** began to introduce cast members on title cards in 1911 that the names of American players would be seen on screen.

The other half of the story of a developing star system involves reception. It was in response to a surge of interest from viewers that US manufacturers first began to release the names of their leading actors. Companies could not continue to ignore the fans who were eager to learn the names of the players they saw on the screen and who

Figure 114 Frame enlargement of Mary Pickford in *The New York Hat* (Biograph, 1912). (Courtesy of the Robert S. Birchard Collection.)

would notice, for instance, that the "Biograph Girl" (Lawrence's first moniker) had become the "IMP Girl." French women began to notice that **Gaumont**'s star, Suzanne **Grandais**, always wore the latest fashions, and in Italy Borelli's bodily movement and attitude gave rise to the term "Borellismo."

The star system meant that fans counted. Companies could not deny box office popularity and finally had to pay higher salaries than they would have liked. Pathé, for instance, had to increase Linder's salary to twelve million francs in 1912, making him the highest paid movie star before **World War I**. In the USA, companies tallied all the letters from fans, including marriage proposals and photograph requests, in order to translate them into salary raises. One indication of how quickly publicity changed from the exclusive promotion of films to the promotion of stars is the case of J. Stuart **Blackton**'s *Motion Picture Story Magazine*. Started in 1911 to promote Vitagraph films, this monthly of plot summaries evolved into a fan magazine by 1912, the same year that saw the launching of what would become the premiere fan journal, *Photoplay*.

See also: framing: camera distance and angle

Further reading

Bergstrom, Janet (1990) "Asta Nielsen's Early Films," in Paolo Cherchi Usai and Lorenzo

Codelli (eds.) *Before Caligari: German Cinema, 1895–1920*, Pordenone: Biblioteca dell''Immagine.

Bowser, Eileen (1990) *The Transformation of Cinema, 1907–1914*, New York: Scribner's.

Dalle Vacche, Angela and Gian Luca Farinelli (eds.) (2000) *Passion and Defiance: Silent Divas of Italian Cinema* (38th New York Film Festival Program), Milan: Grafiche Mariano.

deCordova, Richard (1990) *Picture Personalities: The Emergence of the Star System in America*, Urbana: University of Illinois Press.

JANE GAINES

Starewicz, Wladyslaw

b. 1882; d. 1965

filmmaker, Russia

Hired by **Khanzhonkov** in 1909, Starewicz initially was a regular director and special effects expert and then a pioneer puppet animator. From 1912 on, he was best known for his short films depicting insect life, initially marketed as though enacted by a troupe of tamed insects. These included parodies of fiction films: *Cameraman's Revenge* (1912) parodied a bedroom farce, while *Aviation Week* (1912) mocked a topical **newsreel**; both featured insects cranking a movie camera. Some films even mixed **animation** with live action. In France, where he went to work in the 1920s, Starewicz became famous worldwide.

YURI TSIVIAN

Steiner, William

b. ? d. ?

producer, distributor, USA

Steiner formed Crescent Films with William **Paley** in mid-1904. In 1905, when Crescent ran into trouble with **Edison**'s patent claims, the Paley and Steiner partnership broke up. That year, Steiner organized the Imperial film exchange and later claimed that he was the first to use an automobile to deliver films. In 1910, he formed the Yankee

Film Company, which first released *The Queen of the Nihilists* and issued a **detective film** series featuring a girl sleuth. In 1912, Yankee joined with other independents to form **Universal**. Steiner himself went on to establish the Serial Film Company in 1916 and the Jester Comedy Company in 1917.

EILEEN BOWSER

stereography

Stereography refers to the optical process whereby two-dimensional images are designed to be perceived as having three-dimensional depth. As a technology, its invention nearly coincides with that of **photography**, owing much to Sir Charles Wheatstone's 1838 theory of stereoscopic vision and Sir David Brewster's 1849 development of the lenticular stereoscope. Stereography led to the development of two different viewing practices, one by means of a hand-held device (the stereoscope), and the other, by means of projection upon a screen (the stereopticon). The latter term not only is related to the **magic lantern**'s capacity to create an illusory third dimension but also refers to its ability to dissolve from one image to the next. This sense of the term was frequently bound up with moving picture exhibition since early showmen relied upon both lantern slides and films for their programs and since companies such as Chicago Stereopticon & Film Exchange often handled both media. According to Charles Musser, stereopticons and slides generally played a role in the development of **editing** practices since exhibitors could experiment with sequencing images and build their own stories.

Although stereopticons were directly involved in exhibition, popular hand-held devices such as the Holmes Stereoscope, used to view two slightly different photographic images of the same image, also played a formative role in early cinema's development. Particularly after the mid-19th century introduction of instantaneous photography, interest in the stereoscope grew, peaking in popularity shortly after cinema's emergence. The London Stereoscopic Company, for example, founded in 1854, strove to fulfill its motto, "A Stereoscope in Every Home," by selling nearly 500,000 stereoscopes within two years. In the same period, its catalogue of views increased from 10,000 to nearly 100,000 images. By the turn-of-the-century, the stereograph's status as a mass medium was confirmed: firms such as New York's Underwood and Underwood sold approximately 10,000,000 views per year, including sets on world travel, newsworthy events, and dramatic fictions.

The stereograph's general popularity helped to shape the horizon of expectations for early cinema, just as the systematization of its image production and the refinement of its distribution processes helped to inform film production and dissemination. Pre-1906 moving picture catalogues, for example, are very similar to stereographic view catalogues, particularly in terms of image categories, titling, and sites of tourist interest. Moreover, many pre-1906 *actualités* adapted the compositional conventions of the stereograph (conventions, of course, rooted in wider cultural practices of the period). Rather than rely upon stereographic projection, filmmakers seem quickly to have exploited the illusion of depth created by moving the camera towards the vanishing point (**phantom train rides**) or by allowing traffic to move towards the camera (the **Lumière** effect). Whether because of the film medium's escalation of the terms of visual sensation or because of the rapid spread of home photography, the stereograph faded in popularity during the second decade of the 20th century.

See also: news event films; travelogues

Further reading

Jenkins, C. Francis and Oscar B. Depue (1908) *Handbook for Motion Picture and Stereopticon Operators*, Washington: Knega.
Musser, Charles (1990) *The Emergence of Cinema to 1907*, New York: Scribner's.

WILLIAM URICCHIO

Sterling, Ford

b. 1880; d. 1939

actor, director, USA

Following a wide-ranging career as a circus clown and stage comedian, Sterling entered films in 1911

as a comic actors for Mack **Sennett**'s **Biograph** unit. A founding member of Sennett's **Keystone Film Company**, Sterling was acclaimed for his German (or "Dutch") comic characterizations, for which he sported goatee, frock coat, and top hat. His kinetic performance style perfectly suited the studio's fast-paced humor, and he frequently appeared as chief of the Keystone police. In 1914, Sterling and director Henry Lehrman left Keystone to found the Sterling Comedies unit at **Universal**. The unit was disbanded within a year, and a chastened Sterling returned to Sennett, for whom he worked off and on until 1921.

ROB KING

Stiller, Mauritz

b. 1883; d. 1928

filmmaker, actor, Sweden

One of the leading filmmakers in Sweden during the silent era, Stiller has become particularly well known for his internationally-oriented melodramas and **comedies**.

Born in Helsinki, Finland, of Russian Jewish parents, Stiller came to Sweden as a refugee in 1904, in order to escape the Russian army. By then, he already had been engaged as an actor in Finland. He soon found work in Swedish provincial theaters, after which he returned for two seasons to the Swedish theater in Helsinki and then was engaged in 1911 as a stage director in Stockholm.

In 1912, he was hired as a screenwriter and director by Charles **Magnusson** at **Svenska Biografteatern** shortly before Victor **Sjöström**. Soon, he was established, together with Sjöström and Georg af **Klercker**, as one of the leading filmmakers in Sweden. The close collaboration of Stiller and Sjöström with brothers Julius and Henrik Jaenzon, both cinematographers, has generally been perceived as one of the keys to their success.

During Stiller's first three years at Svenska Bio, he made no less than 28 films (none of which survive) and wrote the scenarios for others. Among his films, melodramas dominated, together with comedies. From 1916 on, Stiller made 15 more films in Sweden. Three films from 1916 are completely or partly preserved: *Kärlek och journalistik* [Love and Journalism], *Vingarne* [The Wings], and *Balettprimadonnan* [The Ballet Primadonna]. *Vingarne* has been considered stylistically advanced compared with other Swedish films of the period, in particular for its use of developed continuity editing. Like later Stiller films, such as *Thomas Graals bästa film* [Wanted, a Film Actress/Thomas Graal's Best Film] (1917) and *Thomas Graals bästa barn* [Marriage à la Mode/Thomas Graal's First Child] (1918), *Vingarne* contains a meta-filmic dimension, in this case a frame story with the director playing the role as himself. The theme of **modernity** is present in many of these films, together with visual gags—evidence of the "Stiller touch" later to become famous as a source of inspiration for Ernst **Lubitsch**'s comedies.

Apart from these explicitly modern films, Stiller made several adaptations of Selma Lagerlöf novels during the so-called "golden age" of Swedish film, from 1917 onwards. He later became well known for his collaboration with Greta Garbo, together with whom he moved to Hollywood in 1925. He returned to Sweden in 1928, the year of his death.

See also: editing: spatial relations; editing: temporal relations

Further reading

Cowie, Peter (1990) *Le cinéma des pays nordiques*, Cinéma pluriel, Paris: Centre Georges Pompidou.

Idestam-Almquist, Bengt (1967) *Stiller*, Paris: Anthologie du cinéma 25.

BO FLORIN

Stokvis, Simon B.

b. 1883; d. 1941

critic, censor, the Netherlands

Stokvis was an Amsterdam theater critic who began to write about moving pictures in 1911, in order to defend the theater against the new threat

of cinema and warn against the decline in aesthetic taste caused by popular entertainments. He founded a committee to fight what he called "bad" cinema and unsuccessfully experimented with what he called "good" cinema programs for a short time in 1912. As a consequence, the **trade press** and film **lecturers** loved to mock him. In *Het Amsterdamsche schoolkind en de bioscoop* [The Amsterdam school kid and the cinema], published in 1914, he investigated the movie-going habits of children.

ANSJE VAN BEUSEKOM

Stollwerck, Ludwig

b. 1857; d. 1922

entrepreneur, Germany

As sales manager of Stollwerck Bros & Co (Cologne), Germany's leading chocolate manufacturer before **World War I**, Stollwerck introduced automatic vending machines with great success, expanding the distribution of sweets into the new sector of mechanical entertainment. Thus Stollwerck came into contact with a series of moving picture pioneers. On 20 December 1892, he signed a contract to purchase phonoscope slot machines from Georges **Demenÿ**, but the latter's financing did not produce commercial results. On 1 March 1895, Stollwerck opened the first **Kinetoscope** parlor in Germany, in Berlin. In June, he also engaged Birt **Acres** to shoot *actualité* footage of the Kaiser Wilhelm Kanal opening for his kinetoscopes. His hopes of exploiting the rights to Acres' **camera** and **projector**, however, again did not pan out. On 26 March 1896, Stollwerck then bought German rights to the **Cinématographe Lumière** and, one month later, screenings began in Cologne. In the autumn of 1896, some ten Cinématographes were earning money in German cities. Each had approximately 1,000 viewers daily, and by the end of the year altogether they had attracted more than 1.4 million viewers to experience the novelty of "living pictures." Although he did not invest further in the film business, Stollwerck remains the first film entrepreneur in Germany.

Further reading

Loiperdinger, Martin (1999) *Film & Schokolade. Stollwercks Geschäfte mit lebenden Bildern*, Frankfurt am Main/Basel: Stroemfeld Verlag.

Loiperdinger, Martin (1995) "Ludwig Stollwerck, Birt Acres, and the Distribution of the Cinématographe Lumière in Germany," in Roland Cosandey and François Albera (eds.) *Cinéma sans frontières/Images Across Borders, 1896–1918*, 165–177, Québec/Lausanne: Nuit Blanche/Payot.

MARTIN LOIPERDINGER

Storey, Edith ("Billy")

b. 1892; d. 1967

actor, USA

Equally adept as a Shakespearian tragedienne, a comedic cross-dresser, and a bonnie Irish lass, Edith Storey reigned as one of **Vitagraph**'s leading players from 1908 to 1917. From her **westerns** filmed while on loan to Gaston **Méliès**, in 1911, through her role as Ellen in a three-reel version of *The Lady of the Lake* (1912), Storey's dramatic flexibility steadily garnered both critical and public acclaim. In 1914, reviewers claimed that her portrayal of Glory Quayle in *The Christian* would never be forgotten. In 1917, Storey left Vitagraph for the Metro Company. She retired from the screen in 1921.

JENNIFER M. BEAN

Stow, Percy

b. ?; d. ?

filmmaker, Great Britain

Stow joined Cecil **Hepworth** as a director of **trick films** in 1901, producing such titles as *How to Stop a Motor Car* (1902) and *Alice in Wonderland* (1903). He left in 1904 and, with another Hepworth employee, H. V. Lawley, formed **Clarendon Film Company**, with studios in Croydon. His Clarendon films are notable for

their creative wit, veering often into social satire. An early title such as *Rescued in Mid-Air* (1906) shows his continued love of camera trickery, but from 1908 onwards (when Stow was in sole charge of Clarendon) there is a marked growth in filmic invention: from the comic absurdities of *A Wild Goose Chase* (1908) or the delightful **Shakespeare film** adaptation, *The Tempest* (1908), to the cross-dressing naughtiness of *Love and the Varsity* (1913). By 1909, while sharing directorial duties with Wilfred Noy and others, Stow introduced the popular *Lieutenant Rose* series; he was still with Clarendon at the start of **World War I**.

LUKE McKERNAN

Svensk-Amerikanska Filmkompaniet

Svensk-Amerikanska Filmkompaniet (S-AF) began as an exchange company, Globe Film, in 1908 and was incorporated early in 1911. The firm had by then added film equipment and material to its line of business. S-AF introduced **illustrated songs** in Sweden in 1909, but without much success. The exchange was headed by Carl Gustaf Albert Sjöberg, who allegedly had several years of experience in the US film business prior to his Swedish enterprise, and his partner, a Mr. Wahlström. Sjöberg later worked for Svenska filmkompaniet and **Pathé Film**, **Pathé-Frères**' Swedish branch. In the 1920s, he was business manager at AB Amerikanska Filmkompaniet.

JAN OLSSON

Svenska Biografteatern

Svenska Biografteatern (SB) was the major exhibition, distribution, and production company in Sweden before its merger with Filmindustri AB Skandia in late 1919, which created AB Svensk Filmindustri.

The company was established as an exhibition concern in 1905, and initially was known as Kristianstads Biograf-Teater, after the town in which it was founded. In 1907, N. H. Nylander, with the backing of Carl Johan Arhén, formed AB Svenska Biografteatern, and in the following year, the company built a new cinema and offices above which a small production studio was installed. SB first ventured into production with a series of *actualités*. In 1909, Charles **Magnusson** was appointed production manager and initiated a series of one-reel dramas that included **historical films** in the *film d'art* style, such as *Regina von Emmeritz och Konung Gustaf II Adolf* [Regina von Emmeritz and King Gustaf Adolf II], adaptations of popular folk dramas such as *Fänrik Ståls sägner* [Tales of Ensign Stål] and *Värmlänningarne* [The People of Värmland], social dramas such as *Järnbäraren* [The Iron Carrier], and emigration dramas such as *Emigranten* [The Emigrant] and *Amuletten* [The Amulet].

Opportunities for expansion and the possibility of bringing new talent from the legitimate **theater** into film were the likely reasons for relocating the company to Stockholm where, by spring 1912, production was re-established in a new, larger glass studio. Over the next few years, growth in domestic exhibition enabled the company to consolidate its position as an exhibitor and distributor in the domestic market and to develop a profitable program of regularized production modelled on that in France and Denmark, supported by the international sale of prints. In 1915, the company opened its flagship cinema in Stockholm, Röda Kvarn.

Georg af **Klercker** was contracted as head of production in 1912 and shortly after, Mauritz **Stiller** and Victor **Sjöström** joined the company as actor-directors. All three had extensive backgrounds in the theater. Although Sjöström's and Stiller's contribution to the development of a national cinema in Sweden occurred primarily after **World War I**, their work on **multiple-reel** films in the early- to mid-teens established a distinct studio style. Sjöström's *Trädgårdsmästaren* [The Head Gardener] (1912), characterized by an autonomous **editing: tableau style**, announced by **intertitles**, figured character subjectivity. These concerns were elaborated in his *Ingeborg Holm* (1913) where **staging in depth** with carbon arc **lighting** was used not only to model space or simulate moonlight but to create pathos. An

alternative to staging in depth achieved by reflecting off-frame characters in a mirror was evident in Konrad Tallroth's *Allt hämnar sig* [Everything Takes Its Revenge] (1917), and lateral **camera movement** as an alternative to inscribing parallel action through cross-cutting was used in Sjöström's *Havsgamar* [Sea Vultures] (1916), where closer shots were also employed to register character subjectivity. Stiller's *Vingarne* [Wings] (1916) featured a framed narrative.

See also: Pathé Film (Sweden)

Further reading

Fullerton, J. (1990) "Spatial and Temporal Articulation in Pre-classical Swedish Film" in Thomas Elsaesser (ed.) *Early Cinema: Space, Frame, Narrative*, 375–388, London: British Film Institute Publishing.

Fullerton, J. (1995) "Contextualising the Innovation of Deep Staging in Swedish Film" in K. Dibbets and B. Hogenkamp (eds.) *Film and the First World War*, 86–96, Amsterdam: Amsterdam University Press.

JOHN FULLERTON

Swanson, William H.

b. ?; d. ?

exhibitor, distributor, producer, USA

Swanson was the first important figure to declare his independence from the **Motion Picture Patents Company** in 1909. His association with movies dated to the 1890s, when he was running a tent show circuit. In 1907 he established a chain of film exchanges based in Chicago (along with several moving picture theaters) and was elected president of the United Film Services Protective Association on 16 November 1907. With Joseph Engel and Edwin S. **Porter** he launched the Defender Film Company in 1910; reorganized as the **Rex** Motion Picture Masterpieces Company in 1911, it was absorbed by **Universal** in 1912.

ROBERT S. BIRCHARD

Sweden

Production

The earliest film produced (though not exhibited) in Sweden was *Komische Begegnung zum Tiergarten im Stockholm* [Comic Encounter at the Zoo in Stockholm] which the **Skladanowsky** brothers shot in August 1896. In the following year, stimulated by the upcoming International Art and Industry Exhibition in Stockholm, **Numa Peterson's Trading Company** produced two films which it screened there. Alexandre **Promio**, representing **Lumière** et fils at the Stockholm Exhibition, also shot a number of *actualités* as well as *Slagsmål i Gamla Stockholm* [Fist-fight in Old Stockholm], filmed against the backdrop of the simulated Old Town recreated for the exposition. A further industrial exposition, held in Helsingborg in 1903, prompted Numa Peterson to produce a series of films synchronized with phonograph cylinders which were shown at Odödliga Teatern (The Immortal Theater). Further waves of synchronized films followed in 1907 and 1908, produced by Christian Svensson, in Stockholm, and Svensk Kinematografen, in Gothenburg; then, in 1909 and 1910, **Svenska Biografteatern** (SB), in Kristianstad, and Frans **Lundberg**, in Malmö, produced a total of over forty-five sound films, combining gramophone-recorded sound with moving images. The earliest years of film production in Sweden were characterized, consequently, by a number of films that employed **synchronous sound** and, in the case of SB, the production of *actualités* which, shot in various towns across Sweden, capitalized on popular topographical views typical of picture **postcards** and **stereographs** to attract local audiences. Thereafter, the development of the **multiple-reel film** put an end to the production of sound films, except for the Stockholm-based company of Nordiska Aktiebolaget Edisons Kinetophone which, in Vienna in 1914, produced fourteen films synchronized with Kinetophone cylinders featuring Swedish artists.

The development of moving picture theaters encouraged a number of exhibitors to venture into production including Lundberg, a cinema proprietor in Malmö and in Copenhagen, N. P. **Nilsson**, who owned a chain of cinemas in Stockholm, Sveafilms in Stockholm, and John

Figure 115 Exterior of the Svenska Biografteatern studio, Kyrkviken, Lidingö, 1912. (Courtesy of John Fullerton.)

Bergqvist's Viking Film in Linköping which supplemented its production of *actualités* and **travelogues** with a short series of features between 1912 and 1913. Of these companies, Lundberg was the most prolific, producing no fewer than twenty-four films between 1912 and 1913, some of which achieved international visibility. Lundberg concentrated on two types of film: "classics" adapted from the tradition of Swedish folk plays such as *Värmlänningarna* [The People of Värmland] (1910), which featured a local amateur cast, and sensational **melodramas** such as *Massösens offer* [The Victim of the Masseuse] (1910), which featured a cast of professional Danish actors photographed by Alfred **Lind**. Such productions enjoyed considerable success in Denmark and Germany where Robert Glombeck's rental agency accorded Lundberg films starring Ida Nielsen high-profile marketing. Of the Lundberg films that have survived, *Kärlekens list* [Love's Stratagems] (1912) is a comedy of disguise and mistaken identity, and *Med dolk och gift* [With Dagger and Poison] (1912), a parody of the Nick Carter **detective film** series, is notable for a special effect in which Lund cathedral is blown up.

In 1912 **Pathé-Frères** commenced production in Sweden, initially in close alliance with SB, including investment in the latter's new studio built on Lidingö. Victor **Sjöström** and Charles **Magnusson** visited the Pathé-Frères studios in Paris in 1912 to gain first-hand experience of French production, and Paul Garbagni traveled to

Stockholm where he directed *I livets vår* [In the Spring of Youth] (1912). Not only did the French company establish a new branch, **Pathé Film**, in Stockholm, but it launched the Phoenix **trade mark** as a production label for films produced in Stockholm by SB and which it could market internationally. SB thus secured world-wide distribution for its films.

The bid for market differentiation which fuelled the development of multiple-reel films caused a number of companies to collapse in 1913, the same year in which, after altercations with the State board of review over its first feature, Pathé temporarily discontinued feature production in Sweden. Suddenly SB found itself the only film producer of any size in the domestic market. With sales secured internationally and a growing circuit of cinemas in Sweden, SB invested in a more ambitious production program. Between 1914 and 1917, investment in production rose more than fourfold as the company sought to capitalize on the international market. In the short term, this strategy proved financially successful, but by the end of **World War I**, when SB's films began to gain international recognition as representative of a national cinema, this investment no longer guaranteed higher returns.

The only other major production company in Sweden, Hasselbladfilm, was established in 1915 by the Gothenburg-based company of Hasselblads fotografiska AB, a producer of lantern slides and picture postcards in the late 19th and early 20th centuries. Appointing Georg af **Klercker** as actor-director and production manager, the company produced thirty films before withdrawing from production in fall 1917. Employing dramatic **lighting** and striking **staging in depth**, Hasselbladfilm typically modelled its narratives on popular detective and romantic novels. Characterized in the **trade press** as "servant-girl romantic fiction" (*pigromanskärlek*), such material helped the company enjoy a short period of success in domestic exhibition before Filmindustri AB Skandia took over the studio in 1918.

Distribution

Four companies dominate the history of film distribution in Sweden before 1909: **Nordisk** and Pathé-Frères as major providers of film imports for the Swedish market, and Numa Peterson's Trading Company and Svenska Biografteatern (SB) as exhibitors and exchanges. Numa Peterson won the concession for the 1897 Stockholm Exhibition where the company operated a cinema with Lumière et fils. It later offered **cameras** and **projectors** in addition to film titles from Lumière and other producers for sale or rental to **itinerant exhibitors**. From 1901, Numa Peterson imported phonograph cylinders to be synchronized with films imported from the French **Phono-Cinéma-Théâtre** company. As in many other European countries, a close relationship developed between moving picture theater owners and distributors/ exchanges during the formative years of exhibition. Numa Peterson initially may have enjoyed sole rights to sell Pathé-Frères in Sweden and Norway, but that did not prevent other exchanges from playing a crucial role in Swedish distribution.

Film catalogues provide the earliest surviving evidence for a number of small exchanges: Nornan in Sundsvall (1906); C. A. **Friberg** in Karlskrona (1907); Hugo Silow in Linköping (probably 1907); Montgomery & Wahlberg in Stockholm and Norrköping (1908); Svensk Films Compani in Jönköping (probably 1908); Svensk-Franksa Handelsaktiebolaget in Stockholm (1909), and **Svensk-Amerikanska Filmkompaniet**, which opened as Globe Films in 1908. The latter company offered titles from American, French, and Italian producers, and ran branches in Copenhagen and Kristiania (Oslo). **Orientaliska teatern** published an extensive catalogue in 1909, listing *actualités*, travelogues, **comedies**, and dramas from the major producers, and Frans Lundberg's exchange included titles by French, American, Italian, Danish. and British companies.

In the summer of 1910, after setbacks in the American market, Pathé-Frères decided to target new markets in Europe. As a component in this strategy, Pathé-Frères opened a distribution outlet in Stockholm, Pathé Film, which subsequently opened sub-branches in Malmö and Gothenburg in 1912 and 1914. In 1910 and 1911, the Stockholm outlet typically bought between one and five copies of each title ordered from Pathé-Frères and its affiliates, and, via London exchanges, American titles, particularly **Biograph** whose output was well regarded in Sweden. Some titles were "sold" to other Swedish exchanges (that is, the exchanges received a distribution option for a limited period, often close to a year, after which they returned the copy), and one or two copies were rented to minor exhibitors. The company also supplied weekly film programs to many exhibitors in addition to selling film stock and film-related equipment.

After moving to Stockholm in 1912, Svenska Biografteatern reached an agreement with Svenska Film Companiet, a rival exchange and exhibition concern, to combine their respective chains of cinemas into Svenska Förenade Biografer. The new company secured Nordisk titles for exhibition by SB via **Fotorama**, and also secured a sales guarantee for all SB titles via Nordisk. This arrangement, while gradually undermining SB's alliance with Pathé, helped the Swedish company consolidate its position in the domestic market in the mid-teens.

Exhibition

As in most northern European countries, the earliest exhibition of moving pictures in Sweden took place in an environment where moving images as a commercial medium were part of a rapidly transforming visual mass culture. Moving pictures were first exhibited in Malmö on June 28, 1896 to considerable acclaim, yet screenings later that summer in Stockholm—by Charles Marcel at Victoria-Teatern in July, by the Skladanowsky brothers at Kristallsalongen in August, and by Anette Teufel at Berns—were not received with such enthusiasm. In 1897, Lumière et fils and Numa Peterson's Trading Company shared a venue at the International Art and Industry Exhibition in Stockholm, where films were exhibited alongside other new technologies—such as interactive X-ray images produced by means of fluoroscopy— as well as popular attractions with a much longer history, such as the panorama and natural history **diorama**.

Few permanent cinemas were established in the period before 1905; instead, traveling showmen incorporated moving pictures in their **magic lantern shows**. In 1897, six traveling showmen toured with moving picture presentations in Sweden; a further twelve, the following year; by 1900, at the height of their activity, thirty-six

itinerant exhibitors were showing moving pictures as far afield as Trelleborg in the south and Luleå in the north, following a seasonal cycle established by the **fairs** and the circus.

Exhibition in the capital was tied, in the earliest years, to the **music hall** or variety theater. Anna Hofmann-Uddgren, a singer and director of variety theater, introduced moving pictures into the program at Svea Teatern in 1898, and at Kristallsalongen and Blanch's the following year. In 1904, Blanch's became one of Stockholm's earliest permanent cinemas. Over the next few years, the number of moving picture theaters in the city rose dramatically: from six cinemas in 1905 to twenty-five by late 1909; by the end of 1912, the number had risen to fifty-six. As in Germany, the boom in cinemas was fuelled by an overabundance of used equipment and films which, traded on a cheap second-hand market, created fierce competition towards the end of the 1900s. New cinemas responded by being more comfortably appointed, and a number of older cinemas were upgraded. By the early- to mid-teens, a handful of **palace cinemas** were opening, a trend which continued after the war: Biograf Palatset (1912) seating 575, Röda Kvarn i Auditorium (1914) seating 1751, and Röda Kvarn (1915), SB's premier cinema, seating 637 in the stalls (including 38 in two loges at the rear) and 226 in the balcony. The development of the palace cinema redefined the experience of film viewing for

Figure 116 Interior of the Lilla Elite Teatern, Härnösand, 1910. (Courtesy of Arkitekturmuseet, Stockholm.)

a mass audience, while the mode of **spectatorship** which characterized exhibition in the earliest years was transformed.

Audiences

"Living photographs," one of the earliest terms used in Sweden to designate moving pictures, entered a public sphere characterized as much by social diversity as by the discourses of **education** and moral uplift which underpinned the cultural reform movements in Sweden at the close of the 19th century. Whether encountering mass-produced stereographs or cheap, stereoscopic slides in Stockholm's Kaiser panorama, the **audiences** that first viewed moving pictures at **world's fairs**, in music halls or variety theaters, or in the shows put on by itinerant exhibitors participated in a burgeoning visual culture that provoked anxiety on the part of the cultural establishment. In particular, the cinema reform movement feared the harmful effects and corrupting influence that "living photographs" might have on children.

Although it is difficult to establish with precision the composition of the audiences that first visited moving pictures on a regular basis, surviving films and photographs taken outside provincial cinemas suggest that they were heterogeneous, if predominantly young skilled and unskilled workers. Culturally prestigious establishments in the larger cities, such as the variety theater, attracted the leisured classes who, in a relatively short period of time, also began to attend moving picture presentations in numbers sufficient to contribute to a crisis of over-supply in entertainment in the capital by the mid-1900s. The new social activity of cinema-going, perceived by some commentators as more democratic than that of the established theater, was a force for cultural redefinition, but one which, in the mid-teens, became increasingly aligned with the cultural establishment.

Regulation

The cinema reform movement, initiated by Pedagogiska sällskapet (Pedagogical Society) in 1908, was part of a wider anti-popular culture movement in Sweden which put pressure on the government to establish a Statens biografbyrå (State board of review) in late 1911. For the leading figures of the cinema reform movement—Marie-Louise Gagner, Walter Fevrell, Dagmar Waldner—the goal of reform was not merely to regulate the conditions of moving picture exhibition but also to regulate content. The reformers promoted moving pictures as an educational medium and thus regarded non-fiction film as the medium's true vocation. However, as multiple-reel films grew in importance, the policy of the board changed, particularly after Gustaf Berg was appointed its head in 1914. Berg encouraged the industry to work with the board to make audiences more discriminating in their preference for fiction film.

Berg's policy had direct repercussions on film-making in Sweden. Images that could be interpreted as providing instruction in criminal activities (such as a close shot of a pocket being picked) were excised by the board, as were shots that showed details of immoral acts or horror effects (such as a close shot of a grotesque facial expression) since such details, it was argued, attracted disproportionate attention. Yet by the mid- to late-teens, as the style of the **classical Hollywood cinema** began to predominate, such distinctions ceased to have relevance, and Statens biografbyrå's influence on film style diminished.

See also: law and the cinema; *phonoscènes*

Further reading

Fullerton, J. (1993) "Intimate Theaters and Imaginary Scenes: Film Exhibition in Sweden before 1920," *Film History*, 5.4: 457–471.

Olsson, Jan (1986) *Från filmljud till ljudfilm: Samtida experiment med Odödlig teater, Sjungande bilder och Edisons Kinetophon 1903–1914*, Stockholm: Proprius förlag.

Olsson, Jan (1998) "Magnified Discourse: Screenplays and Censorship in Swedish Cinema of the 1910s," in John Fullerton (ed.) *Celebrating 1895: The Centenary of Cinema*, 239–252, Sydney: John Libbey.

Olsson, Jan (1999) "Exchange and Exhibition Practices: Notes on the Swedish Market in the Transitional Era," in J. Fullerton and J. Olsson (eds.) *Nordic Explorations: Film Before 1930*, 139–151, Sydney: John Libbey.

Snickars, Pelle (2001) *Svensk film och visuell masskultur*, Stockholm: Aura förlag.

Söderbergh Widding, Astrid (1998) *Stumfilm i brytningstid: Stil och berättande i Georg af Klerckers filmer*, Stockholm: Aura förlag.

Werner, Gösta (1969) *Mauritz Stiller och hans filmer 1912–1916*, Stockholm: P. A. Norstedt & Söners förlag.

JOHN FULLERTON

Sweet, Blanche

b. 1896; d. 1986

actor, USA

Only thirteen when she joined the **Biograph** company, Sweet quickly developed into an accomplished actress for D. W. **Griffith**, epitomized by her descent into madness in *The Painted Lady* (1912). She was awarded the lead in Griffith's first four-reel film, *Judith of Bethulia* (1914), but parted ways with the director soon after she and other personnel had joined him at **Reliance-Majestic** in 1914. Contracted by Jesse **Lasky**, she then worked with Cecil **DeMille**, his brother William, and eventual husband Marshall Neilan in the mid-teens and enjoyed a successful career in features which lasted through the 1920s.

CHARLIE KEIL

Switzerland

The development of early cinema in Switzerland does not significantly differ in chronology from that of Europe as a whole, except that it was a small country that remained an "open market to the world." **Chronophotography** and cinematography began circulating through the traditional channels of scientific popularization. This was the case for the **Edison Kinetoscope** (introduced by **Sivan** in 1895), followed by the **Cinématographe Lumière** (with **Lavanchy-Clarke** as its exclusive dealer, as early as May 1896) and a number of competitors who all offered projections of "moving photographs" throughout the territory in 1896. At the turn of the century these early **itinerant exhibitors** soon found themselves seriously challenged by **fair/fairground** exhibitors (Georges Hipleh-Walt, the Thiélé brothers, Weber-Clément, the Leilichs, Louis Preiss). The business of traveling film exhibition continued, however, in establishments featuring variety shows and in other temporary locations.

From 1908–1909 on, the opening of permanent theaters in the country's major cities accelerated through the exhibition monopoly of Pathé-Omnia's regional franchises presenting **Pathé-Frères** films and the shift from film sales to film rentals. The new spectacle's increasing success soon resulted in the first legal regulations, but these came at the level of the cantons; no centralized censorship was introduced at the federal level. Although the first published text on cinema and the **law**, *Kinematographenrecht* (1909), was written in German by Georg Cohn, a professor at the University of Zurich, the German debates around the Kino-Reform bore little on these regulations, except for the issue of access for school-age children. The pioneering attempt at using moving pictures pedagogically also came at the local parish level, led by Father **Joye** in Basel.

Production began in Switzerland in 1896 with Lumière films that conformed to the imagery of tourism already widespread abroad. Very early on, the country was a privileged destination for cameramen from the most important European companies (**Charles Urban Trading**, **Warwick Trading**, **Weltkinematograph**, Pathé, **Gaumont**, **Raleigh & Robert**), whose precursor was Elizabeth **Le Blond**. They brought back images of picturesque towns, modern vacation resorts, winter and mountain sports, civil engineering works, and folk festivals, all appearing well within the international pool of "outdoor views."

Limited and sporadic domestic production initially was limited to national news (filmed by fairground cameramen) or local events (captured by certain theater owners). In 1914, the few producers present at the National Swiss Fair still could offer only a modest volume of **industrial films** or films promoting tourism. The dominant figure of the period was Frederick **Burlingham**, an American filmmaker based in Montreux, close to cross-border Alpine sites and directly connected to the main continental rail links.

The few feature fiction films produced did not result in sustained activity or constitute anything like a national cinema. They nevertheless set the tone for decades to come, tapping into patriotism with *Wilhelm Tell* (the Interlaken Tellspiele filmed in 1912 and 1914), the "Alpine melodrama" with Eduard Bienz's *Bergführer Lorenz* (1917), or a vague internationalism with Alfred **Lind**'s *Le Cirque de la mort* (1919).

Other lasting characteristics of Swiss cinema also were in place by the 1910s, particularly the economic viability of an artisanal non-fiction cinema. This type entered commercial theaters during the interwar period in the form of a national **newsreel** as well as a variety of **advertising films**.

See also: *actualités*; expedition/exploration films; news event films; travelogues

Further reading

Cosandey, Roland (2002) "Tourismus und der frühe Film in der Schweiz (1896–1918): Elizabeth Aubrey Le Blond, Frank Ormiston-Smith, Frederick Burlingham," *Cinema*, 47: 50–61.

Dumont, Hervé (1987) *Histoire du cinéma suisse. Films de fiction, 1896–1965*, Lausanne: Cinémathèque suisse

ROLAND COSANDEY

synchronized sound systems

From the 1890s to the 1920s, hundreds of systems were invented for simultaneous synchronized presentation of moving images and sound. Early systems sought to synchronize the sound of a phonographic cylinder with film. These include **Edison**'s original Kinetophone, an 1895 version of the 1894 Kinetophone peep-show device, with a cylinder-playing **phonograph** in the cabinet, which patrons listened to through earphones; the 1898 Cinemacrophonograph or Phonorama of Berthon, **Dussaud**, and Jaubert, with projected images and a mechanical connection between the **projector** and phonographs, but still with earphones; and the 1900 **Phono-Cinéma-Théâtre** or Lioretographe of Gratioulet and Lioret, with projected images and sound.

Exploited primarily as novelties, synchronized sound systems did not become commercially successful until Léon **Gaumont**'s disc-based **Chronophone** system, first presented to the French Phonographic Society in 1902. Over the next decade, several hundred *phonoscènes* for the Chronophone were directed by Alice **Guy**, after the sound-on-disc portion had been pre-recorded by others. Exploiting direct connections between projector and phonograph, the Chronophone was soon fitted with a compressed-air amplifier and produced in a two-disc version. During the next few years, many new synchronized systems were developed, including **Messter**'s **Biophon**/Kosmograph, **Spoor**'s Phoneidograph, and Jeapes and Barker's Cinephone. From 1907 to the end of the decade, the American market was actively contested by three systems: the French Chronophone, the British Cinephone, and the American Cameraphone. All of these recorded sound and image separately, until Gaumont succeeded in recording image and sound simultaneously, by 1910.

Synchronized sound systems were installed in hundreds of American theaters. A *Moving Picture World* editorial confidently affirmed "The combination of the phonograph or graphophone with the picture machine has now advanced to such a state of perfection, and is being promoted by so many well-financed concerns, that it is destined to occupy an important part in the moving picture field" (13 March 1909, 293). Nevertheless, several problems prevented synchronized sound systems from taking over the market: while studios suffered from insufficient capitalization, the films had length limitations and poor synchronization, and theaters often had inadequate amplification. Whereas the film industry increasingly was moving toward longer narrative films, sync sound films primarily offered short vaudeville acts.

From 1910 to 1913, Gaumont and Edison competed strongly to capture the sync sound market. With its two-disc system, featuring simultaneous recording of image and sound, with precision connections between projector and phonograph(s),

Figure 117 Gaumont Chronophone advertisement, *Motion Picture World*, 1909.

Gaumont's Chronophone continued to enjoy modest success. Finally introduced in 1913, Edison's **Kinetophone** benefited from an enormous **publicity** campaign but suffered from an exclusive contract to exhibit the new system in **vaudeville** theaters. Though Edison had solved many of the technical woes dogging previous systems, the Kinetophone was eventually condemned by limited exploitation and vaudeville-oriented films. Whether inscribing the sound on cylinders, discs, or film, synchronized sound systems never completely disappeared, but their failure to dominate the industry was not primarily a technical problem. Not until sound films conquered narrative would they triumph.

Further reading

Abel, Richard and Rick Altman (1999) *Global Experiments in Early Synchronous Sound*, special issue of *Film History*, 11.4.

RICK ALTMAN

T

Tachibana Teijiro

b. 1893; d. 1918

actor, Japan

Born in Tokyo and trained as an *oyama* (a *kabuki* actor specializing in female roles) when still a child, Tachibana joined a new-school drama troupe and gained his reputation by the age of twelve. He first entered the moving picture industry in November 1909, and appeared in the films of **Yoshizawa Shoten** and **M. Pathe**. After the **Nikkatsu** trust was formed in 1912, he joined its Tokyo unit, which specialized in making new-school dramas, and soon became the best *oyama* performer in the company. As physically fragile as he looked, he died young.

HIROSHI KOMATSU

Tally, Thomas Lincoln

b. 1861; d. 1945

exhibitor, distributor, USA

Thomas Tally pioneered moving picture exhibition in Los Angeles in 1902 when he opened his Electric Theater, later the Lyric. Already in the summer of 1896, however, Tally managed a phonograph parlor offering both **Kinetoscope** films and the Vitascope for projected moving images. The latter attraction had previously been launched at the local Orpheum Theater. By the early 1910s, Tally was the unrivaled exhibitor in Los Angeles, in command of several spectacular, state-of-the-art moving picture theaters; he also managed a licensed exchange. Later on, he was one of the organizers of First National Exhibitor's Circuit. He retired in the early 20s, only to return to exhibition by acquiring the Criterion Theater.

See also: nickelodeons

JAN OLSSON

Talmadge, Norma

b. 1897; d. 1957

actor, USA

Cast mostly as an ingenue during her first few years at **Vitagraph**, Talmadge graduated to lead roles by 1913 and became the company's biggest star from then on (her career rise coincided with Florence **Turner**'s departure). Although often decorous in her early performances, she became more versatile in her Triangle films of the late teens, developing into a commanding screen presence, renowned for her beauty and **fashion** sense. Her marriage to industry executive Joseph Schenck in 1917 proved mutually beneficial, as he produced many of the melodramas which gained her even greater fame into the 1920s.

CHARLIE KEIL

Tanaka Eizo

b. 1886; d. 1968

filmmaker, Japan

Trained in the European-influenced, naturalist *shingeki* theater, Tanaka entered **Nikkatsu** in

1917, at a time when the more old-fashioned, melodramatic *shinpa* style dominated the conservative company's Tokyo productions. Early works such as *Ikeru shikabane* [The Living Corpse] (1918) revealed innovative uses of film form, but met with resistance from **benshi** and others. *Kyoya eriten* [The Kyoya Collar Shop] (1922) and *Dokuro no mai* [The Skull Dance] (1923), both based on original scenarios, helped shape the social realism that would eventually become the company's style. Tanaka later became an educator.

AARON GEROW

Tannenbaum, Herbert

b. 1892; d. 1958

theorist, Germany

In the midst of the debates in Germany about cinema's social and aesthetic value—sparked by its rivalry with theater—Tannenbaum published a 36-page monograph on *Kino und Theater* (Film and Theater) (1912), which is generally considered to be Germany's most systematic theoretical essay on film before **World War I**. Grounded in Aristotelian standards of unity, it anticipates later important statements by Hugo **Münsterberg**, Rudolf Arnheim, and Béla Balázs in its discussion of film acting and direction. In 1913, Tannenbaum finished his doctoral dissertation on film and **copyright**, one of the very few pre-war dissertations dedicated to film (see also Emilie **Altenloh**).

SCOTT CURTIS

Taylor, Alma and White, Chrissie

b. 1895/1895; d. 1974/1989

actors, Great Britain

From 1910 to 1923, Alma Taylor and Chrissie White were the best known actors of the **Hepworth** Manufacturing Company. They featured in eighteen *Tilly* films, with Taylor playing Tilly and White, her friend Sally. Cecil **Hepworth** himself was very proud of this successful **comic series**. "...the great aim and object in these Tilly girls...was to paint the town extremely red, and the joyfully disarming way in which they thoroughly did it was [their] great charm...." A surviving example is *Tilly and the Fire Engines* (1911), which parodies a typical fire rescue narrative, with the comic duo stealing a fire engine and using the hose to soak the hapless firemen. In all, Taylor featured in over 140 films from 1909 to 1957, was referred to as "the English Mary **Pickford**," and dominated Hepworth's last feature films, *Tansy* (1921) and *Comin' Thro the Rye* (1923). White married her fellow Hepworth player, Henry Edwards (1882–1951), and appeared in over 90 films from 1909 to 1930, including *Blood and Bosh* (1913). Throughout the 1910s, both Taylor and White were promoted in fan magazines, **postcards**, and cigarette cards as Britain's first major film **stars**.

Further reading

Burrows, Jon (2003) *Legitimate Cinema: Theatre Stars in Silent British Films 1908–1918*, Exeter: University of Exeter Press.

FRANK GRAY

Tenkatsu

Tenkatsu was formed in March 1914 in response to the emergence of the **Nikkatsu** trust in 1912. Subsequently, it became the latter's major rival until 1919, when it dissolved. Like Nikkatsu, Tenkatsu had two production units: Old-school dramas were made in the Tokyo studio; new-school dramas, in the Osaka studio. Tenkatsu originated as a company that produced films using the Kinemacolor system. However, with the outbreak of **World War I**, this enterprise quickly failed. After that, Tenkatsu produced conventional old-school and new-school films until the end of the 1910s.

HIROSHI KOMATSU

Thailand (Siam)

As in many other non-industrial countries, cinema was introduced and popularized in Thailand (called Siam until 1939) largely by foreigners and the upper classes or aristocracy. Indeed the first Thai to have any experience of film production and exhibition was the monarch, King Chulalongkorn (who reigned as Rama V, 1868–1910), when he was filmed during visits to Switzerland and Sweden in May and July 1897, and then swiftly afterwards was shown his own moving images on screen. Chulalongkorn was one of the great modernizing monarchs of the end of the 19th century, bringing many western customs and technologies to his country—Siam was one of the few nations in Southeast Asia not to be colonized—including automobiles and **photography**. His interest in cinema was taken up by another aristocrat, Prince Suphakit, who imported a film **camera** in 1900 and used it to record royal events.

It was the upper classes who made up the first audiences for moving pictures in Thailand, when, from June 1897, a number of short films were screened by a traveling showman of unknown origin, S. G. Marchovsky. After this, the country apparently had to wait until 1903 for films to be shown in Bangkok by several foreign companies, including the American Edison Cinematograph Company (named, like so many early film shows, after Thomas **Edison**). The following year another foreign concern, run by a Japanese, Watanabe Tomoyori, exhibited films in the city for several months. Watanabe returned in 1905 and set up Thailand's first permanent cinema, mainly showing films manufactured by **Pathé-Frères**. Watanabe's success encouraged others to enter the exhibition business during the following three years, including Chinese, European, and other Japanese entrepreneurs.

By 1910, movie-going was well-established in Bangkok, with five principal cinemas: the Royal Japanese Cinematograph (run by a Dr. Azawa), the Krungthep Cinematograph (opened in 1909 and managed by Nai Soon Chai), the Phatanakorn Cinematograph, the Siam Phapayon, and the Ratana (destroyed by fire that year). These halls were well appointed and "quite up to the level of those in London," claimed the *Bioscope*. The Phathanakorn was owned by a Sino-Thai, Siaw Songuan Sibunruang, perhaps the most important figure in the early history of Thai cinema. Throughout the 1910s, his company was in bitter rivalry with the Krungthep, until the two concerns merged in 1919.

Royal encouragement continued to be an important factor in the development of exhibition, and in production too, as royal events were regularly filmed. From early on, Watanabe's company was making *actualité* films, including several royal subjects such as King Chulalongkorn's 1910 funeral. The royal family, according to *Kine Weekly*, even had a projection hall installed in the Royal Palace in Bangkok in 1912. That year too marks the debut of Thai fiction films, with a short **comedy** entitled *A Siamese Elopement* that included an extensive chase along roads and waterways. Following this first effort, two more fiction films were swiftly released, also shot in Thai settings. But after this auspicious beginning, production came to a standstill until the early 1920s, when the national rail company began sponsored filmmaking.

Further reading

'B.T.' (1910) "Kinematographisches aus Siam," *Der Kinematograph*, 12 January, n. 159.

Barmé, Scot (1999) "Early Thai Cinema and Filmmaking: 1897–1922," *Film History*, 11.3: 308–318.

STEPHEN BOTTOMORE

Thanhouser Film Company

An independent production company started in 1910 by theatrical producer Edwin Thanhouser, with its principal studio located at New Rochelle, New York. From 1912 through 1916, Thanhouser released its films through the **Mutual Film Corporation**. Charles J. Hite briefly took over operation of the company, but Edwin Thanhouser returned to the helm after Hite's death in 1914. The company disbanded in 1918. Thanhouser's best known production was a **serial**, *The Million Dollar Mystery* (1914). Among the studio's leading players were James Cruze, Marguerite Snow, Florence La Badie and Muriel Ostriche.

ROBERT S. BIRCHARD

theater, legitimate

The legitimate theater stands in a productive, if at times hostile, relationship to early cinema. Actors famous on the legitimate stage were among the first celebrities to be recorded by the medium and among the first to be used in the attempt to synchronize recorded sound with moving pictures. When the new industry began to move away from the **cinema of attractions** after the turn of the last century, the legitimate theater was used to help launch the longer playing fiction films. While this boosted the industry's claim to artistic legitimacy and middle class respectability, it also produced a growing antagonism between the two arts. Theater personnel saw their stars, playwrights, theaters, producers, and public gradually given over to the new "cheap amusement." Commentators in the film industry questioned the need to align moving pictures with another art form. Film theorists and scholars later dismissed the theatrical film as filmed theater. Although attempts have been made to redress this criticism, it is usually the popular theater (conceived as a theater with its roots in mass culture: **music hall**, melodrama **theater**, and **vaudeville**), and not the legitimate theater, which is used to illustrate cinema's theatrical origins.

The first films which featured actors from the legitimate stage were based upon the climactic moments of their most well-known plays. The film was therefore legible to a broad audience and interesting in itself as a visual spectacle. A famous example is the **Edison** film, *The May Irwin Kiss* (1896), which showed May Irwin and John C. Rice re-enact the climax of their successful Broadway musical comedy, *The Widow Jones*. This became the most popular Edison film of the year. In 1898 the first major British actor, Lewis Waller, was filmed in his role as D'Artagnan in the fencing contest in *The Three Musketeers*. In 1899 the first **Shakespeare film** was made with Sir Herbert Beerbohm Tree in *King John*. Featuring a series of climactic excerpts, this film was exhibited in London and in other major European cities at the same time that the play was staged at Her Majesty's Theatre, London. That the film was considered an advertisement for the play made the relationship between the cinema of attractions and the legitimate theater one of reciprocal interdependence.

This interdependence also characterized one of the earliest public attempts to bring recorded sound to film. At the 1900 Paris Exposition, the **Phono-Cinéma-Théâtre** presented a program of short films accompanied by the phonograph. Among the actors featured were Ernest Coquelin (in *Cyrano de Bergerac*), Felicia Mallet (in *L'Enfant prodigue*), Gabrielle Réjane (in *Ma Cousine* and *Madame Sans-Gêne*) and Sarah **Bernhardt** (in *Hamlet*). These roles too already had met with success in established Paris theaters such as the Porte Saint Martin and the Comédie Française. The Phono-Cinéma-Théâtre program thus demonstrates the legitimate theater's early willingness to be involved in some of the more speculative ventures of the nascent cinema.

In 1908, the French **Film d'Art** company was founded with the aim of bringing French culture to the screen. This was also something of a speculative venture since it represented the first time a sustained effort was made to capitalize upon the cultural prestige and literary heritage of a nation. Employing Charles **Le Bargy** of the Comédie Française and playwright Henri Lavedan, it traded upon the idea that the legitimate theater could bring cultural and artistic respectability to the cinema. The first (and most famous) film, *L'Assassinat du Duc de Guise* [The Assassination of the Duc de Guise] (1908), featured Le Bargy, Albert Lambert, Gabrielle **Robinne**, and Berthe Bovy, all well-known actors from the Comédie Française. It also employed the noted scenery designer, Emile Bertin. Filmed before painted sets (but with historically accurate props), from a low camera angle, and at a distance of twelve feet from the players, the film recreated the viewing conditions of the legitimate theater. Given a premiere in the Salle Charras, and accompanied by ads stressing its theatrical origins, the film imitated the conditions under which a theatrical play was given its debut. However, its editing techniques—specifically its use of the cut to emphasize dramatic action—linked *L'Assassinat du Duc de Guise* to the later development of the narrative feature film. In short, the film's more cinematic qualities rather than its theatrical origins are what have attracted the attention of film historians.

In 1911, Film d'Art had to be sold due to debt, but it also released *La Dame aux camélias*

[The Lady of the Camelias], starring Bernhardt and *Madame Sans-Gêne*, starring Réjane. Again, both roles were associated with the famous actresses and had met with enormous success on the Paris stage. Advertised as a double bill in the USA, the films broke box office receipts everywhere. Their success indicates not only the international appeal of these stage actresses, but the extent to which the theatrical film could engage an enthusiastic popular audience.

In France, Film d'Art was not alone in capitalizing upon the renown and respectability of the legitimate stage. **SCAGL**, an affiliate of **Pathé-Frères**, was founded in 1908 with the contractual right to adapt works from Société des gens de lettres. The company used this right to adapt popular works from the theater and **opera**. Like Film d'Art, SCAGL advertised the names of its actors and, in 1909, began to produce longer films as feature attractions. This meant that the **multiple-reel film**—roughly three reels of between 700 and 900 meters—became an established, standardized part of the cinema-going experience. Other companies such as **Éclair**, **Gaumont**, and **Eclipse** followed suit, creating (respectively) the Association des compositeurs et des auteurs dramatiques, Grands Films Artistiques, and Série d'Art to produce higher class "art" films.

Developments in France were repeated across Europe. In Denmark, for example, **Fotorama** engaged actors from the prestigious Aarhus Teater, **Nordisk** filmed plays produced at the Royal Theatre, and a special *film d'art* company, Regia Art Film, was established in 1909. In Germany, Max **Reinhardt**, the famed director—and later owner—of the Deutsche Theater Berlin, directed four films between 1909 and 1914. More significant than these developments, however, was the movement of actors such as Paul **Wegener**, Albert **Bassermann**, and (later) Conrad Veidt and Marlene Dietrich from Reinhardt's stage troupe onto the screen.

In Italy, the production of *films d'art* was spearheaded, in part, by Pathé itself. Founded in 1909, on the model of Film d'Art and SCAGL in France, **Film d'Arte Italiana** produced quality films which featured such famous actors as Alberto **Nepoti** in *Othello* and Vittoria Lepanto (with Nepoti) in *The Lady of the Camelias* (both 1909).

It was the actors themselves, rather than the claims which the companies were making to respectability, however, which began to attract a large and loyal public. This led to the emergence of the diva, a phenomenon which is associated, in particular, with Italian actresses who began their careers in the theater but whose involvement in the cinema—usually in the role of the femme fatale—brought them international fame and popular renown. Pina **Menichelli**, Francesca **Bertini**, and Lyda **Borelli**, all famous divas of the early to mid 1910s, illustrate the way in which fame in the mass medium of film far eclipsed that of the stage. Particularly in the instance of Borelli, female **fashion** and behavior was influenced by her style of dress and arabesque-like acting in films such as *Ma l'amor mio non muore!* [Love Everlasting!] (1913) and *Rapsodia satanica* [Satanic Rhapsody] (1915).

Other actresses from the theater similarly became famous on the screen. One of the best known examples is Asta **Nielsen**. Trained at the Danish Royal Theatre, she made her first film, *Afgrunden* [The Abyss] in 1910. This was an overwhelming international success. Film distributors (in this case, Christoph Mülleneisen) realized the economic profits which could be gained if the exclusive rights to an actor's work was kept within a single film company and, importantly, if these rights were concentrated only on film. Along with Paul **Davidson**, he signed Nielsen for a series of ten films. With this contract, Nielsen was able to focus upon acting for the camera. Although she still drew upon the expressive gestures of Italian diva performance, she became a more "natural" screen actress whose performance style could be associated exclusively with the cinema.

In the USA, the association of the legitimate theater with moving pictures was driven less by the attempt to capitalize upon the nation's artistic heritage than by the attempt to foil civic criticisms of the medium. This produced a turn to established plays and players, an emulation of the more naturalistic Broadway style of performance, and the screening of "quality films" in reputable theatrical venues. These developments were initiated, in large part, by **Vitagraph** and emerged at the same time that the *film d'art* was appearing in Europe. Although quality films represented only a small portion of Vitagraph's output, the release of *Julius Caesar*,

Richard III, Romeo and Juliet, and *Macbeth* in 1908, and *King Lear* and *A Midsummer Night's Dream* in 1909 appeased the criticisms of social reformers and facilitated the emergence of a middle-class audience.

Vitagraph's quality films, however, relied not on stage actors but on its regular players. It was not until Adolph **Zukor** founded the **Famous Players Motion Picture Company** in 1912, that a concerted effort was made to capitalize upon the renown of the legitimate stage star. Securing the distribution rights to Bernhardt's *Queen Elizabeth*, and aided by Daniel Frohman (a respected manager of theatrical actors) and later by Charles Frohman (a Broadway producer), Zukor went on to adapt Broadway productions for film. These were launched with James K. Hackett's appearance in *The Prisoner of Zenda* (1913), and later followed by the engagement of actors such as Lily Langtry, James O'Neill, Minnie Maddern Fiske, and Mary **Pickford**. Such legitimate stage actors helped to promote the rise of the **star system** in the film industry and contributed to the adoption of the feature film format between 1912 and 1915. When Zukor joined Famous Players with the **Lasky** Feature Play Corporation to form the Lasky-Famous Players Corporation in 1916 (a forerunner of Paramount Studios), he led the way in incorporating the legitimate theater into the development of the Hollywood studio system.

Other individuals and companies soon followed Zukor in trying to capitalize on the respectability and renown of the legitimate stage, but not all met with success. In 1913, for example, the theatrical producers, **Klaw & Erlanger**, contracted with **Biograph** to film their stage successes, but poor box office receipts forced them to abandon the undertaking in 1914.

More often than not, the notion that the legitimate theater remained hostile to or failed to cooperate with the film industry persists in film histories. This is because scholars and critics have long sought to validate film's status as a unique and popular art. Cast as a high art form which supposedly retarded, rather than aided, the development of film, the legitimate theater therefore too often gets sidelined in most film histories. The only productive theater-film exchange then gets restricted to more marginal or avant-garde cinemas, such as German expressionism (which emerged in the post-war period). As a consequence, the theatrical origins of all those plays, players, and practices which cycled from the legitimate stage into moving pictures and which were integrated into the daily operation of the industry during the period of early cinema still remain largely overlooked.

Further reading

Abel, Richard (1994) *The Ciné Goes to Town: French Cinema, 1896–1914*, Berkeley: University of California Press.

Altman, Rick (1992) "Dickens, Griffith, and Film Theory Today," in Jane Gaines (ed.) *Classical Hollywood Narrative: The Paradigm Wars*, 9–47, Durham, NC: Duke University Press.

Bowser, Eileen (1990) *The Transformation of Cinema, 1907–1915*, New York: Scribner's.

Brewster, Ben and Lea Jacobs (1997) *Theatre to Cinema: Stage Pictorialism and the Early Feature Film*, New York: Oxford University Press.

Uricchio, William and Roberta Pearson (1993) *Reframing Culture: The Case of the Vitagraph Quality Films*, Princeton, New Jersey: Princeton University Press.

Vardac, A. Nicholas (1949) *Stage to Screen: Theatrical Origins of Early Film: David Garrick to D. W. Griffith*, Cambridge: Harvard University Press.

Waller, Gregory (1988) "Film and Theater," in G. R. Edgerton (ed.) *Film and the Arts in Symbiosis: A Resource Guide*, 135–163, New York: Greenwood Press.

VICTORIA DUCKETT

theater, melodrama

Melodrama was the dominant theatrical genre of the 19th century and, equally, a prevailing mode of framing experience in that period, its characteristics permeating the popular novel nearly as much as the stage. Almost from the moment when a narrative cinema appeared, i.e., offering dramatic plots and the depiction of fictional characters in action, melodrama was inevitably one of the extant theatrical forms referred to and emulated. This much is generally acknowledged.

Historians of cinema have assumed a straightforward appropriation of subject matter and technique but, unfamiliar with the large variety of theatrical possibilities and faced with the obvious problem of unequal duration of stage plays and early films, they also have assumed that moving pictures necessarily abridged stage dramas. Although stage melodramas were chiefly full-length entertainments, usually dramatizing events over a three or four-act span (but occasionally over six or seven acts) and lasting two and a half to three hours, early narrative films rarely played for more than twelve minutes. That observable disparity offered grounds for such assumptions.

To some degree this was true. **Kalem**'s *Ben-Hur* (1907), for instance, sought to represent in six brief scenes the set-piece moments of a six-act stage drama which toured with eight tons of stage effects—most memorably a Roman galley rammed and sunk by pirates and a chariot race with live horses and moving backcloths—and played to large audiences from 1898 until 1915. During the same period, moreover, **British Mutoscope and Biograph**, Herbert Wilcox's London Films, and the **Famous Players Motion Picture Company** all induced stage actors to reproduce some of their better-known roles for the camera. However, the overall relationship between moving pictures and stage melodrama is far more complex than this idea of film melodrama as a scaled-down or photographed stage play.

Melodrama, a theatrical form already known in some of the plays of Euripides and, later, in the tragi-comedies and pastorals of the European and English Renaissance, made its reappearance in France and Britain in the closing years of the 18th century and so passed from Europe onto the American stage. Because theatrical melodrama was superseded by other theatrical genres, it is sometimes assumed that melodrama is extinct. It lives on, however, in many European, American, and "Bollywood" films and also in numerous television dramas. Melodrama, then as now, flourishes in societies where events occur which are not immediately subject to easily comprehended rational explanation or where explanations of phenomena are numerous and contradictory and where the comforting presence and reassurance of divine justice—often expressed as an all-seeing, benevolent regulatory deity—is absent. In place of the absent gods (or God) is a secular explanatory narrative of causality which attributes public disaster and private calamity, peril,

or tribulation to the malign operation of evil seeking to overcome goodness. On stage and in early film, evil is represented through the character and actions of the villain. Unwelcome events are observed to happen because the villain, motivated by greed, avarice, lust, jealousy, and other antisocial impulses, intentionally brings about misfortune to good people. The villain destabilizes the lives of the good characters, often labeled hero and heroine, and, bringing undeserved calamity, danger, guilt, blame, and shame on these good people, forces them from their previously comfortable tranquil existences. Melodrama then requires the hero or heroine to locate the cause of disturbance—the villain—and to punish or expel him or her from the society in which he or she has hitherto acted with malevolence and impunity.

Because melodrama's spectators inhabit a world where crises and calamities (e.g., crime, **urbanization**, industrialization, imperial adventure, war, economic and domestic stress) are continual and random and the causes of further anxiety, dramatists frequently connect the villain to these disturbances. Thus the villain personifies the problem, which may be a source of peril and discord, and serves as a metaphor for the problem. Once the villain is identified and subjected to temporal, if not divine, justice, the greater disturbance is felt to have vanished, consequently, and the audience experiences relief, albeit temporarily, as the current environment is felt to be both safer and more morally coherent. This temporary accord may not be logical, but it is a function of melodrama to make the illogical and the irreconcilable appear both logical and reconciled—as well as morally intelligible—for the duration of the drama, and for some small period thereafter.

Incidental music almost invariably accompanied theatrical melodrama, and its presence prepared **audiences** to respond emotionally and psychologically to the characters and onstage actions they observed. Music was one of the first elements of theatrical performance which transferred to the exhibition of moving pictures, and there too it instructed audiences how to interpret the goodness or malevolence of the characters and actions presented. Music also permitted, and indeed encouraged, the large gestures of melodramatic acting to be incorporated into early film performance. Stage melodramas, although acknow-ledging the "real" world, were not intentionally "realistic" or "naturalistic," and incidental music was a part of the experience which raised melo-dramatic narrative above the everyday into a realm of enjoyable fiction.

Because **music halls** and **vaudeville** theaters quickly incorporated moving pictures as one of a series of variety acts on their programs, it is in such venues that some of the earliest theatrical models for film melodrama may be found. In the latter part of the 19th century, music hall and vaudeville proprietors had increasingly encroached on the privileges of licensed or "legitimate" theaters to present dramatic entertainments alongside variety acts. Theaters offering full-length plays were not licensed to permit smoking or consuming alcoholic beverages in the auditorium; music halls and vau-deville theaters offered these pleasures but were not licensed to stage full-length plays with dialogue. By the mid-1890s a compromise had been reached in which the latter were permitted to exhibit dramatic "sketches." The sketch was a complete narrative, usually a melodrama, presented within an eighteen to twenty-minute time-span. Actors numbered no more than six. The sketch was silent or limited to brief segments of dialogue or, in many instances, explicated by a narrative which was sung rather than recited or spoken. Typical of the dramatic sketch was John Lawson's *Humanity*, introduced in both American and British venues in 1897. Lawson took the role of Silvani, a wealthy Jew who befriends a bankrupt gentile, Cuthbert, and allows him to reside in his home. Cuthbert betrays Silvani's kindness and plans to elope with Silvani's gentile wife, reminding her that Silvani is "only a Jew." Learning of this impending treachery, Silvani sings "Only a Jew," then engages in a ferocious fight with Cuthbert that destroys most of the home's furnishings and causes the staircase to catch fire. Rolling and fighting down the eventually collap-sing staircase, both Cuthbert and Silvani expire, but not before Silvani has avenged this slight to his wife's honor. This brief, almost silent drama com-pressed action and was largely explicable in mime. Music made the characters morally intelligible. Not only were sketches such as *Humanity* commonplace in music halls and vaudeville theaters before nar-rative film appeared, but Lawson, with London's

Magnet Films, subsequently filmed *Humanity* (1913) for exhibition in venues where the live sketch had been previously performed.

Another legacy of stage melodrama visible in early moving pictures is the presence of musical and dance acts within the body of filmed melo-drama. The American stage was adversely affected by a major financial depression in the 1870s which resulted in the failure and closing of numerous "legitimate" and variety theaters. To find an eco-nomically viable formula which would win audi-ences to variety and satisfy spectators who sought more serious entertainments, theatrical entrepre-neurs developed what became known as the "combination company." The combination toured circuits accessible by America's extensive railway system, each company a mixture of actors and variety artists. It thus became standard practice for a touring company to place musical numbers, dancing, and a succession of variety acts within the action of the melodrama. These variety acts could be just as often conspicuously obtrusive and at odds with the plot and tone of the melodrama as they could be well-integrated overall.

The impact of the combination company is clearly visible in two **Edison** films, both directed by Edwin **Porter** in 1903. In *Uncle Tom's Cabin*, filmed using an actual theatrical combination troupe touring New Jersey, one group of actors, some "blacked-up" to impersonate Negroes in key dramatic roles, appear alongside another group of African-American dancers. The African-Americans contribute local color to the scene of a Mississippi riverboat docking as well as a quiet evening of plantation life which they enliven with a "cake-walk," but their exuberant dancing con-trasts sharply with the pathos of a slave auction at which they also appear. We see the combination again in Porter's version of Scott Marble's 1897 *The Great Train Robbery*. After the mail train has been robbed and the guard, fireman, and a passenger have been killed, the essential action of pursuit and apprehension of the bandits is interrupted for a dance hall episode in which a square dance, solo jig, and reel are performed by a separate company of dancers before that pursuit can begin. Audience expectation of such musical and variety elements in straight melodramas extended well into 1930s sound films.

One of the numerous—but also one of the more apparent—links between the content of theatrical melodrama and subsequent appropriation by early filmmakers occurred in narratives of the American Civil War. Less than ten years after the war between the Union and Confederacy had ended, professional theaters began offering dramas that explored the social and domestic disruptions caused by that conflict and that enacted attempts at reconciliation which bridged hostilities and looked to a restored political and cultural consensus. As the war receded, and as veterans' organizations jointly sought to commemorate the conflict and mutual sacrifice in civic monuments, more than a hundred of such dramas, some speaking to the values of the Union, some to the objectives of the Confederacy, appeared on the American stage between 1874 and 1920. By 1908, the formulas, positions, and strategies of Civil War stage melodrama were emerging in films, notably Kalem's *The Days of '61* and **Biograph**'s *The Guerilla*, the first of eleven Civil War films directed by D. W. **Griffith** before 1913. Equally representative were **Vitagraph**'s *A Dixie Mother* (1910) and Kalem's *The Drummer Girl of Vicksburg* (1912) and *The Confederate Ironclad* (1912). Thomas **Ince**'s feature-length *The Battle of Gettysburg* (1913) was even released to coincide with the 50th anniversary of that event and the joint reunion of 54,000 Confederate and Union veterans. All of these films, in concert with further stage melodramas, negotiated a running reappraisal of the Civil War and its significance as a national crisis.

In both Europe and the USA, a similar process occurred in melodramatic stage plays that centered on efforts of imperial Romans to suppress early Christianity and the resistance of Christians to villainous Roman oppression. These "toga plays," with their virtuous Christian heroines and Roman patricians converted by the new faith offered to American and European audiences dramatic metaphors for women's rights, for the laboring man within industrial capitalism, and, above all, for critiques of imperial policy as British, French, Italian, and American governments established commercial hegemonies and actual colonies beyond their territorial borders. Stage melodramas such as *The Claudian* (1883), *The Sign of the Cross* (1895), *Quo Vadis?* (1896), *Ben-Hur* (1899) and various theatrical versions of the novel *The Last Days of Pompeii* (1836) all were successfully realized in moving pictures, a decade or two later, by Italian (chiefly) and American filmmakers.

A further development in the final quarter of the 19th century was enhanced by the new capabilities of moving pictures. Led initially by the English actor-manager Henry Irving, this saw the hero and villain of melodrama fused into a single role. The divided hero-villain, affable and popular with those who knew nothing of his true character, was depicted as secretly criminal, frequently a murderer whose suppurating guilt gnawed at his tattered conscience, causing an inner suffering and remorse that eventually could not be contained. Under pressure from his conscience, his better nature divided from its wicked self. The two conflicted selves struggling for dominance forced knowledge of crime and guilt into the open, and neither self survived. Irving introduced this character in *The Bells* (1871), developed it further in *The Iron Chest* (1879), *Louis XI* (1878), *The Cup* (1881), and *Faust* (1885, 1887, and 1895), and capped it with the double roles of the innocent Lesurques and the thief-murderer Dubosc in Charles Reade's *The Lyons Mail* (1877). Irving's success in these roles then was emulated by the actor-manager Herbert Beerbohm Tree who, with Dorthea Baird, created the roles of Svengali and Trilby in *Trilby* (1896), in which an artist's model was transformed by hypnotism into a remarkable singer by the dangerous, manipulative, but fascinating Svengali. Indeed, both characters in this melodrama had double identities. In the USA, in 1887 actor-managers competed to stage versions of the novelette, *The Strange Case of Dr Jekyll and Mr Hyde*, in which the humane scientist Dr. Jekyll metamorphoses into his deformed, deadly alter-ego Mr. Hyde. These melodramas were frequently adapted as films, not merely in the early period but throughout the silent era and into sound films. Close-ups and **intertitles** made unnecessary the actor's "aside" in which he spoke his true, inner thoughts to the audience, and the transformations of character could be made by stop-action and close-matching or by optical effects.

See also: acting styles; colonialism: Europe; dance films; editing: early practices and techniques;

editing: temporal relations; framing: camera distance and angle; historical films; multiple-reel/feature films; musical accompaniment; musical scores; screenwriting; sound effects; theater, legitimate

Further reading

Mayer, David (1994) *Playing Out the Empire: Ben Hur and Other Toga Plays and Films, 1883–1908*, Oxford: Oxford University Press.

Mayer, David (1997) "Learning to See in the Dark," *Nineteenth Century Theatre*, 25.2: 92–114.

Mayer, David (1999) "Which Legacy of the Theatre? Acting in Silent Film: Some Questions and Some Problems," in Peter Kramer and Alan Lovell (eds.) *Screen Acting*, 10–30, London: Routledge.

Mayer, David (2001) "Opening a Second Front: the Civil War, the Stage, and D. W. Griffith," in Laura Vichi and Leonardo Quaresima (eds.) *La decima musa. Il cinema e le altre arti/The Tenth Muse: Cinema and Other Arts*, 491–506, Udine: University of Udine.

Mayer, David and Helen Day-Mayer (2001) "'A Secondary Action' or a Musical Highlight? Melodic Interludes in Early Film Melodrama Reconsidered," in Richard Abel and Rick Altman (eds.) *The Sounds of Early Cinema*, 220–231, Bloomington: Indiana University Press.

Singer, Ben (2001) *Melodrama and Modernity: Early Sensational Cinema and Its Contexts*, New York: Columbia University Press.

DAVID MAYER

Théophile Pathé

Founded by Théophile Pathé (brother to Charles **Pathé**) and Louis Morénas, the Compagnie des Cinématographes Théophile Pathé became a public limited company (*société anonyme*) in January 1907, replacing the general partnership, Théophile Pathé et Cie, which had been created in July 1906. With a capital of two million francs, the Compagnie Théophile Pathé planned to exploit the patent for Oskar **Messter**'s projecting apparatus. Several key figures in **Cinéma-Halls** and **Film d'Art** were among its stockholders and administrators.

The relationship between Théophile and his brother Charles grew bitter to the point where **Pathé-Frères**, denying anyone else's right to use the name 'Pathé,' took the other company to court, but to no avail.

In May 1908, Théophile Pathé was removed from the direction of his company and Alexandre **Promio** became managing director. In 1913, after its shares had dropped spectacularly in value, the company went into liquidation.

JEAN-JACQUES MEUSY

Thévenon, Etienne

b. 1852; d. 1918

exhibitor, France, Belgium

Born in Lyon, Thévenon seems to have been a technician working for the **Lumière** brothers. In 1897, with a **Cinématographe Lumière**, he began touring a canvas tent theater out of Amiens, but his primary working area soon became Belgium. Although he bought many of his films in France, he also shot many *actualités* himself. Eventually he became the moving picture chronicler of Liège, an important industrial center. There he exhibited moving pictures at the **World's Fair** in 1905, and two years later he opened a permanent moving picture theater in the city.

GUIDO CONVENTS

Thiemann & Reinhardt Company

Founded in 1909 by Pavel **Thiemann**, who had headed **Gaumont**'s Moscow operation, and the wealthy tobacco merchant Friedrich Reinhardt, Thiemann & Reinhardt was a leading Russian distribution and production company. As a distributor, the firm challenged French domination of the Russian market by importing **Ambrosio**, **Nordisk**, and **Vitagraph** films. As a producer, Thiemann & Reinhardt was known for high quality adaptations of literary works, especially its "Golden

Series" of **multiple-reel feature films**. The studio's most famous film was the legendary melodrama, *Kliuchi schastia* [The Keys to Happiness] (1913), based on the eponymous serial novel by best-selling author Anastasiia Verbitskskaia. Co-directed by Vladimir **Gardin** and Iakov **Protazanov**, *Kliuchi schastia*'s 5,000 meter length made it the longest Russian film up to that time. Unfortunately, like most of Thiemann & Reinhardt's films, only a few production stills survive. *Kliuchi schastia* recounts the sexual adventures and ultimate suicide of Mania, a "New Woman" writ large. The film played for nearly six months in various parts of the country and earned a record-breaking 200,000 rubles profit, which enabled the company to build a new studio. Critics particularly praised *Kliuchi schastia*'s "European" production values. More than any other film, *Kliuchi schastia* proved to theater owners that Russian films, if well-made, could be more profitable than the typical four to five picture program of shorter films. This film cemented Thiemann & Reinhardt's position among the top three producers (with **Drankov** and **Khanzhonkov**), where it remained for the next two years.

Like the Khanzhonkov company, Thiemann & Reinhardt early realized the importance of name and brand recognition. This was achieved not only by using sophisticated **advertising** campaigns but also by hiring filmmakers, **screenwriters**, and **stars** whose names (and faces) would be company monopolies. Gardin and Protazanov, writer Verbitskaia, and actress Olga Preobrazhenskaia (who later became an important Soviet filmmaker) were critical to the studio's successes, especially in the heavily promoted Golden Series. **World War I**, however, dramatically changed the company's fortunes, for the worse. Most Russian studios profited greatly from the war, but they were not run by men with German surnames. The addition of a third partner and a new name, Thiemann, Reinhardt & Osipov, did not help. In 1914, the studio was attacked by an anti-German mob, and in 1915, Gardin, Protazanov, and Preobrazhenskaia signed with rival companies. Although Verbitskaia remained loyal, and Thiemann quickly hired new filmmakers, Viacheslav Viskovskii and Aleksandr Uralskii, the firm never recovered.

Thiemann was exiled in 1915, after which his wife, Elizaveta, ran the studio alone. Although circumstances made it impossible for her to save the company, Elizaveta Thiemann's role in Thiemann & Reinhardt's success was pivotal. She was arguably the most important woman working in early Russian cinema, widely admired among her peers for her considerable business acumen. She had been a central figure in the firm from the beginning, responsible for casting and script supervision. She was also Russia's first female filmmaker, co-directing *Ukhod velikogo startsa* [The Passing of the Great Old Man] (1912) with Protazanov. She acted as well, taking on the supporting part of Tolstoi's daughter Aleksandra in this picture. By 1916, the last year for which we have reliable production figures, Thiemann, Reinhardt & Osipov's production had dropped to only 24 films (compared with Khanzhankov's 93). In 1917, after the February Revolution and Pavel Thiemann's return to Moscow, the company ended its days poetically as "Era."

See also: distribution: Europe

Further reading

Leyda, Jay (1960) *Kino: A History of the Russian and Soviet Film*, London, George Allen & Unwin, Ltd.
Youngblood, Denise J. (1999) *The Magic Mirror: Moviemaking in Russia, 1908–1918*, Madison, University of Wisconsin Press.

DENISE J. YOUNGBLOOD

Thiemann, Pavel

b. 1881; d. ?

producer, Russia

The founder of the **Thiemann & Reinhardt** studio, Pavel Thiemann was born in Iurev, Livland (now Estonia) to a Baltic German family. Early drawn to a career in the moving pictures, Thiemann went to Paris in 1902 to learn the business, after which he returned to Russia to manage **Gaumont**'s Moscow operation. In 1909, Thiemann left Gaumont and with the financial support of Friedrich Reinhardt, Thiemann & Reinhardt quickly became an important producer. The outbreak of war in 1914 changed Thiemann's fortunes quite dramatically for the worse. Exiled as a "German" in 1915 to the town of Ufa in the Ural Mountains, Thiemann was not able to return to Moscow until after the first revolution in 1917. His fate remains unknown.

DENISE J. YOUNGBLOOD

Thomas, Arthur Duncan

b. ?; d. ?

showman, Britain

A. D. Thomas was one of the most colorful and incorrigible characters in early British film. As with other showmen of the late 1890s, he graduated from exhibiting **Edison phonographs** to projected film shows, which he shamelessly billed as being provided by Edison-Thomas, even billing himself as Thomas-Edison on occasion. His business flourished, with multiple shows touring up and down the country, using **Urban** films and equipment, until over-expansion forced him to sell out to Walter Gibbons. In 1901, Thomas had two camera crews filming *actualités* in Ireland and the North of England, which were printed and distributed by **Mitchell & Kenyon** (30 titles survive). He subsequently exhibited and filmed in Canada, touring Great Britain once more with his Royal Canadian Animated Photo Company in 1906–1907.

See also: fairs/fairgrounds: itinerant exhibitors

LUKE McKERNAN

Togores, José de

b. 1868; d. 1926

filmmaker, Spain

Togores made his first film at age 46, *La festa del blat* [The Corn Festival] (1914), an adaptation of a play by the Catalan dramatist Ángel Guimerá. Between 1914 and 1916 he managed the Segre Films production company, where he made several Italian-influenced melodramas: *Amor de pescadora* [Fisherwoman's Love] (1914), *Los muertos viven* [The Dead Live] (1915), and *La otra Carmen* [The Other

Carmen] (1915). He worked consistently with Italian cameraman Giovanni Doria and prestigious stage actors. His last work was the much admired *El Golfo* [The Gulf] (1917).

JOAN M. MINGUET

Tokugawa Musei

b. 1894; d. 1971

benshi, Japan

Born Fukuhara Toshio, Tokugawa was well educated but too enamored of **vaudeville** to study for his college entrance exams. He became a *benshi* in 1913 and, working at such prominent foreign film theaters in Tokyo as the Aoi-kan and the Musashino-kan, developed an unobtrusive but artistic narration that aimed to be true to and strengthen the original film. This attitude helped change the *benshi* performance style and endear him to intellectual audiences. Later branching out into acting, radio, essay writing, and, eventually, television, Tokugawa was a prominent "voice" in 20th-century Japanese culture.

AARON GEROW

Tonbilder

A prominent sector of German film production from 1903 to 1910, *Tonbilder* were films of three to four minutes with **synchronous sound** produced by gramophone.

On 29 August 1903, Oskar **Messter** premiered his **Biophon** apparatus in the Apollo theater in Berlin with great success. The Biophon was a patented technique for synchronizing image and sound: a film projector and gramophone were connected via crankshaft and electric motor, and a mark on the record indicated the point at which to start gramophone and projector simultaneously.

Tonbilder were produced in two stages: 1) a song, a musical number, or spoken words were recorded in a sound studio, and 2) a playback scene with the singers, musicians, actors, or their stand-ins was arranged and shot in a film studio.

Up to 1907, the *Tonbild* sector of German film industry was dominated by Oskar Messter who made an agreement with Léon **Gaumont**, his French competitor: Gaumont was to supply no *phonoscénes* to Germany, and Messter was to supply no *Tonbilder* to France; their apparatuses were sold as a common concern under the name Gaumont-Messter-**Chronophone**-Biophon. For subjects, Messter drew almost exclusively on popular singers of the Berlin **operas** and **music halls** and on humorists of the variety theaters; he was even able to engage international stars of dance such as Cléo de Mèrode, Otero, and Saharet. From 1905, special *Tonbild* theaters made well-known German opera and operetta stars available to middle-class **audiences** who could not afford to enjoy their live performances. When the store-front-theater or **nickelodeon** boom arrived in 1907, they were mostly supplied with films of French origin, so that *Tonbilder* contributed a clear German accent within their programs of foreign films.

The facts and figures of German *Tonbild* production still remain unclear. According to Messter himself, by 1913, he had sold 500 Biophon machines to cinema managers and had produced 500 *Tonbilder*. Ads in the German **trade press** account for nearly 850 *Tonbilder* from 1903 to 1911, most of German origin. In 1907, other German companies such as **Deutsche Mutoskop & Biograph**, Deutsche Bioscop, and **Duskes** entered the *Tonbild* sector with their own synchronous sound machines and moving pictures. Instead of expensive stars, they mostly used stand-ins and thus charged far lower prices. Within two years, prices no longer could cover production costs, and the *Tonbild* sector collapsed.

Further reading

Loiperdinger, Martin (2003) "*Tonbilder*. Zur nationalen Ausrichtung der deutschen Kinematographie nach der Jahrhundertwende," in: Jürgen Felix, Heinz-B. Heller, and Karl Prümm (eds.) *Der Film im Ensemble der Künste um 1900*, Vienna: Synema.

Ulff-Moller, Jens (1999) "Biophon Sound Films in Danish Cinemas, 1904–1914: The 'Talking and Singing Movies' in Constantin Philipsen's Kosmorama Cinemas," *Film History*, 11.4: 456–463.

MARTIN LOIPERDINGER

Topical Film Company

Topical was founded in 1911 by William Jeapes, formerly of the **Warwick Trading Company**, and Herbert Holmes Wrench, from the **Wrench** family firm. Its chief product was the *Topical Budget* **newsreel**, which began in September 1911, the third British newsreel after *Pathé's Animated Gazette* and the *Warwick Bioscope Chronicle*. Although lacking the strong backing that its chief rivals, *Gaumont Graphic* and *Pathé Gazette*, inevitably enjoyed, *Topical Budget* survived the over-crowded newsreel market of the pre-war era to last into the 1920s, finally closing in March 1931. The company became most notable for being taken over by the British War Office for the period of May 1917 to February 1919.

LUKE McKERNAN

Toscano, Salvador

b. 1872; d. 1947

producer, cameraman, showman, Mexico

Toscano left a career in engineering for moving pictures, about which he first learned in the French journal, *La Nature*. Beginning in 1897, with a **Cinématographe** purchased directly from the **Lumière** company, he traveled the country as an exhibitor, particularly in areas he had visited as a metallurgical engineer. He amassed a remarkable collection of films that either he or a partner produced or acquired from others. Among the most important was *Voyage to the Yucatán*, a reconstruction of the Mexican president's journey to the peninsula, in which he respects the spatial-temporal sequence of events, a fundamental characteristic of early Mexican cinema. Toscano was active until the 1920s. In 1947, his daughter Carmen created the compilation film, *Memories of a Mexican*, from his surviving footage and documents. His mother's collection of letters about his travels is preserved.

AURELIO DE LOS REYES

Tourneur (Thomas), Maurice

b. 1876; d. 1961

director, France, USA

Influenced by his early career as an illustrator, a graphic designer, and an assistant to Auguste Rodin and Pierre Puvis de Chavannes, Tourneur became known for the pictorial sensibility he brought to his theatrical and cinematic productions. In 1912, he began working on **Éclair**'s ACAD series, first as assistant director to Emile **Chautard**, then as director of such films as *Les Gaîtés de l'escadron* [The Gaieties of the Squadron] (1913) and *Le Friquet* [The Tree Sparrow] (1913). Sent to the USA in 1914 to head Éclair's New Jersey studio, Tourneur became renowned for his American films (1914–1926); *The Wishing Ring* (1914) and *Trilby* (1915) stand out among his early achievements at combining European and American film styles.

KAVEH ASKARI

trade marks

Because all forms of intellectual property—patents, trade marks, and **copyright**—offer a commercial monopoly endorsed by the State, they are of central importance to the development of new technological markets in attracting investment capital. The legal framework that emerged in the early market for moving pictures as the result of disputes over the ownership of intellectual property was of crucial importance in stabilizing and defining a complex and highly competitive environment.

The value of trade marks to early film manufacturers was directly correlated to the degree of control that they were able to maintain over their products. The change, from *actualité* to story films after about 1904, and the concurrent move from sales to rentals of film prints, extended proprietorial rights and encouraged increased use of trade marks as a means of gaining added value and promoting brand identification.

Trade mark registration offering prima facie evidence of ownership was available in Great Britain from 1875, although it was not until 1905 that Congressional legislation gave equal protection in the USA. Early English cases, often initiated by American companies, included *Thomas Edison and the Continental Commerce Company vs. Georgiades and Others* (UK 1895), which prohibited use of **Edison**'s name in connection with the sale of copies of his **Kinetoscope**, and *A & L Lumiére vs. The Anglo Continental Phonograph Company* (UK 1896), which prevented use of the word, **Cinématographe**, to describe a film **camera/projector** not made by the **Lumière** company. The Biograph organization also prevented unauthorized use of its registered name in *Koopman vs. The Manchester Palace* (UK 1897) and *British Mutoscope and Biograph Company vs. Nicole Frères* (UK 1899).

Interchangeability within intellectual property divisions occurred in the interesting case of *Warwick Trading Company vs. Gibbons* (UK 1902). Gibbons had been detected "duping" some of Warwick's films; since a "film" was not recognized at this time in English law, however, no copyright infringement case was possible. Instead the defendant was successfully indicted for forging and "passing off" Warwick's registered trade mark, which had been included in certain of the film's images.

Sometimes a trade mark case achieved solely strategic business objectives. *Warwick Trading Company vs. Urban* (UK 1903) ostensibly was concerned with the unauthorized use of Warwick's registered trade mark, as well as other offenses; but, in fact, the case was brought as part of an ultimately unsuccessful attempt by Warwick to prevent Charles **Urban** from establishing a similar film production and distribution business to its own, whose managing director Urban had once been.

More generally, as **Pathé-Frères** began marketing its products across the globe around 1904, the French company achieved a singular, fixed identity through its trade mark red rooster, a figure that quickly came to guarantee the excellence and dependability of its films to consumers everywhere.

See also: law and the cinema

Further reading

Abel, Richard (1999) "Marketing Films as a Product Category," *The Red Rooster Scare: Making Cinema American, 1900–1910*, 14–19, Berkeley: University of California Press.

Brown Richard (1998) "'England is not big enough . . . .' or American Rivalry in the Early English Film Business: The Case of Warwick vs. Urban (1903)," *Film History*, 1.1: 21–34.

Wilkins, Mira (1992) "The Neglected Intangible Asset: The Influence of the Trade Mark on the Rise of the Modern Corporation," *Business History*, 1: 66–95.

RICHARD BROWN

trade press

A trade press devoted exclusively to moving pictures developed slowly, as might be expected, but was well established by 1914, at least in the USA and many European countries. That development went through several stages and, depending on the specific country, revealed differing alliances between the cinema and other entertainment industries as well as between the press and certain sectors of the industry itself.

In the USA, the earliest trade journal to deal with moving pictures, **The Phonogram** (1891–1893), was allied with the phonograph industry, specifically the **Edison** company. From the late 1890s to the mid 1900s, however, the most consistent sources of information (including advertisements) for the new medium were the *New York Clipper* and *Billboard*, the most widely circulating trade weeklies covering stage performances and cheap amusements. In Great Britain, the earliest trade journal was allied with the **magic lantern** industry: the *Optical Magic Lantern Journal and Photographic Enlarger* (1899–1903) became the *Optical Lantern and Cinematograph Journal* in 1904 and then **Kinematograph and Lantern Weekly** in 1907. In France, by contrast, the earliest trade journals were associated with the **fairs/fairgrounds**— *L'Industriel forain*, where **Pathé-Frères** placed its ads before 1905—or with the Catholic press—*Le Fascinator*, the educational and recreational monthly published by **Maison de la Bonne Presse**.

In both France and the USA, Pathé-Frères (like other manufacturers, it also issued its own catalogues) supported the first trade journals dealing primarily with moving pictures. Pathé partly financed *Phono-Gazette*, which six months after its founding as a bimonthly, in April 1905, became **Phono-Ciné-Gazette** and increasingly gave more attention to the cinema than to **phonography**. Along with **Vitagraph**, the French company also financed **Views and Films Index**, first issued as a biweekly in April 1906, in order to link manufacturers more directly with exhibitors in the USA, especially during the **nickelodeon** boom. Manufacturers in other countries also were involved in financing a trade press: in Russia, beginning in 1915, Alexandr **Khanhonkov** published *Kinematograficheskii vestnik* (The Cinematographic Herald). Yet the trade journals in some countries either originated in or promoted sectors of the industry other than manufacturing. In Denmark, **Filmen** initially was published in 1912 by the major distribution company, **Kinografen**, and then taken over by the exhibitors' association. In Germany, from its beginning in 1908, Die **Lichtbild-Bühne** tirelessly supported small-time exhibitors against all manner of threats to their prosperity. In France, *Le Courrier cinématographique* was edited, from its first issue in July 1911, by Charles Le Fraper, formerly a regional exhibitor.

That the new industry as a whole was developing with more assurance between 1907 and 1910 can be seen in the emergence of relatively "independent" trade journals. In the USA, beginning in March 1907, the weekly **Moving Picture World** sought to chart a course that equally supported both the **Motion Picture Patents Company** and Independent manufacturers; by contrast, **Moving Picture News** appeared in the summer of 1908 as a fierce advocate for the Independents. In France, beginning in August 1908, **Ciné-Journal** gradually relinquished its initial opposition to Pathé and became the chief corporate advocate for the entire French film industry. From its first issues in 1907, *Der Kinematograph* assumed a similar position in Germany (and especially promoted the cinema reform movement there), as did **The Bioscope**, beginning in September 1908, in Great Britain; within another year, **La Ciné-Fono** (partly originating in the south) and *La Vita Cinematografica* (originating in the north) did likewise in Italy.

It was during this period also that other trade papers began to take moving pictures seriously, especially in the USA. In 1908, the theatrical weekly, **New York Dramatic Mirror**, added a section on moving pictures that included some of the earliest important film reviews, a move that *Variety* (a new **vaudeville** weekly first issued in 1905) and then *Billboard* (which covered circuses, amusement parks, and carnivals as well theater and vaudeville) soon took up as well. In 1910, the **New York Morning Telegraph** (a daily specializing in finance, sports, and entertainment) created a Sunday section devoted to moving pictures, also with reviews, which eventually sold as a separate supplement, probably to more subscribers than did all of the other US trade journals combined.

By the early 1910s, as the *Morning Telegraph*'s success suggests, the mass audiences for moving pictures began to be seen as a market that reached far beyond the industry's own members. In July 1912, *Le Cinéma et l'Echo du cinema réunis* adopted a folio format in order to provide current information to movie-going readers throughout France. Months earlier, in the USA, Vitagraph launched the monthly *Motion Picture Story Magazine*, which initially published stories of newly released MPPC films for movie fans. Renamed *Motion Picture Magazine*, it gradually gave more attention to stars than to stories and, along with *Photoplay* (also first issued in 1912), eventually turned into the prototype of the fan magazine (its circulation was over 200,000 by 1914).

Also in the early 1910s, again in the USA in particular, the industry began to view **newspapers** as an extension of the trade press and a valuable venue of **publicity**. In December 1911, the *Cleveland Leader* created a Sunday page of news and ads devoted to moving pictures, initially drawing material from the *New York Morning Telegraph*; over the next two years, other papers in major US cities from Boston to Los Angeles followed the *Leader*'s example. In late 1912, the Scripps-McRae chain of Midwestern newspapers began publishing a syndicated column, sometimes signed by Gertrude Price, whose consistent subject, the individual "movie" personality (most of them active, single women), contributed greatly to the emergence of the **star system**.

Further reading

Abel, Richard (1999) "A Trade Press for the 'World's Greatest Show'," *The Red Rooster Scare: Making Cinema American, 1900–1910*, 80–86, Berkeley: University of California Press.

Abel, Richard (2001) "A Marriage of Ephemeral Discourses: Newspapers and Moving Pictures," *Cinema & cie*, 1: 59–83.

Toulet, Emmanuelle (1989) "Aux sources de l'histoire du cinema... Naissance d'une presse sous influences," *Restaurations et triages de la Cinémathèque française*, 4: 14–25.

RICHARD ABEL

transportation

Transportation technologies such as the railway, the streetcar, the steamship, and the automobile hold an important place in the history of early cinema. At the earliest public demonstrations of projected moving pictures, films of moving trains approaching the camera, such as **Lumière**'s *Arrivé d'un train à Perruche* [Arrival of a Train at the Station] (1896) and **Edison**'s *Black Diamond Express* (1896) helped to demonstrate the novelty of *motion* pictures; simultaneously, they participated in commercialized leisure's provocation and satisfaction of the modern amusement seeker's fascination with shock and speed. In the earliest years of film exhibition, railway technology served another function: it allowed **itinerant exhibitors** and exhibition services supplying **vaudeville** houses, **music halls**, and other venues to present their shows to the populations of most countries, especially in Europe and North America. Later, railroads would prove crucial for the development of **nickelodeons** and larger permanent cinemas, providing the principal means of quickly distributing films and equipment over great distances.

The convergence of the early cinema with transportation technologies also contributed to **modernity**'s annihilation of space and time by bringing films of distant places and times—often shot from a position onboard a moving train or steamship—to the spectator. Shot from the cowcatcher of a moving train, films such as **American**

Mutscope and Biograph's *The Haverstraw Tunnel* (1897) demonstrated the camera's mobility and endowed the spectator with a "traveling" point of view that eliminated the perils of travel itself. Similarly, films such as Edison's *S.S. Coptic Running Against a Storm* (1898), which was shot from the deck of a steamship at sea during a storm, allowed spectators to observe powerful technological forces encounter dangerous natural forces from a position of relative safety. Georges **Méliès'** *Un Voyage dans la lune* [A Trip to the Moon] (1902) imagined a futuristic means of transportation and the "novel" views such a technology might make possible.

In this respect, early cinema's convergence with transportation technologies expanded the availability of what Wolfgang Schivelbusch calls "panoramic perception"—a mechanically mediated, mobile, and enframed point of view first associated with railway travel but structurally similar to the mobile point of view provided by the early cinema. The homology between the panoramic perception of the railway and the early cinema was perhaps most explicit in **Hale's Tours**, a turn-of-the-century amusement in which audiences watched moving pictures through the "windows" of a theatrical space modeled after a railway car. Making its only appearance at the 1900 Paris Exposition, Raoul **Grimoin-Sanson**'s "Cineorama" unsuccessfully sought to exploit the link between panoramas and cinematic visual experience. At the same exposition, both Lumière and Edison cameramen shot several "panorama" films from onboard a far more pedestrian transportation technology—the *trottoir roulant* or "platform mobile"—a moving sidewalk that transported fairgoers through the Exposition grounds.

Other films shifted their focus to the changing behavioral norms and social conventions precipitated by mass transportation technologies as well as the opportunities for crime they presented. Edwin S. **Porter**'s *The Great Train Robbery* (1903) recreates a popular stage play **reenactment** of a notorious train hold-up by bandits. AM&B's *A Railway Tragedy* (1904) dramatizes the dangers of the seclusion provided by European railway cars when a female passenger, alone in a car with a male passenger in disguise, is robbed, beaten and thrown off the moving train. The film concludes with authorities arresting the criminal when the train pulls into the next station. Other films dramatized lesser infractions of decorum. In **Lubin**'s *Streetcar Chivalry* (1903), male passengers graciously offer their seats to an attractive young woman who boards a streetcar. When they fail to do so for a more matronly passenger who boards at the next stop, she takes matters into her own hands: when jostled by the bumpy ride, she allows herself to be thrown upon the male passengers, who quickly abandon their seats.

Other films focus on the tendency of transportation technologies to break down, crash, or run over unsuspecting pedestrians, emphasizing the experience of modern shock and trauma. Hepworth's *How It Feels to be Run Over* (1900) uses stop-motion photography to show a pedestrian—replaced by a dummy at the crucial moment— knocked down in the street by an automobile. Lubin's *The Photographer's Mishap* (1901) features a similar spectacle, although in this film the victim is a photographer who sets his camera up on railway tracks to record an oncoming train. Edison's *A Railway Smash-Up* (1904) takes this genre to the extreme in its documentation of a staged collision between two engines.

Transportation technologies also had a narrative function in the early cinema. In **comedies**, they were featured in the chase sequences that helped delay resolution and in the process extended the length of films. For example, in **Hepworth**'s *Fine Feathers Make Fine Birds* (1905), police give chase when thieves dress up in the touring outfits of wealthy automobile enthusiasts and steal their car. The chase ends when the thieves drive the stolen vehicle into a pond. Later, transportation technologies were crucial to the construction of narrative suspense in one and two-reel sensational **melodramas** made during the transitional era. In D. W. **Griffith**'s *The Lonedale Operator* (1911), shots of a young telegraph operator fending off the assault of hoboes alternate with shots of her engineer boyfriend who races to her rescue in a commandeered engine. While the image of the frantic hero speeding to the rescue suggests that help is on the way, shots of the hoboes breaking through various locked doors to reach the imperiled heroine suggest that he may not arrive in time. Lois

Weber's appropriately named *Suspense* (1912) deftly combines these effects of transportation technologies: a panicked wife telephones her husband's office for help when a hobo breaks into their isolated suburban home. When the hero steals a car in order to race to her rescue, he is mistaken for a thief and chased by the police. In his efforts to elude them and save his family in time, he runs over a pedestrian. In the end, the hero and the police arrive at the house just as the knife-wielding transient breaks into the room where the wife and her baby are hiding.

By 1913, the use of transportation technologies as instruments of shock and as vehicles for chases and last-minute rescues had become so conventional that they either had to be accentuated by novelty, as in the precision bombings from an airplane in **Éclair**'s **crime film**, *Zigomar, peu d'anguille* [Zigomar the Eel Skin] (1913) or in the duels between airplanes in Alfred **Machin**'s *Maudit soit la guerre* [Cursed Be War] (1913). More often, however, they were parodied in comedies such as **Keystone**'s *Barney Oldfield's Race for a Life* (1913).

Further reading

Friedberg, Anne (1993) *Window Shopping: Cinema and the Postmodern*, Berkeley: University of California Press.

Kirby, Lynne (1997) *Parallel Tracks: the Railroad and Silent Cinema*, Durham: Duke University Press.

Schivelbusch, Wolfgang (1986) *The Railway Journey: The Industrialization of Space and Time in the Nineteenth Century*, Berkeley: University of California Press.

KRISTEN WHISSEL

Trautschold, Gustav

b. ?; d. ?

director, scriptwriter, Germany

A writer of popular fiction, Trautschold was hired by Eiko-Film in the summer of 1912 to become its most versatile **comedy** director. He is best remembered for his first film, *Wie sich das Kino rächt* [How the Cinema Takes Revenge] (1912), a playfully self-reflexive satire which turns the moral attacks of the cinema reform movement back on itself and, fuelled by the controversy it entailed, became such a box-office success that a sequel, also written and directed by Trautschold, was produced in 1913. After another half dozen comedies for Eiko, Trautschold radically switched genres and co-directed, with William Wauer and Richard Schott, the prestigious six-reel *Bismarck* (1913–1914), for which renowned composer Ferdinand Hummel wrote an original **musical score**. With *Ostpreussen und sein Hindenburg* [East-Prussia and its Hindenburg] (1916), Trautschold (again in collaboration with Schott and Hummel) made another national epic, this time with overt propagandistic intentions. The first German film ever to be granted a festive premiere at a veritable **opera** house, it combined a semi-documentary account of regional history with a fictional treatment of the life of Germany's highest-ranking military leader of **World War I**.

MICHAEL WEDEL

travelogues

An important kind of early film, travelogues or travel films were a regular part of the moviegoing experience from the cinema's inception through the middle 1910s and beyond. These short films presented glimpses of foreign landscapes, peoples, regional industries, and tourist icons to an audience that was not yet accustomed to world travel. Many parts of the globe were filmed, from Europe to South America, from India to New Zealand, from Mount Fuji to the Colorado River. Travelogues appeared in widely differing exhibition contexts in this period, such as educational travel lectures, commercial **fair/fairground** shows, **Hale's Tours**, or variety programs in small storefront movie theaters. The films' subject matter, however, remained constant no matter what the venue: they were continually concerned with the specificity of place and space, combined with generalized notions of "timeless" scenery and the exotic.

Travelogues grew out of the many pre-cinematic images of foreign lands presented in **stereographs**, **magic lantern shows**, **illustrated lectures**, **world fairs**, and other media. These entertainments catered to a popular 19th-century taste for the exotic. They presented still images of a foreign land (or in the case of the world fairs, actual people and artifacts from a foreign land) paired with a small amount of factual information about the place being represented. But brought alive by the technology of motion pictures, travel film images were highly kinetic, with more **camera movement** than any other genre in early cinema. Despite the uniqueness of the motion inherent in the new medium, however, travelogues remained more like their pre-cinema predecessors in terms of aesthetics and subject matter than most other kinds of films.

Travelogues were shown in non-commercial venues such as public lecture halls throughout the early cinema period, in a pattern of exhibition held over from the 19th-century magic lantern show. Lecturers such as E. Burton **Holmes** and Lyman **Howe** specialized in "high-class" presentations of travel subjects using magic lantern slides. Some travel lectures took a "world tour" structure, covering many different countries in a single evening, while others focused on a single destination, such as Howe's 1903 program set in Egypt, entitled "Scenes and Incidents en route from Cairo to Khartoum." Many lecturers had never been to the places they presented in their talks, and most audience members would never travel to these locations either. These presentations, then, functioned as a kind of substitute travel, fulfilling a desire for knowledge and a curiosity to see what other parts of the world looked like. Travel lectures were endorsed by the bourgeois turn-of-the-century moral code, which suggested that entertainment should also be instructive. These connotations of respectability, derived from pre-cinema traditions, would be carried over to influence the travelogue's status in the new moving picture theaters.

Alongside this non-commercial exhibition, travelogues played a significant role in the development of the early commercial film industry. In the first ten years of the cinema, nonfiction films were more commonplace than fiction. Many *actualités* made by companies such as **Lumière**, **Edison**, or **American Mutoscope and Biograph** depicted foreign locales. Although these were not called travelogues at the time, we can in retrospect view them as an early stage of their development. Travelogues from this earliest period of cinema history were simply individual shots, intended to be combined into a program consisting of multiple views of a given location. For example, Yellowstone National Park was featured in a series of single-shot films made by Edison in 1897, with titles such as *Upper Falls of the Yellowstone*; *Wild Bear in Yellowstone Park*; *Old Faithful Geyser*; *Coaches Going to Cinnabar from Yellowstone*. These single-shot "views" were not self-sufficient; rather they gained meaning through their exhibition context, after the exhibitor arranged them into the order he considered best. Usually such programs would be accompanied by a **lecturer** explaining more about the location being shown.

It was around 1905–1906, when **nickelodeons** came to prominence in the USA, that travelogues solidified into a distinct film genre. As with other genres, by this time they had developed a multi-shot structure that could stand alone in a film program. Although nonfiction no longer dominated as it had during the first decade of moving picture production, travelogues continued to be a major presence on cinema screens. From about 1905 to 1915, they were regularly shown in nickelodeons and the first **palace cinemas** alongside many other film genres as part of early cinema's variety format. A typical forty-minute show might include, for example, several **comedies**, one or more dramas, an **industrial film**, and a travelogue; these films would be interspersed with **advertising** slides or **illustrated songs**. Although a travelogue would not always appear, the genre's existence was in effect assured by this variety format, which was a practice adopted from the variety shows of **vaudeville**. In the USA, travelogues were often released as part of a split reel, sharing part of the standard 1000-foot reel with a short comedy or drama; this too assured the genre's continuance on moving picture **screens**. Travelogues often ran 300 to 700 feet, lasting from four to ten minutes, depending upon the speed at which the **projector** was cranked.

Burton Holmes claimed to have coined the term "travelogue"—a conjunction of travel and dialogue—in 1904, although examples of its usage have been found as early as 1899. While the term was used in the **trade press**, by far the most common trade term for these films in the early period was "scenic." This term indicates the extent to which the genre was more invested in producing generic scenery than scientific facts about specific geographical locations. "Scenic" now no longer resonates as a term, however, while usage of "travelogue" has persisted, which is why we use the word today. A great many other terms also were applied to travelogues in the early years, among them "panorama," "nature study," and "foreign view."

Most early film manufacturers made some travelogues, since they were relatively cheap and simple to film. No actors or elaborate staging were required, and filming in the open air required no special **lighting**. In addition, railroad companies encouraged travelogues by frequently sponsoring their production, since the films were believed to promote tourism. The Italian companies **Ambrosio** and **Cines** made quite a few scenic films, as did the **Warwick Trading Company** and the **Charles Urban Trading Company** in Britain. **Nordisk**, **Éclair**, **Selig Polyscope**, **Essanay**, and **Kalem** also made a number of scenic films. But it was the French companies **Eclipse**, **Gaumont**, and especially **Pathé-Frères** that were most renowned for their travel films. In this era the director and camera operator were still anonymous; it was the manufacturer's name that gave a film its only recognizable stamp of authorship. Exhibitors and audiences grew to appreciate the high quality of these French travelogues, many of which were released in **color**. Pathé's success with the genre was derived in part from its exclusive mechanical stencil-coloring process, which was a precise method for applying multiple colors to individual film prints.

Travelogues were often labeled "genteel." This was in part because of their origins in the illustrated lecture tradition described above, which catered to an educated audience. But it was also a marketing ploy to play up the genre's aura of gentility, part of the drive to legitimate the cinema as a respectable form of entertainment in the face of criticisms that moving pictures catered to "low class" audiences. Travelogues were one of the primary genres to be

held up as an example of film's educational function, and their merits were repeatedly celebrated in the trade press. Reformers and industry businessmen (such as George **Kleine** in the USA) frequently pointed to travelogues as the genre that proved the cinema's ability to "uplift" the values of film audiences. Besides teaching "educational" facts about foreign lands, travelogues also were regularly touted as a substitute for actual travel, "the next best thing to being there."

Unlike fiction films, which developed in conjunction with innovations in continuity editing (crosscutting, close-ups, etc.), travelogues did not require a new "language" with which to articulate foreign landscapes. Instead, cameramen fell back upon the long-established conventions of the picturesque. Although many travelogues have an **amateur** visual sensibility much like home movies, a number of them demonstrate attempts to frame landscapes with picturesque side-screens in the foreground that lead the viewer's eye into a deeply-composed center frame. At the very least, travelogue subject matter was always chosen with an eye for what was pretty, spectacular, or visually striking. Images of smiling children, flowers, waterfalls, and sunsets proliferate in these films. With titles such as Éclair's *Le Japon pittoresque* [Picturesque Japan] (1913), Selig's *Surf and Sunset on the Indian Ocean* (1913), and Pathé's *Ceylan, vécu et pittoresque* [Picturesque Ceylon] (1905), the genre's use of a rather formulaic picturesque aesthetic is made explicit. Colonial lands appear as tranquil as parks; any explicit sense of social conflict is banished from the travelogue world-view. Besides landscape scenery, early travelogues also were filled with ethnographic images of people, often wearing traditional costumes or posed in groups and sometimes preceded by the intertitle "native types."

Although travelogues did not follow the narrative logic of continuity editing, they did follow a different structural logic: that of the collection. Again drawing from pre-cinema models, travelogues were edited as a series of discrete shots joined in a manner that preserves the integrity of each shot, rather like looking at a series of **postcards** or snapshots in a photo album. Travelogues also are characterized by an overwhelming dominance of extreme long shots. Finally, travelogues

Figure 118 George Kleine advertisement, *Film Index*, 4 February 1911.

are filled with movement in just about every shot, either camera movement such as a pan or a tracking shot made by placing the camera on a moving train, or image-movement such as a shot of crashing waves or a crowd of moving people. Indeed, it can be argued that travelogues were the films that first innovated camera movement.

There was a brief moment in the early 1910s when some in the film industry tried to argue that travelogues and other educational films not only could free the movies from their stigma as a cheap entertainment, but also might have more commercial appeal than fiction films. Some exhibitors even experimented with programs comprised exclusively of travelogues and other nonfiction films. It was still unclear, after all, what would best turn moving pictures into a respectable middle-class entertainment. As classical storytelling techniques developed and **multiple-reel/feature films** became more popular, however, this moment of arguing for the box office appeal of the educational film soon ended. The success of the **classical Hollywood cinema** effectively neutralized reformers' attempts to promote the short nonfiction film. Travelogues persisted as an added attraction on movie screens well into the feature film era, but they no longer seemed viable commercial competition for fiction films after the early 1910s.

See also: audiences: surveys and debates; cinema of attractions; colonialism: Europe; dioramas and panoramas; editing: spatial relations; editing: temporal relations; education; ethnographic films;

expedition/exploration films; imperialism: USA; phantom train rides; program formats

Further reading

Barber, X. Theodore (1993) "The Roots of Travel Cinema: John L. Stoddard, E. Burton Holmes and the Nineteenth-Century Illustrated Travel Lecture," *Film History*, 5:1: 68–84.

Gunning, Tom (1995) "'The Whole World Within Reach': Travel Images Without Borders," in Roland Cosandey and François Albera (eds.) *Cinéma sans frontières 1896–1918/Images Without Borders*, 21–36, Lausanne: Payot.

Hertogs, Daan, and Nico de Klerk (eds.) (1997) *Uncharted Territory: Essays on Early Nonfiction Film*, Amsterdam: Stichting Nederlands Filmmuseum.

Musser, Charles (1990) "The Travel Genre in 1903–1904: Moving Towards Fictional Narrative," in Thomas Elsaesser (ed.) *Early Cinema: Space, Frame, Narrative*, 123–132, London: British Film Institute.

Peterson, Jennifer Lynn (2004) *Making the World Exotic: Travelogue and Silent Non-Fiction Film*, Durham: Duke University Press.

Rony, Fatimah Tobing (1996) *The Third Eye: Race, Cinema, and Ethnographic Spectacle*, Durham: Duke University Press.

JENNIFER LYNN PETERSON

trick films

If one assumes that a central aspect of cinematic specificity lies in the motion picture camera's capability of reproducing visible reality, a trick, in the broadest sense of the term, can be considered any kind of intervention which manipulates the exact rendition of the visual impression that an actual scene would provide to an eye-witness. Such interventions can occur at the level of the pro-filmic (e.g. through the use of reduced scale models, fake body parts, etc.), at the level of cinematic devices (e.g. double exposure, stop motion splices, etc.), at the level of post-production (as is commonly the case today), or by combinations of these. In an even broader sense, one might add the practice of the reverse projection of a film, which some of the **Lumière** cameramen used to amaze their audience. With regard to early trick films, however, which techniques are used seems less important than the way in which they function in their mode of address.

Trick films are among the earliest appearing in manufacturers' catalogues: in **Pathé-Frères** sales lists up to 1903, they are grouped under the heading, "*scènes à transformations*," and from then on under "*scènes à trucs*." The former denomination in fact describes a then dominant practice of trick cinematography: namely, the use of a substitution splice in order to instantly transform an object or a person into something or someone else. In another variant of this practice, objects or people suddenly appear or disappear, sometimes in combination with pyrotechnic effects (explosions, smoke). A prototypical example is Georges **Méliès**'s *Escamotage d'une dame chez Robert-Houdin* [Conjuring a Woman at the Robert-Houdin] (1896). Even though Méliès is often credited with the invention, or discovery, of this technique (allegedly due to a camera jam when he filmed at the Place de l'Opéra in Paris), it already had been used in a **Kinetoscope** film produced for **Edison**, *The Execution of Mary, Queen of Scots* (August 1895), where an actor is replaced by a dummy to depict the beheading. However, in Méliès's films, as well as in the "*scènes à transformation*" and "*scènes à trucs*" of other manufacturers, the trick effects are clearly foregrounded. The films are constructed to highlight them: very often there is a stage-like setting with characters such as **magicians**, illusionists, sprites, fairies, or devilish creatures performing their tricks, in a frontal arrangement, sometimes even addressing the camera and thus also the audience. Both the fixed framing and the frontality are in fact essential to the functioning of the tricks, since their effect rests upon the illusion of a temporal continuity that is enhanced by the unchanging spatial arrangement. The same goes for tricks based upon multiple exposures, combining people or objects of different sizes, or multiplying a character within the frame as in Méliès's *L'homme-orchestre* [One-Man Orchestra] (1900). Many early trick films consist of but one tableau, or setting, although during the production there may have been a number of different takes in order to perform substitutions.

Trick films clearly fall within the realm of the **cinema of attractions**. Although they may also present a narrative, the story mainly serves as a pretext for a series of spectacular and elaborate tricks. In this respect, trick films do have a lot in common with *féeries*/**fairy plays**. Both are deeply rooted in stage practices, and **color** frequently enhances their spectacular qualities.

Another important trick technique is the frame-by-frame **animation** (referred to in France as "*mouvement américain*"), producing the effect of inanimate objects moving about as if they were set in motion by invisible forces. James Stuart **Blackton**'s and Albert E. **Smith**'s prototypical and influential *The Haunted Hotel* (**Vitagraph** 1907) proved to be very successful on the international market. This film introduced a new technique to a theme which Méliès had already treated in *L'auberge ensorcelée* [Enchanted Inn] (1897), *Le déshabillage impossible* [Impossible Undressing] (1900) or *L'auberge du bon repos* [Inn of Good Rest] (1903), but mainly using the substitution splice and mechanical stage tricks. The frame-by-frame animation technique was taken up by others, most notably by Segundo de **Chomón**, working for Pathé, and by Emile **Cohl**, working for **Gaumont**. Interestingly, Chomón, too, exploited the same motif in films such as *La maison ensorcelée* [Haunted House] (1908) and *Electric Hotel* (1908). Of course, in many cases the substitution splice and the frame-by-frame technique were combined, Pathé's almost surrealistic *Symphonie bizarre* [Strange Symphony] (1909) being a major example. However, from about 1910, trick films' popularity gradually declined.

Of course, tricks had never been exclusive to trick films. Not only *féeries*, but also **comedies** and dramatic films had made extensive use of them. With the industry's shift to narrative films, their spectacular qualities were increasingly subordinated to the needs of storytelling. More and more, tricks in fact turned into special effects: they now came to function as narrative devices.

Symptomatically, at about the same time this shift began to occur, a number of texts appeared, revealing to a general audience how film tricks actually worked. In March and April 1908, for instance, Gustave Babin wrote two articles for the widely distributed French weekly, *L'Illustration*,

Figure 120 Frame still from *Le Cakewalk chez les nains* [The Dwarfs' Cakewalk] (Pathé 1903).

convincing representation of dramatic action. Not surprisingly, Méliès, true to the ethics of stage magicians, protested making public the tricks of the trade. However, Babin's position fit well within the overall trend in the industry towards a cinema of narrative integration.

Originating in the tradition of stage magic, trick films (or *scènes à transformations* and *scènes à trucs*) thus were a well-established, autonomous "genre" for more than a decade. They are a significant part of the genealogies of two different practices: special effects, on the one hand, and animated films on the other.

See also: editing: early practices and techniques

Further reading

Dahlquist, Marina (2001) *The Invisible Seen in French Cinema Before 1917*, Stockholm: Aura förlag.

Lefebvre, Thierry (ed.) (1999) *1895*, 27, special issue: "Pour une histoire des trucages."

Méliès, Georges (1907) "Les vues cinémato-graphiques," translated in Richard Abel (ed.) (1988) *French Film Theory and Criticism, 1907–1929: A History/Anthology*, 35–47, Princeton: Princeton University Press.

FRANK KESSLER

Figure 119 Production photos of *Magic Bricks* (Pathé, 1908).

explaining in detail different types of tricks. At the same time, Babin outlined a different aesthetics of cinema, in which trick photography in fact mainly would serve the ends of realism. Instead of creating a magical universe of fantastic metamorphoses, he argued, trick effects ought to contribute to the

Turkey/Ottoman Empire

The cinema had an inauspicious beginning in Turkey, when **Lumière** operator, Louis Janin brought a **Cinématographe** to Constantinople in May 1896. He spent several months vainly trying to persuade the authorities to let him project films, and departed before permission was grudgingly granted. The problem was that Sultan Abdulhamed feared **electricity** and so banned the use of all electrical apparatus. Official doubts remained, and cinema was slow to take off in Turkey. Over the following two years, a few shows were given in the cosmopolitan part of the city, Pera, notably by Sigmund Weinberg. Weinberg was Rumanian, and other film pioneers in Turkey tended to be foreign: around 1906, the first permanent cinema in Pera was opened by a Frenchman, while the first in Smyrna was opened in the summer of 1907 by an Italian company.

Some of the restrictions on importing electrical devices were lifted after the Sultan was deposed in the Turkish revolution of 1909. By early 1910, there were eight cinemas in Constantinople (showing mainly French and Italian films), but tight restrictions remained, including a ban on **religious films**, and in the spring of 1911 the police halted a screening of *The Life of Christ*.

Cinema-going did not immediately catch on in Turkey, for the Turkish custom was to stay at home in the evening: in 1911, the US consul reported that only $75,000 worth of films was annually imported into the country. Turkish cinemas tried to entice **audiences**, by offering separate shows for women, for example, and attendance gradually increased. By 1913, there were 19 cinemas operating in the vicinity of Smyrna alone. As the cinema grew in popularity, there was increasing public impatience with French and other foreign **intertitles** that appeared in so many films, and audiences sometimes mobbed cinemas to demand Turkish titles.

Filmmaking was as slow to take off in Turkey as cinema exhibition, again largely due to the pre-Revolutionary restrictions. When British cameraman Henry Howse tried to film there in 1906, he was jailed for his pains. Occasionally *actualités* were filmed, including, bizarrely, a 1908 film depicting the Sultan's harem, and **Ambrosio** and **Raleigh & Robert** released a film of the Revolution the following year. The Balkan Wars of 1912 to 1913 were extensively filmed by foreign cameramen, including those from the Turkish side. But filmmaking in Turkey only began in earnest during **World War I**, when an Army film propaganda unit was established under Weinberg in 1915.

At the dawn of the 20th century, Turkey was the epicenter of a vast Ottoman empire, stretching from what is now Greece to the Middle East and northern Africa, and both film exhibition and production developed quite early in some of these regions. In Turkish-controlled Greece, the cinema arrived when British correspondent Frederic Villiers filmed the war of secession in 1897; and the Manaki brothers shot scenes in Thessaloniki and Monastir in 1905 and 1911. There were four moving picture theaters in Thessaloniki by 1910, mainly screening European films, but within two years American films were the favorites among the city's mix of people. In Tunis, Albert "Chikly" Samama showed Lumière films in 1897, while in Libya there were film shows by 1910. The first screening from Syria is reported from 1908 and from the following year in Baghdad. Because of its Biblical associations **Palestine** was the most attractive part of Turkey's empire for foreign filmmakers, and many cameramen came to the province, starting with the Lumières in 1896. An **Edison** crew came in 1902; Charles **Urban** and cameraman Leo Lefebvre, around 1908; and a **Kalem** unit, in 1912.

See also: Egypt and other Arab countries; Greece; Olcott, Sidney

Further reading

"Correspondence Louis Janin (1896)" (1995) *Bulletin du Congrès Lumière*, 4.

"Il cinematografo in Turchia" (1910) *La Cine-Fono*, 8, 28 May.

Basutçu, Mehmet (1996) *Le Cinéma Turc* Paris: Centre Georges Pompidou.

STEPHEN BOTTOMORE

Turner, Florence

b. 1887; d. 1946

actor, director, USA, Great Britain

One of the pre-eminent stars of the early 1910s, Turner began her career at **Vitagraph**, performing multiple tasks (wardrobe, payroll) in addition to acting. She quickly became an audience favorite, known only as "The Vitagraph Girl," until the company promoted her by name in early 1910. Her American fame peaked several years later, when she was voted most popular **star** in a **trade press** poll. Versatile and capable of emotionally-charged performances, she was featured as the sole performer in *Jealousy* (1911). In 1913, she left Vitagraph to make films in England with Larry Trimble for **Hepworth**, where she enjoyed some success before World War I disrupted that nation's filmmaking.

CHARLIE KEIL

Turpin, Ben

b. 17 September 1874, New Orleans;
d. 1 July 1940, Hollywood

actor, USA

Turpin was a **vaudeville** performer and slapstick comedian, best known for his crossed eyes and an extraordinary ability to take pratfalls, somersaulting from a standing position to land on his face. He worked at **Essanay** for two different periods, 1907–1909 and 1914–1916. Most of his Essanay comedies are lost, except for the 1915 Charlie **Chaplin** films, in which Turpin appeared. After starring in Vogue Comedies, in 1917 he joined Mack **Sennett** for about ten years, where he became famous for his burlesques of movie **stars**. Turpin reappeared in small parts in sound films until the end of his life.

EILEEN BOWSER

U

Umeya Shokichi

b. 1873; d. 1934

exhibitor, producer, Japan

Born in Nagasaki, Umeya believed strongly in Japan's economic and political expansion into Far East and Southeast Asia. Accordingly, he operated several businesses in Malaya and Singapore, including film exhibition. Returning to Japan with a large stock of film prints, he established his own film company, **M. Pathe**, in 1906. After the company was merged into **Nikkatsu** in 1912, Umeya established a new film company, M. Kashii. The film business, however, never became his primary interest. He was more engaged in Asian political movements and supported Sun Wen in his bid for revolution in China.

HIROSHI KOMATSU

Universal Film Manufacturing Company

Formed through an alliance of independent production companies in June 1912, the Universal Film Manufacturing Company is the oldest of the surviving Hollywood studios. Universal's early history illustrates many of the changes of the transitional era, including the demise of the **Motion Picture Patents Company** (MPPC), the rise of studio-based mass production methods, the move westward to Hollywood, and the eventual dominance of **multiple-reel/feature films**.

Universal united several independent production companies operating outside of the powerful MPPC, including Independent Motion Picture **(IMP)**, **New York Motion Picture** (Bison), **Powers**, **Rex**, **Centaur/Nestor**, Crystal and **Éclair American**. These outfits came together shortly after the formation of rival **Mutual Film Corporation**, which had acquired several film exchanges earlier in the year and had begun to distribute the work of competing independents, among them **American**, **Majestic**, **Reliance** and **Thanhouser**. A previous alliance of independents, the **Motion Picture Distributing and Sales Company**, which had opposed the MPPC's distribution arm, **General Film**, fell apart earlier in 1912 as the distribution of new multiple-reel films became an increasing problem for the industry. The realignment of independent companies under the banners of Universal and Mutual also appeared the same year that the federal government filed its antitrust suit against the MPPC, signaling the beginning of Trust's demise. Universal's first president was Charles **Baumann** of the New York Motion Picture Company, but Carl **Laemmle** of IMP soon took control and stayed at the company's helm until 1936.

Initially centered in New York, Universal quickly began to branch westwards where one of its members, Nestor, had established the first Hollywood-based production facility in 1911. Universal purchased a large ranch property on the outskirts of Los Angeles in 1913 and began constructing vast production facilities there. Universal City, as the studio was named, opened in 1915, and the company moved its business headquarters west to the site that same year. Designed to consolidate the company's production operations for maximum efficiency and productivity, the facilities included several large, electrically-equipped indoor shooting stages, standing outdoor sets, an enormous location backlot, as well as film processing labs and editing rooms. Universal City was so large that it became the only studio with its own municipal designation, complete with post office, telegraph office, voting precinct, and police and fire departments.

Under Laemmle's leadership, Universal initially resisted both the move toward feature films, favoring instead a "balanced" program of shorts, **newsreels**, **serials** and dramas. King **Baggot**, Mary **Fuller**, Arline Pretty and Warren Kerrigan, all worked at Universal in the early years, along with serial stars Grace **Cunard** and Francis **Ford**. Many female directors and screenwriters were employed at Universal at a time when women had unrivaled access to positions of creative control within the industry. Lois **Weber**, one of the decade's top-ranked director/screenwriters, worked at the company alongside Jeanie MacPherson, Cleo Madison, Ida May Park, and several others.

Further reading

Edmonds, I. G. (1977) *Big U: Universal in the Silent Days*, South Brunswick, New Jersey: A. S. Barnes.

SHELLEY STAMP

Urban, Charles

b. 1867; d. 1942

producer, distributor, USA, Britain

Urban was born and raised in the German community of Cincinnati. He first flourished as a traveling book agent, before settling in Chicago where he ran a stationery store, and where he saw the **Edison Kinetoscope** exhibited in 1894, and set up his own Kinetoscope parlor early

Figure 121 Entrance to Universal City, c. 1915.

in 1895. He began touring with a Vitascope projector in 1896, but had his own projector developed, the Bioscope. He was hired by the Edison concessionaries, **Maguire & Baucus**, to run their London office in 1897, and brought the Bioscope with him.

Urban quickly rose to the top of the nascent British film industry, with the company renamed the **Warwick Trading Company** in 1898. His success was built on the Bioscope and other equipment largely manufactured by Alfred **Darling**, on the production of **news event films**, **travelogues**, and *actualités*, and on the distribution of such strong producers as **Lumière**, **Méliès**, G. A. **Smith**, and James **Williamson**. In 1903 he broke away to form his own **Charles Urban Trading Company**, and built up through aggressive marketing and an eye for talent a catalogue of **scientific**, travel, and educational films. He gave his educational "Urbanora" shows the memorable slogan, "We Put the World Before You," and worked with photographer-scientists who exhibited a popularizing streak, such as F. Martin **Duncan** and F. Percy **Smith**, and skilled *actualité* filmmakers such as Joseph **Rosenthal**.

Urban broadened his business interests with the creation of the French company **Eclipse** in 1906, and the Kineto company for his science and travel films in 1907. He reached the peak of his success, however, with Kinemacolor, the world's first successful natural **color** film system, invented by G. A. Smith and patented in 1906. Urban's astute selling of Kinemacolor as a prestige experience made him wealthy, although the Kinemacolor franchises in other countries seldom matched the success the system had in Great Britain through the **Natural Color Kinematograph** Company. Urban's greatest success came with the sensational Kinemacolor film of the Coronation Delhi Durbar in 1912.

A court case brought by William **Friese-Greene**, inventor of a rival color system, led to the invalidation of the **Kinematograph** patent in 1914, and as a result of this and other business misadventures, Urban's fortunes started to turn. In 1915, he produced a documentary feature, *Britain Prepared*, and was sent to the USA to get British **propaganda films** on American screens. His success was limited, but he decided to stay, developing a new color system (Kinekrom) and ended the war editing the American propaganda **newsreel**, *Official War Review*.

Urban attempted to revive his fortunes after the war, setting up an ambitious plant at Irvington, New York, and further emphasizing the educational value of the film magazines that he now produced. He also had high hopes for the Spirograph system of viewing films at home on a disk, but his business collapsed and went into receivership in 1925. He returned to Great Britain, and spent his last years in London, and then Brighton.

Further reading

McKernan, Luke (ed.) (1999) *A Yank in Britain: The Lost Memoirs of Charles Urban, Film Pioneer*, Hastings: The Projection Box.

Thomas, D. B. (1969) *The First Colour Motion Pictures*, London: HMSO.

LUKE McKERNAN

urbanization

The USA can serve as a model of urbanization, having been an urban nation since the late 19th century. There, the innovation of moving pictures into cultural, social, and business life came as urbanization was reforming the nation. The cities of the 1880s and early 1890s were crowded, but compact: they were walking cities for most, with horse transportation only for the rich (they had been sited on water so as to serve as "break points" for shipping and long distance travel). The age of early cinema coincided with the expansion of cities due to mass transit. Into the neighborhoods abandoned by new middle-class suburbanites flowed immigrants, redefining the central core of cities. The moving picture show was constrained and prospered as the USA urbanized—from walking cities to vast metropolis built on mass **transportation**, and later the automobile.

Because most cities were ports (from New York City, a sea port, to Albany, a river port), or railroad transfer points (such as Chicago or Indianapolis), their core by 1895 was defined by the railroad station which connected one city to all others (highways were little more than dirt roads useful only for short periods of the year when there was no mud and/or snow). The hub was the port for transoceanic travel, the rail station for internal travel.

Near the rail stations of most cities or towns one found **vaudeville** theaters. By the early 1890s, vast chains of city-based vaudeville theaters controlled the mass market for entertainment in the USA. There was the **Keith**'s chain in major cities in the eastern part of the country, and the Pantages and Orpheum circuits in cities west of the Mississippi. But the standards were set in New York City, then the largest and dominant city. To keep theaters filled, Keith's, Pantages, and Orpheum bookers continuously sought newer acts. One source they looked to was visual spectacle such as magic acts, dance performances, and **magic lantern shows**. Moving pictures appeared as yet another new "attraction" within this category, and thus were presented initially in venues "downtown." They superceded the first **Kinetoscope** parlors which also were located downtown, where vast numbers of new city folks looked for affordable entertainment.

Through the late 1890s, and into the early 1900s, decentralization created by mass transit would prove to be the defining characteristic for the innovation of the moving picture show. The trolley, subway, and elevated train initially enabled the well-off to move to the edge of the city, and commute to employment downtown. **Electricity** supplied the power, and traction trusts laid tracks to sell land at the end of their lines. By the early 1900s, trolleys were carrying about six billion passengers per year, and marked a new phase of urbanization. Formerly separate border towns were knitted together into a single metropolis. This meant that trolley trusts built **amusement parks** at the end of the lines to increase ridership, enabling commuters of all classes to see the moving pictures shown there.

But all trolley lines (and their underground or elevated cousins in the biggest cities) led to the city center. In Chicago, for instance, the elevated "Loop" defined the downtown center of a vast urban area. **Nickelodeons** thus congregated downtown, and along trolley lines, so potential moviegoers would have easy access. This was particularly the case in northeastern and middle western cities. Indeed, the United States Census Department declared in 1910 that the Northeast United States was about three-quarters urban, the North Central region (around the Great Lakes and Mississippi River) was evenly split urban/rural, and the rest of the country was basically still rural. This meant that immigrants and others who lived in border factory towns (from Boston to Toledo) or in ethnic neighborhoods (Chicago had dozens) as well as those crowded into ghettos adjacent to downtown all could see moving pictures at nickel theaters.

Thus with the largest potential audience living in cities, the nickelodeon explosion after 1905 was basically an urban phenomenon. Nickelodeons may have opened in nearly all communities, even those with a population of 1,000 or less, but the greatest numbers came in cities in the urban Northeast and Middle West. Thus from Washington, D.C., to Boston, from Cleveland to Chicago (and St. Louis to Minneapolis), the nickelodeon proved that, in expanding cities, entrepreneurs opening shows which featured moving pictures could make huge profits.

Relying upon mass transit as a necessary condition of their existence, neighborhood nickelodeons also arose in what, at the time, were called "outlying business centers." Often located at an intersection of trolley lines, these served as neighborhood shopping centers where urbanites— before mass electrical refrigeration—did their daily shopping. Many of these nickelodeons catered to ethnic groups who lived within a short distance to make a trip easy and affordable. They prospered in all sections of New York, Chicago, and other growing cities, and offered new immigrant Americans a theater of their own.

This urban success meant that within a couple of years, entrepreneurs in small towns tried and succeeded at what their urban cousins had innovated. It also led urban entrepreneurs to open larger and larger theaters to be able to generate more and more revenue. And until the anti-immigrant laws were passed after **World War I**, cities in the USA grew rapidly. The exhibition business in cities boomed. Entrepreneurs did so well with commercial fare that Progressives such as Jane **Addams** even tried to counter the trend with their own "educational" cinemas.

Figure 122 Central Square, Lynn, Massachusetts, *c.* 1910.

By 1915, all cities were dotted with moving picture theaters. Indeed, in a symbolic conjunction, just as the age of the skyscraper commenced, so did the age of the **palace cinema**. As the logical outcomes of an urbanizing culture, society, and economy, both soon became iconic images of the urban United States.

See also: cinema circuits or chains; migration/immigration: USA; leisure time and space: USA; monopoly capitalism: USA.

Further reading

Fogelson, Robert M. (2001) *Downtown*, New Haven: Yale University Press.

Gomery, Douglas (1992) *Shared Pleasures: A History of Movie Presentation in the United States*, Madison: University of Wisconsin Press.

Levy, John M. (2000) *Urban America*, New York: Prentice-Hall.

Tabb, William K. and Larry Sawers (eds.) (1978) *Marxism and the Metropolis*, New York: Oxford University Press.

DOUGLAS GOMERY

Uruguay

The cinema arrived in Montevideo in 1896, with **Lumière** screenings taking place on July 18, the same day as in Buenos Aires, Argentina. Although still relatively small, Montevideo had an active port and its population was quite attuned to news from Europe and eager to replicate modern experiences. The **Edison Kinetoscope** already had been welcomed in April 1895. Throughout 1896, various locales announced screenings, ranging from the Salón Rouge dance hall to the more prestigious Teatro San Felipe, where moving pictures were shown between acts of traditional *zarzuela* or light operetta. By November 1896, the city had its first moving picture theater.

In 1898, Félix Oliver, a Spanish immigrant, returned from a European trip with a **Cinématographe Lumière** and film stock and shot the first Uruguayan film: *Una carrera de ciclismo en el Velódromo de Arroyo Seco* [A Bicycle Race at the Arroyo Seco Velodrome]. The following year, he shot *Juego de niñas y fuente del Prado* [Girls' Game and the Prado Fountain] and opened his own moving picture theater in downtown Montevideo. After another trip to Europe, in which he encountered George **Méliès' trick films**, Oliver produced his own trick films and various **news event films**. Among the trick films was *Oliver, Juncal 108* (1900), which promoted his sign-painting business.

Around the turn of the century, the Casa Lepage in Buenos Aires (an important photographic supplies and motion picture pioneer) sent a cameraman, M. Corbicier, to Montevideo to shoot *actualités*. Corbicier recorded films of historical significance such as the 1904 Civil War and *La paz de 1904* [The peace of 1904]. In 1908 he produced the country's first **newsreel**, although he was unable to continue regular production.

Later, in 1909, Lorenzo Adroher visited the Lumière factory in Lyons and purchased seven **cameras** and a **projector** with which he established the first Uruguayan production company. Adroher and his brother Juan also opened the Biógrafo Lumière theater, until recently the Cine Independencia. Between 1910 and 1914, they showed their own *actualités* and news event films as well as imported European films. The outbreak of **World War I** and subsequent stock shortages and high costs sharply curtailed their business, and the firm went bankrupt.

Production in Uruguay remained sporadic and artisanal. Its domestic market was simply too small (in 1911, Montevideo had twenty moving picture

theaters, supplied largely by foreign imports), and the presence of Argentina, too strong: those interested in the business tended to go to Buenos Aires, where there were more opportunities. Perhaps the most important films from this period were newsreels produced by the Uruguayan branch of Max **Glücksmann**'s Argentine company between 1913 and 1931, which documented all aspects of national life. Unfortunately, many of these were destroyed in a fire. One of the few salvaged films is *Viaje presidencial* [Presidential Trip] (1924–1925), a detailed record of President José Serrato's trips through the country's interior.

The first fiction film, *Carlitos y Tripín de Buenos Aires a Montevideo* [Carlitos and Tripín from Buenos Aires to Montevideo] (1918), was co-produced with an Argentine studio and directed by Julio Irigoyen (from Argentina). The following year, Eduardo Figari, a store-owner turned film impresario, produced the first **multiple-reel film**, *Puños y noble* [Fists and Nobility], about the popular boxer Angelito Rodríguez; it was directed by Juan Borges and shot by Isidoro Damonte. *Pervanche* (1920), directed by León Ibáñez Saavedra and photographed by Emilio Peruzzi, was unusual in that it was made to raise funds for a philanthropic organization and featured the elite of Montevideo society—the film disappeared in 1925, when the protagonist's husband bought and destroyed all copies in order to eradicate all evidence of her scandalous acting career.

Further reading

Hintz, Eugenio (ed.) (1988) *Historia y filmografía del cine uruguayo*, Montevideo: Ediciones de la Plaza.
Vanrell Delgado, Rafael (1993) *Salones de biógrafo y cines de Montevideo*, Montevideo: Ediciones de la Plaza.

ANA M. LÓPEZ

US patent wars

The first decade of film production was dominated by a series of formative if disruptive patent disputes having to do with the moving picture **camera** and by extension the **projector** and films. Issues such as the economic control of the medium, technological standardization, and attempts to organize the new industry into something like a monopoly were central to these developments. But unintended consequences could be found in film production, where adverse conditions limited creative investment and possibly delayed the widespread emergence of the story film until after **American Mutoscope & Biograph [AM&B]**'s victory over **Edison**'s patent claims in March 1902. The patent wars usually refer to the period of uncertainty between 1900 and 1903, when early producers tried to broker their patents into direct control of the industry. However, the underlying legal disputes can be traced back to Edison's contentious patent application for the **kinetoscope** camera, which the court initially rejected in 1892, opening the way to ever more complicated court wrangling.

Played out on the terrain of the US judicial system, the patent wars had international implications. In 1898, as part of widespread litigation that included suits against Edward Amet, Sigmund **Lubin**, the Eden Musee and **Klaw & Erlanger**, Edison also sued Maguire and Baucus Limited, the American representatives for Charles **Urban**'s **Bioscope** and **Lumière**'s films, and later forced AM&B to temporarily halt the distribution of **Warwick** films. Some companies dropped out of the business, others shifted their activities back to Europe, and still others conformed, paying royalties to Edison. At the heart of the issue was whether Edison's generous interpretation of his patents could be extended to all moving picture cameras and projectors, and thus to the medium as a whole. Other developers of competing camera and projection mechanisms fought parallel battles. Between 1900 and 1902, for example, Armat Moving-Picture Company (owner of the Thomas **Armat**-Charles Francis **Jenkins** patents) threatened patent suits against exhibitors small and large including **Vitagraph**, **Lubin** Film, Lyman S. **Howe**, AM&B, and Edison (winning an injunction against the latter).

The outcomes of the suits were revealing. Initially, when faced with the threat of lawsuits, many smaller companies gave way to the demands made of them. However, convoluted cases, charges of evidence tampering, ever-shifting alliances, and active use of the appeal process slowly eroded the perception of dominance initially accorded to the litigious Edison Manufacturing Company, leading to counterstrikes. Even court victors such as Armat proved reluctant to press their advantage, revealing the diverse motives behind the cases. Armat, for example, sought a strategic and mutually beneficial alliance of Armat, AM&B, and Edison that would put an end to court bickering and enable the three to control the activities of the many start-ups entering (and to his mind, undermining) the industry—an early vision of something like the **Motion Picture Patents Company**. Herman **Casler**, by contrast, wanted to limit the patents' commercial impact and value; the **Latham** brothers sought recognition for his contributions; and AM&B simply wanted to get on with making films without the distraction of endless patent battles.

Further reading

Musser, Charles (1991) *Before the Nickelodeon: Edwin S. Porter and the Edison Manufacturing Company*, Berkeley: University of California Press.

Musser, Charles (1994 [1990]) *The Emergence of Cinema: The American Screen to 1907*, Berkeley: University of California Press.

WILLIAM URICCHIO

USA

Production

Over a period of almost five years, beginning in early 1889, W. K. L. **Dickson** and other engineers employed at Thomas **Edison**'s West Orange, New Jersey, laboratory, developed the first continuous-feed motion picture **camera**—the kinetograph—and an accompanying viewing apparatus—the **Kinetoscope** peepshow machine. The earliest films were taken in a small purpose-built studio dubbed the "Black Maria" (a slang term for a paddy wagon, which the nearly windowless, black-walled building evoked). Commercial film production began in earnest in early 1894, furnishing subjects for dozens of kinetoscope parlors that opened in US cities and **amusement parks** later that year. Of the roughly seventy-five brief (roughly twenty-second) films made in the Black Maria in 1894, virtually all were simple recordings of some type of preexisting popular attraction: displays of boxing, wrestling, and physical culture; comic vignettes drawn from newspaper **comic strips**; specialty dances and other abbreviated **vaudeville** routines; Wild West exhibitions; historical **re-enactments**; and highlights from theatrical comedy hits.

Edison's output fell off in 1895, as the kinetoscope novelty faded and competitors began selling less expensive knock-offs. Within a year, however, new demand was spurred by the invention of **projection** systems, developed independently by a number of different teams, that enabled films to be incorporated into **vaudeville** shows. Having neglected to develop its own projecting mechanism (preoccupied by a more familiar business model based on the precedent of the **phonograph** parlor), the **Edison** company instead acquired rights to the **Phantoscope** projector devised by C. Francis **Jenkins** and Thomas **Armat**. Renamed Edison's Vitascope, it enjoyed a successful New York debut in the spring of 1896, screening short loops of the sort used in kinetoscopes. The hit of the program, however, was not an Edison film, but a British import, Robert W. **Paul**'s *Rough Sea At Dover*. Noting that early audiences delighted in the cinematic medium's intrinsic realism and its capacity to capture scenes of daily life, the Edison company built a portable camera and shifted its production toward *actualité* views of the city and its environs, along with "scenics" or **travelogues**. Proving less expensive to produce than staged films, *actualités* comprised the great majority of Edison's releases for the next several years.

Several other companies emerged as competitors shortly after the Vitascope's debut. Firms like **American Mutoscope and Biograph** (AM&B) and American **Vitagraph** in New York; Sigmund **Lubin**'s Cineograph Co. (Philadelpia); and William **Selig**'s Polyscope Company (Chicago) functioned as complete, self-sufficient purveyors of motion pictures—building their own **cameras** and **projectors**, producing exclusive film subjects, and providing long-term exhibition service for vaudeville houses and other venues. The weekly rental fees paid by vaudeville circuits provided the crucial basis for the early expansion of the US film industry. Until around 1903, their programs were modeled on **newspapers**, mixing views of local interest, *actualités* of newsworthy and sporting events, and comic sketches built around simple gags. A typical **comedy** was AM&B's 1897 *Bad Boy and Poor Old Grandpa* (one of many in the bad boy genre) in which a brat sneaks up behind an old man reading a newspaper and sets it on fire.

AM&B enjoyed particular success before 1900, due in part to its stable projector (less prone to flicker and jump than others) and the high quality of its 70mm-gauge films (providing four times the image surface of the 35mm format adopted by its competitors). By 1899, it was producing nearly 500 films a year, with a relatively high ratio of studio-photographed productions over *actualités*. Lubin had a penchant for mock *actualités*—reenactments of boxing matches, Spanish-American war battle scenes, and other distant news events that were often dubiously marketed as the real thing. Selig, whose exhibition service was regionally prominent for Midwest vaudeville houses, produced many local views, fire department displays, and racial burlesques drawing on Selig's background as a minstrel show manager.

The fledgling industry experienced a production contraction during the years 1900–1903. Competitive pricing eroded profit margins (ultimately forcing AM&B to acquiesce to the cheaper 35mm standard), and firms increasingly tried to disrupt competition and extract revenues through legal warfare. Edison in particular sued nearly all of its competitors for patent infringement, and a tangle of countersuits and appeals involving both technology and **copyright** law generated an overall climate of uncertainty that severely curtailed production activity. The crisis abated, however, around mid-1903, once secure copyright practices had been affirmed by the courts, the main patent infringement disputes had been adjudicated, settled, or abandoned (at least for the time being), and the industry shifted toward longer, more engaging multi-shot fiction narratives. **Chase films**, like AM&B's ten-shot *The Escaped Lunatic* (1903), and sensational **melodramas** like Edison's big commercial hit, *The Great Train Robbery*

(1903), displayed increasing facility with editing techniques conveying continuities of space, time, and action, while continuing to draw upon close intertextual antecedents in American popular culture. By the end of 1905, fiction films running at least half of a 1,000-foot reel (or about eight minutes) had become the dominant product of all five major US production companies—Edison, AM&B, Lubin, Selig and Vitagraph (as well as **Pathé-Frères**, which opened a New York distribution office in mid-1904 and quickly commanded a major share of the US market). *Actualités* were still made in considerable numbers, but their commercial importance dwindled: typically, a company could count on a fiction film selling three to four times more prints than an *actualité* subject.

The **nickelodeon** boom, catalyzed in part by the emergence of film rental exchanges, created skyrocketing demand for films beginning in 1905. Edison and AM&B were remarkably slow to respond to the new opportunities, due partly to internal personnel issues and more generally to the small-scale artisinal nature of the prevailing **mode of production**. Their output actually sagged while demand soared. Vitagraph, whose films were especially popular due to their snappiness and irreverence, fared considerably better. Capitalizing on the strong demand, it set up three production units, instituting an early instance of the central producer system. By 1907, Vitagraph was by far the largest American producer. Lubin also stepped up production, managing to triple output, from one film a week in May 1907 to three a week in September. Two new companies, **Kalem** (New York) and **Essanay** (Chicago), also entered the fray in mid-1907. Nevertheless, US producers fell far short of meeting the needs of the market, resulting in a jackpot for Pathé and other foreign manufacturers. In 1908, over three-quarters of the films distributed in the USA were imports.

One factor behind the production shortfall among US companies may have been the cloud of uncertainty lingering over the industry as Edison continued to exploit its corporate advantage on various legal fronts. In early 1907, following a court-of-appeals ruling that affirmed its patent claims (but, importantly, also bolstered AM&B's

position as a non-infringer), Edison initiated a new round of infringement lawsuits and threatened others. Most companies recognized that they had no choice but to acquiesce to Edison's demand of royalty payments in exchange for patent licenses. Further legal battles between Edison and AM&B loomed, but ultimately the two firms opted to pool their patents and share licensing royalties. The formation in late 1908 of the **Motion Picture Patents Company** (MPPC) joined all the previously warring producers (with AM&B now reorganized as **Biograph**) into one powerful combine, yielding a new level of stability soon reflected in heightened rates of production.

Although the MPPC failed to accomplish its ultimate objective of oligopolistic control, it did succeed in stabilizing production to a substantial degree, primarily by enforcing policies designed to reform distribution practices and then forming its own distribution arm, the **General Film Company**, in 1910. By limiting the circulation time of old prints, eliminating duping, and charging royalties on equipment, the MPPC increased its revenue while also reducing the uncertainties concerning demand. Now that rental exchanges were tied to a predictable release schedule, companies knew exactly when films would be needed; and since films now were pulled from circulation after a predictable amount of time, manufacturers also could produce larger numbers of copies, confident that each reel would find a willing buyer. One crucial reform emerged in late 1908, when producers adopted the 1,000-foot reel as the standard unit of film manufacture. While split-reel subjects were still produced, increasingly the dominant form of narrative film-making was the 1,000-foot single-reel story. This standardized limitation on film length promoted a corresponding rationalization of every phase of production, from narrative construction to shooting schedules to delivery of prints.

While the MPPC's strides in efficiency, standardization, and overall industrial stabilization enabled its members to boost their output greatly, it was still unable to meet the extraordinary demand created by thousands of nickelodeons. Excess demand, coupled with the anger felt by exhibitors forced to pay royalties and by distributors disenfranchised by General Film, led to the steady growth of a competing faction of producers known as the Independents. The ranks of the Independents, or "non-licensed" companies, soon swelled to rival those of the MPPC. By 1911, the burgeoning US production sector consisted of approximately two dozen manufacturers of wildly varying means and standards. Quite a few surfaced only to release a small slate of films before dissolving, but many endured and prospered, including the Independent Moving Picture Company (**IMP**), **New York Motion Picture**, **Thanhouser**, **Reliance**, **American Film Manufacturing Company**, **Solax**, **Majestic**, Powers, **Keystone**, and others. They did so by organizing their own distribution companies—**Motion Picture Distributing and Sales**, Film Supply, **Universal**, and **Mutual**—to supply "non-licensed" exhibitors and with the inadvertent

assistance of a US government anti-Trust court case against the MPPC.

While the overall number of manufacturers increased dramatically and shooting sites became more dispersed after 1908, production practices grew increasingly more similar. A drive toward increased production efficiency becomes more evident during this period, manifesting itself most notably in the adoption of a central producer system by many companies around 1909. Producers developed various measures to help ensure their films met standards of narrative competence while also trying to guarantee their completion in time to meet an unforgiving delivery schedule. Scenario (and, eventually, continuity) scripts functioned as blueprints for filming schedules dictated by the orderly use of sets and locations for all relevant shots; personnel were allocated according to the day's filming

Figure 123 Edison studio interior, Bronx. (Courtesy of the Robert S. Birchard Collection.)

needs; companies were organized into departments, with hierarchical management systems in place. By 1913, stock companies of actors and craft departments were the norm at all but the most marginal of manufacturers and internal promotion allowed some actors to move into directing. Realizing the benefits of product differentiation, many companies began to specialize in particular genres, which led in turn to directors forming their own units and script departments, devising scenarios tailor-made for a specific generic expertise.

The nickelodeon boom and the rationalization of production and distribution by both the MPPC and the Independents generated a spectacular growth in US production, the likes of which have never been seen since. The growth curve was essentially exponential: the number of releases increased 60% in 1909, and then about 50% a year, give or take, for the next four years. In 1908, US studios released 678 films; in 1913, they pumped out over 5,000 titles. By around 1914, imported films had been pushed out of the US market almost entirely, accounting for less than five per cent of all titles distributed.

From 1914 on, virtually every practice of production, distribution, exhibition, and **publicity** underwent profound change as the film industry shifted its primary focus from short films to feature films of four reels and longer. It is important to note that the advent of features in 1913 did not suddenly devastate the production of shorts; indeed, for at least three years, the number of short films continued to climb steadily alongside a rapid escalation in feature film production. But short film production did fall off precipitously in 1916–1918, as **palace cinemas** specializing in star-centered features came to dominate the exhibition landscape, and thousands of small theaters that once prospered showing "variety programs" either acquiesced to a new exhibition model they could barely afford or went out of business. Many short film manufacturers—especially former members of the MPPC (which was ruled illegal on antitrust grounds in 1915)—also went out of business, finding their financial resources dwarfed by those of savvier competitors. Kalem and Lubin ceased production in 1916; Edison and Biograph quit in 1917; and Essanay and Selig closed down in 1918.

BEN SINGER AND CHARLIE KEIL

Distribution

At its simplest, distribution is the process of moving a finished product from its manufacturer to a place where it can be purchased, viewed, or otherwise consumed. For most products this is relatively simple, at least in principle, but film distribution is quite different, and no more so than in the first twenty years of cinema in the USA.

Film distribution developed and changed with great rapidity throughout the period of early cinema. The first model of distribution involved manufacturers sending self-contained production/ exhibition units to exhibitors. **Lumière** began this strategy in 1896, the first year of theatrical exhibition, and it was copied into the first decade of the 20th century by firms such as **American Mutoscope and Biograph** and **Vitagraph**. The initial success of the self-contained unit was undoubtedly because it fostered control over the production, distribution, and exhibition of films. Because the **Cinématographe Lumière** could also be used as a projector and a printer, Lumiere operators needed only the camera, films, and a source of light to function as exhibitors. There were no standard theaters or exhibition sites in this period, so Lumière operators were effectively **itinerant exhibitors**, screening films at local **vaudeville** houses, town halls, **churches**, or other such venues. They also had the ability to shoot and print their own films; although this was relatively rare, as footage was often sent back to France for processing.

Edison introduced a different model of distribution based on selling films to licensed exhibitors. Prices varied, of course, but were based exclusively on the length of the film in feet. In 1898, fifteen cents a foot was a standard rate: a 100-foot film would thus cost approximately fifteen dollars. As vaudeville became a regular, more fixed site of exhibition in the early 1900s, the self-contained-unit system waned. Manufacturers now made their profits in film sales, and their former control over the movie-going experience shifted to the exhibitor. Exhibitors would choose which films to purchase and screen, provide a **lecturer**, edit films to create an overarching narrative, and use **illustrated songs** to create an experience in which the actual films themselves were secondary. They also could turn those choices over to exhibition services such as Vitagraph and George **Spoor**'s Kinodrome which supplied vaudeville managers with a new act each week comprised of a projector, projectionist, and new set of films.

Yet a third model of distribution arose with the first significant film exchanges that appeared in 1903. The **Miles Brothers** purchased a group of old American Mutoscope & Biograph films at eight cents a foot, renting them to exhibitors on the West Coast for a fee substantially less than the purchase price. At approximately the same time, Percival **Waters**' Kinetograph Company began renting films on the East Coast. This jump-started the industry, which had been stymied both by the cost of exhibition and by the presence of old, worn-out films in many theaters. Film exchanges allowed exhibitors to rent more films and change them more frequently, allowing for repeat customers and a better viewing experience. They further allowed manufacturers to deal with only a handful of exchanges rather than hundreds of small exhibitors. Exchanges were one of the major factors, along with the availability of increasing numbers of **Pathé-Frères** imports, in the **nickelodeon** boom that began in 1905–1906, as cheap distribution encouraged inexpensive theaters to open and charge low admission prices.

By 1907, distribution in the USA had centered in Chicago with exchanges like those of George **Kleine**, Carl **Laemmle**, and William **Swanson** renting not individual titles, but an entire weekly supply of films. Film length was generally under ten minutes at this point, so exhibitors needed a number of films to fill out their programs. With the institution of the weekly program, exhibitors needed simply to contract with a single distributor to have their needs met.

This period ended with the formation of the **Motion Picture Patents Corporation** (MPPC) in early 1909. The MPPC began licensing exchanges to distribute its product, in effect forcing theaters to rent films only from associated manufacturers and threatening non-complying theaters (and independent manufacturers) with lawsuits. Along with its distribution arm, **General Film Company**, which purchased the majority of exchanges upon its formation in 1910, the MPPC rationalized the film industry around a program of single-reel or split-reel films, changed either daily or

twice or thrice weekly. One of the key aspects of this program is that the films themselves received little—if any—**advertising**; there was little point for exhibitors to advertise a film that would be at a different theater the next week, or even the next day, while the MPPC simply had little interest in getting in the advertising business. For General Film, as well as many of the independent distributors that followed in its wake, such as the **Motion Picture Distributing and Sales Company**, the make-up and quality of the program rather than individual films was most significant. Furthermore, General Film barely differentiated between theaters in size, location, or prestige: it would rent its programs to any theater that would pay its price.

This system left little room for films that did not fit the short program model, in particular **multiple-reel/feature films**. The term "feature" came from vaudeville, where the feature act was the best and most successful on the program. Because of this derivation, during this period "feature" referred not simply to a film's length in reels—the length of a "long film" certainly varied from 1908–1913—but to a sense that a film could be used as the main act on a program. The feature had to be different from the standard single reel, but perhaps more importantly it had to be differentiated, through practices in production (length, budget, production values, the use of **stars**) as well as distribution.

Certain MPPC companies, most notably Vitagraph, produced a handful of expensive, multiple-reel films even before 1910. Generally these films—such as the five-reel *The Life of Moses* (1909)—were released one reel at a time as part of the standard MPPC program. This made manufacturers less able to recoup their investment in "long" films, but perhaps more importantly it did not produce much differentiation. These factors led to the development of two new distribution strategies that allowed features to be differentiated. The first, roadshowing, came from the legitimate **theater**: a producer or distributor took a film on the road, renting individual theaters on a percentage-of-the-gross basis. This was how Adolph **Zukor** handled *Queen Elizabeth* (1912), starring Sarah **Bernhardt**, how Kleine handled Italian features such as *Quo Vadis?* (1913), and how D. W. **Griffith** initially distributed *Birth of a Nation*

(1915) and *Intolerance* (1916): all among the most prestigious films of the era. While this strategy led to a few notable successes, it was too labor-intensive and risky to become standard.

The second strategy was the state rights system of distribution, which was established for European features such as **Milano**'s *Dante's Inferno* (1909), **Itala**'s *The Fall of Troy* (1910), and **Éclair**'s *Zigomar* (1911) in 1911–1912. In this system, a person or firm would purchase the right to license a film's exhibition in a particular territory. Licensees could then either rent the film to exhibitors in the territory or else subdivide and re-sell the territorial rights further. Although it was possible to sell a film's rights to only one distributor, even the largest state rights firms only covered a portion of the USA, so any widespread distribution required selling a film's rights to a number of different firms.

The state rights system offered several advantages. It could offer films not only a wide circulation but also a long shelf life, allowing them to remain money earners for an extended period of time. Also, unlike General Film and the Sales Company (or its offspring, **Universal** and **Mutual**), state rights distributors could devote a great deal of energy to selling and marketing their films, for most firms dealt with only a few films at a time. Service companies such as General Film, by contrast, marketed their films as indistinguishable commodities, and any film that needed special treatment was likely to get lost in the program. State rights also allowed for extensive advertising, which was crucial for prestige features.

Indeed, both roadshowing and state rights distribution required an enormous increase in the advertising and marketing of films. General Film counted on its program practices, assured that exhibitors and viewers wanted short films differentiated by genre and manufacturer, rather than long films marketed and sold as individual titles. Feature distributors needed to convince potential audience members to come see a specific film, rather than simply "go to the movies." This was one of the factors that led to the emergence of the **star system**, as well as to enormous increases in film budgets and narrative complexity.

The success of features in the early 1910s forced every American film company to rethink its production and distribution practices. To counter the increasing popularity of state rights distribution, for instance, General Film inaugurated its own service, in June 1912, which offered at least one weekly feature that could be exhibited for several days. By 1913, it created an "exclusive service" of feature programs made up of expensive one- to three-reel films, including those of Kinemacolor, in an attempt to reach legitimate and large vaudeville theaters. This service was a combination of General Film's standard program approach with a few new techniques, including an early form of the run-clearance-zone strategy. It would only go to the best theaters, and also to those distant enough from one another so as not to be in competition. Despite such efforts, General Film could not match the weekly programs of features mounted in 1913–1914 by **Famous Players**—and **Warner's Features**, less successfully—as major suppliers of the newly constructed prestigious theaters or **palace cinemas**.

Although the state rights system continued in the industry into the 1920s, it was overshadowed by the emergence of national feature distributors such as Paramount Pictures. Paramount's major distribution innovation was to regularize the system that Famous Players had developed, combining the weekly program format of General Film with the feature marketing techniques of the state rights firms. Beginning in September 1914, Paramount began offering a yearly program of features, consisting of 104 films of four to six reels each, released at the rate of two per week. This was far more features than had ever been released before, making Paramount the first large-scale distributor of feature programs to exhibitors. However, unlike earlier program-based distributors, Paramount heavily advertised its features—emphasizing each film's stars—in an effort to attract new audiences to film theaters. Paramount also innovated a percentage distribution fee, whereby producer and distributor each received a percentage of the gross exhibitor rentals, which allowed the company to share the risks—and the rewards—of expensive feature films. Paramount would become the model for other firms in the **classical Hollywood** period.

MICHAEL QUINN

Figure 124 Laemmle Film Service ad, 1908.

Exhibition

Since at least the mid 1890s, presenting moving pictures has been organized as a business, to maximize profits. Not surprisingly, during the first two decades of the innovation, a number of means of a presentation were tried. It is a myth that Americans instantly embraced the "movie show." That took a decade of entrepreneurial experimentation. But with the coming of the **nickelodeon** in 1905, Americans definitely began their love affair with the movies.

Initially, entrepreneurs figured moving pictures would make the most profits if shown one to a customer. The model was the recent success with the **phonograph**. During the 1880s, the newly invented phonograph was set up in amusement or **penny arcades**, and for a few cents customers could listen to music and speeches through individual ear horns. Thomas **Edison** sought to do the same thing for moving pictures. During the spring of 1894, his first machines reached New York City amusement arcades. The first **Kinetoscope** parlor was a converted shoe store at 1155 Broadway; the initial fee charged was 25 cents per person (later falling to a nickel) for access to a row of five Edison viewers containing 50-foot loops of film which presented moving pictures of vaudeville stars, circus performers, animal acts, dancers, and comics.

Yet an alternative form of mass marketing was already in the works, and the model was the **vaudeville** theater showing to a mass audience. Charge admission at a box office, and project the motion pictures onto a screen. The impetus for this type of presentation did not originate with Edison, but came from Europe, principally from the efforts of the **Lumière** brothers. They sought to develop what we think of today as the projector to fashion a theatrical experience. After a thorough study of the Edison technology, the Lumières constructed their own version of a camera, printer, and projector, the **Cinématographe**. On 28 December 1895, the brothers Lumière held the first public showing of ten short moving pictures—projected on a screen—in the basement of the Grand Cafe in Paris. Within months, they had exported the new system to the USA. Edison responded quickly and presented his own Vitascope projection system to the press on 3 April 1896, and soon thereafter publicly exhibited at Koster and Bial's Music Hall, a noted vaudeville theater located near Herald's Square in New York City.

Quickly entrepreneurs found halls in which to show moving pictures. This occurred in city after city. In Washington, D.C., on New Year's Day, 1897, the Cinématographe was first used to project films in Willard's Hall, at 14th and "F" streets, in the heart of Washington's white downtown. For 50 cents (25 cents for children) exhibitions were presented at 2:00 pm, 4:00 pm and 8:00 pm. Three short scenes of Washington itself were presented as well as a number of short subjects of variety acts and noted persons of the day.

Yet with the system for presentation still not finally settled, entrepreneurs tried other venues. For example, late in the 19th century, **amusement parks** were built at the end of trolley lines of most major cities in order to encourage riders to journey throughout the entire system. Amusement park entrepreneurs presented a variety of live acts in order to attract audiences in the summer months. Into that mix they added moving pictures. But this would not be a permanent solution because most amusement parks were only open three to four months per year.

In 1900, much of the USA was still rural, with most of the population living in communities of fewer than 3,000 citizens, lacking an amusement park, but nearly always having a public hall usually called an "opera house." By then, **itinerant exhibitors** serviced vast rural sections of the country. Often a family operation, an exhibitor would poster a town, announcing moving pictures for presentation in the community's "opera house." This public space was often part of a city hall, county court house, or simply a hall for visiting live entertainers to offer their shows. The circuit of opera houses was crucial because they were already in place when moving picture exhibition was being innovated. Also crucial were railroads which allowed entertainers to travel easily from town to town even in the most rural areas of the country. Traveling exhibitors carried a projector, a screen, and some films as they took their show from opera house to opera house. Often these exhibitors would seek to piggy back on another event—such as a fair or holiday—which already would bring crowds into small towns.

If amusement parks had a limited season, and traveling exhibitors a limited market, urban vaudeville theaters represented the very heart of mainstream mass entertainment. The Vitascope and Cinématographe both made their debuts in New York City vaudeville theaters during the established season of 1896–1897 (September to May) as one fifteen minute "act" among the eight others on the bill. Here was an established theatrical base from which to introduce moving

pictures to millions of Americans. Indeed, by the end of the 1896–1897 vaudeville season, the pattern of presenting moving pictures as single acts was well established. This would endure until the coming of the nickelodeon a decade later. In vaudeville, moving pictures had found an American entertainment form with the greatest base in the middle class. Consequently, some early companies such as **Vitagraph** established special operations to service vaudeville theaters.

Moving pictures played their most important role in what was called "family" vaudeville (relatively small houses with short programs of five to six acts) which flourished, in a half dozen circuits, from coast to coast in the early 1900s. Yet it soon became clear that, even there, they occasionally could serve as a specialty act at best and never become more than a secondary part of the vaudeville industry. These conditions offered nickelodeon pioneers an opportunity to create the moving picture show.

There had been something like nickelodeons from the start. **Raff & Gammon**, Edison's agents in the 1890s, franchised a number of business men and women, who in turn rented store fronts and showed moving pictures there. These store front theaters offered brief programs for a small admission charge. But this initial innovation never took off during the first decade that moving pictures were available as an entertainment form. Acceptance—seemingly everywhere at once—would not come until 1905; yet seemingly "overnight" the nickelodeon became the centerpiece of exhibition in the urban USA. By 1910, observers counted almost 10,000 nickel theaters from New York to San Francisco.

The nickelodeon functioned as a small makeshift theater, made over to look like a vaudeville theater. In front, large hand-painted posters—used by the circus and vaudeville industry before nickelodeons—would announced the moving pictures. The interior of the nickel show was more sedate, simple in design even when compared to plain late 20th-century multiplex standards. The auditorium, typically long and narrow, held between 50 and 300 wooden chairs. The "stage" was usually no more than a simple platform positioned up front. The typical nine by twelve foot **screen** was simply attached to the back wall.

A piano accompanied the silent films, but in the better establishments there might be an orchestral ensemble including several stringed instruments. The projection booth was set off in the rear.

Here was a new form of entertainment for urban Americans at a price most could afford. While moving pictures themselves might seem the core of the new innovation, we should not discount the prominent light displays which heralded the attractions, and gave us the term "the great white way." Electric lights flashing a multitude of colors reminded shoppers passing by that this was a modern marvel in an age when most people did not have **electricity** in their homes. By 1907, no industry watcher doubted that gross receipts reached into the millions of dollars. With the urban population growing, chiefly from the unprecedented wave of immigrants flooding into the larger cities, all classes of urban residents embraced the cheap entertainment form. Before 1910 so did their small town cousins. A new era of exhibition had begun.

Yet the "pure" nickelodeon era lasted but a short time. Entrepreneurs quickly sought to raise prices by expanding their programs, building larger theaters, and seeking out middle class audiences. As the 1900s ended, and the 1910s began, theater owners looked for ways to differentiate their shows from those down the street. They might add vaudeville acts, and for a time Marcus **Loew** and others created what was called "small-time" vaudeville circuits. They fashioned "combination" shows with **music**, **illustrated songs**, and sing-a-longs expanding the program. Even schools, **churches**, and Progressive era leaders (such as Jane **Addams** in Chicago) opened "movie" houses or presented moving picture programs to educate as well as entertain.

As demand surged, entrepreneurs funded and built larger and more ornate theaters downtown or in secondary commercial districts and opened smaller ones in neighborhood areas. As the 1910s began, enterprising theater owners such as the **Saxe** brothers sought a more middle-class audience, wooing away vaudeville patrons. By 1912 or so,

Figure 125 Theatre Row, Broad Street, Richmond, Virginia, 1910. (Courtesy of the Curt Teich Postcard Archives.)

entrepreneurs had abandoned the formula of selling "low price," and raised their tickets to a dime or more. Some such as the **Mastbaum** brothers were successful enough to amass regional **cinema circuits**. The new show in a 1,000 seat ornate picture theater now sometimes emphasized orchestral music, following the lead of managers such as S. L. **Rothapfel**, in both special arrangements and accompanying scores, whether to variety programs of short films or to the special attractions of **multiple-reel/feature films**. Legitimate **theater** and vaudeville suddenly had serious competition, and vaudeville's decline as the centerpiece of popular theatrical fare in the USA had begun.

To lure the ideal family trade these pioneering entrepreneurs looked to the "New American woman" and her children. To accommodate shopping breaks and after school hours, theater owners of the late 1900s and early 1910s set up special "tea hour" screenings; if women and children came, the owner had a stamp of respectability that could lead (and did lead) to more money and a more favorable image in the community. Thus women and children saw half-price matinee specials. Moving picture stories also catered to them, drawn not only from respected classics but from illustrated **magazine** stories and best sellers.

In sum, as the era of "early cinema" was coming to a close, more and more theater owners were commissioning and opening theaters designed by professional architects, aimed at middle-class patrons, and costing as much as twenty-five cents for admission. Most were funded by local investors, with bankers raising as much as $100,000. Uniformed ushers assisted "guests" to elegant seats. Cut flowers and potted plants lined lobbies. Vast lighted facades redefined and highlighted the "new" downtown. All this presaged the **palace cinema** era.

DOUGLAS GOMERY

Audiences

Throughout the first twenty years of cinema history, the size and make-up of the audience in the USA depended on the availability of moving pictures and on the changing conditions of exhibition. During 1896–1897, much of the diverse population in cities and small towns throughout the country had the opportunity to experience the novel attraction of moving pictures at local theaters, **churches**, carnivals, and traveling shows. Over the next several years, moving pictures became a familiar entertainment option at a range of sites that addressed quite distinct audiences, for instance, rural folks visiting a small-town opera house, church-going middle-class families at a **chautauqua** assembly, working-class city dwellers spending a day off at an **amusement park**, or a mixed urban population having an evening out at a **vaudeville** theater.

It was only with the emergence of the **nickelodeon** in 1905–1906, however, that a truly national, mass audience began to form, an audience for whom moving pictures were a regular aspect of everyday life. Daily changing programs and affordable ticket prices at storefront theaters encouraged frequent attendance. Competing theaters in close proximity provided additional viewing opportunities. **Illustrated songs** and other live performances on the nickelodeon bill made moviegoers aware of their collective experience as an audience. People who lived within easy distance of a nickelodeon and had enough spare change to cover the five-cent admission charge could "get the habit," as theater ads proclaimed. This was as much the case for first-generation immigrants in urban tenement districts as for small-town residents whose local roots may have gone back generations. In the more rural sections of the USA, the movies were also likely to be available, at least weekly or seasonally. Even under the oppressive conditions of Jim Crow practices, African Americans had opportunities to see moving pictures in churches, "colored" theaters, or from the balconies of racially segregated shows.

The unprecedentedly large, regularly attending, mass audience that the moving pictures had attracted across the USA by 1910 has proven to be difficult to describe in precise demographic terms. There is not even a comprehensive, accurate list of nickelodeons for Chicago and Manhattan, much less for small towns in places like Nebraska or the Mississippi Delta. Neither are there box-office records that take into account the constant turnover of paying customers in picture shows, many of which continuously ran from morning until well into the evening. The limited historical evidence that does exist—principally based on the number and location of moving picture theaters and even on the way exhibitors advertised their product—suggests that the emerging movie audience was by no means homogenous in terms of gender, age, race, region, class, religion, education, occupation, or ethnicity. In the industrialized Northeast, the prime audience tapped by the nickelodeon was working-class, first-generation immigrants or the sons and daughters of these immigrants (see Rosenzweig). Yet members of the so-called "refined" classes in metropolitan areas had the opportunity to view moving pictures at other sites, even before nickelodeons soon began to be replaced by more luxurious and respectable permanent venues designed, in part, to legitimate the movie-going experience. In and out of the small-town picture show, middle-class, church-going families continued to take in moving pictures.

It therefore makes sense to think of movie-going during and after the nickelodeon period in two distinct, if complementary ways: which audiences had access to moving pictures and which audiences were the most frequent, the most "habitual" customers. By 1915, there were not only larger and more well-appointed theaters, but there was also a generation of moviegoers in rural towns as well as urban neighborhoods who had grown up watching moving pictures. Furthermore, the burgeoning cinema industry itself was deeply invested in increasing the number of regular moviegoers, specifically targeting female viewers (see Stamp). In the most general sense, the regular moving picture audience in the USA, which began as primarily male and working-class, had become in the 1910s less homosocial and more middle-class in behavior and in composition (see Hansen). But the precise situation could differ substantially from locality to locality, as the many case studies that examine individual communities and populations demonstrate (see Waller).

The size as well as the particular make-up of the moving picture audience during and after the nickelodeon boom drew considerable attention from contemporary commentators and self-styled guardians of civic and moral values. As a result, the way American movie audiences were represented,

Figure 126 Mutual Movies advertisement, *St.Paul News*, Minnesota (November 1913).

described, criticized, and celebrated is itself a key aspect of early cinema history in the United States. For instance, censorship initiatives and sabbatarian campaigns to stop all Sunday shows highlighted the importance of children and adolescents as frequent moviegoers who were imperiled by this new form of leisure. Fire safety and building code legislation stressed the potentially fatal plight of the crowded and helpless mass audience. Trade journals like **Moving Picture World** applauded any hint of a refined, middle-class clientele for the new art, while insisting that movie audiences epitomized an inclusive democratic America, with businessmen and laborers, housewives and shopgirls sitting side-by-side before the screen. The naive rube, the enraptured fan, the endangered girl, and the newly arrived immigrant becoming Americanized in the movie theater all stand as common stereotypes from this period. Familiar from cartoons, editorials, sermons, and sometimes from the films themselves, these images help to explain the place of the expanding, nationwide movie audience in American culture.

GREGORY A. WALLER

Regulation/censorship

Legal regulation of moving pictures before 1907 was carried out in the main via the imposition of pre-existing licensing laws, often those used to control venues from **fairs/fairgrounds** and carnivals to **vaudeville** houses and town halls, and directed principally at regulating who could show moving pictures and where they could be shown. In November 1907, a specific regulatory arena directed at moving pictures and the new **nickelodeons** emerged, starting with a police censor board in Chicago that paved the way for other municipal boards as well as state censor boards.

Investigations of nickelodeons from late 1906 had suggested that these new ill-lit spaces of commercial leisure encouraged immorality, in particular sexual immorality, and that moving pictures had a worryingly hypnotic power on the seemingly vulnerable and dangerous groups that seemed to make up the majority of nickelodeon audiences: children, lower-class immigrant groups, women. Local authorities established censor boards directed specifically at nickelodeons and moving pictures in the context then of concerns about governing certain population groups. The police censor board established in Chicago followed on from extensive debates about the regulation of moving pictures and nickelodeons in the city throughout 1907. Exhibitors or film exchanges in Chicago now had to submit an application for a permit to screen a film for exhibition and then send a copy of the film to the police board of censors for approval. The board would not issue a license if the film was found to be "immoral, obscene or indecent," consistent with widely held beliefs about the centrality of morality to public order. Late in 1908, an exhibitor challenged the constitutionality of the board. The Illinois Supreme Court dismissed the case, arguing that censorship was important because moving pictures had a capacity for "evil influence" over the young and impressionable audiences who attended nickelodeons. The decision set an important precedent for local and state censor boards.

Also late in 1908, New York City mayor George McClellan called a public hearing to debate the legality and propriety of allowing nickelodeons to open on Sunday and a host of other questions about the safety and morality of nickelodeons and moving pictures. The following day, McClellan ordered all nickelodeons closed pending further investigation, vowing that future licenses would not allow Sunday openings. This was the most extreme measure of regulation in the early cinema period, striking the nascent industry at the core in the most profitable market in the country. Exhibitors responded quickly by banding together and gaining a temporary injunction against McClellan's actions. They approached the civic reform group, the People's Institute, about the prospect of setting up a censorship board in the city. After the People's Institute readily agreed, the New York Board of Censorship met for the first time in March 1909, and quickly changed its name to the **National Board of Censorship**. Estimates suggest it passed on about 85–90% of films circulating in the USA. Early statements of Board standards focused on concerns about "obscenity" and the representation of criminality. Yet the Board recognised that drama frequently was predicated on criminal or immoral acts and that so long as this was carefully represented, and morality was upheld at the close, this was acceptable. In this sense, regulation helped develop certain narrative conventions—such as the happy ending—that shaped the formal properties of American cinema.

Even so, the efforts of the industry to regulate itself and thus deflect state regulation were not entirely successful. Immediately after the Board was established the African-American boxer Jack **Johnson** won the world heavyweight title against a white boxer. Johnson's fights and films were deeply controversial, for the image of a black man defeating a white man was seen to undercut prevailing notions of racial hierarchy and white supremacy. In 1912, the federal government passed the Sims Act to prevent the interstate transportation of **boxing films**, directly aimed at Johnson. The ramifications of this act, the first federal intervention into the cinema industry, were considerable, for the act defined films as "commerce" and so within the jurisdiction of the federal government; in doing so, it set a precedent that suggested cinema was distinct from the press and could not claim constitutional guarantees of free speech. This federal regulation clearly was propelled by racist anxiety, further evident with the passage of the 1913 Tariff Act regulating the importation of foreign films.

The **white slave films** that emerged in late 1913 and the controversy over D. W. **Griffith**'s *The Birth of a Nation* (1915) also caused the National Board considerable problems. In 1914 and 1916, debates were held in the U.S. House of Representatives about the possibility of establishing a federal censor board. In these debates, the National Board was strongly criticized for being too closely tied to the industry, for not reviewing all films, and for reviewing the ones they did with only the metropolitan standards of New York City in mind. Even though no federal censor board was created, ongoing anxiety about the power and effect of moving pictures on vulnerable and dangerous audiences, together with the Board's perceived failures, led some state governments to establish state-wide censorship boards. Pennsylvania led the way in 1911, although its Board did not start functioning until 1914; Ohio set up a board in 1913; Kansas, in 1914; and Maryland, in 1916. As in Chicago, these state Boards had the aim of prohibiting "sacrilegious, obscene, indecent, or immoral" films.

Legal decisions taken with respect to the state censor boards would prove to be critical to the regulation of cinema. Late in 1913, the **Mutual Film Corporation** challenged the legality of the Ohio state censor board and, in separate cases, of other local and state boards. Mutual argued that the boards were unconstitutional and, when the case reached the Supreme Court in early 1915, that the laws contravened the constitutional guarantees of free speech. The Court denied these claims, however, arguing that cinema, unlike the press, could not be inscribed into those guarantees. Cinema was, the Justices claimed, a "business pure and simple" and, furthermore, had a unique "capacity for evil." Film thus became the sole medium of communication in the history of the USA to be subject to systematic legal prior restraint. The decision was perhaps the most important one ever rendered in relation to moving pictures. The industry would have to construct Hollywood as a place of "harmless entertainment" in order to circumvent regulatory concern. In short, debates and decisions about the regulation of cinema in the period of early cinema helped shape what American cinema would become.

LEE GRIEVESON

See also: airdomes; audiences; crime films; law and the cinema: regulating exhibition; leisure time and space: USA; migration/immigration: USA; monopoly capitalism: USA; musical accompaniment; program formats; racial segregation: USA; transportation; urbanization; US patent wars

Further reading

Abel, Richard (1999) *The Red Rooster Scare: Making Cinema American, 1900–1910*, Berkeley: University of California Press.

Balio, Tino (ed.) (1985) *The American Film Industry*, 2nd ed., Madison: University of Wisconsin Press.

Bowser, Eileen (1990) *The Transformation of Cinema, 1907–1915*, New York: Scribners.

Butsch, Richard (2000) *The Making of American Audiences: From Stage to Television, 1750–1990*, 139–172, Cambridge: Cambridge University Press.

Conant, Michael (1960) *Antitrust in the Motion Picture Industry: Economic and Legal Analysis*, Berkeley: University of California Press.

Czitrom, Daniel (1996) "The Politics of Performance: Theater Licensing and the Origins of Movie Censorship in New York," in Francis G. Couvares (ed.) *Movie Censorship and American Culture*, 16–42, Washington: Smithsonian Institution.

Dizikes, John (1993) *Opera in America: A Cultural History*, New Haven: Yale University Press.

Fuller, Kathryn H. (1996) *At the Picture Show*, Washington, D. C.: Smithsonian Institution.

Gomery, Douglas (1992) *Shared Pleasures: A History of Movie Presentation in the United States*, Madison: University of Wisconsin Press.

Grieveson, Lee (2004) *Policing Cinema: Regulating and Shaping Movies in Early Twentieth Century America*, Berkeley: University of California Press.

Gunning, Tom (1988) "From the Opium Den to the Theatre of Morality: Moral Discourse and Film Process in Early American Cinema," *Art and Text*, 30: 30–40.

Hansen, Miriam (1991) *Babel and Babylon: Spectatorship and American Silent Film*, Cambridge: Harvard University Press.

Keil, Charlie (2001) *Early American Cinema in Transition: Story, Style, and Filmmaking, 1907–1913*, Madison: University of Wisconsin Press.

Musser, Charles (1990) *The Emergence of Cinema to 1907*, New York: Scribners.

Quinn, Michael (1998) "Early Feature Distribution and the Development of the Motion Picture Industry: Famous Players and Paramount, 1912–1921," Ph.D. dissertation, University of Wisconsin-Madison.

Quinn, Michael (2001) "Distribution, the Transient Audience, and the Transition to the Feature Film," *Cinema Journal*, 40.2: 35–56.

Rosenzweig, Roy (1983) *Eight Hours for What We Will: Work and Leisure in an Industrial City*, Cambridge: Cambridge University Press.

Singer, Ben (2004) "Feature Films, Variety Programs, and the Crisis of the Small Exhibitor" in Charlie Keil, and Shelley Stamp (eds.) *American Cinema's Transitional Era*, 76–100, Berkeley: University of California Press.

Staiger, Janet (1984) "Combination and Litigation: Structures of US Film Distribution, 1891–1917," *Cinema Journal*, 23.2: 41–72.

Staiger, Janet (1985) "The Hollywood Mode of Production to 1930," in David Bordwell, Janet Staiger, and Kristin Thompson, *The Classical Hollywood Cinema: Film Style & Mode of Production to 1960*, 85–153, New York: Columbia University Press.

Staiger, Janet (1995) *Bad Women: Regulating Sexuality in Early American Cinema*, Minneapolis: University of Minnesota Press.

Stamp, Shelley (2000) *Movie-Struck Girls: Women and Motion Picture Culture after the Nickelodeon*, Princeton: Princeton University Press.

Waller, Gregory A. (1995) *Main Street Amusements: Movies and Commercial Entertainment in a Southern City, 1896–1930*, Washington, D.C.: Smithsonian Institution Press.

Waller, Gregory A. (ed.) (2002) *Moviegoing in America*, Oxford: Blackwell.

V

Valentin, Karl

b. 1882; d. 1948

actor, Germany

The greatest German comedian of the first half of the twentieth century, Valentin made only a handful of films in the silent era, opting instead to focus his energies on his improvisational, Bavarian-flavored variety act with his wife, Liesl Karlstadt. Yet films such as *Der neue Schreibtisch* [The New Writing Desk] (1914), in which the height of a desk is adjusted until there is nothing left, testify to Valentin's uncomfortable and almost nihilistic relationship to inanimate objects, technology, and his own body, an attitude that became popular with Dadaists and the middle class alike.

SCOTT CURTIS

Valetta

After a fruitful collaboration with **Pathé-Frères** from 1908 to 1911, Camille **de Morlhon** founded his own company, Valetta, in July 1912, choosing as its emblem the family coat of arms. For the next ten years, Valetta produced all of de Morlhon's films, with the support of Pathé's distribution. His initial innovation was to shoot two films at the same time, casting the same actors in primary roles, even when that involved traveling to the south of France. Yet he soon resumed sequential production in order to shoot fewer but longer and more complex social dramas. *Une Brute humaine* [A Human Beast] (1913), remains a landmark: exceptionally

long for the time (1950 meters), it sold 200 prints worldwide—as many as Albert **Capellani**'s *Les Misérables* (1912). After a hiatus caused by **World War I**, Valetta resumed production in March 1915, with de Morlhon producing and directing four films a year until 1917. When he began fighting for authors' rights, in opposition to Charles **Pathé**, the company became dormant, eventually closing down in 1923.

Further reading

Le Roy, Eric (1994) "Les relations entre Charles Pathé et Camille de Morlhon: de l'union au désaccord," in Jacques Kermabon (ed.) *Pathé, premier empire du cinéma*, 190–95, Paris: Editions Centre Georges Pompidou.

ERIC LE ROY

Van Goitsenhoven, Louis

b. 1874; d. 1942

exhibitioner, producer, distributor, Belgium

Before Van Goitsenhoven opened the first permanent moving picture theater in Brussels in December 1904, he worked as a businessman selling optical products, **phonographs**, and rubber tires. From 1907 on, he opened more and more theaters in order to receive optimal profits from the films he purchased. After 1908, he also became a film distributor, and a particularly important one by the end of **World War I**.

GUIDO CONVENTS

Vandal, Marcel

b. 1882, Paris; d. 1965, Le Perreux

industrialist, producer, France

Marcel Vandal was one of the first shareholders of **Éclair** (Société française des films l'éclair) which his friend and fellow lawyer, Charles **Jourjon**, founded in 1907. That same year, he became co-director of the company with Jourjon. He also took part (still with Jourjon) in establishing the Union des grands éditeurs de films in 1911. While mobilized during **World War I**, Vandal was replaced in his duties by Perreau Auguste Agnel; when he returned, Éclair was almost moribund. In 1918, Vandal left Éclair to create (with Charles **Delac**) a combined company out of **Film d'Art** and Société générale de cinématographie, and then went on to produce many films during the 1920s and the 1930s.

LAURENT MANNONI

vaudeville

As the preeminent site in the USA for the exhibition of projected moving pictures prior to the **nickelodeon** era, the vaudeville theater significantly influenced the course of cinema history. The nickelodeon boon had a consequential impact on vaudeville due to a subsequent rise in numbers of small-time vaudeville theaters that proved a challenge to the vaudeville establishment. Threatened by a burgeoning feature film movement in the early 1910s, vaudeville managers invested heavily in talking pictures and when that endeavor failed, sought to cordon off their entertainment domain through a blacklist of actors appearing in films. Ultimately, when sound film and radio became the nation's dominant entertainment forms, those new corporate interests acquired the remnants of once-great vaudeville empires.

Vaudeville and moving pictures reflected a number of cultural proclivities found in late 19th-century urban recreational institutions. Both have been identified as "democratic" in essence and "American" in spirit. Proponents of both adopted a rhetoric of refinement, respectability, and progress to promote entertainment forms frequently depicted as "low" and vulgar. By attracting women, children, mixed social classes, and immigrants, both embodied a wider cultural shift from homosocial to heterosocial **leisure** activities. Not only did both encourage habits of spectatorship that exposed new city dwellers to urban consumer culture, but they also displayed hybrid sensibilities that accommodated Victorian and modern attitudes. Both also were marked by **racial segregation**, discrimination, and stereotyping. Both eventually came to be structured as oligopolies, adopted modern business methods, and valued innovation as a competitive strategy. On occasion both functioned to provide public arenas where national issues were addressed.

In its heyday, vaudeville had some 1,000 theaters across the USA. A 1910 study of New York theaters claimed 60% of the vaudeville audience to be working-class and 36% clerical. The estimated number of vaudeville actors during the industry's peak period ranged from 20,000 to 30,000, although jobs seemed to be available for only half as many. Beginning approximately in 1907, vaudeville theaters were classified as either "big time" or "small time," depending on the number of shows per day, admission price, salaries, and whether headliners appeared regularly. Performers strived to reach the "big time," with success often symbolized by a booking at the foremost venue, New York's Palace Theatre.

As a distinct form of entertainment, vaudeville's most characteristic traits were its modular format, its attempt to appeal to a diverse audience, and its dominant mode of direct presentation. Vaudeville programs were composed of interchangeable acts presented with no connective story uniting them. The slogan, "Something for Everybody," advertised the claim that a typical vaudeville bill could accommodate the preferences of a mixed audience by presenting a variety of types of acts. Common types included acrobats, animal acts, singers, dancers, team acts, storytellers, comedians, **magicians**, impersonators, ventriloquists, mind readers, comic sketches, and playlets.

The institution of American vaudeville developed from two immediately antecedent entertainment forms: the **dime museum** and the concert saloon. Popularized in the 1840s by P. T. Barnum and other showmen, dime museums combined pseudo-scientific exhibits of freaks of nature with variety shows featuring types of specialty acts common to minstrel shows. Concert saloons, gaining popularity in the 1850s, presented risqué theatrical entertainment in **saloons** frequented primarily by working-class men. "Waiter-girls" serving drinks in these establishments gained a reputation for prostitution. Following press outcry, the New York state legislature passed the "Anti-Concert Saloon Bill" in 1862, forbidding amusement establishments from selling liquor or employing female waiters. Although the law was widely ignored, later variety theaters took pains to differentiate themselves from the bawdy concert saloons.

Tony Pastor, sometimes called the "Father of Vaudeville," is generally acknowledged as the first variety show entrepreneur to establish a national reputation. A former circus clown turned concert saloon singer, Pastor advertised his Bowery theater in 1865 as a "great family resort." In 1881, Pastor moved near Union Square, then the heart of New York's theater and shopping district, where he would remain active until his death in 1908. Unlike many others in the first generation of vaudeville entrepreneurs, Pastor remained a small businessman with no interest in creating an entertainment empire.

The 1880s saw the first vaudeville theater chains. F. F. Proctor, formerly an acrobat, began a circuit in the 1880s in New York state. The first theater in what would become the West's dominant chain, the Orpheum circuit, opened in San Francisco in 1887. In Boston, dime museum operator B. F. **Keith** instituted a policy of "continuous vaudeville" in 1885, with the slogan, "Come when you please; stay as long as you like." With his general manager Edward F. Albee, later big-time vaudeville's acknowledged "czar," Keith opened theaters in Providence and Philadelphia, beginning what came to be known as the "Sunday school circuit," due to explicit prohibitions against salacious language and undignified behavior.

When, in 1893, Keith acquired the Union Square Theatre, his first in New York City, the country's hub for theater, he hired J. Austin **Fynes**, managing editor of the *New York Clipper*, as general manager. To compete with Proctor's 23d Street Theatre, where a renowned opera tenor was drawing crowds, Fynes brought in dramatic actors and concert performers on a regular basis and convinced established playwrights to create one-act playlets, hoping to attract theatergoers unfamiliar with vaudeville's appeal. Both Keith and Proctor opened their first palatial theaters in the mid-1890s. It was in this atmosphere of competition, innovation, expansive circuit building, palatial theaters, and appeals to refinement and respectability that projected moving pictures were first exhibited in the USA.

The exhibition of the **Edison** Vitascope at Koster and Bial's Music Hall, on 23 April 1896, inaugurated a period in which moving pictures spread quickly to vaudeville programs across the country. Exhibition services, such as the **Cinématographe Lumière**, **American Mutoscope and Biograph**, and **Vitagraph**, competed for profitable vaudeville venues. The demand for weekly program changes fostered the growth of stable companies by providing a dependable market.

In May 1900, in order to gain control over the booking of acts and to drive independents agents out of business, leading vaudeville entrepreneurs formed the Vaudeville Managers' Association (in the East) and the Western Vaudeville Managers' Association, and began to charge performers a fee for hiring them. Outraged, vaudeville actors formed a proto-union, the White Rats of America, and in February 1901 struck theaters in the East and Midwest. The action induced some managers to use moving pictures to replace striking acts. Although the White Rats prevailed, managers reinstalled the booking fee after the actors' collective power dissipated. Intense sporadic battles between organized actors and managers would mark the next two decades.

The managers experienced dissension within their own ranks as Proctor left the syndicate in 1901 and began to book with agent William Morris, a Jewish immigrant from Austria who rose from office boy to head the talent agency that still bears his name. Known for his shrewd dealing, innovative ideas, and fierce independence, Morris encouraged Proctor and other clients to shift from "continuous" to two-a-day programs built around well-advertised headliners, a style that soon became identified with big-time vaudevillle.

As the novelty of moving pictures wore off, vaudeville managers regularly placed them in the "chaser" or concluding position on bills, so that patrons would not leave during more expensive acts. Although inauspicious, the chaser function provided a secure outlet for product. In order to furnish vaudeville theaters with a reliable supply, manufacturers increasingly turned to story films, which could be produced more efficiently than those dependent upon topical events. As this shift continued, exhibition spread to new small-time or "family" vaudeville houses popping up in the West, Northeast, and Midwest. The increased demand also led to a change in distribution policy: film exchanges charging rental fees by the reel began to replace complete exhibition services. The institution of the film exchange, initially supplied largely with **Pathé-Frères**' French films, fostered the proliferation of nickelodeons.

While nickelodeon exhibitors often constructed programs according to the continuous format model, the differences from vaudeville exhibition practices were significant. Nickelodeons were cheaper to operate; cheap admission prices allowed children and working-class families to attend more frequently and afforded single women the opportunity to attend without relying on men to treat them. Boasting no reserved sections, nickelodeons advertised "democratic" seating. Because programs often were changed three or four times a week or even daily, nickelodeons became more integral than vaudeville to the daily lives of masses of people.

While the nickelodeon boom was underway, Keith secured agreements with rival managers to book with his agency rather than with Morris and formed the United Booking Office (UBO), the core institution of the burgeoning vaudeville oligopoly that would exert autocratic control over big-time theaters and performers east of Chicago (the Orpheum Circuit later would achieve hegemony in the West). Morris then teamed with legitimate **theater** moguls **Klaw & Erlanger** and the Shubert brothers to place "Advanced Vaudeville" high-priced shows in legitimate theaters. In response, the UBO instituted a blacklist of performers playing non-UBO houses. After Keith paid the legitimate chiefs a large sum to leave vaudeville for ten years, Morris put together traveling vaudeville units with high-priced headliners and ensemble acts, a development that increased the costs of big-time vaudeville bills.

In 1908, after the **Motion Picture Patents Company** was formed to license film exchanges and theaters, and force licensees to use only MPPC product and equipment, J. J. **Murdock**, a founder of the Western Managers' Vaudeville Association, created the International Projecting and Producing Company (IPPC) to organize independent distributors and importers in order to supply vaudeville theaters without bowing to MPPC demands. Vaudeville manager Percy G. Williams, an IPPC backer, secured a temporary injunction against his MPPC supplier and charged them with violating federal antitrust laws. The injunction was not extended, and after the IPPC failed to supply the quality of product it had promised, vaudeville managers agreed to MPPC terms.

Figure 127 Exterior of Keith's Theatre, Boston, 1894.

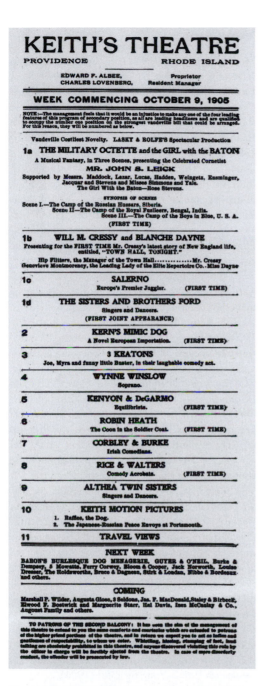

KEITH'S THEATRE
PROVIDENCE   RHODE ISLAND

EDWARD F. ALBEE,   Proprietor
CHARLES LOVENBERG,   Resident Manager

WEEK COMMENCING OCTOBER 9, 1905

NOTE:—The management feels that it would be an injustice to make any one of the four leading features of this program of secondary position, as all are leading headliners and are qualified to occupy the number one position on the strongest vaudeville bill that could be arranged. For this reason, they will be numbered as below.

Vaudeville Costliest Novelty. LASKY & ROLFE'S Spectacular Production

1a   **THE MILITARY OCTETTE and the GIRL with the BATON**
A Musical Fantasy, in Three Scenes, presenting the Celebrated Cornetist
MR. JOHN S. LEICK
Supported by Messrs. Maddock, Lazar, Lucas, Haddes, Weingetz, Ensminger, Jacquar and Stevens and Misses Simmons and Yale.
The Girl With the Baton—Rose Stevens.

SYNOPSIS OF SCENES
Scene I.—The Camp of the Russian Hussars, Siberia.
Scene II.—The Camp of the Royal Fusileers, Bengal, India.
Scene III.—The Camp of the Boys in Blue, U. S. A.
(FIRST TIME)

1b   **WILL M. CRESSY and BLANCHE DAYNE**
Presenting for the FIRST TIME Mr. Cressy's latest story of New England life, entitled, "TOWN HALL, TONIGHT."
Hip Flitters, the Manager of the Town Hall..............Mr. Cressy
Genevieve Montmorency, the Leading Lady of the Elite Repertoire Co.-Miss Dayne

1c   **SALERNO**
Europe's Premier Juggler.   (FIRST TIME)

1d   **THE SISTERS AND BROTHERS FORD**
Singers and Dancers.
(FIRST JOINT APPEARANCE)

2   **KERN'S MIMIC DOG**
A Novel European Importation.   (FIRST TIME)

3   **3 KEATONS**
Joe, Myra and funny little Buster, in their laughable comedy act.

4   **WYNNE WINSLOW**
Soprano.

5   **KENYON & DeGARMO**
Equilibrists.   (FIRST TIME)

6   **ROBIN HEATH**
The Coon in the Soldier Coat.   (FIRST TIME)

7   **CORBLEY & BURKE**
Irish Comedians.

8   **RICE & WALTERS**
Comedy Acrobats.   (FIRST TIME)

9   **ALTHEA TWIN SISTERS**
Singers and Dancers.

10   **KEITH MOTION PICTURES**
1. Raffles, the Dog.
2. The Japanese-Russian Peace Envoys at Portsmouth.

11   **TRAVEL VIEWS**

NEXT WEEK
BARON'S BURLESQUE DOG MENAGERIE, GUYER & O'NEIL, Burke & Dempsey, 3 Mowatts, Perry Corwey, Bloom & Cooper, Jack Norworth, Louise Dresser, The Holdsworths, Bruce & Dagneau, Stirk & Londan, Nibbe & Bordeaux and others.

COMING
Marshall P. Wilder, Augusta Glose, 3 Seldons, Jas. F. MacDonald, Staley & Birbeck, Elwood F. Bostwick and Marguerite Starr, Hal Davis, Ines McCaulay & Co., Auguast Family and others.

TO PATRONS OF THE SECOND BALCONY: It has seen the aim of the management of this theatre to extend to you the same comforts and courtesies which are extended to patrons of the higher priced portions of the theatre, and to return we expect you to act as ladies and gentlemen of respectability, to whom we cater. Whistling, hissing, stamping of feet, loud talking are absolutely prohibited in this theatre, and anyone discovered violating this rule by the usher in charge will be forcibly ejected from the theatre. In case of more disorderly conduct, the offender will be prosecuted by law.

Figure 128 Keith's Theatre program, Providence, Rhode Island, 1905. (Courtesy of Keith–Albee Collection, Special Collections, University of Iowa Library.)

By the end of the decade, small-time vaudeville expanded considerably when Marcus **Loew**, William **Fox**, and Siegmund **Lubin** opened large theaters with mixed vaudeville and film programs at low prices, usually 10 to 35 cents, as compared with big-time ticket prices of 25 cents to one dollar. Loew contracted with Morris to supply big-time talent by drawing on a pool of more than 800 acts that the UBO had blacklisted. These neighborhood theaters, much like nickelodeons, functioned more integrally within their communities than did more cosmopolitan venues.

As Loew expanded westward, he received financial backing from the Shuberts, then gained control of Morris's booking agency and all but one of his theaters, which he converted to small-time. To attract patrons away from Loew, the UBO began their own "family vaudeville" booking unit, dropped their lowest ticket prices to 10 cents, and upgraded talent in theaters near Loew's. They also formed the American Talking Picture Company in 1912 to exhibit Edison **Kinetophone** sound motion pictures, but projection difficulties and other considerations limited the innovation's viability.

Loew's theaters sporadically played **multiple-reel/feature films** beginning in 1912. Keith houses followed suit the next year. Features became a standard portion of the small-vaudeville bill by mid-decade, reducing the number of live acts used. Although the **palace cinemas** built in the 1910s for features often modeled their architecture, decor, and modular format on big-time vaudeville practices, vaudeville theaters lost importance as film exhibition venues when features became the dominant form of production. In 1914, after legitimate actors had begun to appear in features based on famous plays in which they had starred, Albee decreed that he would not book any actor appearing in pictures. His edict acted to further separate the once-interdependent realms of vaudeville and motion pictures.

See also: audiences: surveys and debates; labor movement: USA; leisure time and space: USA; monopoly capitalism: USA; music halls; Poli, Sylvester; synchronized sound systems; urbanization

Further reading

Abel, Richard (1999) *The Red Rooster Scare: Making Cinema American, 1900–10*, Berkeley: University of California Press.

Allen, Robert C. (1980) *Vaudeville and Film, 1895–1915: A Study in Media Interaction*, New York: Arno Press.

Gilbert, Douglas (1940) *American Vaudeville, Its Life and Times*, New York: Whittlesey House.

Kibler, M. Alison (1999) *Rank Ladies: Gender and Cultural Hierarchy in American Vaudeville*, Chapel Hill: University of North Carolina Press.

McDonnell, Patricia (2002) *On the Edge of Your Seat: Popular Theater and Film in Early Twentieth-Century American Art*, New Haven: Yale University Press.

Musser, Charles (1990) *The Emergence of Cinema: The American Screen to 1907*, New York: Scribner's.

Slide, Anthony (1994) *The Encyclopedia of Vaudeville*, Westport, CT: Greenwood Press.

Snyder, Robert W. (1989) *The Voice of the City: Vaudeville and Popular Culture in New York*, New York: Oxford University Press.

ALAN GEVINSON

Velle, Gaston

b. 1872; d. 1942

filmmaker, France, Italy

An illusionist by training, Velle specialized in **trick films** and *féeries*/**fairy plays** such as *La Poule aux oeufs d'or* [The Hen with the Golden Eggs] (1905) for **Pathé-Frères**. In July 1906, he left the company, taking his set decorators and cameraman, to become artistic director at **Cines**. The films he made in Italy plagiarized some of the work he himself had done previously. In late 1907, he returned to Pathé to make several more films and write others such as Camille de Morlhon's *Cagliostro* (1910). A remake of *La Poule aux oeufs d'or*, in 1913, signaled the failure of his attempted comeback.

LAURENT LE FORESTIER

Venezuela

Moving pictures appeared early in Venezuela, at a screening in Maracaibo, 28 January 1897, where **Lumière** films and, rather surprisingly, two shorts filmed locally by Manuel Trujillo Durán were shown to great acclaim: *Muchachos bañandose en la laguna de Maracaibo* [Boys Bathing in the Maracaibo Lake] and *Un célebre especialista sacando muelas en el Grand Hotel* [A Celebrated Specialist Pulling Teeth in the Gran Hotel]. Durán was a photographer, journalist, and world traveler and, while in New York, apparently convinced **Edison** to sell him some Vitascope equipment with which he shot his films and premiered the system throughout the country.

Despite the fact that foreign equipment and films were imported by different impresarios who set up makeshift theaters, national production was slow to take off. ***Actualités*** were shot in Caracas in the late 1900s and through the 1910s: at least two recorded the annual carnival festivities; others documented views of the city and civic events of significance. The first Venezuelan fiction film, González Vidal's *El fusilamiento de Piar* [The Lynching of Piar] (1913) led to the first cinematographic scandal: because of its historical inaccuracies, the film was seized by the authorities and its two Spanish theater actors were deported. Henry Zimmerman imported equipment from the USA and established the first Venezuelan laboratory, Studios Venezuela. He also directed *La dama de las cayenas* [The Lady of Cayenas] (1913), the first **multiple-reel/feature** film and a parody of **Film d'Art**'s *La dame aux camelias*. With Lucas Manzano, he directed another **comedy**, *Don Leandro el inefable* [Den Leandro, the Ineffable] (1918). Other significant films of the period were Vidal's *Siete fusileros* [Seven Assassins], Edgar Anzola and Jacobo Capriles' *La Trepadora* [The Climber] (1924), the first adaptation of a Romulo Gallegos novel, and their apparently sophisticated melodrama, *Amor, tu eres la vida* [Love, You Are Life] (1926).

An unusual phenomenon was a cycle of **religious films** in the late 1910s and early 1920s produced by Nostra, a company established by two Spanish actors/entrepreneurs, Francisco Martínez and Prudencia Grifell. With extraordinarily moralistic stories and religious themes, films such as

Zimmerman's *La pasión* [The Passion] and *El ángel de la guarda* (The Guardian Angel) were popular at the box-office and reflected the conservatism of the period.

Perhaps the most unusual filmmaker was Amábilis Cordero, a photographer from Barquisimeto (in the state of Lara, west of Caracas), who shot and exhibited at least four fiction films and a series of documentaries and promotional subjects locally between 1928 and 1931. Cordero's films—*Amor y fé a la Divina Pastora* [Love and Faith in the Divine Shepherdess] (1928), *La cruz de un angel* [The cross of an Angel] (1929), *Los milagros de la Divina Pastora* [The Miracles of the Divine Shepherdess] (1929), *La Tragedia de la Escuela* [The Tragedy of the School] (1933) plus documentaries and fragments of unfinished films—and all his filmmaking equipment survive and offer a remarkable portrait of life in Barquisimeto and the aspirations of an amateur filmmaker who captured the spirit of the epoch. Revealingly, his films were exhibited not only throughout Venezuela but also in the neighboring islands of Curaçao and Aruba as well as in Colombia.

Further reading

Cronología del cine en Venezuela (1989) Caracas: Cuadernos de la Cinemateca Nacional.

Marrosu, Ambretta (1985) *Exploraciones en la historiografía del cine en Venezuela: cambios, pistas e interrogantes*, Caracas: ININCO.

ANA M. LÓPEZ

Venkaiah, Raghupati

b. ?; d. 1941

exhibitor, producer, India

Venkaiah was a wealthy businessman and photographer before he began exhibiting films in South India, and he is credited with establishing the first permanent cinema in Madras in 1914. After **World War I**, he sent his son, Raghupati Prakash, to learn filmmaking in Europe and set up the Star of the East Studio, where they made *Bhishma Pratigya* [Bhishma's Vow] in 1921. Only R. N. **Mudaliar** preceded the filmmaking efforts of the Raghupati duo in South India. While Venkaiah continued as a leading exhibitor until his death in 1941, his son had an illustrious career as director and cameraman for the next three decades.

SURESH CHABRIA

Veyre, Gabriel

b. 1871; d. 1936

cameraman, France, Mexico

The son of a notary near Lyon, Gabriel Veyre graduated with a degree in pharmacology in 1895, a profession which he left in order to work with the **Lumière** company, and then with Ferdinand "Bon" **Bernard** in Mexico. A skilled mechanic, he solved technical problems caused by strong electrical currents, which allowed him to record and present moving picture performances in Mexico City before the arrival of **Edison**'s Vitascope. Among the films he shot in Mexico City, seventeen have survived, among them *The President on Parade* and *The Duel With Pistols*. In January 1897, he embarked on a filmmaking trip to Cuba, Panamá, Colombia, and Venezuela, from which he returned to France. Two years later, again for the Lumières, he traveled to Canada, Japan, and Indochina. His mother's collection of letters about his travels is preserved.

AURELIO DE LOS REYES

Vidali, Enrico (Giovanni E. V. Novelli)

b. 1869; d. 1937

actor, director, Italy

A stage actor with Ermete **Zacconi**, Vidali was a comedian of international caliber before turning into a Shakespearean actor. Four years after a brief stint as an actor at **Ambrosio** Film, in 1912 Vidali began working as an actor and director for **Pasquali**, creating such grand **historical films** as *Spartaco* [Spartacus] (1913) and *Jone* [The Last Days of Pompeii] (1913)—the latter in direct competition with the Ambrosio Film version. After 1916, he specialized in adaptations of Carolina Invernizio's popular literary melodramas for short-lived companies he helped found (Italica and Vidali Films).

GIORGIO BERTELLINI

Vietnam

The earliest films were shot in Vietnam in 1896 and 1899, respectively, by **Lumière** camera operators, Constant Girel and Gabriel **Veyre**, whose mission was to promote the **Cinématographe Lumière**, take footage of the Indochinese colonies, and expand the company's archive of moving pictures. The versatility of the Cinématographe also allowed Veyre to project films in Hanoi on 6 May 1899 at the Cercle de l'Union, transformed for the evening into a movie theater. Aware that the Cinématographe could be a powerful propaganda apparatus, the Governor General of Indochina, Paul Doumer commissioned Veyre to shoot 500 films to showcase the Indochinese colonies at the 1900 Paris Exposition.

From 1896 to 1902, Doumer embarked on an ambitious plan to develop Vietnam's urban infrastructure. The Cinématographe captured the labor of the anonymous Vietnamese workers who transformed Indochina into the "Pearl of the Orient," as exemplified in Girel's extraordinary *Coolies à Saigon* [Coolies in Saigon] shot in December 1896. This desire to archive everyday practices is also evident in scenics or **travelogues** such as *Le Village de Namo: Panorama pris d'une chaise à porteurs* [The Village of Namo Seen from a Portable Chair]. The first public showings that targeted an indigenous audience were improvised in makeshift locations such as **fairs/fairgrounds**, markets, and festivals. This was the era of a **cinema of attractions**, manifest in the presence of the Grand Cinématographe: "Théâtre des Illusions" at the 1902 Colonial Exposition held in Hanoi. In the early 1900s, no permanent movie theaters were built; instead, the cinema would find a temporary home in the

Cercle Franco-Annamite, the Hanoi Theatre, and other theatrical spaces frequented by the natives.

An incipient official "film policy" emerged in 1917 when the Government General created the "Mission Cinématographique" dedicated to "Make France known in Indochina and Indochina known in France" through moving pictures. For four years the Mission filmed, distributed, and exhibited *actualités* to recruit natives for the French war effort against Germany and to showcase France's grandeur and prestige. By the 1920s, cinema had made solid gains in urban areas: in Hanoi, the Pathé movie theater opened in 1920; the Tonkinois, in 1921. In April 1924, the Government General and the newly created Société Indochine-Films et Cinémas signed an agreement that encompassed all aspects of production, distribution, and exhibition in the Indochinese colonies and made the cinema a legitimate colonial propaganda apparatus. In addition to producing **propaganda films**, the company also opened a network of movie theaters in Bienhoa, Cantho, Cholon, and Saigon. By 1930, the Société and its new French rival, the Société des Ciné-Théâtres d'Indochine, were having to import silent (and sound) films from France in order to contend with the success of American and Chinese films. In 1924, Frenchman E. A. Famechon shot the first **multiple-reel/ feature films**, promoted as "the first Indochinese films with native actors and costumes," another sign of the control exerted by the French, and which inhibited the rise of an autochthonous Vietnamese cinema.

It was not until 2 September 1945, and the filming of Ho Chi Minh's independence declaration, that a truly Vietnamese cinema emerged.

Further reading

Anon. (1924) *Marché de Gré à Gré entre le Gouvernement Général de l'Indochine et la Société "Indochine Films et Cinéma,"* Hanoi: Imprimerie d'Extrême-Orient.

Aubert, Michelle and Jean-Claude Seguin (1996) *La Production cinématographique des frères Lumière*, Paris: Bibliothèque du Film/Edition mémoires du cinéma.

Pham Ngoc Truong (2001) "A Brief History of Vietnamese Films," in David Hanan (ed.) *Film in South East Asia: Views from the Region*, 59–82, Hanoi: SEAPAVAA.

Touzet, André (1919) *Une Oeuvre de Guerre et d'Après-Guerre: La Mission Cinématographique du Gouvernement Général de l'Indochine*, Hanoi: Imprimerie d'Extrême-Orient.

PANIVONG NORINDR

Views and Films Index

(1906–1911)

The first trade weekly in the USA devoted to moving pictures. Chiefly financed by **Pathé-Frères** and **Vitagraph**, *Views and Films Index* (*VFI*) linked manufacturers directly with exhibitors; it strongly supported the **nickelodeon** boom and promoted the regulation of renters and exhibitors. By early 1908, *VFI* was closely aligned with the Film Service Association (dominated by **Edison**); later that year, it became *Film Index*, the mouthpiece of the **Motion Picture Patents Company** (MPPC). As rival weeklies appeared and Independents emerged to challenge the MPPC, its influence waned, until it was acquired by **Moving Picture World** in early July 1911.

RICHARD ABEL

Vita Cinematografica, La

(1910–1933)

An Italian bi-monthly, based in Turin, widely respected for its serious, informative, and cultured coverage of film news and aesthetics. Growing to thirty-two pages in 1912, *La Vita Cinematografica* included long essays on the transition to **multiple-reel films**, US commercial dominance, film iconography and public customs, written by, among others, Giuseppe **De Liguoro**. In 1913, the journal conducted an inquiry among leading writers, including Nino **Oxilia** and Grazia Deledda, about films' artistic potential. The survey confirmed Italian cinema's penchant for prominent theatrical

and literary sources. Concurrently, the journal led a strenuous campaign for the unionization of film exhibitors.

GIORGIO BERTELLINI

Vitagraph Company of America

The Vitagraph Company of America was for the second half of the period covered by this Encyclopedia, the largest film-producing company in the USA, and the second largest in the world (after **Pathé-Frères**).

Vitagraph was founded in 1899 by James Stuart **Blackton**, Albert E. **Smith**, and William T. "Pop" **Rock**. The former two were English-born New Yorkers with experience as concert-party entertainers and in two earlier, short-lived moving-picture ventures, the Edison Vitagraph Company and the Commercial Advertising Bureau (both founded in 1897). Rock had owned the **Raff & Gammon** Vitascope license for Louisiana and exhibited moving pictures in New Orleans. Vitagraph had a roof-top studio in New York City, where Blackton made short sketch films and reconstructed *actualités*; Smith shot *actualités* on location—notably, he was the first cameraman present after the disastrous 1900 floods in Galveston, Texas. Before 1905, Vitagraph was deterred from offering films in the market by threats of litigation from **Edison**; it sold some film through Edison, but the bulk of the company's revenue came from providing a complete projection service (varying programs of films, **projectionists**, and projectors) to **vaudeville** circuits.

In 1905, Edison's position was weakened by a number of court decisions, which led Vitagraph to decide to enter the market in strength on their own behalf. It built a large glass-roofed studio in Flatbush, Brooklyn, and expanded production, primarily of fiction films. It was thus well placed to cash in on the **nickelodeon** boom of 1906–07, and began a decade of rapid expansion, all of it financed out of sales revenue. Vitagraph was a founding member of the **Motion Picture Patents Company** in 1908 (Smith owned one minor projection-related patent) and contributed more footage than any other licensed producer except

Pathé to the Licensed program, distributed from 1910 by **General Film**. At the beginning of 1909, the company contributed 2,000 feet a week to the program; this rose to 3,000 in February 1910, 4,000 in July 1911, 5,000 in September 1911, 6,000 in September 1912 (not including some weeks when a two- or three-reel film put the footage a thousand or more feet higher—the first Vitagraph two-reeler, *Auld Lang Syne*, directed by Larry Trimble, was released in November 1911). By 1913, the footage varied as the number of **multiple-reel films** increased, but was rarely less than 8,000 feet a week. The studio expanded until there was at least three times the area under glass as in 1906.

The company's sales were handled by Rock; Smith ran the financial side of production; and Blackton supervised production. Vitagraph was the first American producer to have its own overseas sales outlet, when it opened a Paris office and printing plant in 1908. As a result, its European sales were particularly strong, and it is perhaps for this reason that more Vitagraph films survive in European collections than in American ones, and that so many Europeans, from Victorin **Jasset** to Victor **Sjöström** single out Vitagraph in discussing the influence of American films on European cinema. Problems with accounting for this foreign income brought Vitagraph into conflict with the IRS; Price, Waterhouse was hired in 1913 to resolve the dispute, and the experience contributed largely to the accounting standards for the film industry that were published in 1915.

In 1911, Vitagraph opened a studio in Santa Monica, California, under Rollin S. Sturgeon, which moved to a bigger site in Hollywood in 1913. Vitagraph released its first feature-length film, *One Million Bid*, directed by Ralph **Ince**, on 7 February 1914, and hired the Criterion Theatre on Broadway, New York City, renaming it the Vitagraph Theatre, to showcase this and its other features for the next two years. In 1915, the company sponsored the formation of VLSE to distribute its features along with those of **Lubin**, **Selig**, and **Essanay**.

The rest of the company's history falls outside the period covered by this encyclopedia; suffice it to say that a 1916 attempt to leverage Vitagraph into a dominant position in the American feature-film industry failed, and the resultant debt left

the company as a secondary producer-distributor, which was eventually sold to Warner Bros. in 1925.

While Blackton was the overall supervisor of production in the Flatbush studio throughout the period covered, so much was produced and he had such a light hand, that individual directors vary a great deal in their style. Important directors include Van Dyke Brooke, William Humphrey, Ralph Ince, Charles Kent, William V. Ranous, and James Young. Ince was a pioneer of a highly edited film style, as well as an actor remarkable for his underplaying. Van Dyke Brooke used a low and close camera and staged scenes in depth allowing front characters to turn their back to the camera.

So many actors well-known at the time or later began their careers at or passed through Vitagraph that it would be impossible to list them. Here I will single out Florence **Turner** (the "Vitagraph Girl"), her frequent partner Maurice **Costello**, John **Bunny** and his frequent partner Flora **Finch**, Helen **Gardner**, Clara Kimball Young, Anita Stewart, and Mr. and Mrs. Sidney Drew.

Because the company rarely deposited more than fragments of its films for copyright purposes, and because no pioneer **archive** was concerned to save its negatives, Vitagraph's films have been unfairly neglected in comparison with those of **Biograph**. Yet Vitagraph films were more likely to

Figure 129 Vitagraph studio exterior, Brooklyn, *c.* 1907. (Courtesy of the Robert S. Birchard Collection.)

be seen in American moving picture theaters in the years before **World War I** and, as a whole, they were more typical of the early American cinema.

Further reading

Cherchi Usai, Paolo (ed.) (1987) *Vitagraph Co. of America: il cinema prima di Hollywood*, Pordenone: Studio Tesi.

Gartenberg, Jon (1984) "Vitagraph before Griffith: Forging Ahead in the Nickelodeon Era," *Studies in Visual Communication*, 10.4: 7–23.

Musser, Charles (1983) "The American Vitagraph, 1897–1901: Survival and Success in a Competitive Industry," in John L. Fell (ed.) *Film Before Griffith*, 22–66, Berkeley: University of California Press.

Slide, Anthony (1987) *The Big V: A History of the Vitagraph Company*, revised ed., Metuchen, NJ: Scarecrow Press.

Uricchio, William and Pearson, Roberta E. (1993) *Reframing Culture: The Case of the Vitagraph Quality Films*, Princeton: Princeton University Press.

BEN BREWSTER

Vitascope

Established in 1907 in Berlin, *Vitascope-Theater-Betriebsgesellschaft* operated movie theaters in and outside Germany, before it was converted into the production and distribution company, Deutsche Vitascope, in 1909. Initially, the company produced short films of fiction and non-fiction and promoted producer Jules Greenbaum's sound picture system, the Synchronoscope. In 1912–13, boosted by Greenbaum's PR-talent and Herrmann Fellner's connections to the theatrical establishment, Vitascope became a leading brand name, at first cashing in on the vogue for *Autorenfilme*. With directors like Viggo **Larsen** and Max **Mack** as well as stars like Albert **Bassermann** and Hanni **Weisse** under contract, Vitascope also made its reputation in popular drama and **comedy**. In December 1913, it opened a new "glass house"

studio in Berlin-Weissensee but, within months, was taken over by **PAGU**.

MICHAEL WEDEL

Vitrotti, Giovanni

b. 1882; d. 1966

cameraman, director, Italy

Regarded as one of Italian cinema's greatest cameramen, Vitrotti spent most of his career at **Ambrosio** Film (1905–13 and 1918–20). He shot about six hundred films for the company, from **comedies** and nonfiction films to such ambitious features as *Gli ultimi giorni di Pompei* [The Last Days of Pompeii] (1913). Appreciated for his eye for landscapes, he made *actualités* in Russia where the Turinese company maintained commercial links with **Thiemann & Reinhardt** (1909–11). Founder in 1914 of the unsuccessful company, Leonardo Film, he worked in Naples in 1915 and in Germany in the 1920s.

GIORGIO BERTELLINI

von Herkomer, Sir Hubert

b. 1849; d. 1914

painter, filmmaker, Great Britain

A German-born painter who made his reputation in Britain with the realistic portrayal of social subjects, von Herkomer was elected to the Royal Academy in 1890 and knighted in 1907. He had experimented with "pictorial music plays" before announcing in 1913 that he was renouncing **painting** in favor of cinema. With his son Siegfried, who had worked for **Pathé-Frères**, he started production in a small garden studio, starring in his first film, *The Old Wood Carver* (1913). Three more followed before his death, none of which survive, leaving open the tantalizing question of how successful British cinema's most distinguished early convert might have been.

IAN CHRISTIE

von Woringen, Paul

b. 1859; d. 1928

director, author, producer, Germany

Born in Rotterdam, the son of German parents, Ernest Guillaume Paul von Woringen began his career as an artistic supervisor at **Deutsche Mutoskop & Biograph** whose managing director he became in January 1911. Backed by his wife, the variety star Nora Gilis, he oversaw the company's transition to **multiple-reel/feature films**, discovered actor Max **Mack**'s potential as a director, and from 1913 on also directed his own films. His first and still best known film, the *Autorenfilm Die Landstrasse* [The Country Road] (1913), was based on an original script by Paul Lindau and is notable for its idiosyncratic use of long takes and parallel editing to create strong visual rhymes and abrupt shifts in narrative rhythm. From 1915, he directed, and sometimes also wrote, melodramas and **detective films** for the company's major female star, Lotte Neumann. Von Woringen retired as head of Deutsche Mutoskop & Biograph in 1921 and died in Portugal.

MICHAEL WEDEL

Wales

The arrival of the **Edison Kinetoscope** brought moving pictures to Wales where **photography** had flourished in the 19th century with the pioneering work of John Dilwyn Llewellyn, John Thomas, and Rev. Richard Calvert Jones. Two Kinetoscopes appeared in November 1894 at the Philharmonic Hall, Cardiff, managed by Oswald Stoll (later to run Britain's biggest film studios in the 1920's), and three machines were installed at a venue in Swansea in 1895. In April 1896, London- based Birt **Acres** projected the first moving pictures in Wales at a Cardiff Photographic Society private show. On May 5—one week before Felicien Trewey presented the **Cinématographe Lumière** at Cardiff's Empire **music hall**—Acres opened the first commercial moving picture show in Wales at the Cardiff Fine Art, Industrial and Maritime exhibition in Cathays Park. On June 27, he shot the first Welsh film—a visit of the Prince of Wales to the exhibition. R. W. **Paul** (or his representative) also shot Cardiff street scenes in 1896.

Faced with fierce religious opposition, especially in rural areas, moving pictures gained popularity relatively slowly in Wales; by 1910, however, 162 venues were screening films. Before 1911 and 1912, when permanent cinemas became common, most residents of the industrialized south or rural mid and north Wales first experienced moving pictures in **fair/fairground** bioscopes or in music halls. In the heyday of **itinerant exhibitors**, bioscopes run by Welsh-based families of fairground showmen—notably, Studt, Danter, Haggar, White, Dooner, Crecraft, and Wadbrook—competed for business at the great Welsh fairs in Neath, Portfield at Haverfordwest, and Pembroke. The flourishing bioscope era coincided with the career of eminent Welsh-based filmmaker William **Haggar**. In the larger towns—Cardiff, Newport, and Swansea—moving pictures were first shown at Stoll's Empire music halls.

Indigenous filmmaking began in 1898, with *actualités* shot by Arthur **Cheetham**, and continued with fiction films made by Haggar and showman John Codman (c. 1905–1909). Yet despite Haggar's achievements, in particular, Wales remained largely barren of "home" filmmakers in the pre-1914 period. Popular **news events** or *actualité* films of the early 1910's featured renowned Welsh boxers Freddie Welsh, Peerless Jim Driscoll and world flyweight champion Jimmy Wilde, as well as the charismatic politician, "Welsh wizard" David Lloyd George (Prime Minister, 1916–1922). Although mining was the principal industry, early **newsreels** rarely hinted at the realities or turbulence of coal field or quarry life.

Fiction films set in Wales but made by either London film companies or units of US studios, immediately post-Haggar, were mainly bucolic romances. Almost all are lost, including the intriguing feature directed by Henry Edwards, *A Welsh Singer* (1915), one of three films adapted from novels by Welsh writer Allen Raine and starring the former "**Vitagraph** Girl," Florence **Turner**. William Haggar Jr.'s feature, *The Maid of Cefn Ydfa* (1913) survives in truncated form, and some extant actualités make impressive use of photogenic Welsh locations—e.g., **British Mutascope and Biograph**'s *Phantom Train Ride to Conway Castle*

(1898) and **Charles Urban Trading**'s *North Wales, England: Land of Castles and Waterfalls* (1907).

DAVE BERRY

Further reading

Berry, David (1994) *Wales and Cinema: The First 100 Years*, University of Wales Press.
Curtis, Tony (ed.) (1986) *Wales, The Imagined Nation*, Poetry Wales Press.

Walker, William

b. ?; d. 1937

bookseller, optical lanternist, filmmaker, Scotland

In 1896, Walker purchased a set of moving pictures to augment his **magic lantern shows**. The following year, he hired cameramen Paul Robello and Joe Gray to film local subjects, using a **Wrench** camera. In 1898, Walker was called to Balmoral to present his films to Queen Victoria, the first of thirteen such presentations, earning his company, Walker's Cinematograph, the epithet "Royal." He produced a large number of *actualités* and **news event films** thereafter, the most ambitious being *Aberdeen University Quatercentenary* (1906). The business folded in 1911, whereupon Walker severed his ties with moving pictures.

JANET McBAIN

Walthall, Henry B.

b. 1878; d. 1936

actor, USA

One of the most popular and respected actors of the period, Walthall achieved his greatest fame as the "Little Colonel" in D. W. **Griffith's** *The Birth of a Nation* (1915). He had worked with Griffith since 1909 at the **Biograph** Company where he played the lead in numerous one-reelers and became skilfully adept at performing the new more "realistic" **acting style**, which was then replacing the older "theatrical" style. In 1913, he also starred as Holofernes in Griffith's first four-reel film, *Judith of Bethulia*.

ROBERTA E. PEARSON

Walturdaw

Walturdaw Company was formed out of the surnames of J. D. Walker, E. G. Turner and G. H. Dawson. Walker and Turner had toured Britain with **Edison Kinetoscopes** and **phonographs** in 1896, before graduating to cinema shows and, thereafter, to renting out their large collection of films. Joined by Dawson (a teacher and former customer), they formed the Walturdaw Company in 1904 and effectively pioneered film distribution in Britain. Walturdaw moved into film production the following year, and in 1907 launched its Cinematophone **synchronized sound** film system. Yet renting remained at the heart of the company's business until the mid-1920s, when it turned to the supply of film equipment, where it was modestly successful for a number of decades.

See also: distribution: Europe

LUKE McKERNAN

Warner brothers

Harry (Hirsch): b. 1881; d. 1958

Albert: b. 1884; d. 1967

Sam: b. 1888; d. 1927

Jack (Jacob): b. 1892; d. 1978

exhibitors, distributors, producers, executives, USA

In 1895, the Polish immigrant Warner family settled in Youngstown, Ohio. After brothers Harry and Sam spent months touring moving pictures in eastern Ohio and western Pennsylvania, they opened a **nickelodeon** in New Castle in 1907. Soon, along with brother Albert, they built up a circuit of theaters and opened a rental exchange, Duquesne Amusement & Supply, in Pittsburgh. They prospered until 1911 when, under pressure from the **Motion Picture Patents Company** and **General Film** (which bought out their rental exchange), the brothers sold the theaters and separately moved into distribution—in 1913–1914, Albert released a weekly program of **multiple-reel films** through **Warner's Features**—and eventually together, after several years of financial difficulties, into feature film production. By the late 1920s, through the innovation of sound, Warner Bros. ranked as one of Hollywood's great studios.

DOUGLAS GOMERY

Warner's Features, Inc.

A distribution company established in 1912 by the **Warner brothers** and formally incorporated on 1 August 1913, with Albert Warner as vice-president and Pat **Powers** as president. Originally an importer of foreign films, Warner's Features eventually distributed moving pictures made by several American independent producers including Gene **Gauntier Feature Players**, St. Louis Motion Picture Co., and the American branch of **Gaumont**. The company provided an important bridge between the **single-reel** and **multiple-reel/feature film** eras by offering a regular weekly service of atleast three-reel films during the 1913–1914 season, but its success was spotty. The firm was reorganized as United Film Service in November 1914.

ROBERT S. BIRCHARD

Warwick Bioscope projector

Charles **Urban**, along with engineer Walter Isaacs, claimed to have co-invented the Bioscope projector—an efficient 35mm fast-pull-down, beater-movement machine apparently based on earlier Georges **Demenÿ** patents. When Urban joined **Warwick Trading** in England in 1897, he imported the Bioscope from the USA for resale. Early versions, which projected both slides and films, had a 'spoolbank' attachment enabling very short films to be repeated continuously. Later models were manufactured for Warwick by the Prestwich Company and sold throughout Europe. Cecil **Hepworth**, for instance, lectured with and demonstrated the Warwick Bioscope in the late 1890s. After leaving Warwick Trading, Urban marketed his own version, the Urban Bioscope.

STEPHEN HERBERT

Warwick Trading Company

The Warwick Trading Company was formed in 1898 out of the British branch of the American firm, **Maguire & Baucus**. It took its name from its London street location, Warwick Court. Frank Maguire and Joseph Baucus headed the business, but the company's dynamism came from managing director Charles **Urban**, who built up the company's nonfiction output, its reputation for quality equipment (based on the **Warwick Bioscope** projector, manufactured by Alfred **Darling**), and its distribution of the output of other producers, notably **Lumière** and **Méliès**. Warwick soon dominated the British market, to the extent of either producing or distributing as much as three-quarters of the films in Britain at the time. Many showmen in Britain and abroad began their film businesses with a Warwick Bioscope projector and a selection of **travelogues**. Films of the Boer War (1899–1902), mostly taken by Joseph **Rosenthal**, especially built up Warwick's reputation. Other notable cameramen included Urban's brother-in-law Jack Avery, member of the landed gentry John Benett-Stanford, South African **music hall** agent Edgar Hyman, mountaineer Frank Ormiston-Smith, and the Reverend Gregory Mantle, who filmed the 1902–1903 Delhi Durbar. Warwick's processing was initially done by Cecil **Hepworth**, who also shot its first fiction films; he was replaced by G. A. **Smith**, whose creative **trick films** also were handled by Warwick.

Clashes with Maguire & Baucus caused Urban to break away in 1903, taking a number of key staff with him. Warwick was never the same force again, although it was brought back to prominence as a producer of **news events** and *actualités* in 1906, with the arrival of the fiery Will **Barker** as manager. Barker left to form his own company in 1909. Warwick showed interest in the new form of news event films, **newsreels**, and the *Warwick Bioscope Chronicle* (first issued in July 1910) became the second British newsreel on the market. Yet the company's fortunes waned still further, and it was purchased by the naturalist filmmaker Cherry **Kearton** in 1913. After some notable early coverage of **World War I**, particularly through Kearton's creative war newsreel, *The Whirlpool of War*, characterized by hand-held camerawork using the innovative **Aeroscope** camera, the company succumbed to debts and went into receivership at the end of 1915.

Further reading

Barnes, John (1996–1998) *The Beginnings of the Cinema in England 1894–1901*, Exeter: University of Exeter Press.

Low, Rachael (1949) *The History of the British Film: 1906–1914*, London: George Allen & Unwin.

LUKE McKERNAN

Waters, Percival Lee

b. 1867?; d. 1942

exhibitor, producer, executive, US

Waters entered the film business in alliance with **Edison Manufacturing**, as founder of the Kinetograph Company, which provided an exhibition service to **vaudeville** houses in the Northeast and Canada. With the rise of **nickelodeons**, the company turned into a rental exchange. By 1910, Waters was general manager of the **General Film Company**, and a major stockholder. Along with J. J. **Kennedy**, he resigned in 1912 to form a second Kinetograph Company, which briefly competed as a distributor of **Motion Picture Patents Company** films. In 1914, Waters returned to General Film, but soon left to become president of the Triangle Film Corporation.

RICHARD ABEL

wax museums: Europe

Wax museums flourished throughout Europe in the 1880s and 1890s and functioned as significant presentation venues for many late 19th-century media practices, including early forms of motion pictures. The later rise of narrative cinema turned this initial symbiotic relationship into a more competitive one. Indeed, many of the institutions founded in moderately sized European capitals in the heyday of the wax museum did not survive the competition and closed in the first decades of the 20th century.

To the long and varied history of wax modeling, the 19th century contributed the establishment of public wax museums in permanent urban locations pitched at middle-class visitors. Madame Tussaud's establishment in London, founded in 1835, is the most long-lived and famous museum of this sort, but in the closing decades of the century, other European cities with metropolitan aspirations regarded the establishment of a wax museum as a crucial component of a well-rounded urban entertainment repertoire.

The name for wax museum in the Germanic parts of Europe, *Panoptikum*, underscores the implicit ambition to gather in effigies, objects, and sights from all corners of the earth. Castans Panoptikum, founded in Berlin in 1871, mixed the familiar miscellany of the curiosity cabinet and **dime museum** with its display of wax effigies, and became the most prominent wax museum in Germany.

More direct connections with early cinema could be found at the Parisian wax museum, the Musée Grévin, founded in 1882. This museum served as an important nexus for new media in Paris, offering itself as a "living newspaper" on the one hand and hosting **electricity** demonstrations and telephone concerts on the other. This public profile of the Musée Grévin made it a logical location in 1892 for Émile **Reynaud** to present his *théâtre optique*, projected life-size painted moving images that were important forerunners to screened photographic images.

Also relevant for early cinema studies is the respectable wax museum's relationship to competing forms of wax display—the wax cabinets and anatomy shows that for years had toured the marketplaces, **fairs/fairgrounds**, and rented halls or storefronts of Europe, and continued to do so through the turn of the century. These spectacle-oriented wax displays had much in common with the **cinema of attractions**, including an itinerant mode of circulation, a slightly disreputable class standing, and an undisguised fascination with the mediated body. The Musée Grévin's historical ties to the Paris Morgue demonstrate this common genealogy of visual sensation. But the Paris wax museum and its emulators, such as the Scandinavian Panoptikon in Copenhagen, also prefigured many of cinema's later strategies of cultural legitimation by developing luxurious interiors, a meticulous system of mise-en-scène, and an emphasis on narrative content and the tableau series.

See also: amusement parks; audiences: surveys and debates; dioramas/panoramas; editing: tableau style; magic lantern shows; museum life exhibits; vaudeville

Further reading

Sandberg, Mark (2003) *Living Pictures, Missing Persons: Mannequins, Museums, and Modernity*, Princeton: Princeton University Press.
Schwartz, Vanessa (1998) *Spectacular Realities: Early Mass Culture in Fin-de-Siècle Paris*, Berkeley: University of California Press.

MARK B. SANDBERG

Weber, Lois

b. 1881; d. 1939

scriptwriter, actor, director, USA

The foremost female director of the 1910s, Weber reached the peak of her career at **Universal** where she directed a **multiple-reel film** adaptation of Shakespeare's *The Merchant of Venice* in 1914, and the only screen appearance of famed Russian dancer Anna Pavlova. Believing that films of social conscience were the key to cinema's uplift, Weber also wrote and directed features on drug addiction, capital punishment, contraception, and wage equity for women. In 1916, she became the first woman granted membership in the Motion Picture Directors' Association, a precursor to the Directors' Guild of America.

See also: Rex; Smalley, Phillips

SHELLEY STAMP

Wegener, Paul

b. 1874; d. 1948

actor, director, Germany

A noted character actor under Max **Reinhardt**, Wegener made his screen debut as the student Balduin in Stellan **Rye** and Guido **Seeber**'s *Autorenfilm*, *Der Student von Prag* [The Student of Prague] (1913). He soon became a major force behind German cinema's obsession with fantastic and fairy tale motifs as actor-director of *Der Golem* [The Golem] (1915), *Rübezahls Hochzeit* (Rübezahl's Wedding) (1916) and *Der Golem und die Tänzerin* [The Golem and the Dancer] (1917). In his 1916 lecture, "The Artistic Possibilities of Film," Wegener outlined his approach to a distinctively "national" cinema, advocating a fusion of German Romantic motifs and special effects cinematography.

MICHAEL WEDEL

Weisse, Hanni

b. 1892; d. 1967

actor, Germany

A former stage soubrette, Weisse was discovered by Max **Mack** who promoted her as one of German cinema's leading film **stars** before **World War I**. After regular appearances in dramas and **comedies** for the Eiko company, she followed Mack to **Vitascope** in 1912, where she played opposite Albert **Bassermann**. In 1913–1914, she was given her own series, designed to exploit her tomboyish charm and nimble vivaciousness in burlesque comedies such as *Die Berliner Range* [The Berlin Street-Urchin] (1913), *Die Tango-Königin* [The Tango Queen] (1913) and *Zum Paradies der Damen* [A Ladies' Paradise] (1914).

MICHAEL WEDEL

Weltkinematograph/ Express-Film

Founded in 1906, Weltkinematograph Freiburg (also Welt-Film or WKF) started out as a cinema chain and shifted to film production in 1908. It specialized in non-fiction, turning out *actualités*, **industrial films**, educational films, views of nature, and local films, the latter being produced on commission only. Weltkinematograph thus catered to the needs of the program format of short films prevalent at theaters of the time.

In 1910, Express-Film was founded as a spin-off of Weltkinematograph. Express also specialized in non-fiction and produced more or less the same kind of films as Weltkinematograph. In fact, in terms of film style and content, the two companies could hardly be distinguished from one another. Weltkinematograph was more productive, releasing some 460 short films between 1908 and 1919. In November 1911, Express launched its short-lived **newsreel** enterprise, *Der Tag im Film*, whose objective (never accomplished) was a daily newscast for the screen. At the same time Express tended to make fewer but longer films. *4628 Meter Hoch auf Skiern— Besteigung des Monte Rosa* (1913), shot with the participation of young Arnold Fanck, was a precursor of the German mountain films of later renown.

With **World War I** the films of both companies became decidedly patriotic. Express's *Mit der Kamera in der Schlachtfront* (1913, 1160 meters), shot by Robert Schwobthaler during the Balkan war, was cited as an exceptional (anti-)war documentary. Schwobthaler, a native of the Freiburg region, was the co-founder of **Raleigh & Robert** and had close ties to Express. WKF responded to the war with short features like *Deutsche Soldaten im Felde*, *Die tapfere deutsche Marine zu Lande und zu Wasser*, *Des deutschen Heeres Entstehung* (all 1914), but continued producing shorts in other kinds of non-fiction as well: *Blütenpracht*, *In den Vogesen*, *Die Sächsische Schweiz* (all 1915), *Valencia*, *Am schönen deutschen Rhein*, *Bernhardinerhunde* (all 1916). Nevertheless during the war both companies declined. WKF stopped advertising its films in 1917, and what became of the company is not known, although it was dissolved in 1924. Express continued making films mostly of patriotic and military content, covering all theaters of war. In addition it made **travelogues** such as *Mit der Kamera im ewigen Eis* (1914, 1077 meters), *Indien, das Land der Hindus* (1914, 900 meters), and *Afrika, der schwarze Kontinent* (1915, 1030 meters). Express stopped advertising late in 1916. Since many of the Express films were later distributed through the Ufa-Kulturabteilung, it is very probable that the company merged with Ufa after the war.

Both WKF and Express were significant contributors of non-fiction films to German screens at a time of French, Italian, and Danish market hegemony. Their activities peaked when the Kino-Reform movement was in full swing, and their films exemplified an alternative to those (feature fiction) films targeted for censorship by the conservative intelligentsia. It is not clear, however, why neither benefited from the radical market changes World War I brought about and which boosted the German film industry as a whole.

See also: propaganda films; scientific films: Europe

Further reading

Dittrich, Wolfgang (1998) "Fakten und Fragmente zur Freiburger Filmproduktionsgeschichte 1901–1918," *Journal Film*, 32: 100–109.

Jung, Uli (2001) "Entdeckerfreude und Schaulust II: Die Freiburger Filmproduktion vor dem Ersten Weltkrieg," *Filmblatt*, 16.

ULI JUNG

Werner, Michel and Eugène

b. ?; d. ?

exhibitors, France

As early as 1893, Michel and Eugène Werner and their father Alexis were distributing **Edison**'s phonographic equipment in France. In October 1894, they created a company called "Le Kinetoscope Edison" and opened the first French **Kinetoscope** parlor at 20 boulevard Montmartre in Paris. Three months later, Michel Werner founded another company in order to exploit kinetoscope parlors across the country. Their businesses, however, faced severe competition as **fairground** showmen were able to find cheaper kinetoscopes or counterfeit machines, first from R. W. **Paul** in London and then Charles **Pathé** in Paris. The exploitation of Edison's machine was not lucrative for the Werners: indeed, their store at 85 rue de Richelieu was taken over by Pathé in 1899.

LAURENT MANNONI

West, Alfred

b. 1858; d. 1937

photographer, filmmaker, lantern lecturer, Great Britain

In the 1890s, Alfred West worked for the photographic firm, G. West & Son of Southsea, which specialized in portraiture and maritime subjects. In 1897, he began to make films of the Royal Navy in and around Portsmouth, which led to the creation of his "patriotic" film and **magic lantern** entertainment, "Our Navy." In late 1899, West established the show at the Polytechnic in London, where it played for the next fourteen years. Its early success led to three national touring companies as well as a colonial company for Canada, Australia, and South Africa. "Descriptive commentary" and **sound effects** were distinctive features of the show, which served as an effective recruiting agent for the Royal Navy.

See also: colonialism: Europe, lecturer

FRANK GRAY

West, T. J.

b. 1855; d. 1916

exhibitor, producer, Australia

Thomas James West toured with slide programs in Great Britain beginning in1878, and with moving pictures from 1899 on. He arrived in New Zealand in 1904, with the Brescians musical company, and first visited Australia in March 1906, eventually operating several **itinerant exhibition** companies, and building some of the first permanent cinemas. He made nonfiction films such as *Living Sydney* (1906), and contracted for the screening rights to **Pathé-Frères** films, which meant exhibiting Australia's first locally-produced **newsreel**. He did not live in Australia, but visited frequently until 1912, when his company became part of **Australasian Films**.

INA BERTRAND

westerns: cowboy and Indian films

What has become known as the genre of the western was not so named during the period of early cinema. Among the labels that circulated were: western comedy; cowboy picture; Indian romance; **historical film**; military picture; Frontier

drama; or just plain **comedy**, drama, or topical film. Besides borrowing familiar themes, stories, and images from cinema's pre-history—Wild West shows, **paintings**, **photography**, dime novels, melodrama **theater**, and popular myth—such films displayed the new possibilities of the medium: thrilling action, liveness, and shooting on location. The early history of the western thus consists of a conglomerate of films whose main common element was an outdoors setting signifying the American West (and in some cases even the American East). They drew on a wide variety of western imagery, from *actualités* and **ethnographic films** to stage plays and exciting adventure stories.

There is not always a clear story line in the earliest films, yet they all foreground "westernness" in motion. The grandiose landscapes of western America were sometimes the subject of films that seem to put picturesque **postcards** in motion. Examples of early titles are *Canyon of the Rio Grande* or *California Orange Groves, Panoramic View* shot by **Edison**'s cameramen in 1898. **Phantom train rides** and **travelogues** also gave the urban film viewer a tourist-like accessibility to panoramic vistas. Ethnographic films documented life in the West, as in Edison's *Wash Day in Mexico* (1897), *Branding Cattle* (1898), and *Rocking Gold in the Klondike* (1901). Other Edison films recorded, for **Kinetoscope** viewing, spectacular acts performed by members of Buffalo Bill **Cody**'s Wild West in front of the camera in the Black Maria: e.g., *Sioux Ghost Dance, Buffalo Dance, A Bucking Bronco* (all 1894). In another kinetoscope film bearing her name, Annie Oakley shows her dexterity at firing a rifle. An early Edison *actualité* featured Buffalo Bill and his troupe of cowboys when they paraded in the streets of New York City in 1898.

These recordings or **re-enactments** focused almost exclusively on performance, not story. Yet, where the performance involved shooting, the story of fighting almost inevitably lurks in the wings. In this sense, the pre-history of the western cannot be extricated from the emergence of the suspenseful, captivating film of adventure. There are historical reasons for westerns' prominence in the fiction film's uneven development from short acts on **vaudeville** programs to **multiple-reel and**

feature films. The myth of the West, increasingly popular as the frontier closed and became a thing of the past, was soon fleshed out with stories of real or fictive events. The distinction between (historical) fact and imaginative stories (fiction) was not clearly established. Nostalgia for the wildness and virgin nature of a West that no longer existed as such made these stories a suitable projection screen for the longings of the urban population in the USA, caught up in the accelerating rhythms of **modernity**, **urbanization**, immigration, and industrialization. Because nostalgia for the recent past as an unreachable other space fed into the films set in that space, the western assumed a prominent place in the social-cultural history of American cinema.

This prominence plays itself out especially in what were often called Indian films. These mixed ethnographic display with captivating events that sent a thrill of excitement and fear through spectators viewing these far-away scenes. A family resemblance definitely linked such films and theatrical spectacles such as Wild West shows as well as **world's fairs** and other public exhibitions. Indians were by definition *on show*. Ethnographic elements predominate in these films, and can be seen as simple recordings of a supposed knowledge in danger of disappearing. While Indians were shown in their otherness from eastern, largely white movie-goers, they were deprived of their liveliness by their resemblance to exhibits in world fairs, as well as by their actual juxtaposition with **dioramas** and other artifacts shown at the fairs. It is perhaps in this ambiguity between moving image and display that we best assess the ambiguous "othering" that inheres in westerns.

This risk of rigidifying the image of the Indian as other looms over such films as Edison's *Esquimaux Village* (1901), recorded at the Pan-American Exposition in Buffalo, New York. This type of staged ethnographic display is akin to the **life exhibits** in museums of natural history. But this kinship poses the problem of taxonomy. Indians as racial others were displayed in ways similar to those used for displaying animals and vegetation, in a mummifying that pins cultures up like rare butterflies. *Sham Battle at the Pan-American Exposition*, also filmed in Buffalo, reveals how the

battles of the recent past are repeated over and over again.

The habit of using white actors, made-up to play Indians, adds to the ambiguity characteristic of these films. Some American Indians—James **Young Deer**, Princess Red Wing, and Chief Dark Cloud—earned popularity and respect through their acting talents. Although the public must have been sensitized to the difference between "real" and "fake" Indians, this did not prevent the practice from continuing. There were even arguments for the greater authenticity of white actors because they allegedly produced Indianness better as an *effect*. This is explicit in a generic **trade press** comment on **Essanay**'s *An Indian Girl's Awakening* (1910): one hesitates whether the girl isn't really Indian, however, the acting is so good that "no Indian could have done it."

Finally, the representation of Indians was thoroughly ambiguous in one more way: when the film's story line had the problematic of assimilation as its theme, as in 101-Bison's *The Lieutenant's Last Fight* (1912) or Kay Bee's *The Last of The Line* (1914). Related to these stories are capitivity narratives. The fear of Indians capturing white women or children often was expressed as an excessive fear of their *becoming* Indian, strongly symbolized by the threat of miscegenation through rape. This fear could be soothed by stories that emphasize the lack of success of this endeavor, as in films where a white woman or child is rescued and brought back to their roots in white civilization.

Another reason for the profound categorical ambiguity of what we now call westerns is that cowboy and Indian pictures shared a family resemblance with other kinds of films. One obvious example is the adventure story involving a struggle with other ethnicities, specifically Mexicans, who mostly were cast as villains, as in **Biograph**'s *A Temporary Truce* (1911) or **Vitagraph**'s *At the End of the Trail* (1912). It is but one step from these to the more fictional western where border-crossing between the USA and Mexico is a favorite game for cattle thieves. Certain historical films drive the point of this affiliation even more clearly home. **Selig**'s *The Witch of the Everglades* (1911) is set in the 17th century, at a time when the frontier was on the margins of the East. Here, in Florida, Seminole Indians attack a pioneer community and abduct a white child to console an Indian mother deprived of her own. The white mother ends up retrieving her daughter, so that the happy ending seems to mitigate the savagery that drove her mad.

Other affiliated genres include travel films, where the same inventive techniques are used as in fiction films. Cameras mounted on trains to produce so-called phantom rides occur frequently in both. Jungle films—a specialty of Selig, a major producer of westerns—display another link with the incipient western. They too are sensational **melodramas** about the transgression of a similar kind of frontier between wildness and civilization. An actor such a Tom **Mix** starred in both, so that the films were also readily recognized as similar through the recognized face. That the jungle film fades, whereas the western "blooms" is evident in Mix's decision to devote his talents more exclusively to westerns in the late 1910s.

Westerns also were not produced exclusively in the USA. In France, **Gaumont** used the beautiful scenery of the French Camargue to stand in for the prairies of the West in such films as *Le railway de la mort* [Greed for Gold] (1912). In this and other westerns for **Éclair** and **Eclipse**, Joë **Hamman** became a French cowboy **star**. Germany and the Netherlands produced cowboy films as well. These European westerns should not be confused with later "spaghetti" and "curry" westerns. Although the latter especially are marked by an integral mix of western conventions and local traditions, these two sub-genres emerge from an emulation of the long-dominant American film industry.

This comparison with westerns from other countries raises the question of whether the western is an American genre per se. For the cinema, the early 1910s is an era of increasing internationalization on the one hand and of a dynamic multinational film market on the other. In such a climate, national "point of origin" can become a kind of shifter term. Thus, films *about* America are sometimes "made in the USA" and sometimes elsewhere. Furthermore, the modes of representation and

Bison's "The Indian Massacre"—Ravenwing Communes With Her Dead Child.

Figure 130 Frame still from *Indian Massacre* (Bison-101, 1912). (Courtesy of Madeleine Matz)

narration that typify the film industry in a particular country can lead to a sense of, for example, an American-style film. A sense of cultural ownership is involved in this. Manufacturers other than American companies also can deploy this mode, however, so that a bundle of features that connote "American-ness" can accrue to all kinds of films set in the West (or elsewhere). The French-American westerns of **Pathé-Frères** present an interesting case of how complex this question really is. More than any other company, Pathé demonstrated that "nationality" can be the product of internationality.

Interestingly, this issue of nationality is made explicit in reviews. The trade press, for instance, questioned the authenticity of Pathé's *Justice of a Redskin* (1908) because it was a "foreign film product." Two years later, the same company's *Cowboy Justice* (1910), shot in New Jersey, provoked a criticism over its lack of realism in setting and acting. Only when Young Deer began producing westerns for Pathé on location around Los Angeles did the trade press declare these to be adequate "American" films. Since the notion of "western" is itself based in geography, and thus suggests the division of the globe into regions that underlie nationality, a rather complex "sense of nation" inheres in those films that seem at first simply characterized by their shooting outdoors.

From the back yard in New Jersey or the flats of the French Camargue to the majestic panoramas of Colorado or California, the scenery may vary from cardboard backdrops to real prairies and mountains, but it is against such "outdoors" backdrops that the moving image of the West was created. It is only in hindsight that so many different films can be unified under the rubric of "westerns".

See also: audiences: surveys and debates; imperialism: USA; migration/immigration: USA

Further reading

Abel, Richard (1999) *The Red Rooster Scare: Making Cinema American, 1900–1910*, Berkeley: University of California Press.

Abel, Richard (2003) "The 'Imagined Community' of the Western, 1910–1913," in Charlie Keil and Shelley Stamp (eds.) *The Transitional Era in US Cinema*, 131–170, Berkeley: University of California Press.

Brownlow, Kevin (1979) *The War, The West and the Wilderness*, New York: Alfred A. Knopf.

Buscombe, Edward and Roberta Pearson (eds.) (1998) *Back in the Saddle Again: New Essays on the Western*, London: British Film Institute.

Griffiths, Alison (2002) *Wondrous Difference: Cinema, Anthropology, and Turn-of-the-Century Visual Culture*, New York: Columbia University Press.

Quaresima, Leonardo, Alessandra Raengo, Laura Vichi (eds.) (1999) *La nascita dei generi cinematographici* (The Birth of Film Genres), Udine: Forum.

Verhoeff, Nanna (2001) "Die Bedeutung des Nationalen in den amerikanischen Pathé-Western 1910–1914," *KINtop*, 10: 29–59.

Verhoeff, Nanna (2002) "After the Beginning: Westerns Before 1915," Ph.D. dissertation, Utrecht University, Enschede: PrintPartners Ipskamp.

NANNA VERHOEFF

White, James Henry

b. *c.* 1873; d. ?

exhibitor, filmmaker, executive, USA

In the summer of 1894, White was hired by the Holland Brothers to install and maintain **Kinetoscopes** in Boston and New York. After briefly exhibiting Kinetoscopes with Charles Webster, he joined **Raff & Gammon** in 1896, as a technician and officer of the Vitascope Company. From October 1896 until February 1903, he supervised film production for the **Edison Manufacturing Company**. White improved the quantity and quality of **comedies** and dramas, led filming expeditions to Asia and Europe, and added Edwin S. **Porter** to the camera staff. In 1903, he was sent to Europe to manage Edison's film and phonograph interests.

PAUL SPEHR

White, Pearl

b. 1889; d. 1938

actor, USA

Pearl White was arguably the US cinema's first international female celebrity. A popular player in short **comedies** and other subjects at Powers and Crystal between 1910 and 1914, White's fame catapulted to unprecedented heights following her gutsy performance in the sensation action serial, *The Perils of Pauline* (1914). Throughout the decade, White starred in ten **serials** for **Pathé-**Exchange, ranging from *The Exploits of Elaine* (1915) to *The Lightening Raider* (1919), and was touted as the studio's most profitable box-office draw. Beloved for her frank personality and her exceptional feats of daring, White became an icon for the French surrealists, Ballets russes, and early Soviet avant-garde filmmakers.

JENNIFER M. BEAN

white slave films

A series of films on white slavery released in the USA in the early 1910s capitalized on wide-ranging fears that young women travelling alone in American cities risked being kidnapped and sold into prostitution. Among the earliest feature-length films, they were also among the most sexually explicit and the most popular of their day, raising concern within the film industry and the culture at large.

When a white slavery panic swept the USA in the early 1910s, cinema stood at the heart of the scandal: dark theaters were said to be one of the chief sites where vice traffickers captured unwitting female victims, just as a rash of sensational white slave films began drawing crowds of young women to cinemas, the very sites where they were supposedly endangered. Many white slave films claimed to be based on vice reports commissioned by municipalities during these years, often capitalizing upon broader cultural fears surrounding **urbanization**, immigration, commercial leisure culture, and women's growing independence.

The vice film craze began in November 1913 with the New York premiere of **Universal**'s *Traffic in Souls*, followed two weeks later by the release of *The Inside of the White Slave Traffic*, a much more explicit and controversial film. By early 1914 many imitators appeared in theaters, including a screen adaptation of the best-selling novel *The House of Bondage* (1914). Although the phenomenon began to wane by March of 1914, film versions of popular Broadway plays, like *The Lure* (1914) and *The Fight* (1915), along with later incarnations like *Is Any Girl Safe?* (1916) and *Little Lost Sister* (1917), cautioned women against white slavers well into the decade.

"Slavers," as they were known, drew records crowds to movie theaters, alarming many in the industry at a time when the film medium was making a concerted bid for greater respectability. Senior **trade press** commentators like Louis Reeves **Harrison**, Stephen W. **Bush** and Epes Winthrop **Sargent** all condemned the cycle. While some voices in the progressive reform community praised the educational quality of white slave films, noting their ability to warn young women about the dangers they faced on urban streets, many others worried about explicit treatments of sexuality and prostitution on screen. Screenings of *The Inside of the White Slave Traffic* where shut down by New York police on obscenity charges, over the objections of local anti-vice crusaders. White slave films also encountered marked scrutiny from the **National Board of Censorship** which issued a "Special Bulletin on Social Evil" in early 1914, carefully delineating the limited circumstances under which it would permit depictions of the vice trade. Even with Board approval, many vice films were banned in cities across the country.

See also: melodrama, sensational; migration/immigration; multiple-reel/feature films; women's movement: USA

Further reading

Staiger, Janet (1995) *Bad Women: Regulating Sexuality in Early American Cinema*, Minneapolis: University of Minnesota Press.

Stamp, Shelley (2000) *Movie-Struck Girls: Women and Motion Picture Culture after the Nickelodeon*, Princeton: Princeton University Press.

SHELLEY STAMP

Figure 131 Minnesota moving picture theater exterior be-decked with posters for white slave films, *c.* 1913.

Wiener Kunstfilm

Founded in November 1911, by Anton Kolm, Louise **Kolm**, Jakob Fleck, and Claudius Veltée, Wiener Kunstfilm, as the name of the firm suggests, was influenced by the *film d'art* movement. Most of the company's productions were adapted from successful stage plays, with actors engaged from the Viennese theaters and with the mise-en-scene following theatrical patterns. The first film was *Der Müller und sein Kind* [The Miller and His Kid] (1911), followed by *Der Unbekannte* [The Stranger] (1912), a drama intended for an international audience. In 1913 and 1914, the firm was successful enough to produce more than 30 films.

PAOLO CANEPPELE

Williams, Kathlyn

b. 1884; d. 1960

actor, scriptwriter, director, USA

After a brief stint at **Biograph** in 1909, Kathlyn Williams moved to **Selig** and became the

company's leading actress, often playing opposite wild animals in jungle subjects from *Lost in the Jungle* (1911) to *The Leopard's Foundling* (1914), the latter of which she also wrote and directed. Williams' acclaim as a player of serene courage and natural charm accelerated with her intrepid performance as the eponymous serial heroine in *The Adventures of Kathlyn* (1913–1914), as well as her winsome portrayal of the dance-hall girl in *The Spoilers* (1914). In 1915, Williams starred in five successful dramatic features under the direction of Colin Campbell before joining the Oliver Morosco Photoplay Company in 1916.

JENNIFER M. BEAN

Williams, Randall

b. 1846; d. 1898

exhibitor, Great Britain

Randall Williams was the pioneer of moving picture exhibition in British **fairs/fairgrounds**. Born into a fairground family, Williams exhibited Pepper's Ghost on the fairground circuit from

1873 on. By 1890, he was touring the largest Ghost show in the United Kingdom, with a seating capacity of 1000. In December 1896, he first exhibited moving pictures for the annual "World's Fair" at the Royal Agricultural Hall in London. For the next two years, he then toured the fairgrounds with two booths showing moving pictures. While attending the Grimsby Statues Fair, he contracted enteric fever and died in November 1898.

VANESSA TOULMIN

Williamson, James

b. 1855; d. 1933

businessman, filmmaker, manufacturer,
Great Britain

Born in Scotland, Williamson trained in London to become a master chemist; in 1886, with his wife and family, he moved to Hove, East Sussex, to establish a pharmacy. For the next decade, Williamson developed a keen interest in **photography** and optical entertainments and, as an **Eastman Kodak** agent, he acquired a good understanding of the technical and chemical nature of photography. In 1896, he introduced X-ray photography to Sussex and, in November that year, presented the first program of moving pictures to the Camera Club at Hove Town Hall.

In 1897, Williamson began to make his own films, and his first catalogue (1899) listed 60 titles, the majority of which were single shots between 60 and 75 feet in length. After a summer of inspired filmmaking by G. Albert **Smith**, his Hove friend and counterpart, Williamson conceived and executed *Attack on a China Mission* (1900), his first edited multi-shot narrative film.

Williamson's next significant multi-shot film, *Fire!* (1901), made on the streets of Hove, exploited the popularity of "fire" dramas then found in melodrama **theaters**, **magic lantern** shows, newspaper reports, and *actualités*. Comprised of five shots running a total of 280 feet, it also reflected his understanding of the rescue narrative and his ambition to find the means to develop a more complex and arresting film

structure. By designing a work of fiction which employed the engines and staff of a real fire brigade, used both location and a set, and evidenced careful shot construction, Williamson created a film which was simple in form yet radical for its time. His subsequent social dramas, *The Soldier's Return* (1902) and *A Reservist Before the War and After the War* (1902), and his ingenious **trick films**, especially *The Big Swallow* (1901), continued this spirit of innovation.

In 1902, the Williamson Kinematograph Company opened its first purpose-built film production studio and film processing works in Hove. His family played a distinctive role in the new business by participating in writing scenarios, making sets and **costumes**, and taking both small and major acting roles. Tom Williamson's part in *Our New Errand Boy* (1905), as the anarchic boy upsetting the pillars of society, expresses his family's enthusiasm for filmmaking as well as his father's provocative imagination. The eldest son, Alan, would become more involved in the company's business affairs, being responsible for opening its New York office in 1907. Williamson himself began to withdraw from film production in 1909 as a result of changes in the world film market. In 1910, the company moved to London where it devoted itself successfully to the manufacture of **cameras** and printers.

See also: editing: spatial relations; editing: temporal relations

Further reading

Barnes, John (1996–1998) *The Beginnings of the Cinema in England, 1894–1901*, vols. 2–5, Exeter: University of Exeter Press.

Gray, Frank (1998) "James Williamson's 'Composed Picture': Attack on a China Mission—Bluejackets to the Rescue," in John Fullerton (ed.) *Celebrating 1895*, 203–211, Sydney: John Libbey & Co.

Sopocy, Martin (1998) *James Williamson: Studies and Documents of a Pioneer of the Film Narrative*, London: Associated University Presses.

FRANK GRAY

Wolf, Nathan Hyman

b.1872; d. 1942

critic, editor, the Netherlands

As a critic of the visual arts, legitimate **theater**, **opera**, and **music hall**, Wolf began writing seriously about moving pictures in the art weekly, *De Kunst*, from 1911 on. For him, film became an art equal to the other arts in 1912, when moving pictures were included in the new Dutch **copyright** law. Films, therefore, deserved to be the subject of art criticism. Especially charmed by Italian divas such as Francesca **Bertini** and by the films of D. W. **Griffith**, such as *Judith and Bethulia* (1914), he grew ever more attracted to the cinema. In 1922, Wolf became chief editor of the trade weekly *Kunst en Amusement*.

ANSJE VAN BEUSEKOM

Wolff, Philipp

b. ?; d. 1899

distributor, manufacturer, filmmaker, exhibitor, Germany

This former textile agent founded the eponymous company, the first large international moving picture firm with offices in Paris, Berlin, and London by late 1896, to handle a huge selection of films from leading filmmakers including Georges **Méliès**, **Lumière**, Robert **Paul**, G. A. **Smith**, and many others. Wolff also offered a filmmaking service, an exhibition service, and an all-metal Maltese Cross (Geneva) projection apparatus designed by Karl Grahner. The firm languished after Wolff's sudden death from influenza in 1899, and ceased trading with a very old stock around 1901.

DEAC ROSSELL

women's movement: Europe

Although many women's movement organizations made a considerable effort to transcend national borders and create a unified struggle towards such shared goals as female voting rights, wage equality and social welfare, nationally specific historical and socio-political conditions proved problematic for international alliances, whether transcontinental, as between North American and European movements, or inter-European. Thus race was a prominent issue in distinguishing women's movement organizations in the USA; whereas social status and class were the most important aspects for the diversification of women's clubs and societies in Western European countries. Within Europe, national specificities as, for example, legal conditions in Germany which prevented an openly political struggle for women's rights modeled on the British suffragette's example, caused marked differences in the agendas, strategies and politics with which women across Europe struggled for equality. As limitation of space prevents a comprehensive account of the various national articulations of the women's movement in Europe, the following account focuses on Germany as an illustration of the formation of the women's movement in one European country by outlining the movement's historical development, organizational structure, agendas and relation to cinema.

While the years 1888–1908 mark the heyday of the German women's movement, its beginnings date back to the bourgeois revolution of 1848. The range of women's clubs and societies which previously had been devoted mainly to philanthropic and patriotic purposes now included organizations promoting women's equality as it was then being advocated in a growing number of periodicals, beginning with *Die Frauen-Zeitung* (The Women's Newspaper) founded in 1849. While the First Women's Movement never questioned the assumption of an essential difference of gender, it advocated the equality of women, particularly in terms of women's education and their participation in the labor force. Efforts to unify the vastly heterogeneous groups began in 1865 with the foundation of the Allgemeiner Deutscher Frauenverein (General Women's Association) and culminated in 1894 in the Bund Deutcher Frauenvereine (Democratic Women's Association), modeled after the General Federation of Women's Clubs in the USA and boasting 500,000 members. The federation's broad range of member societies and the predominantly bourgeois background of its members resulted in a moderately liberal agenda. Within this bourgeois wing of the movement, female workers were regarded less as equal political allies than as objects of reformist social politics that combined the alleviation of social hardship with the propagation of bourgeois values.

German unions and trade organizations did not, as a rule, accept female members, and legal restrictions operative between 1850 and 1908 prevented women from joining political groups and meetings. As a consequence, women formed their own workers associations, often headed by bourgeois leaders and focusing their efforts on the effects rather than causes of social injustice. However, the Social Democratic Party or SPD (founded in 1875) offered an alternative when it initiated women's committees in 1889 and, when the law against women's participation in political organisations was lifted in 1908, was one of the first to grant its female members equal rights. The beginning of the proletarian women's movement is closely associated with Clara Zetkin, its first leader and founder of the periodical, *Die Gleichheit* [Equality] (1891), as well as Gertrud Guilleaume-Schack, who founded the Verein zur Wahrung der Interessen der Arbeiterinnen (Association for the Defense of Female Workers' Interests) in 1895. In contrast to their bourgeois counterparts, the socialist women's organizations saw patriarchy as secondary to unequal property distribution as the prime cause of women's inequality. Although there were affinities between the left-wing proletarian and the liberal bourgeois groups concerning their common goal of women's equality and shared notions of gender difference and of mothering as women's primary task, cooperation was precluded by ideological gaps that became most apparent in the debate over working conditions of domestic servants—an issue which brought female workers' demands right to the doorstep of the movement's bourgeois advocates.

Yet the split between the conservative and the radical wing resulted not only from disagreement about socio-economic issues but also about women's right to vote and the demands for sexual reform. The sexual reform movement, headed by Helene Stöcker, was organized in the Bund für Mutterschutz und Sexualreform (Union for the Protection of Mothers and Sexual Reform) and

addressed such issues as the sexual liberation of women, prostitution, unwed motherhood, and homosexuality. Although the bourgeois wing of the women's movement, with its emphasis on women's education, access to universities (which was granted around the turn of the century), and philanthropic and pacifist activities, dominated the movement, it was the radical groups which had a stronger presence in the mass media. In addition to pamphlets, their publications included a range of periodicals devoted to the women's cause such as *Die Staatsbürgerin* (The Female Citizen), *Der Abolitionist* (The Abolitionist), *Die Neue Generation* (The New Generation), *Die Frauenbewegung* (The Women's Movement), and *Frauen-Stimmrecht!* (Women's Vote!). A number of activists such as Stöcker, Hedwig Dohm, or Franziska zu Reventlo also made use of the novel to publicize their demands.

In the light of this active and conscious use of the press and literature as mass media tools for the propagation of women's issues, it is all the more striking that the cinema, whose first decade coincides with the heyday of the women's movement in Germany, is hardly ever mentioned in these writings, let alone embraced as a political tool. This disregard or outright rejection of the cinema by the German women's movement must be attributed to bourgeois reservations against a burgeoning mass culture, be it popular novels or moving images. As bourgeois cultural and educational ideals were not only advocated by bourgeois leaders in female workers' associations but also by the majority of social-democrat workers, cinema's only usefulness was seen as a tool, as a source of information. Thus local women's societies might include a film screening—e.g., *Mütter, verzaget nicht* [Mothers, Don't Despair, (1911), with Henny Porten]—together with lectures, prayers and songs in an evening program devoted to child care, yet their use of the new medium differed in no way from screenings during the social and educational events of other groups such as, for example, Audubon or colonial societies. The only explicit discussion of cinema in a women's movement journal, *Die Lehrerin* (The Schoolmistress), in 1913, addressed its readers not as potential movie audiences but as educators sharing the reform movement's rejection of the new medium as a moral and physical danger to youth, a topic which was further explored in Ike Spier's book-length publication *Die sexuelle Gefahr* [The Sexual Menace] (1912–1913).

This disregard or outright rejection of the cinema by the women's movement is all the more striking considering the fact that early cinema was not only immensely popular with female audiences from all social strata and was economically dependent on female patronage, but it also dealt extensively with women's issues that were of central concern to the women's movement such as poverty, single women as wage earners, prostitution, women's right to love and sexuality, unwed motherhood, and gender relations in general. Early cinema not only articulated female experience but often addressed men as well, making them part of the emancipatory and educational project of rethinking traditional gender relations. In the cultural realm, cinema thus complemented the social and political agenda set by the women's organizations, offering a different way of probing women's experiences and opening up new modes of self-reflection. In addition, cinema offered its female clientele access to public spaces and participation in the public sphere. Yet the dominance of bourgeois reformist discourse on cinema prevented the women's movement in Germany from embracing the potential of the new medium as a powerful ally to further its cause.

The women who did take the new medium seriously were not part of the women's movement proper. They belonged to the first generation of university-educated, emancipated women as, for example, the women writing for the periodical *Bild und Film* (Image and Film), or, as in the case of the former critic Resie Langer, published book-length works on cinema. Yet the most prominent treatise on cinema by a woman was Emilie **Altenloh**'s ground-breaking study, *Zur Soziologie des Kinos* (The Sociology of the Cinema), published in 1914 and recently translated into English in an abridged version, which investigated the tastes and interests of movie audiences in terms of age, gender and class. The findings of her empirical research, which are free of the reigning reformist bias, highlight the fact that it was above all women who frequented the cinema, and that women irrespective of their social status favoured certain genres, above all melodrama, quite unlike the class-specific diversification of tastes and preferences of male

viewers. Altenloh's study explains the popularity of cinema with its female clientele not only on the basis of subject matter and treatment which addressed women across class divisions, but also gives a detailed account of the way in which cinema caters to the class-specific needs, interests and everyday life patterns of women, from bourgeois housewives to clerical, retail and factory workers.

While both the bourgeois and radical wing of the women's movement ignored early cinema and the way its images and stories spoke directly to the changing experiences of women, it was the feminists of the Second Women's Movement in the second half of the 20th century who would acknowledge cinema's potential as a political tool and explore it as filmmakers, critics, and theorists.

See also: labor movement: Europe

Further reading

Altenloh, Emilie (2001) "A Sociology of the Cinema: the Audience (1914)," trans. K. Cross, **Screen**, 42.3: 249–293.

Fout, J. C. (ed.) (1984) *German Women in the 19th Century*, New York: Holmes and Meies.

Frevert, Ute (1986) *Frauen-Geschichte. Zwischen Bürgerlicher Verbesserung und Neuer Weiblichkeit*, Frankfurt/Main: Suhrkamp.

Rupp, Leila J. (1997) *Worlds of Women: The Making of an International Women's Movement*, Princeton: Princeton University Press.

Schlüpmann, Heide (1990) *Unheimlichkeit des Blicks. Das Drama des frühen deutschen Kinos*, Frankfurt/Main: Stroemfeld.

EVA WARTH AND HEIDE SCHLÜPMANN

women's movement: USA

Cinema's earliest decades coincided with a period of extraordinary change in the lives of American women and marked activism surrounding female voting rights, contraceptive rights, and wage equity. As women became increasingly visible in political life, in the paid labor force, and in leisure culture, commentators everywhere noted the phenomenon of the "New Woman," associating the changes of **modernity** chiefly with shifting gender roles.

The burgeoning women's club movement provided an early basis for women's growing engagement in civic affairs. The General Federation of Women's Clubs (GFWC) brought together more than 200 clubs and 20,000 women in 1890. Membership quickly grew to 150,000 women by the turn of the century and nearly a million by the late 1910s, comprised mainly of educated, married middle- and upper-class white women. The National Association of Colored Women brought together African American women's clubs in 1896, uniting black women barred from joining GFWC branches. Clubs were initially devoted largely to literary and cultural pursuits, but many became more politically active in localized crusades for urban parkland, public health, child labor laws, and mother's pensions.

Settlement houses providing aid to urban working women were another key aspect of women's growing social engagement. By the turn of the century most major US cities had settlement houses based on early models like Hull House, founded in one of Chicago's impoverished immigrant neighborhoods in 1889, and the Henry Street Settlement which opened on Manhattan's Lower East Side in 1895. Established by college-educated middle-class women, settlement houses furnished housing for single working women, childcare services for families in the community, along with leisure activities for residents and neighborhood children. Working and living alongside their constituents, settlement founders were often active in their communities, struggling to improve municipal services and working conditions, and to fight political corruption.

Perhaps the most visible feminist movement during these years was the crusade for women's suffrage, around which many aspirations for gender equality crystallized. The National American Woman Suffrage Association (NAWSA), founded in 1890, began to revise older arguments for female voting rights, moving away from traditional claims of gender equality and individual rights. Instead, activists began to stress the importance of including a feminine perspective on modern urban problems, a process NAWSA vice-president Jane **Addams** described as "civic housekeeping." The

movement also sometimes resorted to racist rhetoric, arguing that white women ought not to be denied a privileged of citizenship already granted African American and immigrant men. The more radical Women's Political Union broke away from NAWSA, choosing to follow the lead of militant British activists in staging pageants and demonstrations. While the campaign had limited success around the turn of the century, the movement accelerated in the early teens: several states granted or proposed women's enfranchisement between 1910 and 1912, and the U.S. Congress debated the issue for the first time in 1913. The Nineteenth Amendment to the Constitution would not guarantee women the vote until 1920.

Increasingly visible in civic and political affairs, women were also transforming the modern work force. By the turn of the century, forty percent of black women and twenty percent of white women worked outside their homes in the paid labor force. Nearly half of all single women were employed, many from immigrant families, and of these close to half did not live at home with their parents. Although their married counterparts comprised a smaller portion of the working public, a significant portion of female wage earners were married, and among black women the numbers were much higher. Jobs in traditional fields like domestic labor were increasingly replaced by clerical, retail and factory positions. University graduates entered growing female professions like teaching and nursing, as the number of college-educated women grew dramatically: women comprised one-fifth of all college graduates by 1900, a number that would climb to forty percent by the end of the 1910s.

Like their middle-class counterparts involved in clubs and political groups, working women were active in union campaigns at a time when they were largely ignored by the American Federation of Labor. The Women's Trade Union League, formed in 1903, inaugurated a series of massive strikes by female garment workers demanding better working conditions. The National Consumers League united working women with the growing body of female consumers in 1899 by publicizing the arduous conditions under which sales women and factory laborers worked, and by fighting for minimum wage legislation, workplace safety laws, improved working conditions, and shorter hours.

The evolving demographics of family life illustrate how substantially the changes in women's lives affected the nation overall. Many college-educated women chose not to marry at all, while among married women birth rates declined sharply, especially for those of the native-born middle-class. A growing number of activists promoted the right to "voluntary motherhood," introducing the modern birth control movement during a time when it remained illegal to disseminate contraceptive information. Pioneers like Margaret Sanger were repeatedly arrested and imprisoned during the 1910s. Feminist Charlotte Perkins Gilman decried the "separate spheres" doctrine, claiming it stifled women's creativity and intelligence by relegating them to the home, while sex radicals like Sanger and Emma Goldman advocated "free love" outside the bounds of marriage and heterosexuality. Divorce rates, low in the nineteenth century, doubled in the first two decades of the twentieth century.

Recreation culture also drew women into public life. New commercial leisure venues like dance halls, **amusement parks**, and **nickelodeons** allowed young, single men and women to interact more freely outside the supervision of their parents by engaging in the new practice of "dating." Just as single "bachelor girls" enjoyed the new urban nightlife, married middle-class women took part in daytime urban pleasures offered by **department stores**, restaurant luncheons, and matinees. Playing tennis and golf, riding bicycles and swimming, athletic "Gibson Girls" helped redefine the very image of femininity in the popular imagination.

See also: fashion; leisure time and space; migration/immigration; star system; women's suffrage films

Further reading

Cott, Nancy F. (1987) *The Grounding of Modern Feminism*, New Haven: Yale University Press.
DuBois, Ellen Carol (1998) *Woman Suffrage and Women's Rights*, New York: New York University Press.
Kessler-Harris, Alice (2001) *In Pursuit of Equity: Women, Men, and the Quest for Economic Citizenship in 20th-Century America*, Oxford: Oxford University Press.
O'Neill, William L. (1989) *Feminism in America: A History*, rev. ed., New Brunswick: Transaction Books.

SHELLEY STAMP

women's suffrage films

America's two leading women's suffrage organizations used motion pictures to promote their cause in the early 1910s, as the fight for voting rights escalated nationwide.

The Women's Political Union (WPU) produced a one-reel **comedy** *Suffrage and the Man* with **Éclair American** in 1912, making light of a young man who learns to value his fiancée's political activism. That same year, the National American Woman Suffrage Association (NAWSA) produced *Votes for Women* with **Reliance**, a two-reel drama that included documentary footage from the 1912 suffrage parade in New York, along with screen appearances by the organization's leader, Dr. Anna Howard Shaw, and its vice president, Jane **Addams**. **Edison phonograph** recordings of the women's speeches were apparently included in some versions of the film.

More ambitious **multiple-reel films** followed. The WPU's four-reel drama, *Eighty Million Women Want—?* (1913), featured noted British activist Emmeline Pankhurst addressing viewers in its prologue. WPU leader, Harriot Stanton Blatch, played herself in the dramatic portion of the film, helping the film's heroine lead the group in a victorious campaign. After witnessing the success of **serials** with younger female viewers, NAWSA joined with **Selig Polyscope** in Chicago, producer of *The Adventures of Kathlyn* (1914), to make its feature, *Your Girl and Mine*, in 1914, hiring Gilson Willets, author of the *Kathlyn* serial, to draft the suffrage feature. NAWSA president Dr. Anna Howard Shaw again made an appearance in the film.

Both suffrage organizations employed novel exhibition strategies to promote their films in

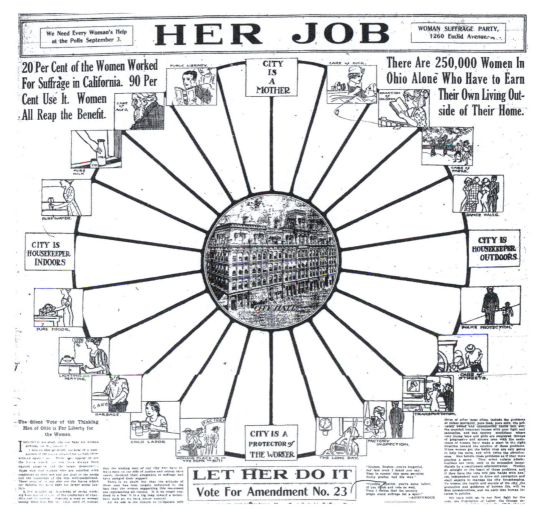

Figure 132 Ohio Woman Suffrage Party advertisement, *Cleveland Leader* (1 September 1912), Metropolitan Section, 4.

commercial and non-commercial settings, with suffrage leaders often appearing in person at screenings to introduce films and to field questions afterwards. While some exhibitors felt these female-oriented educational screenings contributed to cinema's "uplift" during the teens, others were alarmed by the politicization of screening spaces and female **audiences**.

A host of comic shorts were also released on voting rights during these years. Many lampooned conservative anti-suffrage advocates, such as a series of films shot on location in London, England by the Edison company, including *A Suffragette in Spite of Himself* (1912) and *How They Got the Vote* (1914). Many more comedies caricatured suffrage activists, notably the 1914 **Keystone** short, *A Busy Day* (a.k.a. *A Militant Suffragist*), where Charlie **Chaplin** appeared in drag as an especially obstreperous activist.

Motion pictures thus played a vital role during a pivotal moment in the suffrage crusade. Several states granted or proposed women's enfranchisement between 1910 and 1912, as these films began to appear, and the U.S. Congress debated the issue for the first time in 1913. Still, the Nineteenth Amendment to the Constitution would not guarantee women the vote until 1920.

See also: women's movement: USA

Further reading

Sloan, Kay (1988) *The Loud Silents: Origins of the Social Problem Film*, Urbana: University of Illinois Press.

Stamp, Shelley (2000) *Movie-Struck Girls: Women and Motion Picture Culture after the Nickelodeon*, Princeton: Princeton University Press.

SHELLEY STAMP

Woods, Frank

b. 1860; d. 1 May 1939

critic, scriptwriter, director, USA

Woods probably was the first American film critic, writing as "Spectator" for the **New York Dramatic Mirror** from June 1908. He revealed a rare understanding of the creative efforts of early filmmakers and, in particular, D. W. **Griffith**, with whom he began a friendship that became a professional association. Woods wrote scenarios for **Biograph** and other companies before becoming a director for Kinemacolor and then for **IMP**. In 1913, he joined Griffith at **Mutual**, as general manager and head of the scenario department. Subsequently, Woods held that position at other studios, notably **Famous Players**-Lasky.

EILEEN BOWSER

World Film Corporation

World Film Corporation was organized in 1914, with Lewis J. Selznick as general manager and theatrical entrepreneurs William **Brady** and Lee Shubert as production managers. Created as a distributor of independent feature productions,

control of production gradually was centralized with most done in Fort Lee, New Jersey. Brady and Shubert produced film versions of plays, but other branches of the company created original productions. A number of well-respected filmmakers made films released by World, the best known being Maurice **Tourneur**. The company faltered after **World War I**: Selznick and Brady formed separate companies, and Selznick eventually absorbed World into his own.

PAUL SPEHR

World War I

Although cinema has been an international phenomenon from its beginnings, historiography still tends to be driven by national considerations. Consequently, a concise comparative analysis of cinema history during World War I does not yet exist. However, it is possible to trace some general trends, based on studies that describe certain areas of film production and exhibition between 1914 and 1918, especially within the most important European countries involved in the war.

During the war, cinema increased its dominating market position as the cheapest and most easily accessible mass entertainment, due partly to the escapist needs of suffering populations on the home front as well as to the propaganda needs of psychological warfare. Movie-going rose significantly in nearly all countries. In Great Britain, still the most densely industrialized country, 18 million tickets were sold weekly, which means that around half of the population went to the movies every week. Moreover, hundreds of temporary cinemas were established on both sides of the war front for showing moving pictures exclusively to soldiers. Thus, by the end of World War 1, cinema had become the leading medium of mass entertainment, for both sexes, for all ages, and for all social strata of the population—even in a country such as Germany, where cinema had been widely disapproved by the educated elites as well as by **labor movements** before 1914.

Film production and film distribution, however, were deeply affected by the war. The four leading French film producers—**Pathé-Frères**, **Gaumont**,

Éclair, and **Eclipse**—suddenly were cut off from their Central and East European markets. Yet it seems that border-closings resulting from the outbreak of war simply enforced ongoing trends that already had shown declining French and Italian exports in favor of American imports. While Pathé and Gaumont tried to survive by transferring important components of their production to the USA, the invasion of American films that had conquered Great Britain by 1914, also now flooded France, the pre-war stronghold of global film production. Next to the USA, in terms of the film industry, Germany was the winner of World War I: the state-sponsored founding of Ufa in late 1917 established a film trust which dominated the film markets of Central and Eastern Europe up to and through World War II, whereas French film companies never recovered from World War I and Great Britain and Italy largely became Hollywood domains. In order to establish Ufa as a conglomerate, the German government had major banks covertly buy up the largest film companies (**Messter**, **PAGU**, etc.) at no less than 25 million Reichsmark. When the state's share of this sum eventually surfaced in 1920, it caused a major political scandal that ultimately led to Ufa's privatization.

At least in Germany the market dominance of French **newsreels** ended with the outbreak of the war. They were replaced with *Eiko-Woche* and *Messter-Woche*, along with a few other, rather short-lived, ones. These newsreels were distributed with German and foreign language **intertitles** and exhibited on the front and the "home front" as well as in friendly and neutral states. The war also had at least one other effect on nonfiction films. Founded in 1916, the Deutsche Lichtbild GmbH (DLG) was the first company to attempt a systematic production of films promoting the capability and efficiency of German manufacturers, as well as the beauty of German landscapes and the dignity of the German people. This commercial enterprise was strongly influenced by Alfred Hugenberg, later to become the owner of Ufa, and was managed by Ludwig Klitzsch, a close affiliate of Hugenberg's, who would later follow him to Ufa as its managing director.

Due to various commercial interests and the entertainment needs of the public in order to withstand the sufferings of war, feature films increased their position as the main attraction on cinema programs. During the war, the variety program of short films finally gave way to the "classical" **program format** of the long fiction film, accompanied by **advertising films**, a **newsreel**, perhaps a short **comedy**, and a short nonfiction or **animation film**. The principal genres and aesthetic styles of the long fiction film, including lengthy historical epics such as *Cabiria* (1914), had already been worked out before the war, as had the promotional mechanism of the **star system**. The fashion for patriotic fiction films ended early in 1915 in Germany, but not until 1916 in France, and soon **detective films** turned out to be most successful on both sides of the front, whether in **serials** such as Louis **Feuillade**'s *Les Vampires* (1915–1916) and especially *Judex* (1917) in France or Ernst **Reicher**'s *Stuart Webbs* series (which encompassed nearly 50 films) in Germany. Depending on the "seriousness of the situation," censors took care to cut out crime scenes in detective films that might undermine public morale. Although they received considerable attention at the time from propaganda offices and in retrospect from historians, war films such as D. W. **Griffith**'s *Hearts of the World* (1918) were few in number and usually not warmly welcomed by the public.

When it became clear by 1915 that the unexpectedly long war could not be won without strong support from their populations, the warring countries established institutions for visual propaganda activities. In France, *actualités* filmed by the four major companies initially were gathered into a weekly newsreel, with the permission of the military, by the Chambre syndicale française de la cinématographie. In Great Britain, the government first authorized the newly organized British Topical Committee for War Films to perform a similar function. In Germany, it was Messter that gradually gained control of distributing *actualités* on the war through its newsreel, *Messter-Woche*. Eventually, the production and distribution of nonfiction war films was taken over by the state: French Section Photographique et Cinématographique de l'Armée (SPCA), the German Bild und Filmamt (BuFA), the British War Office Cinema Committee (WOCC), and the US

Committee on Public Information and Film Policy (CPI), when that country finally entered the war in April 1917. In contrast to the others, BuFA and the Austrian Kriegspressequartier engaged in a unique strategy to have special military units of the German and Austro-Hungarian armies cover the war front. BuFA's seven specially equipped war reporter units deployed to the various theaters of war consisted exclusively of military personnel, lead by an officer, ensuring that all censorship obligations of the German High Command would be honored. Although the impact of these propaganda efforts on cinema **audiences** is rather doubtful, they did establish the film medium as a useful means for psychological warfare for the ruling elites that previously had expressed reservations about cinema.

Whereas the commercial and aesthetic innovations of the feature fiction film had already been prepared before the war, nonfiction films thus underwent a significant shift from the attraction of description or observation to the polemics of argument. World War I marks a watershed between the descriptive "views" of early nonfiction films such as *actualités* or **travel films** and the concept of documentary film that John Grierson later described as the "creative treatment of actuality" and yet had been invented by propaganda filmmakers during the war. For filmmakers increasingly presented the war events shot by their cameras as visual evidence for statements often explicitly expressed in the intertitles. The emergent trend towards discursive presentation had two main sources. First, most statements on the course of military engagements could not be shown, because the modern battlefield offered a barely recognizable view to film cameras. Thus, war events could not be recorded and projected with the immediacy of the *actualité* but usually had to be shot as **re-enactments**. Second, the warring countries need to calm their civilian populations and mobilize them against the enemy. Thus, propagandistic claims regarding troop morale or the evil nature of the enemy were illustrated by more or less appropriate pre-existing footage or fictionalized scenes. In both cases, moving pictures took on the status of discursive texts or documents that could lend credibility to claims written in the intertitles. Most famous among documentary war films which purport to show battlefield scenes in order to back a propagandistic point-of-view was the British *Battle*

of the Somme (1916), the first "major" film to link fictionalization with the representation of fact. Although the climax of this film clearly is a re-enactment, it would be wrong to deny its authenticity. It was precisely this "fake," the so-called "over-the-top" sequence showing British soldiers leaving the trenches for attack, which contributed so decisively to its impact on British audiences as an "authentic" filmic report of the famous battle.

See also: multiple-reel/feature films; propaganda films

Further reading

DeBauche, Leslie Midkiff (1997) *Reel Patriotism: the Movies and World War I*, Madison: University of Wisconsin Press.

Dibbets, Karel and Bert Hogenkamp (eds.) (1995) *Film and the First World War*, Amsterdam: Amsterdam University Press.

Renzi, Renzo (ed.) (1993) *Il Cinematografo al campo. L'Arma nuova nel primo conflitto mondiale*, Ancona: Transeuropa.

Rother, Rainer (ed.) (1994) *Die letzten Tage der Menschheit. Bilder des Ersten Weltkrieges*, Berlin: Deutsches Historisches Museum/Ars Nicolai.

Véray, Laurent (1995) *Les Films d'actualité français de la Grande Guerre*, Paris: SIRPA/AFRHC.

Wood, Richard (ed.) (1990) *Film and Propaganda in America: A Documentary History I: World War I*, Westport CT: Greenwood Press.

ULI JUNG AND MARTIN LOIPERDINGER

world's fairs

World's fairs or international expositions were monumental exhibitions of manufactured goods, works of art, products of science, and peoples generally held in specially designed parks and pavilions near urban centers. Between 1851 (London) and 1939 (New York), fairs were held at least every few years in a European or American city. Expositions are associated with the period of modern **industrialization**, imperialism and **colonialism**; they were opportunities to showcase both national imperial policies and the market rewards of capitalism. The first world's fair, the Crystal

Palace Exhibition, was held in London in 1851. Its success led to more fairs—Paris in 1855, London again in 1862, Paris in 1867, and Vienna in 1873. The first exposition held in the USA was the Centennial Exposition in Philadelphia in 1876. Thereafter, expositions continued almost annually somewhere until the outbreak of **World War I**. Although expositions continued sporadically after that and through the Cold War, many culture critics agree that they had been replaced in function first by the cinema and then by electronic media as the primary means for teaching the masses about consumer goods, scientific progress, and modern life in general.

Moving pictures first appeared at the Paris Exposition in 1900, but not as an independent showcase. Rather, they were offered as one element of a larger spectacle in concert with **panoramas** and other effects. Earlier, in 1893, it was once thought that the Thomas A. **Edison Kinetoscope** appeared at the **Electricity** Building of the Chicago World's Columbian Exposition. At that same fair, Eadweard **Muybridge** definitely showed his motion studies of people and animals with the help of a Zoopraxiscope that animated their movements.

The 1900 Paris Exposition and the 1901 Buffalo Pan-American Exposition were the first world's fairs that were themselves filmed as *actualités*. Cameramen from various manufacturers filmed panoramic views of each, showcasing the architecture, crowds, and electric illuminations: e.g., *Vue prise d'une plate-forme mobile* [View Taken from a Moving Sidewalk] (**Lumière**, 1900), *Panorama of Paris Exposition, From the Seine* (**Edison**, 1900), *Opening, Pan-American Exposition* (Edison, 1901), *Pan-American Exposition by Night* (Edison, 1901). Of special interest is *A Trip Around the Pan-American Exposition* (Edison, 1901), a ten-minute film taken from the front of a moving gondola as it toured the canals that wound through the exposition. Other films featured the more lurid amusements available on the midways: e.g., *Couchie Dance on the Midway* (**Lubin**, 1901), *Wedding Procession in Cairo* (Lubin, 1901). Lubin also screened moving pictures on the midway in Buffalo.

After 1901, moving pictures were a more regular feature at expositions, and the expositions—and their many exhibits—were regular subjects for *actualités* and **news event films**. Edison filmed the groundbreaking ceremonies of the 1904 Saint Louis Louisiana Purchase Exposition, and **Selig** filmed the dedication ceremonies. Numerous films were shown at different concessions at the Louisiana Purchase Exposition, and **Hale's Tours** and Scenes of the World made its first appearance there.

See also: amusement parks; travelogues

Further reading

Rydell, Robert W. (1984) *All the World's a Fair: Visions of Empire at American International Expositions, 1876–1916*, Chicago: University of Chicago Press.

Toulet, Emmanuelle (1991) "Cinema at the Universal Exposition, Paris, 1900," trans. Tom Gunning, *Persistence of Vision*, 9: 10–36.

LAUREN RABINOVITZ

Wrench Film Company

Wrench was a minor film producer but a leading equipment manufacturer in the early years of the British film industry. J. Wrench & Sons was a long-established London optical company that expanded its **magic lantern** business to include cinematograph equipment. Alfred Wrench patented a Wrench projector in 1896, which was highly popular. Wrench worked with Alfred **Darling** on an improved camera/projector in 1897, and in 1899 they invented the 17.5 mm Biokam camera for **amateur film** use. The Wrench Film Company flourished during the 1900s, and was represented at the European Convention of Film Makers held in Paris in 1909. The company ceased film production by 1914 and was absorbed by another firm in 1925.

See also: cameras; projectors

LUKE McKERNAN

Y

Yermoliev, Iosif

b. 1889; d. 1962

distributor, producer, Russia

Yermoliev was born to a wealthy and distinguished Moscow merchant family. After attending Moscow University, he joined **Pathé-Frères** in 1907, as a translator turned business executive at the French company's distribution agencies in Moscow, Rostov-on-the-Don, and Baku. As Pathé curtailed its activity in Russia, Yermoliev was encouraged to launch his own business. In 1911, he co-founded an independent distribution agency in Rostov and, in 1912, started his own production company in Moscow, where he built a technically advanced studio and published a trade journal, *Proektor* (Projector) to promote his films. With Pathé's continued assistance, he soon became one of three main players in Russia's film industry.

Yermoliev's first productions were mainstream **crime films**—*In the Maelstrom of Moscow* (1914)—but soon after managing to contract **Thiemann**'s best director, Yakov **Protazanov**, and **Khanzhonkov**'s principal **star**, Ivan **Mosjoukine**, the company developed a distinct studio style guided by Yermoliev's notion of what was currently fashionable. Whereas earlier he had appeared in a variety of comic and romantic roles, Mosjoukine now was cast as a neurasthenic male with a steely gaze and broken eyebrows separated by a doleful vertical wrinkle, complemented by the shadowed eyes and blasé manner of his female partner, Natalia Lisenko. The company's prestige productions were high-culture screen versions of literary classics such as *The Queen of Spades* (1916), after Pushkin, or *Nicolai Stavrogin* (1915), adapted from Dostoievsky's *The Demons*, but Yermoliev was best known for his penchant for stories with a decadent flavor—*Let Him Who Is Without Sin Cast The First Stone* (1915)—or satanic twist—*Satan Triumphant* (1917)—often titled after popular variety stage love ballads—e.g., *Already The Chrysanthemums Are Long Faded In The Garden* and *True Love's Strength Is Not The Passion Of A Kiss* (both 1916). One of Yermoliev's last hits was *Father Sergius* (1918), (after Leo Tolstoy), the story of a sexually tempted, self-mutilating monk played, of course, by Mosjoukine.

Owing to Yermoliev's legendary business acumen and the unceasing support of Pathé, after the Bolshevik revolution, he managed to move his company to Yalta and then to France in 1920, where most of his staff and principal players launched their second, equally successful careers through Films Ermolieff.

Further reading

Anon. (1916) "I. N. Yermoliev," *Vsia kinematografiia. Nastolnaya I spravochnaya kniga*, (All Cinema: Desktop Handbook), 10–12, Moscow: Chibrario de Goden.

Anon. (1962) "Iosif Nikolaevich Yermoliev [Obituary]," *Russkaya mysl*, 17 March, 1813.

YURI TSIVIAN AND DENISE J. YOUNGBLOOD

Yokota Einosuke

b. 1872; d. 1943

exhibitor, producer, Japan

In 1897, after the **Cinématographe Lumière** was imported into Japan by Inabata Katsutaro, Yokota Einosuke exploited and exhibited the apparatus in several cities. As part of a delegation from Kyoto at the Exposition Universelle in Paris in 1900, Yokota bought many prints from **Pathé-Frères**. After returning to Japan, he founded Yokota Shokai, which exhibited the French films he had bought in France. Soon after that, the company began to make its own films. In 1912, when Yokota Shokai was merged into **Nikkatsu**, he became an executive and later the new company's president.

HIROSHI KOMATSU

Yokota Shokai

This company was founded in 1900 to exhibit the French films of **Pathé-Frères** that **Yokota Einosuke** had bought in Paris. The company's real expansion occurred, however, in 1904, when films about the Russo-Japanese War were an attraction everywhere in Japan. Forming several touring troupes, the company presented cinema programs throughout the country. By 1908, Yokota Shokai had a studio in Kyoto where it could produce its own films, with old-school dramas directed primarily by **Makino Shozo**. In 1912, Yokota Shokai was merged into **Nikkatsu**.

HIROSHI KOMATSU

Yoshizawa Shoten

Yoshizawa Shoten originally was a shop that sold **magic lanterns** and photographs to Japanese customers and exported ukiyo-e and Japanese stamps to foreign markets. Founded by Kawaura Kenichi, the shop moved to the Ginza district of Tokyo in 1894. An Italian brought a **Cinématographe Lumière** to the shop in late 1896 or in early 1897. With this machine, Yoshizawa Shoten began to exhibit moving pictures; soon the shop was importing motion picture machines and films and expanding into film production. In 1908, it built the first glass house studio in Tokyo. Yoshizawa Shoten was the biggest and most stable film company in Japan until the formation of **Nikkatsu** in 1912.

HIROSHI KOMATSU

Young Deer, James

b. ?, Dakota City, Nebraska; d. 1946

actor, scriptwriter, director, USA

A Winnebago Indian, married to the actress Princess Redwing (also Winnebago). After starring in Wild West shows and several **westerns**, Young Deer was hired to manage **Pathé-Frères'** West Coast studio in Los Angeles in 1910. Although he wrote, directed, and starred in over 100 films made for the company before 1915, most of them Indian and cowboy films, Young Deer is largely forgotten as the first Native American director. Because he was often not credited as actor or director, it is difficult to identify his many films today.

NANNA VERHOEFF

Z

Zacconi, Ermete

b. 1857; d. ?

actor, Italy

Born in Montecchio near Reggio Emilia, Zacconi had a successful acting career on stage, in part with Eleonora **Duse**, long before his limited appearances in cinema. For the most part, he played father figures, as in Gino Zaccaria's *Padre* [The Palace of Flames] (1912), one of **Itala**'s first feature films; but he also took on other roles, such as the self-sacrificing hero in *Lo Scomparso* [The Vanished One] (1913). In his last film, Febo Mari's *L'Emigrante* [The Emigrant] (1915), Zacconi again played a father forced to separate from his young daughter (Valentina Frascaroli).

ANGELA DALLE VACCHE

Zecca, Ferdinand

b. 1864, Paris, France; d. 1947, Vincennes, France

actor, filmmaker, producer, France

A **café-concert** artist, Ferdinand Zecca was hired in 1898 by Charles **Pathé** to make recordings using phonograph cylinders. In 1900, he attempted to make a short film that synchronized with the text of *Le Muet mélomane* [The Dumb Music Lover]. The success of this experiment led Pathé to offer him to work at **Pathé-Frères** related to film production.

Over the course of a few years, Zecca made numerous 40-meter films (up to two a day) for which he would devise subjects, paint sets, and operate the camera. In addition, he sometimes acted in films by other filmmakers as they requested his collaboration. His own works tended towards a certain realism, as in *Histoire d'un crime* [The Story of a Crime] (1901).

In 1903, Zecca left Pathé-Frères to work for **Gaumont**. His activity there lasted but a few months, during which he shot a series of **trick films**, including *Illusionniste renversant* [The Amazing Illusionist]. Upon his return to Pathé-Frères in 1904, the Vincennes studios were being reorganized, and films now were being shot in a new Montreuil studio. Zecca soon took over their direction, and from then on a large part of Pathé's output was placed under his control. Still, he continued to make films such as *Bain des dames de la cour* [Court Ladies Bathing] (1905).

His responsibilities were further extended when he replaced Dupuis as head of the Vincennes studios. As a consequence, he was supervising the entire Pathé production by 1906–1907. This meant that he accepted or rejected proposed scripts, determined the length and budget of the films as well as the duration of shooting, and even devised recording rules for cameramen, favoring full-length framing. Zecca also was engaged in hiring directors, set decorators, and actors. His regular presence on the set made it possible for him to control the shooting and to ensure that what was being executed corresponded to what had been planned. In short, this work probably made him the world's first film producer. Whenever he was more involved in the creative process, his name would appear clearly on **publicity** materials, as with the series he made with René **Leprince** in the early 1910s. This was the case for projects such as the scripting of a Michelin commercial that was never filmed in 1908.

As Charles Pathé's right-hand man, Zecca was entrusted with the most important missions: he made numerous round trips to New York to take care of the company's activities in the USA and even became the managing director of Pathé-Exchange briefly in 1918. He also collaborated on launching the Pathé-Baby system in the early 1920s.

See also: modes of production: issues and debates

Further reading

Pathé, Charles (1970) *De Pathé-Frères à Pathé-Cinéma*, Lyon: SERDOC

Sadoul, Georges (1948) *Histoire Générale du cinéma II: les pionniers du cinéma, 1897–1909*, Paris: Denoël.

LAURENT LE FORESTIER

Zhang Shichuan

b. 1890; d. 1954

filmmaker, China

Zhang was the co-founder of several early Chinese film companies (**Asia**, Huanxian and Mingxing), and director of nearly 150 silent and sound films. Before embarking on his film career, Zhang worked in the famous New World Amusement Complex. His short-lived Huanxian Company made *Heiji yuanhun* [Victims of Opium] (1916), adapted from a popular stage play. With the establishment of Mingxing in 1922, he collaborated with **Zheng Zhengqiu** on numerous films, although his production philosophy was inclined to entertainment rather than didacticism. After the destruction of Mingxing by Japanese bombing in 1937, Zhang continued his prolific career until 1948.

ZHEN ZHANG

Zheng Zhengqiu

b. 1889; d. 1935

filmmaker, China

Called the "father of Chinese cinema," Zheng first worked as a theater critic and then began film-making in collaboration with the **Asia Film Co.** in 1913. He was the co-founder of the Mingxing Company in 1922, for which he wrote and co-directed the three-reel *Laborer's Love* (1922), the earliest extant Chinese narrative film. Combining "business with conscience," Zheng's films were popular among the urban lower and middle classes, especially women, and also among the overseas Chinese. Zheng wrote and directed more than 40 films, ranging from silent melodramas and martial arts films to early sound films.

ZHEN ZHANG

Zukor, Adolph

b. 1876; d. 1976

entrepreneur, exhibitor, producer, USA

Born in Hungary, Zukor immigrated to the USA in 1888. After several years in the fur business, he invested in a **penny arcade** in New York City in 1903, eventually opening a chain of arcades throughout the city. In 1905, Zukor turned his penny arcades into **Hale's Tour** theaters, and shortly thereafter into **nickelodeons**; five years later, he became treasurer of Marcus **Loew**'s chain of **vaudeville** houses in New York. In 1912, along with theatrical producer Daniel Frohman and Edwin S. **Porter**, he formed the **Famous Players Motion Picture Company** with the aim of producing and distributing **multiple-reel/feature films**. Four years later, Zukor became president of Paramount Pictures Corporation, which under his reign would become the first vertically-integrated motion picture company in the USA.

MICHAEL QUINN

Bibliography

Abel, Richard (1994) *The Ciné Goes to Town: French Cinema, 1896–1914*, Berkeley: University of California Press.

Abel, Richard (ed.) (1996) *Silent Film*, New Brunswick: Rutgers University Press.

Abel, Richard (1999) *The Red Rooster Scare: Making Cinema American, 1900–1910*, Berkeley: University of California Press.

Abel, Richard and Rick Altman (eds.) (2001) *The Sounds of Early Cinema*, Bloomington, Indiana University Press.

Abel, Richard and Lorenzo Codelli (eds.) (1993) *Griffithiana*, 47—special issue devoted to the Éclair Film Company.

Albera, François, Marta Braun, and André Gaudreault (eds.) (2002) *Arrêt sur image, fragmentation du temps* (Stop Motion, Fragmentation of Time), Lausanne: Payot.

Allen, Robert C. (1980) *Vaudeville and Film, 1895–1915: A Study in Media Interaction*, New York: Arno.

Allen, Robert C. (1990) "From Exhibition to Reception: Reflections on the Audience in Film History," *Screen*, 31.4: 347–356.

Altman, Rick (1996) "The Silence of the Silents," *Musical Quarterly*, 80.4: 648–718.

Altman, Rick (2004) *Silent Film Sound*, New York: Columbia University Press.

Altman, Rick and Richard Abel (eds.) (1999) *Film History*, 11.4—special issue devoted to global experiments in synchronized sound.

American Film Institute (1988) *Catalog of Motion Pictures Produced in the United States, A: Film Beginnings, 1893–1910*, Berkeley: University of California Press.

American Film Institute (1988) *Catalog of Motion Pictures Produced in the United States, F1: Feature Films, 1911–1920*, Berkeley: University of California Press.

Anderson, Gillian B. (1989) *Music for Silent Films (1894–1927): A Guide*, Washington, D.C.: Library of Congress.

Aubert, Michelle and Jean-Claude Seguin (eds.) (1996) *La production cinématographique des frères Lumière*, Paris: Centre national de la cinématographie, Bibliothèque du Film, Librairie du Premier Siècle.

Ball, Robert (1968) *Shakespeare on Silent Film: A Strange Eventful History*, London: George Allen & Unwin.

Balshofer, Fred and Arthur C. Miller (1967) *One Reel a Week*, Berkeley: University of California Press.

Bardèche, Maurice and Robert Brasillach (1943) *Histoire du cinéma*, 2nd ed., Paris: Denoël.

Barnes, John (1983) *The Rise of the Cinema in Great Britain*, London: Bishopsgate Press.

Bean, Jennifer M. and Diane Negra (eds.) (2002) *A Feminist Reader in Early Cinema*, Durham: Duke University Press.

Bergsten, Bebe (ed.) (1971) *Biograph Bulletins, 1896–1908*, Los Angeles: Locare Research Group.

Bernardi, Daniel (ed.) (1995) *The Birth of Whiteness: Race and the Emergence of United States Cinema*, New Brunswick, NJ: Rutgers University Press.

Bernardini, Alberto (2003) *Cinema muto italiano: I film "dal varo" 1895–1914*, Gemona: La Cineteca del Friuli.

Binet, R. and G. Hausser (1908) *Les sociétés de cinématographe: Etudes financières*, Paris: La France Economique et Financière.

Birett, Herbert (ed.) (1980) *Verzeichnis in Deutschland gelaufener Filme: Entscheidungen* der Filmzensur, 1911–1920, Berlin/Hamburg/München/Stuttgart: Saur.

Birett, Herbert (ed.) (1991) *Das Filmangebot in Deutschland, 1895–1911*, Munich: Filmbuchverlag Winterberg.

Blom, Ivo (2003) *Jean Desmet and the Early Dutch Film Trade*, Amsterdam: Amsterdam University Press.

Bordwell, David, Janet Staiger, and Kristin Thompson (1985) *The Classical Hollywood Cinema: Film Style and Mode of Production to 1960*, London/New York: British Film Institute/Columbia University Press.

Bottomore, Stephen (1995) *I Want to See This Annie Mattygraph: A Cartoon History of the Coming of the Movies*, Pordenone: Le Giornate del cinema muto.

Bottomore, Stephen (ed.) (1998) *Film History*, 10.1—special issue on cinema pioneers.

Bottomore, Stephen (ed.) (1999) *Film History*, 13.3—special issue on early cinema.

Bottomore, Stephen (1999) "The Panicking Audience: Early Cinema and the 'Train Effect'," *Historical Journal of Film, Radio and Television*, 19.2: 177–216.

Bottomore, Stephen (1999–2000) "'Every Phase of Present-Day Life': Biograph's Non-Fiction Production," *Griffithiana*, 66–70: 147–211.

Bousquet, Henri (ed.) (1993–1996) *Catalogue Pathé des années 1896 à 1914*, Bassac: Henri Bousquet.

Bousquet, Henri and Laurent Mannoni (eds.) (1992) *1895*, 12—special issue devoted to the Éclair Film Company.

Bowers, Q. David (1986) *Nickelodeon Theatres and Their Music*, Vestal, NY: Vestal Press.

Bowser, Eileen (1973) *Biograph Bulletins, 1908–1912*, New York: Octagon Books.

Bowser, Eileen (1979) "The Brighton Project: An Introduction," *Quarterly Review of Film Studies*, 4.4: 509–538.

Bowser, Eileen (1991) *The Transformation of Cinema, 1907–1915*, New York: Scribner's.

Brewster, Ben and Lea Jacobs (1997) *Theatre to Cinema: Stage Pictorialism and the Early Feature Film*, Oxford: Oxford University Press.

Brownlow, Kevin (1979) *The Hollywood Pioneers*, London: Collins.

Brownlow, Kevin (1990) *Behind the Mask of Innocence. Sex, Violence, Prejudice, Crime: Films of Social Conscience in the Silent Era*, Berkeley: University of California Press.

Burch, Noël (1990) *Life to Those Shadows*, Berkeley: University of California Press.

Cahiers de la cinémathèque (1987) 48—special issue devoted to Louis Feuillade.

Carou, Alain (2002) *Le Cinéma français et les écrivains: histoire d'une rencontre, 1906–1914*, Paris: École nationale des chartes/AFRHC.

Chabria, Suresh (ed.) (1994) *Light of Asia: Indian Silent Cinema, 1912–1934*, Pordenone/New Delhi: Le Giornate del cinema muto/Wiley Eastern Ltd.

Chanan, Michael (1980) *The Dream That Kicks*, London: Routledge and Kegan Paul.

Chardère, Bernard and Guyad Marjorie Borgé (1985) *Les Lumière*, Lausanne: Payot.

Charney, Leo and Vanessa Schwartz (eds.) (1995) *Cinema and the Invention of Modern Life*, Berkeley: University of California Press.

Cherchi Usai, Paolo (ed.) (1991) *A Trip to the Movies: Georges Méliès, Filmmaker and Magician (1861–1938)*, Rochester, NY: George Eastman House.

Cherchi Usai, Paolo (ed.) (1999–2008) *The Griffith Project*, London: British Film Institute.

Cherchi Usai, Paolo (2000) *Silent Cinema: An Introduction*, London: British Film Institute.

Cherchi Usai, Paolo and Lorenzo Codelli (eds.) (1990) *Before Caligari: German Cinema, 1897–1920*, Pordenone: Biblioteca dell'Immagine.

Cherchi Usai, Paolo and Yuri Tsivian (eds.) (1989) *Silent Witnesses: Russian Films, 1908–1919*, Pordenone: Biblioteca dell'Immagine.

Coissac, G. Michel (1925) *Histoire du cinématographe: de ses origines jusqu'à nos jours*, Paris: Cinéopse.

Cooper, Mark Garrrett (2003) *Love Rules: Silent Hollywood and the Rise of the Managerial Class*, Minneapolis: University of Minnesota Press.

Corey, Marie-Sophie, Jacques Malthête, Laurent Mannoni, and Jean-Jacques Meusy (eds.) (1998) *Les premiers années de la société L. Gaumont et cie: correspondance commerciale de Léon Gaumont, 1895–1899*, Paris: AFRHC.

Cosandey, Roland (1993) *KINtop Schriften I: Film um 1910, or Welcome Home, Joye!*, Basel: Stadtkino, Stroemfeld.

Cosandey, Roland (2002) "Le cinema en Suisse, le vingt premières années," in Rémy Pithon (ed.)

Cinéma Suisse muet: lumières et ombres, Lausanne: Antipodes & Cinémathèque Suisse.

Cosandey, Roland and François Albera (eds.) (1995) *Cinémas sans frontières/Images Across Borders, 1896–1918*, Lausanne/Québec: Payot/ Nuit Blanche.

Cosandey, Roland, André Gaudreault and Tom Gunning (eds.) (1992) *Une invention du diable? Cinéma des premiers temps et religion/An Invention of the Devil? Religion and Early Cinema*, Québec/ Lausanne: Presses de l'Université de Laval/ Payot.

Crafton, Donald (1982) *Before Mickey: The Animated Film, 1898–1928*, Cambridge: MIT Press.

Crafton, Donald (1990) *Emile Cohl, Caricature, and Film*, Princeton: Princeton University Press.

d'Agostino, Annette (1995) *An Index to Short and Feature Films Reviews in the Moving Picture World: The Early Years, 1907–1915*, Westport/ London, Greenwood.

d'Agostino, Annette (1997) *Filmmakers in the Moving Picture World: An Index of Articles, 1907–1927*, Jefferson, NC: McFarland.

deCordova, Richard (1990) *Picture Personalities: The Emergence of the Star System in America, 1907–1922*, Urbana: University of Illinois Press.

de Kuyper, Eric (1995) *Alfred Machin: cinéaste/film-maker*, Brussels: Royal Belgian Film Archive.

Deslandes, Jacques (1963) *Le boulevard du cinéma à l'époque de Georges Méliès*, Paris: Cerf.

Deslandes, Jacques (1975) "Victorin-Hippolyte Jasset," *L'Avant-Scène Cinéma*, 163: 241–296.

Deslandes, Jacques and Jacques Richard (1968) *Histoire comparée du cinéma, II: du cinématographe au cinéma*, Paris: Casterman.

Dibbets, Karel and Bert Hogenkamp (eds.) (1995) *Film and the First World War*, Amsterdam: Amsterdam University Press.

Dickson, W. K. L. (1970 [1895]) *History of the Kinetograph and Kinetophonograph*, New York: Arno.

Dickson, W. K. L. and Antonia Dickson (1894) *The Life and Inventions of Thomas Alva Edison*, New York: Thomas Y. Crowell.

Doane, Mary Ann (2002) *The Emergence of Cinematic Time: Modernity, Contingency, the Archive*, Cambridge: Harvard University Press.

Ducom, Jacques (1911) *Le cinéma scientifique et industriel*, Paris: Geisler.

Dupré la Tour, André Gaudreault, and Roberta Pearson (eds.) (1999) *Le cinéma au tournant du siècle* (Cinema at the Turn of the Century), Lausanne/Québec: Payot/Nota bene.

Elsaesser, Thomas (ed.) (1990) *Early Cinema: Space, Frame, Narrative*, London: British Film Institute.

Elsaesser, Thomas (ed.) (1996) *A Second Life: German Cinema's First Decades*, Amsterdam: Amsterdam University Press.

Elsaesser, Thomas and Michael Wedel (eds.) (2002) *Kino der Kaiserzeit: Zwischen Tradition un Moderne*, Munich: edition text + kritik.

FIAF (ed.) *Le Cinéma français muet dans le monde, influences réciproques*, Perpignan: Institute Jean Vigo.

Fell, John L. (1974) *Film and the Narrative Idea*, Norman: University of Oklahoma Press.

Fell, John L. (ed.) (1983) *Film Before Griffith*, Berkeley: University of California Press.

Ford, Charles (1984) *Albert Capellani, précurseur méconnu*, Bois d'Arcy: Service des Archives du Film.

Frazer, John (1979) *Artificially Arranged Scenes: The Film of Georges Méliès*, Boston: G. K. Hall.

Fuller, Kathryn (1996) *At the Picture Show: Small-Town Audiences and the Creation of Movie Fan Culture*, Washington, DC: Smithsonian Institution.

Fullerton, John (ed.) (1998) *Celebrating 1895: The Centenary of Cinema*, Sydney: John Libbey.

Fullerton, John and Astrid Söderbergh Widding (eds.) (2000) *Moving Images: From Edison to the Webcam*, Sydney: John Libbey.

Gaudreault, André (ed.) (1979) *Les Cahiers de la Cinémathèque*, 29—special issue devoted to early cinema.

Gaudreault, André (ed.) (1988) *Ce que je vois de mon ciné . . . .*, Paris: Méridiens Klincksieck.

Gaudreault, André (ed.) (1993) *Pathé 1900: fragments d'une filmographie analytique du cinéma des premiers temps*, Québec/Paris: Presses de l'Université Laval/Sorbonne nouvelle.

Gaudreault, André (1998) *Du littéraire au filmique: système du récit*, Paris/Québec: Armand Colin/ Nota bene.

Gaudreault, André (ed.) (Fall 2003) *CiNéMAS*—special issue devoted to Dispositif(s) du cinéma (des premiers temps).

Gaudreault, André, Germain Lacasse and Isabelle Raynauld (eds.) (1999) *Le cinéma en histoire: Institutions cinématographiques, réception filmique et reconstitution historique*, Paris/Québec: Méridiens Klincksieck/Nota bene.

Gaudreault, André, Catherine Russell, and Pierre Verroneau (eds.) (2004) *Le Cinématographe, nouvelle technologie du XXᵉ siècle (The Cinema, A New Technology for the 20th Century)*, Lausanne: Editions Payot.

Gili, Jean, Michèle Lagny, Michel Marie, and Vincent Pinel (eds.) (1995) *Les vingt premières années du cinéma français*, Paris: La Sorbonne nouvelle.

Graham, Cooper *et al.* (eds.) (1985) *David W. Griffith and the Biograph Company*, Metuchen/London: Scarecrow.

Grau, Robert (1910) *The Business Man in the Amusement World*, New York: Broadway.

Grau, Robert (1914) *The Theater of Science*, New York: Broadway.

Grieveson, Lee and Peter Krämer (eds.) (2004) *The Silent Cinema Reader*, London: Routledge.

Griffiths, Alison (2002) *Wondrous Difference: Cinema, Anthropology, and Turn-of-the-Century Visual Culture*, New York: Columbia University Press.

Guibbert, Pierre (ed.) (1985) *Les premiers ans du cinéma français*, Perpignan: Institut Jean Vigo.

Gunning, Tom (1986) "The Cinema of Attraction: Early Cinema, Its Spectator, and the Avant-Garde," *Wide Angle*, 8.3/4: 63–70.

Gunning, Tom (1989) "An Aesthetics of Astonishment: Early Film and the (In)credulous Spectator," *Art & Text*, 34: 31–45.

Gunning, Tom (1991) *D. W. Griffith and the Origins of American Narrative Film*, Urbana: University of Illinois Press.

Gunning, Tom (2003) "Loïe Fuller and the Art of Motion: Body, Light, Electricity and the Origins of Cinema," in Richard Allen and Malcolm Turvey (eds.) *Camera Obscura, Camera Lucida: Essays in Honor of Annette Michelson*, Amsterdam: Amsterdam University Press.

Guy, Alice (1976) *Autobiographie d'une pionnière du cinéma*, Paris: Denoël, Gonthier.

Hamman, Joë (1962) *Du Far-West à Montmartre*, Paris: Editeurs français réunis.

Hammond, Paul (1974) *Marvelous Méliès*, London: Fraser.

Hansen, Miriam (1991) *Babel and Babylon: Spectatorship in American Silent Film*, Cambridge: Harvard University Press.

Hansen, Miriam (1993) "Early Cinema, Late Cinema: Transformations of the Public Sphere," *Screen*, 34: 197–210.

Hendricks, Gordon (1961) *The Edison Motion Picture Myth*, Berkeley: University of California Press.

Hendricks, Gordon (1972 [1966]) *The Kinetoscope: America's First Commercially Successful Motion Picture Exhibitor*, New York: Arno.

Hendricks, Gordon (1972 [1964]) *The Origins of the American Film*, New York: Arno.

Hepworth, Cecil (1897) *The ABC of the Cinematograph*,

Herbert, Stephen (ed.) (2000) *A History of Early Film*, London: Routledge.

Herbert, Stephen (ed.) (2000) *A History of Pre-Cinema*, 3 vols., London: Routledge.

Herbert, Stephen and Luke McKernan (eds.) (1996) *Who's Who in Victorian Cinema*, London: British Film Institute.

Hertogs, Daan and Nico de Klerk (eds.) (1994) *Nonfiction From the Teens*, Amsterdam: Nederlands Filmmuseum.

Hertogs, Daan and Nico de Klerk (eds.) (1996) *"Disorderly Order": Colours in Silent Film*, Amsterdam: Nederlands Filmmuseum.

Hesse, Sebastian (2003) *Kamera-Augen und Spürnese: Der Detektiv im frühen deutschen Kino*, Basel: Stroemfeld/Roter Stern.

Higgins, Steven (1984) "I film di Thomas H. Ince," *Grifffithiana*, 18–21: 155–203.

Holman, Roger (ed.) (1982) *Cinema 1900–1906: An Analytical Study*, 2 vols., Brussels: International Federation of Film Archives.

Hopwood, Henry V. (1899) *Living Pictures: Their History, Photoduplication and Practical Working*, London: Optician and Photographic Trades Review.

Hulfish, David S. (1914 [1911]) *Cyclopedia of Motion-Picture Work*, Chicago: American Technical Society.

Jacobs, Lewis (1939) *The Rise of the American Film*, New York: Harcourt, Brace.

Jeanne, René (1965) *Cinéma 1900*, Paris: Flammarion.

Jeanne, René and Charles Ford (1947) *Histoire encyclopédique I: Le cinéma français, 1895–1929*, Paris: Robert Laffont.

Jenkins, C. Francis (1898) *Animated Pictures*, Washington: H. L. Mcqueen.

Jenkins, C. Francis and Oscar B. Depue (1908) *Handbook for Motion Picture and Stereopticon Operators*, Washington: Knega.

Jenn, Pierre (1984) *Georges Méliès cinéaste*, Paris: Albatros.

Jesionowski, Joyce (1987) *Thinking in Pictures: Dramatic Structure in D. W. Griffith's Biograph Films*, Berkeley: University of California Press.

Keil, Charlie (2001) *Early American Cinema in Transition: Story, Style, and Filmmaking, 1907–1913*, Madison: University of Wisconsin Press.

Kermabon, Jacques (ed.) *Pathé, premier empire du cinéma*, Paris: Centre Georges Pompidou.

Kessler, Frank (ed.) (2002) *Historical Journal of Film, Radio, and Television*, 22.3—special issue on early nonfiction cinema.

Kirby, Lynn (1997) *Parallel Tracks: The Railroad and Silent Cinema*, Durham, NC: Duke University Press.

Komatsu, Hiroshi (1992) "Some Characteristics of Japanese Cinema Before World War I," in Arthur Nolletti and David Desser (eds.) *Reframing Japanese Cinema*, 229–258, Bloomington: Indiana University Press.

Kress, Ernest (1912) *Conférences sur la cinématographie*, 2 vols., Paris: Cinéma-Revue.

Lacassin, Francis (1972) *Pour un contre-histoire du cinéma*, Paris: Union générale d'éditions.

Lacassin, Francis (1995) *Maître des lions et des vampires: Louis Feuillade*, Paris: Pierre Bordas.

Lant, Antonia (ed.) (2004) *The Red Velvet Seat: Women's Writing on Cinema, the First Fifty Years*, London: Verso.

Lastra, James (2000) *Perception, Representation, Modernity: Sound Technology and the American Cinema*, New York: Columbia University Press.

Lauritzen, Einar and Gunnar Lundquist (eds.) (1976) *American Film Index, 1908–1915*, Stockholm: Film Index.

Lefebvre, Thierry, Jacques Malthête and Laurent Mannoni (eds.) (1999) *Lettres d'Etienne-Jules Marey à Georges Demenÿ, 1880–1894*, Paris: AFRHC.

Leglise, Paul (1970) *Histoire de la politique du cinéma français: le cinéma et la IIIe République*, Paris: Librairie générale de droit et de jurisprudence.

Leyda, Jay (1986) *Kino: A History of the Russian and Soviet Film*, 3rd ed., Princeton: Princeton University Press.

Leyda, Jay and Charles Musser (eds.) (1986) *Before Hollywood: Turn-of-the Century Film from American Archives*, New York: American Federation of the Arts.

Library of Congress (1951) *Catalog of Copyright Entries: Motion Pictures I, 1894–1912*, Washington: Library of Congress/Copyright Office.

Library of Congress (1953) *Catalog of Copyright Entries: Motion Pictures, 1912–1939*, Washington: Library of Congress/Copyright Office.

Liesegang, Franz Paul (1986) *Dates and Sources: A Contribution to the History of the Art of Projection and to Cinematography*, trans. Hermann Hecht, London: Magic Lantern Society.

Lindsay, Vachel (1970 [1916]) *The Art of Moving Pictures*, New York: Liveright.

Loiperdinger, Martin (ed.) (2003) *Celluloid Goes Digital: Historical-Critical Editions of Films on DVD and the Internet*, Trier: Wissenschaftlicher Verlag Trier.

Low, Rachael (1948–1979) *The History of British Film*, 6 vols., London: George Allen & Unwin.

Malthête-Méliès, Madeleine (ed.) (1984) *Méliès et la naissance du spectacle cinématographique*, Paris: Klincksieck.

Mannoni, Laurent (1994) *Le grand art de la lumière et de l'ombre: archéologie du cinéma*, Paris: Nathan; also (2000) *The Great Art of Light and Shadow: Archaeology of Cinema*, trans. Richard Crangle, Exeter: Exeter University Press.

Mannoni, Laurent (1996) *Le Mouvement continué: Catalogue illustré de la collection des appareils de la Cinémathèque française*, Milan/Paris: Mazzotta/La Cinémathèque française.

Mannoni, Laurent (1999) *Etienne-Jules Marey, la mémoire de l'oeil*, Milan/Paris: Mazzotta/La Cinématographie française.

Mannoni, Laurent and Jacque Malthête (2002) *Méliès, magie et cinéma*, Paris: Paris-Musées.

Mannoni, Laurent, Marc de Ferrière le Vayer, and Paul Demenÿ (1997) *Georges Demenÿ, pionnier du cinéma*, Douai: Editions Pagine.

Mannoni, Laurent, Thierry Lefebvre and Jacques Malthête (eds.) (2000) *Lettres d'Etienne-Jules Marey/Georges Demenÿ*, Paris: AFRHC/Bibliothèque du film.

Mannoni, Laurent, Marie-Sophie Corcy, Jacques Malthête and Jean-Jacques Meusy (eds.) (1998) *Les premières années de la société L. Gaumont et Cie, corresponance commerciale de Léon Gaumont, 1885–1899*, Paris: AFRHC/Bibliothèque du film/Gaumont.

Marie, Michel and Laurent Le Forstier (eds.) (2004) *La Firme Pathé-Frères, 1896–1914*, Paris, AFRHC.

Marks, Martin M. (1997) *Music and the Silent Film*, New York: Oxford University Press.

Maugras, Eugène and Maurice Guégan (1908) *Le cinématographe devant le droit*, Paris: V. Giard et F. Brière.

May, Lary (1980) *Screening Out the Past: The Birth of Mass Culture and the Motion Picture Industry*, New York: Oxford University Press.

McDonnell, Patricia (ed.) (2002) *On the Edge of Your Seat: Popular Theater and Film in Early Twentieth-Century American Art*, New Haven/Minneapolis: Yale University Press/Weisman Art Museum.

McMahan, Alison (2002) *Alice Guy Blaché: Lost Visionary of the Cinema*, New York: Continuum.

Meusy, Jean-Jacques (1996) *Paris-Palaces ou le temps des cinémas (1894–1918)*, Paris: CNRS.

Mitry, Jean (1967) *Histoire du cinéma I: 1895–1914*, Paris: Editions universitaires.

Mitry, Jean (1967) "Max Linder," *Anthologie du cinéma*, 2, 289–348, Paris: L'Avant-Scène Cinéma.

Mottram, Ron (1988) *The Danish Cinema Before Dreyer*, Metuchen, NJ: Scarecrow.

Munsterberg, Hugo (1970 [1916]) *The Photoplay: A Psychological Study*, New York: Dover.

Musser, Charles (1984) "Another Look at the Chaser Theory," *Studies in Visual Communication*, 10.4: 24–44.

Musser, Charles (1991) *Before the Nickelodeon: Edwin S. Porter and the Edison Manufacturing Company*, Berkeley: University of California Press.

Musser, Charles (1991) *The Emergence of Cinema to 1907*, New York: Scribner's.

Musser, Charles (1994) "Rethinking Early Cinema: Cinema of Attractions and Narrativity," *Yale Journal of Criticism*, 7.2: 203–232.

Musser, Charles (1997) *Edison Motion Pictures, 1890–1900: An Annotated Filmography*, Washington, DC: Smithsonian Institution.

Musser, Charles and Carol Nelson (1991) *High-Class Moving Pictures: Lyman H. Howe and the Forgotten Era of Traveling Exhibition, 1880–1920*, Princeton: Princeton University Press.

Nasaw, David (1993) *Going Out: The Rise and Fall of Public Amusements*, New York: Basic Books.

Nissen, Dan *et al.* (2002) *Preserve the Show*, Copenhagen: Danish Film Museum.

Niver, Kemp (1968) *The First Twenty Years*, Los Angeles: Artisan Press.

Olsson, Jan (1986) *Från ljudfilm till filmljud: Svenska experiment med Odödlig teater, Sjungande bilder och Edisons Kinetophone 1903–1914* (From Film Sound to Sound Film: Swedish Experiments with Immortal Theater, Singing Images, and Edison's Kinetophone 1903–1914), Stockholm: Proprius.

Olsson, Jan (1990) "I offentlighetens ljus—några notiser om filmstoff i dagspressen, 1896–1919" (In the Public Sphere—News Items on Film in the Daily Press, 1896–1919), in Jan Olsson (ed.) *I offentlighetens ljus: Stumfilmens affischer, kritiker, stjärnor och musik* (In the Public Sphere: The Posters, Critics, Stars, and Music from the Silent Era), 211–272, Stockholm and Stehag: Symposion.

Pathé, Charles (1970) *De Pathé-Frères à Pathé-Cinéma*, Paris: SERDOC.

Pearson, Roberta (1992) *Eloquent Gestures: The Transformation of Performance Style in Griffith's Biograph Films*, Berkeley: University of California Press.

Peiss, Kathy (1986) *Cheap Amusements: Working Women and Leisure in Turn-of-the-Century New York*, Philadelphia: Temple University Press.

Popple, Simon and Vanessa Toulmin (eds.) (2000) *Visual Delights: Essays on the Popular and Projected Image in the 19th Century*, Trowbridge: Flick Books.

Popple, Simon and Joe Kember (2004) *Early Cinema: From Factory Gate to Dream Factory*, London: Wallflower

Pratt, George (1973) *Spellbound in Darkness: A History of the Silent Film*, Greenwich: New York Graphic Society.

Quaresima, Leonardo and Laura Vichi (eds.) (2001) *The Tenth Muse: Cinema and the Other Arts*, Udine: Forum.

Rabinovitz, Lauren (1998) *For the Love of Pleasure: Women, Movies, and Culture in Turn-of-the-Century Chicago*, New Brunswick, NJ: Rutgers University Press.

Ramsaye, Terry (1926) *A Million and One Nights*, New York: Simon & Schuster.

Rosen, J. (1911) *Le cinématographe: son passé, son avenir et ses applications*, Paris: Société d'éditions techniques.

Rosenzweig, Roy (1983) *Eight Hours for What We Will: Workers and Leisure in an Industrial City, 1870–1920*, Cambridge: Cambridge University Press.

Rossell, Deac (1995) "A Chronology of Cinema, 1889–1896," *Film History*, 7.2.

Rossell, Deac (1998) *Living Pictures: The Origins of the Movies*, Albany: SUNY Press.

Rossell, Deac (2004) *The Magic Lantern*, Stuttgart: Füsslin Verlag.

Sadoul, Georges (1947) *Histoire générale du cinéma 1: L'invention du cinéma*, Paris: Denoël.

Sadoul, Georges (1948) *Histoire générale du cinéma II: Les pionniers du cinéma, 1897–1908*, Paris: Denoël.

Sadoul, Georges (1951) *Histoire générale du cinéma III: Le cinéma devient un art, 1909–1920*, Paris: Denoël.

Sadoul, Georges (1985) *Lumière et Méliès*, rev. ed., Bernard Eisenschitz, Paris: Lherminier.

Salt, Barry (1993) *Film Style and Technology: History and Analysis*, 2nd ed., London: Starword.

Sandberg, Mark (2003) *Living Pictures, Missing Persons: Mannequins, Museums, and Modernity*, Princeton: Princeton University Press.

Sandfeld, Gunnar (1966) *Den stumme Scene* (The Silent Scene), Copenhagen: Nyt Nordisk Forlag.

Santos, A. Videira (1990) *Para a Historia do Cinema em Portugal. I. Do diafanorama aos cinématografos de Lumière e Joly-Normandin*, Lisboa: Cinemateca Portuguesa.

Savada, Elias (ed.) (1995) *The American Film Institute Catalog of Motion Pictures Produced in the United States A: Film Beginnings, 1893–1910*, Meutchen/London: Scarecrow.

Schultze, Brigitte (2003) *Humanist and Emotional Beginnings of a Nationalist Indian Cinema in Bombay*, Berlin: Avinus.

Schwartz, Vanessa (1998) *Spectacular Realities: Early Mass Culture in Fin-de-siècle Paris*, Berkeley: University of California Press.

Singer, Ben (2001) *Melodrama and Modernity: Early Sensational Cinema and Its Contexts*, New York: Columbia University Press.

Slide, Anthony (1994) *Early American Cinema*, 2nd ed., Metuchen, MJ: Scarecrow.

Sloan, Kay (1988) *The Loud Silents: Origins of the Social Problem Film*, Urbana: University of Illinois Press.

Smith, Albert E. (1952) *Two Reels and a Crank*, Garden City: Doubleday.

Sopocy, Martin (1998) *James Williamson: Studies and Documents of a Pioneer of the Film Narrative*, Madison, NJ: Farleigh Dickinson University Press.

Spehr, Paul (1977) *The Movies Begin: Making Movies in New Jersey, 1887–1920*, Newark: Newark Museum.

Spehr, Paul (1996) *American Film Personnel and Company Credits, 1908–1920*, Jefferson/London: McFarland.

Staiger, Janet (1995) *Bad Women: The Regulation of Female Sexuality in Early American Cinema, 1907–1915*, Minneapolis: University of Minnesota Press.

Stamp, Shelley (2000) *Movie-Struck Girls: Women and Motion Picture Culture After the Nickelodeon*, Princeton: Princeton University Press.

Talbot, Frederick A. (1912) *Moving Pictures: How They Are Made and Worked*, New York: Lippincott.

Thompson, Kristin (1985) *Exporting Entertainment: America in the World Film Market, 1907–1934*, London: British Film Institute.

Toulet, Emmanuelle (1988) *Cinématographe, invention du siècle*, Paris: Gallimard.

Trimbach, Pierre (1970) *Quand on tournait la manivelle . . . il y a 60 ans*, Paris: CEFAG.

Trutat, Eugène (1899) *La photographie animée*, Paris: Gauthier-Villars.

Tsivian, Yuri (1994) *Early Cinema in Russia and Its Cultural Reception*, London: Routledge.

Turconi, Davide (1987) "La produzione Vitagraph dal 1905 al 1916," in Paolo Cherchi Usai (ed.) *Vitagraph Company of America*, 443–634, Pordenone: Studio Tesi.

Uricchio, William and Roberta Pearson (1993) *Reframing Culture: The Case of the Vitagraph Quality Films*, Princeton: Princeton University Press.

Vardac, A. Nicholas (1949) *Stage to Screen: Theatrical Method from Garrick to Griffith*, Cambridge: Harvard University Press.

Waldekranz, Rune (1976) *Så föddes filmen: Ett massmediums uppkomst och genombrott* (How Film Was Born: The Origins and Breakthrough of a Mass Medium), Stockholm: Norstedts.

Waller, Gregory (1995) *Main Street Amusements: Movies and Commercial Entertainment in a Southern City*, Washington, DC: Smithsonian Institution.

Williams, Christopher (ed.) (1996) *Cinema: The Beginnings and the Future*, London: University of Westminster Press.

Youngblood, Denise (1999) *The Magic Mirror: Moviemaking in Russia, 1908–1918*, Madison: University of Wisconsin Press.

Index

À *Biribi* (1907) 258, 482

Aaronson, Max *see* Anderson, Gilbert M.

L'Abandonée (1917) 40

Abel, Richard 163, 443–4

Aberdeen University Quatercentenary (1906) 684

Los abismos de la vida (1929) 514

The Abyss (*Afgrunden*) (1910) 68, 164, 175, 263, 273, 280–1, 390, 426, 453, 455, 480, 609, 627

ACAD (Association cinématographique des auteurs dramatiques) 112, 198, 236, 237, 350, 636

Academy of Motion Picture Arts and Sciences 372

access 1–2, 36

Acevedo e Hijos 136

Ackerman, C. Fred 182, 314, 515

Acque miracolose (1914) 447

Acres, Birt 2, 17, 18, 62, 76, 96, 197, 244; celluloid 107; chronophotography 118; film contact printer 238; Hepworth 297; music hall acts 460; news event films 474; Paul partnership with 510; sports films 604; Stollwerck 612; Wales 683

L'acrobate (1907) 577

Across Africa on Film via Rhodesia to Katanga and Lobito Bay: The Tanganyika Concessions at Work (1912) 137

Across the Balkans 58

acting styles 2–5, 129; divas 426; *film d'art* 236, 295; intertitles 328; Le Bargy 378; melodrama 421–2; Netherlands 471; Nielsen 481; Onoe Matsunosuke 489; Pathé-Frères 508; Porten 526; projectionist influence over 536; Protazanov 541; Sawamura 564; Shakespeare films 588; Walthall 684; Xinmin Theater Research Society 115

The Active Life of Dollie of the Dallies 262

actualités 5–6, 309, 474, 475, 476; AM&B 21; Ambrosio 19; animal films 25; Argentina 38; Asia Film Co. 39; Belgium 64; Bergqvist 67; biblical films 68, 69; Bitzer 74; Blackton 75; Bonine 78; Botelho 79; Buckwalter 86; Butcher's Film Service 88; Calcina 90; camera movement 92; Canada 98; Cheetham 113; China 115; Chómon 116, 600; cinema of attractions 124; Colombia 135; colonial films 137; Comerio 145; Commercial Press Motion Picture Department 150; compositional depth 605, 606; consumer cooperatives 153; Cuba 159; Cuesta Valencia 161; decline of 455; editing techniques 204, 211; education 214; Egypt 216; Elfelt 219; Esoofally 220; ethnographic films 222; fairs 227; "fake newsreels" 547–8; fashion 230; fiction writers 449; Finlandia Film 243; Fitzhamon 244; framing 246; France 249, 703; Froelich 260; Gaumont 118, 265, 268; Gelabert 269; Germany 274; Gladtvet 279; Glücksmann 280; Gottschalk 280; Greece 287; Green 287; Hepworth 297; Higgins 298; Hirtz 298; India 318, 582; industrial films 321; intertitles 327; Iran 331; Italy 334, 337; itinerant exhibitors 341; Japan 344, 363; Krüger 364; Leal 379; Lubin 396; Lumière 477, 495; Lundberg 399; Luxemburg 400; Maître 411; Mason 415; Méliès 419; Mexico 431; Milano Films 436; Mitchell & Kenyon 437–8; modes of production 443; Mullens brothers 452; Natural Color Kinematograph 468; Netherlands 469, 470; New Zealand 473; Nöggerath Sr. 482; Norway 484; Notari 485; Omegna 489; Ouimet 491; panoramic views 529; Pathé-Frères 506; Paul 510; Peru 513; Phalke 514; photography 519; Poland 522; popularity of 547; program formats 534; Prószynski 541; Py 544; Quebec 101; Requião 551; Rosenthal 554; Russia 505, 557, 558, 559; Santos 563;

Scotland 572; Seeber 579; Segreto 580; Sfinks 587; single-shot films 207; stereography 611; Stollwerck 612; Svenska Biografteatern 614; Sweden 615, 616; Thailand 625; Thomas 634; travelogues 641; Turkey 646; United States 657; Urban 651; Uruguay 654; US imperialism 315; Venezuela 676; Vietnam 678; Vitagraph 679; Vitrotti 681; Wales 683; Walker 684; Warwick Trading Company 685; Weltkinematograph 687; westerns 689; World War I 703, 704; world's fairs 705; see also documentaries; news event films; newsreels

Les Actualités ouvrières (1914) 123

Addams, Jane 6–7, 315, 652, 664, 699, 700

Addio Giovinezza (1918) 343

Admiral Cigarette (1897) 7–8, 9

Adorno, Theodore 439

Adrienne Lecouvreur (1912) 428

Adroher, Lorenzo 654

Advance of the Kansas Volunteers at Caloocan (1899) 315

The Adventures of Dollie (1908) 348, 414

The Adventures of Kathlyn (1914) 26, 581, 583, 694, 700

The Adventures of Mijntje and Trijntje (1913) 79

The Adventures of Prince Achmed (1926) 588

advertising 7–9, 459, 542, 641; Austro-Hungary 52; *Autorenfilme* 55; *Ciné-Journal* 121; fashion 230; IMP 312; Laemmle 370; Laffitte 371; multiple-reel films 456; penny arcades 511; Pickford 520; Russia 557; Thiemann & Reinhardt Company 633; US 660

advertising films 7, 9–10, 17, 50, 52, 321, 620, 703; churches 120; Gladtvet 279; Hepworth 297; Lowenstein 394; Mesguich 429; Müller-Lincke 452; Phalke 514; Pinschewer 521; Rossi 555

Aeroscope camera 10–11, 355, 474, 685

"aesthetics of immobility" 61

L'Affaire Dreyfus (1899) 419, 540

L' Affaire, Dreyfus (Dreyfus Affair) (1899) 5, 419, 474, 477, 540

L'Affaire du collier de la Reine (1911) 167

Afgrunden (The Abyss) (1910) 68, 164, 175, 263, 273, 280–1, 390, 426, 453, 455, 480, 609, 627

AFRHC *see* Association française de recherché sur l'histoire du cinema

Africa xxix; Belgian colonies 11; British colonies 12; colonial films 136, 137, 138; colonialism: Europe 136–138; expedition/exploration films 224; French colonies 13; German colonies 13–14; safari films 25

African Hunt (1912) 25, 222, 224, 307

The African World and Cape Cairo Express 11

African-Americans 381, 421, 432, 433, 434, 435, 545, 630, 665, 699; *see also* black cinema: USA; racial segregation: USA

Afrika, der schwarze Kontinent (1915) 688

Afro-American Film Company 75

After Death (1915) 61

After Many Years (1908) 288

Agadati, Baruch 499

AGC (Agence Générale Cinématographique) 14–15, 91, 170, 237, 254, 467

AGFA (Aktien-Gesellschaft für Anilin-Fabrikation) 15, 107, 270, 508

Agnel, Perreau Auguste 672

La Agonía de Arauco (1917) 114, 278

Agrippina (1910) 127

Aguglia, Mimì 414

Ah! Ah! die Oscar! (1905) 452

Ah le salle gosse (1906) 143

Aherne, Eugene 597

Ai no kyoku (1919) 200

Aida (1911) 262

L'aide des colonies à la France (1917) 13

L'Aiglon (1914) 112

Aimez-vous (1925) 102

'Ain Al-Ghazal (1924) 217

airdomes 15–16, 22

The Airship Destroyer (1909) 109

Aitken, Harry 16, 20, 61, 260, 403, 549, 582; Mutual 305, 412, 447, 464–465; Triangle Film Corporation 317, 356, 473

AKGT *see* PAGU/AKGT

Aktiebolaget Hälsans gåva (1916) 362

Aladdin ou la lampe merveilleuse (1906) 140, 233

Alam Ara (1931) 220

Alarming Queen's Company of Grenadier Guards at Omdurman (1897) 12

Albania 58

Albee, Edward F. 355, 675

Alberini, Filoteo 16, 127, 169, 334, 336

Alberti, P. A. 173

Alberts Frères 63, 452, 470, 594; *see also* Mullen brothers

Albrecht, Joseph 138
El alcalde de Zalamea (1914) 290
Alexandre, René 384, 512, 553
Algeria 13, 215, 216, 217
Ali Baba et les quarante voleurs (1902/1907) 232–3, 249, 327
Alibaba and the Forty Thieves (1904) 555, 582
Alice in Wonderland (1903) 613
Alkali Ike 24
All-Star Features 368
Allefex machine 598
Allen, Jay 99
Allen, Jules 99
Allen, Robert C. 46–7
Allt hämnar sig (1917) 614
Allumeur-Marche 192
Alma sertaneja (1919) 165
Alma-Tadema, Lawrence 70, 494
Almirante Manzini, Italia 16–17, 333, 334
Almost a Wild Man (1912) 144
Alonen, Oskar 242
Alpha Trading Company 17
*Already the Chrysanthemums
   Are Long Faded In
   The Garden* (1916) 707
Alsace (1916) 467, 529
Altenloh, Emilie 17, 46, 271, 698
Des Alters erste Spuren (1912–1913) 302
Althusser, Louis 42, 601
Altschuler, Modeste 463–4
Alva, Carlos 17, 431
Alva, Guillermo 17, 431
Alva, Salvador 17, 431
Am schönen deutschen Rhein (1916) 688
Amalgamated Pictures 49, 50
Amalia (1914) 38
amateur film 17–18, 215, 410, 642, 705
Amberg, Adolphe 400
Ambrosio, Arturo 18, 19–20, 336, 404, 489
Ambrosio film company 15, 18–19, 40, 333, 500;
   Belgium 64; Bonnard 78; Capozzi 104; Caserini
   105–6; Collo 135; colonial films 138; comic
   series 147; costumes 156; D'Annunzio 164;
   De Riso 167; Duse 194; Fabre 225; Frusta 261;
   Gundersen 291; historical films 299; India 318;
   Italy 336, 337; Maggi 404; Morano 447;
   New York Motion Picture Company 472;
   Omegna 489; Oxilia 491; Rodolfi 553; set
   design 586; Thiemann & Reinhardt Company

632; travelogues 642; Turkey 646; Vidali 677;
   Vitrotti 681
Âme d'artiste (1925) 25
American Biograph (France) 20
American Bioscope 63, 227; *see also* Bioscope
   projector
American Film Manufacturing Company 16, 20,
   195–6, 220, 260, 305, 464, 649, 658; Dwan 194–
   195
American Kinetograph 14, 15, 124
American Mutoscope and Biograph (AM&B) 20,
   21, 71, 96, 327, 328, 439; amusement parks 22;
   archives 36; Biograph 70 mm projector 538–539;
   Bitzer 74; Bonine 78; boxing films 81, 82; *Buffalo
   Bill's Wild West Parade* 132; camera movement
   92, 93, 94; Canada 98, 99; catalogues 542; chase
   films 110, 111; comedies 142, 143; comic series
   145; copyright 111, 154; copyright lawsuit
   against Edison 111, 154; dance films 163–4;
   department stores 177; detective films 178, 179,
   180; Dickson 186, 200; Edison 201, 658; editing
   techniques 210, 211, 212; electricity 218;
   ethnographic films 222; exhibition 340; film
   developing, printing, and assembly 239; Finland
   243; Gauntier 269; Hale's Tours 294;
   intermittent movements 326; Keith 355;
   Kennedy 355; Kleine 361; Lauste 373;
   lighting 385, 387; Long 393; McCutcheon 417;
   Marion 413; Marvin 414; Miles Brothers 436;
   Moore 446; music halls 460; Netherlands 469;
   news event films 474; patent wars 203, 448, 655;
   penny arcades 511; phantom train rides 514;
   Philippines 515; projector 73, 538–9;
   propaganda films 540; Quebec 101; Raleigh &
   Robert 546; Sandow 562; scenarios 576;
   scientific films 570; sports films 605; transpor-
   tation 638–9; travelogues 641; United States
   656, 657; US imperialism 314, 315; vaudeville
   673; *see also* Biograph 70 mm camera; Biograph
   70 mm projector; British Mutoscope &
   Biograph; Dutch Mutoscope & Biograph
The American Soldier in Love and War
   (1903) 315
American Tobacco Company 7
America's Answer (1918) 308
Amet, Edward H. 604, 655
Amleto (1908) 145, 589
Amleto (1910) 589
Amongst the Central African Natives 12

Amor de pescadora (1914) 634
Amor, tu eres la vida (1926) 676
Amor y fé a la Divina Pastora (1928) 677
Amour et science (1912) 151
Amuletten 614
Amundsen, Roald 523–4
amusement parks 15, 21–3, 93, 124, 383, 445, 561, 655, 663, 665, 700; Canada 98; Cuba 159; electricity 218–19; Green 287; Hale's Tours 293; Japan 344; Jones 349; leisure time and space: USA 380–1; Lubin 395; Miles Brothers 436; Quebec 101; Russia 555; Schenck brothers 566; Spoor 604; urbanization 652
Der Andere (1913) 55, 60, 404
Anderson, Gilbert M. 23–4, 201, 220, 318, 439, 527, 580, 604
Andra, Fern 363
Andréani, Henri (Gustave Sarrus) 24
Andresen, Momme 15
Andreyor, Yvette 24–5, 252, 266
Andriot, (Camille-) Josette 25, 80, 198, 347, 583
El ángel de la guarda 677
Animal Locomotion (1887) 465, 570
animal pictures 25–6, 109, 297, 521, 581
animation 17, 26–9, 126; advertising films 10; Argentina 38; Blackton 75; Chómon 116; Cohl 132; color 35; comic series 147; Furniss 262; Gaumont 266; Gladtvet 279; itinerant exhibitors 342; Khanzhonkov & Co. 357; Starewicz 610; trick films 644; World War I 703
Ankerstjerne, Johan 29, 175
Die Ankunft Sr. Majestät Kaiser Wilhelm II. in Port Victoria am 8. November 1902 (1902) 182
Annan, John 118
Anschütz, Ottomar 29–31, 33, 95, 118, 119, 270, 325, 519
Antamoro, Giulio 128
Anthar 467
anthropology 221–2
Antoine, André 39, 84, 103, 168, 176, 177, 364, 467, 565
Anzola, Edgar 676
Apfel, Oscar 171
El apóstol (1917) 38
L'Appel de la liberté (1918) 102
Appleton, Victor 451
Appointment by Telephone (1902) 578
Appollinaire, Guillaume 450

Les Apprentissages de Boireau (1907) 169
Aquila Films 15, 31, 399, 552
Arab countries 215–17
Araki Kazuichi 343
L'arbre creux (1910) 400
Arbuckle, Roscoe ("Fatty") 32, 108, 148, 164, 312
archaeology of cinema/pre-cinema 32–5, 133
Arche, Alto 35–6, 52
archives 1, 36–7, 197, 241, 416; *see also* collections; preservation
Argentina 37–8, 654
Arhén, Carl Johan 614
"Aristos" 385, 388
Aristotle 129
Arizona Bill series (1912–1913) 199, 266, 294
L'Arlésienne (1908) 103, 178, 236, 565
Armat, Thomas 34, 38–9, 96, 203, 519, 538; patent wars 655; Phantoscope 348, 515, 546, 656
Army Life, or How Soldiers Are Made (1900) 307, 510
Arnaud, Etienne 39, 199, 291
Arnheim, Rudolf 624
Arquillière, Alexandre 39, 198
The Arrest of a Bookmaker (1896) 585
Arrest of a Pickpocket (1895) 2
Arrest of a Shoplifter (1903) 177
Arrival of Governor General Lord Minto at Quebec (1902) 101
Arrival of a Train at the Station (1895) 92, 638
Arrivée d'un train à La Ciotat 207
Arrivo del treno nella stazione di Milano 335
L'arroseur arrosé (1895) 142, 149, 576
Arsin, Jean 102
art 336, 458; *see also* dioramas and panoramas; museum life exhibits; painting
Artigas, Jesús 563
The Artist and the Flower Girl (c.1901) 496
The Artist's Dilemma (1901) 496
An Artist's Dream (Bray, 1913) 28
An Artist's Dream (Edison, 1900) 496
As Seen Through a Telescope (1901) 205, 208, 595
Asano Shiro 344, 363
Asia xxix; colonial films 136, 137, 138; expedition/exploration films 223
Asia Film Co. 39, 115, 710
Asian-Americans 432, 433, 434, 435
L'Assassinat du duc de Guise (1908) 84, 91, 236, 237, 250, 299–300, 378, 508; acting style 3, 236;

Bedding review 62; costume 586; Denmark 173; framing 247; legitimate theater 626; musical score 463; Robinne 553; screenplay 578; set design 586; staging in depth 606

L'Assassinat du Grand Duc Serge (1905) 482

Assault on the South Gate (1901) 182

Assembling and Testing Turbines (1904) 218

Association française de recherché sur l'histoire du cinema (AFRHC) 241

L'Assommoir (1909) 103, 565

Assunta Spina (1915) 68, 340, 414, 582

Astaix, Maurice 14–15

Astrakhan Fish Factory (1908) 505

At the End of the Trail (1912) 690

At Twelve O'Clock (1913) 582

Atelier Apollo 39–40, 243

L'atelier d'artiste (1898) 496

Athalie (1910) 105, 565

L'Atlantide (1921) 467

Atlantis (1913) 29, 55, 76, 175, 271, 488, 587

Atop of the World in Motion (1913) 523

Attack on a China Mission–Bluejackets to the Rescue (1900) 137, 695

Attack on a Mission Station (1900) 438

Au Congo 13

Au pays des lions (1912) 26

Au pays des ténèbras (1912) 251, 347

Au pays noir (1905) 248

L'auberge du bon repos (1903) 644

L'auberge ensorcelée (1897) 644

Aubert, Etablissements L. 40, 189, 254

Aubert, Louis 40, 41, 546

audiences 41–48; advertising 7; Altenloh 17; bourgeois 390; boxing films 81; Cambodia 91; Canada 98; France 255–7; Germany 46, 275–6; Great Britain 282, 283, 284; intertitles 328, 329; Ireland 333; modernity 440, 441; music halls 459–60; New Zealand 473; nickelodeons 479; Oceania/South Pacific 487; program formats 534, 535; Quebec 102; reception 323; regulation 375, 377; rise in ticket prices 455; Russia 557–8; Sweden 618; *Tonbilder* 635; travelogues 642; United States 368, 665–6; women 698, 701; *see also* spectatorship

Auf dem Paradeplatz in Luxemburg am Sonntagmittag (1902) 400

Die Augen des Ole Brandis (1914) 55

Auld Lang Syne (1911) 456, 680

Auler, William 48–9, 83, 158, 241, 584

Aunt Sallie's Wonderful Bustle (1901) 156

Aura o las violetas (1923) 136, 183

Aurora Cinema 49

Aus dem Kriegsleben in Süd-Westafrika 14

Australasian Films 49, 50, 51, 298, 348, 502, 554, 604, 689

Australasian Gazette 50

Australia 49–51

Australian Life Biograph 50

Austro-Hungary 51–4, 227

authentication 37, 54–5

L'Auto grise (1912) 258

Autorenfilme 55–6, 60, 61, 76, 165; Delmont 170; Denmark 175; Duskes 195; Ewers 223; Germany 271, 273; Hofer 302; Mack 404; Nordisk 483; Reinhardt 548; Rye 560; set design 586–7; Vitascope 681; von Woringen 682; Wegener 687

Autoscope Company 59–60

Autour d'une cabine 552

avante-garde artists 46, 440, 497

The Avenging Conscience (1914) 289, 412, 465

Aventure sur la plage d'Ostende (1904) 64, 65

Les aventures de Don Quichotte de la Manche (1903) 577

Les aventures de Robinson Crusoé (1902) 419

Avery, Jack 685

Aviation Week (1912) 610

Axelrod, Natan 499

Axt, William 464

Aylott, Dave 460

Ayres, Sydney 20

Azaria, Pierre 267

Azcue, Eusebio 159

al-Azhar al-mumita (1918) 216

Azzuri, Paulo 589

Babin, Gustave 644–5

Babson, Herman 449

Babushka russkoi revoliutsii (1917) 193

Babylas series 146

A Baby's Shoe (1909) 607

Bacigalupi, Peter 484

Bacio della Zingara (1913) 17

Back to God's Country (1919) 591

Bad Boy and Poor Old Grandpa (1897) 656
The Bad Boy's Joke on the Nurse (1901) 143
Baden verboten (1906–1907) 564
Badet, Regina 87
Baga, Ena 241
Bagarre entre journalists (1899) 606
Baggot, King 57, 312, 650
Bagni di Diana (1896) 335
Baharotis, Kostas 287
Bailly, Vincent de Paul 411
Le Bain des dames de la cour (1904) 525, 709
Le Bain d'une mondaine (1895) 349
Baird, Dorthea 631
Le Baiser de Judas (1909) 91, 237
Bajo el cielo antioqueño (1925) 136
Baker, F. W. 88
Bakshy, Alexander 57
Balaban, A. J. 57, 122, 312, 354, 498
Balaban, Barney 57, 122, 354
Balagny, Georges 107
Balaoo (1913) 25, 158, 347
Balász, Belá 481, 624
Balettprimadonnan (1916) 612
Balkans, the 58, 223, 646
Balshofer, Fred J. 58–9, 87, 316, 437, 472
Bamforth 59, 387
Bandarli, 'Aziz 216
Los bandidos de Sierra Morena (1911–1912) 161
Il bandito nero (1908) 31
De Banneling (1912) 482
Banvard, John 188
Bara, Theda 156
Baracchi, Nilde 225
La Baraja de la Muerte (1916) 114
Barattolo, Giovanni 337
Barbe bleu (1900) 206, 207
Barcelona y sus misterios (1916) 299, 414
Barcinógrafo 59, 290, 599
Barcus, James S. 449–50
Baree, Son of Kazan (1917) 26
The Bargain (1914) 295
Bargain Day (1903) 177
Bargain Fiend, or Shopping a la Mode (1907) 177
Barker Motion Photography 59, 60, 284, 595
Barker, Reginald 295
Barker, Robert 188
Barker, William George 59–60, 589, 595, 685
Barnes, John 133, 477
Barnes, William 133

Barney Oldfield's Race for a Life (1913) 640
Barnstijn, Loet C. 470
Barnum, P. T. 187, 672
Baron, Auguste 60
Baron, F.-A. 195
Barré, Raoul 28
Barrymore, John 165
Barrymore, Lionel 72
Barthes, Roland 42, 601
Bartling, Georg 60
Barua, P. C. 264
Bassermann, Albert 55, 60, 404, 548, 627, 681, 687
Bataille, Lucien 194, 199, 444
Battle of Bunker Hill (1911) 300
The Battle of Elderbush Gulch (1913) 586
The Battle of Gettysburg (1913) 300, 316, 465, 472, 631
The Battle of Manilla (1913) 315
The Battle of San Jan Hill (Universal, 1913) 315
The Battle of San Juan Hill (Edison, 1899) 315
Battle of the Somme (1916) 417, 704
The Battle of Waterloo (1913) 84, 284–5
Baucus, Joseph D. 359, 411, 685
Baudelaire, Charles 383
Baudry, Jean-Louis 601
Bauer, Evgenii 60–1, 109, 357, 447, 505, 558; camera movement 92, 94; dances 164; domestic melodrama 423; framing 248; Kuleshov 558; set design 587; staging in depth 607
Baumann, Charles O. 59, 61, 316, 317, 355–6, 371, 447, 464, 472, 473, 549, 649
Bay, Maria 147
Bayley, Laura 460, 595
Bayne, Beverly 87, 220
Bayyumi, Muhammad 217
Bazar de la Charité disaster 256, 257, 349
Bazin, André 248, 519
BBFC *see* British Board of Film Censors
Beal, Frank 20, 180, 196
Beatrice Cenci (1909) 105
Beaufort, Douglas 540
Bébé series (1910–1912) 104, 146–7, 235, 415, 530
Bébé adopte un petit frère (1912) 415, 530
Bébé n'aime pas sa concierge (1913) 415
Becce, Giuseppe 61, 463
Becerril, Guillermo 62

Bedding, Thomas G. 62, 451
Beery, Wallace 148
Begum, Fatma 362
Belasco, David 171, 288, 490, 520, 586
Belge Cinema SA, La 62, 64, 254, 364, 403
Belgium 62–5; colonial films 136, 137; colonies
    in Africa 11; consumer cooperatives 152;
    labor movement 366
Bell & Howell studio camera 65, 97
Bell, Alexander Graham 484
Bell, Chichester 517
Bell, Donald 604
La Belle au bois dormant (1902) 482
La belle cuisinière 518
La Belle-mère (1914) 512
The Bells (1871) 631
Bellwald, Jacques-Marie 399–400
Belot, Charles 63, 64, 65
Ben Dov, Yaakov 498–9
Ben-Hur (1926) 87
Ben-Hur (Kalem, 1907) 154, 295, 353, 374, 488
Ben-Hur (play, 1899) 631
Bendon, Prince 572
Benett-Stanford, John Montague 12, 18, 685
Benetti, Olga 582
Bengal Partition Movement (1905) 404
Benitez quiere ser torero (1910) 161
Benjamin, Walter 42, 383, 439, 440
Bennell, J. J. 572
Benner, Alex 295, 470
Bennett, Colin N. 358
Benoît-Lévy, Edmond 65–6, 80, 170, 194,
    236, 507, 516
Benoît-Lévy, Jean 66, 244
benshi 66–7, 134, 345, 346, 363, 379, 624, 634
Benson, E. F. 378
Benson, Frank 588, 589
Bentley, Thomas 296
Berg, Gustaf 362, 618
Berger, Grete 55
Berger, Henning 449, 450
Bergfilm 298
Bergführer Lorenz (1917) 620
Bergman, Bo 449
Bergman, Hjalmar 449
Bergman, Ingmar 592
Bergqvist, John 67, 615
Berliner, Emile 517
Die Berliner Range (1913) 687

Bernard, Alexandre 333
Bernard, Ferdinand "Bon" 67, 430, 677
Bernède, Arthur 235
Bernhardinerhunde (1916) 688
Bernhardt, Sarah 67, 250–1, 300, 428, 489,
    516, 543; Famous Players 229; Film d'Art 236,
    237, 608, 627; legitimate theater 626, 660;
    Shakespeare films 589
Berst, Jacques A. 67, 503
Bertho, Paul 199, 250
Berthon, 620
Bertin, Emile 626
Bertini, Francesca 68, 135, 156, 229, 277, 340,
    468, 608–9, 627; Cines 128; Cuba 160;
    De Liguoro 166; De Riso 167; diva films 339;
    erotic melodrama 426; fashion 230; Film
    d'Arte Italiana 238, 608; multiple-reel films 3,
    454; Oxilia 491; Roberti 552; Russia 559;
    Serena 582; Shakespeare films 392, 589;
    Wolf 696
Bertolini, Francesco 337–8, 436
Besley, Captain 223–4
Besnier, Alfred 267
El beso de la muerte 59
Betrayed by a Handprint (1908) 179
Bettini brothers 279
Betty of Greystone (1916) 196
Betz, Georg 429
Betzwood Film Company 394
Beynon, George W. 463
Bhakta Vidur (1921) 362
Bhatavdekar, Harishchandra Sakharam 68,
    318, 581
Bhavnani, Mohan 362
Bhishma Pratigya (1921) 677
Bianchi, Joseph 68
La Bibbia (1913) 31
biblical films 68–71, 126, 300, 327; Andréani 24;
    Capellani 103; churches 120; Gaumont 266;
    India 465, 514; multiple-reel films 453;
    painting 494; Palestine 498; *see also* Passion
    plays; religious films
Bibliothèque nationale 579
La Biche au bois (1896) 244, 268
"A Bicycle Tour Through
    Europe" (1897) 307
Bidamant, Yves 123
Bidel, François 63
Bidwell, George 278

Biegaski, Wiktor 523
Bienz, Eduard 620
Big Game Hunting in the North Pole Icefields (1913) 523
The Big Swallow (1901) 695
Bigorno series (1912–1914) 79, 150
Bijou Theater (Boston) 131, 480
Bilet Pherat (1921) 264, 319
Bilwamangal (1919) 404
Binger, Maurits Herman 71, 79, 303, 470
"biógrafos" 77
Biograph 4, 15, 16, 21, 63, 71–2, 202, 373, 441, 472, 657; 70mm camera 71, 72–3, 74; 70mm projector 73, 74, 182, 524, 562–3; animation 27; archives 680; Bedding reviews 62; Bitzer 74; Cabanne 89; Canada 98; comedies 144; detective films 179; Dwan 196; editing techniques 208, 211, 213; *film d'art* 236; film festivals 241; Finch 242; Gish 279; Griffith 288, 289; IMP 312; Ince 316; Johnson 348; Kennedy 355; Klaw & Erlanger 360, 628; Kleine 361; labor movement 368; Lawrence 377; Leonard 383; McCutcheon 417; Mace 403; Moore 446; Normand 483; Olcott 488; Pathé-Frères 507; Pickford 412, 520; Portugal 528; Reliance 549; religious films 69; Sennett 582; sensational melodrama 425; sound effects 596; South Africa 599; staging in depth 605; star system 609; Sterling 611; Sweden 616; Sweet 619; theater, melodrama 631; trade marks 636; US patent wars, 196, 654–5; Walthall 684; westerns 690; Williams 694; Woods 702; *see also* American Mutoscope and Biograph
Biokam 18
Biorama 73, 174
The Bioscope (journal) 73–4, 625, 637
Bioscope camera: urban 73
Bioscope Company of Canada 73, 98–9
Bioscope projector: Darling 164, 651, 685; Demenÿ 170; Urban 651, 685; Warwick 297, 546–7, 651; 685; *see also* American Bioscope
Bioskop projector (Skladansky) 172, 191, 270, 460, 593
Bird's Custard Powder 9
Biribi 123
The Birth of a Flower (1910) 594

The Birth of a Nation (1915) 74, 132, 279, 289, 299, 300, 301, 348, 465, 501; Aitken 16; costumes 156; distribution in the United States 660–1; musical score 462, 463, 464; National Board of Censorship 667–8; racism 301, 545, 599; Walthall 684
Birtles, Francis 50, 223
Bismarck (1913–1914) 640
Bison 15, 59, 61, 355, 472, 543
Bison-101 213, 244, 300, 316, 317, 355, 473, 690
Bitzer, Wilhelm ("Billy") 27, 74, 99, 186, 289, 314, 410, 414, 605
Blaché, Herbert 265, 291, 595, 596
Black, Alexander 112, 307
black audiences 47, 48
black cinema 74–5, 245, 349, 381, 545
Black Diamond Express (1895) 92, 638
Black Diamonds or the Collier's Daily Life (1904) 438
The Black Hand (1906) 180, 427
Blackburn Market on a Saturday Afternoon (1897) 438
Blackburn Rovers vs. West Bromwich Albion (1898) 113
Blacksmithing Scene (1893) 358
Blackton, the Evening World Cartoonist (1896) 75
Blackton, J. Stuart 75–6, 150, 410, 417, 553, 575, 594; animation 27, 28, 29; Edison against 201; *Motion Picture Story Magazine* 75, 609; trick films 644; Vitagraph 679, 680
Blackwell, Carlyle 353
Blair Camera Company 76, 106, 107, 197, 198, 428
Blair Camera Company, European 76, 96, 107, 502
Blair, Thomas Henry 76
Blanket Tossing a New Recruit (1898) 314
Bläser, Ivan 227, 400
Blatch, Harriot Stanton 700
Die blaue Maus (1913) 404
Blazing the Trail (1912) 213
Blechynden, Frederick W. 201
Blom, August 29, 76, 175, 483, 488, 585, 587
Blood and Bosh (1913) 624
Bloomfield, Albert 84
"Blue Laws" 120
Bluebeard (1901) 27
Bluebird films 362
Blumen Arrangement (1898) 211

Blütenpracht (1915) 688
Boarding School Girls (1905) 22, 94
Boaro, Giuseppe 335
Boccioni, Umberto 497
Boersma, Feiko 471
Boggs, Francis 76–7, 580
La Bohème (1896) 496
Boireau a mangé de l'ail (1908) 169
Boireau series 144, 145, 169, 265, 298, 482, 507
Bois, Curt 147
Boitler, Arkadi 147
Bold Bank Robbery (1904) 247
Le Boléro cosmopolite 192
Bolivia 77
Bolten-Baeckers, Heinrich 55, 78, 195, 271, 278, 426, 452
Bombardment of Taku Forts (1900) 547
Bonifacio (1912–1913) 436
Bonine, Robert Kates 78, 487, 523
Bonnard, Mario 78, 106, 280
The Book of Nature (1914) 572
Bool, W. 523
Booth, Walter 109, 510
Bopp du Pont, Maxime 487
Borelli, Lyda 78, 106, 167, 280, 338, 339, 543, 606, 608–9; 627; Cines 128; domestic melodrama 421, 422; erotic melodrama 426; fashion 230; Mexico 431; multiple-reel films 3, 454; Novelli 485; Oxilia 491; Russia 559
Borges, Juan 654
Borgnetto, Romano 333, 338
Boris Godunov (1907) 489
Borthwick, Jessica 58
Boruss, Geo 523
Bos, Annie 71, 79, 303, 471, 609
Bose, Anadi Nath 49
Bosetti, Roméo 27, 79, 146, 150, 194, 251, 266, 291, 431, 460
Bosnia 58
Le Bossu (1913) 40, 252, 298, 393
Bosworth, Hobart 77, 79
Botelho, Alberto Mâncio 79, 82, 584
La bous-bous mées (1909) 144, 163
Bouclette (1918) 428
Bouly, Léon 33, 34
Bourbon, Ernest 79–80, 143, 146, 169, 194, 250, 431
Bourchier, Arthur 589
Bourdieu, Pierre 42

Bourgeois, Gérard 80, 250, 399, 508, 569
Bourgeois, Jeanne-Marie *see* Mistinguett
"bourgeoisification" thesis 42–3
Bout-de-Zan series (1912–1916) 147, 235, 415, 530
Boutillon, Edmond 80
Bouton, Charles Marie 188
Bouwmeester, Louis 303
Bouwmeester, Theo *see* Frenkel, Theo
Bovy, Berthe 103, 626
Bower, B. M. 449, 450
Box Office Attractions 457
boxing films 5, 71, 74, 80–2, 155, 348, 604–5; censorship 468, 667; Clune 132; dime museums 187; Germany 273; itinerant exhibitors 341; Kinetoscope Exhibition Company 359; Latham brothers 372; program formats 533; re-enactments 548; Spencer 604; Wales 683; *see also* sports films
The Boy the Bust and the Bath (1906) 208
The Boy Detective (1908) 179
Bracco, Roberto 340, 414
Bracconot, Henri 106
Brackett, Robert 132
Bradford, F. Guy 73
Brady, William Aloysius 82, 155, 293, 497, 702
Brahm, Otto 60
Branding Cattle (1898) 689
Brandt, Aage 73
Bray, John Randolph 28–9, 150
Brazil 82–4
Breil, Joseph Carl 462, 463, 464
Bréon, Edmond 530
Bressol, Pierre 198
Breteau 84
Brewster, Ben 421–2
Brewster, David 610
Brewster's Millions (1914) 171
Brézillon, Léon 84
Bridgwood, Florence Annie *see* Lawrence, Florence
Brigadier Gerard (1915) 59
Brigandage moderne (1905) 158
Brighton Conference (1978) xxx, 37, 241, 379
The 'Brighton School' 164, 595
Brignon Cinema 91
Brignone, Mercedes 436
Britain Prepared (1915) 651
British & Colonial Kinematograph Company 84–5, 223, 284–5, 417
British Board of Film Censors (BBFC) 60, 283–4

British Co-operative Cinematograph Company 588
British Dominion Films 264
British Gaumont 85, 135, 265, 282, 293, 460, 589
British Journal of Photography 62
British Mutoscope & Biograph 20, 21, 85, 324, 417, 474; *actualités* 6; program formats 533–4; Shakespeare films 588; theater, melodrama 629; trade marks 636; Wales 683–4
British South Africa Company 12
Briton vs Boer (1900) 243
Brittanicus (1912) 167
Broca, Auguste 567
Broken Blossoms (1919) 279
The Broken Coin (1915) 180, 245
Bromhead, Alfred 85, 282
Broncho 300, 316, 355, 473
Broncho Billy series 23, 24, 220
Broncho Billy and the Baby (1909) 220
Broncho Billy's Christmas Dinner (1911) 24
Broncho Billy's Narrow Escape (1912) 24
Brooke, Van Dyke 607, 680
Brooks, Peter 421
Brown, Charles 203
Brown, Clarence 350
Brown, Theodore 18, 85, 279, 357, 358
Brownlow, Kevin 134, 536
La Broyeuse des coeurs (1913) 251, 508
El brujo desapareciendo (1898) 105, 159, 185
Brulatour, Jules E. 85, 371
Une Brute humaine (1913) 167, 671
Bruto (Brutus) (1911) 127, 290
Bruxelles-Scies-Némas (1907) 64
Bucking Broncho (1894) 132, 689
Buckland, Wilfred 171, 386, 586
Buckwalter, Harry H. 85–6, 580
Buell, Kenean 353
Buffalo Bill (1894) 132
Buffalo Bill Cody's Visit to Rhyl (1903) 113
Buffalo Bill's Wild West Parade (1902) 132
Buffalo Dance (1894) 132, 689
Bulgaria 58
Bull, Lucien 33, 86, 119, 482, 566, 568
Bullock, William 479
Bumptious series (1910–1911) 147
Bunny, John 86, 144, 148, 242, 391, 483, 680
Bunny series 148
Buñuel, Luis 444

Bünzli, Henri René 86, 127, 154, 290, 502, 506, 508–9; glass-plate projectors 279; Pathé-Frères 502, 506, 508–9, 510
Burch, Noël 42, 46, 93, 125, 206, 379, 602
Burguet, Charles 87, 252
Burial of the Maine Victims (1898) 159
Burlesque on Romeo and Juliet (1902) 589
Bürli, Georg 14
Burlingham, Frederick 87, 223, 620
The Burning of Joan of Arc (1895) 495
Burns, Bobby 148
Burns, Lou 156
Burroughs, Edgar Rice 451
Busch, Wilhelm 148
Bush, Pauline 20, 196
Bush, W. Stephen 87, 451, 597, 693
Bushman, Francis X. 87, 220
A Busy Day (a.k.a. *A Militant Suffragist*) (1914) 701
A Busy Day for the Corset Models (1904) 177
The Butler (1913) 75
Buy Your Own Cherries (1905) 569

A cabana do Pai Tomás (1909) 83
Cabanne, W. Christy 89
Los cabellos blancos (1914) 290
Cabiria staging in depth (1914) 17, 299, 333–4, 338, 339, 454, 703; camera movement 92, 94; Chomón 117; intertitles 329; Japan 362; marketing strategy 164; musical score 463; Pagano 493; Pastrone 501; set design 586; staging 607
Cabourn, John 73
Il cadavere vivente (1913) 469
La Caduta di Troia (The Fall of Troy) (1910) 299, 333, 338, 501, 586, 661
Caesar Film 166, 337, 339, 552, 582
cafés-concerts 89–90, 253, 257; Frau 259; Froissart 261; Gaumont 266; Italy 335; Pathé-Frères 506; program formats 533; Zecca 709
Cagliostro (1910) 676
Caillard, Adrien 565
Cajus Julius Caesar (1914) 127, 290
Cake Walk (1903) 182
Cake-Walk Infernal (1903) 163
Le Cakewalk chez les nains (1903) 645
Calcina, Vittorio 90–1, 334–5

Calino series 79, 194, 431, 444

Calkins, Earnest Elmo 8

Called Back (1911) 50

Calmettes, André 91, 236, 237

La Calomnie (1913) 167

Calvario (1911) 500

Calvo, Máximo 136

Cambodia 91–2

camera movement 92–5, 248, 611; Bauer 61; *Cabiria* 299; diva films 3; Germany 271; Hale's Tours 294; Pathé-Frères 507; editing: spatial relations 207; Svenska Biografteatern 614; travelogues 641, 643

camera obscura 32, 35

"cameraman" system of production 442

Cameraman's Revenge (1912) 610

Cameraphone 620

cameras 95–7, 519; Acres model 2, 18; Aeroscope 10–11, 355, 474, 685; animation 26; Anschütz 30, 95; authentication 55; Baron 60; Bell & Howell 65, 97; Bianchi 68; Biograph 71, 72–3, 74; Biokam 18; Bioscope 73; Blair Camera Company 76, 96, 106, 107, 197, 428; Bünzli 86; Continsouza 154; Darling 164–5; de Bedts 166; Debrie "Parvo" 96, 168; Demenÿ 170–1; Dickson 186; Donisthorpe 191; English pattern 219; Ernemann 14, 18, 96; fast-motion 86, 482, 568; Gaumont 118; Hepworth 18; Junior Prestwich 18; Konishi Photographic Store 363–4; Lenses 246–8; Le Prince 378; Lux 399; "Maltese cross" 86, 96; Marey 33, 95, 413; Mendel 427; Messter 429, 430; Newman & Sinclair Reflex 10, 97, 474; Parnaland 499; Pathé- Frères 168, 506, 508–9; Paul 510; Prószynski 541; Schneider 566; US patent wars 654–5; Williamson 695; Wrench 684; *see also* Celluloid; Cinématographe Lumière; Edison Kinetograph camera; Edison Kinetoscope; photography; projectors

Cameroon 13

Camille Desmoulins (1911) 529

Caminos de la venganza (1922) 513–14

Campbell, Colin 694

Campbell, James Pinkerton 50

Campos, Antônio 83, 97

Canada 97–100; lecturers 379–80; Quebec 97, 100–3

Cannock, Frank 591

Canudo, Ricciotto 103, 336

Capellani, Albert 3, 103–4, 158, 178, 208, 233, 236, 249, 250, 366, 671; domestic melodrama 506; lighting 386; multiple-reel films 453–4, 508; Napierkowska 467; SCAGL 565

Capellani, Paul 103, 104

Capellaro, Vittorio 97

Capelli, Dante 589

Le capitaine Rascasse (1927) 294

monopoly capitalism 368; advertising 7; leisure time and space 380–3, 382; USA 444–6; world's fairs 704

El capitán mambi o los libertadores y guerilleros (1914) 185, 563

Capozzi, Alberto 19, 104, 500

Caprice (1913) 447

Capriles, Jacobo 676

Captain Macklin (1915) 156

Carbutt, John 197

Cardini, Eugenio 38

Un careca (1899) 580

A Career in Crime (1902) 178

Carl, Renée 104–5, 235, 266

Carleton, LeRoy 184

Carli, 'Flip' 320

Carlisle, Wilson 120, 549

Carlitos y Tripín de Buenos Aires a Montevideo (1918) 654

Carmen (1915) 171, 490

Carmen o la hija del bandido (1911) 299

Carmen van het noorden (1919) 79

Carnaval en Curityba (1910) 551

O Carnaval na Avenida Central (1906) 580

Carnegie Museum Expedition film 523

Carney, Augustus 147–8, 220

Caro, Adrien 123

Carpenter, Philip 406

Carpentier, Jules 105, 127, 166, 267, 268, 398, 510

Carré, Albert 553

Carré, André 58

Carré, Benjamin 199

Carré, Michel 103, 105, 236, 565

Una carrera de ciclismo en el Velódromo de Arroyo Seco (1898) 654

Carter, Sydney 347

Carter, William 121

cartoonists 26–7, 28, 150

Caruso, Enrico 182, 490

Carvallo, Joachim-Léon 566, 568

CASA *see* Club des amis du septième art

Casa Lepage 38, 280, 544

Casasús, José 105, 159, 185

Caserini, Mario 40, 78, 105–6, 127, 279, 338, 491, 606

Caserini-Gasperini, Maria 127

Cash, Edward 550

Casimir series (1913–1914) 199

Casino de Paris 20

Casler, Herman 21, 73, 96, 360, 655

Cass, Godfrey 389

Cast Ashore 525

Castillo, Luis G. 77

Castle, Irene 164

Castle, Vernon 164

The Cat and the Canary (1927) 242

La Catedral de Lima (1899) 513

Caught in a Cabaret (1914) 108, 483

Cavalieri, Lina 490

Cawood, Albert E. 523

Cazzulino, Domenico 279

Un célebre especialista sacando muelas en el Grand Hotel (1897) 676

Célerier, Émile 237

celluloid 15, 96, 106–7, 119, 238; animation 29; Anschütz 31, 95; Blair Camera Company 76; Eastman Kodak 197, 198; Edison Kinetograph 200, 203; intermittent movements 325; Kinetoscope 358, 519; Lumière 398, 519; Marey 33, 413; Pathé-Frères 506; Phantoscope 515

Cendrillon (1899) 155, 205, 231, 249

Cenere (1916) 19, 194

censorship 43, 134, 375, 468; Austro-Hungary 53, 54; boxing films 81, 348, 605; Bush 87; Cambodia 91–2; Canada 99, 102–3; Colombia 135; crime films 158; Denmark 172, 173–4; Egypt 216; Finland 243; France 258; Germany 276–7, 688; Great Britain 283–4; Hoder 302; India 319; Indonesia 320; Italy 338; Japan 345–6; Malaya 413; Norway 484; Oceania/South Pacific 487; Philippines 516; Russia 559; Spain 600; Sweden 361, 592; United States 666–8; white slave films 693; *see also* National Board of Censorship; regulation

Les cent trucs (1906) 116

Centaur/Nestor 108, 304, 649

Central America xxix, 30

"central producer" system of production 442, 443

Ceram, 35

Cerf, Camille 62, 469

Ceylan, vécu et pittoresque (1905) 642

Chaliapin, Feodor 490

Chalmers, J. P. 451

Chaney, Lon 196

Chaplin, Charles 108–9, 142, 144, 148, 460, 520; AGC 15; archives 36; costumes 156–7; dances 164; Essanay 220; Linder 390; Mutual 465; Turpin 647; women's suffrage films 701

Chapman, Frank M. 521, 571

Chapuis, André *see* Deed, André

Chapuis, Pierre 334

Charcuterie mécanique (1895) 584

Chardynin, Petr 109, 357, 426, 558

Charles, Louis 410, 418, 551

Charles Urban Trading Company (CUTC) 12, 25, 62, 73, 109–10, 651; Canada 98; colonial films 137; Darling 164; Eclipse 199; France 250; Frenkel 259; Great Britain 282; Haggar 293; Khanzhonkov & Co. 356; Mesguich 429; news event films 475; Quebec 101; Switzerland 619; travelogues 642; Wales 684; *see also* Urban, Charles

chase films 2, 110–12, 128; AM&B 21; amusement parks 22; animal pictures 25; Arnaud 39; Bitzer 74; British Gaumont 85; Chaplin 108; Collins 135; comedy 142, 143; comic series 145; crime films 157; detective films 178; editing techniques 206, 207–8, 210, 212; Fitzhamon 244; France 249; Gaumont 265–6; Griffith 288; Haggar 293; Hepworth 296; Heuzé 298; Japan 345; Lubin 396; McCutcheon 417; Pathé-Frères 506; staging in depth 606; United States 656

Chase, Walter Greenough 570

Chasse au marabout en abyssinie (1911) 403

Chasse au tigre dans la province de Nam Dihn, Tonkin (1913) 138

Le Chat botté (1903) 80

Chautard, Emile 104, 112, 198, 199, 636

Chautauqua 112–13, 119, 533, 553, 665

Dem chazons tochter (1913) 364

The Cheat (1915) 171, 386

Cheetham, Arthur 113, 683

Chegada do Dr. Campos Salles a Petrópolis (1898) 580

Chekhov, Anton 422
Cher, John 74
A Chess Dispute (1903) 246
Le Cheval emballé (1908) 265, 507
Le chevalier mystère (1899) 205
Chevenay, Julio 114
Chevroton, Lucienne 567, 568
Chew Chew Land (1910) 10, 461
Chez le magnétiseur (1898) 84
Chiba Yoshizo 199–200, 345
Chicago Film Exchange 113
Les chiens contrebandiers (1906) 158, 213, 296
children: Germany 275, 276; nickelodeon
    audiences 43, 45, 46, 479, 665, 666, 667;
    Russia 558; United States 665, 666, 667
Children of the Age (Deti veka) (1915) 61, 357
Children Who Labor (1912) 368, 540
Chile 113–15
China 115–16; Indonesia 320; religious
    filmmaking 550; shadow theater 115, 587
Chinese Laundry Scene (1894) 584
Chomón, Segundo de 116–17, 233, 249, 599, 600;
    animation 26, 27, 28, 29; Itala 333, 501;
    "Panoramic Views" (1901) 414; trick films 27,
    94, 644
Christensen, Benjamin 29, 61, 117, 164, 175,
    386, 607
The Christian (1914) 613
Christianity 549–50, 631
Christie, A. L. 108, 304
Christophe Colomb (Bourgeois, 1919) 80
Christophe Colomb (Pathé-Frères, 1903–1904) 299
Christopher Colombus (1912) 299
Christus (1916) 292
Chronochrome Gaumont 117, 141, 198, 531
Chronophone Gaumont 118, 192, 265, 291,
    429, 620–1
chronophotography 32, 33–4, 95, 118–19, 439;
    Anschütz 30; de Bedts 166; Demenÿ 170;
    Duncan 194; intermediality and modes of
    reception 324; Marey 413, 566; Parnaland 499;
    sports films 604
Chulalonghorn, King of Siam (Thailand) 625
Church and Country: An Episode of the Winter at
    Valley Forge (1912) 300
churches 119–21; Canada 98, 102–3;
    Howe 305; itinerant exhibitors 341, 659;
    United States 659, 664, 665
Il Cid (1910) 386

El ciego de la aldea (1906) 161
Cine Colombia 136
Ciné Multiphone Rousselot 598
Cine Parvus 91
Cine-Fono e la Rivista Fono-Cinematografica, La 121,
    336, 637–8
Ciné-Journal 121, 157, 194, 254, 347, 419, 518,
    543, 578, 637
cinema of attractions 7, 9, 70, 110, 124–7, 128,
    626; China 116; comedy 143; editing: spatial
    relations 206; féeries 232; framing 246; Hofer
    302; modernity 440; projectionists 211, 536;
    spectatorship 602; trick films 644; Vietnam 678;
    wax museums 686
cinema circuits or chains 121–3, 173, 176; Atelier
    Apollo 39; Balaban 57; Fox 245–6; Loew 392;
    Luxemburg 400; Lyyra filmi 400; Mastbaum
    brothers 415, 665; Norway 484–5; Pathé-Frères
    507; Ramos 546; Raymond Animated Picture
    Company 547; Saxe 564–5; Shepard 590
Cinéma du peuple, Le 123, 153, 366–7, 540
Cinéma et l'Écho du cinéma réunis, Le 123, 638
The Cinema (journal) 73
Le Cinéma (journal) 393
Cinéma-Halls, Compagnie des 15, 123–4, 237,
    371, 632
Cinemacrophonograph 620
cinemas see cinema circuits or chains;
    nickelodeons; palace cinemas
cinemateca 36
cinémathèque 36, 37
Cinémathèque française 133, 134
cinematograph definition 34
Le Cinématographe des Colonies 11, 137
Cinématographe Lumière 16, 21, 95–6, 127, 239,
    249, 252, 291, 397, 398, 522, 538, 539;
    actualités 5; amateur film 17–18; Austro-Hungary
    51; Belgium 62; Bünzli 86; Canada 98; Cardini
    38; Carpentier 105, 267; Chile 113; Clément-
    Maurice 131; Cuba 105, 159; Doublier 191;
    editing techniques 204; Egypt 215–16; Finland
    242; France 255–6, 257; Fregoli 259; Germany
    270, 272, 273; Great Britain 510; India 318;
    intermediality and modes of reception 324, 325;
    intermittent movements 325; Isola 333; Italy
    334, 335; Ivens 342; Japan 343, 708; Lavanchy-
    Clarke 373; magic lanterns 405; magicians 410;
    Méliès 418; Mexico 67, 430; Minier 437; music
    halls 460; Netherlands 469; news event films 474;

Peru 513; Philippines 515; photography 519; Poland 522; Poli 524; projectionists 535; Raymond 546; re-enactments 547; Redfern 547; scientific films: Europe 566; Seeber 579; shadow theater 588; South Africa 598; Spain 599; Stollwerck 612; Switzerland 619; Toscano 635; trade marks 636; Turkey 646; United States 659, 662–3; Uruguay 654; vaudeville 673; Vietnam 678; Wales 683; Yoshizawa Shoten 708

La Cinématographie des microbes (1910) 567

Cinematophone 684

Cinéorama 93, 639

Cinephone 620

Cines 15, 16, 19, 68, 127–8, 333; Aubert 40; Belgium 64; Borelli 78; Caserini 105; colonial films 137; comic series 147, 225, 259, 336–7; costumes 156; dances 163; Ghione 277; Guazzoni 290; Guillaume 290, 500; Gys 292; historical films 299; Italy 336, 337, 338; lighting 386; Martoglio 414; Menichelli 428; Negroni 468; Oxilia 491; Rossi 555; Serena 582; set design 586; Shakespeare films 589; travelogues 642; Velle 676

Les Cinq Sous de Lavarède (1913) 40, 393

Le Cirque de la mort (1919) 620

Civilization (1916) 464

Claeys, Philippe 63

Clair, René 25, 108, 444

Clarendon Film Company 15, 85, 128, 588, 613

Claris, Edmond 578

Clark, Alfred 494–5

Clark, Marguerite 165, 229

Clark, May 296

Clark, Palmer 464

Clarke, Jack 353

classical Hollywood cinema xxix, 124, 128–31, 536, 643; editing techniques 206, 212; Hofer 302; Japan 346; lighting 386–7; mode of production 442; monopoly capitalism 445, 446; Paramount 661; spectatorship 46, 600, 602; Sweden 618

The Claudian (1883) 631

Clement, Josephine (Mrs Edward) 131

Clément-Maurice (Clément Maurice Gratioulet) 131, 192, 195, 489, 499, 516

Cleopatra (Gardner, 1912) 264, 456

Cleopatra (Gardner, 1918) 264

Cléopatre (Pathé-Frères, 1910) 163, 508

close-ups 125, 225–6, 609

Club Africain-Cercle d'Etudes Coloniales 11

Club des amis du septième art (CASA) 103

Clune, William H. 132

Cocciutelli (1911–1912) 436

Cochrane, Robert 312, 370

Cock Fight (1896) 25

Coco series 147

Codina, J. M. 161, 299, 414, 599, 600

Codman, John 683

Cody, William F. ("Buffalo Bill") 132, 200, 222, 315, 439, 689

Coeur de femme 384

Coeur de Gavroche (1916) 167

Le Coeur et l'argent (1912) 266

La Coeur n'a pas d'âge (1913) 552

Coghlan, Rose 589

Cohen Collects a Debt (1912) 472

Cohen's Fire Sale (1907) 527

Cohl (Courtet), Emile 27–8, 29, 132, 145, 150, 199, 266, 644

Cohn, Alfred 174

Cohn, George 619

Coil Winding Machines (1904) 218

Coissac, Guillaume-Michel 32, 132–3, 411, 549

Cole, Lewis 571

collections 133–4, 350; *see also* archives

The Colleen Bawn (1911) 354

College Chums (1907) 151, 527

Collier, John 134, 382

Collings, Esme 164

Collins, Alfred 85, 134–5, 460

Collins, John H. 203

Collins, Pat 282

Collo, Alberto 135, 485

Colombia 135–6, 183–4

Colonel Heeza Liar's African Hunt (1914) 29

Colonel Theodore Roosevelt's Expedition into the Wilds (1916) 307

colonialism: Europe 136–8, 217; Ireland 332; propaganda films 540, 541; Quebec 101; world's fairs 704; *see also* imperialism

color 138–41; animation 35; archives 37; Blackton 76; Chronochrome Gaumont 117; cinema of attractions 124; costumes 155; *féeries* 233; Gaumont 266, 267; Italian travelogues 340; newspapers 476; newsreels 478; Pathé-Frères 506; Pathécolor 505; postcards 528; preservation 531; stencil 54; travelogues 642; trick films 644; *see also* Kinemacolor

Colored Championship Base Ball Game 75
Comandon, Jean 141–2, 199, 567,
    568, 569, 571, 572
Come Along, Do (1898) 496, 510
Come Le Foglie (1916) 343
Comédie Française 3
comedies 142–5, 434; AM&B 21; Ambrosio 19;
    American Film Manufacturing Company 20;
    amusement parks 22; Aquila Films 31; Asia Film
    Co. 39; Bamforth 59; Bauer 61; Bitzer 74; black
    cinema 75, 245; Bolten-Baeckers 78; Bonnard 78;
    Bos 79; Cambodia 91; Capellani 103; Caserini
    106; Chile 114; China 115; Cines 127; Clarendon
    Film Company 128; Collins 135; costumes 156–7;
    department stores 177; detective films 180;
    Deutsche Mutoscope & Biograph 182; dialogue
    accompaniment 184; editing techniques 211,
    213; Fabre 225; Feuillade 235; France 249; Gas-
    nier 265; Gaumont 265; Germany 271; Gloria
    Films 280; Guy 291; Haggar 293; Hofer 302; IMP
    312; India 319; Iran 331; Italy 336–7, 339–40;
    itinerant exhibitors 342; Japan 345; Kalem 353;
    Keystone 356; Klercker 361–2; Larsen 372; Linder
    390; Lubin 394, 396; Mace 403; Mack 404; Mar-
    vin 414; Menichelli 428; Mitchell & Kenyon 438;
    Monca 444; Morano 447; Mosjoukine 447;
    Mullens brothers 452; Müller-Lincke 452;
    Netherlands 469; Nordisk 483; Normand 483;
    Norway 484; Paley 499; Paul 510; Perret 512; Peru
    513; Pickford 520; Porten 526; program formats
    641; Protazanov 541; Riche 552; Rodolfi 553;
    Roland 554; Russia 557, 558; Santos 563; Sargent
    564; SCAGL 565; Selig 32, 580; Sennett 72; set
    design 585; slapstick 126, 441; Smith 595; Stiller
    611; Sweden 616; Thailand 625; Trautschold
    640; trick films 644; Turpin 647; United States
    656; Venezuela 676; Vitascope 681; Vitrotti 681;
    Weisse 687; White (James Henry) 692; White
    (Pearl) 693; Wiener Kunstfilm 52; women's
    suffrage films 700, 701; World War I 703; *see also*
    comic series
Comerio Films 15, 145, 169, 435
Comerio, Luca 145, 336, 337
Comic Faces (1897) 143
comic series 145–8, 582; Ambrosio 19; Anderson 24;
    Aquila Films 31; Arbuckle 32; Blackton 75;
    Bosetti 79; Bourbon 79; Comica 150; Deed 169,
    501; Durand 194; Éclair 199; Fabre 225; Feuil-
    lade 235; Finch 242; Fitzhamon 244; France
    250; Gaumont 266, 431, 530; Grandais 281;
    Guillaume 290; Heuzé 298; Italy 336–7; Linder
    390; Mary 415; Milano Films 436; Mistinguett
    437; Monca 444; music hall 460; Nalpas 467;
    Nonguet 482; Pasquali 500; Pathé-Frères 507;
    Perret 512; Poyen 530; Prince 532; racialness
    434; Rodolfi 553; SCAGL 565; Taylor and
    White 624; *see also* comedies
comic strips 29, 142, 147, 148–50, 417, 440, 582;
    detective films 178; United States 656
Comica 79, 146, 150, 251
Comin' Thro' the Rye (1916) 296
Comin' Thro' the Rye (1923) 624
The Coming of Columbus (1912) 581
*Comme une lettre nous parvient des grands lacs de
    l'Afrique Centrale* (1911) 403
*Comment se fait le fromage de
    Holland* (1909) 320
Commercial Press Motion Picture Department
    116, 150
La Commune! Du 18 au 28 mars 1871 123, 366
communication technologies 150–2; modernity
    439; US imperialism 313; US monopoly
    capitalism 445
Compagnie Générale du Cinématographe 40
O comprador de ratos (1908) 379
Compson, John 147
Conan Doyle, Arthur 178, 179
La Concierge (1899) 291
Coney Island at Night (1905) 22
The Confederate Ironclad (1912) 463, 631
Confidence (1909) 4
Congo 11, 136, 137
Congrès International des Editeurs de Films
    (1909) 254
Congrès International des Exploitants du
    Cinématographe (Paris, 1912) 84
Conklin, Chester 108
Conscience (1912) 386
consumer cooperatives 152–3; *see also* labor
    movement: Europe
consumerism 382, 603
La contessa Sara (1919) 552
Continental-Kunstfilm 55, 153–4, 168, 270, 373,
    404, 437
Continsouza, Pierre-Victor 86, 96, 105, 127,
    154, 538; Grimoin-Sanson 290; glass-plate pro-
    jectors 279; Pathé-Frères 502, 506, 508–9, 510
La conversion du braconnier (1910) 400

Coolies à Saigon (1896) 678
Cooper, Arthur Melbourne 9, 17
Cooper, Miriam 353
"Cooper-Hewitts" 385, 388, 389
copyright 1, 65, 111, 154–5, 374, 548, 578, 636;
    Edison 201, 656; intertitles 327; Kalem 353;
    Lubin 396; Netherlands 696
Coquelin, Ernest 626
Il coraggio della paura (1911) 166
Corbett and Courtney before the Kinetograph (1894)
    80, 155, 604
Corbett, James J. 80, 81, 82, 155, 372, 604
The Corbett-Fitzsimmons Fight (1897) 81, 155, 341
Corbicier, M. 654
Cordero, Amábilis 677
Cordero, Pedro Pérez *see* Sienna, Pedro
A Corner in Wheat (1909) 72, 288, 421
The Coronation of King Peter of Serbia
    (1904) 590
Corra, Bruno 336
*Corrispondeza Cinematografica dal teatro della guerra
    italo turca* (1911–1912) 137
Il Corsaro (1923) 485
Cosmopolitan 104, 415
Cossacks of the Don 505
Costa, Júlio 528
Costello, Maurice 4, 155, 589, 680
costumes 155–7, 230, 586; biblical films
    70; cinema of attractions 124; *féeries* 233;
    Gardner 264; India 319; music hall 460;
    paintings 493; Williamson 695
Couade, Maurice 242
Le Coucher de la mariée (1896) 360, 522
Le Coucher de la parisienne (1904) 525
Couchie Dance on the Midway (1901) 705
The Count of Luxemburg (1909) 489
The Count of Monte Cristo (1912) 527
A Country Cattle Show (1899) 484
The Country Doctor (1910) 72, 74, 94, 288
Un Coup de vent (1907) 143, 212
Un Coup d'oeil par étage (1904) 208
La Coupable (1912) 422
A Couple in Trouble (1913) 115
Courrier cinématographique, Le 157, 244, 637
Le Courrier de Lyon (1911) 104, 158, 250, 300, 386,
    453–4, 508
La course à la perruque (1906) 145, 169, 298
La Course aux potirons (1908) 39, 145, 265–6
Courteline, Georges 154

Cousture et Carré 40
cowboy and Indian films *see* westerns
Cowboy Justice (1910) 692
The Cowboy and the Shrew (1911) 589
Cox, Frederick 550
Crafton, Don 143
Crahan, Thomas 523
Crane, Frank 102
Cranz, Carl 568
Crary, Jonathan 439
Crassé, Charles 58
Crawford, O. T. 479
Crawford Shoe Store (1897) 9
Crescent Film Company 59, 610
Cretinetti series 145, 147, 169, 225, 336, 501
The Cricket on the Hearth (1915) 57
Cricks & Martin 40, 223, 322
The Crime of Carelessness (1912) 369
O crime de Cravinhos (1919) 555
Le Crime de M. Lange (1936) 384
O crime dos banhados (1913) 563
Le Crime du Bouif (1921) 529
Le Crime du grand-père (1910) 512
crime films 151, 157–9, 179; Andreyor 24; Andriot
    25; Aquila Films 31; Auler 49; Bolten-Baeckers
    78; Brazil 83; Cuesta Valencia 161; Delmont
    170; Drankov 193; Éclair 543; Feuillade 235,
    425–6, 464, 468; Finland 243; France 251;
    Gaumont 266, 425–6; Gottschalk 281; India
    319; Itala 333; Italy 339; Leal 379; May 416;
    multiple-reel films 454; Pasquali 501; serials 582;
    Yermolíev 707; *see also* detective films
Os crimes de Diogo Alves 528
Crispijn, Louis Sr. 79, 303, 470–1
Cristiani, Quirino 38
Croatia 58
Crowd on St. Catherine Street (1901) 98
Cruickshank, George 494
La cruz de un angel (1929) 677
Cruze, James 625
The Cry of the Children 370
Cuba 159–60, 185; IMP 312; US imperialism 314
La Cuccagna (1917) 135
cue sheets 160–1
Cuesta Valencia 161, 599
A cultura do Cacau em Sao Tomé 528
cultural studies 42, 48
Cunard, Grace (Harriet Mildred Jeffries) 161,
    179, 180, 244, 650

The Cup (1881) 631
Cupid and the Comet (1911) 291
The Curtain Pole (1908) 147
Curtis, Edward 307
Curtiz, Michael 54
CUTC *see* Charles Urban Trading Company
Cymbeline (1913) 589
Cyrano de Bergerac 626
Die Czernowska (1913) 168

da Costa Veiga, Manuel Maria 528
d'Abruzzi, Duc 223
Dæmonen (1911) 291
Dagmar, Berthe 194
Dagover, Lil 271
Daguerre, Louis J. M. 32, 188, 519
Dalagang Bukid (1919) 516
d'Alcy, Jehanne 419
Dalrymple Henderson, Linda 439
Dalton, Sam 460
Dam, Albert 450
La dama de las cayenas (1913) 676
Damaged Goods (1915) 20
La Dame aux Camélias (1911) 67, 104, 237,
    251, 608, 626–7, 676
La Dame de Montsoreau (1913) 198
Dammann, Gerhard 153
Damonte, Isidoro 654
Dampier, Lily 554
Dan Duyu 116
Dança de um baiano (1899) 580
dance films 118, 163–4, 261
dance halls 380, 381, 382
Dania Biofilm 117, 164, 175
Daniel, Henri 123
D'Annunzio, Gabriele 78, 164, 329, 334, 339,
    436, 501, 525
Danse indienne (1898) 101
Dansk Biograf Kompagni 117, 164, 175
Dante's Inferno (1909) 87, 661
Darah dan Doa (1950) 320
A Daring Daylight Burglary (1903) 110, 151,
    157, 590
Darley, Felix 495
Darling, Alfred 96, 109, 164–5, 219, 594, 651,
    685, 705
Darrow, Clarence 369
Dary, René *see* Mary, Clément

A Dash for the North Pole (1908) 523
The Dashing Merchant (1909) 505
Dave, Mohanlal G. 502
Davesnes, Edouard 333
David, Adam 224
David Copperfield (Hepworth, 1913) 296
David Copperfield (Pathé-Frères, 1912) 509
David, Jean Louis 495
Davidsen, Hjalmar 175
Davidson, Paul 165, 270, 273, 480, 493, 608, 627
Davignon, A. 253
Davis, Harry 165, 187, 478, 479, 511
Davis, Michael 381
Davison, Emily 478
Davy, Humphrey 406
Dawley, J. Searle 165, 201, 203, 386, 527
Dawson, G. H. 684
Day Dreams (1915) 94
Day, William Ernest Lytton 32, 133, 134
The Days of '61 (1908) 631
de Albuquerque, Ernesto 528
de Baños, Ricardo 82, 299
de Barros, Luis 83, 165
de Bedts, George William 34, 76, 95, 96, 166,
    253, 333
de Broglie, Pauline 256
de Chapais, André *see* Deed, André
De France, Maurice 63
de Gastyne, Marco 468
De Grandsaignes d'Hauterives, Henry 101, 166
de Jongh, Florence 241
de Kempeneer, Hippolyte 64
de Kerstrat, Marie 101
De Liguoro, Giuseppe 166, 280, 337, 338, 436, 679
de Lorde, Alfred 158
de Maio, Vittorio 82
De Man, Henri 152
de Mille, Beatrice Samuel 171
de Mille, Henry C. 171
de Mille, William C. 171, 619
de Morlhon, Camille 138, 166–7, 251, 508,
    671, 676
De Riso, Camillo 19, 167, 340, 447
De Roberti, Lydia 500
De Windt, Harry 223
*The Dear Boys Home for the
    Holiday* (1903) 143
Death of Narayanrao Peshwa (1915) 502
The Death of Nathan Hale (1911) 300

Death's Marathon (1913) 289
Debrie, Andre 167–8, 539
Debrie, Joseph 167–8, 539
Debrie "Parvo" camera 96, 168
Les Débuts de Max au cinématographe
    (1910) 247
Decauville, Paul 516
Decaux, Léopold 268, 518
Décharge d'un revolver (1914) 86
Decla 271–2, 488
Decourcelle, Pierre 168, 236,
    290, 428, 565
Le Decouverte du Pôle Sud (1912) 524
Decroix, Charles 168, 182
Deed, André (Chapuis, André a.k.a. de Chapais,
    André) 168–9, 179, 225, 250, 460, 482, 507;
    comedy/comic series 142, 143, 145, 147;
    Itala 333, 336; Pastrone 501
Defender Film Company 614
Défilé de policemen 207
Le Déjeuner du savant (1905) 567
Del Colle, Ubaldo Maria 169,
    436, 469, 491, 500
del Diestro, Alfredo 136
Delac, Charles 15, 169–70, 237, 250, 467
Delacroix, Eugène 494
Délano, Jorge 114
Deledda, Grazia 679
Delhi Coronation Durbar (1912) 318, 582, 651
della Porta, Giambattista 32, 35
Delluc, Louis 176, 529
Delmont, Joseph 170, 182, 271, 426
Delvair, Jeanne 565
Demaria, Jules 170
Le déménagement (1908) 27
Demenÿ, Georges 29, 33, 95, 96,
    170–1, 334, 393, 413, 519; chronophotography
    118, 119, 166, 515, 566; Gaumont 265, 267,
    268; intermittent movements 325; Société
    générale du Phonoscope 373; sports
    films 604; Stollwerck 612;
    Urban Bioscope 685
DeMille, Cecil B. 171, 230, 372, 386, 396, 490,
    494, 586, 619
Denham, Clifford 73
Denizot, Vincenzo 333
Denmark 172–6; acting styles 3; archives 36;
    censorship 172, 173–4; exhibition and
    distribution 172–3; legitimate

theater 627; multiple-reel films 453; production
    174–6; trade press 637
Dennery, Armand 123
Denola, Georges 103, 176, 565
Dentler, Martin 176, 273
department stores 176–7, 218, 230, 381, 382;
    advertising 7; museum life exhibits 459; Pathé-
    Frères 506–7; women 700
Depue, Oscar 487
Derba, Mimí 177
The Derby 2
Les Dernières cartouches (1896) 139
Desfile de un tiro de Guerra (1907) 79
Desfile militar de 15 de novembro de 1907 (1907) 551
Desfontaines, Henri 103, 177–8, 250, 294, 428
Le déshabillage impossible (1900) 644
Desmet, Jean 178, 227, 278, 341, 470, 534
Le Desperado (1908) 294
Der Desperado von Panama (1914) 170
A Desperate Poaching Affray (1903) 110, 157,
    293, 341
Le Destin des mères (1912) 235
Destinn, Emmy 490
detective films 159, 178–81; dance 163; Denola
    176; Duskes 195; Ford 244; France 250;
    Germany 271; Hofer 302; India 319; Larsen 372;
    Mistinguett 437; multiple-reel films 454;
    Nordisk 483; Perret 512; Piel 521; Reicher 153,
    548; Russia 558; SCAGL 565; sensational
    melodrama 425; serials 582; Sweden 615; von
    Woringen 682; World War I 703; Yankee Film
    Company 610; *see also* crime films
Deti veka (Children of the Age) (1915) 61, 357
La Dette de l'aventurière (1914) 167
Deutsch de la Meurthe, Henry 167
Deutsche Bioscop 14, 270, 356, 373, 452, 579, 635
Deutsche Lichtbild GmbH (DLG) 703
Deutsche Mutoskop & Biograph (German
    Biograph) 168, 181–3, 270, 272, 635, 682
Deutsche Soldaten im Felde (1914) 688
Des deutschen Heeres Entstehung (1914) 688
Les Deux chemineaux (1913) 512
Les Deux soeurs (1907) 421, 507
Les Deux Timides (1928) 25
Deux voleurs qui n'ont pas de chance (1907) 578
Devant, David 324, 410, 510, 540, 588
The Devil in the Studio (1901) 497
Dewar, Thomas 224
Dewar's Scotch Whisky (1897) 322

Dewey, John 215
DeWindt, Harry 58
Di Doménico family 135, 136, 183–4
Di Ruggerio brothers 183
O diabo (1908) 97
dialogue accompaniment 7, 184–5
The Diamond from the Sky (1915) 20
Diaro colombiano 183
Díaz, General Porfirio 17, 430, 431
Díaz Quesada, Enrique 105, 159, 160, 185, 563
Dibble, John 341
Dick Turpin (1912) 84
Dick Whittington and his Cat (1913) 291
Dickson, William Kennedy Laurie 186, 195, 197, 200, 203, 296, 324; AM&B 21, 85; celluloid 106; Kinetoscope 95, 358, 519, 655; Latham brothers 372; news event films 474; religious films 549; set design 584; synchronized sound system 517
Dieterle, Wilhelm 526, 589
Dietrich, Marlene 363, 627
digital technology 531
Dillon, Eddie 144
dime museums 69, 186–7, 355, 672–3, 686
Dingjunshan 115
Dintenfass, Mark M. 187–8, 396
dioramas 5, 35, 188, 335, 458, 617, 690
"director" system of production 442–3
"director-unit" system of production 249, 442, 443
Dirks, Rudolph 28, 148, 149
The Discordant Note (1903) 212
Disinherited Son's Loyalty (1909) 472
Dislocation mystérieuse (1901) 169
The Dispatch Bearers (1900) 438
distribution: Europe 8, 188–91, 445, 446, 534; Austro-Hungary 53; Belgium 64; Brazil 83; Canada 99, 100; Denmark 173, 245; Gaumont 266; Germany 189, 190, 272–3; Great Britain 282, 284–6; Italy 335–6, 337; multiple-reel films 457; Netherlands 470; newspapers 476; Russia 556; Sweden 616–17; United States 657, 659–61
Ditmars, Raymond L. 521, 572
Ditya Bol'Shogo Goroda (Child of the Big City) (1914) 61, 164, 423, 607
divas 68, 78, 106, 292, 334, 339, 608, 627; acting styles 3; Mexico 431; multiple-reel films 454; sensational melodrama 426
Divekar, V. P. 502

Divers at Work on the Wreck of the "Maine" (1898) 547
Divine Comedy 435
Diving Lucy (1903) 438
Dix Femmes pour un mari (1905) 110, 212, 506
A Dixie Mother (1910) 631
DLG see Deutsche Lichtbild GmbH
Dobbs, Beverly B. 523
Docteur Phantom (1909) 347
documentaries 5; Botelho 79; Brazil 83; Cambodia 92; Colombia 135; Peru 514; Portugal 528; Quebec 100, 103; Santos 563; United States 308; Wiener Kunstfilm 52; see also actualités
De Dødes Ø (1913) 175, 280
Dødsvarslet (1912) 73
Dog Outwits the Kidnappers 244
Dog Sleighing (1902) 101
Dohm, Hedwig 697
Dokuru no mai (1923) 624
Dollard des Ormeaux (1913) 102
Domino 316, 356, 473
Domitor xxx, 241
Don Juan de Serrallonga (1910) 299
Don Juan heiratet (1909) 278
Don Juan Tenorio (1908) 299
Don Leandro el inefable (1918) 676
Don Pedro el cruel (1911) 414
Don Q (1912) 84
Don Quichotte (1913) 167
Donisthorpe, Wordsworth 95, 191
Dora Film 191, 340, 485
Doré, Gustave 70, 494
Doria, Giovanni 634
Dörmann, Felix 52
Dorothy's Dream (1903) 327
Dorraine, Lucy 363
D'ou vient-il (1905) 211
double-film-band projectors 191
Doublier, Francis 62, 191–2, 243, 469
Douglas, Bill 133
Doumer, Paul 678
Down the Hudson (1903) 211
Doyen, Eugène-Louis 131, 173, 192, 499, 567
Dr. Jekyll and Mr Hyde (1912) 57
El drama del 15 de Octubre (1915) 135, 183
Drama po telefonu (1914) 423, 541
Drama v kabare futuristov (1914) 497
Un Drame au fond de la mer (1901) 424, 585
Un Drame de Venise (1906) 208, 246–7

Un Drame en express (1906) 151
Dranem (Armand Ménard) 118, 192, 225, 460, 518
Drankov 61, 192–3, 357, 490, 558, 633
Drankov, Aleksandr 192, 356, 556
Drat that Boy! (1904) 143
Dream of a Rarebit Fiend (1907) 149, 417, 527
Dream of Toyland (1908) 17
Dressler, Marie 144, 394
Drew, Sidney 680
Dreyer, Carl 303
Druhot, Léon 419
The Drummer Girl of Vicksburg (1912) 631
The Drunkard's Reformation (1909) 74, 386, 561
Du Caire au Centre d'Afrique (1906) 137
The Duel (1910) 505
Un duel à la dynamite (1908) 169
The Duel with Pistols (1896) 677
Un duelo a orillas del Almendares (1907) 159
Duhamel, Sarah 144, 146, 150, 193–4, 250
Duis, Perry 561
Duke of York at Montreal and Quebec (1901) 101
Dulac, Germaine 25, 39, 467, 568
Dulay, Arthur 241
A Dull Razor (1900) 225
Dumb Sagacity 244
Duncan, Bud 148, 353
Duncan, Francis Martin 109, 194, 521, 567, 594, 651
Dupont, E. A. 416, 526
Durán, Manuel Trujillo 676
Durand, Jean 79, 146, 150, 194, 266, 431, 444
The Durbar in Kinemacolor (1912) 307
Dureau, Georges 121, 194
Duse, Eleonora 19, 78, 194, 338, 526, 609, 709
Duskes, Alfred 78, 195, 270, 272, 635
Dussaud, François 195, 592, 620
Dutch Mutoscope & Biograph 195, 469
Duvivier, Julien 39
Dwan, Allan 20, 195–6, 220
Dyer, Anson 150
Dyer, Frank L. 196, 202, 203
The Dynamiter (1911) 368

1812 (1912) 505
The Eagle's Nest (1909) 349
Eakins, Thomas 118, 570
Eames, Owen A. 191

early cinema studies (ECS) 41–4
East Lynne (1913) 59
Eastman, George 18, 76, 85, 106, 197, 254
Eastman Kodak Company 15, 18, 95, 197–8, 413, 519; Brulatour 85; celluloid 106, 107; Pathé-Frères 507, 508; safety film stock 198, 215; Williamson 695
Éclair 15, 198–9, 350; amusement parks 22; Andriot 25; Arquillière 39; Belgium 64; bourgeois class 123; censorship 258; Chautard 112; Cohl 28, 132; colonial films 138; comic series 147, 250; communication 151–2; crime films 158, 454; detective films 179, 180; Duhamel 194; Fabre 225; *film d'art* 236, 237; France 250, 251, 252; Frau 259; Gundersen 291; Hartlooper 295; Hatot 296; India 318; Japan 345; Jasset 347; Khanzhonkov & Co. 356; labor relations 368; legitimate theater 627; newsreels 477; opera 489; Parnaland 499; Pommer 271; scientific films 214, 572; sensational melodrama 425; serials 583; Tourneur 636; transportation 640; travelogues 642; United States 661; Vandal 672; westerns 691; World War I 703
Éclair American 39, 192, 199, 649, 700
Éclair-Journal 198–9
Eclipse 15, 109, 199, 448; Belgium 64; colonial films 137; Desfontaines 178; detective films 179; *film d'art* 236; France 250; Hamman 294; industrial films 323; Jasset 347; legitimate theater 627; Mercanton 428; newsreels 477; Rogers 553–4; scientific films 214; Shakespeare films 589; travelogues 642; Urban 651; westerns 691; World War I 703
Ecole du malheur (1907) 421
Edamasa Yoshiro 199–200, 346
Eden Musée 69, 187, 314, 527, 585, 655
Edipo Re (1910) 166
Edison Home Kinetoscope 18, 200, 202, 215
Edison Kinetograph camera 16, 107, 200, 203, 374, 397, 655; Dickson 186; Dyer 196; Heise 296; scientific films: USA 571
Edison Kinetophone 202, 342, 355, 358, 458, 615, 620, 621, 675
Edison Kinetoscope 2, 95, 200, 203, 358–9, 474, 519, 655–6; amateur film 18; Anschütz 30; archaeology of cinema 33–4; Argentina 37; Belgium 62; boxing films 155; Brazil 82; Canada 97, 98; celluloid 76, 107; counterfeit 349, 427, 460, 502, 506, 688; dance films 163; de Bedts

166; Dickson 186; Dyer 196, 374, 655; editing techniques 204; Foersterling 244; Great Britain 282; Heise 296; historical films 300; intermediality and modes of reception 324; Iran 331; Italy 334; Ivens 342; Japan 66, 343; Jenkins 348; Lumière brothers 398; Maguire & Baucus 411; Moore 446; music hall 460; Netherlands 469; New Zealand 473; North American Phonograph 484; paintings 494–5; Paul 297, 510; penny arcades 511; Phantoscope 515; Poland 522; program formats 533; Raff & Gammon 546; Seeber 579; South Africa 598; sports films 604; Stollwerck 612; Switzerland 592, 619; Tally 623; trade marks 636; United States 662; Urban 650; urbanization 652; Uruguay 654; Wales 683; Walturdaw 684; Werner brothers 688; White 692; world's fairs 705

Edison Manufacturing 23, 200–3, 609, 659; advertising 8, 9, 10; AGC 15; amateur filmmaking 215; amusement parks 22; animal films 25; animation films 27, 28; archives 36; Belgium 64; biblical films 68; Biograph with 71, 72; Bonine 78; boxing films 80, 81; camera movement 92, 93, 94; Canada 97, 98, 99; catalogues 542; celluloid 106, 107, 197; chase films 110, 111; Cody 132; color 139; comedies 142, 143; comic series 145, 147; comic strip 149, 150; copyright 111, 154, 374; Costello 155; costumes 156; crime films 157; Cuba 159; cue sheets 160; dance films 163; Dawley 165; distribution 189, 659; domestic melodrama 421; editing techniques 204, 205, 206, 207, 209, 210, 211, 212; ethnographic films 222, 689; facial expression films 225; film perforations 127; Film Service Association 679; Foersterling 244; Fuller 262; Furniss 262; Gilmore 278–9; Gregory 287; Griffith 288; Gundersen 291; historical films 300; Indonesia 320; industrial films 321; intertitles 327, 328; Kennedy 355; Kleine-Edison-Selig-Essanay 220, 361, 581; Lawrence 377; legitimate theater 626; lighting 218, 385, 387; McCutcheon 417; Mexico 431; modes of production 443; Motion Picture Patents Company 503; Mullens brothers 452; music halls 460; news event films 474; opera 489, 494; Palestine 498; Paley 499; phantom train rides 514; Philippines 515; phonography 417, 484, 516, 634; polar expedition films 523; Powers 530; propaganda films 540; Quebec 101; re-enact-ments 547; Russia 556; Sandow 562; scientific films 569; screenplays 578; sensational melodrama 424; serials 582; set design 584; Shakespeare films 589; sports films 604; synchronized sound systems 620, 621; Thailand 625; trade press 637; transportation 639; travelogues 641; trick films 644; Turkey 646; United States 656, 657; US imperialism 314, 315; US patent wars 341, 361, 373, 391, 447, 448, 564–5, 566, 580, 581, 610, 679; Venezuela 676; Waters 686; Werner brothers 688; westerns 689, 690; White 692; women's suffrage films 700, 701; world's fairs 705

Edison, Thomas Alvin 21, 200, 203–4; Blackton 75; capitalism 445; chronophotography 118; Dickson 186; dime museums 187; Dyer 202; education 214–15; electricity 218; Jenkins 348; Kinetoscope 358–9; phonography 517; photography 519; scientific films 570, 572; trade marks 636

Edison Vitascope 21, 200, 201, 203, 305, 538, 656; Argentina 38; Armat 39; Canada 98, 287; Chautauqua 112; Chile 113; Colombia 135; dime museums 187; Italy 334; Japan 66, 343; Mexico 430; musical accompaniment 461; Peru 513; Porter 527; Tally 623; United States 662, 663, 673; Urban 651

editing: and acting styles 2, 3, 4; analytical 130, 149, 179; camera movement 92; Capellani 103–4; classical Hollywood cinema 129, 130; continuity 83, 130, 212–13, 418, 484, 555, 595; early practices and techniques 204–6; and film developing, printing and assembly 238; Gaumont 266; Germany 271; Griffith 288; Hofer 302; India 318; intertitles 326; moral reformation 561; parallel 17, 54, 72, 130, 158, 208, 211, 213, 288; parallel editing 151; sensational melodrama 425; spatial relations 206–9, 210; spectatorship 602; sports films 604; staging in depth 607; stereography 610; Svenska Biografteatern 614; tableau style 2, 3–4, 207, 209–10, 327, 422, 614; temporal relations 211–14; "Tramp" films 145

education 214–15; archaeology of cinema 32; Charles Urban Trading Company 109; churches 120, 121; consumer cooperatives 152, 153; Edison 572; ethnographic films 221; Germany 275; magic lantern shows 406–7;

phonography 517; Poland 522; program formats 533; Sweden 618; travelogues 642; *see also* scientific films

Edward VII coronation 5

Edwards, Henry 296, 624, 683

Effets d'un coup de rasoir (1906) 585–6

Les Effluves funestes (1915) 167

Effondrement du pont de Québec (1907) 491

The Egg-Laying Man 410

Egypt 215–17, 499, 641

Eidoloscope 186, 187, 201, 372, 373, 604

Eiffel, Gustave 267

Eighty Million Women Want–? (1913) 700

Eiko-Film 170, 270, 404, 640, 687

Einstein, Carl 451

Eisenstein, Sergei 124, 213

Ejército General de Bombas (1902) 113

Ekspeditrisen (1911) 585

Electric Hotel (1908) 117, 644

The Electric House (1924) 219

Electrical Wonder Company 30, 31

electricity 22, 217–19, 652; Cuba 105; lighting 388; modernity 439; Turkey 646; US monopoly capitalism 445

Electrocuting an Elephant (1903) 22, 25, 218

Electrotachyscope 30, 33; *see also* Schnellseher

Elfelt, Peter (Lars Peter Petersen) 96, 172, 174, 219, 359

Elmendorf, Dwight 307

Elphinstone Bioscope Company 49, 404

Emerson, Alice B. 451

Emerson, John 329–30

L'Emigrante (1915) 333, 709

Emigranten 614

Empire Express 92

L'Empreinte (1908) 467

En Afrique Centrale: Fachoda 13

En defensa propia (1917) 177

L'Enfant de la folle (1913) 176

L'Enfant de Paris (1913) 248, 251, 512

L'Enfant prodigue (1907) 65, 105, 236, 516, 626

L'Enfant Roi (1923) 294

Les enfants du capitaine Grant (1914) 295

Engel, Joseph 551, 614

Engelein (1913) 481

English pattern cameras 219

Engström, Frans 40

Enhver (1915) 280

Entrée du cinématographe (1896) 51

Entretien de Dreyfus et de sa femme à Rennes (1899) 386

Entsagungen (1913) 373

Epileptic Seizure (1905) 570

An Episode from the Life of Dmitri Donskoi (1909) 505

Epoch Producing Corporation 16

L'Epopée Napoléonienne (1903–1904) 299, 300, 452, 506

L'Epouvante (1911) 437

Eräs elämän murhenäytelmä (1916) 243

Erlanger, Abraham 360

Ermler, Fridrikh 558

Ernemann camera 14, 18, 96

Ernemann Imperator projector 219–20, 539

erotic films 52, 76, 175, 426, 453, 484, 525, 564; *see also* pornography

Erreur du Port (1904) 144

Escamotage d'une dame chez Robert-Houdin (1896) 419, 644

The Escaped Lunatic (1903) 110, 143, 212, 417, 656

L'Escarpolette tragique (1913) 167

Escenas callejeras (1900) 38

Esoofally, Abdulally 220, 318

Esquimaux Village (1901) 690

Essanay Film Manufacturing Company 20, 24, 87, 220, 448, 581, 659; Anderson, G. M. 23; Chaplin 108; Cody 132; comic series 147, 148; Dwan 195; editing techniques 208; Kleine-Edison-Selig-Essanay 220, 361, 581; Linder 390; Shakespeare films 589; Spoor 604; sports films 605; travelogues 642; Turpin 647; United States 657; Vitagraph-Lubin-Selig-Essanay 220, 394, 581, 680; westerns 690

L'Essor (1920) 281

Estévez, Andrés 563

Esther (1910) 512

Estlander, Erik 243

Os estranguladores (1906) 83, 158, 379

Etablissements L. Aubert 40, 189, 254

ethnographic films 221–2, 459, 642; dances 163; Khanzhonkov & Co. 357; Omegna 489; westerns 689

Étiévant, Henri 3–4, 103, 167

Etre légume 192

Étude des mouvements browniens (1907) 567

Eugene Onegin (1911) 489

eugenics 433

Evangeliemandens Liv (1914) 303

Evans, Fred ("Pimple") 222–3, 460–1
Evans, Will 461
Everett, Anna 433
Everson, William K. 134
Everybody Works but Father (1905) 142
Ewers, Hanns Heinz 55, 223, 560
The Ex-Convict (1904) 527
Excentric Club (1913) 437
Une excursion incohérente (1910) 117
Execution of Czolgosz with Panorama of Auburn Prison (1901) 157, 218, 527
Execution of Mary Queen of Scots (1895) 212, 300, 495, 547, 644
O exemplo regenerador (1919) 83, 418, 555
La exhibición de todos los personajes ilustres de Bolivia (1906) 77
exhibition xxix; audiences 41–48; churches 119–21; modernity 439; music halls 460; Quebec 102; regulating 374–7; *see also* airdomes; amusement parks; chautauquas; cinema circuits and chains; itinerant exhibitors; nickelodeons; palace cinemas; vaudeville
Exhibitors Trade Review 87
Expedição Roosevelt a Mato Grosso (1914) 548
expedition/exploration films 223–4, 355, 523–4
Expiation (1918) 167
The Exploits of Elaine (1915) 425, 583, 693
Une Extraordinaire aventure de Boireau (1914) 144
eyeline match 54, 130

Les 400 coups du diable (1905) 231
4628 Meter Hoch auf Skiern—Besteigung des Monte Rosa (1913) 688
Fabre, Marcel 19, 147, 225, 337, 460
Fabrication Malgache des Sobikons 13
facial expression films 30, 94, 143, 225–6
Facial Expressions (1902) 225
Fadren (The Father) (1912) 481, 491
Faes, Charlotte 419
Fahrney, Milton 108
Fairbanks, Douglas 196, 229, 319, 329–30, 464, 520
fairs/fairgrounds 47, 121, 226–8, 226–8; 408, 439, 440; attractions 124; audiences 459; Austro-Hungary 52; Bartling 60; Belgium 62, 63, 64; cinema of attractions 124; colonial films 137; Denmark 172; Dentler 176; Desmet 178; Dutch Mutoscope & Biograph 195; Europe 226–8;

facial expressions 225; France 248, 256; Gaumont 266; Germany 273–4, 275; Great Britain 281, 282; Green 287; Holland 303; Italy 335; itinerant exhibitors 340–1; Komatsu Shokai 363; Krüger 364; lecturers 379; Luxemburg 400; magic lantern shows 327; Méliès 420; Mendel 427; Mullens brothers 452, 470, 594; Netherlands 469, 470; Norway 484; Olsen 488; Pathé-Frères 189, 502, 506, 507; *phonoscènes* 518; program formats 533, 534; Russia 556; Scotland 573; sound machines 598; Sweden 617; Switzerland 619; trade press 637; travelogues 640; United States 667; Vietnam 678; Wales 683; wax museums 686; Williams 694–5
fairy plays *see féeries*
"fake newsreels" 547–8
Falena, Ugo 228–9, 238, 338, 392, 469
The Fall Guy (1913) 75
The Fall of a Nation 464
The Fall of Troy (*La Caduta di Troia*) (1910) 299, 333, 338, 501, 586, 661
Falsely Accused 244
Famechon, E. A. 678
The Family Jar (1913) 10
Famous Players Motion Picture Company 165, 203, 229, 361, 372, 447, 457, 488; Caruso 490; DeMille 171; Dwan 196; legitimate theater 628; Pickford 520; Porter 527, 551; Ramos 546; Schuberg 566; theater, melodrama 629; USA 661; Woods 702; Zukor 67, 710
Fanck, Arnold 688
Fänrik Ståls sagner 614
"fantasmagoria" 32–3, 35
Fantasmagorie (1908) 27
Fantômas films (1913–1914) 104, 158–9, 179, 180, 235, 251, 266, 426, 454, 468, 558, 583
Faraday, Michael 406
Farfalle (1907) 163
Farnum, Dustin 171, 229–30
Farnum, Marshall 230
Farnum, William 230
Farrar, Geraldine 490
fashion 8, 78, 156, 230–1, 478, 623, 627
The Fashion Shop (1915) 230
Fassini, Alberto 127, 337
fast-motion shooting 86, 482, 568
Fat Jack and Slim Jim at Coney Island (1911) 22
The Fatal Hour (1908) 425
The Fatal Wedding (1911) 50

Father Sergius (Otets Sergii) (1918) 541, 559, 707

Fatty and Mabel series 32

Fatty and Mabel Adrift (1916) 32

Fatum (1915) 278

Faure, Jean-Louis 567

Faust (1885/1887/1895) 631

Faye, Hervé 343

feature films *see* multiple-reel films

Feddersen, Wilhelm 118

Fedora (1913) 31, 166

La fée printemps (1907) 233

Feeding the Hippopotamus (1903) 25

Feeding the Otters (1905) 25

féeries (fairy plays) 61, 103, 231–4, 327; animation
    29; Cines 127; color 139, 140; costumes 155;
    Floury 244; France 249; Gaumont 266; Ger-
    many 274; Méliès 97, 125, 418, 419, 584;
    Nonguet 482; Pathé-Frères 506; Smith 595;
    trick films 644; Velle 676

Felicetti, Francesco 335

Felicitous Rebellion 554

Fellini, Federico 291, 447

feminism 699, 700; *see also* women's movement

La Femme du saltimbanque (1911) 176

Fengtai Photography Studio 115, 234

Ferner, Antonin 147

Feron-Vrau, Paul 411

Ferrer, Francisco 366

Ferrez, Julio 82, 83, 234–5

Fertner, Antoni 523

Fescourt, Henri 25, 235

La festa del blat (1914) 634

Los festejos de la Caridad en la ciudad de Camagüey
    (1909) 159, 185

Le festin Balthazar (1910) 163

Festival Infantil de Bohemia (1912) 185

Le Feu qui brûle (1918) 102

Feuillade, Louis 40, 43, 104, 235–6, 249, 347;
    animation 27; comic series 146, 530; crime
    films 24, 158, 180, 464, 468; Decroix 168;
    domestic melodrama 421, 422; Fescourt 235;
    Gaumont 265, 266, 268; Grandais 281; Guy 291;
    Levesque 384; lighting 386; Mary 415; Monca
    444; multiple-reel films 454; Napierkowska 467;
    Perret 512; sensational melodrama 425; serials
    25, 583, 703; Shakespeare films 589; staging in
    depth 607

Fevrell, Walter 618

Feyder, Jacques 92, 444, 467

Fi Bilad Tut 'Ankh Amun (1923) 217

FIAF *see* International Federation of Film Archives

Fiala, Anthony 223, 523

Fielding, Romaine 394

Figari, Eduardo 654

The Fight (1915) 693

La figlia perduta (1912) 333

Figner, Federico 38, 82

Figures de cire (1914) 198

Fiji 487

Filippi, Giuseppe 334–5

La Fille du Margrave (1912) 235, 299

Fille-Mère (1917) 40

Fillis, Frank 598

Le Film Biblique series (1911) 24

film d'art 55, 236–7, 250; ACAD 112; Decroix 168;
    Denmark 173; Gottschalk 280; Jasset 347;
    legitimate theater 627; Maître 411; Malaya 412;
    opera 489; Pathé-Frères 508; Russia 295;
    SCAGL 565; set design 586; Svenska
    Biografteatern 614; Wiener Kunstfilm 694

Film d'Art 65, 236, 237–8, 503, 507, 508; acting
    styles 3, 4; AGC 15; Calmettes 91; color 140;
    Compagnie des Cinéma- Halls 124; costumes
    156; Dania Biofilm 164; Decroix 168; Delac 170;
    Desfontaines 178; framing 247; France 250, 252,
    257; Gaumont 266; Gual 290; Laffitte 371; Le
    Bargy 378; legitimate theater 626–7; Linder 390;
    literary adaptations 329, 543; Nalpas 467;
    Napierkowska 467; opera 489; Pouctal 529;
    Robinne 553; SCAGL comparison 565;
    screenwriting 578; set design 586; staging
    in depth 606, 607; star system 608; Théophile
    Pathé 632; Vandal 672

Film d'Arte Italiana (Pathé-Frères) 68, 83, 128,
    236, 238, 251, 336, 337; color 140; costumes
    156; Falena 228–9; Gasnier 265; legitimate
    theater 627; Lo Savio 392; Maggi 404;
    Nepoti 469; Serena 582; Shakespeare films 589;
    star system 608

Le Film de ma vie (1926) 290

film festivals and occasional events 1, 240–1

Le Film (journal) 298

The Film Parade (or The March of the Movies) 76

Film Service Association 679

Film Supply Company 456, 473, 530, 596, 658

filmarchiv 36

filme cantante (sung films) 49, 79, 83, 241, 584

Filmen 173, 242, 637

Filmfabrikken Danmark 175, 176, 280, 390
filmoteca 36
filmoteka 36
Die Filmprimadonna (1913) 481
films dal vero 191
films sonores 242
Le Fils prodigue (1912) 167
La Fin du jour 39
Finch, Flora 144, 148, 242, 680
Fine Arts 89, 196, 356
Fine Feathers Make Fine Birds (1905) 639
Finkelstein, Henryk 364, 522
Finland 227, 242–3
Finlandia Film 243
Il finto storpio al castello Sforzesco (1896) 335
Fire! (1901) 140, 494, 695
De fire Djaevle (1911) 164, 360, 390
fire regulations 283, 376, 479, 557, 666
Fireside Reminiscences (1908) 213
The First Violin (1912) 247, 607
Fischer, Carl 160, 463
Fisher, Bud 147, 150
Fiske, Minnie Maddern 628
Fitch, E. H. 107
Fitts, J. B. 598
Fitzgerald, Charles W. 223
Fitzhamon, Lewin 243–4, 296, 297, 460, 540
Five Minutes to Train Time (1902) 211
Five o'clock Tea 518
Flaherty, Robert 5, 222
flânérie 383
Flaschenträger, Alexandre 400
flashbacks 213
Fleck, Jakob Julius 52, 363, 694
Die Fledermaus 489
Fleming, George S. 201, 527
Les fleurs animées (1906) 116
Flickorna på Solvik (1926) 362
flip books 8, 9, 26
Floury, Edmond Louis 244
fluoroscope 571
Flying Train (1903) 515
Den flyvende Cirkus (1912) 390
Il focolare domestico (1914) 469
Foersterling, Hermann 96, 244, 270, 272, 469, 538, 593
Folies Bergère 20, 168, 257, 333, 506
A Fool and His Money (1912) 291
För fäderneslandet (1914) 362

För hem och härd (1917) 362
For the Honor of the 8th Ill. U.S.A. (1914) 75
Les Forbains (1907) 507
Forbes-Robertson, Johnston 296, 589
Ford (O'Fearna or Feeney), Francis 161, 179, 244–5, 316, 472, 650
Fordism 381, 383
Les Forgerons (1895) 584
Forst, Willi 363, 526
Förster, Franz 365–6
Foster, Edwin Dunham 120–1
Foster, William 75, 245
Fotoplayer 598
Fotorama 172, 173, 174–5, 245, 390, 593, 617, 627
The Foundling (1915) 196
Foundling Hospital Sports Day (1899) 484
Four Beautiful Pairs (1904) 177
The Four Seasons (1904) 210
Fox, William 122, 245–6, 286, 432, 445, 446, 457, 479, 675
framing 246–8, 574; acting styles 3, 4
Francastel, Professor 34
France 248–59; *actualités* 5–6; advertising films 9; archives 36; cafés-concerts 89–90; Cambodian cinema 91, 92; censorship 258; colonial films 136, 138; colonies in Africa 13; consumer cooperatives 152–3; crime films 158, 159; fairs 226, 227; *féeries* 231, 233; historical films 299–300; Indochina 91, 92, 136, 678; labor movement 365, 366–7; legitimate theater 627; magic lantern shows 406; modes of production 444; multiple-reel films 454; newsreels 477; propaganda films 540; and Quebec 100, 101; sensational melodrama 425–6; trade press 637, 638; World War I 703
France, Anatole 257
La France contre les beni-Snassem (1914) 137
Francesca di Rimini (1910) 229, 247, 328
Francesco Ferrer 123
Francis, David 37, 133
Franco-Film 15, 41
François-Franck, Nicolas C.E. 33, 567
Frascaroli, Valentina 169
Frau, Raymond 127, 147, 259, 337
Frazer Canon (1902) 514
Fred Ott's Sneeze (1894) 225
Frederick, Pauline 490
Free Trade Versus Fair Trade (1905) 540
Freeman, Frank N. 215

Freer, James Simmons 98, 259
Fregoli, Leopoldo 259, 324, 335, 460
Freire Correia, Joao 528
Frelinger, Gregg A. 463
Das fremde Mädchen (1913) 55, 271
Der fremde Vogel (1911) 453
Den Fremmede (1914) 280
Frenkel (Bouwmeester), Theo 259–60, 278, 468,
    471, 482
Les Frères corses (1917) 364
Freud, Sigmund 383
Die freudlose Gasse (1925) 481
Freuler, John L. 16, 20, 260, 305, 464, 465
Friberg, C. A. (Carl August) 260, 616
Fridolín (1914) 290
Friedberg, Anne 93
Friedrich, Adolf 14
A Friendly Marriage (1911) 607
Friere, Octave 224
Friese-Greene, William 33, 134, 141, 191, 260,
    564, 595, 651
Le Friquet (1913) 636
Frith, William 494
Froelich, Carl 260, 271, 526
Frohman, Daniel 229, 628, 710
Froissart, Georges 89, 253, 261
Fröken Julie (Miss Julie) (1912) 481, 491
From the Cape to Cairo (1907) 137–8
From Dusk to Dawn (1913) 369
From the Manger to the Cross (1912) 69, 70, 71, 353,
    354, 463, 488, 498, 550
From Rhodesia via Katanga to Angola, Bulawayo to
    Elisabethville and Kamboveto
    Lobito Bay (1913) 11
Frusta, Arrigo 261
Fuchs, Josef 52
La fucina (1919) 261
Fukuhodo 200, 261, 345, 362, 481
Fuller, Loïe 163, 261, 446
Fuller, Mary 262, 650
The Funeral Arriving at Hyde Park (1901) 205
Il Fuoco (1915) 428, 501
Furkel, Georg 14, 96
Furniss, Harry 74, 150, 262
Furtado, Cardoso 528
El fusilamiento de Dorrego (1910) 38, 263
El fusilamiento de Piar (1913) 676
Futurism 336, 497
Fynes, J. Austin 262, 673

Gabet, (Baron) Francisque
    (François Marie) 263
Gachet, Maurice 505
Gad, Urban 165, 175, 248, 263, 270,
    280, 453, 480
Gaevert 107
Gagner, Marie-Louise 618
Les Gaîtés de l'escadron (1913) 198, 636
Gal-Ezer, Joseph 499
Gallet, Maurice 123
Gallo, Mario 38, 263
Gallone, Carmine 128, 485
Galvanic Fluid or, More Fun with Liquid Electricity
    (1908) 218
Gambart, Henri 150, 169, 415
Gammon, Frank 359, 546
Gance, Abel 11, 117, 467, 512
Gandolfi, Alfredo 18, 19
Ganguly, Dhirendranath 264, 319
Ganz, Thomas 133
Garbagni, Paul 504, 592, 615–16
Garbo, Greta 612
García Cardona, Angel 161, 599
Gardien de la Camargue (1910) 266
Gardin, Vladimir 264, 357, 558, 633
Gardner, Helen 264, 456, 457, 680
Garry, Claude 167, 565
Gärtner, Adolf 264–5
Gaskill, Charles 456, 457
Gasnier, Louis 265, 390, 437, 503, 599
Gaudí, Antonio 290
Gaudio, Tony 312
Gaudreault, André 124, 211, 232, 602
Gaumont 15, 24, 63, 265–7, 448; animal films 26;
    animation 27–8; Aquila 31; Arnaud 39; Austro-
    Hungary 53; Belgium 64; biblical films 69;
    Birtles film 50; Bolten-Baeckers 78; Bosetti 79,
    146; Bourbon 79; boxing films 348; Breteau 84;
    Canada 102; Carl 104, 105; Chronochrome
    Gaumont 117, 141, 198, 531; Chronophone
    Gaumont 118, 192, 265, 291, 429, 620–1;
    Chronophotographe 538; Cohl 132; colonial
    films 13, 137, 138; color 140; comedies 142, 144;
    comic series 145, 146, 147, 431, 530, 553, 568;
    crime films 158, 425–6; dance films 163; de
    Barros 165; Decroix 168; Durand 194; Edison
    Kinetoscope 166; editing techniques 204, 211,
    212; expedition/exploration films 223; fashion
    230; *féeries* 231, 233; Fescourt 235; Feuillade 235;

film d'art 236; film developing, printing, assembly 240; Floury 244; framing 247; France 154, 249, 250, 251, 252, 255; Goncharov 280; Grandais 281; Greece 287; Guy 291; Hamman 294; historical films 299, 300; India 318; intertitles 327; Iran 331; Italy 335; Japan 344, 363; Jasset 347; Kinora 360; legitimate theater 627; Levesque 384; lighting 385, 386; Luxemburg 400; Mary 415; Messter Biophon 429; Mitchell & Kenyon 438; Modot 444; Monca 444; multiple-reel films 454; Musidora 464; Navarre 468; news event films 475; newsreels 477, 478; Oceania/South Pacific 487; Péon 512; Perret 512; *phonoscènes* 490, 518; Piel 521; Portugal 528; projectors 538, 539; religious films 549; Russia 556; scientific films 214, 572; screenwriting 577; serials 180, 583; Shakespeare films 589; Smalley 594; Solax 595–6; Spain 599; star system 609; Switzerland 619; synchronized sound systems 620–1; Thiemann 632, 633; travelogues 340, 642; trick films 644; Warner's Features 685; westerns 691; World War I 702–3; Zecca 709

Gaumont, Léon Ernest 105, 249, 254, 265, 266, 267–8, 508; Chronochrome Gaumont 117; de Morlhon 167; Demenÿ 170–1; Guy 291; *phonoscènes* 518; *Tonbilder* 635

Gauntier, Gene (Genevieve Liggett) 269, 332, 353, 425, 488, 608, 685

Gauvreau, Georges 101, 269
Gavault, Paul 237
Gavin, Agnes 269
Gavin, John 50, 269
Gavroche à Luna-Park (1912) 22
Gavroche series (1912–1914) 199
The Gay Shoe Clerk (1903) 125
A Gay Time in Old Quebec (1912) 102
La Gazette des sept arts 103
Gaz'irli, Fawzi 216
Das gefährliche Alter (1911) 453
Der geheimnisvolle Klub (1913) 170
Die geheimnisvolle Villa (1914) 548
Gehrts, Meg 138
Gelabert, Fructuoso 269, 599
Gémier, Firmin 39, 84, 103
General Film Company 72, 229, 269–70, 448, 456, 464, 472, 649; Berst 67; Canada 102; Dyer 196; Hodkinson 302; Kennedy 355; Kleine 361; Laemmle 370; Long 393; Lubin 394; Milano

Films 436; USA 655, 657, 660; US monopoly capitalism 445, 446; Vitagraph 680; Warner Brothers 684; Waters 686

Geni, Louis 51
Genie tegen geweld (1916) 260
Genina, Augusto 128, 343, 436
El genio del mal (1910) 185
German Biograph *see* Deutsche Mutoskop & Biograph
German Expressionism 280
Germany 46, 270–7; *actualités* 6; Anschütz 30; archives 36; *Autorenfilme* 55–6; colonial films 136, 137; colonies in Africa 13–14; comic strips 148; fairs 226, 227; distribution: Europe 189, 190; framing 248; labor movement 365–6; legitimate theater 627; multiple-reel films 453; newsreels 477; Nordisk 483; sensational melodrama 426; trade press 52, 637; women's movement 696–8; World War I 702, 703, 704
Germinal (1913) 104, 250, 364, 366, 565
Gérôme, Jean-Léon 70, 494, 495, 496
Gertie (1914) 28, 417
La Gerusalemme liberata (1911) 338
Gerval, le maître de forges (1912) 198
Das Gespenst von Clyde (1912) 437
Gestoorde hengelaar (1896) 593
Der gestreifte Domino (1915) 265
Geyer, Karl A. 181
Ghione, Emilio 277, 339, 468
Ghuillaume Tell 299
Giambastiani, Salvador 114, 277–8, 591
Giampietro, Josef 278
Giblyn, Charles 472
Gibson, Helen 353
Gibson, W. A. 348
Gifford, Fred 293, 294
Gigolette (1920) 529
Gilbreth, Frank 571
Gildemijer, Johan Hendrik 278, 470
Gilis, Nora 682
Gillon, Léon 198
Gilman, Charlotte Perkins 700
Gilmore, William E. 200, 202, 203, 278–9
Ginna, Arnaldo 336
Ginzburg, Samuel 364
Le Giornate del Cinema Muto xxx, 241
Giraud, Jean 576
Girel, Constant 373, 678
Girel, François 344

The Girl Detective series 554
The Girl of the Golden West (1915) 490
The Girl and Her Trust (1912) 94, 151, 158
The Girl and the Motor Boat (1911) 424
Girl Spy series 425
The Girl Strike Leader (1910) 368
A Girl of Yesterday (1915) 196
Gish, Dorothy 144, 156, 196, 279
Gish, Lillian 72, 156, 196, 230, 279, 288, 292
La gitanilla (1914) 290
Giunchi, Eraldo 147
Giunchi, Lea 337
Gladtvet, Ottar 279, 484
Glasbläser 36
A Glass of Goat's Milk (1909) 128
glass-plate projectors 279, 538
Gli ultimi giorni di Pompei (*The Last Days of Pompei*)
  (1908) 19, 156, 299, 336, 404, 500
Gli ultimi giorni di Pompei (*The Last Days of Pompei*)
  (1913) 19, 40, 78, 454, 464, 586, 596, 681
Gliewe, Max 279, 429
Glimpses of Bird Life (1910) 521
Glombeck, Robert 399, 615
La Gloria de la Raza (1926) 77
Gloria Films 78, 246, 279–80, 337, 339, 606;
  Caserini 106; De Liguoro 166; De Riso 167
Gloria Transita (1917) 278
The Glorious Adventure (1922) 76
Glücksmann, Max 38, 280, 654
Die Glückspuppe (1911) 363
Glückstadt, Vilhelm 175, 242, 280
Goddard, Pliny E. 221
God's Country and the Woman (1915) 590
Goerz, C. P. 30
Goethe, Johann Wolfgang von 494
Gohar 362
Going Through the Tunnel (1898) 514
Goitizolo, Jorge Enrique 513
Gold is Not All (1910) 421
Goldberg, Rube 150
The Golden Chance (1916) 171, 386
Goldenberg, G. 115
Goldfish (Goldwyn), Samuel 171, 372, 396,
  432, 488
Goldman, Emma 700
Goldwyn, Sam *see* Goldfish, Samuel
Der Golem (1914) 579, 687
Der Golem und die Tänzerin (1917) 687
El Golfo (1917) 634

Goncharov, Vasilii 280, 356, 489, 558
Goncharova, Natalia 497
Goo Goo Eyes (1903) 143, 225
The Good Bad Man (1916) 196
Good Little Devil (1913) 520
Goodness Gracious (1914) 211
Gordon, Julia Swayne 4, 589
Gorky, Maxim 325, 494
Gory Glory (1913) 505
Gottschalk, Ludwig 273, 280–1
Gounod, Charles 494
Gourdinne, Ernest 11
Graatkjaer, Axel 29
Grahner, Karl 96, 279, 696
The Grain of Dust 369–70
Gramsci, Antonio 42
Il granatiere Roland (1911) 19, 104
La grand bretèche (1909) 156
The Grand Old Flag (1913) 315
"Grand Spectacles Aquila" series (1913) 31
Grandais (Gueudret), Suzanne 147, 235, 252,
  266, 281, 428, 512, 559, 609
Les Grandes Films Populaires 24, 298
Grandin, Ethel 316
Grandma's Reading Glass (1900) 206, 208, 595
The Grandson (1925) 320
Grant, Madison 434
Granville, Fred 523
"graphophonoscope" 60
Grasso, Giovanni 414
Grau, Robert 281
Grauman, Sid 281
Graustark (1915) 220
The Gray Automobile (1919) 554
Gray, Joe 684
Gray, Robert Duncan 191
Great Britain 281–6; advertising films 9;
  animation 27; archives 36; Canada film industry
  98–9; colonial films 137; colonies in Africa 12;
  consumer cooperatives 152, 153; distribution:
  Europe 189–90; fairs 226, 227; itinerant exhi-
  bitors 438; labor movement 365, 366, 367;
  magic lantern shows 406; music halls 459–60;
  newsreels 477; propaganda films 540, 541; sports
  films 604; theater, melodrama 629, 630;
  trade press 637; World War I 702, 703, 704
Great Depression 22, 23
A Great Game (1909) 160
The Great Kimberley Diamond Robbery (1910) 599

The Great Train Robbery (1903) 6, 8, 157, 201, 424, 440, 639, 656–7; Anderson 23; camera movement 93; cinema of attractions 125; costume 156; editing: spatial relations 206, 207; Hale's Tours 294; melodrama, sensational 424; screenwriting 577; Porter 527; theater, melodrama 630
The Great White Silence (1924) 525
The Greater Love (1912) 208
Greater New York Film Rental Company 245, 286
Greece 286–7
Green, George 227, 287, 341, 438, 572, 573
Green, John C. 287
Green, Tom 460
Greenbaum, Jules 270, 681
De Greep (1909) 482
Gregg, John 517
Gregory, Carl Louis 287–8
Gréhan, René 250
Grétillat, Jacques 103
La Grève des domestiques (1912) 512
Grezy (1915) 423
Gribouille redevient Boireau (1912) 169
Grierson, John 5, 704
Grifell, Prudencia 676
Griffin, John J. 288
Griffith, David Wark 4, 16, 21, 43, 71, 132, 288–9, 441, 527; Biograph 355; Bitzer 27, 74; black cinema 74; Cabanne 89; *Cabiria* 339, 493; camera movement 94; color 140; comedies 147; communication 151; continuity editing 83, 130, 555; controversy of *Birth of a Nation* 301, 348, 667–8; costumes 156; crime films 158; Dawley 165; domestic melodrama 421, 422; Dwan 196; editing techniques 72, 83, 130, 208–9, 213, 555; fashion 230; Feuillade 266; *film d'art* 236; film festivals 241; Fine Arts 356; Gish 279; Grau 281; historical films 299, 300, 301; intertitles 328, 329; Johnson, Arthur 348; Keystone parodies 582; Leonard 383; lighting 386; McCutcheon 417; Marvin 414; Moore 447; musical score 462; Mutual 464, 465; Pickford 520; Quebec 102; Reliance-Majestic 412; religious films 550; saloons 561; sensational melodrama 425, 427, 639; set design 586; South African film 599; staging in depth 607; Sweet 619; theater, melodrama 631; Triangle Film Corporation 317, 473; USA 660–1; Walthall 684; war films 703; Wolf 696; Woods 702
Grimoin-Sanson, Raoul 64, 93, 170, 289–90, 639

Grivolas, Claude 86, 154, 502, 506, 510
Grönroos, J. A. W. 242
Gross, Edward Meyer 516
Grossmann, Edward B. 293
La Grotte des supplices (1912) 26
Grumbach, Jane 167
Grünkorn, Henri 63
Grünwaldt, Arthur 242
Gual, Adrià 59, 116, 290, 600
Guan Haifeng 115, 116
Los guapos de la Vaquería del parque (1905) 269
Os guaranis (1916) 97
Guardia, Julio 474
Guazzoni, Enrico 40, 127, 277, 290, 292, 338, 339
Guérard, Robert 123
The Guerilla (1908) 631
Guerra, Armand 123
La guerra e il sogno di Momi (1916) 117
Guest, Arthur 487
Gugenheim, Eugène 168, 236, 290, 428, 565
Le guide (1910) 400
Guillaume, Ferdinando 127, 147, 156, 225, 290–1, 336–7, 460, 500
Guilleaume-Schack, Gertrud 697
Gundersen, Jens Christian 291, 484
Gunning, Tom 124, 125, 126, 232, 440, 441, 602
Gurney, Edmund 594
Die guten Hosen (1911) 182
Guterl, Matthew Pratt 433
Guy Blaché, Alice 231, 235, 249, 265, 291–2; comic strips 149; *phonoscènes* 490, 518, 620; Solax 595, 596; *La Vie du Christ* 69, 347, 549
Guzmán, Martín Luis 600
Gyldendal 164
Gys, Leda 167, 292, 340, 582

Hackett, James K. 369, 527, 628
Haddock, William 418
Haddon, Alfred Cort 221, 223
Hadley, Edwin 341
Haevnens Nat (1916) 29, 117, 164, 607
Häfker, Hermann 293, 372
Hafner an der Drehscheibe 36
Haggar, William 85, 110, 135, 157–8, 293, 341, 460, 683
Haishi (1921) 116
Halbritter, Josef 52
Hale, Alan 394

Hale, George C. 293, 294
Hale's Tours 22, 93, 94, 293–4, 344, 515, 639;
    Loew 392; world's fairs 705; travelogues 640;
    Zukor 710
The Half-Breed (1916) 196
Halka (1913) 364
Halla, Josip 58
Halme, Kaarle 401
Ham series (1914–1915) 148
Hamilton, Lloyd 148, 353
Hamlet (1920) 481
Hamlet (British Gaumont-Hepworth, 1913)
    296, 589
Hamlet (Lux, 1910) 589
Hamlet (Méliès, 1907) 588
Hamlet (Nordisk, 1910) 589
Hamlet (Phono-Cinéma-Théâtre) 516, 626
Hamman, Joë (Jean) 199, 250, 294–5, 444, 691
The Hand of Justice (1912) 426
Hands of Justice (1913) 271
Hank and Lank series 24, 147
Hansen, Kai 295, 411, 505
Hansen, Miriam 46, 440, 602–3
"*Happy Hooligan*" series (1897) 585
Harbeck, William 523
Hårdh, Hjalmar 40
Hardy, Oliver 394
Harmsworth, Alfred 476
Harris, John 165
Harris, Neil 321
Harrison, Louis Reeves 295, 451, 693
Harron, Bobby 72, 288
Hart, William S. 229, 295, 439
Hartlooper, Louis 295
Harvesting Alfalfa in New Mexico (1912) 320
Harzer, Curt 181
Hasluck, P. N. 282
Hasselbladfilm 362, 616
Hatot, Georges 69, 84, 249, 296, 347, 495,
    506, 549
The Haunted Hotel (1907) 75, 644
Hauptmann, Gerhart 55, 271
Der Hauptmann von Köpenick (1906) 78, 195
The Haverstraw Tunnel (1897) 514, 639
Havsgamar (1916) 592, 614
Hawaii 487
Häxan (1922) 29, 117
Haynes, Hunter C. 75
Hayward, Henry 473

The Hazards of Helen series (1914–1917) 180, 304,
    353, 425
Heath, Stephen 601
Hearst, William Randolph 28, 148–9, 476, 581
The Heart of Nora Flynn 386
Hearts of the World (1918) 703
Hecht, Hermann 34, 35
Heffer, Charles 31, 40
Heiji yuanhun (1916) 115, 710
Heise, William 200, 201, 203, 296, 358
Heisses Blut (1911) 270, 453
Hell's Hinges (1916) 295
Det hemmelighedsfulde X (1914) 117, 164, 386
Henri, Victor 567
Henriques, Fini 175
Henry, Gale 180
Henry VIII (1911) 59, 284, 589
Henschel, James 274
Hepp, Joseph 287
Hepworth, Cecil 119, 282, 297; chase films 157;
    comic strips 149; editing techniques 204, 212;
    film developing, printing, assembly 240;
    Le Blond 378; phantom train rides 595;
    Tilly series 624; trick films 613; Warwick
    Bioscope 685; Warwick Trading Company 685
Hepworth Company 25, 40, 296–7; comedies 143;
    editing techniques 208; Fitzhamon 243, 460;
    Frenkel 259; Khanzhonkov & Co. 356; Rossi
    555; scientific films 567; Shakespeare films 589;
    Taylor and White 624; transportation 639;
    Turner 647
Hepworth, T. C. 18, 297, 406
Her Great Adventure (1918) 291
Herbert, Victor 464
Herd of Sheep on the Road to Jerusalem (1903) 68
Hermansen, Thomas 245
Hérodiade (1910) 347
Heroes of the Cross (1909) 513
A Heroine of '76 (1910) 437, 551
Heron, Edward Thomas 358
Herriman, George 28
Hertz, Aleksander 522, 587
Hertz, Carl 49, 410, 538, 598
Hertz, Henry 112
Hertzberg, S. G. 115
Hervé, Jean 167
Hervil, René 428
Herzl, Theodor 498
Hesekiel, A. 272

Heuveldorp, L. 320

Heuzé, André 145, 251, 296, 298, 506

Hiawatha 312

Higgins, Arthur 50, 298

Higgins, Ernest 50, 298, 604

Hilde Warren und der Tod (1917) 416

Hill, H. J. 98

Hindustan Cinema Films Company 298, 318–19, 411, 514

Hinemoa (1914) 473

Hintner, Cornelius 298

Hirdt, 400

Hirtz, Eduardo 82, 298–9

His New Lid (1910) 316

His Phantom Sweetheart (1915) 386

Hispano Films 40, 299, 414, 599

L'Histoire du cinéma par le cinéma (1927) 290

Histoire d'un crime (1901) 84, 157, 178, 210, 249, 577, 585, 709

L'Histoire d'un Pierrot (1913) 68, 277, 468

Histoire grivoise racontée par une concierge (1902) 192

historical films 299–301; ACAD 198; Ambrosio 19, 104; Andreyor 24; Barker 59; biblical films 68; Capellani 103, 104; Caserini 105; Chile 114; Cines 127; Clarendon Film Company 128; dances 163; Feuillade 235; France 185; Gallo 263; Gaumont 266; Gloria Films 280; Guazzoni 290; India 319, 411, 502; intertitles 327; Itala 333, 334; Italy 336, 338–8; Krauss 364; Maggi 404; Milano Films 436; multiple-reel films 452–3, 454; Nonguet 482; Pasquali 500, 501; Pathé-Frères 506, 508; Rodolfi 553; Russia 505; SCAGL 565; Svenska Biografteatern 614; Vidali 677; World War I 703; *see also* re-enactments

Historien om en gut (1919) 400

Hite, Charles J. 16, 260, 305, 625

L'hiver, Plaisirs de riches! Souffrances des pauvres! (1914) 123, 366

Ho Chi Minh 678

Hodkinson, W. W. 229, 302, 457

Hofer, Franz 61, 271, 302–3, 607

Hofmann-Uddgren, Anna 481, 491, 617

Hoke, Sam 8

Hold-up on the Rocking Mountain Express (1906) 94

Holger-Madsen 175, 303, 483

Holland, Andrew 359, 484

Holland, Annie (née Payne) 303, 341

Holland brothers 97, 98, 484

Holland, George 484

Hollandia 71, 79, 303, 470–1

Hollandsche Film (Pathé-Frères) 303, 403, 470

Hollywood *see* classical Hollywood cinema

Holmes, Elias Burton 222, 303–4, 307, 487, 553, 641

Holmes, Helen 180, 304, 353

El hombre de acero (1917) 114, 591

Home, Sweet Home (1914) 279

Homeland (1915) 461

Homier, Joseph-Arthur 102

L'Homme aimanté (1907) 235

L'Homme aux gants blancs (1908) 158, 507

L'Homme qui à mangé du tareau (1908) 151

L'homme-orchestre (1900) 644

homosexuality 525

Hongfeng kulou (1921) 116

L'Honneur d'un père (1905) 506

Honnoji Kassen (1908) 412

Hooligan in Jail (1903) 94

The Hope Diamond Mystery (1921) 361

Hope, Laura Lee 451

Hopkins, Albert A. 324

Hopson, Violet 296

Hopwood, Henry Vaux 304

"The Horitz Passion Play" (1897) 307

Hornung, E. R. 179

Hornung, E. W. 449

Horrible fin d'un concierge (1903) 143

Hors la loi (1912) 258

Horse Shoeing (1893) 358

Horsley, David 108, 304

Horsley, William 304

Houdin, Robert 33

The House of Bondage (1914) 693

The House of Darkness (1913) 213

House Divided (1913) 291

The House Fly (1912) 572

The House of Hate (1918) 425

A House in Kolomna (1913) 109, 541

The House That Jack Built 595

How a French Nobleman Got a Wife through the New York Herald Personal Columns (1904) 110

How It Feels to be Run Over (1900) 639

"How the Other Half Lives and Dies" (1888) 307

How She Won Him (1910) 264

How They Do Things on the Bowery (1902) 527

How They Got the Vote (1914) 701

How to Stop a Motor Car (1902) 613
How Washington Crossed the Delaware
    (1911) 300
Howe, Lyman H. 112, 119, 184, 222, 304–5, 308,
    341, 590, 596, 641, 655
Howell, Bert 604
Howse, Henry 498, 523, 550, 646
Huber, George 187
Huet, M. 599
Hugenberg, Alfred 703
Hughes, Robert 450, 451
Le Huguenot (1909) 235
Hulcup, Jack 296
Hulfish, David S. 15, 305
Hull House 7
Humanity (film, 1913) 630
Humanity (play, 1897) 630
Hummel, Ferdinand 640
Humorous Phases of Funny Faces (1906) 27, 75
Humphrey, William 680
Hunt, Jay 472
Hunt, William Holman 494, 496
Hunter, John Danby 460
Hunting Big Game in Africa (1909) 25, 580
Hurd, Earl 29
Hurley, Frank 524
Hurrah! Einquartierung (1913) 271, 302
El húsar de la muerte (1925) 114, 591
Hutchinson, Samuel S. 16, 20, 260, 305
Huygens, Christian 32, 405
Den hvide Slavehandel (The White Slave Trade)
    (1910) 40, 76, 174, 245, 453, 483
Hyatt, Isaiah Smith 106
Hyatt, John Wesley 106
Hyman, Edgar 598, 685
The Hypnotist's Revenge (1907) 164

I kronans kläder (1915) 362
I livets vår (1912) 616
Ibáñez Saavedra, León 654
Ibérico 117
The Iconoclast (1910) 368
ideology 46, 600, 601
Ikeru shikabane (1918) 624
Illusionniste renversant 709
illustrated lectures 70, 73, 112, 307–8;
    ethnographic films 221; Holmes 304;
    program formats 533; travelogues 641

illustrated magazines 7, 137, 301, 308–10, 476;
    advertising 542; cinema of attractions 124;
    industrial films 321; Munsterberg 457–8;
    Pickford 520; United States 665
illustrated songs 7, 15, 32, 209, 310–12, 461;
    churches 120; Green 287; intertitles 327;
    Joyce 350; Mason 415; nickelodeons 479, 664;
    program formats 533; Shepard 590; Svensk-
    Amerikanska Filmkompaniet 613; United
    States 659, 664, 665; US imperialism 314
L'Illustre Mâchefer (1914) 384
Im Deutsche Sudan 14
Imigração e comércio (1910) 83
immigrants 432–5, 603, 667; audiences 43, 45, 46,
    47, 479, 665, 666; illustrated songs 311; law and
    cinema 377; leisure 381; leisure time and space
    382; urbanization 651, 652, 664
IMP (Independent Motion Picture Company) 57,
    62, 312–13, 316, 412, 464, 579, 658; Laemmle
    370, 447; Lawrence 377; multiple-reel films 457;
    Pickford 520, 609; star system 608; Universal
    649; Woods 702
Imparcial Film (1919) 38
L'imperatore (1908) 31
imperialism: USA 313–16, 515; modernity 439;
    world's fairs 704; *see also* colonialism
L'Impressionniste fin-de-siècle (1899) 205
IMR *see* Institutional Mode of Representation
In the Bishop's Carriage (1913) 527
In den Vogesen (1915) 688
In the Gray of Dawn (1910) 472
In the Maelstrom of Moscow (1914) 707
In Old Kentucky 94
Inabata Katsutaro 343, 708
Inaugeraçao da Avenida Central (1905) 580
The Inauguration of the Commonwealth (1901)
    50, 562
*Inauguration par Guillarme II du monument de
    Guillarme 1er* (1896) 107
Inazuma goto (1899) 344
Ince, Ralph 316, 386, 607, 680
Ince, Thomas H. 16, 244, 295, 300, 312, 316–17,
    356, 371, 579; New York Motion Picture
    Company 464–5, 472; theater, melodrama 631;
    Triangle Film Corporation 412, 473
Incendie de la rue Notre-Dame (1906) 491
The Independence of Romania (1912) 58
Independents 447, 448, 458, 649,
    657–8, 659

India 318–20; colonial films 137; mythologicals 465; religious filmmaking 550; shadow theater 587

An Indian Girl's Awakening (1910) 690

Indian Massacre (1912) 316, 691

Indian War Council (1894) 132

Indian War Pictures (1914) 132

Indien, das Land der Hindus (1914) 688

Indiens et cow-boys (1904) 93

Indo-British Film 264

Indonesia 320

Indrasabha (1925) 319

industrial films 5, 9, 320–3; advertising 10; Bergqvist 67; churches 120; ethnographic films 221; Gladtvet 279; Johnson and Gibson 348; program formats 641; Selig 580; Switzerland 619; Weltkinematograph 687

L'Inferno (1909) 169

L'inferno (Milano, 1911) 337–8, 386, 436, 454

The Informer (1911) 72, 288

Ingeborg Holm (1913) 386, 592, 607, 614

Ingram, Henry B. 311

An Innocent Magdalene 196

Inoue Masao 323–4, 346

Inquisitive Boots (1905) 208

Die Insel der Seligen (1913) 55, 548

The Inside of the White Slave Traffic (1913) 180, 693

Institutional Mode of Representation (IMR) 602

Interior N.Y. Subway, 14th Street to 42nd Street (1905) 515

intermediality and modes of reception 324–5

intermittent movement 95, 325–6, 388, 538; Bell & Howell studio camera 65; Biograph camera 72; Biograph projector 73; celluloid 107; Ernemann Imperator projector 220; Nuremberg toy projectors 486; Power's Cameragraph No. 5 projector 530; *see also* projectors

International Federation of Film Archives (FIAF) xxx, 1, 36, 241

International Film Company 9

International Film Service newsreel 28

International Projecting and Producing Company (IPPC) 458, 674

The Interrupted Picnic (1906) 438

intertitles and titles 2, 54, 129, 171, 183, 239, 326–31, 380, 422, 631; D'Annunzio 164; Denmark 174; Egypt and other Arab countries 216; *féeries et les quarante voleurs* 232; Finland 242; framing 247; Germany 703; illustrated lectures 307; India 319; industrial films 322; Japan 345; lecturers 379; Netherlands 470; newsreels 478; Nordisk 483; Pathé-Frères 507; Philippines 515; Poland 523; preservation 531; screenwriting 578; sensational melodrama 427; Shakespeare films 589; Svenska Biografteatern 614; Turkey 646

Intolerance (1916) 130, 132, 329, 339, 362, 404, 493, 661

The Invaders (1912) 316

Invernizio, Carolina 678

IPPC *see* International Projecting and Producing Company

Ippolitov-Ivanov, I. M. 193

Iran (Persia) 331–2

Irani, Ardeshir 220

Ireland 332–3

Irigoyen, Julio 654

The Iron Chest (1879) 631

Irving, Henry 494, 586, 631

Irwin, May 143, 225, 626

Is Any Girl Safe? (1916) 693

Isaacs, Walter 685

Isensee, Hermann 141

Ismail, Usmar 320

Isola, Emile 333, 410

Isola, Vincent 333, 410

Itala 15, 16, 333–4, 336, 337, 338; Brazil 83; Chómon 117; Collo 135; Deed 145, 147, 169, 225; historical films 299; Khanzhonkov & Co. 356; New York Motion Picture Company 472; opera 489; Pastrone 164, 501; Remmert 555; Roberti 552; set design 586; Union des grands éditeurs 350; United States 661; Zacconi 709

The Italian Sherlock Holmes (1910) 180

Italy 334–40; archives 36; fairs 226, 227; historical films 299; lecturer 380; legitimate theater 627; multiple-reel films 454; propaganda films 541; set design 586; star performers 3, 608; trade press 637–8

itinerant exhibitors 47, 340–2, 445, 536; Austro-Hungary 51, 53; Belgian Congo 11; Boutillon 80; British colonies in Africa 12; cafés-concerts 90; Cambodia 91; Canada 98; churches 119–20; Denmark 172; Dentler 176; distribution: Europe 189; Elfelt 219; Esoofally 220; fairs/fairgrounds 226–8; France 253, 256–7; French colonies in Africa 13; German colonies in Africa 14;

Germany 270, 273–4, 275; Great Britain 438; Green 28; Indonesia 320; Italy 335; Japan 344; Jeffs 347; Jury 350; Krüger 364; lecturers 379; Lubin 395; Luxemburg 400; Marro 414; Mullens brothers 452; music halls 460; Netherlands 469; Norway 484; *phonoscènes* 518; Poland 522; Portugal 528; projectors 538; Robertson 553; Schnellseher 30; Schuberg 566; Serrador 584; Slieker 593; South Africa 599; Sweden 616, 617; Switzerland 227, 619; transportation 638; United States 659, 663; Wales 683; West 689
Ivanhoe (1913) 57
Ive, Bert 50
Ivens, Cees A. P. 342
Ivens, Joris 342

J. & N. Tait 49, 50, 348
Jack and the Beanstalk (1902) 201, 527, 577
Jacob, Richard 505
Jacobini, Maria 229, 343, 469, 491, 500
Jacobs, Lea 421–2
Jacobs, Lewis 281
Jacobson, Matthew Frye 435
Jacques L'Honneur (1914) 393
Jaenzon, Henrik 592, 611
Jaenzon, Julius 592, 611
Jane Shore (1915) 59
Jang-e Golha (1900) 331
Janin, Louis 646
Janker, Robert 568
Jannings, Emil 271, 526
Janssen, Pierre-Jules-César 33, 343
Japan 343–6; *benshi* 66–7, 134, 345, 346, 379, 624, 634
The Japanese Silk Industry (1914) 320
Le Japon pittoresque (1913) 642
Järnbäraren 614
Jasset, Victorin-Hippolyte 39, 179, 180, 198, 250, 251, 258, 347; comic strips 149; crime films 25, 158; Guy 291; multiple-reel films 454; sensational melodrama 425; serials 583; Vitagraph 680
Jaubert, Léon 267, 620
Jealousy (1911) 647
Jeane, René 167
Jeanne d'Arc (1900) 419
Jeanne Doré (1916) 428
Jeapes, William 635

Jeffries, James J. 81, 82, 273, 605
Jeffries-Johnson Fight (1910) 81, 273, 348, 605
Jeffs, Waller 347–8
Jenkins, C. Francis 34, 38, 96, 348, 395, 519, 538; chronophotography 118; Phantoscope 484, 515, 656; US patent wars 655
Jenny the Maid (1918) 541
Jerusalem's Busiest Street Showing Mount Zion (1903) 68
Jeux d'enfants (1913) 235
A Jewish Dance at Jerusalem (1903) 68
Jews 396, 432–3, 498–9
Jim le glisseur (1908–1909) 27
Jimeno, Eduardo 599
Joan of Arc (1895) 300
Johnson, Arthur 156, 348, 384, 394
Johnson, George P. 349
Johnson and Gibson 49, 50, 348
Johnson, Jack 81, 348–9, 604, 605, 667
Johnson, Martin 25, 222
Johnson, Millard 348
Johnson, Noble M. 74, 349
Johnson, Osa 25, 222
Johnson-Ketchel Fight (1909) 348
Johnston, Lorimer 20
Jolicoeur (1910) 31
La Jolie Bretonne (1914) 553
Joly, Henri Joseph 96, 195, 256, 349, 427, 509, 538, 566, 598; Blair film stock 76; chronophotography 34, 118, 502; Lux 399; Mexico 431; Pirou 522
Jone o gli ultimi giorni di Pompei (*The Last Days of Pompei*) (1913) 500, 501, 677–8
Jones, Aaron J. 349, 479
Jones, John 517
Jones, Juli *see* Foster, William
Jones, Peter P. 75
Jones, Richard Calvert 683
Joslin, Margaret 147, 220
Joubé, Romuald 167
Jourjon, Charles 198, 250, 350, 499, 672
Le Journal du ciné-club (1920–1921) 176
Joyce, Alice 312, 350, 353, 354
Joyce, James 58, 332
Joye, Abbé Joseph 134, 549, 619
Joye, Joseph-Alexis 215, 350
Juan sin ropa (1919) 38
Judex (1917) 24–5, 40, 235, 384, 464, 530, 583, 703

Judith of Bethulia (1914) 71, 156, 289, 586, 619, 684, 696
Juego de niñas y fuente del Prado (1899) 654
Le Juif errant (1904) 419
Julius, Adam 52
Julius Caesar (1908) 627–8
Julius, Harry 50
Jumonji Daigen 66
The Jungle (1914) 368
jungle films 581, 691
Junior Prestwich 18
Jury, Sir William Frederic 282, 350–1, 475
Just a Shabby Doll (213) 213
"Just to Live the Old Days Over" (1909) 311
Justice of a Redskin (1908) 692
Juve contre Fantômas (1913) 24, 180, 607

Kaapstad, van een trem-ker gezien (1898) 598
Kachusha (1914) 345
Kaeriyama Norimasa 345, 346, 353
Kahn, Albert 141
Kalem 15, 71, 353–4, 361; boxing films 348; Canada 99; comic series 148; copyright 154, 353, 374; detective films 179, 180; ethnographic films 222; Gauntier 269; historical films 300; Holmes 304; Ireland 332; Joyce 350; Long 393; Marion 413; musical scores 463; Olcott 488; opera 489; Palestine 498; religious films 69, 550; Roland 554; sensational melodrama 425; star system 608; theater, melodrama 629, 631; travelogues 642; Turkey 646; United States 657; US imperialism 315
Kalich, Berta 490
Kaliya Mardan (1919) 298, 318
Kamiska, Ester Rachel 523
Kamm, Leonard Ulrich 18, 279, 354
Kammermusik (1915) 302
Kandinsky, Wassily 497
Karadjordje (1910) 58
Karalli, Vera 357, 559
Karandikar, A. P. 502
Karenne, Diana 104
Karim, Muhammad 216
Kärlek och journalistik (1916) 611–12
Kärlekens list (1912) 615
Karlstadt, Liesl 671
Karno, Fred 460
al-Kassar, 'Ali 216

Kastor, Paul 15
Katz, Sam 57, 312, 354, 498
The Katzenjammer Kids series (1912) 148
The Katzenjammer Kids and the School Marm (1903) 143
Kawaura Kenichi 708
Kay-Bee 61, 300, 316, 355, 356, 473, 690
Kaye, Alfred 12, 137
Kearton, Cherry 10, 12, 109, 138, 224, 355, 475, 521, 685
Keating, Patrick 387
Keaton, Buster 32, 219
Keechaka Vadham (1917) 452
Keil, Charlie 94, 213
Keith, Benjamin Franklin 131, 262, 355, 458, 503, 524, 652, 673, 674, 675
Kellogg, C. R. 521
Kemmler, Guillaume 505, 522
Kemp, President 572, 573
Kennedy, Jeremiah J. 71, 355, 686
Kenning, 77
Kent, Charles 589, 680
Kenya 12
Kenyon, James 437–8
Kern, Stephen 439
Kerrigan, J. Warren 20, 220, 650
Kertesz, Michael 363
Kessel, Adam 59, 61, 316, 317, 355–6, 447, 464, 472, 473, 549
The Keys to Happiness (*Kliuchi schastia*) (1913) 264, 541, 557, 558
Keystone Film Company 16, 142, 143–4, 356, 658; Arbuckle 32; Chaplin 108, 220; comic series 146, 148; dances 164; Holmes 304; Ince 316; Mace 403; New York Motion Picture Company 61, 355, 472; Normand 483; Sennett 582; Sterling 611; transportation 640; women's suffrage films 701
Al-Khala Al-Amirikaniyya (1920) 216
Khalil 362
Khanzhonkov & Co. 193, 264, 280, 356–7, 610, 633, 707; Bauer 61, 587; Chardynin 109; Mosjoukine 447; Pathé russe 505; Russia 556, 558
Khanzhonkov, Aleksandr 356, 637
Khatim Sulayman 217
Kholodnaia, Vera 61, 357, 558, 559
Kidnapping by Indians (1899) 438

Kid's Auto Race (1914) 108
Kienzl, Hermann 440–1
Kinema Industries 17
Kinemacolor 12, 110, 141, 260, 531; Belgium 64;
   Bergqvist 67; Frenkel 259; Murdock 458;
   Natural Color Kinematograph 468; news
   event films 475; Raleigh & Robert 546; Smith
   (F. Percy) 594; Smith (George Albert) 595;
   Tenkatsu 624; traveling shows 342; United
   States 661; Urban 651
kinemathek 36
Kinematograph, Der 358, 637
Kinematograph and Lantern Weekly 73, 74,
   357–8, 637
Kinematograph Manufacturers Association
   (KMA) 282, 283
Kineto 15
Kinétographe (Méliès) 166, 418, 551; *see also*
   Theatrograph
Kinetophone 202, 342, 355, 358, 458, 615, 620,
   621, 675
Kinetoscope *see* Edison Kinetoscope
King Charles (1913) 128
King, Henry 394, 554
King John (1899) 588, 626
King Kong (1933) 222
King Lear (Thanhouser, 1916) 589
King Lear (Vitagraph, 1909) 628
King of Paris (1917) 61
King Shriyal (1918) 502
Kingdom, Dorothy 591
Kingston, Winifred 230
Kinografen 174, 175, 242, 359–60, 390, 399, 637
Kinora 360
Kinoreformbewegung (cinema reform movement)
   55, 272
Kipling, Rudyard 449
Kircher, Athanasius 32, 405
Kirchner, Albert (a.k.a. Léar) 360,
   411, 522, 549
Kiriki, acrobates japonais (1907) 116
The Kiss in the Tunnel (1899) 595
Klaw & Erlanger 69, 72, 360,
   628, 655, 674
Klaw, Marc 360
Kleine, George 265, 300, 337, 353, 360–1, 393,
   413, 445, 448, 660; Biograph 72; educational
   films 120, 214, 215; fashion 230; musical scores
   464; travelogues 642

Kleine Optical Company 154, 353, 361, 555,
   572, 580
Kleine-Edison-Selig-Essanay (K-E-S-E) 220,
   361, 581
Kleiner, Arthur 241
The Kleptomanic (1905) 177, 328
Klercker, Georg af 361–2, 504, 592, 611, 614, 616
Kling, W. 400
Klitzsch, Ludwig 703
Kliuchi schastia (The Keys to Happiness) (1913)
   264, 541, 557, 558, 633
KMA *see* Kinematograph Manufacturers
   Association
Kobayashi Kisaburo 261, 362
Kobayashi Shokai 324, 346, 362
København ved Nat (1910) 73
Kodak *see* Eastman Kodak
Kohinoor Film Company 319, 362, 502
Kohlhiesels Töchter (1920) 526
Kohlrausch, Ernst 95, 118
Kolm, Gustav Anton 52, 363, 694
Kolm, Louise Veltée 52, 363, 694
Kolowrat-Krakowsky, Alexander "Sascha" Joseph
   52, 363
Komada Koyo 66, 344, 363
Komatsu Shokai 345, 363
Komet-Film 270
Komische Begegnung zum Tiergarten im Stockholm
   (1896) 615
König Menelaus im Kino (1913) 394
Konishi Photographic Store 363–4
Koopman, Elias B. 21, 85
Le Korrigan (1908) 39
Korsten, Lucien 410, 418, 551
Kosmofilm 364, 522, 587
Kosmograph 620
Kosto on suloista (1913) 401
Koszarski, Richard 108
Kracauer, Siegfried 439, 519
Krauss, Henry 3–4, 103, 298, 364, 508, 565
Krayn, Robert 18, 279
Kremer, Theodore 424
Kress, Eugène 578
Kreuger, Ivar 411
Kri Kri 127, 147, 259, 337
Krüger, Fréderic 63, 64, 341, 364
Kruger, G. 320
Kühlmann brothers 335
Kuleshov, Lev 558

Kun onni pettää (1913) 243
Kürturnen der Schüler der k.k. Franz Joseph-Realschule 36
Kyoya eriten (1922) 624

La Badie, Florence 625
La Fontaine, John de 552
La Ricci, Léonardo 216–17
Labanca, José 83
labor movement: Europe 365–7; Germany 702; Italian 580; projectionists 536; United States 6, 368–70; women 697, 699; *see also* consumer cooperatives
Laborer's Love (1922) 710
Lacan, Jacques 601
LaCava, Gregory 28
The Lad From Old Ireland (1910) 332
Laddé, Machiel Hendricus 593
Lady Baffles and Detective Duck (1915) 180
The Lady of the Camelias (1909) 627
The Lady of the Lake (1912) 613
The Lady and the Mouse (1913) 208–9, 279
Lady Raffles series (1913) 179
The Lady of Shalott (1912) 495–6
Laemmle, Carl 370–1, 432, 445, 446, 457, 660; IMP 312, 313, 316; Lawrence 377–8; Motion Picture Distributing and Sales Company 447, 464, 530; nickelodeon 479; Pathé Cinematograph 503; star system 608; Universal 188, 649, 650
Laffitte, Paul 91, 236, 237, 371, 378
Lagerlöf, Selma 411
Lahiri, Nitish C. 264
Lallement, François 14–15
Lamb, Thomas 575
Lambert, Albert 3, 626
Lamster, Johann Christian 371–2
Le lancer du disque de l'athlète Jean Bouin 482
Landau, Friedrich 52
Landau, Samuel 523
Die Landstrasse (1913) 271, 682
Lang, Edith 463
Lang, Fritz 54, 416, 586
Lange, Konrad 372
Langer, Resie 698
Langlois, Henri 133
Langtry, Lily 628
Lanka Dahan (1917) 465

Lantini, René 150
Larionov, Mikhail 497
Larraín Lecarios, Luis 278
Larraín Lecaros, Arturo 114
Larsen, Viggø 3, 248, 302, 372, 483, 681
Lasky, Jesse 171, 229, 230, 372, 386, 396, 457, 490, 619, 628
L'Assommoir (1909) 39
The Last Days of Pompeii (Paul, 1899) 510
The Last Diva (1982) 68
The Last of the Line (1914) 690
Latham, Gray 34, 96, 155, 186, 187, 372–3, 604, 655
Latham, Otway 34, 96, 155, 186, 187, 372–3, 604, 655
Laudet, Georges 118
Laurel, Stan 24, 460
Laurier, Wilfred 98
Lauste, Eugene 12, 20, 372, 373
Lautensack, Heinrich 55, 153, 373
Lavanchy-Clarke, François-Henri 373, 592, 619
Lavedan, Henri 236, 237, 300, 578, 626
Laveuses, Baigneurs dans l'Oued Senia 13
Lavigne, Marguerite 530
law and the cinema 373–7; *see also* regulation
The Law and the Outlaw (1913) 439
Lawley, H. V. 613
Lawrence, Florence (Florence Annie Bridgwood) 57, 144, 147, 312, 348, 371, 377–8, 394, 589, 608, 609
Lawson, John 630
Lazarev, Evan 426
Le Bargy, Charles 3, 91, 103, 236, 237, 378, 626
Le Blond, Elizabeth Alice Frances 378, 619
Le Bret, Suzanne 512
Le Couteur, John 85
Le Fraper, Charles 157, 637
Le Lieure, Henri 334
Le Prince, Louis Aimé Augustin 33, 95, 188, 378
Le Somptier, René 87, 467
Leal, Antônio 234, 379
Leaving Mass at the Pilar in Zaragoza 599
Lebanon 215, 217, 499
Leben und Treiben in Tangka 14
Lebiedziski, Piotr 522
lecturers 7, 44, 125, 327, 379–80, 531–2, 577; *benshi* 66–7, 134, 345, 346, 363, 379, 624, 634; Bush 87; Canada 98, 100; consumer cooperatives 152; Finland 242; Hale's Tours 93;

Hartlooper 295; India 319; Iran 331; labor movement: Europe 367; magic lantern shows 406; Netherlands 470; program formats 533; Quebec 100, 102, 166; Silvio 591; tableaux 209; travelogues 641; United States 659

Lecuona, Ernesto 160

Lederer, Franz 526

Lefébvre, Léo 13, 646

Legaert, Henri 11

Légende des phares (1909) 235

La légende du fantôme (1908) 116–17

Le Legionnaire (1914) 138

legitimate theater 43, 230, 266, 626–8; Bernhardt 67; declining attendances 574; electricity 217–219; *film d'art* 236, 237; France 257; Germany 275; Howe 305; Lasky 372; Loew 392; star system 608; Svenska Biografteatern 614; United States 660, 665; vaudeville 674

Léglise, Paul 34

Lehrman, Henry 611

Leilich, Philipp 400

Leino, Eino 401

leisure 150, 309, 476; saloons 561; United States 380–3; vaudeville 672

Lekhaim (1910) 411–12, 505

Lemke, Hermann 275

Lenepveu, Jules Eugène 495

Leno, Dan 460

Lenz-Levy, Paul 384

Leonard, Marion 383–4, 608

The Leonard-Cushing Fight (1894) 604

Leonardo da Vinci 494

Léonce series (1912–1916) 147, 281, 512

Léonce à la campagne (1913) 512

Léonce et Poupette (1914) 512

Leone, Vincenzo *see* Roberti, Roberto

The Leopard's Foundling (1914) 694

Lepage, Enrique 38

Lepanto, Vittoria 627

Lépine, Charles-Lucien 384

Leprince, René 103, 250, 384, 553, 710

Let Him Who Is Without Sin Cast The First Stone (1915) 707

Let Me Dream Again 595

Leutze, Emmanuel 301

Leuville, Gabriel-Maximilien *see* Linder, Max

Leuzinger, Willy 227

Lever Brothers 9

Levesque, Marcel 194, 384, 464, 467, 512

Levin, A. 557

Lévy, Benoît *see* Benoît-Lévy, Edmond

Lewis, Max 113

Lewitzki, Ladislas-Victor 62

La leyenda del charco de Güije (1909) 159

L'Herbier, Marcel 428

Li Minwei 115

Lisbon, the Fish Market (1806) 528

Li Ting Lang (1924) 320

Libya 646

Lichtbild-Bühne, Die (journal) 384, 637

Lickmann's Cigar and Photo Store (1898) 9

Liebelei (1914) 55

Lieutenant Daring films 84

Lieutenant Ergunov (1910) 505

Lieutenant Rose films (1909–1914) 128, 613

The Lieutenant's Last Fight (1912) 690

Life of an American Fireman (1902–1903) 201, 206, 212, 424, 527, 577, 602

The Life of Buffalo Bill (1912) 132

The Life of Charles Peace, The Notorious Burglar (1905) 157–8, 293, 590

The Life of Christ 646

Life in Death (1914) 447

A Life for a Life (*Zhizn za zhizn*) (1916) 61, 357

The Life of Moses (1909–1910) 69, 70, 71, 456, 494, 586, 660

A Life for the Tsar (1911) 489

Life on the Zambeze River 12

Liggett, Genevieve *see* Gauntier, Gene

The Light That Came (1909) 328

The Lightening Raider (1919) 693

lighting 218, 384–7; Bauer 61; Belasco 171; Bitzer 74; Christensen 117; classical Hollywood cinema 130; Dwan 196; Germany 271; Hasselbladfilm 616; historical films 299; Hofer 302; Holger-Madsen 303; Jasset 347; Klercker 362; melodrama, domestic 422; museum life exhibits 458; Perret 512; photography 519; Reinhardt 548; Reliance 549; set design 584, 585; staging in depth 605; Svenska Biografteatern 614

lighting apparatus 385, 387–9

Den lille Hornblæser (1909) 173, 593

Lily van Java (1928) 320

Lincoln & Parker Film Company 203

Lincoln Motion Picture Company 74, 349

Lincoln, W. J. 50, 389–90

Lind, Alfred 164, 174, 175, 245, 291, 360, 390, 615, 620

Lindelöf, Oscar 40

Linder, Max (Gabriel-Maximilien Leuville) 108, 179, 250, 390–1, 507, 532, 559, 608, 609; comedy/comic series 142, 144, 145–6; costume 156; Cuba 160; de Barros 165; Deed 333; framing 246; Gasnier 265; Leprince 384; Nonguet 482; Shakespeare films 589

Lindsay, Vachel 391, 561

The Line-Up at Police Headquarters (1914) 180

Lines of White on a Sullen Sea (1909) 383

Linienlaufe unter dem Aequator 14

Le Lion 15, 64, 138, 250, 296, 347

Liquid Electricity: or, The Inventor's Galvanic Fluid (1907) 211, 218

Lisbon, the Fish Market (1806) 528

Lisenko, Natalia 707

l'Isle-Adam, Villiers de 448–9

Literaria-Film 78, 195

Little Ellie (1918) 541

Little Lost Sister (1917) 693

Little Moritz series (1911–1912) 79, 138, 146, 150, 193

Little Moritz Soldat d'Afrique (1911) 138

Little Nemo (1911) 28, 417

"Little Tich" 460, 550–1

Little Willy series (1912–1914) 147, 199

Liu Zhonglun 234

Living Canada series 73, 99, 101

Living London (1904) 348

Living Sydney (1906) 689

Llewellyn, John Dilwyn 683

Lo Savio, Gerolamo 228–9, 238, 338, 392, 469

The Loafer (1911) 208

Löbel, Léopold 399

Locher, Jens 242

Locked Out (1911) 368

Lockwood, Harold 229

Locura de amor (1909) 414

Loetoeng Kasaroeng (1926) 320

Loew, Marcus 122, 245, 369, 392, 446, 479, 497, 511, 566, 664, 675, 710

La Loi du pardon (1906) 420–1, 506

Löjtnant Galenpanna (1917) 362

Lomas, H. M. 109

Lombard, Thomas 484

Lombardi, Giselda *see* Gys, Leda

Lombardo Film 169, 340

Lombardo, Gustavo 292, 337

Lomon, André 142, 568, 571

Londe, Albert 33, 118, 324, 393, 519, 567

London Day by Day 595

London National Film Theater 241

The Lonedale Operator (1911) 72, 140, 151, 288, 422, 639

The Lonely Villa (1909) 151, 158, 213, 219, 422

The Lonely Villa (Protazanov remake) 423

Long, Samuel 353, 361, 393, 413

Longford, Raymond 50, 298, 393, 604

Looking for John Smith (1906) 150

Loos, Anita 329–30

The Looters of Liege (1914) 59

Lordier (Lévy), Georges 40, 123, 251, 393

Lorent-Heilbronn, V. 233

Lorenzino De' Medici (1908) 145

Lortac 150

Lost in the Jungle (1911) 25, 694

Louis XI (1887) 631

Louisiana Purchase Exposition (1904) 287, 705

Love in an Apartment Hotel (1912) 151

Love, Bessie 291

Love in the Suburbs (1900) 74, 93

Love and the Varsity (1913) 613

Love and War (1899) 205, 206, 209, 212, 314

Løvejagten (1907–1908) 372, 483

Lowenstein, Hans Otto 394

Lubin Manufacturing Company 63, 94, 96, 394–5, 448, 570; Balshofer 58, 472; boxing films 81, 155; catalogue 577; chase films 110; copyright 154, 374; crime films 158; ethnographic films 222; framing 247; Hale's tours 294; India 318; Ireland 332; Johnson (Arthur) 348; Johnson (Noble M.) 349; Lawrence 378; opera 489; Philippines 515; Quebec 102; Sargent 564; "Tramp" films 145; United States 656, 657; US patent wars 655; Vitagraph-Lubin-Selig-Essanay 220, 394, 581, 680; world's fairs 705

Lubin, Siegmund 25, 69, 187, 394, 395–6, 479, 538, 655, 656, 675

Lubitsch, Ernst 147, 165, 271, 396, 493, 526, 548, 612

Lucha de corazones (1913) 600

Lucia Di Lammermoor (1908) 490

Lucille Love, Girl of Mystery serial (1914) 161, 244

The Luck of Roarin' Camp (1910) 262

Lucrezia Borge (1912) 392

Lugosi, Bela 298

Lukacs, Georg 439
Lumholtz, Carl 221, 223
Lumière 30, 34, 125, 188–9, 249, 396–8; *actualités* 5, 477; Arab countries 216; Argentina 37–8; Australia 50; Austro-Hungary 51; Balkans 58; Belgium 64; Bernard 67; biblical films 69; Blair Camera Company, European 76; Bolivia 77; Brazil 82; Breteau 84; Brulatour 85; Calcina 90; camera movement 92; Canada 97, 98; catalogues 542, 577; celluloid 76, 107, 197; chronophotography 118; colonial films 13, 136; color photography 139; comedies 142; comic strips 149; crime films 157; dance films 163; Doublier 191–2; Edison 201; editing techniques 204, 207, 210, 211; ethnographic films 222; Foersterling 244; Germany 273, 274; Greece 287; Hatot 296; illustrated lectures 307; India 318; intermediality and modes of reception 324; Ireland 332; Japan 344; Kinora 360; Lavanchy-Clarke 373; Luxemburg 400; magicians 410; Maguire & Baucus 411; Mesguich 428; Mexico 431; Minier 437; modes of production 443; music halls 460; Netherlands 469; news event films 474; Numa Peterson's Trading Company 485; opera 489; paintings 495; Palestine 498; photography 519; Portugal 528; program formats 533; projectors 510, 593; Promio 540; Quebec 101; Raymond 546; re-enactments 547; Redfern 547; religious films 549; Russia 555; Santos 563; screenwriting 576, 577; set design 584; shadow theater 588; sound effects 596; Sweden 615, 617; Switzerland 619; trade mark cases 636; travelogues 641; trick films 644; Turkey 646; United States 659, 662; US patent wars 655; Urban 651; Venezuela 676; Veyre 677; Vietnam 678; Warwick Trading Company 685; Wolff 696; world's fairs 705; *see also* Cinématographe Lumière
Lumière, Antoine 131, 252, 396, 397, 398
Lumière, Auguste 101, 252, 397, 398–9
Lumière, Louis 34, 101, 105, 396, 397, 398–9, 419
"Luminous Pantomimes" (1889–1892) 26
Luna-Film 270, 302
Lund, Fernand 513
Lundberg, Frans 399, 615, 616
Luperti, Conrad 523
The Lure (1914) 693
Lure, S. V. 559
The Lurking Peril (1920) 425

La Lutte pour la vie 384
Lux 15, 250, 255, 399; Belgium 64; Bourgeois 80; Durand 194; *féeries* 233; Hamman 294; Joly 349; Misu 437; Shakespeare films 589; Union des grands éditeurs 350
Luxemburg 399–400
Luz, Ernst J. 462
Lyell, Lottie 50, 393
Lykke-Seest, Peter 279, 400, 484
The Lyons Mail (1877) 631
Lyyra Filmi 243, 400–1

M. Kashii 345, 649
M. Pathe 344, 345, 403, 481, 623, 649
Ma Cousine 516, 626
Ma l'amor mio non muore! (Love Everlasting) (1913) 3, 78, 106, 167, 246, 280, 339, 421, 422, 454, 606, 607, 608, 627
Ma Tante (1902) 192, 225
Mabel's Dramatic Career (1913) 144
Mabel's Strange Predicament (1914) 108, 483
Macbeth (Cines, 1909) 589
Macbeth (Film Industrie Gesellschaft, 1913) 589
Macbeth (Pathé-Frères, 1909) 589
Macbeth (Vitagraph, 1908) 589, 628
McCay, Winsor 28, 29, 150, 417
McClellan, George B. 376, 667
McClellen, Charles 120
McCutcheon, Wallace 71, 74, 201, 413, 417, 527
McDonnell, Claude 523
McDowell, Clare 72
McDowell, John Benjamin 84, 85, 417
Mace, Fred 143, 403
Macedonia 58
McGowan, J. P. 304
Mach, Ernst 568
Machin, Alfred 12, 13, 62, 64, 138, 403–4; comic series 146; Comica 150; expedition films 224; Hollandsche Film 303; transportation 640
Die Macht des Gesanges (1913) 490
Macintyre, John 568, 573
Maciste (1915) 493
Maciste all'Inferno (1926) 493
Maciste Alpino (1916) 493
Mack, Max 55, 153, 182, 271, 278, 404, 452, 681, 682, 687
Mack Sennett Comedies 356
MacKaye, Steel 188

MacKenzie, John 58, 109, 223
McKinley, William 74, 218, 314, 540
McNamara, John 369
Macnamara, Walter 457
MacPherson, Jeanie 650
McRae, V. H. 417, 516
Mad Musician (1909) 590
Madame Butterfly (1915) 490
Madame a des Envies (1906) 291
Madame Dubarry (1919) 396
Madame Loretta (1919) 216
Madame Sans-Gêne (1911) 91, 237, 250–1, 626, 627
Madame Tallien (1911) 167
Madame Tussaud's 458, 686
Madan, Jamshedji Framji 49, 220, 318, 404
Madan Theatres Limited 319, 404, 555
Das Mädchen ohne Vaterland (1912) 248
Madeleine de Verchères (1922) 102
Madieu, Léon 503
Madison, Cleo 650
magazines *see* illustrated magazines
Maggi, Luigi 19, 78, 338, 404, 491
The Magic Box (1951) 260
Magic Bricks (1908) 645
magic lantern shows 119, 247, 307, 404–8, 652;
    Canada 287; Great Britain 281, 282; Hofer 303;
    India 318; intertitles 327; labor movement 365;
    lecturers 379; Palestine 498; Pathé-Frères 507;
    phonography 517; Saunders 564; screens 573;
    sound effects 596; Sweden 617; travelogues 641;
    Walker 684; West 689
magic lanterns 8, 26, 205, 210, 212; 238, 405–7,
    408–10, 549, 610; archaeology of cinema 32, 33,
    34, 35; biblical films 70; Bijou Theater (Boston)
    131; collections 133; color 139; consumer
    cooperatives 153; education 214; Furniss 262;
    intermediality and modes of reception 324;
    Japan 343; Joye 134, 350; Lubin 395; Maison de
    la Bonne Presse 411; Norton 484; paintings 494;
    Philipsen 172; pornography 525; projectors 538;
    shadow theater 587; Smith 594; Spencer 221;
    Strindberg 449; trade press 637; US imperialism
    314; Wrench Film Company 705; Yoshizawa
    Shoten 708
magicians 112, 261, 324, 410, 418, 510;
    Australia 49; Isola brothers 333; Poland 522;
    Smith 594; trick films 124, 644; vaudeville 672
Magnetism (1912) 572

Magnussen, Fritz 592
Magnusson, Charles 361, 410–11, 592, 611, 614, 615
Maguire & Baucus 279, 297, 411, 484, 546, 651, 655, 685
Maguire, Franck Z. 359, 411, 685
Maharashtra Film Company 319, 411
The Maher-Choynski Fight (1897) 187
The Maid of Cefn Ydfa (1913) 683
Mailboat Munster's Arrival at Holyhead (1898) 113
Main de fer series (1911–1913) 151, 281, 512, 583
Main de fer: L'Evasion de forçat de Croze (1913) 94
"Maine" incident (1898) 5
Mairi, Romance of a Highland Maiden (1913) 573
Maison de la Bonne Presse 120, 123, 132, 214, 307, 360, 411, 549, 637
La maison ensorcelée (1908) 644
Maisons du Peuple 152
Maître, Maurice André 295, 411–12, 505
Majestic 16, 403, 412, 447, 464, 520, 658;
    Cabanne 89; Mutual 649; Sweet 619
Making Bamboo Hats in Java (1911) 323
Making a Living (1914) 108
Makino Shozo 344, 412, 481, 489, 708
Maksimov, Vladimir 559
A mala sinistra (1908) 234, 379
Les Maladies nerveuses (1920) 567
Malaya 412–13
Malfasi, Umberto (Dorès) 216
Mallet, Félicia 516, 626
Malombra (1918) 485
"Maltese cross" projectors 86, 105, 127, 154, 220, 268, 290, 326, 430, 530, 538, 539, 696
The Man and his Bottle (1908) 244
The Man With a Weak Heart (1901) 160
Manaki brothers 58, 287, 646
Manhattan Madness (1916) 196
The Maniac Chase (1904) 212
Del manicomio al matrimonio (1913) 513
La manigua o la mujer cubana (1915) 185, 563
Mann, Hank 108
Der Mann im Keller (1913) 271
Mannoni, Laurent 133–4
Le manoir du diable (1896) 576
Manon Lescaut 490
Mantle, J. Gregory 550, 685
Manuel García, o el rey de los campos de Cuba (1913) 185
Manuel Rodríguez (1910) 114

Manzano, Lucas 676
Mara (1910) 505
Marasem-e Moharram va Qamehzani (1901) 331
Marcantonio e Cleopatra (1913) 127
Marcel, Charles 617
Marché à Biskra 13
Marchovsky, S. G. 625
La Marcia Nuziale (1915) 485
Marek, Andrzej 523
Marey, Etienne-Jules 29, 30, 86, 95, 265, 413,
    519; animal pictures 25; archaeology of
    cinema 33, 34, 35; chronophotography 33, 34,
    118, 119, 324, 566; Demenÿ170; intermittent
    movements 325; Janssen 343; Muybridge 465,
    570; Noguès 482; scientific films: Europe 566,
    568, 569, 571; sports films 604
Mari, Febo 194, 485, 709
María (1921–1922) 136
Maria Rosa (1915) 171, 490
Marie Antoinette 299
Marie Stuart (1908) 364
Marinescu, Gheorghe 58, 567
Marion, Frank J. 71, 353, 354, 361, 393, 413
Mark, Mitchell H. 413–14, 511
Markgraf, William 201
Marro, Albert 116, 299, 414, 599, 600
Marsh, Mae 72, 288, 353
Marshall, E. M. 523
Marshall, Eric 223
Marta of the Lowlands (1914) 490
martial arts films 115, 116, 710
Martin, Benjamin 405
Martin, Clyde 462
Martinet, Marcel 366
Martinetti, William 527
Martínez, Blanco y 160
Martínez Casado, Luisa 105
Martínez, Francisco 676
Martoglio, Nino 338, 340, 414
A Martyr to His Cause (1911) 369, 540
The Martyrdom of Nurse Cavell (1916) 269
Les Martyrs de l'Inquisition (1905) 94
Marvin, Arthur 74, 186, 314, 414
Marvin, Harry 21, 414–15
Marx, Karl 442
Marxism 366
Mary, Clément 146, 235, 250, 266, 415
Mary Jane's Mishap (1903) 207, 226, 247, 595
Marzullo, Francisco 379

Mascagni, Pietro 78, 491
Maskelyne, John Nevill 410, 418, 490
Mason, Bert 415
Mason, J. C. Bee 521
Masques et grimaces (1902) 143
The Massacre (1912) 74
Massart, Léontine 167
Massösens offer (1910) 615
Mastbaum, Jules 122, 229, 415, 665
Mastbaum, Stanley 122, 229, 415, 479, 665
Master, Homi 362
Matas, Rudolph 570
Le matelas alcoolique (1906) 265
Mathias Sandorf (1920) 25
Mathieu, Julienne 116
Mathot, Jacques 350
Un Matrimonio interplanetario 151
Matrimony's Speed Limit (1913) 291
La Mattchiche 518
Matuszewski, Bóleslaw 37, 415–16, 522, 540, 567
Maudit soit la guerre (1913) 403, 640
Maurel, Victor 516
Maurice, Georges 131, 198
Maurice, Léopold 131
Mauro, Humberto 83
Max amoureux de la teinturière (1912) 391
Max et son chien Dick (1912) 144
Max Linder contre Nick Winter (1911) 391
Max pédicure (1914) 508
May, Allen 101
The May Irwin John Rice Kiss (1896) 143, 225, 626
May, Joe 153–4, 271, 416, 548
May, Mia 416
Mayer, Hy 150
Mayer, Louis B. 392, 432
Meccheri, Giovanni 337
Mecklenburg, Adolf Friedrich zu 137
Med dolk och gift (1912) 615
Le Médecin du château (1908) 151
The Medicine Bottle (1908) 151
Medina, José 83, 418, 555
Medlinskij, 567
Meet Me at the Fountain (1904) 110, 111
Mei Lanfang 150
Der Meineidbauer (1915) 363
Meir Ezofowicz (1911) 587
Meissonier, Jean-Louis 570
Méliès, Gaston 113, 244, 417, 418, 419, 473,
    487, 613

Méliès, Georges 5, 17, 30, 150, 249, 418–20, 448, 540; advertising films 9; AGC 14–15; Belgian Congo 11; Canada 98; Chómon 116; cinema of attractions 124–6; color 139; Congrès International des Editeurs de Films 254; costumes 155; Cuba 159; dance 163; Debrie 168; Deed 169; editing techniques 204, 205, 206, 207, 210, 212; facial expression films 226; fake newsreel 548; fantasmagoria 33; *féeries* 125, 231–2, 233, 234, 418, 494, 584; Italy 335; lighting 385, 386; magicians 410; Mexico 431; music halls 460; opera 489; Paley 499; Paul 510; Porter 527; projectors 96, 528, 538; propaganda films 540; re-enactments 474, 477, 547, 548; Relph 551; Reulos 551; screenwriting 576, 577; set design 584, 585; Shakespeare films 588; South Africa 598; staging in depth 606; transportation 639; trick films 97, 124, 125, 151, 159, 584, 644, 645, 654; Urban 651; Uruguay 654; Warwick Trading Company 685; Wolff 696

melodramas: acting styles 2; AM&B 21; American Film Manufacturing Company 20; Andriot 25; Aquila Films 31; Bertini 68; Bonnard 78; Bos 79; Brazil 83; Capellani 103; Chile 114; China 115, 116; classical Hollywood narrative 128; Colombia 136; Delmont 170; dialogue accompaniment 184; domestic 115, 244, 420–3, 425, 506; Drankov 61; Duskes 195; erotic 76, 175, 426, 453, 484; Film d'Arte Italiana 238; Fitzhamon 244; France 249, 251; Gaumont 266; Germany 271; Gottschalk 281; Grandais 281; Gundersen 291; Haggar 293; historical films 300; Hofer 302; Itala 333; Kalem 353; Khanzhonkov 356; Kinografen 360; Klercker 362; Lautensack 373; Leonard 383; Lind 390; Lubin 394; Mack 404; narrative/attractions dualism 126; Notari 485; Pasquali 500; Pastrone 501; Pathé-Frères 506, 507; Peru 514; Piel 521; Protazanov 541; religious themes 68–9; Russia 505, 557, 558; Serena 582; Stiller 611; theater 128, 626, 628–32; von Woringen 682; westerns 689; women 698; Zheng 710; *see also* dramas; serials; sensational melodrama

Memories of a Mexican (1947) 635–6
Mendel, Georges 63, 242, 253, 349, 427, 489–90
Mendoza, David 464
Menichelli, Pina 17, 127, 334, 339, 428, 436, 469, 485, 501, 609, 627
Menschen und Masken (1913) 521

Menu, Paul 58
Meravidis, Dimitris 287
Il mercante di Venezia (1910) 392
Mercanton, Louis 178, 428
The Merchant of Venice (1914) 687
Mères françaises (1917) 428
Mericke aus Neu-Ruppin kommt nach Berlin (1911) 264
Merson, Billy 461
La Merveilleuse Vie de Jeanne d'Arc (1929) 468
Méry, Jean 198, 505
Merzbach, Georges 290, 428, 502, 565
Merzbach, Saül 290, 428, 502, 565
Mesa, Carlos 77
De mésaventures van een Fransch heertje zonder pantalon aan het strand te Zandvoort (1905) 452
Mesguich, Félix 9, 12, 131, 137, 195, 216, 243, 428–9, 519
Meskal le contrebandier (1909) 347
The Messenger Boy's Mistake (1903) 23
Messter Biophon 429, 620, 634, 635
Messter consortium 55, 63, 76, 147, 260, 429, 608; Germany 270, 271, 272; Hofer 302; India 318; multiple-reel films 453; *Tonbilder* 270, 272, 278, 280
Messter, Oskar 61, 96, 195, 211, 244, 264, 274, 430; Biophon 429; Gliewe 279; Netherlands 469; opera 489; Porten 526; Portugal 528; projectors 538, 539; scientific films 567; Théophile Pathé 632; *Tonbilder* 270, 489, 634, 635
Messter-Projection/-Film 270
Metro 89, 104, 288, 613
Metro-Goldwyn-Mayer (MGM) 267, 392
Metz, Christian 42, 124, 601
Meusy, Jean-Jacques 565
Mexican-Americans 432, 433, 435
Mexico 430–1; political filmmaking 62; westerns 690
Meyer series 147
MGM *see* Metro-Goldwyn-Mayer
Micard, Henri (Henri de Fleurigny) 62
Michault, Théophile 14–15
Micheaux Book and Film Company 74
Micheaux, Oscar 74
Mickey (1918) 483
A Mid-Winter Night's Dream; or, Little Joe's Luck (1906) 75, 589
middle class 42–3, 46–7, 329, 441, 455, 543, 561; *Autorenfilme* 55; Canada 99; Germany 275;

Great Britain 284; Italy 335, 337; legitimate
theater 626; leisure 381, 382; music halls 460;
nickelodeon 479; Quebec 102; *Tonbilder* 635;
United States 663, 664, 666; vaudeville 663,
664; women 699, 700
Middle East xxix
A Midsummer Night's Dream (Azzuri, 1913) 589
A Midsummer Night's Dream (Reinhardt/Dieterle,
1935) 589
A Midsummer Night's Dream (Vitagraph, 1909)
155, 589, 628
Migé, Clément 79, 143, 146, 169, 194, 250, 431–2
migration/immigration 6, 432–5; *see also*
immigrants
Mikkelson, Captain 223
Los milagros de la Divina Pastora (1929) 677
Milano Films 15, 87, 145, 336, 337, 435–6;
De Liguoro 166; Decroix 168; lighting 386;
Maggi 404; multiple-reel films 454; Negroni 468;
United States 661
Miles Brothers 81, 436, 590, 660
A Militant Suffragist (a.k.a. *A Busy Day*) (1914) 701
military films 10
Millais, John Everett 494
Millefleurs, Lina 436
Miller, Arthur C. 436–7
The Miller's Daughter (1905) 527
Milling the Militants (1913) 128
The Million Dollar Mystery (1914) 583, 625
Les Millions de l'orpheline (1912) 552
Milton (1911) 178
Mine at Last (1909) 247
Mingozzi, Gianfranco 68
Mingxing Company 115, 710
Minier, Louis 101, 437
Le Miracle (1913) 105
Mirakel (1912) 437
Mirbeau, Octave 449
Mirographe 551
Mirska, Maria 523
mise-en-scène 230, 339, 508, 547; Linder 390;
Méliès 419; melodrama 420; staging in
depth 606; wax museums 686
Les Misérables (Pathé-Frères, 1912) 3, 104, 236,
250, 364, 437, 454, 508, 565, 671
Les Misérables (Vitagraph, 1909) 456
Les Misérables serial (1925–1926) 235
Les Misères de l'aiguille (1914) 123, 366
Miss Julie (1912) 481, 491

Misteri de dolor (1914) 290
Mistinguett (Jeanne-Marie Bourgeois) 437, 467,
532, 565, 608
Misu, Mime 153, 437
Mit der Kamera in der Schlachtfront (1913) 688
Mit der Kamera in Ewigen Eis (1914) 523, 688
Mitchell & Kenyon 85, 287, 341, 347, 437–8, 474,
477, 532, 573, 604, 634
Mitchell, Robert A. 18
Mitchell, Sagar J. 437–8
Le Mitron (1904) 192
Mix, Tom 438–9, 580, 691
Mizoguchi Kenji 481
mobile projection booths 52
Modelle (1908–1910) 564
Modernism 57, 116, 290
modernity 46, 100, 276, 449, 536; critique of 450;
and early cinema 439–42; gender roles 699;
Japan 345, 346; leisure 381; spectatorship 603;
Stiller 612; transportation 638; United States 435,
690; urban 383
modes of production 442–4, 578–9, 657, 658–9
Modot, Gaston 444
Mohler, Guy 148
Moigno, Abbé François 307, 406, 551
Moise sauvé des eaux (1911) 69
Moissi, Alexander 55
Moisson, Charles 51, 191, 398
Molchi, grust, molchi (1918) 357, 558
Momijigari (1899) 344, 346, 363
Monca, Georges 103, 250, 444, 532, 565
The Money God 437
Monopolfilm 175, 183, 190, 273, 429, 453
monopoly capitalism 444–6
Monsen, Frederick 222, 307
Montagu, E. H. 503
Montenegro 58
Montpensier, Duc de 223
Montt, Pedro 114
Moore, Alex T. 201
Moore, Annabelle 163, 446
Moore, Owen 312, 446–7, 464, 520
Moore, Tom 350, 353
Moorhouse, A. H. 598
morality 258, 561, 667
Morano, Gigetta 19, 167, 337, 340, 447, 553
Moray, Isidore 64
Mordet paa Fyn (1907) 173
Moreira, Alberto 49

Morénas, Louis 123
Morgan le pirate series (1909–1910) 198, 250, 347
Morocco 13, 215, 217
Morosco, Oliver 694
Morris, William 673, 674, 675
La Mort du Duc d'Enghien (1909) 508
La Mort du Marat (1897) 157, 495, 547
Mortal Flowers (1918) 216
Mortier, Paul 490
Moscow Clad in Snow 505
Moshajereh ba Arab 331
Mosjoukine (Mozzhukhin), Ivan 357, 447, 541, 559, 609, 707
Motazedi, Khanbabakhan 332
The Mothering Heart (1913) 279, 288
Motion Picture Distributing and Sales Company 447, 464, 530, 551, 596, 649, 658, 660; Brulatour 85; Laemmle 370; Miles brothers 436; Nestor 108; New York Motion Picture Company 472–3; popularity of Independents 448
Motion Picture Patents Company (MPPC) 4, 16, 21, 72, 447–8, 451, 472, 507; anti-Trust court case 658; Armat 39; Bijou Theater 131; Blackton 75; boxing films 81, 348; Canada 99, 102; Centaur 108, 304; cinema chains 122; Collier 134; demise of 649; distribution 189, 229; domestic melodrama 425; Dyer 196; Edison 202, 203; Essanay 220, 604; Fox 246; Freuler 260; Gaumont 265; General Film Company 269; Griffith 288; IMP 312, 313; Italy 337; Kalem 353; Kennedy 355; Kessel 355; Kleine 361; Laemmle 370; "Latham Loop" 373; licenses 20, 260, 286, 464, 660, 674; Long 393; Lubin 394, 396; Marvin 414; Méliès 419; modes of production 443; National Board of Censorship 43; Nordisk 483; patent wars 655, 657; Pathé Cinematograph 503; regulation 375, 376; Saunders 564; Schneider 566; Selig 580, 581; Supreme Court 24; Swanson 614; trade press 637; US monopoly capitalism 445, 446; *Views and Films Index* 679; Vitagraph 679; Warner Brothers 684; Waters 686
Motion Picture Story Magazine 75, 310, 609, 638
motion studies 567, 568, 571
Motion-Picture Theater Management (1911) 15
The Motorist (1905) 510
Mottershaw, Frank 58, 110, 590
Mounet-Sully, Jean 236, 589

mountaineering films 87, 378
Le Mouvement (1894) 568
moving picture fiction 448–51
Moving Picture News 451, 462, 564, 637
Moving Picture World 10, 120, 380, 451, 462, 637; advertising 543; airdomes 16; Bedding 62; Bush 87; expedition films 223; Harrison 295; middle-class audiences 666; nickelodeons 478; Pickford 609; projectionists 536; Richardson 552; Sargent 564; Saunders 564; screens 573, 574; screenwriting 578; synchronized sound systems 620; *Views and Film Index* 679;
Mozzhukhin, Ivan *see* Mosjoukine, Ivan
MPPC *see* Motion Picture Patents Company
Mr Delaware and the Boxing Kangaroo (1895) 25
Mr Hurry-up of New York (1907) 211
Mrs Jones Entertains (1908) 242
Muchachos bañandose en la laguna de Maracaibo (1897) 676
Mudaliar, R. Nataraja 318, 451–2, 677
Los muertos viven (1915) 634
Le Muet mélomane (1900) 242, 709
Mülleneisen, Theodore 153–4
Mullens, Bernard (Albert) 63, 452, 470, 594
Mullens, Willy 63, 452, 470, 471, 594
Müller, Friedrich *see* Sandow, Eugene
Müller, Karl 13–14
Der Müller und sein Kind (1911) 694
Müller-Lincke, Anna 452
multiple-reel films: acting styles 3; Ambrosio 19; animal pictures 26; Aquila Films 31; Argentina 38; Australia 50, 502; Balkans 58; La Belge Cinema SA 62; biblical films 71; Biograph 72; Bosworth 79; Bourgeois 80; boxing films 81, 155; Brazil 83; British & Colonial Kinematograph Company 84; Butcher's Film Service 88; Calmettes 91; camera movement 94; Canada 100, 102; Capellani 103; Caserini 106; China 115; Cody 132; crime films 157; Denmark 172; Desmet 178; detective films 179; distribution 189; domination of 582, 649; Edison 202, 203; Europe 3, 452–6; Famous Players 229; France 250; Gardner 264; Germany 271; Gish 279; Great Britain 284; Hepworth 296, 297; historical films 299; illustrated lectures 307; intertitles 328; Italy 337–8; itinerant exhibitors 342; Jasset 347; Keystone 356; Khanzhonkov & Co. 357;

Kinoreformbewegung 55; Klaw & Erlanger 360; Lubin 394; melodrama 421; Messter 429, 430; modes of production 443; MPPC 448; Mutual 464; Netherlands 470; Nordisk 40; Notari 485; Pasquali 500; Pathé-Frères 508; Perret 512; popularity of 643; program formats 534, 535; Robinne 553; Rolfe 554; SCAGL 565, 627; Scotland 573; screens 573, 575; screenwriting 578; Selig 581; Sfinks 587; Shakespeare films 589; Solax 596; South Africa 599; Svenska Biografteatern 614; Sweden 615, 616; Thiemann & Reinhardt Company 633; United States 446, 456–7, 660, 665, 675; Uruguay 654; US imperialism 315; vaudeville 675; Venezuela 676; Vietnam 678; *La Vita Cinematografica* 679; Vitagraph 680; von Woringen 682; Warner's Features 684, 685; Weber 687; westerns 689–90; women's suffrage 700; Zukor 710

Mulvey, Laura 601
Münch, Ludwig 569
Mundviller, Joseph 505
municipal cinema system 484–5
Munsterberg, Hugo 45–6, 457–8, 624
Muratore, Lucien 490
Murdock, John J. 458, 674
Murià, Magí 59, 600
Murphy, Robert Cushman 523
Musco, Angelo 414
Musée Grevin 6, 157, 187, 210, 506, 551–2, 577, 686
museums 37, 133; dime 69, 186–7, 355, 672–3, 686; ethnographic films 221; film festivals 241; life exhibits 458–9, 690; *see also* wax museums
music halls 214, 408, 440, 459–61; AM&B projector 539; Austro-Hungary 52; Belgium 62, 63; Biograph 70mm projector 73; British Mutoscope & Biograph 85; Chaplin 108; Cinématographe screenings 131; Collins 134; colonial films 137; comedies 143; costumes 155; Deed 168; Denmark 172; distribution 189; Dutch Mutoscope & Biograph 195; Evans 223; France 89, 248, 259, 261; Germany 273; Great Britain 281; Krüger 364; magic lantern shows 327; Mistinguett 437; Napierkowska 467; Netherlands 469, 470; news event films 474; North Africa 13; Norway 484; Pathé-Frères 506; popular theater concept 626; program formats 533; Scotland 573; South Africa 598; sports films 604; star system 608; Sweden 617, 618; theatrical melodrama 630;

Tonbilder 635; transportation 638; Wales 683; Warwick Bioscope 546–7
The Music Master (1908) 74, 213
Musica cromatica 336
musical accompaniment 241, 461–3, 531–2, 596; audiences 43, 44; black cinema 75; Canada 98; cue sheets 160; Finland 242; Germany 274; India 319; program formats 533; Russia 557; theatrical melodrama 629–30; United States 664
musical scores 241, 312, 328, 462, 463–4; Becce 61; *Bismarck* 640; *Cabiria* 334; Kalem 353; opera 489
Musidora (Jeanne Roques) 25, 235, 366, 464
Musser, Charles 93, 125–6, 212, 440, 443, 610
Mutoscope 181–2, 186
Mutt and Jeff series (1911) 147, 150
Mutter und Kind (1933) 526
Mütter, verzaget nicht (1911) 697
Mutual Film Corporation 16, 20, 72, 230, 260, 464–5, 473, 649, 658; Aitken 412, 447; challenge to state censorship board 668; dominance of 456; Gish 279; Griffith 289; Horsley 304; Hutchinson 305; Keystone 356, 582; newsreels 478; Powers 530; serials 583; Thanhouser Film Company 625; Woods 702
Muybridge, Eadweard 25, 30, 33, 118–19, 324, 413, 465, 519, 569–70, 572, 604, 705
My Cousin (1918) 490
La Mystère des roches de Kador (1912) 251
La Mystère du pont Notre-Dame (1912) 112
Les Mystères de New York (1915–1916) 168
Les Mystères de Paris (1913) 104, 250, 565
Mysteriet natten till den 25:e (1917) 362
The Mysterious Rabbit 410
The Mystery of House #5 (1912) 505
mythologicals 318, 411, 452, 465, 502, 514

90° South (1933) 525
NAACP *see* National Association for the Advancement of Colored People
Nahw al-hawiya (1917) 216
Nalpas, Louis 87, 237, 250, 467, 562
Namibia 13, 14
Nanfu nanqi (1913) 39
Nanook of the North (1922) 222
Nansen, Peter 164
Napierkowska, Stacia 163, 467, 508, 565
Napoléon (1927) 11, 117
Napoleon Man of Destiny (1909) 213, 495

narrative 125, 126; classical Hollywood cinema 128–9, 131; detective films 178, 179, 181; dialogue accompaniment 184; domestic melodrama 421; intertitles 328, 329; lecturers 380; projectionist influence 536–7; screenwriting 577; sensational melodrama 424
A Narrow Escape (1908) 158, 208, 219, 507
Nasanu naka (1916) 323–4
Nashorn Jagd in Deutsch Ostafrika 14
Nat Pinkerton series 179
Natan, Bernard 467–8
The Nation 57
National American Woman Suffrage Association (NAWSA) 699, 700
National Association for the Advancement of Colored People (NAACP) 545
National Board of Censorship (NBC) 43, 87, 134, 375, 376, 377, 448, 468, 507, 561, 667, 693
National Film and Television Archive (NFTVA), London 350
Nationoscope theater 269
Native Americans 222, 434, 435, 690, 708
Natural Color Kinematograph 109, 137, 468, 595, 651
naturalism 2, 346, 623
nature 575–6
Navarre, René 104, 158, 235, 266, 468
La Nave (1921) 19
La nave dei leoni (1912) 19
NAWSA *see* National American Woman Suffrage Association
Nazimova Productions 104
NBC *see* National Board of Censorship
Neame, Elwin 495–6
Ned med Vaabnene (1915) 303
Nederlands Filmmuseum xxx, 37, 241
Negocio al agua (1913) 513
Negri, Pola 396, 587
Negro, Camillo 567
Negroni, Baldassarre 135, 277, 292, 337, 338, 436, 468
Neilan, Marshall 196, 353, 490, 619
Nekes, Werner 133
Nelly la Gigolette (1914) 339
Nemye svideteli (1914) 248
neorealism 160, 194, 414, 485
Nepomuceno, Jose 516
Nepoti, Alberto 469, 491, 627
Nernst lamps 388

Nerone (1909) 19, 104, 336, 404, 586
Nerone e Agrippina (1914) 280
Nestlé 9
Nestor 108, 147, 150, 304, 499, 649
Netherlands 469–71; distribution 470; fairs 226, 227; Indonesia 320; Nederlands Filmmuseum xxx, 37, 241; production 470–1; revolutionary socialists 367
Der neue Schreibtisch (1914) 671
Neufeld, Adolf 498
Neumann, Josef 52
Neumann, Lotte 682
La nevropatologia (1908) 19
A New Hat for Nothing 244
New York City 46–7, 375–7, 382, 383, 478–9, 497, 575
New York Dramatic Mirror 472, 543, 638, 702
The New York Hat (1911) 230
New York Journal 149, 314
New York Morning Telegraph 472, 638
New York Motion Picture Company 16, 370, 447, 464, 472–3, 549, 658; AGC 15; Balshofer 59; Baumann 61, 649; Ford 244; Ince 316–17; Kessel 355; Keystone 355, 356; Miller 437; westerns 543
New Zealand 473
Newhan, Charles 473
The Newlyweds (1913–1914) 28, 150
Newman & Sinclair Reflex camera 10, 97, 474
Newman, Arthur Samuel 474
news event films 5, 142, 474–6, 477; Australia 50; Autoscope Company 59–60; Bhatavdekar 68; black cinema 75; British & Colonial Kinematograph Company 84; British Gaumont 85; China 115; cinema of attractions 124; Colombia 135; Cuba 159; Dutch Mutoscope and Biograph 195; Egypt 216; German Biograph 182; Great Britain 285; Higgins 298; Iran 331; Johnson and Gibson 348; McDowell 417; Natural Color Kinematograph 468; New Zealand 473; Poland 522; popularity of 547; Santos 563; Serrador 584; Sfinks 587; Smith 595; Urban 651; Uruguay 654; Wales 683; Walker 684; Warwick Trading Company 685; world's fairs 705; *see also actualités*; newsreels
newspapers 7, 149, 475, 476–7, 478; advertising 542; audience research 42; biblical films 71; Buckwalter 85–6; Chile 114; cinema of attractions 124; ethnographic films 221;

industrial films 321; Italy 336; New Zealand 473;
Pickford 520; Poland 522; publicity 638;
sensational 157; serials 583; United States 656
newsreels 5, 323, 475, 477–8; Argentina 38;
Aurora Cinema 49; Australasian Films 49;
Australia 50, 502; Belgium 64; Botelho 79;
Brazil 83; British Gaumont 85; Chile 114;
Colombia 135; *Diaro colombiano* 183; Éclair 199;
Express-Film 688; "fake" 547–8; fashion 230;
France 250, 366; Gallo 263; Gaumont 266, 512;
Germany 272, 273, 703; Glücksmann 280;
Great Britain 284, 285, 509; India 591;
International Film Service 28; Iran 332; Kearton 355;
Leal 379; Luxemburg 400; Mason 415;
Medina 418; Messter 260, 429, 430; Natan 467;
Pathé Cinematograph 503; Pathé-Frères 508,
509; Rossi 555; Russia 558; Selig 581; South
Africa 599; Switzerland 620; Topical Film
Company 635; Universal 650; Urban 651;
Uruguay 654; US labor movement 369, 370;
Wales 683; Warwick Trading Company 685;
World War I 703; *see also actualités;*
news event films
Le Nez de Rigadin (1911) 507
NFTVA *see* National Film and Television Archive
Nhô Anastacio chegou de viagem (1908)
83, 234–5
Niblo, Fred 87
Nicholas II, Tsar of Russia 557
Nick Carter series (1908) 179, 198, 250, 347,
425, 454, 615
Nick Carter versus Zigomar (1912) 180, 347
Nick Winter series (1911) 80, 94, 151, 179
Nick Winter: le pickpocket mystifié (1911) 94
Nickelodeon/Motography (magazine) 305
nickelodeons 113, 445, 478–80; advertising 7, 8;
airdomes 15; anti-drink campaigns 561;
audiences 42, 43, 46–7, 368, 440; Balaban
brothers 57; biblical films 70, 71; black
cinema 74; Brady 82; Canada 99, 288;
churches 120; cinema chains 122; comedies 144;
earliest 511; electric streetcar 219; ethnographic
films 221; expansion of 72, 128, 202, 448, 659,
660; Fox 245; Fynes 262; Hale's Tours 93; illustrated songs 311; immigrants 433; Jones 349;
Keith 355; Laemmle 370; lecturers 44, 379;
Lubin 395; magic lantern shows 327; marketing
543; Miles Brothers 436; modes of production
443; musical accompaniment 160, 461;

New York regulation 376, 377; Norway 484;
Oceania/South Pacific 487; Pathé
Cinematograph 67, 503; Pathé-Frères 507;
Pittsburgh 165; Porter 527; program formats
534; projectionists 536; Rothapfel 555; Saxe
brothers 564; screens 573; sensational
melodrama 425; sound effects 596; sound
machines 598; *Tonbilder* 635; transportation
638; travelogues 641; United States 380, 657,
662, 663–4, 665–6, 667, 674; urbanization 652;
US imperialism 315; *Views and Films Index* 679;
Vitagraph 679; Warner Brothers 684; Waters
686; women 700; Zukor 710; *see also* theaters
Nicolai Stavrogin (1915) 707
Nielsen, Asta 165, 175, 248, 280, 426, 453,
455, 480–1, 559; erotic dance 164; Gad 263;
Germany 270, 271, 430; Gildemijer 278; Italian
divas 68, 339, 609; *Monopolfilm* 190, 273; mul-
tiple-reel films 3, 454; PAGU 493; performance
style 627; Porten comparison 526; Seeber 579
Nielsen, Ida 615
Nielsen, Søren 73, 227
Niepce, Nicéphore 32, 35
De Nieuwe Prikkel (1899) 195
Niewolnica zymysłow (1914) 587
Nigeria 12
A Night Out (1908) 247
Nikkatsu 345, 362, 363, 412, 481, 564, 623–4,
649, 708
Nikolainkadun koulun koulunuorisoa välitunnilla
(1904) 243
Nilsson, Axel 481
Nilsson, N. P. 481, 491, 615
Nissen, R. C. E. 11, 12, 137
nitrate film 1, 36, 37, 54, 106; color 139, 141; fire
risk 283; French regulation 258; *see also* celluloid
Nitzsche, Johann 60
Nizza 79
Njai Siti (1930) 320
No país das amazonas (1921) 563
Noble, Charles Rider 58, 109
La nobleza gaucha (1915) 38
El nocturno de Chopin 59
Nöggerath, Franz Anton Jr. 470, 471, 482
Nöggerath, Franz Anton Sr. 469, 482
Noguès, Pierre 33, 482, 566, 568
Nonguet, Lucien 80, 249, 258, 444, 482, 506
Nordisk Films Kompagni 29, 31, 40, 482–3;
Autorenfilme 55, 271; Blom 76; Brazil 83;

Denmark 172, 173, 174–5, 176; expedition/
exploration films 223; Fotorama legal case 245;
Germany 270, 488; Gundersen 291; Holger-
Madesn 303; India 318; Larsen 372; legitimate
theater 627; Lind 390; Lykke-Seest 400;
multiple-reel films 453; Nielsen 608; Olsen 488;
opera 489; Psilander 542; sensational melo-
drama 426; Shakespeare films 589; Sherlock
Holmes series 179; Sjöström 592; Sweden 616,
617; Thiemann & Reinhardt Company 632;
trade mark 54; travelogues 642
Normand, Mabel 32, 108, 143–4, 148, 164,
464, 472, 483
Normand, Maurice 6, 449
Normandin, Ernest 349, 522, 538, 598
North Africa 13
North American Phonograph 484
North Side Dental Rooms (1898) 9
*North Wales, England: Land of Castles and
Waterfalls* (1907) 684
Northern Photographic Works 107
Northrop, Henry Evans 307
Norton, Charles Goodwin 484
Norway 484–5
Notari, Elvira Coda 191, 340, 485
Notari, Nicola 191
Notre Dame de Paris (1911) 104, 236, 250,
300, 364, 454, 467, 508, 565
Novelli, Amleto 127, 229, 392, 485
Novelli, Ermete 238, 589
Novelli, Giovanni E. V. *see* Vidali, Enrico
Noy, Wilfred 613
Nozze d'oro (1911) 19, 104, 261
Nuchberg, Emil 148
nude scenes 165
Nuit de noël (1908) 158, 426
Numa Peterson's Trading Company 485–6, 615,
616, 617
Daß nur für mich dein Herz erbebt (1908) 182
Nuremberg toy projectors 486, 538
Nylander, N. H. 614

Oakley, Annie 200, 689
Oberdan (1915) 135
Oborona Sevastopolia (1912) 280, 356, 357
Les obsèques du citoyen Francis de Pressensé (1914) 123
The Ocean Waif (1916) 291
Oceania/South Pacific 487–8

October (1927) 213
Os óculos do vovô (1913) 563
Odette 166
L'Odissea (1911) 436
Odyssée d'un paysan à Paris (1905) 384
Officer Henderson (1913) 291
O'Galop 150
Oger, Edmond 63
Oh! You Dirty Boy! (1905) 247
Ohlmanns Kinematograph 14
Olcott, Sidney 269, 332, 353–4, 488, 498
The Old Guard (1912) 102
Old St Pauls (1914) 128
The Old Wood Carver (1913) 681
Oliver, David 488
Oliver, Félix 654
Oliver, Juncal 108 (1900) 654
Oliver Twist (1912) 296, 297, 585
Olsen, Ole 172, 174, 372, 482, 483, 488
Olympic Games 605
Omegna, Roberto 19, 337, 488–9, 567
L'onde de choc 86
One A.M. (1916) 465
One Hundred Years After (1911) 213
One Million Bid (1914) 680
O'Neill, James 527, 628
Onésime series (1912–1914) 79–80, 144, 146, 194,
266, 431, 444
Onésime horloger (1912) 80, 144, 211, 568
Onésime se marie, Calino aussi (1913) 431
The Only Son (1914) 171
Ono ga tsumi (1908) 345
Onoe Matsunosuke 344, 346, 412, 489, 564
Onschuldig veroordeeld (1912) 482
Op hoop van zegen (1918) 79
opera 325, 489–90, 608; acting styles 2; China 115,
116, 234; Chronophone Gaumont 118;
Commercial Press Motion Picture
Department 150; costumes 156; Faust story 494;
Film d'Arte Italiana 238; Fuller 262; Gallo 263;
Germany 272; Grau 281; Pathé-Frères 508;
phonography 517; *phonoscènes* 518;
Prószynski 541; *Tonbilder* 635
opera houses 663
The Opera Martha (1897) 187
Opper, Frederick Burr 28
optical intermittent projectors 490–1, 538
Optical Lantern and Cinematograph Journal 85,
357, 637

"Optima" machine 168
L'Orage (1917) 167
Orde, Julian 20
Orfanelli, Alvise 216, 217
Orientaliska teatern 491, 616
Ormiston-Smith, Frank 109, 223, 685
The Orozquista Rebellion (1912) 17
L'Orphelin de Paris (1924) 530
Ors, Eugeni d' 491, 600
Ortuño, Gregorio 38
Ostpreussen und sein Hindenburg (1916) 640
Ostrich Farming, South Africa (1914) 572
Ostriche, Muriel 625
L'Otage (1912) 138
Otello (1909) 238, 392, 627
Otets Sergii (Father Sergius) (1918) 541, 559, 707
La otre Carmen (1915) 634
Ottalinghi 15
Otto e mezzo (1963) 447
Ottolenghi, Camillo 31
Ottoman Empire 498, 646
Ouimet, Léo-Ernest 99, 101–2, 103, 288, 415, 491
Our Mutual Girl serial (1913–1914) 230
Our Navy (1900) 307, 347
Our New Errand Boy (1905) 695
The Outlaw of the Sudu Mountains 14
Overfaldet paa Postaapnerens Datter (1913) 279
overlap editing 206, 208, 212
Oxilia, Nino 128, 338, 343, 469, 491, 679

Pabst, G. W. 54, 481
Pacchioni, Italo 335
Pacht, Vilhelm 172
Pacto de lágrimas (1915) 600
Padovan, Adolfo 337–8, 436
Padre (1913) 333, 501, 709
Pagano, Bartolomeo 3, 334, 339, 493, 501
PAGU/AKGT 165, 270, 271, 273, 274, 493;
  Autorenfilme 55, 56; Gildemijer 278; Misu 437;
  Nielsen 480, 608; Nordisk 483; Reinhardt 548;
  Union Theater 488; Vitascope 681
Pahlavi, Reza Shah 332
La Paimpolaise 518
The Painted Lady (1912) 4, 619
Painter, Baburao 319, 411
painting 35, 54, 493–7; acting styles 2; Italy 336;
  museum life exhibits 458; racialness 434;
  set design 586; US Revolutionary War 301;

von Herkomer 681; westerns 689;
  see also art
palace cinemas/theaters 43, 46, 497–8, 582;
  Aubert 40; *Autorenfilme* 55; Balaban brothers 57;
  Denmark 173; Finland 242; Germany 274,
  276; Grauman 281; Italy 337; Mark 414;
  Mastbaum brothers 415; Moscow 193, 356,
  357, 556; multiple-reel films 455; musical
  directors 161; Pathé-Frères 508; Rothapfel
  555; screens 575; Serrador 584; Skouras
  593; Sweden 617–18; travelogues 641;
  United States 659, 661, 665, 675;
  urbanization 653
Le Palais des Mille et une nuits (1905) 139
Palermi, Amleto 128, 280
Palestine 215, 217, 498–9, 646
Paley, William ("Daddy") 187, 201, 314, 418,
  499, 610
Pan-American Exposition (1901) 705
Pan-American Exposition by Night (1901) 218, 705
Pankhurst, Emmeline 700
panning shots 93, 94
Panorama of the Bay of Fundy (1900) 98
Panorama de Beaulieu à Monaco I, II, et III 205
Panorama de Constantine 13
Panorama de Curytiba (1909) 551
Panorama en Guinée 13
Panorama of Esplanade by Night (1901) 218
Panorama of Paris Exposition, From the Seine (1900) 705
Panorama of the War 187
panoramas 5, 35, 188, 335, 639, 705
Panzer, Paul 589
Par le trou de la serrure (1901) 249
Paramount 16, 229, 446, 661; Balaban
  brothers 57; Bosworth Film 79; capitalization
  464; Hodkinson 302, 457; Olcott 488;
  Pickford 520; Sennett 582; Zukor 710
Paris 89–90
Paris: les souverains russes et le président de la République aux Champs-Elysées (1896) 204
Paris Exposition (1900) 192, 195, 256, 400,
  516, 550, 705; Cinéorama 93, 639; colonial
  films 136; electricity displays 218; Grimoin-
  Sanson 289; legitimate theater 626; Méliès 419;
  opera 489; postcards 528
Park, Ida May 650
Parker, J. W. 224

Parkes, Alexander 106
Parnaland, Ambroise-François 131, 192, 198, 253, 350, 499–500, 516
El parque de Palantino (1906) 159, 185
Parsifal (1904) 489
Une partie de cartes (1896) 419
Pas possible s'asseoir (1908) 27
Un paseo en el Prado el día de todos los santos (1906) 77
La pasión 677
Pasionaria (1915) 600
Pasquali & co. 19, 104, 147, 169, 290, 336, 337, 491, 500, 582, 677
Pasquali, Ernesto Maria 338, 500–1
Passengers Alighting from the Paddle Steamer "Brighton" at Manly (1896) 50
La Passion (1906) 291
Passion du Christ (1897) 360, 411
The Passion Play of Oberammergau (1898) 69, 187, 307, 585
Passion Play (Pathé, 1903) 126, 210, 452
Passion Play (Pathé, 1907) 69, 249–50, 503
Passion Play (Pathé, 1913) 412
Passion plays 69–71, 87, 120, 126, 210, 212, 327, 360, 549
Pastor, Tony 673
Pastrone, Giovanni 17, 61, 117, 339, 469, 501; camera movement 92, 94, 299; D'Annunzio 164; Deed 169, 336; intertitles 329; Itala 333, 334, 338; Menichelli 428; Pagano 493; Pasquali comparison 500; Rossi 555; staging in depth 607
Patankar Friends & Company 502, 591
Patankar, S. N. 318, 362, 502
patents 96, 107, 195, 374, 447–8; Dyer 196; Edison 203; Kleine 361; pooling 445, 448; US patent wars 21, 196, 654–5, 656, 657
Paterson, Andrew 573
Pathé (Australia) 49, 50, 502
Pathé, Charles 103, 167, 249, 253, 254, 502–3, 506; Berst 67; cameras 508–9; counterfeit Kinetoscopes 349, 688; Gasnier 265; Lépine 384; Maltese-cross projectors 154; Méliès 419; Mendel 427; *Phono-Ciné-Gazette* 516; Prince 532; SCAGL 428, 565; Valetta 671; Zecca 709, 710
Pathé Cinematograph 28–9, 67, 251, 503–4
Pathé, Emil 502, 506, 509
Pathé Film (Sweden) 361, 362, 504, 525, 613, 616
Pathé Journal 79, 250, 477, 478, 508
Pathé Kok projector 18, 215, 504

Pathé russe 251, 504–5, 586
Pathé-American 265
Pathé-Baby 18, 91, 710
Pathé-Exchange 20, 67, 458, 503, 504, 582, 693, 710
Pathé-Frères 72, 439, 448, 502, 505–8; *actualités* 5; AKGT 165; amateur filmmaking 215; Andréani 24; animal films 26, 521; animation 27; Austro-Hungary 53; Bauer 61; Belge Cinema SA 62; Belgian Congo 11; Belgium 64; biblical films 69; Bolten-Baeckers 78; Bosetti 79; Bourgeois 80; bourgeois class 123; Boutillon 80; Brazil 82; Breteau 84; Bush 87; camera movement 93, 94; cameras 96–7, 168, 506, 508–9; Canada 98; Capellani 103; catalogues 542; celluloid 107, 257–8; Chardynin 109; chase films 110; Chómon 94, 116; Cohl 132; colonial films 136, 137, 138; color 140; Comandon 141; comedies 142, 143, 144; comic series 145, 146; Comica 150; Continsouza 154; copyright cases 154; costumes 156; crime films 157, 158; dance films 163; de Morlhon 167; Decroix 168; Deed 169, 501; Denmark 174; Denola 176; Desfontaines 178; detective films 178, 179; distribution 189; domestic melodrama 420–1, 422; Dranem 192, 460; Duhamel 193; Durand 194; Duskes 195; Dussaud 195; editing techniques 208, 210, 211, 212, 213; Egypt 216; ethnographic films 222; Fabre 225; facial expression films 225; fairs 227; fashion 230; *féeries* 231, 232–3, 234; Ferrez 234; *film d'art* 236–7; film festivals 241; *films sonores* 242; Finland 243; Floury 244; framing 246–7, 248; France 248, 249–50, 251, 253–4; Froissart 261; Fuller 261; Gabet 263; Gasnier 265; Gaumont rivalry 265, 268; Germany 270, 271, 274, 275; Goncharov 280; Great Britain 282; Greece 287; Hansen 295; Hatot 296; Heuzé 298; Hintner 298; historical films 299, 300; India 318, 404; Indonesia 320; industrial films 320; intertitles 327; Iran 331; Italy 335; Japan 345; Jasset 347; Khanzhonkov & Co. 356–7; Krüger 364; Lamster 372; legitimate theater 627; Lépine 384; Leprince 384; lighting 385; Linder 390, 609; Lordier 393; Luxemburg 400; Machin 303, 403; Maître 411; Malaya 412; Mary 415; Méliès comparison 419; Merzbach brothers 290, 428; Mexico 431; Migé 431; Miller 437;

Mistinguett 437; Misu 437; Monca 444; multiple-reel films 452, 453–4; musical scores 463; Netherlands 469, 470; New York 67; news event films 474, 475; newsreels 477, 478; nickelodeon boom 527; Nonguet 482; North Africa 13, 216; Numa Peterson's Trading Company 485; Oceania/South Pacific 487; Omnia-Pathé theater 65; opera 489; parallel editing 17; parody of "The Unseen World" films 567; *Passion Play* 69, 87, 126, 212, 412, 503; Philippines 515; Pike 521; Poland 522; Popert 525; pornography 525; Portugal 528; print inscriptions 54; projectors 63, 86, 105, 127, 506, 509–10, 538, 539; Relph 551; rental system 253–4, 255; Riche 552; Rossi 555; Russia 192–3, 556; Sandberg 562; scientific films 214, 567, 572; screenwriting 577, 578; sensational melodrama 424; Serbian royal murder 58; serials 180, 583; set design 585, 586; Shakespeare films 589; Sjöberg 613; Sjöström 592; sound machine 598; Spain 599; sports films 605; star system 608; Svenska Biografteatern collaboration 592; Sweden 615, 616; Switzerland 619; telephones 151, 219; Thailand 625; Théophile Pathé 123, 237, 250, 540, 632; trade mark 54, 636; trade press 637; travelogues 340, 642; trick films 644; turnover 256; United States 657, 660, 674; Valetta 671; Velle 676; *Views and Films Index* 679; von Herkomer 681; West 689; westerns 692; World War I 702–3; Yermolíev 707; Yokota 708; Young Deer 708; Zecca 709

Pathé-Frères (Great Britain) 509

Pathécolor 505

Pathe's Animated Gazette (1910) 50

Patin, Charles 35

Patria (1915) 17

Patrizia e schiava (1909) 386

Patwardhan, Mahadeo Gopal 318

Pätzold, Theodore 279

Paul J. Rainey's African Hunt (1912) 25, 222, 224, 307

Paul, Robert William 2, 282, 497, 510–11, 569, 598; *actualités* 5; archives 37; Argentina 38; art subjects 496; Blair film stock 76; cameras 93, 96; Canada 97; colonial films 137; comedies 143; counterfeit Kinetoscopes 349, 688; exhibition 340; Faust story 494; Fitzhamon 243; framing 246; illustrated lectures 307; Kinetoscope exhibit 297; music halls 460; Netherlands 469; news event films 474, 595; program formats 533; projectors 538; *Rough Sea at Dover* 656; set design 585; sports films 604; Theatrograph 96, 133, 287, 334, 410, 418, 538; Wales 683; Wolff 696

Pauvre Pierrot! 552

Pauvres gosses (1907) 577

Pavlova, Anna 687

The Pawnshop (1916) 465

Los payasos se van (1921) 278, 591

The Paymaster (1906) 269

Payne, Annie *see* Holland, Annie

La paz de 1904 654

Paz dos Reis, Aurélio 528

Paz e amor (1910) 49

Paz y Paz, Horacio de la 563

Pearson, George 509

Peau de chagrin (1909) 178

La peccatrice (1916) 31

Peeping Tom (1901) 585

La película (1917) 38

Pelouzé, Théophile-Jules 106

Le Pendu (1906) 391

penny arcades 132, 181–2, 382, 511; Fox 245; Great Britain 281; Jones 349; Loew 392; Lubin 395; Mark 413; nickelodeons 479; Schenck brothers 566; United States 662; Zukor 710

Péon, Ramón 160, 512

Pepper, John Henry 406

Perdida (1915) 165

Perego, Eugenio 292

Pereira, Arthur 137

Pérez de Léon, Herminia *see* Derba, Mimí

The Perils of Pauline (1914) 265, 425, 437, 503–4, 583, 693

Perkins, Sandon 523

Perojo, Benito 599

Perret, Léonce 61, 151, 248, 250, 266, 347, 512–13; camera movement 94; comic series 144, 147, 553; Grandais 281; lighting 386; Piel 521; serials 583; staging in depth 606

La Perricholi (1928) 514

Perry, Joseph 473, 513, 562

Pershing's Crusaders (1918) 308

Personal (1904) 74, 110, 111, 143, 417, 452

Pertierra, Francisco 515

Peru 113, 513–14

Peruzzi, Emilio 654

Pervanche (1920) 654

Perversidade (1920) 418

Peter the Great (1910) 505

Petersen, Lars Peter *see* Elfelt, Peter

Peterson, Storm 150

Le petit chose (1912) 444

Petit, Georges 89, 253

Le petit poucet (1905) 320

Petit, Valentine 512

La Petite Rosse (1909) 507

Petrolini, Ettore 135

Petronille series (1913–1914) 194

Petrova, Olga 291

Des Pfarrers Töchterlein (1912) 265

Pfeffer, W. 521, 568

Phalke, Dhundiraj Govind 298, 318, 319, 362, 411, 451, 465, 514

Phalke Films 298, 502, 514, 549

Phantasmagoria 405, 406, 408, 409

Phantom Train Ride to Conway Castle (1898) 683–4

phantom train rides 21, 74, 125, 440, 514–15, 689; camera movement 92, 93, 94, 611; compositional depth 605; Dickson 186; Hale's Tours 294; Smith 595; spatial relations 207

Phantoscope 348, 484, 515, 546, 656

Philémon et Baucis (1911) 552

Philidor, Paul 405

Philippe, M. D. 460

Philippines 314, 315, 515–16

Philipsen, Constantin 172, 173

Phoneidograph 620

Phono-Ciné-Gazette 65, 121, 170, 253, 516, 637

Phono-Cinéma-Théâtre 131, 516, 550, 616, 620, 626

Phonogram, The 417, 516–17, 637

phonography 10, 203, 325, 517–18; Belgium 63, 65; Chronophone Gaumont 118; Dussaud 195; Gallo 263; Howe 305, 341; McRae 417; Mendel 427; musical accompaniment 461; North American Phonograph 484; Pathé 502, 505, 506, 525; *Phono-Ciné-Gazette* 65; Py 544; sound machines 598; trade press 637; United States 662

phonoscènes 38, 39, 118, 291, 490, 518, 544, 620, 635

Phonoscope 33, 170

Phonoscope, The 519

Photo-Drama of Creation (1914) 550

The Photographer's Mishap (1901) 639

Photographie electrique à distance (1908) 151

photography 519–20; animation 29; Anschütz 29–31; Atelier Apollo 39; Bamforth 59; daguerreotype 32; Dickson 186; Eastman Kodak 106, 197–8; ethnographic films 221; expedition/exploration films 223; Grimoin-Sanson 289; history of 35; illustrated magazines 309; Janssen 343; Le Prince 378; lighting 385, 388; Londe 393; Lumière 397, 398, 399; modernity 439; postcards 529; Wales 683; westerns 689; Williamson 695; *see also* cameras; chronophotography; film

The Physician of the Castle (1908) 213

physics 35

Picasso, Pablo 497

Pickford, Mary 72, 132, 144, 165, 387, 520; Dwan films 196; Famous Players 229; fashion 230; Griffith 288; Gys comparison 292; IMP 312–13, 609; Ince 316; Laemmle 371; legitimate theater 628; Lindsay poems 391; Majestic 412, 447, 464; Olcott 488; opera 490; plays 171; Porter 527; star system 543

"picture setting" 574–5

The Pictures (magazine) 310

Picturesque Russia 505

Piel, Harry 521

Pik-Nik (1911) 31

Pike, Oliver 521, 594

Pikovaia dama (The Queen of Spades) (1916) 541, 558, 707

Pilgrim's Progress 464

Pimple in the Whip 223

Pimple's Battle of Waterloo (1913) 223

Pinocchio (1911) 290

Pinschewer, Julius 10, 28, 521

Pinthus, Kurt 521–2

Pippa Passes (1909) 386

Pirandello, Luigi 450

Pirate's Gold (1912) 102

Pirou, Eugène Louis 360, 522

Pitman, Isaac 517

Pizon, Antoine 568

Place des consuls à Alexandrie (1897) 216

Place principale à Tunis 13

Planchon, Victor 107, 197, 398

Platzman, Eugene 463

Pleograph 541

Plimpton, Horace 202

Plumb, Hay 296

PMR *see* Primitive Mode of Representation

Pöch, Rudolf 137, 221

El poder de los ñanigos (1917) 185

Pohjanheimo, Hjalmar V. 400–1

Pohjoismaiden Biografi Komppania 243
The Poisoned Flume (1911) 196
Poland 522–3
polar expedition films 523–4; *see also* expedition/ exploration films
Polaski, Benjamin 39, 115
Poli, Sylvester 524
La policière (1907) 577
Polidor (1912–1915) 500–1
Polimanti, Osvaldo 567
political filmmaking 62
Pollyanna (1920) 520
Polo, Eddie 319
Polonskii, Vitold 559
Pommer, Erich 271
I pompieri 335
Pont, Juan José 513
Ponting, Herbert 474, 524–5
Poona Races '98 (1898) 318
The Poor Little Rich Girl (1917) 520
Poorlucks series 244
Popawski brothers 522
Popert, Siegmund 504, 506, 525
pornography 126, 258, 360, 525–6; *see also* erotic films
Porten, Franz 182
Porten, Henny 260, 264, 271, 273, 302, 429, 430, 526, 559, 608, 609, 697
Porter, Edwin S. 6, 9, 23, 94, 526–7, 639; animation 27; combination company 630; comic strip adaptations 149; costumes 156; Dawley 165; Defender Film Company 614; Edison 201, 202, 203, 692; editing techniques 206, 207, 213, 602; facial expression films 226; Famous Players 229, 710; incandescent lighting 218; intertitles 129, 327; *The Kleptomanic* 177; lighting 386; narrative 125, 126; opera 489; Rex 551; sensational melodrama 424; Simplex projector 591; story films 577; tableaux 422
Portugal 136–7, 527–8
A Portugese Railway 528
Posadas, Alejandro 38
poses 2, 3, 4, 61; *see also* tableaux
Posnasky, Arturo 77
postcards 7, 142, 528–9; audience research 42; Bamforth 59; color 139; erotic 525; Hepworth 297; mass production of 238; Russia 557; Sweden 615; Taylor and White 624; westerns 689
posters 8, 71

Potel, Victor 147, 148, 220
Pouctal, Henri 237, 252, 467, 529
Les Pouics 146
La Poule aux oeufs d'or (1905) 94, 140, 163, 234, 506, 676
Pour un collier! (1907) 158, 507
Pour voir les mouquères (1912) 167
Powell, Frank 414
Power, Nicholas 529, 530, 539
Power's Cameragraph No. 5 projector 529, 530, 539
Powers, Patrick A. 320, 371, 530, 649, 658, 685, 693
Powrót birbanta (1902) 522, 541
Poyen, René-Georges 144, 147, 235, 250, 266, 415, 530
La Prairie en feu (1912) 294
Prakash, Raghupati 677
Prampolini, Enrico 336
pre-cinema 34–5
Les précieuses ridicule 516
Precipice (1913) 109
Prehistoric Peeps 244
Preobrazhenskaia, Olga 633
La presa di Roma (1905) 16, 127, 169
preservation 1, 36, 139, 530–2
The President on Parade 677
Prestwich, J. A. 18, 96, 219, 260
Pretty, Arline 650
Pretty Mrs. Smith (1915) 490
Price, Gertrude 638
La prigione infuocata (1911) 500
A Primitive Man's Career to Civilisation (1911) 138
Primitive Mode of Representation (PMR) 602
Prince, Charles 142, 146, 242, 250, 390, 437, 444, 460, 507, 532, 565, 608
The Prince of Graustark (1916) 220
Princess Nicotine, or The Smoke Fairy (1909) 75
Princess Tarakanova (1910) 295, 411, 505
Pringle, Ralph 347, 438, 532
Prinsenschaums Kino 14
La prise deTaza par les troupes françaises (1914) 137
The Prisoner of Zenda (1913) 229, 527, 628
La Procession du Saint Sang à Bruges (1901) 64
Proctor, F. F. 262, 673
production, modes of 442–4, 578–9, 657, 658–9
La Profecía del lago (1925) 77

program formats 43, 533–5, 641, 703; feature films 312; Germany 274, 275; Great Britain 283; Russia 557

Progressivism 376, 381, 540, 652

projectionists 211, 283, 298, 341, 535–7; illustrated songs 311; labor movement 367, 369; regulation 99, 374, 375, 377; Richardson 552; Russia 556; Vitagraph 679

projectors 95, 96, 531, 537–40; Acres model 2; AM&B 21, 656; Armat 38–9; authentication 55; Belgium 62; Biograph 73, 74, 182, 524; Bioskop (Skladansky) 172, 191, 270, 460, 593; Canada 98; changeover 1; Continsouza 154; Darling 164–5; Demenÿ 170; double-film-band 191; Edison Home Kinetoscope 18, 200; Eidoloscope 186, 187, 201, 372, 373, 604; Ernemann Imperator 219–20; Foersterling 244; French regulation 257; Friese-Greene 260; Gaumont 118, 265, 268; glass-plate 279, 538; Great Britain 282, 283; Grimoin-Sanson 289–90; Howe 305; Kamm 354; Lubin 395; magic lanterns 405, 409; "Maltese cross" 86, 105, 127, 154, 220, 268, 290, 326, 430, 530, 538, 539, 696; Méliès-Reulos 528; Messter 429, 430; Mirographe 551; Nuremberg toy projectors 486, 538; optical intermittent 490–1, 538; Paley 499; patent wars 655; Pathé Kok 18, 215, 504; Pathé-Frères 63, 105, 127, 506, 509–10; Paul 510; Phantoscope 348, 484, 515, 546, 656; Pirou-Normandin 522; Power's Cameragraph 529, 530, 539; Schneider 566; Selig 581; "showman" era 536; Simplex 527, 539, 591; Spirograph 85; sponsored films 10; Spoor 604; Theatrograph 96, 133, 287, 334, 410, 418, 538, 598; Urban Bioscope 651, 655, 685; variable speed 1; Warwick Bioscope 164, 297, 546–7, 685; see also Cinématographe Lumière; Edison Kinetoscope; intermittent movement

Prolo, Maria Adriana 133

I promessi sposi (1908) 145

Promio, Alexandre 13, 58, 92–3, 216, 485, 519, 540, 599, 615, 632

promotion see publicity

propaganda films 540–1; Blackton 75; Müller-Lincke 452; Philippines 516; Pinschewer 521; Urban 651; Vietnam 678; World War I 704

Prószynski, Kazimierz 10, 355, 522, 541

Protazanov, Jakov 61, 264, 422, 423, 541–2, 558, 559, 633, 707

Protéa (1913) 25, 198, 347, 583

Protéa II (1914) 80

Protéa IV (1917) 80

Proust, Charles 518

Prouty, Olive Higgins 449

proximity 206, 207–8

Psilander, Valdemar 3, 175, 483, 542, 559

psychology 45, 46

Les P'tits pois 192

publicity: Austro-Hungary 53; Bedding 62; Belgium 63; black cinema 75; Cabiria 334; Eden Musee 69; India 319; issues and debates 542–4; Italy 338; Kinetoscope 359; Lawrence 378; Motion Picture Story Magazine 75; music halls 460; newspapers 638; Olsen 488; Pathé-Frères 189, 608; Russia 557; sensational melodrama 425; serials 582, 583; set design 586; United States 659; Vitagraph 301

Puccini, Giacomo 490, 496

La puce (1904) 525

Pugliese, Lino 31

Pugliesi, Benedetto 183

Pulitzer, Joseph 148

Pundalik (1912) 318

Puños y noble (1919) 654

Pure Film Movement 345, 346, 353

The Purple Mask (1917) 245

Purviance, Edna 108

Put Yourself in Their Place (1912) 102

Py, Eugenio 38, 280, 544

Pygmalion et Galathée (1898) 496

Pyke, Montague Alexander 544

Les Pyramides 207

Qajar, Muzzafared-Din Shah 331

Quadrilla no Moulin Rouge (1901) 580

Quality Pictures Corporation 59

Quaranta, Lydia 333

Les quat'cents farces du diable (1906) 231

Quebec 97, 100–3, 166, 379–80

Quebec Winter Carnival Series (1902) 101

Queen Elizabeth (La Reine Elisabeth) (1912) 67, 178, 229, 251, 300, 428, 456, 463, 628, 660

The Queen of the Nihilists (1910) 610

The Queen of Spades (1910) 109

The Queen of Spades (*Pikovaia dama*) (1916) 541, 558, 707
The Quest (1915) 20
Quirk, Billy 520
Quo Vadis? (1913) 68, 290, 299, 300, 338, 454, 660; Aubert 40, 41; costumes 156; Kleine 361; set design 586; success of 127
Quo Vadis? (play, 1896) 631

Rabinbach, Anson 439
race 382, 432, 433–5, 667, 696
A Race for Life (1904) 424
racial segregation: Malaya 412; United States 74, 375, 545–6, 665, 672
racism 74, 301, 348, 433, 599, 667
Raff & Gammon 38–9, 200, 201, 278–9, 348, 484, 546, 663, 679, 692
Raff, Norman 359, 546
Raffles, the Amateur Cracksman (1905) 23
The Railroad Porter (1913) 75, 245
A Railway Collision (1898) 510
Le Railway de la mort (1912) 294, 691
A Railway Smash-Up (1904) 639
A Railway Tragedy (1904) 639
Rainey, Paul 12, 25, 222, 224
Rainey's African Hunt (1912) 25, 222, 224, 307
Raja Harishchandra (1913) 318, 411, 465, 514
Raleigh & Robert 15, 31, 137, 138, 546, 688; distribution 189; Jasset 347; Switzerland 619; Turkey 646
Raleigh, Charles 546
Ram Vanvas (1918) 502
Ramona (1910) 607
Ramona (1914) 132
Ramos, Antonio 115, 116, 515, 546
Ranch Life in the Great Southwest (1910) 438
Ranchinho do sertão (1909) 299
Rank 85
Ranous, William V. 680
Rapée, Erno 463, 464
Rapsodia Satanica (1917) 78, 491, 627
Rathod, Kanjibai 362
Ratnakar (1921) 49
Raymond, Matt 546–7
Razboinik Vaska Churkin series 193
Razzi, Francesco 121
Re Lear (1910) 589

re-enactments 5, 474, 477, 547–8, 704; battles 315; boxing films 74, 80, 81; Cambodia 92; crime films 83, 157; Cuba 159; Czolgosz execution 218; dime museums 187; Duskes 195; framing 246; intertitles 327; Japan 344; multiple-reel films 453; Netherlands 469; Nonguet 482; Paul 510; Philippines 515; Rossi 555; Santos 563; transportation 639; United States 656; westerns 689; *see also* historical films
Reader, Ronald 75
Realidad (1921) 512
realism 184, 266, 656; Dora Film 191; "fantastic" 39; France 250; intermediality and modes of reception 324, 325; Italy 340, 414; Lumière 125; mythologicals 465; "natural" 576; Sjöström 592; spectacular 425; spectatorship 602; Tanaka 624; trick photography 645; vision scenes 585
Realization of a Negro's Ambition (1916) 349
Rebecca of Sunnybrook Farm (1917) 520
reception: modernity 441; modes of 324–5; spectatorship 601; *see also* audiences
Das Recht auf das Dasein (1913) 271, 426
Recordando (1960) 114
Rector, Enoch J. 81, 372, 604
Recuerdos del Mineral El Teniente (1918) 114, 278
The Red Circle (1916) 554
Red and White Roses (1913) 4
Red Wing, Princess 690, 708
Rédemption (1912) 347
Redfern, Henry Jasper 547
Regina von Emmeritz och Konung Gustaf II Adolf 614
La Règle du jeu (1939) 248
regulation 374–7; Austro-Hungary 53–4; Belgium 64; "Blue Laws" 120; Canada 99; competition 447–8; Denmark 172–3; fire safety 283, 376, 479, 557, 666; France 257–8; Germany 276–7; Great Britain 283; India 319; monopoly capitalism 445; Norway 484; projectionists 536; Spain 600; Sweden 618; United States 666–8; US anti-immigrant laws 652; *see also* censorship
Reicher, Ernst 154, 265, 426, 548, 703
Reicher, Karl 567
Reid, Wallace 20, 196, 229
La Reine Elisabeth (Queen Elizabeth) (1912) 67, 178, 229, 251, 300, 428, 456, 463, 628, 660
Reinelt, Léon 11
Reinhardt, Friedrich 632, 633

Reinhardt, Max 55, 60, 105, 165, 396, 548, 589, 627, 687
Reiniger, Lotte 10, 588
Reis, Luís Tomás 548–9
Réjane, Gabrielle 237, 250, 516, 529, 626, 627
Reliance 16, 61, 348, 368, 472, 549, 658; Cabanne 89; Leonard 383; Majestic 412; Mutual 464, 649; Smalley 594; Sweet 619; women's suffrage films 700
Reliance Roller Film & Dry Plate Company 107
religious films 549–50; India 319; Kalem 354; regulation 375; Turkey 646; Venezuela 676–7; see also biblical films; Passion plays
Relph, Harry ("Little Tich") 460, 550–1
Remmert, Guglielmo 555
Renoir, Jean 248, 384, 444
rental rights 15, 189, 190; France 253–5; Great Britain 284; Italy 337; Netherlands 470
Repas de bébé 207, 399
Reproduction, Coronation Ceremonies – King Edward VII (1902) 548
Reproduction of the Fitzsimmons-Jeffries Fight (1899) 81
Requião, Aníbal Rocha 82, 551
The Rescue of Capt. John Smith by Pocahontas (1895) 300
Rescued by Rover (1905) 25, 157, 212, 243, 282, 296
Rescued From an Eagle's Nest (1907) 165, 527
Rescued in Mid-Air (1906) 613
research: access to film 1; audiences 41–5; see also archives
A Reservist Before the War and After the War (1902) 695
Le Retour d'Ulysse (1909) 91, 237
Retratos de personajes históricos y de actualidad (1904) 77
The Return of Wrangler Paranjpye (1902) 68
Reulos, Lucien 18, 167, 410, 418, 528, 551
Reumert, Poul 455
Rêve d'artiste (1898) 496
Le rêve de Dranem (1905) 192
Reventlo, Franziska zu 697
A revolta da esquadra (1910) 79
La revolución de Mayo (1909) 38, 263
Revolutionens Datter (1918) 279
Rex 437, 527, 551, 594, 608, 614, 649
Reyes, Alfonso 600

Reynaud, Emile 26, 33, 34, 519, 551–2, 588, 686
Rhoads, W. M. 380
Rhodesia To-Day (1912) 12
Rhodesia (Zimbabwe) 12
Rice, John C. 626
Richard, Félix-Max 267
Richard III (British Co-operative Cinematograph Company, 1911) 299, 588
Richard III (Broadway Film Company, 1912) 589
Richard III (Vitagraph, 1908) 628
Richard Wagner (1913) 260
Richardson, Frank Herbert 536, 552
Riche, Daniel 552
Richelieu (1914) 196
Richer, Paul 567
Ricketts, Thomas 108
Ries, Julius 568
Riesenfeld, Hugo 464
Riffle Bill series (1909) 250, 347
Rigadin series 390, 437, 444, 507, 532, 565
Rigadin, garçon de banque (1912) 578
Righelli, Gennaro 343
The Right to Labor (1909) 368
Riis, Jacob 307
Riña en un café (1897) 269
Ringvall på äventyr (1913) 362
Riozzi, Carmine 470
Il ritorno delle carrozze da Montevergine (1900) 335
Rittberger, Max 153
Rituais e festas bororo (1916) 548–9
The Rivals (1907) 149
roadshowing 660, 661
Rob Roy (1911) 573
Robbery of the Mail Coach (1903) 590
Robello, Paul 684
Roberti, Roberto (a.k.a. Vincenzo Leone) 31, 552
Roberts, David 494
Robertson, D. W. 112, 119, 341, 552–3
Robertson, Etienne Gaspard 406
Robinet series (1910–1915) 147, 225, 337
Robinne, Gabrielle 384, 553, 565, 626
Robinson, David 133
Rocambole series (1913) 176, 565
Rock, William T. ("Pop") 553, 679, 680
Rockefeller, John D. 445, 446
Rocking Gold in the Klondike (1901) 689
Rodolfi, Eleuterio 19, 78, 167, 340, 447, 553
Rodríguez, Francisco 159, 185
Rodríguez, Manuel 591

Rogers, George H. 109, 199, 553–4
Le Roi au village (1911) 589
Le roi des dollars (1905) 116
Roland, Ruth 353, 554
Rolf, Siegward 182
Rolfe, Alfred 50, 298, 554
Rollini, G. 506
Roma Film 40, 582
Le Roman d'un mousse (1914) 606–7
Romance of the Rail (1904) 8
Romania 58
Rome, Stewart 296
Romeo e Giulietta (1911) 589
Roméo se fait bandit (1909) 589
Roméo series (1912–1913) 79, 146
Röntgen, Wilhelm 567–8
Roode Bioscoop (Red Cinema) 367
Roosevelt, Theodore 12, 223, 224, 307, 314, 315, 355, 540, 548, 580
Roosevelt's Rough Riders (1898) 314, 315
Roques, Jeanne *see* Musidora
Das rosa Pantöffelchen (1913) 271, 302
Rosalie series (1911–1912) 79, 146, 150, 193
Rosalie et sa phono (1911) 193
Rosalie et ses meubles fideles (1911) 144
Rosas, Enrique 160, 177, 554
Rose of Salem Town (1910) 288
Rosenberg, Carl 164
Rosenberg, Murray 498
Rosenfest in Luxemburg (1905) 400
Rosenthal, Joseph 73, 101, 109, 554, 651, 685
Rosenzweig, Ralph 440
Rosher, Charles 304, 387
Rosito, Victor 217
Rossetti, Dante Gabriel 494
Rossi, Carlo 333, 336, 384, 555
Rossi, Gilberto 83, 418, 555
Rothapfel, S. L. ("Roxy") 131, 498, 534, 555, 575, 665
Rough Sea at Dover 656
Rousby, Erwin 527–8
Roux, Paul Joseph 199, 553–4
Roveri, Ermanno 147
Roy, Surendra Narayan 49
Royal Adelaide gallery 406
Royal Bioscope 555, 581
Royal Panopticon of Science 406
Royal Polytechnic Institution 406
Royal Visit to Calcutta (1912) 582

Royal Visit to Conway (1899) 113
Royal Visit to Victoria (1901) 562
Le Royaume de fées (1903) 125, 139, 249
Roye, Yvette *see* Andreyor, Yvette
Royston, Harry 296
Rube and Mandy Go to Coney Island (1903) 22
Rübezahls Hochzeit (1916) 687
Il Rubino del destino (1914) 436
Rucabado, Ramón 491, 600
run-zone clearance system 446
The Runaway Match (1903) 135
rural areas 47, 663
Le Ruse de mari (1907) 507
Rusi Khan, Mehdi 331
Russia 555–60; audiences 557–8; censorship 559; domestic melodrama 422, 423; exhibition 556–7; production and distribution 556; projectionists 536; sensational melodrama 426, 505, 557; trade press 637
Russo-Japanese war 541, 553, 554
Ruttmann, Walter 10
Rye, Stellan 560, 687

2nd Special Service Battalion Canadian Infantry Embarking for South Africa (1898) 101
16th Century Wedding in Russia (1908) 356
S. Francesco, Poverello d'Assisi (1911) 277
S. M. Küstenpanzerschiff "Odin" im Gefecht (1900) 182
Sabinski, Czeslaw 505, 586
Die Sächsische Schweiz (1915) 688
Le sacre d'Edouard VII (1902) 419
Sadoul, Georges 125, 160, 164, 512, 595
safari films 25, 224, 580
Saffo and Priapo (1921/1922) 525
Sahhafbashi-e Tehrani, Ebrahim Khan 331
Saída do pessoal Operarario da fabrica Confiança 528
A Sailor's Heart (1912) 102
St. Kilda, Its People and Birds (1908) 521
Saint-Bonnet, Jeanne 530
Sairandhri (1920) 411
Salainen perintömääräys (1914) 401
Salaviinanpolttajat (1907) 39
Salis, Rodolphe 587
Salomé (1910) 229
saloons 120, 382, 479, 561–2, 673
Salt, Barry 93, 207, 385, 386, 387, 585
Salten, Felix 55

Le Salut de Dranem (1901) 192
Salvation Army 50, 119, 407, 473, 513, 550, 562
Salvation Army International Congress Cosmorama (1904) 513
Samama, Albert "Chikly" 646
Sambo and Dinah (1914) 75
Sampat, Dwarkadas 362, 502
The Sampson-Schley Controversy (1901) 314
San Giorgio cavaliere (1912) 436
San Paolo (1910) 436
Sandberg, Serge 40, 157, 467, 468, 506, 562
Sanders, Willy 147, 199, 250
Sandow, Eugene (Friedrich Müller) 2, 200, 562–3
Sandow, Raja 362
Sanger, Margaret 700
Sangre y azúcar (1919) 185
Sangue bleu (1914) 68, 339, 491
Sani al-Saltaneh, Ebrahim Khan Akkasbashi 331
Sans famille (1913) 444
Santa (1931) 177
Santana, Alberto 514
Santarellina (1912) 106, 447
Santoni, Dante 127, 169, 336
Santos, Francisco 563
Santos, Pablo 563
Santos, Silvino 563
Santos y Artigas 159, 160, 185, 563
Sapène, Jean 468, 562
Sardanapalo, re dell'Assiria (1910) 436
Sargent, Epes Winthrop 394, 451, 563–4, 578, 693
Sarkar, Jyotish 404
Sarll, Thomas 58
Sarrus, Gustave *see* Andréani, Henri
Sascha-Filmfabrik 52, 363
Sashka seminarist (1914) 558
Satan Triumphant (1917) 541, 707
Satana (1912) 78, 404
Satanella (1913) 469
Saturn Film 52, 525, 564
Saturnino Farandola (1914) 225
Satyawadi Raja Harishchandra (1917) 404
Saunders, Alfred Henry 357, 451, 564
The Sausage Machine (1897) 142
Saussure, Ferdinand de 601
Sauvons nos bébés (1918) 102
Savari Geraftan-e Kutuleh az Arab 331
Saved By the Telephone (1912) 425
Savitri (1912) 318, 502

Savkari Pash (1925) 411
Savoia 169, 337, 343, 491
Sawamura Shirogoro 346, 564
A Sawmill Hazard (1912) 425
Saxe, John 122, 479, 497, 498, 555, 564–5, 664
Saxe, Thomas 122, 479, 497, 498, 555, 564–5, 664
SB *see* Svenska Biografteatern
SCAGL 65, 257, 502, 503, 507, 565, 586; Arquillière 39; Bolten-Baeckers 78; Capellani 103, 104; Carré 105; color 140; crime films 158; Dania Biofilm 164; Decourcelle 168; Decroix 168; Denola 176; Desfontaines 178; *film d'art* 236, 237, 250, 508; France 250; Gugenheim 290; historical films 300; Krauss 364; legitimate theater 627; literary adaptations 329, 543; Merzbach brothers 428; Mistinguett 437; Monca 444; multiple-reel films 453; Prince 532; Riche 552; Robinne 553
The Scarlet Letter (1911) 57
Scena op de Kaapsche Spoorweg (1898) 598
scénario definition 576
Scène d'escamotage (1898) 84
Scènes de la vie cruelle series 384
Scènes de la vie moderne series 384
Les Scènes de la vie telle qu'elle est (1911–1913) 104, 235, 250, 266, 281, 386, 421, 454
"scenics" *see* travelogues
Scheff, Fritzi 490
Schenck, Joseph 392, 566, 623
Schenck, Nicholas 392, 566
Schering Chemical Company 107
Schertzinger, Victor L. 464
Schivelbusch, Wolfgang 439, 449, 639
Schmidthässler, Walter 153, 154, 302
Schneider, Eberhard 566
Schnellseher 30, 95, 325
Schnitzler, Arthur 55
Schomburgk, Hans 14, 138
Schönbein, Christian Friedrich 106
Schönwalder, Paul 52
Schott, Richard 640
Schram, Charles 62
Schröder, Karl Ludwig 175
Schuberg, John 98, 566
Schuhpalast Pinkus (1916) 396
Schuldig (1913) 61
Schumann, Robert 14
Schwartz, Maurice 150, 193, 250

Die schwarze Katze (1910) 302
Die schwarze Kugel oder Die geheimnisvollen Schwestern (1913) 302, 607
Das schwarze Los (1913) 55
Die schwarze Natter (1913) 302
Schwarzer, Johann 564
Schwarzes Blut (1912) 521
Schwebebahn 515
Schwobthaler, Robert 287, 546, 688
Sciamengo, Carlo 333
scientific films 5, 323; Ambrosio 19; animal pictures 25; Cambodia 91; Charles Urban Trading Company 109; Éclair 199; education 214; ethnographic films 221; Europe 566–9; France 250; Froelich 260; Germany 272; Italy 337; Khanzhonkov & Co. 357; Omegna 489; Paul 510; United States 569–72; Urban 651; *see also* education
scientific management 122, 571
Lo Scomparso (1913) 333, 709
Scotland 287, 572–3
Scott & Van Altena 311
Scott, John 406
Scott, Robert F. 524–5
The Scottish Covenanters (1909) 513
The Screaming Shadow (1920) 425
screens 7, 531, 573–6; airdomes 15; archaeology of cinema 33; nickelodeons 479, 663
screenwriting 295, 576–9; Cines 127; Hofer 302; intertitles 330; Japan 345; Khanzhonkov & Co. 357; Méliès 419; Sargent 564; Shipman 590; Thiemann & Reinhardt Company 633; Xinmin Theater Research Society 115
Scrooge, or Marley's Ghost (1901) 510
Le sculpteur express (1907) 27
The Sculptor's Nightmare (1905) 74
The Sculptor's Nightmare (1908) 27
Scuola d'eroi (1914) 428, 485
SDGL *see* Société des gens de lettres
The Sea Lions' Home (1897) 25
The Sea Wolf (1913) 79
The Sealed Room (1909) 383
A Search for Evidence (1903) 178, 179
Seaver, George 516
Sebel, Stanisaw 523
Sébert, Hippolyte 33, 118
The Secret of Box Letter A (1915) 490
"Secrets of Nature" series 594

Le séducteur (1910) 400
Seeber, Guido 10, 270, 481, 521, 560, 579, 687
Segreto, Afonso 82, 579–80
Segreto, Paschoal 82, 579, 580
Sei no kagayaki (1919) 346, 353
Selecting the Tsar's Bride (1908) 356
Selig Polyscope Company 24, 25–6, 76, 448, 580–1; Arbuckle 32; Bosworth 79; Buckwalter 86; comic series 148; editing techniques 213; end of production 659; ethnographic films 222; Greece 287; Hale's Tours 294; historical films 299; industrial films 320, 321; jungle films 691; Kleine-Edison-Selig-Essanay 220, 361; Mix 438; Roosevelt film 224; serials 583; Shakespeare films 589; travelogues 642; United States 656, 657; US imperialism 315; Vitagraph-Lubin-Selig-Essanay 220, 394, 581, 680; westerns 690, 691; Williams 694; women's suffrage films 700; world's fairs 705
Selig, William Nicholas 69, 580, 581, 596
Sellier, Louis Josep 599
Selznick, Lewis J. 702
Sen, Hiralal 318, 555, 581–2
Sen, Motilal 555
Sennett, Mack 72, 144, 316, 403, 582, 647; animation 27; Keystone 108, 142, 146, 356, 472, 483; New York Motion Picture Company 472; production methods 501; Sterling 611; Triangle Film Corporation 317, 412, 473
sensational melodrama 55, 126, 423–7; Ambrosio 19; Aquila 31; Belasco 586; crime films 157, 158; Delmont 170; detective films 180; Feuillade 235; France 251; Germany 271; Grandais 281; Gundersen 291; Itala 333; jungle films 691; Kalem 353; Khanzhonkov 356; Kinografen 360; Klercker 362; labor relations 368, 369; Lind 390; Lubin 394; Pathé-Frères 506, 507; Piel 521; popularity of 441; Protazanov 541; racialized 434–5; Russia 426, 505, 557, 558; serials 583; Sweden 615; transportation 639; United States 656–7
The Sentimental Bloke (1918) 393
Séparation des soeurs xyphopages Doodica and Radica (1902) 567
Sepulchre, Emile 62
sequencing of films 534
Seraphin, François Dominique 587
Serbia 58
Serena, Gustavo 340, 392, 500, 582

serials 582–4; American Film Manufacturing Company 20; Argentina 38; Burguet 87; costumes 156; Del Colle 169; Desfontaines 178; detective films 180; Fescourt 235; Feuillade 235; Ford 244–5; Holmes 304; India 319; Italy 339; Japan 346; Kalem 353; Lubin 394; May 416; multiple-reel films 453; Nalpas 467; Navarre 468; Roland 554; Russia 558; Selig 581; sensational melodrama 425, 427; stunts 441; Universal 161, 650; White 693; women's suffrage films 700; World War I 703
series photography *see* chronophotography
La serpe (1920) 552
Serpentin series 194, 384, 467
Serpentine Dance (1896) 139
Serra, Antonio 83
Serrador, Francisco 79, 83, 165, 241, 580, 584
Servaes, Ernest 250
Serviss, Garret P. 307
Sestier, Marius 50, 318
set design 584–7; Bauer 61; biblical films 70; cinema of attractions 124; classical Hollywood cinema 129; *féeries* 233; Griffith 288; historical films 299; Méliès 419; melodrama 422; paintings 493; Perret 512; staging in depth 606
Setu Bandhan (1932) 298
The Seven Ages (1905) 210, 386
sex 426, 427, 525
sexual reform movement 697
SF *see* Svenska filmindustri
Sfinks 364, 522, 587
Shackleton, Ernest 523, 524
shadow theater 28, 35, 587–8; Cambodia 91; China 115, 587; Hofer 303
Shakespeare films 2, 299, 588–90; Blackton 75; Bush 87; legitimate theater 626; Lo Savio 392; screenwriting 578
Shakuntala (1920) 591
Sham Battle at the Pan-American Exposition 690
Shamama, Albert (Chickly) 215–16, 217, 646
Shaw, Anna Howard 700
Sheffield Photo Co. 151, 157, 590
Sheffield United vs. Derby (1899) 547
Sheffield United vs. Liverpool (1898) 547
Shepard, Archibald 341, 479, 590
Shepherd, David 134
Sherlock Holmes Baffled (1900) 178
Shibata Tsunekichi 344, 363
Shipman, Nell 590–1

Shirha-ye Baghvahsh-e Farahabad (1900) 331
Shocking Stockings (1904) 177
Short, Henry 510, 528
Show, Harold 599
Shubert, Lee 457, 702
Shumway, L. C. 394
Shunsui Matsuda 134
Shylock (1913) 178
A Siamese Elopement (1912) 625
Siaw Songuan Sibunruang 625
The Sick Kitten 206–7
Sidqi, Amin 216
Le Siège de Calais (1911) 24, 585
Sienna, Pedro (Pedro Pérez Cordero) 114, 278, 591
Siete fusileros 676
Die Sigifälle in Cameroun und Togo 14
The Sign of the Cross (1895) 631
La signora dalle camelie (1915) 582
La silhouette animé (1907) 27
Silks and Satins (1916) 386, 387
Silow, Hugo 616
Silvio, Alexandre 102, 591
Simmel, Georg 439
Simon, Walter Cleveland 463
Simplex projector 527, 539, 591
Simulacro de un incendio (1897) 159
Sinclair, James A. 474
Singapore 412
Singer, Ben 47, 440
Singh, Suchet 318, 591
Sinhagad (1923) 319, 411
Sinn, Clarence E. 462, 463
Sioux Ghost Dance (1894) 132, 689
Sir Douglas Mawson's Marvelous Views of the Frozen North (1915) 307
Sister Mary Jane's Top Note (1907) 244
SITCIA 216
Sivan, Casimir 195, 592, 619
Sixty Years a Queen (1913) 59, 595
Sjöberg, Carl Gustaf Albert 613
Sjöström, Victor 361, 386, 400, 411, 504, 592–3, 607, 611, 614, 615, 680
Skaarup, Frede 173, 245, 593
Skladanowsky, Emil 172, 270, 273, 469, 484, 593, 615, 617
Skladanowsky, Max 25, 34, 172, 191, 270, 273, 460, 469, 484, 593, 615, 617
Sklar, Robert 47
Skouras, Charles 593

Skouras, Spyros 593
Slagsmål i Gamla Stockholm 615
Sleighing in High Park (1902) 98
Slieker, George Christiaan 469, 593–4
Sloman, Edward 394
Slovenia 58
Smalley, Philip 79, 551, 594
Smallwood, Ray 316
Smirnov, Dmitri 490
Smith, Albert E. 188, 199, 201, 324, 553,
    594; Blackton 75, 76; spatial relations 206–7,
    208; trick films 644; Vitagraph 679, 680;
    Williamson 695
Smith, Dr J. H. 107
Smith, F. Percy 109, 521, 594, 651
Smith, George Albert 164, 226, 327, 460, 484,
    594–5, 651; Blair film stock 76; camera
    techniques 205, 247; Kinemacolor 141; trick
    films 685; Wolff 696
Smith, John William 595
La smorfia del destino (1912) 436
Smultronstället (1957) 592
Snakeville 24, 148, 220
Snow, Marguerite 625
social class 42–3, 45, 46–7; Bijou Theater 131;
    France 257; Germany 275; labor movement 366;
    Russia 557; women 696, 698; *see also* middle
    class; working class
Socialists 152, 366, 367, 369–70
société anonyme xxx, 40, 123
Société des Auteurs des Films 87, 167, 552
Société des gens de lettres (SDGL) 565, 627
société en nom collectif par actions xxx
Société générale du Phonoscope 373
The Society Raffles (1905) 179
Soga kyodai kariba no akebono (1908) 345, 403
Un sogno di Kri Kri (1913) 147
Sokolovsky, Noah 498
Solax 265, 291, 595–6, 658
Soldat et Marquise (1910) 167
A Soldier of the U.S. Army (1909) 315
A Soldier's Courtship (1896) 460, 585
Soldiers of the Cross (1901) 50, 513, 550
Soldiers of Fortune (1914) 229–30
The Soldier's Return (1902) 695
Song About Kalashnikov the Merchant (1908) 356
Sonka zolotaia ruchka (1914) 193, 558
Sorel, Cécile 3
Sortie d'usine (1895) 5

La Soubrette ingénieuse (1902) 247
sound effects 295, 462, 531–2, 596–7; Carleton
    184; Hale's Tours 93; Howe 305; itinerant
    exhibitors 342; lecturers 379; magic lantern
    shows 406; Pathé-Frères 507; *The Story of the
    Kelly Gang* 50; West 689
sound machines 596, 598
La Souriante Madame Beudet (1923) 39
Sous la mitraille (1913) 287
South Africa 12, 14, 186, 598–9
South America xxix; expedition/exploration films
    223–4; Schnellseher use 30
South Pacific 487
Southern Cross Motion Pictures 50
Spain 599–600; Philippines 515; US imperialism
    314, 315
Spartaco (1913) 500, 501, 677
Spartacus 464
spatial relations 206–9, 210
Specht, Georges 266, 512
special effects 126; biblical films 70; Chómon 116,
    501; Kri Kri films 259; *see also* trick films
spectatorship 42, 46, 293, 383; Bakshy 57;
    fiction 449; issues and debates 600–3; Japan 345;
    Sweden 618; vaudeville 672; *see also* audiences
Le Spectre du passé (1910) 167
Spencer, Cozens 49, 50, 51, 298, 487, 604
Spencer, Walter Baldwin 50, 221, 222, 223
Sperduti nel buio (1914) 340, 414
Spergiura! (1909) 19
Lo Spetrro di Jago (1912) 31
Spier, Ike 698
The Spirit Awakened (1912) 69
Spirograph 85, 279, 651
A Splendid Romance (1918) 490
The Spoilers (1914) 230, 581, 694
Spoor, George K. 24, 220, 370, 604, 620, 660
sports films 5, 478, 604–5; *see also* boxing films
La sposa del Nilo (1910) 127
Sposa Nella Morte (1915) 490
The Squatter's Daughter 244
The Squaw Man (1914) 171, 230, 295, 372
S.S. Coptic Running Against a Storm (1898) 639
Staffa, Giacomo 83
stage acting 2
staging in depth 3, 209, 605–8; Bauer 61;
    Capellani 104; Gaumont 266; Haggar 293;
    Hasselbladfilm 616; historical films 299, 300;
    Holger-Madsen 303; Klercker 362;

melodrama 422, 454; Sjöström 592; Svenska
  Biografteatern 614
Ståhlberg, K. E. 39
Ståhlberg, K. J. 242
Staiger, Janet 126, 442, 443, 444
Stamato, João 83
Stampfer, Simon 270
Stanford, Leland 118, 465, 569–70, 604
Star Film 113, 249, 418–19, 551
The Star of the South (1910) 599
star system 8, 543, 608–10, 661, 703; Brazil 83;
  diva films 339; Famous Players Motion Picture
  Company 229; intertitles 328; Japan 346;
  legitimate theater 628; *Monopolfilm* 273;
  multiple-reel films 454; newspapers 638
Star Theater (1902) 182, 211
Starewicz, Wladyslaw 28, 357, 558, 610
Stark, Curt A. 265
Stead, W. T. 476
Der Steckbrief (1913) 302
Steimberg, José 38
Steiner, William 341, 499, 610
Stenka Razin (1908) 193, 556, 558
The Stenographer's Friend (1910) 10
stereography 119, 465, 610–11, 615, 641
stereopticons *see* magic lanterns
stereoscopy 35, 303, 399, 409, 610
Sterling Camera and Film Company 59
Sterling, Ford 144, 611
Stern, Samuel 370, 371
Stewart, Anita 312, 316, 680
Stieringer, Luther 218
Stiller, Mauritz 361, 400, 411, 592, 611–12, 614
Stöcker, Helene 697
Stoddard, John L. 70, 304
Stokvis, Simon B. 612
Stolen by Gypsies (1904) 94
Stoll, Oswald 683
Stollwerck, Ludwig 2, 244, 270, 272, 273, 373,
  612–13
Stonehouse, Ruth 220
Stoop, Jules 471
Stop Thief! (1901) 205
stop-motion shooting 86, 204, 568, 594, 639
Storey, Edith 613
A Storm at Sea (1900) 204
The Story of the Kelly Gang (1906) 50, 348, 596
The Story of a Mosquito (1912) 28
Stow, Percy 128, 243, 297, 613

Stowe, Harriet Beecher 421
The Strange Case of Dr Jekyll and Mr Hyde
  (plays) 631
Stratemeyer Syndicate 451
Streetcar Chivalry (1903) 639
The Strength and Agility of Insects (1911) 109
Strindberg, August 449, 481, 484, 491
stroboscopy 33, 35
strong men 501, 562
Stuart, Dan A. 81
Stuart Webbs series (1914–1926) 154, 179, 426,
  548, 703
Studdy, George 150
Der Student von Prag (1913) 55, 223, 560, 579, 687
Stull, Walter 148
Sturgeon, Rollin S. 208, 680
subcultures 382
Subject for Rogues Gallery (1904) 94
Un successo diplomatico (1913) 553
Sudan 12, 13
El sueño de un estudiante de farmacía (1910) 185
Suffrage and the Man (1912) 700
A Suffragette in Spite of Himself (1912) 701
Sugiura Rokuemon 363
Sul Sentiero della Vipera (1912) 17
Sulochana 362
Sultana 362
La Sultane de l'amour (1919) 87, 467
Die Sumpfblume (1913) 248, 372
Sumurun (1909) 548
The Sunlight Soap Competition (1897) 9
Sunny South 461
Superstition andalouse (1912) 117
Suphakit, Prince 625
Surf and Sunset on the Indian Ocean (1913) 642
surgical films 192
Survage, Léopold 497
Suspense (1913) 94, 640
Sutto, Leopold 487
Suzanne series (1916–1917) 428
Svensk-Amerikanska Filmkompaniet 55,
  613, 616
Svenska Biografteatern (SB) 243, 361,
  400, 411, 504, 592, 611, 613–14,
  615, 616, 617
Svenska Filmfundet (Stockholm, 1933) 37
Svenska filmindustri (SF) 260, 411
Svenska Förenade Biografer 617
Svensson, Christian 615

Swain, Mack 108

Swanson, Gloria 464

Swanson, William H. 341, 371, 479, 551, 614

Sweden 615–19; audiences 618; censorship 174; distribution 616–17; exhibition 617–18; fairs 227; regulation 618

Sweedie series (1914–1915) 148

Sweet, Blanche 4, 391, 619

Switzerland 227, 619–20

Sylvani, Gladys 296

Sylvi (1913) 401

Symbolism 494, 496, 497

Symphonie bizarre (1909) 644

synchronized sound 14, 44, 242, 550, 620–1; Baron machine 60; Costa 528; Dickson 517; Gaumont 267; Hepworth 297; Kinetophone 358; Krüger 64; Mendel 427; Messter Biophon 429; Mullens brothers 452; musical accompaniment 461; opera 489; Sweden 615; Walturdaw 684; *see also Tonbilder*

Syria 215, 216, 217, 499, 646

Di sztifmuter (1914) 364

10th US Infantry 2nd Battalion, Leaving Cars (1898) 314

Tabata Kenzo 261

tableaux 2, 3–4, 207, 209–10, 233, 327, 422, 458, 614; *see also* poses

Tachibana Teijiro 345, 623

Der Tag im Film (1911) 688

Tahiti 487

Tainter, Charles 517

Tait, J. & N. 49, 50, 348

Talbot, F. A. 214

Talbot, William Henry Fox 35

Taldykin, A. G. 193

A Tale of Two Cities (1911) 155, 299

Tallroth, Konrad 243, 614

Tally, Thomas Lincoln 341, 478, 623

Talmadge, Norma 312, 623

The Taming of the Shrew (1911) 589

Tan Cheng Kee 413

Tan Xinpei 115, 234

Tanaka Eizo 346, 623–4

Tanenzapf, Nathan *see* Natan, Bernard

Tango criollo (1906) 544

Die Tango-Königin (1913) 687

Tannenbaum, Herbert 624

Tansy (1921) 624

Die tapfere deutsche Marine zu Lande und zu Wasser (1914) 688

La Tare (1911) 235, 386, 422, 454

Tarlarini, Mary Cléo 19, 104, 500

Tarr, George 473

Tate, Alfred O. 359

Taylor, Alma 244, 296, 297, 624

Taylor, Frank 119

Taylor, Frederick W. 571

Taylor, J. Hay 357

Taylor, Stanner E. V. 384

Taylor, William 282

Technicolor 141, 531

The "Teddy" Bears (1907) 27, 149

telegraphy 151, 476

telephones 151–2, 219

The Tempest (1908) 588, 613

temporal relations 211–14

A Temporary Truce (1911) 690

Temptation (1915) 490

The Temptation of St. Anthony (1898) 598

"Ten Years in Manitoba" 259

Tenebre (1916) 31, 552

Tenkatsu 200, 345, 346, 353, 362, 363, 564, 624

Tennyson, Alfred 496

Teodora (1914) 31

Teodora (1922) 19

Terje Vigen 592

Terminfilm 272–3

Terribili Gonzales, Gianna 127

Terrible angoisse (1906) 151

The Terrible Kids (1906) 143

Terrible Teddy, The Grizzly King (1901) 142, 527

"Terrore" series (1913) 31

Terry, Paul 29

Terwilliger, George 472

Tesla, Nikola 218

Tessier, Valentine 167

Testa, Dante 333

Teufel, Anette 617

textual approaches 42

Thailand (Siam) 588, 624–5

Thalberg, Irving 371

Thanawalla, F. B. 220

Thanhouser, Edwin 625

Thanhouser Film Company 213, 288, 368, 464, 543, 583, 589, 625–6, 649

That Fatal Sneeze 244

Thé chez le concierge (1907) 235
theaters: acting styles 2; anti-drink campaigns 561;
    Australia 49; Austro-Hungary 53; Belgium 63,
    64; Boutillon 80; Brézillon 84; Canada 99, 288;
    Chile 113; China 115; circuits/chains 121–3;
    Cuba 159–60; Denmark 172, 173; electric
    streetcar 219; 'family' 382; Fox 245–6; France
    15; Gaumont 266; Germany 272–3, 274, 275,
    276, 277; Great Britain 283, 284; Greece 286;
    illustrated songs 311; Iran 331–2; Ireland 332–3;
    itinerant exhibitors' 341; Jones 349; Katz 354;
    Keith 355; Luxemburg 400; Malaya 412, 413;
    Mark 413–14; melodrama 128, 626, 628–32;
    multiple-reel films 456; Nationoscope 269;
    Netherlands 469, 470; Norway 484; Peru 513;
    promotional campaigns 543; Quebec 102; reg-
    ulation 375; Russia 556–7; Saxe brothers 564–5;
    Spain 599; Tally 623; United States 659;
    Uruguay 654; Warner Brothers 684; *see also*
    airdomes; legitimate theater; nickelodeons;
    palace cinemas/theaters; screens; vaudeville
Le théâtre du Petit Bob (1906) 27
Le théâtre électrique de Bob (1909) 117
Theatrograph 96, 133, 287, 334, 410, 418, 538, 598
Théophile Pathé 123, 237, 250, 540, 632
Thévenon, Etienne 63, 64, 632
Thiemann & Reinhardt Company 193, 264, 541,
    556, 557, 632–3, 681
Thiemann, Elizaveta 633
Thiemann, Pavel 632, 633–4
Thirty Leagues Under the Sea (1914) 288
Thomas, Arthur Duncan 347, 438, 532, 634
Thomas Graals bästa barn (1918) 612
Thomas Graals bästa film (1917) 612
Thomas, John 683
Thompson, E. P. 382
Thompson, Frank H. 342
Thompson, Maude 368
Thompson, William Gilman 118
Thornton, F. Martin 468
Those Awful Hats (1909) 230
The Three Musketeers (1898) 626
Thunderbolt (1910) 269
Tiber Films 468
Tigre reale (1916) 469, 501, 607
La Tigresa (1917) 177
Tigris (1913) 179, 333, 501
Tilden, Samuel J. 372
Tillie's Punctured Romance (1914) 144, 356

Tilly and the Fire Engines (1911) 244, 624
Tilly series 244, 296, 624
tinting 139–40, 141
Tire au flanc 40
Tissot, Jacques Joseph 70, 494
Titanic In Nacht und Eis (1912) 153, 437
titles *see* intertitles and titles
Toboggan Slide (1902) 101
Todd, Harry 220
Togo 13, 14
Togores, José de 634
Tojo no himitsu (1915) 323
Tokugawa Musei 346, 634
Tolstoi, Lev 541, 559
Tom Butler (1912) 25, 39, 158
Tom the Piper's Son (1905) 74, 576
Tommy Atkins in the Park (1898) 585
Tonbilder 182, 195, 634–5; Froelich 260;
    Messter 270, 272, 278, 280, 429, 489;
    Müller-Lincke 452; Porten 526; *see also*
    synchronized sound
Le Tondeur galant (1912) 192
toning 140
Tontolini series 127, 147, 290, 336–7, 500
Toodles and Her Strawberry Tart (1903) 142–3
I Topi Grigi (1918) 277
Topical Film Company 635
topicals *see* news event films
Le Torrent (1917) 428
La Tosca (1908) 489
La Tosca (1909) 3, 237, 250, 378, 508, 606
Toscano, Salvador 431, 554, 635–6
Die Toten erwachen (1915) 265
Tour du monde d'un policier (1906) 163, 178
Tourists Taking Water From the River Jordan
    (1903) 68
Tourneur, Maurice 85, 94, 198, 199, 223, 252, 386,
    387, 457, 607, 636, 702
toy projectors 486, 538
Toyo Shokai 200, 345
tracking shots 92, 93, 94
trade cards 7, 9
trade marks 8, 9, 154, 356, 542, 636–7; authenti-
    cation 54, 55; Gaumont 415; Keystone 582;
    Pathé-Frères 506; Reulos 551; Star Film 418–19;
    Svenska Biografteatern 616
trade press 637–8; acting discussions 2; animated
    cartoons 28; Argentina 38; Baggot 57; biblical
    films 70–1; Bijou Theater 131; *The Bioscope* 73–4;

Chile 114; ethnographic films 221; *féeries* 231;
Germany 52; Hasselbladfilm 616; Hofer 302;
intertitles 328; Lubin 396; musical accompaniment 160; musical suggestions 462; Native
American Indian actors 690; nickelodeons
478–9; Pathé-Frères 508; Pickford 520; Poland
523; projectionists 536; publicity 543; Russia
556–7, 559; sound effects 596; Stokvis 612;
Tonbilder 635; travelogues 642; United States
321; westerns 690, 692; white slave films 693

trade unions *see* labor movement

Trädgårdsmästaren (1912) 592, 614

Traffic in Souls (1913) 94, 151, 180, 427, 450,
457, 693

Una tragedia al cinematografo (1913) 127

La Tragedia de la Escuela (1933) 677

A Tragic Elopement (1903) 438

The Tragic Tenth 554

Tragödie eines Streiks (1911) 265

Trail of the Lonesome Pine 386

trailers 8

Train Arriving at Bombay Station (1898) 318

The Train Wreckers 288

The Trainer's Daughter; or, A Race for Love (1906)
424

trains 92, 94, 294

Tram Ride (1898) 484

"Tramp" films 145

The Tramp (1916) 220

The Tramp and the Bather (1897) 145

The Tramps and the Artist (1899) 438

The Tramp's Dream (Edison, 1901) 145

The Tramp's Dream (Lubin, 1899) 145

The Tramp's Surprise (1899) 438

Tramullas, Antonio 599

transportation 9, 125, 638–40; camera
movement 92–3; comedies 639; electric modes
of 218–19; modernity 439; spectatorship 603;
traction companies 22; urbanization 651–2;
US imperialism 313

Der Traum eines österreichischen Reservisten
(1915) 363

Trautschold, Gustav 640

Travail (1919–1920) 529

travel 10, 478

travelogues 5, 9, 321, 323, 640–3, 689; Ambrosio
19, 340; audiences 43; Bonine 78; Cambodia 91;
camera movement 93; Charles Urban Trading
Company 109; China 116; churches 120;

Cines 128, 340; Commercial Press Motion
Picture Department 150; consumer cooperatives
153; education 214; ethnographic films 221;
Express-Film 688; France 250; Gaumont 265;
Hepworth 296; Holmes 304; Italy 337, 340;
itinerant exhibitors 342; Kalem 353; Khanz-
honkov & Co. 357; Machin 403; Maître 411;
Natural Color Kinematograph 468; New
Zealand 473; Palestine 498; Pathé-Frères 372;
Poland 522; program formats 533; promotional
542; Russia 558; Selig 580; Sweden 615;
United States 656; Urban 651; Vietnam 678;
Warwick Trading Company 685; *see also*
phantom train rides

Tree, Herbert Beerbohm 59, 588, 589, 626, 631

La Trepadora (1924) 676

Tressell, Robert 365

Trewey, Felicien 324, 460, 546, 588, 683

Triangle Distributing Corporation 16, 457

Triangle Film Corporation 196, 317, 356, 412, 465,
473, 686

Il Triangolo Giallo (1917) 277

Tricentenaire de Québec (1908) 491

trick films 2, 17, 26, 27, 151, 643–5; Arnaud 39;
Autorenfilme 56; biblical films 70; Bitzer 74;
Blackton 75; Charles Urban Trading Company
109; Chómon 94, 116; color 139; comedies 143;
dance 163; Deed 169; department stores 177;
detectives 178; direct audience address 124;
editing techniques 204, 212; *féeries* 231–2, 233;
Feuillade 235; Fitzhamon 244; framing 247;
France 249; Haggar 293; Hepworth 296, 297;
Hopwood 304; Japan 346; lecturers 327; Méliès
9, 97, 124, 125, 159, 249, 418, 419, 584;
mythologicals 465; Pathé-Frères 506; Paul 510;
Russia 558; Stow 613; Uruguay 654; Velle 676;
Warwick Trading Company 685; Williamson
695; Zecca 709; *see also* special effects

Trilby (1896) 631

Trilby (1912) 363

Trilby (1915) 636

La Trilogia di Dorina (1917) 469

Trimble, Larry 647, 680

A Trip Around the Pan-American Exposition
(1901) 705

A Trip on the Rhodesian Railway 12

Tripoli (1912) 19

Les Trois Mousquetaires (1913) 91, 237, 252

trolley lines 652

Troncone, Roberto 335
Le Trou de mon quai 192, 518
Il Trovatore (1911) 238, 463
True Love's Strength Is Not The Passion Of A Kiss (1916) 707
The Truth About the Pole (1911) 523
Tsar Ivan Vasilyevich Groznyi (1915) 490
Tsivian, Yuri 422, 536
Tsuchiya Tsunekichi 344
tuberculosis 569
Tucker, George Loan 94, 180, 457
Tunisia 13, 215, 216, 217
Turkey/Ottoman Empire 498, 499, 646
Turner, E. G. 684
Turner, Florence 4, 608, 623, 647, 680, 683
Turovskaya, Maya 423
Turpin, Ben 220, 647
Tuschinski, Abraham 470
La tutela (1913) 190
Två bröder (1912) 361
Twain, Mark 315
Twentieth Century Fox 245, 246, 593
Twilight of a Woman's Soul (1913) 61, 94, 505
Twin Sisters Double cycle 161
Two Little Dromios (1914) 589
Two Memories (1909) 520
The Two Orpans (1907) 76
The Two-Gun Man (1911) 24
Tyndall, John 406

Ubirajara (1919) 83, 165
UCI *see* Unione Cinematografica Italiana
Ucicky, Gustav 363
Ueda Tsunejiro 66
Ufa 430, 483, 703
Uguarte, Luis 514
Uittenboogaart, Daniel Louis 195
Ukhod velikogo startsa (1912) 633
L'ultimo dei Frontignac (1911) 19
Umeya Shokichi 345, 403, 649
Der Unbekannte (1912) 694
Uncle Remus' First Visit to New York (1914) 75
Uncle Tom's Cabin (Edison, 1903) 126, 129, 163, 207, 209, 320, 327, 421–2, 527, 630
Uncle Tom's Cabin (Vitagraph, 1910) 421, 456
Uncle Tom's Cabin (World Film Corporation, 1914) 421, 457
The Unclean World (1903) 567

Under the Stars and Stripes (1910) 315
Under Western Skies (1910) 24
undercranking 211
Ungerleider, Moritz 52
Union des grands éditeurs 15, 255, 350
Unione Cinematografica Italiana (UCI) 128, 500
Unitas 40
United Film Service 573, 685
United States xxix, 655–69; acting styles 4; advertising films 9; airdomes 16; amusement parks 21–2, 23; animation 27; archives 36; audiences 42–4, 45, 46, 47, 368, 665–6; biblical films 70–1; black cinema 74–5; Canada 100; capitalism 444–6; censorship 666–8; Chautauqua 112–13; churches 120; cinema circuits/chains 121–3; Civil War 631; comic strips 148–9; detective films 159; distribution 657, 659–61; domestic melodrama 421, 422–3; education 215; exhibition 662–5; framing 247; historical films 300–1; illustrated songs 310–11; imperialism 313–16, 515; labor movement 6, 368–70; legitimate theater 627–8; leisure time and space 380–3; migration/immigration 6, 432–5; multiple-reel films 456–7, 578; musical scores 463, 464; newsreels 477, 478; patent wars 21, 196, 654–5, 656, 657; Pathé-Frères 506, 507; production 655–9; propaganda films 540; racial segregation 74, 375, 545–6; regulation 666–8; scientific films 569–72; screens 573–5; serials 583; sports films 605; star system 608; theatrical melodrama 629, 630, 631; trade press 637, 638; travelogues 641; urbanization 651–3, 664; vaudeville 672–6; white slave films 693; women's movement 698–700; women's suffrage films 700–2; World War I 703, 704; *see also* westerns
Universal Film Manufacturing Company 447, 464, 649–50, 658; Baggot 57; *Bluebird* films 362; Brulatour 85; comic series 147–8; Cunard 161; Defender Film Company 614; detective films 179, 180; Dintenfass 188; dominance of 456; Dwan 196; Gauntier 269; Holmes 304; Horsley 304; IMP 313; labor relations 369; Laemmle 370–1; multiple-reel films 457; New York Motion Picture Company 355, 473; newsreels 477; Philippines 515; Powers 530; Rex 551; serials 583; short films 260; Smalley 594; Sterling 611; US imperialism 315; US monopoly capitalism 446; Victor brand 378;

Weber 687; westerns 349; white slave films 427, 693; Yankee Film Company 610

An Unseen Enemy (1912) 156

The Unseen World (1904) 109, 194, 567, 569

Unsere Polizeitruppe in Togo 14

Unter Palmen und ewigem eis (1914) 298

Unwritten Law (1907) 158

Up San Juan Hill (1909) 315

L'Uragano (1911) 500

Uralskii, Aleksandr 633

Urban & Moy 219

Urban, Charles 12, 76, 96, 109, 254, 650–1; Balkans 58; 'Bioscope' 685; 'Brighton School' 164; developing machine 240; Duncan 194, 567; Eclipse 199; editing techniques 211; educational films 120, 214; expedition/exploration films 223; fake newsreel 548; glass-plate projectors 279; Great Britain 282; Hepworth 297; India 318; Kinemacolor 260; Maguire & Baucus 411; Méliès 419; missionary films 550; Mitchell & Kenyon 438; Natural Color Kinematograph 468; news event films 475; North American Phonograph 484; Rogers 553; Rosenthal 554; scientific films 572; Smith (F. Percy) 594; Smith (George Albert) 595; Thomas 634; trade mark cases 636; Turkey 646; *The Unseen World* 194, 567, 569; *see also* Charles Urban Trading Company

urbanization 6, 313, 375, 651–3, 664, 690; leisure 381; modernity 439; spectatorship 603; white slave films 693

"Urbanora" 109, 110

Urrutia, Edmundo 114

Uruguay 113, 653–4

Urzúa, Adolfo 114

US Cavalry Unloading Supplies at Tampa (1898) 314

US Troops and Red Cross in Trenches at Candaba (1899) 315

Valencia (1916) 688

Valentin, Karl 271, 671

Valentino, Rudolph 488

Valetta 167, 251, 508, 671

Vallade, Fédier 114

Valle, Federico 38

Valli, Alida 343

Vallot, Louis 267

Les Vampires (1915–1916) 25, 235, 366, 384, 426, 464, 467, 530, 703

Vampyre der Großstadt (1914) 302

van Dommelen, Caroline 482

van Dommelen, Jan 303

van Gehuchten, Arthur 567

Van Goitsenhoven, Louis 64, 671

Van Loan, Charles E. 450

Van Neck, Louis 63

Van Rayvon, Baron 591

Vandal, Marcel 170, 250, 350, 672

Vanderlyn, John 188

Vanity Fair (1911) 264, 456

Variety (magazine) 563–4

Värmlänningarne (1910) 614, 615

Vaser, Ernesto 19, 147, 333, 337, 460

vaudeville 15, 21, 113, 187, 408, 445, 573, 672–6; AM&B projector 539; animation 29; anti-drink campaigns 561; Arbuckle 32; attractions 124, 126; audiences 43, 47; Australia 49; Balaban brothers 57; Belgium 63, 64; Biograph projectors 73; black performers 74–5; British Mutoscope & Biograph 85; cafés-concerts 89; Canada 98, 288; chase films 110; 'cheap' 382; churches 120; circuits 122; classical Hollywood narrative 128; Clune 132; comedy 142; dance films 163; detectives 178; distribution 189; Fynes 262; Grau 281; Grauman 281; Hale's Tours 93; illustrated songs 310; Ince 316; intermediality and modes of reception 324; Italy 335; itinerant exhibitors 340; Japan 344; Keith 355, 458; Kinetophone 358; Lasky 372; lecturers 379; Loew 392; Lubin 395; McCay 417; magic lantern shows 327; Méliès films 125; Messter 271; Mexico 431; Miles Brothers 436; modernity 440; *New York Morning Telegraph* 472; New Zealand 473; nickelodeons 479; phonography 517; popular theater concept 626; program formats 533; promotion 542; Quebec 101, 102; racism 433; Russia 556; Sandow 562; Smith 594; star system 608; synchronized sound systems 621; theaters 497; theatrical melodrama 630; transportation 638; travelogues 641; Turpin 647; United States 380, 656, 659, 662, 663, 664–5, 667; urbanization 652; Vitagraph 679; Waters 686; westerns 689

Le Vautour de la Sierra (1910) 198

Ved Faengslets Port (1911) 76, 542

Veeder Manufacturing Company 239

Veidt, Conrad 271, 627
Veijola, Yrjö 401
Velasco Maidana, José María 77
Velle, Gaston 24, 27, 127, 249, 506, 676
Veltée, Claudius 694
Eine venezianische Nacht (1913) 55, 548
Venezuela 676–7
La Vengeance de Jean le loup (1910) 552
Venkaiah, Raghupati 677
Venture, Marie 3–4
La Vénus de Luxembourg 518
Venus Victrix (1918) 467
Verbitskaia, Anastasiia 633
Verettömät (1913) 401
Verirrte Seelen (1911) 182
Veriscope 81, 155, 341
Verne, Jules 449
Het vervloekte geld (1912) 303, 403
Vesuvio Films 40
Veyre, Gabriel 67, 92, 101, 105, 135, 159, 344,
    364, 430, 519, 677, 678
El viaje del Doctor Campos Salles a Buenos Aires
    (1900) 38, 544
Viaje presidencial (1924–1925) 654
Victime du quinquina (1911) 507
Les Victimes de l'alcool (1911) 80, 508, 569
Les Victimes de l'alcoolisme (1902) 327, 569
Victor, Alexander 410, 504
Victoria 40
Vidal, González 676
Vidali, Enrico 338, 500, 677–8
La Vie de Christ (Guy, 1899) 69, 347
La Vie de Moise (1905) 69
La Vie drôle series 384
La Vie et la Passion de Jésus-Christ (Lumière, 1898)
    69, 84, 210
La Vie et la Passion de Jésus-Christ (Passion
    Play) (Pathé-Frères, 1903) 126,
    210, 452
La Vie et la Passion de Jésus-Christ (Passion Play)
    (Pathé-Frères, 1907) 69, 249–50, 503
Vie et Passion de Notre Seigneur Jésus-Christ 84
Vienna 51, 52, 53, 54
Vienna Club of Cinematography 36
Viens Poupoule 518
Vietnam 138, 678–9
Le Vieux docker (1914) 123, 366
*View from an Engine Front – Train Leaving
    Tunnel* 595

Views and Films Index 451, 462, 503, 511, 564, 596,
    637, 679
Vignola, Robert 353
Viking Film 67, 615
Villa, Pancho 478
*Le Village de Namo: Panorama pris d'une chaise
    à porteurs* 678
Villiers, Frederic 287, 646
Vingarne (1916) 612, 614
Vinter, Georges 80
The Violin Maker of Cremona (1909) 520
Les Vipères (1911) 235
La virgin de la Caridad (1930) 512
The Virginian (1914) 171, 295
Visit to Australia of the American Fleet 50
A Visit to Peek Frean and Co.'s Biscuit Works
    (1906) 322, 323
Visita do imperador Guilherme II da Alemanha 528
Viskovskii, Viacheslav 633
Vita Cinematografica, La 336, 638, 679
La vita delle farfalle (1911) 19
Vita futurista (1916) 336
Vitagraph Company of America 4, 15, 23, 261,
    448, 679–81; amusement parks 22; animal
    films 26; animation 27; Belgium 64; biblical
    films 69, 70, 71; Blackton 75, 76; boxing films
    81; *Bulletin of Life Portrayals* 160; Bunny 86;
    cafés-concerts 89–90; Charles Urban Trading
    Company 110; comedies 144; comic series 148;
    Costello 155; costumes 156; Criterion theater
    575; Cuba 159; Delmont 170; department
    stores 177; detective films 179; distribution 189,
    659, 660; domestic melodrama 421; editing
    techniques 208, 211, 213; exhibition 340, 445;
    Feuillade 266; *film d'art* 236; film festivals 241;
    Finch 242; framing 247; Fuller 262; Gardner
    264, 457; Greater 361; historical films 299, 300–
    1; IMP comparison 312; Ince 316; India 318;
    intertitles 328, 330; itinerant exhibitors 341;
    Joyce 350; Kalem 354; Khanzhonkov & Co.
    356; legitimate theater 627–8; lighting 385, 386,
    387; *Motion Picture Story Magazine* 609; multi-
    ple-reel films 456, 457; musical accompaniment
    461; newsreels 477; Normand 483; opera 489;
    paintings 494, 495; patent wars 655; Poli 524;
    Quebec films 102; re-enactments 477; Rock 553;
    Rodolfi 553; Scandinavia 291; serials 583; set
    design 585, 586; Shakespeare films 588, 589;
    Shipman 590; Singh 591; Smith 594; staging in

depth 607; star system 608; Storey 613; Tal-
madge 623; theater, melodrama 631; Thiemann
& Reinhardt Company 632; trade mark 54;
trade press 637, 638; trick films 644; Turner 647;
Union des grands éditeurs 350; United States
656, 657, 663; vaudeville 663, 673; *Views and
Films Index* 679; westerns 690
Vitagraph-Lubin-Selig-Essanay (V-L-S-E) 220,
394, 457, 581, 680
Vitascope 681; *Autorenfilme* 55, 56;
Germany 270; Mack 404; PAGU 493;
Weisse 687; White 692; *see also* Edison
Vitascope
I Vitelloni (1953) 447
Vitrotti, Giovanni 19, 337, 489, 681
Vittoria o morte (1913) 333
V'la le rétameur 192
Vlès, Fred 568
Voina i mir (1915) 558
Vol d'une mouche ordinaire (1903) 86
Le voleur invisible (1909) 117
von Bergmann, Ernst 567
von Bussenius, Gabriela 114, 278
von Harbou, Thea 416
von Herkomer, Sir Hubert 497, 681
von Hoffman, Carl 223
von Hofmannsthal, Hugo 55, 271
von Ledenfeld, Robert 118, 568
von Reitzner, Victor 95, 118
von Sternberg, Josef 54
von Stroheim, Erich 54
von Suttner, Bertha 303
von Woringen, Paul 182, 271, 682
De Voortrekkers (1916) 599
Votes for Women (1912) 700
Vot'permis? Viens l'chercher! (1905) 384
Le Voyage à la lune (1902) 125, 226, 231, 249,
419, 639; costumes 155; editing techniques 206,
210, 212, 213; production photo 232;
screenplay 576, 577; set design 585; staging
in depth 606
Voyage à travers l'impossible (1904) 231, 577
Voyage au planète Jupiter (1909) 117
Voyage to the Yucatán 635
Voyages et grandes chasses en Afrique 13
Le vrai Jiu-Jitsu 192, 518
Vrignault, Marguerite 516
Vue prise d'une plate-forme mobile (1900) 705
Vues de Soudan, Français-Tombouctou 13

Waldner, Dagmar 618
Wales 113, 683–4
Walgensten, Thomas Rasmussen 405
Walker, J. D. 684
Walker, William 572, 684
Walkirie (1903) 541
Waller, Lewis 626
Walthall, Henry B. 4, 72, 220,
289, 383–4, 684
Walturdaw 84, 417, 438, 489, 684
war films 5, 703, 704; Bolten-Baeckers 78;
dialogue accompaniment 184; Mitchell &
Kenyon 438
Warde, Frederick 589
Warner Brothers 76, 415, 530, 594, 680, 684–5
Warner, Harry 396, 479, 684
Warner's Features, Inc. 155, 661, 684, 685
Warning Shadows (1923) 588
Warren, Low 358
The Warrens of Virginia (1907) 171, 520
A Warrior Bold (1910) 160
Warwick Bioscope projector 164, 297, 546–7, 685
Warwick Trading Company 12, 18, 59, 60,
297, 685–6; Belgium 64; colonial films 137;
distribution 189; Hyman 598; India 318;
Jeapes 635; Kearton 355; McDowell 417;
Maguire & Baucus 411; news event films 475;
Nöggerath Sr. 482; patent wars 655; polar
expedition films 523; Raleigh & Robert 546;
Smith (George Albert) 594–5; Smith (John
William) 595; Switzerland 619; trade mark 636;
travelogues 642; Urban 109, 651
Wash Day in Mexico (1897) 689
Washburn, Bryant 220
Washington Library of Congress 1, 37
Washington Under the American Flag (1909)
301, 495
Washington Under the British Flag (1909) 301
Wasserman, Jakob 55
Wasström, Erik 28
Watanabe Tomoyori 625
The Water Nymph (1912) 472
Waterhouse, John 496
Waters, Percival Lee 660, 686
Wauer, William 260, 640
wax museums 63, 458; Canada 98; Denmark 172;
Europe 5, 686–7; France 157, 257; tableaux 210,
577; United States 527
Way Down East (1920) 279

Webb, George R. 490

Weber, Lawrence 81

Weber, Lois 79, 94, 551, 594, 639–40, 650, 687

Weber, Max 439

Webster, Charles 692

Wedding Procession in Cairo (1901) 705

Wedekind, Frank 373

Wegener, Paul 55, 548, 560, 627, 687

Das Weib ohne Herz (1912) 302

Weihnachtsglocken 1914 (1914) 302

Weinberg, Sigmund 646

Weisenburg, Theodore 570

Weiss, Akiva Arieh 498

Weiss, Joseph Leon 369

Weisse, Hanni 681, 687

Weixler, Dorrit 302

A Welsh Singer (1915) 683

Weltkinematograph/Express-Film (WKF) 274,
    619, 687–8

Werner, Eugène 688

Werner, Michel 688

Werther (1910) 168, 529

West, Alfred 347, 688–9

West, George 463

West, T. J. 49, 51, 473,
    487, 689

westerns 179, 689–92; American Film
    Manufacturing Company 20; Anderson 24;
    Balshofer 59; Bison 355, 543; Blackton 75;
    Buffalo Bill films 132; Cines 128; costumes 156;
    Essanay 220; Farnum 230; fiction 449, 450;
    Fitzhamon 244; Ford 244; framing 248;
    France 250; Fuller 262; Gaumont 266;
    Hamman 294–5; Hart 295; Holmes 304;
    Ince 316; Ivens 342; Kalem 353; Larsen 372;
    Lubin 394; Méliès (Gaston) 418; Mix 438–9;
    Modot 444; New York Motion Picture
    Company 355, 472; Norway 484; Paley 499;
    Pathé Cinematograph 503; popularity of 316;
    racialized 434; Roland 554; Selig 580;
    sensational melodrama 425; serials 582; staging
    in depth 607; Storey 613; Universal 349;
    US imperialism 315; Young Deer 708

Westinghouse, George 92, 388

Weule, Karl 14, 137

Wexelsen 14

What the Curate Really Did 244

"What a Funny Little World This Is" (1911) 311

What Happened to Mary? (1912) 262, 582, 583

What Happened in the Tunnel (1903) 23

What Is To Be Done? (1914) 369

Wheatstone, Charles 610

The Wheel of Death (1913) 425

Wheeler, DeWitt C. 311

When Daddy Comes Home (1902) 143

When Macbeth Came to Snakeville (1914) 589

The Whip (1917) 607

The Whirl of Life (1915) 164

The Whirlpoool of War (1914–1915) 355, 475, 685

The "White" Caps (1905) 527

White, Chrissie 244, 296, 297, 624

The White Goddess 138

The White Goddess of the Wangora 14

White, James Henry 201, 296, 692

White, Pearl 156, 180, 319, 394, 504, 583, 693

White Rats of America 673

white slave films 76, 174, 245, 427, 453, 468,
    667, 693

The White Slave Trade (*Den hvide Slavehandel*)
    (1910) 40, 76, 174, 245, 453, 483

Whitehouse, A. H. 473

Whitford, Annabelle 2

Whitney, Claire 291

Who Pays? (1915) 554

Who Will Marry Mary? (1913) 262

The Whole Dam Family and the Dam Dog (1905)
    142, 226

Why? (1913) 368

Wicks, Monty 296

Wie Ninette zu ihrem Ausgang kam (1913) 394

Wie sich das Kino rächt (1912) 640

Wiene, Robert 526

Wiener Kunstfilm 52, 363, 694

De wigwam (1912) 342

Wilcox, Herbert 629

Wild Bear at Yellowstone (1897) 25

A Wild Goose Chase (1908) 613

Wilder, Samuel (Billy) 54

Wilhelm Tell (1912/1914) 620

Wilkie, Edmund H. 407–8

Wilkins, George H. 523

Willard-Johnson Fight (1915) 81

Willets, Gilson 700

Willett, C. A. 312

Williams, J. D. 49, 51

Williams, Kathlyn 581, 694

Williams, Linda 421

Williams, Percy G. 674

Williams, Randall 227, 341, 694–5

Williams, Raymond 42

Williamson, Alan 695

Williamson, James 31, 96, 164, 288, 378, 460, 494, 521, 695; colonial films 137; color tinting 140; editing techniques 205, 595; English pattern camera 219; facial expression films 143; urban 651

Williamson, Tom 695

Wills, Frederick Charles 50

Willy, Louise 360, 522

Wilson, Charles 202

Wilson, Harry Leon 451

Wilson, Mortimer 464

Wilson, Woodrow 301

Winans, Walter 523

Winning the VC (1900) 438

Winsor McCay (1911) 28

A Winter's Tale (1910) 589

The Wishing Ring (1914) 94, 636

The Witch of the Everglades (1911) 690–1

Wizard/World series (1915) 148

WKF *see* Weltkinematograph/Express-Film

Wo ist Coletti? (1913) 271, 404, 452

Wolf, Nathan Hyman 696

Wolfe, Frank 369

Wolff, Philipp 96, 272, 279, 538, 696

Wolff, William Almon 450

women: audiences 43, 45, 46, 47, 48, 479, 665, 666, 667; department stores 177; fashion 230; *flânerie* 383; as key consumer group 542; leisure 381, 382; low incomes 382; projectionists 536; repression of 526; spectatorship 601, 603; United States 665, 666, 667; Universal 650; white slave films 693

women's movement: Europe 696–8; United States 698–700

women's suffrage 7, 700–2

Wong brothers 320

Woodruff, Eleanor 156

Woods, Frank 472, 702

Worcester, Alec 296

working class 42, 45, 46, 47, 440; consumer cooperatives 152; Great Britain 283; Ireland 333; Italy 335; leisure 382; low incomes 382; nickelodeon audiences 479; Quebec 102; regulatory concerns 376–7; saloons 561, 673; United States 368, 369, 666; vaudeville

audiences 672; women's movement 699–700; *see also* labor movement

The Workman's Lesson (1912) 369

World Film Corporation 62, 82, 199, 702; Brulatour 85; Capellani 104; fashion 230; melodrama 421; multiple-reel films 457

World War I 702–4; Ambrosio 19; amusement parks 22; animation in Europe 27; Aquila 31; Aurora Cinema 49; Belgian Congo 11; Benoît-Lévy 65; British & Colonial Kinematograph Company 84–5; Canada 100; China 115; comic series 147; Denmark 172, 174, 175–6; Drankov 193; Finland 242, 243; French army films 13; Froelich 260; Gaumont 268; Germany 271, 275; Great Britain 285; Hepworth 296, 297; Heuzé 298; hygienist films 142; Jury 350–1; Kearton newsreel 355; Kolowrat-Krakowsky 363; loss of foreign markets 203; Lowenstein 394; Lubin 394; Machin 403; McDowell 417; Messter 429, 430; Netherlands 470, 471; news event films 475; Pathé 503; projectionists 536; propaganda 521; Rolfe 554; Russia 559, 560; Sandberg 562; shortage of film stock 39; Thiemann & Reinhardt Company 633; Turkey 646; US documentaries 308; US film industry 316; US theaters during 543; Warwick Trading Company 685; WKF 688

world's fairs 21, 704–5; Berlin (1896) 60; Brussels (1897) 63, 136; Chicago (1893) 30, 188, 465, 528, 562; electricity 218; ethnographic films 221; industrial films 321; London (1896) 227, 695; Lumière programs 533; modes of visual consumption 459; postcards 528; simulated travel 93; Sweden 618; travelogues 641; US imperialism 314; westerns 690; *see also* Paris Exposition

Het wrak van de noordzee (1915) 260

Wray, Cecil 538

Wrench, Alfred 705

Wrench Film Company 283, 635, 684, 705

Wrench, Herbert Holmes 635

Wright, Wilbur 429

Wyckoff, Alvin 171, 386

Wykolejeni (1913) 587

Wzlot aeroplanu w Warszawie (1909) 587

X-ray film 567–8, 570–1, 573
Xinmin Theater Research Society 115
Xirgu, Margarida 59, 600

Yan Ruisheng (1921) 116
Yan Shanshan 115
Yankee Film Company 610
Yasunao Taizumi 523
Yearsley, Albert 516
The Yellow Menace (1916) 425
Yellowstone National Park 641
Yermolíev, Iosif 193, 357, 447, 541, 556, 558, 560, 707
Yin Mingzhu 116
Yokota Einosuke 344, 708
Yokota Shokai 344, 345, 362, 412, 481, 489, 708
Yoshizawa Shoten 199, 344, 345, 481, 564, 623, 708
Youdale, William Henry 18
Young, Clara Kimball 104, 680
Young Deer, James 503, 690, 692, 708
Young, James 680
The Young Rajah (1924) 320
Your Country Needs You (1914) 59
Your Girl and Mine (1914) 700

Za Gostinoi Dveriami (1913) 426
Za la Mort serial 277, 339
Zaccaria, Gino 709
Zacconi, Ermete 333, 338, 501, 677, 709
Zahn, Johannes 405
Zamecnik, J. S. 463
Zangenberg, Ejnar 360
Zapatas Bande (1914) 481
Zaza (1915) 490
Zecca, Ferdinand 84, 232, 384, 460, 482, 569, 709–10; Andréani 24; Capellani 103; Chomon 27; "director-unit" system 249; films sonores 242; Hatot 296; intertitles 327;

Pathé-Frères 502, 506; Riche 552; Robinne 553; screenwriting 577; set design 585
Zetkin, Clara 697
Zeugfärberei 36
Zhang Shichuan 39, 115, 546, 710
Zheng Zhengqiu 39, 115, 710
Zhizn za zhizn (A Life for Life) (1916) 61, 357
Zhongyang Film Company 546
Zhuangzi shiqi (1913) 115
Ziegfeld's Follies (1907) 446
Zigomar (1911–1913) 25, 39, 158, 198, 347, 454, 583; distribution in the United States 661; Japan 345, 362; master criminal genre 179, 180; sensational melodrama 251, 425
Zigomar contre Nick Carter (1912) 180, 347
Zigomar, le peu d'anguille (1913) 347, 640
Zigoto series (1911–1912) 194
Zille, Heinrich 150
Zimbabwe (Rhodesia) 12
Zimmerman, Henry 676, 677
Zimovoi, V. 148
Zingara (1912) 343
Zionism 498–9, 549
Ziyarat al-khidiwi li-masjid al-Mursi Abu al-'Abbas bi-l-Iskandariyya (1907) 216
Zoograph 63, 64, 170
Zotti, Laura Minici 133
Zubeida 362
Der Zug des Herzens (1912) 302
Zuhra (1922) 217
Zukor, Adolph 67, 302, 372, 413–14, 432, 479, 511, 710; Brady partnership 82; critique of Porter 527; distribution 446, 660; Famous Players 229; legitimate theater 628; multiple-reel films 456
A Zulu's Devotion (1916) 138
Zum Paradies der Damen (1914) 687
Zweimal gelebt (1912) 373
Zwischen Himmel und Erde (1913) 373